ADLAI STEVENSON AND THE WORLD

BY JOHN BARTLOW MARTIN

THE PANE OF GLASS
THE DEEP SOUTH SAYS NEVER
BREAK DOWN THE WALLS
WHY DID THEY KILL?
MY LIFE IN CRIME
BUTCHER'S DOZEN
INDIANA
CALL IT NORTH COUNTRY
OVERTAKEN BY EVENTS
ADLAI STEVENSON OF ILLINOIS

JOHN BARTLOW MARTIN, born in Ohio, became one of America's most distinguished journalists in the late 1940s and 1950s. He wrote extensively for *Harper's* and *The Saturday Evening Post,* winning four times the Benjamin Franklin and twice the Sigma Delta Chi awards for best article of the year. Many of his prodigiously researched pieces became important pioneering books on such subjects as prison reform, desegregation, and mental health care. He worked as a writer for and adviser to Adlai Stevenson and was twice a presidential envoy—for John Kennedy and Lyndon Johnson. Mr. Martin was U. S. Ambassador to the Dominican Republic from 1962 to 1964, and out of this dramatic experience came his classic ambassador's report, *Overtaken by Events.* He is a professor at Northwestern University's Medill School of Journalism.

ADLAI STEVENSON AND THE WORLD

*The Life of
Adlai E. Stevenson*

JOHN BARTLOW MARTIN

Anchor Books
Anchor Press/Doubleday
Garden City, New York
1978

Quotations by Dean Acheson, reprinted by permission of David C. Acheson: Interview from "Face the Nation" is contained in Volume 3 of "Face the Nation" Transcripts. Copyright © 1972, CBS, Inc. (Available through Scarecrow Press). Reprinted by permission. Quotations by Alistair Cooke, reprinted by permission. Quotations by Senator Alan Cranston, reprinted by permission. Quotations by John Foster Dulles were excerpted from "How Dulles Averted War," by James Shepley, *Life* magazine. Copyright © 1956, Time, Inc. Reprinted by permission. Quotations by Cyrus Eaton reprinted by permission. Quotations by Dwight D. Eisenhower reprinted by permission of Colonel John S. D. Eisenhower. Quotations by Ralph Ginzburg, reprinted by permission. Quotations from "The Godkin Lectures" reprinted in *Call to Greatness*, reprinted by permission of Harper & Row, Publishers, and Laurence Pollinger Limited. Stanza from "Stopping by Woods on a Snowy Evening," from *The Poetry of Robert Frost*, edited by Edward Connery Lathem, copyright 1923, © 1969 by Holt, Rinehart and Winston, Inc. Copyright 1951 by Robert Frost. Reprinted by permission of Holt, Rinehart and Winston, Inc., and Jonathan Cape Limited. Quotations by Estes Kefauver, reprinted by permission of Gail Kefauver. Quotations by Herbert H. Lehman reprinted by permission of John R. Lehman. Quotations by Robert Murphy reprinted by permission. Excerpts from May 5, 1957, "Meet the Press" Interview, reprinted by permission of the National Broadcasting Company, Inc. Quotations by James Reston reprinted by permission. Quotations by Eleanor Roosevelt reprinted by permission of Franklin D. Roosevelt, Jr. Quotations by Richard Russell reprinted by permission of the Executors of his Estate, Hugh Peterson, Jr., and Richard B. Russel III. Quotations by James P. Warburg reprinted by permission of Joan M. Warburg. Lines from "Princeton," by Alfred Noyes. By permission of Hugh Noyes, Lisle Combe, Ventnor, Isle of Wight, England.

Originally published in hardcover by Doubleday & Company, Inc. in 1977 Anchor Books edition: 1978

again,
to Fran

CONTENTS

ADLAI
STEVENSON
AND THE
WORLD

PART ONE
THE NATION

CHAPTER ONE

Leader in Exile:
His Finest Hour
1952-1955

On November 5, 1952, Adlai E. Stevenson was still Governor of Illinois but yesterday he had lost the presidency of the United States. He was getting bald and putting on a little weight, but his blue eyes were brilliant as ever. He was fifty-two years old, at the peak of his capabilities. Many forces had shaped his life—boyhood in the small town of Bloomington, Illinois; a grandfather who had been Vice President of the United States; his parents' unhappy marriage; a glamorous marriage of his own that ended in divorce; the country club atmosphere of Princeton in the 1920s; the opulent life of Lake Forest and the comfortable life of a country gentleman in Libertyville; the dusty practice of law in a conservative Chicago firm; speeches on foreign affairs; a taste of life in Washington during the New Deal; a successful term as Governor of Illinois; and the lost presidential campaign. What now would he do with the rest of his life?

It was a question he had faced often. In his twenties he had wanted to run his family's newspaper, the Bloomington *Pantagraph,* but his family had lost control of it to his cousin's family, so he had finished law school. He had been restless in law practice, escaping to civic deeds in Chicago and to Washington whenever he could, finally as the principal staff assistant to the Secretary of the Navy during the war. After that he had tried to buy the Chicago *Daily News* but had failed. He had again escaped the law to go to work for the State Department at the founding sessions of the United Nations. That finished, he was increasingly bored by the law and suburban social life; he made serious efforts to get into politics, something he had wanted to do since at least 1930. In 1948 he wanted to run for the Senate, but that year his party needed him to run for Governor, and he did, reluctantly, and won overwhelmingly. Now his term was nearly over. Only a few months ago he had been nothing but another Midwest Governor, virtually unknown outside Illinois. Then in a few incandescent weeks he had suddenly become a national, even an international, figure. His

1952 presidential campaign had run on his brilliant speeches and his gallantry against the odds.

A presidential campaign is possessive, obsessive, even. To everybody in it, nothing else matters. They talk and think of nothing else. How close is New York? What speech is next? Who made *this* itinerary? Then, suddenly, Election Day; and after that everything comes to a crashing halt. The telephones do not ring. There is no speech to write, no schedule to make, no issue to confront. There is, quite simply, nothing to do at all. A whole cosmos in which one lived those months has vanished, as though it had never existed. One does not fly by charter; one flies commercial, at the mercy of a timetable. One deals with everyday matters, not affairs of state. It is all over, and with finality.

Few periods in life are harder than the interregnum which Stevenson now faced—the time between his defeat November 4 and his departure from the governorship January 12. A world, and all the dreams, had come to an end. The cheering, enchanted millions had gone away, disappeared into their own concerns. No more crowds at the airport, no more gigantic rallies, no more bands and bunting and balloons. Nothing to talk about, nothing to prepare for. Nothing.

Yet he must plan. It had been four years since he had been a private citizen. As Governor, he had managed the affairs of a great and populous state. Now he must return to his own affairs. He had had a car and a driver, and thousands had deferred to him. Would he now take the train from Libertyville to a Chicago law office with all the other commuters? If not, what should he do? Somehow he must re-enter private life. But how? It is not easy for thousands of public men who face the re-entry problem each time a national administration changes. And Adlai Stevenson had special problems. He had little private life to return to—no wife. Millions still looked to him to lead—but how could he lead, alone and out of office? Some men, defeated for the presidency, lapse into relative obscurity —McGovern and Landon come to mind. Was that in store for Stevenson?

It seemed unlikely at that time but as things turned out in the years ahead, just as Illinois had shaped him, so would Adlai Stevenson help to shape his country and his world.

2.

The day after the election Stevenson, together with three key men on his staff, Carl McGowan, William McCormick Blair, Jr., and Newton N. Minow, began looking through the pile of telegrams and letters, seventy or eighty thousand of them, and Stevenson said, "We're having fried post-mortem on toast." He told Minow to supervise answering them but he read many himself and answered some. Alicia Patterson, one of the great loves of his life, had sent him a telegram and a letter; he told her, "I've no regrets; did the best I could, didn't trim, equivocate or clasp dirty hands.

But the 20 years, the moribund Dem. organization, Korea (a disposibile [despicable?] & dangerous thing to have put into the campaign!) etc etc were too much. I really don't know, but many newsmen etc. dropping in to say good-bye seem to feel that HST's campaigning hurt far more than it helped by raising the target again and diluting my coverage. Sometime we will talk again—maybe by the black river." (They often talked by a river on her plantation in Georgia.) That letter may not represent his considered retrospective judgment but we can be sure that, like nearly all his letters to Alicia, it truly revealed his private thoughts at that moment.

To his old friend Harriet Welling, who had written that he had grown through adversity, he wrote, "I am sure that the ordeals of the past may be a bit of philosophy that I have unwittingly accumulated and made this one that much easier." To his cousin Bud Merwin: "I am a little tired but not the least bruised and have no regrets about the election. I must say I was bitterly disappointed about the State ticket in Illinois and the people will have cause to regret it." The election of Stratton as Governor was painful to Stevenson—he thought William G. Stratton epitomized the worst in the Illinois Republican Party. Stevenson's boyhood friend, Joe Bohrer, was so downcast by the election result that he went into a severe depression; Stevenson tried to cheer him—"we'll live to fight another day." He told his friend Lloyd Garrison, a New York lawyer, "I hope we can meet to talk some time about the future of our party. I have no regrets except for the disappointment of my friends."

Bernard DeVoto said the campaign was the best in American history; Stevenson replied, "The simple facts are that I am the beneficiary of the hearts and minds of many people who made this campaign which you call mine. . . . For me it was an adventure for which I shall be eternally grateful to my party and to the good and the wise who rallied to our standard." Arthur M. Schlesinger, Jr., who had returned to Harvard after working on Stevenson's speeches during the campaign, wrote Stevenson, "I wish I could report verbatim the many conversations I have had the last few days —the tributes to you and to the level of the campaign and to the role of leadership which you will have in the next years (and quite a lot of specific talk about 1956). In Cambridge, for example, the Volunteers do not wish to disband and are planning some form of continuing organization." (This was going on all over the country; Stevenson always attracted die-hard supporters.) "I can not put much stock in the belief of the Alsops, Reston, etc., that the 'real' Eisenhower will now emerge. . . . I think this last campaign amply disclosed the real Eisenhower—a man with little content of his own, infatuated with the idea of compromise as a solution to everything." Stevenson underlined that. "If this is so, it makes it all the more urgent that we have a vigorous and responsible opposition. . . . You are the man who must set the tone and the line for this opposition."

The mail from the famous and the obscure was extraordinary. Winston Churchill wrote of Stevenson's "distinguished campaign." Bernard Baruch

wrote, "You have brought a new light to the national scene." Albert
Einstein: "It is a pity that it was possible to mislead the people in this
critical time." Carl Sandburg: "Yours is a high name now and for a long
time." Eleanor Roosevelt expressed her distress at his defeat but added
that he would be "free to do many things in the international field and I
am sure that is where you can be most useful." General George C.
Marshall sent a longhand note: "I send you my sympathy over the results
of the campaign. You fought a great fight. Your political speeches reach a
new high in statesmanship. You deserved far better of the electorate, but
you will be recognized increasingly as a truly great American."

Disappointed students at Columbia University put the flag at half mast.
A New York show girl wrote: "The papers keep saying that all the women
in the country voted for Ike. I just want you to know that I and all my
girlfriends voted for *you*. We are singers and dancers in a Broadway show
and we are gorgeous and 100% women. All 16 of the girls in my dressing
room voted for you and half of us spent money and time working for
you. We gave out pamphlets in hotel lobbies, talked on TV, and met
your train when you came to Harlem. We love you because you respect
our intelligence, because you have courage and honesty, and because you
have more sex appeal than any candidate for office we have ever seen.
PLEASE run again."

A San Antonio precinct worker said Stevenson's campaign had given
her "the feeling of exaltation that we were working for a great statesman."
A woman in San Jose, California, wrote: "In four years please lead us to
victory." A woman in Beverly Hills: "I learned more during 14 weeks of
listening to you than in all my 62 years as a naturalized citizen." A Vassar
graduate: "I consider it the greatest privilege of my life to have been able
to cast my first ballot for you the Woodrow Wilson of our generation. I
look forward to 1956." A couple in Los Angeles: "You remain the guardian and spokesman of America's conscience."

Stevenson issued a statement saying that it was impossible to reply
personally and promptly to the writers, that he was nonetheless grateful,
that his first concern must be the party deficit, and that he hoped the Volunteers for Stevenson would continue to participate in regular Democratic
Party politics. The task of answering the letters went on far into 1953,
months after Stevenson had left Springfield and the governorship. The staff
carded the names and addresses, by states, of people who said they wanted
to work in Stevenson's behalf in 1956.

3.

On November 9, Stevenson went to Alton, across the river from St.
Louis, and in a speech long promised dedicated a tablet to the memory of
Elijah P. Lovejoy, the martyred abolitionist editor. He said Lovejoy had

served "a greater cause" than abolition: "This greater cause was the right
—and the duty—of the individual to speak out for the truth." On November 12, Stevenson left with the McGowans and Wilson Wyatts for a long
weekend near Tucson, Arizona, at the ranch of a friend, Dick Jenkins,
hunting, riding horseback, playing tennis, sleeping, resting. Four reporters
and two photographers showed up; he was asleep. When he appeared, he
looked drawn and weary, one thought, but told them, "I should hope very
much that the Democratic Party will take a position of positive and intelligent opposition. To the extent that I can help make the party a useful instrument of the nation, I will be glad to do so." He flew back to Springfield
November 17.

Newt Minow was working on the campaign files and a new legislative
program. "A more depressing task there isn't," Minow says, "than closing
the headquarters of the defeated candidate." He asked members of the administration to pull together recommendations for a legislative program—
Stevenson had to make a farewell address to the legislature in January.
Having inventoried the files, Minow prepared a memorandum recommending that the financial files from campaign manager Wilson Wyatt's
office be sent to the Democratic National Committee, that Stevenson keep
the speech files the writers had accumulated at the Elks Club, and that the
correspondence files be used to form the nucleus of a mailing list.

Stevenson was receiving stacks of invitations to speak at universities
around the country and in England, to political groups—about 300 invitations in November and December. He declined all for the time being. He
was trying to decide what to do. The press was full of speculation about
his future. Immediately after the election Wyatt had proposed his candidacy in 1956, and the political writers took up the theme. But what to do
between now and 1956? Newspapers seemed in general agreement that
Stevenson and Eisenhower, too, must "revitalize" their parties but they
noted that Stevenson would be out of office, and party leadership would
reside in the Democratic National Committee and the congressional leadership. Some suggested that Stevenson lead by going on national television
regularly.

Offers to write were pouring in from newspaper syndicates, magazines,
and book publishers. *Look* magazine proposed that he take a trip around
the world and write about it. Ultimately he agreed. Lloyd Garrison was
negotiating with New York publishers who wanted to publish a collection
of Stevenson's campaign speeches. He reached agreement with Random
House. Before those plans were made final, however, Stevenson seriously
considered returning to the law. He thought of entering several firms—
George Ball's, John Miller's, Ben Heineman's—and of establishing his
own firm with McGowan, Minow, Blair, and others. Ed McDougal, his old
friend and law partner, suggested that Stevenson's old Sidley firm bring
him back and put his name into the firm. But that might have caused
problems with some of the other partners. And in any case Stevenson did

not want to return to active law practice, he did want a Chicago base of some sort, and in the end the Sidley firm gave him office space for himself, Bill Blair, and two secretaries. "We were proud to have him around," Edwin Austin, a senior partner, has said. That became his headquarters after he left Springfield. He wanted to keep McGowan and Bill Flanagan, his press secretary, with him but saw no way to arrange it. Flanagan went to a public relations firm and McGowan to a law firm which represented the People's Gas Light & Coke Company, the gas utility of which Stevenson's old friend, Jim Oates, was chairman.

Schlesinger went to Springfield December 9 and found Stevenson in good spirits, though "somewhat fussed" by the volume of mail and his files. He speculated whether he would have been re-elected Governor but did not berate himself or anyone else for accepting the presidential nomination. Schlesinger prepared a list of about eighty-five campaign speeches which should be considered for inclusion in Stevenson's book. Stevenson would make the final selection and write an introduction. Schlesinger urged him to go away to do it, preferably to Ronald and Marietta Tree's winter estate in Barbados. Although Stevenson was saying nothing publicly about his political future, it seemed clear enough. Schlesinger noted in his journal, "He showed every determination to stay in politics and to work to assert leadership in the party. He sees himself obviously as the unifying influence and would deplore the forcing of issues which would split the party." Stevenson gave high priority to winning the South back and feared labor might try to take over the party in the North. At the same time he spoke of "the business community" as a distinct and probably hostile element and he was much concerned over the combination of the mass media, the business community, and the Republican Party. He wanted to establish a party strategy committee made up of himself, congressional leaders, the national chairman, and others. He chortled over a newspaper story quoting President Truman as calling President-elect Eisenhower's trip to Korea, just ending, demagoguery.

Senator Hubert Humphrey strongly urged him to continue as the Democratic Party's leader and spokesman in order to uphold the liberal faith and combat party reactionaries. Stevenson replied, "Some time we must talk about this 'leadership' business. I am a little perplexed. I should like to do what I can, consistent with earning a living, to be of future help to the Party. . . . Much will depend, of course, upon our coherence and purposefulness in Congress. . . . I agree that restaffing the National Committee for its new mission is the first order of business—besides cleaning up the national deficit." A powerful Southern Senate Democrat, Burnet R. Maybank of South Carolina, declined to say he would recognize Stevenson as titular leader of the party for the next four years. Instead he considered Senator Richard B. Russell and other Southerners "caretakers of the party." It was widely predicted that Lyndon Johnson, as Senate leader, would support President Eisenhower's program and offer little opposition leadership. If Stevenson wanted to lead, he would have to fight.

Stevenson's relations with President Truman were improving. Truman invited him to visit the White House so they could "discuss political matters to our hearts content without fear of interruption or being overheard." He wanted Stevenson to "revitalize" the National Committee and offered to help. Both privately and in public, he made it clear that he regarded Stevenson as the head of the party, that he would cooperate with him, and that he was confident of victory in 1954 and 1956.

Schlesinger predicted an increase in McCarthyism by Republicans who hoped to destroy the Democratic Party by demonstrating that it was "honeycombed with communism and treason." He suggested to Stevenson that they make McCarthy "the acid moral test" and try to split off from Eisenhower decent Republicans who could not abide McCarthy. He reported that Averell Harriman was convinced Stevenson must stay out in front and prepare for 1956. He passed on a suggestion from Walter Lippmann: that Stevenson, like Franklin Roosevelt, make himself "a powerful national figure" in the party simply by writing a great many letters to Democrats. At about this same time, on November 25, Senator Russell was quoted as saying that, while Stevenson was the titular head of the party, Democratic policy making would be done in Congress during the next four years. He said he hoped Congress' efforts could be "coordinated" with Stevenson's. It was the beginning of a long struggle.

4.

Stevenson took a party of friends to a football game at the University of Illinois on November 22. He went duck shooting at a friend's hunting lodge. Planning a trip East, he tried to arrange to see Alicia Patterson. Marietta Tree invited him to Barbados. The day after he wrote in longhand to Alicia Patterson, Stevenson replied with a typewritten dictated letter to "My dear Marietta": "I have read and re-read your thoughtful and heart-lifting letter of November 21. Actually, my heart needs little lifting and I feel more like the victor than the vanquished. But I am distressed by the disappointment of so many friends. Your own heroism I shall never forget. Indeed it would be hard to forget you regardless of campaigns! I shall live in hopes of the Barbados, but the future is misty." He closed, "Ever yours," not a common closing. His staff filed it

Pol '52—Post election ltrs
Tree, Mrs. Ronald

but it was hardly an appropriate category. She would become one of the most important figures in his life. It had been a long time since he had heard from Dorothy Fosdick. The tone of his letters to Alicia Patterson had changed too. Soon Marietta would move to the fore. She was a remarkable woman, intelligent and sensible, tall and blonde, elegant and beautiful. She was born in Lawrence, Massachusetts, and raised in Chestnut Hill, Philadelphia. Her grandfather had founded Groton and been its headmaster fifty-six years. Her brother, Endicott Peabody, became Governor of Massachusetts. She was educated in Pennsylvania. She visited Groton frequently as a young girl. Bill Blair, Stevenson's young friend and aide, met her while he was in boarding school, and they became "great friends," as she has said, by the time they were about sixteen. Their families spent summers at resorts in Maine. She once said, "I became a Democrat years before Bill did. About 1942. I always told him I'd give him a party the day he became one." Marietta was a model at Wanamaker's department store. In 1939, during her junior year in college, she married a New York lawyer. He went into the Army as a private and she went to work for *Life* magazine to support their daughter. She has said, "I shared an office with Earl Brown, the first Negro I ever met. That's how I saw what it was like to be a Negro in America. So I started civil rights work." Working at *Life* as a researcher, she became a shop steward in the Newspaper Guild. In the 1944 presidential election she was vice chairman of the CIO-PAC in New York, working for Roosevelt—"I was tremendously politically oriented." After the war she and her husband were divorced. In 1947 she married Ronald Tree, some years older than she, and they went to live in England. In 1949 they moved back to New York to stay. Marietta became Democratic county and state committeewoman and head of research for the Democratic State Committee. After 1952 she tried to bring the Volunteers into the Democratic Party.

The New York *Post* reported that the resignation of New York State Chairman Paul Fitzpatrick had created a vacuum in the "declining and decaying" party that might be filled by such leaders as Senator Herbert Lehman, Harriman, FDR, Jr., Robert Wagner, Jr., and Secretary of the Air Force Tom Finletter; and it linked such liberal state leadership to Stevenson's liberal national leadership. Stevenson, despite his conservative leanings, had become in less than twelve months the pre-eminent leader of the liberal wing of the Democratic Party. He was adopting the conventional view of his defeat: he wrote to a classmate, "I think [the campaign] may have served a useful purpose to some at least. And I agree that the project was hopeless from the start, made the more so by the General's use of Korea." He told Jim Doyle, Democratic state chairman of Wisconsin, that he wanted to capitalize on post-election enthusiasm for the party but "do not wish to have it all focus around me and endanger the Congressional unity and coherence which is so indispensable to statesmanlike opposition in the Congress." Senator Clinton P. Anderson of New Mexico urged Stevenson to retain Steve Mitchell as National Committee chairman in order to rid the party of graft. Stevenson thought Mitchell would stay on and, as for himself, "I do not see it with any clarity, but I certainly want to do what I can and I am taking prompt steps toward the reorganization of the National Committee."

5.

When Stevenson arrived in New York on Tuesday, December 2, he was surprised to be met by a crowd of reporters and photographers. He joked with them and declined to comment on Eisenhower's trip to Korea. He visited his sister-in-law, Mrs. Ralph Hines. Next day he went to Atlantic City to address the CIO convention. It was an unhappy crowd; it had lost the election and lost its leader—Phil Murray had died a few days after the election. Walter Reuther was the foremost candidate to replace him. Stevenson's speech eulogized Murray and said, "While there are inequities and injustices in our laws that still demand remedy, labor's long battle for status and recognition has been largely won. Violence and ruthlessness by employers and unions alike are now obsolete. . . . Labor has been afflicted with Communist infiltration. It has been afflicted with hoodlums and racketeers. These battles for clean unions have been fought and will be fought as long as necessary. But the bigger job of the future is the proper exercise of organized labor's vast responsibility, not just to the workingman but the country." The delegates cheered him heartily.

From Atlantic City, Stevenson flew to Washington and was met not only by White House staffers but by several hundred members of the Stevenson-Sparkman Clubs of Alexandria and the District of Columbia who nearly mobbed him, shouting, "We want Adlai." Personal friends who had come to welcome him could not get near him. A reporter thought he seemed "exuberant" and "touched and gratified" at the reception. President Truman greeted him under the portico at the north entrance to the White House. Stevenson apologized for being an hour late. They went into the White House arm in arm.

A little later a newspaper columnist, Robert S. Allen, said that during their talks Truman warned Stevenson that unless Stevenson assumed leadership of the party its reactionary leaders would, with disastrous effect. Allen wrote that Stevenson assured the President he had no intention of allowing the party to languish or his own position in it to wane. He intended to help Democratic candidates vigorously in the 1954 congressional campaign. He hoped to work closely with Democratic congressional leaders, especially liberals. Truman warmly approved.

After dinner President Truman and Stevenson talked until about 11 P.M., then Stevenson went to bed in the Lincoln Room. He wrote to his old friend Jane Dick the following night—he stayed two nights—from the

White House: "After this I shall inscribe a message to Eisenhower as follows:

> "Dear General—
> > "I got here first, pal!
> > > "Yours,
> > > "AES"

He described how he had been sleepless in the Lincoln Room: "First I read a bit and then the trouble commenced when I tried to go to sleep— the ghosts and shadows that fill that room, bits and pieces of imperishable words that were conceived, perhaps written here on this table where I am sitting this moment—the very table on which he signed the Emancipation Proclamation after all those months of torment. As if these reveries were not enough—the whole room filled with ghosts—strange faces some of them, bearded, some ugly, some good—all manner of clothes. They seemed to fairly jostle each other for my attention to the imperatives of their speechless mouths. And then it all receded and the portraits came marching up the stairs and down the halls and into my room, or did I leave my room and walk thru the halls and down the stairs and pass them all one by one? I don't know. But behind each in some strange dimension stretched out all the miseries, the burdens, the doubts and anguish that afflicted him here in this house. At 3 A.M. I gave up and took a sleeping pill and then another for good measure. And this morning they had to wake me up and there were Pres. & Mrs. T. patiently waiting outside for breakfast with their irresponsible guest."

That morning he met with President Truman, the White House staff, and party officials—Steve Mitchell, Clayton Fritchey, Dwight Palmer, the party treasurer. Afterward Roger Tubby took him to the White House press room for a press conference. He said he did not favor opposition for opposition's sake. Rather, he thought the interest of the Democratic Party "must be subordinated to the interests of the nation and the dispatch of the public business." He went on, "And it is not our intention to influence the Democratic members of Congress to obstruct, delay, or in any way impair or imperil the new Administration's programs in so far as is compatible with the views of the party. The instrument of doing this and of being a constructive and wholesome influence in our public life will, of course, be the Democratic leadership in the Congress." He was asked if he had discussed party leadership with Southern Congressmen. He repeated that legislative leadership must reside in congressional Democrats and said he did not think all Democrats would "take a vow of silence and wait to hear what I say." Asked about the movement to collect money to keep him on TV and radio, he said he was grateful but the campaign deficit came first. A reporter asked how soon he would speak out on the new Administration. He said he saw "no point in talking until there was something to talk about." He repeated what he had said so often as Governor, that "good government is good politics." A reporter asked if he would not lack a forum. He said this did not worry him. Asked if he and Truman had discussed why he had lost, he laughed and said reporters were better equipped to say. He said he and President Truman had agreed that Steve Mitchell would stay on as National Committee chairman. He described the morning meeting as "desultory discussion" and "jollification." He and President Truman had spent the previous evening in the President's study, discussing party and world affairs. He said he had no firm plans but had not had a vacation in twelve years and was considering traveling abroad.

President Truman held a press conference later that day. Asked about his talks with Stevenson, he said, "I think the Governor pretty well covered the ground this morning." Asked about Eisenhower's Cabinet, he said, "I have no comment. You want to give these people a chance to operate." Had he and Stevenson decided why the Republicans won? "No. I am leaving that up to you. You fellows know all about everything."

That night he had dinner with President and Mrs. Truman, nearly all Truman cabinet members and former members and their wives, Chief Justice and Mrs. Vinson, Associate Justice and Mrs. Clark, General and Mrs. Marshall, former Vice President and Mrs. Wallace. His brother-in-law and sister, Ernest and Buffie Ives, were there. The President and his wife received in the East Room, the Marine Band played in the north corridor, the guests sat at a U-shaped table in the state dining room, and they had coffee in smaller reception rooms. At dinner Truman offered a toast to "the best Cabinet any President ever had." Chief Justice Vinson responded with one to "the best President any Cabinet ever had."

On Friday, December 5, Stevenson, working at a desk in the White House press office, held a series of political meetings. He saw, among others, Oscar Chapman, Francis Biddle, and the national chairman and chairman of the executive committee of the ADA. He also talked to several members of Congress by telephone. He stayed that night with Tom Finletter, still Secretary of the Air Force. After his visit the Washington *Post* praised him and Truman for subordinating the interests of the Democratic Party to the national interest. Cabell Phillips wrote in the New York *Times* that Democrats were optimistic about 1956 because they had come through a defeat with high morale and unified—so inevitable had the Eisenhower sweep been that Democrats had no disposition to blame each other.

Back in Springfield, Stevenson wrote to Dwight Palmer, the party treasurer, about the deficit and offered to do anything he could to help erase it, including making a TV broadcast asking for contributions. He suggested that Steve Mitchell ask selected party leaders, such as Jim Finnegan and Paul Butler, to make a state-by-state survey of the party's prospects for new blood, new leadership, issues, and programs. He was pursuing Senator Richard B. Russell of Georgia—regretted they had not met in Washington, invited Russell to come to Springfield to talk about the party. Senator Estes Kefauver told a newspaperman he recognized Stevenson as the party's "titular head" but went on, "However, he has no right of or in himself to dictate or determine party policy. That is for a policy committee—the national committee and its executive committee and perhaps others. But his views should carry a lot of weight in policy consultations."

Stevenson had asked Norman Cousins of the *Saturday Review* for his views on his future role. Cousins sent a long memorandum saying Stevenson was obligated to "articulate America to the rest of the world," permit his followers to "rally around you" as "Custodian of the Public Conscience," and "rebuild" the Democratic Party. Stevenson replied, "You try me sorely!" He said he agreed that his power within the party was likely to flow from leadership he exerted outside the party, as a citizen. He was unwilling to arrange to speak regularly on TV because he would have to talk whether or not he had anything to say, or to become a magazine editor because he would be "stuck" with everything it printed. He expressed interest in a proposal from an independent Chicago truck drivers' union that he become the public member of a trusteeship to supervise a proposed health and welfare program. Robert Kintner, president of ABC, suggested the possibility of "giving you a regular time period as a representative of the Democratic National Committee," though he would probably have to offer equal time to the Republicans. ABC was interested in exploring the idea of his appearing under commercial sponsorship. Stevenson responded, "I think very well of the idea of allotting time for both parties and would be glad to discuss it with you [later]. . . . For the meanwhile, I shall be saying little if anything."

He told Alicia Patterson he was thinking of going around the world "for self education & to escape while Congress is in session, before I put my foot in it with some of my beloved Democratic brethren." He told her and Brooks Atkinson that the country was in a period of mistrust of liberals and intellectuals.

He went back to Washington and met Adlai III, and together they called at the White House, and President Truman took them on a tour of it. Stevenson and Vice President-elect Nixon were the principal speakers at the annual dinner of the Washington press corps's Gridiron Club. More than 500 attended, including foreign diplomats, members of the Truman Cabinet, members-designate of the Eisenhower Cabinet, Supreme Court justices, members of Congress, and leaders in government, journalism, and business. Young Adlai went with his father; Truman stayed away, leaving the limelight to Stevenson. The program kidded both Democrats and Republicans. It was a gay evening, and Stevenson was at his best. His speech was a Stevenson triumph. His opening line was his best: "A funny thing happened to me on the way to the White House." He recalled the Gridiron Dinner of four years ago: "I, a Democrat, had just been elected Governor by the largest majority ever received in Republican Illinois. And here I am, four years later, and just defeated by the largest majority ever received in Democratic America. . . .

"As you all know, I just love to make speeches. Especially lighthearted speeches. For laughter most of all distinguishes us from the lower—or untamed—animals, and I was much relieved that the Republicans evidently decided not to prohibit humor in politics by federal law. . . .

"I was a little baffled by the emergence of that word 'egghead,' to describe some of my supporters—a word which I am glad to bequeath to the nation's vocabulary. . . . I am happy to note that you refrained from saying of the eggheads that the yolk was on them! . . ."

Of the letters he received during the campaign, Stevenson said: "We gave up counting before long and began to weigh them. So many of them were from people who voted for the General, and evidently felt that they owed me an explanation; curious why people will go to all that trouble to write a long letter when a little X in the right place would have been so much easier. . . .

"But, whatever happens to the Republicans, the Republic will survive. I have great faith in the people. As to their wisdom, well, Coca-Cola still outsells champagne. . . .

"As to you, the press, a last word. It is the habit of journalists, as of politicians, to see the world in terms of crisis rather than continuity; the big story is turmoil and disaster, not the quiet spectacle of men working. I trust that there will be none among my party who will hope for just a small, dandy little catastrophe to vindicate us. I am aware of the thesis that bad news sells papers. But neither politicians nor publishers have the right in this age to hope for the worst. Every newspaperman has talked at one time or another of how to handle the story of the end of the world; but who will be around to buy the 'extra'?

"Every lesson of history is that democracy flourishes when speech is freest. No issue is more important—and more troublesome—in this time of conflict with massive repression than the preservation of our right, even to bore each other. (I was flattered, by the way, by an unsigned letter last week that said: 'Please start talking again, Governor, or we'll be bored to death before we're starved to death.') Never was the responsibility of the majority press greater to make clear that it is concerned about the freedom of all Americans, and not merely about its own liberty to agree with itself. Your typewriter is a public trust. Its sound may be the most beautiful noise you know, but it has meaning and justification only if it is part of the glorious symphony of a free society."

6.

Back in Springfield after the weekend, Stevenson worked at his plans and political correspondence. Mayor Joseph S. Clark, Jr., of Philadelphia, said "a somewhat uneasy truce" existed between Jim Finnegan and Dick Dilworth, a rising, independent Democratic politician there. Finnegan, with Francis Myers, controlled the regular ward organization. Finnegan, as president of the City Council and chairman of the City Committee, had been "an enormous help" to Mayor Clark but he had to represent "the people who are in politics for revenue only." A strong independent group, including the ADA and several labor unions, had rallied around Dilworth and Clark. Dilworth wanted to run for Governor in 1954 and Clark would support him. The regular organization and Dave Lawrence were not enthusiastic. Finnegan and Myers were anxious to get Stevenson to Philadelphia soon for a major political address to help pay off the City Committee's deficit. Were Stevenson to go under their auspices, Clark said, "a number of noses will be out of joint." Clark hoped he would come under the joint sponsorship of the City Committee, the Democratic labor unions, and the independent group headed by ADA, which had organized Volunteers for Stevenson. Meanwhile, Clark hoped Stevenson could "drop by here informally or even incognito" so they could talk. Clark offered to see Stevenson in Chicago. It was an example of the maze Stevenson would have to thread in the coming years. He declined this one. Jack Fischer of *Harper's* once wrote that Stevenson had retired to "the private practice of politics."

Christmas was coming on. Stevenson was sending Christmas gifts to campaign associates—an engraved silver cigarette box to Steve Mitchell, for one. He sent Christmas greetings to Senator Russell and received a reply that might have been a form letter. He spent Christmas in the Mansion with his family. He gave a reception for two hundred friends. He thanked his old friend Dutch Smith for a Christmas check to help pay off the deficit.

A New York friend, Frank Altschul, urged him to assume party leadership. In one of his frankest letters about his political future, he replied, "I have concluded, confidentially, to work as best I can through the National Committee staffing and then keep out of the way for the present session of Congress, meanwhile reflecting and educating myself a bit. This is not to say that I have not had some talks and will not have more with individual members of the Congress and the leaders but, as you well know, it is a perilous business and I want to lay at rest any feelings of suspicion about personal ambition, etc. The South has the bit in its teeth and will bite the harder if it has anything to bite."

The path of leadership would be thorny. Nationally, the party was split into three segments. President Truman led the segment represented by the big-city machines and conservative labor unions. The Congress, with Southerners ascendant, was determined to retain leadership. And the ADA, liberal unions such as Walter Reuther's, and the liberal-academic-intellectual community looked to Stevenson. In addition, in nearly every big state, including New York, Pennsylvania, Texas, and California, local leaders were vying for power. All this made Stevenson's role extremely difficult and explains why he kept referring to "leadership" as an ambiguous thing. He still had his man as the national chairman, Steve Mitchell.

But Mitchell's influence on the national committeemen and state organizations was not great, and his influence on Congress perhaps even less— the National Committee is traditionally White House-oriented, not Congress-oriented, and, besides, Mitchell was not the man to conciliate the South. Were Stevenson to yield to his ardent admirers' importunities to speak out frequently and to arrogate leadership to himself, he almost surely would find himself the target of all the other elements in the party— Southern Senators, big-city machine leaders, some labor leaders, and assorted state and local leaders. They were probably powerful enough to destroy him. They would accuse him of trying to seize control of the party to promote his own ambitions instead of permitting the party to find its own role of opposition. Thus his apparent reluctance to lead was the best evidence that he was thinking—and cannily—of his own political future. And his decision to work quietly through Mitchell, to stay out of the line of fire during the first session of Congress under Eisenhower, and to exert pressure on the party by exercising leadership outside the party—through speaking and writing only occasionally—was almost surely the best way to promote his own ambitions. In a few words, he was now, after the 1952 election, doing almost exactly what he did before the 1952 convention: achieving leadership by not openly seeking it. It was good politics. And it came naturally to him. It was the position he had laboriously reached during the interregnum.

Stevenson hoped to start a world tour March 2 by boat from San Francisco. He had thought of writing magazine pieces on it cast in the form of letters to his sons—"light treatment, geography, what I saw, who I talked to, what I heard, etc., reserving the more ponderous thought about world problems" for a second book. He asked Lloyd Garrison's views. Garrison would negotiate with publishers. Gardner Cowles, president and editor of *Look,* after a long talk with Garrison, on December 30 proposed that Stevenson write ten articles of about 3,500 words each on the following countries or regions: England, Germany, Italy and the Vatican, Israel, the Arab world, India and Nehru, Indo-China, Formosa and Chiang Kai-shek, Korea and Japan, and a summary piece. He suggested that Stevenson take one person along as his personal aide. *Look* would send a photographer and its European editor, William Attwood. *Look* would pay the expenses of the party. *Look* wanted Stevenson to write the articles en route and cable them back for publication while he was still abroad. It would not alter or censor them; Lloyd Garrison could approve final proofs and layouts. It would pay $50,000 for first world publication rights and would not share in reprint or book rights. It would not want Stevenson to write for any other big publication while the series was appearing in *Look*. In order to permit Stevenson to spread the *Look* payment over three years, it suggested that he write another separate piece in the first half of 1954 and another in the first half of 1955, on subjects to be agreed upon at the time and for $5,000 each. Thus the total *Look* commitment of

$60,000 could be spread as $20,000 each year in 1953, 1954, and 1955. It was a fair offer. It would commit him to a great deal of writing.

On New Year's Day, Stevenson held open house at the Mansion as always, and Mrs. Ives acted as hostess; some 2,000 people turned up, many telling him they hoped he would run again in 1956. On January 5, Stevenson held a press conference, his last as Governor. He announced his plans for the world tour. "This is something I wanted to do for years and this seems to be the logical time to do it, when my present job ends and before starting out on a new one." Asked if his trip would not be helpful to him as titular leader of the party, he said, "I think this trip obviously would help me understand our problems in the Orient. It would be necessary if I were to continue to speak and write on world affairs." He said he had no "political plans or ambitions." He had received many job offers but would accept none until after his trip. He would move to Libertyville next Monday—January 12, the day he officially left office; then vacation in the West Indies and start for the Far East March 1. He did not intend to make regular speeches as leader of the opposition but "shall certainly speak infrequently when both a suitable occasion and something useful to say converge."

On January 7 he delivered his final message to the Illinois legislature and, that night, his final radio report to the people. To the legislature he expressed his gratitude for having been allowed to serve as Governor and his regret at departing. He said much the same thing in his radio report to the people, but closed:

"Illinois, where my family have lived and prospered for a century and a quarter, means a great deal to me, and I am humbly thankful for the opportunity that has been mine to serve it. I leave my high office content in one respect—that I have given to it the best that was in me. It has been a richly rewarding experience, and the satisfactions have far outweighed the disappointments. . . . And now, with a full heart, I must bid you all good-by."

On Sunday night, January 11, his last in the Mansion, he wrote to Alicia Patterson: "Alicia dear—This will be my last screed from the dear old Mansion. Tomorrow my successor is inaugurated and I retreat to Chicago for a few days, then N.Y. about Saturday, and Barbados . . . to try to write the wretched book of speeches I've promised. I shall hope to see you in N.Y."

Next day he attended the inauguration of his Republican successor, Governor Stratton. He greeted Stratton at the Mansion at about 11 A.M. and they rode together in the motorcade a few blocks to the Armory, where Stratton took the oath before the legislature. Crowds lined the streets, the weather was springlike, and Stevenson smiled and waved. Stevenson completed his duties, then went to take the train to Chicago. A small group of friends saw him off. As he reached the train steps he said, "I feel as I used to, that I'm just arriving and am expected to make a speech." His friend, the Rev. Richard Paul Graebel, told him he never looked better and his eyes were "bluer than Jack Benny's." That night he went to a play starring Katharine Cornell, *The Constant Wife,* and slept at the Chicago Club. Tuesday he drove out to the house in Libertyville. Bill Blair and his secretaries, Carol Evans and Phyllis Gustafson, went to the four-room law office on the nineteenth floor at 11 South LaSalle in the space provided by the Sidley firm. A reporter noted that it appeared as "chaotic" as an election headquarters, with books, files, and papers stacked everywhere. He saw friends, made phone calls, wrote a few letters, cleaning up odds and ends. To Larry Irvin, of Bloomington, the staff aide who had handled downstate patronage for him, and who now had written a farewell note, Stevenson wrote, "It was a lovely letter and I shall keep it always—and with it memories of a loyalty and a devotion to a common purpose that meant more to me than perhaps you realize." He recommended members of his administration for jobs. He sent a farewell letter to President Truman: "My heart is very much with you and Mrs. Truman on the eve of your departure from that House and that post where you found so much of anxiety, of misery, of misunderstanding, and also of joy and triumph. Having just left my residence in Springfield, I have tasted something of what you are feeling, but I pray that your spirit is serene, that you are content, confident that as these troubled crowded years recede there will emerge a recognition and gratitude for the wisdom and the courage of the great decisions that were yours." He described his travel plans. Truman replied graciously and added, "I am glad you are going to the Far East because that part of the world needs our understanding and cooperation more than any other part of this great globe. Best of luck."

7.

Stevenson had entered the Executive Mansion in Springfield when he was not quite forty-nine years old. He left it when he was not quite fifty-three. They are important years in a man's life. He had entered it virtually unknown in 1949. He left it a figure of national and international renown, a renown won in a few months. This would be his role the rest of his life. But it was not an easy one to sustain, particularly not in the 1950s, out of office, lacking a forum.

It may be well to pause and look backward at where he had come from, at the 1952 campaign and the reputation it gave him as an intellectual, and to glance forward at the national and international weight he came to carry in the years ahead.

Carl McGowan once said, "He hit a rising curve in 1948 and everything went great. He made the most of it. But in terms of calling on him for courage and so forth, it was not very demanding. It never is when you're riding the crest. Adlai deserves a great deal of credit for the way he con-

ducted himself in the life he led after the 1952 defeat. He was *not* riding
the crest then. It's tough to be precipitated from the successful sleigh ride
he had been on to a position where he found himself in 1953. The great
likelihood was that in 1960 the party would turn to a new face. The whole
thing was pretty bleak. But those were the days from which came his leadership on McCarthy, on restraint in the Far East, on the nuclear test ban.
He aroused the interest of a lot of people in politics and public life who
had not had either one before. He kept the lights alive for a lot of people
during a pretty shabby period in American history—the 1950s. For example, the McCarthy speech in Miami," which Stevenson delivered in 1954.
"A lot of younger people might have gotten pretty discouraged about what
seems to win out and take over in the direction of foreign policy. Stevenson was a reassurance. When historians sit down to deal with the Eisenhower administration, it's going to be a pretty damned sad tale. When you
lay out the story of national leadership in those years, historians will note
the paradox that the most solid leadership was provided by a twice-
defeated candidate. This is not the usual thing."

Stevenson's hard-sought and hard-fought role as opposition leader in the
Eisenhower years of the 1950s contrasted sharply with Nixon's during the
Kennedy-Johnson years of the 1960s. Nixon spent his time attending Republican functions, making political friends all over the country, corralling
delegates who would nominate him in 1968 and local leaders who would
elect him that year. For the most part, he avoided the great divisive issues
of policy, preferring to antagonize no segment of his divided party. Stevenson, on the other hand, while he too attended innumerable party functions,
spoke out on the great issues, and frequently on the unpopular, or at least
impolitic, side of them—on McCarthyism, on Quemoy and Matsu, on
others. He was careful and skillful in handling his purely political problems with his divided party—his relations, for example, with such powerful and divided Senators as Russell and Humphrey, Johnson and Kennedy.
But he did not permit purely political consideration to control when he decided to assert leadership on a big issue.

McGowan went on, "I used to feel quite sorry for him during those
Chicago years. It was a tough life he was leading. It's very easy to throw in
your hand and quit worrying about all these things. Take it easy—quit
fretting about speeches. It must have been sour to see the Eisenhower honeymoon, knowing what a lousy thing it was. Yet he never seemed to get
embittered about it. I'm not sure I was with Stevenson during the period of
his more lasting claim to fame, though most people say so." That is, most
people think Stevenson's most lasting claim to fame was his 1952 campaign. McGowan was suggesting that Stevenson's most important years
were those between 1953 and 1960. "A lot of non-vocal intelligent people
looked to Stevenson to articulate their hopes and thinking. This had a tremendous impact on young people. After he died, I received letters from

people like Senator McGovern on this. When issues are floating around, it helps to have someone take a position."

Barbara Ward, the economist and writer, once said, "Despite two appalling personal defeats, he did re-create the Democratic Party—and Eisenhower in victory destroyed the Republican Party. Triumph through defeat —he beat the man who was in." Cook County political leader Jack Arvey put it somewhat differently: "Between 1952 and 1960 Stevenson was the most sought-after man in the party. Were it not for him, John F. Kennedy couldn't have been elected. Because Stevenson maintained a steady, loyal opposition. He was articulate. He kept the liberals together ready for the time to make another fight. He did a great service to the party and to the voters by keeping the programs alive. Stevenson's leadership between 1954 and 1956 was greater than ever before. I speak as a politician. His greatest value to the country was in attracting fine young people to politics and persuading them to assume a role in politics and to realize that only through politics can one be effective in shaping the destinies of the country. A political party not only selects candidates but it also puts forth a platform, policies, takes the message to the people of the country through the members of the party. Stevenson did more of this than anyone since Franklin Roosevelt."

After the 1952 campaign little groups of Volunteers went into the regular Democratic Party or tried to hang on as independent entities. Most were young people previously uninterested in politics. In 1953, not long before Stevenson left on his world tour, several young men who had worked for Stevenson, including Newt Minow, Bill Rivkin, Jim Clement, Dan Walker, and Angelo Geocaris, gave a farewell lunch for him at the Standard Club. They were forming the Committee for Illinois Government, the CIG, to keep watch on Governor Stratton. Stevenson encouraged them; he was bitter toward Stratton. Abner Mikva, a young independent Democrat and admirer, a political admirer of Stevenson, later a member of the Illinois legislature and of Congress, once said, "The CIG's real effect was to keep together and create a place for people Stevenson had brought in and who couldn't get excited about ward organization." The CIG was issue-oriented and presented policy alternatives. Stevenson always encouraged it. Out of it in the late 1950s came the Democratic Federation of Illinois, an activist movement to set up an independent wing of the Democratic Party in Illinois, in areas where the regular party was moribund. Stevenson steered clear of it, since it posed a threat to the regular organization.

The 1952 campaign had given Stevenson a reputation as an intellectual. Was he? Not really, if one considers an intellectual to be one given to creative thinking and interested in ideas for their own sake. Stevenson was interested in ideas for what they could accomplish. He did not so much create ideas as synthesize the ideas of others, as he once told Jane Dick.

And this resulted at least in part from the nature of his work as a politician. From 1948 on, and indeed earlier at the Council on Foreign Relations and with Colonel Frank Knox, he had spent a great deal of his time writing and delivering speeches. Anyone doing this is obliged to read almost exclusively for the purpose of picking up speech material. He has no time for the luxury of creative thinking. Stevenson often said he wished he could go off by himself and think. But he did not, and such inactivity would have bored him, for he was restless to be where things were happening. William Benton said that Stevenson was "a compulsive writer," not a compulsive reader. It is an acute distinction. Once, in preparation for a trip to Latin America, Benton collected reports from the State Department, the CIA, and an independent expert; on the plane he and Stevenson had two seats apiece, one to hold the reading material of each. Benton would be reading away and he would look over and see Stevenson writing on a yellow pad. He would ask, "What are you doing?" "Writing Agnes Meyer [a wealthy Washington friend]," Stevenson would reply. Benton would say, "For Christ's sake, stop it and read this briefing material." Stevenson refused. During these years Stevenson did, however, collect about himself some of the ablest and most original scholars and thinkers in the United States. He brokered their ideas—brought them to public notice. Thus did he lay the groundwork, in the 1950s, for the New Frontier and the Great Society of the 1960s.

Scotty Reston of the New York *Times* once said, "The most important thing he did in the 1950s was that he had a hell of a lot of influence on the Kennedys." Newt Minow said, "I think in perspective it will be said that his most important contribution was in the bridge-making role that he played. Historians will say that when the Franklin Roosevelt years ended the Democratic Party lost its way, bringing to disunity the alliance of university intellectuals, the labor movement, the traditional minority groups that built the Roosevelt majorities—Irish, Jews, Catholics. It was made worse by the frustration and dissatisfaction with the Korean War and the desire of people to get back to a comfortable life under Eisenhower. So Eisenhower was the choice. What Stevenson did was to keep intact and to extend into another generation, one, respect for politics and politicians in young people; and, two, the objectives to win and unite the Democratic Party; and, three, the restoration of policy. And he kept alive the commitment to internationalism and the changing role of America in the world. And finally and most important, the bridge to the Kennedy administration. He made it possible for the New Frontier programs to succeed. All the staff that was hammered out in the '52 and '56 campaigns of Stevenson went into the New Frontier. Basically I think that is how history will regard him. Plus maybe the UN. As to specific issues, nuclear testing was the most important. All great controversial issues take time to change public opinion. He hastened that decision. That one may turn out to be his monument. The great issues of the sixties he set the pattern for in the fifties—civil rights, federal government in education, managing the economy—his thought became law and policy later. And a lot of the people he brought into politics and government wouldn't be in it except for him. If it was not for Stevenson I wouldn't have been attracted to politics. Basically that was the Governor's role—to lead the way to what eventually happened, both on policy and staff. It often baffled me to wonder what kind of a President would he have been? I tell you honestly I'm not sure at all. In the long run it may be that the role that he did fulfill was a better one. The country needed an Eisenhower for a while. I subscribe to the Arthur Schlesinger, Sr., view—the cyclical view of history. Thank God the Gov was in there. He kept alive the ideals until the country got out of that cycle. He was a place to repair to while they were out. George Ball, Fred Dutton, Arthur Schlesinger, Dave Bell, Bill Blair, [Willard] Wirtz, Martin —all these were his legacy to JFK. The Kennedy program was all Stevenson except for the Peace Corps. So it was program and people—a great contribution. I'd hate to think what would have happened if one of the alternatives had occurred in 1952. For example if Barkley had been nominated. I didn't want Stevenson to run in 1952 or 1956. For him I was right—but for history I was wrong. As to his own life, I never met anyone who somehow managed to bring out the best in people as he did. When you were around him—with all his faults, and there were plenty of them— it was always fun and a good time. He was able to bring people to think better of themselves."

Carl McGowan said in a speech about Stevenson that President Kennedy had valued Stevenson's integrity and credibility highly; asked what integrity and credibility mean, he then said, "For me, they merge into something best defined by an answer to the question of whether a particular public figure is as honest with others as he is with himself. . . . Since we are all so conscious of the extent to which we are constantly fooling ourselves as well as those around us even in the concerns of private life, we are greatly complimented when the public man, who must depend on our uncertain favor, appears to be telling us exactly what he is telling himself. Throughout Adlai's lengthy career in the public eye, he persisted in doing just this. . . . He simply found it more natural to operate without guile. It was the easier way for him, although it seemed on occasion recklessly to invite pressure and attack. He appeared to find these consequences less painful than the personal discomfort of blurring an issue by sweeping an inconvenient fact under the rug, or by tailoring his view of it to that which his hearers might be expected to hold. . . . He proved that one can, although denied power, make of integrity and credibility a great national asset. That is the kind of accomplishment which speaks to the young in accents their elders cannot always hear."

Various members of the Eastern establishment on foreign policy held Stevenson in contempt on public questions. Acheson, a friend once recalled, was "bitter and mean" toward Stevenson. But Reston said, "If you will give me a list of all the men who have been regarded by some of our fellow countrymen since the war as having a knowledge of foreign affairs, Acheson has had trouble with them all—Stevenson, Harriman, Fulbright, Rusk, all of them. Acheson is an attractive curmudgeon. But he is quite unfair to his associates who have struggled through these ghastly troubles." Acheson's attitude toward Stevenson was more than one stemming from policy disagreement. Although it probably started with Stevenson's refusal to defend Acheson in the 1952 campaign, Acheson's antagonism grew after that, sometimes in policy disagreement, sometimes in personality clashes. Agnes Meyer once recalled that Acheson published a book and gave it to Stevenson with a warm inscription, whereupon Stevenson said, "Oh, Dean, do I have to read this?" Acheson related the story bitterly to her. "Adlai couldn't resist those deadly little shots." (Mrs. Meyer once gave Stevenson a book of her own and he told her later he'd never read a word of it.) Yet during the 1952 campaign Stevenson mentioned to George Ball only a single person he was considering appointing to his Cabinet if he won: John J. McCloy as Secretary of State—McCloy, a Republican who helped mold the tough-minded cold-war Europeanist Eastern establishment school of thought.

Although Stevenson went to Libertyville from Springfield, he stayed less than a week; and although he considered Libertyville home thereafter, he was gone so much that, in effect, his years as a country squire were over, had been over, indeed, since 1948. His next-door neighbor, Glen Lloyd, had the impression that after 1952, on the somewhat rare occasions when Stevenson was actually in the house in Libertyville, his guests were more likely to be national or international figures than neighbors.

As time passed, Stevenson's interests broadened, until at the end, Carl McGowan said, "No one had a monopoly on Adlai Stevenson. One of the striking things about his life is that he lived it at so many levels. Journalism, law, politics, private practice, public office, business and finance, social and civic causes, private organizations, charitable foundations, education, literature, the worlds of the university and the arts, the sporting field—he was at home in all and known in all. . . . And . . . these many lives of his were led not only in this country but abroad. His foreign friendships alone were astonishing in their number and variety." Stevenson himself told a friend late in life, "I think I can safely say that I have known every famous man and woman of my time in the world—and that may sound like bragging, but it isn't meant that way." This, he felt, was the greatest reward of his own fame. McGowan maintained that Stevenson "was a vital and interesting man wholly apart from his public fame. The calcium lights in his case did not operate a personality. They rather focused a wider span of attention upon one that existed in its own right and by its own force." This, taken together with Stevenson's integrity and credibility, explained, McGowan thought, "how and why it was that this one of our number—a little-known lawyer who rambled around the Loop on the same dusty errands as our own—became a renowned figure whose death was genuinely mourned by high and low alike around the globe."

Because Stevenson lived so many lives and because his personality had so many facets, each of scores, even hundreds, of people thought he himself was Stevenson's best friend. After 1952 the Stevenson legend grew rapidly. A great many people remembered seeing Stevenson in a little flash scene, usually at Libertyville, wearing sneakers and moving books around and talking in wide-eyed terms about politics. Draper Daniels went to see him one day after Daniels had won the party chairmanship in Stevenson's home county, Lake. "He met me at the door of his house on a Saturday morning. He was wearing sneakers. He had been moving books from the library. He said, 'How the hell did you do it?'" Daniels recalled too that in 1956 Stevenson agreed to give a reception in his house at Libertyville for Lake County precinct captains. He happened to be entertaining Marc Connelly, the playwright, as his house guest at the time, and Connelly stood in the receiving line with Stevenson. Daniels recalled that several times, as a precinct captain came down the line, Daniels would turn to introduce him to Stevenson, only to discover that Stevenson and Connelly had gone off somewhere to talk to each other. Such stories are numberless. His friends remember Libertyville fondly. Jim Oates used to play tennis with him there and at the Onwentsia Club. "He was a darn sight better than he looked. Very nimble. He loved Libertyville. The hotter the better." He liked to sun-bathe on the lawn or on the sun deck outside his bedroom.

He often told friends he wanted to remarry but added, as he once did to Bill Benton, "How would I ever find a way to get to know a woman well enough to know if I should marry her?" Minow recalled, "I think he would have liked to get married but he didn't want to feel accountable to anybody." Politics may have deterred him. A divorced and remarried candidate would stand little chance with Catholic voters. Bill Blair asked Stevenson about his favorite audience. "Women," he said, "especially if they've had a couple of drinks." Once a woman said to him after a speech that it was the greatest she'd ever heard—"it was absolutely marvelous." Stevenson said he liked it himself and had thought of publishing it posthumously. "Oh," she said, "I do hope you do, and the sooner the better." At the 1952 convention a pregnant woman at the convention hotel carried a sign, "Harriman's the man." Stevenson used to tell this story about himself. Women were crazy about him. Benton once said, "He had a special talent for women. I introduced him to a bevy of the best women in New York and they went wild." Benton thought that Stevenson's only real friends may have been women, that no man ever was so close to him as Alicia Patterson, and as Barbara Ward and Marietta Tree became. He thought that Stevenson gave more of himself to women than to men, was less "egocentric" around them, allowed himself to become absorbed in their family problems. He seemed to confide in women more than in men. After 1952 he had little time to himself. Quarreling in his own family bothered him a great deal. He had a string of strong women in his life—his mother, his sister, his wife, Alicia Patterson, Dorothy Fosdick, Mary Lasker, philanthropist and widow of Albert D. Lasker, Marietta Tree. He developed a close relationship with Mary Lasker in the fifties. She contributed heavily to his political projects, entertained him and his friends in her beautiful town house on Beekman Place and her country house. Benton once remarked that Stevenson "had a thing" about rich women. He estimated that Mary Lasker, Ruth Field, and Agnes Meyer alone gave Stevenson a million dollars for his political campaigns, probably an exaggeration. Once at a Democratic dinner Mrs. Ives told Stevenson to be nice to Mrs. Lasker, who had said to Mrs. Ives that Stevenson was rude. After the dinner he hailed Mrs. Lasker and asked her for a ride home—then at the last minute invited a newspaperwoman to come along.

Time and again Stevenson seemed a puzzling, contradictory man. When he first arrived in Chicago as a young man he gave the impression of coming from a family with more money than it had. Later as a national figure he read far less than his intellectual admirers thought. One recalls his father, with his promoter's flair and grandiose projects. Each Christmas during his last years Stevenson would telephone Mary Lasker, Mrs. Roosevelt, a dozen others to wish them Merry Christmas. He was ebullient at such times. One wonders if, lonely, he was using them as a substitute family. When one walks in the cemetery at Bloomington, one thinks of Spoon River—behind the friendliness of the town, its cruelty; behind the façade of respectability and success, secret acrimony and misery. He had early escaped the small town's cruelty. He could never entirely escape the bitterness and bickering of his childhood family life.

8.

The historian's task is nearly impossible in an electronic age. (Perhaps it always was.) He cannot know, for example, what was said on the telephone between Stevenson and Lyndon Johnson, two inveterate telephone users, at the end of 1952 and the start of 1953. He has only scraps of documentary evidence, supplemented by interviews; and politicians commit few of their innermost thoughts to paper, and their memories are notoriously inaccurate. It is therefore impossible to put together each piece of the mosaic encompassing Stevenson's position in the party of 1953 and during ensuing years. Only the broad outlines can be sketched.

Any change in the national administration is momentous. When the change is from one party to the other, it is for the outgoing party cataclysmic. Now in 1953 the Democratic Party was obliged to assume a role unfamiliar since the time of Hoover: opposition. How it played that role, and who led it, would determine not only the party's future but, to a considerable extent, the country's.

The Democrats had lost control of both houses. The Republicans had a

48 to 47 majority in the Senate; they had a 221 to 213 majority in the House. (There was one independent in each house.) When the parties caucused January 2, the Taft wing won control of the Republican majority in both houses, with Taft himself the Republican leader in the Senate. And among the Democrats, too, the conservative wing, heavily Southern, took control. In the House, Sam Rayburn became Democratic floor leader. Another Texan, Senator Lyndon B. Johnson, was elected Democratic leader in the Senate. The East and far West, which for years had supplied the bulk of Democratic votes, were largely unrepresented in the Democratic congressional leadership, just as conservative Midwest Taft Republicans dominated the Republican congressional leadership. Thomas L. Stokes, a columnist, wrote, "The people, including many Democrats, voted for Gen. Eisenhower. What they get in Congress is Senator Taft. Likewise, what might be called the 'Stevenson element' in the Democratic party . . . is much in the minority in Congress so far as power and voice is concerned."

Lyndon B. Johnson was a Senate man. He had come to Washington in 1931, at the age of twenty-three, as an assistant to a Texas Congressman. Appointed Texas state director of the National Youth Administration, he was elected to Congress himself in 1937 on an all-out New Deal platform and became something of a protégé of FDR. He was defeated for the Senate in 1941 but elected to it in 1948 by a margin of 87 votes out of nearly a million cast. It was a controversial election—Jim Wells County, predominantly Mexican-American and run by a banker, at first reported its returns incomplete, then turned in an additional 203 votes, all but one for Johnson. Johnson survived efforts to unseat him and in Washington went on to become majority whip in 1951 and now in 1953 minority leader. Reporters covering Johnson thought he had grown increasingly conservative with the years. He himself was reported to have said, "I'm damned tired of being called a Dixiecrat in Washington and a Communist in Texas." It was—and is—hard to be a liberal from Texas. Johnson had supported Stevenson in the election (as had Rayburn) despite Governor Shivers' defection but he was a close associate of the powerful Southern leader, Senator Russell of Georgia. Johnson had cosponsored the Kerr natural gas bill, voted for the McCarran immigration bill, and voted for the offshore oil bill which Truman had vetoed and Stevenson had denounced. When Johnson was elected minority leader, the New York *Times*'s correspondent wrote, "Mr. Johnson, who is basically a 'regular' Democrat, is expected to form a bridge between the all-out Southern conservatives like Senator Harry F. Byrd of Virginia and the Northern Democrats."

In the House, Sam Rayburn was one of the few powerful Southern politicians who had given Stevenson all-out support and never broken with Truman. He was virtually his own policy committee; whether House Democrats would support Eisenhower would depend almost entirely upon Rayburn.

It seemed clear that Stevenson could have little influence in either house

with Rayburn and Johnson in command. But Johnson, an extremely astute
Senate politician, was aware of the suspicion with which Northern liberal
Democrats eyed him. Accordingly, in organizing the Senate, he persuaded
several Southerners with seniority on important committees to make room
for young Northern liberals, a break with tradition and a characteristic
Johnsonian move in reaching for "consensus." (He made other moves,
too, such as inviting Arthur Schlesinger to Washington and asking why
Northern liberals mistrusted him. After nearly two hours of Johnson's persuasion, Schlesinger came away exhausted and convinced that Johnson
was "more attractive, more subtle, and more formidable" than he had expected.) Walter Lippman had written early in the campaign, "Both [Ei-
senhower and Stevenson] are outsiders. . . . Only one of them, the winner of the election, will be able to hold on to the leadership of his party.
The loser must expect to lose all his power and most of his influence
within the party; he may be lucky to be invited to speak at the 1956 convention. . . . The losing party will be run from Congress by the senior
Senators and Congressmen."

Nonetheless, Stevenson involved himself in the leadership fight in the
Senate. In doing so he aroused the antagonism of Lyndon Johnson. Jim
Rowe, a close associate of Johnson who had done advance work for
Stevenson, told Carl McGowan he was "disturbed" by relations between
Stevenson and Johnson. A few days after the election Rowe's own Sena-
tor, Mike Mansfield, had been the first Northern liberal to swing publicly
to support Johnson as minority leader, Rowe said; this had wrecked the
incipient liberal rebellion against Johnson which was being organized by
Paul Douglas and J. W. Fulbright. "At the moment," Rowe wrote, "Lyndon Johnson is the darling of the Northern liberals because he took care
of them so well. In the process he antagonized a few of the older Southern
Senators but thinks that is only temporary. His purpose is plain. He is attempting to unify the Democratic Party in the Senate to make it an effective instrument on most issues." Rowe said that in recent conversations
Johnson had "made some critical remarks" about Stevenson, and Rowe
asked what the trouble was. Rowe wrote, "So far as I can gather it is this:
while Johnson was putting the finishing touches on his campaign for minority leader, which carried with it the two posts of the Chairman of the
Steering Committee and Chairman of the Policy Committee, Governor
Stevenson telephoned Sam Rayburn, Senator Russell, and Senator Kerr to
suggest the three jobs be split up with different leaders as the Republicans
do. The three men the Governor called are Johnson's closest friends and
mentors and, of course, they immediately reported the phone calls to
Johnson." Johnson thought Stevenson had a poor opinion of Johnson's
ability, Rowe said, and believed Johnson's enemy, Senator Fulbright,
had helped Stevenson form that opinion. Stevenson had asked him
to come to Springfield; Johnson declined. Stevenson planned to confer
with Senators on February 15 in Washington; Johnson said he would ar-

range a committee of "handsome-looking men" to confer with Stevenson, implying Stevenson would have no influence on policy.

Whether Stevenson made the phone calls—they would appear to have been a crude effort to diffuse Johnson's power by appealing to the ambitions of his closest associates—it is impossible to ascertain. In any case the incident bears on the continuing and shifting relationship between Stevenson and Johnson—one that stretched on through the years in the wilderness, the 1960 convention, and Stevenson's tenure as Ambassador under President Johnson.

On January 16, when Johnson made his committee assignments and before Rowe wrote to McGowan, Stevenson had telegraphed Johnson, "Delighted with your success with committee assignments for the Democratic minority. My congratulations on your triumph. Regards." Johnson replied, "I was greatly strengthened by your warm-hearted telegram. I am tackling this job to the best of my abilities in the hope that the bonds which have always united Democrats can be forged even stronger in the future."

The day he sent that telegram, Stevenson went to New York on his way to Barbados. He spent the weekend there with his sister-in-law, Betty Hines, and told reporters he had declined a suggestion that he become Democratic National Chairman. Over the weekend and on Monday, Stevenson attended to his writing contract for the world tour, went on two parties, and had Mayor Clark of Philadelphia to dinner at Mrs. Hines's house to talk politics. Clark was willing to help Steve Mitchell keep control of the party machinery in the hands of Stevenson people and ensure that it was not captured by the South or the big-city machines. This would not be easy in Pennsylvania—Finnegan had said many party leaders opposed Mitchell, and Clark feared an effort to unseat him while Stevenson was gone.

Stevenson left for Barbados shortly before noon on Tuesday, January 20, at almost the very hour that Eisenhower was being inaugurated. At the airport he told reporters, "I have no regrets that it is Ike and not myself. I think Ike probably envies me today." He added, "Seriously, my prayers are very much with General Eisenhower and his associates." Flying with him were Marietta Tree and Jane Dick. Arriving at Barbados, Stevenson told reporters that Eisenhower's inaugural address was "an eloquent and splendid restatement of what have been peaceful purposes and principles of the government and people of the United States for many years." From Barbados, Stevenson told Mrs. Ives that he had "loafed" all his first day and hoped to get to work tomorrow "but I'm fearful that this luxurious and languid place was not contrived for work!" Life for him—he stayed three weeks—was a combination of writing, swimming, and partygoing. The Finletters were there for a time; so were Barry Bingham, the liberal Louisville civic leader and publisher and strong Stevenson supporter, and his wife. Marietta Tree said, "Instead of relaxing, he worked in the pink cottage. He went over the speeches and wrote the introduction. The rest of us would have a rum punch before lunch, but he would refuse and work on the speeches, for the whole three weeks. He went off to play tennis only about twice a week." Once she, Jane Dick, and Stevenson were walking together on a nearby public beach, wearing swimming clothes. "Suddenly he took off his swimming trunks and ran naked into the surf. I was shocked. I ran up to the house to get a big bath towel and take it down to him, so he could use it both to dry himself and cover himself with. He had absolutely no modesty." She recalled another incident at Barbados. "One night Jane got some things for a picnic but Ronnie [Marietta's husband] and I had to go to a dinner party next door. Jane and Adlai and the others ate their picnic out on our terrace. Afterward he and Jane and Eddie Dick crept through the shrubbery and watched us. I think he really had wanted to go to the dinner party. The only reason we hadn't included him was that we thought it would bore him. He was always dying to go where the action was."

Stevenson wrote the introduction to his book of speeches in longhand.[1] It was the closest he ever came to writing an autobiography. He related how wartime Italy had inspired him to go into politics, how later he had been with the United States UN delegation at San Francisco and London and New York, how "some of the Democratic leaders asked me to run for governor" in 1947. "This was a new departure indeed," he wrote. "I had never run for office, had never wanted any, had never been active in city or state politics and knew almost none of the party leaders in Chicago or downstate. Moreover, 1948 didn't look like a very good year for Democrats anywhere. . . . But I accepted. Why? I don't know exactly; perhaps it was because of Father and Grandfather Stevenson and Great-Grandfather Fell who had all served Illinois; perhaps it was restlessness about settling down again after eight feverish years of war and peace; perhaps it was the encouragement of some determined friends; and perhaps the public-opinion poll I saw in Italy had something to do with it."

An English friend wrote to Ronald Tree expressing British irritation with Dulles' prospective European policy (and indicating that Tree might have sounded him out about an Oxford degree for Stevenson). At about

---

[1] The title of the first book was *Major Campaign Speeches of Adlai E. Stevenson, 1952. Call to Greatness* (1954), a collection of Stevenson's Godkin lectures at Harvard, sold about 38,000 copies (plus about 17,500 copies in paperback). *What I Think* (1956) and *Friends and Enemies* (1959) each sold about 15,000. *The New America* (1957), a collection of Stevenson's 1956 campaign speeches and position papers, sold only about 3,500 copies. *Looking Outward* (1963) sold about 15,000. *Putting First Things First* (1960) sold 20,241 copies. Random House published the 1952 speeches and *Putting First Things First;* the rest were published by Harper. In 1953, Stevenson's first full year in private life after the governorship, he reported income of $61,599, of which $38,762 came from investments (including $27,847 from the *Pantagraph*) and $20,178 from *Look.* In 1954 he reported just under $48,000, all from investments.

the same time Arthur Schlesinger, after talks with Bob Tufts of Oberlin (Stevenson's foreign policy adviser in the 1952 campaign) and Henry Kissinger of Harvard, told Stevenson that the Dulles policy was seriously endangering our alliances in Europe and Asia. Joe Alsop, the columnist, Schlesinger wrote, thought he perceived a "preventive war logic" behind the Dulles policy but Tufts put it down to Dulles' "ignorance and stupidity." Schlesinger hoped Stevenson would talk about it in his speech to a Democratic dinner in New York February 14.

Stevenson returned from Barbados to New York on Wednesday, February 11. Reporters asked for comment on a trip Dulles had made to Europe. He said, "I am all for unification of European defenses, but if this is an indication of the commencement of dollar diplomacy, then it is the surest way how not to make friends and influence people." He was asked about the removal of the Seventh Fleet from the Formosa Strait separating Formosa from mainland China. (The Eisenhower administration talked about "unleashing Chiang Kai-shek" by removing the fleet.) He said, "I don't know what it means. . . . I only hope it doesn't mean it will uncover Formosa to invasion by the Chinese Communists." He announced a partial itinerary for his world tour and said he would be accompanied by Bill Blair, Barry Bingham, Bill Attwood of *Look,* and Professor Walter Johnson of the University of Chicago.

On Saturday party leaders from the eleven Eastern states giving the dinner met at the Waldorf with Stevenson and Mitchell. The Waldorf ballroom was crowded that night with 1,700 politicians and Volunteers. They heard brief speeches by Margaret Truman, Averell Harriman, Sam Rayburn, Lyndon Johnson, and Herbert Lehman and saw Mrs. Roosevelt introduced as "the first lady of the free world." Stevenson delivered the major address. He said:

"I have questioned my qualifications to be speaking here this evening. My most recent distinction, after all, is the dubious one of being the first Democrat defeated since Al Smith twenty-four years ago. But I derive some personal satisfaction out of being associated with Al Smith—even in misfortune! And, while I make no prediction, I would remind you that the Democratic Party made a very rapid recovery after the disastrous election of 1928." He was gratified that there had been no recriminations over his defeat. He talked about the role of the opposition:

"We shall fight them to the end when we think they are wrong. But our central purpose, our guiding light, must be something different: it must be to keep on working positively and constructively for the good of the country. Of course, it is easier to express these lofty sentiments than to practice them. Undoubtedly we will have our partisan moments. But let us never be content merely to oppose; let us always propose something better. . .
But we wear in common the seamless garment of love of country. The government is our government as well as theirs.

"May I say, then, that we wish President Eisenhower, his official family,

and the Congress, Godspeed in the awful trial they face. Our prayers go
with them in the dark, evil-haunted night they must traverse, confronted
with an enemy whose massive power is matched only by its malevolent
purpose."

He praised Rayburn and Johnson, then said: "But the Congress will not
be the only place where the Democrats write their record. Democrats hold
many offices in states and cities—and we are going to hold many more, I
will add, a couple of years from now." The party must offer good candidates, good programs, good organization at every level. Last fall men and
women took part in a campaign who had never before been active in politics. "These people are the new blood of our political life. We need them.
And to keep them we must have programs and candidates which will command their active allegiance." The Republican Party was attempting something not tried for a long time—government by businessmen. It deserved a
fair test. It faced its test under favorable conditions owing to prosperity
the Democrats had created. "But history warns us, I think, that government by a single group, no matter how high-minded and patriotic it may
be, exposes government to genuine dangers. There is always the tendency
to mistake the particular interest for the general interest—to suppose, in
the immortal thought recently uttered before a committee of Congress,
that what is good for General Motors is good for the country." Thus early
did he make a major issue for 1954 and 1956.

And another—European policy. He spoke of Soviet ambition, then
said:

"The last thing we want, I would suppose, is to stand alone against this
threat. . . . Our allies share with us not only bases and raw materials and
manpower but—more important—the common faith in the worth of free
men which is our most potent weapon. We need them as they need
us. . . .

"I hope I have misread the signs of the revival of the discredited 'dollar
diplomacy.' I hope we are forging no silver chains. We have heard much
about the new 'Psychological' offensive; but we will frighten no Russians
by threatening financial sanctions against our allies. . . . A genuine partnership operates through consultation and persuasion. There is no room in
it for the Big Stick or the ultimatum, be it a small or medium ultimatum,
or the large economy size. Ours must be the role of the good neighbor, the
good partner, the good friend—never the big bully."

He declared the Democratic faith: "We cannot enlist the support of ordinary people abroad if we do not trust them at home." And the liberal
faith: "Our farms and factories may give us our living. But the Bill of
Rights gives us our life. Whoever lays rough hands upon it lays rough
hands on you and me. . . . Only a government which fights for civil liberties and equal rights for its own people can stand for freedom in the rest of
the world. Only a people who can achieve the moral mastery of themselves
can hope to win the moral leadership of others."

Schlesinger and Dave Bell had contributed to the speech. It was a success. It moved Gould Lincoln of the Washington *Star* to write, "Adlai Stevenson has taken up the load of the minority party leadership" and "if the [1956] party nomination were set for tomorrow . . . Stevenson would undoubtedly be the overwhelming choice." The Governor of Rhode Island was "deeply impressed." Truman called it a "great speech" and said he was "more than happy" that Stevenson was assuming party leadership. He added that his daughter Margaret "thought it was about the best she had ever heard and she was talking to her Dad when she said that." It raised $274,000. Scotty Reston of the New York *Times* criticized Stevenson for attacking Dulles too soon; George Ball took Reston to task.

At President Eisenhower's first press conference on February 17, he was asked if he shared Stevenson's fear that "your Administration might become a 'Big Deal,' because of the businessmen you have appointed to office." He replied, "Do you?" Then he said, "Look—let me make myself clear, and I don't mean to brush off a question that easily. First of all, I am not going to engage in any semantics that are directed toward gaining fancied political advantage. I haven't time. What I should like to point out is this: I have lived with the American people. I have lived very intimately with those people, these youngsters, that we have sent out to fight our battles. I can't conceive of having to answer the accusation that I am not concerned with 158 million Americans." Then he said that if savings were to be made at the Defense Department "businesslike practices" were needed, and he had deliberately appointed the men who had made "the biggest record for efficiency in business," but in other departments he had paid no attention to whether or not his appointees were in business.

After the speech Stevenson left New York for Washington by train, arriving about eight-twenty on Sunday morning. (He noted on his schedule, "Came from N.Y.C. on private car." He told Marietta Tree and her husband that he had gone to Washington "by special train." Stevenson to the end retained this somewhat touching and boyish pride in the perquisites of power.) His three days—Sunday, February 15, through Tuesday, February 17—were hectic. About thirty admirers gathered in a drizzle at Union Station outside his private car. He did not appear. After a time a railroad official said he wasn't up yet. They groaned and, after about forty minutes, began chanting "We want Adlai—badly." He came out, said a few words to them, and went back. Inside the car he was having breakfast with Senator Johnson, Sam Rayburn, Senator Kerr, Averell Harriman, and others. Afterward he and Blair called on the Ambassadors of several countries they intended to visit, had lunch at Rayburn's residence with the House Democratic leadership, and went to a reception at the Women's National Democratic Club given by Steve Mitchell and his wife for Democratic members of the Senate and House. Stevenson told reporters he had been invited to the White House and he would not run for Paul Douglas' Senate seat in 1954—"I wouldn't run against him under any circumstances."

Would he run for anything in 1954? "I might run for cover." How about 1956? "It may not be necessary." That evening Stevenson gave a dinner for Democratic Senate leaders and Mitchell.

Monday's schedule was even more crowded—breakfast for liberal House Democrats, visit to National Committee headquarters, visits to more embassies, visit to the Capitol to see a bust of his grandfather, meeting with Senate Democrats, reception at the Women's National Democratic Club for campaign contributors, another political dinner. A reporter wrote that he had received "the sort of reception on Capitol Hill generally reserved for a presidential winner" and said Republican leaders had joined Democrats in welcoming him to the House and hundreds of legislators and staff aides had lined up to shake his hand. About four hundred greeted him in the caucus room of the old House Office Building, including the Republican Speaker, Joseph Martin, and Stevenson said, "If this sort of Republican courtesy goes on much longer, I won't have a hatchet left." Sam Rayburn stood beside him in the receiving line. When he went to the Senate side, Lyndon Johnson presented him to hundreds who had waited outside the Senate Democratic conference room, and thirty-four of the forty-seven Democratic Senators showed up, the only significant absentees being Daniel, Byrd, and McCarran.

On Tuesday morning Stevenson met with Secretary Dulles and four other high State Department officials for briefings on areas of Asia and Africa he would visit. At midday he went to the White House for a half-hour private talk with President Eisenhower; Eisenhower gave a lunch for him and a score of congressional leaders from both parties. Reporters and photographers met him as he entered and left the White House, and he joked with them and expressed his gratitude to the President—who was "very cordial and courteous and anxious to be of any assistance he could" on Stevenson's world tour. Asked repeatedly whether he would run again, he said, "I think I could just about survive another campaign—but that's not saying I want to." He told Marietta Tree and her husband privately that his talks with Eisenhower had been "uninformative."

Stevenson stayed on an extra day, then flew to Chicago on Wednesday, February 18. On the surface, at least, it had been a triumphal weekend, both in New York and Washington, certainly not the cool reception Rowe had warned that Johnson planned. What the facts were beneath the surface was more difficult to say. Political writers thought the Democratic congressional leaders had made it clear to Stevenson that, while they recognized him as titular head of the party, they would not permit him to make party policy, particularly on such issues as offshore oil and FEPC. One writer said that already Senator Russell was leading an undercover move to get rid of Steve Mitchell. Back in Chicago, Stevenson wrote Truman he had found the Democrats in Washington "in better spirits" than he had expected. He said Mitchell "seems to be winning more confidence and respect as he goes along." He was trying to win Truman's support for Mitchell. And Northern liberal support for him—that same day, he wrote Mayor Clark of Philadelphia, "I was . . . much pleased by your reaction to Steve. There is some objection to him, of course, but I was amazed to find during my three days in Washington such a very wide area of approval and satisfaction, particularly in the Congress. . . . I hope you will keep in close touch with him." A few days later Stevenson had lunch with Mitchell and an appointment with John F. Kennedy. Stevenson feared that if Mitchell was forced out a new national chairman controlled by Southerners and other conservatives might replace him. This hidden struggle for the party chairmanship went on a long time.

After putting his affairs in order, Stevenson went to California on February 26. He spoke that night in Los Angeles at a Jefferson-Jackson Day fund-raising dinner, calling Washington "Homburg Heaven," a reference to the businessmen in the Eisenhower administration. Then, contrary to advice to avoid abrasive issues, he took up offshore oil and warned against giving away "our great public domain." It would be an issue in 1954 and 1956. After the dinner he went to Palm Springs where he rested and dictated letters to various Democratic leaders.

At this time Stevenson and Steve Mitchell were interested in strengthening the party in Illinois while it was out of office. They wanted to make Larry Irvin the paid executive director of the downstate headquarters in Springfield. Stevenson now told Dick Daley, who had been Stevenson's staunch political ally during his governorship and was now the rising power in the Cook County Democratic machine, that he had been "disturbed" to hear from the Illinois state chairman, Jim Ronan, that he was having trouble hiring Irvin. Stevenson presumed the opposition to Irvin came from legislators who really opposed Stevenson, not Irvin. He wrote with feeling of the need to "rehabilitate" the party, improve local leadership, get better candidates, and welcome independents. He strongly urged Irvin's appointment and sent copies of the letter to Irvin, Jim Ronan, and Joe Gill, the caretaker Cook County chairman who had succeeded Jack Arvey. It was all in vain—Ronan's motion before the State Central Committee to hire Irvin was narrowly defeated. Irvin, in fighting for the slating of Sherwood Dixon for Governor when Stevenson left the ticket, had earned the enmity of the John Stelle-Paul Powell faction of downstate spoilsmen and their ally, Eddie Barrett, and it was they who now rejected him. That a few Chicago committeemen defected and also voted against Irvin convinced Irvin that Daley had not given him all-out support (Daley had other fish to fry—he was moving to become Cook County chairman himself and to run for Mayor of Chicago). It was a blow to Stevenson.

From Palm Springs, too, on Sunday night, March 1, Stevenson wrote to Alicia Patterson:

> Dearest—I didn't call you in N.Y. because I wanted to see you at your house or the hotel and no opportunity developed. . . . Barbados

was good, perfect, except I had to work so damn hard to get that
book in shape for Cerf. . . . Then N.Y. & that damn speech with
people coming and going—then Wash & Chicago for a few days and
more of the same—then Los Angeles and still more . . . before leaving San F. tomorrow for my long and weary journey that has gotten
completely out of hand, I'm afraid. I don't know what's happening to
me, but the election didn't seem to open any vistas of serenity. Oh,
what the hell, I want to go to the Black River. . . . God—Lauren
Bacall has just walked in and I'm not even packed with an hour to
plane time. *Please* send me a scrap now and then. . . . Don't worry
about Newsday—I had hoped, of course, but I also understand your
situation vis a vis Harry [Guggenheim, her husband]—and also your
journey thru the valley of the shadow. Let's, for God's sake, not talk
of "friends" that are hard to come by. If you're not that & I'm not
that—and much more—then past [?] 30 years are an ugly blank. But
they aren't! My love—are they?

Be strong, well, happy, tender—A

He had not written to her in that tone for a long time.

On March 2, after a round of parties and public appearances in San
Francisco, Stevenson sailed for the Orient. He would go around the world,
returning to New York August 20.

9.

Two girls, Bertrande Benoist, the daughter of a wealthy Californian,
and Ellen Davies, daughter of the chairman of the board of the steamship
line, were aboard the S.S. *President Wilson.* Ellen Davies helped Stevenson with his correspondence en route to Honolulu. Bertie Benoist, who
was about John Fell's age, remained a friend of Stevenson's for many
years. While Stevenson was en route to Honolulu, Stalin died, and soon the
post-Stalin purge began. It seemed to offer hope of a thaw in the cold war.
The Honolulu *Star Bulletin* solicited Stevenson's views by radiogram; he
replied, "Aloha, weather fine, aloha." From aboard ship Stevenson wrote
to Mrs. Ives: "Its been a restful voyage, even tho I've been at my desk
most of the time trying to clean up the monstrous accumulation of mail
mostly from the west coast where my followers were many and aggressive.
Tomorrow we reach Honolulu and I must step again into the clamor, entertaining and 'appearances.' I'm afraid that will be the case all the way,
but we are determined to do all we can to minimize it." He had been so
busy answering mail that he had had time "for almost none of the preparation & reading I had planned," that is, background reading on countries he
would visit. But then, he never did.

At Honolulu he saw Bud Merwin. (He had asked Merwin to help Larry
Irvin find a job and had complained about the *Pantagraph*'s publishing the

David Lawrence column. Merwin said the editorial committee considered Lawrence better than Lippmann, Childs, or Mowrer.) Stevenson's notes on Honolulu, made in pencil in a little dime-store notebook, were sketchy, beginning: "2 days—Garden spot—smothered in Leis" and giving the menu of a Hawaiian dinner, a few notes on Pearl Harbor, notes on crowded beaches and transportation problems and statehood; names of people he saw, including Admiral Radford, then: "Handshakes, photos, speeches, sun, water. Off—at midnight—'team' PanAm." They stopped at Wake Island, where he noted the "gaunt rusting spectre" of a torpedoed Japanese warship, pillboxes, tanks, burned-out vehicles. The airport was busy because of the huge airlift to Korea. He wrote, "Coral atoll like so many I saw during the war." He was reliving his wartime trip to the Pacific with Knox. Then on to Tokyo, first major stop.

They arrived on March 10 and spent five days in Japan. Hurrying from the airport to the Imperial Hotel and then to the U. S. Embassy, Stevenson managed to scribble a few impressions: "Bicycles, motorcycles, crowded street cars. Takagawa family cemetery Gateway—one of few remaining old Tokyo landmarks. . . . Huge new office bldg—solid black—eight stories . . . inner city and the monstrous Palace grounds." Robert Murphy, the U. S. Ambassador to Japan, and his staff briefed Stevenson and his party on the politics, military establishment, economy, culture, and public opinion of Japan. Stevenson took full notes. He was also briefed on Korea—its military situation, its economy, its politics ("Rhee—ruthless dictator, but hates [Communism]"). His attention appears to have wandered during the briefing; he wrote: "Shrill flute noises of the noodle sellers."

After the briefing Stevenson held a press conference. Reporters asked why he was making this trip. For self-education, he replied, adding that, as a result of circumstances beyond his control last fall, he was unemployed and had a chance to travel. A reporter asked if he thought the death of Stalin would make the Soviets easier to deal with. He thought it would be "dangerous indeed" for the world to expect drastic changes in Soviet rearmament, one of the most sensitive issues in Japan, and he said he thought it imperative to develop strength in the free world but thought the Japanese would "do what is in their own best interest" and hoped "their conclusions coincide with the interests of my country."

In the following days, his companions—Walter Johnson, Bill Attwood, and Barry Bingham—talked to a great many people, fact-finding, and Stevenson did too, sometimes with them, sometimes alone. He called on the Japanese Prime Minister, dined with the Foreign Minister, talked with Japanese government officials and politicians, with embassy people, and with U.S. military leaders. He visited a university, went to Kyoto and Osaka. Everywhere he went to markets. His notebook reads: "Markets— colorful packaging. . . . Octopus—ugly greyish white—come out steaming pink. Grinding up tons of sharks for fish balls; dry skins on top for soup." And: "Enroute Osaka—along the blue sea coast—mountainous down to the water once beyond the plain of Tokyo-Yokahoma. Every speck of land cultivated." Everything interested him—the sights and smells any tourist observes as well as the most momentous information imparted by high officials. Once he roused Walter Johnson and Blair and took them, with a State Department man, to visit a fish market and vegetable market. He wrote to the Dutch Smiths from Kyoto, "My 'team' is fit and well fitted!—and they keep the poor old man hopping. I've 'done' every one but the Emperor and take him on when we get back from Korea. Then to Formosa and on and on. Just when I'll do any writing I hardly see and perhaps I'll end up owing *Look* money—Love Adlai" To Mrs. Ives: "So far so good—altho I'm getting a little tired already. We flew here in Ambassador Murphy's plane after some hectic days in Tokyo. . . . Tomorrow we go to Korea—[General] Mark Clark is sending his plane for me and I have no complaints about the reception I've had here. This is a lovely old city, full of shrines & antiquities, but Tokyo is hideous." One can almost imagine his mother—or his father, or even he himself as a young man traveling—writing such a letter.

While in Tokyo, despite his repeated assertion that he had come to listen and learn, not to speak, Stevenson addressed the Japan-American Society, repeating what he had said previously—Asia was the "area of decision." His party arrived in Korea about 2:30 P.M. on Saturday, March 14. He wrote in his notebook, "[Ambassador] Ellis Briggs. Recep in Pusan. Line of children waving flags—Honor guard." Stevenson was swamped with bouquets and handed them to Johnson and Blair. They motorcaded through Pusan, a port city normally of some 440,000, now swollen by more than a million refugees. Stevenson noted, "Refugee shacks crawling up sides of hills." The dusty streets were lined with school children waving Korean and United States flags, here and there a banner, "Welcome Stevenson." At the embassy Ambassador Briggs and embassy staffers briefed Stevenson and his party. President Syngman Rhee and U.S. aid were all that held Korea together, they said. The United States and Rhee differed on the future of Korea, the United States proposing to bring about a settlement at the 38th parallel, Rhee insisting on a Korea united to the Yalu River lest Communist subversion commence all over again. A military dictatorship might follow Rhee. Briggs discussed the four alternative U.S. policies—pulling out, extending the war, continuing the stalemate, negotiating a settlement. "Should make choice soon," Stevenson noted. "Courage of people phenomenal."

They drove to the Prime Minister's office, where the Prime Minister and Foreign Minister received Stevenson. They took him to meet about thirty members of the National Assembly, and Stevenson spoke briefly. During dinner at the embassy residence the Foreign Minister arrived to bring

Stevenson greetings from President Rhee. After dinner they watched a
program of Korean singing and dancing. On Sunday Stevenson, Blair, and
Bingham visited a UN cemetery, a prison camp, and a training center. On
Monday, March 16, Stevenson's group, Ambassador Briggs, and others flew
to an ROK (Republic of Korea) officer training camp, then went on to
Seoul. There, United Press reported, Stevenson received a "triumphal welcome"—honor guard, band, Korean and U.S. troops, photographers, a
key to the city, a motorcade along streets lined with troops, firemen, children, students, and adults waving flags and holding up banners and signs,
"Welcome Adlai Stevenson," "Drive out the Reds," "Unify Korea."
Stevenson spent about a half hour with President Rhee, who asked for
more U.S. help, both military and economic. They dined that night at
Rhee's home. Throughout the President's conversation ran the threads of
intransigent anti-Communism, suspicion of Japan, and insistence on the
reunification of Korea. After dinner Stevenson and the others spent about
an hour with the press. A Belgian correspondent told Stevenson, "Everyone in Belgium voted for you." Stevenson said, "Thank you. I carried
India too. I think I carried all the places I didn't visit during the campaign.
The trouble is—they don't count those precincts."

Next day, March 17, they left Seoul and flew in four small planes to the
1st Marine Division near the front. General Maxwell D. Taylor was with
Stevenson. They went by helicopter to the command headquarters of the
2nd Infantry Division, then up to the 38th Regiment of the 2nd Infantry
at the front. Wearing flak vests and helmets, they moved up slowly on foot
through trenches to the front line. From a hilltop they could see the Chinese positions, about a thousand yards away. Early that morning the Chinese had attacked, breaking into the main Allied line at Little Gibraltar
Hill. Allied troops had beaten them back in hand-to-hand fighting in the
trenches, a seven-and-a-half-hour battle, the longest and sharpest of the
year, according to the press. Stevenson had been scheduled to visit Little
Gibraltar Hill; the Chinese attack prevented it. But he was close enough:
while he was having lunch in a virtually shellproof bunker, two Chinese
mortar shells landed about three hundred yards away, and soon after that,
on General Taylor's orders, he and the others went back.

Back in Seoul, he attended a cocktail party given by the Mayor of Seoul
and dined with General Taylor. He remarked that Eisenhower had put
himself in an impossible position by, in effect, promising a quick end to
the war; Taylor nodded agreement, according to Johnson. Stevenson
asked what the cost would be if we attacked. Taylor said the ROK troops
were excellent but incapable of attacking because they lacked mobility.
The Fifth Army could not attack alone. Mobilization at home would be
required. More air power and amphibious equipment and—according to
Johnson's notes—atomic weapons would be needed. This could drive the
Communists back to the Yalu; after that no one could predict what would

happen. About a million Chinese were in Korea now; it would be easier to wipe them out here than if they were scattered all over China. Taylor thought Russia probably wanted to continue the stalemate—it was weakening the United States.

Next day Stevenson had lunch aboard the aircraft carrier *Oriskany,* where, while fighter planes were taking off about every thirty seconds, Admiral Joseph J. Clark urged the MacArthur view of Korea—"there's no substitute in war for victory"—while Taylor and other high Army and Navy officers sat silent. A sailor told Stevenson he had worked hard for him in California during the campaign and said, "We'll do it next time." Stevenson said, "Once is enough."

Stevenson flew back to Japan and on March 19 borrowed a formal morning suit for an audience with the Emperor. Afterward he told the press only that they had had a "most interesting talk" about Korea and Japanese-American relations for about thirty-five minutes. After miscellaneous festivities and a press conference he left for Formosa, where once again large crowds and high officials greeted him and where he announced to the throng that he was not campaigning. Ambassador K. L. Rankin took them to the government guesthouse, then to the embassy for a briefing. Then Stevenson and his party, accompanied by the Ambassador, called on Generalissimo Chiang Kai-shek (though the interpreter referred to Chiang as "the President"). Stevenson himself made few notes at the meeting—his notebook shows only: "Meeting with Chiang—eyes—direct —Jasmine tea—fragrant. Prime minister—eyes—frail—not old. Trying to correct errors on mainland." Walter Johnson dictated a fuller account: Chiang strongly urged U.S. support and leadership of an all-out amphibious landing on the mainland to drive the Communist regime from power.

They spent next morning, March 21, studying the work of the Mutual Security Administration, AID's forerunner; and Stevenson began taking full notes again on health, education, and agricultural programs, and on their political implications. After long briefings he went on a field trip to inspect various projects of the Joint Commission on Rural Reconstruction. Moving around the city and its environs, Stevenson made random notes: "No beggars—higher standard of living than Japan. Women do manual labor just like men. . . . Chinese most practical people on earth. . . . Many Russians in Peiping but less conspicuous than Americans always are—keep out of sight. Even in Europe."

Stevenson, at a press conference, praised the Chiang regime's "splendid" progress in recent years and said Formosa was "an essential part" of the free world's Pacific defense. He went with his party to dinner at Chiang's house, together with high Chinese and American officials. After dinner Chiang invited Stevenson to move to a private room with Ambassador Rankin, Foreign Minister George K. L. Yeh, and Barry Bingham. They talked for about an hour and a quarter. Bingham made notes of the conversation. Stevenson began by saying that America and Free China shared the objective of controlling Communist aggressive power and asked Chiang's opinion on how it might be done, taking into account America's world-wide commitments, both military and economic. Chiang replied that the only way to destroy Communist power was to attack it at its roots. This meant an attack on mainland China, coordinated with increased military pressure in Korea and Indochina and backed by U.S. force.

Stevenson asked why Communism had established a grip on the agrarian Chinese masses, whose traditions were opposed to Communist tenets. Chiang replied that the Chinese people still had not generally accepted Communism and would not so long as a beacon shone from Formosa. The danger was among the young: Chinese over thirty would never accept Communism. Stevenson pursued the question—said he assumed that Communism appealed to the Asiatic masses by promising material benefits, land reform, nationalism, and an escape from colonialism. Chiang replied that Stevenson and other Westerners were wrong. Communism's appeal had been political, not economic. The Chinese were the easiest people in the world to satisfy economically. All they wanted was something to eat. Political force, "a naked power play," had captured China. Communism in China had pretended to support the tenets of democracy, then had undermined efforts by the Nationalist government to institute democratic reforms.

Stevenson asked how long Chiang could retain the effectiveness of his army, which was growing old on Formosa. Not more than three years, Chiang replied. Every year that passed made it more difficult to rally resistance on the mainland—the Communists were systematically destroying all opposition. Stevenson remarked that one cannot kill Communism with bullets and that it was necessary to release men's minds as well as their bodies from slavery. Chiang declared that Communism must be fought with bullets first. Stevenson mentioned the Communist problem in Indochina, Thailand, Malaya, Indonesia, Burma. Chiang replied that the only solution was to strike the central force on the Chinese mainland, since all Asian Communist movements were directed by Mao Tse-tung. Repeatedly Chiang sought to learn how much support he had in the Democratic Party. Stevenson evaded.

Late that night a Chinese general went to the guesthouse in secret and, appearing frightened, told Stevenson in strict confidence that Chiang was a ruthless dictator who suppressed thought with his secret police. Next day Stevenson, without revealing his source, told Ambassador Rankin he had heard rumors about the secret police. Rankin said he was not particularly disturbed about it (according to Johnson).

After praising Chiang to the press and saying he had been "much impressed" by what he had seen, Stevenson left for Hong Kong.

10.

From Hong Kong he mailed a postcard to Alicia Patterson: "I've finished Japan, Korea & Formosa & they've almost finished me. A couple of days here with the enemy just over the hills and on we go. Korea was better in a way than I expected, Japan worse, and Formosa—?? Hong Kong of course is heaven on a powder keg." On a later postcard he told her Hong Kong "fascinated & enchanted me as no place else in this teeming troubled part of the world." He also sent a postcard to Tom Matthews, editor of *Time:* "How does one express coherent, orderly, confident views about this vast, tortured, teeming, frightened segment of our world. Anyway I've got to and soon—if superficially to earn my fare—and with a mind full of mush how I dread it!" He told Ernest Ives from Hong Kong that he had seen Ives's son Tim in Tokyo and found him "in fine form." He enclosed some stamps for Buffie. He bought clothing, toured Hong Kong, and paused at the Lo Wu bridge to watch travelers cross to and from mainland China. Chinese border guards photographed him. Hong Kong, he thought, must be held although infiltrated with agents and vulnerable to saboteurs. He made detailed notes on smuggling and on free world shipping. He recorded Hong Kong gossip about conditions inside mainland China—China was struggling to industrialize, it was overcrowded and its people untrained, it lacked unity but nevertheless the Communist government was the first in many years that had been able to enforce its authority in all of China, and it was dangerous to think that most Chinese would rise to an invasion.

On to the Philippines and a dinner on March 26 given in Stevenson's honor by U. S. Ambassador Raymond A. Spruance. The embassy had prepared a long list of invitations and requests for interviews it had received for Stevenson. He avoided everything possible: he had to get started on his first article for *Look*. He went to Baguio, the summer capital, to work on it. It dealt with Japan, Korea, Chiang Kai-shek, and Hong Kong. (Attwood helped with the writing and editing on the trip, sometimes giving Stevenson preliminary outlines or partial drafts, sometimes cutting Stevenson's drafts. He thought Stevenson's writing ability better suited to speeches than reportage.)

On Monday, March 30, Stevenson and the others left Manila by plane for Singapore, which was only a stopover; he continued on to Saigon, arriving Wednesday, April 1. En route he wrote to Jane Dick: ". . . now somewhere over the China Sea en route to Saigon—and the Indo China War. It's just one war after another here. The pace has been too fast and I haven't felt well—to bed last night at 12 (after writing 23 letters of thanks to people along our route) and up this morning at 5—officials, functions, heat, interviewing, writing, packing, unpacking, and the ubiquitous photog-

raphers and newsmen, day after day. Besides, I'm afflicted with a misfortune too embarrassing to mention! I wish I could write you a proper letter.
I've spent every moment of spare time trying to do the first of the damn
Look pieces and after writing some eight thousand words finally got a
superficial newspaper-like thing off from Manila of 4000–5000 more than
their maximum. It's maddening—but it may not be as hard again, trying
to squeeze Korea, Japan & Formosa in one tiny piece when I had enough
material gathered for a book on each. . . . The high point for comfort
was Hong Kong—an exquisite house to ourselves—11 servants—the best
food of the orient—and a soul stirring view of placid quiet sea, junks and
sampans gliding slowly over the water, tumultuous green islands—it was
breathless even leaning against the bamboo curtain, but I hardly got to
look at it what with the work." At Saigon he found a cable from *Look*
asking him to rewrite the piece he had sent from Manila because of "armistice possibility," presumably in Korea. He told Jane Dick, "I could cry
and I think I will."

11.

He had been met at the Saigon airport by French, Vietnamese, and U.S.
officials led by an old friend, Robert McClintock, U.S. chargé d'affaires,
in the absence of the Ambassador. At the embassy briefing the political
officer said that half the 22 million people of Vietnam were under control
of the Viet Minh (later called Viet Cong). Kings reigned in Cambodia
and Laos, Bao Dai in Vietnam with French support. The ordinary people
refused to support either their own governments or that of Ho Chi Minh.
Nationalism was strong. The three governments resented the continuation
of French control. The United States wanted the French to continue
their military efforts but at the same time wanted the three states to
become self-reliant. McClintock emphasized that the war was as much
political as military.

The military attaché said the war lacked a front and was "partly" a civil
war. Guerrillas controlled the southern delta, the central plateau, and
about half the villages in the Red River delta around Hanoi, all behind the
line of fortifications built by the French. Although the French and Vietnamese forces controlled many villages in the Red River delta by day, the
Viet Minh moved in at night. The French had about 225,000 troops here.
The Viet Minh were better organized than the French. French strategy
was static—they manned outposts, bridges, waterways, and towns. The
Viet Minh were mobile—and they were extending their control by means
of propaganda and terrorism. The Chinese were supplying the Viet Minh
with equipment. The Viet Minh had no armor, no air force, and no real
navy. Their propaganda was basically anti-French, though it included anti-
Americanism. The French used planes to supply their outposts, bomb sup-

ply routes, and give close support to ground troops. But the jungle was so heavy and the mountains so high it was hard to know whether the bombing was effective. Nearly all of it might have been said fifteen years later and more.

On Tuesday, Stevenson, Blair, and Bingham, accompanied by McClintock, the chargé, flew to Da Lat to have lunch with His Majesty Bao Dai and other Vietnamese. It was, McClintock reported, a "long and rambling" conversation. In it, Bao Dai gave Stevenson his version of the development of Ho Chi Minh and the Viet Minh. Stevenson repeatedly asked what sustained the Viet Minh in their desperate warfare against the French and Vietnamese. A professional courtier replied that, throughout all Vietnam, Bao Dai was revered as the father of his people. Stevenson and McClintock were skeptical—skeptical too when Bao Dai insisted that everyone in Viet Minh-occupied zones supported the Viet Minh only at bayonet point. Stevenson asked about elections for a national assembly. Bao Dai first said this was useless since half his country was in enemy hands, then said without enthusiasm that eventually a national assembly would come. He failed to respond to suggestions that Vietnamese troops' morale might improve if he were to assume personal command. He said nothing about the fact that about a third of the equipment being brought into his country was American. McClintock thought him eager for the ease of exile in southern France.

Stevenson sent a postcard to Ruth Winter in Lake Forest: "And now we're in burning Saigon in the midst of the strangest war in modern history. The enemy is everywhere, in front, behind, alongside—perhaps in the house. Possibly we see here the shape of things to come if there should be a new world war with communism."

The United States had a consulate at Hanoi at that time, and Stevenson had lunch there with the American consul, Paul Sturm. Sturm said northern Vietnam was the center of Vietnamese nationalism. At the end of World War II, Chiang had sent troops to occupy Hanoi and organize opposition to Ho; but Ho, the wartime guerrilla hero against the Japanese, had been strengthened by Chiang's hostility, since the Chinese were the traditional enemies of Vietnam. The Chinese Nationalists had left in April of 1946 and in December Ho had slaughtered some 3,200 Frenchmen in Hanoi. The French had counterattacked, killing about 10,000 Vietnamese, and the war was on. The French still held Hanoi, though they had almost lost it to the Viet Minh in 1950. Someone remarked that to win this kind of war it was necessary to win over the people. Stevenson agreed and said that the French were fighting the wrong kind of war. They did not trust the Vietnamese troops. Until the Vietnamese soldier was convinced he was fighting for his home and his life, he would not fight well.

In the afternoon Stevenson, Blair, and the consul went to see Governor Tri. He told Stevenson that the militia, though underpaid and ill armed, had fought well in repelling a Viet Minh attack because they knew the territory and felt their own homes were at stake. He thought propaganda should try to identify the Viet Minh with the Chinese and with international Communism. Unfortunately, he said, the Vietnam government was considered an "emanation" of the French. People mistrusted it. The French should permit Bao Dai to organize a true national government. But the French were reluctant. Paris was out of touch. The Vietnam government must realize the war was essentially political, a contest for the people's loyalty, and that to win the Vietnam government must protect the people from the Viet Minh.

On Easter Sunday, April 5, Stevenson's party flew 450 miles to an airstrip at Siem Reap in Cambodia and visited the ruins at Angkor Wat. Stevenson told Jane Dick, "A large old gal was waiting at the gates, camera in hand—'I used to live in Danville; I've been waiting for you. I was going to use my last film on a water buffalo, but I've saved it for you!'" Then they flew on to Phnom Penh, capital of Cambodia, to dine at the palace.

Next day, after a briefing on Cambodia, Stevenson went back to Saigon. There a military officer told him that Vietnam's basic problem was to win the allegiance of the Vietnamese people. The French could not do it until they "signed a public statement" that they would leave Vietnam when the military situation was safe. Vietnamese soldiers got only two hours of indoctrination out of nine months of training; half the Viet Minh training was political. The Viet Minh believed that shooting a rifle was secondary to controlling a mind. French businessmen were making good profits and so did not want the war to end immediately. The new Vietnamese Army must be trained for greater responsibility, but the French refused to train Vietnamese for high officer leadership or for guerrilla warfare—they might turn on the French. The French did not take the offensive themselves for fear of serious political repercussions back home. They did not want the United States to interfere yet did not themselves know how to wage this strange war. A French commander told Stevenson that this war would set the pattern for future wars, with the enemy behind you and around you.

That evening, after an embassy reception, Stevenson and the AP correspondent in Saigon, Larry Allen, walked along the docks in front of the Hotel Majestic, where people were living under the docks and eating on the sidewalk. Like everyone else, Allen emphasized that the French could not win this war without the support of the Vietnamese people, and so far they didn't have it. Probably eighty per cent of the people preferred Ho Chi Minh to the present government or the French. The Vietnamese had no will to fight, no leadership. Bao Dai was remote from the people; Ho was close. The Viet Minh probably could not win either because of foreign support for the government. No one thanked the United States for its material aid, much of which was stolen. French soldiers even said they were tired of fighting America's wars. This was a hopeless war, a war without end, unless the Vietnamese people supported it. It was already seven years old and still without hope of victory for either side.

Stevenson spent most of Tuesday, April 7, working on his next *Look* article, taking time out to tell Jane Dick: "It's all very strange—hard to understand, harder to explain. The enemy is all around—in front, in back, along side. The French Governor in Cambodia was stabbed to death by a servant—the enemy—in his house the other day . . . . fascinating & elusive —what to do, how to do it . . . a civil war in which both sides are backed from the outside—Viet Minh by Red China, Viet Nam by France and the U.S., but there seems to be little heart for the war among the natives on our side—just why isn't too clear, nationalism, anti French, no understanding of Communism, no leadership by the little Emperor Bao Dai— with whom I spent a long time without a word of thanks to U.S. etc etc."

On April 8, Stevenson left Saigon for Indonesia. In view of what Stevenson learned about Indochina—and the United States Government knew more—it is all the more remarkable that the United States persisted there through the 1960s and early 1970s. The answer seems to lie in something Stevenson wrote in that second magazine piece:

"From a look at the map, we can readily see why Indochina must be held. The rice-rich associated states are the strategic gateway to all of Southeast Asia.

"If Viet-Nam falls, all of Indochina is doomed; Thailand and Burma would be in mortal danger; Malaya and Indonesia would be exposed and vulnerable. If this vast area of the world, with its 175,000,000 people, its tin, rubber, minerals and oil, is absorbed into the Moscow-Peking empire, the still vaster nations of India and Pakistan would quickly lose any freedom of action. All Asia would slide behind the Iron Curtain." Thus did Stevenson anticipate Eisenhower's domino theory.

12.

When he arrived at Djakarta April 9, he was met by Chester Bowles, who was being replaced as Ambassador to India by an Eisenhower man and had gone to Djakarta on a farewell tour through Asia. Bowles told Stevenson that Russia's economic penetration into Asia was beginning to tell. Russia had recently told Ceylon she would pay thirty-two per cent more than anyone else for Ceylon's rubber and would sell her rice below the world market. Was the United States ready for a trade offensive? At about this same time—Stalin had died, the Kremlin was restless— Schlesinger wrote to Stevenson from Harvard, "We are all currently baffled and astonished by recent Soviet developments. The best opinion around here is that this represents as basic a shift in Soviet tactics as in 1945, or 1941, or 1939, or 1935 (but not, of course, a shift in Soviet strategy)." Perhaps younger men in the Kremlin felt that Stalin had been pursuing an aggressive policy which united the West and sped its rearmament, thereby warding off depression; it was time to take a softer line. Right-wing Republicans were seizing this excuse to cut the defense budget and foreign aid. The views of both Bowles and Schlesinger found their way into Stevenson's writings and speeches. Later, after Stevenson's first two *Look* articles appeared, Bowles congratulated him and reported that Stevenson's press back home had been "generally excellent." Eisenhower was shockingly ignorant of Asia, Bowles said; he seemed to think he could, by tolerance and compromise, unite the Republican Party; and to think that if he gave McCarthy enough rope he would hang himself. But McCarthy's strength had increased. "You have a very big job waiting for you in this country, Adlai." The Democratic Party was "uncertain and frustrated"; Stevenson must revitalize it. How often that phrase appeared before and since.

After an embassy briefing—in poor, backward Indonesia, nobody knew how strong the Communists were but feared the worst—Stevenson called on President Sukarno, who told him that Indonesia was preoccupied with West Irian, the portion of New Guinea claimed from the Dutch by Indonesia, and said that if the United States would recognize that claim it would earn Indonesia's undying gratitude. Stevenson regarded this as blackmail. Sukarno compared Indonesia's revolution with America's. He said that the PNI, the principal nationalist party, and the Moslem party would come out about equal in a free election, that trade unions were developing free of Communist control, that after the war with the Dutch many veterans could find no jobs so had taken up arms and gone to the jungle to fight the government as guerrillas. The recent drop in rubber and tin prices had badly hurt Indonesia's economy. He had fought the Communists in 1948. Now Chinese Communists were infiltrating the country but posed no serious threat. Indonesia would have elections for a constituent assembly this year. Her economic problems could be solved by resettlement, but it would take a long time. Meanwhile the Communists were gaining strength among the urban unemployed, while nationalist guerrillas roamed the hinterland. Sukarno wanted economic assistance from the United States.

Stevenson had lunch with the Foreign Minister and the Finance Minister. The Finance Minister, educated at The Hague, told him his troubles —resistance to austerity, corruption, little economic literacy. Stevenson noted, "Extraordinary ignorance about US. Newspaper editor who said our soldiers were so well paid everyone wanted to go in army. General impression of bottomless wealth in US.—money with no strings. . . . Friendly, cheerful, delightful people. No thanks as usual."

After lunch Stevenson went to the home of a leading newspaper publisher who said that if he were an American he would shut down America's synthetic rubber plants. Stevenson explained they were needed for national defense. An editor of the newspaper said bluntly that the Indonesians did not want to get involved in the Soviet-American cold war, wanted instead to pursue their struggle for independence. The publisher asked what America's objectives were in Asia. Stevenson said that America wanted Asia to be independent. Previously, he went on, the threat to Asiatic independence had been colonialism; now it was Communism. The United States wanted nothing here save peace and freedom for Asians. The publisher said Asia had to live on its raw material exports, he hoped the United States would buy Indonesian exports, and he preferred trade, not aid. (That last would become a theme of Stevenson's 1956 campaign.)

Stevenson responded with "quite an eloquent five-minute statement," Walter Johnson noted, saying the danger was not that Americans wanted to run the world but, rather, that they would refuse further aid and retreat to isolationism unless the peoples of such countries as Indonesia did something for themselves. He said the United States was spending money to try to help Indonesians and others "get on your feet." It was not enough, the publisher said.

Next day Stevenson went touring. His notes read: "Country infested with [Communist] hamlets in large areas. Many ex-soldiers of revolution —discontented, no jobs. Some Dutch think difficulties will overwhelm & Indo will drop back in their laps. Forlorn hope." He wrote that "great volcanic peaks march in row down the center of Java. . . . Great Plume of white smoke rose vertically from the cone of Merad [Merapi?]—rising 10,000 feet above Jogjakarta. Rice paddies climb high up the sides of the green mountains to waste none of the rich volcanic soil. . . . Cloud of bicycles, horse drawn carts, rickshaws & horses. 'Horses'—size of ponies. . . . Woven bamboo houses." He visited a monastery whose records went back to the fourth or fifth century and visited a peaceful town inhabited by Buddhists, Moslems, Christians, and animists.

Back in Djakarta, Stevenson talked to more government officials and Indonesian politicians. He concluded privately that if democracy could work here it could work anywhere. But he did not say so publicly—instead, when he held a farewell press conference on April 13, he praised Indonesia as the only Asiatic nation to win independence through revolution and to maintain it by suppressing a Communist coup d'état. He found disturbing Indonesians' ignorance about the United States and he explained U.S. purpose. He and his party left Djakarta about 11 A.M. and arrived at Singapore about 1 P.M.

They stayed at the Ocean Park Hotel and that night had dinner at the home of the Right Honorable Malcolm MacDonald, Commissioner General for the United Kingdom in Southeast Asia, impressive and well informed, and their conversation ranged widely.

On April 14, Stevenson and his companions left Singapore at 8:15 A.M. aboard a U. S. Air Force DC-3 for Kuala Lumpur, capital of the federation of Malaya. They flew over thick jungle along the Malacca Straits, over heavily timbered mountains, over tin mines. Stevenson stayed with the High Commissioner, General Sir Gerald Templer, and for an hour and a half Templer told him about Malaya.

Communists had been here before World War II, their roots in China and Russia, but they had done little. Then had come the Japanese, a savage occupation. The Chinese had gone into the jungle and built private armies, the best Communist-controlled, and, together with the British, carried on guerrilla warfare against the Japanese. When the war ended the Communists felt they had liberated Malaya, and so when the British returned in 1945 the Malayan Communists fought them. They seized control of labor unions but could do no more, and in June of 1948 they fled to the jungle to commence guerrilla war against the British.

At that time the police were only 7,000 strong; they and the tin mine operators and rubber planters bore the brunt of terror for several months. The guerrillas were well armed; the British had given them weapons to fight the Japanese. Today there were between 4,000 and 6,000 guerrillas. Probably ten per cent were well-trained Communist leaders, irreplaceable, principal targets of the British. About forty per cent were thugs, forty per cent fugitives from justice, and ten per cent were teen-age boys and girls. Only about 350 terrorists came into contact with British forces in a month. The rest were seeking food. The British would win by controlling the food supply. Four fifths of Malaya was jungle, trees two hundred feet tall, like a cathedral at night, and food would not grow under such trees; the terrorists made clearings to grow tapioca, and the British spotted the clearings and bombed them. The guerrillas were not succeeding, partly because they terrorized people friendly to the British. Guerrilla morale was sagging. The British were using airborne loudspeakers over the jungle. They were handicapped by not really knowing what jungle people thought. Why had they gone to the jungle in the first place? Why did some come out?

It was a frustrating war. The terror had been worst from 1948 to 1950. Witnesses dared not testify against terrorists, fearing reprisal, so the British had resorted to arrest on suspicion and to concentration camps. This year the number in concentration camps had been reduced from 9,000 to 3,000. Some had gone back to normal civilian life, some to life restricted to their villages, some to rehabilitation centers, and some to the jungle to fight their former comrades. In recent months the government had been resettling a half million squatters and deporting thousands to mainland China. It was a secret and nasty business but the government wanted to get rid of the hard-core Communists without killing them. Now and then the police arrested Communist agents who had entered Malaya illegally from China. Sometimes when British troops closed in on Communists near the Siamese border the Communists simply walked across it into sanctuary, then, when the British left, returned—"a damned nuisance," Templer said.

Stevenson wrote to Mrs. Ives on stationery reading, "King's House,

Kuala Lumpur, Malaya": "Staying with General Templer in this boiling capital of Malaya—but in spite of war and worries life goes on in the elegant routine of great British houses. . . . Have had to work too hard on this journey—we planned too much too quick and the magazine writing—in such superficial and condensed form—irks me no end." He added, "I think now that I will go to Austria & Yugoslavia after Italy—the news value—places."

On Wednesday, April 15, Stevenson and his party went on a long tour of Malaya, traveling in four cars with two scout cars mounting twin Bren guns. They visited a state housing development, a tin mine and refinery, a rubber plantation where they had lunch, a resettlement village and agricultural experiment station, a leper hospital where they had tea, and an aborigine village where Stevenson was given a blowpipe and arrows—he declined to try it out, saying he would not shoot until he saw a Republican. Next day they left the airport at 9 A.M. in two helicopters for Ulu Langat in the jungle, where Borneo Dyaks were tracking down guerrillas. They waded a stream, watched a ten-man British patrol emerge from a nightlong vigil in the jungle. They flew to a forest preserve and circled over it, watching paratroop training, went to a jungle camp occupied by the Queen's Own Royal West Kent Regiment, then went on to land in a jungle clearing so small that only one helicopter could get in at a time. They ascended again, and in about two minutes the helicopter carrying Stevenson, Bingham, Johnson, and a British officer started to smoke, the motor died, and the rotor blades slowed and idled. A short distance ahead was a small clearing, an abandoned rice paddy. The pilot maneuvered skillfully and though losing altitude fast managed to skim the great trees and bring the helicopter down in the rice paddy. Stevenson stepped out into mud to his knees. He said, "Where's my prang [dagger]? I want to kill a bandit." They had only one gun, and the area was full of guerrillas, cobras, pythons, and tigers. A road ran close by, and in a few minutes a Canadian officer joined them with a second gun. The second helicopter, having watched them land safely, went back to the clearing they had left, dropped Blair, Attwood, and a reporter, and came back to rescue them and take them to Kuala Lumpur, where General Templer, alarmed by radio messages, met them. Blair and Attwood returned an hour later by jeep. No one was hurt.

After a press conference, Stevenson flew to Singapore, arriving at 6:10 P.M. and staying at the Consul General's.

In the morning he worked on his third *Look* article and rested while Blair and Johnson went into Singapore to send cables. At 3 P.M. he received a half dozen University of Malaya students. They asked whether the West had shifted from a position of favoring independence for underdeveloped nations to one of nation-building in order to fight Communism. They wondered whether they were fighting a war for independence or merely a war against Communists. The British had said they would be given independence when they were ready for it but who was to decide when they were ready? They wanted a democratic socialist nation. Students everywhere at that time were saying much the same.

A half hour later a dozen pro-Chiang Chinese called on Stevenson to declare that Communism was attempting to dominate the world and that to save Asia the United States must save China. Stevenson said they wanted America to spill its blood in Korea, the French to spill their blood in Indochina, and the British in Malaya—and then asked how many Chinese had volunteered to fight the Chinese Communists in the jungles here. "Great consternation" followed, Johnson reported, and for several minutes the delegates talked to each other in Chinese before answering. The answer was weak: that if Indochina fell, Malaya and Siam would be next, and the Malayan government should allow Chiang's troops to join the fight. Stevenson persisted: How many of those present had volunteered to fight? More consternation; then they said the police here included 20,000 Chinese. Stevenson said the British were fighting here, the Americans in Korea, why didn't they fight here, it was their country. After delay, the answer came: To join the army here one must be a British subject and speak English. Stevenson said there were many Chinese who were British subjects and spoke English but few were fighting. They said, as the meeting broke up, that if they could organize a separate Chinese army supported by Chiang they would fight, and Stevenson told them if they really wanted to fight they should tell General Templer and he would put them at it so the British could leave. Afterward the Consul General said it was not true that the British had imposed restrictions that prevented them from fighting.

With his companions, Stevenson left on April 20 for Bangkok, capital of Thailand. They spent a miserable evening and first night there—were taken from the airport to the home of the MSA mission chief for a dinner that was supposed to be small and private only to find about sixty people present, some of the women in floor-length dresses; and at the government guesthouse they were kept awake all night by railroad trains, barking dogs, and mosquitoes. In the morning Stevenson called on the Foreign Minister, then went to an embassy briefing. Here as elsewhere in Southeast Asia the war in Vietnam hung over the conversation. When Stevenson called on the Prime Minister, Marshal Phibun Songgram, the Communist danger again dominated the conversation, as it did at a long cabinet lunch and a state dinner given by the Foreign Minister.

Stevenson got everybody up at five-thirty next morning to visit the floating market. The river was crowded with boats, houses built on stilts out into the water, temples along the banks, people bathing in sarongs and washing their teeth in a canal, yellow-robed priests in little boats begging for food, children waving. After breakfast they toured the royal palace with its teakwood and mother-of-pearl furniture and the temple of the emerald Buddha, with murals depicting the history and mythology of the country, all giants and demons. Posing for pictures beside one, Stevenson said, "It's not a demon, it's just a Republican." Before leaving Bangkok on April 23, the Associated Press reported, Stevenson urged all possible American military aid to Indochina to stop a Communist Viet Minh offensive.

They went that day to Rangoon, Burma, and made the usual rounds— an embassy briefing, a wreath at the tomb of a Burmese hero, a gold-leaf pagoda, a call on Prime Minister U Nu, lunch with the President, meeting with the Minister for Land Nationalization, tennis at a party, dinner and dancing at the President's house, an embassy buffet. They flew to Mandalay, and Stevenson told a press conference that Vietnam troops could assume the main responsibility for defending Indochina against Communists "within a year."[2]

13.

Stevenson spent sixteen days in India, the longest in any country on his trip, and ten in Pakistan, the second longest (with England). He started in Calcutta April 28, and the first notebook entry reads: "Calcutta—Dum Dum Airport—Reporters—Recog of Red China. Two white cows lying in front of biggest bank in shade—grazing in the streets everywhere." He heard about the divisions within India and the problems of divided Pakistan. Even farms were cut in half by the boundary between Pakistan and West Bengal, and the line was dotted with police outposts on both sides— "ridiculous." He was told about the Damodar Valley hydroelectric and irrigation project. Much of the digging was done by hand; some 60,000 men were employed. In his notebook Stevenson wrote, "Appalling contrasts between wealth & poverty . . . great palaces of the Imperial past & fine houses of today. . . . Few women, as elsewhere—they stay at home—Horrible! Use manure from the white cattle wandering everywhere in streets for fuel. Bullock carts, human carts & modern trucks all together. Horse carts, miles of stalls—selling everything—Moslem section no trouble. . . . Danger spot Darjeeling dist. Chinese Commies coming thru Nepal & Thibet. Hill people timid, easily misled, like to side with winner."

He went next day, Wednesday, to Asansol in the naval attaché's plane and toured the Damodar Valley project, modeled on TVA: "All paddy land—now dry & burning hot. Skinny white cattle grazing in dry paddy

---

[2] It was during this 1953 trip that Stevenson first met U Thant, later Secretary General of the UN, at that time Minister for Broadcasting and Information in the Burmese government. U Thant once recalled the 1952 American election: "I followed it closely. I listened to the radio to 1 A.M. The announcer said the first returns show General Eisenhower so many votes, Governor Stevenson so many, please don't forget to brush your teeth with Colgate."

fields. Fine homes for executives of steel plant surrounded by mud, tile & thatch huts. Tribesmen carrying bows & arrows . . . in shadow of modern steel plant. . . . *Women carry great rocks . . . 110°—25¢ a day."* From there he flew to Benares, India's holiest city, and noted: "First thing— dead body on a litter carried by 4 men en route to Ganges—Lord how hot it is!"

On Thursday, April 30, by boat to New Delhi. One entry in his note- book: "No one laughs, smiles, in this intense mass of acrid smelling hu- manity, struggling, shoving together to get into the golden temple to wor- ship after a bath in holy Ganges. . . . Sunbaked, whitish soil, dotted with small clumps of trees—villages. Air opaque with dust—*sky and earth blend."*

On to Delhi by plane. He was met by the new U. S. Ambassador, George V. Allen, and a large crowd. He said he had always wanted to come to India and admired its accomplishments. He repeated that, although the countries he had visited appeared to be winning their "battle against ag- gression," the free world must be wary of Russia. He said he regretted the "Soviet" invasion of Laos, and a reporter asked if he meant to use the term "Soviet." He replied, "We'll call it Communist. Call it Viet Minh if you like. No, call it Communist." He thought New Delhi the most modern and most Western city he had seen in Asia, with tall air-conditioned build- ings and green trees and spacious streets; but always *"Heat—*shimmer- ing." He picked up mail at the embassy. Lloyd Garrison told him that RCA Victor was bringing out a record containing excerpts from his cam- paign speeches—Stevenson would receive royalties—and Newt Minow sent him a review of his book of campaign speeches by Scotty Reston: "something extraordinary in the political literature of the Republic . . . undoubtedly the finest collection of speeches made by any Presidential candidate since Wilson and maybe in this century . . . surely among the finest ever crowded into a single Presidential election by a single individ- ual."

Stevenson and his party left Friday, May 1, to relax on a houseboat in Kashmir. He described the journey vividly in his notebook and wrote, "Climbing up out of terraced valeys—air cooler—at last! over sharp wounded spines of lower ranges, follow route of the road—ancient route between hot plains of India and the blessed valley of Kashmir that kings have contested for time out of mind—and still are. Suddenly the great jag- ged white wall of the Himalayas rises up—close in front—150 mi—to the East is 26000 ft Nanda Davi—cross pass above the zigzagging road Banihal pass at 11500 feet—road 9000. Drop steeply down far side— Kashmir valley! White jagged mountains—peaks rising above the clouds encircling it—wet paddy fields—green fields, trees enfolding little villages —and a placid green river winding thru it—*here dwell the happy* people— *and one of the worst political problems of these days.* green green green!

Srinagar surounded by its famous lakes nestling against the N side of the valley. Temple on hill overlooking city. . . . *From 107 to 75—in 45 minutes.*"

Next day he had a long lunch with Sheikh Abdullah, Prime Minister of Kashmir, who explained the quarrel between Pakistan and India over Kashmir and the role of the UN. Both sides had accepted a plebiscite in principle but each wanted the other out beforehand; Abdullah wanted both out. Kashmir feared that Pakistan might attack; the UN guarantees were worthless without a UN force. Abdullah was impatient with the UN. He was attacked in India as a Moslem and in Pakistan as a stooge of the Hindus. He told Stevenson, "I don't mind if I am killed in the struggle. All world teachers have to suffer." Stevenson was greatly impressed.

That night he visited a group of refugees from Communist China—200 of 350 Kazak tribesmen who had survived an exodus of 20,000 or 30,000 from Sinkiang north of the Himalayas to escape Russian and Chinese Communists. They had left in 1949 and reached Kashmir in November 1951. Stevenson visited them in an old government guesthouse once used by traders' caravans from Tibet. He noted, "Girls in ancient costume sang their folk songs while we sat on rugs surrounded by headman of Tribe. Pure Turks. Speak Turkish. Origin of Turks. Look exactly like Ghengis Khans mongols—more Asiatic than the Kashmiri Aryans with their long oval faces and long hooked noses. Chairs in courtyard—rugs. I seated in center—Chief made fine speech of appreciation for my visit; for refuge of Indian govt; for [those] . . . who died on the way. I responded—U.S. admires a people who value freedom more than life. Applause."

Sunday, May 3, dawned as a "cloudless, blue & white day. . . . And there on garden lawn by houseboat was a delegation from the Kazaks"— the chief wanted to thank him again for visiting them: *"they had no friends but America;* Indians didn't want them; didn't want to go to Turkey, wanted to go home. Many of their people wanted to escape but India wouldn't let them in."

Stevenson arrived in New Delhi in time to call briefly on Nehru, have lunch with Ambassador Allen, call on the President and Vice President, see the Mosque and the Red Fort, and dine alone that night with Nehru— "2½ hrs of talk," he told Jane Dick, "and what talk! Surely here *is* a remarkable man—and then I think of McCarthy, Bridges, Bricker—and even some Democrats!" who criticized him. His only notes on his conversation, all underlined, read: "China doesnt want to play Moscows game. Russian line was not pro Commie in China at first. Wants to settle in Korea. Doesnt dare risk world war by invading S E Asia." He wrote to Jane Dick that night, "And now it's 11 and I am back in my room in the utterly fantastic Residence the British built for their Viceroys—air conditioned, a bed 10 feet wide, literally, silver fittings, chandeliers, Roman bath tub. Ho Hum I wonder how I made do in that Executive Mansion so long! God, it's late and I'm tired, and here's Bill with 50 more letters!" He sent his sons his revised itinerary. He suggested that Borden meet him in Israel. "About John Fell, I shall merely express my disappointment about his French. . . . I am not sure he should come abroad because he gives me no information about what he plans to do except to travel with me. . . . Have any arrangements been made about living with a French family?"

They set out early next morning to visit a community development project some eighty-five miles from Delhi, accompanied by an Indian official who said that the hardest task had been to persuade the villagers to participate in the work—Moguls and British had taught them that work was degrading. In all vast India, work on roads, schools, and wells had only begun. And leadership was scarce. Stevenson noted, "200 million cattle—wandering & useless . . . can't slaughter—eat a lot. As caste system was abolished—this will be solved—but not yet." William Manchester of the Baltimore *Sun* went along and reported that Stevenson, wearing an open shirt and cotton pants, traveled by jeep and "strode down narrow alleys between mud huts, peering in now and then at Indian housewives cooking over open fires with dried cow dung as fuel." Everywhere he was greeted cordially.

Like so many who visit India, he seemed overwhelmed by its heat, dust, vastness, and problems. On Thursday, flying southward, he wrote to Jane Dick: "We're en route to Madras across the endless red, grey, brown, barren expanse of India, over the myriad villages and ruins of cities and civilizations that have long since had their hour and passed away—even as this one will which they and we too are struggling so desperately to strengthen. All India looks pretty much alike to me, physically at least so far, and all of it trembles in this pitiless sun! Now Hyderabad—it will be at least 110°." Attwood, he wrote, had been ill and Johnson not well—they stayed in Delhi while Stevenson, Bingham, and Blair went south. "Bingham and Blair were against it—but the old man came to see and by God he's going to see!!" He also told Jane Dick that he might not write again for a long time—Blair insisted he send some three hundred political postcards. He told her about the boys' travel plans, less to inform her than to unburden himself—and closed, "It's hellish hard to manage from this distance & all communication with Ellen has ceased as you know. Divorce is hell."

In Madras he was mobbed by about fifty Indian reporters who backed him against a wall and asked his opinion on everything from his political ambitions to how to fight Communism (raise the standard of living). An American woman rushed up and told him how hard she had worked for him in New York. A horde of autograph seekers waited at his hotel. He made official calls, and, after each, crowds gathered. He insisted on driving through the slums, swarming with people, then went to an ancient temple. Wherever he went, naked children with outstretched hands followed. He was warned that alms might mean a riot but dug into his pocket anyway, only to find it empty. William Manchester wrote, "Stevenson, who left America with conviction he could travel obscurely as an ordinary citizen, had ample evidence today he is regarded in South India as a world figure."

On May 8, Stevenson went from Madras to Trivandrum. In reply to a welcoming address by the Mayor at a garden party, he invited the 185,000 citizens of Trivandrum to accept honorary membership in the Democratic Party of the United States. He told them that while America valued peace as highly as India she valued one thing more than peace—freedom. At the end of the day the crowd was so great that he turned on the light inside his car so the people could see him. He stayed at a "fine guest house," canceled various functions, reported himself "indisposed," and went to the beach to swim. The land here along the coast was densely populated—up to 2,500 people per square mile, families of ten or fifteen living off an acre or so—"can't be done," he noted.

On to Bombay—heavy security precautions were taken to protect him, for the South had a large Communist minority, and when he went swimming, a dozen detectives disguised as fishermen roamed the beach.

Now at mid-point in his world tour, he summed up his impressions for Manchester of the *Sun*. India might be the "area of decision" in the Soviet-West struggle; it was the vast underbelly of the Soviet empire. While the two great powers were concentrating in the Far East and Europe, where the balance of power was static, the future might be decided in the arc running from Hanoi to Istanbul, comparatively neglected by both East and West. The hottest spot in the arc was Southeast Asia. Burma and Thailand were reluctant to identify with the British in Malaya or the French in Indochina. Guerrillas on the Thailand-Malaya border would make Malaya vulnerable were Thailand and Indochina to fall to the Communists. The Communist movement was under control in Malaya but at great cost. The government of Thailand was not strong or stable and might be overthrown by a coup d'état. The French should clearly state their intentions so the Vietnamese would help combat the Viet Minh; Vietnam needed better leadership than that of Bao Dai. Indonesia, though ably led, was in an economic slump. Burma, like Indonesia, had young leadership which contributed to stability.

In Bombay, Stevenson made many notes: "Irrational factors as important as rational ones in the conflicts between nationalism, the haves & have nots, the colonial powers and the colonized peoples. All nations *can* cooperate peacefully. But . . . the world needs & must have checks on errant nationalism. Some say world Federalism." He wrote that most Indians did not understand Communism, considering it just another political party rather than an aggressive imperialism. He was told that Nehru was not pro-Communist, though he admired the Soviet's accomplishment in pulling up a backward country by its bootstraps, and that Nehru felt a "poetic sentimentality" about long-exploited China, but China's invasion of Tibet had shaken him badly. He was "very much upset by noisy get tough chauvinism of Dulles & Ike."

In Delhi, Stevenson talked to Nehru for an hour before dinner. Nehru discussed conflicting refugee claims between India and Pakistan, said negotiations over Kashmir were bogged down over the forces to be left by both sides before the plebiscite, and said the anti-Communist position of the United States would attract no one in Asia. He said the idea of Communism—equality, the realization of people's hopes for a better life—had great appeal for the impoverished Asian masses. Nehru did not favor neutralism for India but, rather, "non-involvement"—he wanted to be left free to build his own country. He did not fear invasion by China or Russia. Stevenson noted, "Rather elementary diagnosis of world situation—old bal of power maintained by Br. Now R & U.S. Fancies role of non involved peacemaker I think. *'Will not be neutral in conflict between tyranny and freedom.'* Evidently thinks U S thinks war inevitable. Wants peaceful co-existence. Evidently not convinced that even [Russia] let alone China will press onward toward world domination. Our position too rigid & inflexible."

At a press conference, Stevenson called a question about Senator Joe McCarthy "awkward," then said that in so far as McCarthy was truly hunting subversives he enjoyed wide support, but "when it comes to his means, guilt by association, irresponsible accusations and methods of that kind, I don't believe he has any widespread support."

Thursday, May 14: Stevenson and his party left India for Pakistan. "Karachi—first thing you see *camels pulling carts with rubber tires.* Camels replace bullocks in dry desert of Sind. Desert—almost—between Delhi & Karachi." Embassy people met them, and so did the press, and Stevenson said that "war is unthinkable" between India and Pakistan over Kashmir. He called on Prime Minister Mohammed Ali and his Cabinet and noted, "They think Nehru & Indians have never accepted principal of Pak. indep. . . . Explained wheat needs of one million tons this year—long drought & 2 crop shortages. No equivocation about where they stand between freedom and tyranny." He stayed with the Governor General in his "vast new house" and called on the Foreign Minister, Sir Zafrulla Khan, who a decade later would become an associate of Stevenson at the UN.

They took off at 7 A.M. on May 16 in the embassy's plane for the Northwest Frontier, leaving Bingham and Attwood behind, Bingham to return to the United States, Attwood ill. At Lahore, Stevenson noted, "Greener and contrast to arid Karachi. . . . ancient brass cannon where Kim was playing in front of museum when Kipling's father was curator. Fine parks. Shalimar gardens. Not so many refugees. . . . Fine old immense mansion of Gov. of Punjab—Dining room was tomb from Mogul period. Swim in pool—cool water from deep well—11' deep! As usual the

Br. rulers of the past certainly made life spacious and comfortable!!" They lunched, talked, dined, and were given receptions by U.S. and local officials. Once Stevenson slipped away to go sightseeing and told Walter Johnson, *"This* is what I prefer, I would walk all day in these crowded streets."

They went off by air on Monday, May 18, to "Peshawar and the Kyber Pass!—across the well watered plain of fertile East Punjab into the more arid and treeless 'western' country getting rough as we approached the rugged rocky barren mountains . . . looks so much like vast areas of the SW and the dry Rocky Mountain approaches." They could see Afghanistan in the distance, high snow-covered mountains; they flew over tribal territory stretching to the Afghan frontier.

They drove toward the Khyber Pass and stopped twenty-eight miles from the Afghan border at the village of Jamrud, entrance to the pass. An honor guard of frontier scouts was drawn up to meet him, and so were a group of tribal chiefs. Garlands of flowers were thrown around Stevenson's neck, and he was given decorated sandals, a homemade revolver, and an ammunition bag. (Stevenson later gave the revolver to the Governor of Alabama.) The tribal chieftains who encircled him for twenty minutes "gave him the works" on Kashmir. They wore cartridge belts and beards. "Alexander's army passed this way to invade India 350 BC—fought over from time immemorial—and still do! . . . Mud walled, fortified villages, watch towers, Kyber villages. What do they live off. . . . Kyber means fort." They were driving on into the pass. Until a few years ago the tribesmen had been ferocious. Now, however, they wanted schools. Stevenson noted, "Tribal belt 1000 miles long . . . Greeks, Bacterian, Persians, Moguls, Turks, Mongols,—even lost Tribe of Israel! Arabs. Border barrier— Afghan guards. . . . Officers mess of the Kyber Rifles—behind mud walls grass, trees, flowers—skewered goat meat, and great book of the Regiment —Douglas MacArthur & fathers names in 1906. Colonel of Reg.— ferocious mustaches—horribly disfigured face, wounded at Singapore— and perfect Oxonian English." Stevenson got out and for an hour walked through the Peshawar bazaars.

Next morning they flew to Rawalpindi along the Kabul River to its junction with the Indus—"Great Mogul Fort," Stevenson wrote, "strategic place where all conquerors have crossed the Indus to invade India. . . . 3½ hrs to go 60 miles up to Governor's summer home 9000 ft. Built by British. Most perilous and beautiful mountain road. Latter part in dark thru rain and clouds—unguarded sides and precipices. Cold in seersucker suit! Pushed other car over slippery place in dark. Attwood & secy from Embassy joined us at Pundi. If she was scared to death so was I. Stopped at twilight on mountain ridge in soft rain for driver to break his fast. Huddled around charcoal cook fire in shack while Moslem ate his soggy grey wheat pancake & bright, handsome, ragged young man, 'police officer' recognized me as 'chief of Democratic Party.' "

For three days Stevenson stayed at Nathis Gali and dictated correspondence and worked on a *Look* article on India and Pakistan. Attwood, Johnson, and Blair helped from time to time. When the piece appeared, Chet Bowles thought it "really outstanding." At about this same time Schlesinger was writing to Stevenson on the state of the Union. The Eisenhower administration was cutting the defense budget dangerously, the welfare state was being replaced by the giveaway state—the Secretary of the Interior gave away Hell's Canyon to a private power company—and McCarthy remained unchecked by Eisenhower. Eisenhower seemed more interested in playing golf and bridge and in painting than in being President, seemed to regard the presidency as a reward for past achievement. John Kenneth Galbraith, the Harvard economist, McGowan, and Schlesinger had been talking of reviving the Elks Club—the group that had handled issues and written speeches in the 1952 campaign—to brief Stevenson when he returned. Schlesinger urged Stevenson to issue a statement when he returned on the adverse effects abroad of arms reduction and McCarthy and to make a TV speech.

14.

On Sunday, May 24, Stevenson flew commercial to Dhahran, Saudi Arabia—"4½ hrs along strange coast of Baluchistan & Iran—ghastly long parallel rows of jagged mountains—no vegetation—burning empty deserts and spiny saw toothed mountains—across Persian Gulf and Bahrin Island at sunset into big airport at Dahran." Ambassador Roy Hare, whom Stevenson had known at the UN, greeted them, along with Arabian officials and American employees of Aramco, the oil company. Driving to the air-conditioned Aramco guesthouse, a "typical American suburban home," they passed a night baseball game, and the sky was lit with burning gas. They dined with the Ambassador. He said Saudi Arabia had existed in a vacuum until oil came in—out of the stream of history for centuries, visited not even by Greek, Roman, Turkish, and other conquerors. Now oil concessionaires paid the Saudi Arabian Government about $175 million a year. No real government and no real business existed. The King was wise politically but not economically. He and his royal family and advisers lived at Ar Ruwaydah. Nothing else was there. Saudi Arabians, like other Arabs, felt the United States had hurt itself by supporting Israel but said little about it because they had no Israeli border. King Ibn Saud was obsessed with preventing Iraq, Jordan, and Syria from making common cause, nor did he like Naguib's setting up a republic in Egypt. The Saudis had almost no armed forces. Things were beginning to change a little—people were petitioning the government, and to quiet them the King paid subsidies to scattered tribes. The Ambassador found them people of great personal charm but frustrating to deal with.

Next morning they attended a briefing at Aramco—oil, relations with the United States, development of the country. At 11:30 A.M., they flew to Ar Ruwaydah in Ibn Saud's plane, given him by President Roosevelt, manned by an American crew. Stevenson described the royal palace as a compound of mud buildings apart from town and surrounded by a mud wall. He wrote, "Camels and Cadillacs; goat skins for water; tiled bathrooms; servants sleeping in the courtyard; armed retainers, slaves, whole roast sheep! gardens, swimming pools, bedouins. Rugs plugging hole in window behind the throne!" The Deputy Foreign Minister said Saudi Arabia needed America's friendship and America should understand Saudi Arabia's desires. Stevenson said America was proud of the Saudis' friendship, knew there were difficulties in the Middle East, hoped for their patience just as they wanted ours. The Saudis passed out American cigarettes and frozen grapefruit juice, then Stevenson and his party went to their air-conditioned palace rooms, carpeted with Persian carpets. Walter Johnson wrote, "About this point the Governor began to agitate to get out to see the town and the people and not be imprisoned in the palace." Ambassador Hare arranged it, not without difficulty, and they drove through "the narrow walls of this mud-brick fortress city." At Stevenson's insistence and over the protests of the security officer, they left their cars and walked the streets.

After lunch they called on King Ibn Saud, a big man with a strong face and expressive hands, old, sitting in a wheel chair, wearing glasses, his voice almost inaudible, yet somehow impressive. He spoke at length about friendship, saying that a friend tells you when you are wrong and supports you when you are right. He did not say so but he meant that he thought the United States should help the Saudis force British troops away from an oil-rich British protectorate in the south claimed by Saudi Arabia.

Stevenson's party called on Ibn Saud's brother and on Prince Faisal. The King's brother forthrightly denounced British and French imperialism and said if the French did not get out of Indochina and North Africa those areas might well go Communist. He wanted the United States to help North Africa, Egypt, Jordan, Iraq, and the southern Arabian protectorates win independence. He appreciated U.S. help in getting the French and British out of Syria and Lebanon. Stevenson said he himself had worked on that negotiation. The world was making progress in ridding itself of the old imperialism. They said not the Middle East—the UN talked a great deal but did little without U.S. support. Stevenson insisted that imperialism was shrinking but Communism expanding, and they should beware of it. They said Islam was strongly opposed to Communism, they returned to imperialism. After about an hour of this, a royal counselor told Stevenson not to forget the "cancer" the United States had placed in Arab hearts. He meant Israel. But they all seemed more preoccupied with the British than with Israel.

That evening they dined with King Ibn Saud at a long table holding twenty-two roasted lambs, set out on a balcony under the moon. As a concession to Westerners, Ibn Saud had provided butchers to slice the lamb instead of requiring his guests to tear off chunks of meat with their hands. After dinner they went to another balcony, where the King sat at one end with Stevenson and the Ambassador flanking him and the rest strung out down the sides, together with some forty bodyguards with rifles, pistols, and curved swords. They drank coffee in tiny cups (and had not enough cups to go around). A man sprayed rose water on their hands, then brought in a charcoal brazier to blow incense-perfumed smoke into their faces. He sprayed the guests' hands again with perfume. It all lasted about an hour. (Stevenson told Jane Dick, "Two Arabs stood behind me waving filthy towels to drive away the flies. But you know the Stevenson appetite.")

On the way back to their quarters the Ambassador told them that each man was supposed to have only four legal wives, but as the wives reached the age of about twenty-five, the man declared them ex-wives, and so ended with many more than four. They also were permitted concubines. Age thirteen was considered the matrimonial age for girls; few married past fourteen. King Ibn Saud had about thirty-six sons who lived to maturity; nobody kept track of his daughters. Slavery still existed, including a slave market.

At about 9:30 P.M. they went to the Crown Prince's palace, a few miles out of town, with gardens he had planted from the five continents. It was moonlight, and the roses and gladioli were in full bloom. He had a swimming pool in his own quarters and one in the women's quarter. No outsider was permitted to see the women's faces.

They walked through the gardens, then had a fruit supper, and one of the Crown Prince's sons said he had been in the United States during the election campaign and thought Stevenson the greatest orator of the twentieth century and predicted Stevenson would win if he ran in 1956.

At last Stevenson and his party returned to their own palace and upstairs were met by the King's major-domo, who presented Stevenson with a sword in a gold case. Stevenson said weakly to Johnson, "It's pretty, isn't it?" At this point a vast oriental rug was unrolled and given to Stevenson. At the airport on arrival Stevenson had exclaimed at the beautiful rugs, and the Ambassador had warned him he would get one, but he hadn't believed it. When now the rug was presented to him, his big eyes showed sheer disbelief. He asked Hare if he couldn't thank them and refuse it. The Ambassador said he had to take it. They gave him an Arab costume, too.

Next day, Tuesday, May 26, they returned to Dhahran and that day and the next talked to Arabian leaders and oil men, visited hospitals and Aramco installations, heard about the nomadic poverty-stricken existence of most Saudi Arabians. And they talked, too, about what Stevenson noted as the "rising expectations" among the people—Stevenson would bring the phrase "revolution of rising expectations" into the language.

They flew to Cairo. Stevenson was told at the embassy that the Prime Minister, Mohammed Naguib, had cleaned up corruption and Secretary Dulles had told him that Egypt looked like a good prospect for U.S. aid if Egypt wanted it. The Egyptians wanted to build a high dam on the Nile at Aswan to increase Egypt's arable acreage by about one third. They were less concerned about Israel than Syria, Lebanon, or Iraq but were obsessed with ending British control of the Suez Canal and getting them entirely out of Egypt. Every politician since 1922 had exploited this issue, and the louder they cried "The British must go" the more successful they were. The embassy thought it would be helpful if Stevenson could persuade the Egyptians to regard Suez not as a matter of sovereignty but rather as an administrative or managerial problem.

Off he went at eleven to see the Foreign Minister, Mahmoud Fawzi. Stevenson suggested that such issues as Suez and Israel were distractions which took Egyptian minds off their real problem—economic development. The Foreign Minister said Stevenson must understand that they had had British occupation for many years—if the British left, Egypt would develop into a strong ally of the West, not of the Communists, but if the British stayed, Egypt would remain weak and perhaps the whole Middle East would turn against the West. They would be willing to use British technicians to manage the canal, if necessary, but they must be employees of Egypt, not of England.

At noon Stevenson talked alone with the Prime Minister, Colonel Naguib, who impressed him. Stevenson wrote in his notebook, "Genial, friendly, modest, soft spoken, hard-bodied soldier. Deep mistrust of Br.— Really don't intend to leave at all. Regional def. pact based on Arab League *after* Br. go. Complains about 80,000 [British] troops vs. treaty limit of 10; that Br. didn't train E. army or leave any equip.; that E. *can* supply the technicians in time." Naguib said the British as well as the Communists here were spreading rumors that the Naguib regime was unstable, stirring discontent among the masses, while Naguib was creating enmity by commencing reform at the expense of the rich. At the end of their meeting Naguib took Stevenson to his car, and to reporters swarming around him Stevenson said only, "He gave me a good cup of coffee."

British officials told Stevenson that if they did not reach agreement with the Naguib regime it might fall, and its successor might be less reasonable. The British had a billion-dollar investment in the base at Suez, it supplied the entire Middle East, and if the British did withdraw they wanted to be sure the base was maintained and ready for action in case of war. The British welcomed American involvement here.

The U. S. Ambassador told Stevenson that Churchill and other Tories were making the Egyptian problem unnecessarily difficult and had not yet worked out a policy to replace colonialism. Egypt would commit "national suicide" if pushed to it. Naguib was a modest man. A colonel named Gamal Abdel Nasser was brighter and more aggressive. The British now realized they must do something. They wanted the United States to underwrite any agreement they reached with Egypt. The question was: How could Britain maintain a base here for the defense of the Middle East against the wishes of the whole Middle East? The answer was: She could not, except by force. Was it worth while? And how could the Egyptians and others learn, except by experience, that Soviet imperialism was worse than British?

Stevenson went by Egyptian government plane sightseeing to Luxor. He noted: "Along narrow green valley of Nile—many pyramids— then over Eastern desert to Valley of Kings, colossi of Memnon, Karnak & Luxor (Thebes)—greatest city in world in time of Amenhotep (New Kingdom) in 1411 BC—richest & mightiest city in world—now sleeping peacefully by the Nile in the shadow of its mighty monuments of the distant past which for more than a hundred years have been the center of archeological work of world." They went in the heat to a hotel in Luxor, then, accompanied by an archaeologist and the plane crew and local dignitaries, crossed the Nile in a "caravan of ancient autos" to inspect the ruins. "Awful thirst," Stevenson wrote. Borden had joined them, and Stevenson noted, "Bordie seemed really interested in antiquities." Stevenson called on Nasser. Like all other Eygptians, Nasser talked about the British—the canal and the base. Stevenson warned them not to push the British too hard—the British too had a public-opinion problem. He tried without success to persuade them to view Suez as a managerial problem.

On Tuesday, June 2, Stevenson and his party left for Beirut, Lebanon. En route he wrote, "Port Said—ships coming & going. Beirut—beautiful city—Blue Med Wooded hills rising above clean modern city." Here the Israel issue sharpened. The U. S. Ambassador said that anti-Israel emotion on the streets was "terrific," that United States-Lebanon relations had been impaired by U.S. support of Israel, that Lebanese nationalists were determined to get rid of the British and French in the Middle East and North Africa, that they identified the United States with British and French imperialism, and that the American national interest required a policy that did not favor Israel but, rather, stood for equal treatment for all and preference toward none. Both sides were unreasonable, and he saw the future gloomily, fearing bloodshed—already incidents were occurring daily between the Israelis and Jordanians. University professors told Stevenson that the United States had taken too active a role in establishing the state of Israel, that Arabs never would feel secure so long as the United States continued to support Israel, and that the United States should push in the UN for internationalizing Jerusalem, fixing boundaries, and repatriating the Arab refugees. Stevenson doubted all three could be accomplished and sought grounds for compromise. It was hard going. At

the Foreign Office, Georges Bey Hakim told him that the great force in the
Arab world was nationalism and therefore leaders did not dare compromise publicly on the Israel question—to do so would be regarded as treason.

On June 4, Stevenson and his party went overland across the border
into Syria and on to its capital, Damascus. There he heard much the same
thing he had heard elsewhere in the Arab world. The Syrian strong man,
General Shishikli, did not think the United States should help Syria "throw
Israel into the sea," Israel was here to stay, but the United States should
help deal with the refugee problem, the boundary problem, and the internationalization of Jerusalem.

After a stop in Amman, Jordan, Stevenson spent five days in Israel.
Prime Minister David Ben-Gurion told him that Israel had three purposes
—to rescue those Jews who could not safely stay where they were and
provide them with a home, to rebuild the desert land of Israel, and to
build a civilization based on Hebrew ethics and modern technology. It
"can be done because it has to be done," he said. Stevenson noted, "Survival as Jewish people depends on it." Ben-Gurion said Israel wanted to
live in "friendly cooperation" with her Arab neighbors. She had been
ready to accept a UN decision but the Arabs had made war against her.
"Our aim is peace," he said. To arm the Arabs was to arm them to fight
Israel, not fight for their own freedom. The United States must "re-
educate" Arabs who had "lived in bondage" for centuries. The Arabs
would not fight for democracy; they would fight only the people they
wanted to fight—Jews. Stevenson noted and underlined that he said, *"If
for sake of peace have to give up Jerus., any of our little terr. we won't do
it. Have enormous terr. they haven't done anything with for centuries. UN
decision doesn't exist morally any more. No one helped us we fought for
lives. . . .* Would have been no refugees if Arabs had accepted UN dec.
Willing to cooperate to help resettle. If Ref. [refugees] came back means
des. of state of Is. because surrounding Arab states are hostile; boycott."

Stevenson told Jane Dick, "I'm so weary. I've never felt this way before. . . . I want to come home so bad and be left alone—and talk and
talk and talk—quietly, on my back instead of my bottom. . . . I want
to get in grass again—oh the hot delicious swoon of the mid-summer
noon, when the year is brought to prime by the bees in the thyme. Do you
have any thyme?" He added, "1 A.M.—as usual."

15.

In Cyprus, where he stayed three days, he worked on his *Look* article
on the Middle East and held official functions to a minimum, though he
could not escape bundles of telegrams from Greek Cypriots asking him to
help them win union with Greece and from Turkish Cypriots opposing

union, nor could he fail to call on the Archbishop and hear his views on Cyprus' problems. He talked to Walter Johnson about writing a book when he returned, not a travelogue, Johnson noted, but a book that raised "philosophical and general questions—such things as (1) are people more stirred by hunger or religious and emotional issues, (2) what is gained for these people by improving the standard of living, (3) the importance of anti-Colonialism and anti-Western imperialism, (4) what form of government is most suited to these nations, (5) what attitudes do these nations have toward the United States." He never wrote the book, though Johnson prepared drafts for it and Stevenson fussed over it well into 1960, saying many times he wished the "wretched book" never had been proposed. Indeed, throughout his life, Stevenson never completed a book-length manuscript; all his books were collections of speeches and articles.

Stevenson received word from home. Invitations to speak were pouring in; Blair was declining all except a suggestion by Steve Mitchell of a homecoming in Chicago about September 10. (Mitchell reported that Al Horan and other Chicago machine leaders—except Arvey—were critical of Stevenson; Mitchell wanted to demonstrate Stevenson's national strength to them.) Blair thought Stevenson should make a statement and answer "a few" questions when he arrived in New York and then "get out of circulation" for two or three weeks. Blair asked Mitchell for suggestions as to what he should say on arrival. He added, 'The Gov."—the rest of his life, Stevenson was referred to as "the Gov." by his close associates—"has refrained thus far from hitting McCarthy on this trip and I think this has been wise. However, the question of McCarthyism comes up all the time and it is undermining our position and losing us respect in most of the world. I don't think that the Gov. should waste any time in telling this to the American people." At about this same time Harry Truman told reporters he would "work in the ranks"—Stevenson was the party's leader.

Stevenson went to Turkey on June 17 and stayed with the U. S. Ambassador, George McGhee, a Texas Democrat with whom he talked politics. (McGhee later became Undersecretary of State in the Kennedy administration.) McGhee said that Turkey's admission to NATO was highly significant, the first time the Turks had been accepted as Europeans. Ataturk had imposed a European state here and imposed its control over religion. Through his Republican Party he had operated a dictatorship, and so had Inonu. During those years, however, Turkey had moved into the twentieth century, with U.S. aid. Turkey had been the first country to volunteer in the Korean War. The Turks, with U.S. support, had stood firm against the Russians. The economy was developing, foreign investment welcomed. This was one country where massive U.S. aid had paid off.

Stevenson spent next morning working on his *Look* article, then met with the Turkish Prime Minister and Foreign Minister. He found them proud of their progress, grateful for U.S. aid, and contemptuous of the chauvinistic and emotional Arab governments, including Egypt, which they considered too impatient on the Suez question. Saudi Arabia had no government at all, they said—only a King and oil. Royalty had looted Egypt and now General Naguib was a front man for a divided revolutionary committee. Jordan was a tribal society, not a nation. Little Lebanon was just a few wealthy families. Syria had had coup after coup. Iraq was more stable but it too was divided. The Foreign Minister threw up his hands and said, "This is the Arab world." He added that the United States must strengthen the Arabs to check subversion—but no matter how much the United States strengthened the Arabs, they would never be as good as three Turk divisions. Stevenson made a note: "Strong confident men."

Before leaving on June 22, Stevenson held a press conference, praising Turkey's emergence as a strong, self-reliant, and democratic state, "one of the wonders of modern history." He arrived in Belgrade late that afternoon and was met by the U.S. chargé, several Yugoslav officials, and a number of Americans, including a Princeton man with his class banner. He noted, "Over the 'guerilla mountains,' Macedonia & into Belgrade where I landed 27 yrs ago in open two seater converted French fighter plane and had to buzz the cows off the landing strip. . . . High officials at airport. 'Guest of State.'" After driving to the Majestic Hotel, Stevenson, Blair, Johnson, and Borden walked down the main street of Belgrade, and while Stevenson was peering into a store window, a man touched Johnson on the shoulder, pointed, and asked, "Stevenson?" Johnson thought it the only English word he knew.

They dined with the chargé, Woodruff Wallner, who a decade later worked closely with Stevenson at the UN. Stevenson spent the next day at an embassy briefing and in talks with Yugoslav officials and American correspondents. Touring the city, he was struck by the absence of automobiles—"fewer than anywhere in Asia." The official lunch was "very lively, good food!" and he told his hosts, "I wish I had a Communist cook." Everywhere he heard about Tito's break with the U.S.S.R. Yugoslavs were jubilant—Russia had proposed they exchange ambassadors. They were worried about a decrease in U.S. aid, however.

On Wednesday, the twenty-fourth, Stevenson and his party flew to Zagreb in a Yugoslav Air Force plane. They went to an "elaborate" lunch with the president of the Council of Croatia, then drove around town—"charming city much more attractive than Belgrade"—visited an ethnographic museum, the Yugoslav Academy, nearby villages—"much wine!" —then flew to Pula "over fertile plains—strips of crops long and thin everywhere in Yugo—into wooded mountains where partisans fought. . . . Fine new hotel replacing old one bombed in war. Beautiful place— opera setting. . . . Prince Paul's fine yacht . . . taken over by Tito in harbor. Superb dinner and good sleep—thank God."

Next day Stevenson would see Tito. "Off by carriage—fine old open carriage of royal family with two men up behind. . . . Long—3¼ hrs— talk with Tito, Vilfan interpreting. Then joined by others & photographers! Then lunch upstairs in his new, modern, air conditioned villa. Fine food, wine and astonishing long & frank talk in presence of others followed by drive around island—deer, pheasants, Roman ruins, beautiful views, sol- diers! He even drove back to Hotel with us & deposited us with a flourish & warm farewell. By his spanking newly converted MTB launch to Pula at 36 knots p.h. preceded by an MTB escort. Out of boat into autos to air- port—grass runway & off in his plane to Dubrovnik along beautiful, rug- ged Dalmatian coast after one of most interesting visits of my life."

During the hour-and-a-half plane ride Stevenson and Attwood, who had joined them for lunch after Stevenson had been alone with Tito, made notes on the talk.

Stevenson thought Tito looked "hard & fit," sunburned, well dressed in gray; firm, stern, intelligent, with an assured confident manner. He reminded Stevenson of one of the "public utility brigands" Stevenson had represented as a lawyer years earlier—hard-living, hard-drinking, breezy, confident. He answered Stevenson's questions without evasion. He thought the shifts in the Kremlin meant a change in Soviet tactics, not in ultimate objectives. The new leaders were likely to be more flexible than Stalin, a tyrant surrounded by sycophants. The signal of real change would come not from foreign policy pronouncements but from within—when force and violence were replaced by consent and cooperation inside Russia. At pres- ent Communism did not exist in either Russia, an autocracy, or in Yugoslavia, a democratic socialist state. Tito saw good prospects for a pe- riod of peace in Europe; Russia's real objective was Asia. China, he thought, was not a Soviet satellite though Russia had talked her into the Korean adventure, to her later dismay. India was highly important—the West would be in serious trouble if ever Russia, China, and India became allied. Riots had recently occurred in East Berlin because people there felt themselves exploited unfairly by the Soviets. Tito spoke well of United States policy in general. He welcomed U.S. aid and said he hoped he would need no more after two more years. He thought our aid unappre- ciated in Italy and France. He did not fear U.S. imperialism. He thought Senator Joe McCarthy did the United States great harm. He would like to visit the United States but did not think McCarthy would let him in. (Stevenson remarked he wasn't sure McCarthy would let Stevenson back in and asked if he could settle down in Brioni.) Tito discussed Yugoslav internal affairs and was not offended when Stevenson told him he sounded "just like an American capitalist." He toasted 1948—the year Tito broke with Russia and Stevenson got into politics. Stevenson offered to go on a lecture tour of the United States with Tito.

After Dubrovnik, Stevenson noted, "A day that will not be forgotten & a place to revisit." It was the first time during his entire trip that he had written "a place to revisit." He retained an affection for Yugoslavia all his life.

16.

And on to Greece, Italy, and Austria. He arrived in Rome on June 30 and stayed a week in Italy. John Fell, by now seventeen, joined him, and so did Mr. and Mrs. Ives. John Fell once recalled, "I was mainly sightseeing. I remember one big press conference at the embassy and some dinners in the evening." He laughed, an engaging laugh that always amused Stevenson. "I remember he loved telling stories on me. Apparently when we arrived in England the press asked what I liked best about England and I said I liked it because they spoke English. Then, another thing, we were out at the race track and we went to see the Queen in her box and she invited us to tea between races. She must have asked me would I like something and I said yes, a glass of milk. He told those stories for quite a while."

Italy was in one of its recurrent political crises, with the Communists threatening to win power. Prime Minister Alcide de Gasperi spoke to Stevenson of the lassitude of the democratic center, the potential resurgence of the Fascist right, and the "unbelievable" bitterness of the Communists who had been imprisoned by the Fascists. "Without the Marshall Plan and arms," De Gasperi said, "we would have nothing in Europe." Stevenson had a private twenty-minute audience with the Pope. Since the U. S. Ambassador was a Republican, Clare Boothe Luce, wife of Henry Luce, the publisher, Stevenson limited his social engagements severely and went to a seaside resort to spend a weekend on correspondence and a *Look* article on Turkey, Yugoslavia, and Greece.

Stevenson wrote, "The caravan proceeds with ever increasing fury and frenzy but the Atlantic draws nearer, thank God!" Returning to Rome, he told a press conference that current anti-Communist riots in East Berlin were as significant as anything that had happened in Europe since World War II. (Tito had said it to him.) He went to Venice and took an overnight train to Austria. "July 8," Stevenson noted, "Arrive Vienna—big crowd at station including Amb. Llewellyn Thompson—old friend. Elegant old 'Bristol' [Hotel]—reminds me of 'Reunion in Vienna' [a play by Robert Sherwood]." He stayed three days—briefings and interviews—and made a brief radio broadcast for Radio Free Europe aimed at citizens of the Soviet satellite countries: "I want particularly to tell my listeners in Czechoslovakia of the warm admiration with which Americans learned of the recent brave conduct of the workers in many cities of that republic. In my own city of Chicago, there are hundreds of thousands of Americans of Czech, Slovak, Polish, and Hungarian origin who have a very intimate interest in the fate of their relatives in their former homeland. Beyond this, we Americans—we all have a direct interest in the cause of freedom everywhere."

In Berlin, after a U.S. briefing, an official reception, and a tour of West Berlin, Stevenson crossed into the Soviet Zone, accompanied by Cecil B. Lyon, a State Department official, and an escort officer. A short distance beyond the Brandenburg Gate they stopped at the ruins of the bunker where Hitler died and clambered over the rubble, Blair and Attwood taking pictures of Stevenson. As they returned to their cars, about ten East German policemen and soldiers appeared, parked a vehicle in front of their cars and another behind them, blocking escape, and when they got into their cars, a German officer said in German, "If you move, we will shoot," and one of his men loaded his submachine gun and pointed it at them and said in English, "You move and I shoot." Lyon, the State Department man, said he was the representative of the U. S. High Commissioner's office and demanded to see the Soviet Ambassador. After discussion, in which the Germans said the Americans should have known they could not take pictures there—it was well known that foreigners were forbidden to take pictures in America—the officer made a telephone call. Stevenson paced up and down, asking about slogans on banners on nearby government buildings, and as he did so two East German policemen followed with Soviet-made machine pistols slung in front of them. At length another policeman arrived with instructions to confiscate the Americans' film and release them. They did. Stevenson called it "an advantageous experience." He insisted on continuing his tour of the Soviet Sector, visiting Stalin Allee, where the recent riots had started, and a Soviet war memorial.

Returning to West Berlin, Stevenson told the press that the people in East Berlin looked shabby, little reconstruction had been accomplished, large numbers of police and soldiers were patrolling empty streets, and East Berlin was much more drab than Belgrade. Next day he was interviewed on Radio Free Europe. He described his encounter with the police in the East Zone. Asked if he saw a "common denominator" in the East Berlin riots, unrest in Czechoslovakia, the "bloodless reform" in Hungary, the fall of Lavrenti Beria, Stalin's secret police chief, he said that tensions were accumulating in the satellite states and that "proud people" would not forever remain "vassels" of "an imperialist power." Had he observed differences among the Western Allies? "Free countries by the very nature of their freedom have differences of opinion" but from Japan to West Germany they were agreed "completely" to keep themselves free of the "new imperialism." At a press conference that same day he said, "While I salute the remarkable recovery of West Berlin, I also salute the indomitable spirit and the brave defiance of the East Berliners. When tanks shoot down workers in a workers' paradise, it is no paradise." Asked about McCarthy, he said, "I am distressed by the injury to the American respect and prestige that I have observed all the way from Tokyo to Berlin," but said if he had more to say about McCarthy he would say it in the United States. Winston Churchill had recently proposed a four-power conference without fixed agenda. President Eisenhower, however, had adopted a go-slow attitude. Stevenson, asked for his views, said he always believed in keeping the door open to negotiation but thought a four-power conference now might be unproductive, since Beria's fall indicated tension and perhaps a power struggle inside Russia. Headlines in the United States read, "Stevenson Backs Ike's Big 4 Stand." Two days later in Bonn he seemed to reverse himself: the New York *Times* headlined its account of his press conference there, "Stevenson Favors Parley of Big Four" and quoted him as saying that four-power talks were to be sought at every possible opportunity.

In Bonn on July 13 he lunched with the U. S. High Commissioner for Germany, James Bryant Conant, then spent two days talking with American and German officials. Everywhere the talk was of German reunification, Soviet intentions, the Big Four conference, and the European Defense Community. On Tuesday he took a trip on the Rhine, then held a press conference. He was asked the usual questions about McCarthy, a four-power conference, the European Defense Community, U.S. foreign policy in general. Asked about the admission of mainland China to the UN, he replied, "As of the moment, I could hardly conceive of Red China being admitted to the UN as long as it is fighting the United Nations 'tooth and toenail.' . . . Furthermore, I point out that Red China is also supporting the Communist rebellion and civil war in Vietnam, and under these circumstances I think any discussion of admission is entirely premature." The same applied to U.S. recognition of the Mao government.

He went to Paris on Wednesday, July 15, and stayed in France a week. His first three days were crowded with briefings, a visit to SHAPE, and interviews with government officials and politicians. He saw, among others, President Auriol, Premier Joseph Laniel, Pierre Paul Schweitzer, Pierre Mendès-France, and Jean Monnet. He saw Paul-Henri Spaak of Belgium. His talks ranged widely. He was told that France was becoming increasingly dependent on U.S. aid, increasingly weary of the Indochina war, and was increasingly making it clear that she intended to postpone decision on EDC as long as possible. French nationalism was rising. The French wanted to become independent of the United States, to recapture their former glory, and to become strong enough to stand alone, but they could not become strong while the Indochina war continued, and they feared the rapid resurgence of Germany. And trouble was looming in North Africa. The French were tired. They were unimpressed with the argument that the free world must oppose Communism; they would be glad to have the United States do it for them. They wanted a strong army of their own but Indochina was destroying their best officers. Mendès-France thought

France should jettison Indochina. Stevenson disagreed forcefully—
Southeast Asia was a prime Russian target, a Russian-Chinese-Indian alliance would be a "nightmare."

In Paris as nowhere else on his tour, Stevenson was besieged by intellectuals. A French edition of his book of speeches had just been published,
and his publishers gave a reception for him. J. J. Servan-Schreiber, then a
rising young French intellectual who only gained international attention
some years later, wanted to arrange a small dinner for Stevenson. Arthur
Schlesinger urged Stevenson to see Nicolas Nabokov, executive director of
the Congress for Cultural Freedom. Julius Edelstein, executive assistant to
Senator Herbert Lehman, urged Blair to have Stevenson talk with James
T. Farrell, the novelist living at that time in Paris, and Farrell did meet
Stevenson at a reception and became a lifelong—and prolific—correspondent. Bill Attwood arranged a dinner with a group of American correspondents, including Theodore White. White found Stevenson "most
unimpressive," as he later recalled; "he seemed to be a political tourist
asking strange ethereal questions. I expected him to be tougher. This serious melancholy questioning man—if he was a correspondent for the *Partisan Review*, I'd have expected it." White later changed his mind after
hearing Stevenson speak in Illinois.

After three days of Paris, Stevenson and the others moved out to Ver-
sailles for a long weekend in a house belonging to Ambassador David
Bruce where Stevenson worked on his correspondence and next article.
("Like a spring freshet after a long freeze, Western Europe is bubbling
and struggling with new ideas and new forces in this seventh summer of
the cold war. . . . [But] the cold war is not over. Good relations with our
European allies are still vital to our mutual security.") He received a long
letter from Jane Dick describing a Lake Forest dinner party at which a
man furiously denounced criticism of McCarthy—his rage frightened her,
and she said she would not say another word as long as she was in Lake
Forest.

Stevenson returned to Paris and held a press conference on July 22. He
opened with light remarks—his world tour had been "fascinating, fatiguing and fattening," he had "spent so much money" that he was flying tourist class to London tonight. He then invited questions. The first one was
on McCarthy—what had been his effect on U.S. relations with other countries? Stevenson replied, "That is what I call an easy question. Perhaps I
can answer it in one word: 'Bad.' I have, as I said before, been disheartened by the precipitate decline in American prestige and leadership
abroad, to which this current infirmity has contributed." What about U.S.-
China relations? The question, he said, would have to be faced but it was
premature at this time. On the Soviet Union, he cautioned the reporters to
distinguish between tactics, which had changed since Stalin's death, and
strategy, which had not. Asked if he brought back "any new ideas on the

mission of America as a great democracy," he replied, "Yes, I did, but as long as none of you can vote in the United States, I am not going to make my speech here."

He flew to London that night and dined with Ambassador and Mrs. Winthrop Aldrich.

17.

Stevenson loved England, and on this trip did many things and saw many people there—attended a garden party at Buckingham Palace and was presented to the Queen, sat in her box at the races, spent a weekend with the Acting Foreign Secretary, Lord Salisbury, and time with such old friends as Herbert Agar and Douglas Fairbanks, Jr., and T. S. Matthews, lunched with leaders of the Labour Party, sat in the House of Commons and met with the British-American Parliamentary Group in the Members Dining Room, had cocktails with American correspondents, made a brief speech to the English-Speaking Union, was interviewed on the BBC, dined with Lady Astor, and much more. But beyond doubt the most memorable event was lunch with Sir Winston and Lady Churchill at Chequers. Churchill was old and ill, unable to perform his duties as Prime Minister, and Anthony Eden was his heir apparent; but he was still vigorous and lucid. At the embassy briefing Stevenson had been told that Churchill was "only half the man he was but he was four times a man." Now at Chequers he talked with Stevenson, and Stevenson later made notes on what the great man said.

Churchill reminisced emotionally about World War II, Britain's sacrifices and losses. Now, he said, Britain was treated "like a beggar"; it "makes me downright angry" to see Britain treated like Haiti or Hawaii, and he wept—he had always wept easily and now, aging, could not control his tear ducts. He feared that people had not thought through the implications of war. He wanted to talk about it to Malenkov, a younger man now one of the new Russian leaders. He spoke of Britain's exposed position— Russia could strike her easily. The best hope for peace, he thought, was America's hydrogen bomb. The United Nations was disappointing, weaker even than the League of Nations, and he would have preferred a regional grouping of states rather than universalism; yet he was grateful that this time the United States had joined. Korea, he thought, ought not be considered "a draw." Instead, it was really something very great—for the first time, collective security had worked and, moreover, Korea had rearmed America.

Of McCarthyism, he said he believed deeply in democracy and its corrective devices and thought them already at work to undo McCarthy. He spoke of the American Civil War, the battlefields he had visited, and wondered if Stevenson had come originally from the South. He himself had written an unpublished history of the English-speaking peoples, including 60,000 words on the American Civil War. He made the point that the British Empire contained 80 million white English-speaking people, that the United States contained 130 million white English-speaking people, that together they were the most powerful influence on earth—"no dog dare bark" without their sufferance. He had been taught, he said, to draw the color line. Today it was unfashionable. "I am glad to call any man my brother," he said, "but not my brother-in-law."

America, he said, in World War II had "saved us all." He had a low opinion of the French—a beautiful country filled with all manner of good things but governed by politicians who passed around the premiership and agreed on nothing save that Germany should make no contribution to European defense. On Britain's recognition of mainland China, he had favored doing it de facto, but the socialists had done it de jure. Similarly, he had not favored all-out independence for India but, rather, a constituent assembly in India empowered to secede whenever it wished. He respected Nehru as a man who had conquered mankind's "two greatest enemies," fear and hate, but thought him "very free with other people's property," especially the Portuguese enclave of Goa (that would trouble Stevenson nearly a decade later at the UN). As for Indochina, he did not care about sustaining the French there and took it less seriously than the United States did. He "perked up," Stevenson noted, at mention of Malaya. But after all he felt that the solution to all problems lay at the center—in Moscow. He asked if Stevenson had known President Roosevelt and said simply, "I loved him." Americans, he said, had thought ill of him when he first spoke (at Fulton, Missouri, with President Truman) of an "iron curtain"; a few years later they thought he had not gone far enough. "People have short memories." He was proud of being a member of the Society of the Cincinnati, a descendant of a colonial officer in the American Revolution, and he introduced his grandson to Stevenson as the ninth lineal descendant in the male line from an officer of Washington's army. The American Revolution had separated America from Britain as a microcellular organism divides, but if they had not separated they would not have experienced "the joy of reunion." Today, he said, Britain wanted nothing from America but trade. He feared the Eisenhower administration might not understand that, might make it hard for Americans to buy from Britain. Dulles, he thought, was "a cold cruel man." He thought he saw eye to eye with Stevenson and told him confidentially that his own wife had been a Stevenson partisan in the last election. Churchill too thought Stevenson would have "done the right thing." But then so would Eisenhower, or at least try. And he reverted to the Great War and its terrors. Again: "I want to talk to Malenkov—tell him about war. I can't now. I am not well. A month ago I could not walk. A month hence I shall be strong again."

In the evening after his lunch with Churchill, Stevenson said in a BBC interview that the warmth of his reception in England led him to think "that maybe I ran for office in the wrong country." Questioned about Korea and mainland China, he asked Englishmen to remember that the United States had spent billions of dollars and suffered 140,000 casualties in Korea and could hardly be expected now to "promptly embrace the [Chinese] enemy whom we have fought so desperately for so long." Asked about his remark in Paris that U.S. prestige had declined, he said, "I think that many people—due to what we call McCarthyism, the sense of repression and fear, that has slipped over the United States—are very apprehensive that the United States has lost confidence in itself." Furthermore, while American aid had been necessary to rehabilitate the postwar world, it inevitably "has caused a feeling that one has for his creditor." Did he think U.S. foreign aid was coming to an end? Stevenson replied, "Have you any little questions you'd like to ask me?" then went on to say that few nations wanted aid if they could support themselves, that foreign aid had placed a "terrible burden" on the American taxpayer, and that he hoped and believed that economic assistance would soon end, although military assistance would continue. His questioners persisted: If aid ended, trade must take its place—and the United States had imposed import restrictions. Stevenson said "a large body of opinion" in America recognized that trade was a two-way street. Did he see any sign of relaxation of the cold war in Europe? He replied, "A softer wind is blowing from the steppes of Russia and from Moscow." Asked if he would run again in 1956, he replied, "I'm obliged to say to you that if I could answer your question, which I can't—I wouldn't."

Stevenson spent the weekend bridging July and August finishing his last *Look* article, a summation:

"There is no reliable evidence yet that Russia is ready to abandon her goal of world domination; the non-Communist world is by no means a harmonious household and includes every variety of attitude; there is a growing sentiment in Europe and Asia for meeting the Russians 'half way' (half way to what, the Europeans and Asians don't exactly know) and, finally, faith in American leadership is shaken as confidence declines in America's self-confidence."

The trip was over. A public assessment of his position began. The pro-Stevenson New York *Post* said that a little more than a year ago Eisenhower was "probably the biggest man in Europe" but today his stock had never "been so low" while Stevenson's had skyrocketed. An article in the *New Leader,* however, said that during Stevenson's stay in London "neither his person nor his views have left a sharp imprint on the public mind" and that an "emotional let-down" had followed his one major press conference. Political reporters in the United States were predicting a struggle for control of the Democratic Party. The AP reported from the annual Governors' Conference that Democratic Governors did not believe Stevenson could beat Eisenhower in 1956. Arthur Krock in the New York *Times* praised Stevenson for having compiled "an impressive record . . . of thoughtful and penetrating accounts of global conditions" during his travels, for having upheld the American "liberal" tradition in foreign policy, and for having avoided many pitfalls. He would return with "increased stature." Nevertheless, "practical politicians" were discussing the advantages of a different candidate in 1956, and Stevenson would be hard pressed to hold the limelight against incumbent Senators and Governors. *Time* magazine said the Democratic Party was "disorganized, in debt and leaderless," the big city machines in New York and Chicago were "backfiring rattletraps," in California only one Democrat, Attorney General Edmund G. (Pat) Brown, held important office; Stevenson was "the titular head" but had long been out of the country, while Truman was exerting no leadership and "Into this leadership vacuum has blown a tornado from the Southwest." Lyndon Johnson was "the key Democrat" at present, a skillful operator. Under his leadership the Democratic Party must make the record on which it would face the voters next year.

18.

Stevenson's plane landed at 8 A.M. at Idlewild Airport (later JFK), and he disembarked with Bill Blair and John Fell. Leading New York Democrats met him, including the State Chairman Richard H. Balch and Averell Harriman. Before television and newsreel cameras, wearing a dark blue suit and blue-striped shirt, he looked tanned and lively. He went to the Biltmore Hotel and held a press conference attended by some 250 reporters and photographers. He "displayed the quick wit and turn of phrase that had made him one of the most articulate campaigners in American political history," the *Times* said. First, he read a statement saying he had traveled tens of thousands of miles by various means, including camelback, and talked to "everyone" in thirty countries, "from cobblers to kings." He expressed his gratitude to his foreign hosts and to the Eisenhower administration and its ambassadors who had eased his way. "There is no substitute for seeing with your own eyes and hearing with your own ears. . . . And what I have seen and heard is both encouraging and sobering."

Americans could not be complacent as long as the "inscrutable men" of totalitarian Russia and China decided on peace or war. "But there are grounds for hope. The policy of building the economic and military strength of the non-Communist world has worked well." Communist insurrection in the Philippines, Indonesia, and Burma had failed. Guerrillas in Malaya were losing. South Korea had been liberated. The spread of Communism had been "arrested." Cracks were opening in the Iron Curtain, especially in East Germany. Since Stalin's death the Soviets seemed to have changed tactics and begun "a cautious retreat" but it was by no means certain that their strategic goal of world domination had changed.

Europe's recovery was "phenomenal." Governments everywhere were turning to free institutions to solve economic and social problems. "In short, we have been winning the cold war step by step. . . . In consequence the danger of world war has diminished. . . . But this is no time to relax or lower our guard." Given this central success, one might expect the Western Allies to be united. Instead, many tensions existed—Kashmir, Suez, Arab unrest, Trieste, Indochina, and others, as well as neutralism in Asia, political instability in France and Italy, and uncertainty about the future of Germany and the unification of Europe. The Communists would exploit every Allied division. Not everybody shared America's "views of Communism and its menace" nor did they think America all-wise, all-powerful, and always right.

America was much misunderstood abroad. Her prestige and moral influence had declined. "There is an impression that we are inflexible and erratic; that faith in cooperation is being replaced by belief in unilateral action—a readiness to go it alone. It is hard for them to reconcile our view of the danger with a cut in our defense buildup. There is an impression that 'trade not aid' is becoming no aid and no trade. Book burning, purges, and invasions of executive responsibility have obscured the bright image of America; and when we give the impression that we are scared and freedom of speech and freedom of expression are on the defensive in the United States, we put the United States on the defensive. But I doubt if anything has been lost that cannot be regained. President Eisenhower's administration faces many acute problems," and he mentioned Korea, Indochina, China, Germany, trade. "While abroad I have never criticized the Administration's handling of our foreign affairs; rather I have sought to explain American attitudes and positions when I had to and as best I could. . . . In conclusion, let me add that while I have not been able to follow events here closely during my absence, I do know that the Democratic minority in the Congress has made a record of which I for one am proud and thankful, and for which the President should be even more thankful. This has been opposition at its best."

His own plans were indefinite—he had to make a living and wanted to do many things, including "some reading and some plain, ordinary, quiet living, which has eluded me for the past thirteen years. . . . I want to do everything I can to keep our country free and strong; a land to which all people in the world can look in the future, as in the past, with respect, confidence and, if I may say so, with love."

Asked about McCarthy, he said he had been asked more often about him around the world than about anything else. He intended to have more to say about McCarthyism now that he was home. He declined comment on the Korean peace conference—"there are enough cooks stirring that broth."

Stevenson was in New York only about eight hours, leaving on a 4:06 P.M. flight to Chicago and going on to Libertyville. A columnist reported that Stevenson telephoned Truman, Johnson, and Rayburn "within a matter of hours of setting foot on his native soil." Murray Kempton, pro-Stevenson columnist in the New York *Post,* wrote, "Adlai Stevenson came home today, jaunty as ever, casual as ever, lonely as ever and aching more than ever with the sense that from here on in, his destiny has no room in it for the peace and the privacy that have escaped him for the last year." It was the Stevenson idolater's stereotype.

In Chicago that night, Stevenson was met by Jack Arvey, Steve Mitchell, State Chairman Ronan, Mayor Kennelly, and reporters. He told them he thought the Democrats' chances of winning the off-year 1954 election were "excellent." Under no circumstances would he run against Paul Douglas for the Senate. Eisenhower had invited him to visit. He would support Mitchell against reported efforts to replace him as national chairman.

Stevenson's world tour had been a triumph. It had enlarged his own knowledge and horizons. It had kept him out of Democratic power struggles early in the Eisenhower years. Newspaper reports had conveyed the impression that he was warmly received wherever he went and was regarded as an unofficial ambassador of the United States to the world. *Look,* and the tour itself, had given him a platform. He had seen virtually every important world figure outside the Sino-Soviet sphere and often had been a guest of state. When one consorts with statesmen, one is likely to be termed statesman. A statesman can speak with authority, carries his built-in platform about with him, and can elevate himself, when he chooses, above partisan infighting (or can join in it at will). The trip had kept him on the national and world stages, places he would have left had he slunk back to a LaSalle Street law firm after his brief hour in the national electoral spotlight. He was no defeated politician, he was a leader, albeit of what was not precisely clear.

On Monday, Stevenson went to his office on LaSalle Street. He dictated correspondence—asked Lloyd Garrison to send him a bill for his services as literary agent (he did—$10,000, about what any agent would have charged), thanked Secretary Dulles for courtesies and promised to see him when he was next in Washington, asked his secretary Margaret Munn in Springfield to have his dog Artie brought to Libertyville. At the office he found some 450 speaking invitations.

Archibald Alexander of New Jersey urged him to lead the Democratic Party, in danger of being sundered by its Southern and Northern liberal wings, and to run again in 1956. Stevenson's reply took a position reminiscent of the one he had taken in the spring of 1952—reluctant to run, willing to serve. It was both in character and appropriate to the times. The *New Republic* published a long "report to Stevenson." It said that Democratic leaders would come to Chicago for his speech and their two-day meeting September 14–15 in a "show us" spirit. All the elements he must contend with would be there—Senators, the National Committee, ex-President Truman and some of his Cabinet, intellectuals, labor leaders. Many wished him well—but most were "frankly skeptical that you can be an active political leader" without alienating some group essential to victory in 1956. The race had already begun: the candidates were Kerr, Kefauver, Williams, Harriman, Symington, and Stevenson.

Dave Bell sent Stevenson a draft for his September 15 speech. Schlesinger sent him a bundle of material on issues, including statements by Dave Bell, Paul Douglas, and Marriner Eccles (former chairman of the Federal Reserve Board) on Eisenhower's fiscal and monetary policies, and a paper by an expert on Social Security. He said that Bob Tufts was sending Stevenson a statement on foreign policy, Galbraith would send one on agriculture, and he expected that Wirtz would prepare one on labor. Schlesinger would also send a draft for the September 15 speech. Stevenson was getting conflicting advice on whether to speak out against McCarthy.

Work was closing in; he spent the Labor Day weekend at Libertyville, working on his speech. Paul M. Butler of Indiana told Stevenson he would be available for a private talk during the Chicago two-day meeting. Jonathan Daniels, the Southern editor and Democratic policy advisor, told him that "these Southern rumblings" were "manufactured by people who were against us in the election and still are, and who will be against us in 1956." On September 12, Senator John F. Kennedy married Jacqueline Bouvier, and Stevenson sent them a telegram. On the eve of the September 14–15 meeting, Scotty Reston wrote in the New York *Times* that Stevenson had "apparently charmed everybody from the Emperor of Japan to the Queen of England" but faced a sterner test now in Chicago: "Democratic politicians out of office charm hard." Stevenson might be a statesman thinking of the next generation but Democrats were thinking of the next election. "Nobody since Bryan has been able to do what Adlai Stevenson is now apparently setting out to do—win a second nomination with nothing but character and eloquence."

Richard Rovere reported in the *New York Times Magazine* that Stevenson was "taking his ease on the Libertyville terrace, reading and talking and thinking, but mostly, or most importantly, thinking." He sometimes played tennis or golf or did some gardening. Rovere received the impression not of a man who craved repose but, rather, "of a man who feels that he has crowded too much experience into too short a time. What he needs now and is getting is time for assimilation." His staff shielded him (though one night a group of Yale students en route to New Haven from the West Coast had found their way to Libertyville and requested the pleasure of his company for an evening; they got it). He feared that if he attacked Administration policy, as he felt he should, his attacks would be misread abroad as a repudiation of American ends, not criticism of the Administration's means. "Our prestige is low enough as it is," Stevenson was saying, according to Rovere, "and I don't want to be used to depress it even

more." Should he return to the law? Write a book? Travel? Where—
Africa? South America? Should he attack McCarthy? Some thought
McCarthy was in trouble, having run out of targets that would make headlines, and a Stevenson assault would only help him. He was reaching no
categorical decisions. He was not that sort. But, Rovere wrote perceptively, "It would be misleading in the extreme to picture Stevenson merely
as a walking mass of indecisions and hesitations. Though the uncertainties
of his position are currently occupying most of his thoughts, there are
broad areas in which he is not beset by any doubts as to what he wants to
do. He unreservedly welcomes the opportunity he is going to have,
whatever his political fortunes may be, to play a leading part in the
revitalization of his party. And he looks forward eagerly to the job of
helping American liberalism to restate its ends and to seek new, appropriate means. The latter undertaking is particularly to his liking." He
hoped to enlist the help of the intellectuals he had attracted in 1952
(though those who insisted on making a cult of him alarmed and re-
pelled him).

On Saturday evening, September 12, Stevenson had dinner with President Truman. Truman urged him repeatedly to take over active leadership
of the party. Stevenson kept protesting his lack of qualifications. Truman
finally said, "Well, if a knucklehead like me can be a successful President,
I guess you can do all right." Stevenson would give two speeches at the
Democratic meetings. He would use Schlesinger's draft Monday night at a
Democratic dinner in Chicago. His big speech would be Tuesday night in
the Civic Opera House in Chicago, nationally televised and sponsored by a
"Stevenson Report Committee" of people active in the Volunteers and IVI
(Independent Voters of Illinois). Stevenson had written a draft himself,
then George Ball (Stevenson's old friend and law associate and a political
adviser in 1952—later Undersecretary of State), Clayton Fritchey, Wilson Wyatt, Barry Bingham, and Phil Stern (Democratic National Committee idea man) had come to town and gone to work on it, and Stevenson
was unhappy with the result.

On Sunday he had breakfast with Oscar Chapman and lunch with
Truman and Steve Mitchell. Averell Harriman was in town, confident that
Robert Wagner "had a chance" in Tuesday's New York mayoralty primary, an opinion widely considered evidence of Harriman's ama-
teurishness in politics. (He turned out to be right.) The national press was
arriving, and so were national Democratic leaders. What had begun as a
Stevenson homecoming was turning into a major between-elections Democratic conclave. Stevenson complained to Schlesinger that Ball, Fritchey,
Wyatt, Bingham, and Stern had "wrenched my ideas all out of focus. I
wanted it to be an Asia speech; now it is a Europe speech. Also there are
things in it I just don't feel that I can say. I've never had such a terrible
time with any one speech." Monday night's Democratic dinner was long
and, Schlesinger thought, tedious. Harriman was hurt at not being on the

dais. Rayburn gave a dull speech, Schlesinger thought, and Truman "a rather routine one," and most others spoke tediously. By the time Stevenson's turn came "the room was filled with sodden and restless Democrats." But when he began "they all sat up as if an electric current had been shot through them. His speech was a triumph."

It was a purely political speech and a skillful one. He praised the "strong and wise" leadership of Johnson and Rayburn, responsible opposition at its best, and said he hoped Eisenhower realized he himself had been "the greatest beneficiary" of the Democratic Party. He said that although the Republicans during the campaign had promised to sweep away "the last vestiges" of the New Deal, so far they had done nothing but postpone every issue. He moved to the attack—"hollow" political gestures, cuts in defense, low morale in the Foreign Service, "reckless smears" at home and weakened alliances abroad. He closed with a ringing endorsement of Senator Paul Douglas of Illinois, up for re-election next year.

After the speech various notables went to Stevenson's suite. Later Stevenson read parts of the next day's speech to Senator John Sparkman of Alabama. Sparkman approved a statement on negotiations in the Far East but was unhappy about a call for a mutual security pact with Russia, and thought Stevenson should instead advocate a non-aggression pact. Sparkman left. Stevenson was "depressed and apprehensive about the speech." Schlesinger promised to rewrite it later that night and, to cheer him up, told him that a correspondent for *Newsweek* was writing that the meetings had already demonstrated that Stevenson was clearly the leader of the party. Stevenson, undressing, said, "Can't these people understand that that is the last thing I want to be?" Schlesinger thought this nonsense though he did not say so. He thought Stevenson, except in his fretful moments, in "fine form," well, not tired, "reasonably eager to play the political game."

On Tuesday, Stevenson saw various Democratic leaders from around the country and that night, to a packed Civic Opera House and a national television audience, delivered his report. It described his tour graphically, country by country, and made the observations and drew the conclusions already noted. He said he was "skeptical" of China's intentions, "but when we search for settlements we have to *search*." He adopted the "domino" theory of Southeast Asia. Germany, he said, was the most urgent European problem. On the whole, America's postwar policy of resistance and assistance had succeeded. But many people abroad saw America as intemperate, inflexible, and frightened; many resented U.S. influence. Moreover, "everywhere people think they recognize the dominant American mood is what is called 'McCarthyism,' now a world-wide word. Inquisitions, purges, book-burning, repression, and fear have obscured the bright vision of the land of the free and home of the brave." Arms control and limitation were stalemated. As things stood, "we seem now to be taking the initiative in unilateral disarmament"; Stevenson opposed. In the past new initiatives had had little impact on the Kremlin. But Stalin was dead, Western Europe was strong, the West had met force with force in Korea, and so now "we should press forward" to confer and reduce tensions and restore hope. The responsibility was the President's, and if it brought him a personal success, Democrats would rejoice.

At the conclusion of his formal televised speech, Stevenson ad-libbed briefly as though talking to his Chicago friends. He explained why he had gone. He said, "My cup of defeat, therefore, has been sweet indeed. After all, General Eisenhower has been to Colorado, but look where I've been." He feared that most Americans really would prefer no foreign involvement at all—that the ideal was isolation but the reality was involvement, "total involvement." He said, "Foreign affairs has been and will be the most important and the most difficult, the most intricate problem for the Administration in Washington and for us citizens for years to come." It did not help that too often we used foreign policy "to get attention and to win votes, by playing on fears, prejudices, and often ignorance. We don't help, my friends, we don't help, by loud talk, by threats, by posturing, by epigrams, abuse, and accusations, and by bad manners that foreigners take seriously. They don't always understand; for we are not talking confidentially in America, and what we say is heard round the world." Foreign leaders of new states were far more reasonable in private conversation than in public utterance, where they were forced to talk to "the street." He talked about frictions among the Western Allies. "But there will always be conflicts. Even after settlements with Russia and China, if, pray God, that is possible. It is not likely that the Communist idea of indoctrination and subversion will evaporate for a long, long time to come. For my part, I am not afraid of the contest of ideas and I am confident that the great strength of America in the future as in the past will be that it wants nothing for itself that it doesn't want for all mankind." Many in the audience thought his last remarks better than his formal text.

Truman, who had to "run to catch a train" after the speech, telegraphed later, "Last night's speech was a great one." The meetings had been a success. Monday night's hundred-dollar-a-plate dinner had raised nearly $150,000 of the remaining $275,000 campaign debt. Democrats appeared to have been determined to show that the party was strong and united, and they did. Steve Mitchell's tenure seemed more sure. No civil rights dispute had erupted. Leslie Biffle, former secretary of the Senate and a shrewd politician, predicted Democrats would regain control of the House next year by at least forty votes and would even win control of the Senate. (This seemed wildly optimistic at the time but in fact they did win the House with a margin of twenty-nine votes and the Senate by a single vote.) Stevenson had taken and held the spotlight. Symington, too wise to get out in front early, attended, shook hands, and kept still. Kefauver electioneered. Hubert Humphrey was given an unexpectedly warm ovation at the Monday dinner, and a reporter detected signs of presidential ambition.

Few people thought Stevenson reluctant to run. Columnist Max Lerner wrote that the Chicago meetings had "a quality of jubilee" and that Truman's and Stevenson's speeches showed that "the Democrats are no longer scattered nomads doomed to spend their lean years in the desert. In less than nine months of popular undisputed rule, the Republicans have managed to turn hope to disillusionment, prosperity to a case of economic jitters, U.S. prestige abroad to defensiveness, and national optimism to a drab pessimism." From this September meeting in 1953 through the conventions of 1956, Democratic optimism about 1956 steadily rose.

19.

Something else remarkable was going on. Richard Rovere had touched its edge when he wrote that Stevenson welcomed the opportunity to find new approaches to new issues. In late August and early September several of Stevenson's friends and advisers were, independently, turning over in their minds the question of how to find those new approaches and they were, independently, reaching the same conclusion: that they ought to form a study group to prepare positions. In part, the idea originated in Stevenson's "leadership" problem; in part, in the usual post-election hangover of losers; but it was more than that—it was an inchoate sense that the old New Deal-Fair Deal liberal programs were inadequate to the problems of the 1950s and, further, that to survive (or at least to survive as the liberal vehicle) the Democratic Party must come up with new solutions.

On August 25, Chet Bowles wrote to Stevenson, urging him to run in 1956, enumerating the Eisenhower administration's mistakes and saying the Administration's policies could not longer go unchallenged, Stevenson must speak out, and Bowles wanted to talk with him about issues. Stevenson replied that he would probably go East late in September "and perhaps we could foregather at your place and with George Kennan [former Ambassador to the Soviet Union] for some more deliberate talks." He agreed that the time for opening up criticism of the Administration "probably" was approaching but the next session of Congress would be "the real test," with the congressional elections lying ahead. On the same day, August 31, Stevenson asked Kennan for a speech Kennan had given and said, "I hope very much that we have an opportunity to talk sometime this autumn." That day, too, Tom Finletter told Stevenson he wanted to talk to him about the effect of the Eisenhower budget cuts on foreign and military aid. In his view they were "threatening our military security and the political solidarity of the Atlantic Alliance." Stevenson replied that he would be East near the end of September—"could we have an evening, perhaps with some others, for some skull practice." Finletter, Galbraith, and Schlesinger were talking about the need to expose Stevenson to ideas on issues between elections in order to "help him to overcome his upbringing," as

Schlesinger once put it (the Lake Forest influence). "Finletter," Schlesinger went on, "on domestic issues was a true radical. All-out. He was never perturbed by things that perturbed Stevenson—civil rights, economic policy, and so forth. He was older than all of us. He was identified with air power and hard-nosed things like that. This gave weight to his views that Ken Galbraith and I did not have with Stevenson." Finletter, a rather slight man born in 1893, growing bald, with penetrating eyes and a penetrating mind, was a highly successful lawyer in a big distinguished New York law firm, Coudert Brothers. He himself had had a distinguished career, moving to and fro from private practice to government service—special assistant to the Secretary of State during most of World War II, consultant to the U.S. delegation to the San Francisco Conference on the United Nations, Truman's Secretary of the Air Force (and later Kennedy's and Johnson's Ambassador to NATO), as well as the author of several legal textbooks and books on foreign policy, a Europeanist, an Eastern establishment figure without the stuffiness that phrase sometimes implies.

Stevenson had talked to Charles S. Murphy, of Truman's White House staff, at the Democratic meetings in Chicago, and Murphy now wrote that he had given thought to the question Stevenson had raised about using "available brain power" to work out policies for the future. Murphy was inclined to think that such a policy planning program should be lodged in the Democratic National Committee's research division, would need Stevenson's leadership, but should not be operated as a personal vehicle for Stevenson, since that would expose him to charges of empire building. He foresaw another problem: when a good paper was produced, what could be done with it? When Truman was President he would have made a speech or sent a message to Congress. Today Democratic ideas would find outlet through speeches of Stevenson and others, through legislation introduced in Congress, and through publication in the *Democratic Digest,* the National Committee's magazine edited by Clayton Fritchey and Phil Stern. Murphy had a source from which he could get funds, probably conditional upon his own participation in the project, and he would be willing to participate if paid. Stevenson suspected the private source was the CIO, and that may be why Stevenson ultimately decided not to establish the project in the National Committee and why Murphy played no large part in it.

On September 23, Galbraith told Stevenson that he had talked with Averell Harriman "about a problem that has long been troubling me" and that had also, he discovered, been on Harriman's mind, as he knew it had been on Schlesinger's—"How can we do the most to keep the Democratic Party intellectually alert and positive during these years in the wilderness? We have all told ourselves that mere opposition is not enough. Yet it would be hard at the moment to say what the Democratic Party is for. On domestic matters we are for good and against evil and for tidying up the unfinished business of the New Deal. We want an expanding economy but there are few who could be pressed into any great detail as to what this means or takes. We are solidly opposed to Hooverism and depression, but there wouldn't be much agreement and fewer new ideas as to what prevention or cure might require. In fact, we are still trading on the imagination and intellectual vigor of the Roosevelt era and that capital is running thin. You will remember yourself the number of times during the last campaign when you found yourself rejecting (or on occasion reciting) ancient and flea-bitten clichés in the absence of anything involving thought." This, Galbraith thought, was "the disease of opposition parties, for initiative and imagination ordinarily lie with responsibility for action." Galbraith thought a party should present a program to the people. Moreover, Democrats needed ideas if they were to attract and hold young voters and offer an alternative to Republicanism. And disunity plagued a party without a central core of ideas.

The solution, Galbraith thought, was "some organization in or adjacent to the Democratic Party" to formulate and discuss policies. He tentatively suggested that a study committee be attached to the National Committee under the chairmanship of some able Democrat not considered a presidential candidate. The committee members should reach out to specialists for position papers. One of the party's "truly great resources" was the many people who were "accomplished students" of national problems and would welcome such an opportunity. "As the party of the well-to-do, the Republicans do not hesitate to make use of their dough. As the party of the egg-heads we should similarly and proudly make use of our brains and experience." Papers would be "sifted, discussed and worked over." As to end product, Galbraith thought "we should keep an open mind"—discussion itself was more important than the product. Possibly the end result might be policy formulation similar to that of British opposition parties. More likely it would be a reservoir of ideas and speech material for members of Congress and candidates. Stevenson told Galbraith, "It is a perfect statement of our problem, which I have thought about for a long time."

On September 21, Stevenson told Finletter he was coming to Washington and New York and had wired Bowles. Those three, joined by Kennan, met the weekend of October 3 and 4 at Bowles's house in Connecticut. This was the birth of what came to be known as the Finletter Group, one of the most important, influential, and notable movements of modern American politics.

Finletter recalled years later, "I'd left the Air Force January 20, 1953, and had arranged with my law firm not to come back for a while. I went to Maine to write a book until the fall of 1953. The idea of a 'cabinet,' an organization in opposition, a shadow organization, was in my mind for a long time. I was always horrified at the party in opposition being unable to find out what the policies were and so on. That weekend we went up on the train and spent the night and talked about the idea. From then on it was a fact. I remember coming down on the train talking to Adlai and he asked me to get it organized—I was the one that called the meetings and saw to it that the papers got written and so on. I was living in New York. I remember Kennan's including himself out, he felt he had to stick to his knitting in Princeton. Usually the meetings were in my apartment at 45 East 66th Street. They were ad hoc meetings—I remember one in Chicago with Stevenson. Once we had a full-dress meeting at Cambridge and Ken and I got Stevenson to come. I never worked with more intelligent and devoted people in all my born days. Not everybody wrote papers. The Gov did not attend. We couldn't get him to the meetings. We sent the papers to him. I only remember he attended two meetings—one at Galbraith's and one in Chicago. [Actually, he attended more.] He may not have even read the papers. But they provided the basis for talking. The papers were written and discussed and sent back again and again for revision. It was not real orderly. We just made ourselves a place where the best views of the Democratic Party were assembled. The quality of the discussion was the important thing. We spent *hours* together. These were men with first-class brains."

Oddly, in September, at about the same time the Finletter Group was on the verge of being launched, John Sharon, a young lawyer in George Ball's law firm who had worked in the campaign, proposed to form a group of lawyers in Washington who would prepare papers on various issues for Stevenson's use. Stevenson hesitated to encourage him but did so anyway. Stevenson wrote to George W. Mitchell, formerly in Stevenson's gubernatorial cabinet and now vice president of the Federal Reserve Bank in Chicago, asking him to get in touch with Finletter and join the group. Finletter told Stevenson that Galbraith would prepare a position paper on agriculture and another on the budget and taxes for the Group's first meeting, about two weeks hence. Stevenson said on October 16, "I am so glad things are moving." He always felt the need of speech material and research support, was always questioning facts. The very existence of the Finletter Group helped keep him from fretting. On October 26, Finletter reported that the Group would meet on Saturday, October 31, to discuss Galbraith's paper on agriculture. He said Harriman would be there and so would Paul Appleby, an academician who had served in Roosevelt's Department of Agriculture, and Richard Bissell, an MIT economist who had been Harriman's aide in administering the Marshall Plan under Truman. Finletter hoped George Mitchell and Richard Musgrave of the University of Michigan would come. Galbraith would bring Schlesinger; Finletter had invited Clayton Fritchey. They had in mind the following subjects: fiscal matters (the budget and taxes) by Musgrave; foreign trade by Bissell, though George Ball and John Ferguson, an academician with State Department experience, should be consulted; power by DeVoto and Harvard University professor Arthur Maass. They intended to avoid foreign policy and defense policy for the present unless Stevenson wished otherwise.

A little earlier, on September 30, William Shannon, then in the Washington Bureau of the New York *Post,* had suggested to Schlesinger that Stevenson make a national TV speech on defense. Schlesinger had passed the letter along to Bob Tufts; Tufts had outlined a speech. Schlesinger sent the correspondence to Stevenson on October 15 saying he thought it deserved "serious consideration" and adding that he had been in contact with scientists at the Massachusetts Institute of Technology who would contribute. Stevenson responded on October 28: Stevenson wanted a draft of a speech from Schlesinger and Tufts and the MIT scientists without committing himself in advance to delivering it. He felt disorganized. He spoke to a friend of "that silly little office" on LaSalle Street—it cost Stevenson about $50,000 a year to maintain it—where Bill Blair, Carol Evans, Phyllis Gustafson, and Florence Medow were answering the hundred-odd letters that came in every day. He seemed in good humor, though he felt a need to work.

After the Finletter Group's first meeting, Finletter on November 2 reported to Stevenson. The Group—Finletter, Galbraith, Roy Blough (a University of Chicago economist who had been a member of Truman's Council of Economic Advisers), Harriman, Schlesinger, Bissell, Fritchey, Appleby, Musgrave—had approved Galbraith's paper on agricultural policy with some changes and Galbraith would send it to Stevenson. The Group also had approved a paper by Musgrave on budget and fiscal matters subject to certain changes. They had assigned topics to writers.[3] They were leaving labor and foreign policy to Stevenson and his Chicago staff.

Schlesinger told Stevenson that the first meeting had been "uncommonly fruitful" and he felt that the Democratic program of firm price supports for agricultural products was sound economically as well as politically and that the Eisenhower administration's policy, as laid down by Secretary of Agriculture Ezra Benson, could be shown to be disastrous both to the farmers and to the country at large. Galbraith concurred.

Stevenson, thanking him for his "splendid memoranda," added, "I wonder, however, if to do our job properly your group should not also enlist contributions from those with conflicting views so as to get all sides of the questions and the alternatives. But I am sure that is old stuff to you." It was a Stevensonian suggestion, and he followed it up with a note to Finletter: "I think Galbraith's farm paper fine, but it would serve the purpose I had in mind better if we had heard from the other side and got a better picture of the controversy and arguments." One wonders whether, had he

[3] Foreign trade, Bissell; natural resources, DeVoto; monetary policy, Alvin Hansen, a leading Harvard economist; public power, Arthur Maass; expanding economy, Chet Bowles; defense, Roswell Gilpatric, formerly Truman's Undersecretary of the Air Force, later an important figure in the Kennedy administration.

These men were by and large men with academic backgrounds who had government experience and belonged to the Roosevelt-Truman Democratic establishment.

been elected President, he would not have behaved in much the same way with his Cabinet. Soon Schlesinger urged Stevenson to see Leon Keyserling, former chairman of President Truman's Council of Economic Advisers, who felt that the Democratic Party should cast its domestic program in terms of the expanding economy. Stevenson would—he was attracted by Schlesinger's assertion that Keyserling had been "a leading proponent within the Truman administration of government-business cooperation."

The Finletter Group was interested in politics as well as policy. On December 7, Schlesinger told Stevenson about a meeting at Harriman's house attended by Harriman, Murphy, Sam Rosenman (counsel to and speech writer for Roosevelt, special counsel to Truman), Ben Cohen (close adviser to and speech writer for Roosevelt, Truman's representative before the World Court, and disarmament strategist), Finletter, Fritchey, Phil Perlman (Truman's Solicitor General), George Backer (quiet but highly influential New York liberal Democrat, a Harriman friend and supporter), Julius Edelstein (head of Senator Lehman's staff), and Schlesinger to consider how to combat continuing accusations by Republican rightists that the Democrats were "soft on" Communist subversion. They agreed to set up in the National Committee a staff which would research existing cases of purported subversion and anticipate future cases. They thought they also should consider a large-scale counteroffensive which would redefine the subversion issue as a threat to American freedom. Drafts were in progress. Who would sign such a statement? The Group felt that Stevenson should, together with Truman, Johnson, Clement, Rayburn, and McCormack, and possibly other contenders at the 1952 convention, Kefauver, Harriman, Russell, Kerr.

Stevenson asked Finletter to have his Group work on wiretapping legislation and the Bricker Amendment[4] (and suggested Dean Rusk, then President of the Rockefeller Foundation, later Kennedy's and Johnson's Secretary of State, might be helpful on the latter), hoping the Democrats could develop solidarity on those issues in the next session of Congress. Finletter told Stevenson that George Ball was already at work on wiretapping and he would talk to Rusk about the Bricker Amendment. He apologized for the delay in completing position papers—"the reason is that our friends are argumentative" and all the papers were being rewritten after the criticism of the December 17 meeting. The next meeting would be January 5; could Stevenson attend? He could not. "If I could, it would only confuse things, so perhaps it is just as well."

By the end of 1953 the Finletter Group had approved only four papers —Galbraith on agriculture, Bowles on full employment, Keyserling on

---

[4] The Bricker Amendment to the Constitution would have strengthened the power of Congress and weakened executive power in the making of treaties and would have weakened America's adherence to the United Nations.

"full employment in an expanding economy," and Musgrave on "the fiscal outlook." In 1954 it produced a flood.[5]

George Ball, while acknowledging that the Finletter Group contained "some of the brightest people in the United States," said years later that too often the meetings lacked focus because of Stevenson's absence. "We could never get Adlai to do his homework," he said. Some of the papers were technical; their detail bored Stevenson. It seems likely, however, that Stevenson absented himself at least in part to avoid the impression that he was building a personal political organization, which would immediately crystallize opposition. Schlesinger felt that the Finletter Group did much to prepare issues for 1956 and also obliged Stevenson to at least start thinking about them, especially economic issues. A Schlesinger phrase came out of the Finletter Group's discussions, "the quality of American life," much used by Stevenson (as well as Presidents Kennedy and Johnson, not to mention President Nixon) and intended to convey the distinction between quantitative liberalism—food, clothing, shelter—and qualitative liberalism —equal justice, personal freedom, leisure, and a better life than mere necessities provide. Stevenson himself probably had more influence than anyone else on the Group's work on foreign policy. Schlesinger was always surprised that the Group contained nobody from the University of Chicago or Northwestern University—Stevenson was not "wired into the universities out there," as Schlesinger put it.

The Finletter Group labored on through 1954 and 1955 and into 1956. It was remarkable in several ways. It clearly demonstrated Stevenson's ability to serve as a rallying point for men of talent whose ideas might otherwise have been lost. In the wake of most losing election cam-

---

[5] Keyserling on "Detail of Economic Objectives for 1960" and on "Five Hundred Billion Dollars by 1970"; Hansen on "Monetary Policy" and "The 1954 Tax Program"; Finletter on "Bipartisanship in Southeast Asia"; Maass on "National Power Policy"; Paul Nitze (director of the State Department's Policy Planning Staff, later an important Defense-State Department figure in the Kennedy administration) on "U. S. Policy toward Indochina"; Ben Cohen on "Disarmament"; Musgrave on "The Budget Message"; George Ball on "Wire Tapping" and "Government Loyalty-Security Programs"; Schlesinger on "Foreign Policy Alternatives"; Roswell Gilpatric on "Economy and the Air Force"; three papers by experts on their fields, Edward G. Miller on "The Latin American Policy of the Eisenhower Administration," Arthur J. Altmeyer on "Your Stake in Social Security," and Gale Johnson on "Agricultural Price Policy"; and a long list of papers by Seymour Harris, an outstanding Harvard economist and enthusiastic and well-attuned Stevenson admirer and adviser, on "America's Health," "Government and Education," "Outlays for Security and the Bankruptcy Issue," "The Improved Distribution of Income 1930s to 1950," "The Expanding Economy and the Responsibility of Government," "Economics of the Guaranteed Wage," "Monetary and Fiscal Policy Since the Middle of 1952," "The Economics of Medicine," "Merit Rating," "Financing of Old Age Insurance and the Reserve Problem," "The Interest Controversy," "An Economist Examines the Promises and Performances of the Republican Administration," "Current Issues in Financing Income Security," and "Another Version of What Every Economist Should Know about Medicine."

paigns, the candidates' supporters briefly cast about to continue the fight but in a few months return to private pursuits. Not these followers of Stevenson—they were serious men, determined to promote the ideas and ideals they believed in. Stevenson was again acting as a broker to the public of other men's ideas—and inspiring the men to produce the ideas—and for nothing save devotion to him and their cause.

The Finletter Group laid the groundwork for the 1956 campaign—Stevenson and his writers would draw heavily on the papers. After 1956 the Finletter Group as such dissolved—but a Democratic Advisory Council sprang up to take its place and continued to hammer out papers on issues. And then, when the Democrats returned to power in 1960, these position papers, with their roots in the Finletter Group, became the basis of the New Frontier and the Great Society. Indeed, much of the legislation that became the law of the land under Presidents Kennedy and Johnson, particularly social legislation, can be traced back to those discussions in Tom Finletter's apartment. It was not that all the ideas produced by the Finletter Group were original. Many had been in the air a long time. But these men got them on paper in agreed language, and Stevenson gave them public currency.

Thus did Stevenson, twice defeated in the 1950s, indirectly exert great influence on policy and American society in the 1960s. It was one aspect of his leadership during the Eisenhower time—and it was those years, Carl McGowan observed later, that were probably Stevenson's most important, a contribution to American life more lasting than even the better-known 1952 campaign.

20.

Stevenson lived in Libertyville that fall, working on correspondence, declining most speaking invitations, fussing with the doomed book on his world tour. To a man who wanted to infuse Volunteer blood into the Democratic machine in Chicago he wrote, "Conceivably there could be some way to bring organized impact on the party, but if you could leave me out of it for the present I would be grateful." It was one of many attempts during the 1950s and 1960s to break the grip of the old-line machine leaders. Stevenson always shied away from the attempts. Schlesinger urged Stevenson to open a law firm with McGowan, Blair, Newt Minow, and one or two others "to do the work"—"law is the best of all covers for writing or for politics." A picture of Stevenson was emerging in the national press that was to remain the stereotype of him throughout this life. It originated in the 1952 campaign; it was now becoming more sharply etched. Alan L. Otten of the *Wall Street Journal* expressed it. He wrote that Stevenson's candidacy in 1956 might be as undecided as in 1952, for "he wants to be free to calculate the risks right up to the last possible moment" and he was a "highly intellectual, moody person," "extremely self-conscious about having no permanent job," "quite likely to become depressed," "still given to soul-searching and to vacillation," "still self-deprecating." There was a certain amount of truth in this, one might argue, but it was by no means all the truth. To the many people who that fall urged him to lead the Democratic Party, Stevenson was replying, as he did to one Californian, "I certainly have no intention of deserting [the party] much as I would welcome a little serenity." And he was busy receiving journalists, politicians, publishers, and others in public life.

Accompanied by Blair, Stevenson went to Washington on September 30. He had lunch with President Eisenhower the next day. He had told a friend he intended to speak to Eisenhower "most emphatically" about "demoralization in the State Department" caused by McCarthy and he subsequently told Secretary Dulles, with whom he was still on good terms, that he had "said something" to the President about it, and the President had asked him to report it to Dulles. Dulles replied that "the personnel problem" was "a difficult one" made worse by budget cuts and pressure to bring in new people to replace ones disloyal to the Administration. He said nothing about McCarthy. He added that he hoped to talk with Stevenson about his world tour and that he hoped "we could discuss foreign policy as a bipartisan effort." Stevenson regretted that "appointments in New York" had prevented him from spending an evening with Dulles. Eisenhower was asked at a subsequent press conference whether he and Stevenson had discussed Stevenson's proposal, advanced in his Chicago speech, of non-aggression pacts in Europe, including one with Russia. Eisenhower replied, "The Governor—I think he said this; I am certain I am betraying no confidence—suggested several ways in which he thought approaches could be made where some of these tensions could be relieved in the world; among them was assuring all nations that we were ready to enter non-aggression pacts under acceptable conditions. I merely explained to him that everything of that kind was being studied in the State Department, and I was sure they would like a greater explanation of his particular ideas. And I am sure that he is giving them." When Stevenson returned to Chicago he told friends he was "appalled" at Eisenhower's lack of understanding or even interest in foreign affairs and said Eisenhower seemed more interested in the World Series.

The "appointments in New York" that night of October 1 which prevented him from spending the evening with Secretary Dulles were, really, a dinner honoring Dulles' predecessor, Dean Acheson, given by the Woodrow Wilson Foundation at the Waldorf. Among the speakers were Stevenson, Finletter, and Acheson himself. Stevenson said that on his world tour he had seen the fruits of Acheson's efforts—in Greece and Turkey, Berlin, Korea, NATO and EDC, in the results of the Marshall Plan. "I have, therefore, always been a little bewildered that even his bitterest critics have charged Mr. Acheson with all the ugly words that deface our political vocabulary—appeasement, blindness, softness toward Commu-

nism. . . . But his record of successful frustration of Communist designs
has won him a place among Russian historians as one of the greatest enemies of the great conspiracy of our century. . . . It is sad that a man's
service and patriotism can be measured in hate. . . ." Stevenson wrote the
speech himself, in longhand. Acheson thanked him for "the kind and generous things which you said about me."

21.

A sudden political squall blew up. Attorney General Brownell, speaking
in Chicago with the knowledge of Sherman Adams, James Hagerty, and
President Eisenhower himself, revived the almost forgotten case of Harry
Dexter White, charging that President Truman in 1946 had appointed
White, then Assistant Secretary of the Treasury, executive director of the
International Monetary Fund despite knowledge of an FBI report that accused White of spying for the Soviet Union. The chairman of the House
Committee on Un-American Activities, Congressman Harold Velde, immediately subpoenaed former President Truman, as well as former Secre-
tary of State Byrnes and former Attorney General Tom Clark, to testify
before the committee on the White case.

Stevenson on November 11 issued a statement calling the subpoenas
"reckless," disrespectful "partisan showmanship." Byrnes refused to honor
the subpoena on states' rights grounds; Truman and Clark refused on constitutional grounds. Truman went on national radio and TV to say that
Brownell had lied and attempted to impugn his loyalty. Stevenson's statement: "It is infamous that [Truman] the man who has done more than
anyone else to organize and fortify the free world against Communism
should be subjected to such malicious political attack." Others joined the
loud controversy. Some thought Brownell and Chairman Velde were simply trying to take headlines away from McCarthy and Jenner. At a press
conference Eisenhower said that he would not have subpoenaed Truman
or Clark, that it was inconceivable that Truman would knowingly do anything to damage the United States, and that he had left the decision on the
speech to Brownell. Since Truman had mentioned McCarthy in his speech,
McCarthy demanded and got equal TV time and, replying, said the White
case was only one of numerous failures of the Truman administration to
get rid of Communists in government and predicted the issue would be important in the 1954 elections. Senator Jenner's Internal Security subcommittee held hearings, and Brownell said that the FBI had warned Truman
in 1945 and 1946 of spy rings in government and insisted that, while he
was not charging Truman with disloyalty, Truman and his staff had been
unwilling to recognize the dangers of Communist espionage. J. Edgar
Hoover testified that memos on White had been sent to the White House
before Truman nominated White for the IMF job in January 1946.

Schlesinger saw in the affair a Republican strategy, directed by Brownell and Leonard Hall, to get a bill passed permitting the use of wiretapped evidence in espionage cases and then indict one Democrat a month until the next election. Democrats should charge that the Republican technique was a "desperate effort to cover up their present bankruptcy and confusion." Luckily, Schlesinger thought, the 1954 elections were twelve months away, the Brownell strategy probably could not be sustained so long. But Brownell might hurt the Democrats with Catholic voters, and "it might be a good idea" for Stevenson to hold "quiet and candid talks with Catholic Democrats." Stevenson received a fair amount of mail on the subject, some hostile. Leonard Hall, Republican national chairman, announced that Communism would be the "big issue" of the 1954 campaign.

Blair, often more aggressive politically than Stevenson, agreed with Schlesinger's disgust at the White episode and added, "I think it is about time that Ike was held responsible for what his subordinates do." Stevenson seemed to be coming around to this view. He told a fan, "I agree with you that the Democrats should not sit idly by without protest in the present climate of affairs in our country."

Stevenson left by plane for Atlanta, Georgia, on Monday, November 23, accompanied by Blair and Ernest Ives. Georgia had never voted Republican for President and had given Stevenson his biggest majority in 1952. He was met at the airport by Governor Herman Talmadge. At 2 P.M. Stevenson held a press conference. Employing golfers' language— Eisenhower often played golf in Georgia—he said the Democrats intended to shoot 108—"Out in 52, back in 56." He predicted that Democrats would carry a Solid South in 1954 and 1956. He resisted efforts to draw him into discussion of civil rights. What did he think of TVA? "Well, I don't think it's creeping socialism," as Eisenhower had described some of its activities. Through the afternoon he had appointments with, among others, Ralph McGill, an outstanding Southern liberal editor in Atlanta, Ellis Arnall, the former Governor of Georgia and a leading Southern liberal, CIO and AFL leaders, and Senator Russell. He attended receptions by a Negro group and a Princeton group and spent the night with Governor and Mrs. Talmadge. Next day, Tuesday, November 24, he addressed a joint session of the Georgia General Assembly at noon in front of the Capitol. Governor Talmadge introduced him.

Stevenson began (as McGill had suggested) by praising graciously and at length Georgia and Georgians, and the South's progress in labor relations, public health, agriculture, and "minorities": "Negroes were long our most depressed minority. Happily, their position has enormously improved." For years experts had predicted that "the North-South cleavage" would tear the Democratic Party to pieces but today it looked more united than it had in a long time. The Republicans were more deeply divided. Their leaders refused to support Eisenhower. After the Civil War the Republicans had maintained power by "waving the bloody shirt." Now they were trying to do it by recklessly waving "the Red Shirt" at Truman

(Schlesinger's formulation). "Government by postponement is bad enough, but it is far better than government by desperation. General Eisenhower promised the people a new morality. But his lieutenants have chosen their weapons without regard for their effect on America's position in the world, or on the level of political debate in our own halls. . . . They have taken McCarthyism away from McCarthy. What an end to the Great Crusade." Of course Communists must be exposed and removed from government. Past mistakes should be admitted. "But for the love of heaven let us do it with dignity, objectivity, and justice, and with some better motive than partisan strife. . . . No one wins this way."

Stevenson went to Montgomery, Alabama, to spend the night with Governor Persons, as Steve Mitchell had urged. Persons and Senator Sparkman met him at the airport. With Borden and John Fell, he spent the night with a college friend, Hamilton "Monk" Hackney. It was Thanksgiving, and other friends were on hand. Former Senator Tydings of Maryland took him duck hunting—"the ducks were not there," Stevenson said, "but we had a good time all the same." He went on to Washington and wrote Alicia Patterson, "There was a lot of money . . . in the Georgia trip, but there will always be people in the North who would rather have no party harmony or effectiveness or even any party, than to go to Georgia. Horrors!" Charles S. Murphy told Stevenson he was "doing a very skillful job in tying Democrats from North and South together."

He wrote again to Alicia Patterson, addressing her, "E dearest," as in the old days, and calling her "the tormented soul I've loved so long." He corresponded with Brown Brothers Harriman about investments. Not all his mail was pleasant. He received a slanderous—and anonymous—letter accusing him of being homosexual. To a woman who took him to task for using the phrase "for the love of heaven" he wrote, "Thank you for your note. I suppose the phrase 'For the love of heaven' has become something of a habit with me. I am sorry if it offended you." A Brooklyn woman, Edith Gifford, was, as a labor of love, preparing scrapbooks for him; acknowledging Volume II, Stevenson said, "There may come a time when I shall find more leisure to enjoy them and relive my departed glories." He also told her, "I emphatically agree with you about the decay of the American editorial. . . . Isn't it dreadful what has happened to our language?" She continued making scrapbooks into the 1960s. To a man who proposed him for president of the University of Illinois he wrote that he was "flattered," had "the utmost respect and pride in" the university, but doubted his becoming its president was feasible "in the harsh partisan atmosphere . . . in which we seem to be living." He did not refuse to consider the appointment. Another man proposed him for president of Princeton, and he was interested, but nothing came of it.

On December 11, a Friday, he went to Philadelphia where the Democratic Party was holding a weekend meeting—workshops, speeches, parties. Marietta Tree recalled that she began seeing Stevenson often after this Philadelphia meeting. "It was all very exciting," she said. "I went there because I had become active in Democratic Party politics after the 1952 election, trying to get the Volunteers to enter the regular Democratic Party in New York." Stevenson spoke Saturday night at a fund-raising dinner. He said the liberty bell "gives an uncertain sound in the confusing clamor of these times. The Bill of Rights is besieged, ancient liberties infringed, reckless words uttered, vigilante groups are formed, suspicion, mistrust, and fear stalk the land, and political partisanship raises strange and ugly heads, the security of secret files is violated, and the spectre of a political police emerges. We begin to resemble the very thing we dread."

On Sunday, Stevenson went to New York by train. Marietta Tree was aboard, and Stevenson invited her to join him in his compartment. "Bill Blair was furious," she remembers, "because he wanted the Governor to work on the train." In New York that Sunday he received a Doctor of Laws degree at a Yeshiva University banquet and spoke briefly about "the great split in the soul of twentieth-century man—intellectual expansion and moral contraction."

On Monday, Dag Hammarskjold, Secretary-General of the United Nations, gave a lunch for him. Stevenson discussed the problems of Communists in government with the U. S. District Attorney in New York, then went back to Chicago. Claude Bowers, the historian, congratulated him on his Atlanta speech, and Stevenson invited him to send along "bits and pieces" of speech material. Harry Truman had listened to his Philadelphia speech and wrote, "It was a good speech and needed to be said at this time. I think we have these Republicans on the run and I think you put them there."

Christmas was approaching. He occupied himself with correspondence, family, and friends. On Christmas Eve he attended the annual luncheon of his old law firm, the Sidley firm, and that night attended a young people's party. The Iveses spent the holidays with him at Libertyville, as did Borden and John Fell.

Between Christmas and New Year's he worked on correspondence and spoke to the Association of American Law Schools luncheon. His speech dealt with the reputation of the government, and in it he first used a line that became famous a little later when he used it in his Godkin lectures: "In words that never occurred to Horace, 'Dura est ovicipitum via'—or, the way of the egghead is hard." He sent a Christmas gift to Jack Arvey, and Arvey thanked him warmly in longhand: "You gave me the consciousness of having introduced to public life a great man. Whether you are President or voted ⚡486 in your precinct, you have contributed greatly to the intellectual awakening of the American electorate, and you will always be an articulate architect of American history. For the small part I played in bringing you into public life, I shall always be proud. . . . If you had become President, I would have retired from *all* public activity, as my life would have been full." Stevenson replied, "I have read and reread your letter. It touches me deeply, and I know from long experience the depth of its sincerity. I only wish I had proved a more genuine hero, but my failings are not the measure of my appreciation for your loyalty, support and counsel since you first talked to me about running for public office in the winter of 1947." That had been only six years ago—six years, and a lifetime.

<h2 style="text-align:center">22.</h2>

Nineteen fifty-four—the year of the mid-term elections. Arthur Schlesinger wrote later, in *A Thousand Days,* ". . . in a sense, Stevenson had made Kennedy's rise possible. The Democratic party had undergone a transformation in its eight years in the wilderness. In the last days of Truman the party motto had been, 'You never had it so good.' The essence of the party appeal was not to demand exertions but to promise benefits. Stevenson changed all that. His lofty conception of politics, his conviction that affluence was not enough for the good life, his impatience with liberal clichés, his contempt for conservative complacency, his summons to the young, his demand for new ideas, his respect for the people who had them, his belief that history afforded no easy answers, his call for strong public leadership—all this set the tone for a new era in Democratic politics. By 1960, the candidates for the Democratic nomination, and Kennedy most of all, were talking in the Stevenson idiom and stressing peril, uncertainty, sacrifice, purpose. More than either of them ever realized or admitted, Kennedy was emerging as the heir and executor of the Stevenson revolution." President Kennedy once said to Schlesinger, "It's very impressive, the way Stevenson managed to keep the leadership of the party without holding public office." Schlesinger thought Stevenson more akin to William Jennings Bryan than to Clay and Webster, who held public office to operate from. He said, "Nixon is regarded as an expert political technician but he did not lead the party or the country when he was out of office. Also, Stevenson was not tied to one issue. He was tied to an attitude toward politics. The atmosphere, the freshening of the spirit. It is a highly intangible thing."

Nineteen fifty-four was the first real test of Stevenson's leadership. He began it with a New Year's Day statement on the preservation of human freedom and followed that with a New Year's broadcast proposing that the Democratic Party resolve in 1954 to "distinguish between the occasion for partisanship and the time when peril demands unity," to "hold fast to our liberal humane traditions," to offer constructive alternatives and "the best candidates," in campaigning "to appeal not to emotion but to reason," and, finally, "may we never forget that the Democratic Party is more important than any individual and that America is more important than any political party." His lofty pronouncements were drowned out by a noisy quarrel between Steve Mitchell (the party chairman) and the ADA. It was a recurring problem. Stevenson tried to help paper it over and managed to escape public—but not private—discomfort.

Although Stevenson had dinner New Year's Day with the Edison Dicks and went to a fashionable wedding in Lake Forest next day, politics was taking nearly all his time. Senator Paul Douglas was up for re-election that year, and Stevenson would help him and other candidates. Richard L. Neuberger of Oregon would run for the U. S. Senate if he could raise campaign funds, and Stevenson wrote in his behalf to Marshall Field. Senator Estes Kefauver wrote a long letter to Senator Lyndon Johnson, proposing that Democrats in Congress refrain from partisan utterance on foreign policy and push a Democratic domestic program. Kefauver sent a copy to Stevenson, who responded with general agreement, though he thought the Democrats might "ridicule" such slogans as "liberation" and "unleasing Chiang Kai-shek." Senator Mike Monroney, one of Stevenson's most loyal supporters over the years, came to see him and urged him to seek nomination in 1956. Stevenson said he did not have "quite the enthusiasm for running again" that a newspaper columnist had attributed to him.

On January 12, Secretary Dulles, speaking to the Council on Foreign Relations in New York, launched a "new look" in defense policy. While acknowledging the efficacy of various Democratic policies adopted in emergencies, Dulles said the Eisenhower administration had concluded it was not sound "permanently to commit U.S. land forces to Asia to a degree that leaves us no strategic reserves," or "to support permanently other countries," or "to become permanently committed to military expenditures so vast that they lead to 'practical bankruptcy.'" He said, "We need allies and collective security. Our purpose is to make these relations more effective, less costly. This can be done by placing more reliance on deterrent power and less dependence on local defensive power. . . . Local defenses will always be important. But there is no local defense which alone will contain the mighty land power of the Communist world. Local defenses must be reinforced by the further deterrent of massive retaliatory power." The Administration, he said, had made a basic policy decision. The United States would no longer respond to every enemy challenge. Instead, it would put the Communists on notice that the United States would "depend primarily upon a great capacity to retaliate, instantly, by means and at places of our choosing."

This was the famous Dulles policy of "massive retaliation"—to replace Truman's policy of local containment of Communist expansion with a threat that if Russia or China started local wars they could expect a nuclear attack on themselves. It was a high policy decision and it touched off a long and widespread debate. Five weeks later Hamilton Fish Armstrong, editor of *Foreign Affairs,* wrote about it at length to Stevenson, proposing that Stevenson write an article. Armstrong asked: Did Dulles mean that

U.S. support against local attack was to consist solely in its ability to attack the Soviet Union with atomic bombs? Who was to decide whether to react —the United States alone, or the United States with its NATO allies or with the UN? Might not all this lead to U.S. isolation? What would happen when the Soviets achieved the ability to deliver heavy atomic attack on the United States? And Bowles had told Armstrong he felt the Dulles policy failed to take into account the question of the third world, specifically India.

Stevenson was committed to addressing a fund-raising dinner in Miami late in February. He asked for the Finletter Group's suggestions—he himself was inclined to assail the Bricker Amendment. Finletter thought it not a bad idea but he also was perturbed by the new Dulles policy, and his Group would take it up. He had sent other papers prepared by the Group, and Stevenson read them and wrote, "I was profoundly impressed." Two days after Dulles spoke, Charles Murphy told Stevenson he was deeply disturbed by the new Dulles policy—he felt it would lead the United States to only two choices: to lose the cold war or start an atomic war. He considered it a "new form of isolationism," a new version of the "fortress America" idea. Who was going to decide "on what day to drop the atomic bomb, and at what place"—when new Chinese weapons showed up in Indochina? When Chinese volunteers turned up there? Stevenson responded, "Much of what you say coincides precisely with my own first reactions, even though I think my alarm is perhaps a little more moderate than yours. I had thought to say something about all this in a speech, but suddenly I find myself with some feeling of insecurity." He invited further views of informed people in Washington. He added, "How we can 'retaliate' against 'civil wars,' which most of us have come to feel . . . is the approved Communist method, I hardly see."

Stevenson solicited George Kennan's views. He continued to be unsure. On January 20 he asked Clayton Fritchey for suggestions and said, "The new 'retaliation' concept of defense has left me somewhat troubled and anxious. I am loathe to say anything until I know more about its implications." On January 22, Finletter sent him a brief technical analysis of the defense budget, emphasizing that the news stories out of Washington were misleading—the Air Force budget "does not and cannot give the proper air-atomic power to back up" Dulles' massive retaliation policy. Stevenson asked Fritchey to document that idea (but did not attribute it to Finletter). Paul Nitze, then at the School of Advanced International Studies of Johns Hopkins, sent a critique of Dulles' speech to Stevenson. Stevenson read it "with the utmost interest" and asked for "further refinements." He went on to make Finletter's point about the Air Force budget (again without crediting Finletter), then said he had to speak in Florida and invited Nitze to help draft a speech.

Then Stevenson thanked Finletter for his analysis of the defense budget and said, "I wish I understood all of this better." Finletter responded with a long lawyerlike letter. He said that the Administration's speeches and budget presentation indicated "a new emphasis on air power" but "the practice is very different from the speeches." Dulles was saying that the United States was so disturbed by France's failure to ratify EDC that we might stop military aid to the French and other European nations and, with his talk of "agonizing reappraisal," giving the impression that we might pull out of Europe entirely. But the facts were, Finletter said, that the U. S. Strategic Air Command needed NATO intermediate bases, we could not protect ourselves from Russian air-atomic power if we dissolved NATO, and Dulles' "rough handling" of the French was inconsistent with his concept of retaliatory power—"retaliatory power will not be able to retaliate unless the NATO organization holds firm."

Furthermore, Finletter wrote, Dulles seemed to be saying that the U.S. retaliatory force would be used to hold the Chinese in check in the Far East as well as to block the Russians in Europe. This was new policy. Truman had relied on local war to stop the Communists in Korea and had resisted Republican efforts to widen the war. Truman had conceived of using U.S. atomic power against the Russians, not the Chinese, and, further, only in retaliation after the Russians struck first. Now Dulles seemed to be abandoning the idea of keeping war local. He had announced that if war were resumed in Korea it would not be localized. He had said that if Chinese armies attacked Indochina the war could not be limited to Indochina. Then on January 12 in New York Dulles had made a general threat that aggression anywhere by the Chinese would be met by "instant retaliation." Finletter thought Dulles right in thinking that local war could not hold the Chinese in the Far East and that American public opinion "would or should sustain American troops joining the fighting in Indochina." But he thought Dulles wrong "in issuing ultimata to the effect that we will bomb somebody—it is not clear whom—if the Chinese advance further in the Far East." Summing up, Finletter said that the Dulles line was "to strengthen the emphasis on retaliatory striking power and to hint at our withdrawal of American troops both from local war containment in the Far East and from NATO in Europe." Then he analyzed the defense budget in detail, demonstrating that, despite misleading statements by Dulles and President Eisenhower himself, Air Force appropriations were insufficient to build the kind of Air Force needed as we approached the time of great Russian air-atomic power. The Air Force budget certainly did not square with Secretary Dulles' policy of "massive retaliation." Instead, it raised the question: Retaliate with what?

Stevenson recognized a good piece of work when he saw it. He told Finletter, "[Your letter] reduces this complicated business to terms that even I can understand. Indeed, it is a masterful brief."

On January 27, Charles Murphy again urged Stevenson to speak on the Dulles policy. Acheson was "available for consultation," Murphy said, and so was Ball. Stevenson said he would welcome a draft for the Miami speech. (Murphy produced a draft but it was not used.) Stevenson again solicited Kennan's views. Averell Harriman told him February 1 that the Finletter Group had discussed defense policy at its last meeting and would do so again at the next. All were "gravely concerned" about the Dulles policy. Harriman considered it a "rationalization of a decision to retrench [financially] for domestic reasons rather than an expression of a decision based on our security." But how, tactically, should the Democratic Party deal with it? Harriman thought congressional Democrats should demand bipartisan consultation. In his own speeches Harriman was saying that the "new look" was really a dictatorial attitude toward our friends which, coupled with McCarthyism, could only cause concern abroad. Harriman did not want to take a more specific position until he knew more about the attitude of Democratic leaders and the Administration. He too seemed unsure.

Stevenson replied on February 2, "I agree that the 'new look' is disturbing, and to me it is also confusing. On the basis of the new obligational authority"—again he did not credit Finletter—"requested in the budget it doesn't look as though there was any conspicuous emphasis on the Air Force, even if they do propose to rely on retaliation, which looks to me like a retreat to the pre-1950 situation. It is all very bewildering, and I wish I knew just what the effect was abroad. I have been loathe to say much, but I thought in Miami . . . I might advert to the new foreign policy with some questions at least." He added a significant postscript: "If they seek bi-partisan support for the new policy—and if it *is* a new policy —I should think we should be very loathe to volunteer much help. I am afraid bi-partisanship to this administration means support for what they previously decided. I could tell you something about what the President said to me in our meeting in late September about his hope for bi-partisanship from the 'inception' of policy. But I see no evidence that this has come to pass."

Frank Altschul on February 10 sent Stevenson a paper he had written about the Dulles speech. He also said he was glad that Democrats in Congress had begun to speak out against Republican suggestions that all Democrats were tinged with treason and thought Stevenson ought to consider making a major speech on it. President Eisenhower, asked about this at his press conference that day, said he had seen no such statement but would consider one "very unwise" even from a political standpoint—"who would be so foolish as to call all of another great group treasonous to the United States of America?" Stevenson replied that he doubted Eisenhower would do anything effective to halt the extremist attacks.

Throughout this period, January and February, Stevenson was keeping a heavy appointment and correspondence schedule, spending several days a week in Chicago. He appeared, from the house in Libertyville, on Edward R. Murrow's nationally televised interview program, "Person to Person." A friend who produced television films proposed that he make a series of TV appearances. He was interested but said it would be months before he could decide. Another friend at the University of Texas Law School told him, "A great hunger is developing for you despite everything our masters can do." Stevenson in reply described his old "horrid conflicts" between "strange political thoughts" and "yearning for an orderly life and some satisfying work." Wilson Wyatt asked if Stevenson could deliver a lecture at the University of Louisville and mentioned a safari to Africa. Blair replied that "we are all intrigued by Africa" but that Stevenson could not speak at the university—he was overcommitted and "a good many of us think that the Governor is making too many speeches in the South and not in the North." Stevenson asked T. S. Matthews, then in London, for help on two commencement addresses—Vassar and Columbia. He acknowledged a note from Alistair Cooke which had described Stevenson as "alternately troubled and cheerful, spruce and sleepless, and always that 'gallant, slightly waddling figure' which we followed via radiophoto around the world." He told John Mason Brown he had not yet written a word on "the damnable" Godkin lectures, which he had to deliver in March, but had read "omniverously—too much." He dreaded disappointing his admirers in Cambridge; the Godkin lectures had to be good. And how could they, with no time for thought?

Jim Rowe sent Carl McGowan a valuable analysis of the Democratic Party and Stevenson's position in it. About one night a week Rowe talked for a long time by telephone with Lyndon Johnson, even though Johnson suspected Rowe of being friendly to Stevenson. From these conversations and from other sources, Rowe concluded that Senator Russell was rounding up 1956 convention delegates and that if he held them to the first few days of the convention, then threw them to Symington, "times are going to be tough" for Stevenson. Johnson complained that he "had not heard a word from" Stevenson since his return from his world tour. Rowe recommended "a little cultivation" of Johnson, even though Johnson's heart belonged elsewhere—Northern liberal Democrats were attacking him increasingly, and he felt them insensitive to the fact that he had to run in the Texas primary in June: Texas was "reactionary as the devil and pro-Eisenhower" and Johnson "just has to be conservative." Rowe wrote, "He is coming more and more under attack and he bleeds rather easily. I would think, therefore, that a few kind words from his titular leader . . . might well pay dividends in the future. It has always been a source of mystery and amazement to me how human tough politicians really are. My old master Roosevelt never forgot it for a moment." Rowe said the Washington press considered Stevenson "the darling of ADA" while the party regulars were moving to Symington. This worried Rowe. Steve Mitchell had achieved a "nice balance" between the ADA and the Southerners—"and then he kicked it all away under what must have been very minor pressure." Rowe said Stevenson's strongest supporter in Washington was Sam Rayburn. Russell, Symington, and Johnson were wooing Rayburn; Stevenson should assiduously cultivate him. Rowe said that of course Stevenson might reply to all this by saying he wasn't interested—but Rowe predicted that "fate and circumstance" would make him so eventually.

During this period Stevenson's attitude toward Johnson was one of derision. Johnson's toward Stevenson was the same, but more savagely so. He was likely to say, "That fat ass, Stevenson—he's the kind of man who squats when he pees."

Blair, planning Stevenson's spring schedule, corresponded at length with Schlesinger, who recommended that when he came to Harvard to deliver the Godkin lectures he spend his free time politicking in the Boston area, Rhode Island, and Connecticut, not at academic functions. "And, in general, let the Governor associate with Irish and Italians whenever possible, and not spend a lot of time with old Republican friends from Dedham." Blair responded, "I will do my best to fend off the Social Register group, but you know the Governor."

For some time Stevenson had been worrying about the Bricker Amendment to the Constitution which the Senate was debating. On January 28 he issued a statement: "I think this is a dangerous, a radical and unnecessary proposal. . . . It would shift the treaty-making power, and, in effect, the conduct of our foreign relations, from the President to the Congress, and even to the forty-eight states. . . . It would cripple the President and his Secretary of State. . . . It is unnecessary because a treaty cannot violate the Constitution. . . . And it is a reactionary proposal, too, because when we deal with other nations we must speak and act as one. . . . Yet this reactionary amendment would restore to the states the very power to nullify treaties which they relinquished when they adopted the Constitution."

Finletter reported on his Group's January 27 meeting. Several members had reservations about the item veto.[6] With Harriman vigorously leading the way, the Group thought Democrats, and Stevenson specifically, should strongly demand bipartisanship in foreign policy. The Group thought Kefauver's suggestion of a joint committee on investigations was only one approach to the wider problem of "security vs. civil liberties"; they would prepare a paper. Schlesinger suggested that Stevenson add Jim Lanigan, a New York liberal Democratic political operative and Harriman supporter who had aided Wyatt in Stevenson's 1952 campaign, to his staff. "As you know there are two basic and distinct staff functions—the Louis Howe function and the Jim Farley function. Bill is a superb Louis Howe, but the days simply are not long enough for him to do the Farley work too; and he must stick close to you, while the Farley should be occasionally roaming about the country on political pursuits." Stevenson replied, "The Lanigan problem interests me but presents many questions which can only be resolved, I suppose, by some basic decisions on my part which I dread to make. There is also the compensation problem."

[6] A proposal to empower the President to veto a specific item or items in a bill without being forced to veto the entire bill. It was not enacted.

Cyrus Eaton offered Stevenson a directorship on the Chesapeake & Ohio Railway; he declined. Steve Mitchell and Jack Arvey engaged in an acrimonious quarrel over division of party funds and other matters; Stevenson carefully kept out of it. Galbraith asked if Stevenson, while at Harvard to give the Godkin lectures, could meet with the Finletter Group. Blair noted that a Gallup poll showed 67 per cent of Democrats wanted Stevenson in 1956. A friend told Stevenson that "the best way to insure another defeat is to keep reminding people that you lost the last election," as Stevenson had done recently. He replied, "I shall try to behave better, but somehow I have trouble taking this 1956 business seriously." When he appeared on Murrow's television show, he commented briefly on McCarthyism, and a fan urged him to speak out more fully, and he replied, "I too am apprehensive about the public climate, but I have difficulties finding time and strength for speech writing. . . . I shall do the best I can." William S. Dix, Princeton's librarian, thanked Stevenson for a copy of his grandfather's book, *Something of Men I Have Known,* and said he hoped that someday Stevenson would give Princeton some of his manuscripts and papers. Stevenson did not respond at the time but did later, and after his death Stevenson's papers became Princeton's largest manuscript collection of an individual.

To person after person at this time Stevenson said he was "making no progress on the damnable [Godkin] lectures." He gave brief, rather routine speeches. He thanked Alicia Patterson for a birthday note and said he had been living "like a hermit in Libertyville" this winter, a couple of days a week in town, occasional public appearances, "trying desperately to keep up with the appalling load of mail, visitors etc." Where would she be between March 6 and 17—when he was due at Harvard? Might they possibly meet at the Black River?

23.

At this time Senator Joe McCarthy, as chairman of the Permanent Subcommittee on Investigations of the Senate Committee on Government Operations, had hired Roy M. Cohn as chief counsel to the Subcommittee, and Cohn had recruited G. David Schine as "chief consultant." They had embarked on various investigations of the armed services. At the end of January, McCarthy in closed session questioned Major Irving Peress, a dentist at Camp Kilmer, New Jersey. McCarthy said that Peress refused to answer questions about his alleged Communist activities; he demanded that Peress be court-martialed. The Army gave Peress a promotion and an honorable discharge. And so began the great outcry, "Who promoted Peress?" It seemed at the time as though the fate of the Republic hung on the answer. On February 18, Army counsel John Adams and Brigadier General Ralph W. Zwicker refused to give McCarthy the names of those who had ordered Peress discharged. McCarthy released a transcript of the Zwicker testimony. He had told Zwicker that he was "not fit to wear that uniform" and hinted he did not have "the brains of a five-year-old." McCarthy ordered Zwicker to appear before him again on February 23. Secretary of the Army Stevens the same day issued a statement saying he had directed Zwicker not to appear again before McCarthy's committee. He said he was "unwilling to have so fine an officer . . . run the risk of further abuse" and announced that he himself would appear in Zwicker's place. On February 24, Secretary Stevens had lunch with McCarthy and the three other subcommittee Republicans. They subsequently issued a "memorandum of understanding" which stated that Stevens would give McCarthy the names of those who had played a part in discharging Peress, that McCarthy had a right to question Zwicker or other Army officers, that "Communists must be rooted out," and that Secretary Stevens' appearance before the subcommittee was canceled. To the press, this looked unmistakably like the surrender of the Eisenhower administration to McCarthy. That same day, February 24, Stevenson issued a statement: "I am shocked but hardly surprised that even the Army has been forced to surrender by the Administration. The abuse and humiliation to which General Zwicker has been exposed has now been officially condoned. I think that fine soldier and hero of the war deserves an apology, not a betrayal."

Faced with news reports calling his "understanding" with McCarthy a capitulation, Secretary Stevens said at the White House that he would not permit Army officers to be "browbeaten." On March 3, President Eisenhower held a press conference and read a long statement "about the Peress case." The Army had made "serious errors in handling the Peress case" and Secretary Stevens had said so. The Army was "correcting its procedures. . . . Neither in this case, nor in any other, has any person in the executive branch been authorized to suggest that any subordinate . . . violate his convictions or principles or submit to any kind of personal humiliation when testifying before congressional committees or elsewhere." The country must be vigilant against "subversive penetration," it must use methods that conformed "to the American sense of justice and fair play," and the Congress would serve as "the conscience of America" in deciding whether the government was "exercising proper vigilance without being unfair." Successful government required cooperation between the executive and legislative branches, and cooperation was possible "only in an atmosphere of mutual respect." During Eisenhower's own military service, he had seen nothing but mutual respect between the military and the Congress. He paid tribute to the loyalty, dedication, courage, and devotion of the military services and their leaders, including General Zwicker by name. At the same time, every governmental employee in the executive branch, civilian or military, "is expected to respond cheerfully and completely" to congressional committees. Executive branch leaders had "my unqualified support in insisting" that executive branch employees "be treated fairly" by congressional committees. He expected the Republican majority in Congress to assume primary responsibility for seeing to it that congressional procedures were "proper and fair." William Knowland, Senate majority leader, had told him that the Republican leadership was already taking "effective steps . . . to set up codes of fair procedure." He regarded it as "unfortunate" when the nation was diverted from its grave problems "through disregard of the standards of fair play recognized by the American people." He concluded, "And that is my last word on any subject even closely related to that particular matter."

Three days later, on March 6, 1954, Stevenson spoke at Miami Beach. He had considered devoting at least a part of his speech to the expanding economy. But as time passed economics receded in his mind and he began to focus on the defense budget and Secretary Dulles' policy of "massive retaliation." And all this while, during January and February, the McCarthy issue had been boiling. A draft of Stevenson's speech dated February 24, a week before Eisenhower's press conference—and much of it written in Stevenson's longhand—concentrated heavily on McCarthyism. The speech went through at least eight drafts, on half of which Stevenson himself worked. The final draft did not depart basically from the February 24 draft and incorporated much of the language in Stevenson's own handwriting. As delivered, the speech was half a slashing attack on McCarthyism, half a questioning of "massive retaliation." The audience was a fund-raising dinner called the Southern Conference of Democrats meeting at Miami Beach. Stevenson's speech began with a joke but almost immediately turned serious:

"This has been a fateful week in the history of American government. We are witnessing the bitter harvest from the seeds of slander, defamation, and disunion planted in the soil of our democracy.

"I do not propose to respond in kind tonight to the calculated campaign of deceit to which we have been exposed of late, nor to the insensate attacks on Democrats as traitors, Communists, and murderers of our sons."

Americans had hoped for an era of good feeling. Instead they had discord, hostility, division, misrepresentation, and timid leadership.

"The loyalty and patriotism of a whole political party, of one half of the nation, has been indicted. Twenty years of bipartisan effort, highly intelligent and highly successful, has been called 'twenty years of treason'— under the auspices of the Republican National Committee. . . .

"That such things are said under the official sponsorship of the Republican Party in celebration of the birthday of Abraham Lincoln adds desecration to defamation. This is the first time that politicians, Republicans at that, have sought to split the Union—in Lincoln's honor."

America's political system, he said, depended on mutual trust. "Extremism produces extremism, lies beget lies. . . . And those who live by the sword of slander also may perish by it, for now it is also being used against distinguished Republicans. We have just seen a sorry example of this in the baseless charges hurled against our honored Chief Justice. And now, too, the highest officials of the Pentagon are charged with 'coddling Communists' and 'shielding treason.' General Zwicker, one of our great Army's finest officers, is denounced by Senator McCarthy as 'stupid, arrogant, witless,' as 'unfit to be an officer,' and a 'disgrace to the uniform.' For what? For obeying orders. This to a man who has been decorated thirteen times for gallantry and brilliance; a hero of the Battle of the Bulge. And this from a man whom the Republican National Committee sends around the country to sow slander and disunion—in memory of Abraham Lincoln.

"When demagoguery and deceit become a national political movement, we Americans are in trouble; not just Democrats, but all of us.

"Our State Department has been abused and demoralized.

"The American voice abroad has been enfeebled. Our educational system has been attacked; our press threatened; our servants of God impugned; a former President maligned; the Executive Departments invaded; our foreign policy confused; the President himself patronized; and now the integrity, loyalty, and morale of the United States Army have been assailed. . . .

"And why, you ask, have the demagogues triumphed so often?

"The answer is inescapable: because a group of political plungers has persuaded the President that McCarthyism is the best Republican formula for political success. . . .

"A political party divided against itself, half McCarthy and half Eisenhower, cannot produce national unity—cannot govern with confidence and purpose. And it demonstrates that, so long as it attempts to share power with its enemies, it will inexorably lose power to its enemies.

"Perhaps you will say that I am making not a Democratic but a Republican speech; that I am counseling unity and courage in the Republican Party and Administration. You bet I am!—for as Democrats we don't believe in political extermination of Republicans, nor do we believe in political fratricide; in the extermination of one another. . . .

"We were told last October by the White House that 1,456 government employees had been removed as security risks. The President later raised the figure to 2,200. And we were told—by the Governor of New York, the Postmaster General, the counsel to the President, and countless other Republican leaders, that most of these were 'subversives,' 'spies and traitors' who had been 'kicked out of government.' Some of these orators even suggested they had been planted in the government. . . .

"The figure has now been raised to 2,427; but the only thing we know for sure is the government's reluctant admission that out of more than two million federal employees only one alleged active Communist has been found.

"It looks as though the Great Crusade has practiced a Great Deception. They may consider this good politics. But it is vicious government. . . .

"The President says he disapproves all these goings-on—this slander and deceit, this bitterness and ugliness, these attempts to subordinate a nation's common purposes to a divided party's political ambitions. He has said so repeatedly in statements to the press—but the nation's ideals continue to be soiled by the mud of political expediency."

Stevenson then turned acidly to the "new look" in foreign and defense policy:

"It has been presented to us as a program for more for our money, national security in the large economy size, 'a bigger bang for a buck.' . . .

"All this means, if it means anything, is that if the Communists try another Korea we will retaliate by dropping atom bombs on Moscow or Peiping or wherever we choose—or else we will concede the loss of another Korea—and presumably other countries after that—as 'normal' in the course of events.

"Is this a 'new look' or is it a return to the pre-atomic 1950 atomic deterrent strategy which made some sense as long as we had a monopoly of atomic weapons together with a Strategic Air Force? Yet even then it didn't deter attack, and brought us to the brink of disaster in Korea where atom bombs were useless. And we were only saved by heroic exertion to recreate conventional ground forces.

"But, you say, we did not use the bomb against Russian and Chinese targets for fear of enlarging the war. Exactly; and if we should now use them in retaliation that way it would certainly mean World War III and atomic counterretaliation. For the Russians have massive power of retaliation with atomic weapons just as we do, and our cities are also susceptible to destruction.

"And if air-atomic power is our policy, what are we doing to build up the Air Force, let alone continental defense? Last year they cut the Air Force five billion dollars below President Truman's request and said it would actually strengthen the armed forces. Which reminds me of Senator Russell's remark: 'Why not cut out ten billion and double our strength?' "

He went on to attack further defense budget cuts, using Finletter's material skillfully. Then:

"Another question: What if we are confronted with something less than a clear case of overt aggression?

"What if we had relied exclusively on a policy of 'massive retaliation' since the close of World War II? Would we have resorted to global atomic war in order to meet the Communist threat in Greece and Turkey? To counter the Berlin blockade? To resist aggression in Korea? . . .

". . . Are we leaving ourselves the grim choice of inaction or a thermonuclear holocaust? Are we, indeed, inviting Moscow and Peiping to nibble us to death?

"This is the real danger. This is the real problem. Will we turn brush fires and local hostilities into major conflicts? Will our allies go along? . . .

"Was the Administration caught between two conflicting sets of promises—to reduce the budget and also strengthen our defenses? Did it choose the former because the one thing that could not be cut, the *sine qua non* of our security, were the new weapons and air power?

"I don't know, but if true bipartisanship in the formulation of policy in matters of such grave import is impossible, at least we are entitled to the facts and the truth unadorned."

It was one of Stevenson's toughest, most important, and most effective speeches. It produced about two hundred letters from the public, by far the most since the election, and many who praised him were Republicans, though one began, "Mr. Alger Stevenson."

The speech did far more than produce fan mail, however. It definitely re-established Stevenson's stature as a powerful national political leader. And it moved events. The New York *Times* said editorially, "Mr. Stevenson, as we have learned to expect, spoke as something more than a partisan. He spoke as a conscientious American citizen. When he said that he was 'counseling unity and courage in the Republican party' he meant it. . . . This speech will have to be answered by some Republican whom the people know and respect. It compels an early and definite decision on the McCarthy issue—which will be awaited with interest." The St. Louis *Post-Dispatch* said, "The proper role of the party out of power is to provide constructive criticism. That is what Adlai Stevenson has produced." The Daytona Beach *Evening News* of Florida said, "Adlai Stevenson was not just making a political speech. . . . Adlai was looking to the future of America. . . . Here, then, is a leader."

Carl McGowan, years later, thought that this speech represented Stevenson's finest hour. "This is the period in which he was the first truly national political figure to look at Joe McCarthy and to observe out loud that the Emperor appeared to have no clothes on. This later became visible to most people. . . . It was Adlai, the losing candidate, who helped greatly to set in train the ultimate deliverance of the Eisenhower administration from the biggest albatross it had, in the process of winning, hung around its own neck."

McGowan was not at all sure that Stevenson was conscious of any personal heroism in doing this. But it took political courage. Why? After a bitter wrangle with McCarthy over the confirmation of "Chip" Bohlen to be Ambassador to the Soviet Union, Senator Taft had told President Eisenhower that he would not again fight for anyone McCarthy opposed. Many Senators were convinced McCarthy could decide the outcome of elections. Several Senators who had criticized McCarthy had lost their seats in 1950. Between then and 1954 few Senators had spoken ill of him publicly. Early in 1954 a Gallup poll found that 50 per cent of Americans held a "favorable opinion" of McCarthy and only 29 per cent held an "unfavorable opinion." At the time Stevenson spoke, many Democrats, including some of the most powerful men in the party, thought it unwise to attack

McCarthy and even more unwise to criticize Eisenhower. And some Democrats wanted to permit McCarthy to destroy the Republican Party. On March 9, three days after Stevenson spoke, Democratic leaders in the Senate met in caucus and decided to fight the forthcoming fall congressional campaign almost wholly on economic issues. They made no move to support Stevenson's attempt to make McCarthyism, and Eisenhower's tolerance of it, a major issue. Lyndon B. Johnson and Richard B. Russell were in control.

Republicans were more responsive. Stevenson had spoken on Saturday, March 6. McCarthy immediately demanded equal television time to answer Stevenson. But on Monday the Republican National Committee designated Vice President Nixon, not McCarthy, to reply to Stevenson. On Tuesday, the day the Democratic caucus ignored Stevenson, Senator Flanders, a Republican from Vermont, charged McCarthy with "doing his best to shatter the G.O.P." On Tuesday, too, Defense Secretary Charles Wilson, the chairman of the Joint Chiefs of Staff, and the Secretary of the Navy all spoke in response to Stevenson's attack on the "massive retaliation" policy. Secretary Wilson said that Defense was not relying exclusively on any one weapon or any one strategy and denied that the United States was prepared to launch an atomic attack on Moscow or Peking in the event of another incident such as the Korean War. Admiral Radford, chairman of the Joint Chiefs, said that defense planning did not subscribe to the notion that "massive atomic retaliation" could meet all security needs. Secretary Anderson said the "new look" in defense policy should not be identified with "any single weapon or any single strategy." Even the New York *Herald Tribune* applauded these utterances and Stevenson's role in precipitating them. On Wednesday, at his press conference, President Eisenhower himself went further than ever before in rejecting McCarthy. He said Nixon would speak on Saturday for the Republican Party and he, Eisenhower, concurred "heartily" in the choice of Nixon. Asked if he agreed with Senator Flanders, he refused to endorse Flanders' "every word" but he did say: "And when Senator Flanders points up the danger to us [the Republican Party] engaging in internecine warfare, and magnifying certain items of procedure and right and personal aggrandizement, and all such questions, to the point that we are endangering the program of action that the leadership is agreed upon and we are trying to put across, then he is doing a service."

Through the rest of the week, various newspapers said that Republicans were stiffening against McCarthy as a consequence of Stevenson's speech. The Chicago *Sun-Times,* for example: "It is all very well for President Eisenhower to describe as nonsense Stevenson's charge that the GOP is 'half McCarthy and half Eisenhower.' But if Stevenson had not made that statement, setting off the chain of events that will culminate in Vice President Nixon's speech Saturday night, the situation might have drifted to a point where the scales would be tipped in McCarthy's favor. Stevenson's challenge forced a quick side-choosing by the Eisenhower administration and responsible Republicans in Congress." Senator Sparkman told Stevenson, "I fully believe it was your speech that furnished the spark to set off these explosions of the last few days!"

On Saturday, Nixon spoke. He defended the Administration's defense policies, Eisenhower's leadership, and the Administration's anti-subversive program, which he said had resulted in the departure from government of more than 2,400 people—and he described their files: "subversive activities or association," "information indicating sexual perversion," "convictions for felonies or misdemeanors," "information indicating untrustworthiness, drunkenness, mental instability or possible exposure to blackmail." But he went on to officially and publicly scold McCarthy (though not by name): "Men who have in the past done effective work exposing Communists in this country have, by reckless talk and questionable method, made themselves the issue rather than the cause they believe in so deeply."

Stevenson promptly telephoned a statement to Clayton Fritchey at the DNC: "At Miami Beach I said that McCarthyism was injuring the government, dividing the nation, and diverting attention from the real issues. Last night Vice President Nixon, speaking for the President and the Republican Party, said precisely the same thing. He also assured us that the President was the 'unquestioned leader' of the Republican Party. That is fine, as far as it goes. But will the Republican National Committee continue to use Senator McCarthy as a party spokesman?" He went on to accuse Nixon of again playing a "numbers game"—reciting misleading statistics on the number of subversives in government—and of reaffirming the massive retaliation policy which had been disowned by the Administration in the middle of the week. He was careful to cover himself on Eisenhower: "As to the President, I repeat that the coequal status of the branches of government must be maintained and efforts to restore order and honesty in his own house and the nation should command the support and sympathy of everyone, Democrats and Republicans alike. His burdens are immense. I hope the kind of revolting diversions we have witnessed so long won't be one of his or our burdens much longer. If his leadership is resolute and undivided, as the Vice President says, it will be good news throughout the world we must lead." Privately, Stevenson told former Senator Millard E. Tydings of Maryland, "I . . . suspect the Administration of reluctance to administer the *coup de grâce*" to McCarthy. By no means all the Democrats in Congress approved Stevenson's Miami Beach speech. The commander was out in front of his troops. All that spring and summer and on into the fall and beyond the elections, the McCarthy controversy continued. It ended in McCarthy's downfall. It is not too much to say that Stevenson's Miami Beach speech set in train the events that prepared that downfall.

24.

Stevenson was staying with the Averell Harrimans at Hobe Sound, Florida, resting and working on the Godkin lectures. He told Bob Tufts that "certainly this charming vacation spot is no place to work." Later, thanking Mrs. Harriman for her hospitality, he said, "I shall never contrive again such a happy combination of working conditions, playing conditions and spirited conversational divertisements!" He had a heavy schedule—the three lectures on the evenings of March 17, 18, and 19; a dinner at the Faculty Club with Dean Edward S. Mason as host before the first lecture; lunch with Governor Roberts in Providence, Rhode Island, and a reception at the Statler Hotel in Boston before the second lecture and, after it, a reception by Harvard's president, Nathan Pusey; and, on the day of the third lecture, a speech at Boston College and a long meeting with the Finletter Group at Galbraith's house.

The three Godkin lectures, taken together, comprised a review of America's position in the world and were later published as a book, *Call to Greatness*. He began the first one, entitled, "Ordeal of the Mid-Century," by saying,

"More than a year ago in a lighthearted careless moment I accepted your invitation to give the Godkin lectures this year. . . . I have spent more time wondering nervously why I undertook to do these lectures than in doing them. My conclusion, in case you are interested in the rise and fall of political meteors, is that after the election of 1952, with gracious and intoxicating applause ringing in my ears from many centers of learning, my lecturing at Harvard did not seem as absurd to me as it does now, and it shortly will to you, I fear."

After more pleasantries, he launched into substance. We lived, he said, in a time of world revolution "of which Communism is more the scavenger than the inspiration." The time was long past when America could stand isolated and aloof. The world was like a drum—"strike it anywhere and it resounds everywhere." He traced the shift in world power from the Tigris and Euphrates to successive centers of civilization, ending with the "two new colossi," the United States and the U.S.S.R. He discussed at length Russian expansionism and Russian anxiety about her border security, noting that the United States had ringed Russia with a system of bases and alliances that "must look imperialist to the Russians." He reviewed European imperialism and said we should not be surprised if most of the non-Western world found the West "guilty of aggression as charged in the Communist indictment." Today Communism was reaching for the revolutionary masses left in the wake of European empire. Newly independent states were emerging rapidly in Asia and Africa while Eastern European states had lost their nationalism to Russia—"an unparalleled growth and an unparalleled decline of national freedom." He cast up a world-wide balance sheet of individual freedom and democratic government. He reviewed U.S. foreign policy since World War II and described his own world tour—a tour of three worlds, really, he said: the Communist world, the Allied world, and the uncommitted world. He described the effects of McCarthyism and the roots of various misconceptions of America abroad —our militarism, materialism, wealth, impulsiveness, recklessness, unreliability, and division. "Ignorance, propaganda, and our own behavior discolor and distort the vision of America. . . . I came back persuaded that America would stand or fall not just by the tangibles, but by the intangibles of American power and character." In the past, "rough-and-tumble American political manners" had been only an "interesting curiosity" for the few foreigners interested. But today all was changed, and what we said at home reverberated powerfully around the world.

In this second lecture, entitled "Perpetual Peril," Stevenson said the two dominant facts were "the revolution of rising expectations" and the threat of Communism to national independence and to our concepts of political freedom and individualism. The West tended to watch Moscow to the exclusion of the developing revolutionary world. That world was more preoccupied with its own affairs than with the Communist danger. Communism would exploit revolutionary nationalism. He described the condition of the people in the underdeveloped areas—poverty, illiteracy, a feudal system, a people greatly impressed by Russia's achievements. "I think it can be said, briefly and soberly, that we have survived the major crisis, that an unsteady equilibrium has been established in Europe and, if Indochina is saved, in Asia as well, but that no settlement or security is in sight and we are now settling down for a long endurance contest." He surveyed the struggle between Communism and freedom around the world and said the United States must be committed to the struggle as long as it lasts—and it would probably last a long while. The West had been unable to achieve a preponderance of power but had achieved a balance of power. That balance must be maintained "until we can move on to a satisfactory international system for the limitation and control of military power, and ultimately, let us pray, to the realization of our dream of peace by the concerting of all interests among all nations, great and small." Since threats of "massive retaliation" had not prevented Korea or Indochina, conventional forces "may well be of more importance than ever in the clouded days ahead." We should encourage European independence and European unity.

In the third lecture, called "America's Burden," he discussed the similarities between Soviet and czarist aims—the "implacable expansionism" of both—and wondered if a similar imperialist spirit has been awakened in China. In the Far East the burden "falls largely on the

United States." The situation in Asia was far more complex than in Europe. In the long run, freedom could only be established in Asia "by the will and work of the people themselves"—not by the United States or the UN. India and Japan were "the anchors of the free world" but India's "unrealistic but persistent neutralism has been particularly irritating to us." As for mainland China, her growing power was the central fact of Asia, and she might well in time become "an even greater influence for good or evil" than Russia. We must face it. He stopped short of advocating China's admission to the United Nations.

Summing up, he foresaw the long twilight struggle and said Americans could no longer assume that all problems can be solved and that every story has a happy ending. "So the first step in learning our new role in world affairs is not one which can be taken by technicians in the State Department, or even by political leaders. It has to be taken by individual Americans, in the privacy of their own homes, hearts, and souls. It involves a conscious acceptance of Christian humility—a recognition that we are never going to solve many of the hard problems of the world, but will simply have to learn to live with them, for years and maybe for centuries. When we have accomplished that step, we will no longer call out a posse to find the traitor who was responsible for 'our' loss of China. . . . In youth, everything seems possible; but we reach a point in the middle years when we realize that we are never going to reach all the shining goals we had set for ourselves. And in the end, most of us reconcile ourselves, with what grace we can, to living with our ulcers and arthritis, our sense of partial failure, our less than ideal families—and even our politicians! Maybe America, as a nation, is approaching that point.

"The ordeal of our times . . . is a challenge to American maturity and American responsibility. Nowhere is this testing more fundamental than in the field of the free mind. For never has an external threat required more clear-headed analysis, more hard and sober thought and more bold and unterrified vision than the threat we confront today. And yet the very existence of that threat has created strains and tensions, anguish and anxiety, which beat upon the free mind, surround it, torment it, and threaten to smother it. . . . Anti-reason is the spirit of the shouting, chanting crowds we remember so well in Hitler's Germany. . . . In recent years we have even seen the contagion of unreason and anti-intellectualism spreading among ourselves. . . . America's greatest contribution to human society has not come from her wealth or weapons or ambitions, but from her ideas; from the moral sentiments of human liberty and human welfare embodied in the Declaration of Independence and the Bill of Rights. America's life story is the record of a marvelous growth of body, mind, and character. Now at maturity we shoulder the heaviest burdens of greatness. In bearing burdens, in ennobling new duties of citizenship, is the greatness of men and nations measured, not in pomp and circumstance.

How shall we bear what Providence has assigned us? In Keats' *Hyperion* are these lines:

> "for to bear all naked truths,
> And to envisage circumstances, all calm,
> That is the top of sovereignty.

"And so it is."

The lectures would have been a triumph if they had done nothing more than demonstrate Stevenson's pulling power among university faculty and students—one young lady arrived with a sleeping bag on the steps of Memorial Hall more than twenty-four hours before the first lecture to spend the night and assure herself a place at the head of the line. She was dissuaded, but a line began to form shortly after noon on the day of the lecture, many people bringing box lunches and camp stools. Some 1,400 people got into Sanders Theater, where Stevenson spoke, and about as many more listened over loudspeakers in two other halls. Nobody knows how many gave up and went home. Dean Mason introduced Stevenson. Each evening he received four ovations—one when he entered the hall, one when he rose to speak, one when he finished, and another when he left. On the second evening he had a sprained ankle and cut the lecture short. After the final lecture he answered questions from the audience. Asked if he thought McCarthy should be suppressed by the legislative or executive branch, he replied, "I would not be so narrow as to limit that function to any one person or group."

But the lectures did more. They summed up what he had learned and what he had said about foreign affairs over many years. They provided a framework, they laid a groundwork, for what he would say in the future. They gave currency to a phrase, "the revolution of rising expectations," which, if Stevenson did not coin, he brought to public attention, interested as he always was in the problems of underdeveloped nations. *Call to Greatness* sold better than any other book of his. (The Harvard University Press wanted to publish it but Stevenson gave it to Harper's in lieu of the book on his world tour.) He dedicated *Call to Greatness* to his companions on the tour, Johnson, Bingham, Blair, and Attwood. There was always a certain consistent continuity in what Stevenson did. He now had, within two weeks, moved with skill and power to the front of national politics with his Miami Beach attack on McCarthyism and "massive retaliation" and, at Harvard, enhanced his position as a world statesman with deep appeal to students and academicians. It was by such means that, though lacking office, Stevenson maintained authority.

During Stevenson's visit to Cambridge, Seymour Harris tried to convert him to Keynesian economics and followed up their talks by sending him

papers on the subject. It was at Harvard, too, that Stevenson met Barbara
Ward, or Lady Jackson, wife of Sir Robert Jackson, a planning expert and
adviser to India, Ghana, and other countries. Miss Ward, a well-known
and prolific British writer, knew Ken Galbraith, who introduced her to
Stevenson at Dean Mason's house. "We all had known about him from
1952, of course," she once said. "He had become the idol of Europe."
Miss Ward, a slight bright quick woman, interested Stevenson, and he invited her and her husband to visit him in Libertyville later in the spring.
They went but found Stevenson in Passavant Hospital so stayed with Jane
and Edison Dick. Miss Ward spoke at the Chicago Council on Foreign
Relations, and she and her husband went with the Dicks to visit Stevenson
at Libertyville, propped up on a sofa just after leaving the hospital. From
this time to the end of his life, Stevenson maintained a close association
with Barbara Ward. She was deeply interested in Africa and lived for a
time in Ghana. Marietta Tree said, "He loved Barbara Ward. He was
deeply devoted to her." She wrote speech drafts for him in the 1950s.
During the 1960s when he was at the United Nations, Barbara Ward was,
according to Clayton Fritchey (Stevenson's aide there), the single most
important influence on his thinking. Stevenson's interest in underdeveloped countries often opposed him to the Europeanists in the State
Department; Miss Ward fortified this interest. Opinions of her varied
widely. She was popular on the lecture circuit and was read with avidity by
persons interested in foreign affairs but not directly involved, such as
members of the Chicago Council on Foreign Relations, and was generally
respected in academic circles. On the other hand, such Europeanists as
George Ball, with actual responsibility for the employment of U.S. power
in the 1960s, had little use for her and considered her a bad influence on
Stevenson during his UN years. Ball once said, "He had an evil spirit floating over him. This bunch of women [in New York]. Barbara Ward was a
terrible influence on him. She's a soup-head. She has a gift for facile writing but there's nothing more." In Cambridge, too, Stevenson met a number of academic people who later became helpful to him and still later entered the Kennedy and Johnson administrations. One such was Walt W.
Rostow, who, having met Stevenson at Dean Mason's house, sent him several policy essays. Early in 1960, John F. Kennedy, preparing to enter the
presidential primaries, wondered how he could tap the academic resources
that Stevenson had drawn on in the 1950s.

On March 19, in Milwaukee, McCarthy counterattacked Stevenson, accusing him of using "the Communist method of attack" on McCarthy and
declaring that the Democratic Party represented "twenty years of treason
—twenty deeds of betrayal," listing twenty deeds ranging from U.S. recognition of Russia to the Korean War. As he listed the "indictments,"
McCarthy called on Stevenson to "plead guilty or not guilty." The next
day, a Saturday, Stevenson, arriving at LaGuardia Airport in New York

from Boston, was asked by reporters to comment on McCarthy's charges. He replied that he was "not going to stoop to the Senator's level" by answering. Norbert Wiener of Massachusetts Institute of Technology wrote, "I greatly admire your courage in stepping on the head of a political snake."

Next day, March 22, Stevenson went to Princeton to speak to the senior class banquet. It was a graceful, sentimental speech. Martin had drafted it, drawing on earlier speeches. It opened by poking fun at the students, President Dodds, and himself, then recalled the hopeful state of the world in 1922 when Stevenson had graduated from Princeton. He spoke of a happier, more hopeful world then, the noble concept of the League of Nations, the twilight of kings, the end of war, then said hope had dissolved in depression and world war and now in "the confusion of world revolution." But, he said, he could not guide the seniors—"What a man knows at fifty that he did not know at twenty is, for the most part, incommunicable. . . . The knowledge he has acquired with age is not the knowledge of formulas, or forms of words, but of people, places, actions—a knowledge not gained by words but by touch, sight, sound, victories, failures, sleeplessness, devotion, love—the human experiences and emotions of this earth and of oneself and other men; and perhaps, too, a little faith, and a little reverence for things you cannot see."

He spoke then at length of their importance. Educated young Americans "dare not" withhold from government their talents. They must work actively to put good men in public office and to defend them there against abuse. The United States had placed all its faith in education. The question was whether we had reached the pinnacle of world power too soon, "before we have sufficiently elevated our national mind to lead the world wisely." Anti-intellectualism, which had been rising in America in recent years, was all the more dangerous. He urged the seniors not to be afraid of unpopular positions, of change. "Don't be afraid of being out of tune with your environment, and above all pray God that you are not afraid to live, to live hard and fast. . . . For yours is a great adventure at a stirring time in the annals of men.

"You have a better chance than many people to give a lot and therefore to take a lot of life. If we can't look to people like you . . . then where can we look?

"And before you depart from this campus that you and I have known and loved, stay a moment, my young friends, and think a bit, inquire— these halls, this campus, our university, what do they mean? 'University' is a proud, a noble and ancient word. Around it cluster all of the values and the traditions which civilized people have for centuries prized most highly. The idea which underlies this university—any university—is greater than any of its physical manifestations; its classrooms, its laboratories, its clubs, its athletic plant, even the particular groups of faculty and students who

make up its human element as of any given time. What is this idea? It is
that the highest condition of man in this mysterious universe is the freedom of the spirit. And it is only truth that can set the spirit free.

"The function of a university is, then, the search for truth and its communication to succeeding generations. Only as that function is performed
steadfastly, conscientiously, and without interference does the university
realize its underlying purpose. . . .

"The university in America is the archive of the Western mind, it is the
keeper of Western culture, and the foundation of Western culture is freedom. Princeton, or any other unversity, great or small, has the obligation
of transmitting from one generation to the next that heritage. The faculty
and administrators of a university can do that only if they are free. . . .

"I came here last night in darkness, after not having been here for some
four or five years. I came with an old friend and an old classmate. We
drove a little through the campus, after dusk. It was soft, the air fresh, the
beginning of spring. I thought of some words that I read here long ago,
written by an English poet, Alfred Noyes, who stayed on the Princeton
campus for a few years. They went something like this if I am not
mistaken:

> "Now lamp-lit gardens in the blue dusk shine
> Through dog-wood red and white,
> And round the gray quadrangles, line by line,
> The windows fill with light,
> Where Princeton calls to Magdalen, tower to tower,
> Twin lanthorns of the law,
> And those cream-white magnolia boughs embower
> The halls of old Nassau.

"Sentimental? Yes. Nostalgic, childish? Perhaps. Yet lovely, beautiful,
true. Your days are short here; this is the last of your springs. And now in
the serenity and quiet of this lovely place, touch the depths of truth, feel
the hem of heaven. You will go away with old, good friends. Don't forget when you leave why you came."

The ending was his own, one of the most graceful touching passages in
all his speeches.

25.

From Princeton he went to Mr. and Mrs. Ives's place at Southern Pines,
North Carolina. While riding horseback there with Jonathan Daniels, he
had a kidney attack—not his first—and entered the Duke Hospital at
Durham. He returned to Chicago on Monday, April 5, and within an hour
of his arrival wrote to Alicia Patterson, describing his travels, and ending,
"Are you coming this way and when. I need a little of that cold impersonal

wisdom of yours—not to mention an xxx." Blair was handling much of his political correspondence. Stevenson spent an evening with Hubert Humphrey, who had changed his mind and now heartily approved Stevenson's Miami speech, though other Senators did not. Bob Tufts sent a critique of Dulles' defense policy. Stevenson responded, "I confess I share your bewilderment about the 'new look,' but have concluded to say no more about it in view of the fact that the administration seems to have been at pains to assure us that there is no new look in fact. . . . I intend to take them to task about the everlasting merchandising and misrepresentation."

Lloyd Garrison, having read about Stevenson's illness in North Carolina, asked Stevenson to tell him privately "how you really are." Stevenson wrote, " 'Privately', and evidently not much more privately than the front page of the newspapers, I have a stone below the kidney on the left side which bit me savagely the other day in North Carolina and I was carried off half unconscious to a distant hospital. Whether to have the thing operated on, which would mean a month of incapacity at least, or to live with it against the hope that it will pass away or be more accessible as it works down, is the question. I am suffering no pain at the moment, never felt better, but the ugly monster can strike again without warning and it is sort of a nuisance when you are traveling and trying to maintain difficult schedules, etc." Estes Kefauver sent Stevenson a sympathy note on his hospitalization. Stevenson and Kefauver were on reasonably good terms, though Stevenson had taken the nomination away from him in 1952. Four days after his return from North Carolina, Stevenson entered Passavant Hospital for observation. While there, he talked to Blair and Carol Evans and directed answers to his mail. On April 12 he underwent major kidney surgery. His office put out a press release: "Mr. Stevenson had a successful operation this morning. A stone was removed from the left ureter." The surgeon, Leander W. Riba, was not, however, entirely reassuring and suggested the possibility of recurring trouble. Stevenson received a sizable amount of "get-well" mail, and the Sidley firm sent flowers.

When Stevenson left the hospital he remarked to reporters that the country needed "a little lockjaw"—the Administration had been issuing conflicting statements. On April 22, the showdown Army-McCarthy hearings began. That day in Libertyville, Stevenson began dictating to Carol Evans replies to accumulated correspondence. He referred repeatedly to "the wretched operation." He anticipated a six-weeks' convalescence. He had a strong constitution but his recovery from this operation was slow. John Bartlow Martin, who visited him on May 7, thought he looked bad, was in pain, and walked with considerable discomfort. He said, "They cut me to ribbons in that hospital," and indicated the area of a fourteen-inch incision. He was fretting about his forthcoming schedule. He had to attend National Hillbilly Day at Meridian, Mississippi, on May 26—"the Governor has asked me down so many times and after all Mississippi was loyal in '52 and I have to go"—and in early June he had several important speeches scheduled in the East, the principal one being an address closing Columbia University's bicentennial celebration on June 7 (President Eisenhower would open it). He wanted to help on that speech and others. At Columbia, he said, he wanted to emphasize "Hooray for America"—there had been too much talk about McCarthyism and what was wrong with America; he wanted to sound an optimistic note. He was still fretting about "that wretched book" and about having promised the same, or similar, articles to different magazines. Martin advised him (as Lloyd Garrison had) to get a literary agent and recommended Harold Ober, one of the most respected of literary agents and a great admirer of Stevenson. Stevenson asked how much an agent's commissions were (ten per cent) and whether it was worth it. He said he had to write to make money—"that silly little office downtown is taking all my income and all it does is answer mail." He complained he couldn't write because of interruptions.

As his convalescence progressed, he began seeing friends at Libertyville and Chicago. The Finletter Group had produced a mass of memoranda but he lacked time to read it. He needed a writer, he said. He had asked Bob Tufts to work for him for a few weeks during the summer—speeches for the fall congressional campaign. He intended to campaign heavily. He was already sounding like a candidate for 1956. When, in a discussion of the Columbia University speech, it was suggested that Americans didn't spend enough on education, he said that was true but he wasn't sure he ought to say so "because people say the Democrats always want to spend money," hardly the remark of a non-candidate. He agreed that he never again should get into the position of 1952, when he suddenly became the candidate but without staff, program, files, or other preparation. Yet he avoided any direct reference to whether he would be a candidate.

Look published a short piece by Bill Attwood saying flatly that Stevenson was running again. Stevenson, he wrote, would spend the rest of the year making speeches, talking to party workers, and making friends. He was "beginning to realize that if he wants the Democratic Presidential nomination in 1956, he'll have to fight for it in the primaries." Attwood had visited Stevenson and found him "more relaxed, more articulate and more self-assured" than when he returned from his world tour. He was sure the Democrats would win control of the House and possibly the Senate this fall. Being in opposition had strengthened and unified his party, Stevenson thought. He believed the Republicans would ignore Eisenhower's counsel of moderation and use the Communists-in-government issue again this fall but that it would fail unless the current recession ended. Stevenson thought American common sense would "take care of McCarthy" but feared "our prestige abroad will be further impaired." Attwood suspected Stevenson might be happier as a university president than as a politician but had "gone too far to turn back." *Look* had held confidential interviews with the 48 Democratic Senators and found that 33 of them thought Stevenson would be nominated, 6 thought someone else would be, and 9 were uncertain. Asked whom they wanted as the candidate, 25 named Stevenson, 8 a "new" face, 5 Symington, 5 Russell, 1 Johnson, 1 Kefauver, and 3 had no preference. (*Look* added that neither Kefauver nor Johnson named himself.) Stevenson wanted to get married, Attwood reported. Stevenson told a friend, "I am afraid Mr. Attwood was writing for his editors, not for his conscience."

Stevenson thought perhaps he should meet with Schlesinger, Galbraith, Tufts, Martin, and others to discuss the issues for the fall, then assign the issues and distribute the Finletter Group's memoranda among the writers to do speeches. He would have to get some money from the National Committee "or somewhere."

Already he was thinking about the issue that later he would make and that would become one of the landmarks in his career: how to control the hydrogen bomb. The United States had recently exploded three bombs in the Pacific, bombs so powerful they had surprised and frightened the public and were coming to symbolize nuclear peril. Stevenson felt pressure to issue a statement declaring, on moral grounds, that the United States would never use the hydrogen bomb. Asked for his opinion, Martin opposed the statement at this time, saying that Stevenson, as a private citizen and defeated candidate, could exercise no effective leadership in this area and could only hurt himself politically—open himself to attack by advocates of a strong defense. Stevenson seemed to agree and in fact did not make the issue until 1956. Lewis Mumford wrote a letter to the editor of the New York *Times* urging that the United States cease all further experiments with the H-bomb and sent a copy to Stevenson, asking him to speak out. Stevenson replied at length: "I share your sense of urgency concerning the problems raised by these dreadful weapons. I must confess, however, that I do not see that any form of unilateral action or renunciation by the United States or by the free nations will have much effect except to worsen our predicament." Mumford, Stevenson wrote, apparently thought that unilateral renunciation by the United States would somehow restrain the Soviet Union. Stevenson thought this estimate "recklessly optimistic" and said weakness would tempt aggression. "Until we can establish some form of effective international control, in short, I do not see how we can concede the atomic race to the USSR and cease atomic experimentation while the Soviet Union prosecutes it." He hedged a bit—spoke of the "moral dilemma," said he was not sure he had "thought these problems through," said we must persist in seeking disarmament or arms limitation.

He was thinking about state politics, too. He intended to help Paul Douglas as much as possible in his campaign for re-election and told him so and sent him $500. He took Bud Merwin to task for the *Pantagraph*'s endorsement of Joe Meek, a conservative Republican and professional lobbyist, in the senatorial primary. Merwin said he was under heavy pressure to support Meek against Douglas in the fall election.

During May the Geneva Conference on Far Eastern Affairs was meeting —the Foreign Ministers of nineteen nations. Free elections in Korea foundered on Communist objections to UN supervision. In May, too, the Viet Minh army of Ho Chi Minh took Dienbienphu, the key French fortress in northwest Vietnam. A little later an armistice ended seven and a half years of war in Indochina with French withdrawal from Vietnam; Cambodia and Laos became independent too. William vanden Heuvel, in the American Embassy in Thailand, sent Stevenson a report on conversations he had with survivors of Dienbienphu. They said the Viet Minh had been willing to pay so high a price to take the fortress because they wanted to discourage any Chinese temptation to desert them at Geneva and to show the Geneva powers that the Viet Minh had a regular army capable of fighting in division strength, not merely a few guerrillas. Vanden Heuvel had bought tableware Stevenson had requested.

Stevenson wrote to Alicia Patterson on April 30, beginning almost lyrically, "Thanks for your yellow scrawl from Ga—& here's a white one from Libertyville—where all is green and bursting with beauty and the lambs are ba-a-aing, the larks larking, my wound healing, my spirits mending, my health restoring!" He asked her to come there in mid-May. Then, enclosing an editorial, he wrote at length about Indochina: "Will you admit this is a *really* silly edit, or must I convince you. Do you *really* think the French who have been fighting the commies in Indo-China for 7 years don't 'realize that is one more step on road to world conquest'; or that the British who have been fighting 6 yrs in Malaya don't understand the score. I marvel—and so does most of the rest of the world—at the smug asininity of Americans and especially American editors who didn't know Viet Nam from Kuala Lumpur two or three years ago and are now telling the Br & the Fr who had been there 100 yrs all about the importance of S. E. Asia and the menace of communism that they were fighting before most of our editors could find Korea on the map."

Unable to attend a New York dinner celebrating President Truman's seventieth birthday, Stevenson sent a check for $70 to the Truman Library Fund and a letter saying, in part, "I venture to say that President Truman will find in the temperance of time a unique place in our annals. History assigned him some of our most grave national decisions and he made them decisively and wisely, I think. . . . I am disappointed not to be there to do honor on a birthday of traditional significance to a great American whom I am proud to call my friend." Increasingly during the 1950s, Stevenson was invited to attend such functions all over the country. More often than not he sent a message instead, usually (though not always) drafted by someone else but approved by him or Blair. Such messages took an inordinate amount of time. He received, too, numerous proposals of marriage from utter strangers. One at this time, offering to marry him even if he was not elected President in 1956, prompted Bill Blair and Carol Evans to get Stevenson's consent to a form letter in reply, signed by Miss Evans and saying that such letters fell into her "department" and that if the writer wanted to meet Stevenson socially she would surely agree that the "best and proper way" would be to find "some friends in common" who would introduce her to him.

Stevenson returned to the hospital for postoperative tests. Lloyd Garrison, in a sympathy letter, wrote, "From the day I saw you on the train to Princeton to this moment I have been overwhelmed with the Oppenheimer case[7] and unable to do another thing. We had nearly four weeks of continuous hearings in Washington and now I am up to my neck in a brief. It has been a grim and arduous affair, and while I am as convinced as I was at the beginning that Oppenheimer should be cleared, on the merits, and in the national interest, I am not too hopeful of the outcome." Stevenson replied briefly, "I find it almost impossible to believe that Oppenheimer will *not* be cleared. But, of course, I know nothing but what I read in the paper. I shall hope for the best, and I know how your heart has been in the *cause celebre.*"

He told Bill Benton that John Fell could not go on a yacht trip on which Benton had invited him—he had to spend time with his mother, and Stevenson wanted his company on a trip to Alaska. Unable to attend the Jefferson-Jackson Day dinner in Washington, Stevenson wrote to Lyndon Johnson a few days later, "I have at last had an opportunity to read what the others heard in Washington. It was a grand speech and stirred my blood and funnybone. I only hope it doesn't stimulate the kidneys. I can't stand much more!" Johnson replied, "Coming from a master of wit and rhetoric that is high praise indeed! I only hope that whatever it stimulates, you will be up and about again and doing your always great job for the Democratic Party." Schlesinger, who had attended the dinner, told Stevenson he suspected a plan by Senator Symington, as treasurer of the Senate Campaign Committee, to create the impression in the fall that the Senators, not Steve Mitchell, were the men to be looked to for money and support. Schlesinger thought Johnson might replace Symington as the "real candidate." Schlesinger also proposed a division of labor among himself, Sydney Hyman, and Martin on speeches.

Stevenson told Truman, "I have read your speech to the Birthday Dinner in defense of the Executive. I think it an utterance of enduring conse-

---

[7] The security clearance of Robert Oppenheimer, the eminent physicist, had been withdrawn by President Eisenhower, and the Atomic Energy Commission was holding hearings on various charges, including that he had associated with Communists and opposed development of the hydrogen bomb after President Truman ordered development to proceed. Oppenheimer denied the latter but not the former. The case was, in the view of liberals, one of the most outrageous manifestations of the McCarthy mania. Garrison represented Oppenheimer at the hearings.

quence regardless of the timeliness of the context." Truman, thanking him, wrote, "I hope you will hurry up and get well and tell us exactly what we ought to do to win the congressional and the presidential elections when they come along. I shall always regard you as the leader of the party." (But Stevenson, in replying to Schlesinger, had said, "As to my speeches, I seem to be drifting for the present in agreeable aimlessness. Somehow I'll have to snap out of it." He was, in part at least, dissembling. But he did not sound like the firm leader Truman wanted.)

Now in May associates were coming to see him. His calendar became busy: Averell Harriman, Henry Steele Commager, Max Ascoli, a Citizens-for-Douglas open house, Marquis Childs, Senator John F. Kennedy. Later (in 1955) he told Agnes Meyer, "I promptly overdid after a kidney stone operation a year and half ago and it was a long time before I recovered my strength and confidence."

On May 17 the U. S. Supreme Court unanimously declared racial segregation in public schools unconstitutional. Stevenson, with a speech scheduled in Mississippi on May 26, made no comment for ten days, then, on May 27, the day after his Mississippi speech, issued a statement there which he drafted himself in longhand. It said, "It seems to me that much of the talk since the Supreme Court decision has missed the most important point: the South has been invited by the Supreme Court to share the burden of blueprinting the mechanics for solving the new school problems of non-segregation. In effect the South, one section of our country with great complexities in race relations, has been asked, invited, challenged to share in writing the decree; to share in the planning and blueprinting, to share the burden with the court. The rest of the country should extend the hand of fellowship, of patience, understanding, and assistance to the South in sharing that burden. We should harness the resources of the federal government, the United States Office of Education, all the technical skills of our great universities—in short our brains and hearts north and south —to help one another work out this problem, because it isn't just a Southern problem, it's a national problem, even as the Constitution governs us all."[8]

It was a curious statement from a man widely considered a liberal. True, it was prophetic in proclaiming the problem a national, not exclusively a Southern, one. But it contained no praise of the decision, no call for all to support it. Indeed, its heaviest emphasis seemed to be a plea for understanding of the South's difficulties. Perhaps the fact that he wrote it in Mississippi influenced it. Or perhaps it merely reflected his lifelong feelings. Marietta Tree has recalled, "Once I pushed him hard on civil rights. He

[8] He also wrote but did not issue the following paragraph: "From what little I know I don't believe the ultimate solution is going to be either as difficult, explosive or dangerous as some of the highly colorful reports of an embattled South would indicate. And I do know that the responsible leaders of the Negro communities want to see this new legal principle worked out in harmony."

said the NAACP was pushing the Mayor of Atlanta too hard." Years later while he was at the UN and the Negro revolution has begun, he told a friend, Beth Currie, that if he had been President at the time of the 1954 Supreme Court decision he would have begun to hold meetings at national, state, and local levels to educate people and plan for desegregation. It bothered him, she later said, that people did not understand his stand on civil rights. He said he felt strongly about the question and feared a "bloody revolution" if something was not done but had been told he was "too moderate". or "old-womanish." By that time he felt that not enough emphasis had been put on job training for Negroes. He was not sure that white youngsters were right in going to jail during the civil rights demonstrations of the early 1960s. But once Stevenson said in a speech at Colby that such an arrest record had become a "badge of honor." At the UN he was concerned about black racism among African delegates. He thought it understandable but wrong. He knew many young African leaders, having met them during his travels in the 1950s, and admired them. They were proud and intelligent men, he thought, but lacked parliamentary training; he tried to help them.

Stevenson's approach to school desegregation matched that of the Supreme Court—it should be accomplished "with all deliberate speed." At that time many liberals believed the Court's Fabian approach a mistake—thought it gave Southern resistance time to mobilize, thought the Court should have ordered immediate desegregation and the President should have enforced that order. Stevenson thought otherwise. In view of the turbulent history of America in the 1960s, with its racial polarization and black separatism and white backlash one must leave it to history to decide whether Stevenson was wrong, with his emphasis on equal opportunity, better education, better job training, and voting rights rather than on the enforced integration that some of his liberal friends demanded.

In his speech at Meridian, Mississippi, Stevenson called the then current televised Army-McCarthy hearings a "shameful spectacle," said their cost to the taxpayers had been high—but the cost in money "is as nothing compared to the cost in American prestige around the world." As for Eisenhower's role in the McCarthy controversy, he said:

"No one who has thought for a moment about the burdens of the presidency in the modern era can fail to have a deep sympathy for President Eisenhower as he deals with the awesome things that crowd against him. . . .

"Our danger has been very real. In the last sixteen months, Republican freebooters, acting from the force of irresponsible habit, have raked their presidency fore and aft—with everything from the Bricker Amendment to intimidation of our diplomats and slander of the Army.

"And while this has been going on, what of the President's inaction? Was he persuaded that appeasement was the best policy; that you can have your cake and eat it too; that you can have the political advantage of demagoguery without the demagogues? I don't know, and I shall say no more, save this: he is sensitive, I am sure, about the dignity of his office and he has spoken often about decorum and refusal to indulge in personalities and name calling. I think he was right. But was it decorous, was it dignified, for his Attorney General to charge that President Truman, the source of most of General Eisenhower's appointments, had knowingly appointed traitors to high office?

"And President Eisenhower has spoken about national unity and his role as a party leader. Once again I think he was right. But did it contribute to national unity for the Republican National Committee to sponsor charges that the Democrats were the party of treason? Did it contribute to national unity for his closest associates to call Democrats 'sadists' and falsify the true picture of security risks in the government?"

Laird Bell, a Chicago lawyer and Stevenson's old friend and supporter, reported a surplus of $394.51 in the account of the committee which had organized his homecoming speech at the Opera House. Stevenson suggested it be used to help defray his expenses in connection with the Godkin lectures. He replied to a letter from Truman: "As to telling *you* what to do to win the Congressional elections; well, I have tried a lot of foolish things in my life, but I shan't try that! I think you have done much on this trip East to set the tone and the direction for the campaign. I hope I can hew to that line. The bipartisanship problem seems to me infinitely complicated by both the Republicans' political indifference to bipartisanship in the past and their present apparent reluctance to use Democrats in policy forming positions. . . . I hope we can talk . . . before long." Truman replied, "Just bear in mind that I am at your call whenever you feel that I can make a contribution to the Democratic party and the election this fall."

Schlesinger told Blair that Elmo Roper, the pollster, had become so disturbed about the nation's course that he was prepared to take a year off to help Stevenson and had written to him, asking for an interview, but received only perfunctory replies. Schlesinger invited Stevenson to contribute to an ADA political handbook and said he was pleased that Stevenson was to meet with a group of Chicago atomic scientists. Blair, who had just returned from California and Las Vegas, said he was arranging an interview for Roper with Stevenson. He would speak to the Governor about the ADA handbook but predicted Stevenson would not be too "enthusiastic." He said Stevenson "apparently" had told Walter Johnson, the University of Chicago history professor who had accompanied Stevenson on his world tour, he would meet with the atomic scientists without informing Blair. "The Governor was appalled at what he had done and at the moment the thing is up in the air." Time and again Stevenson made commitments to people privately; time and again Blair had to extricate him from them. Blair did it with good grace and aplomb. He had a lighthearted offhand manner that concealed a deep devotion to Stevenson and a firm grasp of political tactics.

Stevenson told Bill Benton that Steve Mitchell probably would "insist on getting out" after the fall elections—Stevenson could not try to persuade him to stay "because I must avoid giving the appearance of trying to keep control of the party machinery for my own benefit. At the moment I have no ambitions—except to earn a living!" Chester Bowles was discussing a draft position paper on Southeast Asia with liberal Democratic Senators. Stevenson discouraged him: "I rather hope . . . they don't issue a draft statement just now. . . . I feel that we should miss no opportunity to point out the incessant political attacks of the Republicans on the foreign policy of Roosevelt and Truman. . . . Actually, it seems to me that 'bipartisanship' is never binding when a policy works out badly and yet can never be really successful unless it eliminates foreign affairs from the arena of irrational partisan controversy."

The speech to be given June 5 at Columbia University was the product of many hands—Hyman, Schlesinger, Martin, Stevenson himself. It was the most important speech of that season. The text was not yet finished when Stevenson left for New York. He stayed in Benton's apartment at the Savoy Plaza. His speech, delivered to a large and distinguished audience and broadcast on television, glorified America's achievement and called for greater efforts to enhance the quality of American life. He listed America's accomplishments—material progress, mass production, increase in wealth and its equitable distribution, a fluid society. He reviewed social legislation of this century. "Too many of our people still dwell in wretched slums or on worn-out land. Once again our top soil, our national skin, is blowing away out on the plains. Our schools and hospitals are overcrowded; so are our mental institutions and our prisons. Too many of our cities are wasting away from neglect. And how can we boast of our high estate when more than one of every ten citizens still do not enjoy fully equal opportunities? Nonetheless our progress has been astonishing." Since 1900, America had changed her foreign policy as much as her domestic policy—renounced imperialism and isolation, assumed the burdens of world leadership. Then:

"So, having said: 'Three cheers for America—you've done a great job of work,' we have to add: 'But look out, America, your work has just begun; though you've nobly grasped the present you could meanly lose the future.'" He warned against ignorance and fear, "the most subversive force of all."

To at least one of Stevenson's aides, the speech, as televised, seemed below Stevenson's standards and less good than Eisenhower's, which had opened the bicentennial conference. It seemed to ramble, to wander, to lack substance. Other admirers, however, thought it one of his best efforts. It was not unusual, throughout his career, for opinions to vary so. It was at Columbia that Stevenson first met Agnes Meyer, wife of Eugene Meyer, owner of the Washington *Post*. She was a handsome older woman of regal bearing not unlike his mother. Irving Dilliard, of the St. Louis *Post-Dispatch*, introduced them. Mrs. Meyer recalled years later, "We were instantaneous friends. To show you what a born politician he was, he said, 'I've just finished reading your article on secularism and democracy.' We didn't talk politics at first. It was a very personal friendship. It was a beautiful and incredible friendship. It was harder than a love affair. I miss him more than anyone." She remained his great friend and supporter until his death. In 1955 she told him, "You have the same depth of character as [Chief Justice] Warren, but this never came out clearly in your last [1952] campaign. The instant recognition of this, when I first met you face to face, was a startling revelation. I had already decided that you were the only alternative to this heartless Administration but with no great enthusiasm." Ultimately, she knew him well. Reminiscing years later, she said, "The secret of his life was that he was a mother's boy. He never once mentioned his father to me. His sister was important because she tried to play the mother's role."

Stevenson stayed in and near New York a week. He kept a heavy schedule—his appointment calendar for one day reads:

9:30—Jack Fischer and Cass Canfield [of Harper Brothers, publishers]
10:30—Harold Ober [literary agent]
12—Mr. D'Alesandro [artist]
12:15—Lou Cowan [television producer]
12:30—Chester Bowles
2:15—Roger Stevens [Democratic money man]
2:30—Miss Hirsch (*Collier's*)
2:45—Frank Karelsen [lawyer, educationist, ADA board member]
3:00—Mr. Stewart (Arizona)
3:15—Jim Farley
3:25—Lloyd Garrison
4:15—Wayne Morse [Democratic Senator from Oregon]
evening—dinner and show; Leonard Lyons [gossip columnist].

He saw friends—saw Tom Finletter at Marietta and Ronald Tree's house and took a walk and played tennis with him, attended a barbecue at Alfred Gwynne Vanderbilt's where he played baseball in the middle of dinner and was photographed with Bernard Baruch. He gave a cocktail party in Benton's apartment. He recorded a television interview with Drew Pearson and in it accused the Eisenhower administration of wrecking bipartisanship in foreign affairs and confusing the country and its allies. From New York he went to Vassar to deliver a commencement address, stopping en route to see Franklin D. Roosevelt, Jr., at his farm. At Vassar he talked about conformity and said, "I hope you live curiously

—independently, and emancipate yourselves from the deadening compulsion 'to belong.'" He said that women were less prone to conformity than men and in matters of principle and conscience frequently exhibited a "moral toughness and resistance to conformity that embarrasses the stronger sex, so called." He added, "As for women in public life, from my point of vantage (or disadvantage), I have seen women's organizations take unequivocal positions on controversial issues far more frequently than comparable men's groups, and I have seen individual women enlist with greater alacrity and enthusiasm in 'causes' and reform movements."

Stevenson was politicizing. He visited Princeton, received an honorary degree, and attended a lawn party at the Governor's Mansion, the guest of Governor Meyner. He promised to campaign in New Jersey in the fall if asked to by the National Committee. Heading back to the Midwest, he stopped at Detroit June 16 and, met by Neil Staebler, the state chairman, and Margaret Price, the national committeewoman, and others, went on to Lansing, stayed overnight with Governor Williams (sleeping in Williams' eleven-year-old daughter's room filled with rag dolls and teddy bears). Next morning he held a press conference at Williams' desk to open, as the Detroit *Times*'s political editor put it, "his one-day campaign in Michigan in behalf of Gov. Williams and the Democratic Party." Asked about the Army-McCarthy hearings, he said, "I am delighted that this melancholy spectacle is nearing its end." He plugged for the Democratic senatorial and congressional candidates. Asked what he considered the issues, he replied that nobody knew who was running foreign policy, that people were "disturbed" by legislative invasion of the executive and by "inadequate and indecisive leadership," and that TVA was an issue in the South. Asked if he would support Williams for President if he himself were not the candidate, he said, "I would be delighted to be associated at any time with Governor Williams but I hadn't heard his ambition is to run for President." Expressing hope that unemployment was diminishing, he took a line he often used: "Neither Governor Williams not I can get any satisfaction out of the misfortunes of the country and the dangerous signs of trouble. At the same time we cannot be indifferent to the frailties of the Administration. As I have said many times before, I wish the Republicans well." He thought the Dixiecrats were "evaporating." He returned late to Chicago and told Alicia Patterson:

That week in N.Y. was a horror & how I yearned for orchards, tennis courts—and thee. I got back more dead than alive last night after a hideous day of factory inspections, press conferences, parties, barbecues, handshaking & 3 speeches in Mich . . . and now . . . Indiana, Spfd, Pac. NW, Alaska & back here Aug 7—prepared to receive you en passent full of news of my adventures & eager for yours. It was wonderful but what a brief moment—A

26.

During his Michigan trip Stevenson had attacked, though lightly, Ezra Taft Benson, Eisenhower's Secretary of Agriculture. Benson was unpopular with many farmers, and Stevenson and other Democrats intended to make him a prime target in the forthcoming campaign. Arthur Maass sent Stevenson a paper, a product of the Finletter Group, on Republican power policies, unpopular in the Northwest, for use on his coming trip. He took with him, too, documents Chet Bowles sent him. His briefcase was always full of raw speech material, some read, some unread, some used, some not.

President Truman entered a hospital, and Stevenson sent him a telegram, "Enjoy the sense of delicious total detachment that comes with surgery while you can because you will be up and at it again soon enough. Best wishes from a veteran." Cyrus Eaton wrote again to protest the concentration of financial power in Eastern banks. He was a maverick industrialist, immensely wealthy himself yet with a strong streak of populism, forever traveling to Russia and trying to promote U.S.-U.S.S.R. détente. Stevenson did not respond eagerly to Eaton's initiatives.

Bill Benton had recommended Carl McGowan to Encyclopaedia Britannica Films as its Chicago counsel. Now he wondered if Stevenson intended to establish a law firm in the fall and, if so, whether McGowan would join it—Stevenson might become counsel to "the Britannica itself." Stevenson replied uncertainly—he intended to resume practice after the congressional elections "with a very small operation of my own, taking only a few clients," but McGowan, unfortunately, would not be with him, since "I do not feel that I can ask him to give up the security of a large firm, with a good income, to take his chances with me with an uncertain professional future."

On Saturday, June 26, Stevenson was in South Bend, Indiana, for receptions, luncheons, cocktail parties, and dinners. Governor Schricker and Paul Butler of South Bend, Indiana's Democratic national committeeman, were with him almost constantly. At a press conference, Stevenson said he esteemed Butler "highly" and considered him an acceptable prospect for national chairman. When Schricker gave him a white hat (Schricker's political trade mark) to throw into the 1956 ring, he merely held it and looked at it for the photographers. He plugged hard for John Brademas, a young former Rhodes scholar running for Congress, later a friend and aide to Stevenson, still later elected Congressman and re-elected several times, one of the bright young men Stevenson helped bring into national life.

From South Bend on Sunday he went to Springfield, Illinois, and there on Monday spoke to the Democratic State Convention. He jeered at the Republicans and said that *Time* magazine, "as vigorous a supporter" as

Eisenhower had in 1952, recently had said, "The mess in Washington will be the major issue of November 1954."

Back in Chicago on Tuesday, June 29, he saw Bob Tufts and Bill Wirtz. They would work on fall speeches while Stevenson was traveling in the Pacific Northwest and Alaska. Stevenson told Lauren Bacall—"Dear Betty"—that he could not go to California on this trip but might in October, campaigning—"Evidently some of the candidates still think I am useful, although I suspect their good judgment." He saw his surgeon on Wednesday and on Thursday, July 1, left for Denver, the Pacific Northwest, and Alaska. Blair had worked out their schedule from July 1 through August 7. He had not only arranged plane, boat, and hotel accommodations; he had worked out a detailed program for each stop, and nearly every one involved delicate political judgments. The effort that goes into arranging such a trip is almost unimaginable, and so was Blair's skill at it.

Stevenson attended a reception in Denver and next day spoke at a Democratic lunch. After praising the candidates he assailed "this squalid, disgraceful spectacle," of the Army-McCarthy hearings and "the developing crisis in the conduct of our foreign relations." He said, "An Administration which cannot unite its own party on essentials, at least, can hardly hope to unite and lead the free world." The Administration "has failed to take the necessary measures to protect itself against the blackmail and brigandage of irresponsible people. On the contrary, even as recently as Lincoln's Birthday, the Republican National Committee was paying the traveling expenses of Senator McCarthy to travel all across the United States to speak about 'twenty years of treason,' while they were asking our help in the Congress and speaking of a bipartisan foreign policy." Former Governor Dewey and Vice President Nixon had been doing the same thing. He called Nixon's speeches "McCarthyism in a white shirt" (on other occasions Stevenson said "McCarthyism in a white collar"). Effective government had almost broken down.

"For many months it has been evident that the next test of Western strength and resolution was bound to come in Indochina." Secretary Dulles was "an able man" but he had "an almost fatal taste for slogans and for bold words." Promises of "liberation," to "unleash" Chiang Kai-shek, "capturing the initiative," "agonizing reappraisal," and "massive retaliation" had come to nothing—and at the same time the Administration had proposed to reduce the Army. Then as the Indochina crisis mounted, "a Republican platoon system took over. . . . Secretary of State Dulles has one day told us that Indochina is indispensable to the salvation of all of Southeast Asia. Then he has reassured us that that was not the case after all. Secretary of State Dulles' statements are very promptly superseded by statements by Secretary of State Knowland. . . . Then Secretary of State Nixon usually expresses his point of view. You recall that he promised us in March that there were going to be no more small wars. . . . And within a month he was talking about sending troops to Indochina. And now, now I really think he must be competing, and rather successfully, for the title of history's most irresponsible exalted statesman. He is now announcing to audiences throughout the east that the plight of the French in Indochina is due to the Democrats in Washington. I fear that this babble of voices has baffled our allies far more than it has intimidated our enemies."

Stevenson flew that afternoon to Portland, arriving at night unannounced and greeted by only a few party leaders and candidates. People recognized him as he passed through the airport and applauded spontaneously. The State Democratic chairman, Howard Morgan, drove him away, and Stevenson grinned when he saw a bumper sticker on Morgan's car: *Don't Blame Me. I Voted Democratic.* He stayed overnight at the Hotel Roosevelt and held a press conference next morning, attacking Senator Knowland for saying the United States should withdraw from the UN if mainland China was admitted to it. He met with Dick Neuberger, senatorial candidate, and other Oregon Democrats, then went to the Alfred Corbett ranch at Camp Sherman, Oregon. He stayed there a week, sleeping, fishing, riding, and working on speeches and correspondence. Paul Butler of Indiana had written a long letter at Stevenson's request giving the reasons why he thought Steve Mitchell's successor as national chairman should be a Catholic. (Butler himself was a Catholic.) Stevenson replied that he was impressed "immensely" with the argument but "the trouble is that, beyond yourself, the field seems to me sharply limited."

On July 10, Stevenson ended his holiday and spoke at Eugene. After praising Neuberger handsomely, he attacked the Administration for producing "the lowest farm prices and the highest cost of living in years all at the same time" and said our predicament was "unemployment spreading, Asia tottering, the hydrogen bomb ticking away, our alliances disintegrating, and our leadership faltering at home and abroad in a perilous period." He devoted the rest of his speech to power and natural resources. He attacked the Administration for dropping not only the Hell's Canyon dam on the Snake River but the Libby Dam which it had said could substitute for Hell's Canyon. He attacked the Administration for making "a riod." He devoted the rest of his speech to power and natural resources. policy for almost half a century." Falling into a rather unattractive (but understandable) habit, he said, in effect, "I told you so"—reminded his audience that in 1952 he had warned that the Republican policy of relinquishing offshore oil would establish a dangerous precedent for giving away other public resources. He attacked the Administration's "local partnership" policy "whereby the government and the private utilities will build the project and the private companies get the profitable part, the electricity, and the government, you and I, get the flood control, storage, and reclamation part." The Administration had undermined TVA, REA, Soil Conservation, the park and forestry services, the public domain—it all added up, he said, to the fact "that our government has intervened for the benefit of the few at the expense of the many." It was a long and eloquent partisan speech.

In Spokane, Washington, and Coeur d'Alene, Idaho, he met with Democratic leaders; spoke briefly at an AFL convention; toured Grand Coulee Dam. On Monday, July 12, having been joined by John Fell, he arrived in Seattle in the evening. It had been a twelve-hour day not unlike a campaign day. He told reporters the House was "almost certain" to go Democratic and the Senate was "close." He said Neuberger might well win (Oregon had not elected a Democratic Senator in forty years). On July 13 he held a press conference. The Geneva powers were meeting, and Secretary Dulles had just gone to Paris, and a reporter asked his views. He applauded Dulles' trip and said, "I hope and pray that we can hold the bastion in Indochina, the most important geographical area in Southeast Asia." But it would be "exceedingly difficult"—"you are asking a people to save themselves who do not choose to be saved" because they regarded white colonialism as a greater menace than Communism. He was asked "what could be done to implement" the Supreme Court's desegregation decision. His answer was long and fuzzy: "My goodness, this is a monstrous order. Well, I have said from time to time and will say again that the problem isn't just a local one, the problem isn't just a Southern problem—the problem is of course a national problem in that we all in states where there isn't segregation, which I dare say is the case in Washington, are in sympathy, [and should offer] our advice, counsel and help and certainly our understanding to the states in which this is a problem, a very acute problem, a problem of an inherited attitude and tradition of a hundred, two hundred years. The sociological resources, the resources of our universities, of our institutions of all kinds should be made available to the Southern states. . . . I am confident that within the course of time we are going to be able to work this out without disorder and violence; and that there has been a great deal of intemperate talk. . . . That with tolerance and understanding, particularly in the North with the Southern problem, this thing can be brought about to the advantage of both races concerned."

Stevenson was joined by Dutch and Ellen Smith, two of his oldest and closest Lake Forest friends and supporters, Francis Plimpton, the New York lawyer who had been his roommate at Harvard Law, and Plimpton's wife. The party disembarked at Juneau on July 17, dined with Governor Gruening, and breakfasted with Alaskan Democrats. They went on to Anchorage, where Stevenson had a heavy schedule. At the time, Alaskans were pushing for statehood. His speech said that Eisenhower, before he was elected President, had favored statehood for Alaska but after he was elected had changed his mind. He reviewed at length what Democratic administrations since 1900 had done for Alaska. He himself came out for statehood if Alaskans wanted it. He attacked McCarthyism and the Eisenhower-Dulles foreign policy heavily—the Administration had not been prepared to fight for nor could it negotiate about Indochina.

The next day, with his companions, Stevenson departed on a five-day fishing and sightseeing trip. John Fell thought it hectic: "I remember a fishing camp and a lot of mosquitoes and a PBY flying between the mountains and fishing for a day or two. He seemed to enjoy it." But he was, really, no fisherman: "He wouldn't know one rod from another." He was, instead, a sightseer. "He had never been to Alaska and he thought he had to see everything. We flew all the time. . . . Every day was crammed." A friend told Stevenson that after his Alaskan trip and one made by Eisenhower's Secretary of the Interior, Douglas McKay, several Republicans who favored statehood switched parties. Alaska at that time was considered Democratic (and Hawaii Republican). That fall Alaska went Democratic, and the Territorial Treasurer told Stevenson, "I am really convinced that your visit gave the people the big push that culminated in the landslide."

His fishing trip over, Stevenson found the fall campaign closing in on him. Blair received a long letter about Stevenson's schedule from Hy Raskin at the National Committee, formerly Steve Mitchell's law partner. Raskin proposed to meet Stevenson and Blair in Great Falls, Montana, on August 2. He would bring them up to date before the Kansas City speech, scheduled for August 6, then would go ahead to advance Omaha.

In Great Falls, Stevenson spoke at a Democratic luncheon. Bernard DeVoto joined them at Missoula to show them "the dry country."

While Stevenson and Blair were traveling, Carol Evans was the anchor at Chicago, transmitting both political and personal messages. Mrs. Ives intended to go to the State Fair for Democratic Day on August 18. She hoped Adlai III, "Adlai's girl" Nancy, Borden, and John Fell would go to the fair too. Miss Evans had talked with Adlai III; he was in Louisville with Nancy; Miss Evans suggested he might want to meet his father's plane on Saturday night, August 7, and he said he would. Miss Evans was informed that Frank Holland, Stevenson's farmer at Libertyville, was leaving. She began looking for a replacement and also for a housekeeper—she hoped to have a housekeeper "with food in the house and things in order" for Stevenson's arrival. Blair called from Montana and said Stevenson was "in a stew" about Frank Holland's leaving. From Missoula on August 5, Stevenson wrote, "Dear Miss E[vans]—All the news about the Hollands is very distressing and I'm exhausted from this everlasting travel—with still more ahead!" He asked her to refill the prescription for his kidney pills—he had run out. Blair thought the trip had been wonderful but fatiguing. "I think the prospects for victory this fall are good although the Republicans have not as yet opened up with their big guns." Blair was always realistic, sometimes more so than Stevenson.

On August 5, flying from Great Falls to Denver en route to Kansas City, their commercial plane was struck by lightning. No one was hurt. The plane landed at Billings, Montana, and stayed two hours to repair the radio, then proceeded. To a friend who wrote about the incident, Stevenson replied, "I seem to be tempting fate too often, but as the sergeant said:

'Do you want to live forever?'" Stevenson attended a fund-raising affair, together with President Truman and Steve Mitchell, at the Muehlbach Hotel in Kansas City, Missouri, on August 6 and spoke next day in Omaha to about 600 Nebraska Democrats. He said, 'I don't like the way the Republicans have dealt with the problem of Indochina of late. They bluffed and that's dangerous, especially when you can't or won't back up your bluff. . . . But even so the Republicans are not responsible for the Communist victories in Indochina. . . . The truth about Indochina is that the will and the ability of the French and Vietnamese to defend the country has not, even with American help, proved equal to the will and ability of the Communists to press their attack. That is a sobering thought. . . . We ought, as Americans, to be talking seriously about the problem of Indochina and what we can and ought to do about it. But the Republican contribution to this debate is to charge their own Secretary of State with appeasement and to call the Democrats nasty names—as usual. Yes, and to charge the French with selling us out."

He returned to Chicago August 7, 1954. Adlai III met him. Testimony at Ellen Stevenson's incompetency hearing later described Adlai III's own homecoming from Korea.[9] He arrived at Midway Airport and as he started down the stairs from the plane he saw his mother at the bottom waiting for him. A photographer standing near her called to him, asking him to pause on the step for a picture. Immediately Ellen began berating the photographer, saying he should be taking her picture, not her son's; saying Adlai III was a mere publicity seeker whereas she was Mrs. Adlai Stevenson; going on and on, even in the car with Adlai III on the way to her home. It was then that Adlai III began to realize there was something serious wrong with her.

While overseas, Adlai III had been corresponding with Nancy Anderson, of Louisville, whom he had met while in training at Fort Knox. Soon after returning from Korea he told his mother he wanted to visit Nancy. Again she exploded—said it was outrageous, he should be seeing her, his mother, not some girl in Louisville, and, moreover, having been overseas he had not seen American girls for a year and should not become unduly attached to one until he had seen many.

Nevertheless, Adlai III and Nancy soon became engaged and, that August, Nancy went to visit Adlai III and his father at Libertyville and his mother at her house in Half Day, not far from Libertyville. The visit to Ellen was a disaster, according to Nancy's later testimony. Ellen told Nancy that Adlai III should not be getting engaged so soon. She called Nancy ambitious and aggressive. She telephoned Nancy's parents and told them they were social climbers. A little later Ellen suggested they go to the

[9] In 1966, Ellen Stevenson's sons (Adlai III, Borden, and John Fell) and her mother (Mrs. Carpenter) brought suit in Probate Court to have her declared incompetent. A conservator was appointed to manage her financial affairs, to disburse money provided for her support by her family, and to prevent her from going into bankruptcy.

garden and pick some corn for Nancy to take home with her. The three of them went out and set to work, and Ellen was gay and vivacious, making a game out of the corn picking, behaving as she had many years ago when she and Stevenson were first married. But of a sudden her mood darkened, she turned on Nancy, she demanded harshly, "Why are you stealing my corn? Why are you taking all my corn from my garden?"

The visit with Stevenson was a great success. Adlai III took her to the house in Libertyville, and she and Stevenson hit it off from the start. She was young and pretty and gay, as Ellen once had been, but she was also sensible. Stevenson drove them down to Bloomington and on to the State Fair at Springfield, and en route he talked to her about the Illinois prairie, pointing proudly to strip-mining land reclaimed during his governorship, to a shelter belt of trees planted at his behest, talking about the ecological chain and about the history of Illinois and its meaning. Her first impression of him was of his deep blue eyes and that he was "easy"—easy to get to know, making her feel at home at once, giving her no reason to feel the slightest bit nervous despite his high position and her youth.

That fall Adlai III enrolled at Harvard Law School.

27.

Stevenson had only a few days at Libertyville and in his Chicago office before the fall campaigning. His response to a friend who suggested he visit Russia was that Africa and South America must come first. Agnes Meyer told him he was "giving the country what little intellectual leadership it has of an outstanding character." Stevenson thanked her courteously. Their correspondence would increase in volume. He wrote to various politicians around the country, received more papers from the Finletter Group, worked on his 1954 campaign itinerary (though Blair did most of the actual planning), discussed his speech needs with various writers.

Jim Rowe, though no admirer of Steve Mitchell, told Schlesinger he thought it would be a mistake to allow Mitchell to resign as national chairman—the Stevenson forces would lose control of the National Committee and hence of 1956 convention arrangements. Schlesinger passed it on to Blair, who replied that Mitchell's decision to resign was final. "The best bets" to replace Mitchell, Stevenson thought, were Mike DiSalle of Ohio, Paul Butler of Indiana, or Jim Finnegan of Philadelphia; and of these, Stevenson preferred Butler. Stevenson said, however, that he himself must not appear to intervene in the selection of a successor to Mitchell.

Stevenson went down to Springfield on August 18 to speak for Senator Paul Douglas on "Democratic Day" at the Illinois State Fair. It was, for Stevenson, the opening of the 1954 congressional campaign. The feeling was widespread among Democrats that this was "a Democratic year." Indeed, Stevenson in his speech warned against overconfidence. Why, only two years after Eisenhower's landslide victory, were the Democrats so confident? In large part because (though Stevenson did not say so in his speech) the McCarthy controversies had hurt the Republicans and seemed to have hurt the President himself: because (as Stevenson did say) the Republicans were deeply divided and unemployment was high. He praised highly the way in which the Democratic Party had met the "acid test of opposition . . . it has shown itself stalwart, courageous, and responsible in office." He claimed credit for the Democrats for the constructive achievements of Congress. Noting that President Eisenhower was due in Springfield the next day, he hoped that Eisenhower would make it clear to "Republican campaigners that their campaign this fall is not to be just smile and smear—his smiles and their smears" but he doubted it. He praised Paul Douglas without restraint. And he tucked into the middle of his speech a characteristic Stevensonian passage: "But with the fire of Communism's greed and passion burning brightly, with the hydrogen bomb ticking, our great coalition of the free nations imperiled, with millions of Americans unemployed and more in anxious confusion, surely there are some things more important than which party organizes the Senate."

Theodore H. White, the political writer, was on hand. Later he recalled, "Down from Chicago comes the Cook County machine. Stevenson spoke. Wow! He grabs 'em—Gill and Arvey and all of them. Adlai changed the entire tone of American politics." White was seeing another side of the Stevenson he had met in Paris earlier. "He knew the nuts and bolts [of politics] too. In Paris he'd sounded fey. In Springfield he was getting across."

Three days later Stevenson went in the afternoon to a fund-raising cocktail party for Senator Douglas at the lake-front home of Angelo Geocaris in Winnetka, then on to a box supper at Lake Forest College, then to an evening rally at Waukegan. His theme, as always in Illinois this fall, was Douglas: "The interest of the whole nation has been focused upon . . . Illinois. . . . For this is to be no ordinary choosing between two columns of circles and squares on a ballot. . . . The issue is being drawn here between two basically different meanings of democracy. What we are going to decide in Illinois with its premier Old Guard delegation in Congress is whether democracy will hang on to yesterday or meet tomorrow; whether democracy, if you will, is to stand still or to go forward. . . . Yesterday cannot be democracy's yardstick. America—its economy, its freedom, its security—must either grow or stumble and fall."[10] As he did many times,

10 It was Stevenson's formulation of John F. Kennedy's 1960 campaign theme: "This is not merely a contest between Mr. Nixon and myself. In a very real sense it is not just a contest between the Republican Party and the Democratic Party. It is a contest between all citizens of this country who believe that progress is our most notable product, who believe it incumbent upon us as the chief example of freedom to build a strong and vital society, and between those who wish to stand still. I ask your help. I ask you to join us. I ask you to help us move this country forward."

Stevenson spoke haltingly for the first five or six minutes, and one wondered whether he would be able to get through it; then somehow he caught the feel of the crowd, he took off, and he was good. Paul Douglas offered a striking contrast. People tended to think of them as similar— both Democrats first elected to high office the same year, both liberal, both articulate and educated, both honest, both good-government men. Yet their speaking styles could hardly have been more different. Where Stevenson was cool, even reserved, unemotional, speaking in accents foreign to Midwest ears, Douglas was all heart, waving his arms, sweating, chopping the air, leaning forward as though to overpower the audience, a gutter fighter mounting a tough attack on his opponent, taking an underdog position against the kept press and the wealthy Republican TV experts, crying out for the people's help. Stevenson was urbane, witty, cerebral; Douglas was deadly serious, emotional, appalled at the iniquity of the opposition. The speeches over, the crowd began to leave, and Douglas suddenly jumped up again and yelled, "Let's have victory November 2," and the crowd roared, and he yelled again, and they roared again. They were his, in a sense they were never Stevenson's.

Stevenson corresponded with Warwick Anderson, father of Nancy, Adlai III's girl, about the announcement of their engagement. But he had little time for anything but campaigning. He was leading the 1954 Democratic congressional campaign for control of the House and Senate (and the capture of governorships). He set forth at the end of August, speaking August 27 and 28 in Sioux City, Iowa, and Sioux Falls, South Dakota; and thereafter with only a few days off, most of them spent with politicians, he delivered some thirty speeches all across the country, from New York to California, from Minnesota to New Mexico, attacking Secretary of Agriculture Benson and the Administration's indifference to unemployment, then standing at five million. He spoke five times more for Douglas.

Traveling, he told an Associated Press reporter that he was considering opening a law firm after the 1954 elections and that "I'm not taking any position on 1956." Marlene Dietrich, thanking him for his photograph, said she hoped he would not practice law, even though that would make it easier for her to visit him. She wanted to see him, she said, but it was impossible because it would be publicized. She would leave it to him to find a way. He told Lauren Bacall he could not come to dinner when he visited California.

At a Democratic dinner in Harrisburg, Pennsylvania, on September 8, he opened the Democratic campaign in that state. He denounced "false, accusing cries of treachery and murder and treason," particularly New York Governor Dewey's earlier recommendation "to think of Democrats when you think of American boys murdered in Korea"; declared that Democrats' task this fall was "to give direction again to a foreign policy which wallows aimlessly and dangerously"; criticized Secretary Dulles' and other Republicans' substitution of slogans for policy and their rejection of bipartisanship in foreign affairs; hammered at the split in the Republican Party; and denounced as false Republican claims to prosperity.

Schlesinger visited him in Libertyville September 10 and found him in a strange mood. Blair had warned Schlesinger to expect to find Stevenson in a "negative" state of mind and had said wearily, "You know, it sometimes gets a bit tiring," coping with Stevenson's moods. Schlesinger noted that Stevenson seemed harassed by his sons, who were overdue at a party at Ellen's. After they left, he relaxed. Schlesinger reported that Averell Harriman, running for Governor in New York, had a good chance of winning. (He won an extremely close election.) Stevenson was optimistic about Hubert Humphrey's chances in Minnesota and said, "I don't know any Senator who seems to me more intelligent than Hubert, or more engaging, or more fun to spend an evening with. Nor do I know any Senator who is more ambitious—or more tough and ruthless in pursuing his ambitions." (Humphrey won rather easily.) As to the national chairmanship, Stevenson still favored either Paul Butler of Indiana or Jim Finnegan of Philadelphia but was unwilling to line up votes for either, which Schlesinger feared abandoned the field to "the Senate crowd" led by Lyndon Johnson. Oscar Chapman had recently offered to take charge of rounding up Stevenson delegates for the 1956 convention; Stevenson had said he could not stop him but would not encourage him. Now he told Schlesinger that he would not seek the nomination in '56. He "definitely" would not enter the primaries. If drafted he would accept but did not think it likely. What he really would like to do in 1956 was run again for Governor of Illinois or be appointed Secretary of State. At present he felt constrained by the Democratic Party line and wanted to feel free to bespeak his conscience. "My present position," he said, "is morally repugnant, emotionally unbearable, and intellectually inconsistent." Schlesinger asked where the Democratic line constrained him (outside farm policy—Blair and Phil Stern had had to prevent him almost by force from inserting into the Sioux Falls speech a tentative approval of experimenting with flexible price supports). Stevenson said he would like to hit labor every Tuesday—there was too much violence and intimidation in labor relations. Otherwise, he admitted, the Democratic line was his own. Schlesinger was "somewhat shocked by his evident determination" not to seek the nomination. Stevenson even wondered whether he couldn't issue a statement after the present campaign taking himself out of 1956. "Yet he listened," Schlesinger noted, "to arguments against this fairly cheerfully. And later he would assume unconsciously in a conversation that he would be the candidate in '56 or the President thereafter. I am perplexed." Such perplexity was not uncommon. Or, rather, it should have been more common: Stevenson sometimes spoke in contradictions, or voiced views he did not believe, and this led to serious misunderstanding more than once, including immediately before his death, when journalists misunderstood his position on Vietnam.

He told Senator Fulbright he wished he could talk to him about "this damnable campaign"—"I am a little perplexed as to just what I am doing and how to do it." He asked Tom Finletter to put somebody to work on "more positive proposals in the health field"—he doubted if it would suffice any longer to cling to the far-reaching proposals of Oscar Ewing, Truman's former Social Security administrator, or to denounce Eisenhower's. Soon he received a paper on it from Seymour Harris. Yet though his mood was one of uncertainty and irritability, this fall campaign of 1954 was really one of Adlai Stevenson's triumphs. The tempo increased through September and October until, at the end, he was speaking every day and sometimes more than once a day. Moreover, the speeches were successful, his reception good almost everywhere.

He attended Adlai's and Nancy's engagement party in Louisville and spent a couple of days there, seeing, gaily, the Wilson Wyatts, the Barry Binghams, and other friends, and becoming acquainted with Nancy's parents, the Andersons. Then he drove to Cincinnati and on September 15 delivered, on behalf of the Democratic candidate for the Senate, his standard anti-Administration speech, this time with emphasis on economic issues. From Cincinnati he went to Oberlin, then on to Indianapolis to open the Democratic campaign in Indiana. His speech there on September 18 was less harshly partisan than previous ones but he did not hesitate to criticize the Administration's foreign policy or its "giveaway" policy in national resources and its policy of transferring bounty "from the many to the few" in taxes, atomic energy, TVA, Hell's Canyon, the Dixon-Yates contract,[11] tariffs, REA. "Have we lost our old vision of a nation strong, tranquil, and free? I say that this vision is not dead; that while we have suffered a setback, the tide will turn." The Indianapolis speech attracted wide attention. President Truman congratulated him and said, "I think we have the Republicans on the run and I think we are going to keep them running." Tom Matthews wrote that he was "moved" by the speech and said that whether or not Stevenson became President it was his "unavoidable destiny to be a voice for America."

He was corresponding with Premier Mendès-France of France about the European Defense Community. Chafing under the load of political speeches, he told Tom Finletter he would like to "change my life" after the elections—speak "very infrequently" and "earn a little money on the fringes of the law"—and he would like to make one thoughtful, affirmative, non-partisan foreign policy speech in December. He hoped to distill the thinking of Finletter, Bowles, Nitze, Kennan, and others, "our best people." During that summer and fall, starting when he was recuperating

---

[11] The Dixon-Yates contract was an Eisenhower administration proposal (as Democrats saw it) to block expansion of TVA by authorizing the Atomic Energy Commission to make a contract subsidizing the construction by a private power combine of a steam generating plant whose electric power would replace power furnished by TVA to AEC installations.

from his operation, Stevenson had held conversations with Bill Blair, Bill Wirtz, and Newt Minow about opening a law firm after the campaign ended. He felt he could not go on forever as he had since the 1952 campaign. He needed a firmer base of some sort. The law offered it. Wirtz pressed the idea on him. Newt Minow once recalled, "One day he called me and asked me out to the farm to talk about something. We walked down to the river. He said that he had been thinking about his life and been talking to Wirtz and Blair and had tentatively decided to organize a new law firm. He had some clients, he thought. They wanted me to join the firm. Wirtz would continue teaching at the Northwestern Law School part time. Stevenson said, 'If I were your father, I'd tell you not to do this. You've got a good position in a fine firm'"—Minow had gone back to Mayer, Meyer, Austrian, and Platt—"'and you're going to advance and do well. What I'm suggesting is very precarious. But if you want some adventure and excitement and something unconventional, we hope very much you'll come with us. I've grown very fond of you and trust you.' I said I'd like to think about it and I did. I talked to Jo [Mrs. Minow] and we decided to do it."

To a Connecticut man who admired his speeches but didn't think he sounded "mad enough," Stevenson wrote, "If I haven't sounded as belligerent as I should it is due to emotional inabilities which have always made extraversion difficult for me. I am afraid I shall never be a good political orator." To Kefauver, disturbed by efforts to promote difficulties between them, Stevenson replied that he had heard nothing about it and would not have believed it anyway. Ken Galbraith tried to reassure him about Democratic farm policy, and Stevenson told him that in such rich states as Illinois he detected no great farmer hostility to the Republicans. He added, "The political news everywhere is good to the point of perplexity."

The intense October campaign began. On October 1, Stevenson spoke at Rockford, next day in Detroit. He declared that since Eisenhower had taken office the economy had shrunk instead of grown, unemployment had risen, the cost of living was at an "all-time peak," the average weekly earnings of industrial workers had declined, "the squeeze is on the farmer too," and per capita disposable income was down and so were corporation profits. Worse still, the Republicans were complacent about it. He struck Eisenhower himself a glancing blow: Eisenhower, he said, had recently "joked derisively about intellectuals" but instead he ought to be listening to them, for it was they who had made possible advances in science, medicine, agriculture, and industry. It was necessary, he said, "to arrest the drift and assure the steady growth of our economy" (again the 1960 theme of John F. Kennedy, put less forcefully). He bespoke the need for housing, schools, teachers, hospitals, highways, and conservation to ac commodate the population explosion.

Edmund Muskie won in Maine, the first Democratic Governor Maine had elected in years, and Stevenson, heading West, took it as an omen and crowed repeatedly, "As Maine goes, so goes the nation." At Wichita, Kansas, on October 7, he used Maine to argue that Kansas too, needed a two-party system. The Wichita *Beacon*'s news story began, "Adlai E. Stevenson Thursday night administered a shot in the arm to Kansas Democrats the likes of which they haven't experienced in 22 years."

Stevenson went to Los Angeles to speak in the huge Hollywood Bowl. He was working on speeches as he traveled. Eisenhower was campaigning now too, and Stevenson told Harry Ashmore, editor of the Arkansas *Gazette,* who had submitted a draft for Los Angeles, that he had not been able to use it because he had had to take account of Eisenhower's speeches. It was hard, campaigning by commercial plane; he had to make his schedule fit the airlines', he had less room to move around in, fewer writers and less research material along.

Congressman Emanuel Celler of New York had urged him to criticize the Administration's sending arms to the Arab states in his Los Angeles speech. The speech, however, originally intended as a major foreign policy speech, turned into a plug for Democratic candidates, a general attack on the Administration and its handling of McCarthy, and the most direct attack yet on Eisenhower himself.

Noting that Eisenhower had said there had been no scandal or corruption in his administration, Stevenson listed three minor scandals and the Dixon-Yates contract. Recalling Eisenhower's statement that he rejected the idea that America "must always spend more than it has," Stevenson said that the federal deficit this year would be $4.6 billion. Eisenhower had said, "We have a prosperous economy," a statement which Stevenson said "will be interesting news to a few million people looking for work and to a lot of farmers who don't overlook that we have the highest living costs and the lowest farm prices in a long while at the same time."

Stevenson said he had been "amazed" that Eisenhower claimed a bipartisan foreign policy: "The facts are that not only have no Democrats been appointed to policy-making positions in the State Department and our foreign activities, but they don't even want Republicans who worked for the Democrats, regardless of competence. . . . I hope I don't sound frivolous when I say that the fact of the matter is that they haven't even been able to establish bipartisanship within the Republican Party." Eisenhower said "if you can believe it: 'For the past twenty months there has been harmony unprecedented in our time, between the Executive and the Congress.' The fact is that in the squalid McCarthy-Army spectacle, which delighted our enemies and revolted our friends, the Greek ship deal, the almost daily contradictions of Administration policy by Administration leaders in Congress, the demoralization of our far-flung foreign service, the Bricker Amendment, the Republican challenge of the Bohlen appointment, and many others, are only the public revelations of the extent of the challenge and the invasion of the executive domain and the prerogatives of the presidency. But what the political scientists have been calling the gravest constitutional crisis in many years President Eisenhower calls 'harmony unprecedented.' And I was surprised and a little saddened when the President referred to the 'useless shooting' and 'the futile sacrifices' in Korea. I had not thought that those were his views of that greatest collective effort to halt the Communist imperialism. . . . But I've saved for the last . . . the most extraordinary words of all: 'Over the world we have brought strength where there was weakness. We have brought realism where there was wishful thinking. We have brought frankness, candor, and force to foreign policy which at last insists on distinguishing words from deeds.' I wish it were so. And I suspect the President also wishes it were so. But what they have brought to our foreign policy is a long procession of ringing slogans that lie forlorn but not forgotten, unhappily, along the winding path of the past two years—'liberation,' 'unleashing Chiang Kaishek,' 'seizing the initiative,' 'massive retaliation,' the 'new look' in defense policy. . . . To be sure it is not his fault that the senior Senator from this great state [Knowland] talks of war with China while his President talks of co-existence with the Communists; that he didn't get a single Republican vote for his foreign trade policy, that the foreign policy statements and contradictions from the White House, from Secretary Dulles, and from the part-time Secretaries of State, Nixon and Knowland, have bewildered us Democrats, let alone our friends around the world. The harsh fact is that in twenty months of bluff and bluster, confusion and contradiction, we have lost influence and friends faster of late than at any time since Warren Harding and the Republican repudiation of international cooperation after the first war. All around the world American prestige—our good name and the respect of both friend and foe—has suffered and any pretense to the contrary is misleading and dangerous." Eisenhower, Stevenson said, was going around the country arguing that he needed a Republican Congress. "The sober fact, of course, is that when the President denounces the Democrats as enemies of his program he must know that on many key measures—foreign trade, housing, health, the conduct of foreign relations—the Democrats were far better supporters [of him] than the Republicans. . . ."

He stopped off in Taos, New Mexico, for a few days' rest at Steve Mitchell's home. Blair and Carol Evans were with him, and he caught up on correspondence. To a Chicagoan who had voted for him but now criticized him for repeatedly attacking the Administration instead of making constructive proposals, Stevenson replied, "The press for the most part, including, unhappily, the wire services, pick out just the contentious portions [of my speeches]—which seems to be the contemporary concept of news." The fact was that in many of his speeches he had indeed been attacking the Administration—which was exactly what he should have been doing.

Stevenson spoke at Albuquerque on October 15 and thereafter till Election Day, two weeks hence, he spoke almost constantly. At San Francisco on October 17 the Civic Auditorium, which holds about 8,000, was packed for him. Stevenson always did well in San Francisco; it was, somehow, his kind of town, as Los Angeles was not. After the campaign he told a friend, "The California trip which I had dreaded, turned out to be almost the best of the campaign."

Again and again as the campaign drew to an end he went out of his way to urge the election of Democratic candidates for Senator, Congressman, or Governor, thus piling up political IOUs. Betimes he was trying to plan a Thanksgiving holiday with Bill Benton, but it was hard: Ellen insisted on having the boys with her on Thanksgiving. "It's hell trying to manage a family and a campaign simultaneously!" He told Mrs. Warwick Anderson that he thought Nancy and Adlai III should get married next June, not this Christmas, so that Nancy could finish college and Adlai III his year of law school.

On October 26 he opened his final Eastern swing. On October 26 he spoke in Rochester and, during his introductory remarks of gratification at the size of the crowd, said, as he was doing increasingly, "I almost wish I were running myself." He heartily endorsed Averell Harriman, running for Governor. Harriman, one of the most sensible and durable Democratic leaders of the 1950s and 1960s, recalls, "All through this period, even when I challenged him in 1956, he and I never took it personally. I always felt relaxed with him." Later, during the UN years, Harriman would often prove a staunch ally of Stevenson.

By now Stevenson had focused on half a dozen issues: the "loss" of Indochina, which he called the "greatest disaster" to the free world since the fall of China; the decline of U.S. prestige abroad: the "hopelessly" divided Republican Party; the Administration's "giveaways"; the "character assassination" of Democrats by Administration leaders, especially Nixon; and a plea for a restoration of responsibility to political campaigning. And in some places the economic issues—unemployment in industrial areas, farm recession in agricultural regions.

On to Brooklyn, then Wilmington, then Trenton, New Jersey, with a breather at Princeton. Now in the final week of the campaign each formal speech was surrounded by a collection of other affairs—factory visits, receptions, brief extemporaneous speeches in small towns, television appearances. That Wednesday, Eisenhower told a news conference he knew nothing about the efforts of Nixon, Dewey, and other Republican orators to associate Democrats with Communism. At Trenton, Stevenson interpolated into his released text, "Surely this must be the first time in history that the President, the leader of his political party, doesn't even know, let alone influence, his party's campaign. Surely this must be the first time in history that the President and the Vice President of the United States aren't even on speaking terms." In the closing days the campaign was nasty. Steve Mitchell held a press conference to say that the Republicans were relying more than ever on "smear" tactics—in Wyoming were calling Senator Joseph O'Mahoney a foreign agent, in Montana were circulating pamphlets portraying Senator James Murray as a red spider, in Illinois were attacking the loyalty of Paul Douglas, in New York were impugning the integrity of Harriman. The leader of all this was Nixon. And on Thursday, Eisenhower had lent his name to the whole endeavor by inference— had sent "a warm letter of congratulation to Mr. Nixon on his 'effective work' in the campaign."

Now in the final days Eisenhower himself was making airplane stops across the country, campaigning for "peace and prosperity," declaring that U.S. prestige was at "its record peak," calling for bipartisanship in foreign affairs, claiming that unemployment was decreasing (as it was). Vice President Nixon, in a statement released on Saturday, said: "Mr. Stevenson has been following his usual tactics of covering up the record and failing to answer the facts by screaming 'smear, slur and slander.' His principal target seems to be me. All I have done since September 15 is to cite the hard facts from the record so that the American people can make an intelligent choice on Election Day between going forward with the Eisenhower program or electing a Congress which has been committed by its national chairman to go back to the policies of Harry Truman.

"1. The Acheson foreign policy, which in seven years lost 600,000,000 people to the Communists and left the United States in a war in Korea we were not allowed to win and which had no end in sight.

"2. Blindness and ignorance on the threat of communism which resulted in clearing and hiring of over 6,000 security risks which this administration has investigated and fired.

"3. An economic policy of high taxes, high spending, inflation and controls which in twenty years was never able to provide prosperity in peacetime and which left the United States with 10,000,000 unemployed in 1940. . . .

"4. An administration which was committed to programs which would socialize medicine, housing, water and power, agriculture, and atomic energy. . . .

"5. In the Truman administration people in high places covered up and condoned the incredible dishonesty of their friends and cronies; that in this administration there is not one instance of unpunished corruption. . . .

"6. That the ADA, the cell of left-wingers, which has spawned Mr. Stevenson's speech writers, has a record on the internal communism danger which does not inspire confidence; that is has constantly sniped at J. Edgar Hoover and the FBI; that it has attacked the Presi-

dent's security program; that it called for the abolition of the committee that exposed Alger Hiss; that it called for the recognition of communist China just before the Korean War.

"7. I suggest that Mr. Stevenson in his speech tonight to the American people, instead of answering with his usual quips and with the
shop-worn cry of 'smear' discuss this record. I challenge him to
name one misstatement of fact I have made during the course of this
campaign.

"It is clear that the issue today is exactly what it was in 1952. We
have the same spokesmen, Mr. Stevenson, Mr. Mitchell and their ADA
bedfellows calling for the defeat of President Eisenhower through the
election of an anti-Eisenhower Congress.

"I am confident that millions of Democrats, as in 1952, will realize in
1954 that this clique of starry-eyed opportunists with their feet in the
clouds and their heads in the sand does not represent the true principles of
the Democratic Party and that the Eisenhower program should be supported by members of both parties." Nixon released the statement to Saturday afternoon newspapers, shortly before Stevenson was to speak at
Cooper Union in New York.

Stevenson's reception in the New York garment district at noon on Friday had been tumultuous, as though he himself were running. And Blair,
far more given to understatement than hyperbole, thought the Saturday
rallies in Nassau and Westchester counties "about the best the Governor
has ever participated in." Alicia Patterson's *Newsday* had helped get a
crowd out. A rally in Harlem Saturday afternoon was disappointing, one
of the smallest in years; Congressman Adam Clayton Powell, Jr., did not
show up; it rained, and the meeting was moved indoors. But that night the
final major speech of the campaign, delivered to a packed hall at Cooper
Union, was a great success. Stevenson was staying in Benton's apartment
at the Savoy Plaza, and on Friday night he and Blair had received telephone calls from all around the country from friends incensed at Eisenhower's performance in recent days and urging Stevenson to move to the
attack on Eisenhower directly at Cooper Union. He did.

He taunted Eisenhower: "Our President, who a few months back
disclaimed all thought of active participation, has just completed an inspection of a series of selected airports." He taunted Nixon: "The Vice
President is finishing up his extensive tour—an ill-will tour, you might call
it." He gathered around himself the Democratic campaigners whom he
had led: "I doubt if the Democratic Party has ever been represented by so
many able and eminent men and women as their candidates for public
office," and praised Harriman highly as the apostle of "twenty years of
Reason." He recalled that Eisenhower had said a Democratic Congress
would start a "cold war" between the Congress and the White House but,
Stevenson argued, "the coldest warfare waged within living memories" be-

tween the Hill and the White House had been the attack on the Eisenhower administration by Senator McCarthy and his followers. He expatiated on the contradictions of the President by his majority leader, of one cabinet member by another, of the Vice President by the Secretary of State.

He said that the best way to avoid such confusion was to elect a Democratic Congress. It alone had "rescued" Eisenhower from his own party. "But more disturbing is that not just the Vice President and the Republican campaigners but now the President himself has affirmed the proposition that our prosperity has been achieved in the past only at the price of war and bloodshed. This of course has been standard Communist propaganda for years. . . . I am sure that the President must have spoken thoughtlessly and carelessly."

He expressed dismay at the degeneration of the campaign. "When the campaign began, the President said that the only issue was the record of his administration. But when it became evident that this was a very poor issue the Republican leaders, led by the Vice President, launched their reckless campaign of smear, misrepresentation, and mistrust. . . . A few days ago, when the President was asked what he thought of this kind of a campaign, he said that he had not heard about it. But within twenty-four hours—and despite his earlier protestation that Communism was not an issue in the campaign—he wrote Vice President Nixon expressing gratitude and admiration for his contribution to political enlightenment. And yesterday on his airport tour the President himself found it in his heart, or in his script, to take up these themes himself. This is the end of the great crusade."

If ever, he said, America needed the politics of reason, not innuendo, it was now. "Instead, I fear that irresponsible politicians, tearing the nation apart in the search for votes, have recklessly damaged our freedom, our self-respect, and our unity of national purpose. The challenge is not just to win elections. The greater challenge is to live as a proud and free nation in a future so precarious and so threatening that we can risk no missteps or miscalculations. We need to unite our country, not to divide it; to heal wounds, not to enlarge them. The times demand, not mistrust and suspicion and fear, but more mutual respect and confidence and understanding than we have ever before had in our history." Campaigns such as this threatened to "corrupt the very processes on which the functioning of democratic government depends. To say that one or another American lacks patriotism or favors Communism or wants to subvert our freedom— when his only crime is the crime of disagreement—is to shake our system to the foundation. If we lose our faith in each other, we have lost everything; and no party victory is worth this. . . . I would plead with all Americans to cleanse their minds of suspicion and hate; to recognize that men may differ about issues without differing about their faith in America or their belief in freedom. . . . If we do justice on Tuesday to our own conscience and sense of responsibility, then alone can we do justice to the nation we love; then alone can we make our beloved nation a symbol and shrine of hope and faith for all free men."

It was about as close as he ever got to the eloquence and imagery of the 1952 welcoming and acceptance speeches. It was broadcast over nation-wide radio and television. The crowd in the Great Hall of Cooper Union interrupted frequently with applause, booed the names of Dewey, Nixon, and McCarthy (but not of Eisenhower), and gave Stevenson a standing ovation when he finished.

After the speech there was a party at Benton's apartment. Marietta Tree has said, "He asked me to invite people. I asked his devoted slaves in New York that he wouldn't think of." He saw Alicia Patterson that weekend and wrote to her on Election Day, saying he hoped to go South next week and perhaps visit her at "the Dark River"—the letter was typewritten. Schlesinger came down to New York that final weekend to work on speeches. Stevenson was in a bad mood. He later wrote to Schlesinger, "Before I do anything else . . . I must record again my gratitude for your rescue mission to New York. I am apologetic about my ill temper on Sun-day, but somehow this long, uninterrupted ordeal has all but drained my reserves, including self-control." His nerves were indeed ragged. Stevenson originally had intended to make eight speeches during the fall and ended up making more than thirty. That last Saturday night in Benton's apart-ment he said, "Thank God, that's over." But it wasn't—unbeknownst to Stevenson, Bill Blair had arranged a Monday night nationwide radio hookup with David Dubinsky and other labor leaders. "They thought," Blair has recalled, "that the Democrats should do well and they wanted the Governor to get the credit." Blair now told Stevenson about it at the party on Saturday night. Stevenson said he would not deliver the speech— "if anyone does, you'll have to." And he went into his bedroom and slammed the door. It was one of the few times he was really angry, Blair recalled. "But in the bedroom he made some notes for a speech and soon he came out and said, 'Maybe if we can get a draft it will be all right.'" Blair, of course, had a draft ready.

After his Election Eve broadcast, Stevenson went home to Libertyville and, in his living room at the farm, surrounded by friends and aides, watched the returns on television. Carl McGowan was there, and Bill Wirtz and Bill Blair and Newt Minow and Martin, with their wives (ex-cept Blair, a bachelor then); so were Bill Flanagan and Dick Nelson from the governorship days. So were a few of Stevenson's Lake Forest friends, the Dicks, the Smiths, others. During the summer and early fall most of them had thought it was "a Democratic year" but in the last week or so they had become uncertain, with unemployment decreasing and Eisen-hower himself campaigning. Could Eisenhower transfer his prestige?

That night Stevenson seemed relaxed, with the air of a man who had done what needed doing and now awaited the results. He was less tense, or seemed so, than his guests. He showed his usual solicitousness for his guests' comfort (and his own belongings—put an ashtray on his white rug on the floor beside a woman sitting in front of the television set). Around eleven o'clock, informed that the twelve-year-old daughter of one of his guests (Martin) would not go to bed until she knew Paul Douglas had won, he telephoned her and told her to go to bed—Douglas would win.

Across the nation the vote had been heavy. Early in the evening the returns were mixed. But before midnight a Democratic trend was obvious. And when the votes were counted it became clear that the Democrats had made a striking comeback. They won control of both the House and Senate, picking up nineteen seats in the House (to give them a 232–203 majority) and one in the Senate (to give them a 48–47 majority, with one independent, Morse of Oregon). Douglas won re-election by more than 240,000 votes—received 53.6 per cent of the total cast. Harriman, with decisive help from the Liberal Party, squeaked through to win the New York governorship by about 11,000 votes out of five million cast. The Democrats gained three seats in the House from Illinois, two from Michigan, one from Minnesota, one from New York, three from Pennsylvania, and so on—not a landslide (the California delegation remained unchanged), but a solid victory. Alben Barkley was elected to the Senate, and so were Pat McNamara, Richard Neuberger of Oregon, Strom Thurmond of South Carolina. Senators Humphrey, Murray, Anderson, Kerr, Green were re-elected. Indeed, the Democrats won twenty-two regular seats out of thirty-two that were open. They did even better in the statehouses. Including Muskie's victory in Maine on September 13, Democratic Governors replaced Republicans in nine statehouses; the Republicans failed to take a single Democratic seat. Thus the gubernatorial balance shifted from 30–18 in favor of Republicans to 27–21 in favor of Democrats. Besides Harriman, the winners included Abraham Ribicoff of Connecticut, Orville Freeman of Minnesota, and George M. Leader of Pennsylvania. This was considered highly significant for 1956—Governors, and the courthouse machines which help elect them, control large amounts of patronage. The Democratic organization would be far stronger the next time.

From the house in Libertyville, Stevenson received, and made, telephone calls all over the country that night. In the ensuing days he received, and sent, congratulatory messages. He told Robert Sherwood, "I haven't felt that I was on the right level during this campaign." But he had been. In fact, his campaign this year had recalled more his 1948 campaign for the governorship than his 1952 campaign for the presidency. Now as in 1948 he had been on the outside, attacking; and he was good on the attack. Only in the Cooper Union speech did he revert wholly to his 1952 style. The rest was straight politics, and it succeeded. He had made the issues. He centered his fire on Nixon—and provoked an intemperate response. His effectiveness surely had helped draw President Eisenhower himself into the most extensive off-year campaign any President had ever made; and Eisenhower had been unable to transfer his own popularity. Stevenson had put his prestige on the line and thus forced Eisenhower to do the same. And all this put Democrats around the country in Stevenson's debt and greatly strengthened his position as his party's leader. There were few if any who left his house in Libertyville Election Night with any doubt that Stevenson would seek, and probably get, the Democratic nomination in 1956. And many thought he might well win.

28.

Truman issued a statement of praise, and Stevenson drafted a reply in longhand: "I am grateful to Pres T. for his confidence & good will, but I have no present plans for future political activity. I've done what I could for the Democratic party for the past two years. And now I shall have to be less active and give more attention to my own affairs." Nevertheless, already he was laying plans for the meeting of the Democratic National Committee in New Orleans in December.

He fulfilled two obligations—spoke at a Bonds for Israel dinner honoring Jack Arvey in Chicago on November 6 and at the dedication of Libertyville High School. He wrote out the latter in longhand, a rather touching little speech showing his love for Illinois and for learning. " 'Ignorance,' " he closed, 'is the curse of God,' wrote Shakespeare, " 'knowledge, the wing whereby we fly to heaven.' May this great school, long serve this great & growing community—and may it serve it greatly." Schlesinger urged Stevenson to get in touch with Acheson, and he did visit him a few weeks later. Stevenson thought of an engagement party for Adlai III and Nancy at Onwentsia at Christmastime; her parents seemed cool to the idea. Borden was entering military service. An article by Stevenson entitled "Must We Have War?" appeared in *Look,* part of his contract. He talked more about the new law firm.

On November 13, Stevenson left Chicago for Southern Pines, where he stayed briefly. "Six days of mist and one of sunshine," he told Jane Dick, "but great fun withall what with deer hunting, duck hunting and riding and only two speeches!" The Finletter Group was scheduled to meet, and he wanted to talk politics in preparation for the National Committee meeting in New Orleans in December. Stevenson was leaning toward Paul Butler of Indiana for national chairman but was careful to avoid offending Mike DiSalle, who also wanted the job. Tom Finletter gave a dinner party for him in New York. Finletter had promised it would be non-political, though it could hardly be. Afterward Marietta Tree had a drink with Stevenson, and he talked about running for President in 1956. "I had learned not to give him advice. It maddened him that I wouldn't. I told him, 'You already know what you want to do.' This freed him to talk to me, I think. I'd just listen, I was a sounding board, I'd ask him questions. It was academic anyway, he was going to run and he knew it. He just enjoyed talking about himself."

He spent Thanksgiving with Bill Benton at Southport, Connecticut. Benton had other guests and showed a number of Britannica films, and after each one Stevenson made a little speech, each fascinating, Benton thought. He asked Stevenson where he had learned so much about so many subjects. Stevenson replied, "Bill, I have spent my life collecting useless information." This led Benton, while taking a walk with Stevenson before Thanksgiving dinner, to invite him to go on the Board of Directors of Britannica and the Britannica Films. He subsequently agreed, and received a fee of $25,000 a year. (Other Board members received $5,000 a year plus expenses to the annual Board meeting in Chicago.) Benton's and Stevenson's was a long relationship and not a wholly satisfactory one to either. Stevenson admired Benton's courage in opposing McCarthy but he felt Benton was too demanding, that he wanted to run Stevenson's life, and he once advised Newt Minow not to go to work for him. The Board itself was stimulating, and Benton was a good client, taking Stevenson abroad at Benton's expense.[12]

Stevenson sent Adlai III a list of people to invite to "this wretched party" in Nancy's honor at Onwentsia "which I am beginning to wish I never started." At this same time, on December 2, the Senate voted to censure Joe McCarthy. A few days later, in a speech in Chicago, Stevenson praised Democratic unity in "the act of the Senate this week in reffirming its dignity" and said the censure would "go a long way in restoring not alone our self-confidence and self-esteem but also the respect of our friends." It was, effectively, the end of McCarthy.

The night of the censure Stevenson, accepting an award at the Weizmann Institute of Science in New York, walked the tight wire he and other American politicians walked in the 1950s and 1960s during the Israeli-Arab conflict: "Yet as a friend of Israel since its inception, you will permit me to counsel patience and a broad perspective. In all fairness, one must see the Israel-Arab conflict in the context of the whole Middle East and

---

12 In the end Benton came to feel he had not received his money's worth. He once said, "The Governor didn't take an active role on the Britannica Board of Editors. He served as a member and attended meetings and occasionally made a contribution. . . . We valued him because of his occasional insight, and his presence on the Board, we thought, added prestige to the company. His more important role was as chairman of the Board of Consultants of Britannica Films." Indirectly, of course, Stevenson helped Benton: he helped enlarge the federal government's commitment to education, which in turn helped the Britannica. And his prestige was indeed worth something. Benton has said that Stevenson received no direct compensation during his years as Ambassador to the UN, but did receive "deferred compensation" earned before he became Ambassador which by the time of his death amounted to about $100,000.

Far East security program. One must, I think, accept the over-all assumption that an Arab world with a friendly orientation to the West is better for Israel than an Arab world with a friendly orientation in the other direction. One cannot, in good faith, take issue with the striving of our officials and other Western nations to improve relations, cooperation, and confidence in the Arab world. This would be a major goal of any administration in Washington. But one can inquire whether tensions are lessened or accommodations advanced by sending military equipment to Arab states if there is any ambiguity about the purpose of such assistance—which is defense, not offense, peace, not war. Perhaps it would help to allay rising apprehension for Britain, France, and the United States to reaffirm their policy, declared in 1950, of preventing aggression in the Middle East and to strengthen it with guarantees. And certainly any general security system in the Middle East must take into account the military potential and the democratic vitality and reliability of Israel."

From New York he went to New Orleans, where the National Committee was meeting to select a successor to Steve Mitchell. Accounts of backstage maneuvering there vary widely. There were the three leading candidates—Paul Butler of Indiana, Jim Finnegan of Pennsylvania, and Mike DiSalle of Ohio. DiSalle was considered Truman's candidate. Finnegan was favored by Jack Arvey of Ilinois, James Curley of Massachusetts, Carmine G. De Sapio of New York, and Dave Lawrence of Pennsylvania—the Northern big-city machine leaders. Mitchell favored Butler and urged him on other national committeemen as one of themselves, unbossed by the big-city machine leaders. Butler had been campaigning for the job by telephone. The night before the balloting in New Orleans, Jack Arvey was surprised to hear Sam Rayburn say that Finnegan was "a little too Irish-sounding but Butler is okay." Not until two years later did Arvey learn why Rayburn had said it: Butler, according to Arvey, had written a pledge on the back of an envelope and given it to Southern leaders, including Rayburn, promising he would not consider it his duty as chairman to go into the question of civil rights. It was this Southern deal, Arvey said, that gave Butler the Southern committeemen and the job. When the roll was called, Butler did indeed have the votes of Alabama, Georgia, Louisiana, Mississippi, North Carolina, South Carolina, and Texas, as well as most border states and such Northern industrial states as Michigan and such agricultural states as Minnesota. The vote was 71 for Butler, 18 for DiSalle, and 16 for Finnegan. Arvey contended that later, at almost every meeting of the National Committee, Butler raised the question of civil rights, contrary to his pledge to the Southerners. Arvey said that he continually asked Butler, "Why must we do this?" Arvey considered it a divisive tactic, designed to get the presidential or vice presidential nomination for Butler. Mitchell, who had long fought with the big-city bosses, including Arvey, was pleased with Butler's victory. So were Stevenson and Blair. Arthur Schlesinger considered Butler "the best Democratic national chairman of modern times." He said, "He was issue-oriented. He could talk on television. He got the Democratic Advisory Committee going when the congressional leadership were trying to smother issues."

Stevenson's speech to the National Committee on Saturday, December 4, dealt with the recent campaign, the role of the party in opposition, and foreign affairs. He said, "As Democrats, we must not merely rejoice in what victory has done for our party; rather we must look forward and ask what our victorious party now can do for the country." In Congress, the Democratic opposition should work for bipartisanship in foreign policy. Eisenhower's eventual success would depend upon his success in leading his own party—he would have to conclude "a non-aggression pact" with Senator Knowland. In another passage that presaged one of John F. Kennedy's, he said, "If we do not stand unequivocally at home for civil freedom, we cannot hope to stand as the champion of liberty before the world. If we do not stand at home for equal rights for all our citizens, regardless of race or color, we cannot hope to stand as the champion of opportunity before the world. If we do not stand at home for economic growth and widening social welfare, we cannot hope to stand as the champion of progress before the world."

Thus he moved to foreign policy. The enemies of world peace remained "the implacable power of the Soviet Union" and "the new turbulence and attraction of Communist China." He believed that "we are witnessing today an important shift in Soviet tactics." Checkmated by U.S. rearmament after 1950, the Soviets had turned "to the social and economic battlefield" in order to divide the West and subvert the underdeveloped world. We were "falling behind" on our efforts to counter theirs. We must rebuild our strength, militarily and diplomatically and morally; we must reassure our allies; we must regain our international prestige—and "the act of the Senate this week," the censure of McCarthy, would help greatly. Then he said: "We must recognize the limitations of American military power in any situation short of a world war." When his broadcast time ended, he said a few words more to the national committeemen and committeewomen: "As in the past I have no political ambitions—except to serve my country and the Democratic Party as my circumstances permit. . . . But now I must devote more time to my own concerns. So if, henceforth, I cannot participate in public and party affairs as vigorously as in the past, I hope you will understand and forgive me."

Just two days later Lloyd Garrison sent Bill Blair a long letter about raising money to finance Stevenson's political efforts with a view to his running for President in 1956, a letter that made it clear Stevenson had already discussed the fund-raising effort with Garrison. On November 30 a Garrison memo had said that Stevenson had studied a list of potential contributors and favored "a simple unincorporated association to be called the 'Illinois Volunteers for Stevenson,'" run by Dutch Smith, Jane Dick, and Carl McGowan. Garrison had talked to Smith and McGowan by phone

Stevenson was "relieved" to know that the association would handle the funds and employ the staff. He did not think he could find "a writing man" capable of drafting major speeches. Rather, he thought he would have to turn to various individuals who had helped him in the past and could not leave their present occupations. He would like to compensate them on an ad hoc basis. He did think he needed a full-time writer to help Blair prepare the agenda for meetings with experts, make notes on the meetings, prepare analyses of various subjects, write minor speeches, statements, and messages, important letters, and so on. This would lower the budget for a new "writing man" and add to the budget for stipends for major speeches. It would leave the total budget about where it had been—about $60,000.

Smith would approach the Chicago donors. Garrison and Finletter would approach the New York donors. Who would approach those in California, Texas, and Richmond? How, Garrison asked, should they approach the donors? "Presumably, wherever possible, we should see each one in person instead of writing, and leave with him nothing in writing." Each donor should be shown a list of other donors and the budget, and be told its purposes. In addition, he should be told that the initiative came from Dutch Smith and other friends of Stevenson, not from Stevenson himself, though he would welcome it, since it would relieve him of "a burden that will be too great for him to bear"; that he would not want anyone to contribute if doing so would cut off or reduce contributions to the National Committee; and that "AES cannot make any final commitment, even to his closest friends, to be a candidate. If for any reason he should withdraw or decline to run, he would not want his friends who had contributed to feel that he had let them down. He is most anxious that we should make this clear." All this should be done soon—Stevenson's "present burdens weigh considerably upon him." Garrison urged Wyatt, Bingham, Smith, and Finletter to telephone their ideas to him. He would act as a clearinghouse. Stevenson and Blair would recruit the staff. Smith and his associates would receive and spend the money. Garrison and the others would concentrate on money-raising.

Now in his letter of December 6 to Blair, Garrison said that Stevenson had approved a list of possible donors. Garrison and the others would not actually solicit anybody until they heard from Blair. Garrison had, however, talked in a preliminary way with George Backer of New York, and Backer thought that a contribution of $2,500 to $3,000 in addition to a man's normal contribution to the party would not be obtained except from a very few people. Garrison wondered if they should lower their sights to $1,500, $1,000, or even $500 per person (though obviously the lower they went the more people they would have to solicit). A few days later Wyatt reported to Garrison that he had mentioned the project to Elmo Roper, the pollster, and Roper, who was, Wyatt said, "very dedicated to Adlai," had offered to subscribe $1,000 to "the undertaking."

Just before the election, Stevenson had told Congressman Michael J.

Kirwan of Ohio that he intended to "fade out for a bit and try to recover my strength, my equilibrium, and my fortunes." He told others the same, privately. And, as we have seen, he said it publicly at New Orleans. But the fact is that Stevenson, while intending to become less visibly involved in Democratic affairs in the next year or so, had no intention at all of getting out of politics or out of contention for the 1956 nomination. Blair kept in touch with political leaders. Stevenson received graciously the praise of party leaders and saw them from time to time. The Finletter Group resumed its work. Stevenson approved. Spurred by a letter from Jack Fischer of *Harper's,* Stevenson suggested to Finletter that the party might need "a more formal program research project with an executive secretary . . . full time" which would study problems, apply imagination to them, and come up with answers. Stevenson considered it essential "if we are going to have anything resembling a coherent, well thought out party 'program' a year or a year and a half hence," i.e., in time for the 1956 presidential campaign. Senator Fulbright, observing that the Democratic Party was now "in the best shape nationally" in his time, proposed that Stevenson meet informally now and then for supper with members of the Senate and House—many of them "would like to feel that they know you as an individual person in addition to knowing you as a political leader." Stevenson replied, "I should like very much to do precisely what you suggest" and asked him for further and more concrete suggestions.

Stevenson was in a strong position in the party. The new national chairman, Paul Butler, was his man. Stevenson had helped the party mightily in the 1954 election and put local Democrats, Governors, Senators, and Congressmen in his debt. He had staked out the issues. He had shown he could draw crowds. He commanded the party's intellectuals. He had eclipsed, at least for the time being, the Southern wing in the Senate which had seemed to oppose and threaten him in 1953. (But the Southern Senators were still powerful, which may account for the eagerness with which he accepted Fulbright's suggestion, perhaps seeing Fulbright, mistakenly, as a bridge to the Johnsons and Russells.) Now he could well become less visible for a time, seeming to retire from the spotlight while he was at apogee, yet privately, almost secretly, continuing to politicize. He would, in short, bank the political fires.

Newt Minow was looking for office space: Stevenson intended to open his new law firm at the first of the year. He planned to take on only a few clients in order to "have a little leisure for my health and peace of mind." One was the Radio Corporation of America: he was retained as counsel in a $16-million anti-trust suit brought by Zenith Radio Corporation against RCA. He told a fellow lawyer that the RCA matter "looks like an exceedingly difficult case."

He was making Christmas plans. He began the practice, continued until his death, of sending a card containing an inspirational message to everyone from whom he received a card. Sometimes he appended a personal

note. That year's card contained a quotation from a Christmas letter of
Fra Giovanni in Florence in 1513. It said:

> I salute you. . . .
> There is nothing that I can give you which you do not possess; but
> there is much, very much that, while I cannot give it, you can take.
> No heaven can come to us unless our hearts find rest in it today; Take
> Heaven! No Peace lies in the future which is not hidden in the present
> little instant; Take Peace!
> The gloom of the World is but a shadow. Behind it, yet within our
> reach, is joy. There is radiance and glory in the darkness, could we
> but see, and to see, we have only to look.
> And so, at this Christmas time, I greet you, with the prayer that for
> you, now and forever, the day breaks, and the shadows flee away.

The shadows did not flee for Stevenson, nor could he take peace. He
had wanted Adlai III to accompany him to a fathers-and-sons dinner at the
Commercial Club but Adlai wanted to go to Louisville. Stevenson accepted it understandingly. He decided to join Adlai III in Louisville at the
Andersons' on December 23, taking John Fell; all would return to Lake
Forest for the reception at Onwentsia on Sunday, December 26. After
Christmas, on the day they were to leave for Lake Forest, Nancy and her
mother were packing Nancy's suitcase in her bedroom when Ellen Stevenson telephoned. Mrs. Anderson answered. As Nancy later testified, "She
said to Mother, 'I forbid you to come up here, and I forbid you to . . .
capitalize on the Stevenson name. You are just social climbers.' And I
could hear this because her voice was very loud and it carried through the
telephone into the room and—well, my mother was understandingly very
upset." As a result, neither Mrs. Anderson nor her husband attended the
Onwentsia party. The Lake Forest crowd, Stevenson's law partners and
secretaries, and Adlai III's and Nancy's friends were there. Immediately
after New Year's Day of 1955 Stevenson opened his law office.

29.

The law office was located in a ponderous old building at the foot of
LaSalle Street, No. 231, housing the Continental National Bank, and other
distinguished lawyers' offices. Stevenson's offices on the eighth floor were
modest—two reception rooms, four offices for the lawyers, and two for the
secretaries. The walls were walnut-paneled and hung with autographed
photographs and political mementos. Blair always had a collection of toy
donkeys on his desk. The offices were heavily carpeted, richly furnished,
lit with subdued lighting. Blair's office guarded Stevenson's, and next to it
were offices for Wirtz and Minow. The place looked old, conservative, respectable. It might have housed one of the oldest law firms in town. Next

door was the law firm of Dwight Green, the Republican whom Stevenson had defeated for Governor in 1948. (When Stevenson opened his office Green paid a call.) Stevenson's own office overlooked the Board of Trade and financial district. It was furnished with leather-covered sofa and chairs. Scattered about were copies of the *American Bar Association Journal,* the *Democratic Digest,* several literary magazines. The bookcases contained the Illinois statutes, an encyclopedia, biographies, bound copies of Stevenson's 1952 campaign speeches, books on public affairs in America, France, Africa, and Alaska. The only pictures on the wall were of his sons and of Abraham Lincoln. On one wall was a map of Virginia and Maryland dated 1745; on another was a facsimile of the Lincoln autobiography requested by Jesse Fell.

The partnership agreement between Stevenson and Wirtz set forth that they would become law partners as of January 3, 1955; that Stevenson would contribute $10,000 and Wirtz $5,000 into the partnership account; that all fees received and all expenses incurred would be paid into and out of that account; that if additional funds were needed Stevenson would provide two thirds and Wirtz one third; that each month Stevenson would withdraw $4,000 and Wirtz $2,000 if they wished; and that at the end of 1955 they would divide the firm's earnings, taking into account their "respective responsibilities for the retainers coming to us and for our discharge of the obligations involved." It added, "If our expectations prove illusory we shall adjust these arrangements. . . . The obvious gaps in this understanding as it is here expressed will be filled in by the exercise of mutual good will." They signed it January 1, 1955. At the end of that first year the firm had received $126,528 in fees. Of this, $14,270 came from labor arbitration cases, which Wirtz handled. The rest, $112,258, came from seventeen clients. Stevenson himself was active in handling five of those clients.[13]

Newt Minow has said, "The law firm was happy and successful from the start. Bill Wirtz and I were the real lawyers in the office. The Governor was a very good lawyer but so damn many demands were made on his time that it was hard to get him to focus on anything. He and I did work together on the RCA anti-trust case. We often went to New York to meet with the RCA lawyers. He was terrific. He wrote a brief like he'd write a book. Every word was sweated out." Friends told Francis Plimpton later

---

[13] According to papers Stevenson left at the time of his death, the five were RCA (the biggest client, with a fee of $34,000); Lambert and Co. (a French company, $25,000); Leon Tempelsman & Son (diamond importers and toolmakers on whose behalf Stevenson went to Africa that year, $25,000); Lindsay Chemical Company (a Chicago company, $2,000); J. Henry Schroder Banking Corporation (international investment bankers, $500). He participated to a lesser degree in representing Edward C. Cabot (a family trust dispute, $15,000); Illinois Bell Telephone Company ($4,500); Burr Tillstrom (a television puppeteer, $950); and several others, including the Fund for the Republic and the St. Louis *Post-Dispatch* ($207.50 and $175, respectively). A Reynolds Metals fee of $25,000 was paid in 1956.

that Stevenson had handled the RCA case very well indeed. Everything he did was closely watched by the press, and when he took the RCA case, Drew Pearson wrote that his willingness to take "this tough and unpopular anti-trust case" led some people to believe he did not plan to run again, or did not realize what he was getting into. Schlesinger took this as an "opening Kefauver salvo." Blair assured him that Stevenson was concerned solely "with a procedural point in the RCA case," not its substance. "Of course," Blair added, "it is too much to expect that anyone will make this fine distinction."[14]

Stevenson's law practice consisted mainly in negotiating and counseling. Minow recalled, "The grubby details bored him. But he was a good negotiator. He did very well for Reynolds Metals. They had interests in making alumina in Ghana and Jamaica, and the Gov went there for them. He went to Africa to negotiate with the De Beers syndicate on behalf of a client, Maurice Tempelsman, a man in the industrial diamond business. He would not be your first choice of lawyers if the problem you had was an underwriting. But if you gave him a corporate problem, a negotiation, he could handle it well. Later he got involved in the Field Foundation and became president of it." There was trouble between the New York Fields, principally Marshall Field's widow, and her stepson, Marshall, in Chicago. Minow went on, "Stevenson was brought in to make peace. Benton brought him into the Encyclopaedia Britannica as a director, and I later became general counsel of the film company and started doing legal work for the Encyclopaedia Britannica itself, a good deal of it on Federal Trade Commission problems. We did some work for the Illinois Bell Telephone Company—he had worked for them at the Sidley firm. We did some work for Marietta Tree—Bill and I are guardians of one of her children. Roger Stevens on real estate, financing an American company in Israel, we did very well on financing. We tried a lawsuit for the airline pilots' association. We worked on other offbeat things. Wirtz worked on labor arbitrations. Blair did some work for Mrs. Lasker. Whenever there was a contract or a brief of a corporate matter, Wirtz or I'd end up doing it." Stevenson discussed problems of overseas investment with various firms. He once said, "It's all damn interesting. And profitable too." Minow thought he had more imagination and resourcefulness than most lawyers. Handling a large estate, he looked at "the human aspect" of the heirs more than most lawyers would, Minow thought. Once a friend sent to Minow a

[14] Two federal district courts in different parts of the country were presently trying the same issues between the same parties. To avoid wasteful duplication of protracted litigation, RCA was asking the Supreme Court to intervene. Blair wrote, "RCA contends that the present situation destroys the orderly, efficient, and economical administration of justice—and Adlai Stevenson for a fat fee agrees!" Minow once recalled, "He became absorbed in the RCA case and its problems for their own value, as an intellectual challenge. It was terribly complex litigation and he astonished the other lawyers with his knowledge of it." It interested him because it involved the efficient administration of justice. The Supreme Court, however, refused to intervene.

young man denied an honorable discharge from the Army because it considered him a security risk. Minow became convinced the young man was unjustly accused but he hesitated to defend him because of Stevenson's political position. He asked advice. Stevenson said, "Are you sure he's telling the truth?" Minow was. Then, Stevenson asked, what was the problem? Minow said, somewhat diffidently, that he was concerned about embarrassing Stevenson politically by taking on a loyalty case. Stevenson, looking astonished, said, "If I ever succumb to that, I might as well quit practicing law." Minow took the case and won it.

Stevenson refused many more clients than he accepted. He said at the time, "I only want enough to make some money and get my foot back in the door in the law business. I don't want to try to do more than I can handle." Among clients he refused were people with personal injury cases, people with claims against the government, a woman who claimed she was being kept illegally in a mental institution. Blair referred such people to other lawyers or to the Bar Association. Stevenson also refused several clients who patently hoped to exploit his political prominence. One man accused of making "windfall" profits in federal housing offered him any amount of money "in six figures." Blair did not even let him see Stevenson. Blair once said, "I had no idea how much money a man in the Governor's position could make if he wanted to." Stevenson could, of course, have permitted his practice to expand enormously and, had he chosen to, might over the years have developed his firm into a leading Chicago law factory. He chose otherwise. As Minow put it, "Before '55 was out, people were planning toward the election of 1956. Nobody said this to me at the start but I assumed that his political life was going to continue."

Stevenson still received about a hundred and fifty letters a day. Carol Evans answered many personal letters and letters from strangers. Blair handled speaking invitations, appointment requests, and political correspondence. The mail, which had tapered off after the 1952 election, suddenly rose in December 1954 to protest his supposed retirement from politics. People wrote to him from all over the world, asking his blessing on their projects or telling him what they thought he stood for. Men wanted him to loan them money, women wanted to marry him. His files were filled with such correspondence (and with some 60,000 index cards giving the names and addresses of his political supporters, arranged by state and city). A woman in Scarsdale named her new parakeet "Adlai" and asked how to pronounce it. A woman asked Stevenson to write to her sick son to speed his recovery. (He did.) People wrote to him under the impression he was still Governor of Illinois or some other state. One woman moving from one New York county to another asked him to transfer her pension. Whenever it was announced that Stevenson would speak in a distant city, strangers there invited him to visit in their homes—"if you want a quiet evening, we will have the record player going and we can sit on the floor and talk about books." They had no way of knowing what the life of a public figure was like. People traveled great distances to see him. One woman in the East arranged her vacation so as to be in Chicago when he spoke there. Strangers sent him gifts and cards on his birthday and at Christmas. Many asked money for their churches or charities. Authors sent him their books and manuscripts. People asked for autographs, photographs, or copies of his books and speeches. Some asked for his neckties. Some seemed simply to want to encourage him—"it is comforting in these times to know that a country which produces a McCarthy, a Velde, a Jenner, and a Hall also has [you]." Many tried to imitate his prose. Some sent him long unsolicited memoranda on various public questions. They seemed to feel helpless to deal with the world's problems themselves and thought he was in a position to act.

Stevenson spent an inordinate amount of time reading and pondering his fan mail, too much time, some thought. He received about ten invitations a day to speak. Sometimes, declining an invitation, he sent a message of greeting. Some groups asked no more than a message in the first place. He sent thousands of such messages to local Democratic organizations, Jewish groups, veterans' groups, labor unions, farm groups, testimonial dinners, fund-raising dinners, dedicatory ceremonies, anniversary observances, cornerstone layings, convocations. A typical request, one from a group of foreign-born citizens, read:

> My dear Mr. Stevenson:
> In the opinions of the 100,000 freedom-loving _____
> living in the United States, you are the most respected Democrat leader of the American nation today. Have you a short but stirring message (within 100 or 150 words) for them?

For a time Blair had written the messages. In January, Stevenson asked the present author to write messages and speeches on a part-time basis. Stevenson usually cleared them. Democratic groups and Jewish groups led all others. Democratic and Catholic groups frequently wanted to auction off an autographed copy of one of his own books or some personal memento as a fund-raising device. One Democratic group auctioned off his sweat shirt. Carol Evans said the pressure on his time was as great as when he was Governor. His telephone rang constantly. She and Blair protected him as much as possible. But it was surprisingly easy to drop in on him, and sometimes Stevenson, if he became interested in what a visitor was saying, would keep him for an hour, disrupting that day's schedule.

He was living at the house in Libertyville, commuting by train to Chicago only one day a week if possible, and Blair and Miss Evans tried to crowd all appointments into that one day. Often it proved impossible. He frequently sent out for lunch in a brown paper bag and ate it at his desk; if he had a lunch appointment he merely ordered an extra sandwich. Sometimes he lunched at the Chicago Club, a citadel of Republicanism, or the Attic Club. He commuted to New York once or twice a month. Fre-

1 In the 1950s and 1960s, as Adlai Stevenson won world renown and became ever more deeply involved in foreign affairs, he sometimes seemed to be bearing almost alone the terrible problems of mankind. He once told a friend he had nightmares about nuclear holocaust. It is as this man of sorrows that Ben Shahn, a Stevenson admirer and a great artist (whom the present author is proud to call collaborator and friend), conceived him.

2 During the 1952 presidential campaign General Eisenhower had proclaimed that, if elected, "I shall go to Korea." After the election Stevenson, beginning his famous world tour, went to Korea too. Neither accomplished much. Here Stevenson is shown (March 17, 1953) in a trench accompanied by General Maxwell D. Taylor and (rear) General Paul Kendall, I Corps commander.

3 Lest this photograph of Stevenson and Generalissimo Chiang Kai-shek be taken to indicate that Stevenson was Chiang's warm supporter, one should remember that during his visit to Formosa in 1953 Stevenson also talked secretly with one of Chiang's generals who told him that Chiang was a totalitarian ruling with a secret police. Stevenson informed the American Ambassador, who seemed indifferent.

4 On a later trip, one to South America in 1960, Stevenson, as he had on his 1953 world tour, talked not only with statesmen but with the poor. Here he is shown with his supporter, traveling companion, and sometime employer, William Benton, in the slums of Lima, Peru.

5 In 1954, Stevenson, though out of office, undertook to lead the Democratic Party in the off-year congressional elections. And lead it he did, as perhaps no other defeated presidential candidate in American history ever has. Between political chores, he paused to deliver a "non-political" speech—as though a politician ever delivers one—at Columbia University. Here he is shown with (from his left) President Grayson Kirk of Columbia and three others who, with Stevenson, received honorary degrees: Queen Elizabeth the Queen Mother, Chancellor Konrad Adenauer of West Germany, and Chief Justice of the United States Earl Warren.

6 It was at the Columbia convocation in 1954 that Stevenson first met Agnes
Meyer, wife of Eugene Meyer, then publisher of the Washington *Post*. A
formidable force in Washington life in her own right, Mrs. Meyer became
Stevenson's friend, supporter, and contributor.

7 Adlai E. Stevenson III, Stevenson's eldest son and later U. S. Senator from Illinois, married lovely Nancy Anderson of Louisville in June 1955. Stevenson's divorced wife, whose mental condition was deteriorating, wore black. Stevenson, young Adlai, and Nancy, shown here, put on a good face for the photographers, betraying in public no hint of private anguish.

8 The happy warrior. Almost immediately after the 1952 defeat it was clear that Stevenson would run again in 1956. He knew he would have to fight for the nomination and he began early. Here he waves to a crowd at a rally in Miami in 1955. He often grumbled about the "ordeal"—and the nonsense—of campaigning but at the same time something in him loved it, and occasionally he did indeed look like a happy warrior.

quently in New York he ate at a lunch counter, and he enjoyed riding the subway. Once he got lost on it and was late for an important appointment. He resumed seeing his Lake Forest friends—dinner parties, dances at Onwentsia, debut parties for friends' daughters. He was frequently invited to the homes of people at the University of Chicago but rarely went. He said he went out as little as possible; actually he went out a good deal and enjoyed it. "My friends have been very kind," he once said, "they've let me come back into it pretty much on my own terms. I can go as much or as little as I please. They view me as a sort of eccentric uncle who may forget to come or may telephone at the last minute and say he can't make it."

Minow and other friends considered Stevenson's constant self-deprecation a gambit to disarm people. "He knew he was very capable," Minow said. Minow thought two impulses were constantly at war within Stevenson. "There was the gentleman, a high-class civilized intelligent intellectually minded man. The other was the desire to hold public office in a particular country where the candidate has to comply with the ground rules. They were always in conflict. It was consistent with the former to groan and moan about the political demands on his time—'the precinct captains in the Morrison Hotel.' He could tell Lake Forest, *I have to* go do this.' Then with the politicians he'd say, *I have to* go to Onwentsia for the wedding.' There was a diversity of friendships. One beauty of the Gov's life was that somehow he managed to keep them all. He could go to Lake Forest and yet have dinner with Jack Arvey and Abe Marovitz—or he could go to Oxford or to LaSalle Street—or to the Democratic Advisory Council—or worry about the problems of the world—or on New Year's Eve take a girl to the theater. It was most unusual. Many who progress kiss their old friends good-by. He never did that. He never closed a door. It's the mark of a good politician or a good diplomat or a good person, however you want to look at it. Buffie used to irritate him sometimes but he'd never foreclose a warm feeling for her. He would never say no to an invitation. Desbarats [where the Dutch Smiths had a house]— he put on a big act about, 'Oh, God, I'd rather read a book' but he'd go there. Wanting to read a book was something to talk about but not do. He was not really an intellectual. He brought to politics, one, a restoration of the Roosevelt respect for the mind; and, two, a unique respect for the language; and, three, a courage in being willing to be honest about most of the issues even if it meant losing. He stood up more often than most politicians. In his personal relationships, I never met anyone who somehow managed to bring out the best in people as he did. When you were around him—with all his faults, and there were plenty of them—it was always fun and a good time. He was able to bring people to think better of themselves. He was a good listener. He had the habit of grumbling constantly. Maybe it was the constant frustration that there just wasn't enough time. The priorities were all mixed up. Handshaking, cocktail parties, he sort of liked to shake hands, but he never found time for high-level conversations with people whose judgment he valued. He groaned under the burden of trying to do everything. Maybe this explains his restlessness too. Always having to be on the move, doing something, never getting it done. He was always groaning if he couldn't find someone to play tennis. He was not a bad sport, though—he did not feel sorry for himself." But he was, Minow thought, "driven by a desire for public office even at the expense of family life." He was good with children, other people's children. That year Penelope Tree, daughter of Marietta, sent him a picture of herself amid flowers inscribed, "I love you and you know it." Stevenson wrote on it, "And I love *you*—and do *you* know it? Governor Stevenson," and sent it back to her.

On January 2 he wrote to Alicia Patterson:

Thanks for that sweet note from Kingsland and those dear, dear words. I love all the moments and moods, but the rare moments of softness are best. And I wonder as I get older and more scarred and bruised if such moments are not the only really perceptive ones—if the mature heart isn't a better organ of vision than the eye—vision of what's most important which must be the spirit—tenderness, loyalty, love. I hope '55 has more of what's really important for you my dear —and I long for the Black River, in vain I guess

Affec—

AES

Nancy, his daughter-in-law-to-be, wrote a long thank-you note for his visit to Louisville and his reception for her and Adlai III at Onwentsia, a remarkably perceptive and affectionate note for one so young. She was an attractive girl, almost beautiful; she was bright and clever but she had a great deal of common sense too. She would make Adlai III a wonderful wife, so good that many friends of the family wished Stevenson himself had been so lucky. She now wrote, "A heart full of thanks for coming to Louisville—you left a lot of warmth and comfort to be pushed around by children, fuss and noise and you are a dear to put up with it. . . . Your party [at Onwentsia] was a gay success for me—I loved seeing you kissing all the 'wimmen,' Ad beating all his old friends on the back—and for myself—meeting a lot of people who will, I hope, be future friends. I hope you know how very much the farm is home to me—having seen it in two seasons intensifies the feeling of last summer. Fires instead of cocktails on the lawn, Christmas decor instead of flowers from the garden, the tree with the grubs surrounded by snow—the new memories round out happy thoughts for the future. . . . I wanted to find us alone for a minute to tell you a lot of things—and always felt each moment not quite right for 'a talk.' Ad and I have, I think, a very deep base of calm loving underneath our 'shocking' deeds. This won't be shaken. I understand many things about Mrs. Stevenson—I hope you won't worry about my feelings—mine are more easily protected than Ad's. We will try to keep from being disturbed. Another matter is our wedding. All of the Andersons can fight a bit on the top without bothering the inside core—if you change your mind and feel that the present plan would be rude or in any way hurt you—a change can be made. Oh—enough of all this—they are stumbling sentences which are, in a sense, just a round about way of saying that I love Ad very much, you've given us a great deal and we love you." Stevenson replied, "It was a wonderful holiday for me, and a new daughter is the best thing that has happened to me or any of us for a long while, especially one who is so understanding and patient with all the difficulties she has encountered. Ad is not the only one who loves you—we all do." Nancy's mother, whom Stevenson addressed as "Mary San," told him Nancy had thought the Onwentsia party a great success, regretted she had not been there, and said she and her husband would be visiting in Glencoe, a Chicago suburb not far from Libertyville, the next weekend. Stevenson invited the Andersons and their hosts to dinner.

30.

That January he spent more time in Chicago and his calendar was filled with legal and political appointments. Nearly every evening he had a dinner date. Meticulously he recorded the hours he spent each day on the RCA case (including four on one Sunday and six on another and eight on a weekday, but more often one and a half or two a day).

But he kept in touch with political leaders. And he took the initiative in telling Senator Fulbright he would be in Washington February 1–4 and hoped Fulbright could arrange one or two supper meetings with Congressmen. Fulbright promptly arranged a stag supper on February 2 with Lyndon Johnson, Richard B. Russell, Henry M. Jackson, George Smathers, and John Stennis and said that Senator Lister Hill would have a similar dinner the following evening and would invite Senators Holland, McClellan, Scott, Hennings, Mansfield, O'Mahoney, and Ervin. Stevenson thanked him and added he would also want to see Sam Rayburn, Paul Douglas, and John Sparkman; he could arrange it upon arrival.

Ben Cohen sent Stevenson a memorandum on the Administration's inflexible position in the Far East. In December the United States and the Formosa Chinese government had signed a mutual security treaty. Democratic critics feared the Chiang Kai-shek Nationalists might provoke a situation leading to U.S. involvement in general war. On January 18, Communist forces seized the offshore island of Ichiang, 210 miles north of Formosa, and seemed prepared to invade the nearby Tachen Islands. President Eisenhower, in a special message to Congress on January 24, asked for explicit authority to use American armed forces to protect Formosa, the Pescadores, and "related positions and territories." It was essential to

U.S. security, he said, that Formosa "remain in friendly hands." Congress should "make clear the unified and serious intentions" of the nation "to fight if necessary." Enactment of the resolution would prevent a Communist miscalculation. But neither Eisenhower nor Dulles clarified his intent regarding Quemoy, Matsu, and other offshore islands. Chiang, fleeing to Formosa with his troops before Mao's army, had stopped to fortify Quemoy and Matsu, small islands close to the Chinese mainland coast and about 150 miles apart, which effectively blocked the harbors of Amoy and Foochow. Chiang maintained he wanted to use the islands as springboards for his return to the mainland. When Communist Chinese began shelling them, he claimed they were doing so as a prelude to an attack on Formosa itself, some 100 miles farther offshore. President Eisenhower's message implied that he might commit U.S. forces to repulse an invasion of Quemoy. Democrats thought the offshore islands belonged to mainland China, not to Chiang's government on Formosa, and feared he might use this "fatal ambiguity" to involve the United States in general war.

Stevenson told Cohen he agreed with much of what he said and added that the United States "should be trying to . . . bring about a separate status for Formosa and a unanimity of view in the non-Communist world to that end." Cohen's memorandum became known, and his appointment to the UN delegation was blocked because of it, and Stevenson, indignant, wanted to tell the press so. This was the beginning of a long correspondence Stevenson had with Cohen, Bowles, Wyatt, Warburg, Schlesinger, Tufts, Acheson, Nitze, Fritchey, and others about United States Far Eastern policy, a policy that would result in crisis that spring.

He agreed to conduct four seminars on law and society at Northwestern University's law school that term. He spoke January 13 at a dinner to promote judicial reform and legislative reapportionment in Illinois, causes in which his friend and political adviser Lou Kohn was deeply interested. On January 14 in Evanston he spoke at a dinner honoring Albert Schweitzer. He issued a statement praising the Organization of American States for supporting the democratic regime of José Figueres of Costa Rica. (Blair, to whom fell the task of distributing the statement to the press, reported that one newspaperman responded, "Well, what does the Governor think about the plight of the whooping crane!") He found time to approve a co-author for a book Mrs. Ives was to write, *My Brother Adlai,* and to observe that the advance royalty payment seemed small.

But he was balking at endorsing Dick Daley, running for Mayor for the first time. Daley, Cook County Democratic chairman, was running in the primary against the Democratic incumbent, Martin Kennelly. Kennelly, it will be recalled, had been elected in 1947, and though slated by the Cook County machine had stood apart from it and was considered an independent reform-minded good-government man. His slating and election had helped pave the way in 1948 for the election of Stevenson and Douglas. During his incumbency, however, Kennelly had disappointed his supporters, being more disposed to reign than to rule, and as a consequence, while he exerted little leadership in Chicago and Springfield during Stevenson's governorship, the crooks in the machine stole everything that was not nailed down. Kennelly had been re-elected in 1951 and now wanted a third term. But the machine had had enough and had slated Dick Daley to oppose him in the primary. Stevenson was under heavy pressure from both sides. Machine men urged that he owed it to the organization and to Daley personally to support Daley. Good-government people considered Daley a hack and thought Stevenson should support the high-minded Kennelly. Stevenson was reluctant to do anything, and his silence hurt Daley. Blair, Minow, Martin; Abe Marovitz and other leaders of the party; leaders of the IVI who had originally supported Kennelly but had become disillusioned; and many others pointed out to Stevenson that Daley had served Stevenson well in Springfield while Stevenson was Governor and, moreover, that Daley had worked hard for Stevenson in 1952. On the other hand, an old friend of Stevenson and a civil libertarian, John Lapp, told Stevenson he hoped the report was not true that he was coming out for Daley and the Morrison Hotel crowd. Stevenson replied, "Thanks for your letter, which, frankly, surprises me. I had not thought with your long experience hereabouts that you could so readily believe the current libels about [Daley] one of the best politicos who has emerged here to my knowledge, and who has to his credit already mighty rough tactics with the organization in the judicial campaign in 1953, plus the best ticket ever in 1954. Which is not to say I don't think well of Martin Kennelly—or of an old and valued friend, John Lapp!"

Finally, on February 1, with considerable misgiving, Stevenson issued a statement: "I have not taken sides in the Democratic primaries anywhere in the country, and I had intended to follow that practice in the Democratic Primary for Mayor. I think the people of Chicago are fortunate to be able to choose from three[15] such good men as are competing for the Democratic nomination. But I am moved to say—emphatically—that the continual attacks on Dick Daley are, in my opinion, unfair and misleading." Daley, he said, as county chairman, had given Cook County "the best slate of candidates in many years" last year. He had served Stevenson and the people well as state Director of Revenue and the party well as county chairman. A few weeks ago all three candidates "would have eagerly welcomed" the machine's support. Now the others denounced Daley for having it. "The notion that active participation in party organization somehow disqualifies a citizen from public office is wrong and dangerous. . . . What we need is not less but more participation by more able and honest people of Mr. Daley's type. . . . Aside from my personal

15 The third was Benjamin Adamowski, a lawyer whom Stevenson had known in his early days in Chicago. Adamowski, a maverick, later switched to the Republican Party and ended up with relatively little support anywhere.

respect and friendship for him, I think Dick Daley's contributions as a political leader and a public official commend him highly to the confidence of the voters of Chicago."

It was not an all-out endorsement, but it was helpful. The *Sun-Times* attacked Stevenson heavily for putting himself "in bed with the worst element of the city's Democratic political machine who long have opposed all that Stevenson purports to stand for." On February 17, Bill Blair wrote a rare letter, a long indignant one, to Marshall Field protesting the attack. Blair was unable to understand why the *Sun-Times* questioned the motives of those who supported Daley. It had called Stevenson's statement "a transparent excuse to project himself into the Chicago picture"; Blair asked if it was any more "transparent" than the *Sun-Times*'s efforts to discredit and weaken the Democratic Party. Bob Merriam, son of Stevenson's old friend at the University of Chicago and a young man who himself had helped Stevenson with speeches while he was Governor and had been a Democratic alderman, had this year switched parties and would run for Mayor as a Republican against the winner of the Daley-Kennelly primary fight; and Blair pointed out that the *Sun-Times* had already announced it would support Merriam regardless of whom the Democrats nominated. Blair reminded Field that previously the *Sun-Times* had spoken well of Daley; now it had turned on him, presumably to help elect Merriam. Blair accused the *Sun-Times* of using Joe McCarthy's technique of guilt by association when it said that Stevenson was "in the same corner with" nefarious Democratic machine leaders. So great was his ire that he appended four postscripts.

Lloyd Garrison had begun soliciting contributions to the Stevenson political fund, including Marshall Field, Frank Altschul, and George Backer; the first two would give $3,000, he thought, and the last $1,000. Bill Benton told Blair that he, Sidney H. Scheuer, Alfred Stelsin, Roger Stevens, and Marshall Field had "put up the money for Tom Finletter," presumably the money to finance the Finletter Group, and asked him to persuade Stevenson to thank them.

Stevenson left on Wednesday, February 2, for Washington where he stayed at the Metropolitan Club the rest of the working week. He attended the dinners arranged by Senators Fulbright and Hill. At Hill's dinner for Senate liberals, Morse and Lehman made the liberal criticism of the Formosa resolution with little dissent from the others. They had, however, voted for the resolution and to ratify a mutual security resolution. At the Fulbright dinner, smaller but representing greater senatorial power, Stevenson was told that the Democrats, having for years insisted on presidential supremacy in foreign policy, had no choice but to support Eisenhower's requested resolution despite grave misgivings. They told him Eisenhower wanted peace and needed help to withstand warlike pressure from Knowland, Bridges, Admiral Radford, and possibly Dulles himself. Stevenson had breakfast with Senator Douglas and lunch with Sam Rayburn. He filed a brief before the Supreme Court in the RCA case. He met with Paul Butler and Matt McCloskey of Pennsylvania, the party's money man at that time, then went up to New York. Saturday was his birthday, and friends gave a party; among those present was Lauren Bacall. Over the weekend he had lunch with Averell Harriman to meet the Shah of Iran, recorded a broadcast for NBC, had dinner with Marietta Tree, and saw Mary Lasker. He spent Monday with RCA executives and dined that night with John J. McCloy. The rest of the week he was equally busy—his schedule included meetings with Mayor Wagner, Lloyd Garrison, Eric Hodgins, the *Fortune* author and editor, Franklin D. Roosevelt, Jr., and others; a cocktail party at Benton's apartment to meet the former Parliamentary Secretary in the Ministry of Education in the British Labour government; lunch and dinner with a French client, Jean Lambert, suggested to him by George Ball; a meeting with Schlesinger, Cass Canfield, head of the Harper publishing house, Gardner Cowles, and Maurice Tempelsman about a trip to Africa that would include both legal business for Tempelsman and writing for *Look* and perhaps a book for Harper; lunch with an AT&T executive and dinner with Tom Finletter and Frank Altschul; and, on Friday, a morning and luncheon meeting with the Finletter Group, then dinner with Alicia Patterson.

He went up to Cambridge for the weekend, visiting Adlai III and Nancy, who came over from Smith College, staying with the Archibald MacLeishes, and seeing Barbara Ward and others. Back home, he told Adlai III to wear Borden's overcoat—Borden was in the Army, and Adlai should get rid of "that hamster bait" he was wearing and "consign your coat to charity, if possible, and the ash can if necessary. If Borden's does not suit, get a new one." Nancy sent him a long letter: "Our weekend with you was *superb* fun. . . . Visions of you and Miss Ward eating my tasteless eggs & Ad's delicious artichokes late that night will always dance through the head." She gave him advice he had solicited about a commencement speech at Smith.

After a series of conferences among Steve Mitchell, Wyatt, Blair, and Raskin, Mitchell on February 14 drafted a memorandum proposing that a Stevenson for President Committee be established. It would carry out a campaign for the nomination among both regular Democratic organizations and volunteers, work on preliminary arrangements for the convention, plan for the fall campaign. Nothing was said about Stevenson's entering the primaries. The memo went on to more specific plans—groups of experts on issues, public opinion polls on Stevenson and the issues, finances, possibly a motion picture about Stevenson's 1953 world tour, hiring a public relations man, and opening a committee office with full-time staff. Although Mitchell was important at this time, his importance declined.

Arthur Schlesinger told Stevenson an aggressive Democratic candidate would have an "excellent" chance of beating Eisenhower in 1956, but if Stevenson allowed the nomination to come to him through the "drift of events and in the absence of alternatives," he would have a hard time winning—the single "important doubt" the American people had about Stevenson was whether he really wanted to be President. Agnes Meyer told Stevenson that Eisenhower, whom she had seen recently, was unhappy in his job and might not run again; she guessed the Republicans would probably nominate Nixon or Knowland. She wrote at length about aid to education, a subject she cared about deeply (as Mary Lasker cared about public aid to health, especially mental health). Stevenson told her he might make a speech on education in June.

En route home from a stay in Jamaica with Richard S. Reynolds of Reynolds Metals, Stevenson stopped at Miami Beach. Jack Arvey was giving a dinner there that night for a dozen Republicans and, meeting Stevenson at the airport on short notice, told him he could dine alone, work, or dine with the Republicans. He dined with the Republicans and, Arvey later recalled, "charmed them all." As a result of the meeting, Arvey sent a fundraising letter around the country to help Stevenson's cause.

Back in Chicago, Stevenson found a letter from a friend in Spokane who thought the Washington delegation at the convention would be unanimously for Stevenson and who also thought there was a "50-50 chance" Eisenhower would not run. Stevenson replied that "regardless of what he *thinks* he is going to do, or even wants to do, he will most certainly run, and gladly, when the time comes." John Steele of the *Time-Life* Bureau in Washington reported on March 11 that the Democratic leadership, in both the National Committee and Congress, believed that Stevenson "will be nominated at Chicago virtually by acclamation on the first ballot" and that he "cannot duck running" against Eisenhower in 1956, though some of his fervent supporters hoped he could.

Stevenson's statement on Daley had not been enough. On March 22 he did more—spoke at a Volunteers for Daley dinner put on by many of the same young people who had worked for Stevenson in 1952. By now Daley had won the primary against Kennelly and was opposing young Bob Merriam for the mayoralty. Merriam was conducting a shrill campaign, showing photographs on television of gangsters' bodies in the trunks of cars and suggesting that somehow the "gangster-dominated" Democratic machine was responsible, denouncing "the Morrison Hotel politburo," thus by implication linking the corrupt Cook County machine with softness on Communism in Truman's White House.

The Merriam family and Stevenson had long been friendly. The whole episode was painful. Stevenson, however, after much prodding, went down the line for Daley and the machine: "A man who has so long served the public so well deserves not deprecation and vilification but honor and respect. They say now that he is a captive and creature of an evil Democratic machine. It was different last November when the people overwhelmingly elected the blue ribbon ticket presented by the same machine—headed by Dick Daley. Then they applauded; now they denounce. . . . Neither party has a monopoly on virtue—corruption is not a Democratic problem, it is not a Republican problem, it is a human problem. But the Republican candidate denounces Dick Daley as 'the front man for a pack of jackals who have been feeding off the city for the past twenty-four years.' Well, I have been Governor of this great state and am not unacquainted with jackals, nor would I or anyone deny the mistakes, faults and failures of the Democratic organization in Chicago. But such intemperate language is its own answer, and I never expected to hear anyone assert, let alone this candidate on the Republican ticket, that sin in Chicago began with the defeat of Big Bill Thompson twenty-four years ago!" (Thompson was a corrupt Republican Mayor of the 1920s; he lasted until 1931, when the modern Democratic Chicago machine swept to power and elected the Mayor—as it has ever since.) "Perhaps I should also remind my friend, the Republican candidate and former Democratic alderman, of what his distinguished father, Dr. Charles Merriam, said in his book *Chicago:* 'Personal contact with the alderman quickly dissipates any idea that one race, religion, class, section or party possesses a monopoly of honesty or ability. There are reliable and unreliable Republicans and Democrats, as well.' Perhaps a moratorium on name calling, slander, and mass indictment would not hurt at this late hour, especially from a party which has confessed its own bankruptcy by handpicking a Democrat to try to beat a Democrat." Like Daley himself, Stevenson moved to the defense of Chicago's reputation: "Nothing is easier than to promise 'reform' by painting Chicago as an ugly, depraved city—despoiled by thieves and criminals and politicians. But this is not true," and he extolled Chicago's virtues and declared that Chicago would become what its leaders made it: "No man can do it alone, but a political leader, sustained by vision, by principles, by party and public confidence can. Dick Daley is such a leader. He is the same Dick Daley who has served this community as public official and political leader so well. And he will be the same Dick Daley—mark my words—he will *still* be captain of his soul—two years from today—or two weeks from today when he becomes the next Mayor of Chicago."

Daley was elected easily. A few days after Stevenson's speech Daley thanked him for it and for his "generous contribution" to the Volunteers for Daley. Stevenson, replying to a letter from a man who said he understood why Stevenson had to support Daley but who hoped that "in your private, secret heart you also hope that Bob [Merriam] makes it," said that he had not been forced to support Daley but had done so out of conviction. Merriam's mother wrote a stinging letter to Stevenson, saying that many people were blaming him for Merriam's defeat and that she could more easily bear that defeat than bear her loss of admiration for Stevenson. Stevenson replied, "I am sorry you feel so bitterly about my fidelity to the Party that has offered me its highest honors . . . and about a man, Mr. Daley, who has served me well and really done so much to make my party a better, cleaner, more useful political instrument. I am, as I think you know, an admirer of your son, and I shall continue to count myself his friend in spite of the intemperance of his campaign. . . . I still hope to see him an active Democrat again."

Daley's campaign strategy had been to shrug off Merriam's attacks, wrap himself in the mantle of Chicago's fair name, and speak constantly to the ward committeemen and precinct captains. Merriam ran highly visibly, in the press and on TV; Daley ran almost invisibly in the wards, with the machine. He would be re-elected in 1959, 1963, 1967, 1971, and 1975. During those years he became one of the most powerful Democrats in the nation. He could not carry Illinois for Stevenson in 1956 but he carried it—narrowly—for John F. Kennedy in 1960; and during the Kennedy years and the Johnson years he exerted great influence on Administration policy. He helped rebuild Chicago during those years, too, and for a time he enjoyed the support of every newspaper in town. Republican businessmen as well as liberal Democrats considered him one of the best, if not the best, mayors Chicago ever had. He restricted (relatively) the activities of organized criminals and crooked politicians. At a time when New York and other big cities seemed to be falling apart, Daley made Chicago work. Only a few liberals pointed out that at the same time Chicago had become the most racially segregated city in the nation. (Daley's blind spot where Negroes were concerned resulted both from his having lived lifelong in an Irish community near the stockyards where Negroes seemed to threaten Irish jobs and property values and his having risen in the machine during the years when it was able to control Negro votes—and Negro actions—through political patronage, favors, and money.) It was not until the 1968 Democratic Convention that Daley, having previously badly misread the Negro ghetto problem and now handling badly the young people who protested at the convention, fell from grace—fell, that is, nationally: at home, although criticized by liberal Democrats, he maintained strong support among the mass of Chicagoans. By that time he was virtually the last of the big-city bosses. Stevenson earlier had called him "one of the finest public servants I will ever know." In many ways, he was. He was smart and shrewd. He understood power better than almost anyone. He had few if any confidantes. He talked little. He was a plain man and a sentimental man—in 1969, at his sixty-seventh birthday party, called on for "a few words," he almost broke down when he recited his blessings—friends, parents, wife, children, labor leaders, businessmen, churches, universities—and said, "Above all, I've been given an opportunity to serve in this great city. And I'd like to say to my kids and to my people here before me: When the curtain comes down, and it's bound to someday, I'll just say I did the best I could." He did.

31.

Stevenson was making plans. He would leave for Africa on April 18. He had to be in Washington the night of Saturday, April 16, for a dinner in honor of Speaker Rayburn. He hoped to get Borden up to Washington from his military camp in North Carolina and Adlai III and Nancy down from Massachusetts and to get together with them on Sunday, before departing for Africa, "to discuss all our family plans and problems," including plans for Adlai III's and Nancy's wedding, about which Stevenson had been corresponding at length. He wondered whether in Washington some of them could stay with his friends Dr. and Mrs. Paul Magnuson, or perhaps with Senator John F. Kennedy. (As suited his convenience, Stevenson sometimes declined invitations to stay with friends on the ground that photographers and reporters would be a nuisance, or, contrariwise, asked friends to put him up so he could escape photographers and reporters who hounded him at hotels.) And there were other arrangements, all, as usual, complicated. Adlai III and Nancy were planning a camping honeymoon in Canada. Stevenson wrote, "The plans for the honeymoon sound promising, but if I was a bride I might have some reservations about sleeping bags, tents, lanterns and gasoline stoves." He was worrying about wedding gifts, guest lists, the minister, whether the bridegroom and ushers should wear morning suits.

The mainland Chinese were shelling Quemoy and Matsu, Chiang was reinforcing the islands, a crisis was building up, and, to many people, large-scale war in Asia seemed imminent, with America deeply involved. Stevenson sought the views of Chet Bowles and others. Bowles met with a group of Senators and reported their misgivings and reluctance to speak out—and the increasing regret of some that they had not spoken out sooner. Bowles suggested that Stevenson speak, treating Quemoy and Matsu only as evidence of bankrupt policy, and sent a memo and speech language. James Warburg complained that the Democratic leadership in Congress, by supporting Eisenhower, was throwing away issues for 1956 and urged Stevenson to take "this bull by the horns."

Stevenson tried Senator Sparkman and others, testing the Washington climate. If he did speak out, should he clear the speech with Senator Lyndon Johnson, Senator Walter George of Georgia, chairman of the Foreign Relations Committee, and other Democratic congressional leaders? They did not seem to want to be consulted. In the past Stevenson had taken care not to offend congressional leaders, especially Southerners, for he felt he must never seem to try to tell the party what to do in Congress, and this policy had succeeded: by now Johnson, Rayburn, Mansfield, and others felt it almost certain he would be renominated in 1956. But could he speak out on Quemoy-Matsu alone? Aside from its effect on his own future, doing so might split his party or provoke extremist reaction that could conceivably lead to war. On Saturday, March 26, Clayton Fritchey at the National Committee telephoned Stevenson and suggested he "hold everything" until President Eisenhower's meeting with congressional leaders on Wednesday or Thursday. Stevenson told Bowles that if nothing resulted from that meeting he himself was inclined to go ahead. He felt now that the speech should have been given "a fortnight ago"—Eisenhower's meeting would lessen its impact. He was still troubled by the "delicate problem" of consultation with Senator George.

He made notes to call Dean Acheson and Senator Johnson and Speaker Rayburn. His notes for his phone conversation with Johnson said that he was "gravely concerned" about the Administration's "drift and indecision over Quemoy and Matsu," that he was particularly concerned about "the pressures being put on Ike by Knowland, Bridges, and McCarthy to go to war" over those islands, that he was "convinced" he "must speak out and call for a halt to the drift," for "once the shooting starts, it will be too late to talk. We must try to save the peace." The notes continued: "Of course, beyond the need to speak out from the country's viewpoint, there is also a splendid political opportunity to seize the 'peace' position." He had "composed" a speech but since "you and Speaker Rayburn are right on the firing line" he wanted them to see the speech beforehand and would ask Fritchey to deliver copies to them. He would let Johnson decide who else should see it—perhaps Senator George. He encouraged Johnson to telephone any comments or suggestions. He told a friend he was being "pulled hither and yon, mostly yon," on the speech, "by our leaders in Congress." He told a New Yorker who urged him to speak out, "I agree emphatically with your letter and I have had many of similar import." Senator Lehman's assistant, Julius Edelstein, told Blair it was urgent that he see Stevenson's speech on Quemoy and Matsu in advance. The New York *Times* in a story filed from Chicago on Sunday, April 3, said that Stevenson would decide "in the next several days" whether to speak. (Blair maintained close relations with the *Times*'s Chicago correspondent.)

Stevenson spent the weekend and Monday, April 4, at home writing a longhand draft of the speech. He planned tentatively to deliver it on national radio a week hence, on April 11. During this same period Stevenson was dealing with family problems. Adlai III reported that his mother was protesting the Andersons' plan to have two dinners in Louisville before the wedding instead of the usual bridal dinner. Stevenson replied, "I can imagine the trouble you had with Mother. I had it too and the Andersons had it worse than ever before. I talked with Warwick [Nancy's father] yesterday and found him really shattered this time. I think they are worried about Nancy having to be exposed to this sort of thing but I did my best to try to reassure them. I hardly know what to do about the party and I so much wish the whole business had been handled quite differently. However,

there is no point in crying over spilled milk." He and Anderson had decided to leave plans in abeyance, hoping that Ellen's agitation would cool.
"I have no objection to a single party instead of two parties and if she is
properly buttered up you know she will purr like a kitten. All it takes is a
little management. . . . I have been distracted with work and have written
a speech on Quemoy and Matsu."

Adlai replied that he was going to Louisville this weekend "because Mr.
Anderson really is beside himself and because I think that Nancy may
break down if she has to go through much more. Her faith in me conflicts
with her respect for her father I think. . . . I'm getting some professional
advice about mother—I refuse to try to live a married life exposed 24
hours a day to her vindictiveness and she's getting worse."

Stevenson wrote to Warwick Anderson and sent a copy to Adlai III,
telling him, "I hope this doesn't sound too rough, but he really irked me
this time. . . . Now pay attention to your work and forget all this business. It will work out as it always has, and a son who behaved with less
compassion and consideration for his mother than you have I wouldn't
have much use for."

Stevenson's letter to Anderson had indeed been "rough." It had been
prompted by two letters from Anderson. In them Anderson had said Adlai
III was appeasing his mother, temporizing, refusing to face the truth, and
he indicated Stevenson himself had done the same. He had urged that
Adlai III be told the truth and made to face it, that medical advice should
be sought, and that all should join in resisting Ellen's highhanded
demands. The situation, he thought, was becoming intolerable. He cared
nothing about the details of the wedding—if, indeed, there was to be a
wedding—but cared greatly about his daughter's happiness and the success
of her marriage, which he felt was seriously threatened by Ellen. Ellen, he
added, had telephoned a friend of the Andersons in Louisville after midnight and threatened to give the family row to the press.

At this point, on April 8, Stevenson wrote his "rough" letter to Anderson: "In the first place, Adlai knows and has known for a long time literally everything that I know about her case professionally. No one has been
able to induce her to see a psychiatrist since I got her to see one in Boston
in 1942. As to 'appeasing' her, I think a semantic debate would serve no
purpose. I have not thought of it as appeasement nor have I ever seen any
indication on Adlai's part of giving in, although he has frequently cut off
or just withdrawn from the arena, if I make myself clear. I am afraid I
cannot foresee the same disaster to their marriage that you do, although I
have little doubt that she is and will continue to be a source of infinite
difficulty and that that must be a hazard Adlai and Nancy will have to
face. . . . Perhaps he has not 'faced the facts' in their full import, and I
have been loathe to do anything to set son against mother. I thought it better to take its own course than that she or anyone could find confirmation
for her suspicions and justification for her injury in that direction. As for

you and Mary San being 'blackmailed' into appeasement, I certainly would not be, in any way, shape or form. I am quite aware that the separate parties were arranged to accommodate me, and perhaps I was negligent in not finding out what was going on before Mary San wrote to her. At all events, I would strongly recommend that you do precisely what you wish and if she doesn't choose to come to the Saturday night parties, very well. If you would prefer to have no party I am sure that would be all right too. . . . I am sorry to hear that there have been visible damages to the children. I had not detected it in Adlai and I wish I could somehow make amends to Nancy for the unhappy situation which she has become involved in . . . I can only say I am sorry and disappointed, and you are doubtless right that I have not done a very good job of it all." He added a postscript: "I wonder sometimes if you and Mary San would have more respect for Adlai if he had behaved with less compassion and consideration for his mother. . . . After all, she is his *mother.*"

Ellen's own mother, Mrs. Carpenter, was back in Chicago; Stevenson talked to her, and she agreed to talk to Ellen and to Mrs. Anderson. Mrs. Ives told Adlai III that the situation saddened her.

And all through this week Stevenson's speech on Quemoy and Matsu was in the works. On Saturday, April 9, the New York *Times* announced on page one that Stevenson would deliver a major foreign policy speech on nationwide radio on Monday, his first nationwide speech since December 4. Bob Tufts, following a discussion with Paul Nitze, had sent Stevenson a long memorandum on Asian policy. Stevenson sent a first draft of the speech to Acheson, inviting comment and saying he had misgivings about consulting the congressional leadership. He sent a copy of his draft to Fritchey, and Fritchey showed it to George Ball, Ben Cohen, and Paul Nitze, who criticized it rather sharply. Fritchey sent Stevenson a redraft of the speech incorporating changes suggested by Fritchey, Stern, Ball, Cohen, and Nitze. Dean Acheson telephoned his own suggestions.

The day he made the speech, Stevenson wrote to Mrs. Ives to thank her for writing to Adlai III: "It should help him. We have had a bad time lately and I find Mr. Anderson exceedingly emotional about it all, which has made it more difficult for Adlai, and indeed for Nancy. I have thought several times it would be better if they had no wedding affair and got married in a little church in Cambridge immediately after Nancy's graduation. I shall have a good talk with him this week-end in Washington." He added, "After an awful struggle I am making a radio speech tonight." That same day Warwick Anderson sent a cordial reply to Stevenson's letter and said Adlai's weekend visit to Louisville had been helpful. And so back to Quemoy-Matsu and U.S. policy in Asia.

The speech had gone through many drafts and many hands. Stevenson himself had worked on it again and again; obviously he considered it of the highest importance. The final draft as delivered over radio Monday night, April 11, was, essentially, the draft he had originally written out in longhand. He worked on it till the last minute—there was no time to mimeograph it before he delivered it.

He began solemnly: "My fellow countrymen, I have not spoken to you for more than four months. And I do so tonight only because I have been deeply disturbed by the recent course of events in the Far East and because many of you have asked me for my views." The Quemoy-Matsu problem, he said, had now moved to the point where President Eisenhower must decide what to do if the islands were attacked. His judgment that the attack was only an attack on the islands or was the prelude to an assault on Formosa could be only "a guess." Should the question of modern war hinge on such a guess? Many influential Republicans were insisting that Eisenhower pledge us to the defense of the islands lest Asians think us a "paper tiger" and lest we damage the morale of Chiang's troops and endanger Formosa itself. Acknowledging some merit in these arguments, Stevenson thought them overborne by others: "I have the greatest misgivings about risking a third world war in defense of these little islands." They differed from Formosa. They had always belonged to China. (Formosa had belonged to Japan and been ceded by the Japanese peace treaty.) But the President's judgment was final. Stevenson only hoped that "the inflammatory voices" in Eisenhower's party and administration would not decide the critical questions of whether the islands were "essential to the security of the U.S.," whether they were even essential to the defense of Formosa, whether they could be defended without resort to nuclear weapons, whether we were prepared to use nuclear weapons to "incinerate" China to defend the islands, and whether we were prepared "to shock and alienate our Western Allies and most of the major non-Communist powers of Asia by going to war over the islands." He asked, "Are we, in short, prepared to face the prospect of war in the morass of China, possibly global war, standing almost alone in a sullen or hostile world?"

Stevenson said he considered the division of the Western Allies over the Quemoy-Matsu issue "a greater peril to enduring peace than the islands themselves." Some politicians pretended we did not need allies. They were wrong. We held only six per cent of the world's population and needed overseas bases to protect our own territory, strategic materials, and above all "the moral strength that the solidarity of the world community alone can bring to our cause. Let us never underestimate the weight of moral opinion."

Was there any hope of a peaceful solution? Stevenson thought so. He proposed that the United States consult its friends and the uncommitted nations and ask them all to join with us in an open declaration condemning the use of force in the Formosa Strait and agreeing to stand with us in the defense of Formosa against any aggression, pending some final settlement of its status—by independence, neutralization, trusteeship, plebiscite, or "whatever is wisest." We might also invite Soviet Russia to declare its position. With such an international declaration, Chiang would have little further interest in Quemoy and Matsu, and should be willing to relinquish them. Alternatively, we might ask the General Assembly of the United Nations to condemn any effort to alter the status of Formosa by force and to seek a formula for the permanent future of Formosa. Heretofore, we had been making Formosa policy without regard to others. This must stop. If the Chinese Communists insisted on force and rejected peace, the burden of aggression would be on them, and we would not stand alone.

How, he asked, had we ever got into our present position? It had resulted, he said, from the Administration's efforts to please both wings of the Republican Party. Vice President Nixon a year ago had "talked of sending American soldiers" to fight in Vietnam; but nothing had happened. The Administration had talked boldly of "liberation" for Eastern Europe; nothing had happened. Last year the Administration had made "dire threats of instantaneous and massive atomic retaliation"; recently, the President had spoken of "pinpoint retaliation with tactical weapons." The Administration had indulged in "massive verbal retaliation" and those words had "alarmed our friends a good deal more than deterred the aggressors." President Eisenhower's announcement two years ago that he was unleashing Chiang Kai-shek had come to nothing: Chiang could not possibly invade across a hundred miles of water with his small over-age army without "all-out support" of the United States. People had thought it incredible that the United States could be "bluffing," so Eisenhower's "unleashing" policy had caused "widespread anxiety" that we planned to support a major war with China which might involve the Soviet Union. Hence we found ourselves with the Quemoy and Matsu crisis.

What lessons could be learned? We should abandon "the policy of big words and little deeds." We should "renounce go-it-aloneism." We should face the fact that Chiang's army could not invade the mainland unless we were prepared to accept enormous burdens and risks—and accept them alone, for our allies had made it clear that they would not support us in such an enterprise. "Too often of late we have turned to the world a face of stern military power. Too often the sound they hear from Washington is the call to arms, the rattling of the saber. . . . Thus have we Americans, the most peaceful and generous people on earth, been made to appear hard, belligerent, and careless of those very qualities of humanity which, in fact, we value most. The picture of America—the kindly, generous, deeply pacific people who are really America—has been clouded in the world, to the comfort of the aggressors and dismay of our friends. . . . We will be welcome to the sensitive people of Asia, more as engineers and doctors and agricultural experts, coming to build, to help, to heal, than as soldiers. Point Four was an idea far more stirring, far more powerful, than all the empty slogans. . . . So I say, let us present once more the true face of America—warm and modest and friendly, dedicated to the welfare of all mankind, and demanding nothing except a chance for all to live and let live, to grow and govern as they wish, free from interference, free from intimidation, free from fear. Let this be the American mission in the hydrogen age. Let us stop slandering ourselves and appear before the world once again—as we really are—as friends, not as masters; as apostles of principle, not of power; in humility, not arrogance; as champions of peace, not as harbingers of war. For our strength lies, not alone in our proving grounds and our stockpiles, but in our ideals, our goals, and their universal appeal to all men who are struggling to breathe free."

Stevenson considered the Quemoy-Matsu his third important speech since 1952 (the others being the Chicago report on his world tour and his anti-McCarthy speech in Miami Beach).

Secretary Dulles held a press conference next day. In his prepared statement Dulles said, "Mr. Stevenson suggests, as original ideas, the very approaches which the government has been and is actively exploring. The results we all want will not be advanced by publicly prodding friendly governments. On one matter we seem sharply to differ. Mr. Stevenson speaks feelingly about our allies. However he forgets one ally, namely the Republic of China. That alliance, originally created by President Roosevelt, was recently reaffirmed by our mutual security treaty with the Republic of China. Yet Mr. Stevenson seems to assume that that ally can be ignored and rebuffed." As Dulles was questioned, it became obvious that he and Stevenson differed on other points. He thought it unwise to seek a public declaration from Russia. He was far lessing willing than Stevenson to give up Quemoy and Matsu in return for an international commitment to defend Formosa. As for the UN, Dulles said the question was still before the Security Council and so could not appropriately be considered by the General Assembly. (The fact was, however, that under the "uniting for peace" resolution of 1950, which enabled the General Assembly to by-pass the Security Council on Korea, the Formosa question could have been given to the General Assembly since the Security Council seemed unable or unwilling to act.) The New York *Times* reported that Stevenson's speech was "warmly received" in the embassies of America's major allies, some of which seemed puzzled by Dulles' comments. The reaction to Stevenson's speech was widespread and generally favorable.

On April 13, two days after the speech, Stevenson met all day at the Chicago Club with the Finletter Group on health and education. Blair subsequently told Seymour Harris that Stevenson considered it the best meeting of the Group to date. Preparing to leave for Africa, he went over the draft of an article for *Fortune* on the relationship between government and business.

En route to Washington he talked to Dick Daley—both were on their way to attend a big dinner honoring Rayburn. Stevenson had lunch with Sam Rayburn, Lyndon Johnson, and Paul Butler. "Johnson," Stevenson noted in a journal he was starting, "rationalizing why they don't attack Eisenhower's management more, but seemed to approve my criticism re foreign policy this week. Rayburn very critical, but uncertain about political tactics—aging a little and a little indifferent." Borden was in town. and

Adlai III arrived from Louisville in the afternoon, "feeling better about latest crisis with his mother."

Stevenson met with Wilson Wyatt and Archibald Alexander of New Jersey. He attended cocktail parties given by the Illinois and Pennsylvania delegations who had come to Washington—"everyone *very* cordial—even Al Horan!" the Democratic ward boss in Chicago—then went to the hundred-dollar-a-plate Rayburn testimonial banquet intended to raise money for the National Committee. Stevenson sat between Mrs. Roosevelt and Senator George. Mrs. Roosevelt was "now almost motherly," he noted. Senator George was "a little reserved at first; obviously already running for re-election! and scared of Talmadge. By no means 'illiterate' on foreign policy but not very 'keen'—anxious to be constructively critical of adm. but also content to let them lead the way & evidently not dissatisfied with their good will." Stevenson introduced the honored guest, Sam Rayburn, "a man we all admire and love," he said in his opening sentence, then went on to extol Rayburn's virtues, tucking in three "basic things" the Democratic Party must stand for steadfastly: social progress, "equality of opportunity for all," and peace, especially peace in "the hydrogen age." Stevenson wrote in his notebook, "Made good intro. of Sam Rayburn on Radio-TV." He was right: it was brief, eloquent, affectionate. Stevenson thought Rayburn's own speech philosophical but out of character—"written by David Cohn," he thought. "Pres. Truman—looking himself again— also spoke in old attack vein, and as usual caught hell from Rep. press which never even mentioned his criticisms. Very friendly to me."

In New York he arranged through Benton to have Borden transferred from psychological warfare to the Army Signal Corps's motion picture division. He had business appointments with Maurice Tempelsman and Jean Lambert, whom he was to represent in Africa, and had lunch with John Gunther. He also arranged to have Adlai III talk with Dr. Carl Binger, a psychiatrist, about Ellen. Binger was familiar with the case. Adlai III subsequently wrote, "There's no question in his mind but that mother is a paranoid. Uncoupled with depressions, which I've never been able to detect, there's very little hope of the condition ever improving. There's good chance of the condition deteriorating. . . . He says the only thing to do is remove yourself as far as you can in good conscience. . . . He says I should never expose Nancy to her. He says there's fortunately time to consider whether she should even be permitted to come to the wedding—lest she make some cynical remark at the 'forever hold your peace' moment in the ceremony. Mother called the other night and I had to hang up again."

32.

Stevenson and Blair left New York for Africa at 5 P.M. on Monday, April 18. Their first stop was Rome; they arrived there Tuesday evening in the rain. Stevenson went shopping—"prices seemed high" but Rome was "beautiful, cool, fresh and still to me the world's most wonderful and exciting city." He went to lunch on Wednesday with Prime Minister Mario Scelba at Scelba's residence, Villa Madama, "on hill on outskirts overlooking Mussolini's great sports park," Stevenson noted. "Long talk thru interpreter in the *magnificent* Villa Madama. Wants $300 million more annually for 5 years to 'save the south' from communism. Same story—almost —I heard 2 years ago. . . . Scelba firm, pleasant, unpretentious, simple little man—more interested in Italy than the 'world.' His wife plump and pleasant & unaffected. Delicious lunch with foreign minister etc etc—and Mrs. Luce [Clare Boothe Luce, Eisenhower's Ambassador to Italy], who tries hard to be pleasant and considerate. Returned to Embassy with her and talked a bit about the new oil discoveries and the proposed oil law etc shook a few hands—and then to Hotel to . . . polish my poor and long neglected article for Sat Eve Post on party cooperation. Barbara [Ward] & Robt. Jackson arrived in time for late gay dinner at Palassis fine restaurant—Mussolini's modern villa for his mistress. Then a night club! Recognized everywhere—autographs, photos!"

Stevenson spent Thursday, April 21, sightseeing in Rome with "the charming, witty, totally cultivated Barbara" Ward, then left that night for Africa via Athens. On Friday, April 22, he wrote, "Woke up above Khartoum . . . at confluence of Blue & White Nile. Larger town than I expected—green spot surrounded by the endless desert. But as we flew south surprised by vast irrigated farming area. Wheat I suppose. Noticed many scarred faces among natives at airport—Religious or Tribal or ?? . . . Addis Ababa is not far to the East—and this I suppose is as close as I'll ever get to that capital. Desert changes to mountains and as we enter Kenya looks more & more like high dry west of U.S. Turns green & lovely rolling pasture land dotted with trees & patches of red cultivated soil as we approach Nairobi [capital of Kenya]—great clusters of circular thatched mud huts; farmsteads & country residences and the formless sprawling town. Quite a reception of dignitaries at air port—to Norfolk Hotel." There they were joined by Lloyd Garrison and Cass Canfield and their wives. (At dinner one night with the Garrisons on Sixty-fourth Street, Stevenson, leaving the dining room, had said something about his African trip and to Garrison, "Why don't you and Ellen come along?" Garrison said it would be great. Stevenson said to Canfield, "Why don't you join us?" He often issued invitations on the spur of the moment.)

They were taken to the Royal Nairobi Game Reserve by the director of Kenya parks, whom Stevenson described as a "calm, confident, trim & hard Englishman with a military mustache," and Stevenson catalogued meticulously in his notebook the wild animals they saw. Stuck in the mud, they transferred to a four-wheel-drive Land Rover and returned to Nairobi. There they talked to government officials about the problems of multiracial Kenya. Stevenson noted, "In Asia I thought the Chinese were destined to inherit the earth, but when you see the Indian monopoly of trade, their education & cultivation, in Africa and how hard they are prepared to work you wonder what chance the really western races have. . . . Can it be that we too will be driven to self protection against the rising tide of color—brown or yellow first—like the racists of S.A.?" that is, South Africa. European settlers and African preserves took up most of the good land.

Stevenson's account of lunch with the Governor in an "elegant" house and his talk with "the charming, cultivated, aristocrat—Sir Evelyn Baring," successor to "my old friend and host in Fiji—Sir Philip Mitchell," made him sound as though he belonged in the British Foreign Service. He made notes on the cost of the "war" against the Mau Mau, a nationalist anti-white terrorist society, and said his host thought the Mau Mau "is licked, but that Africa is African & little by little they will take over." Stevenson underlined the last. He would remember it later at the United Nations.

After lunch they went by car, accompanied by officials, police, and press, to the great Rift Valley to inspect the villages into which the Kikuyus had been gathered in sanctuary from the Mau Maus. Stevenson noted that they "picked up another of those remarkably handsome, competent and British young career men . . . & his *beautiful* wife also born & raised in Kenya of civil service or missionary parents." Visiting the new settlements, he wrote, "Kikuyo houses all windowless & fluless [?] circular wattle & dark & thatched pointed roof thru which the cooking smoke leaks. People small, spare, not too cheerful, withered & on the whole unattractive. Women as always appear to do *all* the work. . . . An interesting day. . . . Enchanted as always by the British spirit of 'carry on'—while their authority is melting before their eyes." He spent another day at Nairobi. He absorbed everything, stuffed his notebook with facts and snatches of scenery, verbal snapshots of people, the feeling of the place, the political future of emerging Africa.

Garrison, observing that Stevenson's schedule had him seeing all the principal whites but no Africans, went looking for African lawyers. He discovered there was only one African barrister in all Kenya. Garrison called on him. "We talked in his office then had lunch at a restaurant where he could eat then he drove me out to see a Mau Mau prison camp where he had clients." Later, in segregated Southern Rhodesia, Garrison found an African barrister in the compound where he was forced to live. He had married a white woman in London. Garrison took them to see Stevenson, who, Garrison thought, was "a little shocked" by the white wife.

With his companions, Stevenson left Nairobi on April 24, spent the day touring Uganda, and stayed that night at Masaka in what Canfield called "a primitive but decent hotel"—"It wasn't quite up Blair's alley but we had a good dinner, after which Lloyd [Garrison] worked out with the proprietor a day's motor trip, designed to kill off any ordinary traveller. Thus began our custom of arising at 5:30, which persisted with discouraging regularity." By car and riverboat and small plane they toured Queen Elizabeth Park, went on to Lake Kivu in Ruanda-Urundi, went on to the Congo and to Southern Rhodesia and, on May 1, to Johannesburg, South Africa. On the way they were the guests at lunch of the Union Minière du Haut-Katanga, a huge mining company which would figure importantly a few years later in the conflict in the Congo; they observed the dances of the Watusi giants and the orderly town of Elisabethville. They visited a tribe of pygmies, and Blair had his photograph taken with a crowd of naked pygmies and next Christmas had it printed on his card with a message, "Happy New Year from all of us to all of you."

They attended official dinners with complicated seating arrangements. Stevenson sent Alicia Patterson a postcard: "This black continent is seething and fascinating." A Kenyan leader later told Blair how impressed he had been with the "dynamic personality of Mr. Adlai Stevenson." So was Harry Truman back home—in Chicago at about this time he declared that Stevenson was his "choice" for the 1956 presidential nomination. Averell Harriman said the same thing.

Stevenson had business in Johannesburg, and they stayed a week, from May 1 to May 8, with a side trip to Swaziland, where they were entertained by the King and the Queen Mother. Stevenson noted that the King asked, "Who's that young man dancing?" and someone replied, "That's your son, sir." "56 wives," Stevenson noted. The Queen Mother came out on the back porch to greet them, and a crowd gathered, and the Queen Mother filled a big pail with a kind of beer and offered a cup of it to Stevenson. "He was supposed to drain half the pail," Garrison has recalled, "but he limited himself to a very dainty taste." Stevenson regarded the visit as a lark, not a sociological expedition.

The law in South Africa forbade gatherings of more than three or four Africans. Garrison arranged for a dozen Africans to meet clandestinely with Stevenson. They met at night with the lights off in the basement of a private home on the outskirts of Johannesburg—a minister or two, a doctor or two, black intellectuals. "They were not fire-eaters," Garrison recalled. "They were like the American Negroes of that time. It was a very good evening. Stevenson did very well. He was very curious. He was at his best in that kind of gathering—not one to one, not expose his own feelings, be able to learn." A newspaper reported that Stevenson had had "secret" conversations with non-Europeans in Johannesburg. Blair said that Stevenson had met with political leaders in "private," not "secret."

Stevenson wrote in his notebook, "S.A. Closing every possible safety valve. Police etc can hold off trouble long time. Little white leadership for African movement. . . . Just reverse in Congo—opening more & more businesses. 7000 entrepreneurs—own own businesses in Leopoldville. Remarkable for people who 25 yrs ago didn't even know wheels." En route to Swaziland, he wrote, "Along the East Rand across the high veld to Swaziland thru miles and miles of yellow mountains made by man looking for gold. Beyond . . . the high velt & rolling prairies & cane fields looked for all the world like Kansas or Nebraska. Cattle herds sheep. Tsotsi— young hooligans, gangs, 16–25 yrs, terrorize, don't work, steal, drink, dope, killers; potential terrorists. Many younger blacks hopeless, nihilists, cynical."

Later, after long pondering Africa's plight, he summed up colonialism there this way:

Br—Train for self govt—for indep in common[wealth]. So give education & justice.

Fr—Turn Africans into Frenchmen. Give lots of edu. 10% black in Chamber.

Bel—Pure colonial—No pol rts; great benefits.

Port—Pure colonial—No pol. rts; no benefits; no color bar; no ed; no money; very few assimilados.

Union—Others are mixed or plural societies; must work out some coexistence. But Union—white society.

Upon leaving Johannesburg on Sunday, May 8, Stevenson held a press conference at the airport. He said:

"The present generation of South Africans did not make the problem that they confront—they inherited it. But it is for this generation to find the solution. This problem is of such gravity and complexity that you have to come here to appreciate it. I feel for every South African old enough to share the responsibility.

". . . I would express the hope that the people of this lovely land take care lest fear lead them along the wrong path. Perhaps it is always best in human affairs to do what is right and ethical and just to all of God's creatures and leave the consequences confidently to God.

"Responding to specific questions which have been sent me from all sides and speaking with the utmost diffidence, I cannot foresee the success of Apartheid as applied to industry and economic development with any confidence. And let me add I have grave misgivings about efforts to arrest the progress of a whole race when the rest of the world is moving so rapidly in the other direction. It is seldom wise to close safety valves."

In response to questions, Stevenson spoke hopefully of American investment in South Africa and the role American capital could play in its development. He was asked about the effect of the U. S. Supreme Court desegregation ruling. He said the ruling was "the law of the land" and desegregation would "move along" but would "take time."

Not surprisingly, his remarks on Apartheid drew attack. *Die Transvaler* of Johannesburg said editorially, "It is a great pity that Mr. Stevenson's visit to the Union had to end on the sad note of platitudinous and unfriendly remarks about 'apartheid.' By doing so he struck the vast majority of his hosts in the face and attacked their deepest convictions . . . inaccurate . . . unfounded . . . one-sided . . . unenlightened." Members of the Prime Minister's Cabinet joined the attack.

From South Africa, Stevenson flew to Accra, capital of the British colony of the Gold Coast.[16]

He went because Barbara Ward and her husband had a home there and because he was interested in what would become the country's experiment in self-government under President Kwame Nkrumah. He saw Nkrumah several times and later told him, "I shall long remember my delightful visits with you in that exciting and promising land which must look to you and your sound and sensible leadership for enduring foundations. You have certainly wrought well so far." Nkrumah became for a time one of the most important of all African leaders.

Barbara Ward loved Africa and was an articulate champion of Africans, African independence, and aid to Africa. Her views powerfully reinforced Stevenson's own. She often spoke of Africans' "love of life." She once said, "This is why the Africans never were destroyed by slavery as the Caribbean Indians were. Their love of life preserved them and their gift of enlarging and enhancing it in art and dance and love. In Africa, Adlai bought love philters for his friends back home 'because God knows they need it,' he said. The Victorians killed this love of life because they were afraid of the body. Adlai was a very eighteenth-century character."

After Stevenson left Africa, Barbara Ward sent him a long letter about the visit and their conversations. Ten years later, the year he died, he reread it in Libertyville and took it to New York to have a portion of it copied. She wrote: ". . . while you were here, we began to talk of so many things which there was never time to pursue. . . . So I want to write to you quickly while they still turn about in my mind. . . . One morning you asked me how one could stop feeling resentful & bitter over life & distrusting it & being on the defensive & underneath it all, afraid. And I think we agreed that to believe life to be fundamentally good & meaningful is an act of faith—religious faith. For me, it has been so. . . . There, I think, we stopped & I wish we had had more time for I don't believe that is all there is to be said—not by a long way. In spite of all the horrors in the world & apparent areas of complete irrationality & purposelessness, I still think you can make a very rational argument for the belief that goodness & love are the fundamental meaning of the universe." Stevenson penciled a question mark in the margin there. She went on to argue the case. Most people did or did not find happiness in "the small area" of "neighbors & wives (or husbands) & children to love & do good to." And "eggheads like me" underestimated this "unspectacular happiness" which "makes up the

---

[16] In 1957 the colony of the Gold Coast and the trusteeship territory of Togoland became the state of Ghana, with Dominion status, and in 1960 Ghana became an independent republic within the British Commonwealth.

solid ocean of humanity while wars & revolutions aren't much more than high & low tide on the beach." She cited the teachings of various religions to support the view that "man's true centre is goodness. And they all make the same link here between love & goodness. Love is not simply sentiment or emotion or passion. [Stevenson checked that.] It is readiness to seek the good of another human being & to do it consistently & steadily & if necessary against your own inclinations. . . . The people I have known & loved & admired most have been disinterested, unselfish, capable of seeing other people's needs before their own &, on balance, serene & happy. Whereas the smashers & grabbers (among whose number I must frequently include myself) remain enclosed in the narrowing circle of their own self-concern & the more they get what they think they want, the less it seems to satisfy them. [Stevenson put an exclamation point in the margin.]

"Love of others seems to grow by loving & the capacity to give by giving. . . . I cannot help thinking . . . that . . . both of us have every reason to be profoundly content with life, not because it hasn't been difficult (yours far more than mine) but because compared with the vast majority of mankind, it has been so blessed & so much fun. To have health & intelligence, never to worry about the next meal, to be literate & heir to such a culture, to have lived in an age when one can visit the entire world & learn about all its histories & civilizations—there are times . . . when I feel . . . that one can never [repay what] . . . life has given. I am having an extraordinary life—& so are you & I can't see how . . . one can do anything but thank God for it & try with even greater energy to make something of opportunities not given to one in ten million of our fellowmen. . . . And as far as your present position is concerned, I would think you could be unperturbed. I don't mean by that that you need like it. No sane man, I imagine, can relish everything in political life. [Stevenson underlined that and marked it with an exclamation point.]

"What I mean is that your present situation has come to you unsought & is therefore in a special way a condition of Providence. You did not want to run in 1952. And now the reason for running in 1956 is really beyond your control—for isn't it that a leader can't back down because the prospects aren't good enough? . . . If this is cold comfort, oh please remember & console yourself with how much you have done already to keep America's image bright in the world & to restore dignity & reticence & respect to political life. [Stevenson wrote in the margin, "Thanks!"]

"Long before I ever met you, I was one of the millions who felt better about politics because you had appeared. . . . Isn't this contribution something to offset the sense of uncertainty you say you feel? . . . I think part of the greatness of Lincoln was that he had to grope his way to the sense of Divine Providence & wrestle all the time with the doubts which must beset minds that can see more than one facet of truth. [Stevenson marked that heavily.]"

She sent a verse from the great religious poet of seventeenth-century

England, George Herbert, and may have sent it to him with that letter, although when he took the letter to New York ten years later to have it copied he left the verse with a small collection of her personal letters which he kept separate from the mail file of her correspondence. The verse refers to the recovery of hope and confidence after a period of great spiritual turmoil:

> And now in an age I bud again
> After so many deaths I live & write
> I once more smell the dew & rain
> And relish versing. Oh, my only Light
> It cannot be
> That I am he
> On whom Thy tempests fell all night!

Stevenson's homeward-bound plane stopped at Dakar for repairs, and he spent part of the delay in writing a twenty-three-page "Memo to the Boys on the month in Africa." Like nearly everything he wrote, it was scribbled in longhand on a ruled pad, with many passages crossed out, phrases written in between the lines, and large inserts indicated. It showed both his descriptive and analytical powers. "Perhaps," he wrote, "the place to start is where I am—on the edge of the area of French Africa which covers ¼ of the continent. Behind me to the East stretch almost empty deserts and semi deserts for thousands of miles, but to the south, from whence I've just come, lie steaming . . . equatorial rain forests of the Guinea Coast, the slave coast of old—and the rich Congo basin. Beyond the tropical forests and the headwaters of the Congo, 4000 miles to the south and west, the country changes to high 'savanna,' sometimes well watered, green, rolling and lovely, as in the highlands of East Africa, and sometimes impoverished woodland and arid, treeless grassland. . . . Still further south at the tip of this huge, little known continent, lies the healthy, beautiful rolling 'velts' of South Africa, the best known part of all, which is in the shadow of gathering crisis. It seems a little curious that the extremities of this continent, 5000 miles apart, are both restless. Along the northern fringe, in Morocco, Algeria and Tunisia the dominance of a European minority has been violently challenged by Arab-Berber majority. In the far south a dominant European minority is afraid it will be challenged by an African majority. . . .

"It is customary and dramatic nowadays to write of Africa as if it were all 'seething' and 'in ferment,' but I cannot in honesty dramatize the native unrest in the country thru which I have just travelled. Except for the Mau Mau terrorism in Kenya . . . there is no rioting or anti-white or anti-foreign demonstrations or violence as in North Africa.

"But it would be a bold optimist indeed who didn't detect trouble ahead

if the awaking Africans' demands for greater freedom and better economic
opportunities are not satisfied. And it is what is being done in response to
these urges that interested me most. . . . One obvious thing that is happening is the transition to a western money economy everywhere. People
who have known nothing but shifting cultivation by the most primitive
methods; people who have always tended cattle or goats; people who have
produced for subsistence and barter only, have learned about money from
the white man, and how to get pots and pans, bicycles and beer, and those
brightly colored clothes that come from England, India and Japan and
make any market place or roadside in Africa the most colorful anywhere in
the world. European civilization, the missionaries, traders, settlers, planters and industrialists have also brought with them new moral values,
sanitation, disease control, tribal peace, better tools, new skills, a little
education—and also that insensitive partner of order—taxes! But don't
think the African is getting rich. Money incomes probably range from $30
a year in the more primitive areas to $250 in the most developed, the
Union of S.A.

"The consequences of all these things that have been gathering momentum for a century are many, some good, some bad. Population . . . is increasing as the death rate goes down. Cattle are still the measure of wealth
in some places, and you will be interested to hear that the price of wives is
rising alarmingly. But I won't be stampeded into a purchase! Speaking of
wives, women are still doing most of the work. . . . Babies in Africa, by
the way, seldom cry—a curious fact for which I heard no satisfactory explanation."

Population pressures were worst in such areas of white settlement as
Kenya, Southern Rhodesia, and South Africa, he wrote. Europeans had
gained control of the best lands. Landownership was "certainly about the
hottest subject south of the Sahara." The migration of labor into money-
earning centers had disrupted family life and retarded the growth of a
skilled African labor force. More serious than the economic dislocations
caused by the growth of the money economy were the psychological and
political stresses, especially in areas of large European settlement. "For
here the African collides head on with the color bar and economic and political discrimination, as well as social segregation." This meant trouble,
problems that could be solved only by "cooperative and rational African
leadership" as well as by enlightened European leadership. The development of African leadership was difficult. "I often asked Africans in what
order progress should come—economic opportunity, political participation, education, or respect. Almost always the educated ones said recognition and respect. Almost always the illiterate said they didn't know or
didn't understand. . . . But everywhere, with the exception of South
Africa, it is the same—the African is advancing. Indeed, the question is
not *if* he is advancing, but *how* and how *fast*. And that varies from country to country. . . . Literally millions of Africans are voting [in French

Africa]. Public investment is on a large scale. . . . I would hardly have recognized [Dakar] due to the expansion and building I have seen here today. France is spending a lot more than it is earning in these territories. . . . While the British aim is generally the creation of new self governing units, the French objective is political incorporation in the French Union. . . . If anywhere, the experiment in African self-rule should succeed in the Gold Coast where Europeans of all nationalities have been building fortresses and trading for gold, ivory and slaves since the 15th century. . . . The Gold Coast is rich. . . . Like Nigeria, the Gold Coast has an educated urban class. . . . And it has leadership, very able leadership headed by Dr. Kwame Nkrumah. . . . The Gold Coast has no European problem. I mean Europeans never came to settle in West Africa, 'the white man's grave,' as they did in East, central and South Africa. There is no large, settled, dominant white community. . . . But the big hazard is separation, fragmentation. Nigeria is divided into four or five regions and tribes that have little in common except that they have been part of a British administrative unit. How and whether they can subordinate their jealousies and unite or federate effectively remains to be seen. Certainly they cannot afford the luxury of separate states." Thus did Stevenson anticipate the secession of Biafra by a dozen years. And he went on to carefully sort out the problems of other new African nations. "The great Belgian Congo, 80 times as big as Belgium, is the heart of Africa and from its untold riches pours a mounting flood of copper, uranium, diamonds, tin, gold, cobalt, zinc, manganese, vegetable oils, cotton and coffee. And the Congo offers something intensely different from African self-govt. a la the British or the French. . . . For the Congo is frankly a colony and operated with a beneficent paternalism that commands everyone's respect if not everyone's confidence that it is the best solution to 'Africa.' In the Congo they do everything for the African to keep him happy and economically progressive—'give him everything—but a vote.' But the 70,000 Europeans among the 14 million Congolese can't vote either. It takes clairvoyance to foresee the Congo's economic future. Aside from the notorious mineral wealth, agricultural development has only started and the hydroelectric potential is among the greatest in the world. But everyone speculates on the Belgian approach to mutual accommodation with the African population and compares it with the others. In the Congo control is firmly in white hands and there they mean it to stay for the present. How? By, as I say, keeping the Congo for the Congolese and setting no limits on their economic advancement. No European can buy land. Permanent residence is discouraged. Even tourists are not wanted, and Indians, so conspicuous in Br. Africa, are not admitted. Officials of the government, mining and business companies come to work not to stay.

"So the African can have no quarrel with a dominating white settler class in the Congo. Nor can he claim discrimination in employment—a Belgian goes home when an African can take his job and nowhere, I daresay, are Africans performing so many and such advanced tasks and for such good wages as in booming Leopoldville and Elisabethville. . . .

"All this and much more is consistent with the Belgian theory of a lot of economic advancement and a little education first; giving the African a 'stake in the community' before exposing them to dangerous ideas on political power. Sandwiched between total freedom in the Gold Coast and total suppression in South Africa, the hard headed Belgians who run the Congo are confident that their way is best, and they can point with pride to the fact that there is practically no racial tension in the Congo. A Belgian said to me, 'We will be here at least 25 years more. Can you say that about any other colony?'

"It may be that they are right and certainly the performance is impressive. But usually economic development and education bring with them demands for a share in ones political destiny. There are dangers in too long a delay in establishing some political participation and perhaps that is why even in the Congo they are now establishing municipal councils with some African participation."

Stevenson described "the finest scenic motor trip in mid Africa" through Ruanda-Urundi. There he had seen one of the famous Watusi dances. "I can still hear the drums and the thunder of their footbeats in that incredible rhythm. I sat beside the huge chief, resplendent in a saffron toga, and the dancers in the wildest moments never seemed to direct their eyes from his. But they weren't giants!—except for the 'dance master,' a seven footer with the traditional half moon headdress, who pranced around in front evidently urging the dancers to greater exertion. Frequently he flung his spear flat on the ground with a mighty gesture of total anger and indignation. But it signified approval! . . .

"Uganda is tranquil but the authorities are watchful for next door, the other side of Lake Victoria, is Kenya and Mau Mau land. I have neither time nor competence to tell you much about the magnificent, highly civilized 'white highlands' which British settlers have pioneered and where scores have died violently and suddenly, along with thousands of terrified Africans. Mau Mau springs from deep, deep wells—land hunger, nationalism, bewilderment, resentment, paganism, witchcraft and, some say, just plain boredom. . . . Mau Mau with its unspeakable horrors is on the wane now, but the British face the monumental task of de-brainwashing, rehabilitating and protecting from reprisal some 40 or 50 thousand 'infected' Kibuyuo still in concentration camps." He described Kenya at length, saying that Mau Mau had "brutally directed" world attention to the problems of multiracial societies with small dominant minorities and large subordinate majorities. Many solutions were offered. British government men in Kenya had high hopes that a "multiracial" government and society could be established with better education and more job opportunities for Africans and limited voting rights. In the Rhodesias, too, Stevenson heard more about "partnership" and "multiracial" society. "But one thing is sure in Kenya—responsible people realize more and more that the old strong arm methods are not good enough and that development depends on inter-racial cooperation rather than mutual isolation. Cooperation in turn implies the elimination of discrimination, restriction and special privileges, which is just what they are *not* doing in South Africa. . . . [South Africa] appears to be the area that is furthest from a solution of one of the great problems of our century—racial co-existence. Moreover South Africa influences the rest of Africa. What happens there increases African suspicions of attempts to deal with the question elsewhere, and at the same time encourages the more uncompromising and reactionary Europeans not to yield to the 'new ideas.' It is always easy to criticize and often hard to understand anothers views—especially if they conflict with your prejudices! But my impression of much of what I saw and heard of apartheid in practice is summarized by a remark about the new Bantu Education Act: 'Like many other acts of this Government, it gives much that is better and withholds all that is best.' " In a postscript he said he had one disappointment in his African trip: he had not been able to visit Dr. Albert Schweitzer, "whom," Stevenson wrote, "many call 'the greatest living man.' . . . I wanted also to confirm the epitaph he has written in case he is eaten by cannibals: 'He was good to the last.' "

33.

Stevenson arrived in New York on May 17, stayed overnight there, dropped in at an NAACP dinner, and was back in his Chicago law office next day. Events, his staff, and his own ambition were propelling him toward a second presidential candidacy. The polls were showing that Eisenhower could beat Stevenson again but that almost any Democrat could beat almost any other Republican.

John Steele reported a growing feeling among Democratic Senators and Governors that Eisenhower could be beaten next year. Several things heartened them—the 1954 congressional elections and virtually every local election since; feuds among the Republicans not confined to McCarthy and Jenner but involving Knowland, Bridges, Millikin, and Bricker; unity among the congressional Democrats, who supported Eisenhower more consistently than his own party did. Various Democratic Senators and Governors were eying the nomination. Eisenhower, Steele thought, had not made up his mind to seek re-election. All Democratic Governors and national committeemen thought Stevenson could have the nomination if he wanted it—but he could not be drafted, would have to say he wanted it. His astute friends wanted him to delay announcement, Steele thought, while his astute rivals wanted him to declare quickly, hoping thus to force him into the dangerous primaries. Some Democrats wanted their party to attack Eisenhower but others thought continued restraint would encourage

Republican divisions, while attack might unite the Republicans and prove unpopular in the country at large. All in all, Democratic prospects—and Stevenson's—looked good that spring. He spent only a few days in his Chicago office, corresponding with John Fell about his graduation plans and with Nancy and Adlai III about their wedding, then left for the East. He saw Mayor Clark of Philadelphia and spoke there on May 24 to the General Federation of Women's Clubs. Barbara Ward had published a book, *Faith and Freedom,* and some of the ideas, if not the language, Stevenson used seemed to derive from their talks at Accra. He also decried "our recent inclination to turn upon our thinkers, to sneer at intellectuals," and, further, the emphasis in schools on the "the well-adjusted individual," which could lead to "docile support of the status quo." He talked about the hydrogen bomb. "Today either war must become obsolete, or mankind will. . . . Let us . . . place effective arms control at the very core of our diplomacy and at the very heart of our communications with other lands."

John Steele reported that Stevenson's friends thought he would enter the campaign with a good deal more gusto than in 1952. His position in the party had strengthened, too—Southern leaders now respected him, ardent ADA members may have cooled but would quickly warm up again if he ran, he was clearly the most acceptable candidate to both the National Committee and the congressional party. Sargent Shriver sent Stevenson a clipping containing a statement by his brother-in-law Senator John F. Kennedy predicting Stevenson's nomination in 1956.

After a few days back in his office, Stevenson went to Oberlin. (He received three honorary degrees that year—from Oberlin, New York University, and Queen's College of Canada). While at Oberlin he talked with Bob Tufts and Oberlin's president, Bill Stevenson, who was married to a distant cousin of Stevenson. Back home, he told Harry Ashmore, "Things are clarifying a little, but only a little." To Ellen's aunt, Mary Spears, he wrote, "It looks as though that old devil 'destiny' was creeping up on me again." Ken Galbraith, leaving for Europe to write a book, told Stevenson he would be on call if needed. Schlesinger sent a speech making the point that the United States was enjoying abundance in its private economy but starving the public sector.

Stevenson had talked several times with Steve Mitchell since returning from Africa, and now in mid-June Mitchell and several others established a "Steering Committee to Secure AES Nomination in 1956," an outgrowth of the earlier Lloyd Garrison proposals. Between June and November the Steering Committee raised about $50,000, most of it in large sums. From these funds was paid the expanding staff that Stevenson assembled that fall. The original Steering Committee members were Wyatt, Blair, Raskin, and Mitchell. They urged Stevenson to visit critical states in the fall of 1955 for a series of "community conferences" but Stevenson declined. The committee discussed at length when Stevenson should announce his candidacy. Mitchell had decided not to play a major role in Stevenson's next campaign, preferring to try to run himself for Governor of Illinois. In the end Jim Finnegan became Stevenson's campaign manager and Hy Raskin Finnegan's deputy.

During the summer the committee members began actively rounding up convention delegates and discussing what primaries, if any, Stevenson should enter. Political intelligence from around the country was coming in. Raskin was concerned about California. Arthur Schlesinger forwarded ADA reports on Texas. Stevenson maintained some pretense to innocence —he told a friend, "I hardly know what Steve is up to but I am sure your help will be comforting to him"—but it is clear he knew what was going on and approved. He invited Jim Finnegan to meet with him and the others in Libertyville on July 8: "There is much I should like to know and much to discuss before the situation advances much further, I believe, and your counsel would be most helpful to me. . . . I think it might be just as well if this meeting were not publicized." Blair subsequently suggested to Finnegan that he come out on Friday and spend the weekend with Stevenson; he invited Finnegan to suggest an agenda. Stevenson had lunch with Dave Lawrence and Matt McCloskey the day he invited Finnegan and, when he told them about the planned meeting, they were enthusiastic. As it turned out, Stevenson fell ill, and the meeting had to be postponed, but this made little difference. At Barbara Ward's suggestion, Stevenson invited her and her husband to Libertyville or the Smiths' place at Desbarats to discuss campaign issues—"it looks more and more as though I would have to run."

On Friday, June 24, Stevenson flew to Louisville with the Dicks for the wedding of Nancy and Adlai III the next day. Ellen Stevenson had repeatedly telephoned the Warwick Andersons about such matters as whether Adlai's name should appear on the invitation as "Jr." or "III." She wore black to the wedding. Borden drove her to Louisville in a car she had bought as a wedding present. En route, she opened her purse and showed him a small automatic pistol. She said she carried it to protect herself from Chicago politicians. It was not loaded; Borden checked it. She seemed nervous at the prospect of a confrontation with Stevenson. Borden tried to comfort her. The ceremony was outdoors at the bride's home. Her family had hired a photographer to take wedding pictures, and when Ellen saw him she berated him. Adlai III had sent her orchids; she threw them to the ground. She looked unkempt, was wearing a big Mexican shawl. When during the ceremony the minister said, "Do you, Adlai Stevenson, Jr., take this—" she interrupted with, "That is not his name." After the ceremony, Adlai III and Nancy went to greet her, and instead of welcoming Nancy into the family she demanded, "Why is this photographer here at the wedding?" Nancy wept. Adlai III drew her away.

After it was over, Mrs. Ives told Carol Evans they had had a lovely time in Louisville. Miss Evans wrote, "I had such a wonderful time in Louisville, and I am still floating on clouds."

34.

From Louisville, Stevenson flew to New York for business meetings, an all-day meeting with the Finletter Group, lunch with Governor Harriman, and other political errands. He and Harriman agreed that they would appraise the political situation and then support one or the other of themselves (or so Stevenson said later).

Since his return from Africa, Stevenson had been corresponding with Agnes Meyer and had hoped to visit her at one of her homes, the one at Mount Kisco, New York, on this same trip; but she had been obliged to undergo surgery, and the visit was postponed. In later years he visited her often for quiet weekends at Mount Kisco. She went to Libertyville only once—"That kind of scenery bored me to death. Flat." She carried on an enormous correspondence. "I'm a born letter writer, and so was he." She liked his "delicious sense of humor." But "he was very self-centered and that made him careless of other people's feelings. If he thought about it, he was the kindest man in the world. He was a bowl of contradictions. He wanted to be President, and he didn't. He was terribly hurt by his marriage, yet he never knew when he hurt people. His greatest asset was his incredible vitality." Like Mary Lasker, Mrs. Meyer contributed heavily to Stevenson's campaign funds (and he made speeches on their interests, health and education—though he doubtless would have anyway).

Mrs. Meyer considered herself an almost professional politician and did not hesitate to give him political advice. In May she had told him she intended to rebuild the party's women's organization; she had telephoned Katie Louchheim, its leader, and planned to hire "a top-flight professional organizer" to help. She told him that in one speech "you threw off all the nervousness, the humorous defence mechanisms and became for the first time in a public broadcast the self-confident human being you fundamentally are." She addressed him as "Dear friend." She advised Stevenson to announce his candidacy at the "first psychological moment." She said her husband wanted to see him and without her. After conferring with Philip Graham, her son-in-law and publisher of the *Post* since Eugene Meyer had become board chairman, she decided the best place would be their farm at Mount Kisco, New York, and she suggested that Stevenson go there late in June or early in July.

Stevenson replied, to "Dear Mrs. Meyer," "Careful, please; I'm falling in love!" and asked if June 29 would be convenient for him to visit Mount Kisco. On June 16 she addressed him as "Reckless Creature" and said her husband's favorite niece, just back from Europe, had called him up and said, "How are things with you?" Meyer had replied, "We are in a terrible turmoil. Agnes is in love again and this time, it's Stevenson." The niece: "What's wrong with that? Every sensible woman is in love with Stevenson." Meyer: "And when was Agnes ever sensible?" In this letter, Mrs. Meyer described herself as "a woman with a shady past, who has been a pain in the neck to her family for lo, these many years" and said that her enthusiasm for Stevenson aroused nothing but "resistance and suspicion" in Meyer and Graham—"as far as the Washington Post is concerned, I am your greatest handicap." Subsequently Stevenson told her he could not go to Mount Kisco on the morning of the twenty-ninth because he had a lunch date with Harriman, "at which we will eat a lot, drink a lot—I hope —have a good time and settle nothing. By evening I am sure to be flushed, happy and sleepy—when I encounter your suspicious lord and master. Anyway, I had best telephone in the morning when I want the car. I assume that is all right."

On June 20 she advised him in the next campaign to eschew "verbal pyrotechnics" and reveal his true strength of character. In 1952, she thought, "neither [Stevenson nor Eisenhower] knew how to speak to the people. This time you must get mind and heart working together." She advised an emotional speech aimed at women. She wrote, "I admire [Arthur] Schlesinger in spots and love Archie [MacLeish] altogether, but both lads are babes in the woods politically speaking." Stevenson put an X beside that. She wrote, "I hope your ticket will be Stevenson-Harriman."

Stevenson wrote to Harry Truman, praising a speech Truman had given, saying he had seen Truman's "charming daughter" in New York, saying he hoped to see Truman himself soon, asking his plans for the summer, and closing, "I feel an acute need—growing acuter!—for communion with you. I had not thought I would be facing this decision again, and before I say or do anything more about it I should like to talk with you." "Communion" seemed a strange word to address to Truman. Truman replied promptly that he would be in Chicago the following Tuesday, July 12, for a Shrine parade and would be happy to see Stevenson on the thirteenth. Stevenson telegraphed, "Delighted. May I arrange to motor"—another strange word for Truman, but not for Stevenson—"you out to Libertyville for either the night of July twelve or thirteen or shall we meet morning of the thirteenth and lunch at a friend's house in Chicago. Regards." Senator Lyndon Johnson was seriously ill; Stevenson wrote to his wife, "I need not tell you how distressed and anxious I am about Lyndon." Lady Bird Johnson replied, "I read both your telegram and your letter to Lyndon and I don't know of anything that has meant more to him during his illness. He told me to tell you that it was the very best medicine he could have had."

Stevenson hoped Chet Bowles would be available to help. "The image I create now and this fall, if and when I make some announcement, becomes important, obviously." More immediately, Stevenson, nursing a cold, confronted a major speech—one to be given on Wednesday, July 6, at the Chicago Stadium to the National Education Association. He and others had worked on the text long and hard. It contained the outlines of major policy speeches on education he would make next year in the presidential campaign. Federal aid to education was at that time a controversial issue, conservatives fearing it would lead to federal control, liberals hoping to use it to promote desegregation. Stevenson defied both. He said control of public education should be exercised "by local authorities." But educational financing could no longer be taken care of entirely from local "or even from state and local revenues." Property tax revenues were outrun by the expanding population and community income. "Some measure of assistance to public education from the federal purse has now become necessary." That need would increase with time. Eisenhower had done nothing. Schools and teachers, taken together, were "America's No. 1 domestic need." Stevenson proposed a federal school financing policy and program. He set forth the shortages—at least 250,000 classrooms, at least 180,000 teachers. He supported proposals pending in Congress for $400 million of federal funds each year for the next four years for school construction to be matched by state funds. He proposed a federal grant to the states of about $50 million a year (matched by the states) to supply more teachers. States least able to finance education should receive larger grants than wealthy states. Finally, he suggested national scholarships for students who would give some years to teaching. From a political viewpoint, the most important point he made was this: "I hope that what is good for all will not be lost to all by any linking together of the school aid and desegregation issues which would delay realization of our hopes and expectations on either or both of these vital fronts."

The NAACP and many liberals were urging that a desegregation rider be attached to any federal school appropriation bill. Stevenson, characteristically, opposed. Lloyd Garrison commented, "I admire you for sticking to your guns and putting in that sentence opposing riders. You didn't have to do it and I had rather hoped that you wouldn't, but you were right on principle, and now that you have done it, I'm glad." Stevenson said he thought the NAACP was making a "dreadful" mistake: "The philosophy of rule or ruin is no more tolerable among Negroes than whites." Senator Hubert Humphrey congratulated Stevenson but pointed out that Democrats would be held responsible if they failed to pass school construction legislation—and thus far they had failed to act solely because of the segregation issue. Senator Lehman, Humphrey said, wanted to support the NAACP's anti-segregation amendment. That would kill the bill on the floor—Southern Democrats would filibuster against it. Humphrey had tried to reconcile the opposing sides with little success. Stevenson might be able to do it by calling together leaders in education, labor, and Negro groups. He might be reluctant to do it but would certainly have to face the issue in the campaign. (He also advised Stevenson to tell his supporters before January 1956 whether he would run; otherwise, "a rash of favorite son candidates" and "a scramble" by potential candidates would develop. He himself supported Stevenson.) Stevenson replied that he understood the difficulty the NAACP was creating in Congress but said he was "loathe" to take an initiative and actually did not "in the least" sympathize with the NAACP.

Stevenson's meeting with Truman on the following Tuesday had to be shortened when, on Thursday, July 7, the day after his education speech, he was taken to Lake Forest Hospital with bronchial pneumonia. He was released on Monday but had to spend the ensuing ten days at Libertyville recuperating. He did, however, see Truman briefly. Discussing the presidency, Truman advised him to make up his mind he wanted the job and say so. Stevenson replied that he wanted to restore public interest in government and to that end wanted the Democrats' strongest candidate nominated in 1956, whoever he was.

Agnes Meyer sent congratulations on his education speech. "Dearest Adlai—Does that appelation startle you? Nothing less will do just after finishing your speech on education." She had undergone an exploratory operation. She had made several codicils to her will, then realized she had done nothing for her political commitment. "Above all, at this critical juncture, to help you get your campaign off the ground seemed the last best service I could render to my country. . . . It is exhilirating to hope that perhaps I have lifted some of the grinding details of a political campaign off your shoulders." She took it for granted that he would announce his candidacy in September, as he had indicated to her. "But to win, dearest friend, you must want the job. Please don't ever again say to anyone as you said to me, 'I don't want it.' . . . Only you can save us from these budget-balancing blood-suckers. And you can't save the country unless, by God, you want to save it."

Stevenson, replying from his own sickbed, was grateful for her potential contribution. He would probably make no announcement before late fall. He asked her not to think badly of him for "not wanting it," though he acknowledged he might have to indicate publicly that he did. Privately, he maintained, he did not. "To know the proper measure of this task precludes anybody but the lightheaded or ruthless from 'wanting it,' it seems to me. I think we do what we must do, and the job is to do it as well as it lies within us. To summon more savage fervor is, I fear, beyond me." He was groping for campaign themes. "I think we realize that mediocrity, materialism, social indifference and repulsive showmanship cannot be forever disguised by wholesome smiles, golf clubs and a Bible firmly clutched beneath the right arm if seldom read; and somehow I feel that ways and means must be found to get at these imperfectly perceived realities and incomprehensible language by means that touch masses. It will be hard, if not impossible, I am sure, with prosperity, peace and a contented press." What Stevenson needed most, he said, was somebody to handle the press. He asked her for suggestions, though aware, he said, that the best men, such as Al Friendly, managing editor of the *Post,* were unavailable.

In a note to Carol Evans, Mrs. Ives said she was greatly concerned about Stevenson's health. More, Mrs. Ives feared she irritated Stevenson and could no longer help him. Miss Evans tried to reassure her, and Stevenson apparently telephoned her on her birthday, July 16.

Stevenson had sent a collection of speeches to Cass Canfield of Harper's. Canfield proposed to publish them as a book in March. Stevenson wanted them published earlier. They were published under the title *What I Think* in February. (Stevenson considered the most important speech the one he had delivered at Miami Beach on McCarthy.) He did some editing on the book that Mrs. Ives was writing in collaboration with Hildegarde Dolson, *My Brother Adlai*. He was thinking about issues for 1956. He told Agnes Meyer that, with McCarthyism receding, most of the issues would be small ones. He wondered, "Can't we, however, put together a great multitude of small ones somehow and emerge with a large one—general disillusion?" He also seemed worried about his health.

President Eisenhower's prestige was high that summer. He had just returned to great acclaim from the "summit meeting" with Great Britain, France, and the Soviet Union. Stevenson complained to Irving Dilliard of the St. Louis *Post-Dispatch* that when he had proposed just such a meeting two years earlier Republicans had cried "appeasement." He asked Dilliard to help him find a "press man" who could feed such information to the press. The first week in August, Stevenson had lunch with John Steele of *Time* and later asked Steele to become his press secretary but it was impossible: *Time* would not rehire him as a political correspondent if he went to work for Stevenson. (Many magazines and newspapers discouraged their employees from working for any candidate.)

Agnes Meyer told Stevenson liberal lawyers had remarked to her that Harriman was campaigning actively for the nomination but Stevenson was waiting to see what Eisenhower was going to do. They thought Stevenson was showing "the same reluctance to fight for the job" as in 1952. This "irked" Stevenson, and he told Mrs. Meyer he "obviously" would have to move before Eisenhower and, moreover, he had not been indecisive or reluctant to fight in 1952. Bill Blair received word that Teddy White found organization politicians saying that, although Kefauver was hard to get along with, he would run a more aggressive campaign than Stevenson. Archibald Alexander of New Jersey sent Stevenson a long political analysis, concluding that economic depression was unlikely before the election and that the Administration's prestige in foreign policy was at an all-time high. Stevenson agreed and said the prospects of victory were hardly an inducement to run. Blair thought Democratic prospects for 1956 "don't look too rosy at the moment . . . [but] things can change."

Senator Kefauver came to town but, confused about his own timetable, missed Stevenson and, on August 1, apologized, hoping they could meet later in New York. Passing through Washington on September 23, Stevenson tried to telephone Kefauver, but he was on a trip to Russia. Kefauver sent him a note from there and later a postcard from Malaya (misaddressed). They finally talked by telephone and, on October 25, Kefauver sent Stevenson a copy of his speech about his trip. Stevenson thanked him and said he would read it while traveling. On November 1, Kefauver told Stevenson he had heard that Stevenson would be in Washington November 10 or 11 and invited him to dinner. Stevenson, who by then was on the verge of announcing his candidacy, asked Blair's advice— should he accept? He put a note on his desk calendar, "Notify Kefauver re. plans." But on November 8 the Chicago *Tribune* carried a front-page story saying that Stevenson had arranged to meet with Kefauver and a Stevenson-Kefauver ticket was a possibility. Stevenson immediately vetoed the meeting. Soon they were fighting it out in the primaries.

35.

Stevenson held a strategy meeting at Libertyville the weekend of August 5. Among those invited were Wirtz, Blair, Minow, Wyatt, Finletter, Ball, Jane Dick, Congressman Hale Boggs, Archibald Alexander, Roger Stevens, Arvey, Daley, Raskin, Mitchell, and Finnegan. An agenda began, "1. Basic decision: Should AES be a candidate?" After that came many questions. What should Stevenson's "posture" be from now to January 1956? What should be said to political leaders? To the press? What speeches should Stevenson make? When and how should he announce? How should the Steering Committee be expanded and how should it operate? What should the Finletter Group do? How could all this be financed? What polls should be taken? Who would conduct liaison with congressional leaders, Democratic Governors, state organizations, national committeemen and committeewomen? What of the Volunteers? Should campaign headquarters be in New York, Chicago, or Washington? How much TV and radio time should be bought? And what of the primaries?

Minow says of the meeting: "It was a dinner and an evening discussion. Only one or two of us felt that he should run for the Senate. I gave it up very fast. I was against his running for President for the same reason that I had been in '52—I thought it was a lost cause. But the rest all felt he was the party's best; Eisenhower was a disaster; the prospect of Nixon was even worse. He had to run. It was pretty well decided that he was going to do it. But he kept saying, 'Not unless the party wants me.' He was not going to contest for the nomination. He wanted to avoid the primaries and conduct a thoughtful campaign."

Minow's and Blair's notes show that Stevenson opened the meeting by saying the question of his candidacy was open. Finletter responded that he had no choice in so far as his obligation to the people was concerned. Only he had a real chance of beating Eisenhower. A great many Americans wanted him to run. Wyatt agreed and talked at length about "the mantle of leadership." George Ball said, "You run when the opportunity presents itself." Jack Arvey observed that in 1947 Stevenson's chances of winning the governorship seemed far worse than his chances of winning the presidency now. Nonetheless Arvey thought that, as things stood today, the Democrats could not win. Eisenhower was too popular. Arvey found himself "torn." As a Democrat, he would like to see Stevenson run because he was the strongest candidate. But as a friend of Stevenson he would advise him to run for the Senate, not for President, because he thought he could be elected Senator but not President. Wyatt asked him what about 1960? Arvey said he couldn't predict what might happen in 1960. Wyatt said something about "a junior Senator." Mitchell said, "He's got to run for President," and argued the case: Harriman would not stand a chance, Kefauver would be nominated.

Stevenson asked where the party's interests lay. It was nonsense to say that he was "it." "Am I really?" he asked.

Blair said, "Yes, you are."

"I asked a question," Stevenson said. "What is best for the party?"

Arvey responded, "If what is best for the party is the issue, that's easy— that's Adlai Stevenson. But you must be an aggressive candidate. A fighting speech—that's what they want. The world loves a fighter."

Stevenson said, "Nobody is fighting."

He invited Jane Dick to speak, and she said, "I have nothing to add."

Stevenson said he felt his duty to the party was discharged. Arvey said it was the party's principles, not the party as such, that mattered. "You can't abandon your principles." Minow noted: "Left #1 in the air," that is, the question of whether he should run, and Stevenson moved on to the third item on the agenda, the "time and method of announcement," thereby, of course, indicating that at least in his own mind question #1 was settled, he would run—as indeed it probably had been for months. He now asked, "What do I say and when?"

Steve Mitchell suggested he announce at the National Committee's dinner that fall, about a year before the election. Stevenson observed that his announcement statement was "of the utmost importance" and would set the tone of the campaign. George Ball had a memo on what should be in the statement. Arvey thought it should contain a general indictment of the Administration and an announcement of his candidacy. Stevenson thought the announcement should be made in Illinois.

They discussed his campaign organization. Blair would work directly with Stevenson. Under them would be five sections.[17]

Stevenson wanted Carl McGowan brought in. Finletter said, "We need $100,000 quick—between now and the announcement." Led by Roger Stevens, they discussed fund-raising at length.

[17] Political, Mitchell, Finnegan, Boggs, Oscar Chapman; public relations, unstaffed; research, Finletter and Wirtz; money, Benton, Roger Stevens, George McGhee, J. R. Posten, Dwight Palmer, Stanley Woodward, James Bruce; and as for volunteers, Jane Dick, George Ball, Wyatt, and others would study the 1952 Volunteer effort and make recommendations.

Stevenson kept recurring to his need for a press secretary. Wirtz would coordinate research as "editor-in-chief." Research would include programs from the Finletter Group, public relations, speeches, statements. They would try to hire John Brademas, the young congressional candidate from South Bend, to build up a research division. Blair would handle correspondence and draft an organization chart. Finletter suggested hiring Elmo Roper, the pollster. Stevenson wanted to know, "What *are* the issues?" and went on to say he had to reach the low-income, low-education groups. "Is it only peace and prosperity? We must be careful on the questions that are asked in a poll."

Stevenson said, "Now, what about campaign strategy? What counties are crucial? What cities? Second, find out who the Democratic defectors are and why. This is for the political committee to analyze." Raskin would undertake it. They wondered whether the Volunteers should be given a new name, such as "Stevenson for President," "Americans for Stevenson," "People for Stevenson." Headquarters should be in one place, probably in Chicago at the outset, later moving to New York where the money was. They left the question of primaries to the political committee. As for television, Stevenson asked, "What about spot announcements?" and said they needed advice from a top-notch agency or network man. Stevenson asked what the "character" of the campaign was to be, and Mitchell said, "Intensive visits—do away with the aloofness image." Stevenson ticked off six points:

1) go on offensive
2) make an indictment which sets tone of campaign—indignant— vision of future
3) dissipate the myths
4) we need a legion of people out working
5) we must hit low income education levels
6) foreign policy—erratic etc—dangerous—but doubts it is going to be too effective as an issue.

Minow's notes concluded, "Ad agencies won't take Dem Party account. Press—money—govt *all* Republican."

At about this time Stevenson and his staff had before them a paper from the Finletter Group, perhaps written by Arthur Schlesinger, on "The Central Issue for 1956." It said the Democrats could not beat Eisenhower unless they "put a new and positive and inspired program before the electorate." Voters would admire Stevenson's wisdom and personality but would vote for Eisenhower's peace and prosperity. "We need an issue." Public opinion experts said people don't vote on issues. The paper argued, however, that, while it was true they did not vote on the old New Deal-Fair Deal issues, they would vote for a new issue which, though not yet verbalized, was sensed by the populace. "Briefly stated, it is this: *We have a new age, a new prosperity, increasing leisure. Before us there is a vision of a New America. What is the substance of this vision, and what are we doing, what can we do on a large scale, and practically, to realize it? We must act before it is too late, and before the Eisenhower administration sells our national birthright down the river."* The phrase, the New America, became the theme of Stevenson's 1956 campaign.

The paper argued that the Democratic Party must align itself "not with the New Deal, or the Fair Deal, but with the New America." It said, "Everywhere you hear, 'This is a new age.' The old people can observe a vast sweep of social and economic change, culminating in the present society. Those who grew up in the Depression see a new leisure and prosperity, a wonderful new sense of security. Even the young people sense local change, optimism, opportunity. With our prosperity and increasing leisure time, our people are traveling, watching, listening, building, advertising, creating, spending, selling, learning. And they are looking around for the first time at our great nation. It is alive, beautiful. There is a great surge of national self-consciousness. But here is the point: we are rushing around without a clear idea of what we have and what we might have and what we are in danger of losing. The Democratic candidate can provide this clear idea." The United States could spend the money to convert sea water to fresh water and use atomic power to pump it to the dry West, establishing a new green belt in the continental desert. Atomic power could be used in medicine, electricity, home heating, cars and planes and ships. We could develop an imaginative national transportation plan that would prevent the developing "permanent national traffic jam." Recreation areas must be greatly expanded and preserved. The school system was daily becoming less able to handle the increasing number of students. And there was more, much more.

In 1952, the Schlesinger paper said, Stevenson had traveled tirelessly, making clear his position on all issues, a speech on each one. Eisenhower had spoken in generalities about the Great Crusade. Stevenson's campaign, though laudable, had been uninteresting, had not captured the voters' imagination. Appeals to special interest groups, such as farmers, did not produce nationwide enthusiasm. "We must have a central theme that is reiterated everywhere, that makes the candidate a man with a mission. . . . I propose that the New America theme should be the heart of every campaign speech in 1956." Other issues should be fitted into that framework. "The candidate should act like a man with a vision—a practical vision." But heavy research should underpin every vision. Democratic congressional campaigners should be urged to take up the cry.

Stevenson and his staff also had a memorandum put together by Blair from two Schlesinger memos and one by Walter Johnson drawing heavily on a letter of June 24 from Schlesinger. It said that four basic assumptions must be made about 1956: Eisenhower would run, the world would be at peace, no more than 3.5 million people would be unemployed, and therefore "nothing will have happened to shatter Eisenhower's popularity and the national mood of complacency and apathy on which his popularity rests." Nevertheless, there were "substantial Democratic prospects for victory." The Gallup poll had recently reported that 54.3 per cent of all Americans considered themselves Democrats, 34.3 per cent Republicans. In the 1954 congressional elections Democratic candidates had won the largest percentage of the popular vote (52.6 per cent) in any off-year election since 1934; if translated into electoral votes, these results would give 367.5 for the Democrats and 163.5 for the Republicans. State and local elections in 1954 were similarly encouraging. But if Eisenhower was able to win again in 1956, he might well create a genuine Republican majority as Roosevelt had created a Democratic majority after 1934. So what should the Democratic strategy be? It must activate the "normal Democratic majority on a regional and local basis." The Democrats could win by "making the right combination of regional and local appeals—against, of course, the backdrop of a favorable and appealing national party image." In other words, the Democrats could win without a dramatic shift in public opinion.

The memorandum calculated Democratic chances. It assumed the Democrats would hold the 89 electoral votes they received in 1952. Tennessee would return to the Democrats on the Dixon-Yates issue. Missouri and Oklahoma, with Democratic Governors and Congressmen, would return and add 32 votes. If the Democrats hit hard on public power, they had "a good chance" of picking up Washington, Oregon, Idaho, and Montana—18 more votes. If they hit hard on unemployment, they should get back Massachusetts and Rhode Island—20 more. If they did well with dairy farmers, they should have Minnesota—11 votes. That totaled 170, not enough. "If finagling with the South could bring back Texas, Virginia and Florida, that would bring the total up to 210." But 266 were needed. In 1954, Democrats had carried New York, Pennsylvania, Michigan, and Illinois. If in 1956 they could carry any three of those states (or New York and any other), they would win. This left out of account such small, traditionally Democratic states as Delaware and New Mexico and larger states where Democrats had a chance, including New Jersey, Ohio, and Connecticut. All this suggested concentrating hard on crucial issues state by state—Dixon-Yates in Tennessee, public power in the Northwest, unemployment in New England, and so on.

The recent Democratic record in Congress was nearly useless; Congress must make the issues in the forthcoming session. But it could not be counted on. So Stevenson should start to identify himself with "a wide variety of local issues" and might start traveling the country in the spring of 1956, visiting small places that would have to be by-passed in the fall. His trips should be informal, fact-finding, touring, handshaking, short speeches, conferences. That done, he could spend next September and October on national telecasts and on getting out the vote in the big cities. The election was likely to be close. Therefore the vice presidential candidate would be unusually important. Kefauver was the best possibility.

Labor would be nominally for the Democrat but it must be enthusiastically for him, and Stevenson should talk with labor leaders and address "a number" of union conventions in 1955. Negroes should not be taken for granted—efforts since 1952 to woo back the South had caused disaffection among them. The Eisenhower strategy probably would be to minimize the differences between the parties. Therefore the Democrats should emphasize the differences. But they could hardly do so in foreign affairs. Therefore foreign affairs probably would not lend themselves to effective campaigning. The campaign would have to be run on domestic issues.

The day after his Libertyville meeting, Stevenson received Governor John F. Simms of New Mexico. The Governors' Conference would not start officially until two days later, on Tuesday, August 9, but the Governors arrived early, and Governor Simms's visit on Sunday was followed by a series of lunches and dinners at Libertyville for other Governors. Then Stevenson gave a big dinner downtown at the Tavern Club for the Governors and the press, and said he would announce his 1956 intentions in November. Nancy and Adlai III helped him entertain many of the Governors, as did Blair and Minow. All or nearly all the Governors thought Stevenson ought to be the Democratic candidate in 1956. Some may have been enthusiastic because privately they believed that nobody could beat Eisenhower.

On the day Stevenson gave his party at the Tavern Club, his former wife gave an interview, telling the press that Democrats had forced her to cancel a reception she had planned this week for Adlai III and Nancy. "They didn't want the publicity of our divorce ruining the [Governors'] conference," she was quoted as saying. Stevenson was a "Hamlet" who "can't make up his mind" about running for President. "He loves to be dramatic, you know. That's why he hasn't announced whether he'll run for President in 1956. That's why I don't think he'd make a good President." She said he did not want to run against Eisenhower "because he knows he can't beat him. He wants to wait, but he knows if he does he's politically dead."

Blair said privately, "The Governor was upset, but he is beginning to get used to that sort of thing."

In the midst of the Governors' Conference, Stevenson received a letter from Agnes Meyer taking him to task for saying, as he had in a recent letter, "I wish I had a stronger heart for the work ahead." Admonishing him against his own "self distrust," she wrote, "Don't for a moment think that my recognition of who you really are and of the great human being God meant you to be, is feminine sentimentality. A woman who has spent her life being adored by men of genius from John Dewey to Claudel to Thomas Mann to Schweitzer etc—and whose insight into human nature has been further sharpened by years of social research, among the hoi polloi, is nobody's fool when it comes to the evaluation of individual strength and weaknesses. Whether you are elected to the Presidency or not, you are bound to become the nation's outstanding leader if only you can overcome a deep psychopathic fear of your own greatness and destiny. What the origins of this emotional block may be I do not know since I have never had a chance to talk it over with you, but ever since we had our only meeting, I have allowed the passionate and disinterested sympathy I feel for you to stream out towards you. For I realize that whatever my reason, my political training and my wide connections can do for you, —all this is secondary to your need for love and for a faith in you that is far stronger than your own. . . . We can win only if you capture the public imagination in your first pronouncement and do it before too long. . . . Oh, if you knew, how I hate to be so hard on you! But if my demands encourage your bad habit of being sorry for yourself, remember that a critical demanding *love* is the only kind worth having." She told him not to worry about money.

She made an interesting point when she spoke of his fear of his own destiny. He replied, "No, you are wrong, I insist. It isn't just self distrust; it is prior experience and also a genuine anxiety to be sure the Democratic party is doing the best thing for it and its cause, which is the restoration of public interest in government. However, let us not argue about my frailties, of which I have a great many; nor will I argue about my virtues of which I am afraid you see more than there are. I am, in fact, quite ready for the task, if equally ready to see someone else, and I would hope a better man, undertake it. That you feel about me as you do I must add fills me with confidence measured only by my gratitude." He described the weekend meeting and said Roger Stevens would raise $100,000 promptly to enable him to hire a staff. "This, together with your help, gives me a feeling that I can now expand my entourage and relieve myself somewhat of other things." (Mary Lasker had recently sent Bill Blair a check for $3,000 for this same purpose.) He was still looking for a press secretary.

Stevenson, together with Nancy and Adlai III, read a long letter from John Fell, who was traveling. Stevenson advised him to see as much of Europe as possible even though he might be eager to come home—it might be a long time before he would be there again. He was enjoying the house in Libertyville that summer. Often Nancy cooked dinner, and Stevenson would prowl the kitchen, lifting the lids of cooking pots and tasting the contents and suggesting additional ingredients. Once he reproved her for picking the corn as early as 5 P.M.—"don't you know you should pick it just before you cook it?" She explained she had wanted to finish her work in the kitchen in order to help entertain the dinner guests. He said, "After this, I'll pick it myself—you tell me five minutes before you're ready to cook it." He loved his vegetable garden and enjoyed the role of gentleman farmer. He walked around in old khaki shorts and a floppy sun hat. In his travels, he had picked up an embroidered Uzbek shirt, and wore it even to dinner parties. If he had to go to the airport, Nancy and Adlai III insisted on taking him—Stevenson himself was an inattentive and potentially dangerous driver, neglecting the steering wheel to turn around and tell someone in the back seat a story. He invariably got to the airport at the last minute. Knowing this, they would tell him they needed two and a half hours to get him there. He would demur—"You know it doesn't take that long." Well, they would say, all right, two hours, we'll leave at two-fifteen. At two-five they would go into the library and tell him he had only ten minutes. "All right," without looking up. Other warnings at five-minute intervals; he would say, "All right, just a minute, just a minute." Finally they would leave fifteen or twenty minutes late, something they had included in their calculations. He knew it, they knew it, it was a game, he was teasing them about caring.

He was a mean tennis player—splices, cuts, placement shots, good net play. His old asphalt tennis court was crisscrossed with many cracks, out of which weeds grew, but he refused to have it resurfaced—he knew where every crack and every weed was and used them to his advantage. Nancy hired a string of housekeepers for him; one was eccentric, given to using an earphone to communicate with the dead, while the house got dusty, and Nancy asked Stevenson why he didn't fire her and he said, "I was about to but she tells the most marvelous stories about her days as a barker in a circus." When he came home from a trip he would drop his battered briefcase in the hall, walk down to the river and up to the vegetable garden, then go to his desk; and, at dinner, regale Nancy and Adlai III with yarns about his trip, not a lecture, just a series of funny stories. But at the end they realized they had learned a great deal about the place he had visited. After their children were born, Stevenson spent hours holding them on his lap, playing, nibbling at their ears and saying, "These are my cookies." One of them remembered him that way and, after his death, said she missed her grandfather's eating cookies.

Stevenson told Barbara Ward, "Averell has been here, panting with anxiety but gallant, good and gracious as always." Agnes Meyer sent two more letters, saying that Eisenhower had had nothing to do with the relaxation of tensions between the United States and the Soviet Union, promising to sound out the possibility of Kefauver's supporting Stevenson ("K owes me a lot") and advising Stevenson to seek the advice of such scientists as Vannevar Bush on "international control of the bomb." Stevenson replied that he did not completely agree that Eisenhower had nothing to do with the reduction of tensions. Nor did he agree that this was the time to propose a stronger international organization. He said he had seen some twenty-two of the twenty-seven Democratic Governors and that all, "with the possible exception of Ribicoff," had been in favor of his running.

Jim Rowe told Bill Blair he was pleased that Finnegan would manage Stevenson's campaign and that Hale Boggs would work in his behalf in the South—"as you know, Boggs is Rayburn." He advised a letter-writing campaign such as FDR had carried on before the 1932 convention (Schlesinger had advised the same thing earlier), warned Blair not to underestimate Harriman, and said he had been hearing anti-Stevenson talk but thought it would vanish in the fall when Stevenson became active. Lloyd Garrison told Schlesinger that thus far he had been able to do little about developing contacts for Stevenson among Negroes. Stevenson passed on to Finletter a suggestion from Walter Johnson that study be given to refugees and immigration policy and to defense and defense manpower policies. "The draft and reserve programs as of now are not clear." (The draft would be the subject of a major Stevenson proposal in 1956.) Blair and Minow—and others—now thought Stevenson would have to enter the primaries despite his extreme reluctance.

36.

After the Governors' Conference, on August 15, Stevenson went to Desbarats to stay until August 24. Blair was traveling around the country, sounding out Democratic sentiment. Stevenson had discussed with Harry Ashmore, editor of the Arkansas *Gazette,* Ashmore's joining the staff as an idea man and writer. Ashmore now told him that he would do it, that he needed about $22,000 a year, and that he would have to resign as editor of the *Gazette.* Blair forwarded the letter to Desbarats with a memo advising Stevenson to "grab Harry Ashmore without a moment's hesitation," to pay him $22,000 and not worry about getting the money, and to try to get him to Chicago by October 1 or November 1 full time. "All in all," Blair wrote, "I don't see how you could do any better. I think he is first-rate in every respect and could even replace Carl McGowan as your 'conscience.' " Ashmore joined the Stevenson staff in Chicago at the end of September. Ashmore was one of those gifted, garrulous, funny, hyperbolic, Southern raconteurs. He charmed Stevenson with his long tales. As the winter passed and the spring primaries intensified, however, he irritated some staff members, who felt that he talked too much and wrote too few speeches.

Stevenson came back from Desbarats on the night of August 24, and John Fell surprised him by meeting him at the airport. Secretary Dulles sent Stevenson a copy of a speech on the Middle East he planned to make soon, together with a long letter explaining what President Eisenhower would recommend the United States do in order to settle "the Israel-Arab problem." Although Dulles did not say so directly, his letter indicated that he hoped for Stevenson's support of the program. Stevenson replied somewhat warily and sent the speech, Dulles' letter, and his reply to Judge Harry Fisher, one of his Jewish friends, inviting his comments and saying that Dulles' proposals contained little new except to give them "official sanction." Fisher said that people interested in Israel would be "skeptical" of the speech and wondered if it were not politically motivated. He said it was "heartening to know that a friendly relationship exists between you and the Secretary." Stevenson penciled in the margin, "Only on this subject!."

Steve Mitchell sent Blair and Raskin a long memorandum on a conversation he had had with Paul Butler. (Butler, as national chairman, was theoretically neutral among the candidates for the presidential nomination. This memorandum implied that Mitchell was acting as a go-between for Butler and Stevenson.) Blair was receiving other political intelligence. Stevenson kept worrying about issues. He told Chet Bowles that "the peace issue is important" but wondered how it could be taken away from Eisenhower. He was still telling well-wishers he was eager to let someone else run but at the same time would "do what the party wishes and what seems best to its leaders." But he was moving ahead with his planning. John Brademas joined the staff as research director in September at a salary of $7,000 a year. He had lost his campaign for Congress the year before by a narrow margin and intended to run again in 1956. Before long he had put together a formidable research file, building on the Finletter papers.

During the last week in August, Stevenson entertained Pat Brown, Attorney General and later Governor of California, and his wife at Libertyville. Brown became a strong Stevenson supporter. Stevenson talked that week with Jim Doyle of Wisconsin and with Kenneth Davis, who was working on a biography of Stevenson. He kept in touch with Truman by telephone. Governor LeRoy Collins of Florida told Stevenson he thought Truman's "activities and statements should be restrained as much as possible"—he was unpopular in the South and every time he attacked Eisenhower he strengthened Eisenhower's popularity. Stevenson replied, "I understand what you mean about President Truman. The situation, as I am sure you realize, is not for me to handle." Benton sent Blair correspondence with Lyndon Johnson which, Benton thought, indicated that Johnson did not count himself out for the presidency.

On September 6, Stevenson went to New York and spent the next day meeting at the Century Association with the Finletter Group.[18] Finletter had prepared a memorandum for discussion. It presumed that between now and January 1 Stevenson would announce in broad outline his policies and that a "main theme" would run through the speeches announcing the policies; it proposed the theme be decided on soon. It said that in domestic matters the Eisenhower administration made only such concessions to liberalism as it felt essential and used advertising techniques to make things look good. In foreign affairs the Administration pretended to seek peace but at the same time carried on "a campaign of bluster and threats which bring the country to the brink of atomic war." All this

[18] Present in the morning were Finletter, Brademas, Wyatt, Wirtz, and Blair. At lunch and at an afternoon meeting were Arvey, Boggs, Finletter, Finnegan, Mitchell, Ashmore, Raskin, Governor Roberts of Rhode Island, Wirtz, and Blair. (President Eisenhower was a member of the Century, a club, at that time.)

sprang from "a lack of integrity." Once the theme was decided on, a list of subjects for fall speeches should be made up. Material for the speeches could either be produced by the Finletter Group or by having one writer do a first draft alone under Stevenson's direction. (This last was illusory.) There followed a list of subjects on which work was going on or being planned.[19] These subjects, and others, could be tested by polls and checked at regional meetings of Democratic leaders. Brademas would organize the Finletter Group's material and combine it with National Committee research material. As Brademas identified gaps in facts and opinions, the Finletter Group could fill them.

At the Century club meeting that morning, the conversation focused on the foreign policy section of Finletter's memo, no doubt because that was where Stevenson's own interest was keenest. The afternoon meeting was given over to discussion of the form and time of Stevenson's announcement.

Stevenson left the meeting early to go to the Meyers' estate at Mount Kisco. He saw Mayor Wagner and others the next day and then, on September 9, accompanied by Nancy and Adlai III, left by plane for Haiti and Jamaica, where he had legal business with the Reynolds Metal Company. En route he wrote to "My dear Agnes" Meyer. After praising her cuisine and hospitality, he said his visit had "worked a miracle I somehow find it hard to explain. Never before have I dissolved so utterly with another human being. I don't understand your alchemy. But it has worked some magic with my spirit, my confidence and my perceptions of my role. I suppose I needed someone to whom I could unburden. . . . My visit, in short, was an important interlude for me. I can't, and have ceased to try to understand how an older woman, a total stranger, could suddenly, without at least the normal preliminaries of acquaintance give me both feminine understanding and masculine participation, and mental provocation and moral confidence. Its a comfort. It is quite a lot of comfort! And I hope the tonic 'takes' in this frail vessel. Thanks, dear Agnes, and I know better

---

[19] In foreign affairs, a study on Europe by a group headed by Schlesinger; one on U.S. military policy by Roswell Gilpatric aided by high-ranking military officers; one on the Far East and Africa headed by Chet Bowles; and one on disarmament by Charles Bolte, Ben Cohen, and others. In domestic affairs, Wes McCune of the Democratic National Committee was working on agriculture, Bill Wirtz would take over labor, Arthur Maass and Bernard DeVoto had done public power, Keyserling, Paul Samuelson (an economist who served under Truman), and others were working on the expanding economy; Richard Musgrave and others on taxes; Seymour Harris on public spending. Lloyd Garrison was concerned about Negro defections. George Ball could study "the Republican attack on individual rights"—the Republicans should not be permitted to "push under the rug" their acceptance of McCarthyism. Phil Perlman could do immigration; and George Ball "the Eisenhower record of favoritism of big business." Someone should study "the Great Give-Away" of public assets to private interests and "the failure of the President to govern"—"the long vacations, the short workday, the Army staff techniques, and the President's philosophy as to the role of the Presidency."

what people mean by a much abused phrase—'a remarkable woman.' And 'remarkable' reminds me to add that Mr. Meyer's interest, friendliness and helpfulness touched me deeply," and he praised Meyer at length then added a postscript: "P.S. Mr. Meyer indicated that the Washington Post normally endorsed no candidates and that that would be its position, I gathered, next year. I guess that confirms what you suggested." It was the first longhand letter in her collection of his letters.

She wrote to him (in a bold longhand, as she nearly always did) the same day, saluting him, "Adlai, Adlai, Adlai, I must shout aloud the ecstasy of our all too brief encounter while its enchantment holds me enthralled. . . . I was terrified before you arrived. Partly I was afraid 'the shock of recognition' would imperil my normal self-control. At the same time I was apprehensive lest reality could not possibly live up to my extravagant anticipations. Yet these confused emotions were resolved in mutual understanding and acceptance the minute you entered the door." She had never seen her husband "more quickly captivated, more genuinely concerned about somebody he was meeting for the first time." A "threesome" was always, "difficult," and it was a "tribute to your extraordinary gift for eliciting the best from people"—striking how many people said that of Stevenson during his life—"that lent our meeting such sustained interest, excitement and nobility." She felt she had inadequately verbalized her feelings to him. "Frankly, my darling, I was overawed and abashed by the serenity, the harmony, the sheer poetry that hovered about us even when we discussed the most practical matters. But I shall never again be able to look out of my study window over the lake and hills without recalling the silence that reigned between us as we stood there together. A mutually shared silence such as that reverberates in the mind longer and is more sustaining to the soul than the most beautiful avowals." She wrote on about "love of life" and said, "If ever a human relationship had that awesome quality of the miraculous, it is ours." Attached to her letter was a photograph of her as a young woman. Her features were strong and, if not beautiful, handsome; her gaze seemed purposeful.

Receiving Stevenson's letter, she wrote another long one to him. She was "stunned" by the similarity of their letters. She wrote of herself, "This professional, this artist in the 'alchemy'—again your word—of human relationships, has dire moments when she feels for the first time in her life that she is threatened by something she cannot wholly control,—to put it inelegantly but accurately that she may have bitten off more than she can chew."

Stevenson's aides and associates had been busy. Tom Finletter had prepared a paper in response to Stevenson's inquiry at the Century club on "how to seize the peace initiative." Finletter thought the Democrats could not win in 1956 on domestic issues alone. He felt the President had lost control of foreign policy and that elements in the Republican Party were conducting it in such a way as to involve the risk of atomic war.

Most voters, however, thought of the Democrats as the "war party." Therefore the Democrats must, first, argue persuasively the "weakness and warlike nature" of GOP foreign and military policy and, second, strongly state "the case on disarmament." More specifically, Finletter proposed a speech saying that the Republicans had brought us twice "to the brink of total atomic war" at Dienbienphu and in the Formosa Strait, that the danger of atomic war there was still present and would be as long as we relied on military might as the primary means of blocking Communist expansion in the East, that Republican budget cutting had "gravely weakened" the defense establishment, especially the Air Force, and that in the "vital area" of disarmament the Republicans had "moved backward and virtually abandoned any serious attempt to prevent war." They had done so because they believed in congressional, not presidential, government and because the President reigned but did not rule and hence policy was made by men without responsibility. The Democrats should "drive immediately and vigorously" for an enforceable plan of disarmament. (In a detailed section of his memorandum, Finletter said that "it is likely that the Soviets are ahead of us in the intercontinental ballistic missile area." The "missile gap" notion persisted and became an important part of John F. Kennedy's campaign in 1960.)

John Brademas produced a memorandum assigning various issues to various experts as Finletter had suggested. Some papers had already been prepared. Harry Ashmore wrote Stevenson on September 20 saying the Finletter papers had put the staff "in reasonably good shape" on issues. As to "image," Ashmore thought that to eloquence Stevenson, in his speeches, must add "vigor, determination, dedication, human warmth." The next speech would be to the Wisconsin State Democratic Convention. Wes McCune had written a farm speech; Ashmore thought it should also be "a fighting, partisan" speech. A speech in New York should convince the New York politicians that Stevenson would be "tough to handle" in any contest for the nomination. A November speech in Chicago should emphasize the differences between the two parties. "Politics" was the area of Ashmore's "greatest concern." He felt there was little hostility to Stevenson in the party but enthusiasm for him was "spotty," and in some areas apathy existed—and in those areas Harriman and Kefauver men were at work. Stevenson must convince party leaders he would "make a real fight" in the election, and the best way to do that was to convince them he would fight hard for the nomination.

The persistent notion that Stevenson was not a fighter, that he spoke well enough on issues but did not really care about them, had several sources—his posture while Governor as a non-politician, his quest for independent support and rejection of blind partisanship, his instinctive reliance on reason rather than emotion, his often repeated public appeals to intelligence, his protest at the lunacy of campaigning and his professions of weariness and boredom, his gentlemanly language. Yet anyone who has studied his 1948 campaign for Governor, his 1952 campaign for President, and most especially his 1956 campaign knows that Stevenson was indeed highly combative. And if one doubts the depth of his commitment to ideas, one should recall his extemporaneous defense in 1952 on "Meet the Press" of his deposition in the Hiss case, his subsequent attacks on McCarthy and McCarthyism, his private as well as public outrage at John Foster Dulles' "massive retaliation" and "liberation" slogans, his deep disgust with political hucksrering.

An article signed by Stevenson appeared in the September 20 issue of *Look* magazine: "Memo to the President: Let's Make the Two-Party System Work." In it he accused the Republicans, under Eisenhower, of putting party unity ahead of the nation's welfare. He spent Thursday and Friday, September 22 and 23, in his office, having lunch on Thursday with Newt Minow and on Friday with Minow, Blair, and Wirtz. On Saturday, September 24, in Denver, President Eisenhower had a heart attack. Although the illness was described as a "mild coronary thrombosis," he was totally incapacitated for several days, did not return to Washington until November 11, and for a time transacted presidential business from his farm at Gettysburg.

Eisenhower's illness shook presidential politics like an earthquake. Among Republicans, it set off speculation about who would control the party if Eisenhower were unable to run for re-election. Vice President Nixon continued carefully in his role as Vice President. Among the Democrats, Senators and Governors who in August had been unanimously urging Stevenson to take on what looked like a hopeless assignment now in September began reassessments. If Eisenhower were out, the Democratic nomination, which had seemed a poor consolation prize a month ago, suddenly looked golden. Nobody said this out loud at first, of course. But the thought ran throughout the party. Democrats had felt for some time that the Administration had made serious mistakes. But they had despaired because nobody seemed to blame the mistakes on Eisenhower, a revered figure so far above the battle he was almost invisible. Now, if Eisenhower was replaced by some ordinary mortal, such as Nixon, that man could be charged with those mistakes.

Stevenson was at Libertyville that Saturday when Eisenhower was stricken. Blair was ill. Minow, playing golf, received a telephone call from his wife Jo; Stevenson wanted him urgently. Minow called, and Stevenson said Eisenhower had had a heart attack, about thirty reporters were at Libertyville, they thought Eisenhower was dying, they wanted a statement from Stevenson, Stevenson was scheduled to go to Texas to see Lyndon Johnson and Sam Rayburn in a few days, he needed Minow. Minow went. Stevenson spoke to the press briefly and next day read a formal statement to the press and television: "President Eisenhower's health is a matter of concern to the whole world. The news of his heart attack is very distressing, and—as I said yesterday afternoon—I am sure *all* Americans, regardless of our political or other differences, share my anxiety and on this Sabbath day earnestly pray for his speedy and total recovery."

Agnes Meyer had read in the New York *Times* that Harriman was openly seeking the nomination. "I went off like a sky-rocket." She had telephoned Mrs. Roosevelt and enlisted her aid and, acting almost in a staff capacity, advised Stevenson to telephone Mrs. Roosevelt himself. She regarded Harriman as a "rich play-boy." (It is odd how many people around Stevenson at that time seemed to think of Harriman, who proved to be one of the ablest public servants of his time, as a "playboy.") She advised Stevenson to try to get a piece about his private life, including his divorce, published in *McCall's,* whose editor, she said, was friendly. She also advised him, if confronted with the announcement of Harriman's candidacy, to "be as noble as you please but *not* indifferent. We can't get people to die in the trenches for you if you, yourself, don't seem to care." Stevenson replied on the day of Eisenhower's heart attack: "Agnes dear— I want to write you a proper letter; but I can't. The phone rings incessantly; the Pres. is ill; next week I must speak at the Univ of Texas and I haven't even got the accumulation of my last journey cleaned up; a client wants me to go to Europe on a quick trip which would be helpfully profitable, but the speeches stretch out before me and I've promised Harpers the new book and introduction by mid-October. Also there's the MSS of my sister's book to read—last chance. Ho hum. . . . I'm happy and confident, somehow, in spite of the harrassments and anxieties. . . . I've found a new dimension of love, understanding and helpfulness. Could one ask more of life, of womankind? Yes—*companionship;* and that will be difficult, but I've rarely known it anyway." He had called Mrs. Roosevelt.

Mrs. Meyer wrote again. She had decided to straighten out his domestic life in Libertyville. As credentials she presented the comment of Thomas Mann, who had stayed with the Meyers often, that she kept "the best hotels on two continents." "Comfort in your home," Mrs. Meyer told Stevenson, "is essential before the campaign gets hot. You must know that when you get home tired and dispirited, that somebody efficient and concerned is there to take care of you. In a small house this is no problem at all." What he needed was "a good couple who live in," the woman a good cook, the man to keep the place clean, wait on table, and look after his clothes. She would try to locate one. To do things properly she ought to see his house. She proposed to fly to Chicago from Albuquerque October 27—she wanted to see Bishop Sheil anyway. Would Stevenson be in Chicago October 28? This would be the greatest service she could perform. "It is absurd that a man of your importance and capacity should not live in comfort. It is a waste of your energies and when I hear about your cold suppers, I could weep." Stevenson told her he probably would be in Chicago on October 28 though the twenty-seventh would be better. His domestic situation was "somewhat better"—he had "a devoted little colored woman who is good on the telephone and with guests and is learning to cook" but "her husband is a weak reed and exasperates me now and then."

On Tuesday, September 27, Stevenson saw George Backer, a close associate of Averell Harriman. Stevenson told Mrs. Meyer, "I have today had an emissary from Averell. It is all a little obscure and evidently he isn't ready yet to come along all the way; but more of that later." Stevenson later said that in August he had sent Harriman a letter giving him his understanding of their agreement to appraise the situation and then support one or the other. This letter was never acknowledged, Stevenson said; instead George Backer came to Chicago and told Stevenson that Harriman "had decided to go ahead on his own." Stevenson asked whether this meant that the agreement was off. Backer said yes, according to Stevenson —Harriman might support Stevenson later. But for now he was in the race for himself.

37.

On Wednesday, September 28, Stevenson and Minow left for Dallas. Reporters accompanied them. "It was almost like a campaign," Minow once recalled. More reporters met them at the airport in Dallas and again in Austin. At a hotel, Stevenson and Minow had to cope with the leaders in a long-standing Texas Democratic feud—Minow put Stevenson into a bedroom and, while Speaker Rayburn kept conservative Democrats busy in another room, took Ralph Yarborough, the liberal, to see him secretly. They dined with the president of the University of Texas and the dean of its law school. After that Stevenson spoke at the University on "America, the Economic Colossus," a hymn to America's might, a prayer that she use it with humility, and a warning against depression.

Afterward, Stevenson, Rayburn, Minow, and Grace Tully (who had been FDR's secretary and now was Lyndon Johnson's), were driven to Johnson City where, at his home on the Pedernales, Johnson was recuperating from his heart attack. They reached the LBJ ranch very late at night but it was all lit up and Johnson was reclining on a lounge chair in the front yard. His wife was, rightly, angry: his doctors had told him to rest. Unmindful, Johnson said, "Adlai, there's a hell of a lot of newspapermen around here—they've been here all day like vultures—they think Ike is dying and the three big Democrats are sitting here plotting to take over the country. We can't let them think that because we're not going to do that. So we'll be up and out early and tour the farm and they can come with us and interview us so there won't be any secrets." Stevenson said fine. Early in the morning they drove around the farm, then held a press conference. Then Stevenson, Johnson, and Rayburn went into a room to talk alone. Finished, they said good-by, and Johnson took Minow aside and told him,

"You tell your man that he has to be moderate—be moderate on all these issues—the country's moderate." (Paul Butler had been in Texas and had irritated Texas Democrats by pushing the liberal congressional cause as opposed to the Johnson-Rayburn line of cooperation with the President.)

On the plane going home Stevenson said to Minow, "You know what they told me?" Minow said he could guess. Stevenson said, "They told me that I must run in the primaries. They told me that with Eisenhower sick there's going to be a lot of candidates and if I want the nomination I have to go into the primaries." Minow said he thought they were right. Stevenson said, "Then I'm not running. I have no interest in this. I'm not running for sheriff. If the party wants me I'll go run—but I'm not going to those supermarkets." Minow said, "If you don't, you won't be nominated. I guess Eisenhower is not going to run. If he doesn't, there'll be a chance for the Democrats, and everybody and his brother will be in it." Stevenson said, "Then I'm out." Johnson and Rayburn probably had hoped that Johnson would be nominated but Johnson's heart attack, now given emphasis by Eisenhower's, seemed to rule him out. Stevenson was more acceptable to them than several alternatives. Back in Chicago, Blair and Wirtz agreed that Stevenson must enter the primaries. Later Hubert Humphrey told Stevenson the same thing. Stevenson remained obdurate for a time. He consulted various people—Jack Arvey, Jim Finnegan, others. All said the same thing. Finally he consented. By that time Blair and others were already selecting the primaries he would enter.

Now in late September those close to Stevenson thought that, while Eisenhower's heart attack probably would force Stevenson into the primaries, it would almost ensure his election—provided he could get nominated. Suddenly the nomination, not the election, had become the big problem. But even the nomination seemed to pose no insurmountable obstacle. Beyond doubt he had the strongest claim to it. By common consent he was the front runner. His prestige, created by the 1952 campaign, had been enhanced immensely during the years since. He was not only the leader of the Democratic Party; he was its spokesman to the world at large. It would have been a rash man indeed who that fall would have predicted flatly that Stevenson had no chance of becoming President of the United States.

His office space and staff were expanding. Down the hall from Stevenson's office on the eighth floor, his firm took an office, Room 859, that later became Jim Finnegan's, large, bare, with a map of the United States on the wall. Hy Raskin used it too. Down another hall was a large room where a dozen or so volunteers and one or two paid staff workers did mimeographing and handled card files and leaflets and all the paraphernalia of campaigning. Off this room were Harry Ashmore's and John Brademas' offices. Brademas acquired an assistant, Ken Hechler, who, like Brademas, later became a Congressman. Later to an office on the thirteenth floor came the man Stevenson finally hired as a press secretary. Roger

Tubby, who had been President Truman's press secretary for a time, was a rather slight, harried-looking man, quiet-spoken, deferential toward Stevenson, eager to help the press. Tubby acquired an assistant, C. K. McClatchy, of the McClatchy chain of newspapers in California, a young man who had been in the 1952 campaign. Several blocks away, at 69 West Washington Street, was the volunteer headquarters, called the Stevenson for President Committee, with Jane Dick and Barry Bingham as cochairmen.

The October issue of *Fortune* published a piece under Stevenson's name on "My Faith in Democratic Capitalism," arguing that business and government need not quarrel so much as they had. His political schedule grew heavier in October and November. Bill Blair assigned people to states. Steve Mitchell was still important but others were moving in—Finnegan, Arvey, Raskin, Boggs, Wyatt, Blair, Ashmore. Stevenson reserved for himself Tennessee (which meant Kefauver) and Texas (Johnson and Rayburn).

Agnes Meyer told Stevenson she had dined with the Harrimans and Harriman had spent nearly an hour discussing Stevenson and other Democratic candidates. She had asked why Harriman did not support Stevenson, avoid a party fight, and accept nomination for Vice President. Harriman had said he would rather be Secretary of State. He had said that Democratic Governors' support of Stevenson was only "lip-service"—the Governor of Tennessee, for example, had assured Harriman that he had come out for Stevenson only to prove he was against Kefauver. Harriman had said Stevenson had "no real strength with the peepul," as Mrs. Meyer put it, and was not a politician, as Harriman himself was. "In short your great friend Harriman has no glimmer of loyalty to you whatsoever and thinks he can make the grade."

Mrs. Meyer advised Stevenson to *"never, never, never* mention your wife to people who aren't old trusted friends" and related how a woman she knew had told her that she had sat next to Stevenson at dinner in New York a while back and he had "let fly at" his wife. She also told him that Harriman seemed to think the Republicans would draft Chief Justice Warren to run for President in Eisenhower's stead but that she and her husband didn't believe it. She thought that either Christian Herter or Humphrey (presumably Secretary of the Treasury George Humphrey) would be nominated. She wrote again, admonishing him against "coy" photographs of him that appeared as illustrations of excerpts from Mrs. Ives's book in the *Ladies' Home Journal.* She suggested that "this charming sister" live with him and keep house for him. She discussed his mother's photograph at some length: "Your mother is superb both as to looks, mind and character. . . . One of the things your mother wrote you that hit me hard was her advice: 'Let go your hold' as Wm. James says, 'resign your destiny to higher powers.' " She warned him not to allow himself to be distracted nor to belong to anybody: "You belong to your country, to the world, to mankind." She again discussed her visit to Libertyville and again criticized his "conscious preoccupation" with literary style. She asked for a photograph of him. He sent it and took occasion to reassure her that he had not spoken to her friend about his wife. He agreed about the "coy" photographs and hoped she could meet Mrs. Ives. The Libertyville visit would not work out. He agreed he had "painstaking and profitless habits" about writing. As for Harriman, "Further evidence comes from various directions that Averell *is* intent and determined and that your estimate of his intentions was more accurate than mine. I am a little disappointed, and I hope we can avoid any conflict." At the same time he sent a two-sentence typed letter to Alicia Patterson: "Dear Alicia: I hear you passed this way in my absence, without notice. Damn!"

He was giving thought to next year's Democratic state ticket and asked Paul Douglas' advice about running Richard Stengel, a young downstate legislator, or Laird Bell for the Senate against Everett Dirksen. Schlesinger told Blair that except for an occasional speech he would be unavailable this fall and winter and on into next spring, since he had to finish the first volume of *The Age of Roosevelt,* but should be able to give Stevenson full-time help from the convention (or somewhat earlier) until the election —but he quickly added that he did not want Stevenson to feel he had to use him and said "there are probably strong arguments for" Stevenson's assembling a new research and writing staff.

Agnes Meyer—she was writing almost daily—told Stevenson she thought the New York *Times* was "certain to return to its traditional Dem position, despite the fact of a certain unfriendliness to you in Jimmy Reston's columns." She thought she might help persuade Kefauver to settle for the vice presidency. Stevenson encouraged her to see Kefauver: "I am still eager to avoid the waste of a lot of energy and money on a contest." Her daughter and son-in-law, the Phil Grahams, were coming to Chicago early in November; Stevenson invited them to dinner at Libertyville, and Graham wrote later that they had "never had a better evening."

On October 7, Stevenson left for Green Bay, Wisconsin, to speak to the Democratic State Convention there, but bad weather grounded his plane and he could not deliver the speech. It was to have been his first speech since Eisenhower's illness. He was to have said that tradition required "fervent partisanship" at a party convention. "We do not meet tonight, however, in traditional circumstances. Our minds and hearts lie in the shadow of the sad misfortune that has befallen our President. And our anxiety and sympathy are not bounded by party lines. Rising above division of feeling on any public issue is our common hope and prayer that his health will be restored as quickly, as fully as possible." Thus did Stevenson lay down a line which he would follow until election eve of 1956: Eisenhower's health was not an issue. It may have been one of his worst political mistakes. Agnes Meyer reported that Mrs. Roosevelt felt ordinary people, particularly minority groups, considered Stevenson remote. Mrs. Meyer said De Sapio was appealing on Harriman's behalf to Italians, Negroes, Jews, Catholics, and Poles and other people whose homelands were under Soviet domination. She told Stevenson he must do likewise. Stevenson gave her letter to Ashmore with a note, "We must not overlook something of this in the Nov 19th speech," an important one before the National Committee. Mrs. Meyer also said that Cardinal Stritch was coming out for Stevenson by telling bishops "he has you in his pocket." She considered this a part of Cardinal Stritch's "rivalry" with Cardinal Spellman, who had supported McCarthy.

Maneuvering among the Democrats increased. Truman visited Harriman in Albany on October 9 and went out of his way to praise Harriman as qualified to be President. He said he would not exclude other candidates but if he were a citizen of New York he would vote for Harriman. He refused to say whom he would vote for if he were a citizen of Illinois. He added he wanted a free and open convention. Next day Tom Finletter called on Truman. Finletter said his own first choice was Stevenson and his second Harriman. Truman said he felt exactly the same way—but added "that he wanted an open convention." He also said he did not want to use his influence on behalf of any candidate. In relating to Finletter how he, Truman, had procured the 1952 nomination for Stevenson, he said that Sparkman, on Stevenson's instructions, had made no reference to the Truman administration in his acceptance speech. Truman told Finletter that Stevenson "highly disapproved of Mr. Truman's conduct of the presidency," as Finletter put it. Finletter assured him this was not true. "Mr. Truman did say though that all of that was in the past and in no way influenced his views. I am not entirely sure though that this is the case." Finletter asked Truman whether Stevenson should announce his candidacy soon. Truman said he should have announced it a month ago and, moreover, once he did announce, "and gets in there fighting," in Finletter's words, "he will be invincible." Finletter asked about the primaries. Truman thought Stevenson should get into them on a selective basis and should beware local treachery. He went on to say that Governor Dever of Massachusetts foresaw a problem for Stevenson in heavily Catholic Massachusetts because of Stevenson's divorce. But Harriman, Finletter said, had the same handicap. Dever had asked Truman's advice, and Truman had told him to wait until the convention and then get on the bandwagon. But Stevenson had understood that Dever was going to call a five-state New England conference to generate enthusiasm for Stevenson. When Finletter telephoned all this to Stevenson, Stevenson said that the big change was Truman's decision for an "open" convention, which would set the Democrats to fighting among themselves. The cause was Harriman's "personal ambition." Stevenson himself had no personal ambition except to see the Democratic Party win.

Lloyd Garrison called a meeting of Jane Dick, Finletter, Cass Canfield, and Marietta Tree, and they decided to reactivate the Volunteers nationally immediately after Stevenson announced. They would keep Harriman and De Sapio informed, hoping to "avoid increasing the rift." They hoped to enlist the help of Mrs. Roosevelt, Jim Farley, FDR's early political strategist, and others but this could not be done without help "from Chicago," i.e., Stevenson's announcement. Subsequently Finletter and Anna Rosenberg, Truman's former Assistant Secretary of Defense and an influential liberal in New York Democratic politics, became cochairmen for New York. Marietta Tree worked full time, running the headquarters. She said, "We had a good group. We produced most of the money for the campaign here. We worked all day every day."

Schlesinger sent a long political memo to Stevenson. He thought the campaign had entered "a new phase." Truman was "out to get the nomination for Harriman." Dever, after talking with Truman, said that Massachusetts would have an unpledged or favorite son delegation. This was the Truman-Harriman strategy, Schlesinger thought—to tie up as many delegations as possible in unpledged or favorite son situations, to "line up the bosses" for Harriman, and to hope that Stevenson and Kefauver would "kill each other off in the primaries." Truman had thought all along that Stevenson looked down on all politicians including Truman (Stevenson marked this with a question mark), that he was not sure Stevenson was liberal enough or relished political slugging (Stevenson marked this "OK"), but that Stevenson would nonetheless be the strongest candidate; and so he had favored Stevenson. But "with Ike out of the picture" Truman now thought almost any Democrat could win and so he preferred Harriman—he was closer to him, Harriman was more liberal, did not look down on politicians, and would "put on a slugging campaign." Schlesinger thought "we have missed opportunities with HST," but that was past, and anyway Truman probably would not take any irrevocable steps. Truman had moved now in order to interrupt Stevenson's candidacy before it became unbeatable. The result of all this was to put Stevenson in somewhat the same position Kefauver had been in in 1952—he had only the people, while the bosses and Truman were against him. But Stevenson's position was stronger today than Kefauver's then. Stevenson should "play boldly and from strength." He should "give a fast green light" on the formation of Stevenson for President clubs. Blair should call three dozen people throughout the country, mostly regular Democrats, and they should quickly form clubs and issue press releases. Stevenson himself should telephone Dever and Lehman and "however distasteful this might be" ask each for his support (and urge each to run for election himself).

He outlined what Stevenson should say to each. Stevenson should see Kefauver as soon as Kefauver returned from abroad (a fiasco already noted). Schlesinger thought Kefauver should be put on the ticket as Vice President with Stevenson but doubted he would settle for second place at this time. A visit with Kefauver would at least foreclose a Harriman-Kefauver axis. New York was crucial. Efforts should be made to stop Harriman in his own state. The New York *Post* would help. Stevenson supporters should seriously consider putting a Stevenson slate into the New York primary headed by Lehman, Mrs. Roosevelt, Farley, Finletter, and others. (If Harriman's slate won, he would get no credit for winning his own state; if he lost, it would hurt him badly.) Above all, Stevenson should rely on his own instincts, not yielding to professional politicians who "are useful to have around for display purposes, but they live a lot of their life in dream worlds too." Over all, Schlesinger was not unhappy about developments. People might "begin to see you as a happy warrior, not as a brooding Hamlet." The thing to avoid was bitterness that would diminish the value of the nomination.

Stevenson told Alicia Patterson, "I'm a little irked by the goings on in N.Y. . . . . I've done my best for the party & tried to play it straight and impersonally for 3 yrs. I've made no campaign on my own behalf feeling that the leaders about the country should indicate if they want me *again*. And then when they have—almost unanimously—along comes this crafty business. . . . [Harriman] has or is kicking away the first chance in modern times for a major party out of office to agree on its candidate 10 months in advance and concert its effort and resources against the enemy. . . . Ho Hum!" He kept telling people, as he told a friend of Mrs. Roosevelt, "As for the nomination I want it less than I want a Democratic victory." It seems likely Stevenson had convinced himself that he lacked personal ambition, would be a candidate only if his party wished, and was only interested in his party's success. But these protestations were hard to square with all the strategy meetings he had held, all the professional politicians he had consulted and gathered about him, all the careful maneuvers during the past three years, all the recent fund raising and staff building and planning. Nor was there any reason why Harriman, the incumbent Governor of the state of New York, should not seek the nomination without being accused of perfidy. Stevenson might deny personal ambition; but he had shown it all his life. And ambition was no sin.

38.

Stevenson had a heavy schedule the week of October 10. On Tuesday he lunched with Mayor Daley at the Tavern Club and had appointments with a client; Dick Babcock, a young Illinois lawyer drawn into politics by Stevenson; Ed Day, formerly on Stevenson's gubernatorial staff; and others every half hour or oftener through dinner. On Wednesday he saw Bill Evjue of the Madison, Wisconsin, *Capital Times,* then attended a Britannica Board meeting and lunch. Next day he saw, among others, Joseph Alsop; Senator Douglas; Rabbi Jacob Weinstein, of K.A.M. in Chicago; two *Time* reporters; Steve Mitchell; and Harry Ashmore. At the end of the week he left for Toronto to deliver a speech and receive an honorary degree at Queen's University. Before leaving for Toronto, Stevenson

sent Agnes Meyer a hasty note in response to her letters, saying he
hoped to see Dean Acheson while East—Mrs. Meyer had suggested
that Acheson serve as go-between among Stevenson, Harriman, and
Truman. He told Mrs. Meyer he would be glad to see Kefauver but
thought it unwise to "put any suggestions about 'deals' into his head" and
passed along—with disbelief—a rumor that Harriman would finance
Kefauver in order to damage Stevenson on the chance that Harriman
would benefit ultimately. He said he had "always liked" Kefauver. He said
he had been "a little injured by Harriman's behavior and thought
Truman's intervention would slow up the professionals." He was receiving
almost unanimous advice to let Stevenson clubs emerge rapidly along with
endorsements from political leaders. He did not say he was opposed to either. He would be glad to meet George Gallup but "I have never been a
believer in polls." He asked her to "ghost"—his word—an article for *Parents' Magazine* for him setting forth his ideas on schools and welfare in the
hope of reaching women with his views.

Pat Brown told Stevenson he "need have no fears whatsoever" about
beating Kefauver in the California primary—he would have to do only "a
minimum" of campaigning. Brown would try to see to it that only one
slate of delegates was entered in the California primary. Stevenson
thanked him "for your decisive and unequivocal leadership there in this
current 'crisis'" and said it was regrettable but inevitable that with Eisenhower ill "uncontrollable ambitions" had flowered. "For my part, I intend
to go on without any change." George Ball, Wyatt, Fritchey, and John
Sharon met at the Hay-Adams Hotel in Washington on October 14 and
agreed that Finletter should soon call a meeting of Ball, Wirtz, Brademas,
and others to establish the policy line Stevenson should take in his
speeches; that Stevenson should ask Barry Bingham quickly to head the
organizing committee of the Volunteers; that the political committee
should meet soon and name Jim Finnegan chairman; that Stevenson's announcement of his candidacy should be made on the morning of November 19. Ball and Fritchey would draft it and submit it to Stevenson and,
with Wyatt, work with him on redrafting. They thought his November 19
dinner speech in Chicago should be aimed at the nation, not at the immediate audience of politicians. They thought he might want to appear on national television a week or two later to discuss his candidacy. Rather than
making public speeches for the rest of the year, he should travel quietly
and talk with Democratic leaders, they thought.

After Stevenson's speech at Queen's University, which dealt mainly with
U.S.-Canadian cooperation, he went to Cambridge for the weekend. He
managed a family gathering on Sunday with Adlai III, Nancy, John Fell,
and Aunt Lucy. That same day he went to the Schlesingers' big old house.
It was a cold rainy October afternoon. Schlesinger noted that Stevenson
"seemed philosophical about HST," though puzzled by Truman's feeling
that Stevenson considered himself above politicians—his father and grand-

father had been politicians. Stevenson had not seen Truman face to face since July. Just before Truman's recent visit East, Stevenson had telephoned him and told him he was worried about the Harriman problem and hoped that nothing would happen to divide the party. Truman had told him, "Don't worry about that. That's why I'm going to Albany. I want to fix things up." Stevenson now commented to Schlesinger, "He fixed things up all right." Since his visit to Albany, Truman had told both Acheson and Finletter that Stevenson remained his first choice, but Stevenson seemed to doubt this. Schlesinger, withdrawing from the stand taken in his letter, said he thought Truman was "just giving [Harriman] a run for his money and perhaps hoping to stimulate AES into a more militant stance." Stevenson gave Schlesinger the impression that he was not concerned about the political effect of Harriman's candidacy but was "troubled and a bit hurt by the manner of it"—he thought Harriman had planned it this way from the start and had "deliberately deceived" Stevenson about their agreement. He was uncertain about what to do but disinclined to make an open fight. "Obviously," Schlesinger noted, "the Harriman problem concerns him more than anything else at this moment." Stevenson spoke admiringly of Kefauver's well-organized campaign—"the postcards; telegrams; the letter of congratulations from Moscow received by a Wisconsin Democrat on the birth of a child; etc." But he feared that Kefauver would seek to bargain for the vice presidency. He felt Kefauver would be a terrible Vice President—he could not perform liaison with Congress because he was, according to Johnson and Rayburn, "the most-hated man to serve in Congress for many years." Johnson's candidate for Vice President was Hubert Humphrey. (Interesting—nine years later Johnson made Humphrey Vice President.) Stevenson felt that Humphrey would be much better than Kefauver as far as congressional liaison was concerned. Paul Douglas had told Kefauver that despite their friendship he would have to support Stevenson. Stevenson's present plan was to announce late in October or early in November in response to a Minnesota resolution. At the MacLeishes, later that afternoon, Stevenson said the political problem was to meet the great "spiritual hunger" and unrest of the time—a hunger and unrest signaled by Joe McCarthy and Billy Graham.

From Cambridge, Stevenson went to New York. Finletter told him Carmine De Sapio had announced that, because of the President's illness and Truman's announcement at Albany the preceding week, the Democratic National Committee dinner on October 31 would be canceled—this was no time to have Stevenson and Harriman on the same platform. They would hold the dinner January 12 instead under joint sponsorship of the State and National Committees.

At a lunch on October 18, while Stevenson was in town, and at an earlier one, some $80,000 was raised from such politicians and political contributors as Roger Stevens, De Sapio, George Backer, Arnold Grant, and Angier Biddle Duke. De Sapio said it had been a mistake for California Democrats to announce their support of Stevenson just as De Sapio ar-

rived there, as had recently happened. It had been interpreted as "an unnecessary slap" at De Sapio. De Sapio thought it important there be no ill
will between the Stevenson and Harriman camps; Democrats must fight
Republicans, not each other. De Sapio, Garrison, and Finletter would
lunch from time to time to head off trouble. Nor should Stevenson or Harriman people give the impression they were conspiring to pick the
nominee. Neither of them should seek Kefauver's support. De Sapio said
that neither he nor Harriman would finance Kefauver's campaign in order
to stop Stevenson. Stevenson clubs might spring up in New York and nationally, Garrison said; De Sapio offered no objection and added that Harriman clubs might spring up at various places. The New York *Times* had
reported that Senator Lyndon Johnson was planning a Southern coalition
to enable the South to choose the nominee in an "open" convention.
Finletter and De Sapio agreed that competing Northern liberal candidates
might knock each other out and leave the nomination to the Southerners.

Everybody was meeting. A Stevenson-Kefauver ticket was suggested.
George Ball thought it might result in trouble with other potential vice
presidential candidates. Charles Murphy said Stevenson must expect that
Truman was closer to Harriman than to Stevenson. He said Truman
would never support Kefauver. He suggested that Stevenson telephone
Truman before announcing his candidacy, that he see Truman in Chicago
early in November, and that he hire David Lloyd, the former Truman staff
aide and now executive secretary of the Truman Library Committee, as a
speech writer.

All this and more was filtering through Bill Blair. At last they were getting a wider range of political intelligence than Steve Mitchell had offered
earlier. In 1952, Stevenson's political range base had been quite narrow—
little more than Illinois plus the New York-Cambridge-Washington axis.
But in the campaign that year, and in the years since, he had broadened
his political base greatly and now had quiet but effective support around
the country—Hale Boggs and several Governors in the South, Hubert
Humphrey and other liberals in the North, and influential leaders across
the country from Mike Monroney of Oklahoma and Clinton Anderson of
New Mexico all the way to Ed Muskie of Maine, from Pat Brown of California and Dick Neuberger of Oregon to Emanuel Celler of New York and
John F. Kennedy of Massachusetts.

Barbara Ward told Finletter on October 20 that she had seen Senator
Lehman and he was "leaning to Adlai & was disappointed in his talk with
Averell." Lehman felt that New York Democrats' reputation was low and
might be restored by supporting Stevenson. She suggested that discreet
influence be brought to bear on Lehman and that, if he announced for
Stevenson, Finletter and a group of distinguished volunteers announce at
the same time. Finletter told her on November 3, "Well, you and Herbert
[Lehman] did it. And what an effect it has had. It has revolutionized
the New York situation."

What had happened was that the day after Senator Lehman saw Barbara Ward he formally announced his support of Stevenson. He said he had consulted with Harriman, Wagner, and De Sapio before doing it.

Stevenson returned to Chicago on October 20. The next day he asked Jack Fischer of *Harper's* to draft a letter "thanking the State Central Committee of Minnesota for its endorsement, agreeing to enter their primary, and explaining why I am glad to offer myself for the battle against the Republicans." Thus it is clear that by October 21 he had decided to enter the Minnesota primary. Bill Blair and Jim Finnegan chose among other primaries; Stevenson made the final decisions. (Minnesota would be announced November 16; California, Florida, Pennsylvania, and Illinois December 14. Oregon came later.)

On October 21, Stevenson told Roger Kent, chairman of the northern division of the California State Central Committee, that "before too long I suppose I must reach some conclusions about California." He asked Kent to keep him informed about Kefauver's strength there. Roger Kent, a soft-spoken almost courtly man, with an estate in Marin County across the Golden Gate Bridge from San Francisco, was an unlikely politician and a Stevenson idolater. Kent was somewhat reminiscent of some of Stevenson's Lake Forest friends. He was deeply devoted to Stevenson and good government—but, unlike the Lake Forest people, even more deeply committed to Democratic liberalism. He had spoken to California Democratic groups frequently and found them favoring Stevenson eight or nine to one over Kefauver. He was "certain" that a strong Stevenson slate would be elected; still, if a Kefauver slate was entered against him he would "have to come to California and do some campaigning." Kent was considering two big meetings—one in March in Sacramento at the opening of the legislature and the other in mid-February at a meeting of the California Democratic Council, an organization of Democratic clubs headed by Alan Cranston (later a U. S. Senator) that had grown up in the wake of the Stevenson 1952 campaign. The clubs had persevered and now seemed about the closest thing to a Democratic organization that existed in California's swirling politics. The clubs were pro-Stevenson, Kent thought. Pat Brown was considering a try for the Senate.

Stevenson had one week in Chicago before his next trip. It was busy.[20] On Saturday, October 29, he went to Duluth, Minnesota, to speak to a Democratic rally for Hubert Humphrey and Orville Freeman. Between

[20] A tea at his home for Lake County Democrats, Senator John Sparkman and Chet Bowles as overnight guests, a speech to a United Nations luncheon, a picture with Vietnamese students, appointments with such people as Ben Swig of San Francisco (owner of the Fairmont Hotel and a Stevenson admirer), Jim Ronan (Illinois state chairman), Mayor Lawrence of Pittsburgh, Steve Mitchell, Claude Wickard (FDR's former Secretary of Agriculture), Matt McCloskey (treasurer of the Democratic National Committee), Scotty Reston of the New York *Times,* Governor Gary of Oklahoma, and Congressman William Dawson of Chicago, who had controlled a large bloc of Negro votes for many years and done little more to enhance the reputation of Negro politicians than Adam Clayton Powell, Jr.

appointments he kept up his correspondence and telephoning and message-sending. Stevenson, while traveling in the East on October 15, had sent a note to Truman; now home he dictated its substance to Carol Evans: "I want you to know that all the feeling which seems to have been generated by what happened in New York last week-end has in no way affected my regard for you or my respect for your opinion. I am sure your motives are, as always, the best interests of the country and the party. I hear you are to be in Chicago October 29. I guess I am destined to miss you again, as I have a long standing engagement to speak in Duluth that night. If you are coming the day before, however, I hope I can call on you for a visit. I think it can be arranged quietly and without publicity. Also, I should be back by Sunday noon in case you are staying over the weekend." Truman replied on October 24—he understood Stevenson would not leave Chicago until eleven o'clock on the twenty-eighth; he, Truman, would arrive by train "at 7:30 God's time, 8:30 Chicago time if you're still on daylight." He added, "I'll be delighted to see you any time, any place. We can have a lot of fun with the columnists!"

Steve Mitchell told Stevenson on October 24 (with copies to Finnegan and Hale Boggs) that he had talked with Speaker Rayburn the day before and found him "very distressed" at the prospect that Lyndon Johnson would seek to go to the convention as Texas' "favorite son" candidate. Sam Rayburn said he wanted to declare publicly for Stevenson but Johnson's move "puts me in a bind." Rayburn would, however, say publicly he considered Stevenson the strongest candidate and privately would try to discourage Johnson. Schlesinger continued to urge upon Stevenson, Blair, and Wirtz the idea that Stevenson should court labor. *Collier's,* in a piece by Theodore H. White, and the *Saturday Evening Post,* in a piece by John Bartlow Martin, said that Stevenson was undoubtedly the front runner for the nomination. Stevenson seemed pleased by both.

He saw Truman in Chicago on October 29. They met in Truman's hotel suite high above the Chicago Loop, and at one point in the meeting Truman drew Stevenson to the window and said, "Do you know what the issue of the campaign is?" and pointed through the window at a man on the sidewalk and went on, "The issue is: Who's looking after that guy? The people down in Washington aren't looking after him. They're looking after themselves. What we have to tell the country is that we Democrats intend to look after the ordinary guy."[21] What else they talked about is

---

21 This story has been repeated many times in varying versions; this account is based on what Stevenson told Schlesinger a little later. Years later Stevenson told a friend, Beth Currie, that he was irritated at what he considered Truman's misunderstanding of the incident. He said that he, Stevenson, had looked out the window and said he wished he could get through to the people down there. Truman, he said, thought he meant he had difficulty meeting people and getting along with them. All he meant was that he wished he could persuade people to be concerned about issues, not personalities.

not recorded. But reporters wrote that when Stevenson departed he looked grim and replied curtly to their questions. And Truman did not take occasion to say he favored Stevenson.

Senator John F. Kennedy had written Stevenson a few days earlier. A Harper editor had shown him Stevenson's favorable comments on Kennedy's book, *Profiles in Courage,* and Kennedy said, "I certainly am honored and flattered by those very nice sentiments." He went on to talk politics: "In line with our conversation, I am preparing a statement which I will issue calling upon the Democratic Party to nominate you and pledging my own support. I will be glad to release this statement whenever you think it would be most helpful." He regretted he had missed Stevenson in the East but hoped they could meet soon. He addressed him "Dear Adlai" and signed himself "Jack." Thus, as early as October 21, Kennedy gave Stevenson a flat commitment of support for the nomination, in writing. Stevenson replied, "Thanks for your letter. I have talked with Sam Rayburn. He is withholding his statement pending the resolution of some Texas problems which I think you can surmise. He has little doubt that they will work out satisfactorily. Meanwhile, he suggested instead of talking to the majority leader [Johnson] by telephone he will write him a note of the same import. In these confused circumstances I cannot be sure what effect it will have. He was quite candid in saying that the gentleman did not 'like me' and I gathered that it was because of the fact that I was divorced. I trust that you and Paul Dever will proceed as you think best. As to the time of any announcement you care to make, for my part I don't have any strong feeling but the 'advisers' seem to think the sooner the better for all concerned."

Stevenson's speech at Duluth that Saturday night was hard and partisan. It began: "I came here tonight for three good Democratic reasons: [Congressman] John Blatnik, Hubert Humphrey and Orville Freeman." He praised each at length with gaiety and elan and then moved on to "a larger vision of our country and of ourselves." He spoke with asperity about the "loose talk and erratic behavior of the Administration in foreign affairs:

"I mean the threats of massive atomic retaliation as a national defense policy.

"I mean the boast of 'unleashing' Chiang Kai-shek.

"I mean the talk of intervention in Indochina.

"I mean tough talk and timid action; I mean bluff and backdown; I mean blowing alternately hot and cold, and confounding everyone in the process, themselves included."

He said "the great Republican divide between talking and doing stands out just as sharply today on the domestic front" and attacked Administration slogans and inaction in education, security risks, power resources, ethics in government, and agriculture. He attacked big business and the big press and, perhaps echoing Truman, said, "For the government must be the trustee for the little man, because no one else will be."

Stevenson received a confidential report of an off-the-record interview Harriman had given a reporter. Harriman had said (according to the reporter) that he had more grass-roots strength than Stevenson, would run a more efficient and tougher campaign, thought that Stevenson had not made a good speech since Miami, 1954, and said the Democrats would find themselves "with an old tired face on their hands." He disclaimed personal friendship and called Stevenson "a social acquaintance." In wartime Washington he, Harriman, had been working "on a much higher level" than Stevenson. He had had more experience in government than Stevenson or almost anybody else. Stevenson's 1952 campaign had been good, he conceded, but 1956 would be "rougher." He claimed delegates for himself in Arizona, Colorado, Idaho, Montana, Wyoming, Utah. He planned to enter no primaries.[22]

Upon returning from Duluth, Stevenson went into Passavant Hospital for a two-day checkup—"all the horrid tests and Chinese tortures they could contrive," he told Agnes Meyer. She had asked him for advice on what to say when she met with Walter Reuther. Stevenson replied that he had had "some calls" from Reuther lately, but they had been unable to arrange an appointment, and he hoped she could "find out precisely how he feels before he knows too much about how you feel." He added, "Other top CIO people have been here pledging me the usual undying fealty." He thanked the Humphreys and Freemans for their hospitality. Mrs. Humphrey replied—she wanted him to know that their support was based on esteem, though some might misinterpret it as wanting to get on a bandwagon. For many years Humphrey and his wife cherished their association with Stevenson. John Mason Brown begged Stevenson to make a statesmanlike announcement speech *"above* politics." But advice of this kind, so almost suffocating in 1952, seemed to be diminishing. Stevenson this year was in touch with professional politicians and those who, amateurs in 1952, were by now semi-pro. His appointment sheets reflected it during the ensuing ten days before his next trip East—Barry Bingham, Elmo Roper and Ashmore and Blair, Art Moore of the National Committee, Jack Arvey, Congressman Sidney Yates and Paul Simon (a rising young downstate Democrat, later Lieutenant Governor and a Congressman), Tubby, Finnegan, Mitchell, Raskin.

Agnes Meyer sent Harry Truman a long letter giving the reasons she was supporting Stevenson. Stevenson thanked her and told her his own meeting with Truman had been "most agreeable." Truman would remain neutral prior to the convention because of "Averell's ambitions" and in order to serve "as an honest broker" to promote unity. Stevenson was receiving political intelligence on intra-party maneuvers in Arkansas, Oklahoma, and several Southern states. Schlesinger made notes on the strategy meeting at Blair's house November 5–6. Present were Stevenson, Finletter,

---

22 An independent survey at the time showed that Stevenson seemed safe in Arizona, Colorado was uncertain, he was ahead in Montana, and Wyoming was probably safe for him though Senator O'Mahoney was uncommitted.

Blair, Wirtz, Ben Cohen, George Ball, Jane Dick, Ashmore, Fischer, Tubby, Schlesinger, and Brademas. Stevenson and Tubby, coming up from Bloomington, did not arrive until about 9 P.M. The meeting broke up a little past midnight and resumed at 10 A.M. next day, continuing till 1 P.M., "at which time we adjourned for drinks and Lauren Bacall," Schlesinger noted. "The object was to determine the main themes for the campaign, the essential points to be made and reiterated, and the prevailing tones. There was little serious disagreement, and the group reached consensus without too much difficulty. It was concluded that the main emphasis of the campaign should be (1) on 'qualitative liberalism' . . . , (2) on single-interest government . . . , and (3) on the Republican use of chicanery and deceit in the administration's communication with the American people. It was agreed that the essential framework of the campaign should be affirmative and constructive, seeking to unify, not to divide; and that the 'give-em-hell' element, highly necessary to persuade party Democrats that AES is a fighter and can put on a militant campaign, be used but absorbed in the more positive overall strategy. AES himself was in good form. At times he was responsive to the argument for statesmanship, at times not. 'You know what I would really like to do?' he said at one point. 'What I'd really like to do is to attack the administration from A to Z—go down the line, taking up every item in the book: the lies they have told to the people, the raid on the natural resources, the packing of regulatory commissions, the smear and slander, and all the rest. I'd like to call them on every point. I'm tired of this statesmanlike stuff.' Bill Wirtz intervened: 'You might like to do it. But you would hate to have done it.'

"The one serious difference was the extent to which #3—deceit—was really an effective issue. AES felt strongly that it is a real issue—or at least ought to be. TKF vigorously backed him up. But Wirtz, Jane Dick, Tubby and myself all felt that the lies and the broken pledges were mainly of historical interest and would not cut much ice votewise. AES said, 'I think it is time to change my methods. My speeches must be more simple, vivid, concrete. In the past they have been too abstract and philosophical. I've always tried to cover too much. Now I must work hard to get specific instances and examples which will carry over to people and mean something to them.'" Curiously, peace and disarmament, which had appeared as major issues in previous discussions and memoranda all fall, were not mentioned in Schlesinger's notes.

Stevenson was planning to go to Washington on November 10 to see Dean Acheson, Kefauver, Paul Butler, Agnes Meyer, and others. He expected to make his announcement on November 14. Bernard Baruch of New York sent him a memorandum on atomic energy, saying that in negotiations with the Soviet Union the United States should return to its original proposal: International ownership and control of atomic energy with inspection. Stevenson told Charles F. Brannan, once President Truman's Secretary of Agriculture, that he hoped the Democrats "come up with something more than 90% parity in the next session." He asked Ashmore and Wirtz to work hard on his speech for the Democratic dinner on November 19 while he was East. The *Tribune* broke the story about the Kefauver meeting; Stevenson canceled the meeting and suspected the story had leaked because of a wiretap.

From a friend in Denver, Bill Blair received word that Eisenhower aides were developing a tentative strategy to draft Eisenhower for a second term despite his illness. Sherman Adams and Jim Hagerty, "abetted knowingly or otherwise by Doctors Snyder and White," planned to maintain a Republican political vacuum until January or February in order to keep the door open for one final plea to a recovered President to run again. Already Senator Knowland and Governor Knight of California had begun to move; this plan would forestall them. Sinclair Weeks, Eisenhower's Secretary of Commerce, had told a Republican finance meeting that the President was far from being out of Republican planning for next year. So far as could be determined, incredible though it seemed, Eisenhower himself had given the matter no thought, but his wife was known to be firmly opposed to his running. Such professional politicians as Len Hall were not enthusiastic about the prospects of Eisenhower's running again. Shortly before his illness Eisenhower was said to have suggested that Herbert Hoover, Jr., and Robert Anderson of Texas were presidential material. (When he mentioned Hoover, someone said, "The man can't even hear very well," and Eisenhower replied, "My God, what a blessing for a President.") Blair's friend was convinced Eisenhower would not run.

Stevenson, preparing to leave for the East, asked Adlai III and Nancy to come to Chicago for the Democratic affair. "I don't want to embarrass you as I am sure you realize, and I doubt if I will need to impose on you again for a long time, but if you could do it this time without too much inconvenience I will be most grateful." Carol Evans sent a telegram to Barbara Ward in Montreal, "Could you draft for Governor by next Sunday 400 words for announcement explaining why he thinks it important to run and win. He says a purple passage please. Regards." Elmo Roper reported to Harry Ashmore that sentiment in the Midwest indicated people had cooled off somewhat on Stevenson but the tide was setting against the Republicans if Eisenhower did not run. Agnes Meyer said the *Post* thought the ticket would be Stevenson vs. Nixon and would support Stevenson.

Stevenson left early Thursday morning, November 10, for Washington, taking Blair and Tubby. After political meetings there, he drove to Charlottesville where, at the University of Virginia, he delivered a speech opening the Woodrow Wilson Centennial celebration, carried on a nationwide radio network. He spoke of the League of Nations, Wilson's "war against war," his economic justice at home, and his view that a stable world order required justice for the "great masses of people" who demanded a better life. Not mere anti-Communism and self-interest should guide America's foreign policy but unselfishness and magnanimity.

Central to its policy should be "an enforceable system of disarmament." Today "the rosy mists" which had surrounded last summer's summit meeting were dissipating, revealing a security system that was disintegrating. Violence was mounting in the Middle East, Russia had made an arms deal with Egypt, America must offset any Soviet effort to upset the arms balance. "The Middle East has long been an area of Russian ambition. . . . The contagious flames of undeclared war between Israel and her neighbors have smoldered too long. We applaud the peaceful efforts of the Secretary General of the United Nations." The Soviets had recognized the limits of force. We must not allow "their charm policy" to "further weaken" our defenses. "And we must take care, too, lest rigid military-security diplomacy hobble our foreign policy." All that year and next, Middle East tensions mounted, to explode shortly before the American election; it was one of Stevenson's most difficult problems.

Hubert Humphrey passed through Chicago and sat up late, as was his wont, talking to Bill Blair. Afterward he sent him a long letter: "I am a Bill Blair man." Humphrey was impressed with his "loyal friendship" for Stevenson, his political acumen, and, in short, "I like the way you do things" and "I want to work with you Bill and hope that I can have that privilege." In the ebullient, almost boyish way that endeared him to so many people, Humphrey rambled on at length about Stevenson. Stevenson was, he thought, "way out in front for the nomination." No one could stop him barring "some colossal mistake which I am sure will not happen." The party needed leadership and it could come from no member of Congress or former President but only from Stevenson. Between now and next summer Stevenson "should spend a great deal of time visiting with party leaders and particularly the party leadership at the county and state central committee level." This should be done informally, "such as inviting some of these folks to Libertyville for a brief visit. . . . I think it is very important that this atmosphere of informality be developed and impressed. Everyone knows that Adlai Stevenson is brilliant. In fact he is so brilliant that he may occasionally frighten some people away. . . . He does a beautiful job in these receptions and informal gatherings. . . . The word will spread . . . that they met Stevenson and that he is a real guy. . . . Everyone can not stand too much of this keen hard hitting political analysis." Stevenson should not speak too often—every speech offered a target to his enemies. Instead, his supporters should speak for him—Governor Leader, Governor Freeman, Senator Fulbright, Humphrey himself, and others. And he repeated, "I want the country to know the real Stevenson." (How many times, times without number, did Stevenson's staff and friends say this! The feeling would not down that somehow the statesman on the platform, though impressive, was not the warm friendly human being known to his intimates.) Humphrey, in this letter and on other occasions, could not let go of the idea: "Bill, when Stevenson believes that something is wrong he must not only say so in well spoken words, but his very countenance, his whole being must exhibit and emphasize that moral indignation and protest. In other words, he has got to get angry over wrong doings. . . . Yes, I would like to see him slam his fist down on the podium when he knows that the people are being deceived."

39.

Arriving back in Chicago on November 12, Stevenson spoke briefly at an Israel bond rally in the Morrison Hotel. Senators Kefauver, Humphrey, and Douglas spoke too, and Stevenson told a friend, "After the bath of Zionist oratory from the local Zionist leaders and Messrs. Kefauver, Humphrey and Douglas I must have sounded like a very soft wind and felt like a very cold shower." D. B. Hardaman, a Texas politician who was helping Stevenson, reported on an exploratory trip to Florida. It was "far from in the bag, but far from hopeless." Stevenson was on the verge of announcing his candidacy. The chosen date was now Tuesday, November 15, 1955. The National Committee would meet in Chicago from Thursday to Sunday. Stevenson would address it on Saturday night, the nineteenth. The night before he announced, he met in Libertyville with his friends and advisers. On Tuesday at 2 P.M. he appeared in the Boulevard Room of the Conrad Hilton Hotel and, before the press and television and an audience composed of Senator Douglas, Mayor Daley, Jack Arvey, Steve Mitchell, Jim Finnegan, Illinois Congressmen, party leaders, and his old friends and staff, he read his announcement. He had written out the original in longhand. The statement said he would be a candidate because he believed it important to return to Democratic rule, he had been assured that his candidacy would be welcomed, and he believed any citizen "should make whatever contribution he can to the search for a safer, saner world." It was a rather bland statement, setting forth no theme nor any heavy attack on the Administration, probably because of Eisenhower's illness. It left many questions unanswered, such as whether he would enter primaries. The next day he held a press conference, said he would enter the Minnesota primary, said he probably would enter other primaries, ruled out any deals on the vice presidency, said the choice of a vice presidential candidate should be made by the convention with great care, announced that Jim Finnegan would manage his campaign, promised that Eisenhower's health would not be a campaign issue but would be a "consideration," and refused to speculate on whether Eisenhower would run.

He advised his sister-in-law, Betty Hines of New York, to say nothing to the press about his announcement unless asked—to do so might prompt the press to solicit comment from Ellen. If Ellen volunteered anything hostile, Stevenson thought Mrs. Hines and their mother, Mrs. Carpenter, should "promptly issue a statement expressing gratification as citizens with my candidacy and pledging your support." He told a friend from New

York, "I have 'gone and done it,' not with any weary sense merely of doing my duty nor with any great exhiliration, but with a comfortable feeling that it is right and that it has fallen to my lot in my generation to do all I can to preserve the dialogue that makes democracy work and that could even make it better. Moreover, with experience I am less anxious and harrassed than I used to be." It was as close as he came to expressing his feelings upon becoming a candidate again.

The National Committee met Thursday and Friday at the Conrad Hilton. On Friday, Stevenson moved into the Madrid Suite at the Hilton and opened it to visitors. The California delegation was the first. Thenceforward until Sunday, he spent nearly all his time at the suite. His day on Saturday began with a breakfast for a group of New England leaders at 9 A.M. At ten-thirty he saw Jack Kroll of the CIO. At eleven he received a Minnesota group. He fitted Roger Kent into the morning schedule along with a West Virginia group and Matt McCloskey. He gave a luncheon at twelve-thirty for Democratic Governors—Meyner, Roberts, Harriman, Dennis, Williams, Marland, Simms, and Leader, along with Dick Daley. Mrs. Ives was his hostess.

Senator Kefauver charged that the National Committee was favoring Stevenson, giving him top billing and all available radio-television time at the big dinner that night. It was a harbinger of the contest to come.

At five o'clock Stevenson attended receptions at the Saddle and Sirloin Club adjoining the Stockyards. The hundred-dollar-a-plate dinner began there at 7 P.M., in the great Amphitheater where Stevenson had been nominated in 1952. President Truman was there, and so were the various other candidates for the nomination, and, indeed, nearly every important leader of the Democratic Party in the nation. So were the ward leaders of the Chicago machine, and some of them snubbed him. They had no more use for Stevenson now than in 1952, less, indeed—he was no longer Governor, with patronage power. His speech was broadcast on national radio and television. The speech attacked the Administration—but not the President, in whose recovery he said he rejoiced—on both foreign and domestic policies. Peace could not be won by slogans or by vacillation; America's military strength had been reduced. At home, the Administration had proved to be special-interest, big-business government, pursuing policies inimical to the ordinary man in natural resources, agriculture, schools, health, labor, civil rights, and civil liberties. He told, embellished, the anecdote about Truman's pointing out the hotel window at a man in the street. Stevenson's speech became known as his "moderation" speech, for in general he followed the line that Lyndon Johnson and Sam Rayburn had urged on him at the LBJ ranch. Harriman, in his own speech that night, staked out a position to the left of Stevenson, declaring, "There is no such word as 'moderation' in the Democratic vocabulary," a sentence curiously similar to Barry Goldwater's famous sentence in his 1964 acceptance speech.

Mrs. Ives thought Stevenson seemed under strain. She had been with him through the meetings but felt in the way. Leaving, she told Carol Evans she would visit him at Christmas but only if he invited her.

Stevenson remained at the Hilton that night and on Sunday went to church; then he met with people from Virginia at twelve-thirty and, at one, with a Wisconsin group, joined by Finnegan, Minow, Blair, and Raskin. Stevenson left for Libertyville before the meeting ended. On Monday he was back in his office. He had his picture taken at the public announcement of the formation of the National Stevenson for President Committee, as the volunteers were called this year, with Barry Bingham and Jane Dick as cochairmen. He had interviews with a magazine writer. That evening Alicia Patterson came to see him. He told Agnes Meyer that Kefauver, while in Chicago, had expressed to Stevenson his "grave distress" at the leak about their meeting. (Stevenson and Kefauver kept up the charade—exchanged elaborately gracious notes. Kefauver was not yet a declared candidate—only Stevenson was.) Stevenson also told Mrs. Meyer that if nominated he would rather run against Warren than Nixon —"at least I would know that the dialogue would be decent and the system secure." It is hard to believe he really meant it—Warren almost surely would have been harder to beat than Nixon. What he said was safe enough —Warren had taken himself out publicly (and Agnes Meyer was Warren's great admirer).

Lyndon Johnson sent him a photograph of himself, Stevenson, and Rayburn and a note: "Incidentally, as nearly as I can make out this must have been the occasion upon which the so-called 'Southern coalition' was formed. Sam Rayburn is a Southerner and I understand your farm is south of Chicago [it was not] and that puts you among the very few 'Southern political leaders' that I have talked to since I left Washington. It has been rather interesting to watch the stories in the press about what I am doing and what I am thinking and I am wondering just when some of the writers are going to get around to what appears to be the usual expedient of asking me." Stevenson replied to "Dear Lyn": "If you ever find out why writers write what they do about us without asking us, let me know."

John Sharon reported that on the morning after Stevenson's speech a former Truman White House staffer invited him to have a cup of coffee with Truman, and Sharon found Truman with Mrs. Truman, Harriman, Charles Murphy, and Donald Dawson, the last two also former Truman staff men. Sharon was not identified as a Stevenson man. He listened while the others said that Harriman's speech on Saturday night was the best and that Stevenson's speech was "not very good." Harriman said, "Well, Adlai certainly didn't rouse that audience with that kind of a speech. That wasn't the kind of speech they wanted to hear." Dawson said, "I thought it was a terrible speech because it just didn't seem to strike home." Mrs. Truman said, "Yes, that's what we were all saying when we came back here last night." Truman himself said, "Well, it just didn't seem to catch fire as I thought it should have. I think he may have been talking a little over their heads." (Monday's New York *Times* quoted Truman as saying that Stevenson "made the best New Deal speech I have ever heard him make.") Murphy said, "Well, all I can say is that by the time they got around to Mr. Stevenson's speech I had to get up and walk around, I was so worn out." Later Harriman remarked that if he himself had delivered Stevenson's speech he would have been accused of "abdicating everything I stood for" but Stevenson could "[get] away with it." Harriman thought Kefauver's speech far more critical of Eisenhower's foreign policy than Stevenson's but his delivery terrible. He repeated that "moderation is not our course and never has been."

From a source in Texas, Blair received an account of a speech Lyndon Johnson had made at a ten-dollar-a-plate dinner at a small town in Texas. Johnson had presented a thirteen-point "Program with a Heart" which he promised to push in the coming session of Congress and part of which apparently was designed to mollify Northern liberals—Social Security reform, tax reduction, medical research, hospital construction, school construction, highway construction, farm price supports, housing, water resources projects including a high dam at Hell's Canyon, aid to depressed areas, elimination of the poll tax, immigration law changes, and authority to the oil and gas industry to set natural gas prices. (Joe Rauh of the ADA was not mollified: he said it was indistinguishable from "Eisenhower moderation." Hubert Humphrey, however, who was at this point Johnson's bridge to the liberals in the Senate, praised the program.) Perhaps more significant for Stevenson's present purposes, Johnson had departed from his prepared text and shouted into the microphone: "I want it clearly understood with no ifs, ands or buts, Texas should send a Democratic delegation to the Democratic Convention that will fight for its views, but abide by the convention's decision—then come home and make war on the Republican Party and on everybody who works for the Republican ticket." This, of course, was anathema to Governor Shivers and other Texas conservatives.

Senator Richard B. Russell had sent Stevenson an encouraging note: "I think your announcement and present plans assure you the nomination. If we can get a reasonable platform, a unified, militant Democratic Party will elect you President next November." Stevenson, spending Tuesday, November 22, in his office on correspondence, thanked him, said he would "very much like to have a talk with you," and said he would be at Alicia Patterson's place the coming weekend near Kingsland, Georgia, "writing a speech and shooting quail." Rabbi Jacob Weinstein told him, "The *moderate* line seems to me a good one. Perhaps it ought to be tempered with a bit of passion . . . [on] civil liberties or conservation giveaways." Agnes Meyer wrote a long letter on November 23. Phil Graham of the Washington *Post* was for him. She advised him to "crowd out prosperity . . . with the larger issues of peace and a brave new world."

That Wednesday Stevenson entertained Mr. and Mrs. Walter Lippmann at Libertyville overnight. Next day was Thanksgiving, and he went shooting with a friend, then had his out-of-town staff for dinner and, on Friday, November 25, left for Kingsland, Georgia, and Alicia Patterson, taking Bill Wirtz and his wife along. It was the start of a political swing that would take him into Florida, Oklahoma, New York, and Arkansas in the next two weeks—the start, though the unofficial start, of his second campaign for the presidency. The year ahead, from November to November, would be a long one.

CHAPTER TWO

The Great Campaign
of 1956

By the time Stevenson died ten years later, many of his friends and supporters, looking back, felt that his effort to win the presidency in 1955–56 was unworthy of him. They considered the 1952 campaign far superior to that of 1956. They thought he had somehow diminished himself in 1956—that his speeches had been less eloquent, that he had appeared to want the presidency too much, that he had trimmed and compromised, that he had surrendered himself to the professional politicians and had come to seem almost one himself.

Yet if one examines the evidence, one wonders. True, the incandescent flash with which Stevenson had burst upon the political scene in 1952 was gone. Inevitably so—he could be seen for the first time only once. In 1952, unknown, he had startled people with his fresh unorthodox appeal. By 1956 he was a national and international figure, rather expectable. And the situation differed in other respects. In 1952 he had been defending a position, the Truman-Roosevelt position; in 1956 he was attacking a position, the Eisenhower position. Attack almost inevitably sounds shriller, more "political," than defense. (And defense sometimes employs eloquent rhetoric to conceal what cannot be defended.) His 1952 speeches had been eloquent indeed. But his 1956 speeches contained far more substance. It is often said that his 1952 speeches "elevated the political dialogue." What is said less is that his 1956 speeches set forth issues and programs that laid the groundwork for the New Frontier of John F. Kennedy and the Great Society of Lyndon Johnson. One can identify idea after idea that Stevenson made issues in 1956 and that later became law in the Kennedy-Johnson administrations, from nuclear testing to Medicare. Indeed, it may not be too much to say that Adlai Stevenson made his greatest contribution to U.S. policy in the 1956 campaign. In 1952 he had defended the New Deal and Fair Deal—the liberal faith of the 1930s and 1940s. In 1956 he charted a course for the 1960s and 1970s. What was also forgotten later was how hard he had to fight for the nomination in 1956 and how close he came to losing it. No presidential nomination of his time was more vigorously, not to say exhaustingly, contested. Ten years later an impression existed that in 1956 Stevenson was his party's obvious choice, that he had only to consent to receive the nomination. It was not so. He had to fight hard, and often uphill. The idea of a "new Stevenson" plagued him throughout 1956. It arose in part from the image of him which his most ardent admirers had constructed in their own minds during and after 1952. He never was quite what they had thought, and so when he recaptured the limelight in 1956, acting like himself, they were disappointed. They were remembering a 1952 campaign as better than it had been or could have been.

When he began the fight at the end of November 1955 his prospects seemed good—better, indeed, than they really were. Eisenhower was still a sick man, and the Republican managers' campaign to renominate him had not yet surfaced. The Democratic nomination looked very much like a prize worth having. Belief was widespread that if Eisenhower did not run almost any Democrat could win. Stevenson was the only announced candidate. He was far ahead of the field. He had for more than two years assiduously tried to win back the South. He retained the allegiance of Northern liberals and intellectuals. Labor leaders might not love him as they had loved Roosevelt and Truman but they would support him (though how hard they would work for him was as yet unknown). Similarly, nobody knew how many Northern Negroes would desert the Democrats, or how many Jews, Catholics, blue-collar workers of Eastern European descent, and other urban minorities of the old FDR coalition—this might depend in large part on the efforts of labor leaders. The farmers were considered disillusioned with Eisenhower and though no great lovers of Stevenson were believed ready to return to the Democrats. Perhaps best of all (if one was worried about the urban minorities and workers), the Democratic Party's big-city machines were strong—in some places stronger than they had been in FDR's time. They were strong in Chicago, Pittsburgh, northern New Jersey, and Philadelphia. They were considered strong in New York, Boston, and other cities. In Minnesota the Democratic-Farmer-Labor Party was at the apex of its power. Even in preposterous California the Democratic Club movement had mobilized thousands upon thousands of party workers. And finally in the mid-term congressional elections of 1954 the Democrats had captured many statehouses and courthouses, with all the patronage power they contained.

Beyond the party stood the candidate. As a political leader and statesman, Stevenson was head and shoulders over anybody in sight except Eisenhower himself. He seemed to have lost some of the reluctance and uncertainty of 1952. He seemed to have gained not only in stature but in self-confidence. Experience at intraparty infighting had taught him much (and had also taught his closest associates, including Bill Blair). His platform manner had improved, and his television technique. He was no longer a one-term Governor thrust unexpectedly into the pitiless glare of national television. He was a seasoned campaigner, and if he did not always seem it, that was because he was also still Adlai Stevenson.

It became boring to say that this time a thoroughgoing professional, Jim Finnegan, was in charge. Finnegan was a neatly dressed Irishman with iron-gray hair, wearing gray suits, entirely at home as, coming into his office in midmorning, he asked his secretary to start returning his telephone calls, working his way from the East Coast to the West. Finnegan was deeply devoted to Stevenson. But his effectiveness was somewhat limited because Stevenson, better educated, better spoken, wealthier, somehow intimidated him, and Finnegan hesitated to give him the plain-spoken advice he gave others. Below the Butler-Finnegan level—though not necessarily below them in influence on Stevenson—were not professional politicians but Stevenson's own associates. Blair was closer than anybody else, constantly at his side, the only man who could persuade Stevenson to do things he didn't want to do. Bill Wirtz had replaced Carl McGowan in charge of the substance of speeches. Wirtz found it harder than McGowan to say no to Stevenson. Newt Minow was given the title of "campaign coordinator"—straightening things out when they went wrong, all sorts of things, many important. Stevenson probably relied more on Blair, Wirtz, and Minow for advice than on anyone else, though he listened to Finnegan on issues as well as on purely political matters, and also to the advice of such old friends as Tom Finletter and George Ball.

The research and writing operation of 1956 was less happy-go-lucky, less brilliant, but far more solid than the Elks Club of 1952. Grounded in the Finletter Group's work, which had drawn upon some of the best Democratic minds in the country, the research material had been built up mountainously by John Brademas and his associates. The principal writers-on-hand during the primaries were Harry Ashmore and John Bartlow Martin (Martin joined the staff full time after the Minnesota primary). From time to time during the primaries Schlesinger or Galbraith or someone else contributed a major speech. Stevenson listened to Ashmore and Martin along with Wirtz, Blair, and Minow, and to other writers more distant. After the convention Schlesinger came on full time to head the speech writers' group, which during the fall campaign included, part time, Bob Tufts and William Lee Miller. Near the end of the fall campaign, as the speech load became intolerable and the writers were traveling more and more with Stevenson, Tom Finletter came in to administer the writers' group. Galbraith, John Hersey, and others contributed drafts of major speeches.

For a time during the fall Robert F. Kennedy rode the Stevenson campaign plane, hoping to learn how to run a presidential campaign. He later said he had learned how not to run one—he had never seen an operation so poorly run. He should have seen 1952. Of 1956 he once said, "I thought it was ghastly. It was badly organized. More important, my feeling was that he had no rapport with his audience—no feeling for them—no comprehension of what campaigning required—no ability to make decisions. It was a terrible shock to me. In 1952, I had been crazy about him. I was excited in 1956, at the start. I came out of our first conversation with a very high opinion of him. My brother [John] did too. Then I spent six weeks with him on the campaign and he destroyed it all."

Stevenson liked Sargent Shriver but his relations with John and Robert Kennedy were never good. Once during a campaign strategy meeting at Libertyville, Stevenson was called to the telephone to speak to Kennedy's father and, as he took the call, groaned, "Oh, my God, this will be an hour and a half." Robert Kennedy, who was there, almost surely heard him but said nothing.

There were times when John Kennedy's campaign of 1960, and Bob's own primary campaign of 1968, closely resembled the occasional chaos of Stevenson's 1956 campaign. The fact is that any campaign is almost bound to be disorganized. The Stevenson campaign of 1956 was far better planned and executed than his 1952 campaign. The staff was more experienced. It was more purposeful. It seemed less out on a lark than bent on winning an election. Its amalgam of professionals, semi-pros and amateurs worked together better than any outsider supposed. Once during the fall Scotty Reston, eavesdropping outside the door of a hotel suite in Washington during a rare staff meeting, overheard Stevenson saying loudly, "Am I not master in my own house?" Reston concluded that the professionals and amateurs were quarreling over the tone and direction of the campaign, the professionals urging Stevenson to continue his combination of attack and handshaking and reliance on party organization, the amateurs arguing for a return to the lofty rhetoric of 1952. The fact was that Stevenson was quoting sardonically from one of his own speeches in which he said that Eisenhower was not master in his own house; the discussion had to do with expenditures for broadcasting, and Stevenson was making a joke. Actually, when Stevenson sought policy advice on a major issue, the professional politicians, such as Jim Finnegan, often found themselves ranged on the moral side of an issue, while the semi-pros or amateurs, such as Schlesinger and Martin, found themselves taking a hardheaded political view of it. (Thus Finnegan thought Stevenson should press the H-bomb testing issue because it was right—and because it received applause— while Schlesinger opposed because, although it was morally right, it was bad politics—too complicated to discuss in a campaign, challenging Eisenhower in the field of his own expertise.)

2.

Stevenson's schedule in Florida gave him a taste of what was to come in the primaries. (He had not yet announced he intended to enter this one.) They arrived at Gainesville on the afternoon of Monday, November 28, and motorcaded to the courthouse square for a public reception. On Tuesday they went early to the University of Florida cafeteria, had breakfast with students and faculty, toured the campus under the guidance of Young Democratic leaders, went to the courthouse square to walk around and shake hands, went to Ocala for handshaking and lunch with local Democrats, then to Silver Springs and Deland and Sanford for brief stops, on to Orlando, where they attended a reception, then flew to Miami where, mercifully, after an airport reception, they spent the night at the Florida home of Jack Arvey.

On Wednesday, at the annual luncheon meeting of the American Municipal Congress, Stevenson delivered the only set speech of the Florida trip. The Young Democrats gave a reception for Stevenson in the afternoon, and he dined with Arvey that night. On Thursday he went to the University of Miami, walked around it and shook hands; in the afternoon he attended a cocktail party given by Arvey for about fifty people and went to a reception at Bay Front Park. In the morning, Friday, December 2, he flew to Dallas and was met there by Senator Monroney in a private plane and taken to Oklahoma City where he held a press conference and addressed the national convention of the Young Democrats, a partisan attack on the Administration. Late that night, he returned to Chicago.

He had breakfast the next day with Senator John Kennedy. Agnes Meyer told him that his views on the Israel-Arab problem were "too neutral"—her husband thought "we must guarantee the integrity of Israel" if we were to prevent World War III. He thanked Alicia Patterson for the time by "the beloved Black River"—"you were good to take in the Wirtz' who don't have such experiences often." Barbara Ward reported on British opinion about Russia, Asia, and Germany and about reactions she had heard in New York to his Chicago speech. (From now on she would give him the kind of advice that Dorothy Fosdick had given earlier.) On Tuesday, December 6, Stevenson went to New York. He saw Tom Finletter and Anna Rosenberg and Marietta Tree and others late in the afternoon, then went to a fund-raising dinner at Mary Lasker's beautiful town house. On Wednesday he had breakfast with Jim Finnegan and lunch with Matt McCloskey. Subject: money. That afternoon he saw Roy Wilkins of the NAACP and, after him, Abba Eban of Israel, Jacob Potofsky, the labor leader, and David Lilienthal, the first chairman of TVA. Lilienthal arrived before Eban left, and Blair told him that "they" were trying to make it appear that Stevenson was anti-Israel. After this Stevenson went to a small dinner at Lloyd Garrison's.[1]

[1] Present were the Cass Canfields, Harold Hochschild (the board chairman of American Metal) and his wife, Marshall and Ruth Field, Blair, John and Jane Gunther, and Nathan P. Feinsinger, a professor and labor expert. Afterward a larger group arrived to see movies of the African trip, most of them members of the New York Committee for Stevenson, among them Mr. and Mrs. Telford Taylor, Anna and Julius Rosenberg, Simon and Ada Rifkind, Mr. and Mrs. Francis T. P. Plimpton, Jack and Alice Kaplan, Marietta and Ronald Tree, and Dorothy Schiff of the New York *Post*.

Next day, December 8, Stevenson delivered a major speech to the AFL-CIO unity convention at the 71st Regimental Armory. He attacked the Administration for "what appears to be a design to play the ugly politics of group hatred" and said that leading Republicans, including cabinet members, had variously blamed the farmer's depression on the city workers' wage increase, charged labor leaders with organizing "a conspiracy" to take over the federal government, insinuated that labor had become a potent political force in America at about the same time that the Nazi Party arose in Germany, called union men "goons," and proclaimed that labor leaders were "Marxist-Socialist bosses who are trying to take this country down a rathole." Stevenson said, "This, I repeat, is a distressing and dangerous brand of politics. This is divisive and therefore destructive. We in this country are just emerging from a long and shameful interval of hate and fear and slander. Today McCarthyism is out of style. But is a similar hate campaign in the making around distorted images of 'goons' and 'power hungry labor bosses,' ugly phrases we hear almost daily? Must the image of America be further defaced? Is this, indeed, an attempt to stir up class conflict? No election, no office, is worth such a price!"

Labor, he said, would make no demands as a special interest. It would keep Communists and racketeers out of labor unions. The greatest hope of workingmen and all Americans was "for peace, for peace with freedom." Here at home "our central purpose" was "to create fuller lives for all our people." America had made "enormous strides" under Roosevelt and Truman and yet a single company was making a profit this year, before taxes, of over $2 billion while eight million families were trying to get by on $2,000 or less. He went on to press issues for a better life—housing, schools, medical care, Social Security, and strengthened collective bargaining. It was a long distance from Cadillac Square, even farther from Evansville, two cities where, in the 1952 campaign, he had gratuitously offended organized labor by extemporaneously declaring his independence of it.

After the speech Stevenson attended a big fund-raising luncheon at the Hotel Pierre. In the afternoon he saw, among others, Adam Clayton Powell, the flamboyant Negro Congressman from New York, and Alex Rose of the hatters' union. Then he went to Arkansas and spent the next few days hunting with Senator Fulbright and other Arkansas politicians. Back in Chicago on December 12, he received an award from the Women's Division of the American Jewish Congress; the subject of the award—freedom—enabled him to avoid the Israel-Arab question.

3.

He was anxious that Adlai III attend a father-and-son dinner at the Commercial Club on December 22. Brademas was anxious for him to improve his relations with the Farmers' Union leaders. A political friend sent

him a long memorandum urging the importance of cultivating Lyndon
Johnson, suggesting he persuade Truman to visit Asia when he went to
Europe next spring and summer, and advising Stevenson to stay out of the
Florida primary. Stevenson told Mrs. Ives, *"Very* successful visit to N.Y.
—and the same in Arkansas—but more so!" He told her that Christmas
without her and Ernest for the first time in many years "will be difficult
and a little dreary." Nancy and Adlai would be at Libertyville but Nancy's
parents had decided not to come, in part because they did not wish to stir
up Ellen, who had been quiet lately. His Florida supporters reported enthusiastically such comments as "will sweep Florida" and "appeared a
changed candidate" and "very different situation than 1952" (and
also, "Kefauver still can carry a great TV audience"). He asked Larry
Irvin for advice on Illinois delegates to the National Convention, recalling
previous difficulties with Paul Douglas. He told Paul Douglas he thought
Dirksen would be easer to beat (for the Senate) than Stratton (for Governor).

It was mid-December, almost time for Democratic slate-making. Arthur
Schlesinger sent him a letter from James Wechsler of the New York *Post*
complaining because Stevenson had not spoken out against the murder of
Emmett Till.[2] Stevenson replied with asperity, "I return Mr. Wechsler's letter herewith. No one can approve of the Till case, and anyone can say so,
and say it over and over again." He added that Governor White and many
prominent people in Mississippi had done just that. "I hardly know what
Mr. Wechsler would want me to do, unless it was just shout, which helps
things very little." He was concerned about disfranchisement of Negroes
in Mississippi and had asked Roy Wilkins for legal research on it. In another letter he said he had had "a nice talk" with Wilkins and another talk
with Adam Clayton Powell. He said that in 1952 Dorothy Schiff had told
"her" liberals that Stevenson was insufficiently liberal; now they were telling
her so, she said. Stevenson was always prickly on civil rights. He had a long
lunch with John B. Oakes of the New York *Times* to discuss "moderation"
"and finally convinced [him], I think, that labels are useless except item by
item."

On December 14 he issued a statement saying he would enter primaries
in California, Florida, Pennsylvania, and Illinois, in addition to Minnesota. "These primaries," he said, "were selected to provide for expressions
of preference on a regional basis in the East, Midwest, South and West."
He said he had "reached no final decision" on other primaries. Next day
he received a telegram from Senator Kefauver: "I shall announce my can-

[2] Till, a fourteen-year-old Negro from Chicago, was taken from his bed and beaten
to death while visiting relatives in a Mississippi hamlet. Two white men were tried—
Till was said to have "acted fresh" toward one of their wives—and promptly acquitted by an all-white jury. The defense argued that the body found in a river and
identified as Till's was not in fact Till's and said that the whole affair was a plot by
outsiders to help destroy "the way of life of Southern white people."

didacy for the Democratic nomination tomorrow. I want you to know that my effort will be devoted to pointing out weaknesses in the Republican administration and I shall endeavor to keep and improve the unity which our own Democratic Party has today." Stevenson immediately responded with a statement: "Senator Kefauver is an esteemed friend and I say, come on in; the water's fine. I am glad to hear that he wants to increase the unity and strength of our party. Certainly we shall need unity and strength next November for the important contest." He saw his doctor and went home that night, as he told Mrs. Ives, "to find the tree up, decorated, lighted, and the house garlanded and lovely after a visitation by four self-starting angels—Ellen Smith, Betty Welles, Marion Sudler and Rosalind Oates."

He thanked Mayor Joe Clark of Philadelphia for help on his Miami speech. On December 16 he released to the press a letter he had sent to Senator James E. Murray of Montana thanking him for his support and sharing his concern at the Administration's "giveaway" policies. Governor Freeman of Minnesota reported a Minnesota Congressman's opinion that Republicans were succeeding in efforts to make Stevenson's comments on national issues seem "flippant." He told Herbert Lehman that his reception at the AFL-CIO Convention had been "as warm as anything I have experienced in some time" and the fund-raising luncheon in New York had yielded "almost as much money as I spent in the entire campaign running for Governor in 1948." He had heard that Harriman was "rather bitter" and asked Lehman's advice. Schlesinger warned him that two of Stevenson's friends in Washington were planning to put him into the District of Columbia primary, where, Schlesinger thought, Kefauver would easily win.

Agnes Meyer had sent him a long letter, a Christmas letter endeavoring to express her feelings for him. She wrote, "Adlai—what you have learned or are learning is to love yourself, the essential factor in loving other human beings," and she liked to think that she was responsible. On Monday, the nineteenth, he began a long handwritten reply: "Actually it has been a ghastly 3 months and more, and with all this experience with relentless pressure I sometimes wonder how I can deliberately face what's to come. Duty? Can any impersonal honest sense be so compelling? Vanity? I had thought not, having experienced the honor once before and having dealt with it as well or better than I shall ever be able to again. Yet, vanity it must be. And having long denounced, inwardly and certainly, the presumption, arrogance and insensitivity of any one who would *seek* a Presidential nomination, here I am doing just that!" he stopped writing and resumed the next day, Tuesday, December 20: "It seems incredible that we take this means of preparing a man for a Presidential campaign, not to mention that method of preparing a man for the Presidency!" On Israel, he thought "some temperance in talking to Am. Jews and in their thinking—the Zionists—is the imperative of any progress in my judgment There will have to be give as well as take. . . . Frankly I don't think the

Am. Jews have been helping much in that direction lately. I was one of the 10 members of the U.S. delegation to the UN in 1947 which *literally* created Israel and . . . I don't, *confidentially* like the shouting that has been going on lately aided and abetted by some Democratic senators—Kefauver included. . . . I quietly asserted that it should be the policy of this government not to permit any change in the status quo by force—and the more noisy Zionists have been denouncing me as a traitor ever since, and, frankly, I'm getting damn well fed up with it. . . . Moreover I'm about the only leading Democrat left with whom the Arabs will still talk in confidence."

On Wednesday, December 21, as he walked into his office, Stevenson was told that John Fell had been seriously injured near Goshen, Indiana, in an auto accident on his way home from school. John Fell, by now nineteen and a sophomore at Harvard, had been driving his father's Chevrolet on U.S. 20 east of Goshen with three classmates as passengers. As he came over a hill, a truck, passing another, hit him head on. The two students sitting beside John Fell in the front seat were killed. The one in the back seat was seriously injured. John Fell's right kneecap was shattered, his lower jaw broken, several of his upper teeth knocked out, and his mouth severely lacerated. Stevenson was a friend of the parents of the two dead boys. He immediately called them and offered to take them to Goshen with him. They declined. Stevenson, accompanied by Bill Wirtz, Roger Tubby, Mrs. John Alden Carpenter, and a doctor, flew to Goshen in a chartered plane. They stayed overnight, then the next day brought John Fell to Chicago in an ambulance, accompanied by Adlai III. Ellen Stevenson met them at Passavant Hospital.

It was three days before Christmas. Messages of sympathy poured in from, among many, President Eisenhower, Senator Kefauver, the President of Uruguay. Stevenson cabled Barbara Ward in Accra that John Fell was recovering. Bud Merwin wrote, "Poor kid! what a terrifically sad Christmas this has made for all of you—yet how lucky that he is alive." Stevenson told a friend a little later, "As to John Fell, his body is mending rapidly now, but the spirit will take longer. It was a ghastly experience for all of us and I am the most fortunate parent in the world that he is alive." On Wednesday, Stevenson finished his letter to Agnes Meyer: "He will be alright in time—or almost alright—but who knows what the death of two of his dearest friends beside him in the front seat will mean and do inwardly." He did not say so but must surely have remembered his own childhood accident that resulted in another child's death. Mrs. Meyer called when she heard the news. Truman telephoned, a "most affectionate call," Stevenson thought, and a little later wrote; Stevenson, replying, said, "I was most of all concerned about the psychological injury from the death of his friends. But I am sure he returned without any feeling of self-reproach, in view of the circumstances and the tender concern of so many of his friends."

On Christmas Day, Stevenson wrote to the parents of one of the dead boys, a moving, religious letter invoking the power of faith to console them. So many people sent their sympathy to Stevenson that he replied with printed cards: "While his body is recovering rapidly, the spirit will be slower to mend. But faith and love are healing powers, and there is a great reservoir of both in the world. They are lifting John Fell on a warm, sustaining flood and will restore him in time, I know. Our greater anxiety is that the families of all his beloved friends will be given the strength to live through and beyond this tragedy." He sent one to Alicia Patterson, appending a longhand note: "Somehow the wave of spontaneous love and concern that broke over us after John Fell's accident is about the most affecting thing that has happened to me in 'public life.' "

4.

At the end of the year the feeling was rising that Eisenhower would run. His press secretary, James Hagerty, managed to create the impression that Eisenhower was recovering and was running the country. It was obvious, however, that the Republicans were in no hurry to force a decision. Time was with them—as long as matters lay unresolved, the Democrats had nobody to attack. When Scotty Reston in the New York *Times* noted the increasing impression that Eisenhower would run, the editor of *Holiday* magazine, Ted Patrick, a friend of Tom Finletter, wrote a letter to Reston saying that the press ought to tell the people the truth about Eisenhower's physical condition, that no respectable physician would advise Eisenhower to run again, that Eisenhower would almost surely die in office if reelected, and that a standard medical textbook supported his view despite recent public statements by a doctor attending Eisenhower, Paul Dudley White.

Reston replied, "This is a very serious question, one that has disturbed me, I think, as much as anything since I have been in Washington. Like you, I don't feel easy about this; haven't done so since the beginning." For a time he had thought it "a holding operation," and so justified. "In recent weeks, however, as I reported, there is developing a concerted effort to make him run. He is cooperating with it, and by the general silence of the newspapers throughout the country he and the people are being led to believe that there really isn't a big issue there. . . . It is for [a newspaper] itself, and not for its Washington correspondent to state the policy and make clear the points you have made in your letter. . . . I have felt for some time that Dr. White was not only going beyond his proper bounds as a doctor getting into the political realm, but that he was using his new prominence to argue for pet research projects. Both of these things obviously are improper." Patrick passed the correspondence on to Finletter. It was a question that haunted the politics of 1956.

Larry Irvin had warned Stevenson on December 16 that disgruntled downstate Democrats who disliked Stevenson might use Kefauver's candidacy as a vehicle to embarrass Stevenson in the Illinois primary. Irvin thought this made it all the more important that candidates for Governor and Senator who were unquestionably loyal to Stevenson be slated. He favored Steve Mitchell for Governor. Blair replied that Stevenson had had a two-hour lunch with Dick Daley on December 17 but no decisions had been taken.

Finletter told Harry Ashmore that Thomas E. Murray, a member of the Atomic Energy Commission, would be willing to talk to Stevenson on "the political implications of atomic energy." Finletter also took the unusual step of telling Brademas that he thought Stevenson himself should read a memorandum on national defense prepared by Professor Samuel P. Huntington of Harvard. (Stevenson had been swamped by the Finletter Group's production and unable to read much of it.)

Dore Schary advised Stevenson to speak more slowly on television and to resist any efforts by TV "experts" to put pancake make-up on him. He also reported that many people wondered if Truman really was for Stevenson. Stevenson agreed that he should speak more slowly and thought the only solution was to write shorter speeches—"I always attempt to get too much into a speech." He thought Truman would maintain a public impression of neutrality in order to serve as conciliator. He was receiving letters from a variety of people around the country—Congressmen, professors, ordinary citizens—hailing his announcement that he would run. Chester Bowles reported that he had seen General Douglas MacArthur and that MacArthur was "about as" violently opposed to Eisenhower as to Truman, considered Dulles the worst Secretary of State "in several generations," believed Stevenson would "almost certainly" be nominated and elected, and asked if he could see Stevenson next time Stevenson came to New York. Bowles thought such a visit might be risky—"Truman and Harriman would almost surely use it to prove that you are not really a reliable Democrat" but added that, "strange as it may sound, I believe he can be induced to come out for you next fall—and that might influence some votes."

5.

The year 1956, the year of the primaries and general election, was one of the most hectic in Stevenson's life. That spring he campaigned heavily in contested primaries in four states and his name was on the ballot in others. From the end of January until the last primary, on June 5, he traveled almost ceaselessly and made hundreds of speeches. He had not wanted to enter the primaries but felt obliged to because of other candidates and in order to "surround himself with an aura of victory," as Carl

McGowan put it, to dispel any tinge of defeat that lingered from 1952. By his tireless travels and speeches he would also create a picture of a vigorous man in robust health to contrast to the aging and ailing President. Starting on January 4, each day's schedule was crowded—so crowded that one insistent Chicago liberal who managed to see him on January 20, for example, was accorded but five minutes. Earlier in the year he saw newspaper columnists and magazine writers individually, and this way produced many thoughtful essays and "exclusive" interviews but at considerable cost to himself.

In January and February, Stevenson rounded out his staff. On January 15 he entertained several moneyed men at dinner in Libertyville, including George McGhee, Dwight Palmer, George Killion (a West Coast shipping power), Albert Greenfield, and Roger Stevens. Stevens had already begun work as the principal fund raiser. He once said the primaries cost about a million dollars.

During the fall campaign Roger Stevens became chairman of the finance committee of the Democratic Party. He and Matt McCloskey often disagreed but managed to work together. McGhee and George Ball were active in fund-raising too. Stevens recalled that the party spent about $4 million in the September-October general election campaign, including money channeled through several national committees but not including local spending or labor's spending.[3]

In January, Stevenson had dinner at Libertyville with Golda Myerson, then Israeli Labor Minister, later Golda Meir and Prime Minister; Judge Fisher, and others; lunched with the French Ambassador; attended Britannica Board meetings; dined with Finnegan and Raskin; received politicians from various states; saw Barry Bingham with a group from Iowa and a group of farmers' coop leaders, met with Mayor Daley and other Illinois

[3] Among the large contributors were Agnes Meyer, Mary Lasker, Lansdell K. Christie (a mining company executive), George Killion, Ellie Heller (wife of a West Coast executive), and Jacob Blaustein, the oilman. A member of the Reynolds Metals family contributed $50,000 to the primary campaign and $50,000 to the fall campaign, Stevens said. He also said that Stevenson received almost no Texas oil money. "Once Matt [McCloskey] went to Texas with high hopes. I think he got $5,000. We got quite a lot in Washington. Nothing out of Oregon. Chicago was very disappointing. We didn't get really big money out of Lake Forest. New York, according to De Sapio, was the big spot. We took a million and a quarter out of New York. New York was the center of rich liberals, all of whom loved Adlai. It's interesting that a man who is rich and liberal is usually freer with his money than one who is rich and Republican." Stevenson's law firm suffered from his political activity: it received only $89,465 in fees in 1956 compared with $126,527 the year before, and of this two clients contributed $65,000—$40,000 came from Leon Tempelsman & Son and $25,000 from Reynolds Metals Company. The firm had only six other clients—Illinois Bell Telephone Company, $4,500; the Stevenson-Kefauver Campaign Committee, $3,000; the Lindsay Chemical Company, $1,000; Burr Tillstrom, $1,300; McKinney Trust, $300; and Ella Shure Cahen, $200. (Wirtz also served two labor arbitration clients—U. S. Rubber, $14,065, and the Franklin Association, $100.)

politicians, all in preparation for the campaign. Often Bill Wirtz or another close associate sat in on the meetings. The staff prepared a list of Stevenson fans in show business and the arts, including Ava Gardner, Shelley Winters, Lauren Bacall, Vanessa Brown, Yul Brynner, Gottfried Reinhardt, Dorothy Sarnoff, Philip Dunne, Joan Fontaine, Brooks Atkinson, Tallulah Bankhead, and Eddie Fisher. Blair kept in touch with them.

On January 3, Stevenson suggested to Truman that the ex-President travel to Asia in connection with his forthcoming spring and summer trip to Europe, saying that Russia was making progress in Asia and the Administration "would have to publicly welcome" such a trip as "tangible bipartisanship." (Although Stevenson told Truman his letter was filled with "impetuosity and spontaneity," he rewrote it carefully in longhand from a dictated draft.) Truman declined the suggestion: "The present administration's objective obviously is to try to discredit almost every one of my actions, both domestic and foreign."

A friend in Florida warned that truckers there, learning of Stevenson's record as Governor, would work against him in the primary. Stevenson told Blair to ask a friendly Chicago trucker for help, first clearing it with Mayor Daley. Max Ascoli, a Stevenson supporter in 1952, published an open letter to Stevenson in the *Reporter* (of which he was editor), comparing the Stevenson of 1956 unfavorably with the Stevenson of 1952 and saying that many Stevenson men from 1952 were reluctant to support him now because he was reported to be in the hands of professional politicians and in danger of yielding to the pressures of special interest groups. He also urged Stevenson not to fear "talking over the people's heads" and to denounce to the fullest and immediately the Eisenhower-Dulles foreign policy, going far beyond a denunciation of "unleashing" and "agonizing reappraisal," even though advised that nobody was interested in foreign affairs. Stevenson sent Ascoli a private reply on January 3, saying that he was essentially unchanged from 1952 except aged by "time, weariness and long-sustained responsibility." He wrote, "I am not conscious of much pressure from any direction about anything, unless it is that I must spend less time writing and rewriting and more time politicking and talking with people. . . . I suppose you are right about the 'reluctance' of some of my old friends to support me. . . . I am sorry, and I wish I knew what to do about it. But, surely, the reason cannot be any confusion about my views on foreign affairs. . . . After all, I have lectured, talked and published on that subject incessantly for the past three years. . . . Maybe I have misunderstood you, but on that score your piece made me wonder a little if anyone had been listening to me during these long, weary years."

Hubert Humphrey, responding to a Stevenson letter, stated his own position on Israel. He respected Stevenson's "restraint" and "deep concern" but said the United States should "stand by" Israel, should have a "strong economic policy for both the Arab states and Israel," should not be "blackmailed" by Soviet aid into giving Egypt economic aid; should stop acting on the basis of "expediency" and should not start "walking out on Israel and then trying to make a hasty-patchup job of economic and diplomatic relationships with Egypt." Stevenson replied, "I guess *we* don't disagree at all on Israel, but I am afraid that many Zionists in this country disagree with *us*."

Stevenson told Adlai III that John Fell would return to Cambridge on January 8 and asked Adlai III to meet him at the airport and help him get settled back in college. He told Mrs. Ives, who was at Southern Pines, "His right leg is in a cast from the hip to the ankle, and he has some fine temporary false teeth and a sturdy cane. Beyond that, no scars are visible and the healing of the face has been remarkable. His spirits are good and I think he has weathered the emotional trauma well." To Agnes Meyer; "My beloved John Fell I brought home tonight in a cast and sparkling with some fine false teeth. I am the luckiest happiest living mortal this very night." She had sent him a 16-page longhand letter on her sixty-ninth birthday. She discussed his reasons for running: "Neither duty nor vanity is the final answer. In your case as in mine it is the instinctive drive of persons with a distinguished background to exercise their God-given inherited talents and capacities. If you are a natural leader, Adlai, it is not merely a matter of brains and courage and moral fortitude. It is something in the blood. . . . I am sure most of your forebears were distinguished people and so were mine. . . . There is such a thing as 'noblesse oblige.' We are both aristocrats who are as definitely propelled toward leadership as any of the ancient regime. . . . Oh, I too feel pangs of commiseration when I consider the unusually long haul that lies before you. But it's all so gallant, Adlai."

Stevenson asked Bill Blair to talk to Doug Anderson, Senator Douglas' aide, about Illinois delegates to the National Convention. At the same time he sent a memorandum to Mayor Daley asking him to consider appointing to the Illinois delegation Hy Raskin, Dick Babcock, Don Forsyth (a Springfield insurance man), Larry Irvin, and Lou Kohn. In the memorandum Stevenson made cryptic reference to slating candidates for Senator and Governor. He added, "I appreciate your keeping me informed, but I know how busy you are and it isn't necessary. I know you will do what's best, in the long view too." Stevenson asked Ben Swig of the Fairmont Hotel to be his finance chairman in the California primary. Congressman James Roosevelt offered to support Stevenson in the California primary although he had supported Kefauver in 1952. Stevenson replied rather coolly. Former Vice President Wallace offered to help Stevenson after the conventions in a "quiet, non-political way" although he refused to be called either a Democrat or a Republican, insisting he was an independent and would vote for Eisenhower. Stevenson replied noncommittally.

On Sunday, January 8, Stevenson appeared on a CBS-TV network interview program, "Face the Nation." Most of the questions dealt with his candidacy, though he did manage to talk a little about massive retaliations and other Eisenhower slogans he criticized. He said he would not enter the New Hampshire primary because of prior commitments (actually, New Hampshire was Kefauver territory). A reporter on the panel said Stevenson had been asked to shake hands at plant gates in Minnesota—was this "humanizing" activity essential? Stevenson said he had campaigned that way all over Illinois in 1948. Could the President's health be kept out of the campaign? "Well, it certainly will be kept out of my campaign." Could it be kept out by other Democrats? "Well, that I can't say. I can't underwrite that, but I personally pray—and I mean that with all sincerity— for the President's health, not only because he is President but because he is a fine citizen of our country."

Soon, however, Stevenson quarreled openly with his questioners, not only with John Madigan, at that time with *Newsweek* but formerly a gadfly newspaperman in Springfield while Stevenson was Governor, but also with Cabell Phillips of the New York *Times.* At one point Stevenson and the questioners were all talking at once and what they said could not be understood. Phillips and Rowland Evans, of the New York *Herald Tribune,* sought to bring Stevenson into a clear confrontation with Eisenhower on the nation's defense strength, and at length Stevenson flatly disagreed with Phillips' statement that "our system of collective security is stronger now than it was a year or three years ago." Once Stevenson interrupted a question and said stiffly, "Yes. Very well. If you will permit me, I will explain my views." Madigan tried to surprise him with a question about the forthcoming natural gas bill; Stevenson was well prepared for it. Madigan asked if he thought he could carry Illinois after losing it by 350,000 or 400,000 in 1952. Stevenson interrupted: "I carried it in 1948 by 575,000." Madigan said, "For Governor. Do you think you can carry it for President this time?" The nomination came first, Stevenson said.

Afterward, Lawrence Spivak, moderator of "Meet the Press," told Stevenson that if he appeared on "Meet the Press" the panel "will not affront you" as he implied had occurred on "Face the Nation." Stevenson received favorable comment on his appearance. But Arthur Schlesinger, who visited Stevenson at the time, found him "furious" over the treatment he had received. Schlesinger noted in his journal: "[He] felt it was cheap, undignified and useless; and had to be dissuaded from writing a letter to Frank Stanton about it. This led him into a general explosion about the irritations of being a candidate: the things people wanted him to do (as, for instance, going to Minnesota to file as a candidate; or serving as a disc jockey for half an hour for the March of Dimes); the pressures on him to take positions (he seemed particularly annoyed at the Zionists); the staff problems; above all, the question of speeches. At one point he said, 'Strictly off the record and just between us, I would get out of this in a minute if I could!' (I don't think that he really meant a word of this; it was a form of blowing off steam.)" Despite his assurance to friends that John Fell's recovery was complete, Stevenson told Schlesinger, "But he

will always bear the scars of this. It will be an eternal nightmare for him."
He was disappointed at Harry Ashmore's failure to buckle down and
write, as Schlesinger put it; among all the writers, he seemed to have full
confidence only in Wirtz. He was irritated by New York politics, telling
Schlesinger, "Formerly, I was greatly interested in what was going on in
New York, what Averell was up to, what our people were doing. But I
can't follow it any more. It is all too complicated. As for Averell, I have
absolutely no interest in him, his motives or his intentions." He seemed to
fear that Finnegan, whom he otherwise praised highly, "might be somewhat taken in by De Sapio." He spoke strongly about the need to take economic aid in the underdeveloped world out of a military framework but he
said of Chet Bowles, "I always go along with Chet up to a point; then he
becomes too soft and sentimental for me; and he always ends up with the
implication that the solution lies in spending more money." Stevenson said
Bowles had offered to come out in the spring and work full time; he was
inclined to accept his offer but to decline one from George Ball because,
Schlesinger thought, Stevenson felt his own staff opposed Ball. He sympathized with Eisenhower's cuts in the defense budget, said he himself would
not believe anything the generals and admirals told him, and said he would
like to take a large slice out of their budget. He showed more interest in
disarmament than ever before, Schlesinger thought, and seemed interested
in working out a disarmament program and turning it into an important
issue.

That same day, January 8, President Eisenhower held his first press
conference since summer. It took place at Key West on the eve of his return to Washington to assume again the "full duties of the presidency." He
would not say whether he had reached a conclusion about whether to run
again. Sparring with reporters, he said he had "not made up my mind to
make any announcement as of this moment," said "it is a very critical
thing to change governments" in mid-term and he agreed with Dr. White
that "hard work never killed a healthy man," but added, "my mind at this
moment is not fixed." He declined to promise a firm answer in March as
he had promised earlier. He sounded like a candidate.

6.

Senator Lehman now responded to Stevenson's letter of December 17
about Harriman. He had not discussed the political situation directly with
Harriman but had heard he was, unfortunately, not "too happy" about it.
Lehman felt "quite strongly" that for the sake of success in November
every effort must be made to maintain relations on as cordial a basis as
possible. He was sure Stevenson would keep this in mind and urge restraint on his friends in New York whose enthusiasm might lead them to

open wounds that would hurt next fall. Stevenson replied, "I emphatically agree. . . . This is the trouble with primaries."

Look magazine asked Stevenson—and six other candidates—what each would do, as President, if a Southern state refused to comply with a federal court order to desegregate its schools. It was a particularly cruel issue for a candidate running in the primaries of both Florida and California. Minow and Brademas drafted a reply, and Stevenson rewrote it carefully, blurring his position. The final draft said:

"You ask me to assume that Americans will deliberately violate the law of the land. This pessimistic assumption is contrary to our history, our traditions, and our basic concepts of what is right. I once said that I do not agree with those who charge that the South—or any group of Americans —is wedded to wrong and incapable of right. For this itself is an expression of prejudice compounded with hatred.

"There will be a period of time during which the Supreme Court's decision will be implemented in different ways in the various states. In some areas there will be long resistance to any sudden change in ancient customs. But the progress already made in altering traditions and practices older than the Republic is very reassuring. As time goes on all Americans will, I think, accept and abide by the law of the land and the right of every child to equal opportunity for education will be honored in full.

"I cannot foretell what a President would or should do in the hypothetical circumstances you suggest, nor am I fully informed on the law and precedents, if any. But I do know that it is the President's duty under the Constitution to 'take care that the laws be faithfully executed.' "

The last paragraph was nearly all Stevenson's own. Minow and Brademas had written instead: "It seems to me obvious that the man who becomes the next President of the United States—whoever he may be—will act promptly and vigorously to fulfill his duties under the Constitution to 'take care that the laws be faithfully executed,'" a stronger position. Stevenson was turning toward gradualism on desegregation. The issue haunted him through the primaries. This particular reply never saw the light of day. But such requests sometimes occupied staff members for several days and Stevenson himself for many hours. Other politicians and their staffs handled such requests more rapidly and offhandedly. But for Stevenson, anything on paper required close attention, and Stevenson, with his lawyer's training, and his associates with theirs, set great store by what he had already said on the record. If the necessity arose to break new ground on a question on which he had previously taken only a partial position, the task might take days. From his previous utterances his research staff compiled an encyclopedia of his views, issue by issue, and updated it as the spring primaries wore on, so that by summer they had another set of the thick books called the "Adlaipedia."

Vanessa Brown, the actress, urged Stevenson to appear periodically on a television show, using his home as the setting. He replied on January 10,

"While I agree with you that the little details about one's life seem to be a useful means of popularizing a person, I am sure you will agree with me that it is also almost intolerably distasteful to be so perpetually exposed. The newspaper diagrams of President Eisenhower's insides not long ago seem to me to have exceeded the tolerance." That morning, he said, he had looked up momentarily aboard the commuter train and a flashbulb had gone off in his face. The photographer said, "Just wanted to show you riding with the common people, Gov." Stevenson wrote, "I had thought I had been riding with the common people all my life, but I guess we have to prove it every few minutes." To Agnes Meyer on January 11, "You are not only a remarkable woman, you are an heroic Christian—'There is no freedom except through loving and being loved which results from unselfish giving of one's whole soul.' I know this, I really know it; my mother, sister, ministers galore have told it to me. I've, what's more, discovered it for myself. But somehow I needed awfully to be told it again just now. . . . And now Goldie Myerson and a bunch of Zionists are at the gate and I must leap from you and charity, beauty, love, understanding to the statesman role! Can I? 'Yes, you can,' she said. (But can I keep awake is another question.)" After dinner with Mrs. Myerson, Stevenson told Rabbi Jacob Weinstein he had been surprised to find her more rigid than Eban.

He sometimes involved himself in the tasks of organization which were being handled by Finnegan, Blair, and others. He fretted about issues. James P. Warburg, a businessman and prolific writer, urged him to issue short statements on current events, and Stevenson told him he would like to, but "I have little in the way of creative staff to help contrive them." New York continued to be troublesome. Finletter reported that De Sapio was concerned mainly about local primary fights, including one in De Sapio's own assembly district. Finletter assured him that the Stevenson people had no intention of making primary fights. De Sapio also suggested that by about April it should become clear whether Stevenson's or Harriman's candidacy was going well, and if one was not he might support the other. Finletter doubted Harriman would withdraw. He also did not see how the candidates could know who was ahead by April, since by then only the New Hampshire and Minnesota primaries would have been held —Wisconsin was to come in April but Florida, Oregon, and California would vote in May and June.

On January 17, Stevenson flew early in the morning to Minneapolis to file as a presidential candidate in the Minnesota primary. He had been scheduled to shake hands at the Minneapolis-Honeywell plant gate at 6:30 A.M. but canceled that appearance and arrived later, met with Governor Orville Freeman and other Democratic leaders in the Governor's office at the state capitol in St. Paul, filed as a candidate with the Minnesota Secretary of State, attended a luncheon meeting in St. Paul, and, in the afternoon, held a press conference at the state capitol, visited the Ford plant in

St. Paul to shake hands at shift-change time, met with Stevenson Volunteer groups, attended a reception in a hotel from 5:30 to 7 P.M., dined, and returned to Chicago late that night. He told Governor Freeman, "It was a grand day. . . . What's left of me is grateful."

Schlesinger, just back from California, reported that people there thought Stevenson was ahead but must not underestimate Kefauver, who would portray himself as the underdog frozen out by the party organization. Kefauver would have formidable support and plenty of money from various people, including Ed Pauley, an oilman, who wanted to stop Stevenson in California in the hope of nominating Symington. The key question for Stevenson, as Schlesinger saw it, was how to employ the California Democratic Council. Since ward and precinct organizations were almost nonexistent in California, and since California laws encouraged the fragmentation of political parties, the clubs which comprised the Council represented the most important element in the Democratic Party. The Council would hold its convention soon in Fresno, and Stevenson was scheduled to address them, one of the most important of all spring speeches. The Council members were among Stevenson's most ardent supporters; some were restless, eager to endorse him, and a floor motion at their convention for endorsement might sweep the convention, whatever the leadership wanted.

Schlesinger went on, "The tone of the speech might be simple, direct, rather personal; warm and self-revelatory in its approach rather than focussing on issues. And, while praising Kefauver generously and cordially (and he well deserves it for his senatorial record), the speech might well imply a contrast between his approach to the Presidency and your own. . . . What is the status of the Stevenson image at the moment? So far as I can gather, there is a spreading impression something like this: that in 1952 you were a man who said and did what you thought right regardless of political consequences; but that now you are being surrounded by professional politicians and that you are tempering your utterances to political considerations."

Two California issues illustrated the point—natural gas and civil rights. One Californian had told Schlesinger that Stevenson's statement on natural gas on "Face the Nation" had sounded like Eisenhower while, on civil rights, Californians thought that Kefauver was taking a more forthright position than Stevenson. Schlesinger also urged a "revival of the Stevenson wit" and said, "You must appear to enjoy politics, and your humor, I think, is an indispensable part of your appeal."

At about this time Seymour Harris of Harvard found himself at a luncheon sitting next to Kefauver's campaign manager, who innocently revealed Kefauver's strategy: to concentrate on Florida, playing to the "Georgia crackers" who dwelt there upstate. (Harris was embarrassed and gave Schlesinger a memo on the conversation with a note saying he did "not know enough about political morality to know whether this information should be passed along." Schlesinger sent it to Blair with a note, "I have none of Seymour's scruples.") At the same time Bobby Baker, Secretary for the Majority in the Senate, told Harry Ashmore that Senator Smathers of Florida believed Kefauver was making headway in Florida because Stevenson and Blair had offended the working press during their last visit there by making Stevenson inaccessible and because Stevenson had not courted the Jewish people sufficiently in Miami. Ashmore told Baker he had been along on the Florida trip and could not understand the allegation that Stevenson had been rude or unavailable to the press. Baker was offended. Ashmore sent him a mollifying letter.

Stevenson asked Herbert Agar for a draft on "The Image of America" for delivery before the American Society of Newspaper Editors on April 21, a speech which Stevenson regarded as one of his three or four "major efforts" during the primary campaign.

Secretary Dulles discussed in an article in *Life* magazine the "art" of going to the "brink" of war. The article aroused a storm. In it Dulles said that Eisenhower had decided to use tactical atomic bombs against mainland China if hostilities broke out after the truce talks in Korea, that Dulles had recommended sending American ground forces—along with British and French and friendly Asian forces—into Indochina in order to prevent a "domino effect" in Southeast Asia, and that Dulles had drafted the congressional resolution on Quemoy-Matsu, authorizing the President to use U.S. military forces should the mainland Chinese attack Formosa. Dulles wrote, "You have to take chances for peace, just as you must take chances in war. Some say that we were brought to the verge of war. The ability to get to the verge without getting into the war is the necessary art. If you cannot master it, you inevitably get into war. If you try to run away from it, if you are scared to go to the brink, you are lost. We've had to look it square in the face—on the question of enlarging the Korean war, on the question of getting into the Indochina war, on the question of Formosa. We walked to the brink and we looked it in the face. We took strong action. It took a lot more courage for the President than for me." Stevenson promptly called on Eisenhower to repudiate or fire Dulles and in private correspondence referred repeatedly to the "latest Dulles gaffe."

At about the same time General Matthew B. Ridgway, former Army Chief of Staff, said in an article in the *Saturday Evening Post* that he had dissented from the defense recommendations sent to Congress in January 1954—President Eisenhower had said the defense program had been unanimously recommended by the Joint Chiefs of Staff. On January 18, Scotty Reston of the New York *Times* wrote that Eisenhower would have to deal with the questions at his press conference the next day, the first since his return to the White House, and said that the capital had been "bombarded" with questions from foreign offices around the world asking "whether the leader of the free world coalition actually decided, in certain circumstances, to wage an atomic war, without letting them know such a decision was taken." Eisenhower, however, at his press conference on January 19, did not face the questions squarely. He opened by reading a telegram he had sent to an official in New Hampshire, where petitions had been filed qualifying him for a place on the Republican primary ballot. He told New Hampshire that he would interpose no objection to appearing on the ballot but wanted everybody to know that this did not indicate a "final decision" to run. He went on, "It would be idle to pretend that my health can be wholly restored to the excellent state in which the doctors believed it to be in mid-September. At the same time, my doctors report to me that the progress I am making toward a reasonable level of strength is normal and satisfactory. My future life must be carefully regulated to avoid excessive fatigue." After reading the telegram Eisenhower told the press he would answer no "personal political questions." The press asked them anyway, or skirted them. The questioning then turned to the Dulles piece in *Life.* A reporter asked if any decision had been reached to use the atomic bomb in the instances cited. Eisenhower said he had not read the article, refused to dignify a "privately written article" and give it the status of a state paper, refused to discuss decisions taken in the National Security Council, and said he had "complete faith" in Dulles: "I do not know whether they were unfortunate expressions used in that article by him or by someone reporting them. But I know he is devoted to peace . . . the best Secretary of State I have ever known." Asked about the Ridgway article, he denied making a military decision on the basis of domestic politics, referred questioners to Admiral Radford and Secretary Wilson, said for years he had received and disregarded advice from military subordinates, and said, "People in authority must make decisions based on the best advice they get." During the campaign Stevenson frequently criticized Dulles for employing "brinkmanship" instead of "statesmanship."

Stevenson told Agnes Meyer on January 22, "I wonder . . . if the full implications of the Dulles story and the Pres' statement that he didn't know what he said, have been considered. Sometimes I get a little frightened—and when I do I feel very lonesome because no one else does or seems to and I suspect I must get things all out of proportion." He adds a postscript, "How do you think my campaign's going? Honestly? I get a little worried, altho we're beginning to get some money and therefore some staff." And yet another postscript: "Lord—How you can write!!"

On January 23, Stevenson sent a long and carefully drafted message to the forty-ninth annual meeting of the American Jewish Committee. He was on solid ground in praising unstintingly the AJC's work on behalf of civil liberties and against the restrictive McCarran-Walter Immigration Act. When he turned to Israel, his discomfort under Zionist pressure showed. He praised the AJC's efforts "to make secure the State of Israel," recalled his own role at the UN in establishing Israel, said the United States Government should arrest "the frightening tensions in the Middle East, not only for the sake of Israel but its Arab neighbors as well," and recommended, "A first step, as I have said before, should be the re-straining effect of an equitable balance of armed strength between Israel and her neighbors. And I think that the security of all of these states should be guaranteed by the United States, and also by France and Britain who joined with us in the tripartite declaration against change by force. I have suggested, too, that one way to make such a guarantee effective would be to keep Israeli and Arab forces apart by substituting United Nations patrols in the areas of tension and collision on the borders. . . . I think this country should reassert its fundamental friendship for both Israel and the Arab states. . . . Once the Arab states recognize and accept the permanency of Israel, then the real community of self-interest in the Middle East would become apparent and we can help solve the border adjustments, refugee resettlement and other obstacles to . . . peace and economic progress." He had the message mimeographed for distribution in the hope of quieting Zionist criticism.[4]

When Jack Arvey sent Finnegan a sample of anti-Stevenson mail he had been receiving from Jewish friends, saying the letters caused him "nervousness, apprehension and fear," Finnegan responded with mimeographed copies of Stevenson's correspondence with Jewish leaders and the exchange between Rabbis Weinstein and Fine. Finletter showed the letters to Ambassador Eban and reported he was "very pleased." Many Jews, however, remained unconvinced. In 1952, Stevenson had been able to win Jewish votes by his dedication to civil liberties during the McCarthy period. In 1956, however, the fulcrum on which the Jewish vote turned was different: Israel's survival.

Jacob Weinstein years later, after Stevenson's death, recalled, "The newly established state of Israel was still on shaky legs and ardent Zionists were eager to get the firmest commitments from candidate Stevenson. They were so absorbed in the rightness of their cause and so completely persuaded that any right-thinking man would see eye to eye with them that they were often impatient with the Governor's insistence on objectivity and his image of himself as one who might be in the mediator's position as President and therefore not free to show too partisan a hand. . . . He was awkward in the presence of that free-wheeling, loose-lipped camaraderie that floats about Irish politicians in their cups. He was equally awkward in the presence of Jewish emotion."

Tom Finletter thought many people considered Eisenhower "a man of

---

4 At about the same time he wrote to Abraham Feinberg, president of the Development Corporation for Israel, setting forth his position on Israel, and this letter, too, was mimeographed for distribution. Rabbi Jacob Weinstein, no doubt at the behest of Stevenson or his staff, wrote a long letter to a California rabbi, Alvin I. Fine: "When I was with you at the Histadrut rally a few weeks ago, you conveyed to me some of the doubts and criticisms you have been hearing concerning Adlai Stevenson's attitude to Israel. I expressed my firm confidence in his stand . . . and promised you that I would document this judgment." He proceeded to do so, using Stevenson's recent statements and earlier speeches and offering personal testimonials.

peace" and Stevenson one who carried a "big stick": "This peace issue is of absolutely first importance and the more the Governor comes out with a real backing for this disarmament program, the better it will be." Stevenson thought to speak on defense and foreign policy on February 25 at a Jefferson-Jackson Day dinner, but he was urged instead to a more important and non-partisan audience, the American Society of Newspaper Editors on April 21.

7.

On January 23, Stevenson left Chicago and flew westward on his first campaign trip of 1956. He went to Tucson, next day drove to Phoenix and spent a week at Bill Benton's home, writing, answering correspondence, and preparing for California. Blair and Carol Evans were with him. He was traveling by commercial plane. Usually he was unaccompanied by newspapermen. He was operating without expert advance men; instead, he relied on local people to arrange his visits. In Arizona, Blair received a letter from a friend in San Francisco who warned of trouble in California— Republican newspapers would support Kefauver and his claim that Stevenson was the creature of party bosses. Senator Hubert Humphrey warned of the same trouble in Minnesota: "I am irked with Estes. He plays this underdog role to a point where it grates on my nerves. This fellow is going to take a licking in Minnesota. The one danger that we face lies in the possibility of Republicans moving into our primary and voting for Kefauver. . . . Every single newspaper in Minnesota will be giving him the breaks. The Republican high command for the first time in a year sees an opportunity."

Stevenson flew over a flooded area in northern California and in Sacramento held a press conference, attended a farm meeting and a reception, and in the evening spoke at the state fair grounds. On Wednesday, February 1, he saw an executive of the McClatchy newspapers and campaigned in the San Francisco Bay area at a luncheon, receptions, and box supper. His speeches were "image" talks intended not to take up concrete issues but to project Stevenson, the candidate. In his opening remarks at the Oakland Municipal Auditorium he sought at length to identify himself with his audience, saying he was not one who believed that organized labor was a "menace to society" or that all students were "dangerous" or all professors "subversive"—the audience contained all these groups. He returned to the wit of 1952 with the line, "Eggheads of the world arise," followed by "I was even going to add that you have nothing to lose but your yolks." He talked about the growth of California and American society and of the world's population, about "mass education" and "conformity," about the world-wide "rising revolution of expectancy," about Republican failures. He skipped lightly from one point to another, developing none fully. Near the end he said, "But I have neglected to say to you why I am here tonight. I said a great deal—probably more than I intended—but I suppose I should confess that I am here seeking the presidency of the United States [*applause*]. I'm glad you approve [*laughter*]. I did not say that I am qualified for the presidency of the United States and if anyone says to you that he is, will you tell him that he lacks the first qualification, which is humility [*applause*]. But I do say to you that I am available [*laughter*]. I do say to you that there are others like yourself who have urged me again to seek an office that beggars human ambition and that exceeds human capacity. And I shall do so gladly and I hope in good spirit; I hope with wisdom and certainly with an everlasting and patient concern for what lies in the heart of all we undertake in public life in America—and that is, the welfare of the United States and all of its citizens."

He spent that night at the Fairmont Hotel, campaigned in the Bay area the next two days, and then went to Fresno to speak to the California Democratic Council (CDC) convention. This was the most important speech of the trip. Months earlier Alan Cranston, president of the CDC, had invited him to make it; in the interim, no speech had received more attention from Stevenson and his associates.

It turned out to be another image speech, a speech about "our concepts and convictions about America and our time on earth." He referred to the talk about "the new Stevenson which is shortly to be unveiled" and swiftly told a joke as though to defy those friends who advised him to eschew wit. He denounced Republican hucksterism, then said the campaign must "deal with the great issues of our time" and listed them. He briefly attacked Dulles' "intemperance" in the *Life* article and the Republican "drumbeat" that the United States was prosperous and at peace. He attacked complacency, security, and stagnation. He claimed for the Democrats credit for Social Security, public housing, minimum wages, farm income supports, resource development, and federal aid to education and medical care. By quoting Toynbee on "the family of man," and in such phrases as "no nation can survive . . . which dares not dream" and "faith in ourselves, not in dictators or symbols or images, but in each other," he attempted to return to the rhetorical heights of 1952. The speech was a political disaster. Stevenson had come to California with the support of members of the CDC, many of them young, intellectual, and suburban. He had received numerous speech drafts and in Arizona had started putting them together and had ended by writing virtually an entire new speech. Blair said later that he had begun to worry shortly before the speech when Stevenson told him this would be the best speech he ever had given. It was lofty, thoughtful, and almost nobody in California liked it. They referred to it as "the Fresno Fiasco." Kefauver spoke the same day Stevenson did, delivered an all-out attack on the Republicans, and took the CDC by storm. From that day on, all through the long spring primary, Stevenson was fighting to regain the ground he had held before Fresno. On few occasions has a single speech made more difference. It helps explain Kefauver's sudden ascendancy in California in February and March—after the Minnesota primary, Kefauver turned a California trip into a victory tour, for the volatile California electorate, regarding Stevenson as a has-been because of his Fresno speech, turned wholeheartedly to Kefauver.

Eugene Meyer printed the full text in the Washington *Post,* telling Stevenson, "Personally, I may say that I felt it was on a new level." But Stevenson, while thanking Meyer, told Mrs. Meyer, "Here among the intense young liberals it missed the mark. Evidently what they want to hear about is civil rights, minorities, Israel and little else, and certainly no vague futures." Pat Brown loyally told him that the rest of California and the United States had liked the speech even though it had not pleased "the reckless demands of a majority of those at the convention." Stevenson later told Lauren Bacall, "I *was* depressed about the reaction to the Fresno speech when I saw you in Los Angeles. I thought it was good, philosophical, forward looking, and the kind of thing that the eager young liberals would like to hear instead of a sterile recitation of traditional Democratic positions. I was wrong, I guess, but there were plenty of good reactions from the audience around the country, which comforted me."

A Stevenson supporter from Los Angeles told Stevenson he was deserting him for Kefauver because in 1956 Stevenson's speeches "seem to lack the old vigor," Stevenson sounded like a professor of political science rather than a candidate, and "we want to vote for you *because* of Dixon-Yates and *because* Charlie Wilson represents big business rather than the people, not because Dixon-Yates or Charlie Wilson symbolize an undemocratic philosophy of government. . . . I was a little disappointed in Senator Kefauver's corny poetry [in his peroration] . . . but I was aghast at your quoting Arnold Toynbee. Sure, we want a government by egg heads . . . but must we rub the average unsophisticated Democrat's fur the wrong way by being so esoteric?" Stevenson, by then back home, thanked him and said, "I was not informed that the Fresno Convention wanted a speech denouncing the Republicans and reaffirming traditional Democratic party positions. This I have been doing day after day for the past three years," and he enclosed, as he did in letters to other critics, a copy of a letter from a Republican who admired the Fresno speech. No matter. A woman from Pasadena who had attended the Fresno convention said she had seen Stevenson buttons falling there "like autumn leaves."

His friend Gilbert Harrison, publisher of the *New Republic,* criticized the speech in a long letter, saying that Californians thought they knew what he was and wanted to know where he stood. Stevenson began a long reply, "I have had your letter in my pocket for weeks of weary traveling and endless battering in the West." He acknowledged that the speech had failed but said he had been told in advance that "warmed-over New Deal" was not enough and that he should "try to do something 'good, uplifting, forward looking' with these young, visionary Democrats." He said that "the one thing I need is a little advance notice as to my audiences. I am afraid the answer to that would be to make the same speech in a primary —hot partisan and warmed-over New Deal is good enough. But there are sometimes vast radio and TV audiences, such as the one in Fresno. I have to think about that too. . . . I wish to hell you would send me along some textual suggestions that I could use. I am more bereft of writing talent than you suspect, and I usually end up late at night biting my pencil and trying to keep awake, with the press clamoring in the bar nearby for an advance, something some of the other candidates don't have to worry about too much."

From Fresno, Stevenson went to Los Angeles for two and a half days of campaigning on February 5–7: breakfast meetings, luncheons, press conferences, picnics, university visit, receptions, private finance meetings, a birthday party—he was fifty-six years old that Sunday, February 5. One stop was at a breakfast given by Dore Schary and others at the Hillcrest Country Club in Los Angeles, a fund-raising affair for wealthy Jews. Some of the questions verged on the hostile. It was probably of this occasion that Roger Stevens recalled later, "We raised $55,000 or $60,000 but it was very unpleasant. He didn't want to be pinned down on Israel." Newt Minow said years later he had never detected any anti-Jewish sentiments in Stevenson. "He thought the Jews were friendly," he said. "But he resented their pressure on him to make speeches. For that matter, he didn't like pressure from Jewish groups, or unionists or businessmen, or any other pressure group. But look what he did with his own life. He chose me as a partner. He merged later with a firm that's half Jewish. Some years ago I was invited to join the Legal Club. It's the younger lawyers from the bigger firms. It had never had a Jewish member. The president, Ed Stephan, said that they wanted me to be the guinea pig. I said all right. One day I was having lunch with Stevenson and Ed McDougal and they congratulated me. I got the booklet out and turned to the list of past presidents and told them that I saw that both of them had been presidents and I asked, 'Why am I the first Jew? Why didn't you do something about it before this?' They didn't believe it was a conscious policy—they simply had never thought about it."

At Stevenson's press conference at the Beverly Hills Hotel on Monday, February 6, a reporter said that Kefauver claimed to favor federal legislation to intervene "in such things as the Emmett Till case" and asked whether Stevenson agreed. Stevenson took refuge in a legalism—it would be unconstitutional for the federal government to pre-empt state court jurisdiction in a murder case—and, discovering that the reporter was not sure of precisely what Kefauver had said, suggested that Kefauver might have meant voting rights, not murder cases, and slid away by saying that Kefauver "must have been misunderstood." Another reporter, however, asked if it was true that Stevenson was taking a less firm position on civil rights than Kefauver because he feared to alienate Southern Democrats.

Stevenson said, "I am not conscious of any of these anxieties, either the alienation of Democrats or reluctance to enter into the controversies." Another asked if he would "favor public school desegregation strongly in the South?" Stevenson said "Oh yes, it is the law of the land, it has been so enunciated by the Supreme Court." He took a forthright position on the Powell amendment to the federal aid to education bill, an amendment sponsored by Representative Adam Clayton Powell of New York which would deny federal aid to schools that practiced segregation: he was against the amendment—"The objective of such an amendment seems entirely plausible and proper but we mustn't hazard the loss of the whole program to serve such an objective as that. The important thing is education. Things like . . . segregation will yield quickest of all to the spread of education." Was not this inconsistent with his view that the Supreme Court ruling was the law of the land? "No, because the administration of the schools is a local matter." President Eisenhower had taken a similar position a few days earlier and been accused by liberals of advocating "gradualism." A reporter asked Stevenson if he was concerned because some of his admirers at Fresno had considered his speeches over the voters' heads. Stevenson replied, "No. . . . I think the voter's head is a little higher than we give him credit for."

The next morning, February 7, Stevenson went to a meeting of Mexican-Americans and Negroes at the Hotel Watkins at Western and Beverly in the heart of Los Angeles' Negro district. The crowd was singing "Happy Birthday" as he entered, and he thanked them, saying he had been greeted the same way at Bakersfield a week ago, making this "the longest birthday I have ever had." He spoke briefly, then invited questions.

The questions asked from the crowd at a political meeting are nearly always poor—rambling, imprecise, uninformed—and the questions of a minister who now interrogated Stevenson were no exception. He was not hostile, merely vague, as, for example, when he began: "How do you feel about using the Department of Justice to see that the laws that are already on the statute books are enforced?" Stevenson felt obliged to ask for clarification: "Which laws?" And the minister said, "The laws with regard to desegregation." And Stevenson asked, "In the schools?" And so on— the colloquy continued awkwardly for several minutes, until finally Stevenson asked if the minister meant the time had come for the Supreme Court to issue a decree ordering that, unless schools were desegregated within the next six months, federal troops would be sent to enforce desegregation. Yes, the man said, that was what he meant. Stevenson then said, "I think that would be a great mistake. This is exactly what brought about the difficult Civil War and division of the Union. Now, we will go about these things gradually, because it will be the spirit of man that will make the laws successful and make it possible to enforce them continuously. It will not be troops or bayonets. We will have to proceed gradually. You do not upset the habits and traditions that are older than the

Republic overnight. There is, however, a question of what time is tolerable to bring about the family of man in this country. We have been a hundred years almost—it will be a hundred years on January 1, 1963. It will be almost a hundred years from the Emancipation [Proclamation] to the time when I think the spirit of that declaration will be enforced. That is a long, long time."

His questioner seemed sympathetic yet he persisted, and at length Stevenson, grown impatient, said, "I'm not running for this office for the honor of it, my friend." Then he said his party represented all the people of the country regardless of race, and he himself would "do everything I can to bring about [national] unity even if I have to ask some of you to come about it gradually." Other questions on civil rights followed, and he seemed to try to hold them at a distance. Once he called attention to the progress already made in desegregating Southern schools. He again firmly opposed the Powell amendment. He took a liberal position on voting but even there said that federal force should be used "very" cautiously and never beyond the limit to which the public would support its use.

The damage, however, was done: he had opposed federal action to implement school desegregation and called for "gradualism." He had seemed to imply that it would be soon enough if school desegregation was accomplished by 1963, then seven years away and nine years after the Supreme Court school decision. Liberals throughout California and across the country were alarmed. Arthur Schlesinger read William Lawrence's story from Los Angeles in the New York *Times* next morning and promptly wrote to Blair. He said he sympathized with Stevenson's sense of responsibility about the issue but felt he could have made the same points "without projecting—as at the least the Lawrence story does—a pervading sense of coldness about the whole problem." He wished Stevenson had prefaced his remarks about gradualism and force with a strong condemnation of interposition, recent events at the University of Alabama, the failure of justice in the Till case, and so on. This, he said, was what Senator John Kennedy did. "If we can communicate [deep] concern, then we can remain as responsible and uncommitted as we want when it comes to policy." Agnes Meyer told Stevenson that his position on the Powell amendment was right but he should call in NAACP leaders to explain it. Stevenson sent a waspish memorandum to Harry Ashmore, "I think the time has come to try to get some of this stuff straight, and I wish you would put in my hands as promptly as possible a draft statement which I can use in all press conferences hereafter, material with respect to: (1) desegregation; (2) voting (3) violence." Andy Hatcher, a Negro newspaperman who served as Stevenson's local press secretary in California (and later became deputy to Pierre Salinger, press secretary to President Kennedy), told Bill Blair that Kefauver had gained an advantage at Fresno by meeting with Negro delegates to the convention and taking the strong positions they favored. Blair replied that Kefauver "completely switched his position when he got down to Florida." He had not known in Fresno that Negro leaders had asked to see Stevenson. A Beverly Hills attorney who had gone home from Fresno "slightly shaken but still a Stevenson man" said the next day, after reading an account of Stevenson's rejection of federal force to compel desegregation, that he had switched to Kefauver.

Stevenson went briefly to San Diego, then to the home of friends, the George Richardsons, at Rancho Santa Fe for three days, working on speeches, answering letters, and licking the wounds. He told a California Congressman, Cecil R. King, "The journey had been gratifying from the standpoint of the multitudes and the enthusiasm. But I was almost wholly unprepared for the types of pressure and special interests, like minority groups, Zionism, etc., which I encountered. This, and the necessity for appearing more frequently than I had foreseen has not made for the best for my own utterances or news coverage." He told a friend in Escondido that his California week had been "about as intense as any I can recall in my 'long political life'—and virtually without preparation."

To Agnes Meyer, "Estes, after his fashion, told the Negro leaders in private that he would shut off all aid to any segregated school, etc. etc. When it leaked and the press interrogated him he promptly denied it. This state, as you know is a bewildering array of diverse interests, and the Democratic party has little leadership and organization, but my following seems to be large and some of the more sober people realize that to win in November you have to carry more than the minority groups and the Democratic regulars." He was, as always, galled by the pressures of minority groups and regular party men; irritated, he turned on his staff and tried to excuse himself. "I am more tired than I should be, but find a peculiar resilience that I hope endures a few more months of this ordeal. But I do not enjoy it, and what makes me uncomfortable and depressed is the rapid sequence of total surprises with no preparation or previous indoctrination. I have never enjoyed slapstick politics or extemporaneous speaking, and that seems to be all that is contemplated. The result, of course, is that the image comes out confused and the misquotations are at least as numerous as the accuracies. It is an awkward posture for me to be in when I am trying to be the 'responsible' candidate and most of the pressures are either for irresponsibility or banality. . . . I am so thankful for your wire about the Powell Amendment. It illustrates my problem. I have no thoughtful advice on this sort of thing in spite of the fact that Harry Ashmore has been travelling with me continuously. My staff troubles are by no means resolved."

Relations with the press had been confused during the California trip. Tom Wilson, an assistant press secretary, had received the text of the Fresno speech late and could not have it ready for distribution until nearly four-thirty California time on the afternoon of the day Stevenson delivered it, a Saturday. There are early closing deadlines in the East for the big

Sunday papers. Correspondents complained—they received the speeches too late, and Stevenson's speeches were complex, with the newspaper lead, or principal point, often buried, and the press needed time to study them. Wilson proposed that Stevenson decide what he wanted the press to emphasize and release a few straightforward paragraphs on the point. He wondered whether Stevenson "really distinguishes clearly between hucksterism and good, artful communication"—"to hide the lead for newspaper correspondents or make it hard for them to extract it from the text —or to run over 20:30 [twenty minutes and thirty seconds] on the air—is just plain bad communications. And it has nothing to do with content." Stevenson's long series of press assistants struggled with the same problem over and over through the years and never fully solved it.

Alicia Patterson told Stevenson she believed that Harriman was turning sharply left in defiance of the South, that he had his eye mainly on the Negroes and Puerto Ricans in the Northern big-city slums. She told Stevenson not to yield to pressure from professional politicians but "to thine own self be true." How many people, especially women, told him that in his lifetime! Was it because they felt he needed shoring up? Or because it pleased them to bespeak high principle? Stevenson replied: "I am anxious to avoid obscuring my image and that is exceedingly difficult in the type of campaign I have been expected to do here: six or eight talks a day to enormous groups, all wildly enthusiastic, and with a consistently hostile and critical press, and a party element more interested in extremism on the racial issue, Israel, etc. than on winning elections. This element seems to be quite powerful in the Democratic party here and puts temperate behavior in the posture of reaction very quickly. . . . On to Oregon!" he added. He was irritable and tired—and it was only February.

8.

Disquieting word came from Minnesota and New York. Kefauver was said to have made heavy inroads in many areas of Minnesota, including the iron range and the farming region, in part because the Minnesotans thought Stevenson softer on farm price supports than Kefauver and in part because Minnesotans were independent and the Democratic-Farmer-Labor machine of Freeman and Humphrey had moved too quickly in endorsing Stevenson. Lloyd Garrison thought it time for a reappraisal of the Powell amendment and all civil rights issues. Roy Wilkins of the NAACP was satisfied with Stevenson's position on Negro voting rights but was "surprised" at his position on the question of violence. Finletter thought that when Stevenson came to New York in February he should visit headquarters and shake hands—"we need a lift."

Stevenson received a thoughtful letter of birthday greeting from Adlai

III and Nancy, including verses by Nancy, and it pleased him greatly: "What punctilious and thoughtful children you are. I can't recall ever remembering one of my parent's birthdays, but maybe I wasn't brung up right!" On February 8, Finletter told Schlesinger he was "anxious" that Stevenson speak on foreign policy at a big New York Stevenson Committee dinner on April 25. "I do not want a political speech, I want a really serious operation here, well prepared in advance." He wanted it to be specific on such questions as Arab-Israeli affairs. That same day Finletter commented on a Schlesinger memorandum on hydrogen bomb testing. The memo had said that for a time the Russians had seemed inclined to support an Indian proposal for a test ban and that the United States should "call any Russian bluff" by agreeing to negotiate within the UN a ban on hydrogen bomb testing. Although agreement on a test ban seemed unlikely, the United States would hold the diplomatic initiative and should maintain it by proposing that a UN agency monitor and report on tests. Finletter wondered if they did not need "more up-to-date scientific information" before getting specific. Although the idea of banning nuclear tests was in the air at that time—Finletter, as noted, had already called Commissioner Murray of the AEC to Stevenson's attention—Schlesinger's memo is the earliest that has survived in his and Stevenson's and Finletter's papers.

Stevenson spent February 11, 12, and 13 campaigning in Oregon. At a press conference in Portland he said he had not yet decided with finality to enter the Oregon primary. His name had been entered in Alaska but he could not go there. He was discouraging friends from entering his name in New Hampshire. A Gallup poll showed that six out of ten voters favored Eisenhower's re-election, a reporter said—did he agree? Stevenson would not contradict the poll. Did he favor 90 per cent of parity for farm price supports? "I do, sir," he said unequivocally. Did he have any comments on "the Tuscaloosa incident?" (Only a few days earlier, the Supreme Court had ordered Alabama University in Tuscaloosa to admit its first Negro student, Autherine J. Lucy, for postgraduate study. But Miss Lucy, threatened by students and others, had been suspended "for your safety and for the safety of the students and vaculty members.") Stevenson had anticipated the question and written out a statement, which he read:

"The temporary denial of the right of a Negro student to attend classes at the University of Alabama is deplorable. The fact that this came about as the result of mob violence is intolerable. At this point the sovereignty of the state of Alabama became the issue—and there can be only one proper answer. The law must be obeyed.

"But it seems to me the extreme interpretation many people have put on the incident is unfortunate. In the first place, it appears that the officials of the university have behaved responsibly from the beginning. Now Governor Folsom has said that they will have his full backing—that he will never support mob rule over constituted authority.

"Moreover, it appears that the resistance has come from only a small minority of the students of the university and that the real trouble came from outsiders.

"As things now stand I think we can assume that order will be restored on the campus at Tuscaloosa, and that Miss Lucy will return to her classes.

"Finally, I think we should take into account that the unhappy incident at Alabama is only part of the total picture of the South. Negroes have been admitted by the Universities of Virginia, North Carolina, Kentucky, Arkansas, Louisiana, and Texas without incident. This I suggest is news, too, and it shouldn't be obscured by the hot headlines from Tuscaloosa." (A poor prophecy. Miss Lucy was subsequently permanently expelled by the university trustees for remarks she made in federal court. She went to New York for rest and medical attention, did not try to re-enter the university, and was married in April in Dallas.)

A reporter for the Negro newspaper, the Chicago *Defender,* started to ask a question. Stevenson, recognizing him, said, "Well, welcome, brother Elk." The reporter said, "Governor, the opinion prevails that you are committed to gradualism on civil rights," said that after a hundred years gains in Mississippi had been "slow or maybe minute," and wondered if he now had "any idea in mind of stopping this wholesale—" Stevenson interrupted: "I think there are several questions involved. The desegregation of schools pursuant to the Supreme Court decree, the miscarriage of justice— as, for example, the Till case, and the third is the definite violation of civil liberties—the right to vote by economic pressures, or duress or violence or whatever. I don't believe you can answer all of them in the same language, and that is one of the troubles, that we try to emotionalize all of them and talk in packages. They are all entirely different subjects. As to the subject of desegregation, I think I shall issue a statement on that in writing tomorrow. On the subject of interference with the right to vote in the South or wherever it may be, I think it is very sad that people, whoever they are, by intimidation or violence should be deprived of what not only is the right of every American citizen but is the duty of every American citizen—the duty to vote. . . . On the third subject, the violence and the miscarriage of justice in the South. Nobody can view with anything except alarm and dismay and distress any miscarriage of justice anywhere. The trouble is we have a federal system—division of jurisdiction, both criminal and civil, between the states and the federal government. In cases that relate to the states only, as for example the Till case, the boy who was murdered in Mississippi, we have to look to the states to enforce the law. So if you ask me do I have a program as to that I can only say to the extent that the federal laws should be enforced; but in the cases of murder and kidnaping, it was committed wholly within the state of Mississippi."

The reporter asked, "Would it take other federal laws?" Stevenson began, "I think it is a constant problem that we are confronted with—"

The reporter began, "Then they have a right to kill anyone down there whenever they are ready to—" Stevenson interrupted, "I don't want to dispute your statement, but it is an extreme statement that you make."

It was a weekend. On Saturday, February 11, Stevenson had a major Jefferson-Jackson Day dinner speech to deliver in Portland. But he was beset, under pressure, and in trouble on civil rights. Mrs. Eleanor Roosevelt, always one of his most loyal supporters, told him, "I like your statement on Alabama University." But Senator Lehman of New York sent a long letter with "great hesitation," knowing that Stevenson had been "wrestling with your conscience on this question for a long time" and that what he had said in California had not been said lightly or insincerely— but he could not refrain from "expressing my sense of disquietude" over Stevenson's position. "You have been reported as emphasizing 'gradualism' and 'education'"—Stevenson circled and questioned "education" —"as the way to make progress on the human rights front. I do not know whether you appreciate what the word 'gradualism' and the word 'education' mean to Negroes and to White people who are deeply concerned with the civil rights issue. These are words which have been used by apologists for discrimination and injustice for many years. . . . It is difficult to speak of the enlightening effects of 'education' in a situation such as we have in some places, chiefly some parts of the South, where all the *active* education is in the direction of prejudice and discrimination." (Stevenson underlined the last clause and wrote beside it, "No!") Lehman argued that for three quarters of a century, in the absence of outside pressure, Southern segregation had acquired legal sanction, and that what progress had been achieved since 1933 had been achieved not by "education" but by administrative, legislative, or judicial fiat. Today school segregation was only one of the "critical fighting civil rights issues." Others included voting rights, "physical violence and security, and many others." The denial of the protection of the Bill of Rights "must be confronted." (Stevenson underlined and checked the word "confronted.") Lehman understood the commitment of some people to segregation. Obviously, "it will take time" to achieve full civil rights for all. "But the date we set for making a good-faith start toward achieving each of our objectives must be now. . . . To set a distant target date merely postpones for that length of time coming to real grips with the problem." (Stevenson underlined "target date" and penciled "No!" in the margin.) Lehman went on, "I know you are, and will continue to be, subjected to many pressures." (Stevenson underlined "many pressures" and wrote "No!") "I know, also, that you are well accustomed, and well equipped, to resist pressures. This is not an attempt to apply pressure. This is an attempt merely to set forth my feelings and my reactions. I hope you will accept them as such." Lehman closed by sending sympathy for Stevenson's "ordeal." He did not, however, reaffirm his support of Stevenson, whether by accident or intention.

To some Stevenson partisans, the whole problem looked like part of a plot to stop Stevenson. Alicia Patterson sent Stevenson an editorial saying that a few days earlier Truman, Harriman, and Kefauver had conferred to "wreck the policy of 'moderation' which Stevenson had enunciated as the foundation of his campaign and thus prevent his nomination." Alicia said she had received private assurances that organized labor led by Walter Reuther would in the end support Stevenson, but labor leaders' current statements belied it.

On Sunday beleaguered Stevenson issued a statement in Portland clarifying his position. He began by saying that he was surprised that anything he could say on civil rights at "this late date" would still be news. His "attitude" had not changed since he first "had a part in integrating Negroes in the naval service fifteen years ago." He deeply believed that "it is the first obligation" of every citizen "to work for the full realization of the goals stated by our original charter—freedom and equality for all Americans. Freedom, as I understand it, means that a man may advance to the limit of his natural endowment without hindrances because of his race or religion. Equality, as I understand it, means that each citizen shall be judged on his own merits. And particularly it means that every citizen shall be guaranteed equal treatment under the law." Under Supreme Court decisions the "legal base of our civil liberties" had been broadened for a hundred and fifty years until today equal treatment was required in "virtually every public activity supported by public funds," including schools. Therefore the question was "not what we are trying to accomplish but how we should go about it." The Court had recognized "that we cannot by the stroke of a pen reverse customs and traditions that are older than the Republic." It had not set a fixed time for compliance but, rather, had established a "good faith" test to measure progress. Results had been "heartening." In a more than half of the seventeen states which had practiced segregation, integration had been "completed or well begun." In the rest, as the Court recognized, more time was needed. "True integration requires more than the mere presence of children of two races in the same classroom; it requires changes in the hearts and minds of men. No child can be properly educated in a hostile atmosphere." Then he confronted the immediate issue:

"In the five or six states where public opinion does not yet sustain the Court's decision we are faced with one of the ultimate tests of democracy and of our federal system. There we are attempting to secure and protect the declared rights of local minorities in the face of the adverse views of controlling local majorities.

"This condition imposes special burdens on all of us and even heavier burdens on public officials. I can think of no greater disservice to our country than to exploit for political ends the tensions that have followed in the wake of the Supreme Court decision.

"Our purpose must be to attain unity, harmony, and civilized relations, not to set section against section or race against race. And as a practical matter we must recognize that punitive action by the federal government may actually delay the process of integration in education.

"We will not, for example, reduce race prejudice by denying to areas afflicted with it the means of improving the educational standards of all their people.

"Certainly we will not improve the present condition or future prospects of any Negro citizen by coercive federal action that will arm the extremists and disarm the men of good will in the South who, with courage and patience, have already accomplished so much.

"I suggest no slowing down of the effort to bring to reality the American concept of full equality for all our citizens. We must proceed, as the Court has said, with all reasonable speed. [The Court had said 'all deliberate speed.'] But we must recognize that it is reason alone that will determine our rate of continued progress and guard against a reversal of the trend that has made the last three decades the period of greatest advancement for our Negro citizens on all fronts.

"I had hoped the action of the Court and the notable record of compliance that still far outweighs the instances of overt resistance would remove this issue from the political arena and make possible its orderly resolution without the emotional coloration of a presidential contest. I still consider this not only possible but essential."

The controversy did not end. George Meany, president of the AFL-CIO, attacked Stevenson. On Tuesday, February 14, from Seattle, Stevenson sent him a telegram: "I do not understand the statements attributed to you in press reports here. I can only assume you have not read the statement of my position regarding desegregation released in the Monday newspapers. Otherwise, I do not see how you could interpret anything I have said, either as running away from the problem or suggesting that it be postponed forever. What I have said is that I would oppose the use of force, and I think you would, too." On the same day Mrs. Roosevelt issued from Chicago a statement strongly supporting Stevenson. Stevenson telegraphed his thanks.

The issue continued to dog him through the primaries that year (but it was less important in the general election, since Eisenhower's own position, in so far as he had one, did not differ greatly from Stevenson's, except that increasingly as the campaign progressed Stevenson urged the President to use his moral authority to solve the problem, while Eisenhower sought to avoid becoming involved and repeatedly said it was a problem for the district courts). Stevenson was attempting a moderate position, not merely because he was running in both Florida and California but because it came naturally to him. Eric Sevareid said at the time that it required more courage to adopt a moderate than an extreme position—was easier for Harriman to demand federal force in the South and for Senator Eastland of Mississippi to advocate outright defiance of the Court. Stevenson believed he was acting responsibly, and he was. The trouble, as

Arthur Schlesinger had pointed out, was less with the position he took than with the impression he gave—one of almost grudging espousal of the civil rights cause. No doubt some of this proceeded from his natural resistance to pressure from any minority group or special interest. But some of it came from deeper springs. What his friendly critics—those loyal both to him and to civil rights—missed was something he himself probably did not know he lacked: a strong emotional commitment to the civil rights cause. To realize this one has only to contrast Stevenson's cool, rather legalistic and pre-eminently rational approach to segregation with Robert F. Kennedy's passionate outcry a dozen years later: "This is unacceptable." Kennedy felt the civil rights cause in his bones. Stevenson never did. Stevenson mistrusted emotion, tried to keep it out of politics. This is what they blamed him for.

His speech to the Jefferson-Jackson Day dinner in Portland on February 11 was, in contrast to the Fresno speech, a highly partisan attack. Republicans, he said, hoped the voters would "sign a blank check." He welcomed the President's embrace of Democratic proposals but doubted his deeds would match his words. He read the shopping list of Democratic issues—civil liberties, small business, labor, housing, health research, aid to schools, natural resources, fiscal policy, agriculture, expanding on agriculture and natural resources. At Timberline Lodge in Mount Hood, Oregon, on February 12, he caught up on personal correspondence and went for a ride in a snow machine. It overturned, injuring his companions but not Stevenson. Years later he said it had fallen over a drop of about thirty feet. He relished relating how he had had several close escapes in airplanes and wrecked automobiles.

On February 14 he spoke at a Democratic dinner in Seattle, a salvo on Administration foreign policy as one conducted by bluffs and boasts and slogans, and an effort to draw the party line sharply on domestic issues.

9.

Back in Chicago, on February 20, he told Mrs. Ives the Western trip had been "satisfactory" but the schedule had been too full for this early date and the staff now realized it. "I find the primary part of this business distasteful. Moreover, I also find it hard to see how I can improve my position and it is so easy to impair it." Mrs. Ives had seen Agnes Meyer, and Stevenson wrote Mrs. Meyer, "I was delighted that you found Buffie *simpatico*. . . . I haven't seen her for months and months, and I hope she is getting calmed down. . . . I think I am storing up experiences . . . for a political essay on 'How *Not* To Choose a President.'" Senator Lehman had come to lunch, "more pained than indignant, and of course anxious to be helpful." Stevenson went on, "But ultimately we have to face the fact that the ultimate sanction, force, will solve nothing." Nevertheless, his position on segregation still worried him. He asked Mrs. Robert Kintner for the names of "responsible Negro leaders who would express preference for integration by persuasion rather than force."

Thanking Alan Cranston, president of the California Democratic Council, for his courtesies in California, Stevenson said, "I am sorry the speech was so disappointing for that group. I had been ill prepared as to what to expect, and somehow I had the idea they wanted futures and visions rather than warmed-over New Deal." Cranston did not reply for more than three weeks and then said it was not warmed-over New Deal that was wanted but rather "a direct grappling with today's issues—albeit too many of them think New Deal answers will suffice, which they won't." He wrote to Congressman Bill Dawson of Chicago, the long-time Negro leader, "I have been much disturbed by some of the rather extreme reactions, especially on the West Coast, to what I thought were wholly realistic expressions regarding the desegregation of the schools. I am sure you know that they reflected no equivocation about compliance with the decree; nor did I in fact propose any target date for compliance, as reported in the newspapers. But I am of the opinion that to defeat aid for schools for everyone by this route again will not accelerate integration and might cause a serious setback. At all events, I should like very much to have a chance to talk with you."

He put Jim Finnegan in charge of everything except editorial work and research—including correspondence, politics, public relations, press relations, relations with the Volunteers, and so on—and asked Minow to act as Finnegan's administrative assistant. Stevenson wanted to keep "personal direction" of speeches through Bill Wirtz. He sent a noncommittal reply to a man who urged him to work for the reinstatement of Wolf Ladejinsky, a land reform expert in Vietnam, who had resigned under McCarthyesque pressure.

Bill Blair received heartening word from a friend. Senator John F. Kennedy reported that a private poll on presidential preferences among registered Massachusetts Democrats gave this result:

Stevenson	69 per cent
Kefauver	17
Harriman	9
Lausche	5

Stevenson's lead was even greater in Boston—78 per cent.

On Saturday, February 25, Stevenson opened a twelve-day trip, the first half in the East, with a speech at Hartford, Connecticut, a blast at the Administration's record in all fields, with emphasis on civil rights, immigration, and flood control, all of local interest. Stevenson spent the weekend at Cambridge, visiting his sons and seeing friends. Arthur Schlesinger noted in his journal that they talked mostly of civil rights and the Middle East. Stevenson kept saying the basic fact was the difficulty of Southern adjustment to desegregation, that Negro leaders were mistaken in pressing for early implementation, and that their only hope lay in reducing tensions and permitting moderate Southern whites to work out problems gradually. Schlesinger, together with Garrison, Finletter, Jack Fischer, and a Syracuse professor, Stuart Gerry Brown, had drafted a statement for Stevenson taking a position in favor of withholding federal funds from non-complying states. Stevenson obviously was much more in accord with an alternative draft by Ashmore which appealed to Negroes to go slow and to relax tension in their own interest. Schlesinger argued that Negroes never had achieved anything except through pressure and knew it. Further, Stevenson expected Negroes to be more reasonable than he expected white Southerners to be and this seemed unfair. Schlesinger thought he persuaded Stevenson that he could appeal successfully to the Negroes for moderation only if he had first demonstrated an emotional concern over their problems. "But I have a feeling that his basic convictions in this area are very deeply rooted." He found Stevenson "very indignant" at Roy Wilkins, declaring he could never "do business with a man like that," and he denounced an editorial by James Wechsler in the New York *Post* as "a long, rambling, diffuse, schizophrenic, hysterical piece, proving how little Northern liberals understand the real problems" of desegregation.

Schlesinger noted that Stevenson said he had studied the Middle East closely, knew more about it than all but half a dozen other Americans outside the State Department, thought the Arabs unreliable, thought the Jews would be committing suicide if they started a preventive war, and believed that "the only solution . . . was a tough policy of knocking their heads together."

While Stevenson was in New York, on February 29, President Eisenhower announced at a press conference he would run again. Asked whether he would consent to the entry of his name in primaries where his consent was necessary, the President said he had not decided. Asked how he would expect the issue of his health to be handled in the campaign, he said he had not given it any thought but he himself would "try to be just as truthful as I can be." That night he went on radio and television in a nationwide broadcast. He said that in reaching his decision he had "been guided by the favorable reports of the doctors" and described his physical condition. "I am classed as a recovered heart patient. This means that, to some undetermined extent, I may possibly be a greater risk than is the normal person of my age. My doctors assure me that this increased percentage of risk is not great. So far as my own personal sense of well-being is concerned, I am as well as before the attack occurred. It is, however, true that the opinions and conclusions of the doctors that I can continue to carry the burdens of the presidency contemplate for me a regime of ordered work activity, interspersed with regular amounts of exercise, recreation, and rest. A further word about this prescribed regime. I must keep my weight at a proper level. I must take a short midday breather. I must normally retire at a reasonable hour, and I must eliminate many of the less important social and ceremonial activities. But let me make one thing clear. As of this moment, there is not the slightest doubt that I can perform, as well as I ever have, all of the important duties of the presidency. This I say because I am actually doing so and have been doing so for many weeks. . . . Some of the things in which I can properly have a reduced schedule include public speeches, office appointments with individuals and with groups, ceremonial dinners, receptions, and portions of a very heavy correspondence." He would reduce his travel. "All of this means, also, that neither for renomination nor re-election would I engage in extensive traveling and in whistle-stop speaking—normally referred to as 'barnstorming.' I had long ago made up my mind, before I ever dreamed of a personal heart attack, that I could never, as President of all the people, conduct the kind of political campaign where I was personally a candidate. . . . On the record are the aims, the efforts, the accomplishments and the plans for the future of this Administration."

The next day, March 1, Stevenson flew to Minneapolis-St. Paul for a week. The Minnesota primary was only three weeks away. To Stevenson and staff, his principal opponent was Eisenhower, not Kefauver. And to Stevenson, if not to his staff, this meant, to a considerable extent, attacking Eisenhower's foreign policy. Before leaving New York, he asked Geoffrey Crowther, editor of the [London] *Economist,* as he had asked Barbara Ward, for views on "some of the things about America that concern you most." He sought Senator Fulbright's advice on how to run against Eisenhower, and Fulbright replied, "It is not easy to penetrate the protective fog they have created about Ike." Opposing Eisenhower now became all the more urgent after Eisenhower's announcement that he would run. On Stevenson's first day of campaigning at the Minneapolis Labor Temple he made a first tentative effort to make the President's health an issue. He said that foreign affairs could not be "adequately managed" until final responsibility was "clearly fixed once more" in the presidency:

"And that brings me to the new dimension, the new and compelling issue in this campaign: the manner and mode in which the duties of our highest office are to be discharged. I have shared with you the whole nation's concern over President Eisenhower's misfortune. And I share with all of you our pleasure at the progress of his recovery. He had not only the sympathy of our party but our understanding in the weeks following his illness when, of necessity, his activities were severely limited. But now I understand that the condition of his recovery is that the special arrangements made to accommodate him, of necessity, must be made permanent.

"To delegate the functions and, of necessity, the authority of the President on a scale that we have not known in our time represents an issue that is not the personal one of the President's health, but the public matter of how the office of President can and should be conducted. To add to our other vast problems at home and abroad, there appears also to be emerging for the people's careful consideration a re-examination of the nature of the greatest office on earth. It is an office designed to be filled by an executive. Can the functions be altered without significantly altering the structure of the federal government? And the question is the more solid at a time when tensions are rising at home and abroad, when the day-to-day management of our public affairs demands close and exacting attention and a firm and a certain hand."

Stevenson spent the first day in Minneapolis and St. Paul, breakfasting with the Mayors, visiting city halls, attending a Junior Chamber of Commerce luncheon, visiting the Labor Temple, touring the Minneapolis-Honeywell plant, attending a fund-raising reception and a precinct workers' rally, and speaking at the University of Minnesota, where he discussed civil liberties and civil rights—after which Senator Lehman introduced the speech into the Congressional Record and reaffirmed his support of Stevenson. What Stevenson said was this: The United States must hold out "hope and inspiration" to Asians and could do so only by demonstrating that the United States "is still concerned with steadily broadening freedom for all its own people." Americans could "take great pride in the gains of our minority groups over the past two or three decades." But this progress posed "a new threat to the constitutional process" and the world was watching how it would be resolved. "In several states we are now attempting to secure the declared rights of a Negro minority in the face of the adverse reaction of controlling local majorities. We see again the ugly face of race prejudice; we hear again threats of violence and organized resistance. And it is, clearly, a matter of grave national concern when a girl in Alabama is denied her constitutional rights by mob violence or by subterfuge, or when murder goes unpunished in Mississippi or when American citizens are denied peaceful occupancy of their homes in my own state of Illinois, or when citizens are denied, whether by physical or economic coercion, their right—and duty—to vote. But against the failures there is evidence that the process we have undertaken is certain to prevail—that we are managing to change the hearts and minds of men as well as the laws under which they have long lived. . . . The problem of changing a people's morals, particularly those with an emotional overlay, is not to be taken lightly. It is a problem which will require the utmost patience, understanding, generosity, and forbearance, and from all of us, of whatever race. But the magnitude of the problem may not nullify the principle. And that principle is that we are, all of us, free-born Americans, with a right to make our way unfettered by sanctions imposed by man because of the work of God." Stevenson also said, "Before we cast a stone at

Alabama, it might be well for those of us who live in some of the great Northern cities to ask ourselves, in candor, how the Negro minority is faring in our own communities."

After opening day in the Twin Cities, Stevenson spent the rest of the week in the hinterland, the prairies and lakelands of Minnesota. Everywhere he was accompanied by Governor Freeman or Senator Humphrey or both. Congressman (later Senator) Eugene McCarthy accompanied him on some occasions. The schedule was backbreaking. On Saturday he spoke at Big Lake at 8:30 A.M., at the Waverly City Hall at nine-thirty, at the Litchfield Armory at eleven, at Sauk Centre at two-thirty, at a hotel in Little Falls at three-thirty, at St. John's College in Collegeville at six, and on the radio at a rally in St. Cloud at 9 P.M. He rested and went to church on Sunday with Orville Freeman, then on Monday made seven speeches in scattered towns starting at the Worthington Armory at 8 A.M. and spending the night at Fergus Falls. Often he arrived far behind schedule. Frequently he kidded Humphrey and Freeman about the schedule they had set him—Humphrey was in truth one of the most indefatigable campaigners of the times. Once Stevenson said he had intended to talk at length about agriculture but "I shall have to forgo that because I dare say that any moment somebody is going to pull the back of my coat and say, 'Governor, hurry. We are behind schedule.' That has happened until my coat is frayed." He usually spoke extemporaneously and at length. Once he raised the issue of the President's health. "Now, this means that we are being asked to alter the terms of service of the Chief Executive of the United States, and therefore to reconstitute our highest office. If so, this is a very serious and significant constitutional change that we are being asked to make in this casual way. There is, as we know, no way to delegate the critical responsibilities of that office, and yet apparently we are being asked to reduce the stature of the office just as the nation's responsibilities and difficulties increase."

For the most part, however, Stevenson told jokes, tied himself tightly to Humphrey and Freeman, and hammered hard at the farm issue— prosperity on "Main Street" depended on prosperity on the farm; agriculture was America's "number one problem." Occasionally he spoke of foreign affairs, though in general terms, denouncing Administration sloganeering. Consumer credit, inflation, soil conservation, natural resources, small business, depressed areas, urban and rural slums, health, schools, civil liberties, fair labor laws, "grinding conformity . . . anti-intellectualism"—those were issues he touched. Sometimes he asked for his listeners' support; but somewhat tentatively. "If you should see fit to entrust this responsibility to me again," he began one passage, and again, "I am engaged, I suppose, in one of the most responsible and formidable undertakings in which a human being can engage, the pursuit of the office of the President of the United States. It is not, as you know, a new undertaking for me. I was honored beyond my deserts and to the full measure of my party's capacity in 1952, when it elected me as the nominee for the presidency. Here I am again [*applause*]. Thank heavens nobody groaned out loud [*laughter*]."

His crowds were big and responsive. Not once in the recorded transcripts of his speeches did he mention Kefauver or any other candidate for the Democratic nomination. He was running against the Republicans. The speeches seemed routine. They lacked fire, urgency, conviction. And he was holding himself somewhat aloof from his audiences, speaking to them as from a distance. Nowhere did he convey the urgent necessity of his winning the nomination that later John F. Kennedy in 1960 and Hubert Humphrey and Robert F. Kennedy in 1968 conveyed.

But he seemed pleased. Returning home on Wednesday, March 7, he told Mrs. Ives that his trip had been "most successful and encouraging—and exhausting!" He told Agnes Meyer, "I am back after five days of cruel and relentless campaigning through the snow bound western counties of Minnesota. I made as many as eight or ten stops and speeches a day after wild rides over icy roads between the towns. The crowds were enormous and attentive. The politicians were delighted and astonished. The consensus seemed to be that it was a combination of the farm issue, which is acute there, and the curiosity about me, and a vague anxiety that seems to be everywhere apparent." It bothered him that the press reported he had made Eisenhower's health an issue when what he thought he had done was to make not his health but the conduct of the presidency an issue. Stevenson believed the Republican managers would "dump Nixon with no protest from the President." This would make Stevenson's problem more "difficult." John Steele of *Time* reported that Stevenson was "the odds-on choice" to win Minnesota's twenty convention delegates. Danger, of course, lay in this, danger to Stevenson: Kefauver was claiming nothing in Minnesota, and therefore the tiniest victory would appear a triumph, while Stevenson's managers, exuding confidence, would have trouble explaining away the smallest defeat.

10.

Finletter reported on a luncheon at the Century club with Alex Rose of the Liberal Party and Carmine De Sapio. Rose said that, with Eisenhower in the race, the Democrats must agree on their candidate soon—the three-way struggle among Stevenson, Kefauver, and Harriman could help only the Republicans. Nothing, however, could be done at least until after the New Hampshire and Minnesota primaries. They would lunch again on March 22, after Minnesota. Finletter proposed that Harriman and De Sapio attend a big Stevenson Committee dinner on April 25. De Sapio was cool at first but, urged by Rose, promised to try to persuade Harriman to go. From Frederick G. Dutton in California came a report on difficulties between the regular organization and the independents for Stevenson. People emerging as independent leaders were really party veterans who would attract few real independents. Political parties were always fragmented in California, and the divisive primary fight was making matters worse. Dutton thought the Stevenson slate of convention delegates a good one. The meeting which selected them had been an uproar—"for a while there was everything except blood on the carpet."[5]

The day he got back from Minnesota, Stevenson told Ashmore to keep him supplied with material on conservation, Dixon-Yates, and other issues. He asked for an all-purpose whistle-stop speech. Ashmore was reluctant to write it because he did not think Stevenson would use it. He probably was right, but Wirtz thought Stevenson was entitled to have a draft, so several were produced. Stevenson also told Finnegan and Blair that he wanted an opportunity to go over future schedules before they were agreed upon. Newt Minow said, "Once during the Minnesota primary, Humphrey and Freeman wanted the Governor to go to some meeting or other. The Governor was in Chicago. He said no. They called Bill Blair and told him he had to get the Governor to change his mind. Blair went in to see him. The Governor screamed at him absolutely positively 'NO—if you want to go make the speech go ahead.' Bill called them back and said, 'He's coming.' He didn't tell the Governor until the day before. The Governor went. Bill was marvelous. No one else could do that with him."

Awaiting Stevenson when he returned was an enthusiastic letter from Adlai III announcing that Nancy was going to have a baby, and adding, "It's about the best news I ever had." Stevenson received a telegram from Kefauver saying that both candidates could appear on the same platform in Moorhead, Minnesota, on March 17 and he would be happy to do so. The Greater Moorhead Days Committee had no objection but could not consent unless Stevenson agreed. Stevenson's own supporters in Moorhead thought it an attempt to embarrass Stevenson but seemed powerless to stop it. Blair showed them how—dictated a statement for Stevenson's Minnesota committee giving details of Stevenson's itinerary and saying he planned "a major farm policy address" for Moorhead, with radio coverage, adding that since Stevenson and Kefauver both sought victory for the Democratic Party in November they had up to now avoided appearing on the same platform in order not to give the impression that they were debating one another. The committee approved. Stevenson telegraphed Kefauver: "Thanks for your wire. Understand Stevenson Committee in Minnesota has issued statement and been in touch with Greater Moorhead Day Committee. Regards."

---

[5] Dutton, at that time assistant counsel for the Southern Counties Gas Company of California with offices in Los Angeles, was new to politics. He emerged as one of the best of all Stevenson men in California, worked there for John F. Kennedy in 1960, entered the Kennedy administration, and in the 1968 primaries became Robert F. Kennedy's campaign manager.

Stevenson was home only from Wednesday to Saturday, March 10, and on that date spoke to a Jefferson-Jackson dinner at Detroit. Much thought had gone into the speech. Since the staff considered Stevenson sure to win in Minnesota, their thought looked beyond the primaries, looked to how Stevenson would run against Eisenhower, and this was reflected in the Detroit speech. In it, Stevenson said, "The President has announced that he is going to run for re-election under certain conditions—conditions relating to the limitations of time and energy which he can give to this greatest responsibility on earth, and to how this responsibility can be distributed among his associates. But such conditions, as the President stated them last week, sound more like the rules for governing a kingdom or a corporation. They are not the rules for governing a democracy."

He listed various large issues. "And to these must now be added a new issue—whether to permit a fundamental revision of the role of the President of the United States. This is not the question of President Eisenhower's health, but of the nature and stature of the presidency in our system." The President, he said, had declared "in a sentence that must have no parallel in American history: 'In many cases these things can now be done equally well by my close associates.'" After saying he had "nothing except sympathy and concern for [Eisenhower's] well-being," Stevenson took up Eisenhower's proposed "delegation of our highest responsibilities to some 'associate presidents.'" He then turned to them. It was "rumored," he said, that Nixon, "his beloved Vice President," would be dumped, "so we may not yet know who the principal associate president is going to be." He then attacked the other "associate presidents"—Secretary of Defense Wilson, who had cut the defense budget for political reasons; Secretary of Interior McKay, who had proclaimed that "we're here in the saddle as an administration representing business and industry"; Secretary Benson, who "just doesn't believe in doing anything to help the farmer, and it looks as though he is going to prove it even if he gets rid of half the farmers doing it"; Attorney General Brownell, "who has used his high office as a weapon for partisan attack upon the patriotism of loyal Americans"; Secretary of State Dulles, whose statement in *Life* had "stumped the whole free world" and who had presided over various catastrophes in foreign affairs. "Finding peace and security in this seething cauldron of crises is a full-time job for a full-time President," Stevenson said. But the Administration "remains frozen on dead center, immobilized and ineffective." He again called on the President to "assert effective leadership" on civil rights.

Senator Kennedy had announced his support of Stevenson the week before. Governor John F. Simms of New Mexico, who along with Senator Anderson had already announced support of Stevenson, told him it would be a mistake at this time to try to instruct the New Mexico delegation and put them under a unit rule; better to use quiet influence. Jim Finnegan, Hy Raskin, and their aides were putting pressure on various state Democratic leaders, particularly in small states, to come out early for Stevenson, telling them that their votes would not count for much once the big-state bandwagon for Stevenson started rolling but would mean a good deal at this early date. It was the same with those small delegations as it always is with financial contributions: "early money" means more than "late money."

Adlai III told Stevenson Ellen had telephoned him to say that Chicago's city fire and building inspectors, urged on by the Democratic Party, were harassing her with unreasonable demands. She seemed to think that if Stevenson or Daley "would say one word they'd all lay off." Stevenson asked young Adlai to keep him informed about her charges of persecution by the city.

The New Hampshire primary was Tuesday, March 13. That night Stevenson sent Agnes Meyer á postcard: "It's 'New Hampshire evening' and I don't even have enough curiosity to turn on the radio. What a candidate!" Kefauver, unopposed in New Hampshire, took all the delegates. Stevenson told Finletter, "New Hampshire does not trouble me much although I suppose the press will make quite a defeat out of it. Actually, to get more than a third of the vote when they have painted me as too proud to fight and disdainful of New Hampshire seemed to me not too bad." Stevenson told Mrs. Meyer, "Thanks for your letters and the wire re Detroit. I thought it the most 'political' speech I ever made and suspected you might disapprove. So I'm much relieved, but I intend now to say little more about the part-time Presidency and time-and-a-half for undertime, etc. It will filter through, I think. The southern manifesto is very disturbing."[6]

Stevenson asked Thomas Murray of the Atomic Energy Commission to see Benjamin V. Cohen, who had been advising Stevenson on atomic energy. Murray, a month later, said he had been busy preparing disarmament proposals for a Senate subcommittee, copies of which he sent to Stevenson and Cohen, and said he would see Cohen soon.

Chet Bowles had suggested to Stevenson that he, Bowles, form a working committee to meet once or twice a week in New York or Washington to discuss foreign policy issues as they arose. Bowles offered to get the group together and keep it at work providing Stevenson with speech material and press conference statements. He suggested the group include George Kennan on Europe including Russia, Dean Rusk on Asia, Ben Cohen on the Middle East, and Paul Nitze or Roswell Gilpatric on military questions. (Stevenson penciled in Bob Tufts on disarmament.) Bowles could give Stevenson four days a week through the fall election ex-

---

[6] The Southern Manifesto, originally conceived by Senator Strom Thurmond of South Carolina and rewritten by Senator Richard B. Russell and others, was presented in Congress March 12 and signed by eighty-two Southern Representatives and nineteen Southern Senators. It pledged the signers to exert "all lawful means" to reverse the Supreme Court desegregation decision and appealed to Southerners "to scrupulously refrain from disorder and lawless acts."

cept for a couple of weeks. He thought the Democrats might win or lose on foreign policy. He wondered how such a group would work with Finletter's.

Stevenson sent Bowles's memorandum to Finletter, speaking of the "imperative necessity" of having such a group keep in constant contact with Stevenson with suggestions for his comment on developments as they occurred. "It is in this field that the stature and image which we have talked about so often can be best demonstrated. . . . I would have to add that foreign affairs, to my distress, does not provoke the interest at the grass roots level that I would like to be able to breathe into it." He sent a carbon to Bowles with the hope that he would proceed promptly with Finletter. "I hope to heaven that this can work because almost daily now there is something that needs saying, and instead of saying it, I get more oppressed with the multitude of things I have to do." He added a postscript that showed his concern: "I can't overemphasize the importance of being able to issue brief statements that make sense in reaction to spot news. My long, carefully considered, painfully prepared speeches have a mighty meager audience in fact and get into the back country not at all. Even the speech at the University of Minnesota the other day had no press that I could discover on the basic foreign policy points. I frankly get discouraged during this primary period." In a separate note he told Bowles he had written Finletter: "I want to get going on this so much. It has been something I have wanted for years but never quite got out of the Finletter Group operation. Its importance gets greater every day." To George Kennan he complained that Republican editorialists and speakers constantly criticized him for attacking the Administration's foreign policy without offering affirmative alternatives and asked if Kennan could prepare an answer, "a sharp digest of our situation which I hope won't sound more like Kennan than Stevenson." He ruminated that Congress should pass a resolution that the much-traveled Foster Dulles not be allowed to leave the country. He asked James Warburg to draft a simple brief foreign policy statement: "Can you send it to me in the sort of form that is usable in a few minutes in the sort of speech one has to make even in a place like Moorhead, Minnesota or Podunk, Florida?"

On a letter containing a recent statement of Senator Bricker that the Eisenhower administration had promoted economic justice, and defining economic justice as "the policy of recognizing that every man is entitled to the things that are his own," Stevenson penciled cheerfully, "and let there be no more derision of this great thinker."

11.

On Wednesday, March 14, he went back to Minnesota to stay until the primary, only six days away. Again, the schedule was backbreaking. He sent a copy of it to Marietta Tree with a note: "Lest you wonder what I'm doing—this is but a specimen. I don't know whether Kefauver is hunting me or vice versa, but its hellish work in subzero weather and deep snow, and of course every 2 minute appearance turns into a 20 minute speech and then as you leave someone grumbles—'Didn't give us much time did he?'" He began on the Mesabi Range, flying to Hibbing and spending the night at Grand Rapids. On Thursday he spoke at village halls in Grand Rapids and two smaller towns and at Itasca Junior College and at a luncheon at Hibbing; stopped briefly at the town halls and in the evening went to a smorgasbord dinner in the Coates Hotel in Virginia, then spoke at the Eveleth Hippodrome. At the end of the day he flew to southern Minnesota, and on Friday spoke at six towns—Mankato, Waseca, Albert Lea, Austin, Kasson (where he and Eisenhower had spoken on agriculture in 1952)—and in the evening at Rochester. He stayed overnight there, on Saturday spoke at Concordia College in Moorhead on the North Dakota border, then hurried to Chicago to speak at a banquet given by the Irish Fellowship Club of Chicago at the Hotel Sherman, a curious piece of scheduling. He rested on Sunday and on Monday, the day before the election, returned to Minneapolis and St. Paul for radio and television programs and a smorgasbord with Humphrey and Freeman. Agriculture, labor, health, schools, single-interest government, foreign affairs, and again agriculture—these were his topics. He summed up in an Election Eve appearance on television and radio and went back to Chicago.

He was tired—the schedule had been "murderous," the weather terrible. Meetings had been scheduled twenty or thirty miles apart at half-hour intervals and Stevenson had had to be driven to them over icy roads. Once he and his party were using two small aircraft, and the wind was too strong to permit one to take off; Stevenson went on alone and by the time Blair caught up with him in the second plane, Humphrey and Freeman had added four more stops to the itinerary.

On Election Day he answered correspondence. He told a friend in South Africa that he had hoped the Administration, in concert with Great Britain and France, would "take a somewhat more positive position" in the Arab-Israeli dispute but it had not, and "my patience is wearing thin. But I'm still anxious not to appear to aggravate this situation for political advantage." He told Clement Davies, the Liberal Party leader in England, "I fail to understand why Britain and the U.S. could not have long since joined in some much more positive utterances, with France if possible, about Israel." He sent Governor Frank Clement of Tennessee a memo drafted by Newt Minow proposing that in the fall election Stevenson challenge Eisenhower to debate (Clement had made a similar suggestion several months earlier). He told Oscar Chapman, "We are keeping our fingers crossed about Minnesota. It was a long hard grind and the political rebels up there plus Republicans anxious to injure me can cause real trouble."

Indeed they did. At least, someone did—early in the evening, as the first returns came in, Bill Blair, still in Minnesota, told the Stevenson law office by telephone that Kefauver was getting about five votes for every three for

Stevenson. Finnegan, Minow, Tubby, Rivkin, and others felt sure Stevenson had lost. Finnegan was the first to say so—"We're deader than Kelsey's nuts." That night Stevenson's paneled law office was a grim place. Finnegan, his face gray as his suit, sat at Stevenson's desk. Stevenson himself was at home in Libertyville, listening to the returns after a black-tie dinner party to celebrate victory, with Bill Wirtz, Jane Dick, Barry Bingham, Archie Alexander, and others. From time to time Finnegan, receiving returns, called Stevenson to pass them on. As it turned out, Kefauver got 56 per cent of the vote in Minnesota. He won 26 of 30 delegates to the National Convention.

Stevenson's first reaction was anger. "He outpromised me," he said, referring to the fact that Kefauver had promised 100 per cent of parity to farmers up to $7,000 annually, while Stevenson had stuck to 90 per cent, the party's formal position. He also thought that Republicans had crossed over into the Democratic primary to vote for Kefauver in order to stop Stevenson and embarrass Humphrey and Freeman. Finnegan, Tubby, and others took this line with the press, and it had a certain plausibility. It seems likely, however, that Kefauver won because he took the underdog position and thus appealed to the discontent of farmers and others; because the Humphrey-Freeman machine could not deliver; because their support tainted Stevenson with bossism before an electorate notoriously independent; because dissatisfied farmers are more likely to turn to a new face than to an old one; because Kefauver's handshaking and curbside campaigning appealed to the small farmers and businessmen of Minnesota— Stevenson's style served him better at huge urban rallies or on national television than in small country towns. Harry Ashmore, who was in Minnesota with Stevenson, once said that Stevenson frequently holed up in a hotel room instead of shaking hands with the Mayor and other local figures—"every town we went into we lost votes." Finnegan had felt during the campaign that Stevenson was not "getting over."

Finnegan held a staff meeting that night in the law office to consider whether Stevenson should now withdraw from the California and Florida primaries. Roger Tubby thought so. He said that in Minnesota Stevenson had had the local organization as well as the Senator and Governor supporting him, had had a well-organized campaign, had had plenty of money, plenty of TV and radio time, and plenty of time to campaign; and yet Kefauver, who seemed to have "nothing going for him," had won. This being so, Tubby doubted it was worth continuing. He like others was beginning to wonder if Stevenson could ever win an election. Wirtz, on the other hand, felt strongly that Stevenson should continue and was annoyed by any defeatist attitude. One staff member suggested that Stevenson had to stay in the primaries because it was important to keep him alive as a political leader. Finnegan agreed that it was important to keep him alive but was not sure that keeping him in the primaries was the way to do it. Finnegan urged Stevenson not to issue any statement that night, but rather to wait until the next morning at a press conference, scheduled for ten-thirty. Stevenson, however, insisted on saying immediately that he was in the California and Florida primaries to stay and issued such a statement late that night. As on other occasions, he had no intention of quitting.

Next morning Stevenson seemed in excellent spirits, better than anybody on his staff. He went over two drafts of a proposed statement to the press and accepted suggestions willingly. The statement as issued said that, while he was "personally disappointed" at the results, the "real point" of the primary was the heavy Democratic vote, which amounted to a "repudiation" of the Administration and boded ill for the Republicans next fall. He said he would not "conjecture" about a Republican crossover into the Democratic primary. He said, "Senator Kefauver has won the first round and I congratulate him. As for myself, I will now work harder than ever, and I ask my kind friends everywhere to redouble their efforts, too. As I said last night, my plans are not changed, and neither are my ideas. I have tried to tell the people the truth. I always will. I have not promised them the moon. And I never will. This may not be the way to win elections but it is, in my opinion, the way to conduct a political campaign in a democracy."

A reporter said Kefauver's campaign manager had said that morning that Stevenson now could only seriously run for Vice President on a ticket headed by Kefauver. Would he consider it? "Well, I should be glad to consider anything Mr. Donahue says, except that." Did he consider his chances of being nominated slimmer now? "Well, it would seem to me that I'm no longer the front runner." Did he expect Harriman now to become an avowed candidate? He did not know. The Minnesota primary should worry Eisenhower more than Stevenson, he said. Had he been in touch with his California supporters? Pat Brown had telephoned that morning, he said, to say that the Minnesota defeat would "do them good" in California since it would spur Stevenson supporters to work harder. Had other political friends called? "Yes, we've had . . . well, endless calls and telegrams today to that effect. It's been very reassuring and comforting, really." Would he change his campaign tactics? He would not try to cover so much territory so rapidly again. Did he think it important to shake more hands? "There's no doubt but what handshaking—develops an identity between the shaker and the shakee."

A reporter said that Mayor Daley had suggested a Stevenson-Kefauver ticket and asked if this sounded "good." Stevenson said, "I'm sure that Senator Kefauver, as I've frequently said, is well qualified for any office within the gift of the people of this country." Asked if he thought Kefauver's charge of bossism had helped him, Stevenson said, "I'm told that it may have." What would he do in the event of defeat in California or Florida? "I have no intention of withdrawing of any kind. I shall go to the convention and if the party chooses to nominate me I shall be flattered in the extreme; if it doesn't, well, that—that's the party's decision." And then, "I think a point I'd like to make about all this is that—about this—your question about working harder is that when you believe something and you believe it deeply and you feel it strongly and you attempt to say it and you attempt to communicate it to people and you find that they vote against you or that they don't agree with you, all it does in my case is not so much fill me with any sense of—injustice or—defeat as it is a feeling of failure that I have not succeeded in communicating properly and that I must try harder and must try to do it better."

As he turned the press conference over to Jim Finnegan he said, "I hope you'll all come campaigning with me, 'cause we've just begun." His partisans in the room applauded. He had never handled a press conference better; it had been interrupted many times by laughter and bantering. Once again he had shown courage in adversity.

Finnegan threw as much dust into the air as he could. He produced statistics to prove that "well over 100,000" Republican voters crossed over into the Democratic primary. Asked how he could regain the initiative with the score 2–0 in favor of Kefauver, he first denied that Kefauver had won two primaries, pointing out that Stevenson had not entered New Hampshire, then accepted the 2–0 figure and predicted it would be 2–2 after the Illinois and Pennsylvania primaries where Stevenson was entered but Kefauver was not. A reporter asked about "a sixteen-state meeting—a behind-the-scenes thing—a stop-Adlai meeting in the last week or two. He said he had heard about it. Had it occurred? Yes, it had. In Denver. He had heard the meeting was of men from about twelve states, most of whom supported Harriman. Frank McKinney of Indiana, former national party chairman, had presided over it.

Stevenson dictated a letter to Barbara Ward and left it unfinished: "And speaking of consequences, I have just suffered a few myself in Minnesota. Tens of thousands of Republicans moved into the Democratic primary into the cities to discredit the DFL party . . . and incidentally to knock me off if possible. It appears that Mr. Stassen's fine and disarming hand guided the adroit maneuver skillfully." (Harold Stassen had visited Minnesota shortly before Election Day.) Paul Ziffren of California, a Jack Arvey protégé, telegraphed, "The fight has just begun." Eleanor Roosevelt telegraphed, "Better luck next time." Fred Dutton wrote to Blair, "I for one, want to make clear that we all love him—we all want him—more than ever. We want to *fight*. And we hope with all our heart that he will fight, too. We still need to talk sense, but we also need to talk specifics. No promises, but no platitudes, either." Steve Mitchell told Stevenson that a repetition of Minnesota seemed to be developing in California, that Stevenson was "failing to communicate to the average person," who did not want to admire Stevenson's speeches from afar but wanted to know him "as a human being" and as a candidate. He recommended that Stevenson stop making speeches and instead arrange question-and-answer meetings.

To many people, Estes Kefauver was a most attractive candidate. He had something of Harry Truman's common touch. If Stevenson seemed to the ordinary man remote, Kefauver did not. He had taken his law degree at Yale and been a vice president of the American Political Science Association but on the campaign trail he wore a coonskin cap. Television had brought him to national attention when his Senate committee investigated organized crime but he never abandoned his Southern drawl. Many Democratic liberals admired him because he, alone among Southern Senators, had refused to sign the Southern Manifesto, but ordinary voters admired him because he shook so many hands.

Don Bradley, a pro-Stevenson Democratic party manager in San Francisco, reported on a Kefauver press conference. Asked why he had made different statements on civil rights in California and Florida, Kefauver denied he had done it. He said the South would not be able to resist desegregation and the Supreme Court decision was the law of the land. He said the Minnesota results had not been totally unexpected, but he had had to overcome Stevenson's organization support, his use of television, and his commanding position as head of the party. He said he had worked harder than Stevenson, met more people, shaken more hands, and spoken in detail on the issues. He thought the Republican crossover showed that many Republican voters were dissatisfied with Administration farm policy. In California he thought he was the underdog but he had an effective organization, was making great progress, had a good slate of delegates, and thought California looked close. (His manager, Jiggs Donahue, predicted he would sweep the state.) Bradley reported that Kefauver drew nearly 1,000 people in a sidewalk meeting in the Fillmore district, a Negro area. In the Mission district, a polyglot workingmen's area that was pro-Democratic and pro-labor, he drew a big sidewalk crowd and addressed them as friends and neighbors, declared he had not signed the Southern Manifesto, pictured himself as a crusader against crime, plugged old-age security, and "confessed" that he wanted to be President and asked for their votes. He was introduced as "the winning Democrat." After the meeting, which blocked traffic, he shook hands for at least twenty minutes, making much of the fact that he had not eaten and was shaking hands with a sore thumb. His biggest and most enthusiastic crowds were on the streets and in poor neighborhoods, not at hotel receptions.

Herbert Lehman, sending $1,000 for a table for ten at the New York Stevenson dinner, told Finletter, "I do not believe . . . that the battle is by any means over." Senator Kennedy telegraphed that he and Paul Dever would commence at once a write-in campaign for Stevenson in Massachusetts. Without mentioning Minnesota he added, "With all good luck for the future." This time Stevenson responded promptly: "In view of what happened in Minnesota, I feel it might be even more helpful." A friend in New York told Bill Blair that Stevenson "had not been making his old impression," no longer seemed "perpetually exciting and original" as he had from 1952 through 1955, and should "take off the gloves, and slam away as he did earlier." Blair replied that Stevenson had been criticizing Eisenhower and sent copies of recent speeches. But, he added, "I do agree that for some reason he hasn't caught on this year and I don't honestly know what the reasons are. Perhaps Florida and California will be different stories. They had better be."

Truly, the Minnesota primary was a disaster, and many people thought Stevenson never would recover from it. It contained enough confusions, however, to prevent it from becoming the catastrophe that Willkie's defeat had been in Wisconsin or Stassen's in Oregon in previous years. Nonetheless, now he must win, and preferably win easily, in California and Florida if he was to be nominated. Many Democrats thought Averell Harriman was the chief beneficiary of Minnesota. Harriman was staking out a liberal position. He said years later, "I thought we needed a more vigorous statement of our position. Much as I respected Adlai, I felt he was not vigorous enough—I'm of the Harry Truman school. I thought there would be a good chance to win in '60 and as titular head of the party"—which Harriman would have become if he won the nomination in 1956—"I wanted to be in a spot to get it."

12.

Stevenson was more rattled than he appeared. Two days after the Minnesota primary he was scheduled to deliver a speech to a Democratic rally in Decatur, Illinois. Wirtz and Martin spent all day on the speech. Stevenson himself spent most of the day on it, rewriting it interminably, between telephone calls from political leaders around the country. He sent out requests for research material which in the end he discarded; and when he finished the speech it wasn't much good. About 4:30 P.M. he rushed out of the office to deliver it, trembling, overwrought. Yet the speech was for a small audience in a downstate town in Illinois, a minor speech that most candidates would have tossed off extemporaneously. The next day he fussed a good part of the day over the wording of a simple statement Wirtz wanted him to issue criticizing the Administration for opposing Democratic Social Security reforms.

At a staff meeting members of his staff criticized him for wasting too much time on speeches and urged him to speak extemporaneously. He accepted their criticism in good part but countered by pleading again for an all-purpose whistle-stop speech. He promised to work on it with a writer over the weekend (but did not—as before, nothing useful came of this). He asked his researchers to assemble a compendium of all positions he had taken on issues since 1952 and asked his writers to prepare a specific program and a speech on each issue. He also asked for a one-page summary of information about groups he would address and issues he should discuss on his forthcoming trips.

As he traveled, his speaking schedule would be lightened to allow time for him to meet with local leaders. He agreed to continue whistle-stopping —Finnegan thought it important that he keep moving around in order to contrast with Eisenhower's White House campaign—and to appear on local television programs. In his speeches he should try to make only one point and should strive for emphasis and clarity in making it. He should avoid self-deprecation and should answer some of Kefauver's charges. He should use now whatever ammunition he had and not hold back for the fall campaign, since he would not be in it if he didn't win the primaries. He should ask Mrs. Roosevelt to campaign for him in Florida and California.

George Ball told Newt Minow the time had come to bring Wilson Wyatt into the campaign to coordinate and organize it. Minow demurred; Wyatt was a fine, able, enthusiastic man but, if he were brought in, Finnegan probably would resign. The campaign was in terrible shape because nobody had his duties clearly outlined and only Stevenson had any final authority. Theoretically, Finnegan should be coordinator. But Finnegan was so in awe of Stevenson that he hesitated to assert himself. Moreover, some people, such as Jane Dick and Barry Bingham and Harry Ashmore, wanted to work directly with Stevenson, not through Finnegan. After Minnesota, however, Finnegan became more assertive. He had known for months the campaign was disorganized. The writers, for example, had not yet divided up the primaries or the Eastern speeches. This worked itself out—Ashmore took Florida, Martin California, and Wirtz stood over both while also working on the Eastern speeches. A little later Finnegan, too, told Minow to coordinate the entire campaign.

Stevenson and his staff and friends were trying to decide what he could do to diminish the impact of the Minnesota defeat. Word came from California that his supporters were disheartened. Kefauver had hurried there after Minnesota and his journey through California resembled a triumphal tour. Tom Finletter and George Ball came out to Chicago at the end of the week, and Stevenson decided to go to California immediately and deliver a "fighting" speech on television in Los Angeles and San Francisco in order to "put out the Kefauver fire." He wanted the speech to avoid substantive issues, to attack Kefauver, and to be angry and aggressive in tone. Wirtz urged him to be "affirmative" as well as aggressive.

On Monday and Tuesday, while Wirtz, Ashmore, and Martin worked on drafts for the televised speech in Los Angeles, Stevenson responded to Adlai III, who had asked him about an investment and had said, "Cambridge is in mourning." Stevenson wrote, "I shall see what I can do about the investment, but I am a little distracted at the moment." He asked Adlai and Nancy to join him in Florida April 12–15 and then go with him to

Southern Pines. To Agnes Meyer, whom he had hoped to see soon: "Everything about future planning has suddenly been dropped, in view of the present 'crisis.' " To Alicia Patterson in Kingsland, Georgia: he planned to arrive in Jacksonville on April 3 with John Fell and stay at her house until April 6. To Warwick Anderson, "Thank you for your kind note. But the Devil's best tool is discouragement, and I am really not as discouraged as perhaps I should be." And to Chet Bowles: "I feel more and more that I may want at some stage to take some bold, advanced, realistic position in the foreign affairs area."

In New York at the end of February, he had talked with Frank Altschul about proposing a unilateral declaration that the United States would discontinue the testing of thermonuclear weapons. Altschul had thought it politically unwise. He reasoned that Khrushchev had already said Russia was willing to discontinue tests; Eisenhower had not responded; and why he had not could not safely be guessed by anybody lacking access to classified information. He suggested instead urging a buildup of conventional arms so that we would not be obliged to use tactical atomic weapons in brush-fire wars. Stevenson now on March 26 told Altschul, "I had not planned to make the statement [on H-bomb testing], rather to hint at it, having once described the absurdity of building bigger H-bombs when the smallest already surpasses in power many times anything our people know about. The idea would be that this would be meeting the Russian proposal in good faith and putting the cat on their back, if there were further tests, for all the world to see. I had not, however, understood that they were far ahead of us, as you indicate, and if that is the case I think perhaps you are right that I should be cautious about saying anything bold in this field." At the same time Stevenson sent a copy of Altschul's letter to Tom Finletter and, reluctant to drop the matter, said, "I had thought this was an area in which we were ahead, or at least not behind. It seems to me the idea still has merits, at least to enlarge a little on the absurdity of such competition." Finletter replied that he agreed with Altschul—Stevenson would seem to be criticizing Eisenhower for his failure to accept the Russian suggestion, a dangerous position: since Eisenhower was fully informed and Stevenson was not, the public might think he was speaking without adequate information for political purposes and speaking on a subject "they do not want involved with politics." (Finletter also thought but did not say that the idea had little real merit or importance.)

Arthur Schlesinger suggested that Stevenson ask Finletter to come to Chicago and serve as Stevenson's executive officer. On speeches, Schlesinger thought moderation would become useful as a position after the convention but made no impact on people who cared enough to vote in primary elections. Stevenson replied that Finnegan was "the top man" in Chicago and Finletter was needed in New York, and that while Schlesinger was probably right about the speeches, "I confess that I am perplexed about the complaint. . . . Perhaps the explanation is that my language has been too complicated." To another man who sent condolences about Minnesota, Stevenson replied, "I evidently have lost the art of stirring Americans up—but I will keep at it—my way—as best I can." Wallace Deuel, a well-known correspondent of the Chicago *Daily News,* told Stevenson, "We think you're perfect the way you are." Stevenson thanked him and said, "I am up and at 'em again—my way!" He asked Don Forsyth of Springfield to prompt V. Y. Dallman, publisher of the *Illinois State Register,* to run "a good hot editorial" calling upon all Democrats to vote in the Illinois primary. He asked Judge Chalmer C. Taylor of Bloomington to prod the *Pantagraph* into doing the same.

Wirtz, Ashmore, and Martin produced drafts for Los Angeles on Monday. Wirtz's draft omitted any reference to Kefauver, Martin's criticized him but not by name, and Ashmore's attacked him directly. Wirtz and Martin combined their drafts; Ashmore would submit his separately. All three spent most of Tuesday working on the passage dealing with civil rights. Kefauver had been making votes that week in California by coming out strongly in favor of desegregation, taking a line more liberal than Stevenson's. Stevenson would have to move left. At the same time he would not forget that what he said in California would also be read in Florida. It was the most dangerous issue of all, the one that could defeat Stevenson in the primaries. It was at the same time the issue that could rescue him, for it might appear to the Democratic managers at convention time that only Stevenson could prevent the Democratic Party from being torn apart by the desegregation issue. Ashmore, a Southerner, had been talking for weeks to friends in the South. He now reported alarming news. Whites in South Carolina had been armed for a long time, he said, and now Negroes were reported arming themselves. Virginia, by adopting the interposition doctrine, had put its state seal on the resistance movement, and therefore it was no longer possible to separate the Upper South from the Deep South—resistance to desegregation was not merely a Georgia cracker's fight but a Virginia gentleman's fight and therefore respectable all across the South. In Florida the incumbent Governor who had been expected to win re-election easily had said the Supreme Court decision was the law of the land and as a consequence he seemed to be running behind a white supremacy candidate. At the end of Tuesday the writers went over the desegregation section of the speech with Stevenson word by word. He took their drafts, and one of his own that he had been working on, and began putting them together. He asked Martin to go to California with him the next day.

He was due to leave Chicago on an American Airlines flight at 9 A.M. but the weather was bad and the flight delayed. Stevenson and Blair arrived at the airport at about 10 A.M. Reporters and photographers trailed Stevenson back and forth across the airport lobby. When it became apparent the American flight would not take off, Stevenson and his party transferred to a noon flight on United Airlines and went into a United office to work on the Los Angeles speech. The speech was about 250 words too long; he would run over his television time. Blair and Martin took out 257 words, including a paragraph dealing with how hard it was to run for President. Blair and Martin felt Stevenson should never again say he was reluctant to run or anything close to it. Stevenson accepted the cuts. Blair telephoned the speech to Minow, who would telephone it to Los Angeles and have it put on the teleprompter while Stevenson was aloft—there would be no time after he arrived.

From the airport, Blair telephoned Marshall Field at the Chicago *Sun-Times* to ask him to run an editorial urging people to vote in the Illinois primary; Stevenson telephoned Don Walsh of the *Herald-American* asking him to do the same. They agreed. Blair also asked Field for money, and he said he would give it. The Illinois primary was less than two weeks away. Little had been done about it. Suddenly, after Minnesota, it had become important. The Illinois Volunteers had only about $1,500 in their treasury. Newt Minow had telephoned Lou Kohn a few days earlier and asked him to raise more money and promised to spend it on advertising and television spots. Stevenson had made only one speech, at Decatur, and had not planned to campaign in Illinois. But now his staff feared Kefauver might start a write-in movement. If Stevenson's vote dropped below that of the candidates for Governor and Senator and if, at the same time, Kefauver got as many as 30,000 write-in votes, Stevenson might be killed off in his home state. Suddenly receptions were arranged for him in Highland Park, Oak Park, and Evanston, and staffers began exploring the possibility of Stevenson's speaking in the East St. Louis area. He could not appear at the Cook County machine's traditional lunch for its precinct captains at the Morrison Hotel because he would be in Florida that day, and Finnegan proposed to appear in his stead, but Mayor Daley thought it unwise. Now at the airport Blair busied himself on the telephone with Illinois problems.

The plane left at last, about twelve-thirty. Aloft, Stevenson began going through his briefcase, reading several memoranda, handing others to Martin. Stevenson read slowly. He read each memorandum carefully, seeming to attach great importance to it, and Martin became impatient. Stevenson could spend as much as an hour on a memorandum or a long letter. He even did it with casual correspondence—letters from well-wishers he did not know. Stevenson asked what he was going to talk about at a rally and a labor meeting that night in Los Angeles after his television speech. Martin suggested he continue the theme of the television speech—attack Kefauver. He wanted to know what to say when he arrived at the Los Angeles airport. The same, Martin suggested, and began writing out notes. Stevenson wanted to know what he should talk about on television from San Francisco the next night. Martin suggested he repeat the Los Angeles speech—the two television stations reached different audiences. Stevenson demurred at delivering the same speech twice. Martin suggested he talk about labor, Social Security, or foreign policy. As soon as Martin mentioned foreign policy, Stevenson began talking about it at great length. Indeed, they talked about little else the rest of the way to Los Angeles. But in the end Stevenson said he would not have enough time to do it justice in his San Francisco speech, and, anyway, he was always talking about foreign policy there.

He arrived at Los Angeles so late that he had to take a helicopter to the television studio. Finnegan and Martin went to the Biltmore Hotel to watch Stevenson's speech on television. Stevenson liked to use the teleprompter but it made him seem wooden and immobile—he stared straight at it and did not once move his hands or his torso. The camera work was poor, and he was sitting in a high-backed chair which made him seem small and insignificant. The speech itself was good. He had written most of it himself, though he had accepted the desegregation passage and other language from the writers' drafts. Blair was unable to watch, so much did he fear that Stevenson would not finish on time. Without preamble, Stevenson began:

"I have come back to California and to Los Angeles for a brief visit because there are some things I want to say and say promptly to the Democratic voters in this state.

"What I have in mind is prompted, very frankly, by my experience last week in the Minnesota primary—and by my determination to win the presidential primary contest in my native state of California.

"I am not going to make any excuses for my defeat in Minnesota or talk about the massive Republican invasion of the Democratic primary there. I have no alibis.

"But something happened in Minnesota that I must speak about because it has also happened here in California. And other people beside myself are being unfairly hurt by it.

"My candidacy in Minnesota was sponsored by United States Senator Hubert Humphrey, by Governor Orville Freeman and many of the leaders of the Democratic Party. I was honored to have their unsolicited support and confidence.

"Yet Senator Kefauver and his supporters denounced them as 'political bosses'; and as a 'machine' trying to exclude him and to deny the people a choice.

"And the same thing has been done in California. Again my supporters are being described as sinister political bosses who are trying to dictate the people's choice.

"The Senator knows this is not so. I want to be sure you do too." (The released text had used Kefauver's name. Stevenson omitted it in delivery.)

He named several Californians on his slate of delegates and said Kefauver had "personally sought" the support of some of them. "The endorsement of the leaders of our party evidently becomes reprehensible only when the Senator doesn't get it." By discrediting Democratic leaders in California, Kefauver could only "weaken and divide" the party, thereby helping the Republicans. "For four years I've done my level best to unite the Democratic Party, not to tear it apart. And I propose to keep on thinking that the party's welfare is just as important as my own candidacy. So much for this false and divisive boss nonsense. Now let's get down to business—and the things that count."

He said he would conduct "as vigorous a campaign as time permits" in California. He would "not attempt to outbid any other candidate. . . . I will not promise anything I don't believe in or that I don't think is reasonable or possible. . . . There is such a thing as wanting to be President too badly. Another thing: I said in 1952 that my position would be the same in all parts of the country. It was then. And it will be this time, too. And that position will not be changed to meet the opposition of a candidate who makes it sound in Illinois as though he opposed federal aid to segregated schools, in Florida as though he favors it, and in Minnesota as though he had not made up his mind."

He said it made him "mad" to read in the papers that he spent too much time discussing the issues and not enough time shaking hands.

He attacked the Administration. He mentioned a number of domestic issues, ending with desegregation:

"And that reminds us that eliminating segregation in the schools of some of our sister states presents us today with a national challenge to our maturity as a people. For my part, like most Northerners, I feel that the Supreme Court has decreed what our reason told us was inevitable and our conscience told us was right. I feel equally strongly that, whether you agree with that decision or not, it is the law and should be obeyed.

"The Supreme Court has said *what* is to be done. The courts will determine *when* compliance will be expected. The question of *how* we will effect this transition in an orderly, peaceful way remains to be settled. This question is not going to settle itself. And the longer we drift the greater the danger—the danger from those who would violate the spirit of the Court decision by either lawless resistance or by undue provocation.

"I have suggested that the President should promptly bring together white and Negro leaders to search out the way to meet this problem as a united people.

"The fate of the world depends today on unity among Americans. To have that unity we must settle this problem peaceably, honorably and according to our law, our conscience, and our religion. I believe deeply that there is this unity in America's heart; and I believe that no man, North or South, has any greater present duty than to help find the way to unite this nation behind the right answer to this problem."

He spoke briefly on foreign affairs, then closed with as personal an appeal for support as he ever gave.

En route from the television studio to the hotel, the car in which Stevenson was riding had a flat tire, and he was late for appointments throughout the long evening—a meeting with Negro leaders and two speeches. Don Bradley of San Francisco thought the television speech so good that he recommended repeating it the next night in San Francisco. Stevenson was reluctant, and in the morning Martin, after talking with Stevenson, rewrote the Los Angeles speech slightly, strengthening a passage on labor— Bradley said that union leaders in the San Francisco area were lukewarm toward Stevenson—and shortening the passage on foreign affairs, and slightly recasting the "bossism" passage.

Thursday morning Stevenson made several television appearances, met with local leaders, then near noon walked a few blocks from the hotel to the Los Angeles garment district to speak briefly on immigration and Social Security. About 1,000 people turned up, and the meeting went well, but when Stevenson boarded the 2 P.M. plane for San Francisco he seemed nervous and distraught, worried about the San Francisco telecast. He kept jabbing at the speech manuscript with a pencil, changing things for the sake of changing them, and asked, "Why do I have to give them all this crap about labor?" Martin explained, and Stevenson irritably hacked up the labor insert but finally agreed to use part of it. He was irked because Roger Tubby had permitted a stenographer to make a transcript of his extemporaneous remarks at the previous night's rally and had distributed them to the press; he told Tubby never to do it again. He seemed to think extemporaneous remarks unworthy of him, to want to speak only formally and for the record. During the flight he kept saying he couldn't possibly finish working on the speech in time for delivery tonight, and sure enough when he landed he was only about two thirds of the way through. He was angry at himself for having spent so much time on it and at everyone else for not having it ready for him in final form. He was tired.

At the San Francisco airport the crowd pressed closely about him, he lost his hat, he and the press led a procession of supporters up through the airport, then back out again and then up through the lobby and finally to a room where local people said he was to hold a press conference—but the door was locked and nobody could find the key. People were milling around, women were yelling, the photographers were pushing people. He finally held the press conference, doing surprisingly well considering the circumstances, then got into a car in a fast motorcade and with Martin worked on the television speech all the way into the city—Stevenson was trying to rewrite the desegregation passage, Martin urged him not to under these circumstances, he finally agreed.

At the Fairmont Hotel, Stevenson worked on the speech again, while Blair and Martin marked optional cuts in his reading copy which he could make if he was running late. Two Negro leaders waited in an outer room. Stevenson finished with the speech only five minutes before time to leave the hotel for the TV studio, and the Negroes barely had a chance to shake his hand as he brushed past them. He reached the TV studio minutes before his television time. Stevenson then delivered the speech from a manuscript, not from a teleprompter, and was extremely animated throughout: It was one of his best television appearances ever. Afterward he went on to a rally and a labor meeting.

That night a friendly newspaperman described Kefauver's campaign methods to Martin. Kefauver, he said, began his day with a breakfast at 8 A.M. in a women's club. Then he organized his motorcade and took it not downtown but to outlying workingmen's residential areas or shopping centers, and there he said, "They don't like me downtown, so I'm out here with the people. It's the bosses who are downtown. They're with Stevenson. But I'm out here with the people." As he drove slowly along the streets he stopped to shake hands with anybody he could find. At noon he went to a luncheon, often at the Elks Club. He only said a few words, never delivered a long speech, and ended, "Now I'm going to go over and stand by the door to shake hands with every one of you as you are leaving." And he did it. In the afternoon he resumed his motorcade, toured a factory, greeted workers as the shift changed, and dined with another civic group, saying a few words and again shaking hands with everybody, then leaving for his only speech of the day. It was usually twenty minutes long, delivered to some non-political group such as the Postal Clerks' Union or the Grange. He moved fast from one place to another, ninety miles an hour, and he was accompanied by only one secretary and one writer. He was working California by congressional districts. The newspaperman thought it all effective and said that, while Stevenson had the support of the leaders of the California Democratic Clubs, Kefauver had the support of the rank-and-file members. He had won it at Fresno. Stevenson had only a paper organization—club leaders, nothing more, and they could deliver no votes. Kefauver was shaking about four hundred hands a day, and it seemed to be as effective in California as it had been in Minnesota, where a farmer had told the reporter, "I voted for him. I don't know much about him but my cousin over in Sauk Center shook hands with him a week or two ago, and he seemed like a pretty nice fella, so I voted for him." This was Kefauver's strategy and appeal.

The newspaperman thought Stevenson should stay out of Los Angeles and San Francisco and visit small towns and cities and farming centers. He added that Stevenson's labor union backing was also almost wholly paper support: he had the prominent labor leaders but they could not deliver their members' votes. The situation seemed tailor-made for Kefauver. He was running for sheriff, and to most people there was not too much difference between being sheriff and being President. Stevenson, on the other hand, was running for President almost as though he had already been nominated. Such a campaign made little impression on the ordinary California voter, he thought. Kefauver's usual speech line was this: "I want you people to know that if I am elected President of the United States, I want you working men and working women to know that you will have a friend in the White House." And nothing more. He usually knew the name of at least one man at a meeting, and the names of his wife and children, too, and was likely to say, "I sure am grateful to Milton Jones here for working for me. Of course I know it isn't Milton that really does all the work, it's his wife Gladys and his daughter Joanne. Stand up, Gladys, stand up, Joanne, and take a bow." And then he threw his arms around Milton. People thought it wonderful. When he addressed a street-corner crowd he began by asking, "How many of you folks are from Tennessee originally? Five or six hands went up. Then he said, "Well, I guess I better not brag too much about what I did back home." When he did discuss issues, Kefauver took almost exactly the same positions as Stevenson. The difference was in their campaign methods.

Next day Stevenson, Tubby, Finnegan, and Martin took the 9 A.M. plane back to Chicago, Blair staying in California to raise money, and en route Martin reported to Finnegan what he had learned about Kefauver. Finnegan had heard similar things. He was thoroughly disgusted with the Democratic organization in California, disgusted and alarmed too. He said they were "all chiefs and no Indians," perpetually fighting among themselves, and unless somebody came out here and straightened them out, Stevenson would lose California. Like the newspaperman, Finnegan said the Californians were conducting a "public relations campaign" for Stevenson. They would do nothing until Stevenson arrived in California. Then they would get him on television, hold press conferences, issue press releases—and then do nothing further until he returned a month later. Instead of this, of course, they should have been handing out buttons and stickers, getting shop stewards in factories to wear buttons, and performing other organization chores that are routine in Chicago or Philadelphia. To make matters worse, Kefauver appealed strongly to ordinary people of no great education or means who made up the bulk of Democratic primary voters, and Stevenson did not. The tide was running against Stevenson, Finnegan thought, and he had no California organization to stem it. Finnegan might have to go to California himself to build an organization in the two months that remained before the primary.

In the plane Stevenson talked to Martin for two hours about his schedule, what he ought to do and say, and the all-purpose whistle-stop speech. He seemed confused, seemed to want to put everything into the speech. He said it should be divided into an attack on the Administration and a positive program, but whenever he started talking about the positive section he returned to the attack. He was bitter toward the Administration. And on some issues he had no positive program, for he had not really taken a position on the specifics of all issues although he thought he had.

Stevenson said he wanted to draw up an "indictment" of the Administration that would "stick," did not want merely to "plead conclusions." He said he wished the writers would prepare a brief summary of his own experience which could be mimeographed and given to people who were to introduce him, and he listed what he called his own "versatile" and "unusual variety" of experience—candidate for President who got 27.5 million votes, Department of Agriculture, State Department, lawyer, businessman, Governor, traveler, author, recipient of honorary degrees. He repeated several times that his accomplishments, particularly his literary and scholastic ones, set him apart from the ordinary run of politician. He was proud of his books and honorary degrees and of his family's connection with politics. ("Fifteen or twenty honorary degrees in recognition of his wisdom and scholarship and judgment," as he said himself. He said that as Governor he had made a record that was "unequaled" in Illinois history. When he mentioned his experience with Secretary of the Navy Knox he referred to it as having been at "the very top of the Navy Department." At the same time he could be funny and told Martin to omit dates from the memorandum because if they were included the introducer would be fumbling and peering at his memorandum and saying, "Well, it says here 1948, 1947, I don't know, I can't quite read it, I can't make out what he did then," imitating the voice and manner of a befuddled introducer.

Martin suggested that Stevenson, in trying to talk to whistle-stop audiences, should speak against colonialism. Earlier in the spring, on St. Patrick's Day in Chicago at a meeting which Stevenson had addressed, John Kennedy had made a long impassioned speech against colonialism. It had impressed his hearers mightily but Stevenson had been bored. "There isn't any colonialism," he said, "it's all gone." Martin pressed the argument, saying that most people didn't know it was gone and as underdogs would identify with colonial peoples and, hence, with Stevenson. Stevenson said without enthusiasm that perhaps he could say something like, "It is fantastic that we have not yet identified with the peoples in the underdeveloped portions of the world." It was Stevenson's way of abstracting and elevating ideas, thus at the same time broadening and desiccating them.

He returned to the all-purpose speech: he had to have it because if he did not have a manuscript of some sort before him when he spoke ideas would run around inside his head and he could not sort them out and often would start talking about three subjects, get interested in the first, and talk for fifteen or twenty minutes about it, then realize he had no time to go on to the other two, which might be of equal or greater importance. This, he said, bored audiences and made him disgusted with himself.

He spoke acidly of the "moral duplicity" of the Eisenhower administration—"but we'll have to be careful or people will think we're talking about Ike's morals." The Administration had done nothing constructive, had eroded liberty, had failed to lead against McCarthy, and had barely held the New Deal gains. He saw nothing but "rigidity and stagnation" in foreign affairs and thought Russia was "overtaking us in every direction in which we look." He criticized single-interest government by big business and spoke of the rising tensions at home and abroad. He said, "I've got to make some ringing speeches and lift some hearts," and he talked about papers Barbara Ward had written on Asia.

He said he could not outmatch Kefauver in direct appeal but could in reason and sense. He quoted Lincoln: "We must not promise what we should not lest we be called upon to perform what we cannot." "It's easy to come along and say what I'm going to do—but then what respect would you have for me?" he said. "Shaking hands—the candidate has a greater obligation than that. Here's a guy who's got the courage not to say always what you want to hear. To get the poor people, working people, you've got to give 'em a kick or a lift." Labor, he argued, was no different from anybody else. They wanted what everybody wanted—schools, hospitals, highways, health, Social Security, disability insurance. "But most of all labor needs an expanding economy," he said. "I must indicate to them in simple words that I've thought about their problems and my heart is with them."

He said the all-purpose speech should close with a passage from Barbara Ward about the quality of life, should end with inspiration, imagination, and a vision of the future. He desperately wanted the all-purpose speech, said he had tried to get it from Ashmore and Wirtz unsuccessfully and now "simply had to have it." It was a favorite gambit. But he seemed truly shaken and uncertain of himself. His hands trembled and he fiddled with papers and a pencil while talking. At one point, trying to explain something he wanted in the all-purpose speech, he became involved in a long complicated sentence and then suddenly in the middle of it, disgusted, said, "Oh, damn it, I never can say anything simply." Too many people had been telling him that. He had always seemed a calm man supremely confident in himself and sure of what he was about. Not now. Minnesota had changed him. So had the conflicting advice he had received since. Perhaps the rigors of campaigning had too. Martin felt sorry for him but gave him another piece of advice: to drop qualifying clauses from his speeches. In San Francisco he had added to the textual passage calling for repeal and replacement of the Taft-Hartley Act a qualifier that the new labor law would be fair to labor, fair to management, yes, and fair to the public. Stevenson replied he always felt that on television he was talking to many people who were not Democratic voters and would respect him for his stand in favor of the public interest.

Stevenson showed Martin a memorandum from an Eastern friend asking hard questions on foreign policy. Did he favor recognition of the Peking government? Did he favor its admission into the UN? Did he favor immediate shipment of arms to Israel? And so on. Stevenson, looking out the plane's window at the barren Rockies, began musing about the questions and said, "Sometimes I think I ought to go ahead and answer these questions and start talking about them because the people are going to have to face up to them sooner or later. Maybe I ought to go ahead and tell them the truth about these problems. I'm sure it would be the end of me as a politician, but I think it would make my reputation as a prophet." Unhappy and uncomfortable, he paused, as though seriously considering answering the questions publicly. He seemed caught in the ancient dilemma of a politician: the desire to utter the truth as he knows it and the desire to get elected. Stevenson would like to have spoken out on these issues, to have said that of course the United States must recognize Peking and vote for her admission into the UN, for example, but he dared not if he wanted to stay in public life. He returned again to attack the Eisenhower administration, sometimes making fun of himself while doing so.

Finnegan joined the conversation, told Stevenson he was in bad shape in California, and advised him not to enter the Oregon primary. Several Oregon Democratic leaders had urged Stevenson to enter, arguing that Kefauver would run as a write-in candidate and saying they could organize a write-in campaign for him—he need not campaign personally. Finnegan, however, thought Stevenson had enough on his hands in California and Florida and ought not enter another primary where he could not campaign heavily. Moreover, the Oregon politicians had been unable to convince Finnegan that they could deliver. But only in deference to Finnegan had Stevenson withheld a decision to enter.

Finishing their talk, Stevenson seemed glum. He said he wanted to rest on his trip to Jacksonville next week. He also said he did not want to take any staff with him to Florida because of the cost. John Fell, home for Easter vacation, met him at the airport, and they went home to Libertyville together. It was Easter weekend.

13.

The Minnesota primary had affected Stevenson. He had been the front runner for so long, and had received such world-wide acclaim as a statesman since 1952, and had so immersed himself in issues, that it seemed incredible that a lanky man in a coonskin cap whose principal asset was the handshake could beat him. But the Minnesota defeat may have been, as some of his staff came to believe, a good thing. During his two-day trip to California he had delivered more than a half dozen speeches and made many appearances. The two major ones on television had been more hard-hitting than usual, more suited to a primary campaign, recognizing his opponent, attacking him, and speaking pointedly to the issues. The contrast with Fresno was striking. Suddenly he was not the philosopher-statesman of the party setting forth visions of the future but a candidate in a primary fighting for his life. Not since his 1948 campaign for Governor against Dwight Green had he talked that way. If he could succeed, if he could win the remaining primaries, he would go far toward accomplishing what Carl McGowan hoped the primaries would do for him: surround him with an aura of victory. Other friends might prefer him as a statesman. But after Minnesota he had little choice: Kefauver had pulled him off the pedestal and he had to fight on the ground. It helps explain what many admirers later objected to: that his 1956 campaign was less lofty and more political than his 1952 campaign.

Still the advice continued. Paul Douglas made available to Stevenson "the most precious political jewels in my possession"—his "classified" mailing list of some 100,000 Illinois Democrats and independents. Senator Kennedy suggested that Stevenson use Kefauver's absentee record in the Senate vigorously. Eddie Barrett, the Illinois spoilsman now helping Stevenson in the Illinois primary, recommended that Stevenson stay out of southern Illinois, which was lost to Kefauver anyway, and that he "talk plain and simple and climb down from Cloud 7."

Newt Minow was trying to work out a joint statement of support by the Illinois congressional delegation but it had to be cleared with Dick Daley; was buying $5,000 worth of radio and television spots the week before the Illinois primary; and had arranged to mail postcards to about half of Paul Douglas' mailing list. None of the mechanics of campaigning was inspired but all seemed urgent in the wake of Minnesota.

Ashmore greeted Stevenson with a long memorandum on the politics of desegregation. He thought it "a foregone conclusion" that if Southern delegates to the convention did not get what they considered a satisfactory ticket, they would walk out of the convention with consequences to the nominee more serious than in 1948, for they would "certainly" take five states out with them and perhaps as many as nine. Ashmore reported that the Deep South was determined to resist desegregation and had formed Citizens' Councils to lead the resistance. The Upper South had remained calm and had avoided legislative action. The Border South had begun to move toward desegregation. But in June of 1955, when the Court handed down its implementation decrees, liberal leadership in the South had failed, and racists had attracted new support. To the restless white South, the Till case, the Autherine Lucy affair, and the Montgomery boycott were inflammatory symbols of new Negro determination. At present, Southern political leaders who had initially taken moderate positions had, under the pressure of primary campaigning, abandoned them in order to survive. Ashmore argued that the first job to be done in the South was to reduce racial tensions and restore communication between white and Negro leaders. Only a "conciliator" could do it, and Stevenson was the conciliator. Stevenson's nomination had always depended on his ability to hold the Southern support he and Mitchell had won since 1952. Southerners still considered him the lesser of two evils (Kefauver was the other; Harriman was totally unacceptable). If Stevenson lost the primaries, Southern delegates would probably swing to Symington—they hated Kefauver as an apostate. If that failed and the Northern delegates forced through one of their own, perhaps Harriman, the result would be a party split permanently. Therefore the "careful development of the Great Conciliator role is not only good morals but the only possible political course." Stevenson must hold the party together. He should avoid both fringes, the Southern racists and the "Madison Avenue abolitionists," and try to broaden the center.

Kefauver, preceding Stevenson into Florida, made a strong speech in favor of desegregation. Stevenson staff members thought he might have decided he could not win Florida anyway and would at least get credit in California for courage. They thought he had pulled the teeth of Stevenson's charge that he said different things in different places.

While Stevenson was in California, Jack Arvey had told Minow that Stevenson must take a stronger stand on arms for Israel. In the past Stevenson had favored arming Israel but had clouded his stand with qualifying clauses, Arvey thought; now he must take a firm position lest he lose Jewish votes and contributions. Arvey thought Stevenson should say that he personally favored arms for Israel but that the Israel-Arab problem should be given to the United Nations and the UN asked to guarantee Israel's borders. On Sunday, Jim Finnegan told Minow he had just learned that Kefauver would issue a strong pro-Israel statement on Wednesday; Finnegan wanted Stevenson to beat him to it. Finnegan could not reach Stevenson. Neither could Minow. But Minow reached Blair, and Blair told him that Stevenson had already decided to issue a strong pro-Israel statement on Tuesday. As had happened on other occasions, Stevenson had balked for weeks at Minow's urging that he issue a strong statement but then had decided by himself to issue one. He did, in Atlanta, Georgia, that day, Tuesday, April 3.[7]

[7] The United States Government "has no firm policy" in the Middle East, he said, and attacked "the Eisenhower administration" for not having reaffirmed "the Three Point Declaration of 1950 with Britain and France," for not having "made it clear that the State of Israel is here to stay" or that the United States "will not tolerate the use of force by Israel or the Arabs in violation of the UN Charter or the armistice agreement," for having done "little to strengthen the authority of" the UN armistice agency, for having failed "to devise measures to prevent the border clashes which endanger the peace," for having "encouraged alliances and Arab rearmament in disregard of tensions and animosities, thereby opening the area to Communist penetration. . . . Ever since Secretary Dulles presented General Naguib of Egypt with a revolver three years ago, the situation has constantly deteriorated. And now, Russia, with an eye on the oil of the Middle East, is cynically fishing in these troubled waters and war threatens." War must be avoided to save Israel and avert the danger of a spreading war. The statement continued: "Steps should be taken to make it unequivocally clear:

"(1) That Israel is here to stay;

"(2) That we will not tolerate armed aggression by either side;

"(3) That an equitable balance of armed strength should be preserved between Israel and her neighbors. And Israel should not be deprived of the necessary means of defense, and weapons and training should be promptly supplied to restore that balance.

"It is said that to strengthen Israel would be to start an arms race and would fur-

On the same day Secretary Dulles at a press conference said that, in an emergency in the Middle East, U.S. forces might be sent into action without congressional authority. But he added that it was "the disposition" of Eisenhower not to do so without "consultation and concurrence" by Congress. Next day in Miami, Senator Kefauver favored American arms for Israel but said that American troops should be committed there only with congressional approval. Kefauver was campaigning hard in Florida, shaking hands and trying to maintain the underdog position by declaring that Stevenson was still the front runner. Stevenson rested a few days at Alicia Patterson's plantation in Georgia, working on his Jacksonville speech, due Friday.

Meanwhile, most of his aides back home thought he ought to stop delivering set speeches and either speak extemporaneously or merely answer questions at meetings. Finnegan felt strongly that, whatever format Stevenson adopted, he must bring what he said down to the level of the ordinary man: "He's got to get off of Cloud Nine." Unfortunately, he said it to the staff, not to Stevenson. Finnegan, though he dressed like a banker, had a breezy manner when at ease but he was not at ease around Stevenson. He thought that old age, health, and education were the best issues, and a gleam came into his eye when he speculated on how many voters over the age of forty were afraid they might develop cancer. (He later died of cancer.) People tend to think that professional politicians care only about organization, precinct work, and political favors. Finnegan, like Arvey, worried at least as much about speeches and issues. (And people like Schlesinger thought political work more fun than speeches and issues.) Finnegan did not like the Israel statement, thinking its qualifying clauses robbed it of its effect. Arvey, however, was pleased. Ashmore was receiving word from Florida that Kefauver was making real progress and that Stevenson was slipping. Minow was discouraged because he could not get a decision from anybody on anything. Some thought Stevenson's best hope lay in a great international crisis during the primary period. Only this, they thought, would remind voters that a statesman, not a handshaker in coonskin, was what the country needed.

The Wisconsin primary was held that Tuesday, the day Stevenson went to Florida. Stevenson was not on the ballot and write-ins were impossible. Eisenhower ran ahead of Kefauver. Some months earlier friends, including Minow, had urged Stevenson to go into Wisconsin, but a private poll had shown him weak in the farm areas, strong only in Milwaukee, so he had stayed out. Another secret poll, this one in Illinois, showed that if Stevenson ran against Eisenhower in the fall he would lose in Illinois by at least as big a margin as in 1952. The poll showed that he had lost ground all

---

ther alienate the Arab States. That would be a clear misfortune for us and the Arabs as well. But the Russians have already started an arms race, and once the balance of power is roughly restored, I think the United Nations should call on Russia and everyone else, including ourselves, to establish an embargo on the shipment of arms to the area."

over Illinois, that people were beginning to be impressed with Kefauver, and that they were very favorably disposed toward Eisenhower. Eisenhower, indeed, looked just about unbeatable. The survey, based on long interviews with a relatively few people, showed that Chicago Negroes were against Stevenson, were equally against Kefauver, and might vote Republican if they could not have a civil rights Democrat like G. Mennen Williams of Michigan. Farmers paid little attention to politics but if interested at all leaned toward Kefauver. They did not like Eisenhower or Stevenson. Intellectuals in the University of Chicago area were deserting Stevenson. Organization Democrats in Chicago were lukewarm. At least one alderman was telling his precinct captains to forget Stevenson during the primary election next Tuesday. Organized labor had broken away and some labor leaders were considering moving to Kefauver. They and the machine men wondered whether Daley "has his heart in it."

Throughout the state, people seemed to have no pride in Stevenson as a native son or former Governor. They had only the dimmest impression of him as a world traveler. They did not identify him with any of the "gut issues," such as civil rights (except in Negro minds, where he was unpopular), farm depression, unemployment. Many thought him too clever, "a smart aleck." The survey showed that up to now the only thing that had kept Stevenson's candidacy from collapsing completely was the absence of any alternative candidate.

The erosion of Stevenson's support even among liberal Democrats who had idolized him in 1952 was clear at any number of cocktail parties in Chicago at this time. They would, of course, vote for him. But they had lost their enthusiasm. It did no good to argue that he was trying to conciliate North and South and that the alternative to conciliation was civil war. They were convinced that he had tried to straddle the issue to win delegate votes both North and South, and they thought it unworthy of him. It did no good to argue that the Republicans could not bring about reconciliation because they had no strength in the South, or to argue that Eisenhower had worsened the situation by standing silent so long. They only felt the more strongly that the Democratic Party should become, in effect, an abolitionist party. Or so at least it seemed to those still loyal to Stevenson.

That week the Cook County machine's precinct captains attended their luncheon in the Morrison, and Daley read a message from Stevenson. Rather unexpectedly, the precinct captains cheered. At a long staff meeting the Stevenson advisers debated whether he should enter Oregon. Minow argued that, with Kefauver's people organizing an Oregon write-in campaign, Stevenson was, in effect, already in Oregon whether he wanted to be or not and he might as well make a fight of it. Others felt he was in so much trouble in California that he must not dilute his efforts with an Oregon campaign. Further, if Kefauver campaigned there and Stevenson did not and Kefauver won, the effect would be no worse than it had been in New Hampshire, but if both campaigned and Kefauver won, Stevenson would have suffered a major defeat. And in a state with a farm vote Oregon looked too much like Minnesota for comfort. And in a public power state Kefauver had the Dixon-Yates issue—he was investigating it in the Senate. The pro-Oregon view carried the day, however, and soon Stevenson authorized a campaign in his behalf.

He delivered a major speech before the Jacksonville Bar Association on April 6—a counterattack on Kefauver's charges of "bossism," his divisive tactics, and his Senate absenteeism. On desegregation, he repeated in substance what he had said in California, though adding at Ashmore's insistence this language: "The job that has to be done now is to find, even in the conflicting counsel of those who disagree so strongly, the best course by which the Court's decision can be carried out."

14.

Stevenson returned to Chicago that night. Roger Tubby, who had been with him, said that in Florida he had seemed nervous and rattled and short-tempered. He complained that he couldn't seem to think any more, that he needed new ideas and didn't have them, that everything seemed stale to him, nothing fresh. Tubby suggested to him that the times were responsible, that desegregation and the farm program were uppermost in people's minds but there wasn't anything new to say about them. Tubby did not say so but all this, if true, could only result in another Eisenhower landslide.

News from around the country was not good. Reports from Montana were bad. A representative of a railroad union said Stevenson was in "great danger" in California. Charles Brannan, a Truman Secretary of Agriculture, was reported to have criticized Stevenson heavily at a farm meeting. Lower-level farm organization leaders tended to favor Kefauver. An REA official felt Stevenson was only "lukewarm" on public power. That weekend, Martin thought, was the lowest point yet in the campaign. The staff felt that Stevenson's support had not been strong to begin with and that it had left him as soon as it had any reason. Minow decided to throw away the posters and buttons already printed and to substitute for them a photograph of Stevenson, one of him riding in an open convertible, throwing his head back and laughing, a photograph reminiscent of FDR at his most popular. Tubby tried to avoid sitting beside Stevenson on airplanes because it simply wasn't fun to be with him now.

When Stevenson arrived home he went to Bill Blair's house and found a gathering that included Tom Finletter, Arthur Schlesinger, and Marietta Tree, who had flown out from New York that day, and the elder Blairs, Bill Wirtz, and Jane Dick. Schlesinger noted, "He looked exceptionally tired; sad, gentle and charming in manner; and the total impression was rather heartbreaking. We talked some about his attacks on Kefauver. He said that that had been the one part of his Jacksonville speech . . . which he had disliked. (But he returned to the attack at his press conference on Saturday and again on a TV show on Sunday.) Everyone else present felt the attacks were a great mistake."

These people, and many others, had assembled in Chicago for a conference of the national Stevenson for President Committee. Stevenson spoke early Saturday morning. "When he entered there was great applause and a rising ovation," Schlesinger noted. "His speech was quiet and dejected with (it seemed to me) the chill of defeat all over it. There was far less applause when he concluded and left. The delegates were greatly disappointed and let down." Marietta Tree recalled years later, "He was so exhausted he was making no sense, commuting from Florida to California, so tired that it was suggested that he should not address us. But with all those people who had gone there to see him—I was horrified at his condition, so horrified that I almost lost faith in him. We in New York were very depressed, especially Jack Shea [a New York Volunteer leader] and I, by his condition. So was Tom Finletter. Barry Bingham said, 'This is not the man we knew in 1952.'"

Delegates agreed that Stevenson was not "getting over" to the people. Most agreed that nobody knew where he stood on issues—that his positions lacked clarity, cogency, and concreteness, as Schlesinger put it. "The death watch continued through the day and was redeemed only in the evening when Finletter, addressing a dinner meeting, gave his own views on issues, ruthlessly declared that they were Stevenson's views and brought the whole affair to life. Afterward people said, 'If only Stevenson would talk the way Finletter does.'"

After addressing the delegates Stevenson hurried to East Alton, Illinois, across the Mississippi River from St. Louis, Missouri, and delivered a speech about the meaning of the Illinois primary next Tuesday. He asked for a big Democratic vote in Illinois to put pressure on President Eisenhower to sign a Democratic farm bill pending in Congress.

On Sunday, Blair drove the Finletters, Marietta Tree, and Schlesinger out to Libertyville, and the delegates to the meeting in Chicago arrived en masse by bus for a box lunch. Stevenson took Finletter and Schlesinger to an upstairs room to talk about the speeches on April 21 to the American Society of Newspaper Editors and on April 25 to the Stevenson New York dinner. They told him he must give a liberal speech in New York or not go there at all. This led to discussion of civil rights, and as Schlesinger reported, "AES now made an impassioned speech about how his role was that of the conciliator, that this was a role requiring far more courage than pro-civil rights demagoguery, and that making remarks which provoked the South would only delay the eventual achievement of the objective. What did we think, he asked, of the idea of a year moratorium on all further agitation, legal action, etc., in the civil rights field. We discussed the conflict between principle and unity and pointed out that in 1952 he had been considered as the man who stood on principle whereas he is now considered the man who would sacrifice principle to unity. He accepted this and said that, where principle and unity conflicted in this matter, he was bound to stand by unity. I asked whether he thought the Democratic platform could possibly not endorse the Supreme Court decision. He said he didn't know about that, hoped the question could be avoided, and wanted to talk to his southern friends about it. Tom and I both came away deeply disheartened. It seems evident that he does not feel any strong moral issue in the civil rights fight; that he identifies instinctively with the problems of the southern white rather than with the sufferings of the southern Negro; that he feels it to be easy to be what he calls a demagogue on the issue; and that any strong position he might take will be against convictions." Later on that Sunday, Stevenson attended a reception at a high school in conservative Highland Park, a suburb not far from Libertyville, and found a surprisingly large crowd, including many Negroes and Jews.

Stevenson had only a day and a half at home before he resumed traveling, a trip that would keep him on the road almost continually until June 5, the date of the California primary. He spent it on correspondence. The *Pantagraph* endorsed Stevenson in the Illinois primary. On Monday night, Election Eve in Illinois, Stevenson appeared on a television program, and Dick Daley introduced him with an emotional speech that praised his liberalism. Stevenson himself recalled his Illinois ancestry, his work as Governor, and his life in Illinois as a citizen, an effective speech. He spoke with conviction, and it mattered little what he said.

Next morning on his way to his office from Libertyville he heard that Eisenhower would speak in the evening of April 21 to the American Society of Newspaper Editors (ASNE) after Stevenson had spoken to them in the morning. This made that speech all the more important, and he sent a quick letter to Finletter saying so and adding: "I must return to Florida now and I'm afraid I'll have not a tranquil moment to think about this until too late." Governor Ed Muskie of Maine had sent diffident suggestions about projecting warmth to large audiences as he did to small, and Stevenson told him, "I am trying to do something about it and also about more personal contact and less time in speeches." He asked Ernest Gruening to issue a statement supporting him in the Alaska primary. He told Lloyd Garrison he had talked to a New York Negro about coming to Chicago to explore the possibility of joining Stevenson's staff—"I am concerned about whether what I am saying is getting communicated to the Negro community." Blair said that a columnist had quoted Governor Williams as describing Stevenson as "tired, timid, temporizing and despairing" and as saying that moderation was "a good policy for drunks, but not politicians." Blair said the piece had caused "consternation" among Stevenson supporters and he hoped Williams would repudiate it if he did not say it.

Senator Neuberger of Oregon sent Minow a somewhat truculent letter about the Oregon primary. His wife, Maurine, wanted to campaign for Stevenson but he feared trouble if she did—he had pleaded with Stevenson in January to enter Oregon, Stevenson had refused, he had acted as intermediary in arranging for both Stevenson and Kefauver to stay off the ballot, and now if his wife campaigned for Stevenson it would be construed as a violation of the truce. Stevenson aides were already irritated with Neuberger for refusing to campaign in Oregon for Stevenson, recalling that Stevenson had helped Neuberger greatly when he ran for the Senate in 1954. Minow felt that Stevenson had entered Oregon as a write-in candidate only after Kefauver had—"if anyone has departed from any understanding at all, it was Senator Kefauver."

Illinois voted. Stevenson did well. He got fewer votes than the combined total of the two candidates in the contested gubernatorial nomination but he swamped Kefauver, whose write-in vote was small. Stevenson got the big plurality in Cook County that he should have gotten and ran well downstate. His vote nearly equaled Eisenhower's. This actually meant little, of course, since neither had serious competition and neither had campaigned extensively—Eisenhower not at all—in the state. Stevenson headquarters, however, was able to issue a statement claiming that Stevenson had run well in Negro wards and workingmen's wards and downstate which, although largely undocumented, found its way into the press and lifted the hearts of Stevenson adherents. (Stevenson's good showing in Chicago Negro wards meant less than it appeared, for many Negroes there were ineligible to vote in the Republican primary and so could not display their preference for Eisenhower.) Martin, serving up the headquarters line on the primaries at lunch with a group of national political reporters, found them inclined to write off Stevenson's candidacy as lost.

15.

Stevenson now set off on a hard schedule, at least as heavy as the September-October schedule of a presidential campaign. On April 12, in Miami, he delivered a substantive speech on health, one foreshadowing an important issue he would make this year. He called it shameful that the federal government was spending so little on medical research. It had spent $25 million on cancer research the year before although one of every seven Americans would die of cancer. With mental illness costing "incalculable suffering" and nearly $1.5 billion a year, the United States was spending only $11 million, less than one per cent of that cost, on research. It was spending about a penny a person for research on arthritis and rheumatic diseases. Stevenson proposed if elected "to use the powers and resources of this nation to cut down killing and crippling disease with all the vigor we use to stop the killing and crippling which comes from war." He called for "protection" against the "sudden and devastating costs of illness." In over half a million cases, catastrophic accident or illness would take the entire family income. Eight million families were in debt for medical care. "In too many American homes a parent at some time or other looks down at a sick child, knows that something should be done and that there just isn't the money to do it." Something must be done. "I am not in favor of national health insurance. There are other alternatives." Private health insurance programs should be developed to cover low-income families. "I urge further consideration of governmental programs to provide long-term, low-interest-rate loans to groups which are organizing prepayment insurance plans, and perhaps other forms of financial assistance." Social Security should be revised so that its benefits would be paid to people who became totally disabled before reaching retirement age. Moreover, the shortage of doctors was serious, and the federal government should aid in the construction and expansion of medical schools. It should also speed up hospital construction.

In this speech Stevenson was taking a moderate position. The Eisenhower administration opposed some of the programs he favored, and the American Medical Association considered them radical. But he had not gone so far as President Truman in 1949, when Truman proposed compulsory national health insurance under the Social Security system—and saw it killed in Congress after a fight. Stevenson did not spell out his position fully. He would develop it throughout 1956, heading closer to what came to be called Medicare.

He spoke on good government and political ethics to the Tampa Bar Association on April 13. Months later a Southern newspaperman, John Popham, wrote a long letter to Stevenson about Tampa: "Governor, I urge you to keep in mind the mood of the Florida primary, particularly the exciting and ever-important hours of the afternoon in Tampa. I keep recalling to mind that very critical period. You had recently experienced the Minnesota primary, had just racked up the Illinois win, and yet the climate of the fair-weather prophets was gloomy and the sharpshooters were doing their damndest to dig your political grave. But that day in Tampa in the cigar factories was the turning point in a sort of mystique manner. That was the time you broke the schedule of appointments, grabbed at the golden and shining moments at hand and drank deeply of the true electrification of human communication. Lord, I will never forget the twinkle in your eyes, the joy that exuded from your face, your whole body, as you went from floor to floor among those Latinos making the cigars, chatting and laughing so exuberantly, not quips or sallies, but honest earthy language that came from the heart. And right behind you were your son and sweetly charming daughter-in-law, just bursting with happiness at seeing you in that wholehearted role. And then the quick luncheon at the cafeteria with the same people and their families. It was an exciting and uplifting and wonderful few hours. You were never more wonderful in your career,

I daresay. . . . Like all true aristocrats . . . you draw something real and deep from the peasantry or plain folks of this world, and in Tampa you found it that day."

At Pensacola, Stevenson spoke on war and peace. Contrary to Administration claims, all was not well, he said. "The grim facts are that the American position, instead of getting better and better, has gotten much worse recently; that, if present policies continue, our children will grow up, not in a safe and peaceful world, but in a world where Communism advances and where the United States grows weak, insecure, and vulnerable. . . . And, while Communism steadily increases its political, military, and economic strength, there is in one part of the world—the Middle East —a steady and terrible drift to war." President Eisenhower had spoken "with entire satisfaction" about NATO but NATO had never been "so weak and shaky. Foreign policy and the spirit which makes it real has to be made in the White House and sustained by the President. It takes more than golf scores to inspire peoples with a common will to struggle for a better, safer world. . . . To restore the world position of the United States . . . we need a new fighting liberal spirit in our foreign policy."

Bill Wirtz joined Stevenson and Blair at Southern Pines. While Stevenson met with North Carolina politicians, Wirtz talked by telephone with Martin in Chicago, who mailed speech drafts for Pennsylvania. Pat Brown told Stevenson his California campaign was better organized than it appeared and predicted Stevenson would win all the cities except Fresno and Sacramento. Senator Kennedy passed on word from Wyoming that the Wyoming delegation at the National Convention would be for Harriman unless Stevenson or Kefauver acted promptly.

Stevenson's Pennsylvania schedule had swamped the writers; now, as Stevenson went there, Oregon swamped them, and by the time they had finished with Oregon, California would be upon them. The campaign was still disorganized. Finnegan had been in California and was on his way to Pennsylvania and Washington. Raskin was in Oregon working on a schedule. Wirtz was with Stevenson, as was Blair. Nobody from headquarters was in California. The Finletter Group and others had been working on the big speeches for New York and Washington. Too much energy was going into the Eastern speeches—where Stevenson was not entered in contested primaries—and not enough into preparations for Oregon and California, where he was. New Jersey held its primary on Tuesday, April 17, and an unpledged slate of delegates headed by Governor Meyner and considered friendly to Stevenson ran well ahead of a Kefauver slate. It was a minor setback for Kefauver, who had campaigned hard in the state (as Stevenson had not). But President Eisenhower ran far ahead of any Democrat. A small boom began for Meyner as Stevenson's vice presidential candidate. Finnegan thought it unlikely, since Meyner was at that time a bachelor. Finnegan was also opposed to Senator John F. Kennedy for Vice President because he was a Catholic. Other Stevenson people, however, thought Kennedy's presence on the ticket would diminish Catholic disaffection with Stevenson. The quiet boom for Kennedy for Vice President continued. (Blair favored him.) Minow was trying to run the Alaska primary campaign by telephone.

On Tuesday, April 17, President Eisenhower made his first openly political speech of 1956, appealing, in an address before 800 Republican leaders in Washington, to independents and "sound-thinking Democrats" to join Republicans in support of a record "unimpeachable in its concern for people and principles." He set forth eight principles which he said the Republican platform would express—that the individual is "of supreme importance," that "the spirit of our people is the strength of our nation," that "no section or group in America can permanently prosper unless all groups and sections so prosper," that "government must have a heart as well as a head," that "courage in principle, cooperation in practice make freedom positive," that "the purpose of government is to serve, never to dominate," that "to stay free we must stay strong," and that, "under God, we espouse the cause of freedom and justice and peace for all peoples."

Next day, Wednesday, April 18, Stevenson invaded Pennsylvania. He addressed the Press Club of Pittsburgh on "the suppression of public information by the national government." News was suppressed, he said, not because of concern about national security but concern about "the security of the political party now in office." News had been manipulated by the Administration to "cover up some Administration blunder or to put a good face on a bad situation for partisan political advantage." Defense Department news was heavily censored. One agency had refused to tell a congressional committee how much peanut butter the armed services were buying on the ground that the information might enable an enemy agent to deduce the size of the armed forces. At the same time a different agency was reporting regularly on the size of the armed forces. Leading scientists had declared that the present security system was hindering defense development. Scotty Reston had recently written that he detected "a growing tendency to manage the news." Early in the Administration a high government official, C. D. Jackson, had said, "We're going to merchandise the living hell out of the Eisenhower administration." Stevenson said, "I think the record is clear that they have done precisely what they set out to do." The speech, well received, contrasted sharply with Stevenson's "one-party press in a two-party country" speech of 1952.

Mayor Lawrence accompanied him to Harrisburg, and he spent that night with Governor Leader. Next morning, Thursday, April 19, he held a press conference in the Governor's office. The first question was, "I would like to know whether you favor withholding federal funds from segregated schools," and although the questioning, some of it ill informed, drifted to other topics, it kept returning to desegregation; and Stevenson, annoyed, lost patience with the reporters and said, at the end of one of several answers, "Now could we move on?" But the reporters returned yet again to the question, and a barren exchange took place.

Martin and other writers, using the enormous research files of John Brademas, had put together short speech segments on small business, aging, health, foreign policy, and depressed areas, for use in whistle stops. They intended to prepare similar pieces on all other major issues (and thought it was absurd they were still preparing them at this late date). Wirtz now was able to work out with Stevenson a formula for semi-extemporaneous speeches, using these brief segments, and Stevenson tried it in speaking to state employees at the capitol in Harrisburg at noon. He began with a few comments on how glad he was to be there, went briefly into a passage that tied him to the locale—talked about his ancestors who had come from Pennsylvania—moved to a passage on the accomplishments of a local leader—in this instance Governor Leader—then said, "I'd like to say a few words in particular today about one public problem that I'm afraid is getting all too little attention," and used the previously prepared segment on depressed areas (as, in other places, he might use one on natural resources, agriculture, or another issue of local interest). That segment was the only prepared text he had and the only part of the speech that was released to the press, thus, it was hoped, ensuring that the press would emphasize the issue the staff wanted emphasized. Stevenson then repeated an affirmative peroration modeled on the one he had used on TV in California, describing the kind of America he wanted. The speech worked well at Harrisburg—Governor Leader's press secretary thought it the best political speech he had ever heard. Stevenson's writers, faced with an overwhelming burden of whistle stops for Oregon, California, and Florida, took heart.

On depressed areas, Stevenson said that heavy unemployment and severe depression existed in certain areas of the United States, including the coalfields of Pennsylvania, and that only a "coldhearted Administration" could brag about national prosperity at such a time. He said, "The President listed Tuesday night, as one of the fundamental principles in what he called the Republican credo, the proposition that 'America does not prosper unless all Americans prosper.' Well, the people in these towns aren't prospering and a proposition in a Republican credo isn't a check they can cash at the bank or a ticket to a job. We have had enough Republican talk. It's time now for some Democratic action," and he endorsed a proposal to aid depressed areas put forward by Senator Douglas of Illinois and Congressman Daniel Flood of Pennsylvania. Some members of Stevenson's staff thought a "pothole" campaign, appealing to specific disadvantaged areas or disaffected groups, offered the only hope of defeating Eisenhower in the fall.

He was driven to Philadelphia and that afternoon addressed a rally at the Bellevue-Stratford Hotel. There he followed the Harrisburg pattern of speaking half extemporaneously, half from a prepared text, and this time his prepared text was on civil rights, for Pennsylvania political leaders feared his "moderate" line was losing "their" Negro votes. He said essentially what he had said in California and Florida, including the Ashmore language. To the state convention of the AFL that day in Philadelphia, Stevenson again used the Harrisburg formula, this time with a segment of workers' rights. Two days later, on Saturday, April 21, in Washington, Stevenson delivered one of the most important speeches of his life. He delivered it to a luncheon of the American Society of Newspaper Editors (ASNE).

16.

This speech had a long history. Stevenson had discussed it with Tom Finletter, Commissioner Thomas E. Murray of the Atomic Energy Commission (AEC), Frank Altschul, and others. Sometime later Stevenson, asked privately when he first started thinking about H-bomb tests, said, "Not long after Hiroshima." He said that in the Navy Department he had had "some rudimentary understanding of the development possibility of nuclear fission, if not fusion," and had been "quite familiar" with the Acheson-Lilienthal Report on which Carl McGowan had worked at Navy. In the winter of 1956, "probably February or March," he said, he had talked at length in New York with Commissioner Murray of the AEC about "suspending" tests of nuclear weapons in order to arrest development and diminish fallout. He added, "There were doubtless many talks and readings in this field in the interval of my leaving the government in the spring of 1946 and the primary campaign of 1956." Asked whom he had consulted on the question, he mentioned Commissioner Murray. He believed the Pope had indicated concern about nuclear testing. "I concluded after considerable thought" to speak on it to the ASNE. He said he wrote the H-bomb portion of the ASNE speech in Philadelphia, a day or so before it was to be delivered. His "consultants," he said, were Bob Tufts and possibly Schlesinger. Asked if a memorandum by Professor W. R. Hawthorne had influenced him, Stevenson said he could not recall the memorandum.

This account of the genesis of the proposal is at once too simple and too forehanded. It is true that the control of atomic weapons had been in many people's minds from 1946 on. Indeed, it was in that year that Bernard M. Baruch, then U.S. representative on the UN Atomic Energy Commission, proposed international control of atomic energy, whether for peaceful or military purposes, under an International Atomic Energy Development Authority with power to send inspectors into states to watch for violations of the treaty. The U.S.S.R. had said that international inspection as proposed by Baruch was incompatible with national sovereignty. On this basic disagreement arms control talks had languished during the cold war. During these years, too, certain scientists had warned of the dangers of fallout from A-bomb tests, warnings that became more urgent with the advent of the H-bomb. Other nations, including India and Japan, demanded an end to testing but the Eisenhower administration refused, saying that national security required testing. Russia said approximately the same thing. Tests continued in 1956, although the Soviet Union late in 1955 said it would support a test ban. The United States would not.

Nothing in the Stevenson papers during the years shortly after 1946 suggests that he was seriously interested in the problem then. It was not an issue in his 1952 campaign. At the same time, he had advice on it from many more people than he indicated, and he did not simply dash off the speech in Philadelphia—he polished it there, but it had been a long time in the works and many hands had helped in its preparation.

It is difficult if not impossible to trace the genesis of such ideas. They are simply in the air—several people hit upon them at approximately the same time. The single most important and direct influence on Stevenson's thinking was almost surely Murray, the AEC commissioner. After their first talk in New York, Stevenson corresponded with various people about the idea, including Finletter, George Kennan, Ben Cohen, Schlesinger, and others. Only nine days before Stevenson's speech to the ASNE, Commissioner Murray, in testimony before a Senate Foreign Relations subcommittee, urged the United States stop testing hydrogen bombs and limit their size and number in the weapons stockpile. He told the Senators he knew of "no reason why we should develop bombs more powerful than those we now have." The United States, he said, already had enough big bombs to retaliate against any aggression. He favored limitation of hydrogen weapons regardless of what Russia might do. Further tests should be limited to smaller nuclear weapons; "the tests of multi-megaton thermonuclear weapons [should] be stopped."

Schlesinger originally had written a draft for the ASNE on foreign policy and defense. It did not contain a proposal to stop testing H-bombs—Finletter had expressed reservations about the proposal. But Finletter had telephoned George Kennan on April 11 about it, and Kennan responded with a long letter which said, "I can personally see no reason why we should not show a readiness to abandon further tests of nuclear weapons, on a basis of complete reciprocity and some reasonable arrangement for inspection, until the United Nations can undertake a thorough and leisurely survey of the effects of the release of radioactivity through such tests."

Ben Cohen sent a draft. It said the Administration had not taken the people into its confidence—the people were asked to take on faith Administration assurances that tests were essential to national security and were safe, though some scientists disagreed. A test ban, Cohen argued, would be self-policing—there was no possibility of concealing an H-bomb test

from detection. Little of the language but much of the substance of
Cohen's draft survived in Stevenson's final draft. Wirtz took the Cohen,
Schlesinger, and Kennan drafts and put them together. His draft did not
propose unilateral cessation of tests—it proposed an agreement with other
nations to stop them. Wirtz sent this draft to Schlesinger, who criticized it
at length. Stevenson himself worked from a revised Wirtz draft. That draft
continued to use the word "agreement"—that is, an "agreement" with
other nations to stop testing. The day before he was to deliver the speech,
Stevenson was still revising it extensively. It was during this process that
he dropped the word "agreement" and moved to a unilateral cessation of
tests. It is entirely clear that his H-bomb test proposal to the ASNE was
nothing he did on the spur of the moment. The final passage which he
delivered was as carefully phrased as anything he ever delivered.

Stevenson began by reminding his audience that he once had been a
newspaperman. He moved to the Administration: "One of the most serious criticisms I would make of this Administration is that it has had so little respect for the public's right to know. . . . Peace and security are the
nation's most important business. Yet nowhere has our government told us
less and kidded us more. It has used foreign policy for political purposes
at home. Unwilling to admit its failures, it has been unwilling to take us
into its confidence. Reverses have been painted as victories. And if the
Administration has not succeeded in misleading the enemy, it has succeeded wonderfully well in misleading us."

He recalled that three years ago President Eisenhower in a speech to
this same society had endorsed the principles which had guided American
foreign policy since 1945. At that time, Stevenson said, the United States
was enjoying the fruits of "great, creative years" of policy under Truman,
and he mentioned the UN, the Truman Doctrine and Greece and Turkey,
the Berlin airlift, the Marshall Plan, Point Four, NATO, and the Korean
War. Stevenson said, "Compare that extraordinary outburst of creativity
with the sterility of the past three years." Eisenhower had ignored his
own speech. Stevenson asked a series of questions about America's position today as compared with three years ago. Were her relations with her
allies stronger or weaker? Was mounting criticism of the United States
abroad really without foundation? Did Dulles enjoy the trust, respect, and
confidence of the free world? Was the "image" of the United States one
that inspired confidence, respect, and cooperation? Were we "winning or
losing ground in the competition with the Communist world?" Stevenson
said he hoped Eisenhower, in his speech to the same audience later that
same day, would take up these questions.

Where were we today? We lived at "the coincidence of three revolutions:

"(1) the technological revolution that has split the atom, devastated
distance, and made us all next-door neighbors;

"(2) the political revolutions that have liberated and subjugated more peoples more rapidly than ever before in history;

"(3) the ideological revolution, Communism, that has endangered the supremacy of Western ideas for the first time since Islam retreated from Europe."

The Administration had been slow to respond to the mood of change. The Soviets had exploited it adroitly. And he inserted a passage on Khrushchev: "Mr. Khrushchev's remarks in London yesterday on peace and the abolition of arms illustrates the point. He has appealed to this hopeful, peaceful mood again. We would like to believe that he means we are on the threshold of real progress in disarmament at last. At all events, I hope his remarks will be received here with something more positive than derision."

He listed "tension points" in the world—Israel, Algeria, Formosa, Indochina, Indonesia, Kashmir, Cyprus, and "now the whole NATO area." Then he said, "What is more basic and ominous and infinitely harder for us to accept is that in these last three years the United States has come dangerously close to losing, if indeed it has not lost, its leadership in the world—economically, militarily, and worst of all, morally." Millions in revolution looked to Russia, not the United States, for help. Why? It had started with Hiroshima—"since America dropped the first bomb on Asians, and then the Japanese fishermen were burned, America has been unfairly suspected of caring precious little about Asians and peace." More recently, the Administration had boasted to the world about America's virtues, yet dealt with the world in terms of military threats and military alliances. And in the last three years America had lost her air-atomic superiority.

What, then, should be done?

First, Stevenson said, "a decent respect for the opinions of others is still a basic requirement of a good foreign policy. Foreign policy is not only *what* we do, it is *how* we do it. The wisest policy will be poisonously self-defeating if mishandled. Smugness, arrogance, talking big are poison. Impulsive, abrupt actions create the impression that we are impulsive and abrupt." We must stop "boasting about brinks" and massive retaliation, "stop trying to reconcile the irreconcilable wings of the Republican Party," and stop talking "nonsense about the imminent collapse of the Soviet system."

Now Stevenson came to the central point:

"Secondly, I believe we should give prompt and earnest consideration to stopping further tests of the hydrogen bomb, as Commissioner Murray of the Atomic Energy Commission recently proposed. As a layman, I hope I can question the sense in multiplying and enlarging weapons of a destructive power already almost incomprehensible. I would call upon other nations, the Soviet Union, to follow our lead, and if they don't and persist in further tests we will know about it and can reconsider our policy.

"I deeply believe that if we are to make progress toward the effective reduction and control of armaments, it will probably come a step at a time. And this is a step which, it seems to me, we might now take, a step which would reflect our determination never to plunge the world into nuclear holocaust, a step which would reaffirm our purpose to act with humility and a decent concern for world opinion.

"(After writing this last week down South I read last night in Philadelphia that the Soviet Union has protested a scheduled H-bomb test. After some reflection, I concluded that I would not be intimidated by the Communists and would not alter what I had written. For this suggestion is right or wrong and should be so considered regardless of the Soviets.)"

Third, Stevenson said, we should "make greater use of the United Nations as the economic aid agency," remove economic development from the cold war arena, use agricultural surpluses and atomic energy for peace, cooperate responsibly with the U.S.S.R. all over the world, and make aid's primary objective "human betterment," not military alliances. "It is time to regain the initiative; to release the warm, creative energies of this mighty land; it is time to resume the onward progress of mankind in pursuit of peace and freedom."

It was the first major substantive speech he had given in some time. It broke new ground, made a new issue. The New York *Times* put the story at the top of page one alongside the story on Eisenhower's own speech to the ASNE and called Stevenson's speech "the sharpest attack yet made on President Eisenhower's leadership in foreign affairs." The Scripps-Howard newspapers said that "most . . . informed opinion" agreed with Stevenson's assessment of the United States' position in the world, not with Eisenhower's, and noted that the members of the ASNE thought, by a 2–1 vote, America was losing the cold war. The President did not mention Stevenson's speech in his own. He was asked about it at his press conference four days later, and replied, "Well, I usually ask you people not to quote someone else when you want me to talk, because I don't comment on somebody else's opinion. They are entitled to their own opinions. But I do want to point this out: it is a little bit of a paradox to urge that we work just as hard as we know how on the guided missile and that we stop all research on the hydrogen bomb, because one without the other is rather useless."[8]

---

[8] Stevenson, of course, had not proposed stopping "all research" on the bomb, only testing. Eisenhower continued: "So we go ahead with this hydrogen bomb—not to make a bigger bang, not to cause more destruction—to find out ways and means in which you can limit it, make it useful in defensive purposes, of shooting against a fleet of airplanes that are coming over, to reduce fallout, to make it more of a military weapon and less one just of mass destruction. We know we can make them big. We are not interested in that any more. So this whole thing goes together: the guided

William P. Bundy, then with the CIA, later an Assistant Secretary of Defense and of State in the Kennedy administration, told Blair on April 24 that Dr. Rabi and Dr. Lauritsen of the AEC General Advisory Committee, both considered liberals, regretted that Stevenson had raised the H-bomb question and doubted that he had consulted with real experts before speaking. They said they themselves could not consult with Stevenson but suggested he talk to Professors Barker, Ramsey, Zacharias, or Wiesner. Blair replied that Stevenson would be glad to hear their reactions and said that, on the basis of what he knew, he agreed with them. However, he said, Stevenson had had "a memorandum from some MIT atomic scientists." Stevenson sent the Bundy letter to Ben Cohen, said the President and the *Herald Tribune* were doing their best to confuse the bomb and its missile vehicle, and solicited further thoughts "on how to carry on this dialogue." He told Walter Lippmann, who was criticial, "I cannot complain if you did not like my speech before the editors. But perhaps you will permit me to protest the suggestion that it was written in part by others." He told Schlesinger, "I am certain I am on the right track on the hydrogen bomb, but I certainly haven't got it properly put forward yet."

Stevenson did not choose to press the H-bomb issue at this time, although it kept coming up during that spring. But he did make it a prime issue of the fall campaign against Eisenhower. It was one example of how his campaign helped lay the groundwork for the Kennedy-Johnson administrations. Such ideas, of course, had been in the air a long time, but Stevenson brought them to the forefront of national consciousness, and they did not die, though he lost. Of all the issues thus raised in 1956, the H-bomb testing issue may well have been the most important, for though he was denounced for it that year, it flowered in the Limited Nuclear Test Ban Treaty of 1963. Stevenson, pressing the issue in the fall, emphasized the health danger of test fallout, a harbinger of another issue that became important in the 1970s: anti-pollution.

The day after his ASNE speech Stevenson appeared on "Meet the Press." There he was informed that President Eisenhower had told the ASNE the world situation was more promising than three years ago. Did Stevenson agree? He did not. "I think it's very much less promising," and he explained why. He was asked for examples of how the Administration had denied the people the facts, and gave them. He was asked about the Middle East and explained his position in detail. He was asked about his own health and said, "I have no organic disorders. I won't guarantee the

---

missile, with an expensive thing that is a one-shot thing, is really effective because it has a tremendous blow when it gets to the end of it. So if you don't work on one and get the right kind of explosive to use there, why work on the other? So I think research without test is perfectly useless, a waste of money. And, goodness knows, I don't want to do this. If the world would allow us to put the money in schools and all the rest of the things, we all know what would result, the great benefit of mankind. But as long as we have to do it, let's do it right as best we know how."

mental situation." Did he still feel the President's health should not be an issue? "I think the important thing is not the condition of his health; what is very important, in my judgment, is the office of the presidency, and what happens to it." He handled questions on desegregation well. If the United States Government stopped testing hydrogen bombs but the Russians continued, would he suggest the United States resume testing? He said, "We'd have to look at the situation as it developed."

17.

That weekend in Washington, Stevenson saw politicians and friends while Ashmore talked to people from Florida. Ashmore sent Finnegan a memo: "The bandwagon psychology is all important in Florida, and as of now neither the Stevenson nor Kefauver campaigns have it." Stevenson already had endorsements from important political leaders and might get more. "On the word-of-mouth level, Kefauver's people are undoubtedly making hay with Kefauver's ain't-nobody-here-but-us-Confederates approach to segregation. In the Cracker Country the standard technique is a broad wink and the question: who do you think can handle them niggers better, a city fellow from Illinois or a country boy from Tennessee?"

On Tuesday, April 24, Stevenson spoke to the United Auto Workers' seventh international conference on education. It was a taut partisan speech, arguing that nobody in the Eisenhower Cabinet represented the consumer, the workingman, the school children, old people, farmers, the poor. "This isn't a meeting of a people's Cabinet. It is a meeting of a corporate board of directors. What single-interest government has come to mean . . . is simple . . . government without representation." Stevenson recalled a statement in a UAW magazine some years earlier: "It's time to write the lawyers out of the [labor] contracts and write the people back in." Stevenson said, "It is time, I suggest, to write the businessman's administration out of this government and write the people back in."

He went up to New York and held a press conference, then attended a reception for Stevenson workers. At the press conference he tried to clarify the H-bomb issue. He said that the day before, in London, Khrushev had made "the startling claim" that soon the U.S.S.R. would be able to deliver "anywhere in the world an intercontinental missile with a hydrogen bomb warhead." Stevenson said the Administration had been "dangerously dilatory in getting on with a guided missile program," and "I think it is time that we awakened to the fact that the Soviet Union has made enormous industrial and technological strides and that we can no longer assume that we shall be permanently the stronger." Then he said, "I have suggested that we should take a step toward peace by stopping further tests of hydrogen bombs. But the means of delivery, by guided missiles or airplanes, is another question, and it is evident that we must renew our efforts in this whole area." The statement may have muddled the H-bomb issue more than it clarified it.

He met privately with several television people who wanted to help him. They urged him to speak briefly, to address the television audience as "you," to use the word "my," as in "Here are some of *my* ideas concerning *your* problems." Even a local program on a small station could easily reach 125,000 people, far more than he would reach in a high school appearance. Stevenson responded, "I hear a lot about how important it is to project your personality, instead of lecturing and preaching, and that this is best done by interrogation and family trivia. I'm willing to do anything, within reason, short of singing and toe dancing. . . . Every one tells me how warm and endearing [Kefauver] is, but I can't do that sort of thing." He said the point of a campaign for high office was to debate the issues soberly and carefully and complained Kefauver did not do it. One of them said, "He probably does, more than you think," and another, "When you do discuss foreign policy, national defense and other major issues, translate them first into terms of the individual."

On Wednesday, April 25, Stevenson had lunch with Lloyd Garrison and four Negro leaders. That night he delivered his long-planned address to a banquet of the Stevenson for President Committee at the Waldorf. Although Finletter and others had urged him to speak on foreign affairs, he spoke on "freedom in America"—civil liberties and civil rights. He began with a bald statement he was beginning to use frequently this spring: "I have come to New York to ask support for my candidacy for the office of President of the United States." But, unlike John Kennedy and other candidates, he could not let it go at that but had quickly to add an explanation: "But this is too large a thing for any man to seek or ask on a personal basis. And I do not. I come to you rather in the deep conviction that if there is to be peace in the world and freedom in America the reins of our government must be returned to those with the passion for progress and the dedication to the ideal of human dignity which are the qualities of the Democratic faith—of your faith and mine."

The speech was filled with lofty rhetoric: "I see freedom in the world today as the great life-giving river of which America is the source. It will be whatever we are, not more, not less."

Of civil rights: "The achievement of equal rights for all American citizens is the great unfinished business before the United States." (In 1960, John Kennedy would often speak of our "unfinished business.") This would be true whether or not the Supreme Court had ordered school desegregation. That order required social change in some areas, which created "massive problems of adjustment." The Court had "wisely" left the measure of good faith progress to the district courts. "There remains, however, the abiding responsibility of the executive branch of the government. . . . The present Administration, in my judgment, has failed. . . .

The presidency is, above all, a place of moral leadership. Yet in these months of crucial importance no leadership has been provided. The immense prestige and influence of the office has been withheld from those who honestly seek to carry out the law in gathering storm and against rising resistance. Refusing to rise to this great moral and constitutional crisis, the Administration has hardly even acknowledged its gravity. It is the sworn responsibility of the President of this nation to carry out the law of the land. . . . As President, if that were my privilege, I would work ceaselessly and with a sense of crucial urgency—with public officials, private groups, and educators—to meet this challenge in our life as a nation and this threat to our national reputation. I would act in the knowledge that law and order is the Executive's responsibility; and I would and will act, too, I pray, in the conviction that to play politics with the Court's decision and the basic rights of citizens and human beings is wicked." The right to vote was crucial. Political freedom underlay all others. The laws protecting voting rights "should be enforced" and, if inadequate, strengthened. He turned to civil liberties and "the grievous assaults [on the Bill of Rights] that have scarred and stained this interval. The flood stage of hate and hysteria among us, so alien to our nature, reached its crest in 1953 and 1954, the first two years of the present Administration," and he recalled those days "when our government quaked before the junior Senator from Wisconsin." The 1954 election, he said, "marked the turning of the tide." But the evil effects of McCarthyism lingered on. "Who," he asked, "can best clean up the wreckage of this flood? Who can best rebuild the structure of our Bill of Rights?" And answered: "It is . . . the task . . . for those who tried faithfully to defend our liberties even as the flood mounted and rolled over its crest. . . . This is our job—yours and mine —a job, if you will, for Democrats."

He closed with an eloquent peroration:

"Only by such a rekindling of this nation's passion for freedom can we persuade the world that America is genuinely the hope of free peoples everywhere. For, in the end, democracy will triumph or go down, and America will stand or fall, not by the power of our money or of our arms, but by the splendor of our ideals.

"Let it be the obligation of the next Administration in Washington to display that splendor once again in its radiance to all the world."

Adlai III told Carol Evans, "The New York dinner was the best I've ever been to. I've never seen such a polished performance; the old man even finished his speech on time." Next day in Washington, Walter Reuther said at a press conference, "I think that maybe if I were making speeches [on desegregation], I would say things differently than perhaps Mr. Stevenson says them. But I don't think there is any question of where he stands on the basic question of civil rights. . . . And I believe that if he were to become the President of the United States, that he would do everything in his power to correct these wrongs [done to Negroes]." As he was leaving New York for Miami on Thursday, April 26, Stevenson asked Tom Finletter to try to reconcile his proposals to end H-bomb tests and speed up the missile program.

Next, to Miami Beach that night and a program for the aged. He came out flatly for Democratic proposals to broaden Social Security by lowering to sixty-two the age when women would receive benefits and by paying benefits to persons who came totally disabled at age fifty or older. He listed other changes which "ought to be considered"—incentives to old people to work, a retraining program, low-rent public housing, more money for medical research. He was not yet willing, however, to come out for medical care for the elderly.

Martin went to Los Angeles and met with Pat Brown, Don Bradley, Fred Dutton, Alan Cranston, Dick Tuck (a Democratic prankster), and others to prepare for Stevenson's forthcoming trip. Martin would stay there most of the time until Election Day, June 5, working on major speeches, preparing notes and briefing sheets for whistle-stops—"speech advance," or "editorial advance," as it came to be called.

Stevenson, back in Chicago briefly, told John L. Lewis, "I enjoyed our little visit the other afternoon immeasurably, but somehow I forgot to even talk to you about labor." He asked Carl McGowan what he should be saying: "I find myself increasingly incapable of keeping up with the news or translating it into statements, etc." He took time to send a post-card to Penelope Tree, Marietta's daughter, then six years old. He asked Jane Dick's advice on whether to announce publicly that he was about to become a grandfather. She said no—it was too early, Nancy was not even "past the miscarriage stage" yet. She offered other advice: "I don't think you have any idea how tired you are. I do know. I don't think you have any idea how *different* you are when you are tired. I have been deeply concerned. . . . In my considered judgment, this *one factor* of wearing you out, until you are just an animated shell of the *real* Adlai—has been *the major mistake* of the campaign, and contributed substantially to whatever other things have gone wrong." She urged him to tell all this to Blair, who alone could protect him, and to rest whenever possible. Good advice given often by her and others, seldom heeded. She added, "I'll see you one of these days in California. Meanwhile my heart and my prayers go with you. . . . May He take special care of you in the coming difficult weeks!"

18.

Stevenson, having been home in Libertyville only eleven hours, went to Portland on Saturday, April 28, to open his Oregon write-in campaign. He talked with his supporters there on Sunday and on Monday went whistle-stopping in and around Portland. He spoke on single-interest government and came out for the Hell's Canyon dam. (In 1952, it will be recalled, he had refused to endorse Hell's Canyon flatly, saying that to do so was tantamount to putting it into his first presidential budget.) On Tuesday he flew to Medford, then to Klamath Falls near the California border for an evening speech on conservation, natural resources, and Administration "giveaways." The schedule was less crowded in Oregon than elsewhere and the voters less volatile. He wrote a few letters. He told Dick Daley, "My fortunes seem to be prospering," but he was not sure what would happen in Oregon. He asked to be named a delegate at large from Illinois to the convention.

Martin arrived in Klamath Falls on Tuesday, May 1, to join Stevenson. He was preparing briefing sheets for Stevenson to use at California whistle-stops—a page or two on the nature of the occasion, the setting, the size of the expected crowd, its composition (whether farmers, laborers, Negroes, aircraft industry employees, Democrats, general public, and so on), whether the meeting was indoors or outdoors, which issues should be raised and which avoided, which local candidates or party leaders should be mentioned and which avoided, and a few lines on the locale which Stevenson could use to identify himself with the audience. If the issue to be discussed was a new one or a dangerous one in California, Martin would provide language designed to handle it. If it was an old issue, he would simply copy out material from previous Stevenson speeches—enough to remind him. This study of local issues disclosed a number of problems. For example, water was an extremely complicated issue in California, with unnumbered facets, including this one: Los Angeles wanted to divert more water from the Colorado River for its own use, but Stevenson had already said at Salt Lake City that he opposed further diversion and so now he could only dodge the question, which he had to, repeatedly. Most of California's own water was in the north but most of her population was in the south; the south wanted to use northern water but the north was jealous of its water; the issue was easy for a congressional candidate but cruel for a state-wide candidate. The issue was further clouded by the competition among federal, state, and local governments to handle the problem. And agriculture was at least as complicated an issue.

Martin, in writing the whistle-stop speeches and briefing sheets, was trying to stay two or three days ahead of Stevenson. But on some days Stevenson made as many as sixteen whistle-stops, devouring material rapidly, and Martin was working alone. Moreover, he had to stay with Stevenson while Stevenson was in the state, and so those days, largely lost to writing, had to be made up while Stevenson was campaigning in Florida or Oregon. The result was that by June 5, primary day, Stevenson and Martin finished in a virtual dead heat, with speech notes and drafts being prepared hours, or even minutes, before they were delivered.

The night was soft, the air fresh on May 1, in Klamath Falls, a small town in a magnificent setting, and Stevenson returned from his speech feeling good. He had forgotten to use in his speech an insert on treatment of the Indians, drafted after great difficulty by the staff; he joked that he would have to go back and deliver the speech all over. Standing on the railroad platform late that night waiting for the train that would take him to California, he listened to a briefing on California problems. His only complaint was that he had been obliged to say "big business Administration" too much in Oregon and wanted to revert to the softer "single-interest Administration." He said a wealthy contributor in New York had admonished him against attacking the "business" Administration. When Martin suggested that he might tell farmers the Administration was setting workingmen against farmers and vice versa by blaming the high price of farm machinery on labor's wage increases, Stevenson agreed and said, "It might be a pretty good line to take—and besides it might have some truth in it," and laughed. He was relaxed and cheerful. No wonder—the District of Columbia had voted that day, and Stevenson had won every delegate contest over Kefauver.

Next day, Wednesday, May 2, in San Francisco, Stevenson put in one of the best days of whistle-stopping in his life. His schedule was murderous— 9:45 A.M. press conference, 10:30 A.M. Californians for Stevenson headquarters, 11 A.M. Yerba Buena housing project, 12:15 P.M. Union Square, 1 P.M. fund-raising lunch at Clift Hotel, 3 P.M. Geary and Fillmore streets, 3:20 P.M. Spanish-American Stevenson headquarters, 3:40 P.M. Twenty-second and Mission streets, 4:30 P.M. San Francisco waterfront, 7:30 P.M. Night in Italy, 9 P.M. Chinatown, 9:30 P.M. Young Californians for Stevenson at the Fairmont Hotel. It was a lovely day in San Francisco, crisp and sunny. Stevenson was at his best. Don Bradley handed him his briefing sheets one at a time, just before he arrived at each stop, and Stevenson read them, then turned them over and scribbled notes in long-hand, making the pages his own, and he used them, speaking, in effect, extemporaneously from notes, and the crowds liked it. He rode the cable car up Nob Hill, spoke all over town all day long, filled Union Square with more than 2,000 people where 200 or 300 had been expected, told them the UN never should have been moved away from San Francisco—a newspaper headline that stood up all day—and wound up at cheerful gatherings in the Italian quarter and Chinatown. That night his staff felt sure he would carry San Francisco easily and maybe other parts of the Bay area as well. Reporters began writing about "the new Stevenson" who enjoyed campaigning and shaking hands.

His friend and distant relative, Senator Alben Barkley, had died April 30, three days before. Stevenson decided to go to the funeral. It was a purely personal decision, as so many of his were. He was scheduled to campaign the next day, Thursday, in the Central Valley of California, and some of his California managers opposed his going to the funeral, warning that he might lose the Valley and so the election if he canceled his whistle-stopping there. But he said he would not feel right if he did not go to Barkley's funeral. Nor did he want to make political capital of his going; his announcement was short, and he went alone, taking a midnight flight from San Francisco to Chicago, being met there by Newt Minow, chartering a plane to Paducah, Kentucky, returning to Chicago by charter and thence back to Los Angeles, arriving late Thursday night, May 3. Minow thought: "At the funeral, in two rows, were Kefauver, Harriman, Symington, and our candidate. One bomb would have wiped out the Democratic Party!"

Martin had given Stevenson a memorandum on California to read on the plane. Stevenson, it said, was ahead about 2–1 in the cities and behind about 5–8 on the farms. He should run as though he were ahead—should not attack Kefauver, should attack Eisenhower and Nixon. The Waldorf speech on civil rights and civil liberties had helped with California intellectuals. The H-bomb was a good issue in San Francisco. Stevenson's quick trip to California after the Minnesota primary had succeeded in putting out the Kefauver fire. Kefauver had passed his peak, Stevenson was on the way up, in northern California; they were about even in southern California. Fred Dutton, however, feared Los Angeles. He believed that the liberal wing of the party could always win a Los Angeles primary and that Stevenson was in trouble with liberals, Jews, Negroes, labor. Kefauver had been backing away from liberalism lately; Stevenson should now cross over and undercut him by showing, at street-corner meetings, deep concern about Social Security, education, immigration, and housing. And in southern California he should deal with civil rights and civil liberties, attack Eisenhower directly in order to force voters to face the question of which candidate could best oppose Eisenhower in November. Another good southern California issue was the "missile gap"—the notion that the Russians were passing us in missiles and military aircraft. He should attack the big business Administration. In San Diego he should be careful of the issue of dispersing defense plants. At San Pedro tuna fishermen wanted a high tariff on Japanese tuna, and Kefauver had promised it to them.

Stevenson returned to Los Angeles from Kentucky near midnight with Bill Wirtz. Blair and Martin were already there. They gathered in Stevenson's room, and he bit into an apple, as he often did late at night, and said, "All right, brain trust, what do we do tomorrow?" They gave him his schedule and made recommendations, including one that he hit Nixon hard—he would be campaigning near the Vice President's home district. Martin had asked Wirtz to think about it on the plane coming out, and Wirtz had prepared a statement saying that Nixon had poisoned several previous campaigns and could be expected to poison this one. Stevenson approved, Wirtz worked it over after Stevenson went to bed, and the next day Stevenson used it. He would make more than fifty speeches that week.

Before he started out that first morning in Los Angeles, Stevenson listened to Bill Blair trying to deal with the worst problem on civil rights yet. Martin had written a speech line for a whistle-stop in San Francisco saying that Stevenson, if elected, would make it his first order of business to deal with the rising tensions that had followed in the train of the Supreme Court decision. Somebody had told Congressman Sikes of Florida that Stevenson had said he would make it his first order of business to enforce the Court decision. Sikes was now telephoning from Florida and threatening to leave Stevenson's slate of delegates and take most of the rest with him. Nobody could be sure precisely what Stevenson had actually said, since he had spoken extemporaneously. But Blair was able to convince Sikes that he had not said what had been reported, and, mollified, Sikes agreed to remain on the slate. It was well that he did. Without him, Stevenson could lose Florida.

In two days around Los Angeles, Stevenson went to factories, rallies, press conferences, hedge-hopped from one small airport to another, visited shopping centers, campaigned in a middle-class Jewish neighborhood from a flatbed truck, attended a Spanish-American celebration, and spoke in a school auditorium.

In Ontario, a rather conservative suburb not far from Nixon's home town, he declared that Nixon had shown "extreme irresponsibility," that Nixon "slanders and impugns the motives, even the loyalty of those who oppose him and his party," that Nixon had irresponsibly proposed on April 16, 1954, sending American troops to Indochina but then had reversed himself, and that he had "seriously aggravated" the school desegregation problem by claiming the Supreme Court's decision was "a Republican triumph."

Tuesday, May 8, called for campaigning in the Bay area—sixteen speeches, factory visits, a coffee break in a private home, visits to local headquarters, brief stops for photographers, receptions. The most important speeches were at the University of California at Berkeley, at an evening labor rally in Richmond, and to the Ministerial Alliance in Oakland, a Negro group. The Ministerial Alliance had been the most troublesome. It had worried Stevenson's people for weeks. After the Fresno fiasco, Stevenson had been in trouble with Negroes, and Byron Rumford, Stevenson's Negro leader in the Bay area, had been reported prepared to switch to Kefauver. By now he seemed to be back on Stevenson's side but barely. The ministerial meeting originally had been planned as a closed meeting, with Stevenson submitting to questioning. Martin disliked the question-and-answer formula and had feared that, if the meeting was closed, the press would try all the harder to learn what had taken place at it and ministers unfriendly to Stevenson might leak distorted paraphrases to the press. Martin had wanted Stevenson to make a speech. Bradley and the other California managers finally agreed to open the meeting and to have Stevenson make a brief statement, then invite questions. Thus it became a task of writing a statement that would anticipate questions in the hope that none would be asked. After consulting with numerous Californians, Martin had carefully drafted one. Bradley was prepared to break up the meeting by telling Stevenson he was due at another meeting if the questions became embarrassing. Pierre Salinger, another Californian active in Stevenson's campaign around San Francisco, then a magazine writer (later President Kennedy's press secretary), had worked on the statement (and on the Berkeley speech). By the time the entire project reached Stevenson he resisted it strongly. Again, he did not see why he had to repeat himself on civil rights. Late the night before in San Jose, Martin had given him the statement together with a Bill Wirtz draft of a labor speech for Richmond and a draft for Berkeley. Stevenson returned the Ministerial Alliance draft with a note:

> John—
> I'm too hopelessly exhausted to do more tonight—I'll try to get up early—
> I see *no* reason for releasing this—unless we have to after the meeting. It adds nothing to what I've said. And I want to reread before this meeting the N.Y. speech, and the last one or two on this subject.

Stevenson and his staff got only a few hours' sleep that night before arising early to start out to whistle-stop the Bay area aboard a chartered bus. Stevenson sat near the back, somewhat protected from local political leaders. With him were Blair, Bradley, and Martin. Blair nearly always stayed at Stevenson's side but did not need to when Bradley was along, for Bradley handled Stevenson well. Sometimes on such days at whistle-stops, Stevenson used the briefing sheets Martin gave him, sometimes he discarded them and heeded an oral briefing from Bradley, and sometimes he heeded neither but spoke entirely extemporaneously. Many people came to whistle-stops out of curiosity; they did not want to hear him discuss issues, wanted only to see what kind of man he was. He was turning into a good whistle-stop speaker, and the editorial advance work helped keep him on the track. No matter how tired he was when the bus pulled up for a stop, no matter how disgusted he was with the way things were going, when he got off the bus his expression changed and so did his whole attitude, and while he was speaking he seemed to be warm, relaxed, confident, outgoing, a man enjoying himself and seeming, in the cant phrase, to draw strength from the crowd. When he finished he would drift off the platform and shake hands. When he got back on the bus he might be as morose and tired as ever. But the crowds did not know it, only his staff.

Sometimes when he returned to the bus he would make a face indicating that he thought he had done poorly, and he could be funny at it. Once when an oafish man held up a Kefauver sign and thumbed his nose as the bus passed, Stevenson gave him a smile and a little wave, while saying sotto voce through clenched teeth, "Hello, you son of a bitch." At other times, weary, he was irascible. Once on the crowded bus he lost his writing pad, a white letter-size ruled pad. When the bus stopped at a shopping center Carol Evans jumped off and, while Stevenson was speaking, ran all over the shopping center and finally found a stationery store. She bought several pads and, when Stevenson returned to the bus, gave them to him, thinking he would be pleased. They were ruled yellow legal-size pads. Stevenson threw them down in disgust and said, "These are of utterly no use to me—they're too long and I can't use them." Campaign nerves. And yet—once when the bus stopped Stevenson raised himself up from his slouch in a back seat, looking disheveled and hot and sticky and disgruntled and exhausted; he made his way through the clutter of typewriters and mimeograph equipment, through the litter of Coke bottles and paper cups and paper and stencils and accumulated trash on the floor, and, trying to straighten his necktie, said, "Well, boys, here comes your gladiator." And then got off and faced the crowd with a smile.

At Long Beach he got off the bus and instead of going to the speaker's stand went to a park and started playing croquet with several old men there, and he seemed to enjoy every minute of it, one would have thought he had come all the way to California for the sole purpose of playing croquet with these people. Yet a few minutes before on the bus he had been complaining to his staff about his next day's schedule. Many people thought that Stevenson was a man who would turn inward under pressure or when tired and faced with a crowd of strangers. It was not so at all. He turned outward, to the crowd; and when he left the bus he seemed almost a stranger to his staff aboard it, a close friend of the people waiting outside.

That day in May—it was the eighth—he worked the Bay area hard. His crowd was huge at Palo Alto, minuscule at another morning stop. He did well at several small gatherings, then went to the Ministerial Alliance. The room was small and dark and crowded. No lectern had been provided, and Stevenson, who had become increasingly farsighted and sometimes had difficulty reading even a speech typed on a speech typewriter, asked permission to speak while sitting down. About a hundred ministers and others were present, many in clerical clothes. Stevenson followed his prepared text almost exactly: it was a clear restatement of his position on desegregation, followed by brief remarks on other issues.

He invited questions. No one spoke. Byron Rumford, seated near him, asked, "Is everybody satisfied?" No one answered. Stevenson left. Rumford and others thought the meeting went well—no one, they said, could ask any candidate to say anything more or go further on civil rights than Stevenson had gone.

He spent an afternoon whistle-stopping around Los Angeles. Much of the time was wasted. He spent more than five hours on the bus and talked to no more than a few hundred people. Sometimes he rode for as much as two hours without a stop. It was partly bad scheduling, partly Los Angeles' geographic sprawl. Stevenson and the others grew bored and realized how futile the trip was. Yet in the midst of it Stevenson delivered to Negroes one of the most eloquent and moving speeches he ever made on civil rights. He spoke extemporaneously. He said nothing he had not said before. But somehow he put his heart into it, and it was extremely effective. Not more than a hundred persons heard it.

For Long Beach the staff had worked out a paper in which Stevenson attacked the Republican campaign theme of peace, prosperity, and progress, asking, "What peace, what prosperity, what progress?" Stevenson had used it several times in California. But now he rebelled and said, "By God, I'm not going to make that speech again." More than once during the campaign he and the writers would laboriously develop such an all-purpose speech, he would use it several times until he had learned it well, it would work with the crowds—and at about that point Stevenson would tire of it and refuse to use it again. He would insist on having new material —and then would complain that he had no time to learn it. Many times during each day he would turn to Martin and say, "Why do we have to say this?" If Martin had talked to local people, he could present the arguments, and nearly always Stevenson would capitulate and do what needed doing. But it was necessary to be at his side.

Sometimes, whistle-stopping by bus, he would turn away, stare out the bus window, see something that interested him, and ask questions and talk about it at length, to the discomfiture of the writer with him, who knew the bus was only minutes away from the next stop. Frequently local politicians would manage to sit down beside him on the bus, interfering with his work and the writers', though of course talking to a local politician might be far more important than the next speech. Once when a woman sat too long beside Stevenson, Bradley took her by the arm and almost bodily removed her—and when Stevenson saw her go, he said, "You're not leaving me, are you?" and so of course she wanted to sit down again; Bradley had to do it all over.

Once at a shopping center Stevenson abandoned his briefings and launched into a speech on foreign affairs, and, back on the bus, said repeatedly that he wanted to speak on foreign policy. He was grumbling about a speech he had to make at noon next day at the Jewish Community Center at Olympic and Fairfax. The speech had been arranged long ago, and now as the time for it approached, Stevenson and his staff came under heavy pressure from Jewish leaders. They wanted him to speak on the Middle East; they had announced that he would deliver a major foreign policy speech, would speak for half an hour, and would answer questions for half an hour. Some of them had been disagreeable. By the time Stevenson's bus reached Long Beach, he had become petulant at the whole project and was threatening not to appear at all. Martin was to write the speech at the hotel in Long Beach that night. Stevenson went off to the Long Beach rally.

In it he moved closer to Medicare—proposed government encouragement and possible underwriting of private health insurance plans. And in the fall campaign he finally said that if elected he would "urge a thorough investigation by Congress of the possibility of adding a program of hospital insurance for the old to the present Old Age and Survivors Insurance System. It is particularly important, so far as older people are concerned, to take action in this area because most private plans are now closed to older people. We do not want compulsory insurance—but neither do we want older people to be involuntarily excluded from voluntary plans." This was, essentially, the Medicare plan, enacted into law nine years later.

When the party arrived at a hotel Blair would order whiskey and ice sent up to the room, and Stevenson, working on his speech, would have one drink of bourbon, sometimes two, before going off to speak. Blair and one or two other staff members would wait quietly. Sometimes he locked himself in a bedroom to work. They stayed that night in a hotel in Long Beach, and during the evening Martin worked on the Jewish Community Center speech for the next day, again trying to write it so there would be no questions. When he finished the speech he gave it to a girl to retype and slip under Stevenson's door.

Next day, Friday, May 11, Stevenson began at the Wilmington-San Pedro waterfront area, then made a plant gate stop in the Torrance area. The Jewish Community Center was next; he was due at noon. All morning he had complained about going and now he said flatly he would not go. Wirtz tried to persuade him. It was no use. Wirtz told Blair that for once Stevenson meant it—the meeting would have to be canceled. Blair talked to Stevenson alone, then told Wirtz calmly, "It's all right—he'll do it." He did, too. The speech was a long one, repeating his positions on civil liberties, civil rights, and Middle East policy. He closed with an eloquent description of his own visit to Israel.

The Texas primary had just been held, and the moderates there, led by Senator Lyndon Johnson, defeated the right-wing followers of Governor Shivers—a success for both Johnson and Stevenson. Stevenson telegraphed congratulations, and Johnson replied, "This is one year in which we can be sure of a Democratic delegation from Texas to a Democratic National Convention and that is something that will make every Democrat happy." Harry Ashmore, who had been negotiating for a long time with Senator Kefauver's campaign manager, telegraphed Stevenson that they had agreed a Stevenson-Kefauver debate would be broadcast from Miami on May 21 over ABC television and radio. It would be the first election-year debate between two presidential candidates on nationwide television in history.

In the Central Valley of California, his next target, Stevenson was almost sure to be asked about water. He must also speak about agriculture. His major farm speech would come on the second day, Sunday, at a fair at Los Banos, but all day Saturday he would whistle-stop his way northward through farmland. It was a hard place to speak, an area of perishable specialty crops of great variety, one where prosperity and distress alternated. He would talk about his experience with the AAA in the 1930s, assault the Administration generally and Secretary Benson in particular, and offer a rather vague farm program of his own. He would deliver one other set speech, at Tulare on Saturday. When he arrived at Bakersfield late Friday night, sitting in his bedroom with his feet on the bed, eating a bowl of fruit, he muttered about the Jewish Community Center speech. It had gone badly, he said. He had not wanted to make the speech in the first place and when he had finally arrived he had found a tremendous crowd waiting for a formal speech and had found himself without a text of any kind, "totally unprepared," a phrase he used constantly. Martin later asked Wirtz if the typist had failed to put the speech under Stevenson's door. Wirtz said of course not, Stevenson had received the speech and, after Blair's urging, had delivered it almost exactly as written.

On Saturday, Stevenson flew from Bakersfield to Porterville, then went by bus to Lindsay, Visalia, Dinuba, Hanford, and Tulare. It was a hot dusty day. During it Stevenson used a line that Martin had given him about the Tigris and Euphrates—Stevenson had traveled there and found nothing but stony soil because the ancients had not used the water to irrigate the potentially rich land, and the question now was whether the United States had the vision to use its water and soil wisely. Stevenson liked the line because it seemed to elevate him above the rut of whistle-stop politics. He had wearied of denouncing Benson as a scoundrel and promising to make the farmers rich, and late in the day he asked Martin, "Haven't you got another Tigris and Euphrates line?" He used writers when he needed them. But that same day Martin suggested he say that a glass of milk a day for every school child would quickly use up the accumulation of dairy surpluses. It was a line Walter Reuther had used. Stevenson asked sharply, "How much would it cost?" Martin had neglected to find out. Stevenson said, "Then I can't use it."

At Tulare, for the last speech of the day, Tubby thought Stevenson should attack Nixon again—Tubby thought this would make it impossible for the Republicans to drop him. Martin wrote it into the speech and gave it to Stevenson. Stevenson rebelled and said he had better stop attacking Nixon for fear he really *would* force him off the ticket. When he heard the Tubby strategy he delivered the passage. But he had discussed it so long that it did not reach the press in time to make the morning editions, and so was virtually lost. The party flew on to spend the night at Merced, the nearest sizable town to Los Banos. Wirtz was already at Merced. He had been working on the Los Banos farm speech all day. He had liked a suggestion that the speech recount the history of agriculture under Democratic and Republican administrations and had nearly completed a draft when local people told him the speech had to deal with current farm issues and had to attack Benson strongly. At about that point, Wirtz had realized the speech would be delivered on a Sunday, May 6, which was Mother's Day. Kefauver was to speak to the same audience that day. Wirtz suspected that Kefauver would say something like, "Folks, I'm not going to get up and talk to you about the Administration today or about politics. It's Sunday and it's Mother's Day and it just wouldn't be right." And then he would deliver a sermon on motherhood. Stevenson was to speak first. If he delivered a slashing political message, Kefauver could make him look foolish. Wirtz began drafting a Stevensonian sermon. The local people at Merced were vigorously opposed. This had to be a partisan speech. Don Bradley supported them, saying that anybody who attended a political meeting was interested in politics, Mother's Day or not. Wirtz finished the speech, gave it to Stevenson, and early Sunday morning flew home, adjuring Martin to keep watch during the day.

When Martin arrived at the hotel room Stevenson was struggling to get into the cowboy levis and jacket and boots and string necktie that he had to wear in order to ride horseback in the parade at Los Banos before speaking. He looked odd. And knew it. On the way to the elevator he said, "*God,* what a man won't do to get public office." They got into a local farmer's Cadillac and drove off toward Los Banos. Stevenson thought the speech a little soft, not hard-hitting, lacking punch, and asked Martin to fix it. They stopped at the ranch of a Stevenson supporter, and while Stevenson went in to shake hands Martin worked on the speech. Stevenson returned, they drove on, and Martin told him what he proposed to do with the speech, and Stevenson concurred, and when they reached Los Banos, Stevenson got out and got on his horse and rode off in the parade while Martin looked for a car, the secretaries, typewriters, and a mimeograph machine. After considerable confusion he found them at the locked home of a Stevenson supporter. They went to work on the patio, and after a time Stevenson arrived to rest between the parade and the speaking, and Martin took the speech to him page by page.

The party went to the fairground. Stevenson, walking toward the crowd with Martin and Tubby, said, "I don't think you fellows are really in the spirit of this thing," and strode off to shake hands a little grimly with the people in the crowd.

It was hot and dusty, brown hills rising above the valley floor. The others lay down on the grass in the warm sun or went to get something to eat and only then realized that nobody had mimeographed Stevenson's speech and distributed it to the press. They set to work in a fairground administration building. While they were working it caught fire, and a man collapsed, and the fire department and police ambulances arrived noisily. They put the fire out. During this time Stevenson was involved with several beauty queens and Alistair Cooke of the Manchester *Guardian.* The staff finished the press release just before Stevenson started to speak. The speech itself was a compromise between a Mother's Day sermon and a political farm speech. It employed at one point this transition between the attack and programmatic sections: "But we're not going to spend Mother's Day in Los Banos talking about how bad things are. Basically, they're not bad; they're good. But the farm economy is out of kilter right now. What are we going to do about it?" Stevenson delivered the speech well, and it sounded good, but the crowd just stood there. He got almost no applause. His local supporters told him and his staff it was the best farm speech they had ever heard him give. Stevenson left. Martin and other staffers stayed to listen to Kefauver. Kefauver did exactly what Wirtz had predicted: delivered a Mother's Day sermon. But he tucked into it a flat promise of one sentence coming out in favor of the federal government's building of the San Luis dam, and so next day the newspaper headlines in the valley quoted him on that promise, and it appeared that he had delivered a substantive speech on water and agriculture. Newspapermen told Stevenson's staff that in their opinion Stevenson had had the better of the occasion. It was May 13, three weeks before the California primary.

19.

From Portland, Stevenson wrote letters. To Agnes Meyer: ". . . I still struggle and strain to say something better and end up with something worse. . . ." To Adlai III (addressing him as always, "Dear Bear"), "I wish I could write you a proper letter, but I am living in a state bordering on insanity. . . . There is incessant and repeated demand for Nancy to join me in Florida . . . but I am not going to press it because of her 'condition' —not to mention your uxorious claims!" Hubert Humphrey had written that Stevenson seemed well on the road to nomination: "I have walked around in ashes and sackcloth, ashamed that we got you into such a mess [as the Minnesota primary] and even more embarrassed that we were unable to deliver." Stevenson now replied, "Things are going better and better and the direction has all been one way since Minnesota."

Stevenson made a fast swing through Oregon, headed for Florida, with brief stops in California on the way. Oregon voted on Friday, May 18, and Stevenson won, 98,131 to 62,987, a big victory. Raskin had contributed greatly to it. Everybody was heartened. Minow, who had pushed Stevenson's entry into Oregon, felt that Stevenson had recouped the Minnesota loss. He campaigned Florida hard. He did not, however, alter his basic positions on issues.

On Monday, May 21, eight days before the Florida primary, Stevenson and Kefauver engaged in televised debate in Miami. A great deal of thought had gone into preparation for the debate (called a "discussion"). The decision to appear jointly with Kefauver had been a close one, some arguing that doing so diminished Stevenson, others arguing that he simply could not refuse after Minnesota. Everybody thought the debate crucial. Minow, always impressed with the impact of television, thought it might decide the outcome of the entire spring primary campaign. But the debate turned out to be rather dull. Stevenson and Kefauver spent the first part of the program in a fuzzy, blunted discussion of foreign affairs. Moving to domestic policy, both took firm stands on civil rights.

When the broadcast was over Stevenson telephoned Wirtz, Minow, and Martin, who were watching in Minow's home in a Chicago suburb. Stevenson felt he had come off badly. "Totally unprepared," he said, and went on to say that Kefauver had had numerous cards he had spoken from but Stevenson had had nothing. (In truth, Finnegan and Ashmore had spent the last couple of days going over with Stevenson the questions that probably would be asked.)

Wirtz, Minow, and Martin said he had come off better than he thought. Stevenson, however, was not mollified. He told George Ball angrily, "What I should have done was destroy him with some blinding oratory. But I didn't have any notes."

He campaigned unremittingly through the final week in Florida. Finnegan was not optimistic. Stevenson was emphasizing local issues, including the spread of the Mediterranean fruit fly, a pest. The campaign was becoming increasingly acid. Kefauver replied to Stevenson's attacks on his absentee record in the Senate with an attack on Stevenson's record as Governor on old-age pensions. In an interview with CBS, Stevenson said he expected to win and said Kefauver's personal attacks hurt the party and diminished the presidency. Once during the final week a Stevenson supporter, introducing him to a segregationist crowd, implied that Stevenson was a white supremacist at heart. Stevenson, sitting on the platform, working on his speech, did not hear the introduction and simply acknowledged it and began speaking. Later newspapermen taxed him with it, asking why he had not repudiated the introduction. He hastily called a press conference and disavowed the introduction but the damage was done: the story spread through California. In Florida, too, Kefauver people were hinting that Stevenson's people there were tied to Miami gambling interests. Stevenson staffers began gathering material tying Kefauver supporters to Chicago racketeers. In California a Kefauver man again began spreading the story about old-age pensions.

Newt Minow reported on a movement by downstate Illinois Democrats, including Paul Powell, John Stelle, and Scott Lucas, to keep the Illinois delegates unpledged at the convention. Minow persuaded state chairman Ronan to issue a statement saying that Stevenson's 717,000 votes in the Illinois primary represented a "mandate" to Illinois delegates. Minow was struggling with Stevenson's campaign budget. He anticipated a deficit of more than $40,000 by California primary day. The payroll ran to $21,000 a month. Of this by far the biggest single sum was $7,100 for editorial and research help.[9]

[9] The highest-paid staffers were Ashmore at $2,083 a month, Blair at $1,000, Finnegan at $1,250, Martin at $1,500, Raskin at $1,541, Tubby at $1,083, and John Horne in Washington at $1,000. Some thirty-eight people were on the payroll. Minow wanted to cut the staff drastically after the California primary.

Reports from California were cautious. One estimate was that Stevenson was ahead 2 to 1 in the San Francisco area, that he was running behind Kefauver in the Central Valley, and that he was about even or perhaps a little behind in Los Angeles. This added up to a close election. The Stevenson campaign in crucial Los Angeles seemed disorganized, the press wholly hostile, and it was hard to see how Stevenson could make an impact upon the voters in that vast place. One week to go.

He arrived at Los Angeles International Airport late on the afternoon of Monday, May 28. Almost immediately well-laid plans went awry: Mrs. Roosevelt had flown all night from New York to San Francisco, campaigned there all morning, and been scheduled to arrive at Los Angeles airport at the same time as Stevenson so they could hold a joint televised press conference; but she arrived early and went to a nearby motel. Stevenson went there and they held their press conference; then she went off to a rally in the Negro district while Stevenson went to a television studio. Someone told him that Mrs. Roosevelt could not appear with him on television and this, rightly, disturbed him considerably. He seemed tired and disgruntled. He had declared in Florida that he would never again appear on television to answer questions put to him by three supporters, yet here he was about to do it again in Los Angeles. At the studio, as usual, he became very nervous. He met the guests, began fooling with his manuscript, disappeared behind a screen and, as air time approached, could not be found, then emerged and in turn could not find his staff. The pencils needed sharpening; he wanted Wirtz and Martin to work with him on the manuscript. Finally the show went on. Afterward, he watched a film clip of the joint press conference with Mrs. Roosevelt. The show was only fair. Such programs were never good. Nonetheless, the point had been made: he was here, Mrs. Roosevelt was with him, the campaign was in its last week. It was hoped that Mrs. Roosevelt would help with the Negro vote and strengthen his ties to the New Deal-Fair Deal tradition.

From the studio he went to Gus Hawkins' rally in the Negro district— Hawkins was a Negro leader and later a Congressman—and delivered with good grace a speech based on the Oakland Ministerial Association speech. The audience, sizable even though the hour was late, received it well. On the way back to the hotel he said he had heard that the McClatchy newspapers were turning against him and he wanted to know why. Martin tried to explain but Stevenson did not really listen, he only wanted to be angry with the press. (Stevenson had said at Redding he saw nothing wrong in principle with the "partnership" system of joint private-federal water-power development but thought the Eisenhower administration was doing it wrong. "Partnership" was anathema to the McClatchy papers.)

Stevenson awakened early Tuesday morning and set to work on the day's speeches—a recorded speech to an NAACP meeting in Los Angeles and a major luncheon speech to the Press and Union League Club in San

Francisco at noon. The NAACP speech, modeled on the Oakland Ministerial Association statement, was recorded because his managers did not
want Stevenson to appear before the NAACP that day, the day Florida
voted. The speech in San Francisco was well received. He said he would
speak not about this primary but about the fall election. Nobody knew
who the Democratic candidate would be but everybody knew who the Republican candidate would be. Eisenhower had enunciated eight principles
on which he could campaign:

"First, he said he is unequivocally in favor of the supreme importance of
the individual. And I agree with him.

"Second, he proclaims the importance of spiritual values. I take it we
are agreed on that.

"Third, he is unequivocally in favor of prosperity, peace, plenty, and
happiness. Anybody here against that?"

And so on—Stevenson listed all eight points. Then, "I say to you that
however lofty his sentiment, however good his intentions, this is not the
kind of leadership we require as we venture upon the perilous stage of history in the last half of the twentieth century—particularly when there are
lurking in the wings the Vice President he esteems so highly and the Old
Guard stage managers of the Republican Party."

President Eisenhower, he said, "did not say a word about" rising racial
tensions, the plight of the farmer or small businessmen or the aged, dangers in the Middle East and in Russian imperialism.

The prospect for the future was even worse, he said. "For we are now
asked to remake the role of the presidency itself to meet the present unfortunate circumstances. And already we are beginning to see the consequences—

"—the President is kept in ignorance of our lag in guided missile development;

"—the President smiles at Israel while the Russians move into the Middle East and arm her enemies;

"—the President evidently is not informed of the confusion of self-interest in the Dixon-Yates deal and at sundry high levels of his administration;

"—the President gives a clean bill of health to Richard Nixon's California crony—yet the Republican managers discreetly drop him from the
team;

"—the Secretary of State announces in a magazine article, if you please,
that he had led us three times to the brink of war, with the President's approval, but the President says he has not read the article;

"—the President and his Secretary of State issue reassuring bulletins
while Soviet leaders woo Asia;

"—the President is not informed of controversy in the armed services until it erupts in a violent quarrel;

"—the President withholds the immense prestige of his office from those who seek to resolve the crises in civil rights; and

"—in the latest so-called security case the President says he is not familiar with it because, as he puts it, 'They bring before me what has been going on, usually not in terms of names but in terms of numbers. . . .'

"The American presidency is the greatest temporal office on our planet. Its capacity for good or evil, for influence on human affairs, is almost without limitation. When the President leads, billions follow. When the President falters, the world trembles. When the President speaks, the world pays heed. When he is silent or when he is absent, chaos threatens.

"All down the years, in war and peace, in time of trouble and time of need, it is to the White House that the people of our country and the people of the world have looked for leadership—for deeds, not words.

"Today, too, our people at home need many things—schools, pensions, housing, highways, jobs, medical care—and it is of the White House that they ask: When will we get them? How will we get them? . . .

"I suggest to you that it is only in the presidency that the people will find their answers. And I submit to you that on the record the Democratic Party is the one best equipped to lead the nation to the new plateau of the better, safer life only just beyond the horizon."

Stevenson told Wirtz he got more satisfaction out of delivering this speech than out of anything he had delivered since the ASNE speech in Washington. Never before in this campaign had he attacked Eisenhower so hard and so directly. Not for some time had he employed rhetoric at the level of the 1952 acceptance speech.

Afterward, on the bus to Vallejo, he talked about his family's experience in California. The story was around that his uncle had been forced to sell his farm in the Central Valley during the Great Depression. Stevenson now said that his uncle once had had a place out here but had sold it for a pretty good price before the Depression, then had discovered he could have gotten a much better price later. He went on to say that this penchant for buying high and selling low seemed to run in the family—he himself had made some bad investments. Once, he said, while on the *Princetonian*, he had earned nearly $1,000 and had been given the choice of investing it in an enterprise back in Bloomington or in the project of a classmate to start, with Henry R. Luce, *Time* magazine. He had invested in Bloomington and lost his money. *Time* stock would have made him rich. The story amused him. As the bus rolled on he talked about the countryside. As often happened, he knew more about it than those who briefed him. He had traveled widely around America over the years. He had an excellent memory, although he pretended to have a poor one. And he had the ability to keep his mind on several things at one time. Frequently he would be working on a speech manuscript while his aides talked off to one side in low tones, thinking him oblivious; but then it would develop that he had heard and retained everything they had said, yet at the same time had got his own work done—and had been looking out the window betimes, taking in his surroundings.

That night in the hotel at Vallejo the first returns came in from Florida: 71 of 1,778 Miami precincts gave Stevenson 8,849 and Kefauver 7,920. Blair, in Stevenson's suite, spent the evening on the telephone to Florida, receiving returns. They seesawed back and forth. At one point Stevenson was 300 votes ahead. At another he was 2,000 behind. At another he was 1,000 ahead. Stevenson went downstairs to deliver his speech, then came back up and, sitting on the bed, waited while Blair manned the telephone. It began to look as if he was losing. He looked up at Wirtz and Martin and, his big blue eyes round and staring, said, "They're doing it again, aren't they?" He meant Republicans were crossing over into the Democratic primary. He did not seem angry or even disappointed. He simply seemed shocked and hurt, almost like a child who has been unfairly spanked. Near midnight it was clear that the election was a tossup with one district still not heard from, Congressman Robert L. F. Sikes's district, a district of bigoted wool-hat upstate segregationists, that Stevenson was supposed to carry. As it turned out he did carry it and with it Florida— Florida by about 12,000 votes. Thus Stevenson had squeaked through in Florida by carrying a district which, if he was liberal on civil rights, he should not have carried. There was no victory celebration in the hotel that night or ever.

Kefauver's manager, F. Joseph "Jiggs" Donahue, promptly declared in Los Angeles that the Florida election was a "tremendous victory" for Kefauver. He said Stevenson had won with a "measurable margin" only in Sikes's district "where the Stevenson people made segregation an issue" and at Miami Beach where the gamblers exposed by the Kefauver investigation had reopened their business. He said Kefauver's integrity was proved when he refused to modify his position in support of desegregation. Donahue added that Florida was the winter home of "the Chicago Democratic machine and its operating boss, Jack Arvey. "In California, this same combine headed by Arvey's Western lieutenant, Paul Ziffren of Beverly Hills, is making its deals for expedience." Plainly Kefauver intended to make a desperate stand this last week in California. Some Stevenson staffers thought the Florida election had turned out just right. If Stevenson had lost Florida a Kefauver bandwagon might have swept California. If Stevenson had won Florida overwhelmingly the Negro vote in California might have deserted him. There was evidence of a Republican crossover—a Florida newspaper reported that Kefauver had run best in precisely those districts where President Eisenhower was strongest in

1952. One analyst told Finnegan, "The Republicans came very close to up-setting Adlai in Florida. With the genuine Republicans eliminated from our Democratic primary, Adlai would have had a majority of 75,000."

20.

Next day was May 30, Memorial Day, and Stevenson spent it campaign-ing in northern California, including a buffet and cocktail party at Roger Kent's home in Marin County. Stevenson was in good spirits; this was his kind of gathering: pretty women, liberal intellectuals, beautiful surround-ings, a band for dancing. He took time out to go upstairs and record a speech to party workers for state-wide radio. To everyone's surprise he asked why he couldn't repeat the Press and Union League Club speech in San Diego. Martin thought not—by that time they had national press trav-eling with them, and the lead would not be on the speech but on the idea that Stevenson was tiring at the end of the campaign and delivering a speech twice. Stevenson nodded and went back downstairs to talk to sup-porters. Kefauver and Jiggs Donahue were attacking Stevenson in south-ern California as a white supremacist, tool of the political bosses, and enemy of pensions for the elderly. Finnegan, Wirtz, and Martin met to de-cide what to do. They thought Stevenson should "take the high road," ig-nore Kefauver, and leave a reply to him to someone else. Finnegan talked to Pat Brown, who was attending the party downstairs, but he was un-willing to attack Kefauver. So were others whom Finnegan approached. Wirtz and Martin did not think Finnegan should reply—he was too close to Stevenson. They were still discussing it when it came time to leave Roger Kent's.

On the bus they told Stevenson what Kefauver was saying. Stevenson was indignant. He wanted to take out after Kefauver "hammer and tongs." He had wanted to do it previously, when he first landed at Los Angeles airport, but had been dissuaded. The others, including Blair, were less in-dignant than concerned—they suspected that Kefauver might be making headway with Negroes and old people, and furthermore, they had no way of estimating the impact of the bossism charge but knew it had succeeded in Minnesota. They still did not want Stevenson himself to attack. But he took out a ruled pad and wrote out sharp statements about Kefauver, each successive one stronger than the last. Wirtz kept saying, "Wait until to-morrow and make the statement—you can't do it on Memorial Day." Stevenson said, "What argument are you going to use on me tomorrow?" Wirtz said, "I'll think of that tomorrow." Stevenson seemed determined to issue some sort of statement. The bus ride would end at San Francisco air-port, and he would be met by the press. A question arose as to whether Kefauver had actually already attacked Stevenson or whether he was going to that night. Everybody agreed that Stevenson should not attack Kefauver for something he had not yet said. All but Tubby agreed he should not attack him at all. The argument swirled on. Stevenson kept writing bitter statements. At length, just before the bus reached the airport, Martin suggested to Stevenson that, if asked about Kefauver's attacks, he say merely that Kefauver was obviously a bad loser. This was what he did at the airport, though he added a few remarks about the bossism and pension charges, mild stuff compared to what he had written out for himself. He and his party, by now a large one, flew to Los Angeles that night. The argument over how to handle Kefauver continued on the plane.

It was Thursday, May 31. The election would be next Tuesday. Kefauver and Stevenson were crisscrossing each other's trails all over the state. By now, by common agreement, California had clearly become the key to the Democratic nomination for President. At noon that day Stevenson spoke to a Town Hall luncheon in the Biltmore Hotel in Los Angeles. He attempted to define a liberal. The liberal, he said, believed "in the existence of the future, and believes that it can be made a good future"; that "people are all that is important, and that all people are equally important"; that ideals were worth fighting for courageously, as when Wilson spoke of a "fighting ardor for mankind" and Lehman of a "passion for full freedom." Stevenson applied these observations to current issues and turned them to criticize the Administration.

After the speech Stevenson flew to San Diego. There he set to work feverishly on the evening's talk, which he thought contained faulty logic. He left to deliver it in a great flurry with the reading copy unfinished. The speech rebuked Kefauver, defended Stevenson's record on old-age pensions as Governor, discussed Social Security and health, attacked Eisenhower, and closed with a paraphrase of his Florida speech on why he ran for President. Finnegan noticed that Stevenson, delivering it, had the audience "on the edge of their chairs" as he approached the peroration and, had he sailed straight through, would have had them cheering in the aisles at the end. Instead, he paused to tell a joke, broke the tension, and finished to ordinary applause. He had done it before and would do it again. He seemed to try to kill applause. More than once he said impatiently, "What are they applauding for?" He preferred that his audience listen. Once he half seriously upbraided Wirtz and Tubby for counting the applause breaks in a speech. At another point he said, "God, a lot of crap goes into these speeches, doesn't it?" Feeling thus, he often threw cold water on his audience, and Finnegan sometimes referred to him as "my fireman"—an expert at putting out the fire in a hot audience.

He stayed that night in San Diego and spent the next day, Friday, June 1, whistle-stopping his way by bus northward all the way to Los Angeles. It was a long hard day, much of it wasted. That night he spoke to a street rally in El Monte.

Saturday, June 2—only the weekend remained. He flew early from Los Angeles to Fresno. Because of the earlier Fresno fiasco, everyone was nervous about his appearance there now, and his California managers had given conflicting advice about what he should say. He and his staff had in mind not only the fiasco but the need to say something definitive about agriculture and to appease the McClatchy papers on power development.[10]

He left for Stockton, where he made one television appearance and one at a saloon, then flew to San Francisco. He spent Sunday, June 3, in the San Francisco Bay area; that night he flew to Los Angeles. On the plane Eddie Folliard of the Washington *Post* told him he ought to talk about Kefauver's bossism charges and about foreign policy. He agreed—those were the things he most wanted to talk about. Wirtz and other staffers, however, thought he should cover the issues and at the same time deliver an image speech. After he talked to Folliard it took his staff nearly four hours—on the plane and at the hotel in Los Angeles—to persuade him away from the Folliard view. They had written a draft and gave it to him, and he began rewriting it completely along the lines Folliard had suggested. Time and tempers grew increasingly short. In the end he had a reading copy which contained so much foreign policy that he could not possibly finish on time, so Blair and Martin simply removed the foreign policy pages. Unfortunately they failed to notice a sentence at the bottom of a page leading into the foreign policy section so that, on air, Stevenson delivered it and turned the page and found nothing facing him on foreign policy. He stumbled through it somehow, delivered the speech—a shopping list, a talk about the campaign, an image speech. It was one of the worst yet.

Election Night in California—Stevenson had asked Martin to prepare statements "either way"—one for use if he lost, one if he won—but there was no need: it was apparent shortly after the polls closed that Stevenson had a commanding lead. He never lost it. Indeed, he simply overwhelmed Kefauver. He won California with 1,139,964 votes to Kefauver's 680,722. The most optimistic staff estimate had been a 300,000 plurality. He won by 459,000—62 per cent of the vote. He carried Los Angeles County by 488,898 to 238,372; San Francisco 100,015 to 34,868; Alameda (Oak-

---

[10] On water resources, he said: "The Administration is willing to make the taxpayer's money available for what it calls 'partnership' deals but isn't willing to make it available for public projects that would serve the total public interest. This 'partnership' proposition has served, first of all, as an excuse for putting off the construction of needed public power facilities—or, worse still, for developing them to only a fraction of their capacity and thus wasting the great potential that belongs to all people. . . . The drive is on for a 'partnership' deal at Trinity River [in California]. . . . It would appear that, in the case of Trinity, the Republican concept of 'partnership' is less a device for furthering development of this great damsite at lower cost to the government than a means of undercutting the basic principles of public development of our natural resources. These principles can be stated simply: the rivers belong to the people. They must be developed for the benefit of all the people." The speech was not aimed at the immediate audience but at the general public and the McClatchy newspapers, and while it bored many of his listeners it accomplished its larger purposes.

land), 87,595 to 43,864. Kefauver carried only a few counties in the Valley and in the northern mountains where, as Jim Finnegan said, "there are more bears than people." Stevenson won in the farm country, where Kefauver's folksy handshaking had been considered unbeatable, and in areas where old people lived. He carried Negro wards 5 to 1 or more. He won in San Diego, where Kefauver had outpromised him in aircraft building.

This California primary victory was comparable to his landslide in Illinois for Governor in 1948. So big was it that it was hard to understand. In retrospect, it appeared that Kefauver's campaign had been ill advised toward the end. By attacking Stevenson he threw away his own greatest strength—that of the friendly handshaker. Worn out, he went too far in his attacks. He also went too far in his promises—his purpose became transparent and hurt *him*.

Looking back, it appeared that Stevenson had started in California in December with a lead over Kefauver. He had the political leaders and the Democratic clubs, he was better known, it was his kind of state. After the Fresno fiasco, the history of Stevenson's California campaign was that of a precipitous plummeting from the heights and then of a long slow climb back upward. He changed his tactics, shifting from high-level oratory to political infighting at whistle-stops.

If the Minnesota defeat was the best thing that ever happened to Stevenson politically, the California victory was the worst. Minnesota had forced him to stop acting as though he was not seeking the nomination. Minnesota made him abandon rhetoric and take to effective whistle-stopping, where votes are made in a primary. Minnesota fired up his workers elsewhere and drew from them maximum efforts. On the other hand, while the California victory did create a picture of a fighting candidate who came back strongly and won, it also made Stevenson overconfident. As June and July passed he seemed to forget how he had won in California, and as, confident of the nomination, he planned his fall campaign, he seemed to revert to the style of 1952—lofty rhetoric on grand issues. Some of his staff members believed he could defeat Eisenhower only by campaigning the nation as he had campaigned California—whistle-stopping hard in areas of disaffection, a "pothole" campaign, rubbing the raw nerves of discontent in a generally complacent country, maximizing his support among workingmen, Negroes, coal miners, and others. In California, shaken by Minnesota, he had been willing, almost eager, to accept local advice. After California he changed. His advisers, including Finnegan, Wirtz, Schlesinger, Tufts, and Martin, told him that although it might be so that the Eisenhower administration's greatest failures were in foreign policy, there were no votes in that issue. But others, including Bowles and Finletter, talked foreign policy to him. Once Walter Reuther came to Libertyville and talked about almost nothing but India. Stevenson loved this sort of talk, disliked bread-and-butter issues and whistle-stopping, and, confident after California, readily reverted to the role of statesman. Some advisers urged that foreign policy was not only a useless issue but a dangerous one —most Americans believed that in 1952 America had been at war in Korea, Eisenhower had ended the war, therefore Eisenhower must know all about foreign policy, and further, if Stevenson were to persuade them otherwise he could only do it by frightening them half to death over the Soviet menace and this, in turn, would cause them to rally around the President.

Stevenson resisted this reasoning. He laid plans to make foreign policy a leading issue in the fall. He asked Senator Fulbright for suggestions: "While I reluctantly concede that the politicians are probably right, and that there are mighty few votes in it, I am also convinced that the administration is most vulnerable in that area and that it is also the most important area." He told Hubert Humphrey and others, "Planning for the campaign, the issue and themes to be emphasized and how, occupies my attention, I am afraid, at the expense of the delegate hunt." California had given him an enormous lift. He told Nancy's parents, and others too, "I had no trouble with the primaries except in Minnesota and Florida where the Republicans could interfere, and did in a big way, to help Estes dispose of me. Now they will build up Harriman and I will have to go through it all again with a new opponent with the same Republican backing. Ho hum!" He seemed convinced he was the choice of his party. Newt Minow said years later that the nomination was "pretty well set" after California "but we wanted to do it on the first ballot so there wouldn't be any scars and so it would impress the TV audience." Stevenson resisted a proposal that he visit Nevada and Wyoming. Newt Minow told him, "Governor Harriman and Senator Kefauver are cultivating the delegates out there very assiduously." Stevenson replied, "Let them assiduate." Minow said, "They'll assiduate you right out of the nomination." Stevenson said, "Nonsense," and looked incredulous. Only with difficulty did Blair and Finnegan persuade him to make overtures toward delegates.

After the primary Stevenson went to the San Ysidro ranch near Santa Barbara for a few days' rest. Blair was with him, and Marietta Tree came out from New York. One day they toured the MGM studio with Dore Schary. At the ranch Blair was "very protective" of Stevenson, Marietta later recalled. "He would give the Gov a whiskey and tell me, 'Let's you and I go out on the porch.'" Once Stevenson fell asleep on the beach, and Blair took Marietta away, saying, "Let him sleep." Stevenson remembered it was Jane Dick's birthday and sent her a telegram. He talked to a newspaper owner in California, Tom Storke, and some years later considered buying his paper.

He was swamped with telegrams and letters of congratulation. Kefauver sent him a congratulatory telegram, promising to work for the ticket in California in November. Stevenson wrote out a terse reply: "Thank you for your wire. I too hope the campaign has strengthened the party. Best wishes." Blair inserted "very thoughtful" in front of "wire" and sent it. Stevenson was also considering a trip to Russia, or at least to the East European satellite countries, between now and the convention "for education, the 'feel,' publicity of the right kind and escape from what will be the mounting pressures in the delegates' search." He told Mrs. Roosevelt that her one-day contribution to the California campaign "was of more value than anything that happened" and thanked her for pulling in the Negro vote.

He told Bill Benton, "It is the 'morning after' and I am enjoying the hangover," and thanked him for "another fat contribution." He welcomed a suggestion from a contributor, Jack Kaplan of New York, that repeated questions directed to the President would enliven the fall campaign. "I noticed after my American Society of Newspaper Editors speech in April that the President was on the defensive for some little time."

Roger Stevens, chairman of his finance committee, sent him a long memorandum. He had collected about a million dollars and spent it on the primaries and had ended with a $50,000 deficit. It could be covered by $25,000 in the Volunteers' treasury and another $25,000 from new contributions—victory in California would loosen purse strings. No commitments had been made to contributors. Mary Lasker and Lansdell Christie had been "magnificent" in their contributions. The Reynolds brothers and Marshall Field had been "very generous." George Killion and Albert Greenfield, respectively Eastern and Western chairmen of the finance committee, had "come through very well on commitments made at your house at the January meeting. . . . Mrs. Guggenheim"—evidently Alicia Patterson—"did a good job at the New York dinner." Stevenson should thank them all.

If Roger Stevens was to stay on for the fall campaign, what, he asked, would be his relationship to the Democratic National Committee? Planning must begin at once—there were only sixty days between the convention and the election, and financial commitments had to be made in cash thirty days in advance. Stevens' memorandum urged that coordination with the National Committee be arranged by July 1 to avoid "chaos," that Stevenson approve an organizational chart, that Stevenson appoint a deputy with power to act for him, that each department have "a financial watch dog (God help him!)," that campaign headquarters be moved to Washington. The finance committee should have a small dinner on August 11 to pay convention expenses, with contributions of $500 each. Big money for the general campaign would be hard to get unless contributors could be convinced that Stevenson had a good chance to win. "As a theatrical producer, I would like to make some suggestions as to the programs," Stevens wrote, and his first suggestion said this: "Unless some dramatic things are done, we do not have a chance to win." Stevenson needed a Catholic vice presidential candidate. He should make no more than six full-length national television speeches and should spend most of his broadcast money on radio, television spots, and possibly five-minute programs. (This was what the Republicans intended to do.) He should seek the services of the cartoonist Herbert Block (who signed his cartoons Herblock). Unemployed auto workers should go on television to make an appeal. Finally, "Since the *Saturday Review of Literature* last week stated that only fifteen percent of the people of this country even read a book last year, it is important to simplify our programs." Stevens added that none of this was intended to criticize the way the primary campaign had been run. It was thoughtful, realistic memorandum, and some of it was adopted.

21.

The nomination suddenly became more valuable—only a few days after the California primary, President Eisenhower underwent major abdominal surgery after an attack of ileitis. It appeared for a time that he might not run after all, although his aides minimized his new illness. But by August 1 he was telling a press conference he would run anyway. For a time it was uncertain whether he would have Vice President Nixon on the ticket with him again—Eisenhower refused to commit himself to Nixon's renomination and, indeed, gave Harold Stassen leave from his administration while Stassen worked to block Nixon. (But in the end Stassen, at Eisenhower's request, made a seconding speech for Nixon at the convention.)

Stevenson, who returned to Chicago shortly after Eisenhower's abdominal surgery, told Archibald MacLeish, "The real problem is how to attack the incessant irresponsibility of Eisenhower. Instead of using his great prestige to inform and enlighten us he has contributed to our complacent delinquency and a sugar diet leads to fatty degeneration." He told Gerald Johnson, "As to the illness, I have no doubt the attitude will be 'if he can walk he can run.'" He told Ralph McGill, "My secretary just said if the administration kept us as informed about the state of the world and the nation as they do about the state of the President's blood pressure and insides we would be risking little of the hazards of ignorance." He wrote to Eugene Rostow of the Yale Law School about "the basic theme of the President's irresponsibility, call it huckstering, duplicity, deceit or innocence." He had come a long way from his respectful view of the Eisenhower of 1952.

Stevenson reluctantly made some staff changes. Harry Ashmore departed. Clayton Fritchey, deputy chairman of the Democratic National Committee, became press secretary and Roger Tubby his assistant. Bob Tufts joined the staff on a part-time basis. Arthur Schlesinger soon joined the staff full time as head of the writers (under Wirtz). Dawn Clark joined as a researcher (Brademas would have to leave after the convention to run for Congress). The writers for the fall campaign became Wirtz, Schlesinger, and Martin full time; Tufts and William Lee Miller half time; plus several occasional contributors, including John Hersey, John Kenneth Galbraith, Chet Bowles, Seymour Harris, David Lloyd, and Charles Murphy.

During the preconvention period they worked on various drafts of the acceptance speech, on messages from Stevenson to various groups, on platform language, and on a position inventory. Brademas and Hechler drew up a list of some 180 issues; they and the writers prepared policy position papers on each one, raising all the questions likely to be asked, setting forth the Administration position, congressional proposals, other positions, and Stevenson's position if he had one and a recommendation for a position if he did not. The papers were to be used for speeches and in briefing Stevenson for press conferences. A great deal of work went into each one; sometimes a day was spent on a single sentence. The writers were also trying to draft language for the desegregation plank in the platform, most difficult of all. Lloyd Garrison, Stevenson's staff, and others suspected that Harriman and other Northern liberals, encouraged by Republicans, intended to try to force through a civil rights plank that would drive the Southerners from the convention and result in the nomination of Harriman by the remaining half of the party. Stevenson told Mrs. Roosevelt, "I would gladly withdraw from this political contest if it would serve in any manner to save the party from breaking up and enthroning the white extremists in the South or losing the Northern cities and thus the election. Either alternative is sad, but the former the saddest and most injurious to the Negro and his advancement." Lloyd Garrison thought the solution was to write a plank that all but the most extreme Northerners could accept and that, though the Southerners would vote against it, they would "swallow" it to hold the party together and because it was right. Reports from the South showed that Stevenson's delegate strength was respectable though not overwhelming, a good position.

Stevenson had not forgotten the H-bomb issue, nor had others. Archibald Alexander told him on June 14 that the "storage" of radioactive particles in the upper atmosphere reinforced Stevenson's proposal to stop H-bomb tests. William H. Davis of New York told Stevenson that if multimegaton tests could be stopped without detriment to the atomic weapon development program, stopping would impress world opinion more than anything else. Stevenson replied, "I have provoked a host of criticism as a result of my suggestion that we start doing now what we are going to do ultimately—not use hydrogen weapons. I am afraid I am out of step with the current thought."

Near the end of June, Kefauver initiated a move toward a rapprochement. Bill Shannon of the New York *Post* and a New York lawyer named Sidney Davis urged on Kefauver a policy of moderation. They told him he had nothing to gain from a Harriman alliance because Lyndon Johnson would shift to Stevenson in time to prevent a Harriman-Kefauver victory and Truman would make sure that Kefauver would not benefit. They suggested that, instead, Kefauver stop personal attacks on Stevenson and come out for an unbossed convention. Jiggs Donahue, on the other hand, urged Kefauver to continue to attack Stevenson as not electable. Kefauver was to appear on "Meet the Press" on June 17, and when the show began no one knew what he would say. He apologized for his attacks on Stevenson. After the show he told Shannon the next step was up to Stevenson. Schlesinger urged Stevenson to telephone Kefauver and thank him and say that, if Stevenson were doing it over, he "would do some things differently" himself. Blair thought Stevenson should write to Kefauver but should not indicate any regrets over his past behavior. At the same time Stevenson should respond to Kefauver's request for support in restoring $1.1 billion which the House had cut from the foreign aid bill: Blair recommended support in principle but no blanket endorsement of the bill. Martin drafted a "Dear Estes" letter. When Stevenson saw it he said, "I don't like the son of a bitch and I don't see why I should have to write to him." The staff persuaded him. He took Blair's advice, adding, on Jack Arvey's recommendation, the hope that they could meet sometime in Chicago. Soon Kefauver was explaining that he had been in Chicago but too briefly to see Stevenson. A little later he sent a note from Indianapolis, where he was hunting delegates, saying he hoped for "friendly rivalry between now and convention time." He made several moves which some Stevenson supporters took as hints that he would deliver his votes to Stevenson if Stevenson would assure him of the vice presidential nomination. Finally, on July 26, he announced he was withdrawing in favor of Stevenson.

Stevenson asked many people for a draft of his acceptance speech, including Jack Fischer, Archibald MacLeish, Herbert Agar, Norman Cousins, Gerald Johnson, Ken Galbraith. George Ball proposed that his acceptance speech proclaim "the New American Revolution." Stevenson asked Agnes Meyer to get her husband's views on whether he should have a Catholic vice presidential candidate; he himself thought prejudice was still too strong in the back country and that "it is only to be considered if the boldest steps are necessary."

For several years Martin and other Stevenson advisers had been urging him to leave his lofty perch, his arid intellectual discussion of issues, and go among the people to see at first hand their problems—blacks in the Chicago ghetto, farmers on marginal land, coal miners out of work, and so on. He had resisted. Perhaps he was so famous that such visits could not remain anonymous, he would be identified by people on the street, crowds would gather, the whole purpose would be defeated. Perhaps he was too old to learn. Perhaps he already knew. In any case, they now renewed their importunities; and after a Fourth of July speech at Bloomington, Stevenson headed westward by automobile through the drought-damaged farm country of Iowa. It rained steadily for three days during his trip. He had hoped to go unnoticed but this proved impossible—two carloads of reporters and photographers accompanied him. He ended the week in Nebraska and Iowa attending barbecues for convention delegates. The trip was a fiasco.

Schlesinger, arriving in Chicago July 6 to join the staff, found the principal topic of political speculation the identity of the vice presidential nominee. The two leading candidates were Kennedy and Humphrey. Finnegan favored Humphrey and so, reportedly, did Wirtz and Stevenson himself. Blair thought Humphrey best qualified but thought Kennedy might help the ticket more, a view Schlesinger shared. Minow favored Kennedy and had urged his views on Stevenson forcibly, but Stevenson had said, "I like Jack Kennedy, admire him, but he's too young; his father, his religion." Finnegan was firmly opposed to Kennedy, and Minow had told him he was prejudiced, being a Catholic himself. McGowan inclined toward Robert Wagner. There was little talk of Kefauver.

In mid-July, Stevenson went to Maine and spoke at a Democratic clambake on behalf of Ed Muskie's re-election as Governor, terming him "one who stands in the vanguard today of the progressive young leaders." While in Maine he issued a further statement on nuclear testing: "I had hoped that the United States might take some strong initiative in halting the tests of the weapons of total self-destruction, when even the testing may be so dangerous, let alone the use of such weapons. Meanwhile, the scientific work of development could go on against the time when we might have to resume tests if the Russians did not cease, too. This is one area where we could take a step with relative safety toward the disarmament we talk about so much. But evidently we are going to go on and on with the assurance that everything possible will be done 'to assure that radiation will not rise above tolerable levels.' I find little comfort in that, and it was only the other day that an American general testified that if hydrogen bombs are used hundreds of millions of people would be killed, friends and foes alike, depending on the vagaries of the wind."

Finnegan and the rest of the political section were concentrating on delegates. They divided the states among some two dozen men, assigning them states they knew, and began assembling data on delegates. With Finnegan's guidance, Blair, John Sharon, and Minow ran the delegate operation. A card on every delegate showed his name, his family, how he voted in the past, what he did for a living, how to reach him, who his friends were. When the delegates arrived in Chicago for the convention, the assigned Stevenson operatives would arrange for Stevenson to meet them. They were careful not to ask the support of delegates who were committed to someone else, including favorite sons. In mid-July, *Time* ran a cover story on Stevenson which said that he had 432½ first-ballot votes "pledged and indicated" (with 686½ needed to nominate). Kefauver had 195½, *Time* said; Harriman, who had formally announced his candidacy early in June, 140½; Johnson 89; Symington 60½; favorite sons 266; "on the fence" 188.

Because so much effort was concentrated, necessarily, on the convention and nomination, Finnegan and others could give little thought to the fall campaign. But much had to be done. No over-all strategy existed, though the feeling was growing that Stevenson would have to win by appealing to the disaffected. He might have to throw away many states and concentrate where his chances seemed best—for example, Pennsylvania, with unemployment in the coal fields and steel industry; Michigan, with unemployment in the auto industry and a strong labor organization; Illinois, his home state, where the farm vote might be decisive; Massachusetts, with unemployment and a strong Democratic organization, Minnesota, where the farm vote would help; the border states, areas of compromise on desegregation; the Democratic South; California. Instead of campaigning in every state, he might campaign regionally. This argued against a truly national campaign, on the theory that Eisenhower could win a national election; Stevenson would try to win a series of small elections. Yet the National Committee was reserving large quantities of national network television time.

George Ball had recently been appointed director of public relations. Wilson Wyatt was to plan the fall campaign.

One of Schlesinger's first tasks on arriving in Chicago was to make a survey of various opinion polls. The results were devastating—they showed Stevenson in trouble with almost every group in the country with the possible exception of Negroes and Jews, and even these were considered shaky.

Stevenson met on July 26 with Wirtz, Schlesinger, Tufts, McGowan, and Martin. They talked briefly about the vice presidency. Stevenson said that Truman thought Humphrey "too radical," had no use for Kefauver, and dismissed Kennedy as a Catholic. James Farley had told Stevenson, "America is not ready for a Catholic yet." Sam Rayburn had said, "Well, if we have to have a Catholic, I hope we don't have to take that little pissant Kennedy. How about John McCormack?"

Stevenson asked what approach he should take to issues, how he could dent the nation's complacency. He read portions of a letter urging him to attack. Wirtz thought Stevenson should be affirmative, "two words of affirmation for every word of criticism." McGowan favored concentrating on the costs of complacency rather than an indictment of Eisenhower. Tufts favored appealing to the people's latent sense of moral responsibility, invoking our obligations to the children, the aging, allies, and so on. Stevenson was somewhat skeptical. Wirtz asked if it was possible to present a program for peace. Schlesinger remarked that, since the public opinion surveys showed that the Democratic Party suffered from its reputation as the party of war, the more alarmed the people became at the prospect of war the more likely they were to turn to the man and party of peace, Eisenhower and the Republican Party. He thought Stevenson's foreign policy speeches of 1952 had had little appeal because they offered nothing but "bleak vistas of indefinite living with crisis." Might not the issue be turned by making a big issue of disarmament? Tufts suggested criticizing Eisenhower's failure to take advantage of peace-making opportunities. Stevenson asked why he couldn't do more with America's loss of prestige and friends abroad. The staff saw little mileage in this—most people felt that "if the rest of the world didn't like us, so much for the rest of the world." Stevenson wanted to spell out the consequences of our failure in the underdeveloped world; nobody was enthusiastic. George Ball had suggested that Eisenhower might seek to match his "I will go to Korea" announcement of 1952 with a sudden presidential proclamation ending the draft. Schlesinger suggested that Stevenson anticipate this in a speech to the American Legion. They discussed how to link the draft with disarmament. Stevenson was obviously eager to attack Dulles.

Turning to domestic issues, Tufts and Schlesinger favored national health insurance. McGowan and Wirtz, not disagreeing, regarded it as politically unwise. All agreed that Stevenson should favor federal loans to cooperative health insurance plans plus financial encouragement of private voluntary health insurance programs.

The acceptance speech? All thought that Stevenson should write it himself. He mused about his problems, saying, "The trouble with too many of my speeches is that there has not been enough factual justification in what I have been saying. I have been pleading conclusions. The tone of the acceptance should be more in pain than in anger. I might express my dismay over the state of the Union and the world; mention the great historic responsibility of the Democratic Party; then emphasize the critical nature of the decisions we face. Are we to ratify euphoria? Or can we communicate realistically and meet our problems with a determination to achieve peace and well-being? The test of our system is its capacity to preserve the individual in the midst of modern technology. That is all our scheme exists for—to protect the individual, his rights, his opportunities. Our business is getting bigger; our farms are getting fewer; our opportunities are contracting. We are at a watershed. What direction should we go?" And then, "Or maybe it should be a short, cruel political speech."

How to treat Eisenhower? Stevenson said, "Never did anyone make such a success of being a cheerleader. He is a great politician. Sixty-five years old, infirm and ailing, he has contrived to remain politically unassailable. Never in his career has he been identified with an unpopular decision." And he told a story about asking a farmer who, unhappy about the Eisenhower farm policy, was asked, "But why aren't people mad at Eisenhower?" The farmer replied, "Oh, no one connects *him* with the Administration."

The writers had hoped to discuss in detail the American Legion speech, the Labor Day speech, and the first television speech on all three networks, opening the campaign. They had hoped to ask whether Stevenson wanted to make the H-bomb test ban a major issue, whether he wanted to concentrate his campaign in a few states, what should be done about platform planks, what he wanted to do about the President's health. The meeting never reached those items on the agenda.

Some, including Martin, thought the President's health was the overriding issue of the campaign and should be met head on at the outset. George Ball had proposed that other Democratic speakers say they did not know whether Eisenhower was well enough to serve as President and urge voters to ask their family doctors whether a man of sixty-five who had suffered a heart attack and a serious abdominal operation was qualified to serve. He wanted it done commencing with the keynote speech at the convention. Others were dubious. Ball argued that by November everybody would have forgotten about the health issue unless Stevenson made it. The problem continued to haunt the campaign to its end. On July 30, Stevenson, after other meetings, wrote to Truman and suggested that Truman raise the issue of the President's health. "It seems to me that, given the difficulties of attacking his deficiency directly, it should be possible to make vital and appealing a proper concept of the Presidency, and no one can talk about it with range and depth like yourself. Enabling the American people to see exactly how much is involved in the proper operation and concept of the office is both a service to their education and partisan opportunity. . . . The purpose, it seems to me, is to get the people to realize, without necessarily spelling it out in capital letters, that a symbol is not enough and that over-delegation of powers, for any reason, as well as undue inaccessability of the President can be damaging and dangerous. . . . What I am trying to say is that I think we badly need, regardless of the election, some public education about the Presidency. And could there be a better educator than H.S.T.?" Truman replied, "I am very glad to have your thoughts about a possible speech on the Presidency, and I am going to try to follow through on just such a program as that."

Agnes Meyer sent him a long letter, "a spiritual bequest and confession, an attempt to gather the various aspects of our relationship—now that you are being swept ever more rapidly toward a deep and stormy sea where my voice can no longer reach you." She felt a "touch of melancholy" but had always known that if he were elected President—"my dearest wish"—she would have to abandon him. She quoted Richard Hofstadter on Woodrow Wilson's "powerful need for affection," his deep sense of isolation, his "cramped capacity for personal communication." She thought Wilson's own description of his loneliness applied "word for word to your predicament." She sent him a photograph of herself taken when she was twenty-one—"I was in Paris doing graduate work at the Sorbonne. My hair looks dark but it was a tawny gold then!" He replied with an affectionate postcard.

President Nasser of Egypt, retaliating against Secretary Dulles' withdrawal of support for the high dam on the Nile at Aswan, nationalized the

Suez Canal on July 26. Stevenson considered exploiting the issue but did not.

The preconvention pace was stepping up. During the convention Stevenson would have the Skyway Suite in the Conrad Hilton Hotel and two suites in the Stockyards Inn, adjoining the International Amphitheater. Reports were coming in from around the country of delegate selection. So were drafts of the acceptance speech.

When Kefauver withdrew, Stevenson was with some difficulty restrained from commenting ungraciously on Kefauver's activities in the primaries. Stevenson's staff was filled with good feeling, but Stevenson himself remained cool. Agnes Meyer told Stevenson she was "making up" with Kefauver. Stevenson responded, "I have your letter about 'making up' with Estes. I think he behaved well, but why shouldn't he? He had always asserted his confidence in the primaries. There is actually but little support for him for Vice President except among his own former delegations and some 'practical politicians' who feel he has at least a harmony value. I am sure that someone else with a fresh face and greater potential use in the Congress would be far more valuable in the long run—but who!" He added a postscript. "This letter sounds a little ill-tempered. I have never found it in my heart to be bitter about Kefauver, and I am really not. I think he does have good instincts and I've always liked him. Indeed, I could find it in neither my heart nor head to say anything harsh about him in the primary. I only wish he had done the same."

22.

On August 6, Stevenson spoke briefly at a $250-a-plate fund-raising dinner intended to finance his campaign through the convention. Most of those present were old friends from the Chicago area, together with a few machine leaders. It was the week before the convention.

Marietta Tree came out from New York, stayed one night at Libertyville, and when Stevenson's staff opened the Skyline Suite at the Conrad Hilton she, together with Helen Stevenson—a relative of Stevenson who would soon marry Governor Meyner of New Jersey—served as hostesses. "We washed glasses and saw that there was enough soda and gave messages to Bill Blair," Mrs. Tree recalled. "Adlai seemed quite serene and rather liked the role of being the focal figure. As who wouldn't?" During the week she dined with several of the politicians and journalists who at that time enlivened presidential politics—Hubert Humphrey, Arthur Schlesinger, Richard Rovere, Scotty Reston, Jack Arvey, Bill Blair, Joe Alsop, Eric Sevareid, Claiborne Pell, George McGhee, David Bruce. She wore a Stevenson costume and arranged for pretty girls, Mrs. Roosevelt, and Stevenson to pose together for photographs. It was the enjoyable side of politics.

The other side was revealed to Finletter late Thursday afternoon, August 9, when he went to see Truman in his room at the Blackstone Hotel. Stevenson people had hoped for Truman's support after California. Finletter now found him unwilling to speak frankly. He made several remarks which led Finletter to suspect he would support Harriman. To Stevenson himself Truman was noncommittal. Next day Truman held a press conference but refused to support anybody and said he would make his preference known on Saturday. On that afternoon he flatly endorsed Harriman. This brought the Harriman candidacy to life on convention eve. Stevenson in his suite overlooking Michigan Avenue watched the Truman press conference on television with no show of emotion. Finnegan, Blair, Minow, Wirtz, Tubby, and others were with him. Some seemed relieved: the not surprising blow had been struck. Shortly after the announcement Stevenson telephoned Lyndon Johnson, who occupied a nearby suite, and discussed the Suez Canal crisis. Truman had told Johnson what he intended to do just before he did it, adding, "I'm opening this thing up so anybody can get it—including you." A little later Stevenson walked down the corridor to visit Sam Rayburn, looking cool and content. He had always felt Rayburn more firmly behind him than Johnson. He appeared at a Stevenson rally in the Conrad Hilton ballroom, jaunty and confident. Roger Tubby quickly released portions of a telegram from Mrs. Roosevelt strongly endorsing Stevenson.

On Sunday afternoon Stevenson gave a reception honoring Mrs. Roosevelt. Delegates flooded into Chicago that day, the last day before the official opening of the convention, and Stevenson workers sought them out assiduously. At the Mrs. Roosevelt reception, Jo Minow, Newt Minow's wife, saw John F. Kennedy standing, alone and unrecognized, at the end of a long line; she took him to the front of it. Kefauver was helping to hold his delegates in line as some of them threatened to switch to Harriman. Stevenson received delegates and state leaders, including Governors and Senators, in his Hilton suite. In the midst of it all Stevenson told a sidewalk interviewer in an ill-considered moment that the platform "should express unequivocal approval of the Court's decision [on desegregation], although it seems odd that you should have to express your approval of the Constitution and its institutions." This dismayed Stevenson's moderate Southern friends on the platform committee, including John Battle of Virginia, J. P. Coleman of Mississippi, and Sam Ervin, Jr., of North Carolina. But they were able to hold Stevenson's Southern support in line, or at least most of it.

None of the convention's work had been carried on under greater pressure than the platform committee's work on civil rights. In the end the committee drafted a plank which declared the Supreme Court decisions "the law of the land" but made no specific pledge to implement the Court's decisions and denounced the use of force. A move by a Northern liberal group led by Governor Williams, Senator Lehman, and Senator Douglas to insert a pledge to "carry out" the Court's decisions was defeated on the convention floor, and the platform was adopted on Wednesday, August 15. Unlike previous conventions, neither side had seemed badly to want a fight over civil rights.

Even the fight for delegates had about it the air of a foregone conclusion. Harriman's candidacy, despite Truman's thrust, did not really get off the ground. Nor did a move by Lyndon Johnson. Finnegan was telling Southern delegates that Stevenson had the nomination assured by Northern votes and if they wanted to retain any influence on him they should get aboard his bandwagon. At the same time he was telling Northern delegates that the South was for him and they must join in or forfeit control to the South. Mrs. Roosevelt had gone from delegation to delegation with Stevenson, speaking on his behalf, calling him the heir of FDR, smothering the Truman move. On Wednesday night, her work done, she left and Stevenson gratefully took her to the airport in a limousine. He waited with her for her flight and escorted her to her plane, carrying her crocheted handbag with wooden handles. A photographer asked if he would kiss her on the cheek and he said, "Nonsense," and shook her hand, and she left.

John F. Kennedy was to nominate Stevenson, with seconding speeches by Luther Hodges, a liberal Southerner, Lehman, Leader, Edith Green of Oregon, and William Dawson. Schlesinger and Martin had written their speeches. Kennedy did not like his and asked his aide, Theodore Sorensen, to prepare a new one. They spoke, voting began, and on Thursday, August 16, Stevenson was nominated on the first ballot with 905½ votes. Harriman received 210, Johnson 80. It was Finnegan's Pennsylvania that put Stevenson over the top. Newt Minow was on the convention floor "with Dick Neuberger at the moment the nomination occurred. Tears were streaming down both our faces. It had been so hard and so long and when all those balloons let go, even though I again thought, 'Brother, this is another lost cause!' still we'd won the nomination. I was very moved."

Stevenson had spent that morning and early afternoon alone in his law office, working on his acceptance speech. It had gone through many drafts. He went back to a draft of his own. About five o'clock that afternoon Finnegan, Finletter, Blair, Wyatt, Ball, Stevens, Minow, and Wirtz met in Stevenson's law office. Finnegan said Stevenson had decided to throw the convention open to nominations for Vice President instead of picking his own running mate. He would indicate that at least three were satisfactory to him—Humphrey, Kennedy, and Kefauver. They added others to the list —Bob Wagner of New York, Lyndon Johnson, Mennen Williams, Leader, Meyner, Gore of Tennessee, and others. This was a bold innovation; traditionally the presidential nominee chose his vice presidential nominee.

Some time earlier Theodore White had told Ted Sorensen that Bill Blair said Stevenson was considering Kennedy or Wagner as his running mate. Sorensen had taken it as a feeler from Stevenson. During the convention

Sorensen had told Minow and Blair that, if Stevenson wanted Kennedy for Vice President, Kennedy would accept but he would not compete for the nomination. Now, on the floor, Sorensen asked Minow what was going on, and Minow replied that he was on his way to the meeting with Finnegan and the others to find out, and Sorensen said, "If it's open, Kennedy will go for it." The idea of throwing the convention open had been "kicking around for some time," Schlesinger noted, but no decision had been taken till that afternoon. Throwing it open avoided choosing among the alternatives and provided a contrast to the lackluster Republican Convention at which Nixon had been forced on the delegates. Stevenson told a friend several years later that when he threw the convention open he fully expected John F. Kennedy to win the vice presidential nomination. He had wanted Kennedy all along, he said—that was why he had asked Kennedy to nominate him. Throwing the convention open also focused public attention on the vice presidency, which, in a tangential way, centered it on Eisenhower's health.

Late that night Stevenson went to the Stockyards Inn and met with Finnegan, Rayburn, Johnson, Butler, Ribicoff, Battle, Arvey, David Lawrence, and others. Rayburn profanely and contemptuously denounced the idea of throwing the convention open—it violated all sensible political rules. Butler supported him. Johnson was cool. Finnegan argued the other side. Rayburn and Johnson feared that Kefauver would win; he was the only candidate already organized; nobody could catch him with less than twenty-four hours to work in. They also argued that the move would contribute to the public impression that Stevenson was indecisive. The Kennedy people supported Finnegan. The meeting was turbulent. Stevenson stuck to his decision and went before the convention very late that night to announce it. The public received, Schlesinger thought, "the new image of a serious, decisive, masterful Stevenson who was prepared to carry the fight to the enemy." A little later, in his hotel suite, Stevenson told Schlesinger that he regarded the move as a great gamble, that it might result in putting Rayburn or Symington on the ticket, but that it was a risk worth running.

Next morning Harry Truman telephoned Stevenson and asked if he could come down from his fifth-floor suite at the Blackstone to Stevenson's third-floor suite. Stevenson said, "No, no, Mr. President, I'll come up," and did, with Blair, for a few minutes' talk. The Kennedy and Kefauver people and others had worked most of the night, and now on Friday at the convention hall the real fight for the vice presidency began. Schlesinger termed it "the most exciting thing I have ever seen at a convention." For a time, while the maneuvering and balloting were going on, Stevenson worked alone in his law office on his acceptance speech. Then he went into Blair's office to watch the drama on television. He was intensely interested yet somehow detached, a spectator. At one point in the balloting Kennedy seemed about to win and received 648 votes, only 18½ votes short of the number needed. Suddenly votes began to switch. Schlesinger noted, "I was strongly for Kennedy until the moment of climax in the second ballot when Albert Gore announced that Tennessee was shifting to Kefauver. Then I was suddenly seized by an unexpected onrush of emotion and found myself shouting for Kefauver. On reflection, this seemed to me right. Jack, who made himself a national political figure in this convention, will have many more chances. Estes has earned his chance, if anyone has; and we are fielding our strongest possible ticket."

Shortly after Kefauver was nominated Stevenson admitted newspapermen to the reception room of his law offices and said, "I think that what has occurred this afternoon is a clear indication of the vitality of the Democratic Party. I am happy that Senator Estes Kefauver is to be my running mate. . . . He is an old friend and an able leader and I welcome him on the ticket." When Kennedy was not nominated for Vice President, Mrs. Ives, who was attending the convention, said, "Oh, those poor little Catholics." Kennedy himself may have overheard her. That evening Truman opened the convention proceedings with a fighting speech that began, "I am here to give my full support to Adlai Stevenson." Stevenson watched on television at the Blackstone, then drove to the convention hall. Kefauver spoke, a lackluster effort. Then Stevenson appeared on the platform and he was joined by Truman and the other party leaders and the crowd let loose a half-hour demonstration. Schlesinger said, "Stevenson never looked more forceful, and his voice, when he began to speak, was sure and confident. Here seemed the moment to cap the convention by giving the emotional surge of the last 24 hours a fitting expression." Instead, the historian noted, "there came a diffuse mass of words. After a few moments, the sense of excitement was trickling away." If one watched from the rear of the enormous hall, as Martin and his wife did in order to observe the audience's reaction, with balloons and cigarette smoke swirling in the air, Stevenson seemed a remote figure, disembodied, almost a puppet uttering the tired phrases of the Democratic faith—President Truman and Mrs. Roosevelt be praised, "the New America" would be his watchwords, the President's health was not an issue but his conduct of his office was, the Administration had tried to merchandise its candidates like breakfast cereal, the press supported it, the Administration said all was well but farmers and small businessmen and old people were not prosperous, good intentions were not enough, the country was "stalled on dead center"; and he spelled it out in a ponderous litany. It lifted few hearts. He moved to foreign affairs—mentioned lost opportunities, the hydrogen bomb (but without calling for a stop to H-bomb testing); he bespoke anticolonialism and said peace in a nuclear age was "no longer a visionary ideal" but "an absolute, imperative, practical necessity." He spoke further about peace and American ideals.

But the speech simply did not work. During the afternoon Ball, Finletter, and McGowan had gone over his final draft and had made many criticisms but when Wirtz took them to Stevenson he virtually ignored them. Schlesinger noted, "Where McGowan, in moments of stress in 1952, would simply cross things out that AES liked and thus make sure that they would not appear in the speech draft, Wirtz gave up this fight. He is not temperamentally tough enough and he has the weary feeling, 'Well, it's his speech; I guess he has the right to say what he wants.' "

In the hall that night as he spoke one could feel the letdown. The delegates had come to cheer but he gave them nothing to cheer and their applause was mechanical; they seemed bewildered. He had not won in 1952 but he had lifted hearts. Now he did not. Phil Graham of the Washington *Post* said afterward, "You know, I thought that the Democrats had a real chance to win until Adlai began to speak." Fulbright thought it the worst speech he had ever heard Stevenson give. Al Friendly of the *Post* said that in intellectual content the speech was indistinguishable from an Eisenhower speech. Harriman was contemptuous. Schlesinger noted, "One felt that the image of the New Stevenson, this grim, masterful figure had suddenly disappeared and in its place appeared the old Stevenson, the literary critic, the man obsessed with words and with portentous generalization." Late that night in Truman's suite at the Blackstone, Truman, Rosenman, Harriman, George Backer, and others sat "talking darkly" about the candidate and his speech. Thus the convention ended. Stevenson had won the nomination. But he had disappointed his own followers with his acceptance speech and he had alienated Rayburn, Truman, and others by throwing the convention open for Vice President. Johnson had told Rayburn, "It's his decision, he has to live with it, not us." But it all left a sour taste. And now he made another mistake.

Most of his advisers had thought he should replace Paul Butler with Jim Finnegan as national chairman. Tom Finletter had been chosen to carry the message to Stevenson and, supported by Wyatt, had done so, forcefully. Jack Arvey and David Lawrence backed them up. Stevenson seemed to resist—he had asked Butler not to run for Governor of Indiana some months earlier but to stay instead as national chairman, and he also feared the public reaction if he fired Butler as he had fired Frank McKinney in 1952. Moreover (he told Marietta Tree) Butler had pleaded to be allowed to continue because he needed the money and his wife was ill. But Stevenson agreed to replace Butler and, on Saturday morning in his suite in the Blackstone, told him so. The National Committee was meeting in the grand ballroom. Jack Arvey, Carmine De Sapio, and David Lawrence sat in the front row, determined to get rid of Butler. They wanted a single campaign director, not two, as in 1952, and they did not want Butler. They sat silent while resolutions were adopted praising Butler's past services. As rumors ran through the hall that Butler was through, he began to speak, broke down and wept, unable to continue. Arvey, De

Sapio, and Lawrence sat stony-faced. Butler said, "You are writing my political epitaph," and offered his resignation. He apologized for his breakdown. Arvey put through a resolution naming a new executive committee. Another committeeman who wanted time to talk to Stevenson offered a resolution calling on Butler not to resign at this time and it was adopted, though the professionals sat silent. Butler met again with Stevenson, this time with Finnegan present. Rayburn and others urged that Butler be retained. They worked out an arrangement—Butler would stay on as national chairman but would have no power; Finnegan would be campaign manager with full power to run the entire campaign under Stevenson's policy direction. Stevenson went down to the National Committee meeting with Butler and asked the committee to re-elect Butler as national chairman with the understanding that Finnegan was taking over as campaign manager. It was done.

Several of Stevenson's advisers were shocked. Schlesinger noted, "I have never seen Clayton [Fritchey] in so emotional a state. . . . It seemed extraordinary to all of us that AES would go against the advice of everyone on his staff to keep on a man whom he does not know and whom all reliable testimony condemns as a cold, self-seeking, mischief-making egomaniac. The only answer seems to be that he knows his friends won't make a fuss about it and he knows that Butler would; so he chose the easy course. Both George [Ball] and Wilson [Wyatt] feel that this decision raises great questions as to whether they can usefully continue in the campaign. And all of us felt that the incident raised even graver questions as to whether our man is really fitted to be President." (Schlesinger and Fritchey later changed their minds about Butler, who in retrospect they felt turned out to be one of the best national chairmen up to that time.)

Stevenson drove home to Libertyville. There that night a group of townspeople, including the Republican Mayor, welcomed him at the high school. He introduced his family and spoke extemporaneously. "There are moments in our lives which transcend narrow partisanship and neighborliness is one of them," he said. He said that he believed "in the forgiveness of sin" and if any Republicans wanted to step forward and "join with the true faith" he would welcome them. He said, somewhat sadly, "Libertyville is a good place to live, but I always seem to be going away from Libertyville and wanting to come home again." He added that the voters of the nation might decide to "send me home again." After that he stood a long time shaking hands with people who filed by. It was a little like the old days in Hyde Park when Franklin Roosevelt talked to his Republican neighbors. Then he went home to the farm and his first full night's sleep in a week.

On Sunday morning, a cool clear day, he worked, dressed in dungarees and sneakers, on his mail, then in the afternoon began a series of meetings with Finnegan and other members of his staff. Schlesinger was not appeased. "It seems to me that through weakness he has invited a host of troubles for the next vital weeks. So, instead of being in a mood of elation and confidence, I find that the acceptance speech and the national chairmanship fiasco have made me feel quite depressed. The new Stevenson was all too short-lived."

23.

Finnegan announced that the campaign headquarters would be moved to Washington and soon it was.

Despite the staff's suggestion that Stevenson concentrate his campaign in only a few states, despite their intention to run a television campaign, despite Stevenson's own exhaustion from the primaries, Stevenson conducted an even more intensive fall campaign in 1956 than in 1952, covering the entire nation, speaking in small towns as well as great population centers, working unremittingly from late August till Election Day.

The 1956 campaign was, Arthur Schlesinger once recalled, "an ordeal, no fun at all." He meant that many on the staff considered it a losing cause almost from the start, something that had to be played out to the end despite inevitable failure and, further, that the campaign lacked the youthful first-time exuberance of 1952. Jack Arvey once said that Stevenson had no choice but to run in 1956 and added that he might have won if he had picked John F. Kennedy as his vice presidential candidate. (In some Irish Catholic wards in Chicago which the Democrats normally carried by fifteen to seventeen thousand votes, Stevenson won by only one or two thousand. The same thing happened elsewhere, Arvey said, and Cardinal Spellman endorsed Eisenhower.)

This time the campaign was run from Washington. Stevenson was there only on some weekends. Instead of traveling with him, Finnegan spent most of his time in Washington, dealing by telephone with state politicians. Bill Blair traveled with Stevenson. Finnegan, Blair, Jim Rowe, Hy Raskin, and Senator Clinton Anderson of New Mexico worked out the campaign schedule. Bill Rivkin, as a deputy to Finnegan, was in charge of all advance men and helped on scheduling. Clayton Fritchey, aided by Roger Tubby, handled press relations although George Ball was in over-all charge of public relations. Ball, as he did in other campaigns, dealt quietly with important national figures, advised Stevenson, and worked on television and radio problems. Matt McCloskey of Philadelphia, as treasurer of the Democratic National Committee, and Roger Stevens, as Stevenson's own finance chairman, raised money. Wilson Wyatt was a "general coordinator" and prepared for Stevenson an elaborate book on the transition from the Eisenhower administration to the Stevenson administration. Jane Dick, Barry Bingham, and Archibald Alexander handled the Volunteers. Newt Minow was Stevenson's man in Washington while Stevenson was traveling. Minow urged Stevenson to challenge Eisenhower to a television debate. Wirtz opposed. Stevenson was interested but feared it would appear a campaign gimmick and an attempt to capture the President's audience. He did not do it. Wirtz traveled with Stevenson and was the final editor next to Stevenson himself on speeches.

Immediately after the convention Truman had written Stevenson, "I hope that the next time I send you a letter of congratulations I can say Dear Mr. President. . . . Something had to be done to wake up the Party and I undertook to do it. I was in deadly earnest as a Democratic politician, to put some life and leadership into the Party. It was the purpose in 1952 to do just that for you. I am sure that you did not understand that. The Democratic Party and the United States of America never needed a leader as badly as it does at this time. You have all the qualifications for that position if you will just let them come to the top. In California and Florida primaries it began to come out—but complete satisfaction did not come to me until the Convention fight and your victory there. I was not putting on a show at that Convention. The principles of the Democratic Party and the welfare of the nation and the world, I felt, were at stake. The Party cannot exist as a 'me too party,'" an apparent allusion to Lyndon Johnson and the congressional leadership which had supported Eisenhower since 1952. "It must exist as a Party for all the people, rich and poor, privileged and underprivileged. It must be ever ready to see justice done to those who cannot hire expensive representatives to look after their welfare in Washington. Only the President can do that. He must be a fighter and one whose heart is in the General Welfare. I have never had a desire to be a party boss or to be the No. 1 Democrat. I tried to abdicate in 1952. The happenings at Chicago gave you the leadership *on your own*. Now I am ready to do whatever I can to help the Party and its Leader to win. It is up to you to decide what that will be. I do hope you will have a central headquarters and someone in charge who understands leadership in politics. I wouldn't blame you if you never speak to me again—but let's win this campaign and think of that afterwards if it is ever necessary to be thought about."

It was a longhand letter. Stevenson replied on August 23 with a carefully drafted and typewritten letter. "I am deeply grateful for your very kind letter. . . . I confess, as I told you, that I was disappointed by what transpired at Chicago, but I am also much relieved that the results, as you say, were actually so satisfying to you. I note your generous proffer of help during the campaign, and I am sure that ways will be found to take full advantage of it. In 1952, while I was Governor of Illinois I had to continue in my capital. . . . That, of course, is not the case this time and the headquarters will be in the National Committee in Washington. . . . And, finally, together with my thanks for your kind letter, let me assure you again that I appreciate fully the high motives which prompted your course of action at the Convention."

After the convention Stevenson had taken some pains to mend fences with party leaders. He told Lyndon Johnson on August 26, "I think you know that my personal feeling for you goes a long way back. . . . While I know that you and Mr. Sam were displeased by my decision to throw the Vice Presidency open, I had precisely the confirmation I wanted—that you would back me up." Johnson replied, "My misgivings on the decision to throw the Vice Presidency open are not secret. But neither is it a secret that I have absolutely no misgivings whatsoever about backing your candidacy to the hilt." Johnson was pleased that Stevenson had Finnegan with him: "He is the kind of a man that we understand and we feel that he understands us." Stevenson told him he had had good reports from the South except for Virginia. This "comforted" him—he hoped he could rely on Johnson and others "to take care of the South." Johnson wrote, "The Texas situation is still uneasy."

Averell Harriman had telegraphed his congratulations and offer to help. Stevenson thanked him but told Alicia Patterson that Harriman probably would not help the New York organization greatly—a strong volunteer campaign was necessary. He asked John F. Kennedy to speak at the Pennsylvania organization's annual fund-raising dinner in Philadelphia on October 25, and Kennedy put it on his calendar. Stevenson told Kennedy, "I had hoped to see you before you left Chicago, and left, may I say, a much bigger man than you arrived! If there was a hero, it was you, and if there has been a new gallantry on our horizon in recent years, it is yourself." He added a graceless condolence upon Mrs. Kennedy's miscarriage. Kennedy soon sent a detailed account of his fall speaking schedule and offered to rearrange it in order to spend more time speaking in Massachusetts, a doubtful state this year. As the campaign progressed, a formidable array of speakers came forward to campaign for Stevenson.

Opening his campaign, Stevenson wrote Lady Mary Spears, "I have been both emancipated and nominated." He told Agnes Meyer, "Sometimes I wake up at night startled with the thought that I am doing all this again, and I can't say I look forward to it with any bouncing eagerness at the moment. But perhaps that's the consequence of three solid days of making movies, which is hard and tiresome work." (He had been making television spots.) He also said, "I confess I'm tired and don't feel the old urge to say everything just right as I used to. But I like to think my present more philosophical attitude is not without advantages—even if the quality of my 'utterances' won't be at the old level." To Francis Biddle, "I wish it were possible to make a few good speeches instead of a lot of lousy ones." He told Dean Acheson, who, with Paul Nitze, set to work on foreign policy speech material, "Last time—in 1952—I am afraid I spent far too much time on texts, at the expense of politics. It's hard to do otherwise when you have some taste for responsibility and style." Acheson told him he needed speech material less than "a little bit of luck" (the title of a currently popular song). Bill Rivkin sent Schlesinger a note attached to a clipping: "I hear a lot of this sort of thing—that we've lost much of the tone and quality of 1952 utterances. Finnegan prefers it this way—'no more of that damn egghead stuff'—but I think we have to face up to the expectation of greatness from disaffecting admirers."

About the second week in October, a number of people felt the campaign had lost momentum. Stevenson said to one, "As the Republican campaign picks up momentum ours appears to recede and slack off, which is, of course, the calculated risk I took when I decided to start in high gear after the convention." Eugene Rostow wrote him, "I do *not* feel that the Scotty Reston business ('he has abandoned the high-road of '52') has any meaning. The real problem, I feel, is to get down from the general level of contrasting the two parties and their records, to specific issues, treated in some detail." Agnes Meyer told him his speeches this year were "far more effective" than in 1952.

Carl McGowan once said, "I thought that the ideas put out in '56 were more significant than those in 1952. In 1952 we did not set forth a new policy—no new ideas. In 1956 you tried to fill out new departures and new ideas. We went into 1956 with more research effort and thought than 1952. 1956 was heartbreaking. We were wrestling with jelly. The country was very complacent. Though the war hero had been shown wanting, there was no indication that was going to affect the voters." McGowan took little part in the 1956 campaign, probably feeling that his doing so would undermine Wirtz's position.

Scotty Reston said, "There's no comparison between the two campaigns. '52 had spirit. It was Adlai. '56 was Finnegan until the move on disarmament. They said, 'We tried all that elegant stuff in 1952—now let's let the organization run it.'" Barbara Ward thought the 1952 campaign better than 1956. The 1956 program papers were good, she thought, but nobody saw them. Jane Dick said, "Ike was unbeatable. I think the 1952 campaign was the better. In 1956, the speeches stand up, though at the time I didn't think so." George Ball said, "He had a public personality. By 1956 he began to believe in it. You could always pull him out of it by a crack. I remember two nights before the 1956 election coming back from New York, all of us were tired and I was in his compartment, just the two of us, and all at once I thought, 'In two days he may be President of the United States and you've got to stop saying to him, "Look my boy, don't be a God damn fool."' All in all, the 1956 campaign was better on the issues and was better organized than 1952."

Republican managers had obtained Eisenhower's agreement to run for a second term by promising him that he would not have to go "barnstorming," as he called it, but could limit his campaign to a few nationwide television appearances plus appearances at the World Series and at press conferences. When he began to campaign, he seemed to overwhelm Stevenson. He opened his campaign with a radio and television address on September 19 and went out to speak at the National Plowing Matches at Newton, Iowa, in Des Moines, and at Peoria, Illinois. He made a one-day trip to Cleveland and Lexington, Kentucky, on October 1. At about that time the Republican managers believed he had a "medium to hard fight on his hands" but felt reasonably confident he would win without any basic change in campaign strategy.

The party's only asset, virtually, was the President. Reporters visiting Iowa reported a restlessness among farmers but added that those who seemed to be leaving Eisenhower had not yet attached themselves to Stevenson. The Republican managers decided to wait until the last ten days or two weeks of the campaign to determine whether Eisenhower should be asked to campaign more heavily. On October 9 he delivered two speeches in Pittsburgh. On October 12 and 13 he appeared on television. He went to Minneapolis-St. Paul October 16, delivered three speeches there, went on to the Pacific Northwest, spoke to a rally in Seattle on the seventeenth and at Tacoma, Washington, and Portland, Oregon, on the eighteenth, then went down to southern California for two speeches on the nineteenth and stopped off in Denver on his way back to Washington. He spoke to the carpenters' union on October 23 and on radio and television on October 24 and in Madison Square Garden on October 25. During the last week of the campaign he spoke every day but one, three times in one day, visiting Miami, Jacksonville, Richmond, Philadelphia, and speaking on national television and radio. Thus he campaigned more than he originally had intended but undertook nothing remotely resembling the backbreaking schedule of Stevenson, who that year delivered some 300 speeches and traveled some 55,000 miles.

To Stevenson's staff, the most maddening thing about the 1956 campaign was Eisenhower's apparently indestructible popularity. Schlesinger and Harris wrote later, "It was, indeed, more than a question of popularity; it became almost a question of Eisenhower's invulnerability to the kind of candid discussion which up to this time has been normal in our democracy. People who had recognized no limits to taste or truth in their attacks on Franklin Roosevelt and Harry Truman began to act in 1956 as if statements of fact about Eisenhower—e.g., 'He spends a lot of time on the golf course,' or 'He has had a heart attack'—were almost blasphemous." He was almost totally above the battle, unreachable. Moreover, people did not seem to identify him with failures of his administration, and while they might not like things his administration had done, they did not hold him responsible; nor could Stevenson persuade them to, try as he might. Eisenhower was, above all, the man of peace, and no matter how often Stevenson declared that neither party wanted war, the Democrats remained in the public mind the war party. Above all, Schlesinger and Harris wrote, President Eisenhower benefited from public apathy, an apathy they thought understandable—for twenty years, from 1932 to 1952, the American people had been summoned to sustain the worst depression in history, the great World War, the grueling cold war. Their private lives had been invaded and they had been under constant strain. They wanted respite from public affairs. Eisenhower offered it. His speeches, and above all his television appearances, were bland and reassuring. On television people asked him questions, and he answered reassuringly if vapidly (as Stevenson partisans saw it). Where Stevenson was rather ineffectual on television, Eisenhower was devastating. (And the Republicans had more money to spend on it, though not as overwhelmingly much more as Democrats thought—they spent $3,737,000 on television to $2,746,000 for the Democrats.)

Eisenhower had and used the power of the incumbency—issued campaign documents disguised as presidential statements, held press conferences, reported to the people on the crisis at Suez, sent a message to Premier Bulganin of the U.S.S.R. regarding the crushing of the uprising in Hungary. Stevenson could only pursue him madly. Sometimes during the pursuit Stevenson disappointed his admirers. They thought him too "political," not "statesmanlike" enough. They forgot that he had to fight, that he had wearied of the issues during the long primaries, that this time he wanted to win because he had lost faith in Eisenhower, that he knew more about issues than he had four years ago, and perhaps above all that he simply could not delight by seeming fresh, as he had when he first burst upon the political scene in 1952. The novelty was, simply, gone; he was known. And his idolaters expected too much. He once said that he enjoyed approval but disliked adulation because he knew it would be followed by disillusionment. His idolaters, he complained, expected miracles of him, then, discovering that he was after all only human, blamed him for having limited power, for being himself. Arthur Krock of the New York *Times* he numbered among such people, and, in later years, some of the young men around President Kennedy. He once said that one of his greatest disappointments in the 1956 campaign was its failure to "evoke any real debate of issues." He said, "In the climate of opinion which then prevailed it was easy—and politically astute—for my opponents to brush them aside. Yet the illumination of problems, needs and dangers, and alternatives for dealing with them are the very purpose of a campaign, especially for the presidency."

24.

It would be tedious to relate the progress of the campaign in day-to-day detail. It may be more profitable to analyze the campaign and its issues.

It was, really, two campaigns.

It was, unlike the defensive campaign of 1952, an attack. It had to be— the Republicans were in power, and Stevenson's task was to dislodge them.

It was, second, a programmatic affirmative campaign. Stevenson had never been comfortable with the entire New Deal-Fair Deal program. The solutions of the 1930s and 1940s were inadequate to the 1950s. Some of them had become, he thought, mere liberal clichés. The problems were no longer just food, clothing, and shelter but involved the quality of life—better education, better medical care, the defense of civil rights and civil liberties, the problems of children and of the elderly. These were the problems of the new America, as Stevenson saw them, and he developed programs to deal with them. In doing so, he dropped much of the glittering rhetoric of 1952 and delivered speeches that set forth in specific detail programs for the nation's ailments.

As for the attack aspect of his campaign, he laid down most of the attack lines in his speech opening the national campaign at Harrisburg, a speech which disappointed his followers and which he himself considered "a frightful failure." In a sentence that anticipated John F. Kennedy's 1960 campaign, he said, "Indeed, it is a central issue in this election— whether America wants to stay on dead center, mired in complacency and cynicism; or whether it wants once more now to move forward." He said that in "four years of wealth and abundance" the Administration had allowed the shortage of schoolrooms and teachers to worsen, had watched juvenile delinquency increase "at a frightening rate," had done "almost nothing to stop the slum cancer" or to help the poor and the elderly as living costs rose. We had done little to aid medical research or make up the shortage of doctors and nurses. We had done nothing for "the hapless, helpless farmer." The small businessman was "backed to the wall." Instead of developing natural resources for the many, "we have seen them raided for private profit." Abroad, "The Soviets have advanced, while we have fallen back, not only in the competition for strength of arms, but even in the education of engineers and scientists. . . . And today there is doubt in the world about whether America really believes in the freedom which is our birthright and the peace which is our greatest hope." Why had it happened? "It has happened because for four years now we have had a government which neither fully understands nor wholly sympathizes with our human needs or the revolution that is sweeping the world." This was "a businessman's government." Eisenhower had appointed big businessmen to high positions, then had, "partly by choice, partly by a necessity," turned over to them more and more power. They had effectively cut taxes for the well to do and turned over natural resources to private companies. But "where human interests are concerned . . . there no one leads." He respected Eisenhower's "good intentions." The Democrats in Congress had tried to help him. "Everyone shares in sympathy for the circumstances which have created a part-time presidency. . . . But we cannot understand—and we will not accept—turning the government over to men who work full time for the wrong people or a limited group of people." The situation would worsen; Eisenhower's influence would decline, that of his "heir apparent," Nixon, would rise; the President was not "master in his own house."

In a Labor Day speech in Cadillac Square in Detroit he attacked the Administration's claim to prosperity. True, America was prosperous "in part." But prosperity had been built by the workingmen, not by Republican politicians, and "the question is who is going to do the job that remains.

"I say it is wrong that 14 million of our fellow Americans live today in families whose income is less than $1,000 a year.

"I say it is wrong that the 10 million men and women over sixty-five years of age in this country . . . are being forced to live in what ought to be their golden years on an average family income of less than $1,500 a year.

"I say it is wrong that the American farmer is getting this year only three dollars of income for every four dollars he was making in 1952 while his costs have increased."

And so on—farm income dropping, cost of living rising, auto workers laid off—"sorry facts, disgraceful facts, in this richest, most fortunate country in the world."

In Harlem on October 4, Stevenson hit the Administration on economic issues and civil rights, on "four years of shuffling and postponement." He decried slums, low minimum wages, low Social Security benefits. "And, finally, when the President was presented with an opportunity for great national leadership in [the field of desegregation], he was virtually silent. . . . The President of the United States recently said of the Supreme Court decision, 'I think it makes no difference whether of not I endorse it.' As for myself, I have said from the beginning—and say now—that I support this decision!"

In a speech at Walnut Hill, Maryland, on September 15, Stevenson defended civil liberties and said, "The abuse of the security policies under this Administration during the last four years is a shameful chapter in American history which began in consecration to individual liberty." At Newton, Iowa, he attacked President Eisenhower for breaking his farm promises and Secretary Benson for presiding over policies that had brought farm prices down and farm costs up and tightened farmers' credit. At Providence, Rhode Island, on October 6, Stevenson attacked "the Republican presidential candidate" for having broken his 1952 promise to increase employment in the depressed areas of New England. At Great Falls, Montana, on October 9, he attacked the Administration heavily for its record on conservation and resource development—for having given away the people's resources to private interests.

In Milwaukee on September 28, Stevenson laid out in detail the deplorable condition of the schools, called an Administration bill for federal aid to school construction "inadequate," and said, "To sum up, we have had, during these four years, fine words, conferences, and lofty, high-sounding proposals about education. We have had no action and no results." As to health insurance, on October 11 on national television from

San Francisco, he called the Administration's proposal of a reinsurance "utterly useless." As to health research, "Last year the government spent more money for eradication of hoof and mouth disease in cattle than on mental illness—which afflicts 9 million people."

On the theory that the Republican Party was far less popular than its President, Stevenson repeatedly attacked the party—and its campaign methods. "I thought of bread and circuses not long ago when I read about great Republican bandwagons that were going out all over the country, complete with movies, jeeps, girls, and gadgets of all kinds—to sell Eisenhower and Nixon again to a docile, complacent, carefree people all happily chanting, 'Peace, Prosperity and Progress—ain't it wonderful!' The whole aim of all this ballyhoo and thirty-foot balloons, those streamers and bands, is not to excite thought or provoke discussion. It is, in the finest advertising tradition, to get at our electoral subconscious and persuade us to vote, blissfully and blindly, for things as they are."

But he also criticized President Eisenhower for failing to lead (although he denied he was "attacking" him and emphasized he was "not talking about the President's health" but, rather, about his "limited concept of the presidency"). He said that Eisenhower in 1953 and 1954 had proposed legislation "that looked good on paper" but had done little to get it enacted. While Eisenhower "declined to exert presidential leadership, Republican Senate leader Knowland carried on his personal—and belligerent —foreign policy. Republican Senator McCarthy conducted, unhampered, his career as national bully. Republican Senator Bridges rallied Republican Senators in a fight against the Republican President's own nominee as Ambassador to Russia. Republican Senator Bricker pressed his amendment to cripple the Republican President's control over foreign policy. Eighty-four per cent of the House Republicans voted against the President's position on housing. . . [At one point] the President was so discouraged with the Republican Party that he began to talk of forming a third party. And yet . . . the President soon let it be known that he 'favored the election of every Republican over every Democrat for every office any place.'" The question was: "Who's in charge here, anyway?"

So much for the attack section of Stevenson's campaign.

A series of opinion surveys available to Stevenson before the campaign showed that the main strength of the Democratic Party lay in the picture people had of it as the party of "the little guys" against "the big guys." Its principal weakness was the impression that it was the war party. The Republican Party's main strength was that Eisenhower was above all a man of peace. Its principal weakness was that it was the party of big business and the rich. These conditions did not well suit Stevenson. He disliked campaigning against the rich. He believed that the most serious failures of the Eisenhower administration had been foreign failures, that the nation's greatest problems were in foreign affairs, and that if the people were alerted to them they would respond. Moreover, he wanted to talk foreign affairs because he had been talking domestic affairs all spring and now could turn with freshness to foreign affairs. But the polls dictated a campaign heavily emphasizing domestic affairs. Stevenson acquiesced unwillingly. And indeed, when the Suez crisis erupted near the end of the campaign, Stevenson's aides wished they had not advised him to shun foreign affairs all fall. In any case, he campaigned heavily on populist domestic issues for the first three quarters of the campaign. In doing so, he brought to public attention issues that demanded solution, he put forward programs that became a basis for John F. Kennedy's New Frontier and Lyndon Johnson's Great Society.

What were Stevenson's affirmative policy proposals?

Arthur Schlesinger and Seymour Harris, in an introduction to a collection of Stevenson's 1956 campaign speeches published later, wrote, "Sometimes in national elections defeats are more significant than victories. Thus Buchanan beat Fremont in 1856, McKinley beat Bryan in 1896, Hoover beat Smith in 1928—but a few years later the ideas of the winners were repudiated, and the ideas of the losers had conquered."

In the domestic field, Stevenson set forth a number of concrete programmatic proposals. He did it both in speeches and in a series of "program papers," long sober attempts to deal with substantive issues in greater detail than was possible in a fifteen-minute or half-hour speech. They received favorable comment from editorial writers, and some of their ideas found their way into legislation enacted under President Kennedy and President Johnson. Few of his proposals were new. Most had been debated in Congress. But Stevenson now elevated them to the level of presidential leadership. He made them national issues, called them to the attention of the wide public, and thus kept them at the forefront of national debate. In taking up a topic, he usually began with a description of deplorable existing conditions, arraigned the Administration for doing nothing about it, then proposed a program.

His program paper for older citizens, issued September 14, proposed that Congress act on a pending Democratic proposal to establish an office of Older Persons' Welfare in the Department of Health, Education and Welfare, arguing that only nine people on the Secretary's staff at HEW were working at enlarging the opportunities for old people compared with 40,000 working "on the problems of the nation's business concerns." Congress later passed such legislation. He recommended lowering the retirement age for women from sixty-five to sixty-two years and permitting retired persons to earn more than $1,200 without losing their Social Security benefits. Congress later passed such legislation. He recommended federal financing for housing for older people, both public and private. Congress passed the Senior Citizens Housing Act of 1962 under President Kennedy and the program was extended under President Johnson in 1965.

As to medical care, Stevenson advocated "a thorough investigation by Congress of the possibility of adding a program of hospital insurance for the old to the present Old Age and Survivors Insurance system." As early as 1935 liberals had favored including compulsory national health insurance in the Social Security system, and in 1945 President Truman had asked Congress to enact it. Congress had refused. The debate in the 1940s had centered around liberal proposals for a compulsory national health insurance program for persons of all ages. Despite Truman's repeated urging, this plan was never adopted. The American Medical Association called it socialized medicine. In the 1950s its backers shifted to narrower ground: compulsory national health insurance paid for by a payroll tax and covering only persons sixty-five or older. It was in this direction that Stevenson's proposal headed. President Kennedy proposed it when he became President but it failed to pass in his lifetime. It passed the Senate in 1965. Finally, in 1965, under President Johnson, it became law—"Medicare."

Stevenson recommended programs to encourage young men and women to enter medical research as a career, to provide improved laboratory facilities, to provide additional research funds, to build more medical schools and provide federal loans and scholarships for medical education, and to expand the Hill-Burton program of hospital construction. He recommended that Congress consider various proposals to make comprehensive private health insurance available on a voluntary basis to all Americans. Except for insurance, most of this was done over the next nine years. And still later President Nixon adopted Stevenson's insurance proposal.

In a program paper on "the crisis in education" issued October 1, Stevenson urged adoption of a national policy of federal aid to education where local and individual resources could not meet the need. He urged a program of general federal financial assistance to the states for school construction and teacher training, federal college scholarships and fellowships and loans, the expansion of foreign exchange programs on the basis of merit and need, and the expansion of vocational and adult education. Ever since the war, and for several years after 1956, Congress enacted various laws to assist education but only in special ways, as for example with the National Defense Education Act of 1958, emphasizing science and passed in response to Russia's success in orbiting an earth satellite. But Congress refused to enact general aid-to-education laws, some conservative legislators maintaining that federal aid meant federal control and, anyway, it would cost too much. Little progress was made during the Eisenhower and Kennedy administrations. The log jam broke in 1965 under President Johnson—Congress authorized more than $2 billion for revolutionary new education programs to help students and schools at the elementary, secondary, college, and graduate level. It passed a general aid-to-education bill, providing an initial $1.3 billion for elementary and secondary schools, a program of federal scholarships for college students, more than $650 million for college aid including student loans, increased construction funds, grants for library books and material, grants for university extension programs, and funds to help small colleges. Much credit for the bill went to President Johnson. But Stevenson had brought the issue to the forefront in 1956, and John F. Kennedy kept it there in the early 1960s.

In a final program paper issued October 29, Stevenson said he had set forth expensive proposals in health, education, natural resources, old age, and urban renewal and it was only fair to ask where the money was coming from. His answer, in his program paper on the economy, was, basically, the answer later given by Presidents Kennedy and Johnson: "From the great and constantly increasing productive capacity of the United States." The paper spoke of steady economic growth with full employment, the Kennedy doctrine of 1960 subsumed under the phrase, "Get this country moving again." Stevenson criticized the Eisenhower administration for curtailing expenditures for education, natural resources, and technical and economic aid. He proposed to use the power to tax "as a balance wheel to help keep a stable economy"—when economic activity was high and resources fully employed, the government's budget should be balanced, but when capacity to produce rose faster than the market could absorb production, tax cuts and deficit financing were called for.

Stevenson took up another issue that became important years later: poverty. In a speech at Tulsa on September 24 he recounted in detail the history of the Democratic Party's efforts to "push back poverty," starting in 1933 under President Roosevelt. He said the Republicans had opposed most such efforts and would oppose them again, said the families of 30 million Americans today had an annual income of less than $2,000 a year, and said, "I believe with all my heart that we can abolish poverty." He proposed no detailed program to do it, however.

At Wilkes-Barre, Pennsylvania, on October 3, he called for enactment of the Douglas-Flood bill to help economically depressed areas, which had died in the last session of Congress for want of Administration support. The bill subsequently passed and was twice vetoed by President Eisenhower. President Kennedy gave it strong support, as the renamed Area Redevelopment Act, and it was passed and signed during his first year in office. In a speech to the New York State Democratic Convention on September 10, Stevenson uttered the phrase that Kennedy made ring through the nation four years later: "It will require a Democratic Administration to get us back on the track—to start our nation moving again."

25.

At the same time Stevenson raised two issues in the area of national security, the military draft and the H-bomb tests, which later became Republican doctrine though the Republicans derided them at the time.

Stevenson first raised both issues shortly after the convention in a speech to the American Legion in Los Angeles on September 5. He said, "There is not peace—real peace—while more than half of our federal budget goes into an armaments race . . . and the earth's atmosphere is contaminated from week to week by exploding hydrogen bombs. . . . Until there is world-wide agreement on a safe, effective system of disarmament we cannot abandon armed deterrents to war. . . . I have thought that a powerful strategic air force must be the first element in this defense establishment. . . . But exclusive reliance on strategic air power would seem to mean that we are committed to an all-or-nothing strategy. . . . It is clear that we must rethink the problems of military strategy and military requirements in this atomic age. Many military thinkers believe that the armies of the future, a future now upon us, will employ mobile, technically trained and highly professional units, equipped with tactical atomic weapons. Already it has become apparent that our most urgent need is to encourage trained men to re-enlist rather than to multiply the number of partly trained men as we are currently doing. We can now anticipate the possibility—hopefully but responsibly—that within the foreseeable future we can maintain the military forces we need without the draft. I want to say two things about this prospect: First, I trust that both parties will reject resolutely any thought of playing politics with this issue which strikes as closely into every American home as the Korean War did in 1952, and is susceptible to the same political exploitation. Second, I think it is the national will, shared equally by every American—candidate or voter, Democrat or Republican—that the draft be ended at the earliest possible moment consistent with the national safety. I subscribe with all my heart to this purpose. . . . I regret that the Administration chose to casually dismiss my proposal last spring to halt further testing of large nuclear devices, conditioned upon adherence by the other atomic powers to a similar policy. I call attention to the fact that these other nations have subsequently announced their willingness to limit such tests."

In making these proposals about the draft and the H-bomb, Stevenson was on dangerous ground, and realized it soon afterward. He was challenging a popular President who had been a successful wartime general and was widely considered an expert on military affairs. Furthermore, by coupling the two issues in a single speech, he appeared to be—though he was not—carrying water on both shoulders. Finally, he made the mistake of not spelling out in detail what he meant by either proposal. (An earlier version of the speech had explained the draft proposal at greater length. It was unwisely shortened just before delivery.)

The Republicans were quick to accuse him of playing politics with the national security. At a press conference on September 11, President Eisenhower said, "I see no chance of ending the draft and carrying out the responsibilities for the security of this country that must be carried out."

Stevenson replied at his own press conference on September 17, "The Democratic position has always been for a strong defense. . . . What I said in Los Angeles about the draft and the possibility of terminating it was quoted extensively, I gather, with little reference to what I said about our defense needs."

He quoted his Los Angeles speech, then said, "I have read the comments of President Eisenhower and Vice President Nixon. But I, for one, am not content to accept the idea that there can never be an end to compulsory military service. My statement does *not* call for the immediate termination of the draft. It does *not* call for a reduction in the strength of our armed forces or in our ability to deal with any defensive contingency or in our determination to discharge our commitments under NATO or other pacts. What it does call for is a re-examination of our military policy in the light of the recent extraordinary changes in military technology. . . . It should be obvious that the weapons revolution which has transformed the character of warfare has also altered training needs and personnel requirements. The effectiveness of our armed forces depends increasingly upon the technical and professional skills of the men in the service," and he cited expert testimony. "It seems clear that the armed forces of the future . . . will be highly trained, highly mobile, highly professional. And it also seems clear that a draft army, in which men serve very limited tours of duty, cannot meet the specialized requirements of our rapidly changing military technology."

In a speech on September 19, President Eisenhower rejoined, "We cannot prove wise and strong by hinting that our military draft might soon be suspended—even though every family naturally hopes for the day when it might be possible. This—I state categorically—cannot be done under world conditions of today. It would weaken our armed forces. It would propagate neutralist sentiment everywhere. It would shock our allies who are calling upon their people to shoulder arms in our common cause."

In that same speech the President called Stevenson's H-bomb proposal a "theatrical national gesture." He said: "We cannot prove wise and strong by any such simple device as suspending, unilaterally, our H-bomb tests. Our atomic knowledge and power have forged the saving shield of freedom. And the future use and control of atomic power can be assured, not by any theatrical national gesture—but only by explicit and supervised international agreements."

Next day in a speech at Silver Spring, Maryland, Stevenson interrupted his campaign on domestic issues to reply. The President had "dismissed curtly" Stevenson's proposals. He had given them "misleading implications. . . . When he called the proposal to spare humanity the incalculable effects of unlimited hydrogen bomb testing a 'theatrical national gesture,' he indicted churchmen and political leaders the world over, including Pope Pius XII, representatives of the Baptist, Unitarian, Quaker, and Methodist Churches, Commissioner Murray of the Atomic Energy Commission, Sir Anthony Eden, and many other sincere and thoughtful persons in the United States and abroad who have made similar proposals.

If the President intends to foreclose debate on these proposals I think he does the nation a disservice and I must dissent and persist in my efforts to invite public attention to matters of such grave concern as the hydrogen horror and national security."

In Minneapolis on September 29 at the Democratic-Farmer-Labor Party's Bean Feed, Stevenson repeated his proposals to end the draft and H-bomb testing, emphasizing that he favored a stronger, not weaker, defense establishment. "We must not let selective service become our Maginot Line. What I am suggesting is that we ought to take a fresh and open-minded look at the weapons revolution and the whole problem of recruiting and training military manpower. . . . I am distressed that President Eisenhower should dismiss this objective out of hand. . . . I don't see how we can ever get anywhere against the rigid, negative position that we cannot even discuss the matter." Eisenhower's reaction on H-bomb testing was even more distressing. "The testing alone of these super bombs is considered by scientists to be dangerous to man; they speak of the danger of poisoning the atmosphere; they tell us that radioactive fallout may do genetic damage with effects on unborn children which they are unable to estimate. I think that almost everyone will agree that some measure of universal disarmament—some means of taming the nuclear weapons—is the first order of business in the world today. . . . But there must be a beginning, a starting point, a way to get off the dead center of disagreement. I have proposed a moratorium on the testing of more super H-bombs. If the Russians don't go along—well, then at least the world will know we tried. And we will know if they don't because we can detect H-bomb explosions without inspection. It may be that others will come forward with other ideas; indeed, I hope they do. But I say to you that in this field, as in many others, fresh and open-minded thinking is needed as never before. . . . I was shocked when Mr. Eisenhower the other night brushed off my suggestion as a theatrical gesture. I don't believe it was worthy of the President of the United States. I have never questioned his sincerity on a matter that I am sure means more to both of us than anything else in the world—the matter of permanent peace—and I do not think he should have questioned mine. All decent men and women everywhere hate war. We don't want our boys to be drafted. And we don't want to live forever in the shadow of a radioactive mushroom cloud. And when I say 'we,' I mean Democrats and Republicans alike. I mean mankind everywhere. Peace is not a partisan issue. Every American, Democrat and Republican alike, wants peace. There is no war party in this country; there is no peace party. . . . Franklin Roosevelt was not a physicist. . . . I, too, know little or nothing about the mechanics of the H-bomb. But I do know this: if man is capable of creating it, he also is capable of taming it. And nothing —including presidential frowns—can make me believe otherwise."

Republicans counterattacked heavily. On October 3, Vice President Nixon called Stevenson's H-bomb proposal "catastrophic nonsense." He said it lacked "the essential ingredient" of a "foolproof inspection system." Stevenson's draft proposal was "irresponsible." Former Governor Thomas E. Dewey on October 16 said of Stevenson's H-bomb proposal: "an invitation to national suicide." Next day he accused Stevenson of the "most dangerously irresponsible scaremongering by any political candidate." A little later he called Stevenson "a spokesman for the proposals of Moscow." Senator Knowland called him "naïve." Leonard Hall, GOP national chairman, said he had proved himself "incompetent" to be President. Harold Stassen called Stevenson's proposal "unsound" and "dangerous." Premier Nikolai A. Bulganin of the Soviet Union proposed to Eisenhower an immediate United States-Soviet agreement to ban H-bomb tests, using arguments Stevenson had put forward. Neither Stevenson nor Eisenhower welcomed his intervention.

On October 6, President Eisenhower took the unusual step of issuing a presidential statement on the testing of nuclear weapons.

He said he regretted it had been made a campaign issue.

"The manner in which the issue has been raised can lead only to confusion at home and misunderstanding abroad. There is no subject more difficult than this to discuss before an audience of the whole world—which must include those hostile to us. . . .

"I speak as President, charged under the Constitution with responsibility for the defense and security of our nation.

"I therefore must point out the following essentials . . . :

"*One*. The testing of atomic weapons to date has been—and continues —an indispensable part of our defense program. The development of these weapons has been a major, if not decisive, deterrent to Communist aggression in past years. . . .

"*Two*. As part of a general disarmament program, the American government, at the same time, has consistently affirmed and reaffirmed its readiness—indeed, its strong will—to restrict and control both the testing and the use of nuclear weapons under specific and supervised international disarmament agreement. . . .

"*Three*. In terms of our national weapons policy, it is the responsibility of specific officials of the government—notably the Atomic Energy Commission, the Joint Chiefs of Staff, and the President—to weigh, at all times, the proper emphasis on various types and sizes of weapons, their testing and development. Such emphasis necessarily is subject to constant review and re-examination. This specific matter is manifestly not a subject for detailed public discussion—for obvious security reasons."

In recent months, he said, several proposals to stop testing had been considered. "The unwisdom of such action, without proper international safeguards," was emphasized by the Democratic chairman of the Joint Congressional Committee on Atomic Energy, Senator Clinton Anderson, who said, "There is no indication that Russia would stop their tests. Under the circumstances, I do not believe we could call off ours." Thus this was not "a partisan political issue, but an issue raised by one individual." Tests of large weapons could be detected when they occurred—but any test followed many months of research and preparation, so another nation could prepare for a test without our knowledge, and by the time we found it out "our present commanding lead in the field of nuclear weapons could be reduced or even overtaken." The most recent tests had "helped us to know how to make—not weapons for vaster destruction—but weapons for defense of our cities against enemy air attack." Moreover, as a result of recent tests, "we have learned to make weapons which reduce fallout to a minimum and whose destructive effect can be concentrated upon military objectives. . . . In the verbal confusion surrounding these proposals, an attempt has been made to cite, as having made 'similar proposals,' great world figures, even including His Holiness Pope Pius XII." These men, "like this government," badly wanted international arms control agreements. Finally, within the past week, yet another proposal had been advanced. "This proposition denounced the government's 'insistence' on 'perfect' or 'foolproof' supervision of disarmament as a 'danger' imperiling any possible international agreement. I must solemnly disagree. I shall continue this insistence for however long I am charged with chief responsibility for the security of our nation."

Next day Eisenhower issued a presidential statement on the draft. It began, "The recurring political talk about a possible early ending of the draft is, I believe, hurtful to America's security interests throughout the world." The cause of peace was not promoted by suggestions whose effect "would be greatly to weaken our defenses." U.S. power was "mainly what holds the world from general war." Communist power's "fixed determination" was "to dominate the world." For twenty years or more the United States had vacillated between a strong defense establishment and a weak one. "We must not let down our guard again. We must not by weakness invite another war." The United States presently had about 2.8 million men under arms. "For an armed force in excess of 1.5 million men, experience shows that Selective Service is indispensable." The Administration was taking "every advantage of new advances in the technology of modern arms." It had produced "the finest and most powerful military forces in our peacetime history." It had reduced manpower by 20 per cent, 700,000 men, since Korea. It had reduced draft calls from 523,000 per year to 136,000. Voluntary re-enlistments had increased. It was building a strong ready reserve. "The free world looks to the United States for leadership in standing firm against the Communist push. We must not now betray that leadership by loose talk of soon ending the draft. . . . To call the draft wasteful and to term it a Maginot Line evidences either ignorance of our military needs or a willingness to take a chance with our nation's security."

In a speech at Pittsburgh on October 9, President Eisenhower said:

"They—the opposition—have urged stout military defense with greater reliance on modern weapons—but have advised stopping our atomic tests.

"They have promised national security and a bold role in world affairs —while they urge us to start thinking about ending the military draft.

"Now I, my friends, as your President and Commander-in-Chief of the armed forces, cannot and will not make proposals contrary to national interest—nor offer you attractive prospects if they are unjustified by world realities.

"I will not promise that winning a peace based on justice will be cheap and easy.

"The issue of our military draft is no matter of a technical point to be scored in a political debate. It is a matter of the safety of our nation.

"Why?

"Because we need the manpower.

"Because we cannot pretend that rockets and bombs make brains and hands obsolete.

"Because our future military burden must not be borne always and entirely by veterans who have already earned their nation's gratitude.

"Because we cannot encourage our allies in the world to shoulder arms —while we throw down our own.

"Now, let me say, the truth before us is clear.

"Strong—we shall stay free.

"Weak—we shall have only our own good intentions to be written as our epitaph."

Eisenhower's response had been powerful. He had thrown Stevenson on the defensive, forcing him to explain matters. For a brief period Stevenson dropped the issues. But he went to the Far West the second week of October, and every time out there that he mentioned the H-bomb issue the audience cheered wildly, most notably at Oakland, California. He and his staff became convinced that this might be the issue on which the election would turn. It seemed somehow to gather up all the points Stevenson had been trying to make against the Administration—its fearfulness, lack of imagination, complacency, rigidity. As the issue rose to greater and greater prominence about mid-October, Stevenson, who had for some time been restless with domestic issues and populism, determined to move to foreign affairs plus the H-bomb.

He told Barbara Ward on October 13, "The H-bomb has boiled up again. . . . I am sure I am on sound ground here and that the administration is unspeakably culpable in its failure to do anything whatever about the most terrible thing on earth." Dean Acheson told him, "I hear repeatedly . . . that some of your advisers deprecate your talking about foreign policy. I couldn't disagree more. . . . I am for making foreign policy . . . a main theme for the rest of the campaign. . . . The material which Paul [Nitze] and I have been collecting is in hand—two papers are due tomorrow. . . . Our material has to be worked over by someone who knows your needs. Tufts and Martin seem to be against your talking on foreign affairs, so to give it to them seems equivalent to throwing it away." Stevenson replied on October 13, "Confirming as [your letter] does much of my own thinking, I welcome it, and I shall also welcome the materials you and Paul have prepared. I am having a meeting this week-end with some of my 'advisers' and I hope they will have these materials with them." He told Philip Noel-Baker of Great Britain, "The deterioration of our relations over Suez is frightening. I have been in a quandary as to how to handle foreign affairs during this campaign and I am both ill informed and reluctant to cause any embarrassment. But on the H-bomb tests I must stick to my position and convictions." Lyndon Johnson sent Stevenson a letter from a constituent: "I notice by the papers that, if elected, [Stevenson] intends to stop the national Selective Service 'draft' law, and prohibit further research on nuclear weapons. . . . I think that the man must be a complete fool to ever suggest such a thing." Stevenson told the man that, on the draft, he merely thought we should "get the kind of professional forces we need" and, on the H-bomb, he had called for a moratorium on testing, not on research, and only if the Soviets would agree as they said they would.

On October 11 at President Eisenhower's press conference a reporter quoted Stevenson as saying that scientists understood his H-bomb proposal better than politicians and quoted Stevenson (two nights earlier in Seattle) : "Republican politicians, including the President, have little understanding or sympathy with attempts to save man from the greatest horror his ingenuity has ever devised," and the reporter asked for comment. The President replied: "Only this: that I admit I have no great knowledge of the processes of nuclear fusion and nuclear fission, but I have been working with scientists for a very good many years in all of this military field and I have never expressed an opinion involving the scientific parts of it without having the advice and information provided me by scientists in whom I had confidence. Moreover I think for three and a half years the record is there; that we have done everything that is humanly possible, consistent with our own concern for our own national safety, to get this thing under control and use it for peace." A reporter said that, according to "reliable sources," the Administration itself and the AEC had been considering ending both the draft and H-bomb testing before Stevenson proposed it first and that Republican strategists had planned to have Eisenhower announce it during the campaign. Would he comment? The President replied, "You are telling me things about my administration that I have never heard and I am quite sure that it's not true. No one has come up and has suggested to me that we eliminate the draft in my administration. Now, I tell you frankly, I have said my last words on these subjects."

In Chicago, Stevenson conferred with his staff over the weekend of October 14. They felt he had not yet made the H-bomb issue clear. They also thought Eisenhower had put himself in an untenable position by trying to foreclose debate. Accordingly, on October 15, Stevenson devoted a nationwide television studio speech to the H-bomb alone. He said, "Until there is world-wide agreement on an effective system of balanced arms reductions with adequate safeguards, we must maintain our national defense and the defenses of the free world." He called for a balanced defense establishment, not one relying solely on nuclear strength, which might force the nation "to choose between appeasement and massive retaliation . . . between submission and holocaust." Effective disarmament meant universal disarmament. Thus far, efforts to work out a safe, reliable system of inspection had been blocked by the Soviets. "They will not agree to let us inspect them; we cannot agree to disarm unless we can inspect them. And the matter has been deadlocked there for eleven years. . . . We must find means of breaking out of this deadly deadlock. . . . It was with this hard, urgent need in mind that I proposed last spring that all countries concerned halt further tests of large-size nuclear weapons—what we usually call the H-bombs. And I proposed that the United States take the lead."

He had made his proposal, he said, to the American Society of Newspaper Editors, a forum "as far removed as possible from the political arena." Others had chosen to make the proposal a political issue. But this was good—"the issue is mankind's survival, and man should debate it, fully, openly, and in democracy's established processes." The Republicans had been entirely negative. Therefore he wished to restate his proposal.

"First, the H-bomb is already so powerful that a single bomb could destroy the largest city in the world. . . . Second, the testing of an H-bomb anywhere can be quickly detected" and so "H-bomb testing requires no inspection. . . . Third, these tests themselves may cause the human race unmeasured damage. With every explosion of a super bomb huge quantities of radioactive materials are pumped into the air currents of the world at all altitudes—later to fall to earth as dust or in rain. This radioactive 'fallout' carries something called Strontium 90, which is the most dreadful poison in the world. Only a tablespoon shared with all members of the human race would produce a dangerous level of radioactivity in the bones of every individual. In sufficient concentration it can cause bone cancer and dangerously affect the reproductive processes. . . . I do not wish to be an alarmist and I am not asserting that the present levels of radioactivity are dangerous. Scientists do not know exactly how dangerous the threat is. . . .

"Fourth, the dangers of testing by three powers are ominous enough. . . . Last May, Mr. Stassen, the President's disarmament assistant, said that within a year the 'secret' of making the hydrogen bomb would spread around the world. Think what would happen if a maniac, another Hitler, had the hydrogen bomb. And imagine what the consequences would be of a dozen nations conducting hydrogen bomb tests and wantonly thrusting radioactive matter into the atmosphere."

Stevenson said he had proposed that the United States announce its willingness to stop testing, calling upon other nations to follow its lead, and making it clear that if they did not we would resume. Since then, both Russia and Great Britain had said they were willing "to join us in trying to establish the kind of policy I have suggested. What are we waiting for? . . . Therefore, if elected President, I would count it the first order of business to follow up the opportunity presented now by the other atomic powers. . . . In the meantime . . . we will proceed both with the production of hydrogen weapons and with further research in the field. There is little danger to national security."

He took up Republican critics. They said that his plan did not provide for "proper international safeguards." This was not so—we could detect any large explosion anywhere. They said that other countries "might get the jump on us," for they would continue research while we stopped ours. This was not so—Stevenson had not proposed stopping research, only testing. They said the proposal would "somehow reduce or curtail our power to defend ourselves." It would not—we would maintain current stockpiles and add to them as needed; we could continue to develop and test "smaller nuclear weapons." We would continue research and development on guided missiles. Most "disturbing" of all, the President said he had said his "last word" on the subject. "This is one subject on which there cannot be, there must not be, any last word." And, finally, "I say that America should take the initiative; that it will reassure millions all around the globe who are troubled by our rigidity, our reliance on nuclear weapons and our concepts of massive retaliation, if mighty magnanimous America spoke up for the rescue of man from the elemental fire which we have kindled."

Three days later, on October 18, at Youngstown, Ohio, Stevenson pressed the draft issue. He said, "It isn't just that these Republicans lack new ideas. They seem to despise new ideas. When someone makes a proposal for strengthening America, the automatic Republican response is to call the proposal irresponsible, dishonest, deceitful, theatrical, or even wicked." He continued, "We are living in an age of complex new weapons and new military techniques." In that context he had made his draft proposal to the American Legion. "This suggestion has been taken by some— and deliberately misconstrued by others—as a proposal for weakening our armed forces. It is exactly the opposite. It is a proposal for strengthening our armed forces. The point is simply that we already need and will need more and more a type of military personnel—experienced and professional—which our present draft system does not give us. The draft means a tremendous turnover in our military personnel and a resultant high proportion of inexperienced personnel." Some 750,000 men would leave the armed forces this year. To train their replacements would cost $2.5 billion. The draft entailed "incredible waste." "[But] the Republican candidates insist that it should not even be discussed, that this isn't the people's business, and that with a military man in the White House things like this can best be left up to him. Well, I say just this: What is involved here is the security, perhaps the life or death, of this nation. What is involved is the use that should be made of two years of our sons' lives. What is involved here is whether there should be new ways of more effectively meeting new problems. And I say that these are decisions that must be made not by one man—not by one general—not even by one man as President—but by the American people."

Speaking at the Hollywood Bowl in Beverly Hills on October 19, President Eisenhower countered:

"They tell us that peace can be guarded—and our nation secured—by a strange new formula. It is this: simultaneously to stop our military draft and to abandon testing of our most advanced military weapons.

"Here perhaps I may be permitted to speak in the first person singular.

"I, both as your President and the Commander-in-Chief of the armed forces of the United States of America, cannot and will not tell you that our quest of peace will be cheap and easy. It may be costly—in time, in effort, in expense, and in sacrifice. And any nation unwilling to meet such demands cannot—and will not—lead the free world down the path of peace.

"My fellow citizens, we might afford to be tolerant—in an amused sort of way—of the current effort to sell on the domestic front senseless economic panaceas in a political bargain basement. We cannot be very tolerant of the suggestion that the peace of the world can be bought on the same terms and at the same counter. And the man who today dismisses our military draft as 'an incredible waste' is a man who, while I do not question his sincerity, is speaking from incredible folly, or incredible ignorance of war and the causes of war."

On a Republican television program with several women a few days later, on October 24, the first two questions were on the draft and H-bombs, and the President said, "Well, to try to predict how long you would have the draft would be really using a crystal ball, and I don't think I'd be justified in talking about it in terms of months and years. The draft is brought about by conditions." America was prosperous, and young men would rather earn high wages in private employment than volunteer for low-paying military service. America lived in a hostile world and must be strong. "Experience" had shown that it was impossible to keep more than 1.5 million men under arms as volunteers; current strength was nearly 3 million. As for the H-bomb, "We never can have a hydrogen war, as I see it, and still have a civilization such as we now know. It's absolutely mandatory that progress be made. . . . Now, as to the hydrogen bomb, if we are going to remain secure in the type of world we have now, with aggression always possible, we must talk, we must urge agreement from a position of strength. Strength can cooperate with its neighbors and with other people; weakness cannot, weakness can only entreat. So part of that strength is the bombs, because they prevent war, as we see it. They are a deterrent that warns any aggressor, 'Don't attack us, because it would be suicide.' . . . People in our country determine whether or not we should ever go to war. Therefore, we know we are not going to start a war."

That same day the President issued yet another presidential statement "reviewing the government's policies and actions with respect to the development and testing of nuclear weapons." The critical issue was not the question of testing nuclear weapons but of preventing their use in nuclear war. "America has repeatedly stated its readiness, indeed, its anxiety, to put all nuclear weapons permanently aside—to stop all tests of such weapons—to devote some of our huge expenditures for armament to the greater cause of mankind's welfare—to do all these things whenever, and as soon as, one basic requirement is met. This requirement is that we, as a nation, and all peoples, know safety from attack." Until agreement was reached, the nation must maintain a defense strong enough to deter aggression. He had asked his administration to submit to him the record of the past eleven years—years, he said, in which he himself had been involved uninterruptedly "in my successive capacities as Chief of Staff of the Army, adviser to the Secretary of Defense, Supreme Commander Allied Powers of Europe and, since 1953, as your President and Commander-in-Chief of the armed forces." As President, he had sought to "ease the burden of armaments for all the world by establishing effective international control of the testing and use of all nuclear weapons and promoting international use of atomic energy for peace." He explained in detail steps he had taken. Always he had insisted on "indispensable" safeguards and controls. The Soviets had refused to accept safeguards. Therefore, the government had been enlarging its stockpile of nuclear weapons and continuing its development and testing of nuclear weapons.

"The continuance of the present rate of H-bomb testing—by the most sober and responsible scientific judgment—does not imperil the health of humanity. On the amount of radioactive fallout, including Strontium 90, resulting from tests, the most authoritative judgment is that of the independent National Academy of Science. It reported last June, following a study by 150 scientists of the first rank, that the radiation exposure from all weapons tests to date—and from continuing tests at the same rate—is, and would be, only a small fracion of the exposure that individuals receive from natural sources and from medical X rays during their lives." Radioactive fallout, including Strontium 90, resulted from the testing of any nuclear weapons regardless of size, and so the notion that atmospheric poisoning could be stopped by concentrating on small weapons tests was ignorant. A simple agreement to stop H-bomb tests could not be regarded as automatically self-enforcing because, while tests of large weapons would probably be detected, no one could be sure, in view of the vast Soviet land mass.

On October 29, only a week before the election, Stevenson issued a program paper on the H-bomb. In it, he accused President Eisenhower of "hopeless defeatism" when he said that H-bomb tests should not be discontinued, of offering "another do-nothing solution," and of presenting "no more than a campaign pamphlet" in his official statement. He said Eisenhower had attempted to create the impression that Stevenson's proposal would weaken U.S. defense. "He knows better, or at least should know better." Instead, it would strengthen the U.S. position relative to the Soviet Union, since the United States was already ahead of Russia and a freeze on the "H-bomb race" would operate in the United States favor. Eisenhower seemed "insensitive" to the danger of radioactive fallout. Most of the world was sitting on the sidelines, helpless spectators of the nuclear race, and should not be overlooked. He quoted Albert Einstein as saying, "I don't know what terrible weapons will be used in World War III. But I do know the weapons which will be used in World War IV— they will be sticks and stones." Stevenson said, "The modern technology of war has put humanity on the road back to the cave. I believe that humanity has some higher and nobler destiny."

By now partisans of both candidates were issuing statements. Democratic scientists defended the Stevenson position; Republican scientists defended the Eisenhower position. It was all somewhat reminiscent of expert psychiatric testimony at a criminal trial. Newspaper editorialists took up sides. The New York *Times* thought Stevenson "mistaken." Experts disagreed on the detectability of tests, on the dangers of fallout, on nearly everything. Stevenson charged that the Administration was concealing the fact that Strontium 90 was already contaminating the country's milk supply. Kefauver, who had last spring opposed Stevenson's H-bomb notion when he first put it forward, now announced he supported it and declared that hydrogen bombs could "right now blow the earth off its axis by 16 degrees, which would affect the seasons." Soon he was talking about a cobalt bomb.

In retrospect, it appears that both issues, the H-bomb and the draft, were introduced without adequate preparation, and, since they were coupled, seemed contradictory. The H-bomb proposal was vulnerable to demagogic attack although the Administration had secretly been considering making it itself. The draft made Stevenson seem demagogic and false to his own character. The public really did not understand the issues. The H-bomb issue involved disputes among scientists. This, taken together with the differing views of physicians about Eisenhower's health, gave the campaign a bizarre mad-scientist aspect. Stevenson had logic on his side on both issues. But in the end Eisenhower probably benefited politically from them. With his imposing string of titles—Chief of Staff of the Army, Supreme Commander Allied Powers of Europe, and so on—and with his access to secret information, Eisenhower simply overwhelmed Stevenson.

Years after (in 1962), Stevenson told a friend he still resented the violent opposition to his draft and H-bomb proposals. He said he would do the same if he had it to do over and he felt vindicated by history. Ironically, less than two years later, on August 22, 1958, President Eisenhower issued a statement welcoming the "successful conclusion" of a Geneva meeting of American, Soviet, and other experts who had concluded that if an agreement to stop nuclear testing were in effect, "its effective supervision and enforcement would be technically possible." Eisenhower said he was prepared to proceed promptly to negotiate an agreement with other nuclear powers to suspend nuclear weapons tests. If negotiations began, the United States would stop testing for a year unless the Soviets resumed. On "a basis of reciprocity," the United States would suspend testing on a year-to-year basis if "the agreed inspection system" was working and satisfactory progress was being made in arms control negotiations. He would instruct his negotiators to be ready on October 31 to open negotiations.

The Geneva meeting reconvened October 31. Negotiations dragged on, seeking a comprehensive test-ban treaty, while no nation tested. In August of 1959, President Eisenhower extended the one-year test suspension through December. On December 29 he announced that the United States would not resume nuclear testing without giving advance notice. The following day Premier Khrushchev said the Soviet Union would not resume testing unless the Western powers did so first.

John F. Kennedy in his campaign of 1960 made much of arms control, decrying the fact that the United States Government had more people working on the Commission on Battlefield Monuments than on arms control. On September 1, 1961, the Soviet Government resumed testing; it exploded a huge 57-megaton bomb on October 30. President Kennedy announced the United States was prepared to resume atmospheric testing if needed to preserve superiority. In November the test-ban talks resumed. Again they dragged. In April 1962 the United States began a series of atmospheric nuclear tests which ended November 4; on August 5 the Soviet Union began another series of tests.

Early in 1963 talks resumed. In June they began to move—the United States, the United Kingdom, and the Soviet Union announced on June 10 that high-level talks would be held in Moscow to seek agreement on a test ban, and President Kennedy in a speech at American University said that the United States would voluntarily suspend nuclear tests in the atmosphere pending negotiation of a test-ban agreement if other countries would do the same. Finally, on July 25, 1963, the United States, the United Kingdom, and the Soviet Union initialed a treaty outlawing nuclear tests in the atmosphere, in outer space, and under water, and outlawing also underground tests if they resulted in spreading radioactive debris outside the territorial limits of the testing state. The Limited Nuclear Test Ban Treaty was signed in Moscow on August 5. It was ratified by the United States Senate September 24, 1963, and by the end of the year 113 countries had acceded to the treaty. (France and mainland China refused.) President Kennedy considered the treaty one of the most important, if not the most important, accomplishments of his administration. Its origin lay in Adlai Stevenson's 1956 campaign. As for Stevenson's proposal to end the draft and raise a volunteer military establishment, Richard Nixon, campaigning successfully for President in 1968, came out for an end to the draft and the creation of a volunteer Army. As President, he—and Congress—did just that.

26.

Stevenson went into the final two weeks of the campaign weary, with divided counsel, and unhappy with the way things were going. In September he had attacked Eisenhower and peddled a populist line—the Administration belonged to big business, the Democrats were the party of the people. Added to the rapidity of his precampaign regional swing, it had created the impression of a new fighting Stevenson. He had seemed buoyant, expert, and happy, and the party had seemed united, and Kefauver had seemed to be helping the ticket. Stevenson's speeches had been hard-hitting and aggressive. And, since Eisenhower had not yet started campaigning, Stevenson had made all the news. Eisenhower handed him a good issue when he asked in a speech which party had done more to help the ordinary man in his everyday life. This seemed to invite a debate on Stevenson's strongest ground—the Democratic record on domestic policy —and Stevenson took it up gladly.

But soon he was grumbling about talking only on domestic issues, saying the Republicans should not be allowed to pre-empt peace. Moreover, foreign policy was the most important issue. His staff disagreed, arguing that Eisenhower had given him an opportunity to fight on his own ground, that raising foreign policy would shift back to Eisenhower's strongest ground, and that the more Stevenson said the peace was in danger the more likely people would be to turn to Eisenhower for safety. Stevenson continued to argue that he should make a foreign policy speech on national television, and a half hour of television time was purchased for that purpose. At about this time he hit a slump in his campaign, drawing small crowds in Pennsylvania and doing poorly with his crowds in New Jersey.

Barry Bingham felt it was a mistake not to let Stevenson do what he wanted—he treated halfheartedly material that bored him. Finnegan, depressed, felt that if Stevenson turned to foreign policy—and business, as he also wanted to do—he would lose the election. He must, in Finnegan's view, exploit the social issues. But such admirers as Barbara Ward urged him to take the high road and educate the people about the issues of destruction and survival, and he felt ashamed of his attacks on the Republicans as the party of the big interests. In mid-October the H-bomb issue boiled up anyway and Stevenson spoke on it at length from Chicago.

On Tuesday, October 23, Stevenson set out from Chicago on his fifth and next to last campaign trip. He spoke that night in Madison Square Garden, always one of the major rallies of the campaign, and Mrs. Roosevelt and Senator Lehman and Governor Harriman were on hand. He attacked the Republicans' claim to peace, prosperity, and progress: "Progress? When the richest country in the world doesn't have enough schools and teachers for its children? . . . Prosperity? . . . What about the farmer? The small businessman? The distressed areas? The great pockets of unemployment? . . . Peace? When our erratic foreign policy has brought us repeatedly to the brink of war, and now the whole world is in peril over the Suez? When the earth is a trail of gunpowder from Korea to Cyprus? When all humanity lives in the grim shadow of the hydrogen bomb? Yet, when Democrats mention the areas of poverty and inequality in our land, and the goals we have to reach, the President of the United States sarcastically dismisses these human troubles as 'fancied ills.' And when we raise matters literally of life and death—for us all and for all civilization—he tells us that this is a 'theatrical gesture' and 'incredible folly.' But in a free democracy there is no place for the notion that the President can do no wrong." He attacked Nixon—"the man whose idea of political responsibility was to imply that his opponents were Communists and traitors has been miraculously transformed into a high-minded and virtuous statesman."

He spent the rest of the speech on foreign policy and the H-bomb. "We have all been stirred," he said, "by Poland's struggle against Soviet domination"—Poles had rioted recently, and he proposed taking the matter to the United Nations. He said he had kept Suez out of the campaign but Eisenhower himself had introduced it by saying on a paid political television broadcast that he had "good news" about Suez.[11]

"It is not good news that Syria is threatened by a Communist coup. It is not good news that the Western oil interests, so vital to Western Europe,

---

[11] At a press conference on September 17, Stevenson had criticized Dulles' "on-again, off-again negotiations" about the Aswan Dam but had said, "[Suez] is an area of vital concern to us and to our allies and I do not think that any comment or criticism by me at this crucial moment would serve a constructive purpose." On October 19 at Cincinnati he had said, of Eisenhower's remark that he had "good news" about Suez, "But there is no good news about Suez. Why didn't the President tell us the truth? Why hasn't he told us frankly that what has happened in these past few months is that the Communist rulers of Soviet Russia have accomplished a Russian ambition that the czars could never accomplish? Russian power and influence have moved into the Middle East—the oil tank of Europe and Asia and the great bridge between East and West."

are threatened by the fires of nationalism. And it is not good news—it is very bad and sad news—that our relations with our oldest and strongest allies, Britain and France, are more fragile than they have been in a generation."

As for Israel, this was "not a cause to be cynically remembered in late October of an election season," he said. "The first premise of any Middle Eastern policy is that Israel is here to stay—and that she must have the arms, the economic support and the diplomatic guarantees necessary to secure her independence and integrity." He mentioned Indochina, Ceylon, Burma, Afghanistan, and Indonesia; he deplored Soviet gains, said the Western Alliance was in disarray, then asked, "Why don't they at least tell us the truth about the world in which we live? And, I ask, how much longer can we afford the bungling which precipitated the Suez crisis? . . . Do we want four more years of John Foster Dulles?"

Agnes Meyer sent him a telegram that night saying, "Washington *Post* is giving you terrific support on your position on nuclear energy tests." It was that day too that Eisenhower issued his long statement on nuclear policy, together with a White Paper presenting a chronological review of nuclear weapons history. Eric Larrabee, then of *Harper's,* attending the Garden rally, noted that Stevenson received a big audience response on the H-bomb passage and said, "I think this is real issue-making, like Lincoln. It is taking history by both hands, what they said he doesn't do."

Stevenson stayed overnight at the Biltmore and next day spoke at a businessmen's luncheon in the Waldorf. It was the speech he had been wanting to give, trying to demonstrate that the Democratic Party was really business' best friend. He went to Illinois and farther westward. But by the time he got to Albuquerque, he was becoming shrill: "How long will it take the [Soviets] to catch up with our hydrogren bomb technology? And as they do, will the pressure be ever greater on us to increase our own testing and to thrust ever greater quantities of radioactive poison into the atmosphere? Or will all the nations go to still more dire weapons to try to maintain an advantage in the balance of terror? Or, where does this madness end?"

In Washington Square in San Francisco, he returned to the attack on Eisenhower: "He says he's running on his record. What record?" And, "My opponent has come out four square for prosperity, national strength, and national security. And you've got to respect his clear and forthright opposition to inflation, deflation, fission, fusion and confusion, doubt, doom and gloom and fog and smog. Also he is fearlessly for health, right-thinking, happiness, and golf." He said, "He remains a shadow candidate—as he has been a shadow President. . . . My opponent has told you almost nothing about the issues of the campaign," and he listed them, then said, " 'Just trust Ike' isn't enough."

Now his pace was almost frantic. He left San Francisco that Saturday afternoon, flew to Los Angeles, spoke to a rally, left late that night for

Phoenix, and on Sunday flew to Boston. In Los Angeles he dealt with presidential leadership, one of the toughest speeches of the campaign. In 1954, he recalled, Indochina "was falling to the Communists." He had seen "that frightening war in the rice paddies and the jungles" himself. "Hasty voices," including Richard Nixon's, had advocated armed intervention by American troops. The New York *Times* had reported that Senate leaders were alarmed by fears of U.S. involvement and called Administration leaders to an urgent secret meeting. On the same day the *Times* reported that President Eisenhower had gone South on a hunting trip with Secretary Humphrey. Two days later alarm had deepened, and the *Times* reported that Eisenhower was leaving for a six-day California vacation. Secretary Dulles returned from a Four-Power Conference in Berlin and could not report to the President. Next day it was announced that we would airlift aid to Indochina; the President was playing golf in Georgia. A few days later the *Times* said that the United States was considering fighting in Indochina if necessary. It also said Eisenhower was still vacationing in Georgia. On April 18 the papers reported that Nixon had said that the United States might have to intervene with military force. They also reported that Eisenhower had played golf in Augusta. On April 23 it was announced that the last outposts around Dienbienphu had fallen. That day the President arrived in Georgia for a new golfing holiday.

"I could go on," Stevenson said. "The President was away golfing when it was announced early last year that our Air Force had gone on a full war footing as a result of the Formosa crisis. He was shooting quail when we evacuated the Tachen Islands. He was golfing in New Hampshire in June 1954 when the Soviets shot down a U.S. plane off Alaska. In the New York *Times* it said, 'There was no visible evidence that the President had anything on his mind other than having a good time.' . . . The President is an honorable man. So when he smilingly assures us that all is well and America's prestige has never been higher, he just must not know that in fact the American star is low on the world's horizons. . . . This list could go on endlessly. I have left out of the list every case where the President's absence from Washington or his ignorance of crucial facts could be traced to his illnesses. . . . But a President must assume the full responsibility of that high post. He is the Chief Executive. And I say bluntly that I do not agree with President Eisenhower that the United States can be run by a board of directors, with the President presiding at occasional meetings. . . . The price of the President's abdication has been irresponsibility in our foreign policy. . . . Here at home we are in the midst of a great social transition [school desegregation]. . . . But President Eisenhower, far from rising to this challenge of leadership, has not even expressed his views on the decision and the goal itself," and he predicted that the next four years would be worse: "We know from past experience that the President will not lead. We know that if he should try his party will not follow. And into this vacuum would come Richard Nixon—beloved by the most reactionary wing of Old Guard Republicanism," and he recited Nixon's record. "The plain fact is that the people of this country just can't picture Richard Nixon as the leader of the greatest of the world's nations. They can't imagine putting Richard Nixon's hand on the trigger of the H-bomb. They just can't trust him."

Back in Washington, the campaign was assuming cloak-and-dagger aspects. Stevenson staffers were meeting surreptitiously with scientists and friends in the Administration, seeking information on the H-bomb. Tom Finletter summarized the results in a memorandum to Stevenson dated October 27. It seemed certain, he wrote, "that the Administration at the very top level has been considering trying to work out a deal to stop the testing of big H-bombs; that the decision to take the opposite line, as the President did on September nineteenth, has been taken for political reasons only; and that if Eisenhower were to be re-elected, he would again take up the idea as soon as memories could fade a bit. I think here is the great big vulnerable issue of the campaign. . . . I think we can show not only that the whole White Paper is a shocking series of falsehoods and ½-falsehoods, but more than that, that the basic falsehood is that the President himself really believes big bomb testing should be stopped and was indeed ready to propose this to the world as late as September 11. . . . On October twenty-sixth Mr. X, a pretty high official in the Pentagon (I know his name and position) told Mr. Y (I will give you his name) who told me, that Mr. X knew that on September eleventh a meeting was held in the White House . . . where the decision was taken in principle to go ahead with offering the Russians an agreement to stop testing the big bombs. . . . But between September 11th and September 19th the decision was reversed. And on the nineteenth, Eisenhower blasted the Stevenson proposal as a theatrical gesture."

In Boston, at the start of the last full week of campaigning, Stevenson on Monday, October 29, issued his program papers on the H-bomb and the economy. About a week earlier Polish Communist leaders had defied Kremlin leadership, and the Hungarian revolt had begun. Now on October 29, Israel invaded Egypt's Sinai Peninsula. The Suez crisis had exploded. Two days later England and France joined the Israeli invasion. That night Stevenson spoke to the traditional Boston rally in Mechanics Hall, introduced by Senator John Kennedy and broadcast over nationwide television. His prepared speech was again on presidential leadership and included once more his draft and H-bomb proposals, but he inserted several paragraphs on Poland, Hungary, and the Middle East. He praised the Polish and Hungarian people, rejoiced at the news that Cardinal Wyszynski had been freed "only a few hours ago," and expressed hope that Cardinal Mindszenty of Hungary would soon be freed too. On the Middle East, he said, "The government in Washington has been telling us that all is well in the world—that there is peace, that there is—as the President announced only a few days ago—'good news from the Middle East.' These reassurances—as today's news confirms—have been tragically less than the truth."

In this final week Stevenson fought hard for Pennsylvania, Michigan, Ohio, Illinois, and New York. Word came from Michigan that Governor Williams was comfortably ahead but Stevenson was seriously behind. Stevenson left Boston early in the morning on Tuesday, October 30, flew to Baltimore, and spoke at City Hall Plaza, flew on to Philadelphia, motorcaded to Camden, New Jersey, returned to Philadelphia and spoke in the evening at the University of Pennsylvania. It was a harsh, rasping speech; he made others like it near the end of the campaign.

Stevenson left Philadelphia Wednesday morning, October 31, and took a train to New York City where he spoke at a lunch-hour rally in the garment district, a traditional Democratic rally, dampened this year by drizzle. After preliminary remarks about "single interest rule" and civil rights, he said that in its conduct of Middle East policy the "Eisenhower-Dulles administration" had been consistent in only one respect—"it has not told us the truth." Then, "The President has called on Israel and Egypt to find peaceful solutions to their differences. Everyone shares that hope and plea, and prays that the United Nations can deal with the situation effectively and promptly. Surely the United States can never condone an unprovoked attack by any nation on another. But let us, I pray, not be too quick to judge whether there has been provocation, or what Israel has done or what the British and French are doing. We know little. . . . But we do know that the British and the French have commitments to preserve peace in that area and so have we. We know also their dependence on the Suez Canal. And most of us know, I think, that this country has denied arms to Israel while her hostile neighbors to the south and also the north have been supplied by Russia. And by every consideration of law, of moral and spiritual obligation and faith, this nation is bound to support this integrity of Israel. . . . And let us cease to cry, 'Peace, peace,' when there is no peace."

That day France and England bombed Egypt, which had rejected their cease-fire demands. President Eisenhower had been scheduled to campaign in Texas, Oklahoma, and Tennessee but canceled the trip and that evening at 7 P.M. spoke to the people on nationwide all-network radio and television on Eastern Europe and the Middle East. He began, "Tonight I report to you as your President," not as a political candidate. He dealt briefly with Eastern Europe: "In Eastern Europe there is the dawning of a new day." He rejoiced in the moves of Poland and Hungary toward freedom and pointed out that "only yesterday" the Soviet Union had announced it was reviewing its policies in view of the demands of East Europeans for independence. He said the United States Government had already undertaken to assist economically the new governments of Poland and Hungary and had told the Soviet Union that the United States would not look upon them as potential military allies. He turned then to the Middle East.

The situation was "somber." The United States had "labored tirelessly there" for peace and stability. It had been basic U.S. policy "to support the new state of Israel" and at the same time to strengthen American ties with both Israel and the Arab countries. Unfortunately "passion in the area threatened to prevail over peaceful purposes." Fighting had been almost continuous for several years. The situation was worsened recently by Egyptian rearmament "with Communist weapons." Israel felt increasingly unsafe. Great Britain and France feared that Egyptian policies threatened the Suez lifeline. Crisis occurred on July 26 when Egypt nationalized the canal. There were "some among our allies who urged an immediate . . . use of force." The United States had counseled otherwise and prevailed. Negotiations had gone forward in the United Nations. There a solution had seemed within our reach.

"But the direct relations of Egypt with both Israel and France kept worsening to a point at which first Israel—then France—and Great Britain also—determined that, in their judgment, there could be no protection of their vital interests without resort to force." Events had moved swiftly. On Sunday the Israeli government ordered full mobilization. On Monday their armed forces penetrated deeply into Egypt "to the vicinity of" the Suez Canal. On Tuesday the British and French governments delivered a twelve-hour ultimatum to Israel and Egypt. Now they had followed up by armed attack on Egypt. The United States had not been consulted or informed in advance.

"We believe these actions to have been taken in error. For we do not accept the use of force as a wise or proper instrument for the settlement of international disputes." What next? "There will be no United States involvement in these present hostilities." Therefore he would not call Congress into special session, though he would keep congressional leaders "of both parties" informed. The government "will remain alert." Its purpose would be "to do all in its power to localize the fighting and to end the conflict." Already it had gone to the UN with a request that Israeli forces go home and hostilities cease. Great Britain and France had vetoed this proposal. The President hoped that now the matter might go before the General Assembly, where veto was impossible and world opinion might help force a settlement. He believed the UN represented "the soundest hope for peace in the world."

Stevenson, speaking in Pittsburgh two hours and a half later, said, "I trust you have all heard the President's broadcast of this evening. . . . Just before the President made this broadcast I sent him a telegram in which I said that I hoped that the President would not be led into any hasty actions involving the use of American armed forces in the Middle East. Even though the President could not have known of my telegram at the time he went on the air, I am glad that in his broadcast he assured us that he has no present intention of calling Congress into special session or involving the United States in these hostilities. I am not gratified, though, by the fact that the President failed in his broadcast to acknowledge that his foreign policies in the Middle East have been disastrous; that we have not won by this erratic, vacillating policy the confidence of Egypt, which is dealing with Russia, or the Arab states, that we have lost the confidence of beleaguered Israel surrounded by hostile neighbors and now, evidently, desperate; that, thanks to our bewildering appeasements and provocations, the Russian Communists have attained the foothold in the Middle East the czars could not get in centuries; that we have alienated our allies, our oldest and strongest allies, Britain and France; and finally, that the world is on the brink of war again, and we find ourselves on the side of Colonel Nasser, the Egyptian dictator, and the Soviet Union when Communist policy has for years been trying to divide the great Western Allies. . . . And there was no evidence whatever in the President's speech that he knew what was wrong or would have the courage to do what is right—if it is anything more than words of good will."

Minow, dispatched by Finnegan from Washington, met Stevenson in Pittsburgh and told him he should ask for equal broadcasting time to answer Eisenhower. Stevenson was exhausted, stretched out on his bed in the hotel, moaning about "going through all this." He agreed, however, to speak on Suez if Minow and the others could get equal time. Stevenson asked when and where. They would have to cancel part of the next day's schedule and stay in Pittsburgh to prepare the speech. But then it was discovered that Richard Nixon was coming to Pittsburgh tomorrow afternoon and would occupy the same hotel suite. While others worked out the mechanics, Minow and Finnegan stayed up most of the night trying to get equal time. By morning they were nowhere. All three networks referred them to the Federal Communications Commission. The commissioners were in a meeting. Finnegan finally got to one of them who was a relative of Sam Rayburn. The FCC divided on the issue and decided to leave it to the networks. All radio and television networks decided to give him time.[12]

Stevenson sent telegrams to all Democratic members of Congress, Governors, and congressional candidates, urging them to help in "bringing our country a full understanding of the causes and consequences of the Middle Eastern crisis." From Buffalo that night, Thursday, November 1, on all networks, he replied to Eisenhower. He said that the Middle East crisis

[12] The Republicans promptly denounced the networks for having given Stevenson time, arguing that Eisenhower had been speaking as President, not as a candidate, and demanded equal time to reply to Stevenson. On Monday, the day before the election, the FCC reversed itself and decided that Eisenhower's original address had not required reply by Stevenson. This left the networks out of balance, and at least one network, CBS, through Frank Stanton, offered Eisenhower time through Leonard Hall, the Republican national chairman. Hall declined it.

"should be above politics" but he wanted to sum up "the central facts." He quoted that day's New York *Times:* "The United States has lost control of events in areas vital to its security." Stevenson said, "The condition which confronts us is stark and simple—our Mid-Eastern policy is at absolute dead end. And the hostilities going on tonight . . . reflect the bankruptcy of our policy; and they have given the Soviet Union two great victories"—a foothold in the Middle East and the breakdown of the Western Alliance, the Soviets' "supreme objective" since World War II. As a result, the United States found itself arrayed in the United Nations with Soviet Russia and the dictator of Egypt against the democracies of Britain, France, and Israel. "A foreign policy which has brought about these results . . . is a foreign policy which has failed."

He had, he said, three points to make. "The first is that this series of failures could have been averted. . . . The second is that this Administration not only made mistake after mistake in its Middle Eastern policy but has withheld the consequences from the American people. The third is that there are many things which might have been done in the last year to avert war in the Middle East."

When Eisenhower came to office, he said, Communist influence in the Middle East was low and so was violence. Then Secretary Dulles gave General Naguib, Nasser's predecessor, a pistol as a personal gift from Eisenhower, a piece of "fateful symbolism." The Administration adopted a policy of "impartiality" between the Arab states and Israel. The United States, seeking to build up Nasser as a bulwark of stability, pressured the British to evacuate their military base along the Suez Canal. Dulles then "fanned the flames of ambition, nationalism, and rivalry" with the Baghdad Pact. In 1955, Nasser's negotiations for U.S. arms bogged down and he turned to Russia. "We not only failed to stop the introduction of Communist arms into the Middle East, but we refused to assist Israel with arms too." We "dangled before" Nasser the prospect of financing the Aswan Dam but, when Nasser turned out not to be a "bulwark of stability but a threat to the peace," Eisenhower "abruptly and publicly" withdrew support for the Aswan Dam. At this Nasser promptly seized the Suez Canal.

"Driven by our policy into isolation and desperation, Israel evidently became convinced that the only hope remaining was to attack Egypt before Egypt attacked her . . . her tragic decision. Here we stand today. We have alienated our chief European allies, we have alienated Israel. We have alienated Egypt and the Arab countries and in the UN our main associate in Middle Eastern matters now appears to be Communist Russia—in the very week when the Red Army has been shooting down the brave people of Hungary and Poland. We have lost every point in the game. I doubt if ever before in our diplomatic history has any policy been such an abysmal, such a complete and catastrophic failure."

It was "bad enough" to be responsible for such a failure. It was "almost worse" to try and conceal the truth from the people, as the Eisenhower administration had done "systematically." Only "a few days" earlier Eisenhower had told the people that progress was being made in settling the Suez dispute. Nixon had said at the same time, "We have kept the peace." Stevenson said, "Either the President or the Vice President did not know how serious the situation was in the Middle East, or they did not want the American people to know—at least, till after the election."

What now should be done? Stevenson had said at Charlottesville a year ago that UN "guards" should patrol the areas of violence in the Middle East and keep the hostile forces apart. Today Eisenhower was "trying, very properly, to check military action." But this would only restore the *status quo ante* of four days ago, which threatened "strangulation of our European allies, the destruction of Israel, and increasing control of the Middle East by Communist Russia." A mere restoration of the *status quo ante* would be another "setback for the West." Stevenson closed, "I would not condone the use of force, even by our friends and allies. But I say that we now have an opportunity to use our great potential moral authority, our own statesmanship, the weight of our economic power, to bring about solutions to the whole range of complex problems confronting the free world in the Middle East. The time has come to wipe the slate clean and begin anew."

Next day, Friday, November 2, Sam Rayburn sent Stevenson an encouraging telegram praising his position on the Middle East and voicing strong support.

Stevenson went that morning to Cleveland and spoke at noon in Public Square. Russian tanks were re-entering Hungary, hostilities were continuing in the Middle East, the British and French were about to land troops. Stevenson struck again at the Administration's failures in foreign policy. He went on to Detroit and in the evening told a rally and the Michigan television audience, "The President went on a paid political broadcast two or three weeks ago to talk about good news from Suez. When he thought the Suez crisis could be exploited for political advantage, he exploited it, while I refrained from talking about it to avoid any possible embarrassment of our government's negotiations. Now that his policy has ended in failure, he wants to silence discussion." He laid down a four-point program for diplomatic action. "Security must be restored" along Israel's frontiers. The United States should insist that no single country could cut the Suez Canal. It must "launch an all-out attack" together with other nations to settle the Arab refugees. Finally, it must, with other nations, "present a program to improve economic conditions" in the Middle East.

He flew to Chicago late that night. Next day, Saturday, November 3, the final weekend of the campaign, he motorcaded around Chicago and that night led a parade to the Chicago Stadium where he addressed the traditional final rally of precinct captains and other Democrats.

On Sunday, Stevenson released his last paper, one on natural resources. And Nancy bore her first child. Stevenson issued a statement from Libertyville, "I am elated to join all the grandparents. There could be only one other end of the campaign that could please me half as much! I hope this child will make its parents as happy as my boys have made me. And I pray that this baby may live to see a greater America and a more peaceful world." He later told a friend that the campaign "had had its moments," especially the birth of his grandson. Jim Oates saw him at Libertyville that Sunday night. "Adlai was absolutely exhausted. He had lost his light touch. He knew he'd lost."

The Russians were about to complete crushing the Hungarian revolt. Stevenson sent Eisenhower another telegram: "I have been following the developments in Hungary throughout the night, and like all Americans, I am shocked and gravely disturbed over this brutal treacherous attack. I would like to be as helpful as I can and with this in mind, may I respectfully urge upon you a course of action. . . . Premier Nagy of Hungary has already appealed to the United Nations for help. May I therefore recommend that you at once set in motion machinery to activate the Peace Observation Commission which was created in 1950 under the Uniting for Peace Resolution," the resolution which had enabled the United States to circumvent the Security Council and pursue its intervention in Korea under authority of the General Assembly. "This would make it possible for the United Nations to mobilize large teams of official observers and fly them into Hungary . . . and also any other satellite nations, such as Poland, that might welcome or consent to their presence. I believe that this step . . . might help to save Poland from a fate similar to Hungary."

Stevenson had planned to spend Monday at Libertyville and to end his campaign with a nationwide broadcast from there with Kefauver. Instead, on Monday he resumed heavy campaigning. He flew to Minneapolis and repeated his accusation that the Administration was not telling the people the truth and that "the President doesn't run the store. Presidential negligence on questions of peace and war may plunge the whole world into the horror of hydrogen war. And negligence is precisely what we have been getting."

It was Election Eve. He flew to Boston and there ended his campaign with a nationwide broadcast on which various Democratic leaders, including Mrs. Roosevelt, Senator Kennedy, and Governor Muskie, appeared. His staff, flying separately direct from Chicago to Boston, helped draft their speeches, and in Boston, Schlesinger and Martin tried unsuccessfully to persuade Ted Sorensen, Senator Kennedy's aide, that Kennedy in his speech should attack Senator Joe McCarthy. In Boston, Adlai III sent Stevenson a note:

Dear Grandpa,
   Please forgive me for not being at the airport to meet you, but right now is one of the few times I am permitted to be with Nancy.
   I am looking forward with great pride in personally introducing my

son—your grandson—to you. I will be waiting at the hospital for you and hope you can get here as soon as possible before visiting hours are over,

                                                    Love,
                                                    Adlai

Toward the end of his final speech that night Stevenson said:
"And now, one other matter.
"Your choice tomorrow will not be of a President for tomorrow. It will be of the man—or men—who will serve you as President for the next four years.
"And distasteful as this matter is, I must say bluntly that every piece of scientific evidence we have, every lesson of history and experience, indicates that a Republican victory tomorrow would mean that Richard M. Nixon would probably be President of this country within the next four years.
"I say frankly, as a citizen more than a candidate, that I recoil at the prospect of Mr. Nixon as custodian of this nation's future, as guardian of the hydrogen bomb, as representative of America in the world, as Commander-in-Chief of the United States armed forces.
"Distasteful as it is, this is the truth, the central truth, about the most fateful decision the American people have to make tomorrow. I have full confidence in that decision."
When some of Stevenson's own supporters and staff, watching the television broadcast in the hotel in Boston, heard him deliver this passage, they gasped. Where the passage originated is not clear. Something similar is contained in a draft by Finletter written on the plane between Minneapolis and Boston. Schlesinger recalled years later that Wirtz had shown him the passage and asked his opinion. Schlesinger has recalled, "I'm afraid I said, 'It's true, and the people should know it,' or something like that. I wish I had said that it was wrong—because I thought it was. But I gave him some terrible answer like that." It alienated some of Stevenson's Republican friends and tarnished his reputation.
Back in Chicago, Stevenson listened to the returns in the Blackstone Hotel. It was apparent early that he was losing. Finnegan told him. So he went before the television cameras one more time:
". . . For here, in America, the people have made their choice in a vigorous partisan contest that has affirmed again the vitality of the democratic process. And I say God bless partisanship, for this is democracy's lifeblood.
"But beyond the seas, in much of the world, in Russia, in China, in Hungary, in all the trembling satellites, partisan controversy is forbidden and dissent suppressed.
"So I say to you, my dear and loyal friends, take heart—there are things more precious than political victory; there is the right to political contest.

And who knows better how vigorous and alive it is than you who bear the fresh, painful wounds of battle. . . .

"I have tried to chart the road to a new and better America. I want to say to all of you who have followed me that, while we have lost a battle, I am supremely confident that our cause will ultimately prevail. . . .

"And, finally, the will of our society is announced by the majority. And if other nations have thought in the past few weeks that we were looking the other way and too divided to act, they will learn otherwise. What unites us is deeper than what divides us—love of freedom, love of justice, love of peace.

"May America continue, under God, to be shield and spear of democracy. And let us give the Administration all responsible support in the troubled times ahead.

"Now I bid you good night, with a full heart and a fervent prayer that we will meet often again in the liberals' everlasting battle against ignorance, poverty, misery, and war.

"Be of good cheer. And remember, my dear friends, what a wise man said—'A merry heart doeth good like a medicine, but a broken spirit dryeth the bones.'

"As for me, let there be no tears. I lost an election but won a grandchild!"

27.

He had lost by a bigger margin than in 1952, even though he was far better known by then. He carried only seven states, every one except Missouri from the Old Confederacy—North and South Carolina, Georgia, Mississippi, Alabama, and Arkansas. He carried not a single Northern state. For the first time since 1876, Louisiana went Republican. Even Texas, Florida, Virginia, Kentucky, and Tennessee went Republican. So, even, did Rhode Island. Eisenhower received the largest popular vote in history and a plurality second only to FDR's in 1936. The totals showed 35,590,472 votes for Eisenhower (457 electoral votes) and 26,029,752 for Stevenson (73 electoral votes). Eisenhower received 57.7 per cent of the total vote cast. He ran unusually well in Northern urban areas. More Negroes voted Republican than in any election since before the New Deal.

The Eisenhower landslide, however, was not enough to pull his ticket in. Democrats retained control of both houses of Congress. The party switch of Senator Wayne Morse actually added one Democratic vote to the Senate majority, making it 49 to 47. Democrats won Republican seats in Colorado, Idaho, Ohio, and Pennsylvania. Among the newly elected Senators were Javits of New York, Church of Idaho, Clark of Pennsylvania, Morton of Kentucky and Lausche of Ohio. In the House the Democrats actu-

ally added to the 29-seat margin they had won in 1954. The new line-up
showed Democrats 234, Republicans 201. Moreover, the Democrats
gained one governorship, holding 28 to 20 for the Republicans. Clearly
the election was a landslide for a popular President, not for his party.

It seems likely that Suez turned a certain victory for Eisenhower into a
landslide. Stevenson once said that Suez cost him four million votes and
said wryly of the Israelis: "Just think, after all those bond drive rallies I've
addressed they couldn't have waited another week." He said that before
Suez he had detected increasing excitement in the crowds and a feeling
that he was overtaking Eisenhower. It may be that, had Stevenson had his
way and made foreign policy an issue from the start, he could have turned
Suez to his own advantage. As it was, however, it merely alarmed the people and sent them scurrying to Eisenhower for safety. His last-minute use
of the President's health almost surely cost him votes. It would have been
a legitimate issue if he had made it one from the beginning. Coming as it
did on Election Eve, it seemed the last-minute act of a desperate candidate. All in all, however, it is impossible to conclude that Stevenson could
have won, no matter how he had campaigned. Eisenhower in 1956 was
simply invincible.

If few Stevenson advisers had expected him to win, even fewer had expected him to be beaten so badly. Minow once said, "The Governor took
this one hard. He knew he was through in terms of ever being President.
And it hurts to lose bigger than the first time." The day after the election
in Libertyville, Stevenson told Marietta Tree, "Oh, it hurts so badly. It's
even worse than in 1952." She recalls seeing him "a man in torture, bleeding from his wounds. In public he was sporting and gay, but it was a private agony that was worse than '52." Next day Marshall Field died suddenly. When Marietta saw Stevenson at the services he said, "I hope you
will wear a beautiful hat with a veil like that at my funeral." He often
talked to her about his funeral. "He told me how he'd like to have it arranged. He had a melancholy streak. And it was a spur to him, I think. He
was thinking in terms of immortality."

28.

Bill Wirtz once said, "If the Electoral College ever gives an honorary
degree, it ought to go to Adlai Stevenson." Many felt that way. Condolences came in from everywhere, an avalanche, some of the mail heart-
broken. Agnes Meyer wrote, "Adlai, I am no coward. But I am a woman
—who loves you. Please let me see you before too long." Mrs. Roosevelt
wrote, "No one could have done more, but the love affair between President Eisenhower and the American people is too acute at present for any
changes evidently to occur." Nan McEvoy spoke for the die-hard Stevenson Volunteers when she told him, "The campaign is over and with it an

era for us all. For you who lead it's probably the most crucial moment in your life. God be with you. May you find the quiet place, the gentle stream and the new born laughter to start again. . . . Those who were Stevensonians are still deeply glad today there was you to rally behind. You stirred their imaginations and opened a new awareness in them. I don't think they'll forget and I do think they'll act. To me that's winning in a realer better way than mere occupancy of the White House. Today at lunch a couple of dear old gals who were and are violently pro-Adlai, were still refusing to concede defeat. Over the egg and corn muffin course they discussed the President. Such language came forth from very proper ladies that the very antimacassars reverberated. . . . Whether it's the academic world, or better to me a Foundation, I hope you'll find something very satisfying."

Scotty Reston's son Tommy, then about thirteen years old, had been a wildly enthusiastic Stevenson supporter during the campaign. His room was filled with pennants, banners, and other campaign memorabilia. Just before the election Reston had to go up to New York and, leaving, told his son, "Look, when I get back from New York let's put all this stuff up in the attic." When he returned Tommy had not only put his mementos up in the attic but had moved up there with them. His mother found a note he had written: "Mr. Chairman, fellow Democrats, fellow Americans—I accept your nomination in this year of 1980." Reston told Barry Bingham about it, and Bingham told Jane Dick, and she told Stevenson, and he immediately wrote a postcard to Reston, "Fellow Americans, fellow Democrats! In this year of decision—1980—Well, there's *one* Democratic candidate who will be *ready*. Tell him I love him; that I apologize; that in 1952 I didn't *want* to be ready; in 1956 I didn't have time to *get* ready and in 1980 I'll be cheering—here or there." He followed it with a note to Tommy himself: "I want you to know how grateful I am for all of your help during the campaign. You know the Volunteers were very precious to me because most of them really *were* volunteers, just like you. I hope you were not too upset by the election. After all, it was a difficult undertaking at best. But I am sure you will agree that it was worth while keeping up a good, vigorous contest about things we believe in."

Stevenson told General and Lady Spears, "I was doing not badly until the Middle East came apart and then the public was, thanks to years of conditioned ignorance, rushed into endorsing the author of our disaster." He told Kefauver, "Surely this ratification of the Administration's disastrous foreign policy springs from ignorance and not consciousness." To Harry Truman, who had said, "You made a wonderful campaign; only demagoguery and glamour defeated you—nothing else," he wrote, "While defeated, I don't feel particularly bruised. But I am alarmed by the numbers that switched their allegiance in the last few days to support the author of our Middle Eastern crisis. It is a curious irony and must reflect not so much design as ignorance. And that presents a formidable problem to us Democrats!" Congratulating Mennen Williams on his victory in Michigan, Stevenson said, "I hope we can have a talk one of these days about the party's future." Herbert Lehman of New York said, "The election of 1956 was lost before the campaign began. . . . The Democrats in Congress failed to *make* the issues during the eighteen months we were in control." Lyndon Johnson held a press conference three days after Stevenson's defeat, taking no notice of the results of the presidential contest but taking credit in the name of "responsible cooperation" for the continued Democratic control of Congress. Thus in effect he claimed credit for the congressional victory and blamed Stevenson's defeat on Butler.

Stevenson told Congressman Richard Bolling of Missouri, "I know I was right on the H-bomb. . . . I so much hope that we can profit from our past experience and develop an effective and sustained opposition this time." To Paul Douglas: "The readiest answer [to how to enlighten the public] would seem to be a more active opposition role in the Congress for the Democrats." Time and again in post-mortem letters he expressed his concern with "the depth of the public ignorance." He told Lloyd Garrison, "I still have an old fashioned notion . . . that there must be some advantage to truth even in politics, but I am a little shaken." He wrote Tom Matthews, "Vast numbers of people voted in sort of a voter's panic for psychological refuge from the threatening situation in the Middle East. It is more than a little ironic that they took refuge with the authors of the crisis. Yet this is the way it is and reflects how effective the brainwashing and euphoria has been." He told Barry Bingham he wanted to retain "some vestige of influence" on policy. He told the former Governor General of India, C. Rajagopalacharya, "While the President and his party have rejected my suggestion regarding the taming of the H-bomb during the campaign, I have little doubt that we have not heard the end of this problem. . . . While what I proposed during the campaign, both as a liberal program at home and some new initiatives abroad, were rejected, I feel that they are only delayed and ultimately must prevail." Stevenson told Senator John Sparkman, "I really don't believe Eisenhower would have been too hard to beat if he had been chopped up a little beforehand." He asked Frank Altschul, "Do you think I could have cut through four years of euphoria if I had started talking foreign policy earlier and more vigorously?" To another correspondent, "I am quite bewildered about the Negroes."

On November 18 he sent a letter to his sons saying he was leaving that day for Chelsea plantation, Ruth Field's place at Ridgeland, South Carolina, to rest and shoot quail. He assumed that Ellen would spend Thanksgiving with the sons. (Adlai III later reported on Thanksgiving in Cambridge with Ellen: "There were a lot of toasts at Thanksgiving dinner, and mother wouldn't raise her glass when it came turn for Nance to be toasted.") Stevenson suggested to Agnes Meyer an article in the *Post* about the party's indebtedness to Stevenson and his ideas in the hope that it would "enlarge my *ideological,* not political influence." He did not, he said, want to start a "public quarrel" with Lyndon Johnson about what shape the opposition should take. He told John F. Kennedy, "I can think of no one to whom we should all be more grateful than to you."

Stevenson was appointed to the new Democratic Advisory Committee (DAC), a policy steering group established by Paul Butler to counter Lyndon Johnson's leadership of the opposition. He issued a statement saying he would not run again for President. "I intend to resume the practice of law in Chicago on January 1st with my old friends and associates, W. Willard Wirtz, William McC. Blair, Jr., and Newton N. Minow. I will not run again for the presidency. But my interest in the Democratic Party . . . will continue undiminished. I want to be of help wherever I can." Saying he had accepted membership on the DAC, he added, "In my opinion the greatest service the Democratic Party can now render is a strong, searching, and constructive opposition." Thus by inference he aligned himself with those who criticized Johnson's cooperation with Eisenhower. He told a woman in California, "The purpose [of the statement] was to disarm all of the ambitious fellows by disclaiming any Presidential intentions myself, hoping thereby to possibly be of some more welcome influence in the party councils than I would be had I continued in the equivocal position."

Evidence exists that Stevenson might have preferred becoming president of Princeton to returning to private law. From Mrs. Field's Chelsea plantation, he wrote to his old friend from Princeton days, Richard K. Stevens, the Philadelphia lawyer, "I've just been 'interviewed'—between shooting ducks and quail!—again, and again this everlasting question about the presidency of Princeton has arisen—even in Ridgeland S.C.! And now I must go tomorrow to New York and Boston (on business and to see my kids) and I'll get the same inquiry again and again. So I've concluded to turn to you—as all-wise in matters relating to Princeton in the hope that you will tell me or can ascertain if there is any substance to these rumors. If there is, I would be interested of course; if there isn't I wouldn't be surprised!—to say the least." He had told Bill Benton earlier, "I have heard nothing about the Princeton job, but I think it's a myth. I confess it would interest me a lot—almost as much as being editor of the Britannica." The idea had first come up after the 1952 election. In 1956 and 1957 several people proposed Stevenson to a committee that was searching for a new president for Princeton. In the end, however, the committee dropped him because it had previously established a guideline ruling out anybody older than fifty-three.

Stevenson was considering other enterprises and did not put them entirely aside even after he announced he would return to the law. He told

Alicia Patterson that, according to Bill Benton, the Hartford *Courant* could be bought for about $5 million and that, according to other friends, a chain of Texas newspapers could be bought. He declined an invitation to write a newspaper column which, a syndicate guessed, would bring up to $800 a week after the first year. Senator Fulbright proposed him for president of the University of California but the chairman of the Board of Regents, Ed Pauley, doubted he could be elected. He declined a suggestion that he undertake a lecture tour. He told Morris Ernst, a well-known New York lawyer, "I have reflected long and earnestly since the election over various proposals to write newspaper columns, edit magazines and conduct programs of various kinds. Reluctantly I have concluded to decline them all. I think the reason rests in my feeling that I don't want to feel committed to an inflexible schedule."

He planned to attend the first meeting of the DAC in Washington on January 4 and told Agnes Meyer he would join in her birthday party at the same time.[13] Telling Kefauver he would see him at that meeting, he added, "and I earnestly hope that the Democrats in Congress will mount a more effective offensive and opposition than they have in the past." Sam Rayburn had already declined to serve on the DAC, and ultimately Lyndon Johnson, too, boycotted it. Minow told Phil Stern that Stevenson's renunciation statement was intended "to renounce personal ambition but retain party influence. Whether this can be done is now the unresolved question." Political reporters predicted a power struggle for control of the Democratic Party which could lead to a lasting schism between its Northern and Southern wings. In the face of Johnson's and Rayburn's determination to maintain congressional leadership of the party, six liberal Democratic Senators from the North and West announced they would insist on National Committee leadership. It remained to be seen whether Stevenson could effectively lead the liberal revolt.

Finletter, Schlesinger, and Galbraith were corresponding early in December about a resolution Stevenson might present to the DAC. Stevenson had proposed to Finletter in New York that the resolution contain something about the equal use of television and radio by the two parties. Finletter thought the idea needed more study but agreed that the party should

---

[13] Mrs. Meyer told him about the guests she had invited to her birthday party whom she wanted him to meet, "my special loves"—Edward Steichen, the photographer; Rudolf Serkin, the pianist; Gian Carlo Menotti, the composer; Sam Barber, the composer; Harlow Shapley, Harvard astronomer; Harold Taylor, president of Sarah Lawrence College; Otis Wiese, editor of *McCall's;* Fritz Redl, child psychologist; Herblock, the cartoonist; Mrs. Roosevelt; and others. Mrs. Meyer would put Stevenson between her daughter Elizabeth ("my most wicked and gifted offspring") and "the seductive Mrs. David Bruce." The Finletters would be there, as would George Gallup, Mark Childs, Walter Lippmann, James Reston, Frank Kent, Alice Longworth, Chief Justice Warren, Justice Frankfurter, about 140 in all. "Hope to goodness the dinner will be good. Happy New Year!"

propose somehow to limit the power of money in political campaigns.
Thus did they again anticipate an issue of the 1970s. Stevenson told
Ernest Gruening of Alaska, "I wish I were more confident that the [DAC]
was going to be more effective. I am afraid we are at a critical juncture in
our party affairs."

His schedule for the last part of December was a curious blend of the
dim gone past and the uncertain present. He would be in New York from
December 19 through December 21 and would see Lloyd Garrison, Cass
Canfield of Harper's, Lansdell Christie, Mrs. Roosevelt, Robert Sherwood, and Bennett Cerf; would attend a dinner dance, and a meeting with
Finletter and others on the DAC resolution. Back home, he would give a
buffet supper for thirty on December 23; on the day before Christmas he
would attend the old Sidley law firm's annual Christmas luncheon at the
Chicago Club and go to a Tavern Club party. He would be home on
Christmas Day. On the twenty-seventh he could give a party for his campaign staff. On the twenty-ninth the Iveses would give a party at his
house. On New Year's Eve he would go to the Cuneos' party in Libertyville and to the Phelps Kelleys' dinner dance at Shoreacres. His holiday
message, written out in longhand and reproduced in facsimile, was a quotation from the remarks of Louis Pasteur responding to the greeting of the
French Academy on his seventieth birthday in 1892: "You bring me the
deepest joy that can be felt by a man whose invincible belief is that science
and peace will triumph over ignorance and war, that nations will unite, not
to destroy but build, and that the future will belong to those who have
done most for suffering mankind." When his son Borden arrived in Chicago
for his vacation, Ellen would not let him in her apartment, he later testified; he had no money for taxi fare and called his father in Libertyville.
Stevenson told Alicia Patterson the day after Christmas:

> It *has* been fun with two boys and all the gaiety. I yearn to see and
> talk with you—and walk in the snow along the Des Plaines—When
> will you come?

X X X

A.

He telephoned the Magnusons in Washington to ask if he could stay in
their house between January 3 and 6. They were away, but the maid assured him he was welcome. He dictated letters. To Professor Stuart Gerry
Brown, who had analyzed the election, Stevenson wrote, "The misfortune
was, of course, the primary, which exhausted minds, bodies and resources
and also wasted precious time in the wrong places and in the wrong
ways. . . . But don't think I have overlooked your conclusion that the
New America series [of position papers] was the 'genuine contribution of
the campaign.' I think so too!" To Eugenie Anderson, a leading Minnesota Democrat: "I think you are right, and that it has been more a 'tri-

umph for the age of advertising' than an expression of confidence, popularity and approval of the President and his administration, which is the usual conclusion." To W. B. Bryan of the Minneapolis School of Art, "I have few regrets. . . . I had the satisfaction of saying some of the things I felt needed saying and suggested some objectives for our country and my party. That they will come to pass is reward enough."

CHAPTER THREE

A Generation Passes Away
1957-1960

The years between 1956 and 1961 were fallow years, a pause between Stevenson's presidential campaigns and his term as United States Permanent Representative to the United Nations under President Kennedy and President Johnson. During those years Stevenson traveled widely, wrote and spoke rather sparingly, influenced the Democratic Party, and prospered as a lawyer.

In 1957 he was fifty-seven years old. He had publicly renounced any intention of running for President again (but neither he nor some of his friends really put the idea aside until after 1960). In 1957 he used the Democratic Advisory Committee (DAC, later the Democratic Advisory Council) to promote his political ideas, he went on Encyclopaedia Britannica boards and the Field Foundation board, traveled to Europe and Africa and the Caribbean, published a collection of his 1956 campaign speeches under the title *The New America,* widened his law practice, became involved in NATO policy, and gave more attention to his family than he had been giving. Although he traveled a great deal and kept a crowded calendar, he seemed less busy at important public matters than at any time in recent years.

He had been "quite troubled" by Borden during the holidays, he told Adlai on January 2, and had had "a candid talk" with him. "He feels that his 'complexes' are diminishing since Hawaii. . . . I have lectured him about cigarette poisoning, about taking more exercise, going to bed earlier and getting up earlier, etc. I think it would be wonderful if both you and he could arrange to play squash at least three times a week. . . . But most of all I think it might be very helpful if Borden could be induced to spend an evening of forthright talk with Carl Binger," a psychiatrist.

Adlai III was in Cambridge, finishing Harvard Law School. Stevenson's nephew Tim Ives was taking over management of the McLean County farm owned by Stevenson and Mrs. Ives. Stevenson carried on a political correspondence with various people and a business correspondence with the Reynolds Metals Company and others.

On January 4 and 5 in Washington, Stevenson attended the first meeting of the DAC. (On the same trip he dined with Harry Truman, lunched with the Foreign Relations Committee, attended swearing-in ceremonies in the Senate, and issued a statement criticizing President Eisenhower's request for a congressional "blank check" to use armed force in the Middle East.) The DAC ran into trouble from the beginning. At the time of that first meeting Stevenson quarreled with Johnson and Rayburn. He felt the opposition should include Democratic Governors and other officials and party leaders, not just congressional leaders; Johnson and Rayburn replied to him "in very unkind tones," as he put it. Paul Butler had intended to name to the DAC six Senators and six Representatives in addition to Governors, Mayors, national committeemen, and such party leaders as Truman, Stevenson, Kefauver, and Mrs. Roosevelt. Rayburn, however, did not want members of the House to serve, and ultimately all Senators and Representatives except Senator Kefauver and Senator Humphrey declined or withdrew.[1] Not only did congressional leaders oppose or ignore the DAC; it was also split internally with Stevenson, Truman, and Butler all seeking control. Probably the most influential people in the end were Stevenson, Acheson, Galbraith, and Finletter. Stevenson was able to control the DAC because he raised the money that kept it going. The money came mainly from New York liberals. Stevenson had originally seen the DAC as a way to attack the Administration, as Charles Michelson had destroyed Herbert Hoover.[2] Instead, it turned into a policy and program body. It met about every three months and oftener on call. Stevenson attended nearly every meeting. Subcommittees of about 25 people each—some 278 in all—prepared papers, and the DAC members

---

[1] By 1958 the members were Stevenson, Jack Arvey, Paul Butler, Governor Harriman, Senator Humphrey, Senator Kefauver, Mayor Lawrence of Pittsburgh, former Senator Lehman, Harry Truman, Governor Williams of Michigan, California Committeeman Paul Ziffren, national committeemen or committeewomen from Rhode Island, North Carolina, Montana, Louisiana, Minnesota, West Virginia, Michigan, Utah, New Jersey, Alabama, and Colorado, and one other Governor and one other Mayor. The DAC itself had advisory committees, including one on foreign policy headed by Dean Acheson with Paul Nitze as vice chairman and Eugenie Anderson, Bill Benton, Chet Bowles, Barry Bingham, James B. Carey, Ben Cohen, Silliman Evans, Jr., Abraham Feinberg, Dorothy Fosdick, Philip Jessup, Kefauver, Lehman, Edward G. Miller, Jr., Hans J. Morgenthau, David J. McDonald, James G. Patton, Edith Sampson, and Governor Williams as members; another on economic policy headed by John Kenneth Galbraith with John I. Snyder as vice chairman and with Marriner S. Eccles, Henry H. Fowler, Seymour Harris, Walter W. Heller, Joseph D. Keenan, Leon H. Keyserling, Murray D. Lincoln, Isador Lubin, Arnold H. Maremont, Arthur Schlesinger, Jr., Wayne Chatfield Taylor, Robert C. Weaver, Wilson Wyatt, and Paul Ziffren as members; and one on labor policy headed by George M. Harrison of the Brotherhood of Railway Clerks and with various labor leaders, including James B. Carey, Joseph A. Beirne, Harry Bates, Sidney Hillman, Thomas Kennedy, Jack Kroll, David J. McDonald, Jacob Potofsky, and Walter Reuther, as members.

[2] Michelson was publicity director of the Democratic National Committee during Hoover's last years in office and, later, worked in the White House for FDR.

argued them out. The end product was inferior to that produced earlier by the Finletter Group because, to a greater extent than the Finletter papers, each DAC final draft represented a compromise among contending factions. The members would take a subcommittee draft, rewrite it, and, if they could reach agreement, issue it publicly as a policy statement. The worst quarrels were over civil rights (because of the North-South split) and foreign policy (because of an Acheson-Stevenson split). The DAC was cautious on some issues, such as civil rights—President Kennedy and President Johnson in power went far beyond the DAC position. It produced only a few new ideas, but one led to President Kennedy's creation of the Arms Control and Disarmament Agency. Charles Tyroler, the executive director, recalled later that Stevenson worked hard at the DAC, that he had a highly political approach to issues and always looked to see if a statement had political "bite," that he was decisive and often stubborn, and that he kept insisting the Democrats must not be caught unprepared in 1960 as they had been in 1956 because of congressional non-opposition to Eisenhower.

That first meeting in January of 1957 produced statements on the Senate filibuster and foreign policy. In February the DAC issued statements or resolutions on Alaska-Hawaii statehood, civil rights, and foreign policy. On May 5 it dealt with foreign policy, economic policy, right-to-work laws. It issued a statement on the Little Rock school controversy on September 15, one on the Russian satellite on October 11, and others that fall on foreign policy, defense policy, economic growth, civil rights, immigration, and the President's speeches on national security. In all, it issued twelve papers in 1958, twenty in 1959, and fifteen in 1960, covering most important issues of the times. Like Stevenson's campaign position papers of 1956, some DAC papers found their way into the 1960 presidential campaign and into legislation enacted under Presidents Kennedy and Johnson. Stevenson attached considerable importance to the DAC, though frequently he came to meetings without having read the papers in advance. The DAC received much publicity, especially in the New York *Times* and Washington *Post,* and therefore influenced public opinion and congressional policy. Tom Finletter called the DAC an "extension" of the Finletter Group. Scotty Reston once said, "Lyndon gutted it as much as he could."

It was during this period, according to Carl McGowan, that Acheson and Stevenson fell into almost complete disagreement, though the roots of their difficulties ran back to the 1952 campaign. Newt Minow said, "They differed on almost everything. On Germany, for example. Stevenson felt we were being told what to do by the Germans, we were slaves to the German position on Berlin. He didn't think reunification was possible and maybe not desirable. Acheson was uncompromisingly against Soviet détente and China admission. Acheson was a prisoner of the past and of his critics—always trying to prove how tough he was on Communism." As

Averell Harriman saw it, "We knocked Acheson out. The DAC kept the Democratic Party liberal. I took the lead in saying the rough things to Acheson that had to be said. That's one of the advantages of being trained by Truman. On all the things that came up, as I recall it, I was on Adlai's side, though sometimes we hit it from different directions. Usually he was right but didn't fight hard." In 1966 the New York *Times,* saying that the Republican Party was failing its function of constructive opposition, said editorially, "What is needed is a G.O.P. equivalent of the now-defunct Democratic Advisory Council."

2.

James P. Warburg proposed that Stevenson organize a bipartisan citizens' committee "to keep the public alert and informed" about foreign policy. Stevenson declined. He told a friend that people were always telling him to form a group and exercise power but he thought it was nonsense. Just so did he brush aside suggestions that he form a third party.

At Bill Benton's urging he became a member of the Board of Editors of the Encyclopaedia Britannica, a member of the Britannica Board of Directors, chairman of the Executive Committee of the Britannica Film Company, and chairman of its Board of Consultants. The boards met four times a year. Benton seemed to hope Stevenson would give full-time attention to the Britannica, and Stevenson was considering it. Benton told Stevenson the American Britannica would pay his expenses to London and back in May, since he would attend the London directors' meeting there, and the London Britannica would pay his expenses in London. At the same time Stevenson was considering merging his own small law firm with the large Lloyd Garrison firm in New York. He was also considering buying one of several downstate Illinois newspapers. A project of writing a foreign policy book in collaboration with Bob Tufts was receding. Stevenson began planning a business trip to Africa for late spring and, in a letter to Richard S. Reynolds, Jr., of Richmond, Virginia, offered to look into anything that Reynolds Metals might be interested in there. He also reported to Reynolds on a conversation about aluminum development in the Gold Coast that he had had with Sir Robert Jackson, Barbara Ward's husband. As he told Jonathan Daniels, he was "in one of those transitional stages and trying to get a new life organized."

He went to the wedding of Helen Stevenson, a distant relative, to Governor Meyner of New Jersey (and kissed the bride on the mouth and was reproved by Marietta Tree). He denied to Mrs. Ives a rumor that he and Mary Lasker were engaged to marry. At the end of January he went East to talk with Lloyd Garrison about the law firm and with Bill Benton about the Britannica and to visit Adlai III and Nancy in Cambridge. Judge

Walter Schaefer of the Illinois Supreme Court arranged to take Adlai III on as his law clerk after he was admitted to the bar. Stevenson wrote, "Bless you for that letter to my beloved Adlai. He is really a first rate and most conscientious fellow."

Stevenson spoke in San Francisco on February 16 at a regional meeting of the Democratic National Committee. He denied a widespread notion that Eisenhower's re-election was a great personal triumph and that once he had retired the Democrats could easily recapture the presidency. "The Republican candidate, whoever it may be, will be hard to beat. . . . Never before . . . have the vast agencies of big money, big government, and the big press been so concentrated and so united in politics. . . . Nor can we afford to disregard another significant change: the flight to the suburbs . . . [which] has undermined the old basis of Democratic dominance in the cities." The Democratic Party's "image" had been blurred by Republican pretenses to liberalism and Democratic internal conflicts over civil rights. "The Democratic Party must pick its issues, stand by them, fight for them, not only in the lobbies and cloakrooms of Congress, but everywhere and all the time and by all of us—Congressmen, Senators, Governors, Mayors, legislators, officeholders, and private citizens. You cannot win national elections against such obstacles and resources and ruthlessness as we confront in two months. It will be hard enough in four years." On specific issues, he hoped Congress would pass civil rights legislation promptly and thought the United States should pursue its objectives in the Middle East of reopening the Suez Canal and establishing peace between Israel and the Arabs, and preventing Russian domination "even at the risk of war." Strong language, superficially reminiscent of Dulles' brinkmanship; but Dulles had been talking about risking war in Indochina, Quemoy-Matsu, and the China mainland beyond Korea, not about risking it in the Middle East, where Soviet influence had recently increased, thus endangering, as Stevenson saw it, American interests more vital than those in Asia.

On March 2, Stevenson spoke to the Gridiron Club dinner in Washington. It was a risky undertaking—he could hardly surpass his 1952 triumph there with its great opening line ("A funny thing happened to me on the way to the White house"). Now in 1957 he began, "After that sad song about my present friendless state, I am very grateful for your friendly greetings. I feel a little like that famous cow on the cold wintry morning who looked at the farmer and said, 'Thanks for that warm hand.'" He went on, "I hesitate to come back four months after the election to rake among the embers of my funeral pyre, a bonfire which most of your publishers fanned so vigorously, and a funeral at which so few of you mourned! . . . Just what made me think I could do better the second time escapes me now. I have some recollection before the accident, of a noble desire to do what my party wanted me to do. . . . Well, anyway, since the accident, a gallant fellow sufferer in Vermont sent me a verse which neatly summarizes my story, and which I read to some of you here not long ago:

> "Everyone said it couldn't be done,
> But he with a grin replied,
> How do you know it can't be done,
> Leastwise, if you haven't tried?
> And he went right to it and at it,
> And he tackled the thing that couldn't be done,
> AND HE COULDN'T DO IT."

He said he thought of a presidential campaign—"and who has thought of it more?"—as "a chaotic interlude of voluntary frustration sandwiched in between four years of anticipation and four weeks of recuperation. . . . It's a wonderful way to meet a lot of people you wouldn't meet otherwise —at any price! . . . You don't even have to read or write; someone will do it for you." He saluted Arthur Larson, Eisenhower's resident intellectual, and said, "I hope you are enjoying your missionary work among the heathen, Mr. Larson. But I know that there are those who would rather be second in Rome than first in an Iberian village." He went on, "I have had some experience with the perils of writing my own speeches. The price of being yourself in American politics is ruinous—your speeches are always late, the reporters are harassed, you miss their deadlines, and these things are evidently far more important than what the candidate really thinks, writes, and says. And worst of all, when I added what *I insisted* on saying to what my *staff* said *must* be said, I couldn't possibly get off the air before the television time was up."

He said, "Since the election we have done some research, and we find that the shift of a mere four and a half million votes would have changed the result. Those were the votes that Harold Stassen promised us, if Nixon was nominated.

"But Harold didn't count on the Middle East explosion just before the election. Neither did I! Now I don't say that the Administration planned it all; indeed I see no evidence of any planning in the Middle East. But in 1952 General Eisenhower at least had to say, 'I will go to Korea.' This time the Middle East came to him!

"After that I suppose everyone knew that all was lost—except me. I suspect I was like the fellow who hadn't read much Shakespeare . . . who jumped up after the first act of *Macbeth* and announced: 'I'll bet I'm the only person in the theater who doesn't know what's going to happen.'"

Although he took comfort in the fact that the country still had a Democratic Congress, he said he actually was "the defeated leader of a victorious party . . . surrounded by so many more fortunate Democrats." He said, "I feel like the Lone Ranger when he was riding across the country with Tonto and was suddenly confronted with a thousand Sioux Indians. Quickly they wheeled around, and there, behind them, were 2,000 Blackfeet! They turned to the right, only to see 3,000 Arapahoes coming toward them. And on the left they were cut off by 4,000 Apaches. The Lone Ranger said to Tonto, 'It looks bad for us, doesn't it?' Tonto replied, 'What do you mean *"us,"* white man?'"

In the speech's only serious passage, he said, "I remind you once more that your function as truthful, inquisitive reporter and honest, relentless critic is essential to our system of checks and balances. . . . You cannot forever pour molasses on this government or any other without gumming it up."

He went to New York and Princeton and on March 6 left for Barbados. There he had the vacation he had wanted for a long time. It lasted until nearly the end of March. Arthur Schlesinger was there, and the Binghams. They made trips to St. Vincent and Dominica and Martinique. Marietta Tree once recalled, "It was great fun. I remember one time Arthur and Adlai and I were out on the water and we started to laugh and nearly drowned." Stevenson told Agnes Meyer it was "The perfect place—luxury, sea, isolation." He was still—as he had been months earlier—"struggling to read & correct" Kenneth Davis' biography of him.[3] En route to New York on March 26, he thanked the Trees for a perfect holiday. "My woes I forgot, my work I neglected; and certainly I am brown, baked, peach-fed and rum soaked, in short, edible!" He missed Agnes Meyer in New York but met his law partners and Lloyd Garrison's, and returned to Chicago, spent the night at the Wellings', and went to the office on March 28 for the first time in six weeks. Then he sent Agnes Meyer an article from the magazine *Frontier* which said, "The cost of the 1956 election was not that the Democrats lost a presidential election—there will be other elections in the future. The question is, will there be other Stevensons?" It pleased him.

Mrs. Meyer hoped he would run again for President. On April 1 she told him, "I am a political realist but I also know better than most people that our old traditions are gone, including the one that a presidential candidate twice defeated is a dead duck. . . . Let's look at the picture for a moment," and she said Kennedy could not be elected because he was Catholic nor Johnson because he was Texan. She advised him to practice law and let the political situation work itself out. Between now and 1960 she would be a leader among his friends who wanted him to run again.

3.

In April the Stevenson firm was joined with the New York law firm in which his friend Lloyd Garrison was a partner.[4] It was a big firm with

---

[3] It was published by Doubleday under the title *A Prophet in His Own Country*.
[4] The new firm had offices in Chicago, Washington, and New York. In Chicago it was known as Stevenson, Rifkind & Wirtz; in Washington as 'Stevenson, Paul,

what Newt Minow once described as "a diversified practice." He said, "Rifkind is the best trial lawyer in the United States. It is not an old-line firm. It's about half Jewish, half Republicans, half Democrats, uptown, not Wall Street. It has theater clients. It's liberal, people in the firm write books, it's an interesting group of people. They represented Marilyn Monroe. It's nothing like what the Sidley firm used to be in the old days, the 1920s, when Stevenson first got out of law school and joined it—the day-to-day grinding away at routine matters. I was very content. Our practice enlarged. We added Ed McDougal and John Hunt in the Chicago office. We did the Chicago work for the Garrison clients. Stevenson practiced more than he had previously, working out something with foreign businessmen. Once he went to Russia to represent the Authors League. One of my problems was to persuade Congress that the *American Heritage* deserved second-class mailing privileges. We had a big tax case. The Gov became more involved with the Encyclopaedia Britannica and the Field Foundation and so did I." Minow often went to New York with Stevenson during these years. He recalls the visits fondly. "He loved to cook breakfast. Once he made me breakfast. It was so awful I couldn't even look at it. He said, 'Don't you like it?' I said, 'No.' He said, 'Do you mind if I eat it?' Once we had to go down to Wall Street and I said, 'I'll get a cab.' He said, 'Cab? We can take the subway.' I said, 'Do you know how?' He said, 'Sure. Why spend five dollars?' I said okay. Naturally we got lost and wound up in Brooklyn and got to the meeting an hour late. Once we went to the Museum of Modern Art. People recognized him and crowded all around him and asked for his autograph. Wherever you went you always had a good time with him. He went into business deals in California with Ben Swig. We were Pat Brown's first house guests after he became Governor. Once Harry Golden came to our house and I took him to lunch with Stevenson. Those were the good days. Those were the busy years, the prosperous years. I went to Israel and Europe on business. He was enjoying his children. He was enjoying making money. He probably took $70,000 or $80,000 a year out of the firm plus income from his investments." That fall Stevenson moved his Chicago offices to a small suite high in the Field Building, at 135 South LaSalle Street in the financial district, with a view overlooking Lake Michigan. Minow went with Stevenson and John Fell to Elkhart, Indiana, for the trial of the truck driver involved in John Fell's auto accident. Stevenson did not want to go into court; Minow went to protect John Fell's interests. Stevenson hoped the trucker would be convicted—he feared that if he was acquitted John Fell would

---

Rifkind, Wharton & Garrison; and in New York as Paul, Weiss, Rifkind, Wharton & Garrison. Wirtz, Blair, and Minow were partners. In announcing the firm on April 22, Stevenson said, "I have joined together with some old friends in establishing a new law firm. I will continue to be a resident of Illinois, and my principal office will be in Chicago as in the past, but I will also have offices in New York and Washington with my new partners."

feel he himself was guilty. Minow worked with the prosecutor. The trucker had been indicted for involuntary manslaughter; he was convicted on a lesser included charge, assault and battery, and sentenced to two months in the county jail and fined $100 (fine and costs suspended).

Stevenson twice asked Adlai III and Nancy to accompany him to Oxford where he would receive an honorary degree: "Please don't feel that I am insisting if your other plans seem better, but what a comfort it would be to have someone around on this occasion." At the National Guard Armory in Washington he spoke to the Democratic National Committee dinner on May 4, kidding President Eisenhower about his trouble with his own administration over the budget. It illustrated "the feebleness of the Eisenhower administration . . . the easy, careless indifference with which the President and his Cabinet seem to be prepared to abandon their own budget, and thereby the principle of executive responsibility for the budget." He said Democratic members of Congress and Governors must continue responsible opposition—"I wish I sat today where any one of you sits. What a time it is for Democratic leadership in America!" Next day, May 5, he appeared on "Meet the Press." Asked how the DAC would function effectively if it disagreed with the congressional leadership, he said, "I wasn't conscious of the split, sir." He repeated that he was "very much in favor of eliminating the tests of the large hydrogen weapons" and thought large nuclear weapons would not be used in war. Pressed to propose an alternative to the Eisenhower foreign policy in Germany or the Middle East or China, he said, "I think it is fair to say it is not always what you do but how you would do it. Much of the misfortune that we now confront . . . the deterioration of our grand alliance . . . the growing anti-American feeling in Britain and in France . . . the Russians have now penetrated the Middle East . . . the dislocation in the power balance in the world . . . [are] largely due to the errors of this Administration."

Scotty Reston asked, "Are your services available to help correct this situation?" He said, "I would be glad to help in any way I could, but I should want very much to know in what capacity. And I haven't had any offers." Marquis Childs asked if he thought the H-bomb issue had won or lost votes last fall. Lost votes, he said, because "it was misrepresented, not as an honest, sincere proposal, but as a gesture of some kind to get votes and endanger our national defense," but he predicted sharply the issue would surely grow in importance. He repeated that he did not "intend" to run for President again but refused to rule out running for Governor of Illinois. Mark Childs asked, "How broad does your authority extend as titular head of your party, and will it grow or diminish as we near 1960?" Stevenson replied, "I am not sure that it extends from me to you, but it certainly doesn't extend beyond you." Reston asked why the people did not support his criticism of Eisenhower's foreign policy. He replied, "It is quite possible that I am wrong. As to whether the people are listening or not, I don't know. I have sometimes suspected that one of our greatest problems in the conduct of public affairs in this country is the problem of communications. I am sure it is. Foreign affairs are our most intricate affairs. It is extremely hard for the average man to understand both the enormity of their importance and, also, their intricacy, their details."

He saw Agnes Meyer in Washington and afterward wrote to her about the idea that he might marry, something she had discussed with him previously. He said, "I think you are right that I've been so busy most of my life with impersonal things, and still am, that I'm not a very fit candidate for marriage and probably never was. But isn't there something to be said for the proposition that *until* I'm married to the right sort of person I won't get what you call my 'ego-ambitions' (I say, *if any!*) into balance and behave, and love, etc. as you have suggested I must? . . . It would have to be the right kind of person, and there's none in sight!! . . . But, madam! I protest again that 'mother's boy has in self-defense never loved anyone but himself.' He has, he does, love, really love many people." She replied, "Of course you must marry. Eleanor [Roosevelt] and I only wanted it postponed until you were rested. . . . Your dear heart is more than ever set on marriage but your head is already in unison with your drive for loving companionship. Fear not—you will find the mate you deserve."

Now he was making last-minute travel plans. Mr. and Mrs. Ives were going to England separately, and Stevenson told her he would arrive in London May 21 and that weekend would "go to stay with Lord and Lady Albemarle, thanks to Lady Barbara Jackson, in Suffolk. They would be delighted to have you and Ernest too I am sure." He was never hesitant about inviting not only himself but his relatives and friends to stay with people, including British aristocracy. He assumed they would be welcome, and they were, though assuming it showed considerable self-confidence, at the least. He invited Barbara Ward, too, who had sent him a speech draft for Oxford.

4.

He left Chicago on May 15 and flew to New York where he and Borden and John Fell dined with Mary Lasker and attended a musical comedy. (John Fell would spend the summer working on a steamship in the Pacific, an arrangement made by George Killion, Stevenson's friend in San Francisco, head of American President Lines. Borden wanted to go to Hawaii.) On to Paris, where he was met by a car from the American Embassy and one from George Ball's law firm. (Ball had helped arrange his Paris schedule.) After a talk with President Guy Mollet, Stevenson wrote in a notebook which he once more had started to carry with him, "Greeted me warmly & alone. . . . Tough and tired. Algeria—No one likes what's happening and no one—save communists—has really anything else to suggest. . . . Knows that if Algeria were free it wouldn't be long before the communists would take over. . . . Quoted Lenin's advice—don't preach communism in these countries, but nationalism. . . . Vide Indonesia. *Middle East*—More troubled by U.S. policy in M.E. than by Algeria or France's economic crisis. Did we have any policy? What was it? All he could see was support for kings & feudal systems etc., while Russia and the communists worked on the *people.*"

After dinner at the British Embassy he and a party went to the Lido—"my first Paris 'night life' in a long time and the best entertainment I ever saw! To bed 3 A.M.—Horrors!" He was pleased with French-German *rapprochement* and spectacular progress toward unification of Europe but disappointed with Algeria and France's financial difficulties. He found strong opposition to the withdrawal of American troops from Europe.

In Brussels on May 20 he saw Tempelsman, his client with diamond interests in South Africa, and government and business officials. He wrote to Borden and John Fell, "My only unusual experience so far was the long session with the little King in the Palace in Brussels and I found him a shy, sensitive and insecure and thoughtful lad who seemed more concerned that we see the condition of the native in the bush than the development of the cities in the Congo. His grandmother, old Queen Elizabeth, now going on ninety, sent for me and I went to see her in her little chateau in the country. She was a great hero of the First war period and I found her as beautiful and vivacious as I had expected. She weighs probably less than 100 lbs. but is still a musician, sculptress and painter of talent. We had tea alone and then she took me on to the terrace and insisted on taking photographs of me, although I am not sure that she got the camera focussed on the target. Finally I insisted on taking photographs of *her* too and we ended up with much merriment surrounded with Ladies and Gentlemen in Waiting. It was all very reminiscent of a royal era that is past." As his father had advised him so many years ago, he now advised his son Borden: "I hope Borden will have a chance to stop off and see some of my friends in San Francisco on his return from Hawaii. . . . It can't hurt and it might be useful in the future."

He went to London, attended a Britannica film showing, and on Friday, May 24, went to Oxford where he received a degree, Doctor of Civil Law, *honoris causa.* Barbara Ward—she, Blair, Mr. and Mrs. Ives, and Adlai III and Nancy accompanied Stevenson—described the event. "The celebrations began at 4 P.M. with a tea at the Vice-Chancellor's lodgings. I may say it was a day as bitterly cold as only an English May can produce. . . . The Vice-Chancellor, Mr. Masterman, is the archetype of the University Don—gentle, elderly, urbane, witty, a bachelor. He was already in academic dress, morning coat, Geneva bands and voluminous gown. . . . The Public Orator was also arrayed in white bands and robe and he circulated to the few guests the Governor's citation. . . . While we

struggled over the Latin, the Governor was tried out for length in his scar-
let academic gown and for (mental) breadth in his flat black velvet Tudor
bonnet. He looked like one of Henry VIII's rather less staid advisers."
Shortly before five they were driven to "a large covered amphitheatre."
The academic community sat on the floor of the hall facing the Vice
Chancellor's throne. Around him were high benches for invited guests.
Behind and above were the public galleries, "filled to overflowing"—all
tickets had been gone for weeks. They waited about ten minutes. "Then a
hush fell and we all rose to our feet for the Vice-Chancellor's procession.
This entered from a side door. Four macebearers came first, carrying
heavy golden maces, then two unidentified dons . . . in academic dress,
then the Vice-Chancellor looking remarkably shy. He raced through the
arena and with quite remarkable agility hoisted himself up to his steep
chair." He raised his mortarboard to the company; so did they. All sat and
waited. "There were confused sounds outside, a certain amount of cheering and, to the trained eye, the unmistakable flash of light-bulbs in the
grey afternoon light. The great doors at the end of the arena . . . opened
once and a cautious face looked in. Through the crack, we could see the
distant figure of the Governor, gorgeous in scarlet, standing beside the
Public Orator and surrounded by a bedlam of press photographers. . . .
The Proctors arose and marched back between the rows of faculty
members and once again we all got to our feet. The great doors swung
open, the Proctors righted about and stamped slowly back followed by the
Governor, looking pale and moved, and the Public Orator. There was absolute silence until the procession reached the open space before the
throne. There, in clear Latin, the Public Orator read out the citation, very
gracefully, savouring every phrase (and why not, for he wrote it) and then
the Governor advanced and climbed the excessively abrupt steps to the
throne. The Vice-Chancellor (I need hardly say) raised his mortarboard,
then grasped the Governor's hand and declared him a Doctor Honoris
causa." The Public Orator read, "I present to you, for the degree of Honorary Doctor of Civil Law, Adlai Stevenson, amid the strains and stresses
of national and international politics, the champion of humanism in word
and deed, and himself the source." "Thereafter a really very surprising
thing happened—for Oxford at least. The assembled audience raised the
roof. They clapped, they stamped, they banged the benches and the hurri-
cane went on for at least two minutes. Many of the dons were visibly
surprised—and as visibly delighted. I am told that all over the upper tier,
where the undergraduates were thickest, there appeared a rash of Stevenson buttons. The four conspicuous gentlemen perched in their pulpits almost fell to the arena in their excitement."

Stevenson then spoke for nearly an hour. It was, he thought, one of his
most important speeches, ranging over Anglo-American relations, postcolonial problems in the underdeveloped world, Russia, the bomb, the UN,
and the Middle East. It was graceful. He began by referring to himself as

an "unsuccessful politician" and to Oxford as "the mother of lost causes." He recalled having visited "timeless Oxford" when he was nineteen, a student at Princeton. "It was spring then, as it is now," he said. "The first war was over . . . that happy threshold of a new day of universal and perpetual peace. I felt that way then, so many years ago, and I feel that way now —that what unites us is far more important than what divides us." He spoke of his private concern—the problem of "mass communication and mass manipulation of the public mind." In America the people had not always been told the whole truth about American foreign relations. The Suez "misfortune" had given Russia a foothold in the Middle East and weakened the Western Alliance. Some Europeans seemed to regard the integration of Europe as less a way of strengthening the Western Alliance than of escaping from it. They seemed to regard it as a third force between America and Russia. This was "foolish." The Alliance must meet challenges united. The most important challenge was the question of how to preserve the individual in a world where everything was getting bigger. Two immediate political problems existed: a settlement with Russia in Eastern Europe, and Western relations with the free peoples and new nations of Asia and Africa. Colonialism was ended, at least the colonialism of the past. "While Britain has been liberating an empire voluntarily, the Soviet Union has been creating one involuntarily." He praised the way Britain had ended colonialism. The great task of establishing new and better relations with Asia and Africa now lay in devising "ways of restoring some of the props provided by the old order while avoiding any semblance of domination." Anglo-American cooperation was essential. Much aid probably should be channeled through the United Nations. The danger to peace lay not in direct attack but in the expansion of local conflict into general war. The United Nations should intervene in local breaches of the peace. America had to give up a dream of isolation. So did Great Britain—she no longer bore sole responsibility.

Barbara Ward wrote, "At the end, the ovation was as warm as at the start . . . and when the Governor left in procession with the Vice-Chancellor, a small army of students followed him." Mrs. Ives once said, "He loved it," that is, receiving the honorary degree, and Adlai III said, "He never missed a chance to wear those red Oxford robes."

Stevenson stayed in England another ten days, seeing clients, Britannica people, friends and politicians, in and out of office. The names on his schedule were impressive as usual—Geoffrey Crowther, Hugh Gaitskell, Harold Wilson, Tallulah Bankhead, Drew Middleton, Archibald MacLeish, General Bor, the Prime Minister and Lady Macmillan, Clement Davies, Lady Astor, Senator Benton, the Lord Chancellor Lord Kilmuir, Minister of Defense Duncan Sandys, the Duchess of Atholl, Hamish Hamilton, Lady Spears, Foreign Secretary Selwyn Lloyd, Madame Pandit, Ambassador Whitney.

From London he flew to Lisbon and on to Accra, Ghana, and an appointment with Prime Minister Nkrumah. He issued a statement at a press conference: "Whatever happens to Ghana must have a profound effect, for better or for worse, on the rest of Africa and, therefore, the whole world." Diversified economic development was essential. Conditions must be favorable for foreign investment. This meant an "attractive" tax policy and "an honest, stable, sensible government. . . . Any talk of nationalization or expropriation of existing foreign investments in Ghana will quickly frighten away further foreign investments. All these considerations apply decisively, I think, to foreign investment in the Volta project," a hydroelectric plant to supply energy for the development of bauxite in which his client, Reynolds Metals, was interested.

Subsequently he sent a progress report to Walter L. Rice of Reynolds Metals, a report that illustrates how, like many another lawyer-politician, he was using his political connections to benefit his clients and himself, though by no means improperly. He related how he and Blair had stayed with Nkrumah in his sixteenth-century Danish castle; how Sir Robert Jackson, Barbara Ward's husband, soon to become head of the Development Commission of Ghana, had made his appointments; how he had met with cabinet ministers, the acting Governor General, the American chargé d'affaires, leading bankers and businessmen. He wrote, "While the situation leaves much to be desired and isn't as good as I expected to find, due to the decline in cocoa prices and the rise in political foolishness, it is certainly still good enough and hopeful enough to warrant active promotion of the Volta project." Nkrumah had given an option to finance the Volta project to rival interests and seemed "a little sheepish" about it when Stevenson brought it up. Nkrumah professed to be "very irked" by all the "carpet-baggers" that had arrived since independence, but Stevenson suspected his African ministers were flattered. Stevenson also heard "plentiful rumours" about corruption. After the rival option expired and Jackson became head of the Development Commission, Stevenson thought, Nkrumah would feel freer to negotiate seriously about the Volta project. If an existing consortium was not ready to proceed by the first of the year, Ghana would hope to proceed with a larger group including Americans. Stevenson would follow those developments in New York in the fall, when Nkrumah would probably attend the General Assembly of the United Nations. In Belgium, Stevenson reported, he had seen "most of the leaders of the Government and also the King and the old Queen Mother."

Stevenson's plane landed at Dakar and the Governor General of French West Africa came to the airport to greet him and urged him to return on his way back to Europe after July 1. Stevenson said he had made Reynolds' interest in a huge aluminum project in French West Africa well known everywhere and asked Walter Rice to let him know whether he should proceed further. Rice replied that Reynolds was interested in all three projects—Volta, Belgian Congo, and French West Africa—wanted Stevenson to make Reynolds' interest known to Stevenson's unusually good connections, and wrote at length about the projects, which were, indeed, huge.

Stevenson also reported to the J. Henry Schroder Banking Corporation in New York, recounting his trip to Accra and estimating the prospects of development there. "I am afraid I was not very successful in getting any assurances about opening even token accounts with Schroder for the present. They have almost no transactions directly with America and cocoa for the foreseeable future will have to be handled thru London because of the marketing arrangements of the Cocoa Marketing Board." Ghana's balance of payments was a problem, and Stevenson had talked with officials about using foreign investment to produce local substitutes for imported goods. "One can see advantages in the proposed match and cement factories where local materials can be used, but even the soap factory which Unilever is starting doesn't really make too much sense and they are doing it largely to help the country where they have a large investment. . . . Also there are not much American goods evidently that can be imported and sold competitively except the old standbys—automobiles, refrigerators, air conditioning equipment, electrical appliances, machetes, etc. There is more and more competition from Germany and Japan. . . . All in all I can hardly say that I thought that the commercial prospects were very good unless the Volta project goes ahead."

Stevenson had entered the world of international finance and investment. It was a profitable world for one with his entree to men with power. Although he did use his political reputation to advance his clients' interests, more often than not he urged an enlightened view on his clients, as when he told Richard Reynolds he hoped foreign aluminum companies could make "a substantial contribution to political and economic stability" in Africa.

On Wednesday, June 5, Stevenson arrived in Johannesburg. He spent a week in South Africa, representing the Britannica and meeting with local businessmen and editors and politicians, including the Prime Minister. He received a stream of visitors and held press conferences. He sent a letter to Borden and John Fell, dating it "June 6, 1957 (Victory day in Calif. 1956!)" His traveling party increased—Adlai III and Nancy joined him, as did Marietta Tree and her husband and daughter, and Alicia Patterson. Adlai III said years later, "On this African trip, Dad brought both Marietta and Alicia. Marietta brought her husband. Dad really loved Marietta. As he grew older, she made him feel younger."

In South Africa, Adlai III remembers, "From early morning till late at night there were meetings with United States and local government officials and newspapermen. Negro leaders were slipping in the back door. Then we went sightseeing with him with the emphasis on markets and ruins, seeing how the people lived, which he loved." Leaving Johannesburg for ten days of travel through the Rhodesias and Belgian Congo, Stevenson held a press conference and opened it saying, "Honesty compels me to say again that the policy of total racial separation does not seem to me either practical or realistic in a modern industrial state where the European and non-European are interdependent. . . . But I do not question the good faith of the authorities, nor their concern for the well-being of the natives." He said his visit had been "very successful"—he had had some "very satisfactory" talks with business leaders and had been "delighted" to find the Department of Education using Britannica films in schools to help overcome the teacher shortage.

The Stevenson party's travels in the Congo were arranged by the Belgian government. Emerging at length at Leopoldville, Stevenson on June 21 wrote to Mr. and Mrs. Ives, "I think we have seen every kind of indigene, pygmy and giant, and every kind of scenery, jungle, savannah, mountain and marsh, that the world offers. . . . South Africa was beautiful and depressing, more so even than before." He added, "I am afraid [you and I] are getting awfully old but I seem to have a good time and keep interested all the same. I pray that you do likewise and if I did not succeed in telling you how much it meant to have you in England with me, let me do so now! . . . Much love." He told Geoffrey Crowther, "As everywhere in Africa, the race problem is uppermost in [the Belgians'] minds and their efforts to meet and to mold the growing race consciousness is impressive indeed. But few of the thoughtful ones think they can hold out indefinitely. So the question is rather whether they can guide the evolution to independence and some sort of African rule which will preserve order, responsibility, and their investments." "Guidance" failed, and a few years later Stevenson was obliged to try to deal with the bloody result as U. S. Ambassador to the UN.

From Brazzaville they went to Lambaréné to see Dr. Schweitzer, a long-planned visit. Schweitzer's hospital was dirty as well as noisy, and others in Stevenson's party depreciated Schweitzer, but Stevenson defended him. Talking with Schweitzer, Stevenson squashed a mosquito on Schweitzer's shirt, and Schweitzer reproved him—life, any life, was to be revered.

Stevenson made notes of his conversation with Schweitzer:

1st—Must stop nuclear testing. (Story of his radiologist who had two monster children).

2nd—*Then talk about danger of wastes from atomic reactors:* explosion; radioactive cooling water, disposal of wastes. Teller knows all about it! . . .

If eliminate uranium & just use Hydrogen—could tell Arabs to drink their oil!

In addition to his notebook, Stevenson dutifully filled twelve half sheets of paper with notes on what Schweitzer said to him about theology and philosophy, the meaning of life, the "benevolent and enlightened despotism" which Schweitzer practiced, the hydrogen bomb and renunciation of war, his own experiences, and a definition of culture and the politics of the cold war.

Stevenson returned to Leopoldville to confer on behalf of Reynolds with Belgian Congo officials and chartered a plane and flew over the INGA hydroelectric site. He issued a statement to the press saying that Schweitzer was "gratified" by the world's reception of Stevenson's declaration on the dangers of testing atomic devices, that he considered this the "most dangerous" period in history, that he was "much pleased" by a recent anti-testing petition signed by 2,000 American scientists, and that he felt public opinion, led by scientists, would soon influence governments.

Stevenson visited Lagos, Nigeria, in a downpour, stopped briefly in Liberia, and went to Lake Como, where he stayed at the Francis T. P. Plimptons' Villa Balbianello, an area he had visited as a child. From Como, Stevenson traveled to Austria and Germany, spent an evening with Chancellor Konrad Adenauer, went back to Paris for meetings with Reynolds people.

Senator John F. Kennedy made his famous speech criticizing U.S. support for France against the Algerian rebels and said Algeria was no longer a problem for France alone. J. J. Servan-Schreiber, editor of the Paris *L'Exprès*, carried the full text of the speech. Arthur Schlesinger happened to be in Paris and brought Stevenson and Servan-Schreiber together. (They had met briefly while Stevenson was Governor.) The meeting was "a flop," Schlesinger recalled later. "Stevenson thought that Kennedy's speech was terrible and defended the policy of the French government at the time. Servan-Schreiber asked me later, 'Why do you Americans think [Stevenson is] so good? He's conventional.' Stevenson took the establishment view of the French-Algerian question, Kennedy did not." Upon leaving Paris, Stevenson issued a statement: "I think there has been enough preaching to the French. Algeria is a French problem."

He returned to New York on August 6 and issued a statement at the Savoy Plaza summing up his observations of Europe and Africa. On Europe, he said that the Marshall Plan had produced "a bursting energy, progress, and hope unequaled in a hundred years," the new Franco-German friendship was ending old hostility, and there was a growing sense of unity heretofore unheard of—it had "put Communism on the defensive." At the same time, German recovery had created fears among her small neighbors, Algeria was "a running sore" bleeding France, inflation was "a growing menace" throughout Europe, "Russian imperialism still extends to the Elbe," and rich European countries, "notably" Germany, were not sharing in help to underdeveloped nations. On Africa, realistic Frenchmen would advance proposals to meet "the aspirations of the Moslem population" in Algeria but outright independence now would invite more bloodshed and chaos. South African apartheid "does not seem to me either practical or realistic." In Central Africa nationalism and race consciousness were apparent. What should the United States do? "Declare a six months' moratorium on self-righteous moralizing and preaching. . . . Convince Europe that we know what we are doing; that we believe in the Alliance; that we are permanently committed to Europe's lasting security." Finally, we should "pursue a sustained, consistent policy of constructive foreign aid and investment—not just military aid—to insure that the underdeveloped countries can develop." He reiterated his proposal to stop nuclear testing and production. He supported the important Negro voting bill, then pending, with reservations. He criticized an Eisenhower appointment and Eisenhower's failure to support federal aid to education.

5.

Stevenson returned to Chicago late on Sunday, August 11. He sent a long report to Richard Reynolds. At the same time he kept in touch with Lyndon Johnson, J. W. Fulbright, Herbert Lehman, and Walter Reuther. He took Borden to Desbarats, first having a long talk with him which he described to Mrs. Ives as "the best . . . I've ever had." Borden had been seeing a psychoanalyst in Cambridge. He had met a man in Boston who had given away a fortune and was studying to become a Trappist monk and was "the happiest man I ever knew." Borden talked about doing welfare work in Boston or working part time at Harvard. "I'm baffled but delighted!" Stevenson wrote.

On August 28, President Eisenhower announced that the United States, in concert with the United Kingdom, Canada, and France, would propose at the UN Disarmament Subcommittee meeting in London a two-year suspension of nuclear weapons tests. Stevenson, at Newt Minow's suggestion, sent a letter to Eisenhower expressing his "warm approval" of the statement. Eisenhower thanked him courteously.

6.

The law firm's time sheets show that, in September and October of 1957, Stevenson put in 127¼ hours on law business, about sixteen hours a week, less than half time. In November he put in 26 hours, or between five and six hours a week. In December he put in 166¾ hours, or about thirty-eight hours a week—full-time work.

On September 8 he appeared on the CBS News television interview broadcast, "Face the Nation." John Steele asked what he thought about Governor Orval Faubus "flouting" a federal court's school desegregation order by using the Arkansas National Guard to prevent Negro children from attending a Little Rock high school. Stevenson said he was "both distressed and surprised" by what "my friend Governor Faubus" had done. At that time Faubus was an archvillain to Northern liberals, and

Stevenson's calling him friend made them wince. What would he do if he were President? "I don't suppose at this point the President has much that he can do." Asked if he would advocate the use of force to implement the Court's desegregation order, he said, "No, I would not." Not under any conditions? "I think this would be a lamentable state of affairs. . . . We are making progress. . . . I congratulate the President on saying that he would see that the Constitution was complied with, and use all of the agencies at his command. . . . I only wish he had made his position emphatically clear long before." He also congratulated Eisenhower on his espousal of a cessation of H-bomb tests. Asked if he regarded himself as the titular head of the Democratic Party, he replied, "No, sir, I do not." But he would not say who was.

Asked what the issues would be in the 1958 congressional elections, he mentioned foreign policy first and expanded: "I think we have to begin to realize . . . internationally . . . as we have come to realize nationally, that great wealth and great poverty can't exist safely side by side indefinitely. And we have in this world, especially among the newer nations and the underdeveloped nations, many areas of great want, great want and great misery; that the two great revolutions that are sweeping the world is revolution against want and against poverty, and the revolution against foreign domination." He said we had not yet faced up fully to the necessity of meeting the demand for economic development. "I think we ought to think about, in terms of an international development authority, in which the 'have' nations and the 'have not' nations, the contributors and the receivers, would sit down together, some would contribute and jointly they would allocate, very much as we did under the Marshall Plan." Asked if he thought "we have done enough . . . toward pushing for political liberation," he replied, "Yes. I am not too eager, as perhaps you know, too eager about premature independence. I think you have got to learn to walk before you can run." Asked if he would support Senator Kennedy's proposal to ask the UN to solve the Algerian question, Stevenson said he did not think so. Did he intend to enter the 1958 congressional campaign? "I certainly would want to be of any help as a soldier in the ranks." Peter Lisagor quoted a Chicago paper as saying that some of Stevenson's avid Chicago followers were "plotting" to get him to run again for President. Stevenson said, "I am not in on that plot, and let me tell you something, Mr. Lisagor: I am not a candidate, I will not be a candidate, and I don't want the nomination. And what is more, I'm not going to get it." Richard C. Hottelet asked, "Who do you think at this moment would be the strongest Democratic candidate?" Stevenson replied, "Oh, come now, Mr. Hottelet."

The Little Rock situation worsened, and after a fruitless meeting with Governor Faubus, President Eisenhower sent federal troops to Little Rock to maintain order and enforce the Court's desegregation order. That same day Stevenson issued a statement: "At this point the President had no choice. . . . But this is only a temporary solution. We have suffered a national disaster and I hope the President will now mobilize the nation's conscience as he has mobilized its arms."

On September 26, Stevenson—somewhat reluctantly, because of Little Rock—headed South for a long-standing date to speak on education at the University of North Carolina, adding a political-educational visit to Atlanta on behalf of Britannica Films and a visit to Winston-Salem to confer with Richard Reynolds.

President Eisenhower, through his aide, Sherman Adams, asked Stevenson to become a member of the presidential Commission on Civil Rights. Dean Acheson and Tom Finletter advised him to decline; Schlesinger thought it Stevenson's "inescapable challenge and duty" to accept. His other advisers were similarly divided. He declined.

The Soviet Union on October 4 launched into orbit the first man-made earth satellite, Sputnik I. Stevenson said the launching confirmed that the Soviet Union was "ahead of us in some of the most important areas of scientific development. I hope our government will not be content with further misleading reassurances."

7.

Toward the end of October, Stevenson received what he termed "a plaintive plea" from Secretary Dulles to go to Washington for six weeks or so to "work up some means of restoring confidence before the NATO meeting in Paris in December," as Stevenson put it in a letter to Mrs. Ives. Dulles wanted Stevenson's help in working out a political program for NATO and in tightening lines among the allies. Eisenhower might go to the NATO meetings.

Stevenson went in secret to Washington October 30. That evening he talked at length with Dulles, who said Stevenson's collaboration would symbolize national unity. He gave him two tentative working papers. One of the papers set forth his status and duties. He would be designated Special Assistant to the President, would receive political guidance from Secretary Dulles, would have an office in the State Department, would have a staff from State and Defense and the Atomic Energy Commission, and would be expected to devote most of his time for the rest of the year to the job. The job was to develop the U.S. position on points covered in a recent Eisenhower-Macmillan communiqué; to coordinate this position with the U.K., France, Germany, and Italy; to promote support for the U.S. position; and to participate in presenting the position to the North Atlantic Council in December. He would have to do "missionary work" within the government as well as before the country at large. He would devise means of assuring our NATO allies that our nuclear capability would actually be used to defend them. (Stevenson wrote in the margin beside this last:

"Can't be done by this Adm! Asking me to say you can trust Ike! Deeds not words and machinery.")

Stevenson had misgivings about the assignment from the beginning. He consulted Tom Finletter, Lloyd Garrison, George Ball, and others and over the weekend reached a decision. He told Dulles he had "reluctantly" concluded that the problems were so many and so complex that he could not do the work in time for the NATO meeting, let alone in time for the President's meeting with congressional leaders on December 1, and, furthermore, policy formulation was the responsibility of the President and Dulles and no one else could or should undertake it, especially not an opposition leader. "But," he wrote, "I do not want to leave it there. I would be glad to review and discuss your proposals from time to time before they are put into final form. And where we are in agreement, I will do such 'missionary' work as I can," even making a trip to Europe to consult the allies in advance as a "special envoy of the President" if necessary. On that same day he telephoned Dulles and conveyed the sense of the letter. On the telephone Dulles was agreeable, said he thought Stevenson might be right.

On November 7, Stevenson sent Dulles a memorandum containing his preliminary thoughts about NATO and U.S. defense policy and a letter which suggested that President Eisenhower "make some little announcement about calling me in for consultation because of my experience as well as my politics."

Word of his NATO involvement began to leak in the press and, after two unsatisfactory telephone conversations, one with Dulles and one with James Hagerty, President Eisenhower's press secretary, Stevenson on November 12 issued a statement saying he had declined Dulles' invitation to "formulate the President's policies," had agreed to "review and discuss our government's proposals before they were put into final shape," and had agreed to support them if he could and to do "missionary" work for them here and abroad.

Stevenson on November 13 drafted a letter to Dulles saying he was "quite dissatisfied" with developments—he had assumed that when Dulles reached a conclusion about Stevenson's collaboration the President would announce it, "at least expressing his gratification." Instead, Hagerty had made a misleading statement and then had had to correct it. Stevenson requested no further statements be issued without advance consultation with him. He did not send the letter but conveyed most of its content to Dulles by telephone.

Now and in ensuing weeks Stevenson accumulated memoranda, position papers, and notes of conversations with advisers on NATO. They were wide ranging and included Dean Rusk's views on China.

Stevenson went to Washington to see Dulles, and there on November 17 issued a statement about the Russian satellites: "Sputnik has awakened us. I am glad it has. But simply a greater effort in scientific research and missile development is not a sufficient response. . . . We must rebuild mutual confidence between the United States and our allies. . . . More likely than the unlimited nuclear-missile war is limited Communist aggression, as in Greece, Korea, Indochina, and Malaya." That same Sunday night, November 17, he sent a letter to President Eisenhower. Eisenhower had written to him in New York saying, "I am delighted that you and Foster will be getting together on Monday. . . . I share his view that you can be of real help to us in this work. I regret that on Monday I shall be absent from Washington . . . but I am sure that later there will be opportunity for conferences at which we can both be present." Stevenson now thanked him and said that, "while I must be free to seek advice in my informal consultative capacity from persons outside the Department, including leaders of my party, and also to express my views, even where they may differ from the administration, I shall strive to promote national unity in furtherance of the great tasks before us."

Stevenson met with Dulles on Monday, November 18. Next day at his press conference Dulles was asked about Stevenson's role. He referred the questioner to Stevenson's own statement issued in New York. Asked why he had chosen Stevenson, he said, "Well, we picked him because he was the titular head of the Democratic Party, and, in addition, has had a considerable amount of international experience." Would Stevenson go to Paris? "I don't know about that." Stevenson was sworn in as a consultant on November 20. He asked Garrison to separate him from the law firm in order to guard against any conflict of interest. That same day Dulles flew to Chicago to speak to the Council on Foreign Relations, and Stevenson accompanied him.

On November 25 he went to Washington to take up his work on NATO. He stayed there, except for two trips to New York, until December 12, just before Eisenhower left for Paris. Thus his service to the government lasted two and a half weeks. He took Bill Blair and Carol Evans with him. He lived in the elegant home of Florence Mahoney, a close friend of Mary Lasker, and he had an office on the sixth floor of the State Department. He had the choice of being paid $48 per day plus travel expenses or $12 per day (considered "without compensation") plus travel expenses; he chose the latter. For help Stevenson drew upon his friends and advisers from the presidential campaigns. He met with them on a tight schedule in Washington and New York—George Ball, Tom Finletter, Paul Nitze, Arthur Schlesinger, Lyndon Johnson, Jerome Wiesner, Oscar Chapman, Sam Rayburn, Chester Bowles, Walt Rostow, Scoop Jackson, Dean Rusk (but not Dean Acheson). His notes on his talk with Johnson contain this line, "Don't trust Dulles," and, with Rayburn, "They got in mess—get out! But we're Americans." Many of them contributed long memoranda on NATO's problems. He went to dinner parties and receptions and meetings in Washington and New York, functions attended by some of the most influential people in America, politicians, journalists, broadcasters, publishers. There was in the air a feeling that at last he was about to take his rightful place in guiding America. Agnes Meyer wrote to him, "Adlai, my hero, your moment has come. Seize it with that great heart & mind of yours. The future of our country is in your hands."

Others saw it differently. A huge amount of work—much of it by others —went into what he did, but the results were insufficient to justify the labor. George Ball once recalled, "He asked me to drop my law practice to help him. Dulles said I wasn't cleared," that is, did not have security clearance. "Stevenson wanted me with him but I couldn't come into the State Department building. He'd steal the papers and we'd work on them at Georgetown, at Florence Mahoney's house. Then a messenger would bring them back. It was a typical Stevenson operation—all balled up." Schlesinger and Finletter—a tough-minded man—had thought it a mistake to undertake the assignment. Stevenson was gloomy from the beginning. Before he even went to Washington, he told Mrs. Ives, "I shall do the best I can with this miserable assignment. . . . It is a melancholy job, surrounded by people who mean me no good." In letters to Senator Fulbright, Ben Swig, and others he referred to his "melancholy task." He was not, really, a NATO man. Ball recalled, "I thought the central issue that the United States had to face up to was France on the nuclear issue. He was not at all interested. His great interest was in the new countries," that is, the underdeveloped world. "I thought the stuff he wrote was half baked, dilettante. That was the end of it. It was disappointing."

During his stay, Stevenson met with Secretary Dulles and his colleagues several times, but he spent less time in the Department than out of it. Twice he went to New York, once to make a speech and once to confer with the Field Foundation and the Reynolds Metals people, and often he met privately with Walter Lippmann, Marquis Childs, Eric Sevareid, John Steele, Scotty Reston, Clifton Daniel, John Oakes, William Shannon, and Cyrus Sulzberger. He went to a variety of parties.

On his first day in Washington he had lunch with a Dulles aide to discuss Stevenson's "missionary work" among Democratic congressional leaders and at 2 P.M. with Dulles and discussed Dulles' weekend visits with the German Foreign Minister, the difficulty in persuading the Joint Chiefs of Staff to trust the European allies, and the possibility of Stevenson's writing "some paragraphs for the President's speech for the summit meeting communiqué." Stevenson received Department position papers on scientific and technical cooperation, weapons development, and economic cooperation and attended a meeting of a task force of scientists and administration men to discuss them. He had been scheduled to meet with President Eisenhower next day but received a note from Dulles informing him that the President was ill.

Late that first night Stevenson met with George Ball, Bill Blair, and others. Notes taken at the meeting show him rattled, distracted, unsure of himself. Ball recommended that he give Dulles a memorandum for the record saying he lacked sufficient time to bring forward "definitive ideas" and warning against going to the NATO meetings without careful work with Congress. After further conversation, Stevenson said, "I don't know what all this adds up to, as to what *I* do." Finletter had submitted a long, thoughtful, orderly paper on NATO problems, taking up such questions as the placing of missiles in Europe, but Stevenson had not yet read it. Stevenson reported on his day at the Department and said he "didn't have any intelligent question he could ask during the whole meeting." He said, "Most of it is over my head; I can't quarrel with it too much." He rambled over what Dulles had said, seeming troubled. He telephoned Finletter in New York. Finletter was reluctant to come to Washington. Stevenson wanted "two, three or four points" he could "try to get over" to Eisenhower. He wanted to emphasize that "elimination of nuclear weapons should be objective No. 1." He described the task force meeting to Finletter and said a revised paper would be ready tomorrow noon; he suggested Finletter come to Washington and go over it. If he did not, Stevenson probably would "go ahead and approve the whole thing because I don't know any better," the preliminary papers were intricate and related to many things Stevenson was ignorant of. Perhaps Finletter could come down and read the paper in the afternoon and offer comments, which Stevenson could transmit to Dulles the next day. Finletter could read the paper almost anywhere "so long as it gets back to the department to be shut up for the night." Finletter finally agreed to come.

Stevenson was still worrying about his own role and wanted to issue a public statement along these lines: "I am constantly asked about the political implications of my temporary service to the President and Secretary of State in preparation for the NATO meeting. I also hear that there is some resentment among my friends about the way I have been greeted by the Administration. I wish to say that I am not interested in ceremonials, titles, or manners. I came to Washington not for fun or fanfare but to help out—to lend what experience, influence, and confidence I have to my country in a critical hour. I have had a cordial welcome. . . . No limitations on my freedom of speech have been imposed or even suggested. Likewise, I do not want to interfere with anyone's freedom to criticize. I do not speak for the Democratic Party, but for myself alone. . . . I will not participate in purely party activities until my service is terminated. The salary provided by law in my case I intend to give to charity. And now I want to get to work." Blair held the statement up—he thought it "gratuitous." Stevenson drafted two more.

That Thursday was Thanksgiving Day, and Stevenson told Jane Dick, "How I wish I were sharing the festivities on Woodland Road," where she lived. At the end of that first week in Washington, and with a good deal of help from his advisers, on November 29 he prepared for Dulles an interim report of his reactions to the Department's staff papers on NATO. "The paper work I have seen seems to be good and with much of it I agree," he began, and then criticized the papers heavily. A heads-of-state meeting on December 16 seemed to him too early for proper preparation and congressional concurrence. He was "troubled by the lack of a sense of urgency"— he had seen urgent motivation in Washington in 1933 and 1941 but not now. The political differences among the NATO states "are dangerously enfeebling." Our allies wanted political, not mere military, assurances.

He doubted that aggression in Europe could be met with tactical nuclear weapons without precipitating general war. Outside the NATO theater he saw "an even greater need for a conventional force availability, including airlift, to cope with small wars and keep them small." He found the paper on economic assistance inadequate and criticized it in detail. The United States should lead the "capital countries" in accelerating the development of underdeveloped areas. Finally, the disarmament papers did not do justice to the subject "or the opportunity."

Dulles responded immediately. He was glad that he and Stevenson were "in substantial agreement" about "the specifics" of the coming NATO meeting. Some of Stevenson's points, he said, "go beyond" the present task. As to the timing of the meeting, nothing could be done about it. Stevenson probably had noted more urgency in 1933 and 1941 than now because "the circumstances are different." As to political consultation with our allies, "we have more of this than, perhaps, many appreciate." The question of nuclear versus conventional weapons, and general versus limited war, would not come up at the December meeting. As to economic development, more precise figures were needed. "I am very responsive to your paragraphs . . . on Trade Policy and NATO's Larger Meaning."

On December 2 an Associated Press writer reported that Stevenson would not go to Paris, had not been asked, and thought his work with Dulles would be ended by then; his refusal to go to Paris had led to speculation that he had found the Administration's proposals "wanting." Other newspaper stories appeared about the same time, the result of Stevenson's private meetings with reporters. They said he thought the Paris meeting "must transcend the current obsession of both Washington and London with missiles, rockets and weapons systems." The *New Republic* thought Dulles wanted to use Stevenson's reputation to rebuild his own in Europe.

Stevenson seemed more concerned with his political and public position than with substance. When newspaper stories inspired by his secret meetings with journalists began to appear, he professed dismay—on December 3 sent a note to Secretary Dulles: "The inquiries from the press about the Paris meeting and the confusion appear to be endless," and proposed to issue a "little statement" if Dulles approved. The statement said he expected to complete his consultations, which he had undertaken "as a patriotic duty," in about a week. He would not attend the Paris meeting—"I would be without authority and necessarily identified with decisions I might not always agree with and could not publicly oppose. . . . [But] I do not wish to leave the impression of disagreement with our proposed positions at the meeting. On the contrary, I agree with most of them."

That day Stevenson met with Eisenhower and attended his briefing of the congressional leaders. He thanked the President and explained his own statement to the press, saying "Foster" had approved it. Eisenhower thanked him in turn. Dulles issued a press statement of his own: "I regret that Governor Stevenson does not feel that he can appropriately attend the NATO meeting in Paris. President Eisenhower has asked me to express on his behalf, and also I express on my own behalf, our appreciation of Governor Stevenson's contribution."

The whole undertaking was turning into an exercise in public relations, not a substantive collaboration. On December 5, Reston reported in the New York *Times* that Stevenson had "urged the Administration to enlist the cooperation of other North Atlantic Treaty Powers in a new effort to negotiate a general political settlement in the Middle East." Stevenson quickly wrote to Dulles, denying he had made any such "formal proposals to anyone. . . . I am advising Reston that he is misinformed. . . . I cannot apologize for what I have done because I didn't do it, but I feel very badly about it and want you to know it. Let me add that his long recital about what happened at the White House briefing that I attended also must have come from other sources." The fact is that Stevenson had seen Reston and Clifton Daniel late at night on the day he had attended the White House briefing. He had seen Israeli Ambassador Eban that afternoon. Before Stevenson's work ended, Dulles must have felt him a prickly person to deal with.

On the other hand, as John Steele of *Time* reported, "Adlai would be less than human if he was not somewhat annoyed at the extremely backhanded treatment he has received from the White House. Remember Hagerty's original blooper in saying that Stevenson had turned down the Administration request for help; Hagerty's repeated flat 'no' to reporters' questions on whether Adlai would go to NATO; the [Sherman] Adams crack in Chicago that Stevenson was called in because the nation wanted bipartisanship, but that he doubted the services of Democrats would be worth much . . . the secret and unannounced swearing in of Adlai at the State Department." Nonetheless, Steele reported, Stevenson had been pleased by the smooth working relationship he had developed with Dulles. Steele thought Stevenson was pleased at his relationships with the Department but not with the White House.

On December 5, Stevenson met with leading newspaper correspondents at John Steele's house. He told the reporters he had declined an invitation by Eisenhower to go to Paris because he did not believe the Administration genuinely wanted him there, because the President's invitation was casual, because he doubted there would be a real job for him there, because he believed that America's narrowly military objectives would foreclose any broadening of NATO's work into the political and economic fields, because to go would be to sacrifice a part of his position as an opposition critic.

On December 6, Stevenson gave Dulles a critique of the draft of President Eisenhower's opening statement at NATO: he liked parts of it, did not like others, especially those declaring "our total reliance on nuclear defenses," as Stevenson put it. "I wish the President in this speech could loudly declare that he thinks NATO has a larger purpose than defense; that its purpose is peace and progress; that as free nations have gathered together to protect themselves they should also mobilize their resources and skills to help the less fortunate in the human family to advance; that in this shrinking world, as in our communities, the rich must help the poor; and that this is a higher, better goal for NATO than the accumulation of nuclear weapons, however necessary."

On December 12, Stevenson wound up his work and went back to Chicago. The next day, while Eisenhower was preparing to leave for Paris, he dined with the Edison Dicks at Jacques Restaurant and went to the December Ball. Earlier he had penciled on his calendar, *Leave for NATO.*

8.

Stevenson spent the rest of the year on familiar rounds—speaking to the American Civil Liberties Union in Chicago, attending law firm annual parties and the wedding of the daughter of an old friend, attending holiday parties and supper dances given by Lake Forest and Gold Coast friends from long ago at the familiar Chicago clubs, corresponding with Reynolds Metals about their West Africa interests (he agreed to accept $35,000 a year from Reynolds), and spending Christmas in Louisville with the Warwick Andersons—he told Mrs. Ives, "Our Christmas Day in Louisville was an ordeal by tissue paper—but very loving and gay." Stevenson often passed on Christmas gifts he received. Once he gave the Minows a gift from Henry Crown, the Chicago industrialist, identical to the one they themselves received from Crown.

9.

Stevenson's life in the first half of 1958 was relatively uneventful. He was busy practicing law on behalf of the Britannica and Britannica Films, the Field Foundation, Reynolds Metals, the Illinois Bell Telephone Company, and other clients. He traveled often—to New York and Washington and Cambridge, to Ruth Field's Chelsea plantation, to Princeton, to Dallas to confer with a prospective oil company client, to Bloomington for a *Pantagraph* meeting, to Florida for a speech, to Albany, New York, to argue a case before the Court of Appeals. He spent more time at Britannica Board. meetings than at DAC meetings. He made tentative plans to go to "the Black River" with Alicia Patterson but canceled them.

He wrote letters of recommendation to colleges for Marietta's daughter, Frankie FitzGerald, and Alicia's niece, Alice Albright. He saw Agnes Meyer and wrote to her often, sometimes urging her to lobby on behalf of a bill which would promote the use of Britannica's educational films. Barbara Ward, a faithful correspondent whose letters contained useful material on economic development and foreign affairs, came to Cambridge, and Stevenson, there to celebrate his birthday with Borden and John Fell, went to dinner with her at President Pusey's. In New York on various trips, he dined with Mrs. Roosevelt, with Roger Stevens (for whom he was doing some legal work), with the Cass Canfields, with Barbara Ward, with Mary Lasker. In Chicago he gave a dinner at the Casino Club for the John Gunthers, lunched with Dick Daley at the Chicago Club, entertained Mrs. Roosevelt, occasionally saw old friends from Illinois politics. His old law partner, Sidley, died on April 28. The Sidley firm invited Adlai III to join it but he decided to join Mayer, Friedlich, Spiess, Tierney, Brown & Platt (after a year as a clerk to Justice Schaefer of the Illinois Supreme Court). He intended to go into politics. Stevenson advised him to make some money at the law first, then enter politics at the top, as he had, running for Senator or Governor. Instead, Adlai III started at the bottom, working in another campaign and running first in 1964 for the state legislature at the age of thirty-four. Ellen Stevenson closed her 1020 Club and Art Center. It was at this time, young Adlai later said, that he first became concerned about her ability to manage her financial affairs.

Stevenson made a half dozen speeches that winter and spring. On February 22 at a Democratic dinner honoring Harry Truman he praised Truman's candor in office, his "telling the American people the truth about their condition. For politics is essentially an educational process." After the speech Stevenson wrote to Marietta Tree: "Last night's 'Truman dinner' was a sell out. . . . 'Truth' was my text and it worked very well, I think. . . . [Truman] was extremely cordial with me, and Bess even more so. I sat next to Lyndon who complained incessantly about Butler, NDC, DAC, his health, his trials etc. etc. . . . Last night—after the dinner—I stopped to see C. K. McClatchy and fiancee at their very gala dance, but eschewed the Phil Sterns and ten other fiestas and crept off to bed like a good boy, or was it an old man."

He drew on Barbara Ward's material when he spoke to the President's Conference on Foreign Aid: "I don't think this meeting should ever have been held; I don't think it should have been necessary to stir up public support and pressure on Congress to support foreign economic aid which is just as imperative, in my judgment more so, than the defense appropriations that are voted so easily. . . . Does anyone really think that the

Soviet Union . . . would deliberately launch a direct attack against this country? . . . But does anyone doubt that Communist political-economic-psychological probing and penetration will go on and on all around the world?" He spoke again on March 27 to the National Conference of Organizations on International Trade Policy, a speech that began, "Sixty-five years ago this month, my grandfather was inaugurated Vice President with Grover Cleveland, after a campaign in which he incessantly preached the virtues of free trade and the evils of excessive protection." Under Barbara Ward's influence, he was preoccupied at this time with trade and economic development, interests which linked his political views to his law practice and his travels.

On March 30, on a Sunday network television interview program, he repeated he would not be a candidate in 1960 and said he could "hardly conceive" of another draft. Asked if he still "recoiled" at the prospect of having Nixon for President, he said he did. Asked how it felt to be a twice-defeated candidate—"can anything ever really seem the same again," he replied, "Oh yes. Well, it's not the—you couldn't go on living at the emotional level of a political campaign all of your life. I'm sure there's no human being could withstand that trauma, but what happens, if I can reflect for a moment over these years—at least what has happened in my case, is that I've had limitless opportunities to go on expressing views from time to time, too often, I suspect, on public issues; I've had wonderful, exhilarating and exciting, enlightening adventures. I've traveled all around; I've come to know all of the leaders of my time on earth, or most of them. I've had the privilege of participating in some important national decisions, in intervening in congressional campaigns, in national policy formulation. . . . In addition to this I have also been extremely involved in an active and busy law practice. I've had more time for my children. I've had the opportunity to travel, to see, to think, and to read a little. On the whole I've found it both busy and agreeable. What I do lose is any privacy."

Agnes Meyer reported that Roscoe Drummond, a columnist, predicted Stevenson would be nominated in 1960 and that Al Friendly, managing editor of the Washington *Post,* thought that "you're going to hear a lot more of that." She also told him that remarriage would not only hurt him politically but emotionally because of his "emotionally promiscuous nature . . . you get an enormous amount of warmth and stimulus from the numerous adoring females, Barbara [Ward], Jane Dick, Gay Finletter, the beautiful movey actress whose name escapes me momentarily, even myself and numerous others, that you would lose if you were tied up to one female." A little later she reported that Harry Truman had told her privately he agreed with her that Jack Kennedy should not be nominated in 1960 because "the country was not ready for a Catholic President." She had urged on him the view that Stevenson was the strongest Democrat.

On June 15, Stevenson again left for Europe.

10.

During his 1953 world tour he had deliberately skirted the rims of the two great Communist powers, China and Russia. Now he would go to the heart: to Russia. He would be gone all summer. He would combine business with sightseeing, and from the sightseeing would come a series of syndicated newspaper articles on Russia (later published as a book, *Friends and Enemies*).[5] He declined an invitation from Mikhail A. Menshikov, Soviet Ambassador to the United States, to travel as an official guest of the Soviet Union. He told Menshikov he hoped to discuss with Soviet officials in Moscow the matter of royalties to American authors whose works were published in the Soviet Union. He also told him whom he hoped to see in Moscow and where he hoped to go in Asia.

His entourage was large. In addition to himself, his two sons, Blair, and the interpreter Tucker, he was accompanied on parts of the trip by Alicia Patterson and her niece, Alice Albright; Ruth Field and her daughter Fiona; Jane Dick and her husband. His plans to take them to Russia, together with a conversation he had with Agnes Meyer, provoked an angry letter from Mrs. Meyer. She wrote to him on May 1, "Before I sign off completely and forever—for I am now forced to do after the cold, impatient tone in which you informed me that I should stop running you for the Presidency—I want to end our long conversation with a valedictory. . . . I resent your stern command to break off my efforts, because you are running as hard as you can, both consciously & unconsciously. . . . Your orders to me to desist are typical of your ambivalence between ambition and your damnable irresolution. You messed up both previous nominations by exposing this inner conflict to the whole electorate. Now you are repeating the old pattern. I am not implying that you should tell me the blatant truth 'Yes, by God, I want it as much as ever.' But the hypocrisy of saying to a trusted friend 'Stop running me' is sheer callousness . . . . It proved to me that all my efforts to bring about your acceptance of your great, latent capacities and your full sensitivities have been in vain." She criticized him for taking several rich women with him to Russia. A little later she told Carol Evans, "I cannot understand . . . how the girls get along so well with each other—it sounds like a Mormon household and as for Bill Blair,

[5] His trip cost $23,089 and he received $67,523 in fees, including $16,023 from the North American Newspaper Alliance, $50,000 from Tempelsman (the firm's annual retainer), and $9,000 from a foundation. The Britannica paid his plane fare, $873. He charged $139 to Reynolds Metals and $439 to the American-Scandinavian Foundation. John Fell and Borden went along, and John Fell took photographs to illustrate Stevenson's writings. Stevenson paid his interpreter, Bob Tucker, $2,250 in salary and expenses of about $1,051.

I should think that he'd be driven crazy." A few days before leaving, Stevenson asked Marietta Tree or her husband to arrange for him and his companions to stay with friends of theirs in the English countryside.

He spent ten days in London seeing friends and famous persons, transacting legal business, and going to the theater. He stayed at Claridge's. He had dinner with Lady Spears and her husband and Max Beaverbrook ("thank God I don't have to court his favor!" he noted in his diary) and with Conservative leaders. He had lunch with Edmund de Rothschild and his partners and the governor of the Bank of England. He talked with the managing director of Royal Dutch Shell and reported on the conversation to his oil client in Dallas. He went to the theater with Douglas Fairbanks, Jr., and the John Gunthers, dined with Lord and Lady Kilmuir, called on Madame Pandit at India House, had lunch with Princess Aly Khan, and attended Britannica Board meetings and viewed Britannica Films. He went to dinner in the country with Fairbanks in an "ancient house" and afterward went to a dancing party accompanied by his sons, who brought the Fairbanks girls. "Beautiful party!" he wrote. He spent a weekend in the country—Barbara Ward, Warwick Castle, Oxford, and Stratford, where he saw *Romeo and Juliet* and afterward went backstage to see the cast. Busy in Brussels, he had lunch with the King, "who was as shy as last year but remembered everything about my visit & letter re Congo last year," and received three letters from Marietta Tree. He wrote to her: "Brussels will be forever blessed; not one, but three [letters]. . . . I am reminded of some other words: So few who live have life. I think [we] are blessed because [we] have *life,* in so many dimensions."

On June 27 he flew to Copenhagen and was greeted by the American Ambassador, Val Peterson, "who apologized for nasty speech he made in '52 campaign," Stevenson noted. " 'Some stuff prepared by Stassen; sorry I made it.' " Politicians, government officials, editors, businessmen, bankers, sightseeing, night life, official luncheons and dinners and toasts and brief speeches—those were his rounds in Copenhagen and, successively, in Norway, Sweden, and Helsinki.

In Copenhagen he received a call from Chicago: Lauren Bacall, at 3 A.M., in the Pump Room of the Hotel Ambassador East, had decided to telephone him. In Oslo he received word that his second grandchild had been born, Nancy's and Adlai III's daughter Lucy. Trygve Lie met him, and he called on King Olav II. He noted in his diary, "After seeing something of those big Norwegian businessmen, so simple, guileless and smart, I understand why, as one hears, there are no Jews in Norway!" In a letter from Oslo he complained of too much wining, dining, toasts, lunches, speeches: "Not enough time to stand and stare. . . . As to world, as I draw closer to the iron curtain I know less. Is the Kremlin closing its doors again, to be opened only to spew forth more Trojan horses?" (The last sentence was copied from a Barbara Ward letter.) He wrote, "Lange, the

FM, excellent!!! Trygvie calls him, a little contemptuously, an 'intellectual.' Why do I always get along best with the wrong people—intellectual men & married women?"

U.S. News & World Report wrote at this time that Stevenson, in Europe, was telling friends he saw no suitable Democratic candidate for 1960—Kennedy "has three strikes on him: 'religion, too young, too rich.'" Blair later explained to Kennedy that in London a *U.S. News & World Report* correspondent had given a cocktail party for Stevenson. Several reporters told him he should run again because there was no one else. He "made it emphatically clear" that he would not be a candidate and said several good candidates were available, including Kennedy and Humphrey. Someone suggested that Kennedy had "two strikes against him, such as his religion, etc." Stevenson had replied "that he supposed some people would hold your religion and your youth and your money against you, but that he didn't think these were important considerations" and he had said "some very nice things" about Kennedy and three others.

Stevenson found Finland "like upper Mich. or Ontario." He thought the Finns "charming agreeable good looking people" and noted that Borden and John Fell had gone sailing with Alice Albright "& beautiful Finnish girl." To Marietta, writing of himself in the third person, "[He] is a mess. He can't sleep. Perhaps it's the nightless northern nights. He moves thru his crowded routine of the days with zestless determination. Even markets get only a glassy sidelong glance as the remorseless schedule of sightseeing, official palaver and ponderous feasts passes by. . . . I know what's wrong and it rather seems he's right. After all he's been master of heart & head a long time, and then *thought* he was a long time longer than he was, if you can understand that sort of sentence. But now the defenses are crumbling and the poor fellow is weak with wanting. . . . [Please send] *precise* details as to relative merits of arrival & departure dates in Paris, or elsewhere, if any." From Helsinki he flew to Leningrad in a Russian plane.

At the Leningrad airport on July 12 he was greeted by the vice president of the Leningrad Soviet, other officials, and American reporters. After speeches of welcome and bouquets for the ladies, he issued a brief statement: "This is my first visit to the Soviet Union in thirty-two years. We have come to learn as much as we can about life and work in the Soviet Union," and he spoke of the desire of "ordinary people everywhere" for peace. The government had sent a representative of the cultural committee to greet him; he and other officials took Stevenson into the city. "Enormous wide street," Stevenson wrote in his diary: "huge ugly stolid apt. bldgs. rising out of treeless plain on both sides. Astoria hotel on St. Isaac Sq. Ancient splendor of 19th Century—I have a bedroom, dining room, parlor, office & bath!—gilt, brocade & lace. Met U.S. press. Long palaver with our innumerable guides & hosts re plans. Fine dinner—caviar, bortsch, steak & vegs. Lovely twilight walk to Hermitage Sq. along

Neva. People poorly dressed, small but seemed cheerful. J.F. gathered a crowd of young ones. Very gay." Stevenson found a group of students and workers in front of his hotel, gathered to examine "a strange and wonderful sight—a 1956 Buick." He wrote, "Their hair was long, their clothes poor, but they were friendly and good-humored, with a ready laugh when I said we hoped to go to Siberia—'and also to return.' They were intensely curious about America, our education and living conditions. 'How many hours of work to buy this car?' stumped me, but my sons saved me. Some of the eager questions reflected, I thought, obvious mistrust of the information the people were getting from their own sources. When I excused myself to go to bed and left my sons to carry on, I cheerily said something like, 'Well, come to see us in America.' And the wistful 'How?' that greeted me from several eager young men will haunt me a long time."

Next day he went sightseeing—Kazan cathedral, Nevsky Prospekt, Alexander Nevsky church, Tchaikowsky's tomb, the Admiralty, Hermitage, the Winter Palace, the subway. On July 14, Stevenson visited the Smolny Institute, the finishing school for girls of nobility where Lenin had set up his headquarters, and its monastery church and an electrical generating plant and the Young Pioneer playground in the Park of Culture and Rest—"group singing, dancing, games, reading room, swimming; seemed solemn for children, but friendly, even affectionate. The leader—a stern looking bright girl—tied red hank, around my neck & declared me an honorary young Pioneer! Moving experience! Evening with reps. of Len. Academy of Science. . . . Enormous banquet in the bldg. of the Society of Writers—many toasts & remarkably good speeches, including mine, I hope! . . . Even these very distinguished profs. seemed wholly part of system & happy. Are they I wonder? Midnight train to Moscow. Good Train—'Red Arrow'—painted blue."

He spent two days in Moscow, calling on the chairman of the Committee on Cultural Relations to discuss authors' royalties, visiting the Kremlin and Red Square. A crisis was at hand—the United States had landed Marines in Lebanon to prevent the overthrow of a pro-Western regime by forces friendly to Egypt and the Soviet Union—and the American Ambassador was called to the Foreign Office at 10:30 P.M. The newspapers were denouncing American "aggression." Stevenson saw the "Mayor" of Moscow, discussed housing ("hideous great yellow brick structures"), then after an Embassy briefing called on Foreign Minister Gromyko. "Had come in from Dacha 40 km. Very cordial reunion—asked for boys—followed my career. Did I want to talk seriously? What did I think of Lebanon etc? Talked one hour; two stenos recorded every word. Familiar line. Aggression; no outside interference. . . . Told Gromyko not to underestimate unity of Am people behind Pres! etc." He issued a statement: "During our conversation the situation in the Middle East arose. I don't feel at liberty to report our discussion in full but, while deploring the fact that such action was necessary, I did express my confidence that the people of the United States would emphatically support the action of the President. . . . I enjoyed my visit with Mr. Gromyko after so many years, and he was most kind to interrupt his holiday and return to Moscow to receive me."

Aluminum statistics were concealed, but Stevenson obtained guesswork estimates. The Minister of Culture discussed authors' royalties. The Minister said his government felt that books belonged to the people and the first consideration was to distribute them as widely as possible. He would be happy if Russian books were printed and distributed in the United States without royalty payments. The Minister needed more time to study a memorandum by Stevenson and agreed to see Stevenson again. He also promised, at Stevenson's request, to prepare material explaining the Soviet government's use of educational films.

From Accra, Barbara Ward faithfully mailed him two working papers on economics. Stevenson sent a postcard to Marietta Tree: "We leave Moscow for the 'interior' this minute & still no word from [you]." Stevenson sent a cable to the State Department on his meeting with Gromyko and on Thursday morning, July 17, flew for three and a half hours aboard a Russian TU-104 southeast into the Asiatic Soviet Union, to Tashkent, near the Afghan and Pakistan borders, 1,800 miles from Moscow. Out for a walk, "Bright eyed little Uzbek boy asked if Amerikowski—Yes. 'Do you live better? Well, anyway "we are friendly"' and as we left ran after us to shout—'Greetings to children of America!'"

Next day he called on the Mayor, a "humorous little man" who was concerned about housing and "very defensive on subject of Russian domination of sovereign Uzbeck Republic." The city architect showed them around . . . same hideous drab brick modern bldgs. But wide tree lined streets. . . . Eager workers showed us around. Wood carving, painting, embroidery, sports, etc. and chess groups. Hysterics over boy not yet 5 who was chess prodigy—going to Moscow with Uzbeck team—beat editor of 'Michigan Telegraph' quickly. . . . Old Russian woman spoke few words of French to me—very eager, but crowd quickly gathered & I moved on. What story could she have told! Priced skull caps—from 16 to 60 rubles. Crowds curious, correct & quickly responsive to smiles & gestures. Yet Taskent Pravda this morning says 'People of Uzbeckstan wrathful about American aggression in Lebanon.'"

Stevenson had long interviews with the local chief justice and two women jurists and made detailed notes on the legal system. He visited the "shabby small main mosque thru winding streets of old city to be met by deputy Mufti." The believers were "mostly old & ragged men—Uzbecks *all* moslem." He had dinner with the Deputy Mufti—"marvelous melons —kind of Casaba—soup, rice, mutton—tea—ripe figs etc." The meal was long, served by "3 slovenly men," with speeches at beginning and end. The Mufti presented Stevenson and his companions with beaded caps and Stevenson with a silk gown which Blair determined sold for 750 rubles. In the evening they attended a concert, the orchestra dressed in white Western shirts and black ties and black evening trousers and playing "only Uzbeck string & wind instruments—shrill, rather unpleasant." It was "a solemn day indeed," Stevenson wrote, with the U.S.S.R. casting its eighty-fourth veto in the Security Council of the UN and with the local newspapers showing pictures of Russians demonstrating in front of the U. S. Embassy in Moscow against American "aggression." At the dinner Stevenson spoke of peace and said its first condition, according to Khrushchev, was trust and the precondition of trust truth, that the Voice of America had been jammed for the last two nights, and that all American newspaper reports and even Stevenson's own statement had been censored. He asked if they did not believe in "equal treatment in the search for truth," and "the Mayor said 'yes'—and crossed his heart with his right hand in the graceful gesture of the Uzbecks—that has only one peer—the Indian!" Back at the dacha he tried to listen to jammed American broadcasts about the Lebanon crisis and noted, "If this has been going on for 10 yrs. its a wonder we are still at peace."

On Sunday, July 20, he wrote, "At last, at 58, the Golden Road to Samarkand, by air!" Next day they flew deeper into the Asiatic Soviet Union to Alma Ata, snowy and high. They went to the theater that night, "marvellous dancing, ballet, chorus singing," then went back to the dacha "for mountains of strawberries, raspberries—and Voice of America on terrace at midnight by rushing stream—on opposite side of world from Chicago." On July 23 they flew by chartered plane with "4 chaperones" north into what Stevenson called Siberia and landed at Rubtsovsk, a "new pioneer town surrounded by rich farm land & 'new lands' in huge Kolkzs [kolkhozes] & State Farms." Here he found women working in a tractor plant that had been evacuated from Kharkov in 1941. "Met by typical political 'mayor'—go getter, aggressive type always ready with peace speech—now so familiar." He found another political leader "a most unusual & attractive man" who had been raised at a kolkhoz and become a schoolteacher: "In many long talks revealed ignorance & mistrust of Am. Denied censorship, jamming, restricted areas, Am. armed forces figures etc. One party enough when all people united. Amused, incredulous about all we said—and very *intelligent,* parrot of party line. Discouraging experience." A large crowd of curious people had met him at the grassy airport. "I'm first important foreign visitor. Although this is another 'Day of Wrath' over Lebanon smiled and clapped when I spoke to them.

"Driving along Turk Sib Ry to town across vast flat prairie on soft dirt road I felt like a boy in Bloomington again. Wail of steam whistles, dogs barking, chickens crowing, dust on roads, unpaved streets, log cabin villages spread along roads, calfs grazing on road sides—all reminded me of frontier life. Visited great state farm, large Kolkoz, tractor repair station (400 employes) & communities clustered around—like early west except social life around party club house (ornamented with Stalin & Lenin) instead of church—and tractors & thousands of acres instead of horses & hundreds. Big crowds around hotel to see me. Guides always tried to hustle me thru. Very reserved, but as usual quick to smile & clap. Little chance to talk with *people*—also as usual. . . . Everywhere signs—catch up with America."

In Novosibirsk: "Visited machine tool plant—arrogant mgr. angry about trade with U.S. 'Warned you that if you wouldn't sell to us we would make our own—and we have.' They have! Huge drills, presses etc." The theater here, he noted, was the largest in the Soviet Union, and "very handsome." The Siberian People's Chorus performed songs and dances: "Performing arts in R. the best! Went back stage (after audience rose at end—turned to 'royal box' & applauded *me!!*) and joked with jolly, curious cast of 50." He visited factories, met with scientists, observed that the new institutes and university put *"no* emphasis on humanities. . . . Enthusiastic and able men apparently dedicated to development of Siberia for which this impressive undertaking is being created. . . . Banquet with this *very big* and agreeable business man—ruggedest drinking bout yet & the American team lost!"

Next day, July 27, they flew back westward toward Moscow. On the twenty-eighth they were in Kazan on the Volga River: "met by smiling, delightful 'Mayor,' historian of city, deputy minister of culture, Prof of law from Univ. Saw lovely Kremlin built by Ivan after defeat of Tartars in 1552—by full moon. . . . Volga river boat 46 yrs old and a tiny compartment & bed at 3:30 A.M.!" Next morning he woke up on the Volga, "another place I never thought I'd be!" moving upstream: "High bank on one side, low on other. Occasionally stops at villages on high side. . . . Occasional tugs & tank barges, huge log rafts with huts on top. . . . Old peasants selling cucumbers, eggs, bread, raspberries on banks at stops. Moujick types getting rare. Country flat and vast. . . . Children swimming on banks—all in trunks. Women wear regular bras & black panties. Old grizzled toothless peasant—black bread, dried fish—'Our Mother Volga'—with great pride." By mistake, he awakened very early next morning, July 30, and read on deck in the sun until 9 A.M. when the boat reached Gorki. "Large, eager delegation at dock. Up bluff by auto—thank God—to busy lovely old town & ornate old hotel." After an "enormous" dinner with the Mayor and many toasts, they went "reeling to our private plane to Moscow at 7:30."

There, Stevenson issued a statement on his Asiatic journey: "Everywhere we were received with the utmost cordiality and hospitality. . . . I have been deeply impressed by the friendliness of the people. . . . On the other hand, I regret to say that I have found a depressing lack of knowledge and understanding of the United States, our way of life and purposes."

Stevenson and his entourage spent nine days in Moscow, from July 31 to August 8, sightseeing in the GUM department store, monasteries, churches, galleries. Stevenson had "many" conferences with Ambassador Thompson, "lucid re USSR if not strong." He had an interview with Mikoyan, whom he considered "sharp." Like other distinguished visitors, he was summoned with only a few minutes' notice to the walled Kremlin for a meeting with Khrushchev. They talked there for two and a half hours. Stevenson found Khrushchev "friendly, stubborn, shrewd—tired & old," a man whose manner was "unpretentious and jovial," whose laugh was "quick and infectious," and who had an "unmistakable ring of authority in his low voice." Khrushchev had just returned from a visit to Chairman Mao in Peking and made clear Russia's intense preoccupation with China. He probably welcomed America's Lebanese intervention, Stevenson thought, since it diverted attention from Eastern Europe, where Imre Nagy of Hungary recently had been executed. Khrushchev asked repeatedly, "How shall we improve our political relations?" He agreed that big powers should not intervene in the affairs of small ones but he and Stevenson could not agree on what constituted interference, and when Stevenson mentioned Russia's recent "intervention" in Hungary and Yugoslavia, "he let me have it" and denounced America for intervening in Lebanon, Jordan, Guatemala. Khrushchev indicated that what happened inside the Communist bloc was the business only of Communists.

Stevenson gained the impression that Khrushchev and other Russian leaders genuinely feared the United States. "We see ourselves encircled by your bases," Khrushchev said, and mentioned bases in England, Turkey, and Greece and asked how the United States would feel if Russia established bases in Mexico. Of Dulles' "rollback" policy he said, "But history will roll him back. The policy of rollback must be rolled back. You cannot roll us back. On this basis there not only cannot be friendship, there cannot even be good relations." Stevenson said that America's bases represented only an American response to our fear of postwar Soviet ambitions and argued that America had been prepared to continue U.S.-U.S.S.R. wartime cooperation but had been forced to defend Western security against Soviet designs on Greece, Turkey, Czechoslovakia, Berlin, and all of East Europe as well as Korea and the Middle East. He added that his countrymen were eager to find a way to settle differences with the Soviets. Khrushchev said, "This I believe. I have read your speeches. Some things in them are wrong and even offensive . . . but on the whole I think you stand for improving relations and we welcome it."

He stated at length the Communist faith that the world was inexorably "going Communist," as Stevenson put it. Stevenson thought this nearly ruled out détente but took heart from the fact that Khrushchev envisaged the further expansion of Communism as a peaceful process and employed none of "the old fire and brimstone rhetoric." Khrushchev confided that when the leaders of Communist countries got together they always toasted their best friend, Secretary Dulles. Stevenson replied that the Democrats might have to deprive them of that advantage at the next election, and

Khrushchev asked questions about American politics, expressing contempt for Richard Nixon. Khrushchev said Stevenson had not shown that there were any differences in foreign policy between his party and "Mr. Knowland's." Stevenson defended the Republican administration and assured him that Americans were united in some things, including their anxiety about war and their desire to reduce tensions.

Khrushchev mentioned the visit of Roswell Garst, a hybrid corn producer of Coon Rapids, Iowa, to Russia in 1955 and recalled talking about corn and drinking brandy with him in the Crimea. Stevenson pointed to some ears of corn in Khrushchev's office and said it was not bad, but in Illinois they raised much better corn. He suggested, "Perhaps we ought to have a summit meeting in a corn field." Khrushchev approved the idea with delight. Stevenson suggested that joint recognition of equality of power between us might change the political climate and help arrest "the awful waste of the arms race." "The awful danger, too," Khrushchev added.

Khrushchev then sent for Borden and John Fell, who were exploring the Kremlin, and a photographer, and while pictures were being taken said that his youngest son, Borden's age, was working "in the field of rocket launching," his older son had been killed in the war. He then suggested that Borden and John Fell return and marry Russian girls as "a contribution to Russian-American relations." Stevenson reported that his sons were "noncommittal."

Jane Dick recalled the trip years later: "It was a marvelous way to travel. Adlai was very indiscreet. He had a big sitting room in his quarters. He'd have us send for vodka and he'd recount the day's experiences very humorously. The place was probably bugged."

Departing on August 8, he issued a statement: "I leave the Soviet Union full of gratitude to the people of this great country who have been so hospitable. . . . I am especially thankful for the long and intimate talk with Prime Minister Khrushchev which served to measure the gulf which unhappily divides our countries, and also the goals and interests that unite us. We were firmly agreed that the latter must prevail. I have been deeply disturbed by the widespread misunderstanding and ignorance about the United States. . . . I believe we must have a much wider and freer exchange of ideas and information. . . . Let us compete in those areas that construct rather than destroy."

In his syndicated newspaper pieces and the book in which they were later collected, *Friends and Enemies,* Stevenson wrote that the changes in the Soviet Union since he had first visited it as a young man in 1926 did not surprise him much "except that the people were more friendly, their ignorance and anxiety about America greater, and the industrialization more spectacular than I had expected." He saw no evidence of internal weakness or upheaval in the Soviet Union. It was a "vibrant" country whose people dreaded war, which they had known intimately. They were striving unremittingly to "catch up" with the United States and were succeeding, though at heavy cost. The conflicting demands of heavy industry, consumer goods, and military spending suggested that soon the Russians might be receptive to détente and serious disarmament proposals, an opportunity we should not overlook. Could the West compete with Soviet state trading without using state trading itself? Could the American system "prevail in competition with the central planning, control and direction" of the Soviet system? And could we conduct foreign policy "in competition with the speed, secrecy and certainty of the Kremlin? . . . The next ten years, I would guess, will *really* prove whether this nation or any nation so conceived and so dedicated can long endure—and right now the prognosis is not good. . . . In our complacent, happy fashion, we assume that we can't lose—that if we stand firm, persevere and damn the Communists enough, Right will surely prevail in the end. Well, it didn't once before, when Athenian democracy was involved in a similar long, tiresome struggle with Spartan tyranny. . . . Is it happening again?"

Stevenson wrote that when Soviet leaders considered China's population growth they feared that before long vast Russia would appear to crowded China as the largest emptiest area on earth, tempting Chinese expansion, and more than one Russian, Stevenson said, upon hearing that a UN commission estimated the Chinese population at 1.6 billion by the year 2000 raised his vodka glass and said, "Which is another reason for better Soviet-American relations. . . . But," Stevenson concluded, ". . . it would be a very great mistake to underestimate the present solidarity of Russia and China—or, indeed, as Khrushchev implied, of the whole Communist empire."

His party scattered, some of its members to rejoin him later. He went to Warsaw, Prague, and Zurich: "Changed at Zurich—with help of Federal Counsellor, Municipal & airport & consular officials! Can I ever be alone? (And how will I like it when I am!)" He spent four days in Bern, writing newspaper articles, making a couple of brief speeches, and writing to Marietta Tree: "How tiresome all the talk has become! I feel like a soldier just out of trenches at a university seminar on war, or is it peace? . . . No intelligence waiting here although this is spy capital." He signed himself, "Ivan the Tired."

On August 18 he took the train to Florence to join the Iveses and his sons: "Florence—and the beautiful 15th century Capponi villa high on the hill called Arcetri crowned with Gallileo's tower—and golden Firenze beneath the terraced gardens, olive groves and cypress walled pool. Buffy in heaven, at last—and why not!" Borden and John Fell joined him, John Fell driving a new Mercedes en route to Cannes to visit the Aga Khan, with whose son he had roomed at Harvard. John Fell would be paid $10,000 for his Russian photographs, Stevenson noted enthusiastically.

Stevenson went to Paris, saw De Gaulle on September 2, and noted his "singular appearance—long body, narrow shoulders, huge nose, solemn face, eyes enlarged by thick glasses, speech quick, accurate & easily comprehensible, seemed unhurried, no jokes or humor." De Gaulle asked whether Stevenson was optimistic or pessimistic about Russia and spoke of its formidable economic development. He talked at length about developing black Africa. He was curious about China's influence on Russia. A crisis was building once more over Quemoy and Matsu; De Gaulle doubted China would risk war but would try to make the American position embarrassing. He thought the United States would not fight for Formosa except in general war and asked what the United States considered essential to its security. He wished the United States, the United Kingdom, and France could arrive at a common policy toward China. As to Algeria, he thought that "education & industry will create conditions for a political settlement that will be neither integration or independence." Stevenson added: "Will rev. [revolution] wait for this long term settlement?" As to nuclear weapons, Stevenson noted, "Must go ahead and provide for own nuclear competence *unless* there is general nuclear disarmament. I said but it will take long time to set up test inspections & then negotiate first disarm steps. In meantime? Inconclusive answer. Would stop development if any good likelihood of disarmament."

Interviewed, Stevenson was asked if he would again be a presidential candidate. He said, "I will not again seek nomination by the Democratic Party," a softer statement than he had previously made. Stevenson saw Mendès-France, Guy Mollet, Couve de Murville, and others, and on September 6 went to Algiers en route to Sahara oil fields. He noted, "Occupied same room in St. George Hotel where I presented my credentials from FDR, Frank Knox and Henry Stimson to Gen Bedell Smith, Ike's chief of Staff in Nov. 1943. The past rose before me like a dream—for here Ellen & I also stayed just 30 yrs ago—1928—on our wedding trip."

After visiting the oil fields and an oasis in "cruel, rubble desert," he left on September 8 for New York with John Fell—"and so ends 3 months of almost incessant travel . . . and if I missed anything or anyone—well I'm almost glad! How tired I am!—and now the accumulation of months at home—*and* Lucy Wallace Stevenson!"—his new granddaughter.

11.

He arrived in New York Tuesday afternoon, September 9, in the midst of the new Quemoy-Matsu crisis. He said he hoped for negotiation, not war. He regretted we were involved with those little islands. But we must meet our commitment to defend Formosa itself. He said he had found abroad an "undertone of great anxiety of conflict between East and West." He had observed a disposition to look to the United States for leadership and to blame the United States for everything that went wrong; perhaps this was inevitable in view of the "clumsy, erratic, and self-righteous conduct of our foreign affairs in recent years." Democrats recently had won in Maine, and Stevenson said it augured well for the fall congressional campaign, in which he said he would be active. On New York politics, he had hoped Tom Finletter would be nominated for the Senate after Mayor Wagner became unavailable but thought District Attorney Frank Hogan would make "a fine" Senator.

He spent three days in New York, meeting with his law partners, with the Authors League, and with Maurice Tempelsman, and reporting at length by telephone and letter to Reynolds Metals. On September 12 he arrived in Chicago. That day the Supreme Court reversed a lower court decision granting a two-and-a-half-year delay in desegregating Central High School in Little Rock, and Stevenson told reporters he was not surprised and hoped the authorities would cooperate and avoid violence. The *Tribune* reporter, George Tagge, wrote that Stevenson appeared "trim and tanned—and obviously a contender for a third Democratic nomination for President." He went to his LaSalle Street law office and after talking for an hour and a half with Wirtz and Minow sent copies of his 1955 speech on Quemoy-Matsu to several newspaper writers and publishers, calling it still "pertinent."

The fall congressional campaign had begun; Stevenson would be less active in it than in 1954. At a lunch with Wirtz and Martin, who were working on his speeches, he said that several things had been borne in upon him during the summer—the frailty of America's allies, the magnitude of the Russian challenge, and Chinese hatred of the United States. Should he say in a speech, as he believed, that we never should have become involved with Quemoy and Matsu? Or should he say he was unable to discuss it during the crisis? The real question was the ultimate fate of Formosa. He thought he should "say something about"—it was a phrase he used repeatedly—not being a candidate in 1960. He wanted to talk about getting rid of Dulles. He wanted to acknowledge that Communist societies were here to stay, to promote better understanding of what the United States stood for, to assist underdeveloped countries, and to improve education. Wirtz proposed that he say he did not like our involvement in Quemoy and Matsu but we were there and in view of negotiations at Warsaw could say no more. Stevenson thought it would be considered a "dodge." He wanted to discuss America's unwillingness to be dragged into "other people's wars" by Chiang Kai-shek. He saw as a theme the idea of realism, truth, no more myths—Chiang was not going to overrun the mainland, Russia was not going to disintegrate, America's dominant position in the world was diminishing, we should make no commitments beyond our strength.

By now Stevenson had moved his law offices to the Field Building, a tower in the financial district. He was putting on weight but had not yet grown obese as he did toward the end of his life. He frequently ate lunch at his desk with his colleagues and aides, a hurried sandwich; then he would lean back in his chair, swivel to gaze at the lakefront, regard the ceiling, and talk. He seemed in those days a little less ebullient and happy-go-lucky than he had when Governor. He seemed deeply committed as a serious politician, no longer able to look upon politics as a spectator detached, as he had when Governor; and he seemed bowed down by the great problems of war and peace. Nevertheless, he was by no means remote or stuffy, he stood on no protocol, his invitations were still spontaneous. And he was as generous—and at the same time as stingy—as ever. At the end of one afternoon Fran Martin, who was still helping out as a volunteer in his office, offered to drive him home, and he accepted. It was dark by the time they reached the street, and raining. Stevenson asked if she minded stopping by one of his clubs, the Tavern Club—he had given a dinner party there, and two bottles of wine, which he had paid for, had not been drunk, and he wanted to retrieve them. Struggling through rush-hour traffic, Fran finally reached the club. He hurried inside, returned at length with the wine, and they headed home. On the way she proposed that they stop for a drink with Martin. Stevenson agreed, then said, "Why don't you both come home to dinner with me?" They did stop for a drink at the Martins', they did all proceed to Libertyville for dinner, and at dinner they drank both bottles of wine. Over the years, countless others had similar experiences. At such times he was a joy.

Sherman Adams, enmeshed in charges that he had interceded with federal agencies on behalf of a businessman friend, resigned as Eisenhower's principal assistant, and Stevenson issued a statement: "No political party will ever have a monopoly on virtue. But I have nothing to say about Governor Adams' resignation. I don't believe in kicking a man when he is down. I wish him well."

Late in September, Stevenson's aides thought Dulles was headed for war over Quemoy-Matsu, and they urged Stevenson to speak out. Others urged him not to. Dulles made efforts to keep Democrats quiet. Stevenson decided to speak, and the only occasion available was a fund-raising dinner for Clair Engle, senatorial candidate, in Los Angeles September 30. He began by saying he had hesitated to discuss the subject because secret negotiations were under way in Warsaw, then quoted at length from his 1955 speech. But, he said, the country must "get out of the dilemma" that had plagued it throughout the Eisenhower administration—when all was quiet abroad criticism was dismissed as "politics" and when a crisis occurred criticism was called "unpatriotic." He said he had kept silent in 1956 while the Middle East crisis was building and had spoken out only when the Suez disaster occurred. This time, "I must say what I think." He did: "I think that we, the United States, should not be defending these islands right on China's doorstep. If Marshal Chiang wants to that's his business. . . . If we avoid war and the crisis subsides, then I think we should get out and stay out of these islands. But, even more important, I think we must at the first opportunity clarify America's position." To be sound, the American position should be acceptable to our allies and, hopefully, to the uncommitted nations, be militarily feasible, and avoid "either appeasement or provocation." He went on, "I think these conditions would be met by (1) a cease-fire, (2) withdrawal of the Nationalist armed forces from Quemoy and Matsu, (3) joint renunciation by Formosa and Peiping of the further use of force against each other, and (4) the declaration by the United Nations and all concerned that the future of Formosa would be decided by the island's population at a time and under conditions to be determined by the United Nations."

Such arrangements, he said, "would hasten the day of Communist China's admission to the UN and full participation in the world community." If she rejected such a settlement and chose to fight, "her credentials for admission would look far more doubtful to many nations than they do now." Our present China policy commanded little respect or support and should be "reconsidered and restated without delay." We should make it clear that we would fight to defend Formosa but equally clear that we were not "helplessly entangled" with Chiang. We had no commitment to defend the offshore islands; they had always belonged to China, their military value was negligible, they were indefensible except by heavy U.S. involvement, and the fight for them was a continuation of the Chinese civil war in which we should not intervene. Most of our friends strongly opposed our making our stand against Communism at Quemoy and saw in it more domestic politics than "the great principles daily invoked" by Secretary Dulles. Dulles had talked about fighting "by means and at places of our choosing"; instead our friends thought we were committed to fighting at places and by means of Chiang's choosing. Eisenhower's recent comparison of Quemoy with Munich "was hardly worthy of him" and his classification as "appeasers" of all who opposed war with China to keep Quemoy was "below him."

"Of course the United States must fight if need be to prevent Communist aggression in the Far East. We have—in Korea. And we will do so again if need be. . . . To stand fast when you are right is wisdom; to stand fast when you are wrong is catastrophe." Disengaging at Quemoy would not be appeasement. The world would respect us for recognizing mistakes. "It is also said that the loss of Quemoy will bring down Chiang's government and mean the loss of Formosa, and then, like dominoes, Korea, Okinawa, Japan, and the Philippines will all fall. I don't believe it. It doesn't work that way; it didn't in Indochina." Thus did he change his position on the falling domino doctrine, advanced later to justify the Vietnam War.

It was a strong speech, coming close to advocating the admission of mainland China to the UN. It had less impact than he had hoped, in part because, the morning he delivered it, Dulles held a press conference cooling the crisis. Fred Dutton thought the speech indicated that Stevenson was preparing to run in 1960. Martin, who had not discussed the matter with Stevenson, gave Dutton his own opinion: "He will not run for the nomination openly, he would accept it if it came to him, and he would love to have it."

In mid-October, Stevenson spoke in New York on behalf of Averell Harriman. He spoke in Milwaukee on behalf of Senator Proxmire, running for re-election, and Gaylord Nelson, running for Governor, as well as for two Congressmen, Clem Zablocki and Henry Reuss. It was a highly partisan speech, ridiculing a recent Republican manifesto denouncing the New Deal and Fair Deal, a manifesto which Eisenhower had repudiated, whereupon, Stevenson said, the Republican national chairman "quickly repudiated the President's repudiation." He finally compressed his themes into one paragraph: "If this crisis in the Formosa Straits is a needless crisis, so too is the crisis of our educational system. So too is the school desegregation crisis. So too is the economic crisis. All of these things could have been avoided if we had an Administration which took thought in advance—instead of waiting placidly on the fairways until mortal danger is upon us and then angrily calling out the Marines. The tragedy of the Eisenhower administration is that its only weapons seem to be platitudes or paratroops. And this seems to be true whether the situation is Little Rock or Lebanon, South America or Quemoy."

He kept on campaigning for Democrats to the end. On Election Night he listened to the returns in Blair's apartment and went to Democratic headquarters in the Morrison Hotel. Across the nation a Democratic landslide occurred, the biggest Democratic victory since the Roosevelt landslide of 1936. Counting the returns in Alaska (in an election held a little later), the Democrats gained 15 Senate seats and the Republicans lost 13, giving a Senate of 64 Democrats and 34 Republicans. Democrats won seats in California, Connecticut, Indiana, Maine, Michigan, Minnesota, Nevada, New Jersey, Ohio, Utah, West Virginia, Wyoming, and Alaska. Among the new Senators were McCarthy of Minnesota, Dodd of Connecticut, Engle of California, Keating of New York, Hugh Scott of Pennsylvania, and Harrison A. Williams, Jr., of New Jersey. The House would have 282 Democrats, a gain of 48 and the highest figure since 1936. The Republicans dropped from 201 to 154. Republican House losses were heaviest in the Midwest, where they lost 23, and in the East, where they lost 20. Only two incumbent Democratic Congressmen were defeated. The Democrats gained six governorships and now would have 35 to the Republicans' 14. Among Democratic Governors elected were Pat Brown of California (who beat the Senate Minority Leader, Senator Knowland), Mike DiSalle of Ohio, Ralph G. Brooks of Nebraska, Ralph Herseth of South Dakota, Gaylord Nelson of Wisconsin, and J. Millard Tawes of Maryland. The Democrats also re-elected Governor Abraham Ribicoff of Connecticut and George Docking in Republican Kansas. The biggest Republican victory was that of Nelson Rockefeller over Averell Harriman in New York. Republicans also won the Oregon and Rhode Island governorships.

Most analysts blamed the Republican defeat on weak organizations, President Eisenhower's failure to lead the party, economic recession, depressed areas, and farm disaffection. Few mentioned Stevenson's contribution. And it would be unwise to give him too much credit, if only because he campaigned less than usual (or if only because in off-year elections local issues tend to dominate). Nevertheless, Stevenson's constant chipping away at Eisenhower over the years must have had some effect. And chipping away at demonstrable weaknesses in the Administration—its addiction to slogans, not coherent foreign policies; its lack of leadership in civil rights, education, and other fields; its neglect of problems until they all but overwhelmed the country. Six years after 1952 it was no longer possible for a Republican Senator or Congressman to contentedly wrap himself in the Eisenhower mantle. During those years Stevenson, by his responsible opposition—opposition conducted with intelligence and principle—had started the process of turning the country around, of turning it away from the Republican landslides of 1952 and 1956 and toward a possible Democratic victory in 1960. He would not himself finish the process, but he had started it. In this sense, too, just as in his programs set forth in the 1956 campaign, he broke trail for Kennedy and Johnson.

The day after the election Stevenson said:

"This is a happy day for Democrats—and happier than some others I can remember.

"But it also is a sobering occasion. The Democratic Party has received a mandate to produce thoughtful, creative leadership in a dangerous time. I am confident that the Democratic Congress will meet its opportunity with responsibility.

"I am hopeful that the bitterness engendered by the campaign will be soon forgotten. As I have said under quite different circumstances, the things that divide us are infinitely less important than the things that unite us—love of justice, love of freedom, love of peace, love of country."

Thus in a brief statement—which he wrote out himself in longhand—did he manage to refer twice to his own defeats.

12.

His pace did not slacken but the importance of what he did diminished —a trip to Bloomington, a meeting with Mary Lasker's expert on mental health, one with the Finance Minister of Kenya, a local TV appearance, a lawyer's business trip to New York with a packed schedule. His dog Artie, to whom he was greatly attached, died, and Stevenson buried him outside the window of the study in Libertyville. He had dinner before the December ball with Suzie Morton Zurcher, an attractive Chicago heiress who was a friend of Mrs. Welling and lived near her.

In response to an inquiry, he told Senator Joseph S. Clark of Pennsylvania, "As to Presidential candidates, I am eager to hear your assessment but I am afraid there is little I can contribute. I have tried to keep as far away from that and from the plans and ambitions of the candidates as I could, for obvious reasons." He was arranging a dinner party for Geoffrey Crowther of the *Economist,* who would visit Chicago soon. "It will probably be small and dull, but I'll try to dig up a few agreeable spirits. Funny how they get fewer and fewer in my old home town!"

Stevenson worked in his office and had lunch with Carl McGowan on December 30 and spent the rest of the week in Libertyville, working on the introduction to *Friends and Enemies.* He sent Agnes Meyer a birthday greeting containing a postscript: "Wasn't it a pity Ike didn't use that missile to send to the world and heavens some really rousing Christmas message, such as: 'Fear not! I bring tidings of great joy! The next President of the United States will be Richard M. Nixon!' " He never stopped despising Nixon.

David Lawrence of Pittsburgh, who had just been elected Governor, was quoted as saying that Stevenson was "by far the ablest statesman" in America and, though handicapped by two defeats, might emerge again for President. Stevenson wrote to him, "Thanks for 'them kind words,' my dear and loyal friend." Senator Humphrey invited him to testify before the Senate Foreign Relations Subcommittee on Disarmament; Stevenson declined. Mrs. Ives wrote to him, a happy letter reminiscing about the past and urging him to savor each day in his lovely home and each day with his sons, adjuring him not to hurry to get everything done—there would always be things unfinished, what counted was the moment. He replied, "Thank you, thank you, for that lovely letter. And what a glorious Christmas it was." They had grown somewhat apart—he felt she fussed at him constantly, and it made him nervous—but now and then they had a good reunion. Their roots were deep and intertwined.

13.

Like the preceding year, 1959 was tightly scheduled, filled with business, travel, social life, and correspondence but containing little important accomplishment. Stevenson was busy with Britannica and Field Foundation board meetings, correspondence and travel on behalf of Reynolds Metals, work for other clients. He became president of the Field Foundation and was paid $25,000 a year. Since his principal task was to mediate between the Chicago and New York Fields, whose views on the proper work of the foundation differed widely, it resembled diplomacy more than law. (Ruth Field of New York felt that the Chicago foundation—her stepson, Marshall Field, and Dutch Smith, who represented him—wanted to change the liberal direction her husband had set for the foundation. She feared that Stevenson, eager to make peace, might compromise, something she was unwilling to do.) A friend who was close to the problem noticed that "He resented the time it took. Adlai and Dutch got it worked out about the time that young Marshall died." Mrs. Field once said, "He took this on after Marshall died. They'd been friends and he wanted to help me. He had a terrific sense of Old World chivalry—the old lady bereft, damsel in distress. My stepson was very ill. He was a manic depressive. Adlai was the peacemaker."

He was going to parties on the Near North Side and in Lake Forest and to functions of the Council on Foreign Relations, the old group where he had started. When foreign celebrities came to town he entertained them— Anastas Mikoyan, King Baudouin of the Belgians, Tom Mboya of the Kenyan opposition, the Maharaja of Mysore, visitors from India and South Africa and elsewhere. Alfred Lunt and Lynn Fontanne stayed with him at Libertyville; so did Hamish Hamilton, the British publisher, and his wife. At the suggestion of Congressman Charles Porter of Oregon, Stevenson wrote to Fidel Castro on February 24 "[Porter] gave me a most interesting account of his recent interview with you in Havana and also mentioned your charitable words about me. I am honored and grateful. I send you my best wishes and most earnest hopes for the success of your great undertaking in Cuba." Castro had entered Havana only a few weeks before. At that time many other Americans wished him well. Castro was planning to come to the United States "under your wing," as Stevenson put it to William G. Reynolds of the Reynolds Metals Company, and had sent word through Porter "that he would welcome a visit" from Stevenson.

Stevenson traveled often that winter and spring, usually on business, sometimes for pleasure or to make a speech. He went to New York, Washington, and San Francisco; he spent most of a week at Aspen, Colorado, as a guest of the Walter Paepckes. (Paepcke, an old Chicago friend, had converted Aspen from a mining ghost town into a fashionable resort with intellectual and cultural aspirations.) He spent most of a week at Kingsland with Alicia Patterson. He spent more than two weeks in Southern vacationlands, dividing his time between Jamaica and Naples, Florida, where he was the guest of Agnes and Eugene Meyer.

He was devoting time to his private affairs. He was worried about Borden but had a "reassuring" visit with him, as he told Adlai III and Nancy. Benton was trying to help Borden find congenial work. John Fell was working for Roger Stevens' real estate company. (Stevens had owned the Empire State Building.) Stevenson thought of revising his will and consulted Adlai III. He was going through some files regarding Ellen. Mrs. Ives was interested in buying a house in Florida, and Stevenson considered joining her in the purchase.

He was continuing to see or correspond with a large number of women

—Eleanor Roosevelt, Harriet Welling, Agnes Meyer, Jane Dick, Barbara Ward, Alicia Patterson, Marietta Tree, and Suzie Zurcher. A chronological account may indicate the quality of those relationships.

Agnes Meyer told him in a casual note on January 5 that she had been reading "a solemn treatise on the physiology of women" and had found the following: "Someone asked Princess Metternich how long the sex impulse in women lasted. She replied, 'You must ask someone else. I am only sixty.' That should terrify you! Yours for more and better nonsense." Stevenson replied, "I am not terrified—but delighted! Impulsively yours." At the same time he declined a dinner invitation from Mrs. Roosevelt because he was speaking in Lake Forest on the night she would be in Chicago. He invited her to visit him at Libertyville. At that time, too, he wrote to Barbara Ward about a broadcast on which both were to appear and about plans to meet in Aspen or Chicago. He thanked Agnes Meyer on January 23 for the "gala" she had held in his honor. From Aspen on February 4 he wrote to Alicia Patterson about meeting her in New York, Kingsland, or Libertyville. He addressed her as "Elisha" and signed it "Adpai." On January 26, Agnes Meyer recommended that he read an article in the *Bulletin of the Atomic Scientists,* described her own project to rally women of the world to call on male political leaders to ease international tensions, and added, "Well, that's none of my business but visiting your lady friends is a dangerous business, not for you but for them." Leaving for Naples, Florida, a few days later, she wrote, "My public work has burgeoned at an unbelievable tempo. I seem to have arrived at a point in my career when fruitful ideas fall off me as from a tree that has arrived at its period of production."

On February 12, Suzie Zurcher sent him a handmade Valentine containing a photograph of Stevenson doing gymnastics in Aspen. On the twenty-sixth, he wrote to Agnes Meyer about his proposed visit to Naples. Back in Chicago after visiting Alicia Patterson, he told her, "The Black River was glorious—and so are you. . . . Hooray! For our Pres.—Norman Vincent Eisenhower!" He addressed her as "Elisha" and closed, "Love & such A."

Late in 1958 and early in 1959 in Chicago, Stevenson began to take Suzie Zurcher out to dinner. She was politically naïve, divorced, a tall good-looking brown-haired young woman, the daughter of Sterling Morton and heiress to the Morton salt fortune. (Years earlier, Stevenson had known her father.) Her family was Republican. She gave the impression of being nice and unpretentious. Adlai III thought his father lacked any serious romantic interest in her but others had a different impression. Their relationship ended in April of 1961, about two years after it began. Marietta once said, "He told me that he broke it off. She thought she was the only one. She didn't realize there were twenty-two others." Mrs. Zurcher, on the other hand, recalls that it was she who broke off their relationship because of the coterie of New York women with which he surrounded himself when he went to the United Nations and because she had become interested in someone else. When she broke off their relationship he said, "No one has ever done this to me before."

During 1959 and 1960 they saw each other frequently. They had known each other casually for some years, the way people do who move in the same social circle. Now she began a correspondence with him. He told her to mark her letters "PRIVATE PLEASE." (Mail addressed to Stevenson at Libertyville during heavy mail periods was automatically forwarded to his Chicago office. There Carol Evans opened it, respecting, however, the legend "PRIVATE PLEASE" on the envelope.) He took Suzie to receptions and other gatherings. Some evenings she visited him alone at Libertyville. More often than not he sat her down in a chair by the fireplace and gave her a basket of his mail to sort while he went to his study to work. At times he seemed almost wholly committed to work. He often told her he wanted only to sit in Libertyville and "watch the people dance" but after a few hours of solitude he would begin telephoning people around the country. Sometimes she found the house filling with people. He could not be alone, could hardly be with only one other human being. One of his women friends once said perceptively, "To be Adlai's girl, you had to have a husband."

On April 15, Agnes Meyer wrote that Ralph McGill's newspaper column said that "Kennedy would not consider accepting the Vice Presidency with anyone but Stevenson." "The tide is rising! . . . But I do not agree with the remark in Naples that you plan to be out of the country during the Convention." Between now and the 1960 convention, Mrs. Meyer would be in the vanguard of numerous people, most of them women, who wanted him to run for the third time. Suzie Zurcher, by contrast, sent him a piece of doggerel urging him lightly not to forsake her for the presidential campaign.

Stevenson sent Marietta Tree a letter from a woman in Oregon who described recent visits there by Hubert Humphrey, John F. Kennedy, and Governor Meyner and implored Stevenson to run again—the others would not do. (Stevenson told her, "I don't want to get involved again and must pray for the frustration of your schemes.")

Stevenson wrote a sentimental letter about Illinois to a daughter of Lloyd Garrison: "Spring has come, violently as it always does in Illinois. Here we have a lovely long fall, but spring is an erratic season of wild winds, cold days and savage heat, and then comes summer all too quickly. But I fly around the country so fast and so much that I hardly have time to enjoy even the bad weather! I hope it is never that way with you, because the satisfactions of serenity and quiet get more precious as life moves on." On May 19, Agnes Meyer sent details of her plans to visit him at Libertyville, and next day reported that at a "Truman nation-wide telecast" at Constitution Hall "everything was rather quiet until you were thrown on the screen with your address, at which the whole audience broke loose with tumultuous applause."

Barbara Ward wrote on May 23 from London, suggesting means by which he could "escape from the hideous risk of 1960. Make speeches so frank & so careless of selfish entrenched minorities of whatever kind that you become completely unacceptable to all the cautious old pols." She sent a speech draft in her spidery longhand and Carol Evans typed it, as she did other Barbara Ward drafts.

June 1 came and went, and Agnes Meyer visited Libertyville for the first and only time. Back in Washington she wrote to Stevenson: "I feel as if I had been wandering hand in hand with you in the Elysian fields. Nobody, but nobody, can really know you who has not felt your love for those broad, fertile meadows, your deep friendship with each one of your noble trees and your delight in the leisurely meandering of your shadowy, sun-flecked river. Your home is a quite different and yet related revelation of your exquisite personality. Just as the garden, and pastures and woodland reflect your close relationship to nature, so the house reveals your sensitivity to art and to that greatest of all arts, the art of living. In this utterly charming cottage I saw for the first time how warm and sweet it is to live in a small, intimate environment." No record survives of Stevenson's reaction to her well-meant but slighting reference to his "utterly charming cottage." Compared to Mrs. Meyer's own home, which from the outside resembled a public library, Stevenson's house was indeed a "cottage," but he hardly thought of it that way. He told her, "I am off to Europe on the 18th for probably two months, and for once I really find the exertion of further travel extremely distasteful. I suppose there comes a time when age conquers curiosity and the taste for adventure and strange places is satisfied at last. Evidently I have hit it abruptly." On the eve of his departure she sent him a sad letter wishing him a good trip and displaying her own fortitude—her husband was dying.

14.

Politics had not occupied a great deal of Stevenson's time that winter and spring though it claimed a good deal of his attention in correspondence. Dick Daley was running for re-election, and Stevenson supported him publicly. He saw Bill Attwood more than once to discuss speeches (and later Agnes Meyer paid Attwood a salary to write speeches for Stevenson). In January, replying to a letter from Walt W. Rostow, Stevenson ignored a suggestion that he not rule out the possibility of a Stevenson-Kennedy ticket. John Steele reported on January 6 that Stevenson was reluctant even to talk about the possibility of running a third time and had only with difficulty been persuaded even to attend a meeting of the DAC. Bill Benton told Stevenson on January 29 he thought Kennedy would develop enough strength to ensure his nomination for Vice President. He thought that if Stevenson pulled out Humphrey would inherit a large part of Stevenson's strength in the North. Jim Rowe told Blair that Paul Butler was doing everything he could "to make sure that Adlai gets no attention whatsoever." Blair urged Stevenson to attend a Democratic dinner in Washington, signing his interoffice memo, "Your friend and supporter." He did not go. Benton told Stevenson on February 10, "I had an hour with Jack Arvey. . . . Jack adheres strongly to the belief that you are by far the best qualified man for the presidency in either party. He is not equally positive that you would make the best candidate. . . . Lyndon Johnson said to him, 'Any Democratic candidate that can announce to the American people that Adlai Stevenson will be his Secretary of State —is sure of election.' "

Barry Bingham asked Bill Blair for guidance in answering a letter from a Stevenson fan who wanted to draft him for President. Blair replied on February 27 that he and Stevenson were telling people that, "for reasons which we are sure they will understand, the Governor does not intend to be a candidate for the nomination" and that they were discouraging draft-Stevenson movements—"if these committees start popping up the Governor's motives will be even more suspect than they are." He added, "My own feeling is that the only way the Governor can be drafted is if there is a deadlock in the Convention and I don't think we should be doing anything to bring that about. If it happens, it happens."

Stevenson issued a statement discounting the idea that the Democratic Party's chance to win in 1960 had been injured by present congressional leadership. Lyndon Johnson thanked him not once but twice. George Tagge wrote in the Chicago *Tribune,* "[Stevenson] is rated a strong possibility for a third nomination if the 1960 Democratic convention deadlocks over the front runners," whom Tagge identified as Senators Humphrey, Kennedy, and Symington. Secretary Dulles' health was failing, and several people suggested that Stevenson be appointed to replace him. Stevenson replied to one, "I suppose you are right that I would have to take it unless I had a doctor's certificate of disease, preferably communicable. . . . But . . . how could you do that job after all that has gone before without confidence in or of your President!"

Bill Benton predicted a Stevenson-Kennedy ticket. Stevenson spoke at a testimonial dinner in Boston on March 5 to raise money to pay off the campaign deficit of Endicott "Chub" Peabody, a brother of Marietta Tree who a few years later was elected Governor of Massachusetts, and Peabody told Stevenson that Boston Irish politicians thought Stevenson might be the nominee.

John Steele of *Time* had lunch with Stevenson at Libertyville and told him he had a "persistent feeling" that Stevenson would be nominated and, for the country's sake, he hoped so. When Steele recounted his travels with Kennedy, Stevenson said, "Tell me more, a lot more," and then expressed doubts about Kennedy. "Firstly," Steele wrote, "[Stevenson] was not overly sympathetic to Jack Kennedy's great problem, that of overcoming his youthful appearance, his public picture of 'that nice young man from back east.' Somberly, Adlai wondered if Kennedy 'really' has the balance, the judgment to lead the nation. Warningly, he wondered if Jack was not seeking the elusive presidency with far too much passion. Was he pacing himself? Would he really do as the Democratic nominee? . . . Clearly," Steele wrote, "Humphrey is his favorite for the nomination and . . . he is concerned lest Stuart Symington emerge as the nominee. That means Frank McKinney, Sam Rosenman, Harry Truman, Ed Pauley and that whole gamey crowd all over again, he said."

Stevenson told Steele of his own political plans. He would try to stay "utterly aloof" from current maneuvering. Only one thing could make him active before the convention: a conviction that Symington was about to be nominated. In that event he would either try to bring Humphrey and Kennedy together or would endorse one or the other of them to stop Symington. (This last came from Blair, not Stevenson, Steele said.) Stevenson hoped the campaign would bring forth "a reasonable discussion of foreign policy issues," which Steele thought indicated self-interest. Steele criticized a recent foreign policy paper issued by the DAC, and Stevenson agreed, "attributing it," Steele wrote, "to Dean Acheson's vitriolic pen and commenting at some length on how Acheson's frustrations and scar tissue have reduced his value almost to the vanishing point." Stevenson considered Nelson Rockefeller the ablest Republican but expected Nixon to be nominated. Steele concluded, "There is about Stevenson today a certain not previously observed sense of placidity, of willingness to accept the future without particular unrest whether it be a third presidential nomination, an appointment as Secretary of State, or a Chicago-New York-Washington law practice which is beginning to be a lucrative thing." Despite his antipolitical stand, Stevenson was greatly interested when Steele quoted Phileo Nash of Wisconsin as saying, "You scratch a Kennedy man or a Humphrey man and what do you find? A Stevenson man." Stevenson asked, "You've seen Dave Lawrence [of Pennsylvania] lately? What does he say?" Steele thought it revealing.

Secretary Dulles, ailing, resigned, and Stevenson issued a generous statement: "I am extremely sorry. I know of no one who has served his country more diligently and devotedly than Secretary Dulles."

On May 1, John Steele filed a dispatch on presidential prospects. He said Senator Kennedy, heading West that day, was "the current leader by far in the open phase of the race." Kennedy, he said, hoped to do so well in the primaries that it would be hard for the convention to spurn him. Humphrey, unlike Kennedy, who held that the New Deal and Fair Deal were "dead," was staking everything on his reputation as a liberal. But in California, Humphrey had been told painfully, "Hubert, we guess you're okay; but, God, we sure would like Adlai first." Stevenson, Steele wrote, would not lift a hand to be nominated. Nor would he try to throw the nomination to another candidate. Pressure on him would increase if Kennedy defeated Humphrey in the primaries and liberals rejected Kennedy and, even more strongly, Symington. At that point Stevenson would have to take himself out unmistakably or make it clear that he was available for a draft. Stevenson's biggest weakness, as Steele saw it, was that he did not have "the powerful boss support" which he had had in 1952 and, except for Truman, in 1956. But if by the first of the year it appeared that Humphrey could not get off the ground and that Kennedy was "too young and too Catholic," the professionals might well turn to Stevenson. "Adlai is the guy that Hubert and Jack are watching much more than they are watching each other."

Mary McGrory of the *Evening Star* of Washington told Stevenson that "they still love you in California and in fact all through the Northwest." She had been on the West Coast with Humphrey and Kennedy and found that Stevenson still had strong supporters there, most of whom had entered politics because of him. Stevenson replied, "I am constantly meeting folks who say they got into politics on my account. But why don't they get out on my account?" James E. Doyle, a liberal from Madison, Wisconsin, now publicly endorsed him for President in 1960.

Jim Rowe, working on behalf of Hubert Humphrey, called on Stevenson and his Chicago partners in May and asked for access to Stevenson's political files. Stevenson indicated he could have it and added that his state-by-state files would be available to other candidates as well as Humphrey. Rowe thought Humphrey could easily beat Kennedy in Oregon if Stevenson were not on the ballot and proposed that Stevenson be sure he was not on the ballot by filing an affidavit with the Oregon Secretary of State declaring that he was not a candidate. Stevenson indicated he would do it. On a trip to the West with Humphrey, Rowe had discovered "Stevenson strength . . . more of it than I suspected." Rowe later told Stevenson, "In short, I am, as a Humphrey man, moving closer to the necessity for your political assassination. I have no doubt, however, that he is politically your spiritual heir. A few of your voters may go to Kennedy, a few of the 'pros' who supported you may go to Symington, but the 'issue' people are all for Humphrey."

Stevenson was invited to speak at Dartmouth College next January or March but said he "would rather not" go to New Hampshire at the time of the primary there. Secretary Dulles died and, on May 25, Stevenson said: "Personal integrity, patriotism, and stern resolution—these are Secretary Dulles's legacies to the nation he served with such devotion."

15.

Stevenson made a number of speeches that winter and spring. On January 18, delivering the A. Powell Davies Memorial Lecture in Washington, he spoke of Albert Schweitzer's conviction that this was the most dangerous period in human history. "Russia is a vast powerhouse of energy all harnessed to the communal task of building the Soviet dream. . . . And if these people are in deadly earnest, what about the 600 million Chinese?" Why were Russians so dynamic and we of the West so "sluggish"? American policy was "to a depressing degree purely defensive." We offered aid not to help others but to shield ourselves, reacted to countless Soviet initiatives, took few ourselves. "Why this lack of initiative? Why this paralysis of will?" He reviewed the collapse of earlier empires whose leaders were committed to pleasure and profit alone and said, "A nation glued to the television screen is not simply at a loss before the iron pioneers of the new collective society. It isn't even having a good time. No society has ever spent as much as we do on drink and tranquilizers. Can one argue that this is evidence of universal fun?" He spoke at length of poverty and inequality in America and called for more participation in politics by citizens with both moral purpose and a willingness to do the "grinding, boring, tedious work, as well as the glamorous, high-sounding, headline-hitting work."

Speaking at a fund-raiser for "Chub" Peabody in Boston on March 5, Stevenson said Russia had "set the stage for another showdown" at Berlin and he wondered if Russian leaders had underestimated and misunderstood Americans. If so, "let me add my voice . . . to warn them not to drive this nation too far and not to mistake the underlying temper of our people. . . . When the President says we will not give in to force, he speaks for all of us." America must never "forsake" free Berlin. A Russian attack there would mean retaliation by our Strategic Air Force. At the same time we should explore with the Russians a more stable settlement in Europe than the present one.

Stevenson spoke on April 2 at the Sherman Hotel on behalf of Richard Daley's re-election and went all out for him. Daley won overwhelmingly.

Stevenson spent most of a week in April on the Yale campus as a Chubb Fellow, speaking to several classes and attending the *Yale News* banquet and meeting with students and faculty, to discuss among other things Russia, Berlin, China, economic development in underdeveloped countries, disarmament, American government, and colonialism. While he was there the *Yale News* took a presidential preference poll and showed Nixon leading Stevenson by only 11 votes out of more than 1,200 cast, which seemed to indicate a landslide victory for Stevenson in an actual election, since the student body was heavily Republican.

On May 6 at Newark, to the American Council to Improve Our Neighborhoods, Stevenson spoke of urban problems he had witnessed abroad from Damascus to Berlin to Siberia. The American cities' problems could be solved, he said, only by the joint efforts of "private enterprise and public responsibility." (His audience was composed mainly of businessmen interested in urban renewal.) He spoke well of new middle-income housing created by public-private enterprise and ill of "public housing," which, he said, nobody liked. He warned that care must be taken to ensure that subsidized housing did not become racially segregated housing. He proposed the establishment of a federal department of urban development and emphasized the perils of pollution. Thus he proposed a federal department that was to become a cabinet ministry in the 1960s and raised the question of pollution that became an issue in the 1970s.

On May 12 he went down to the University of Illinois at Urbana to speak on foreign policy. There, he denounced recent U.S. policy as lustily as when he had been a candidate and Dulles had been Secretary. He then sketched out two aims for the future—a "world under law," and a satisfactory relationship with "the vast revolution sweeping our planet." But this was not policy; policy must deal with the "hard political realities." The first important reality was the division of the world into three camps, free, Communist, and neutral. How should the United States conduct its affairs with them? Relations with the Communists meant relations with Russia and China, which were "for the time being" bound together. "Years ago" Stevenson had urged that instead of fighting over Quemoy and Matsu we should be discussing the independence of Formosa and the admission of China to the United Nations. Our present policy of isolating China made Russia her spokesman. "I believe we should not veto the admission of Communist China to the United Nations." It was as close as he had come to publicly advocating admission. He advocated independence for Formosa and an undertaking not to use force in settling its future. The United States and Russia should seek equality of power, not superiority. All limited agreements, such as a ban on atomic testing, should be "vigorously supported and extended." No summit meeting could achieve "a fully integrated system of controlled disarmament." We would probably negotiate that "for the next two decades." Areas of tension brought headlines. These were the areas where the interests of the Great Powers overlapped and where the collapse of colonialism had left vacuums, the borders of China, the Middle East, Europe. The solution was "not always" the formation of military blocs such as the Baghdad Pact.

Senator Fulbright told Stevenson after reading the speech, "I cannot refrain from saying 'Amen.' I think it is one of the best you have ever done." Stevenson's outline of a foreign policy, particularly his emphasis on the underdeveloped world and the European Common Market, foreshadowed the foreign policy which would be pursued by President Kennedy after 1961. This was a Kennedy-Rusk foreign policy not as actually pursued but as seen through Stevenson's eyes, with its emphasis on the UN's capabilities, disarmament, and accommodation with the Soviet Union and mainland China.

16.

On June 18, Stevenson left Chicago for London via BOAC to start his summer in Europe. The centerpiece of the trip was the cruise aboard Bill Benton's yacht. And the centerpiece of the cruise was Stevenson. The guest list was composed to please Stevenson—Benton was always eager to please him. In one letter he said, "There is no real importance for either of us being at the Board meeting of Britannica Limited on June 29th—except that it validates the payment of your expenses to London. And your expenses at Claridge's." Benton once said after Stevenson's death that Stevenson probably would have considered Benton his closest associate. Their relationship, however, was far from satisfactory, as Benton himself acknowledged. (Benton once said that Stevenson "never really did anything for" the Britannica, was obsessed with money, and was "supported" by Benton.) A trifling incident of January 1959 throws light on their relationship. Benton had written an article on the Soviet industrial challenge, and a friend called it to Stevenson's attention. Stevenson gave it to Bill Blair with a note, "Bill Benton likes *thank you* letters. Pls read this carefully & congrat. him from me appropriately." Blair subsequently wrote to Benton: "I had an opportunity at long last to read your article . . . and all I can say is that I wish I had written it myself!" He signed Stevenson's name to the letter.

Stevenson spent about ten days in London and at country estates, attending Britannica meetings, dealing with clients, seeing British aristocracy and old friends both American and British. Suzie Zurcher was there, and one day Stevenson took her with him to visit a duke and duchess in their great country house, where Stevenson slept in Marlborough's bed.

Stevenson visited John Steinbeck and his wife, and Steinbeck talked about the Arthurian legends and after lunch took Stevenson to what Stevenson called in his diary "the true Camelot!" He visited Stonehenge, went to dinner with Lauren Bacall, had lunch at Kensington Palace with the Duchess of Kent and went with her to Wimbledon and "sat with her in the Royal Box all afternoon." Sometime after that entry he wrote in his diary, "(And from there on I never made an entry!)" It was true. During the long cruise aboard the *Flying Clipper* he neglected his diary entirely. In earlier years he had been more scrupulous. But then he had been gathering notes for magazine or newspaper articles. This summer he seemed to give himself over to pleasure—as he wrote to Agnes Meyer, "All is sun and sea, crumbling castles and iced wine, laughter, reading, sleeping—and eating."

The cruise began from Lisbon, where Stevenson went on June 30 (and, with Roger Stevens, represented an American client interested in building a hotel).[6] The *Flying Clipper,* a Scandinavian boat, was two hundred feet long and slept about sixteen. The cruise lasted until about August 15, though Stevenson left earlier. She went to such places as Seville, Gibraltar,

[6] At various times—people kept getting on and off along the southern coast of Europe—those aboard included Suzie Zurcher, Marietta Tree and her daughter, the Bentons, their son and his wife, Adlai III and Nancy, the Roger Stevenses, George Ball, the Dutch Smiths, Mr. and Mrs. Harry Scherman (he was board chairman of the Book of the Month Club), the Bruce Goulds (editors of the *Ladies' Home Journal*), the Francis Plimptons, Sir Geoffrey and Lady Crowther, Bill Blair.

Málaga, Valencia, Mallorca, Corsica, Sardinia, Malta, Sicily, Italy. (Bill Blair was also cruising that summer through the Greek islands on a boat which he and two of John F. Kennedy's sisters chartered). Before each stop Benton looked up the port ahead in the *Encyclopaedia Britannica.*

This was the first of two trips Stevenson made aboard the *Flying Clipper.* (Benton remembered them fondly and once gave Stevenson a silver platter engraved with a picture of the *Flying Clipper.*) Benton said, "Stevenson was the most avid tourist I've ever known." John Fell, after an exhausting visit to the Dalmatian coast of Yugoslavia with his indefatigable father, said, "I'm just sick of old stones." Stevenson himself never sickened of them. Suzie Zurcher recalled, "In most places he was recognized. He pretended that it was distasteful to him, but it wasn't. Once in Minorca nobody seemed to know him. We walked through the streets. He was looking queer. He said, 'I guess I'm a stranger here—isn't it wonderful?' I said yes, it was. But pretty soon somebody appeared with a camera and right away he turned on a big smile and looked a little relieved. There was a bullfight in Palma, and a bull was dedicated to him. Benton was an organized cruise director. You found a Cadillac waiting on every dock. Meals on board were long-drawn-out affairs. We would drink sangría, then have lunch after sightseeing, then sleep, then dinner. Then sit on the afterdeck of the boat, a lot of talk, a monologue by Benton." Stevenson told Mrs. Ives, "It is a lovely cruise—eating, sleeping, swimming, sailing—and sight seeing madly. Adlai [III] is relaxed and Nance enchants every one. I have asked Marietta Tree and her daughter to stop in Florence [with you] on their way back from the Middle East."

While he was on the cruise Jane Dick, back home, underwent an operation for cancer. Ruth Winter, an old Lake Forest friend of both, told Stevenson, and he sent a reassuring letter to Jane—"I *know* that everything is going to be alright"—but a far different one to Mrs. Winter: "I'm stunned. . . . And now I'll have something more useful to do in all those great cool, dim churches. . . . And I'll spend some time afloat on my knees too. . . . I've seldom prayed so hard."

Eugene Meyer died, and Stevenson wrote to Agnes Meyer from Mallorca, "I know, dear Agnes, that you *were* prepared; yet when it came I know you were *unprepared.* But know too, as you wrote in that fine farewell to me, that you *can* measure up to all the demands—and *have.* . . . But *now* is when it will be the hardest. . . . I suppose the reaction will set in when intensity and splendor vanish and leave behind emptiness, questions, soul-searching and all manner of melancholy reflections. But there will, mercifully, be adjustments to make, new patterns of living to devise, new demands to meet, new perplexities to solve. And here is where your old ally and loyal friend—WORK—will come to refresh and reinvigorate you. And, little by little, but quickly I pray, the outside world *will* become meaningful again." Then he wrote about the cruise and its pleasures: "Horrors what eating! I've relaxed at last, or maybe decomposed! And I pray that yachting in the Mediterranean is habit forming for my rich friends." (She took him on a yacht trip in the 1960s.)

Stevenson left the cruise and went to Florence to visit Ernest and Buffie Ives July 25. Interviewed on BBC, he said, "I should like most to be remembered for having made some contribution to a higher level of political dialogue in the United States than I found when I came, at the top level." He recalled his childhood: his mother "was always putting rubbers on me and always switching me if I misbehaved and got caught out cold. . . . I used to be afraid I was going to fail my examinations, and I would wake up in the night and worry about that, and I sometimes still do. I'm still taking those examinations, over and over again."

On August 2, Stevenson left Florence with Borden, who had arrived there when he did, and went to Athens to see Britannica Films's new overseas manager. "Car for stay furnished by Foreign Office," he noted on his appointment sheet. He called on the Foreign Minister and Ambassador Ellis Briggs, talked with the Minister of Education about Britannica Films, and made a speech at a showing of them. On August 5 he left with Borden for Istanbul and Ankara to promote Britannica Films and meet an oil man client. They left for Rome on August 10 and went on to Nice and to Mary Lasker's villa. He played tennis with a viscount and went for a cruise "with Onassis and 30 guests on Christina to nudist colony on Isle Levant on cold rainy day! Delightful week—but little work accomplished." On Thursday, August 20, he left Nice for New York, pausing for a midnight conference in Lisbon with a man who was expected to be the next Foreign Minister of Japan and who told him, as Stevenson wrote, "I was the American statesman that commanded greatest respect in Asia."

George Ball had written to him at Mary Lasker's villa on August 8: the political winds were "blowing your way" again, for Humphrey had not "gotten his campaign off the ground," Kennedy was "whirling like a dervish on dead center," Symington was little known, Pat Brown while ambitious himself conceded that Stevenson would carry California in either a contested primary or a general election, and a recent Gallup poll had persuaded politicians that a Stevenson-Kennedy ticket would be the strongest one possible. "All this adds up to the fact that events are beginning to respond to an inexorable political logic as they did in 1952. . . . Logic may, of course, be deflected or derailed. . . . In any event, if the Convention insists on nominating you I am sure it will be because you do nothing about it." Among the Republicans, Ball found some doubt that Nixon would be permitted ascendancy; Rockefeller would announce his intentions by November. (Ball noted that Rockefeller's great accomplishment so far had been to "marry his son off to a Norwegian housemaid" and asked if Stevenson couldn't "induce Borden to marry the beautiful, proud but penniless Italian-Negro daughter of a Puerto Rican Jewish Catholic.") This, then, was the climate in which Stevenson would return to America. Ball sent Stevenson an affidavit disavowing candidacy and recommended he file it with the Secretary of State of Oregon before he returned to America, then he could tell the press he had stated his position fully in the affidavit. Ball hoped he would reschedule his South American trip so as to be out of the country during the primaries. (Stevenson had already decided to postpone a trip to South America, previously scheduled for this fall, until early the following year.)

The political letter from Ball was like a dash of cold water. Stevenson had been lapsing into a pattern of luxury and indulgence that would become set firmly during his years at the UN—yachts, villas, idolatry, food. But at this time he still resisted, and he told Mrs. Ives, "I'm . . . impatient to get back after 2 months of wandering. This visit with Mary has been luxurious and pleasant but a little too much society & people for my taste."

He arrived at Idlewild Airport in New York on August 21. He wrote out in advance answers to questions he expected from the press. He was pleased by the forthcoming Eisenhower-Khrushchev reciprocal visits—"I have long advocated more and less formal talks with the Russians." But nobody should expect any early results—"we will be talking for years. The best hope is to talk this foolish cold war to death." On Nixon's recent visit to Russia, Stevenson said he thought it was "a good thing—especially for Nixon. Several years ago he said I was un-American or disloyal when I pointed out the alarming implications of Russia's rapid economic growth. But now he is saying the same thing, but better late than never. And I believe in adult education, especially for Mr. Nixon. He has also discovered that Khrushchev is tough, quick-witted, and stubborn. Many of us, here and abroad, learned that about the Russians in the postwar negotiations ten to fifteen years ago. Our friends abroad are a little perplexed and amused over the torrent of publicity about the Vice President's observations, but I think they were relieved that he did not prophesy the imminent collapse of the Soviet Union as Mr. Dulles used to do."

On domestic politics he said, "I am flattered that so many people still want me to run for President again. Such continued confidence is the greatest possible reward in public life and I am deeply flattered. But—as I have said since 1956—I will not seek the nomination in 1960. And I hope that all my friends will work for the avowed candidates of their choice. In Oregon, I hope that my dear friends will not enter me in their primary and put me in the false position of being a candidate when I am not." He added, "I have never thought for a moment it was possible for me to be drafted and I have no reason to think it now."

17.

After a few days in New York, Stevenson went home to Chicago on August 24. Bill Benton was talking about a trip to Canada on behalf of the *Britannica,* and Stevenson hoped he would not have to make a major speech. "But if you wanted to go for just a Directors' meeting, with attendant publicity about our being there, I would be quite available. I could, of course, make a call on the Prime Minister or the Foreign Minister and fellows in the other camp like Mike Pearson and Paul Martin, which would make a little publicity."

On August 25, John Steele sent a personal memorandum to Stevenson. (Steele recalled later that his memos to Stevenson constituted his only entry into partisan politics during his journalistic career—"I always felt a little guilty about this unprofessional conduct, but my personal affection and admiration for AES conquered my professional scruples, I fear.") Steele thought Democratic presidential politics fluid. "The Democrats stand, less than a year before their national convention time, actually in search of a candidate." There was no Franklin Roosevelt of 1932 or Adlai Stevenson of 1952 in sight. Kennedy was in the lead, but it was not a commanding lead, and he would have to run against several potential favorite-son candidates in state primaries, with his Senate votes open to scrutiny. The Humphrey campaign had "sadly . . . failed to get off the ground." Symington "remains an enigma" but with plenty of money. Lyndon Johnson "remains a figure in the background," Meyner "a personal enigma to this reporter." Kennedy regarded Stevenson as his most formidable rival and a man with whom he might be willing to run as vice presidential nominee. "The Stevenson strength is a some what strange thing. It prevails even more solidly among the second tier of party workers than it does among the leaders, with the notable exception of Dave Lawrence. . . . The Stevenson attraction . . . is due partially to the lack of any other single, completely attractive candidate who looks like a winner. . . . The Governor's recent statements, including that on his return to this country, are not regarded in political circles here as closing the door to anything."

Stevenson spent the fall as he had spent the spring. Sometimes, in Chicago for an evening, he would stay overnight with Nancy and Adlai III, who by now was practicing law. Like his father, Adlai III did not enjoy the routine practice of law, though he put up with it.

Stevenson gave a party at Libertyville for more than a hundred people in connection with the Pan American Games, and it rained, and the guests crowded into the house and made a mess of it, as he put it. Chet Bowles, now a Congressman, told him that he continued to hear of Stevenson's political strength, and Stevenson replied, "You are right that the continued talk about me is rewarding and a great satisfaction; but all the same I find it very disquieting." He told Alicia Patterson, "If you want to stop off en route East—well, there are clean sheets, green corn, ripe tomatoes and old tennis balls!" He signed it "Aristotle the Yachtsman." She spent the weekend of September 19 with him. Stevenson wrote on his engagement pad, "Gay day!" Alicia wrote to him afterward—she had loved her days with him beside the Des Plaines River, she thought she would never stop wanting to be with him despite his remarks about her tennis and her bad habits.

Stevenson heard that some of Hubert Humphrey's staff regarded Stevenson as an obstacle to Humphrey's candidacy; Stevenson asked Bill Benton to find out how Humphrey himself felt. Jim Doyle asked Stevenson to speak briefly at a Democratic reception in Madison on September 25. Coincidentally Stevenson was planning to visit Madison to speak at a meeting of the Civil War Round Table and was able to put the two together: he told Doyle, "I will do precisely as you wish, although I prefer not to make any formal speech. I have tried to avoid speaking at political gatherings for fear of being misinterpreted." At this same time, August of 1959, other people were interesting themselves in his 1960 candidacy, urging him to move forcefully—Agnes Meyer, Mrs. Roosevelt, Tom Finletter, Stuart Gerry Brown of Syracuse University.[7] Agnes Meyer put up money to advance their efforts. Stevenson was getting help on speeches from Barbara Ward and Bill Attwood of *Look,* paid for by at least two people, Agnes Meyer and Mary Lasker.

Khrushchev was touring the United States and would visit, among other places, the farm of Roswell Garst in Iowa, repaying the visit Garst had paid him in Russia which he had discussed with Stevenson the previous summer. To Stevenson's delight, Newt Minow arranged to have Garst invite Stevenson too, and Stevenson left on September 22 for Des Moines, taking John Fell with him. He attended a banquet for Khrushchev in Des Moines that night, then next day went to the Garst farm at Coon Rapids. He noted on his appointment sheet, "Soldiers everywhere! Did farm sightseeing in advance of K. Met for lunch at Garsts farmhouse. Sat next to K. 45 min. talk—re disarm. etc. Returned to Chicago with JF [John Fell] in evening." On September 24 he issued a statement: "I think Mr. Khrushchev is serious . . . his proposals should be carefully considered, and not dismissed as propaganda."

On September 25, Stevenson, accompanied by Blair and Minow, went to Madison by private plane, held a press conference in Governor Nelson's office, delivered his speech on Jesse Fell and pioneer Illinois to the Civil War Round Table, attended a Democratic reception at a hotel and a party at the Governor's Mansion, where 1,100 people showed up—Stevenson went to bed in the Mansion at 3:45 A.M. Governor Nelson took him around Madison next day and to a football game. Minow once described the trip as one of the best he ever made with Stevenson. "He had a good time. He made a very funny speech. It was typical of the carefree, laughter-filled times." A few months later Jim Doyle's draft-Stevenson movement surfaced in Madison. Minow once said, "I suppose we were dissembling a little—but it was in a good cause. We knew what Jim Doyle was doing. The Governor helped get money for it from Benton and Mrs. Lasker and others. We disavowed it but we always kept in touch with it.

[7] Brown, with Stevenson's cooperation, was working on a book on Stevenson in the 1950s; it was published in 1961 as *Conscience in Politics.*

Often the Gov played dumb and innocent when he really knew all about something. In 1960 he kept saying that he didn't want to run—but he was interested." Wisconsin at this time appeared to be a key state in the 1960 preconvention campaign. The beginning of Stevenson's unannounced third campaign for the presidency could be dated that weekend in Madison.

He had been corresponding for some time with Hamilton Fish Armstrong, editor of *Foreign Affairs,* about a proposed article. Stevenson now asked Barbara Ward, in Ghana, for help on an article on Stevenson's meeting with Khrushchev, disarmament prospects, reunification of Germany, the Middle East, and entry of China into the UN (he thought the United States should desist from leading the opposition to her admission and that there were advantages to admission since China would then be "called to account before the bar of world opinion constantly," but he wanted to be careful not to commit himself publicly to advocating outright admission). He hoped the article could be prepared in time for publication in the January issue, which would be circulated to the large membership of the Book of the Month Club. He added a familiar note—Borden was back in Cambridge "with his Doc. and looking for a job," John Fell was in New York, Adlai was "working too hard—and Nancy is having another baby!" He closed, "I hope you are serene, and know you are. I hope you are well, and I know you are beautiful. Love to all."

A confidential poll of Democratic Governors and state chairmen showed little support for Stevenson's 1960 nomination. Kennedy seemed to be ahead though a good many politicians thought Symington would emerge as a compromise choice. Most considered Humphrey and Johnson weak. Jim Rowe told Bill Blair a close friend had reported that at a dinner party George Meany of the AFL-CIO had spoken with great vehemence against Stevenson—"Meany said 'any of the three'—Humphrey, Symington, Kennedy—would be all right with labor 'but not Adlai.'

18.

On October 18, Stevenson was interviewed on a television program, "Open End," by David Susskind. Susskind asked him to explain why his speeches created such an impression of intimacy yet at the same time he seemed remote and withdrawn from the crowd. Stevenson said he had always been "a very gregarious fellow" but "it's very difficult for me to combine work in the sense of creative work and constant exposure to the diversions of people in the crowd. . . . People have had the impression that maybe I've been a little aloof, a little withdrawn, a little shy about public exposure and I suspect I have. But one of the reasons for it is that I've had to have time to do my own work and my own thinking and this I can't do in a goldfish bowl." He insisted that he enjoyed handshaking and mingling with crowds but always felt he was wasting time he should be spending on more important things, such as writing speeches. Susskind asked if Stevenson credited the people with a higher intelligence and more information than editors and advertising men conceded. He did. But he said he felt contrite when a survey showed that more than a third of all Americans did not know West Berlin was surrounded by East Germany—it made him feel that he and other leaders had failed to communicate. Asked what "lessons and truths" he had learned from his political experience, Stevenson ended a long answer by saying, "I have often thought that if I had any epitaph that I would rather have more than another, it would be to say that I had disturbed the sleep of my generation."

Stevenson went to Boston on October 22 to see Borden and, while there, Arthur Schlesinger asked if he thought he could stay out of the Oregon primary. Stevenson replied he had told Oregon friends that the best way to get the nomination would be to stay out of Oregon. Someone asked if Bill Blair was working for Kennedy. Stevenson looked slightly hurt and said, "I certainly hope not. I have been going along on the assumption that his heart belongs to Daddy!" Schlesinger noted in his journal, "It was the general feeling that he is definitely interested." At about this time Chet Bowles told Stevenson that he had visited Wisconsin and found Governor Nelson strongly in favor of a Stevenson-Kennedy ticket and other Democrats hopeful that Stevenson "could somehow be induced to run." Bowles considered Kennedy strong enough in Wisconsin to beat Humphrey but thought Kennedy would be wise to stay out of Wisconsin. Stevenson agreed—Kennedy would be wise not to challenge Nelson in Wisconsin, Pat Brown in California, or Mike DiSalle in Ohio. "Thank God, I don't have to worry about these things any more!" But Stevenson was worrying about such affairs—Ralph McGill published a column entitled, "Adlai Sees His Program Adopted," and Stevenson thanked him for it.

Time magazine, querying its staff and auxiliary correspondents all over the country, found little more than latent Stevenson strength among leading Democrats. Some who had gravitated to Kennedy or Humphrey, however, confessed privately that their hearts still belonged to Stevenson. *Time*'s Chicago correspondent reported that the situation in Illinois, Iowa, and Ohio was extraordinary—a "huge segment" of "hard core" Democrats was paralyzed, "in limbo, immobilized, frustrated but content to squat on the sidelines and decide nothing until next summer," all because the man they considered best qualified, Stevenson, was doing nothing.

A Texan said, "Adlai's going to have to get on his horse and show his face and his guts before a lot of little people down here are gonna stick their necks out for a ghost of a candidate and incur the wrath of Lyndon Johnson, and then have the ghost vaporize out from under them." A correspondent in San Francisco reported great affection and respect for Stevenson but a feeling that voting for him was "about as fruitful as that old protest ballot for Norman Thomas used to be."[8]

19.

On the evening of October 24, Ellen Stevenson telephoned Jane Dick and talked to her for nearly an hour and a half, a long, somewhat disjointed attack on Stevenson. Mrs. Dick put the conversation into a long memo which Stevenson marked "Destroy." According to the memo, Ellen said Borden was with her and she was going to "rescue" him from the rest of his family. "The two younger boys are trying to escape." She said she could help them because "now I'm worth about a million dollars, and all through my own unaided efforts." (Yet at other times she said she was impoverished.) "Adlai," she said, "is just his father's puppet." She said she had tape recordings of every telephone conversation she had had over the last four years with her sons, her mother, her sister, or Stevenson. Her "bodyguard" had worn a tape recorder on his wrist at face-to-face conversations. "My own family have tried to buy him off! Adlai Stevenson said I'd be picked up and committed. Two of my sons have had nervous breakdowns. They said I went to the wedding with a pistol in my hand in order to kill the bride. I think it better that he not run again. He'd better not. If he'd been presidential quality I'd be helping him. . . . His sister is worse than he is," and she launched a diatribe against all the women who "surround" Stevenson, mentioning by name Marlene Dietrich and Suzie Zurcher. "For the sake of the United States he must never become President."

She went on, "Listen, my dear—I know you're a good person and I want you to know I'm telling you the truth and it's not pretty. The whole family is a pack of wolves. . . . Old Stevenstein ought to marry a Guggenheim or a Lasker and be happy. He won't win anyway. He certainly won't if I publish my paper." She said she had written a clever paper enti-

---

[8] By this time, among the non-professional Stevensonians at Harvard, Ken Galbraith had already openly declared for Kennedy. Seymour Harris was Stevenson's strongest supporter along the Charles River. Schlesinger would like to see Stevenson President but could not bear to see him lose to Nixon. He had great difficulty deciding between Kennedy and Humphrey. He knew Kennedy better and liked him better and Kennedy was his own Senator. But in the old ADA days Humphrey had fought alongside the ADA and Kennedy had not. Schlesinger concluded that so long as Humphrey was a candidate he would not come out for Kennedy; but privately he favored Kennedy and undertook to mediate between him and Stevenson. Martin had a somewhat different problem. Kennedy asked him to join him early in 1960, but Martin felt he could not so long as Stevenson refused to take himself out. He favored Kennedy, doubted Stevenson could be nominated, even doubted he could beat Nixon; but past loyalty held him in suspension. He did agree to join Kennedy once he was nominated or once Stevenson withdrew.

tled "Let's Have a Party": "You're all in it—all the Guggenheims, Dicks, Ronnie Trees, Mrs. Lasker and so on."

Jane Dick expressed sympathy with her and all she was going through (although she didn't really feel sympathetic). Ellen said, "I'm not going through anything. I'm happy. I'm free. All I want to do is to save my sons." She was considering a move to New York or Connecticut, she might arrange for a showboat to anchor in the Chicago River so she could produce plays on it, she had had offers from San Francisco and might go there. "Anyway, Jane dear, I'm not vindictive. I promise you I'm not. I'm free. I'm having fun. No one can hurt me now. . . . Do you remember the last thing I said to you? 'Please take care of Adlai. Just do anything to make him happy so that I won't feel guilty.' Well, you've certainly lived up to it and I thank you. Good-by."

Stevenson, acting in both his capacities as unofficial ambassador to the world and as an attorney for Reynolds Metals, had worked for several months at arrangements for the visit of Sekou Touré, President of Guinea, to Chicago. At 12:15 P.M. on October 30, he went to a luncheon at the Blackstone Hotel's Crystal Ballroom given in Touré's honor by Mayor Daley. He spoke briefly and went back to the office for a little more than an hour while Touré was visiting the African Institute at Northwestern University. Then he left the office for Libertyville, taking Ed McDougal and Walter Rice of Reynolds Metals with him. He would entertain Touré at Libertyville for dinner. It was the night before Hallowe'en.

Newt Minow attended the dinner. "The Gov tells Viola there will be about eighteen for dinner—he would be out there first—the guests would arrive about six-thirty. Then he called back and said there would be about twenty-eight and she would have to get more food. Viola was making beef stroganoff. She had some ham and so she sliced it up and put it in the beef stroganoff. The Governor was delayed at the office. The guests arrived first. They were wearing flowing African robes. Viola went to the door. She thinks they're trick-or-treaters—and she gives them peanuts and fruit and candy and shuts the door. A white girl from the State Department who was their escort rang the bell, Viola opened the door again, the girl came in and said, 'These are not Hallowe'en trick-or-treaters, they are the guests.' Viola lets them in and asks for their hats. That was the second mistake. They refused to take off their hats. In about fifteen minutes the Governor and Blair and I arrive. Touré says, 'What a quaint American custom to serve the guests nuts and apples at the door before dinner.' Well, we all had a drink. The next thing that went wrong was Mrs. Touré. I hear a scream—I look around—her dress had fallen off. It was only held up by one strap and the strap broke. She was naked to the waist. There was nothing under it. She rushes to the bathroom. Well, she came back. The Governor was trying to jolly everyone along. We went in to dinner. There is a lot of excited conversation in French—I can't speak French. I hear somebody say something about pork. The question is: Is there any ham in the stew? The Gov says, 'Oh no—this is beef stroganoff.' Just then the girl from the Department of State says, 'Governor Stevenson, this ham is absolutely delicious.' It might have been Suzie Zurcher. Anyway, these people are Moslems and can't eat pork. At that point the doorbell rings. It's more trick-or-treat, real this time—Marshall Field and his kids come in in flowing robes. Viola invites them in, thinking they were more guests. They joined the party. I tried to save the evening. There was a very good-looking Negro there who spoke English. I said to him, 'You speak English beautifully.' He looked at me and said, 'Why not? I'm the United States Ambassador to Guinea.'" (Minow, in later years, may have embroidered the story. Stevenson probably would have enjoyed the embroidery.)

Stevenson assigned Reynolds Metals eight hours of his time in attending lunch and dinner for Touré. In a note to Agnes Meyer written the next day Stevenson described the incident and said, "They're Moslems, and spotted the ham in the casserole! Horrors!—and if they go communist don't you tell on me. It was all for a client with business in that country—and now I suspect he's going too!" He signed himself "Mr. Fixit!!!"

20.

Throughout the rest of the year ran the thread of the 1960 convention. He was telling his friends, including his law partners, to go to work for the candidate of their choice.

John Steele wrote a piece saying that all potential Democratic presidential candidates, and Nelson Rockefeller as well, were campaigning on a promise to summon the country again to great tasks. Stevenson had started it with his 1956 position papers (and Steele said that every potential candidate he had come across kept a book of Stevenson's 1952 speeches at hand). Russian technology had surpassed American, and the average American did not like to see his country running second. Johnson warned about the missile gap, Symington talked about the lack of national purpose, Kennedy talked about the "corrosion" of luxury, Stevenson talked about the need for national rededication, Humphrey called for "more of everything."

By coincidence, the day after Steele filed that report Stevenson gave a memorandum to Bill Blair: "I expect to talk bluntly at the New York Insurance dinner about the state of stagnation we're slipping into again. But I don't want to do it unless it can be done constructively as well as critically. The indictment is, as always, easy. There were stirrings in the country for a while (after Sputnik), even signs of life earlier this year at the White House (after Adams). But we are back in the doldrums again. Time is running out. . . . Foreign affairs has become a matter of utter superficiality: the visits of Nixon to Russia and Khrushchev here (and that sickening moment of untruth at Los Angeles when they showed K the can-can girls and said this is America!); another summit some place; a brush-fire of internecine Democratic disagreement between Acheson and Kennan about Germany. The country is completely confused about the bomb test-ing—or where we or the Russians stand on it; and now France is getting ready to pollute the atmosphere over the Sahara. There is no real clash of ideas; no new ideas; no ideas at all; not even inching progress toward peace; no thinking, so far as I can see, about the future of a world in which whites are the minority, and likely the have-not minority at that; ev-erybody even afraid to talk about letting the world's largest nation into the U.N. Domestic affairs are even worse. One pitiful cheater on a commercial TV program receives a hundred times the attention paid four or five mil-lion unemployed workers. We shake our heads about tailfins and an affluent society, but don't shake our fists or flex our muscles about any-thing. Concern about civil rights has died down so far most people don't even know—or care—whether Central High in Little Rock is open or closed this year; much deliberation, no speed. We are being brain washed with economy and anti-inflation talk until there is real question whether decent school-hospital-health-housing programs can be gotten off the ground again for years. Taft would be a radical in the Senate today. Nobody has the elementary courage even to whisper that we're going to have to spend more money, which means more taxes. A year's debate on a labor bill centers around [James] Hoffa [head of Teamsters' union] and a few other hoodlums. . . . I want to say some of this—and not feel much concern about how it is going to go down with the business men in that audience or the Democrats (or Republicans) who may hear about it. (. . . And see DDE 11/2 speech about not wanting to pass debts on to his grandchildren. What kind of bequests has he in mind? Slums? Uncured disease? Deformities? Ignorance? More war?!!)" He asked Blair to have someone get up a draft.

The speech he actually gave on December 8 turned out far less crisp and effective than the memo.

Jim Doyle sent a long letter to Blair about a Wisconsin man who wanted to launch a national draft-Stevenson movement. Doyle preferred a scatter-ing of local and state groups. He planned to form a Wisconsin Stevenson committee at the time of the Democratic State Convention in Milwaukee November 13–15. Subsequently he told Blair that several reporters said "the evidence of Stevenson sentiment was the most significant thing about the convention." Doyle thought a "central intelligence agency" should be established to keep track of national political developments affecting Stevenson.

In Washington where he was a member of George Ball's law firm, John Sharon had lunch with two men interested in getting Stevenson nominated; he reported to Blair. The *Congressional Quarterly* polled the nation's editors and found that Stevenson and Nixon were "stronger-than-ever" contenders for their parties' nominations. Allan Nevins, the historian, told Stevenson he hoped the ticket would be Stevenson-Kennedy, thought others were coming to this view, and was urging it on the Kennedys.

On December 7, Stevenson spoke at a black-tie fund-raising dinner honoring Eleanor Roosevelt and other Democratic leaders at the Waldorf Astoria's grand ballroom. The audience was the liberal, moneyed, intellectual—and important—New York wing of the Democratic Party. It was Stevenson's audience, and he made the most of it, delivering an eloquent and moving speech in praise of Mrs. Roosevelt. Stevenson also told a story about a drunk who kept calling the hotel switchboard all night to ask what time the bar would open and, finally informed that in his present condition he would not be admitted to it, he shouted, "I don't want in, I want out." Humphrey spoke well, and Symington gained by joining the DAC in spite of Lyndon Johnson. (Johnson boycotted the dinner.) Governors Williams, Meyner, and Pat Brown inspired few. Kennedy spoke well. Stevenson was treated as a candidate and received the most applause.

On December 11, Bill Benton sent Stevenson a description of a luncheon given in New York for Humphrey on the day after the dinner. "[Humphrey]," Benton said, "had a most remarkable turnout, perhaps 150 people. Averell Harriman was there and pledged a contribution. Tom Finletter and many other of your supporters were there. I publicly pledged $2,500. Hubert put on a most skillful presentation of his case. . . . He will have an impact on the platform. . . . And he will have an impact on the attitude of our candidate, no matter who he may be. . . . Of course Hubert speaks of you with tender regard and deep affection."

Advance copies of Stevenson's article in *Foreign Affairs* were circulating, and the New York *Times* put an account of it on the front page. The article, entitled, "Putting First Things First," was later published in a book of that name which included seven other 1959 speeches and papers. In the article Stevenson said "freedom from war" should be at the top of American foreign policy. But since Korea, he said, "our political leadership" had not acknowledged massive changes in the world scene or devised new policies to meet the changes. "The main lines of American military and foreign policy are still those of 1947–1952," he said, thus directly challenging Acheson—but without naming him: instead, he named Dulles and Eisenhower as those who led the effort to contain Communist power through military alliances. At the same time, the Administration had defined its overriding task as keeping the budget down. And so America had fallen behind. What were the new "realities"? Colonialism had all but vanished; new nations were trying to fill the vacuum. Population was exploding. Scientific advance had created supersonic flight, the nuclear bomb, and space exploration. The "brief day of two-power domination" was passing and "new centers of power are rising from old ashes in Asia." By the end of the century China and India would be industrialized, a unified Europe would re-emerge as a world power, regional unification would take place in Latin America and Africa. Communism was successfully exploiting revolutions around the world. Khrushchev proposed to put down arms and defeat America at peaceful competitive coexistence. It was a safer and surer way to world-wide Communist power than war. The "two most dangerous realities" today were the multiplication of nuclear weapons and the disparity in living standards between rich and poor nations. We must end the gap between rich and poor through supranational institutions. We must work for "a disarmed world under law and organized police power." To achieve all this, we needed "our own creative policy"—not merely the negative policy of stopping Communism. "We cannot live by tail fins, TV and a 'sound dollar' alone." The West must spend at least $5 billion a year for at least forty years to help underdeveloped countries. The United States should work to unite Western Europe, including Britain. The West must remain strong militarily. Trade should be freer. Cultural exchanges between the United States and the U.S.S.R. should be increased. Controlled disarmament should be "at the top of the world's agenda." He regretted that the United States had not taken the lead in stopping H-bomb tests but was glad they had been stopped. Khrushchev's disarmament proposals should not be dismissed out of hand.

Stevenson recommended exploring with Khrushchev the possibility of negotiating with mainland China. Perhaps neither the United States nor the U.S.S.R. was yet willing to negotiate specifics. But no general control of disarmament had "any value" unless it included China. And China in the UN would be accountable to world opinion.

The areas where great power interests collided—Germany and the Middle East—could not be settled by military anti-Communist blocs but by negotiation. In the Middle East we should try "organized non-intervention . . . some international problems are never solved; they just wear out." In divided Europe the key to settlement was disarmament—the only satisfactory solution for divided Berlin was the unification of Germany, the road to unification lay through reduced fear in Russia and the West, and fear would subside only when progress was made toward disarmament.

In all these areas the "first priority" for the West was to "recover the initiative." Today Russia was the world leader in efforts toward peace. Nations could not demonstrate a sense of purpose abroad when they had lost it at home. Wilson had helped shape world thinking because he had pioneered the New Freedom at home. Roosevelt's world-wide liberal prestige was rooted in his New Deal at home. Truman's Marshall Plan and Point Four followed in the train of the Fair Deal. "The link is no less vital today. . . . By our default as much as by his design, Mr. Khrushchev is enabled to continue dictating the terms of the world's dialogue." Our foreign policy had been dominated by fear of Communism, our domestic policy by fear of inflation. He concluded: "I end where I began. I believe the

United States is ready for a new awakening and the achievement of greater goals. . . . It is the task of leadership to marshal our will and point the way."

It was a break with the past, with Acheson and other cold warriors. It was a search for policies for the future. John F. Kennedy would say many of the same things during his presidential campaign later that year and try to put them into practice as President. Stevenson at the end of the 1950s made of himself a bridge between past and future. His grandfather, the Vice President, had performed a similar service on a small scale long ago.

Mrs. Ives told Stevenson Mike Monroney's wife sent word that Monroney thought Stevenson ought not go to the convention but should be near enough to get to it in a hurry if he was drafted. The Iveses intended to go and would contribute $1,000, which would entitle them to two seats at the convention. Stevenson scribbled a note to Blair, "Have I a room the Ives could use at the Convention? I think I may not want to go to the Convention but should have a room pending a decision." Blair said, "I think Mike Monroney's suggestion that the Governor not be at the convention is absolutely mad. I am sure the Governor would be the laughing-stock of the country if he sat back in Chicago or over the border in Tijuana looking as if he was waiting to be summoned—particularly if he was not summoned at all. I am a great believer in doing what comes naturally and, as the leader of the party and the candidate in two national elections, I don't think he has any alternative but to attend the convention."

Arthur Schlesinger, visiting Washington just before Christmas, noted in his journal Phil Graham's outline of the Lyndon Johnson strategy. The Johnson men believed that Kennedy would go into the convention with about 500 votes, Johnson with about 300, nobody else with a sizable bloc; Kennedy would not make it, Stevenson would emerge as the Northern candidate, a struggle would develop between Stevenson and Johnson, and in the end the Northern professional politicians would go to Johnson because they did not think Stevenson could be elected and they disliked him anyway. Right after Christmas, Schlesinger visited Stevenson in Libertyville for several days. One night, after other guests—McGowan, Wirtz, and Martin—had left, Stevenson told Schlesinger, "I have something I want to discuss with you. I am greatly troubled over the general misunderstanding about my attitude toward the nomination. People seem to think that I am engaged in a subtle plot of some sort to get the nomination. No one seems to understand that I really don't want it. I think I ought to issue some sort of clarifying statement before I leave for Latin America." Schlesinger asked what he would say. "I'd like to say that I am not seeking the nomination, that I am not working for it, that I wish others would stop working for me, that I *don't want* the nomination. The question is whether I should go beyond this." He paused. "The question is whether I should add that, if the convention wants me, I could not, of course, decline the nomination." Schlesinger said he doubted that such a statement would clarify anything, since it expressed what most people already thought was his position. Stevenson said he had considered issuing what he erroneously called a "Grant statement"—"interesting Freudian slip," Schlesinger noted, "since Grant wanted to be nominated and Sherman didn't"—but said he feared it would look as though he was running away from a fight. "I'm not frightened, and I don't want anyone to think I am. If defeat could destroy a man, I would have been destroyed long since. If the convention wants me, I will have no choice but to accept the nomination. But *I don't want it,* and I wish people would understand that."

Stevenson still preferred Humphrey, Schlesinger noted, "but wonders about his impetuosity of judgment. He likes Kennedy personally, but is worried about an alleged profound and anti-European prejudice reported to him by Elmo Roper and Barry Bingham." Late on December 29 they talked again at length, and Stevenson talked about the importance of getting a "brain trust" started for the benefit of "whoever is nominated" and asked if Schlesinger would be free to go to Washington if a Democrat was elected. He talked at length about his contempt for Nixon and said, "I don't think I should be the candidate because I despise Nixon so much that I couldn't be trusted not to say something absolutely terrible about him in the course of the campaign. I detest him so much that my true feelings would be bound to come out."

Angier Biddle Duke told Stevenson that, like many others, he was emotionally drawn to Stevenson's candidacy. He had agreed to be chairman of the New York luncheon for Humphrey but had told Humphrey's people that Stevenson was his real candidate always. Stevenson thanked him—"but I think you realize that I feel strongly that I have had enough of such major exertions!"

In Christmas messages to Agnes Meyer, Stevenson said that Barry Bingham had told him about her "activities," presumably to get him nominated, and promised her "no cooperation on your major plot for the New Year." Alicia Patterson had slipped on a rug in her house in New York and broken her foot, and Stevenson wrote Barbara Ward that she would "not be able to walk for a long, long time, and probably never play games again."

21.

Nineteen-sixty—the last chance for a last hurrah. Stevenson was sixty years old. If he was to run again it would almost surely have to be now. What he did and said up until the time of the convention at Los Angeles in July was, except for his South American trip and certain business matters, almost wholly connected with presidential politics.

In retrospect it seems that once again his luck was bad. He was out of step with history. In 1952 he had been obliged to run at the end of the Roosevelt-Truman period and against General Eisenhower. In 1956 he had had his second chance—against Eisenhower. Now in 1960 he was not only twice defeated but he stood at the threshold of a new decade opening at a time when the country, after seven years of lassitude and irresponsibility under Eisenhower, was once again ready for new initiatives, new policies—and new faces. Stevenson, by his opposition to the Eisenhower administration, by his attacks on national complacency and his warnings against national frivolity, had helped prepare the country to commence again the forward movement it had abandoned after Roosevelt and Truman. But it was John F. Kennedy, not Stevenson, who symbolized the exciting youthful surge toward national greatness. Stevenson, older in years and older in the national consciousness, represented not the future but the lost past. As Stevenson had burst on the national scene in 1952, so Kennedy burst on it in 1960. But at the start of 1960 all this was far from clear.

On New Year's Day he sent Alicia Patterson a poem:

For Elisha—on the first day of a new decade—

> Build on resolve and not upon regret
> The structure of the future.
> Waste no tears upon the blotted record of lost years,
> But turn the leaf and smile;
> Ah, smile to see the fair white [illegible]
> That remain to thee—and me

                                                    Adpai

Stevenson wrote Lady Spears, "Nixon is not 'popular' in the usual sense. He is very much a politician's politician and I suspect there is extensive uneasiness and mistrust in people's hearts about him. God knows there ought to be! However, there is no doubt that Eisenhower's sudden excess of energy and total reversal of the Dulles rigidity has given the Republicans a new lease on life and the better of the 'peace' issue—as of now! That one day the press can applaud Dulles for rigid 'firmness' and the next day praise Eisenhower's flexibility in the 'search for peace' is a measure of our current scene. But I am used to that."

Senator Kennedy told Stevenson on January 5 that he had heard that a Professor Latham of Amherst, who was working on issues for Kennedy, was bruiting it about that Kennedy felt Stevenson had treated him unfairly in the contest for the vice presidential nomination of 1956. Kennedy told Stevenson he had not talked to Latham for six months and never about the Chicago convention. "My feeling is wholly the reverse of what he described. . . . I would not write you this except I would not want anything to mar our extremely cordial relationship. I rarely see you, unfortunately, though I do see a good deal of Bill Blair and keep in touch with you

9 His old friend Jane Dick (Mrs. Edison Dick) of Lake Forest had supported him for Governor in 1948 and for President in 1952 and in later years she was ever ready to charge forth on his behalf. Even after he died she strove mightily to make the Adlai E. Stevenson Institute succeed. As he did for so many, Stevenson put an added meaning into her life. Here she is shown in 1956 in San Francisco, organizing for him. The hole in her shoe, intended to remind voters of a famous photograph of Stevenson, was one of the few gimmicks that crept into Stevenson campaigns.

10 The mid-1950s were the years of Adlai Stevenson's greatest leadership. In the 1954 congressional campaign, in his own 1956 presidential campaign, and in his other speeches and position papers in those years, he laid the groundwork for the New Frontier of John F. Kennedy and the Great Society of Lyndon B. Johnson. Here he is shown late in August 1956, fussing as usual over speeches—speeches he would deliver at a series of unusual regional meetings around the nation, cementing politicians' support but also setting forth policy on basic issues.

11 New York City fell in love with Stevenson in 1952, a love affair that endured until his death. Here he is shown at the Madison Square Garden rally near the climax of his 1956 campaign with four other famous Democrats—Governor Averell Harriman, Senator Herbert H. Lehman, Mrs. Eleanor Roosevelt, and Mayor Robert Wagner.

12 Alicia Patterson Guggenheim remained his friend until the end. At her death in 1963, Stevenson showed more personal grief than at any other's.

13
Nikita Khrushchev came to the United States in 1959 and visited, among other places, a farm in Iowa. Stevenson was there.

14 The last hurrah. In the spring of 1960, during the contest for the Democratic nomination for President, various Stevenson advisers urged him to withdraw in favor of Senator John F. Kennedy. Stevenson refused; he wanted a third chance. Here he is shown in Los Angeles amid a happy crowd that welcomed him to what became, for him, a melancholy convention.

15 In December 1960, President-elect Kennedy, at his house in Georgetown, was forming his government. For many reasons he could not give Adlai Stevenson the job he wanted, Secretary of State. On December 8, when this photo was made, he offered him the job of Ambassador to the UN. Stevenson offended him by asking time to think about it. The relations between Stevenson and the young President were never so good as one might have hoped but better than some thought.

16 The relationship between Stevenson and Dean Rusk was not an easy one. When he was appointed Secretary of State, Rusk was virtually unknown; Stevenson was a world figure. Rusk was extremely careful of Stevenson's feelings; Stevenson was less careful of Rusk's but ever mindful of his position. Here, as they enter the White House to meet with President Kennedy early in his administration, Stevenson is walking on Rusk's left, the correct position, according to State Department protocol, for a subordinate.

17 Eleanor Roosevelt was ever Adlai Stevenson's great and good friend. He loved her simply, and when she died he told the United Nations General Assembly, "She would rather light candles than curse the darkness, and her glow has warmed the world." If in the future the world abandons the system of warring nation states and goes the way of Eleanor Roosevelt and Adlai Stevenson, toward internationalism and world order, their towering place in history seems assured. Here they are shown early in the Kennedy administration entering the house of peace, the UN.

18 In perhaps the worst blunder of his administration, President Kennedy authorized the invasion of Cuba at the Bay of Pigs by Cuban exiles managed by the CIA. So doing, he unwittingly compromised Ambassador Stevenson at the UN: his CIA supplied Stevenson with photos of airplanes bearing the forged markings of Castro's Air Force which, the CIA pretended, had been flown by Cuban Air Force defectors to bomb Cuban airfields. Stevenson displayed them to the UN, not knowing they were forgeries.

through him." He wished they could meet before Stevenson went to South
America. Stevenson replied to "Dear Jack": "Thanks for your letter. But
please don't worry; I was sure the Professor was confused." He would be
in Washington in January and would be "delighted" to see Kennedy. He
added a postscript, "You're doing fine!" It was the first of several communications between Stevenson and Kennedy in 1960. Blair kept in touch
with both John Kennedy and Robert Kennedy and he also saw their sister
Eunice Shriver frequently. "President Kennedy liked Blair a great deal,"
Robert Kennedy said. But John Kennedy, he thought, had been partly disillusioned with Stevenson in 1956, and their relationship deteriorated during 1960.

Lewis M. Stevens, a Philadelphia lawyer who had been active in the
Volunteer movement, told Blair that although Stevenson was still his first
choice he intended to work for Kennedy if Kennedy entered Pennsylvania,
since Stevenson seemed unavailable. Blair told Stevens as he told others:
"If I were you I would by all means go to work for Jack. We get a good
many letters similar to yours and without exception the Governor has
urged his friends to go to work for the candidate of their choice. . . . I
think Jack is doing extremely well and I happen to be one of the people
who feel he has an excellent chance of being nominated."

To a friend who had expressed the view that Nixon would be "bad" for
the country, Stevenson wrote, "It seems to me unthinkable that a man with
his background of slander, abuse, innuendo, expediency and resort to all
the most devious political devices should ever occupy an office which we
have tried for generations to exalt in the esteem of young people and the
world. However, strange things are happening here and elsewhere."

Agnes Meyer met with the Roger Stevenses and the Finletters, and they
decided that if the nominees were Nixon and Kennedy, Nixon would win,
and therefore, for the sake of the country, they must work to nominate
Stevenson. "Tom Finletter came up with an idea that is practical, sound
and promising. . . . It is important that you do not know about it. . . . I
promised financial support which is never to be revealed." John Sharon
sent Bill Blair samples of Stevenson-for-President campaign literature together with a price list for bumper stickers, windshield stickers, postcards,
and other materials. He reported that a 1956 volunteer was generating activity in New York and writing to Stevenson men in other states.

Stevenson attended a heavy schedule of Britannica meetings for three
days, then on January 14 went to Washington to call on Latin American
Ambassadors and receive State Department and CIA briefings on Latin
America. He saw Senator Kennedy and Senator Clark. And he saw Ambassador Mikhail A. Menshikov of the Soviet Union at 4 P.M. on Saturday, January 16. They had a most extraordinary conversation.

A few days earlier Menshikov had telephoned him in Chicago and told
him that he had some presents and messages from Premier Khrushchev
which he wished to deliver. Menshikov had volunteered to go to Chicago;

Stevenson had protested that *he* would call on *him;* and now he did, in Washington, at the guarded forbidding Soviet Embassy. They had met several times before. Menshikov was a rather outgoing man, given to diplomatic courtesies as some Russian emissaries were not. They exchanged pleasantries about health and families; Menshikov offered caviar, fruit, other delicacies, and drinks. Then at last he came to the point. He carefully withdrew from his pocket a folded sheaf of notes written in ink on small sheets of paper and began to speak, obviously under tight instructions. Stevenson dictated, on January 25, a memorandum of their conversation ("I hesitated for a week before making any record of this curious conversation"):

"Before returning last week from Moscow, he [Menshikov] had spent considerable time alone with Premier Khrushchev. He wishes me to convey the following: When you met in Moscow in August 1958, he said to you that he had voted for you in his heart in 1956. He says now that he will vote for you in his heart again in 1960. We have made a beginning with President Eisenhower and Khrushchev's visit to America toward better relations, but it is only a beginning. We are concerned with the future, and that America has the right President. All countries are concerned with the American election. It is impossible for us not to be concerned about our future and the American Presidency which is so important to everybody everywhere.

"In Russia we know well Mr. Stevenson and his views regarding disarmament, nuclear testing, peaceful coexistence, and the conditions of a peaceful world. He has said many sober and correct things during his visit to Moscow and in his writings and speeches. When we compare all the possible candidates in the United States we feel that Mr. Stevenson is best for mutual understanding and progress toward peace. These are the views not only of myself—Khrushchev—but of the Presidium. We believe that Mr. Stevenson is more of a realist than others and is likely to understand Soviet anxieties and purposes. Friendly relations and cooperation between our countries are imperative for all. Sober realism and sensible talks are necessary to the settlement of international problems. Only on the basis of coexistence can we hope to *really* find proper solutions to our many problems.

"The Soviet Union wishes to develop relations with the United States on a basis which will forever exclude the possibility of conflict. We believe our system is best and will prevail. You, Mr. Stevenson, think the same about yours. So we both say, let the competition proceed, but excluding any possibility of conflict.

"Because we know the ideas of Mr. Stevenson, we in our hearts all favor him. And you (Ambassador Menshikov) must ask him which way we could be of assistance to those forces in the United States which favor friendly relations. We don't know how we can help to make relations better and help those to succeed in political life who wish for better relations and more confidence. Could the Soviet press assist Mr. Stevenson's personal success? How? Should the press praise him, and, if so, for what? Should it criticize him, and, if so, for what? (We can always find many things to criticize Mr. Stevenson for because he has said many harsh and critical things about the Soviet Union and Communism!) Mr. Stevenson will know best what would help him.

"The presentation concluded with questions about 'Mr. Stevenson's rival,' meaning Vice President Nixon, and repeated declarations of desire not 'to interfere in an American election,' together with many sober statements about the profound 'interest' of the Soviet Union, and of all countries, in the American election. The protestations about non-interference were interspersed throughout the presentation, which I did not interrupt. The distaste and mistrust of Nixon was expressed cautiously but clearly. The Ambassador made a gesture of sad resignation about the Khrushchev-Nixon altercation in the model kitchen at the Trade Fair in Moscow, if not saying, at least implying, that Khrushchev had not realized that such an irrelevant dialogue recorded on television would be shown and taken seriously in the United States, to the great political advantage of Nixon.

"While it was not included in the formal presentation of Mr. Khrushchev's message, it was apparent that they were quite aware of the effect on the Presidential election of the [forthcoming] Summit Conference and Eisenhower's visit to Russia; that a 'success' would redound to the benefit of the Republican candidate which seems to leave them in some dilemma.[9]

"Mr. Menshikov concluded by saying that this interview was the best evidence of the confidence reposed in me by the Premier and his colleagues and that he had no misgivings about my keeping it in confidence.

"At the conclusion, I made the following points:

"(1) My thanks for this expression of Khrushchev's confidence.

"(2) My thanks for this proffer of aid.

"(3) However, I was not a candidate for the nomination and did not expect to be a candidate for the Presidency in 1960.

"(4) My grave misgivings about the propriety or wisdom of any interference, direct or indirect, in the American election, and I mentioned to him the precedent of the British Ambassador and Grover Cleveland. (He in turn implied that President Eisenhower was not above intervention in the British election last fall; nor Dulles in behalf of Adenauer vs. the Social Democratic party in Germany.)

"(5) Finally, I said to him that even if I was a candidate I could not accept the assistance profferred. I believe I made it clear to him that I considered the offer of such assistance highly improper, indiscreet and dangerous to all concerned.

[9] A "summit" conference among Eisenhower, Khrushchev, De Gaulle, and Macmillan was scheduled for the coming May in Paris. It was wrecked after the Russians shot down an American U-2 spy plane.

"In thanking Khrushchev for his expressions of respect for my 'realism and understanding of the Soviet Union' I said that I hoped that I *did* have some understanding beyond the ordinary, and that I was sure Menshikov and Khrushchev had come to understand the U.S. much better, about which I found so much ignorance in the Soviet Union.

"I said that I was aware of some of the difficulties of the Soviet Union, especially with respect to China. At this point, Menshikov said with a wry smile: 'Yes, we may be allies again.'

"His manner was extremely amiable but very serious during his presentation of Khrushchev's message, which was done in a low voice, in a parlor adjoining the family dining room on the third floor. On two occasions when a waitress appeared with food, etc., he interrupted his conversation.

"On January 22, 1960, I wrote Mr. Menshikov the attached letter."

That letter was surprisingly open:

I am most grateful to you and Premier Khrushchev for the splendid gift you delivered to me at the Embassy in Washington last week. So much delicious Russian caviar and wine may not be good for me —but I like it! I hope you will extend my very warm thanks to Premier Khrushchev, and also my best wishes for his health and happiness in the New Year and the New Decade. That the year and decade will see ever closer and constantly improving relations between our great countries is my highest hope, and I am sure you and Mr. Khrushchev have similar sentiments about our common future.

The confidence expressed in me during our conversation and Premier Khrushchev's interest in my views were flattering, and I wish I could thank him in person. But I must repeat that I will not seek the nomination for President again and that I do not expect to be a candidate of the Democratic party this year. Even if I was, however, I would have to decline to take advantage in any way of the confidence and good will I am happy to enjoy among your compatriots. I am sure you and Premier Khrushchev will understand, and I hope respect, my feelings about the proprieties in the circumstances we discussed, and I trust that my reaction will not be misconstrued as discourteous or ungrateful.

With renewed thanks to you and the Premier, together with my hope that we may have further talks from time to time, I am

Cordially yours

Curiously, a day later, on January 23, Scotty Reston wrote in the New York *Times* that the Russians were showing "both a keen interest in the United States and an appalling ignorance of the dangers in commenting about it." He said their controlled press had denounced Rockefeller, and their officials had told him and other reporters they disliked Nixon as well as Rockefeller. "Even the Soviet Ambassador here, Mikhail Menshikov, has been talking freely about his opinions of the candidates and leaving no doubt among his hearers about how the Soviet Union would like to see the election turn out in November. . . . It is the unwritten law of the Diplomatic Corps here that no Ambassador initiates any discussion of Presidential politics," and Reston recalled the intervention of the British Ambassador during the campaign between Cleveland and Benjamin Harrison in 1888. He wrote, "There is not a candidate in the race who would not love to have the hostility of the Soviet Union as an issue."

Stevenson was staying in Washington with Laura Magnuson and evidently told her about the Menshikov conversation. After leaving, he wrote to her, "As I think about it I get more and more indignant about being 'propositioned' that way; and at the same time more and more perplexed, if that's the word, by the *confidence* they have in me. I shall do one thing only *now:* politely and decisively reject the proposal—and pray that it will never leak, lest I lose that potentially valuable confidence. Thanks for housing, feeding and *nursing* me!" (He had burned his ankle painfully by spilling a pot of hot coffee in the kitchen of his house in Libertyville a few days earlier.)

John Steele, who observed Stevenson's visit to Washington but did not know about the Menshikov conversation, reported, "In two days of needlessly frenetic activities here this weekend he presented the picture of an utterly harried, put-upon, almost distraught person. He was not the picture of a man, even in the eyes of his friends, who should be in the White House. It is not, however, an irreparable situation. He needs either a strong-willed wife, a bull-headed secretary, or a prize fight manager—better yet all three. He spun from useless cocktail party to cocktail party, disheveled and breathless. He submitted to the back pounding of people who can help him not at all. He affronted editors who sought to shake his hands as he bolted for an exit. He forgot his papers as he left one Georgetown home heading for another, frantically had to run back. He bitterly complained because no one had supplied him with copies of his recent speeches on which he was to be questioned by a TV panel. He had no time to read the newspapers. He angrily bewailed his fate in missing an opportunity to chat with an important scientist whose advice he sought—the reason, a fat jezebel with dyed red hair pinned him in a corner and verbally raped him. He fought to extricate himself from a meaningless primary (District of Columbia) into which he'd been propelled by self-serving local politicians. He left Washington torn, exhausted, frustrated and saddened. For the moment Stevenson appeared a rather pathetic man— no very real objective, no solid base, few real friends; only chaos. . . . Bill Blair . . . almost has thrown up his hands in despair."

22.

From Washington, Stevenson went up to New York for a few days. Dean Rusk read a paper on "The President" at the Council on Foreign Relations. This paper, published that spring in *Foreign Affairs,* was thought to have influenced President-elect Kennedy in appointing Rusk Secretary of State. Just before catching a plane back to Chicago on January 20, Stevenson dictated a letter to Agnes Meyer about Bill Attwood. Attwood, he said, wanted to work on issues and speeches to be made by somebody prior to the convention. He would ask for a leave of absence from *Look* from February 15 to November 15; Stevenson and Finletter had agreed to pay him monthly at the rate of $22,000 a year, plus travel expenses, not to exceed in total $25,000. Mrs. Meyer had agreed to pay Attwood's salary. Subsequently Stevenson wrote to Attwood, "Excellent men for sharp verbal work in the Senate are Senators Gene McCarthy, Mike Monroney, John Pastore and Warren Magnuson. Why not a profile on Nixon by Steinbeck or John Hersey? . . . I think the operation needs someone with a sense of the ridiculous and who isn't afraid of bloodshed! You know what I mean—'He is a man of no character and we are going to prove it.' One of the most useful things that could be done for the Democrats would be to get some action on the bill for equal television time for the Presidential candidates." John Steele, in a dispatch filed January 28, said that Jim Doyle was about to announce plans for a national draft-Stevenson movement. Steele said that Jack Arvey and Dave Lawrence were veering toward Symington, that Daley was leaning toward Kennedy, that Rayburn would be for Johnson first and Symington second, and that no important state chairmen or national committeemen were working for Stevenson. Many amateur draft-Stevenson movements had sprung up in the country but Steele thought their chances poor unless professional politicians supported them—that had been the history of the successful 1952 draft movement. Stevenson had slipped, Steele thought, but was not yet eliminated.

Stevenson returned briefly to New York on January 27, saw Mayor Wagner and Bill Attwood and some law clients, and, in a speech to the ADA, thinking of Nixon, tried to meet the character issue head on: "Surely the indispensable quality for a President is character. For, as Franklin Roosevelt said, 'the presidency is pre-eminently a position of moral leadership.' " He again attacked the Administration for lulling the people into complacency. Agnes Meyer on February 2 told Stevenson not to "worry too much" about an outline Attwood had submitted—"I shall work with him closely." She enclosed a copy of a letter she had sent Attwood, outlining speeches Stevenson should make when he returned from South America and offering to buy television time if necessary. She went on, "I must emphasize that you have overdone your hands-off policy about political developments. . . . Adlai, you *are* the titular head of your party, candidate or no candidate, and you owe it to the American people . . . to clarify the fact that *the future of our country is at stake in this election.* . . . I would rather see you go down to defeat for the nomination rather than fail to carry out a mission only you can fulfill. . . . Adlai, your greatest moment will come when you return from S.A. . . . . Adlai, I demand that you rise to your greatest self when you come home."

Stevenson's former wife Ellen telephoned Carol Evans on February 4 and said that her mother's home at 1020 Lake Shore Drive and the building she was living in at 1362 Astor Street were being sold and that she had sent an "audit" to which she requested a reply that day. Miss Evans suggested she call Adlai III. Ellen replied (according to Miss Evans' memorandum), "Poor Adlai, I had hoped to keep him and the other boys out of this, I don't think it is a good thing to have things like this turn up in the newspapers because it is so bad for them, the poor boys. Well, I will call up Adlai, I didn't even mention it to him, I didn't send any of my sons a copy as I didn't want them to know about it, I wanted to deal direct with Mr. Stevenson, it is not fair, I won't deal with him through my sons." Miss Evans murmured that she knew nothing about the problem that was troubling Ellen. The house at 1020 Lake Shore Drive was sold for $85,963. The building on Astor Street was sold a little more than a year later for $181,165. Ellen shared the proceeds with her mother and sister.

At about this time, according to testimony given later at a hearing on her competency, Ellen visited the home of Adlai III and Nancy. Nancy testified, "I had asked her to come over. We tried to invite her from time to time so that she would know the children and see them, and I had invited her over to come in the afternoon after they had gotten up from their nap. At this point, we had Adlai [IV] and Lucy. Adlai was about three, three and a half, Lucy was just beginning to walk. She was expected to come at about four-thirty, and the children were . . . waiting for her at four-thirty at the door, eagerly." Ellen did not arrive until about seven-thirty, the children's bedtime. Nancy let them stay up and play with her. For a time it went well. But when Nancy took the children upstairs to put them to bed, Ellen followed, saying, "You are not a fit mother. You are a—you are a little bitch who is trying to take my grandchildren away from me, and you are not a fit mother," and, according to Nancy's testimony, became increasingly abusive. They nearly struggled physically, and Nancy finally asked her to leave. Outside, Ellen stood on the sidewalk for about five minutes shouting abuse.

Friday, February 5, was Stevenson's sixtieth birthday. In letters to friends he said of it, "Horrors!" His friends went to greater lengths than usual this time. The Dicks, the Dutch Smiths, and the Ed McDougals got out printed invitations to help celebrate "Adlai's 60th Birthday" at 7 P.M. at the Smiths' and 10:30 P.M. at the Dicks', an old-fashioned progressive party in the Lake Forest tradition of the 1920s. Barbara Ward came and spent the weekend with Stevenson. The Barry Binghams came from Louisville, others from elsewhere. Jane Dick delivered a long toast, telling several stories about Stevenson's dealings with women and thanking him for enriching her life. The party was large and happy.

Next day Stevenson gave a buffet lunch for the out-of-town guests. Averell Harriman sent Stevenson a birthday telegram: "Welcome to the sizzling sixties."

Buffie Ives sent him a somewhat elegiac birthday letter—it was hard for her to realize how old he and she really were. Stevenson tried to telephone her three times at Southern Pines, North Carolina, forgetting that she was in Florida, and told her, "I must be nuts—or perhaps it is age."

23.

To Latin America: he would be gone two months. He was accompanied by Bill Blair, Bill Benton, John Fell, and Dr. Carleton Sprague Smith, head of the Brazilian Institute of New York University. He would write about Latin America for *Look*. It was his first extended trip to Latin America. John Fell took photographs and accompanied his father to meetings. "I felt that was sort of a chore," he once said. "What we really wanted to see was something else. He would always go to see the markets and the churches and the slums—the city dumps." Benton once said that he paid all expenses of the trip, about $30,000 or $40,000. Benton later wrote a book about Latin America, stringing together notes he dictated en route; Stevenson never read it.

They left Chicago in a blizzard, Stevenson wrote in his notebook, and were met at Mexico City by the American Ambassador, Robert Hill. Stevenson noted that night, "Already impressed with growth and modernization—after 24 years! since last visit to Mexico—with Ellen." Next morning he spoke to 250 members of the embassy staff, then received a briefing. Mexican-American relations were friendlier than in the past, aided by presidential visits, but Mexican news was poorly reported in the North American press, and Americans were appallingly ignorant of Mexico. Yet Mexico City had the United States' largest consulate general, 50,000 Americans lived in Mexico, and 600,000 Americans visited there annually. The government's great objective was land reform, breaking up large estates and reducing foreign control, but so far it had not been notably successful. "No serious domestic communism. . . . Sov Emb largest in LA [Latin America]—125—direct all of LA. . . . *Influence of Castro with students in LA enormous! . . . Little danger of communism in LA. except Bolivia.* Should increase power of OAS and effectiveness—less talk, more facts. . . . *Don't intervene with Trujillo.* Support any movement to increase democ. and protect human rights. *Don't give any help;* moral condemnation." (A few months later, in August of 1960, the OAS imposed sanctions on both Castro's Cuba and Trujillo's Dominican Republic.)

A lunch given in his honor by the Foreign Minister, talks with President López Mateos, lunch with the Cabinet and "BIG businessmen," press conferences, embassy receptions ("a mob scene"), a visit to murals and ruins, speeches and a marimba band and dancing in native costume—he was back on the official circuit, as he had been on his 1953 world tour. He did not seem to weary of it—wrote in his notes that the band playing from a balcony for him was "splendid," that an old church was "remarkably beautiful." On to Mérida, in Yucatán, and the spectacular Mayan ruins at Uxmal and elsewhere—"Reminded of Ankor Wat by these enormous structures covered by scrub jungle for centuries."

In Guatemala City, Stevenson visited President Ydígoras Fuentes, a "gentle, quiet, humorous little man." Ydígoras, he wrote, had been elected in an upset after the assassination of Castillo Armas. People had expected him to be a dictator; instead he had introduced democratic institutions— and now a free press proved it by attacking him, a free judiciary sent no one to jail, and everyone not on the government payroll conspired to over- throw him. "Delightful man with rare touch of genuine greatness but prob- ably not forceful or ruthless enough for these infant democracies. . . . Country's needs like all of them," he wrote, "hospitals, medicines, schools, water supply." Then over mountains and lakes to Costa Rica and "Pepe Figueres, former Pres and one of really significant democratic leaders of hemisphere." (Stevenson had met him earlier through Arthur Schle- singer.) Everywhere the talk was of Castro and Communism. Figueres suggested moving the OAS to Panama, giving it the canal, and renaming the Zone the District of the Americas. Otherwise the canal would always be embroiled in Panamanian politics and the United States would always be the whipping boy. At midnight they started for La Lucha Sin Fin (The Fight Without End), Pepe Figueres' home in the mountains. "Arrived after hair raising trip over rugged mountain road driven by Pepe who talked incessantly about civil war in CR which he led and which restored const. democracy after 8 years of coalition of extreme right who wanted to make money and communists who wanted power. Farm and all blds burned. Stories of Somoza . . . tortures in Nicaragua—squeezing testicles a favorite. Trujillos brutalities. *That these things could be happening in mid-twentieth century!*' . . . to bed at 2 A.M. a little sick with his long reci- tation of our stupidities in LA and toleration of these bastards so long." He slept next morning till nine-thirty. "Beautiful tropical mountain scenery. Very rugged; rope factory; idyllic setting; sweet pregnant wife Karen, Danish-Am; charming bright eyed children. *Incessant and fasci- nating talk from this eloquent, passionate, gentle, sensitive man who hates tyranny and injustice as no one I've ever met! 'What all SA wants is opportunity to develop themselves. . . .'* Re Cuba—never suspected any commie link. *Now only 50-50 chance of saving So. Am continent.* Coalitions of extreme right—money—and extreme left—power."

In Panama, mindful of Figueres' advice, he said, "I can see little objec- tion to raising the flag of Panama alongside ours in the Zone as a visual acknowledgment of Panama's titular sovereignty, provided the Republic of

Panama at the same time reaffirms that the United States has all rights and privileges in the Zone as if it were sovereign, and also that the freedom of access to the Zone should not be used for certain defined purposes, including violence and demonstrations such as occurred last fall. . . . To me the most serious problem of all is the exclusive community of American civilians that has grown up in the Zone and has little contact with the friendly country around them. Steps should be taken to break down these barriers. . . . I have heard it suggested that [the canal be internationalized and] the OAS itself might be moved to this midway point between North and South America and the Zone renamed as the District of the Americas."

Carol Evans was forwarding mail. Agnes Meyer told Stevenson she intended to "sound out" Walter Reuther "about being for Stevenson." The Rev. Richard Graebel of Springfield recommended that Stevenson visit Cuba and talk to Fidel Castro and help him. Stevenson warned Graebel that Latin Americans thought Castro a Communist.

Newt Minow cabled that the New York *Times* had reported from Costa Rica that Stevenson said the amount of money being spent on Senator Kennedy's presidential campaign was "phenomenal," probably the most in history. It also claimed that Stevenson had remarked upon Kennedy's large campaign staff and quoted him as saying, "Sometimes all this spending and show of power is not a good thing politically because people are apt to show natural sympathy for the underdog." Minow said Robert Kennedy had called the law office, "very upset," to protest that he was not spending large sums. Minow urged Stevenson to immediately set things right. Stevenson promptly sent the following cable to Turner Catledge of the New York *Times:*

UNAUTHORIZED QUOTES BY YOUR CORRESPONDENT IN COSTA RICA VERY EMBARRASSING AND INACCURATE. HAVE JUST TELEPHONED MY PARTNER, WILLARD WIRTZ, CHICAGO, AS FOLLOWS: I AM ASTONISHED BY THE NEW YORK TIMES STORY AND NEITHER AUTHORIZED NOR MADE ANY SUCH STATEMENTS. STOP. IN RESPONSE TO A QUESTION BY A COSTA RICAN AT A RECEPTION I AGREED THAT IF THE TIME MAGAZINE STORY ABOUT SENATOR KENNEDY'S CAMPAIGN WAS CORRECT, IT WOULD BE VERY EXPENSIVE AND MIGHT CREATE SYMPATHY FOR HIS OPPONENTS. STOP.

Hubert Humphrey, campaigning in Wisconsin, had said that the Kennedy organization was on a "spending spree." Kennedy, campaigning there too, had challenged Humphrey to sign a "treaty" limiting campaign spending. On a national television interview program, Kennedy now said that Stevenson had repudiated the statements attributed to him by the *Times. Newsweek's* issue of February 29 repeated the Stevenson quotations and said that the publisher of a San José, Costa Rica, newspaper had heard Stevenson utter them at Pepe Figueres' reception, had written a story about it, and had shown it to Bill Blair. Blair had "exploded" and said Stevenson could not possibly have made the statements. Later, Stevenson complained to the publisher, who told him that the *Times* correspondent had also heard him say it and probably had already cabled the quotes to his paper, whereupon Stevenson said in an aside to someone, probably Blair, "Oh, God, a guy [from] the *Times* has filed it." Stevenson had told a *Newsweek* reporter he had thought he was having a "private conversation" with the reporters. They had quoted him out of context, he said.

He flew to Bogotá in the President's plane, he wrote, adding, "Very swank." He wrote, *"Arrived in time for bullfight. . . . Two dedicated to me! Tremendous greeting by crowd! Almost mobbed!!"* Embassy briefers told him that Colombia was a pro-American political democracy with a "great" President. Its main problems were its one-crop economy, political immaturity, political and outlaw violence which had killed 300,000 people in ten years, and the absence of a successor to the incumbent President. Stevenson had lunch with seventy-five government and business leaders in a salt mine. "Incredible—*monstrous cathedral cut out of salt* 500 feet underground in world's largest salt mountain. Deeply impressive —scented with rotting potatoes stored in mine!" President Lleras told him that nothing was as important as resettling people on unused land. If it was not done, they would turn to Castro. Living conditions in the city slums were miserable; the people would return to the country if given land. A labor leader told him that Communists were actively trying to gain control of the labor movement and were gaining.

On February 23, Stevenson received an honorary degree from the National University at Bogotá. He spoke at length: "I would like to see all the Latin American republics declare as one their intent and determination to avoid an arms race, and to progressively reduce the arms burden in this continent. It would be a moral and practical example of what wise, bold statesmanship can do to restore sanity to the world." He also said it should be possible in the next generation "to go forward toward eliminating poverty" in the hemisphere—political conditions were now favorable.

In a postcard sent from Bogotá, Stevenson told Agnes Meyer, "The welcome bewilders me!" (Bill Blair asked a local reporter to cable a story about his "fantastic reception" in Bogotá to the Washington *Post,* New York *Post,* and Chicago *Sun-Times.*) Jim Doyle of Wisconsin sent a political report—Lyndon Johnson had told him that he himself would not be nominated and had expressed high regard for Stevenson; Stevenson's friends in California were lying low out of fear that Kennedy might enter the primary; Jim Rowe thought that if Humphrey fell in the Wisconsin primary Stevenson supporters should move rapidly; Williams of Michigan was expected to get aboard the Kennedy bandwagon if Kennedy won in Wisconsin; Kennedy ran stronger against Nixon in a Minnesota poll than Humphrey; Governor McNichols of Colorado said Stevenson support there was evaporating rapidly, and Kennedy and Humphrey seemed "definitely to be developing some animosity toward one another." In a letter to Marietta Tree, Stevenson referred to his trip as "this South American primary."

On February 25, Stevenson was in Quito, Ecuador, called on President Ponce, a "brisk conservative business man type." Again he found education a basic problem. The American Ambassador "told me nothing of interest about Ecuador all the time I was there except the fishing and shooting!" Former President Galo Plaza took him to a monastery, a school, and a farm and told him that his daughter and other Stevenson supporters had donned black when Stevenson was defeated. He was told that *"400 families own and run Peru. But don't realize pol. and social revol. in S. Am. New leadership can contain this revol. if can put thru social reforms. Galo, Betancourt, Lleras, Frondizi, Alessandri. But Brazil trying to do it by inflation!"* The Foreign Minister said that Castro was "infantile" but that *"any new social order raises an echo among impoverished."* Communist influence was increasing in Ecuador.

Stevenson and his party arrived at Lima at 8:30 A.M. on February 28, "16 hours late, thanks to Panagra!," met with "intellectuals and pol. leaders of three parties." They discussed the boundary dispute with Ecuador, their country's desire for democratic government, the population explosion, lack of economic development, the problem of bringing the Indians into the Peruvian economy. Stevenson spent a day aboard the yacht of one of Peru's leading families. An embassy briefing next day: Democracy had begun only a few years earlier. Support of the armed forces was essential to any government. The government was inefficient. The country's economy was improving after serious inflation. Peruvians considered U.S. import quotas on cotton, sugar, lead, and zinc discriminatory. The government was doing nothing about land reform. Few Peruvians were aware of the danger that the Indians, as they left the stone age, might move toward Communism. Stevenson visited the slums, "about the worst squalor and filth I've ever seen. cf Hong Kong, Calcutta, Karachi, Joburg."

On March 1, Stevenson arose at 5 A.M. to go to Cuzco, capital of the Inca empire in the high Andes. Several Americans including an archaeologist accompanied him. "By car to ferrocarril—narrow gauge—up the Urumbamba valley—Sacred valley of Incas—across magnificent rich wide valley covered with cows and sheep, thru narrow perpendicular gorges more mighty than El Capitan and Yosemite. Indians high crowned white straw hats; miserable poverty, thached adobe on perpendicular pole huts. Very dirty, no apparent sense of cleanliness, refuse all around, guinea pigs all over, mangy dogs, no chimneys. No better than the worst of darkest A! . . . After three hours dismount, cross raging muddy Urumbamba and zig zag up mountain side in busses to Machu Pichu—incredible lost city of Incas—evidently used for religious rites; only female skeletons (Vestal Virgins) found. Marvellous masons. Stones fit so perfectly—can't get knife between them. Dispute as to date. 1100–1400? Enormous stones. How did they move 100 ton stones? . . . Saw my first Vicuna—tied to a stake! Large liquid black reproachful eyes. One of greatest sights on earth—not as impressive structures as Mayan—but setting of verticle mountains and wild scenery—majestic. No rain—blue skies, great white clouds—in middle of rainy season! Wed. Mar 2—Machu Pichu Woke up in black fog and rain at 6. Down mountain from little hotel with singing chauffeur. . . . Down the narrow gauge, in sunshine, to Ollantaitambo—great fortress of Incas. . . . Never taken by Spaniards—Incas folded up due to prophesy of white man with fair hair and blue eyes who would come to rule the Incas. Guns—horses How did conquistadores get thru the Andes to Cuzco!!" Cuzco, he wrote, had had a Soviet government for one day in the spring of 1958. The Soviet Union now was broadcasting an hour a day in an Indian dialect, and the Indians were restless. "Why do all Spanish colonial plazas and streets echo every sound all night—and why must I always have the best (and worst!) corner room! Not a wink of sleep in spite of pills—due to altitude and breathing trouble."

Back in Lima, Stevenson held a press conference—"poor questions"—and met with the Cuban Ambassador, who said the Castro government would be *"very pleased"* to have him visit Cuba. A former candidate for President of Bolivia, in exile now, called on him and warned that Bolivia was "going communist." Fernando Belaúnde Terry, narrowly defeated in the last Peruvian election and later the President, visited him, and Stevenson thought him a "most attractive architect." He said, *"I, too, am a political accident."*

While Stevenson was dressing for the Foreign Minister's elegant banquet at the country club, twenty students arrived, and Stevenson, unable to find his pants, spent a half hour in a bathrobe talking with them. "Mostly communist," he noted. "Leader cold, expressionless, thin ascetic looking 'professional student'—at Univ. eight years—organizing for communists. All law, economics or medical students. Anti Americanism evident; mostly economic questions—why does USSR loan at 2-½% and U.S. much higher? Why do we pay such low prices for Peru goods? Lead, zinc, sugar discrimination. Is Cuba revol. communist? Dictators. (*I always reply by condemning dictatorship of right or left. Only gov't we can approve is one representing freely expressed will of people; and one that can be changed by some expression peacefully—without force.*) They began to smile a little; some (Apristas?) shook hands warmly when I had to leave."

At about this time four young men in New York—David Garth, a television producer; Arthur Blaustein, a restaurant owner; Arthur Woodstone, a newspaper reporter; and Tedson Meyers, a lawyer—formed a "Stevenson-for-President Committee of New York." In Washington, George Ball, John Sharon, Senator Mike Monroney, and his administrative assistant, Tom Finney, had set up a small command post, two telephones and a secretary, in Senator Monroney's office. At the same time an informal group of large contributors was meeting at Robert Benjamin's office at United Artists in New York—such people as Ruth Field, Mary Lasker, Marietta Tree, Tom Finletter, Roger Stevens, Arthur Krim. Russell Hemenway, a young reform Democrat active in the Volunteers, ran an office for them. Soon these groups were in touch with each other and with Jim Doyle. Doyle now reported to Blair and Minow. He said Kennedy had told a friend in a private conversation that if he were not nominated Stevenson would be. Kennedy did not seem concerned about Johnson's chances but was concerned about Symington. Sargent Shriver had tried to persuade Doyle to support Kennedy in the Wisconsin primary. Doyle had been "making some wild guesses" about delegate strength and gave Johnson 448, Kennedy 510, Symington 125, Humphrey 56, with 342 listed as unknown. Given these guesses, Doyle thought that, considering vote shifts after the first ballot, Humphrey had no chance of nomination, Johnson almost none, while Kennedy had a good chance and Symington an excellent one. "The Kennedy and Humphrey people might well move to Stevenson rather than to Symington, and Stevenson support might also be drawn from some Johnson sources."

On March 4, Stevenson and his party left for Chile (he spelled it Chili in his diary.) "Santiago on big broad flat plain at foot of arid mountains—looks like Lima—large—European city—cosmo.—Hotel Carona 14 stories—very fine. *Beautiful women!* Unusual ceremonial welcome at airport—Ike gone two days."[10]

President Allessandri had been elected in a free election by a close margin and was governing with a coalition. Communists were in a Popular Action Front with Socialists and made a strong and articulate opposition. Also in the opposition was the Christian Democratic Party with Eduardo Frei as its leader—"idealistic way to solve country's problems," Stevenson noted. (A few years later Stevenson would come back to Chile to attend the inauguration of Frei as President.) If Alessandri failed to solve the country's economic problems, the country would turn left, though probably not to the Communists. Alessandri emphasized arms control. The military stayed out of politics. Communists had about 10 per cent of the organized labor force. They had 450 paid agents. They were influential in the university. The country's most urgent problem was inflation. Chile complained continually about U.S. ownership of its copper mines. Agrarian reform had not begun. Chile and Uruguay felt they were surrounded by dictators and did not like U.S. policy of non-intervention which led to "support" of dictators. "We dined with Amb and Mrs. Walter Howe, Rep leader and super conserv. . . . Nice, blond, low cut!, wife. Sat next to her and famous Chilean writer and educator. . . . Obviously this is a cosmopolitan country!! *No Indian blood. Much Anglo-*

---

[10] President Eisenhower left Washington on February 22 for South America. The timing of his trip and Stevenson's was pure coincidence.

European mixture. Santiago—no old churches, Spanish colonial houses, Indian ruins—nothing!—*a French city and not gay*—but the *most attractive people in SA! . . .* Usual talk of commies, politics and U S! Ike's trip evidently great *personal* triumph." Stevenson spent about two and a half hours with about fifty students and thought their speeches "very good"—*"not sure I handled it very well but Embassy people seemed delighted. First time anyone had met them."* He toured slums and a banker's hacienda—"Tea on lawn—with watermelons!—like English country house. Charming worldly people of the feudal aristocracy. . . . Fine dinner—enormous lobsters from Juan Fernandez—Robinson Crusoe's island!" Stevenson went by helicopter to visit Valparaiso and Viña del Mar, Chile's great port and resort, "and *landed on a cricket ground adjoining race course just as Sunday cricket match was starting. Big Englishman stepped forward—'Glad to see you again, Sir; last time was in Singapore—wasn't it!' "* He noted *"Barefoot people watching parades of shining boats."* He and President Alessandri talked about arms limitation, the economy, housing, agrarian reform. Stevenson wrote, "Unsmiling— large—tall—Mussolini look—voluble, high loud squeaky voice. Attacks on Marxists, demagogues, Frei, Ch. Dems. . . . *More excited by China than Russia!"*

Stevenson went to the lake country of southern Chile to rest, work on his *Life* article, and catch up on politics and correspondence. Drew Pearson had said in his column that Stevenson and Kennedy had reached "an informal secret understanding to help each other" at the convention. Hy Raskin had brought them together shortly before Stevenson left for South America. Pearson wrote, proposing that Stevenson help Kennedy in the early primaries and balloting; if Kennedy failed of nomination, Kennedy would throw his support to Stevenson; if Kennedy was nominated, he would appoint Stevenson Secretary of State; if he failed, he, Kennedy, would be nominated for Vice President and Stevenson for President.

Jim Rowe, a Humphrey man, sent the Pearson clipping to Wirtz and Minow with a sharp memorandum. Wirtz wrote to Blair in Santiago, "What, if anything, can I tell Jim Rowe? I wish Hy wouldn't talk so much. Or is this really just pure Pearson?" Blair replied that there was "no basis" for Pearson's story: "The Governor and Jack Kennedy did not meet at all before the former's departure and, as a matter of fact, have not seen each other for a year or longer." Someone put a question mark beside that sentence. Stevenson's appointment sheets show that he saw Kennedy in Washington shortly before leaving for South America. Blair told Wirtz, "Jack did call the Governor when we were in Washington just before leaving to see if they could get together but Jack was leaving the following day for Louisville and there was no time. I would appreciate if you could pass this on to Jim Rowe."

The New Hampshire primary took place on March 8, and Kennedy, unopposed, received an impressive 43,300 votes. The next day Jim Doyle called Minow to report that various people in Washington, such as Senators Yarborough, Proxmire, and Carroll, felt that Stevenson should make a series of speeches shortly after his return to the United States. Al Otten of the *Wall Street Journal* had heard that Stevenson would make several important speeches during the spring and that Bill Attwood was involved. Wirtz told him he did not know about it. From the lake country of southern Chile, Stevenson on March 10 wrote Agnes Meyer he had been "quite hurt" by a *Post* article which, he said, gave the impression he expected nomination and would be disappointed if he did not get it. "I [cannot] understand the people who have been saying, 'Adlai is doing just the right thing, the only thing he can do,' and are now saying if Adlai doesn't *do* something pretty soon, show some interest, get busy, it will be too late.' I suppose this curious confusion of counsel . . . is due to the rising fortunes of young Jack Kennedy. . . . I could reply that if they don't like the situation . . . why don't *they* do something. Jim Doyle of Madison, Wis. *is* doing something, I hear, *and very intelligently,* but wholly without my authority."

He wrote, "Yesterday I fished a wild stream around the foot of a snow clad smoking volcano in a rowboat for 10 hours—my only 'day off' in more than a month." The trip had been "immensely satisfactory," the U.S. press had ignored it, his welcome had been like "a long lost brother's," and the embassies had used him relentlessly with difficult groups—labor leaders, students, intellectuals. He spoke of "endless" functions and said, "I've survived somehow, tho there has been little *fun,* and regret that I'm always in the position of defending my country when often my heart isn't in it. . . . The Rep. program has been to make So. Am. safe for American business, and little else. . . . Lord, what a legacy [Eisenhower] and Dulles have left the next president—and if its Nixon—a figure of positive contempt—I fear for our 'hemispheric solidarity.' "

In Buenos Aires the ruinous legacy of Peron was everywhere. Stevenson noted, "Visit and fancy lunch with President Frondizi—foxy looking fellow who has wholly deserted his platform and adopted his opponent's austerity program." He thought Buenos Aires "just like Paris," Mar del Plata a resort "like Atlantic city." They dined at the United States Embassy, and *"Benton gave J.F. [John Fell] $100 to take [the Ambassador's daughter] out—back at 8:30 AM—with more than half the money left!"* He heard, as elsewhere, that the United States was so involved in Europe it ignored Latin America, that *"the OAS was organized to help* the U.S.," that FDR had created a feeling of confidence in Latin America, that the United States should intervene to overthrow Castro, and that "a *terrible* civil war" was coming in Bolivia and it might become a stronger Communist center than Cuba.

From Brazil, he told Carol Evans to send papers relating to a speech he was to make at Charlottesville, Virginia, to him at Caracas or Barbados. He also instructed her to send "my Princeton hood" to the president of the University of Virginia "unless he would like me to wear my Oxford splendor. . . ."

He wrote and sent to Attwood a draft statement on his non-candidacy. He added: "I was troubled about the stories in connection with your work for me. . . . If you have to make any further statements, I think the emphasis had better be on my fitness for the office and your anxiety to further that result, even at the personal inconvenience and without my solicitation or even approval. Otherwise, I think I shall be in a most ambiguous and inconsistent position if it appears that you are ghost writing and actively cooperating with me."

Agnes Meyer wrote on March 23—Kennedy had come to see her. "I must say I was impressed with his political maturity." She considered Stevenson's New York supporters headed by Tom Finletter "very amateurish." They had had Louis Bean make a survey which proved "fairly conclusively" that Stevenson could beat Nixon; she would try to help them get it published. She hoped Stevenson would allow Attwood to meet him in Barbados—otherwise, "how can you get your [Charlottesville] speech ready for the press." On the same day John Steele filed a story saying that Louis Bean found after sampling three key wards in each of New York, Pittsburgh, St. Louis, and Los Angeles, that Stevenson's 1960 chances were "undeniably strong." Bean believed that 1956 voters, given a choice between Stevenson and Nixon, would shift to give 54 per cent to Stevenson and 46 per cent to Nixon.

Arthur Schlesinger, en route to a conference of Midwest Democrats in Detroit, ran into Sam Lubell, another political analyst, who believed that at present Kennedy certainly and Humphrey probably could beat Nixon in Wisconsin but Nixon would beat Stevenson easily. Former Eisenhower voters hesitated to vote for Stevenson now since it seemed to confess error; women were still bothered by Stevenson's divorce. Governor Williams told Schlesinger that he preferred Humphrey but, since Humphrey was not going to be nominated, he was prepared to endorse Kennedy if Kennedy won easily in Wisconsin. Doyle was trying to learn how the delegates felt about Stevenson and to provide a clearinghouse for the various local Stevenson movements. He had observed little movement toward Stevenson but thought Stevenson would be the beneficiary of any Kennedy collapse. The Kennedy people had feared that Stevenson would be entered in the Oregon primary but in the confusion after Senator Neuberger's recent death, each Stevenson group thought that another was filing so none had.

Senator Kennedy and others spoke at a Jefferson-Jackson Day dinner in Detroit, and Schlesinger saw Kennedy privately. Kennedy expected to win in Wisconsin—Humphrey had been making progress but Kennedy's lead was commanding. Humphrey might go into West Virginia. Kennedy hoped not—he did not want to spend the energy or the money, and West Virginia was 97 per cent Protestant. But if Humphrey made a fight inevitable,

Kennedy thought he himself could win. If Humphrey withdrew before West Virginia, Humphrey would be the logical candidate for Vice President. He was the man Kennedy wanted on the ticket with him. Kennedy hoped Schlesinger would see Humphrey the next day and tell him all this, not as a proposition or a deal but as an exploration of possibilities. Kennedy went on to say that, if he was forced into a fight in West Virginia and won, he could not be denied the nomination. He would owe nothing to anybody. But if people supported him between Wisconsin and West Virginia, he would consider himself under certain obligations to them. He meant, among others, Stevenson. If Stevenson came out for Kennedy before West Virginia, and if Kennedy lost in West Virginia, and eventually dropped out, he would feel obligated to support Stevenson for the nomination. If Kennedy won in West Virginia and was nominated and elected, he would feel obligated to give Stevenson a major role in the new Administration. "(State Dept implied but not stated)", Schlesinger noted. Kennedy hoped Schlesinger would tell all this to Stevenson in Barbados.

Schlesinger saw Humphrey on the morning of March 27 and without saying he had talked to Kennedy asked what Humphrey intended to do after Wisconsin if he was badly beaten there. Humphrey said he would go into West Virginia no matter what happened. Schlesinger said that surely Humphrey would not want a Ku Klux Klan victory in West Virginia. He said of course not; he had already turned down the support of anti-Catholic agitators. On the other hand, intolerance had been used as a weapon against him in Wisconsin. Humphrey said he was not bitter toward Kennedy but was "bitter at the use of religion against me in this campaign." Schlesinger suggested that what happened after Wisconsin was of concern to liberals throughout the country and said it might be well if Humphrey were to await Stevenson's return before deciding what to do. Schlesinger then said that if Humphrey withdrew after Wisconsin he would be the "natural" candidate for Vice President with Kennedy. Humphrey replied "with some vigor" that "I have talked this over with Muriel, and I have no interest at all in the Vice-Presidency." Later in the day, according to Schlesinger's journal, Humphrey ran into Kennedy at a UAW rally and told him, "I talked to Arthur about W. Va. It's no use—I'm going to have to go through with it."

From Lake Forest on March 26, during a visit to the Edison Dicks, Barbara Ward sent political advice to Stevenson. "I think you will find that the decline in interest in you and your possible candidacy won't much survive your return . . . [since it is] due to genuine interest and support. . . . It will be also due to the rolling of the Kennedy bandwagon and the desire of a great many . . . people to use you to stop him. . . . You will be in the thick of it." She reported that Eugenie Anderson of Minnesota was certain that Humphrey would stay in the contest after Wisconsin, win or lose, because "the campaign methods being used in Wisconsin have made him so fighting mad that he won't concede anything which might help Kennedy. . . .[11] But if Hubert . . . withdrew, asking liberals to back Kennedy, then the Kennedy people could next look to you, hoping for another push to the bandwagon, possibly the decisive push. The crude arguments for you giving it and coming out for Jack are (1) you would be Secretary of State in a Kennedy Administration . . . and (b) you would get the reversion of Kennedy delegates if the Southerners did contrive to stall Kennedy after all. My *hunch* is that if you were to be [the] candidate, you would need Jack as a running mate to prevent Catholics sitting on their hands or staying with the Republicans. . . . If you backed Jack after Wisconsin, you might slip him the nomination—and thereby exclude yourself. If you did not, you might miss the Secretaryship of State if Kennedy won or lose his considerable following if the Convention passed him over. . . . Jack is too dependent for his political future to refuse a firm draft for the Vice Presidency. . . . My own feeling . . . after working with him . . . is that he is much better than a public relations ballyhoo and his 'extended family' suggest. . . . The polls may be beginning to suggest that Nixon is more vulnerable to any decent Democrat than seemed likely when you went away. . . . I must report that a number of your warmest friends believe that, for the reason of the dilemma I described earlier, you should support Jack. . . . If Kennedy should make it, you ought to be Secretary of State. If he doesn't make it, you ought to be able to have him as Vice President. I don't know what strategy produces this result, but I am certain at least about the need for the result itself. . . . Arthur will put to you the case for supporting Jack. In certain conditions, it is very strong."

On March 24, Stevenson went to Rio de Janeiro, "as beautiful as *advertised!* . . . Copacabanna Hotel—Suite of 5 huge rooms and two gold fitted marble bathrooms. Thank God I'm a guest of state! . . . Cocktail party with 'international set' at Rognan Janner, rich Swede & his lovely Italian wife. . . . Women's waists—look after their figures." President Kubitschek—"brisk, quick sharp slim man—like all Brazilians of mixed descent—Czech & Portugese. Medical doctor who 'fell into politics.' Shamelessly proud of achievements; 'urged to amend const. & run again'— (term expires this year.)—decided not to! *Spoke most graciously about my fatherhood of his ideas and his Democratic partisanship.* Going to buy farm near Brazilia and 'could run for Pres. again in 5 years.'" He went to Brasilia—"V. impress! . . . Huge central avenue. . . . Marvelous Exec. office—white marble, gleaming black glass—no stairs—ramps—huge covered terraces without colums—wide expanse of green rolling country— all half surrounded by huge artificial lake. Pres. residence—600 feet long 2 stories—all glass. . . . Really splendid! . . . What wonders genius of man and the purpose of his leaders hath wrought—in the wilds of Brazil. And if this is the city of the future—I like it. This will be the most talked

---

[11] She was referring to reports that Kennedy was seeking to win in Wisconsin as a Catholic.

490   *Three: A Generation Passes Away*

of city in the world. I *don't* think of what Ghandi said when he saw New Delhi—'what a wonderful ruin it will make'—built on 7 earlier cities. . . . But would Brazil be better off if the same money—no one knows how much—had been used on education?" And, *"Man shot with arrow 15 miles from Brazilia month ago."*

Caracas, Venezuela, was, he said, "Most expensive country in world— *$6 tip to bell boys! Scotch $45.00."* He went to President Betancourt's house for a long private talk. Betancourt was the maximum leader of the non-Communist left in the Caribbean, a vigorous enemy of Trujillo and other dictators. Stevenson noted, "Pres Betancourt—Short, plump round, smiling little man with black horned rim glasses & easy laughter. Plan to invest in productive projects instead of extravagance of dictator: Education, housing, health, agrarian reform, public works, power 2 million illiterates and 700000 child. without schools. . . . Long talk re Castro—He against; FM [Foreign Minister]—for! *All Venezuelans evidently passionate Democrats and Stevenson fans!* Much communist sympathy in Univ." The Foreign Minister did not believe Castro was a Communist and said the Party was stronger in Venezuela than in Cuba. At a press conference Stevenson refused to criticize the Eisenhower administration for allowing the former Venezuelan dictator, Pérez Jiménez, to enter the United States. He wound up his Latin American trip with a brief stop at Trinidad, then went to Barbados to visit Marietta and Ronald Tree and work on his Charlottesville speech.

Latin America interested Stevenson, as did all underdeveloped countries, but from his notes and correspondence one receives the impression he was more deeply fascinated by Asia and Africa. He was, however, quick to perceive the basic problems of Latin America—schools, housing, land reform, unstable or authoritarian politics, inequitable distribution of wealth, coupled with economic backwardness—and much of what he said during and after his trip anticipated President Kennedy's Alliance for Progress. In his later years at the United Nations he found friends and, frequently, staunch allies among the Latin American Ambassadors, some of whom he had met on this trip in 1960.

While he was with the Trees in Barbados, newspapers at home were printing stories again, as they had in 1952, about Mrs. Ives, who would be Stevenson's "First Lady" at the White House if he was elected. Agnes Meyer, on a yacht trip to the Greek islands, wrote, "Of course, I am a terrible contriver. I have even written Kennedy a farewell letter that is a masterpiece of political intrigue. If he should ask to meet with you *privately,* do not refuse. It is my doing." Jim Doyle, in Washington, received the impression that Kennedy was all but certain of the nomination.

Some journalists and members of Congress were for Stevenson but in the absence of his candidacy were confused, "isolated," or leaning toward others. Soon Doyle would meet with leaders of the IVI in Illinois who had helped draft Stevenson in 1952.

The day Stevenson arrived in Barbados, Kennedy won the Wisconsin primary with 476,024 votes to Humphrey's 366,753, about 56 per cent of the votes. But because political analysts had forecast a big Kennedy victory, and because he lost four Protestant districts outright and carried another narrowly (out of ten), and because his majority had come almost entirely from heavily Catholic areas, his victory was not decisive. He would have to do it again in West Virginia.

In Barbados, Stevenson talked endlessly about his trip and about American politics. Blair cabled him on April 8, "Washington press converging on Charlottesville to cover speech. Expecting something great." Jane Dick implored him not to permit the professional politicians—or, "far more dangerous—the amateurs who gloried in believing they were pros"—to take him over again as, she said, they had in 1956.

24.

On April 11, Stevenson went to New York. The Democratic National Convention was exactly thirteen weeks away. That day the amateurs in New York, who were trying to draft him, officially opened their headquarters, and the press crowded the room. Stevenson himself held a press conference at 1 P.M. at the Savoy Hilton and began by reading a statement he had written out about the nomination: "I have had that honor twice, and I neither seek it, nor hope for it, nor expect that it will be offered to me again," but he would continue to speak "in support of a liberal program." In Latin America he had transacted private business and, in Rio, with Benton, had announced a Portuguese-language edition of the Britannica. But mainly he had sought "self-education" in thirteen countries. He was "neither as optimistic, or as satisfied with our relations as President Eisenhower was after he returned last month from his brief visit to four of these countries. Latin America is in revolution. The dictators are being swept aside. Genuine democratic movements are emerging. Most of the continent is still afflicted by illiteracy and poverty and all their attendant ills. Everywhere the demand is for social change and improved living standards for the people. The whole continent is on the verge of great economic development, and they are going to build a new society under our methods of free enterprise, if possible, and if not, under socialism. There is anti-Yankeeism everywhere. . . . Communist activity is also universal. . . . I think the President's visit helped to reassure our neighbors. . . . But it will take a lot more than good-will tours to assure the solidarity of this hemisphere."

He invited questions. Predictably, the first one—would he accept the draft of a deadlocked convention? He replied as he had in 1952—if he answered yes he would appear to court a draft, if he said no he would be a "draft evader," so he would cross that bridge if he came to it and did not expect to come to it. What about reports that the Humphrey candidacy was only "A holding operation for you"? He had never discussed it with Humphrey or any Humphrey representative. Did he consider Kennedy a liberal? Yes. Nixon had said that if Kennedy won in West Virginia he would be assured of the nomination; did Stevenson agree? He did not know. Did he have a "favorite candidate" for the Democratic nomination? No. Would he like to be President? "I have trifled with that thought so long, and so often in the past years, that I think I have reached the point where I can view the possibility that I will never be President with the utmost equanimity."

Asked about President Eisenhower's reaction to recent Negro sit-in demonstrations in the South, Stevenson said, "I wish the President had been much more emphatic about the whole subject of race relations ever since the Supreme Court decision six years ago," then said white Southerners appeared to have "no objection to eating a sandwich alongside of a Negro, if you are standing up, but that if you are sitting down, it is intolerable. I would have to say that seems to me silly. . . . I think these demonstrations are a reminder that our Negro citizens resent this humiliation."

Asked about Castro, he said, "The Castro revolution was very popular throughout South America, almost universally, especially the land reform program. I think it is evidence . . . that a social revolution against the excesses of Dictator Batista was due, and overdue. . . . However, with the passage of time, I think many of the things that have taken place, the mass revenge killings, the expropriation of private property without discussion, the suppression of the press, the assaults on other countries from Cuban territory, armed landings, the irresponsible abuse of the United States, the disdain for the democratic processes of election, all of these things, I think, have combined to create grave confusion, and anxiety, indeed in many cases mistrust of the Cuban revolution under Dr. Castro. . . . I don't know, nor do most of the people I talked to in South America, whether the things that Dr. Castro has done mean that he is a Communist. I personally don't believe that he is. I would be disposed to take his word for it. But the fact of the matter is that many of these actions are characteristically Communist actions. . . ."

Asked about religion as a campaign issue, he said, "It seems to me that the issues of this campaign are too grave for the voters to be distracted by such questions as in what church the candidates pray. I think it would debase the campaign, for example, if so fine an American as Jack Kennedy were to be forced to defend himself against bigots." He thought religion was being overemphasized in the press, radio, and TV. Would he remain neutral to the end or could he foresee circumstances where he would endorse a candidate? "Yes, I don't exclude the possibility that before the nominating convention is over that I might want to express a view and a very positive position on the selection. But I can't at the moment foresee under what circumstances that possibility would arise. . . .

I am just as much opposed to a Stop Kennedy movement as I would be to a Stop Humphrey movement." Asked whom he would prefer for a running mate if he was nominated, he said, "Why did I come home anyway? I was getting along so well down there." He took occasion to say he had read that he had hired himself a speech writer, then clouded the question. Near the end, a reporter said, "Governor, I came in late. Are you a candidate?" Stevenson replied he himself was leaving and courteously closed. He thought the press conference "most successful."

Kennedy won the Illinois primary. A few days later, campaigning in West Virginia, Kennedy said, "If religion is a valid issue in the presidential campaign, I shouldn't have served in the House, I shouldn't be serving in the Senate, and I shouldn't have been accepted by the U. S. Navy." He won primaries in Massachusetts, Pennsylvania, Indiana, and Nebraska. West Virginia, the critical primary, vigorously contested, would vote on May 10. Many people thought that if Kennedy won by a big margin in West Virginia little more would be heard of Stevenson's candidacy, but that if Kennedy lost or won narrowly Stevenson would be propelled into the center of the contest. A friend told Newt Minow that Stevenson must go no further in renouncing the nomination. Wirtz encouraged him to continue on his present course, saying nothing further in the belief that he might be drafted. Stevenson began to get pressure in the other direction from several people close to him. Blair, Minow, and Martin all urged him to take himself decisively out of the race and to endorse Kennedy. They felt that he himself could not be nominated unless he entered the primaries, that even if he were he might lose to Nixon—a personal disaster —that he was impeding Kennedy's candidacy. They argued that if he endorsed Kennedy now he would almost ensure his nomination and that he would have a claim to being Kennedy's Secretary of State. Stevenson refused. He did not favor Kennedy, thought he was too young and, as a Catholic, could not be elected. And he was obligated to Mrs. Roosevelt and others to keep himself available. Or at least this was what he said. They believed that in his heart Stevenson wanted the nomination.

Stevenson appeared before the American Society of Newspaper Editors in Washington to discuss, along with Mike Pearson of Canada and Hugh Gaitskell of Great Britain, the role of the political opposition. The opposition was hampered by a new trend in American politics—most people were comfortable and did not like criticism. "The engine of social progress has run out of fuel—the fuel of discontent. . . . I think the role of the opposition is . . . to shed light on what has been obscured by the incumbents. . . . If the people are complacent and unconcerned about the good health of our system the press must share the blame. . . . A responsible press can be a great help to the opposition by giving it an adequate hearing. . . . The essence, the key to free society lies in the strength and critical effectiveness of the opposition." Two days later Stevenson, on "Meet the Press," criticized the Eisenhower administration, refused to endorse any

Democratic presidential candidate, refused to remove himself from consideration, and deplored the rise of the religious issue. Back in Chicago he told Agnes Meyer he was ending his relationship with Bill Attwood—"I just can't be left in any public ambiguity about ghost writing and political plotting." But he did not really end it.

Some time earlier George Ball and John Sharon had raised money to finance the Louis Bean survey which showed Stevenson beating Nixon, thus dispelling the myth that a two-time loser could not win, and Ball had distributed it to about fifty columnists and eighty Congressmen and Senators, and several newspaper and magazine stories had resulted. Now, working with Jim Doyle, they drafted a letter to delegates over Doyle's signature and on May 2 sent out 4,308 cpies of the letter and the Bean survey. The letter said "Dr. Bean" had come to the conclusion that there was no historically valid basis for the theory that a twice-unsuccessful presidential candidate could not win on a third try. It said Stevenson had lost in 1956 because of Eisenhower's personal popularity and two international crises just before the election. It said Bean's poll showed that 21 per cent of the 1956 Eisenhower voters would now shift to Stevenson, while only 3 per cent of the 1956 Stevenson voters would shift to Nixon. The letter said the poll was made without Stevenson's knowledge or approval. Sharon notified Bill Blair and Newt Minow of all this on May 3 and said they had tried to write the survey and letter in such a way as to offend no one but feared some Kennedy people would be offended anyway.

Stevenson was working at home on magazine articles. Barbara Ward from Accra told him she wanted him to become President or Secretary of State and believed both depended on his relations with Kennedy. The liberals should not divide. "I believe you are the most fitted—but after you, Jack."

25.

On May 5, on the eve of the summit conference in Paris, the U-2 incident occurred. Khrushchev announced in a speech to the Supreme Soviet that on May 1 an American airplane flew over the Russian frontier, continued into the interior and was shot down, and that Russia would protest strongly to the United States. He accused the United States of "aggressive provocation aimed at wrecking the summit conference." In Washington, NASA handed out a CIA "cover story" of a lost weather research plane, while a State Department spokesman said that "there was no deliberate attempt to violate Soviet air space and there never has been." Thereupon, Khrushchev on May 7 demolished the story by disclosing details he had withheld "to see what the Americans would invent." He said the Soviets had captured the pilot, identified him as Francis Gary Powers, said he had admitted being on a reconnaissance mission, listed the plane's equipment, and warned Turkey and other countries not to permit such flights. Caught in a lie, the State Department said the flight "probably" had been undertaken "to obtain information now concealed behind the Iron Curtain" but said that Washington had not authorized it. Had this remained the official United States position the incident might have been forgotten. But Eisenhower advisers feared this would prove Democratic charges that a "part-time" President did not know what was going on in his own Administration. So, on May 9, Secretary of State Herter said that the United States, at the President's direction, had undertaken "extensive aerial surveillance" over the U.S.S.R. to protect against surprise attack. On May 11, President Eisenhower at a press conference took full responsibility. Khrushchev said the same day that Powers would be tried as a spy and rescinded his invitation to Eisenhower to visit Russia. He said, "The Russian people would say I was mad to welcome a man who sends spy planes over here like that."

De Gaulle and Macmillan made no progress in efforts to ameliorate the situation. The United States announced the suspension of U-2 flights. But when the summit conference convened on May 16 for its first (and only) meeting, Khrushchev denounced the "spy flight," demanded U.S. assurances and punishment of those "guilty of such actions," and asked that the summit be postponed for six or eight months—that is, until a new President had been elected. Eisenhower defended the flights, said they would not be resumed, but rejected Khrushchev's other demands and implied that Khrushchev had come "all the way from Moscow to Paris with the sole intention of sabotaging this meeting." The summit meeting broke up. The ensuing uproar was enormous. The episode was at the top of the news and at the heart of presidential politics.

Stevenson was to speak to a Conference on World Tensions at the University of Chicago on May 12. He had originally intended to speak on Latin America but now drafted a new opening on the U-2 incident. No one, he said, questioned the necessity of gathering intelligence. "But our timing, our words, our management must and will be sharply questioned. Could it serve the purpose of peace and mutual trust to send intelligence missions over the heart of the Soviet Union on the very eve of the long-awaited summit conference? Can the President be embarrassed and national policies endangered at such a critical time by an unknown government official? Is it possible, indeed, that we, the United States, who want nothing of anyone but peace and security, could do the very thing we dread: carelessly, accidentally, trigger the holocaust? Doesn't this incident make the reduction of international tensions all the more imperative? What effect will this untimely drama have on the hospitality and confidence of the host countries adjoining the Soviet Union where our bases are situated? And what of our international reputation for honesty, even competence?" He recapitulated the State Department's contradictory statements. "In short, our government has blundered and admitted it. And the blunder has made the President's task at the summit meeting"—it had not yet collapsed—"more difficult. Changes must and will be made. But this is no time for partisan censure. The summit meeting is too fateful for any American to risk making the President's task even more difficult."

He then deplored Eisenhower's announcement on May 7, amid the U-2 uproar, that the United States would resume underground nuclear tests, without consulting the British or Russians. "I hope and pray that the prospect for a test ban agreement at the summit has not been harmed by this confusing announcement just when everything looked as if there was for the first time a real chance—perhaps a last chance—to bring the development of nuclear weapons under reasonable control."

On May 10, Kennedy won the West Virginia primary by a 61 to 39 per cent margin. It had been a campaign envenomed by the religion issue and charges that Kennedy was spending large sums of money. For Kennedy it was a remarkable victory. Defeated, Humphrey withdrew from the race, and with good grace. Shortly after the primary Robert Kennedy telephoned Minow and urged him to persuade Stevenson to come out for Kennedy. Minow agreed, but Stevenson refused. A little earlier Minow had seen Kennedy, and Kennedy had jabbed a finger at him and said, "Your leader Adlai is a candidate." Minow had denied it. Kennedy had said, "Don't kid me. All these friends of his get around him and blow smoke in his face and tell him he's the one." Minow had acknowledged the pressure but pointed to the fact that Stevenson had not entered the Oregon primary as evidence that he was not a candidate—"he could beat you there." Kennedy had seemed persuaded.

On May 14, Kennedy, traveling, telephoned Arthur Schlesinger. Kennedy could not see why Stevenson would not help him—if Stevenson was himself a candidate, "he can get somewhere only over my dead body," and if he was not a candidate, why not say so? Kennedy thought he needed about eighty to a hundred votes and Stevenson could provide them from California, Pennsylvania, Colorado, and Minnesota. "He is the essential ingredient in my combination. I don't want to have to go hat in hand to all those Southerners, but I'll have to do that if I can't get the votes from the North." He said West Virginia had proved to him that it was "absolutely fatal" to have Southern support. "I want to be nominated by the liberals. I don't want to go screwing around with all those Southern bastards." Schlesinger asked him about Governor Williams and Governor Lawrence. Kennedy said Williams "still had ideological misgivings"—he recently had been told that Kennedy had failed to rebuild the party in Massachusetts in a liberal image—and Lawrence was obstinate and old. He said Pat Brown could deliver only two thirds of the California delegation; with Stevenson's support, Kennedy would get it all. Schlesinger told Kennedy he could not expect Stevenson to do things inconsistent with his personal style and past positions. Kennedy said he understood this, recognized the difficulty in seeming to jump on a bandwagon or make a deal; he did not expect an immediate endorsement but would like some assurance that he could count on Stevenson's help at some definite time before the convention. He would prefer public endorsement but private intervention with Lawrence and California delegates "would be a good deal better than nothing."

Next morning Schlesinger called Stevenson in Libertyville and asked for his post-West Virginia reflections. Stevenson said everybody had been calling him—Humphrey, Symington, Johnson, Williams, Nelson. "As you know," Stevenson said, "I think less than nothing of primaries. But the politicians take them seriously." He said he did not think that West Virginia settled everything. Schlesinger asked what he meant. Stevenson thought Symington and Johnson might together hold enough votes to stop Kennedy, although Symington had told him there was no sign of possible collaboration with Johnson. Stevenson said Blair had been pressuring him for a year to come out for Kennedy. Stevenson felt that to do it now would be inconsistent with past positions and his personal style. "It would look as if I were jumping on the bandwagon. Everyone would say, 'There's the deal we told you about.' It would look as if I were angling for a job. I can't do this sort of thing. If I have residual strength, I think it is much more with the people than with the delegates. And I think it will therefore be more useful the closer we get to the convention. One thing that keeps coming through, though I don't have it quite clear in my mind, is a note of 'threat.' I have never had anything like this from Jack, but I keep getting it from his people. The note keeps coming through that I better act now, that delay will get me into trouble, that if I don't act now I won't be chosen as Secretary of State. All this is hard to take. I don't believe that Jack would choose his Secretary of State on the basis of political aid rendered before the convention; I believe he will choose his Secretary of State on the basis of what is good for the nation. I don't give a God damn whether he picks me as Secretary of State unless he thinks it would be best for the country."

Schlesinger told Stevenson that Kennedy understood his problem, did not want him to come out immediately, wanted only some hope of favorable action, preferably public but at least private. Stevenson asked Schlesinger to repeat that, then asked him to send it to him in writing "so that I would have it all clear." Schlesinger asked if he would consider helping Kennedy before the convention. Stevenson replied, "On the basis of present alternatives, I would be quite prepared to do it in terms calculated to preserve as much party harmony as possible. To come out now and kick Lyndon and Stuart in the face and demean my own position of neutrality and aloofness would be an error. Lyndon's candidacy is so improbable and fictitious anyway that the time might come when something could be done with him. Jack will have to work with him if he becomes President; therefore he wants to take care not to alienate him now. Maybe I can help to keep that avenue open to Johnson." He thought it important not to have another Dixiecrat walkout. Oddly, he seemed concerned about getting Southern support for Kennedy, while Kennedy seemed to want to escape it. When Schlesinger said he would like to see Kennedy be the candidate of the liberal wing, Stevenson dissented: "I would like to generalize that—I would like to see him the candidate of the whole party, including the South." Stevenson said he feared there would be more talk about Kennedy's youth and money. Humphrey had told him "atrocity stories" about Kennedy's spending in West Virginia. Humphrey thought Nixon had proof of this.

Stevenson also said that pressures for a Stevenson draft continued to increase—eleven telegrams that very morning. People were saying Kennedy's youth and religion were too crippling, the only solution was a Stevenson-Kennedy ticket. When they asked if they could work for this, Stevenson replied, he said, "Not so far as I'm concerned. If you do anything about this, you must do it on your own." Schlesinger did not think Stevenson was discouraging them hard.

Stevenson testified before a Senate committee in behalf of a bill to permit television broadcasters to give free time to candidates. (Stevenson, with Martin, had written a two-part article for *This Week* on the subject.) He argued that television had become "almost prohibitively" expensive and so the party with the largest campaign fund could purchase the most television time, and that the complexity of television scheduling obliged candidates to employ advertising agencies who, understandably, turned to jingles and spot announcements useful in selling soap but not in enlightening the public. Even occasional televised speeches helped little. "Presidential campaign ritual requires that the candidate be shuttled from coast to coast as many times as possible, assuring maximum physical exhaustion, and minimum opportunity to prepare his statements. The result is the ever greater use of the ghost writer and the ever greater difficulty of knowing the candidate himself." The pending bill would provide that both major parties would be given equal opportunity to present their candidates and their programs, that both candidates would have adequate time to discuss the issues regardless of their budgets, that each candidate would have thirty minutes, scheduled consecutively, to discuss the issues, thus facilitating comparison, that the programs would be scheduled in prime time, and that a series of such programs scheduled in advance would enable candidates to organize their campaigns around them. Stevenson thought that each candidate should have thirty minutes a week for eight weeks. Each candidate must use his time himself, not present a musical extravaganza— "the purpose is not to entertain but to enlighten." The vice presidential candidate could use some portion of the time. The introduction and discussion of this and other bills led that year to the congressional suspension of the "equal time" provision of the Federal Communications Act, and this made possible the famous Kennedy-Nixon debates, the first face-to-face nationwide television confrontation of presidential candidates in the nation's history. Agitation to continue the practice increased, and

Newt Minow, who had helped arouse Stevenson's interest in the problem, was actively engaged.

The same day he testified, Stevenson called on Lyndon Johnson, and Johnson said Stevenson was in the presidential race whether he wanted to be or not and asked why he did not move. Stevenson said his course was clear—neutrality and non-intervention. Johnson asked about the rumor: did he intend to endorse Kennedy? Stevenson said flatly that he had no present intention of endorsing Kennedy before the convention; the chances were very good that he would not do so and that he would maintain his neutrality to the end. He referred sarcastically to "young whipper-snappers" in his own camp and in Kennedy's who were pressuring him to endorse Kennedy. As to moving in his own behalf, he would not—but neither would he repudiate anybody who worked in his behalf. Thus Johnson and Stevenson seemed to be allying themselves—though not explicitly—in an effort to keep uncommitted Governors and other leaders locked in place for the time being and off the Kennedy bandwagon. They agreed that the breakdown of the summit meeting made the race "a new ball game." Johnson said troublemaking newspapermen had spread the false impression that Johnson disliked Stevenson. Stevenson said that, similarly, troublemakers had spread a story saying that he did not want Johnson nominated. It was not true—he had known and respected Johnson as a young Congressman long before he knew Kennedy or other candidates. Johnson said it was in the nation's interest to keep the choice of a candidate open until the convention.

By this time, with Kennedy's primary victories rapidly widening his lead, Johnson was considering ways to stop him. Humphrey must not throw his delegates to Kennedy. Neither must Stevenson flatly take himself out. Johnson had previously described Stevenson as an unacceptable nominee but now on May 16, according to Minow, Johnson told Stevenson something like this: "I'm going to try for it and if I don't get it, it will be you." It may have been on this occasion that Johnson, as Adlai III relates, told Stevenson to go out "and corral some votes," and Johnson would get some and "we'll teach that little ——— a thing or two."

On this same day Jim Doyle sent Blair a long memorandum. He said that an intense effort would be made by "the Johnson and Symington forces" to deny Kennedy the nomination and would probably be joined by others who opposed Kennedy but did not favor Johnson or Symington. Doyle estimated the combined strength of these allies totaled 800 votes. "The Kennedy forces," on the other hand, were aggressively engaged in forcing specific leaders and delegations out of neutrality and into open Kennedy support—Williams of Michigan, Green and Lawrence of Pennsylvania, urban leaders in New Jersey and Chicago, Pat Brown in California. Humphrey's people were divided—some regarded Kennedy's nomination as inevitable and wanted Humphrey to help bring it about, others still resisted Kennedy. Six days after West Virginia, Doyle thought, "the most notable factor is that a stampede to Kennedy is not in evidence." This might or might not reflect strong resistance to Kennedy. The effect of the U-2 affair on the Kennedy candidacy was unpredictable. The chance of Kennedy's nomination, however, now appeared "very strong" and of Stevenson's "very slight." Kennedy would be a stronger candidate in November than Johnson or Symington and "would probably be a better President. . . . The Kennedy campaign has revealed a certain toughness, which probably commends him as a strong executive, but also several signs of gross ambition and even viciousness, which are disturbing." If Stevenson thought Kennedy "worthy of the office," he should probably endorse him and do it at a time when Kennedy thought his endorsement decisive, though not before June 1.

On his trip to Washington, Stevenson also saw Jim Rowe, who told him that Kennedy was likely to be nominated and could be stopped only by Johnson, who was late in trying, and Stevenson, who showed no disposition to try. An aide to Senator Mike Monroney, Stevenson's loyal ally, began consulting with an aide to Lyndon Johnson. As a result of all this, Monroney himself, accompanied by John Sharon, went on a scouting trip around the country—not a stop-Kennedy drive but a start-Stevenson drive. They found the California delegation split, Pennsylvania yearning for Stevenson but leaning toward Kennedy, Daley of Chicago committed to Kennedy, New Jersey holding for a favorite son, reform elements in New York still loyal to Stevenson. They concluded that if Kennedy made a major breakthrough in a big state before the convention he would be unbeatable, but the odds were against it.

On the morning of May 17, the day after he saw Johnson, Stevenson had breakfast in Washington with Supreme Court Justice William O. Douglas. During breakfast Abe Fortas, a prominent Washington lawyer close to Lyndon Johnson, telephoned to say the Johnson office felt something should be done about Khrushchev's declaration of the day before, wrecking the summit. (That same morning the New York *Times,* in a roundup of Washington comment on the summit failure, quoted Stevenson as calling it almost inevitable in view of the Administration's mishandling of the U-2 incident.) Stevenson and Douglas drafted a cable to Khrushchev which said, "As leaders of the Democratic Party of the United States, we earnestly urge you to reconsider postponement of the summit meeting until after the national election in this country. We feel that the implications of total failure of the conference and increasing mistrust on both sides will be serious and deeply disturbing to the whole world. Whatever may have been the mistakes of the past on either side all of the American people earnestly desire peace, an end to the arms race and ever better relations between our countries." The cable went on to say Americans were united. Johnson and Rayburn approved it. Kennedy was not consulted. Stevenson asked them to invite Fulbright, who was traveling in Egypt, to join them in signing the cable and to notify the State Department they were planning to send it at once. Stevenson went home to Chicago at noon. Upon his arrival, Johnson telephoned. The State Department, unable to reach Fulbright, had requested that the cable not be sent—it would further complicate the situation. Undersecretary Dillon had consulted with Vice President Nixon and he had discouraged the project. At 4:30 P.M., however, Johnson telephoned again to report the State Department now approved the cable provided it was transmitted to Khrushchev by President Eisenhower. The telegram was sent, and Fulbright joined in signing it.

Yet another crisis arose on the two-day span of May 16–17. Lincoln White, a State Department press officer, telephoned on May 16 with a message for Blair or Stevenson. Tass, the Soviet news agency, was saying that *Paris-Presse* had published an interview with Stevenson quoting him as saying that Americans "must quit Berlin and Europe" if they wanted peace; that, under Eisenhower, America's real Secretary of State had been Chancellor Adenauer. Stevenson, returning to Chicago on May 17, issued a statement and sent a copy to White: "Report of alleged interview with *Paris-Presse* is grotesque. Have given no interviews to any Paris paper in past year and at no time have made any policy recommendations remotely resembling those attributed to me." He actually had had a reporter for *Paris-Presse* at Libertyville, Robert Boulay, in April; on May 18 he issued a further statement: "My recollection is that the young man was brought to my house by friends. I never give exclusive interviews without request and he would not have received one had he asked in such circumstances. As I recall he wanted to discuss all of the problems of Europe and evidently confused discussion with opinion. What he reports me as saying have, of course, never been my views and are not my views today. The most charitable explanation of such irresponsibility, presumption, and discourtesy is that his English was poor and my French no better." Boulay issued a counterstatement: "I was introduced to Mr. Stevenson on April 16 in my capacity as a newspaperman and at no time did he indicate that the views he expressed had a private character. Mr. Stevenson has seen fit to deny in injurious terms what he said to me. I support in their entirety the terms of my conversation with him as they were reproduced in *Paris-Presse*. Today Mr. Stevenson regrets his declarations to me. I don't regret having reported them." For weeks the incident would not die down. Stevenson suspected that Boulay had been "put up to it" by *Time* magazine and that Nixon, or at least a Nixon aide, had helped disseminate the story widely.

26.

Elmo Roper sent Stevenson copies of correspondence between himself and Kennedy. Roper opposed Kennedy because, among other things, he considered Kennedy "anti-Europe." Stevenson read the correspondence and told Roper, "It certainly bears his father's flavor, and I hope and pray that the young man has come a long way since those days."

John Steele had flown back to Chicago with Stevenson and talked to him most of the way. Stevenson said he had been approached by someone who spoke for Kennedy—he would not say who, but Steele thought it was Robert Kennedy, though Robert Kennedy himself denied it—and who suggested that, inasmuch as Stevenson would no doubt be Kennedy's Secretary of State, he should endorse Kennedy before the convention. (Concurrently, a newspaper reported that, in Oregon, Kennedy had said that "whoever is the Democratic President" would appoint Stevenson Secretary of State.) Still Stevenson had no plan to endorse anybody, he told Steele, though he could change his mind at convention time. Steele received the impression that Stevenson would endorse Kennedy at the convention if the nomination of Johnson or Symington seemed imminent. Steele thought Kennedy was Stevenson's favorite candidate though he had some doubts about Kennedy's ability—once he punched a newspaper and asked, "Can he deal with this?" He meant its headlined foreign news. He exhibited "explosive, barely controllable rage" at the way the Administration had handled the U-2 affair.

On May 18, Finletter sent Stevenson a long powerful memorandum on peace. The candidates were saying nothing about arms control, and the people probably would not listen if they did—yet education of the public was imperative. Since last September, when the British and Russians had placed new proposals before the UN, new hope had arisen, and the United States had reversed its previous negative position. Now the failure of the summit had smothered hope. Stevenson must revive it, Finletter argued.

In 1945 and 1946, right after the war, world leaders had seemed determined to disarm. Gradually their momentum subsided. The Eisenhower administration had rejected the ambitious notions of 1945–46 and urged a partial approach, and by the summer of 1957 disarmament was dead. Then in 1959 had come the peaceful "bombshell"—the British and Russians had called for substantially total disarmament, inspected and enforced by the UN, to be reached in stages, each stage safeguarded so that if collapse came after it had been reached no one would be worse off relatively than at the outset. The proposal had caught the United States by surprise. The UN General Assembly had adopted a resolution stating that general and complete disarmament was the most important question facing the world and expressing the hope that measures leading toward it would be agreed upon "in the shortest possible time." The United States had been obliged to go along, thus repudiating its own partial approach. At a ten-power meeting in Geneva in March of 1960 the United States had joined with France, Italy, Canada, and the United Kingdom in a proposal similar to that of the Russians and British and in April had even adopted the language of "general and complete disarmament under effective international control." This again formally repudiated the old Eisenhower partial approach. Subsequent negotiations by a ten-power group at Geneva had not been notably successful. When the ten-power group recessed, it had hoped that the summit would pick up where it had left off. This did not happen—the U-2 incident wrecked the summit. Finletter believed that the progress between September 1959 and the flight of the U-2 must not be abandoned.

President Eisenhower in commenting on the U-2 affair had stated that in order to protect the United States it was necessary to carry on repeated "acts of war"—Finletter's phrase, not Eisenhower's—against the Russians and the Chinese. Nixon had agreed—and Nixon would be the next Republican candidate for President. This was dangerous. In all of recorded history wars had recurred at "fairly short intervals." Unless the world order was changed "it is going to happen again." Therefore, Finletter wrote, "it must be our national policy to assume that the chances of accidental war are growing and growing, and that the weapons simply must be controlled. In short, what I am saying is that there isn't any argument to the contrary of the proposition that general and complete disarmament under international control has become an imperative for the United States in its own self-interest."

It was false for technical reasons, Finletter thought, to argue that no country could ever strike first and escape terrible retribution. Any pre-emptive attack would be made only when the attacker was at peak strength and with both his interceptor planes and missiles and his population well dispersed about the countryside. "Under these circumstances the United States counterattack will be under some disadvantage in finding and striking at the Russian air power." The planes and missiles would be hard to find and hit. The cities would be there, an inviting target. "And the question is whether the horror of a powerful murderous blow against civilian populations will be enough to deter the Russians. The answer is plainly that it will not be." The United States would be mad in these circumstances to start trading blows against cities; the Russians would be far ahead in population dispersion and civil defense. The chances were that the United States would never have an effective civil defense system; the people did not want it. So American leaders would have to decide to hit Russian cities and kill perhaps ten million people when they knew that the counterblow would produce among the unprotected Americans casualties many times greater.

Finletter thought that no one who really studied the problem would disagree. He concluded: "For we must recognize that what we are saying when we talk of disarmament is that we want a new world order in which the rule of law will be extended to the whole world, a new world order in which war for the first time in history will be eliminated as the final recourse when disputes between nations reach a certain point. I must say I find this argument as persuasive as the one that asserts that disarmament is an imperative if mankind is to survive. . . . It is, I agree, too much of a step to expect to extend the rule of law to the whole world as quickly as is necessary. . . . The other day Arthur Larson compared the situation to a fox chasing a rabbit. The rabbit comes to a tree. The question is: can he climb the tree? The answer is that he can't but if he is scared enough, he will. This will be the situation here. We can't have a world law; but we may have to. I am certain of one thing. We will not get world law, we will not climb the tree without great leadership, by a few men, perhaps by one man. I hope that so far as the Democratic Party is concerned, indeed so far as the country is concerned, you may fill this role. I don't know of anyone else who can and I believe you can if you are convinced that it is the right thing to do. The purpose of this memorandum is to try to convince you that it is the right thing to do and to urge that you start on the educating job the people so much need."

The thoughtful memorandum was reflected in Stevenson's subsequent speeches. Stevenson had long been concerned about the control of nuclear weapons. It was in his mind as the convention approached, and would be later when he had to decide whether to go to the UN, and still later when he and President Kennedy reached an impasse in their views of arms control. Stevenson told Suzie Zurcher he had nightmares about the world's being blown up. Arms control was, for Stevenson, more than a political issue or an abstract ideal. It was an urgent necessity for world survival and at the same time a testing ground for his own ability to lead.

The next day Stevenson received a telegram from the Eleanor Roosevelt Democratic Club of Hollywood: "Stand up. Say something in this crucial hour in defiance of US foreign policy towards spying and the destructive answers of Mr. Nixon. We look to you for leadership. Be our next President. Keep us out of war." (Punctuation supplied.) A number of similar communications came in. He spent most of that day in his office working on a speech he was to deliver that night to the Cook County Democratic Committee dinner and left the office about 6:15 P.M. to give it. The speech aroused more uproar than any he had given for a long time. He plunged straight into his deadly serious subject:

"It appears that this year's campaign will be waged under the darkest shadows that ever hovered over the world—the mushroom clouds of a nuclear war that no one wants. This terrible danger—and how to avert it—will and should overshadow every other issue.

"For the chances of a more stable world, which seemed to be brightening, have been rudely reversed by the breakdown of the summit conference in this historic week.

"Premier Khrushchev wrecked this conference. Let there be no mistake about that. When he demanded that President Eisenhower apologize and punish those responsible for the spy plane flight, he was in effect asking the President to punish himself. This was an impossible request, and he knew it.

"But we handed Khrushchev the crowbar and sledge hammer to wreck the meeting. Without our series of blunders, Mr. Khrushchev would not have had a pretext for making his impossible demand and wild charges. Let there be no mistake about that either."

He went on to relate how the United States had sent "an espionage plane" deep into the Soviet Union just before the summit, how it had first denied it, then admitted it, and how when Khrushchev said he assumed Eisenhower was not responsible "the President proudly asserted that he was responsible." Moreover, we had intimated that espionage flights would continue, then we had reconsidered and called them off, then, "to compound the incredible, we postponed the announcement that the flights were terminated—just long enough to make it seem we were yielding to pressure, but too long to prevent Mr. Khrushchev from reaching the boiling point. And, as if that wasn't enough, on Sunday night when there was still a chance that De Gaulle and Macmillan could save the situation, we ordered a world-wide alert of our combat forces!"

It was a tough, blunt attack. To those who attribute pure political ambition to all politicians, it would appear that Stevenson had found his issue. To those who believe that politicians sometimes are moved by higher motives, it would appear that he had spoken up for what he believed at a time of national crisis. Stevenson had been asked by Daley only to make an appearance—Chester Bowles was the main speaker—but before the dinner Stevenson had called Daley and said he was "damned sore" and had something he wanted to say on foreign policy. Daley gave him five minutes. The politicians listened to his speech—it ran for seven minutes—then cheered more loudly than any audience Stevenson had addressed in years. The speech was published in full in the Washington *Post,* and Congressman Chet Holifield wired congratulations and followed with a letter: "Thank God for your courage and clarity of expression. Thirty-seven Members of the House sent the enclosed letter to the President this afternoon. . . . We want you to know your speech was greatly needed and filled a void other Democratic leaders failed to fill."

Khrushchev had overplayed his hand, seeking to humiliate Eisenhower, and as a result Americans were rallying around the President. Almost alone, Stevenson attacked.

27.

Agnes Meyer told Blair on May 20 that some of Stevenson's best friends on the *Post,* and other newspapermen, wondered if he was an efficient administrator of presidential caliber if he could not even get his speeches out on time. She asked, "Did he keep on changing the text up to the last minute?" Blair replied, "I will show your letter of May 20 to the Governor, but I am afraid there is just nothing we can do about his speeches. I have been with him now for exactly ten years and he will work on a speech up to the last moment whether he has one a day or sixteen a day. I can certainly understand the frustrations of the press, but if the Governor is famous for anything it's his speeches, so I have been consoled by that thought!"

The Oregon primary was held on May 20, and Kennedy won with 51.1 per cent of the votes, defeating the favorite son, Senator Morse. En route East from Oregon, on the morning of May 21, Kennedy stopped in Chicago and went out to Libertyville to see Stevenson. Blair had arranged the meeting—he, Minow, and Schlesinger thought that if the two men came to know each other better they would be natural allies. Blair and Minow met Kennedy at the airport. Driving to Libertyville, Kennedy asked, "Do you think I should suggest the possibility of Secretary of State to him?" Neither Blair nor Minow answered immediately; there was a silence in the car. Then Minow said, "No, I wouldn't." Kennedy asked why. Minow said, "He'll be offended and on top of this you shouldn't put yourself in the position of being committed." Minow asked Kennedy who he thought would be nominated if Kennedy was not. Kennedy thought it would be Johnson. At Libertyville they had breakfast. It did not go well; Stevenson was stiff and hesitant. After breakfast Blair took Stevenson and Kennedy into the study, then left them alone. They were in the study for about a half hour or forty-five minutes. When they came out, Blair and Minow suggested they have a statement ready in case newspapermen learned of the meeting. Stevenson and Kennedy drafted separate statements. They could not agree on a joint statement—the problem related to Stevenson's remaining neutral. Kennedy got back into the car with Blair and Minow. Minow asked if he had mentioned the Secretaryship of State. Kennedy looked surprised and said, "No—you told me not to." Minow worried after Kennedy left and told Stevenson what he had done. Stevenson told him he had been right.

Stevenson's relations with Kennedy were never good. Minow ascribed it to various things. "The Gov had a feeling that here was a rich kid—his father was throwing money around to get him elected. Part of it was his youth." Robert Kennedy recalled the Libertyville meeting—his brother told him about it after it occurred. "It was an important meeting. I don't think he ever asked Stevenson to be Secretary. I would be very, very surprised if he did. President Kennedy always felt that his meetings with Stevenson were unsatisfactory. He just never felt that Stevenson was being frank or candid. He was shocked or surprised that Stevenson would be addressing himself to these matters in this way. President Kennedy felt that he and Stevenson could understandably be guarded when talking to the press but that when they sat down together they ought to be able to speak frankly, as man to man." Kennedy felt that Stevenson did not do so at the Libertyville meeting and on other occasions.

Adlai III, too, recalled the meeting as unsatisfactory but his view of Stevenson's later relations with Kennedy differs somewhat from most. "Later Dad developed a healthy respect for Kennedy, especially as regards his intelligence, what a really quick mind he had. This impressed Dad. Gradually they developed a pretty satisfactory relationship, based on some mutual respect. The age difference was one of the greatest obstacles. This young man had risen so rapidly and passed him by."

Ted Sorensen, too, recalled the meeting as unsatisfactory. "During that spring Stevenson's position had become increasingly clear. Some of his friends hired Bill Attwood to write speeches for him. Doyle was active up in Wisconsin for him and so were others. We knew they wouldn't do that without his knowledge. It was clear to Kennedy that if the Stevenson process would deadlock the convention, it would not benefit Stevenson—it would benefit Symington or possibly Johnson. We used Johnson as a scare-word to the liberals, but we really thought it would be Symington if we didn't make it on the first ballot. Kennedy thought Stevenson was being unrealistic about it and he also thought Stevenson was not being as candid with him in private conversations as he should have been. It's one thing to make public statements but when two men sit down in a room alone face to face they should be able to talk frankly to each other. Kennedy did not think Stevenson was doing that. At Libertyville, in general, Stevenson indicated he didn't want the nomination but he also said he didn't know how he could call his people off." Sorensen said Kennedy had not only supported Stevenson in 1952 and 1956 but had "liked and admired him." In 1960, however, their relations worsened. "He had some questions on his mind about whether the man had the sort of ruggedness that was required for political fighting. Which President Kennedy himself had not had early in his career but had acquired. Their relations became strained. You know, the political air around convention time is always filled with rumors about who is sticking knives in people's backs. We heard all sorts of rumors. We had very good antennae. And we heard a variety of things that Stevenson was supposed to have said about Kennedy. Kennedy discounted most of this. You always hear that sort of thing. But at the same time he knew about his own efforts to get Stevenson to declare himself." Sorensen described the Libertyville meeting in his book, *Kennedy,* as "inconclusive" and wrote that Stevenson had "still talked of a dark-horse liberal, still dreamed of his own election and, according to our intelligence agents, had said of Kennedy to one Democrat, 'If only he [Kennedy] had ten more years.' "

Stevenson's own account of the Libertyville meeting was quite different. It was set forth in a letter to Arthur Schlesinger, written in longhand that same afternoon while Stevenson was aboard a plane from Chicago to New York. Stevenson told Schlesinger:

"You were so good to write me about Jack Kennedy's views that I am sending you this report on our talk at Libertyville this morning—written hurriedly as the airplane approaches LaGuardia.

"He came for breakfast en route from Oregon to Cape Cod for his *birthday* (43rd—hush! hush!) party; looked fine and fat (mirable dictu) and happy of course to be finished with the damn primaries. He defends them now on but one ground, I gathered: an opportunity to get known all over the country and I think he makes a good point, if not good enough to convince me!

"He *seemed* to feel that my reaction to the Summit bungling was correct and that we shouldn't, either for the country or the party, let this one be buried in maudlin mush. But I will wait to see what he *does* with interest.

"He felt that Nixon would take the tough guy with Khrushchev line now, that he *had* to, and his strategy would be to put us on the defensive as the soft on communism party. I have hoped for this and that we can get some generalship and coherence to handle it effectively—thus recapturing the peace issue—and also getting the country in a posture to save the alliance, restore confidence and perhaps sometime make some progress toward peace in fact!

"As to the campaign, Jack reviewed *all* the states and said he was still short 80–100 votes probably; that I was strong especially in Oregon, Wash, Calif, Colo, Pa etc—that I could help him and he wanted the help without specifying *when.*

"I explained that I wanted to be consistent and didn't feel therefore that I could come out for him *now,* but that he could be sure that I would not be a party—overtly, covertly etc.—to *any* 'stop Kennedy' movements; that I had been approached—and *have* I!—with that proposal and had emphatically and unequivocally rejected the overtures; that, further, I would, as in the past (cf. D.C.) do *nothing* to encourage 'Draft Stevenson' movements which could embarrass or weaken him. (And I think my speech here the other night on facing the realities of the Summit debacle has probably effectively taken care of *that!*)

"The meeting was entirely satisfactory from my point of view and I cannot say he seemed disappointed or surprised about my attitude and certainly not elated! The only sensitive point I felt was his response to some remark I made about Johnson and the importance of his [Lyndon Johnson's] cooperation if K was elected. Here the reaction was sharp and certain—that there was only one way to treat Lyndon now—*Beat him!* that he would come along after the election, etc. etc. etc.

"There was *no* talk about Secy of State or deals. 'If I can't make it,' he said, 'we'll have to reappraise the situation at that time,' but no reference or hint about supporting me. There were several references to 'the same people' are 'your friends and mine.'

"I can add that he seemed *very* self-confident and assured and much tougher and blunter than I remember him in the past. We talked a little about the release from the Osservatore Romano, which *shocked* me (as Nixon would say!) and he said if necessary he would repudiate or some such word, publicly the idea of any such dictation or influence in political affairs. I offered to help, as a Protestant layman, on that if I could. And I think—and *hope*—that I left him with a feeling of great good will, determination not to *hinder,* and no doubt about my preference and anxiety to *help* in any way if he is nominated.

"He didn't use the 'liberals stand together' argument; indeed didn't argue at all and was totally correct. As I conclude this I guess the only faint misgiving about the meeting I have is that he may not fully appreciate some of *my* difficulties and how easy it has been and would be [to] give some impetus to a movement for myself which would be largely at his expense and with some of the people he mentioned with such confidence as '*his.*' But perhaps that's hardly surprising in *view* of *his* difficulties."

That letter was written on Saturday afternoon but not received until Monday. Late Sunday afternoon, May 22, Kennedy telephoned Schlesinger to report on his talk with Stevenson. "He said that it had been wholly pleasant," Schlesinger wrote in his journal, "but that obviously AES did not intend to do anything for the moment. Jack said that he was not much impressed by AES's account of why he did not wish to act; but supposed this to be because he did not wish to disclose his real reason—that, if he said nothing, there might still be a possibility that he would emerge out of the scramble as the candidate.

"Jack's particular fear was that AES had been 'snowed' by Johnson—that Lyndon on Monday had told him that, if he stayed aloof, he would be Lyndon's second choice (next to himself), that anything might happen, and that therefore he should do nothing to sew the nomination up for Jack. Speaking with a certain detached bitterness, Jack said: 'I told him that Lyndon was a chronic liar; that he has been making all sorts of assurances to me for years and has lived up to none of them.' Adlai emphasized to Jack the importance of party harmony and his remaining on good terms with Lyndon. Jack made clear that he regards party harmony as no problem at all: 'Everyone will come around the day after the convention; and anyone who doesn't come around will be left out and won't matter. The support of [party] leaders is much overrated anyway. Leaders aren't worth a damn. . . .'

"Adlai mentioned that Monroney, Gore and Carroll all had come out for him. Jack said (I am not clear whether he said also to Adlai) that none of them controlled a single delegate's vote except his own. He added, 'Stevenson has a lot of support, but it's mostly Secretary of State support.'

"Bill Blair told Jack that people were saying to AES that he does not need to come out for Kennedy; that, if Jack fails to make it, he has no place to go but Stevenson anyway. Jack said, 'Well, that may be so; but there would be a lot of difference between going for Stevenson with enthusiasm and just going through the motions.'

"On the Oregon primaries, he pointed out how badly Symington and Johnson had done. 'I don't see how those two bastards can keep their heads above water.'

"His general attitude was rueful but philosophical. 'I guess there's nothing I can do except go out and collect as many votes as possible and hope that Stevenson will decide to come along.'"

On Monday, Blair telephoned Schlesinger, who wrote in his journal:

"[Blair] is evidently fed up with the situation in Chicago. He says that he is regarded with suspicion because of his pro-Kennedy views and is going away to Paris for ten days on Thursday. 'I am regarded with almost as much suspicion as you,' he said. Apparently the argument about liberals-standing-together was a great flop. AES says that, if Kennedy is the kind of man who will seek support from the bosses and the south, we don't want him as President anyway. (Surely a curious position for Stevenson, who had assiduously sought precisely that support in 1956.)

"Bill was concerned about the 'hypocrisy' of the Governor's position— his pretense of being neutral and above the battle, all of which Bill calls 'rationalization.' Kennedy said to Bill after hearing it: 'The Governor ought to know that in this situation no one can be neutral.' Bill thinks it is awful for Stevenson to keep saying that he isn't a candidate while [Mike Monroney and John Sharon are] running around the country on his behalf. . . . 'I have just learned that Sharon and Attwood were in to see him this morning [in New York].' I said that I thought Attwood was out of the picture. [Blair]: 'I thought so too, but I guess that Tom Finletter and Agnes Meyer persuaded the Governor that he had treated Bill unfairly, so Bill is now back.'

"Bill says that Mary Lasker, Agnes Meyer and George Ball are against a Kennedy endorsement; Barry Bingham, Ben Heineman, Newt Minow and himself are for it; Bill Wirtz inclines toward it, but feels that AES ought to be left alone and allowed to make up his own mind.

"Bill says that Lyndon Johnson is exercising great influence on AES. Kennedy's conjecture to me of what J said to AES last Monday was evidently right. According to Bill, J said that his own candidacy wasn't too serious, but that he couldn't stand to be pushed around by a 42-year old kid, etc., and that he favored Adlai next to himself. Johnson also said that Symington would be a stronger candidate than Kennedy, and AES was much impressed by this.

"Kennedy's last word to Blair at the airport: 'Guess who the next person I see will be—the person who will say, "I told you that son-of-a-bitch has been running for President every moment since 1956"?' Blair: 'Daddy.'

"Bill said not to use the liberal argument any more. I asked him what argument he thought would be most effective. He said the general argument that AES had worked for eight years to bring in fresh faces and recast the Dem Party in his own image; that this had largely succeeded;

that Kennedy stood for this and was its beneficiary; and that all the bums and all the people who had opposed him were on the other side. If AES was a candidate, he should say so; but that, if he wasn't, he should help his friends. If Kennedy failed to make it, then he would turn to AES—and it would make a great deal of difference whether he made a perfunctory personal gesture toward him, or whether he pounded the table and demanded that all his people back him. He said that AES would listen to this, though he did not like to hear talk about being Secretary of State."

Schlesinger wrote to Stevenson, reporting on Kennedy's reaction to the Libertyville meeting, and on May 29 Stevenson telephoned Schlesinger and said he was sorry that Kennedy felt "regretful" over their conversation. Schlesinger replied that Stevenson was taking a word in his letter out of context and overemphasizing it—Kennedy was regretful only over Stevenson's reluctance to endorse him forthwith but was "wholly philosophical" about the talk in general. Schlesinger wrote in his journal, "AES said that he obviously made a 'dire mistake' in mentioning Johnson; this provoked the only flash of anger on Kennedy's part. 'Obviously the feeling between the two of them is savage.' AES said again how fiercely Johnson had spoken against Kennedy when they met in Washington. AES said, 'I suppose I made a mistake bringing Johnson up; but I thought that, if I were to serve under Kennedy, it might be helpful if I could keep a personal in with Johnson. If I double-cross Johnson now, it would mean that he had no personal relations with anyone in the new administration.' (The phrase 'double-cross' was interesting: does this mean AES has assured LBJ that he won't endorse Kennedy? Or did he just use the word loosely?)

"He said that he got from Minow and Blair the impression that Jack, after their breakfast together, felt AES to be a candidate and thus competitive with him. 'I was very sorry about that. I don't know what to do about it.' I didn't respond particularly to this.

"AES said that he thought that Kennedy had been 'perfect' in his post-Summit remarks. AES had just received a long cable from Noel-Baker saying that Kennedy's support of AES after Paris had done a great deal to dispel anxieties in England over his possible nomination."

Schlesinger had invited Kennedy and Stevenson to dine in Cambridge June 5. Kennedy now declined because of conflicting speaking engagements but said he hoped that Stevenson could be persuaded to put his delegates behind Kennedy, citing a newspaper survey showing that Kennedy had 620 delegates, Johnson 515, Symington 145, Humphrey 100, and Stevenson 75, and arguing that Stevenson thus had no chance himself and clinging to his delegates would benefit Johnson and Symington.

The pressure got to Stevenson. On May 31 he sent a memo to Minow with copies to Wirtz, Blair, McDougal, Garrison, Finletter, and Adlai III: "Having no public relations management, couldn't you in your way make it clear that *not* coming out for K. is consistent with the policy of four years, and fair to the others; and that I won't be party to any 'stop K. movements.' It is discouraging to read about my 'entourage' all the time always in terms of 'to come out for K. or not to come out—to help *myself* get the nomination.' Couldn't someone suggest that I never had any intention of 'coming out' for anyone—or stopping anyone and it is unrelated to any 'draft Stevenson' movement and exactly consistent with what I've been doing for four years—keeping out of everyone's way and not being a candidate myself."

28.

The Sunday, May 21, New York *Times* carried a full-page advertisement placed by the New York draft-Stevenson committee. Under a banner headline proclaiming, AMERICA NEEDS ADLAI STEVENSON, the ad emphasized the summit and urged readers to work with or contribute to the committee. The ad cost $6,840 and one committee member had mortgaged his house to pay for it. The result was some $46,000 in contributions and many volunteer workers. Committee leaders believed that anxiety over the international situation had suddenly made Stevenson a credible candidate. They held a meeting in a New York school auditorium three days later, and the hall was filled. They urged volunteers to collect signatures on petitions. They began organizing neighborhood clubs in the New York area, and by the end of June about twenty such committees had been set up, all supplied with petitions, campaign literature, and buttons. They began to move up through Connecticut to Boston. There, they formed an advisory board that included John Steinbeck, Melvyn Douglas, Reinhold Niebuhr, Leonard Bernstein, and Max Lerner. "Reform" Democratic clubs in New York were reluctant to join them. Even more reluctant was the regular organization—and it had picked the convention delegates, most of whom were already committed to Kennedy. Meanwhile, Stevenson was under attack from several quarters, including the Chicago *Tribune* and the New York *Daily News* and Jim Farley, for his stand on the U-2 affair. Stevenson sent hostile heavy-handed editorials from the *Tribune* and New York *News* to Alicia Patterson with a wry comment: "Note big drift of News and Tribune to Stevenson by brilliant thoughtful reasoned editorials!"

A number of people, including Dr. Edward S. Corwin of Princeton, a well-known law professor and once Stevenson's teacher, congratulated Stevenson on the U-2 speeches. In an article in the June 6 issue of *Look*, President Truman criticized Stevenson. Stevenson spent the morning of May 25 working on a statement in reply and that afternoon read it for the television cameras: "I respect President Truman—if not his memory of events. But our different recollections of 1952 and 1956 are not important now—and I will make only one further brief comment on his article, because I believe that we Democrats have more useful work to do than to criticize one another. I deeply regret President Truman's criticism of my plea in 1956 for the United States to take the lead in bringing about an international ban on the testing and further development of the lethal hydrogen weapons that could exterminate us all. If he disapproves of trying to rid the world of this hideous danger, I think his criticism should be directed to the Eisenhower administration which suspended tests *two* years later—but *after* the Russians had taken the lead and got the credit among the people of the world whose confidence and respect we are trying to win. Of course, there is no international system of control and inspection yet, but agreement with the Russians was very close before the summit conference collapsed. And I devoutly pray that this first step toward nuclear disarmament and sanity in the world is not going to be a casualty of the disaster in Paris last week."

On May 26 he received an award from his old audience, the Chicago Council on Foreign Relations. Once again he spoke on the subject of disarmament.

On May 31, Alicia Patterson's *Newsday* endorsed Stevenson for President because of "his experience, his wisdom and his ability. . . . He is qualified for many reasons but the one overriding reason is that he would be able to deal with the totalitarian powers." *Newsday* endorsed Kennedy for Vice President. Alicia Patterson signed the editorial and sent a copy to Stevenson.

John Sharon and Senator Monroney telephoned Stevenson on June 1, and he issued a statement repeating his non-candidacy and neutrality, observing, "The doubt about my position has apparently arisen because I have spoken out bluntly on the current crisis in our affairs. I have done so because I think it my duty as a citizen." Hubert Humphrey inserted an article by Stevenson on the national purpose into the *Congressional Record* and told Stevenson, "Is it any wonder that millions of Americans want you to be President and, my good friend, if you don't expect this to happen you better quit writing articles such as this." Stevenson gave Newt Minow a note, "Please write to John Sharon where I am staying in Los Angeles— *if* I go to the Convention—I have no idea!"

On June 1, Stevenson spoke to the Textile Workers Union convention in Chicago. The day before, the Textile Workers had endorsed Kennedy, the first union to do so, and Kennedy would address them the next day. Humphrey had addressed them the day before and had spoken of Stevenson with enthusiasm. Stevenson's speech would be taped for evening coast-to-coast broadcast. In it, he returned to the attack. He said that progress toward a nuclear test ban and a break in the arms race must not be allowed to vanish in the U-2 summit debacle. "I think we need a special agency under the Secretary of State charged with the great, complex, and neglected task of peace and disarmament which will be a symbol of our determination to lead the world away from madness." (President Kennedy established just such an agency after his inauguration.)

Stevenson's friends believed that his recent speeches on the summit and disarmament had put him back into the race for the nomination. The speeches had been dangerous, inviting attack by Nixon that he was appeasing Khrushchev, but they had been effective. They had, however, moved few or no professional politicians, who simply did not want a two-time loser.

On Thursday, June 2, Stevenson went to New York again for a long weekend, attended a fund-raising cocktail party given by the Committee for an Effective Congress on behalf of Senators Muskie and McCarthy, and attended a dinner with DAC people. On Sunday he went up to Boston with Borden and saw Arthur Schlesinger and spent the night.

Schlesinger noted that Stevenson "constantly" insisted that he was not a candidate but was obviously gratified by his reception at the Boston airport. He "fussed a little" about Kennedy, saying again he had made a mistake in talking about Johnson to Kennedy. Stevenson said Johnson had told him he would yield his votes to Stevenson but not to Kennedy or Symington. Stevenson said Kennedy's post-summit statements had been fine but "I don't know whether I would want to be Secretary of State with him or not." The next day Tom Finletter called Schlesinger to say he was enthusiastically for Stevenson because of the way Stevenson had seized the peace issue. "He is the only one who really understands the disarmament question." He said he admired Kennedy, too, but thought Kennedy would leave Stevenson out of his Administration since he had not supported Kennedy before West Virginia. (Kennedy, elected, appointed Finletter Ambassador to NATO.)

The Chicago *Daily News* reported that Schlesinger, Ken Galbraith, Joe Rauh, and Henry Steele Commager were endorsing Kennedy. Stevenson had been Schlesinger's house guest only forty-eight hours before; Schlesinger had said nothing about it. When the story leaked, Schlesinger was mortified.

Earlier, during the Wisconsin and West Virginia primaries, Schlesinger had been neutral. He had told both Kennedy and Humphrey that he thought the winner of those primaries would be entitled to united liberal support. After West Virginia a Kennedy man had reminded Schlesinger of this and asked him to sign a pro-Kennedy statement also signed by Commager, Walt Rostow, and others. Schlesinger had said he was ready in principle to come out for Kennedy but did not like the text of the statement. Joe Rauh and Commager had not liked it either and prepared further drafts. In the meanwhile the U-2-summit affair had suddenly revived interest in Stevenson. This had made Schlesinger hesitate. There was still no agreed draft, and he had hoped the matter would lie dormant until he left for Berlin, as he was scheduled to do in a few days. Because nothing seemed imminent, he did not discuss the matter with Stevenson when he stayed with the Schlesingers; he intended to leave for Berlin without signing and to tell Stevenson well in advance that he intended to sign. He did urge Stevenson again to consider coming out for Kennedy, but said nothing about his own plans.

When the story broke, "I felt sick about it," Schlesinger noted. He issued a statement saying that Stevenson was best qualified but that, since he was not a candidate, he was for Kennedy. Bill Blair told him that, if he had been free, he would have done the same thing. George Ball and Tom Finletter were disapproving but amiable. John Sharon was angry. Kenneth Davis, an author, and others felt that, as an intellectual, Schlesinger had no business engaging in political calculation and should settle for nothing less than the best. Schlesinger knew that, ironically, he had come to the private conclusion he would rather have Kennedy as President than Stevenson—though Stevenson was "more thoughtful, more creative," he "had been away from power too long; he gives me an odd sense of unreality. . . . I felt in Barbados and in Cambridge this strange feeling that he had been away from things too long. I find it hard to define this feeling—a certain frivolity, distractedness, overinterest in words and phrases? I don't know; but K in contrast gives a sense of cool, measured, intelligent concern with action and power. I feel that his administration would be less encumbered than S's with commitments to past ideas or sentimentalities; that he would be more radical; and that, though he is less creative personally, he might be more so politically. But I cannot mention this feeling to anyone. At any rate, I felt terribly all week (still feel so). My greatest affection is for AES; my greatest debt is to him; if he were a declared candidate I would of course, despite all misgivings, be for him. I wrote him a letter trying to set forth my position. He replied a few days later, rather casually, I thought; a little cool and hurt? I fear so. I would have been in his place. Judging from my mail, I was much more hurt than he by this defection; the intellectuals as a whole are faithful to Adlai."

The letter from Stevenson said, in its entirety:

Dear Arthur:
I confess I was surprised by the announcement that greeted me on my return after my visit with you. However, your letter is most reassuring. I only hope your telephone has not been burning like mine! I doubt if it is, but it will all subside quickly enough.

I have only now uncovered in a mass of neglected mail your letter of March 2 about Harold Fruchtbaum [a student of Schlesinger's who was researching Stevenson's position on the H-bomb] and I enclose a memo which I am afraid is quite inadequate. If he would like something more, tell him not to hesitate to let me know. I believe, by the way, that my utterances on this subject have been researched before.
Yours, hurriedly.

It was as though, by reaching back to a letter neglected since March, Stevenson was closing the books on Schlesinger. Schlesinger's secretary, Julie Jeppson, wrote to Stevenson, and he replied, "Bless you for that angelic letter. What a dear friend you are. I am afraid I have been more distressed by all that has happened—and for quite different reasons, namely, that it has upset the Schlesingers, and you, and so many good friends. As for me, I am not upset in the least!" The cruel dilemmas of the spring of 1960 hurt many people.

A few days later, on June 12, Schlesinger, his wife, and Galbraith went to Hyannisport to spend the day with the Kennedys. They found Kennedy and his wife Jacqueline playing croquet on the lawn on a hot, overcast day. During daiquiris on the terrace and a ride on the Kennedy launch, they discussed issues, and Schlesinger and Galbraith could discover none on which they disagreed with Kennedy. Schlesinger said he had recently had dinner with Joe Alsop. He was about to say Alsop had told him that he had convinced Kennedy he should appoint Acheson Secretary of State —which, if true, probably would have led Schlesinger to withdraw his endorsement of Kennedy—but Kennedy interrupted to say, "I'm fond of Joe, but I guess we have to face the fact about him that he is an Achesonian," and made it clear that he, Kennedy, was not. Kennedy went on, "Do you know one man who is hoping for an open break between Stevenson and me? Chester Bowles." Of Stevenson he said, "One reason I admire him is that he is not a political whore like most of the others. Too many politicians will say anything which they think will bring them votes or money. I remember in 1956 when Adlai met with Judge Dewey Stone and some other big contributors in Boston a few days after Suez. They wanted him to say certain things about Israel and Egypt. If he had said them, he could have had a lot of money out of that room; but he refused to say them. I admired that."

Kennedy seemed confident he would be nominated. He said Humphrey was his first choice for Vice President. He regarded Johnson as his main rival for the nomination, called him a "riverboat gambler," and said he resembled Peel, who was omnipotent in Parliament but lacked popularity in the country.

They discussed Kennedy's campaign staff. Schlesinger thought Kennedy seemed aware that Ted Sorensen "feels threatened" by the addition of new people. Schlesinger and Galbraith urged Kennedy to make Archibald Cox of Harvard his chief of staff. Kennedy asked whether they would help. They said he should "consider carefully before he takes over the Stevenson team."

He wanted to work out the "major themes" of the campaign soon. They discussed civil rights. Galbraith suggested Kennedy announce dramatically that if elected he would try to prevent Senator Eastland of Mississippi from being chairman of the Judiciary Committee. Kennedy said, "I couldn't do that. It wouldn't be in character for me to do that."

Stevenson did not resent the desertion of Galbraith and Schlesinger and, after the convention, Martin, to Kennedy—or, if he did, did not show it. "There was a largeness about him," Schlesinger once said. "He could be small and mean, but not when it mattered. This was why we forgave him his smallness and meanness. This was why we loved him."

29.

For several days starting June 8, Stevenson attended social functions for the children of friends—weddings, a bridal dinner at Onwentsia, lunch at the Dicks' house, a dinner dance at Onwentsia. His own children gathered, John Fell and Borden, and Nancy and Adlai came out to Libertyville. Stevenson attended a cocktail party for the Aga Khan at the Racquet Club in Chicago, then took him to Libertyville for the night. Mrs. Ives was there part of the time. So was Theodore White, the journalist, who subsequently wrote that Stevenson seemed far more concerned about foreign policy than about politics. While White and Stevenson were talking, Stevenson received a telephone call from New York and was told that Mrs. Roosevelt was about to insist publicly that he declare whether or not he sought the Democratic nomination. He seemed annoyed and rattled and angry. He felt his position was clear. He had stated it repeatedly. He received more phone calls from the East. White wrote, "One had the sense of a distant clamor calling for executive leadership. Yet he would not act. He would wait."

Mrs. Roosevelt endorsed him publicly, the impression got around that he was a candidate or about to become one, and he wrote a statement: "I am not a candidate," and she became honorary chairman of the New York draft committee, which by mid-June had about 7,000 volunteers and some 250,000 signatures on petitions. It had moved to a former USO center in mid-Manhattan rented for $500 a month and hung out a five-story banner proclaiming "STEVENSON-FOR-PRESIDENT HEADQUARTERS." Inside, crowds of volunteers were enlisting new workers, handling petitions, stuffing and mailing envelopes, talking and planning.

Albert Schweitzer in a letter dated May 29 urged Stevenson to be active in politics as a candidate for President or as an independent politician in the cause of peace. On June 10, Stevenson dictated a letter to Lloyd Garrison over Carol Evans' signature—he dictated it but Miss Evans signed it as if it were her own—suggesting: "If Dr. Schweitzer made a public statement expressing his regard for the Governor and confidence that more than any other American he could conduct fruitful negotiations with the Russians and advance the prospects for peace, it might be helpful to a better understanding of what the Governor is trying to do, i.e., keep our attitude towards the Soviet Union rational. It occurred to me that Clara Urquhart [a Schweitzer associate] might get some statement out of Dr.

Schweitzer which could be sent to someone promptly or released by Dr. Schweitzer for the wire services in Africa or Europe. Forgive me for intruding, but I am sure you see the possibilities here." It was a devious maneuver reminiscent of some he had made as a young man. What is perhaps most surprising is that he dissembled to Lloyd Garrison, his old friend and close associate.

Pat Brown told Agnes Meyer that Kennedy had made "remarkable progress" in California and indicated he feared a Stevenson movement might deadlock the convention and nominate Johnson. Mrs. Meyer, sending the letter to Stevenson, dismissed this thesis and said the crowds she addressed were "tepid" when she spoke of Kennedy but enthusiastic when she endorsed Stevenson. Stevenson wrote Barbara Ward on June 21, "Here the papers all over the country are blossoming with full page 'draft Adlai' advertisements and children are filling tin cups with pennies and young people 'madly for Adlai' are circulating petitions. . . . Kennedy's tactics are coercive, but effective, and if he is nominated, as I suspect he will be, all will be well, but if he slips the victims will turn upon him like wolves, I fear. He has made an excellent foreign policy speech and verbally handles everything well. But the entourage is ruthless and tough beyond the virtues of that word, I fear." He told Agnes Meyer he had not followed the delegate count but felt that "our young friend" might be nominated on the first ballot. "I really don't know and find strength in the fact that I don't seem to care. I am afraid this will make you angry."

On June 22, leaders of the draft-Stevenson movements in Wisconsin, Washington, and New York met at Washington to set up a coordinated headquarters—Jim Doyle, Senator Monroney, John Sharon, Tom Finney, and David Garth and others from New York. They decided to build local campaigns wherever possible before the convention and to put pressure on convention delegates. Doyle would head the volunteers at the Los Angeles convention. Tedson Meyers would go there at once to set up a headquarters. The Washington people, led by Monroney, would plan convention moves, communicate with party leaders and with Stevenson, and work the floor. They would assemble a staff to handle political intelligence, press relations, and delegate relations. They would raise money for the convention operations. In Los Angeles they located a building, the old Paramount Building, strategically situated directly across Pershing Square from the Biltmore Hotel, official convention headquarters, and rented it. By convention time a "STEVENSON FOR PRESIDENT" sign ten feet high and a hundred feet long dominated the area. By the end of June some three hundred local committees existed, though only the New York and Washington groups were able to mount large-scale efforts. The movement throughout the nation had little direct effect on delegates but it did demonstrate rank-and-file Stevenson support.

On June 23, Stevenson addressed the Illinois State Bar Association, meeting in Waukegan in his home county. He called for "a full and frank" discussion during the coming campaign. The discussion must be carried on "in a political atmosphere free of accusation, of innuendo and of irresponsibility. . . . We must keep in mind that our chief problem is still how to deal with the Russians and the Chinese. It is not a matter of who is soft and who is hard, but of who is wise and who is stupid." The greatest danger of nuclear war was not that Russia would start it but that it would happen accidentally. The only deterrent to accidental war was disarmament. "I don't know whether Khrushchev wants to help elect Nixon or not —nor do I care. . . . I suggest that both presidential candidates this year pledge themselves in advance of the campaign to keep Mr. Khrushchev out of our national debate." His audience, which contained many Republicans, gave him a standing ovation. Senator Fulbright inserted the speech into the *Congressional Record* and told Stevenson he hoped the draft-Stevenson movement would prosper—it would be "a tragedy" if the voters had to choose between Kennedy and Nixon.

Estes Kefauver, in a hard primary fight in Tennessee, asked Stevenson for help, and Stevenson sent a letter to about fifty Democratic contributors in New York. But the crushing volume of mail of an active candidate was no longer his—it was only three weeks before the convention, and he found time to answer fan mail promptly and to inquire about a Russian edition of his book describing his trip there. Jack Ryan of Little Rock told him he believed that Russian missile bases were being built in Cuba, or soon would be. Stevenson replied, "While I have no doubt the Soviet Union would be delighted to establish a missile base in Cuba and retaliate for our bases all around Russia, I would find a transmitter station much more significant and dangerous." It was not the way President Kennedy would react two years later.

Stevenson received a form letter from Chet Bowles urging the nomination of Kennedy. "As you know, I am serving as foreign policy adviser to Senator John Kennedy—and I am convinced that he is the man who can inspire the Free World to regain the initiative for peace." (Months earlier, when Kennedy, reaching for liberal support, had asked Bowles to become his foreign policy adviser, Bowles had consulted Stevenson, with whom his heart lay. Stevenson had told him to join Kennedy—Kennedy's position on foreign affairs had not yet crystallized, Stevenson thought, and Bowles might help nudge him in a liberal direction.)

Stevenson would arrive in Los Angeles on Saturday, July 9, and would stay at the Beverly Hills Hotel until Monday, the eleventh, the day the convention opened, when he would move to the Sheraton West Hotel. He had the presidential suite at the Sheraton West and so could entertain easily. He would keep the Beverly Hills bungalow for a "hideaway." Agnes Meyer had taken an estate in Pasadena to serve as an informal Stevenson base and was planning a large preconvention cocktail party for him. She would invite, among others, sixty friendly members of the California delegation "to encourage these shepardless sheep that we mean business no matter what Brown does—I invited Brown a week ago. I bring up the size and importance of the party because I hope you can come direct from the plane. . . . It would be a flop if all these delegates, state governors, Senators etc (to say nothing of local chairmen) had to wait to greet you. This time please cooperate and act secretly like a serious minded candidate."

On June 29, Stevenson went to New York and Washington, deep in the troubles of the Field Foundation and attending a fund-raising party for Hubert Humphrey, who was running for re-election to the Senate. (Stevenson gave him $500.) It was the last week before the convention.

On July 5, Stevenson wrote a long stiff letter to Mrs. Ives: "Although I have not discussed it with her, I have been painfully aware of your hostility to Jane Dick, though not fully aware of the reasons. . . . My old and loyal friends—those to whom I can talk freely—are essential to me. I number among these Eddie and Jane. . . . But with them, as in case of some other people, your resentments or tensions have not been helpful to my relationships. After three campaigns Jane has a large acquaintance and a political insight that are important and your cooperation with her can be most helpful to me. I have never understood why we should not enjoy and use, reciprocally, our friends as fully as possible. . . . I was pleased to feel that your relations were mending. I hardly need add how much *you* can help me in times of need, and one of the most important ways would be to relieve me of any anxiety about your relations with my friends on whom I am so dependent, whether you like them or not. This is hurried and not well considered, and hope it doesn't irritate you." He sent a copy to Jane Dick.[12] It was as though, almost on the eve of the 1960 convention, he returned to earlier days, withdrew to personal relationships.

The New York *Post* had endorsed Stevenson for President and Kennedy for Vice President on June 29. On July 5, Stevenson thanked Mrs. Dorothy Schiff, with a carbon to James Wechsler: "I had thought to telephone you both to thank you, but on second thought I concluded to do it this way and not risk the excessive emotion. Somehow as I get older I get more sentimental. . . . I will cherish this editorial always as a precious reminder of my momentary political resurrection in 1960." There was something elegiac about these days. One recalls Schlesinger's comment that Stevenson seemed out of touch with power and reality. The truth seems to be that Stevenson had a firmer grip on reality than his supporters, though not on power. And the reality was that his political day was over.

On July 5, Lyndon Johnson officially announced his candidacy and at a press conference refused to rule out the vice presidential nomination, though said he expected the presidential nomination.

A California magazine, *Frontier,* endorsed Stevenson, and Stevenson told its editor it made him blush: "and a very pleasant sensation it is— even for an old man!" Stevenson spent most of Friday, July 8, working on speeches for the convention. He recorded an interview with CBS. Asked

---

[12] The rift healed after the campaign; Jane and Buffie remained friends.

why he had not sought the nomination, he replied he had felt it not "fitting and proper" to seek a third nomination—he should "stand aloof, step aside and let the party decide." He would accept a draft but thought one "unlikely, quite unlikely." What, then, was his reaction "to this great surge of Stevenson sentiment" in the past month? "I had no idea that there was such an extensive grass-roots support and confidence in me still, and it's been deeply moving, deeply touching, and very gratifying." He hoped this support would rally to the candidate whoever he might be. In another statement Stevenson said that if he were nominated he would campaign "with vigor and a sense of real purpose," and told Anthony Lewis of the New York *Times* he would accept a draft and do "my utmost to win."

That same day, July 8, Stevenson sent Barbara Ward copies of speeches he expected to deliver upon his arrival in Los Angeles—"where some five or ten thousand shouting, banner waving, undaunted Madlys for Adlais will greet me"—and at Democratic dinners there. He said, "I have little doubt that Kennedy will be nominated, perhaps promptly." Suzie Zurcher was in Santa Barbara and sent him a letter that is fully understandable only if one knows that she is descended from Pocahontas: "Would that my forest domesticity might comfort you a little in this ordeal. Happily would I find you wild berries and cool spring water, roast you trout and chestnuts, fan your sleep with grey goose feathers. . . . Look for me and —you alone—will see that I am holding aloft a campaign placard, a light blue one that says, in creditable calligraphy, WINGAPOH, ADLAI, I LOVE YOU!"

30.

Stevenson left for Los Angeles. It would be, one reporter wrote, "a tough week," for Stevenson. He would be under conflicting pressures— Monroney and his associates would advise him to stay in contention until the end; others would advise him to get out entirely and save himself embarrassment; others would advise him to endorse Kennedy and be made Secretary of State. John Steele wrote, "It is hard to watch the younger generation take over and that seems about to happen here." Paul Butler had reluctantly assigned Stevenson's workers cramped space in the Biltmore Hotel, two small and almost inaccessible rooms known to reporters as "Butler's pantry."

Stevenson's New York, Washington, and California supporters had arrived at the convention scene several days earlier and set up headquarters and were at work on delegate files, a daily newspaper, and "Stevenson girls" for demonstrations. Senator Monroney became the principal leader of the Stevenson forces and Doyle their spokesman. By the end of the week they believed that on the first ballot Kennedy would have 600 votes —with 761 needed to nominate—Johnson between 450 and 500, Syming-

ton between 100 and 150, and Stevenson a firm 45 to 50 and a possible
75 to 80. If Kennedy reached 700 on the first ballot, a few switches would
put him over. Thus it was necessary to keep uncommitted or favorite-son
delegates firmly uncommitted or behind their favorite sons in order to
deny them to Kennedy. Among the crucial states were Pennsylvania, California, New Jersey, Minnesota, and Illinois. Whether Stevenson wanted it
or not, his supporters were obliged to try to stop Kennedy on the first
ballot if they were to have a chance. Yet they would have to avoid the appearance of doing so if they hoped to pick up Kennedy's supporters once
he was stopped. If Stevenson appeared in the role of the stopper, embittered Kennedy people would support Johnson rather than Stevenson.
Johnson's interests lay in using Stevenson as a Kennedy stopper. His aides
tried to swing delegates to Stevenson in, among other states, California. By
convention eve, although he had few solid votes of his own, Stevenson appeared as the principal obstacle to Kennedy's nomination.

Stevenson's plane arrived late. He was greeted by a large crowd,
variously estimated at between 5,000 and 10,000, wildly enthusiastic people buoyed up by his statement the night before that if nominated he
would campaign hard. He went to Agnes Meyer's party. His ardent supporters there told him he would be drafted. Ken Galbraith was there, and
a loyal Stevenson supporter angrily accused him of "the worst personal betrayal in American history"—Galbraith was supporting Kennedy.

Blair went to a big splashy dinner party in honor of Senator Kennedy at
the home of Kennedy's sister Patricia, then married to Peter Lawford.
Most of the guests were movie stars. Senator Kennedy greeted Blair
warmly, asked if there was any chance Stevenson would withdraw, and,
when Blair said he was afraid not, responded, "Look, I understand." Robert Kennedy was only a little less understanding. But when Blair went up
to their father to pay his respects, the senior Kennedy stared at him stonily
despite their long and good relationship and clenched his fist and said,
"Your man must be out of his mind." Blair mumbled something to the effect that perhaps this was not the place to talk politics. The senior Kennedy said, "You've got twenty-four hours," and turned away.

On Sunday in his bungalow at the Beverly Hills Hotel, Stevenson saw
Phil and Katharine Graham, and Graham raised the question of Stevenson's placing John F. Kennedy's name in nomination. "He was quite apa-
thetic to this," Graham later wrote, "insofar as the Kennedy people had
urged it as a means to avoid his being 'humiliated' by an unsuccessful draft
effort. Simultaneously, he seemed willing to be tempted if only this course
were urged as a way to unify the Party. But he expressed the feeling that
he could not nominate Kennedy unless Johnson and Symington concurred,
because he had assured all three avowed candidates that he was not a candidate and would not help any candidate in the race."

Stevenson saw Walter Reuther—labor had endorsed Kennedy. Senator
Monroney, John Sharon, and Tom Finney told him what they were doing

in his behalf and urged him to actively seek the nomination—he must act, and act quickly, they said, for the serious business of the convention, state caucuses and private meetings of leaders, was going on this same Sunday in hotel rooms all over town. Newt Minow was present. "Senator Monroney and Sharon and Finney were giving him statistics on how he would be nominated. I said, 'Governor, can I see you for a few minutes?' There were people in the bedroom. We went into the bathroom. I took out my sheets and said, 'You can listen to what you hear from those people or to me—and Illinois is caucusing in fifteen minutes and it's almost one hundred per cent for Kennedy.' Stevenson said, 'Really?' I said, 'Really.' Stevenson said, 'What do you suggest?' I said, 'I suggest you not go out of here a defeated guy trying to get nominated a third time. I suggest you come out for Kennedy, be identified with his nomination, and unite the party.' Stevenson said, 'I know you're right but what can I do with people like Mrs. Roosevelt—kick 'em in the ass?' I said, 'You're getting kicked in the ass this way. You don't believe me. Why not get some of the pros whose judgment you respect? Get Arvey and Lawrence—they'll tell you.'"

Stevenson visited his headquarters and seemed "overwhelmed" at its activities, according to Robert Hirschfield, a student of the movement. That evening Stevenson appeared on the television interview program "Face the Nation." He did not deny that his supporters were counting delegates. He was "very flattered" by talk about his becoming Secretary of State and said he would accept if his views coincided with the President's. He did not rule out running for Vice President with Kennedy though hoped he could serve his party in some other capacity.

That same afternoon Illinois caucused, and when the caucus ended Daley announced that Illinois would cast 59½ of its 69 votes for Kennedy, 2 for Stevenson, 1 uncommitted, and the rest for Symington. It was a powerful boost for Kennedy. Mrs. Roosevelt had telephoned Daley and asked him to support Stevenson, but he had told her his delegates were already committed to Kennedy. (During the spring, according to Newt Minow, Daley had said to Stevenson, "Tell me if you're a candidate—I've had trouble with the delegates before but I'll try if you are a candidate." Stevenson had said he was not.) At a fund-raising dinner that night Blair and Minow sought out Arvey and Lawrence. Pennsylvania would caucus tomorrow morning. Arvey and Lawrence agreed with Minow's assessment —Stevenson should come out for Kennedy. Arvey thought that even a convention deadlock might not nominate Stevenson—might, instead, nominate Symington. Lawrence thought the Illinois caucus had sunk Stevenson. At 2 A.M., Lawrence went to see Stevenson and urged him to withdraw and make the nominating speech for Kennedy. "But the Governor was just not going to do it," Minow recalled. "After he said no to nominating Kennedy, Blair and I tried to help him get the nomination himself. We knew that we owed him everything."

On Monday, Pennsylvania caucused and gave Kennedy 64 votes,

Stevenson 8, the rest scattered, and Lawrence announced for Kennedy. This almost surely clinched the nomination for Kennedy, giving him more than 700 votes on the first ballot. California was virtually Stevenson's only hope. California would caucus on Tuesday. Stevenson began visiting delegations that were still open. Now he was trying for the nomination in earnest. Minow recalled, "I went with him to the New York delegation. To me it was just heartbreaking. Just what we didn't want. We did it anyway." Schlesinger, with Bill Rivkin, watched Stevenson speak to the Minnesota caucus. Before he arrived, Monroney had made a powerful plea for Stevenson, including attacks on the Kennedy movement. Stevenson spoke, and Schlesinger found himself in tears. He later wrote, "Stevenson's talk was polished, graceful, courtly, charming, rather noncommittal; in its substantive passages, it rehearsed the litany of Dulles-Eisenhower foreign policy errors, beginning with the pledge of 1953 to unleash Chiang Kai-shek. Something was holding him back, that old pride which prevented him from giving the audience what it was waiting for. I think the delegates were a bit let down; there was less applause at the end than at the start." Over the weekend, New Jersey had clung firm to Meyner but the favorite sons of Kansas and Iowa had released their delegations to Kennedy.

At the convention's opening session on Monday night a chain of Stevenson supporters ringed the hall, yelling and chanting, setting up a subdued roar, marching, carrying banners: "Adlai Is a Moral Man"; "Adlai Is a Lousy Golfer"; "A Thinking Man's Choice—Stevenson"; "Win With Adlai"; "Stick with Stevenson"; "We Want Stevenson." It was an impressive demonstration—Theodore White wrote, "It was more than a demonstration, it was an explosion"—and on Tuesday more demonstrations occurred in Pershing Square outside his headquarters and his suite in the Sheraton West. Rumors spread that the Kansas and Iowa delegations were in revolt, threatening to reject Kennedy and revert to their favorite sons. Stevenson's supporters persuaded him to hold a press conference in the Biltmore Bowl, and Mrs. Roosevelt agreed to introduce him, and it was the biggest press conference of the convention, for reporters had heard that he would announce his active candidacy. Instead he arrived late, said a few nice words about Mrs. Roosevelt, and departed, a great letdown to his supporters.

Nevertheless, the enthusiasm of the continuing Stevenson demonstrations infected even him. His suite was boiling, people coming and going. He asked Marietta Tree if he ought to take his seat on the convention floor. She had thought his chances of being nominated slight but now she too was being swayed by the crowd. He went to the convention hall to take his place as a member of the Illinois delegation. This was, ostensibly, to show that he was not a candidate—candidates traditionally do not appear on the floor before the nominations are over. It erupted into a wild cheering, marching demonstration. The galleries were packed with Stevenson people. The galleries "went mad," Schlesinger reported, and pandemonium broke out on the floor as well. Stevenson was finally taken to the rostrum. He might have commanded the hall. Instead, he told a bad joke—"after going back and forth through the Biltmore today, I know who's going to be the nominee of this convention—the last man to survive." The audience went flat. Then he spoke a few words, more a personal message of gratitude than a call to arms, and subsided.

Agnes Meyer saw it. "Mrs. Roosevelt and I sat there—we and Finletter had worked hard for the demonstration—we had the applause there—but then he went up on the platform and throws it out the window. He could have swept that Convention. I could have murdered him. I could see Bobby Kennedy running around on the floor trying to hold his delegates. He should have told us he wouldn't fight." Benton's opinion was that "he wanted it, but he didn't have the stomach to fight for it." Humphrey told Benton on the floor that Stevenson would have been nominated if he had made a move only a week before. Most of the leaders of the Stevenson draft movement thought that if he had made any speech of substance he could have been nominated. But the truth was that the delegates were giving him what delegates always give a man when they cannot give him votes —an ovation. Barkley had received the greatest ovation of the 1952 convention—but not votes. At that time Barkley had been the old man whom time—and the convention—had passed by. Now it was Stevenson's turn.

It was not yet clearly so, however. That evening the California delegation caucused, and it split: 30½ for Kennedy but 31½ for Stevenson, the rest scattered. The Stevenson votes were produced by Eleanor Roosevelt and Jim Doyle. Stevenson people thought they could count on 12 additional California votes after the first ballot. Now they had a nucleus. They knew, too, that Iowa, North Dakota, and Alaska were unit-rule states which Kennedy held by only a half vote. Kansas, also a unit-rule state, and Iowa were already reported in doubt. The switch of a vote or two in those delegations could switch entire states and start a snowball rolling, adding mass to the California nucleus of 31½ votes. Several New York delegates were reported caucusing at the Ambassador Hotel to reassess Stevenson's chances. Stevenson's managers invited friendly delegates to a room in the Sheraton West that night, and more than 150 delegates and alternates showed up (and paid for their own drinks). Senator Monroney spoke to them, and so did Bill Benton. But they wanted Stevenson. Past midnight his managers persuaded him to come down to the party from his suite, and he did and spoke briefly. Once more he explained his inaction. He was grateful for their loyalty; it obliged him to rethink his position. He closed, quoting a poem by Robert Frost (which was also a Kennedy favorite):

> "The woods are lovely, dark and deep,
> But I have promises to keep,
> And miles to go before I sleep,
> And miles to go before I sleep."

Then he left them. They thought he might yet lead.

Next morning Hubert Humphrey declared for Stevenson. Robert Kennedy, convening a meeting of his aides, told them he wanted their delegate counts and wanted facts, not guesses or generalities. They counted 740 votes, 21 short of a majority but enough to trigger switches that would nominate Kennedy. Robert Kennedy warned that they must make no mistakes today. This was Wednesday, the day the nominations would be made and the voting would begin. Robert Kennedy believed that his brother had to win tonight or not at all. Stevenson support was mounting. The convention hall was again ringed by men and women chanting for Stevenson. An afternoon newspaper headline said, KENNEDY BANDWAGON FALTERS and another: KENNEDY TIDE EBBS.

That morning Stevenson tried to telephone Dick Daley to see if he had support in the Illinois delegation. Daley would not take the call. Stevenson kept trying and finally reached Jack Arvey, who in turn found Daley on the convention floor and urged him to return the call as a matter of courtesy. Reluctantly, Daley did. Stevenson said he knew the Illinois caucus had given Kennedy 59½ votes and Stevenson only 2. He wanted Daley to know it was true that he had not sought the nomination, that he would if nominated campaign vigorously against Nixon, that he was the first Illinoisan to be considered for the presidency since Lincoln. He hoped the delegates' vote might merely indicate they thought he was not a candidate. Daley told him that he had no support. Stevenson asked if this meant no support in fact or no support because the delegates thought he was not a candidate. Daley replied that Stevenson simply had no support. He reminded Stevenson that earlier Stevenson had told him he was not a candidate. He added that Stevenson had had no support in the 1956 delegation either, but Daley had held it together for him.

This was the real end of the Stevenson candidacy, although demonstrations continued, for if he could not get the support of his home state his candidacy was doomed. Arvey remembered it as one of the most painful experiences of his life.

Stevenson's name would be placed in nomination that day along with the names of Kennedy, Johnson, Symington, and the favorite sons. Stevenson later told a friend, Beth Currie, that a number of delegates had urged him to allow his name to be put in nomination in order to prevent a first-ballot nomination of Kennedy. He had permitted it, he said, because only by being put in nomination could he become available as a compromise candidate. The Kennedys, he said, had sought to persuade him to nominate Kennedy and not to allow his own name to go before the convention. He had refused. Adlai III said Stevenson refused to nominate Kennedy because he felt as titular leader he should remain neutral, perhaps he doubted Kennedy was the best man, and perhaps "subconsciously he hoped for the nomination himself." Robert Kennedy, when asked later about Stevenson's relationship with President Kennedy, said, "The Democratic Convention was a tremendous shock to the President—that Stevenson behaved the way he did. There were a number of conversations between President Kennedy and Stevenson before the convention and there were several meetings in Los Angeles. He thought that Stevenson was not being realistic or exercising good judgment. He wanted the nomination but he wasn't willing to fight for it. He wanted to keep his options open for Secretary." Ted Sorensen agreed that the gulf between Stevenson and Kennedy widened at the convention because, when Kennedy sent word asking Stevenson to nominate him, a reply came back that Stevenson thought it a good idea but he just did not see how he could do it, he was "a helpless pawn with all these forces," as Sorensen put it. "Kennedy's reply was profane. He said if he didn't know how to do this, he's got no business being here."

Stevenson's name was placed in nomination by Senator Eugene McCarthy of Minnesota. It was a moving speech: "Do not reject this man. Do not reject this man who has made us all proud to be Democrats. Do not leave this prophet without honor in his own party." Perhaps it was not all pure loyalty. Some Democrats think McCarthy had come to Los Angeles supporting Johnson and now was doing Johnson's work of building up Stevenson support in order to stop Kennedy. (If a deadlocked convention nominated Johnson, he could use a Northern liberal Catholic such as McCarthy for his Vice President.)

The Stevenson managers had arranged to pack the galleries. Given only about 150 tickets officially, they had asked all members of the $1000 Club, who received two tickets each, for their unused tickets, and had collected about 1,000 tickets. They had picked up most of California's host party's share, 1,000 tickets. Learning that the Kennedys expected to receive 2,500 tickets from the regular machinery, they sent their followers to stand in line wearing Kennedy buttons; thus they had stolen some 1,500 tickets from the Kennedy bank. In addition, they infiltrated the security apparatus of the convention, and at the crucial moment a guard at a utility entrance to the hall was called away and replaced by a student for Stevenson wearing a guard's uniform, and he allowed hordes of Stevenson volunteers into the hall, wearing Kennedy buttons as a cover but carrying Stevenson banners under their coats. So it was that when McCarthy finished his speech nominating Stevenson the galleries and the convention floor itself exploded. Paper banners unfurled in the galleries, a huge papier-mâché ball bounced up and down over the demonstrators, the demonstrators tore state standards from delegations and paraded through the hall led by California, chanting "WE WANT STEVENSON" in thunderous waves. The convention chairman, LeRoy Collins of Florida, called for order, so did McCarthy, so did Mrs. Roosevelt, but the demonstrators kept marching and chanting. The band struck up through amplifiers; it did no good. Collins ordered the lights turned off; this made no difference either. Not since Wendell Willkie was nominated at Philadelphia in 1940 had spectators so threatened to stampede a convention's delegates—or so it appeared, though the truth was otherwise: Kennedy had the votes, Stevenson had only the ovation. The demonstration lasted nearly a half hour and made no difference. Kennedy was nominated on the first ballot. The vote before switches was Kennedy 806, Johnson 409, Symington 86, Stevenson 79½, Meyner 43, Humphrey 41½, Smathers (Florida) 30, Barnett (Mississippi) 23. The draft-Stevenson movement, unlike the Volunteers of 1952, disbanded on the day after the nomination as quietly as it had begun.

Stevenson had watched the balloting on television with his family and a few friends. Laura Magnuson, who was one of them, recalled that, when the balloting ended, Stevenson stood up and said, "I'll go and write a little purple prose now."

During the complicated maneuvering over the selection of a vice presidential candidate, Kennedy consulted Stevenson, among many others, regarding the choice of Lyndon Johnson. Stevenson said later that he thought it a mistake to "bury" Johnson in the vice presidency—Kennedy wanted Johnson "out of his hair," he said. On Friday, the last day of the convention, Stevenson introduced Kennedy for his acceptance speech, on the "New Frontier." Despite their differences, Adlai Stevenson, by his campaigns and other endeavors of the past eight years, had made that moment possible. Hubert Humphrey once said, "Adlai gave us all a little class. He set the tone."

31.

Stevenson was exhausted after the convention. People around the world were wondering whether he would be Secretary of State. So was he.

He spent Sunday night at Santa Barbara, then drove north toward San Francisco accompanied by John Fell, Borden, Adlai III and Nancy, and Alicia Patterson. He encountered Scotty Reston, and they talked about Stevenson's chances of becoming Secretary of State. Stevenson wanted it badly, Reston thought. On Saturday, July 23, Stevenson flew back to Chicago and was in his office on Monday, the day the Republican Convention opened in Chicago.

Bill Blair said that, for the first time in a long time, "I feel in my bones that we can win." He had not enjoyed the convention but thought the ticket a strong one. He had lunch with Stevenson, Wirtz, and Minow; in a few days he was going to visit the Kennedys, and he urged Stevenson himself to visit the Kennedys soon. Stevenson did, at the end of the week. Benton invited Stevenson to cruise the Baltic aboard the *Flying Clipper* but Stevenson wired, "Baltic [beckons] but so does Kennedy. Deep regrets." Robert Hutchins passed on a report that Stevenson might be too

Europe-oriented to be Secretary of State, that Kennedy would prefer Chet Bowles because of his experience in Asia and Africa, and that Stevenson probably would be offered the job of Ambassador to the United Nations. Stevenson replied, "I suspected something like this might be cooking, although I have spent far more time in Africa, South America, the Middle East and the Soviet Union than the gentleman named," that is, Bowles.

On July 26, George Ball sent Stevenson a long letter containing similar news and warning that if Kennedy won and offered Stevenson the UN Embassy and Stevenson rejected it embarrassment would result on all sides. "You and I know that the function of the United States Ambassador at the United Nations is largely ritualistic and ministerial but the public does not know this. Your refusal to undertake the responsibility could easily be interpreted by a none-too-friendly press as sour grapes on your part. I think, therefore, that you might be well advised to clarify your position with Jack [now]."

Any firm commitments at this time would be "inappropriate" and perhaps even illegal, Ball said. But Stevenson should let Kennedy know now that he was interested "solely" in "the post of major responsibility," that is, Secretary of State. Ball thought that the Republican ticket would be Nixon and Lodge, both with foreign policy experience, both able to claim that "they can argue with" Khrushchev. In this area the Democratic ticket was weak. As a result, Kennedy would "need desperately to associate you as closely as possible" with his campaign. "This means that your bargaining position will probably never be higher than it is at the moment." Therefore Ball suggested that Stevenson indicate to Kennedy not only his willingness to campaign in certain areas "but also the desirability of your setting up an ad hoc group to formulate a specific foreign affairs program for execution during the first months of next year." This proposal was adopted and became the well-known Stevenson task force report to Kennedy on foreign policy. In this letter Ball said that, with matters deteriorating under Eisenhower, the new Administration must move fast and decisively once it took office. It must give evidence of its ability to "regain the diplomatic initiative" and transform America's reputation around the world. Ball likened the first days of the new Kennedy administration, which would take office during foreign policy crisis, to the first hundred days of the Roosevelt administration in 1933, which began amid domestic crisis. Kennedy must take office with a well-prepared program to deal with the foreign policy crisis. Stevenson should offer to prepare a program. It should have two objectives—specific actions to be undertaken in the first six months to restore American leadership, and fresh formulation of long-term objectives of policy. Ball concluded, "Whatever you have to say to Jack, I am sure that this is the time to say it." It was good advice, given at the right time.

Stevenson told Gerald Johnson, the author, he was somewhat troubled by the impression some people had that he had been "hoping for the nomination" but went on to say: "My problem now is my future with the Kennedy administration—if any." He told an Alabama publisher, "I do not know what the future has in store for me, but I will help with the campaign, of course, and serve Kennedy's administration if at all possible. Having served in the United Nations for three years long long ago, I am afraid that is of no interest to me whatsoever." The publisher had only remarked casually upon the UN job; Stevenson had quickly picked it up, missing no opportunity to try to foreclose it. He told Lady Mary Spears, "Kennedy is an able man and there should be no possible question in your mind about his superiority to Nixon—one of the few people in my life I really deeply distrust and dislike. Kennedy has asked me to come to see him this week and I have no doubt he will want me to campaign most extensively this fall." Wirtz discouraged a woman idolater's efforts to organize a chain-letter writing campaign to pressure Kennedy into appointing Stevenson Secretary of State.

On Wednesday afternoon, July 27, Stevenson went to New York. He dined there with Marietta Tree and spent the next day in his office, seeing Attwood alone and, jointly, Mrs. Roosevelt, Agnes Meyer, Senator Lehman, and others, all to talk about his role in the campaign. He was driven to Mount Kisco to spend the night with Mrs. Meyer. On Friday he went on to Hyannis. From Mrs. Meyer's he sent Barbara Ward a letter saying he was on his way to see Kennedy. He wrote, "Kennedy is going to send me out to campaign very actively. . . . I am planning to agree to eight major speeches, two in California, two in New York, Philadelphia, St. Louis, Denver and somewhere else. Doubtless more will be added later. I will concentrate on foreign policy, of course. He will badly need the 'Stevenson people' who number several million and who are a little disaffected at present for a variety of reasons. He will, of course, try to delay any indication about the Secretary of State and may not want me at all, also for a variety of reasons. But in any event I must and want to help as best I can even without assurances on that score." He urged her to send speech drafts—he would have no staff except Wirtz and Attwood.

At Hyannis, Stevenson was met by Evangeline and David Bruce—Bruce would be appointed Kennedy's Ambassador to the United Kingdom—and Eunice Kennedy Shriver and (as he noted) "200–300 Adlai addicts." They drove to the Bruces' home at Oyster Harbor for swimming, a dinner party, and the night. Bill Blair was staying with the Kennedys. On Saturday, Arthur Schlesinger and his wife took Stevenson to Chatham. En route, they had a confidential talk. "He said that he had no expectation that he would be appointed Secretary of State," Schlesinger noted, "that he wasn't even sure that he wanted it or could serve with Kennedy. He felt Kennedy to be cold and ruthless though he readily differentiated Jack from his brother in this respect and in certain contexts (especially foreign policy) expressed a high opinion of Jack. His mood was one of essential relaxation and composure, tinctured by fairly mild streak of suspicion and resentment. As for himself, he did not wish to campaign as much [he said] as the Kennedy people had asked him to do; and he was especially anxious not to be cast as an anti-Nixon hatchet man. He wants to give four or five high-level speeches, primarily on foreign policy. (This is a somewhat artificial problem. I can guarantee that, when the moment comes, no one will take a more harshly anti-Nixon line than AES.)" In a letter to Marietta Tree, Stevenson described Schlesinger—who, as we have seen, had earlier followed Stevenson's own advice and come out for the candidate of his choice, Kennedy—as "sheepish" and said, "I could detect no contrition in [Schlesinger] who now seems tentatively persuaded that it is 'a strong ticket,' that Kennedy will be 'good on the issues,' tho he has been 'a little disappointing' on handling people. I would say that his anguish is about over and that he is *'growing'* rapidly. The words liberal or liberalism were never mentioned—obviously a sign of maturity!"

Stevenson spent the night at Chatham at the home of Lorna Underwood Sagendorph, whom he had known in college. On Sunday morning she drove him "to Jack's at Hyannisport," as Stevenson put it to Marietta Tree, "and there followed five hours in the bosom—or the sharks teeth— of the Kennedy family ashore and afloat. Even the Black Prince [apparently Robert F. Kennedy] and wife were there. Jack talked of the campaign, the Jews, the Negroes, the farmers, the N.Y. situation. He wants me to campaign extensively but details were deferred until his and Johnsons schedules are worked out. I promised him a memo on how to meet the Rep. attack on his youth and inexperience. And he also eagerly accepted my suggestion that he put someone to work on a post election and inauguration program of legislation & pronouncements to immediately take firm and resolute hold of foreign policy. And guess who got the job? There was no hint of post election plans re Sec. State etc. and I said nothing. So that remains where it was." He wrote with some relish about difficulties he anticipated Kennedy would have with Stevenson's ardent supporters in New York. "There is so much to report; but one final morsel —Jackie—soto voce 'I can't bear all those people peering over the fence. Eunice loves the whole horrible business. I may abdicate.' Adlai—likewise soto voce, 'Steady kid; you ain't seen nothin' yet.' But what a fortunate fellow he is to have that large team of competent dedicated family around him—all knowing what to do! Shriver looked to me like the ablest and carrying the heaviest load. He's got a good business committee—cf. the advantage of running when there's a chance of winning! But they claim there is money trouble and asked *us* for a list of 100 who might give $5000 each!!! The primary expenditure really WAS shocking."

He had lunch on Kennedy's boat with Kennedy, Jacqueline Kennedy, Sargent and Eunice Shriver, Mrs. Ted Kennedy, Prince and Princess Radziwill, and Bill Blair. They decided that Stevenson would campaign mainly in California and New York, by now his areas of strength. (Interestingly, Illinois was not such an area.) Kennedy promptly accepted Stevenson's suggestion of a foreign policy task force. He did not discuss policy with Stevenson. He later told Schlesinger the Stevenson visit was satisfactory. Somewhat to his surprise, he found Stevenson's political advice shrewd and realistic. Kennedy told Schlesinger he would not ask Stevenson to help him now if he did not think of him "as playing a role" in his administration. He said rather sadly that he wished he had more rapport with Stevenson. He had rapport with Blair, he said, and Stevenson had it with Jacqueline. "If you were me, would you appoint Stevenson Secretary of State?" Schlesinger said he would and gave reasons. Kennedy listened with interest but without disclosing his feelings. At the end of the meeting between Kennedy and Stevenson they held a press conference, and Kennedy issued a statement which Stevenson had drafted: "Governor Stevenson will be advising me on foreign policy and on campaign strategy generally. I want to take advantage of his presidential and foreign experience. I expect to see him periodically and will talk with him by telephone from time to time. Because of his recent experience in Latin America and extensive travels in Africa I have sought his views on the current crises in those areas. I have also asked him for a review of the principal problems that will confront a new President."

During the press conference Stevenson talked more than Kennedy. He urged his supporters to support Kennedy, said he would campaign hard for him in New York and "elsewhere," and said—and Kennedy agreed— that the pre-eminent issue would be foreign policy and how to marshal Western resources against Communist countries without war or surrender, not how to talk back to Khrushchev (as Nixon was bragging he had done). Stevenson seemed disconcerted when reporters asked about his supporters' pressuring Kennedy to make Stevenson Secretary of State—at first he said he did not understand the question, then said he and Kennedy had not discussed cabinet appointments and would not until "later."

After this visit Stevenson spent ten days in the East, mostly in New England, visiting friends, sailing, playing tennis, attending luncheons and dinners and house parties—Agnes Meyer ("or was it with her chef and vintage wines?"); Lloyd Garrison ("a really noble man and perhaps the noblest I know," he told Marietta); Mary Lasker ("There are so many people working around here—mostly picking up withered petals—that solitude is to be found in the WC only!"); the Finletters; Walter Lippmann; Ruth Field. During a house party at Ruth Field's he wrote Marietta Tree, "Impatient to get home and end this road show. . . . Have slept in 16 different beds since LA. . . . Alcoholic dinner concluded by Winthrop Aldrich to a 'great American whom I would have voted for this time regardless of party'—followed by 'and I don't care who knows that I think our present choices are tragic.' Much too much talk about Jacks girls— Clayton [Fritchey] told episode of watch & girl. Why she didn't slap his face no one explained to me."

He returned to Chicago August 9 and, except for a trip to Youngstown,

Ohio, to attend the wedding of Edison and Jane Dick's son and a short business trip to New York, spent the rest of the month in Chicago and Libertyville, working on correspondence and speeches and writing an article for *Look* on Latin America. Once he went to a night club to see a comedian, Mort Sahl, whose low-keyed political satire was popular at the time, and he had Sahl to dinner one night.

Agnes Meyer told Stevenson, "I am working now for Kennedy, without conditions. I promised before the convention I would. But I have many strings to pull to make you Secty of State. I wrote to Phil [Graham] about it immediately after our conversation. If he made Lyndon V.P.—as he did —he can help to make you Secty of State."[13] She referred to Robert Kennedy as "that incipient dictator" and to Nixon as "that other dictator." She refused to continue paying Bill Attwood, who wanted to divide his speechwriting time between Kennedy and Stevenson. Attwood would discuss working for Kennedy with Archibald Cox, who was heading a Kennedy writers' group in Washington. (The group produced great quantities of papers but, as usually happens to speeches written at headquarters while the candidate is traveling, little of them found their way into Kennedy's speeches, which for the most part were written aboard his plane by Sorensen and Richard Goodwin.) A little later Mrs. Meyer wrote Stevenson, "I have just finished my first job for Kennedy. . . . What I cannot face is that wisdom, maturity, experience have been set aside for pure efficiency. . . . Today unless you are as scurrilous as Nixon, you can succeed only by being as shrewd and organization conscious as Kennedy. . . . You are the last of the great artist-statesmen, such as Churchill, Roosevelt, Wilson. The era of engineer-statesman has begun."

Porter McKeever, a leader of the Stevenson Volunteers in 1952, told Blair he feared that a campaign to make Chet Bowles, not Stevenson, Secretary of State might succeed—Stevenson was being termed indecisive and therefore unable to direct the necessary reorganization of the State Department, but, on the other hand, eloquent and therefore invaluable at the United Nations. Blair replied, "I couldn't agree with you more and I only wish I knew what to do." Blair had thought it inappropriate to broach the subject with Kennedy at Hyannis but made it clear to others close to him that Stevenson "would not be interested in" the UN job.

The first meeting of the foreign policy task force had taken place at Mary Lasker's. That was, according to one of its members, the only task force meeting that Stevenson attended. Stevenson had asked Ball to help prepare the report, and Ball had asked Harlan Cleveland (later Assistant Secretary of State for International Organizations) and others to help. Theodore White later thought the foreign policy task force report Steven-

[13] Phil Graham's account of his role at the 1960 Los Angeles convention can be found in the appendix to *The Making of the President 1964* by Theodore H. White.

son's most important contribution to the Kennedy campaign. The report—
a collection of papers, really—was given to Kennedy after the election.
According to Ted Sorensen, Kennedy liked the papers and asked that task
forces be set up to pursue various questions further. Actually, Stevenson
had little to do with the report, though it bore his name. Ball and others
did the work. Ball once said, "I couldn't even get Stevenson to read it, let
alone write it."

On August 5, a few days after the meeting at Mrs. Lasker's, Ball sent
Stevenson a preliminary outline, said he had talked with David Lloyd and
would soon see David Bruce, proposed that during the next two weeks the
task force concentrate on culling previously published documents, and said
he himself was studying thirteen reports made to the Senate Foreign Relations Committee, reports of the Rockefeller Foundation, a Brookings Institute study of "Presidential Transitions," the speeches and papers of
Kennedy and Bowles, the Rand Corporation's study of Berlin, and fifteen
or twenty books on foreign and economic policy. Stevenson replied, "[I]
marvel at the rapidity with which you have seized hold of this assignment." He described the task force to Barbara Ward as an extremely small
and secret working party and said, "We are largely preoccupied now with
Castro and the Congo. At last the administration is waking up to the necessity of doing something about Latin America. It is also a late and lamentable response to Khrushchev's penetration in Cuba. But the Congo is
something else, and here the feeling seems to be that the UN is our only
hope for the survival of order and reason. . . . From what little I have
heard, even Lumumba seems to be an unknown to our State Department. . . . If there are things we should be saying and doing about Africa
now, and especially in this campaign, I would welcome them particularly."

On August 24, Stevenson sent Ball a memorandum on atomic energy
and a letter from Peter Grothe, a foreign relations consultant to Hubert
Humphrey, proposing "a Peace Corps of 5,000 dedicated young men . . .
to work in development projects in Asia, Africa, and Latin America."
Stevenson suggested to Ball, "Perhaps this should go in your lesser ideas
file."

A little later Kennedy appointed Paul Nitze, David Bruce, and others to
study national security, and Stevenson, visiting Washington, asked him if
this would not overlap and confuse the work of the foreign policy task
force. Kennedy said it would not—Nitze and the others would be studying
only national security, not foreign policy, which remained the province of
the Stevenson group. Stevenson passed this word along to David Bruce,
who discussed the question with Nitze and Bowles. They saw no need for
confusion. Bruce, however, remained unconvinced. Stevenson met with
Ball and wrote to him several times during the fall campaign, usually asking to be "brought up to date" on the papers Ball was preparing.

On August 11, Stevenson told Barbara Ward he was in a "state of black
depression. . . . I can't seem to get on top of my mail, my visitors, my

phone calls and, of course, the article on South America. . . . Meanwhile, my time is almost gone and I am desperate—also as always." Agnes Meyer told Stevenson that Mrs. Roosevelt would see Kennedy next weekend and would tell him "firmly" that he must "play up to you" if he wanted the Stevenson vote, that Chet Bowles would not do as Secretary of State but would do well at the UN, and that Stevenson would not take the UN job if Bowles was made Secretary. About August 12, Kennedy phoned Stevenson to say that Chet Bowles, against Kennedy's advice, was withdrawing from the congressional race in Connecticut after polls showed him running far behind, that this would create speculation about Bowles's appointment as Secretary of State, and that such speculation was groundless. "[Kennedy] has asked me to prepare a statement of some kind about my collaboration with Kennedy on foreign policy," Stevenson wrote Bill Benton. "I am sure I have no idea what he has in mind eventually and I am not sure he does either!" That weekend Stevenson wrote to Marietta Tree: "No news re me and Sec State—except that Kennedy called to warn about Bowles getting out of Connecticut race. . . . Mail like 1952 all over again. Keeps my eyes misty, heart full and mind alive with wonder that there can be so much perception, feeling and devotion, for an unknown man. . . . Speaking schedule prepared by K. people heavy— probably end up doing 12–13 'majors'—and no staff, ideas, inspiration. Think I'll ask Mort Sahl if he'd like to try ghosting! *Discretion* indicated about Jack's personal life."

At her meeting with Kennedy on August 14, Mrs. Roosevelt did not ask him for a firm commitment to appoint Stevenson Secretary of State but she did tell him he needed Stevenson votes to carry California and New York, two states he needed because he could not hold the solid South. Kennedy remarked that he had not fully realized until recently how deep the North-South split in the party was. He said the newly elected Governor of Florida had come to see him and said, "I want you to know that I am a conservative, I am against integration, and I am for the right-to-work law." Kennedy replied, "Why don't you join the Republicans?" He now told Mrs. Roosevelt about the foreign policy task force. She replied that this "was not enough"—that he would have to give Stevenson's supporters "the assurance that they were working together," for as everybody knew Stevenson would not accept the office of Secretary of State unless his and Kennedy's views were similar. She told Kennedy that he must quote Stevenson during the campaign, appear on the same platform with him, and emphasize that he was counting on him for advice. She hoped he would do the same thing with respect to Bowles. Kennedy "agreed and said he would try to do this," as Mrs. Roosevelt recalled it. Mrs. Roosevelt thought Kennedy liked Bowles and found him easy to work with but thought he sometimes acted impulsively, which made Stevenson all the more valuable. She wrote in a memorandum of conversation, "Now, I have no promises from him, but I have the distinct feeling that he is planning to work closely with Adlai. I also had the feeling that here was a man who could learn. I liked him better than I ever had before. . . . I think I am not mistaken in feeling that he would make a good President if elected." On Monday, Mrs. Roosevelt telephoned Stevenson and reported on this conversation, and in his own memorandum of that conversation Stevenson wrote, "She seemed to feel that he realized that he could not win without me."

Norman Cousins, publisher of the *Saturday Review,* told Stevenson on August 17, "They've asked me to join the writing team for Kennedy. This is something a fellow ought to do only if he has his heart in it. I don't—at least not now. Oh, I'll vote for him all right; but it would help if I could think of a good reason for becoming enthusiastic. What I mean is, does Kennedy really have stature?" At this stage of the campaign many liberal Democrats, including friends and followers of Stevenson, felt that way about Kennedy. He differed so markedly from Stevenson, not merely in his youth and personality, but in his approach to issues, a hard pragmatic decisive approach that contrasted sharply with Stevenson's thoughtful discursive careful explorations and ruminations. Indeed, so many Democrats felt as Cousins did that Arthur Schlesinger, Jr., wrote a campaign book entitled: *Kennedy and Nixon: Does It Make Any Difference?* Jack Fischer of *Harper's* told Stevenson he should soon make a speech about the citizen's duty to participate in politics in order to overcome the refusal of his own idolaters to work for Kennedy. "They regard themselves as Old Guard Stevensonians, they feel hurt and bitter that you didn't get the nomination, and they express their resentment by maintaining that if they can't work for you they won't work for anybody. This . . . is . . . a touching tribute to you—but it doesn't seem to me to make much sense politically. . . . A lot of these people are acting like spoiled children." Stevenson replied that he agreed "emphatically."

Stevenson told his old friend Harry Hochschild, "I yearn to talk with you about the Congo and Katanga. If the Belgian technicians are driven out of the copper belt, is it possible they could be replaced from Northern Rhodesia to keep the mines operating and the natives employed? Have you ideas about what we should be doing there at this time? It seems to me that the UN has done extremely well in the circumstances and that there is little the United States can or should do outside the UN. Am I wrong?" It was a question that would confront Stevenson with immediacy in the next year. His business trip to New York at this time was mainly to see Dag Hammarskjold and Andrew Cordier at the UN about the Congo on behalf of his client, Maurice Tempelsman.

His speaking load during the campaign would be heavier than he had anticipated. On August 24 he wrote to Barbara Ward. "Staffing," he wrote, "is more difficult than ever in view of the paucity of people who have not already been recruited by Kennedy's enormous operation. . . . All this is preliminary inquiry as to whether you could stop off here for a while en route to Australia. . . . And if you could hole up in New York or Libertyville for a while to do some writing."

Agnes Meyer told Kennedy that "the Catholic issue should be combatted at once." She asked Stevenson what he thought of her proposal to have a prominent Protestant bishop make a television broadcast on the subject. Stevenson noted on the letter, "just aggravates—may hang selves." Presumably Stevenson would have advised Kennedy to ignore the religious issue. What Kennedy actually did was to meet it head on—"I am not the Catholic candidate for President. I am the Democratic Party's candidate for President who happens also to be a Catholic. I do not speak for my Church on public matters—and the Church does not speak for me."[14]

On August 29, Stevenson sent Kennedy a paper which he said he had written, pursuant to their conversation, on the "age and experience" issue. It said that Kennedy should not voluntarily take up the issue himself. Anything he said would be defensive and self-defeating. As for age, Kennedy should not try to appear older than he was, or argue that William Pitt and Napoleon were younger. Others could make these arguments. If the issue was raised Kennedy could say that the difference between forty-three and forty-seven (Nixon's age) was inconsequential and that not years but ability, convictions, and character were what the presidency required. The "experience" issue was more serious. It could, however, be argued that since 1928 the Republicans consistently had nominated presidential candidates with less experience in government than the Democrats, that Nixon had had no executive experience, that nobody could be trained for the presidency in any event. Kennedy's behavior should demonstrate capacity for firm, thoughtful, courageous decision making. He should avoid any suggestion of petulance, argumentativeness, defensiveness, or over-confidence. In the proposed television debates he should give easy answers tersely and directly but "the harder answers [should] reflect full realization of the difficulties involved." Since the Republicans would make much of Nixon's "kitchen debate" with Khrushchev, Kennedy should make clear that dealing with Communists required more than shaking a finger in a dictator's face.

Kennedy was receiving letters from Stevenson partisans urging him to appoint Stevenson Secretary of State. To one such man, Kennedy recited his past associations with and campaigning for Stevenson in 1952 and 1956, assured him that he and Stevenson would "work closely together in this campaign" and had already had a long meeting on foreign affairs at Hyannisport, said that Stevenson had agreed to speak on Kennedy's behalf and to work actively in developing foreign policy issues and program. He added that "I cannot at this time" select a member of the Cabinet—doing so would create pressures to select more, and "the folly of making

---

[14] Kennedy said it on September 12, 1960, in a speech to the Greater Houston Ministerial Association at the Rice Hotel in Houston, Texas. It was one of the most dramatic and important moments of his campaign.

cabinets in advance was never clearer" than in 1948 when Dewey did it. "I do expect, however, that Mr. Stevenson will have a significant role in our future affairs."

At a press conference announcing formation of the four-man group headed by Paul Nitze to consult with him on national security, Kennedy emphasized that President Roosevelt and President Truman had brought to public service "many distinguished Republicans" and, in appointing the Nitze commission, Kennedy was continuing the bipartisan tradition. Ball called Stevenson and said that, in response to a question as to whether Stevenson and Bowles would work with the Nitze group, Kennedy had said, "As I stated in Hyannis Port, there would be talk with Governor Stevenson during the period on the problems of foreign policy, and I will do so. Of course, Congressman Bowles has been very helpful. However, as I said, this group will carry on a non-partisan consultation. Mr. Nitze's effort will not be connected with the campaign in any way." He left the impression that Stevenson's role would be to advise on foreign policy during the campaign itself rather than on future foreign policy. Ball thought all this embarrassed members of the Stevenson task force and proposed that Kennedy clarify matters at another press conference. Stevenson wrote out in longhand a draft of a statement which he proposed Kennedy deliver. It said, "In July I asked Governor Stevenson to develop a program of action on the problems of foreign policy I would confront if elected. He is doing this work and will make recommendations to me after consultation with Congressman Bowles and others. Mr. Nitze's group of consultants are concerned with problems of defense and national security and the restoration of non-partisanship in these matters. Their work will not conflict with Governor Stevenson's." He telephoned Kennedy, and next day, September 1, Kennedy did hold a press conference but said nothing about Stevenson —he dealt principally with civil rights.

On that day Stevenson addressed the American Bar Association in Washington. (He was substituting for Nixon, who was in the hospital.) It was a non-partisan speech, ranging widely over foreign affairs, extolling the strength of and calling for increased unity of the "grand alliance" of the West, emphasizing the "total interdependence" of nations and the danger of nuclear war, declaring the importance of the underdeveloped nations, and urging the export of freedom as the best counter to Communist imperialism. British lawyers were in the audience, and Stevenson later told friends he had designed the speech "to reassure them about our attitude in the event of Senator Kennedy's election." Agnes Meyer thought it a superb speech—"If you, Adlai, will go on fighting on this high level, we cannot lose. . . . You kindle in me such hopes, such vigor, such confidence that I could slay giants after reading one of your speeches. Be assured, my hero, that you have the same effect on all the other battlers for Kennedy." Stevenson, back in Libertyville for the weekend with Marietta Tree and

John Fell, wrote to Alicia Patterson, trying to arrange to meet her soon and telling her ebulliently: "Made *great* speech to American Bar Assoc."

32.

On Labor Day, September 5, Stevenson went to New York with Wirtz and Ball and spent all the next day in a meeting in his New York law office with a group of campaign writers—Bill Attwood, Charles Bolte, Jack Fischer, Tom Matthews, Charles Darlington, and Norman Cousins. On September 7 he returned to Chicago and that evening spoke to the Illinois State Democratic Convention, opening his campaign for Kennedy. He praised Dick Daley and pleaded for support for Kennedy and the state ticket, headed by Otto Kerner for Governor (he won), and congressional candidates, including Senator Paul Douglas, up for re-election (he won).

On September 10, Stevenson spoke to a Democratic dinner in Milwaukee, asking for support for Kennedy: "I hear this year more than usual a kind of talk . . . that the candidates are pretty much alike and that it doesn't even make much difference who is elected President. I want to say first, as a Democrat, that this is false and wrong, and that the political cause it threatens is the Democratic cause."

Kennedy was campaigning furiously. He traveled light, with a small staff in a small private plane, while Robert Kennedy ran the national headquarters in Washington. Kennedy often blithely threw away the advance texts of speeches and spoke extemporaneously, something Stevenson almost never did. Kennedy spent far less time in preparing speeches and far more in seeing people and being seen. He repeated the same speech over and over. Everywhere he went he was surrounded by hordes of young people jumping and squealing as they never had for Stevenson. The journalists traveling with him were nearly all for him, as they had been for Stevenson. Kennedy was particularly effective in whistle-stopping. Sorensen, who wrote most of Kennedy's major speeches, had long admired Stevenson's speeches and often adopted and improved on certain Stevenson mannerisms, such as parallel phrasing. Most of Kennedy's speeches sounded better than they read. Many Stevenson speeches, on the other hand, read better than they sounded. Where Stevenson's delivery tended to be choppy but cool and restrained and somewhat stiff and distant, Kennedy gestured forcefully, almost seemed to seize the audience physically, and threw himself wholly into every speech and upon every audience. Kennedy speeches were easier for newspapermen to write and they stuck in the memory better than Stevenson speeches if only because their structure was simpler and they usually contained a four-point or a seven-point or a ten-point program, clearly outlined. If the phrasing was sometimes less graceful than Stevenson's, it was often more effective. Kennedy's 1960 campaign speeches did not soar and capture the imagination as Stevenson's 1952 speeches had but they and his own behavior got his message across—that he was young, vigorous, and would get this country moving again, as he reiterated tirelessly. Stevenson had often been criticized for employing humor; Kennedy was not, perhaps because humor befit the young man but not the old.

Stevenson seemed to be enjoying himself. He called or wrote to Marietta Tree almost daily during the 1960 campaign. "He told me every day what happened and how people reacted. He'd say the crowd in 1960 was as big as 1956 and tell me how they applauded. He was laughing all the time. He spent a lot of his time trying to make people laugh. It was part of his charm. He was a great showman. A master of timing."

Robert Kennedy visited Stevenson at Libertyville on September 11, and the next day Stevenson mentioned it in a letter to Mrs. T. S. Matthews as evidence that the Kennedys were counting heavily on him. He said he disliked deprecating the UN but "I simply don't want to work there myself. Perhaps it is because I don't like to carry other people's briefs any more."

Stevenson had been corresponding with Dr. Henry Van Dusen of Union Theological Seminary, who had heard that Kennedy was sexually promiscuous. When Stevenson asked if this was fact or rumor, Van Dusen replied that the stories had first come to him from Reinhold Niebuhr, who said he had asked Galbraith and Schlesinger about them and said they had dismissed the matter as inconsequential. Stevenson sent the letter to Schlesinger with a remark that he wished he could "keep a mile away from such matters." Schlesinger felt the same way. He said that if such stories were true they did not bear "essentially" on Kennedy's capacity to be President; that the stories were "greatly exaggerated" and usually heard in Northeast Harbor, Fisher's Island, East Hampton, and "all those circles where, in the past, vicious and lying stories have been told about Woodrow Wilson, Franklin Roosevelt, Harry Truman and you." Schlesinger thought that after the war Kennedy had believed he had only a few years to live and "meant to enjoy these years to the utmost"; that the turning point in his life had come in the winter of 1955–56 when he had a series of back operations which nearly killed him; that as soon as he knew he had a full life to live he settled down to prepare himself for the presidency. Finally, Schlesinger questioned "the purity of Dr. Van Dusen's own motives," for he had written a "nauseating" book entitled *The Spiritual Legacy of John Foster Dulles*. "I think you should give Van Dusen hell for circulating rumors which are (a) out of date, (b) largely unsubstantiated and (c) even if true and contemporary—which they are not—would hardly seem crucial when the alternative is Richard M. Nixon." Stevenson on September 13 wrote to Van Dusen and took the Schlesinger line, adding, "Having been the victim of ugly rumors myself, I find this whole business distasteful in the extreme!"

On September 14, Stevenson went to New York to open the campaign officially, taking Blair with him. He attended an affair at the Waldorf arranged by Bob Benjamin, an important New York Stevenson contributor, to introduce Kennedy to his New York friends—the Eastern liberal establishment. After that both Stevenson and Kennedy addressed the Liberal Party dinner at the Commodore Hotel. For a time Stevenson had considered not speaking for fear of overshadowing Kennedy—the Liberal Party of New York was one of the strongest Stevenson bases in the nation. He began by calling the Liberal Party "the best audience in the world": "I have often thought that I would rather speak to the Liberal Party of New York than at an inaugural ceremony in Washington. My envy of our honored guest tonight is that he will do both." He poked fun at the Republicans: "Isn't it funny how nothing ever changes in the Republican Party? In 1952 it was Eisenhower meeting at dawn with Taft on Morningside Heights; in 1960 it is Nixon moving under cover of darkness—so the President won't know he is out—to rendezvous with Rockefeller on Madison Avenue. As the night wears on, lighted only by flash bulbs, the clandestine conspirators finally emerge to announce unity and harmony on the bridge of the Grand Old Ship; that it is ready to sail again with experienced navigators in the chart room but with bold new hands at the wheel. The good flag 'Dynamic Conservatism' is run up at the mast, and away she goes. But—four years later—we always find the old square-rigger right where it was before. The trouble is they never pull up the anchor."

He praised Kennedy's liberal record on domestic and foreign issues and said, "I commend John Kennedy to you as a representative of the highest traditions, as I know them, of the Democratic Party and of the Liberal Party of New York. This man we honor tonight was already in Congress when I first became active in politics. I have worked with him ever since that time—with an increasing admiration which led me to ask him to place my name in nomination at the 1956 Democratic Convention. It is this same admiration which makes it a privilege for me to support him in this election with all my strength and heart." This of course was the point, what he had come for.

He went further—it was a strong and generous endorsement. Then he went on to touch the issues, to voice the liberal faith, and to close: "This is what this campaign is all about: languor or leadership; stagnation or strength; fear or faith—this and the revindication of American power and American purpose."

Kennedy in his own speech poked fun at Republicans and conservatives, quoted Stevenson's 1952 joke before the Liberal Party about the "pause in the Republican occupation that's known as the Liberal Hour" and mentioned Stevenson's name three other times—included him twice in the Democratic litany of Wilson, Roosevelt, Truman, and Stevenson; and said, after having "saluted" Senator Lehman and George Meany, "And tonight we [also] salute Adlai Stevenson as an eloquent spokesman for the effort to achieve an intelligent foreign policy." The core of his speech was a passage on the "proper" relationship between the citizen and the state. At the end he said, "Some pundits are saying that it's 1928 all over again. I say it's 1932 all over again. I say it is the great opportunity that we will have in our time to move our people and this country and the people of the free world beyond the new frontiers of the 1960s."

In a real sense, the torch of which President Kennedy would speak in his inaugural address was passed to the new generation that night at the Liberal Party dinner.

33.

Next day, September 15, Stevenson made a recording with William vanden Heuvel (a Kennedy coordinator running for Congress in New York), saw a law client, toured Washington Square with Vanden Heuvel, dined at the Garrisons', and in the evening spoke to a Brooklyn rally staged by the New York Citizens for Kennedy and Johnson Committee. Once again his main emphasis was on support for Kennedy and Johnson, though he also attacked Nixon.

Bob Benjamin told Stevenson that Kennedy had been impressed by Stevenson's Liberal Party speech.

Alex Rose, leader of the hatters' union and the Liberal Party, told Stevenson that the Liberal dinner was one of the best affairs he had participated in. Agnes Meyer berated Stevenson for saying to her he did not know whether he wanted to be Kennedy's Secretary of State, which she called "shilly-shallying." Stevenson replied, "It has nothing to do with 'shilly-shallying' and a great deal to do with conditions in which it would be possible to work for or with anyone. Perhaps it is because I am more concerned with what you term 'the sake of the country' than my 'own sake.'"

A woman in Connecticut asked sixteen friends to join her in writing letters to Kennedy urging him to appoint Stevenson Secretary of State. She sent a copy to Stevenson. This time he did nothing to discourage the letters. Stevenson told Benton that "a lot of rich Catholics" opposed his appointment as Secretary of State "and their voice is audible in [Kennedy's] councils although I don't think they have voted Democratic for a long time." Agnes Meyer reported that Phil Graham felt optimistic about both Kennedy's election and Stevenson's appointment as Secretary of State.

Stevenson wrote to Alicia Patterson on September 23, "Why the hell don't you let me know your plans—if any! I'm a busy man—and a *bored* one!"

He was concerned about the religious issue. He thought, however, it might backfire if Protestants pressed it too hard. Early in September a group of prominent Protestant clergymen had formed the National Conference of Citizens for Religious Freedom and after a daylong closed meeting had issued a statement challenging Kennedy on several issues and making it clear that his religion made him unacceptable as a President: He could not free himself of his church's hierarchy's "determined efforts . . . to breach the wall of separation of church and state." Norman Vincent Peale, a prominent clergyman, author, and lecturer—and a friend of Richard Nixon—acted as the conference's chairman and spokesman. Many people reacted sharply to the statement, and Peale announced he was withdrawing from the conference. He said he had no disagreement with it but had had no relationship to it except his attendance at one meeting. Stevenson, comparing Peale with St. Paul, said he found Paul appealing and Peale appalling. Privately, he thought this might be the backfire he had predicted. The Peale incident helped set the stage for Kennedy's courageous and widely publicized confrontation with the Protestant ministers in Houston.

By September 23, Kennedy had been campaigning hard every day but one in September, making fifteen speeches some days. Stevenson had made forays into Milwaukee and Minneapolis and a more extended one into New York but that was all. Now on Friday, September 23, accompanied by Blair and Attwood, Stevenson set forth on a two-week trip to Washington, Utah, Colorado, and California. On Saturday night in Seattle, Stevenson spoke at a big $100-a-plate Jefferson-Jackson Day dinner in the Olympic Auditorium, his speech broadcast live on state television. He had told Tom Finletter that he felt Kennedy's "constant emphasis on defense" needed "a counterweight on peace." That night he made peace his central theme, speaking on disarmament and his 1956 proposal for a stop to H-bomb testing.

In California he attacked Nixon heavily, concluding, "I call it dangerous to entrust the presidency of the United States in the nuclear age to such a man."

Jim Doyle, touring California with Schlesinger, found that relatively few Stevenson supporters were turning their backs on Kennedy. Most merely wanted to be reassured that Kennedy was liberal.

On September 27, Stevenson spoke twice in San Francisco, once at a fund-raising buffet in the Fairmont and once at a theater rally, where he said, "The real question is not who can stand up or talk back to the Russians. That's too easy. The real question is who can sit down with them at the bargaining table and negotiate with them from a position of strength and confidence. The real question is not who is tough and who is soft. The real question is who is wise and who is foolish, who likes to play with words and who likes to get things done."

On September 28, Stevenson was at the outdoor Greek Theater at the University of California in Berkeley. He promised to pay homage to the tradition by giving both parties equal time—ten minutes of praise for the Democratic Party and ten minutes of his opinion of the Republicans. Our greatest handicap in dealing with the Russians had been "the defensive and negative nature" of our policies. We must begin anew, with the Marshall Plan our example, to guide into constructive channels the revolutions in India, Latin America, and Africa. America's allies and friends must help. At home, we must "recover the rhythm of economic growth." John Kennedy, in his campaign and later as President, said many of these same things. If Stevenson was not entirely comfortable later on as a member of the Kennedy administration, it was not because he was out of sympathy with its purposes. On the schedule sheet he carried with him Stevenson noted that 10,000 heard him at Berkeley: "Best."

He flew to Los Angeles that afternoon and spoke that night at the Shrine Auditorium, attacking Nixon and praising Kennedy.

On September 29 he attended a tea for (he noted) "1500" women and made a speech—"Good!" He spoke at a fund-raising lunch at the Beverly Hilton Hotel—"poor." He flew to San Diego that afternoon with Pat Brown and spoke to a rally that night—"2000-Good!" then returned to Los Angeles at noon. Late in the morning on September 30 he spoke at the University of California at Los Angeles, and 6,000 attended— "Good!"

On Saturday, October 1, Stevenson went to Salt Lake City and held a press conference and, he noted, "spoke at large meeting—no standing room—good!" That night he spoke to 1,500 people at Grand Junction, Colorado, then drove to Aspen, arriving at 1:30 A.M. He spent a weekend holiday there with the Walter Paepckes. He had lunch with Bill Stevenson, formerly of Oberlin College, and worked with him on a Field Foundation project. On Monday he went to Denver by chartered plane and that evening addressed a "large overflow rally at East Denver High—*very good,*" he noted. Next day he held a press conference, taped a television show, and flew back to Chicago. There he recorded TV tapes of spot announcements for Citizens for Kennedy, dealt with autographs and personal invitations, sent a note to Alicia Patterson: "LaBelle Paepcke reports you in Wyo. and buying her house in Aspen, and visiting the Stevensons—and all the time I've been waiting to hear where you were. . . . Faithless wretch!" For a signature he drew a skull and crossbones. He added a postscript, "Only a telephone call to Empire 2-4466 [his telephone number at Libertyville] with *exact* date can possibly save you!" Two days later, on Thursday, October 6, Alicia came to see him and stayed at Libertyville.

In Chicago, Stevenson spent time on Britannica affairs. It was October 11, the campaign was nearing its climax, the election was precisely four weeks away, and Kennedy was campaigning hard in the East and preparing for his third TV debate with Nixon. Stevenson found time to attend a reception for Congressman Sidney Yates of Chicago. Nothing could comment more powerfully on Stevenson's role in the national campaign. Suzie Zurcher invited him to watch the Kennedy-Nixon debate in her apartment on Thursday. Stevenson took time to cast his ballot for persons to be elected to the Hall of Fame for Great Americans.[15]

Minow told him that recently when Chet Bowles had been asked what he would do about something when he became Secretary of State, he had replied, "Let me make it clear that my first choice for Secretary of State is Adlai E. Stevenson."

34.

On Friday, October 14, Stevenson flew to New York to resume campaigning. He recorded a speech, met at length with George Ball, Tom Finletter, and others in the foreign policy task force, went to a reception for the King and Queen of Denmark, called on Ruth Field, dined at the Finletters'. On Monday he spoke at an "Adlai on Broadway" rally at the Morosco Theater—Melvyn Douglas was master of ceremonies, Mort Sahl was on hand, and so were such people as Tallulah Bankhead, Lauren Bacall, Bette Davis, Myrna Loy, and Henry Fonda, all gathered to hear Stevenson give his reasons why they should join the Kennedy campaign. To Kennedy's style, he contrasted Nixon's dexterity, elusiveness, and evasion: "Governor Rockefeller says America is going too slow; Senator Goldwater says it is going too fast. Vice President Nixon says we shouldn't talk about it." The speech contained nothing more than humor, praise of Kennedy, and the assault on Nixon.

Next day, Tuesday, October 18, Stevenson made the major speech of his New York trip at a dinner given in the Hotel Commodore by the New York Citizens for Kennedy/Johnson Committee. His address was a summing up of what he had been saying all fall, with heaviest emphasis again on Kennedy, foreign policy, and peace. At one point he lapsed into his habit of quoting himself. (Subsequently, Bill Blair sent the second draft of the speech, containing Stevenson handwriting, to Fred Dutton, who indicated he knew a man willing to pay $1,000 for it. The cult would go on.)

At about this time Bill Benton saw Dean Rusk and told a friend, "I asked him [Rusk] whether he was prepared to return to the Department in the event of a Democratic victory. He stated flatly that he can't afford it. He referred to his problems with his children. . . . [But Secretary of State] is an appointment he couldn't resist. And Jack Kennedy could do worse. If the forces who are opposing Governor Stevenson's appointment

---

[15] He voted, his notes indicate, for Jane Addams, Thomas A. Edison, Oliver Wendell Holmes, Jr., and Henry David Thoreau, passing up Luther Burbank, Andrew Carnegie, Jefferson Davis, William James, Edward MacDowell, Herman Melville, Sylvanus Thayer, and Orville Wright. He also wrote in longhand three additional names not on the submitted list: Winslow Homer, Emily Dickinson, and Junípero Serra.

are successful—I think these same forces would prevent the appointment of Chet Bowles or Averell." At about the same time Benton wrote to Stevenson, setting forth at length his own qualifications to be Ambassador to Great Britain. It was the only job in the Kennedy administration Benton wanted, and he tried hard to get it.

After speeches in Philadelphia and North Carolina, after a weekend with Mrs. Ives at Southern Pines, Stevenson on October 24 went to Baltimore to appear as a surprise guest and to speak at the seventieth birthday celebration of Gerald Johnson at the Enoch Pratt Free Library. (Kennedy was campaigning hard that day in downstate Illinois.) Next afternoon Stevenson spoke in Bethesda, Maryland, outside Washington, D.C., on Cuba and the campaign. (The Bay of Pigs was only six months in the future. At this time neither Stevenson nor Kennedy knew of the plans afoot, though Nixon did.) "The Vice President has found a new issue—Cuba." Cuba was a problem because of "an angry, young dictator who is evidently taking advice from Moscow." Castro had led a popular revolution against the rightist dictator, Batista, whom the United States had embraced. Nixon, in Havana earlier, had praised the "competence and stability" of the Batista dictatorship. The United States did not appoint an Ambassador to Havana "for months" after Castro came to power. The United States did not try to guide the revolution in a democratic direction; the Communists beat us to it. What should be done now? Castro was an inter-American problem. The United States should do nothing without her treaty partners in the OAS—unilateral action "will only revive the cry of Yankee imperialism." Kennedy had been suggesting joint action. "He wants us to encourage democratic forces throughout Latin America—including Cuba. He wants us to be sympathetically identified with the new generation of leadership in Latin America that believes in social reform, economic development, and a new deal for the people of South America. . . . He is concerned with making Latin America safe—not just for American business—but for American ideals. And he knows that the solidarity of our hemisphere is a mighty bulwark against the extension of Communism." He reviewed the Administration's record. "After years of courting hated dictators and ignoring the rising social unrest among the people, after years of their pleading for economic aid, the Administration finally came up with a hastily conceived program—just three months before this election, after Castro and Khrushchev had carried the cold war to our doorstep. . . . And now this Administration has taken unilateral action by imposing an economic embargo on Cuba twenty days before our presidential election! No other country has joined us in this embargo. We are going it alone, which certainly offends the spirit of the Charter of the Organization of American States. The fact is that the main effect of this embargo will be, first, to drive Cuba further into the Soviet orbit; and, second, to alarm other Latin Americans. . . . And the embargo will no more overthrow Castro than Mr. Dulles' economic sanctions against Egypt overthrew Nasser in 1956. . . . So the Administration has embarked on a dangerous course. But Mr. Nixon wants to give the impression that he has a plan to get rid of Castro—regardless of how this impulsive action affects our relations with the rest of Latin America. But this is Mr. Nixon's impulsive, dangerous way."

A Kennedy administration would undertake "prompt and intimate consultation" with Latin American states to plan joint steps to "cauterize the Castro infection." The United States must join all Latin America in a "cooperative economic development program that will hasten long-delayed reforms." Latin America was in revolution; the United States must join it, not resist it as in Cuba. The Cuban people would "take care of Castro" as repression and economic depression increased under his dictatorship while the rest of Latin America made progress with U.S. help. What was needed was leadership, and the country would not get it from the party "that has neglected Latin America and its problems for eight years," and he went on to criticize Nixon's record. At one point he had this to say of the man who eight years later would be elected President of the United States (an event which, it seems safe to say, would have dismayed Stevenson almost more than anything else could have): "It seems to me that Mr. Nixon endeavors to project an 'image' rather than express a point of view. I perversely enjoy the thought of the Vice President and his advisers getting together, with pads and pencils on their knees, looking for just the right recipe for just the right 'image.' A pinch or two of maturity. Yes, but a dash of humility. A dollop of experience. A heaping tablespoon of austerity and sagacity. And let's not forget 'good-guyism.' As the Vice President has admitted to one of his journalistic admirers, he wants to be thought of as a good guy—i.e., to project the image of one. Hence he woos athletes, and even—though this came as an afterthought—scholars. Stir the mixture, and you get the Nixon of the moment. Something which is so fragile, though, can easily come apart, and any moment—today or if he becomes President—recipes might quickly change. Such gambling makes me very uncomfortable. I don't think any one man has shown so many different faces to the American public since the death of the lamented Lon Chaney."

On October 26 and 27, Stevenson campaigned in New Jersey and Westchester County, New York, and on the following day went home to Chicago where he dictated and worked on speeches. He told Mrs. Ives he was home only long enough to repack his suitcase. He thanked Barbara Ward for speech language and told her he thought Kennedy would win "an easy victory. . . . But it will be as much a defeat for Nixon as a victory for Kennedy. . . . The debates (my proposal, as you know) have paid off heavily for Kennedy, and there is no surer way to lose confidence in Nixon than to see him, which was also foreseeable. With the recession advancing apace, Kennedy has another break. And, finally, with the anti-Catholics overdoing it even that handicap has been neutralized to some extent. I have had wildly enthusiastic crowds and find the Stevensonians still emotional and moving. Most of them are staying with the party and many of them working actively for Kennedy and the ticket. A handful are irreconcilable and are recommending 'Vote No on November 8 and keep the White House empty for another four years.' In many places they have 'Stevensonians for Kennedy' bumper tags and similar devices. My own efforts have been unqualified, and I assume will not be overlooked or underestimated in the Kennedy camp. But I can assure you that the candidate's 'foreign policy advisers' neither see, hear nor advise the candidate! I think he has been extricated from his appalling blunder about Cuba[16] and, in short, is in excellent shape and riding a rising tide. But what to do after the election? The problems that are arising all around the horizons are staggering. . . . If you have ideas as to the priority problems a new President should be prepared to meet I would love to know how you rate them."

Stevenson, in his Chicago office on October 28, found time to write to Stanley de J. Osborne, president of Olin Mathieson Chemical, about developments in Guinea in which Reynolds Metals was interested. By October 30 he was in Portland, Oregon. Next day, after more appearances on behalf of Kennedy's candidacy and the senatorial candidacy of Maurine Neuberger, widow of Senator Richard Neuberger, Stevenson flew to Los Angeles. There, from the Beverly Hills Hotel, he wrote to Marietta Tree: "I've just arrived in this familiar place after a) triumphant affair in Portland and (one of the *best speeches!*)—preceded by a TV show and followed by a $50 'supper' fund raiser, b) a sleepless night at the dear Corbetts, c) a beefsteak breakfast at eight chez Corbett, d) a hotel breakfast with 200 'business people' cum speech, e) a TV press conference with Maurine for 45 minutes, f) a speech to convocation at Reed College, g) greetings to the Kennedy Hqrs, h) ditto to the Woodworkers of America, i) lunch with faculty of Portland Univ cum speech, and j) speech to convocation of Portland Univ!!! But Maurine was delighted; and Wayne Morse flew out from the UN to introduce and went overboard in a burst of passionate oratory—'I had converted him to the Dem party; *every* Dem in Oregon was a Stevensonian; I was high on his list of the 25 greatest Dems etc!' (I guess he's running for re-election already!). . . . Jane [Dick] just telephoned—this minute—to report rising agitation and indignation that I had not been invited to the Chicago rally Friday. . . . Ho hum! I wish I were there—you were here—we were—?

"—we have no home,
    only a beauty, only a power,
        Sad in the [one word illegible], bright in the flower,

---

[16] Kennedy had proposed strengthening Cuban "fighters for freedom." Since Kennedy was ignorant of the plans for the secret operation that became the Bay of Pigs, Schlesinger has said this was only an oratorical flourish designed by the Kennedy staff to take the offensive after Kennedy's supposed soft position on Quemoy and Matsu.

        Endlessly erring for its hour;
        But gathering as we stray,
        A sense of life so lovely and intense,
        It lingers when we wander hence:
        That those who feel behind their back
        When all before is blind,
        Our joy, a rampart to the mind."

The following day, Tuesday, November 1, exactly one week before the election, he gave Kennedy a remarkable and rousing introduction at a climactic—for Stevenson—rally at the East Los Angeles College Stadium. In the motorcade that pulled up to the stadium, Stevenson's car was dark, and he sat in the back seat staring stolidly into the blackness. Kennedy's car was lighted, and he leaned forward so that the light fell full on his hair; he wore it like a halo. At the end of his speech Stevenson said, "Do you remember that in classical times when Cicero had finished speaking, the people said, 'How well he spoke'—but when Demosthenes had finished speaking, the people said, 'Let us march.' Well, when Election Day is over we Americans will march forward once more under the leadership of the next President of the United States, John F. Kennedy."

Kennedy, responding, began by saying, "I am grateful to our distinguished leader, Governor Stevenson, for his warm and generous introduction tonight, as I am grateful for his support and counsel in this campaign. I am glad to be marching on his side, and we are going to march forward together for success and victory. [Applause.]" Then he plunged straight in: "Governor Brown, Senator Engle, Members of the Congress, the people of California, I come here tonight and ask your help in this campaign. [Applause.] I come here tonight and ask your support in moving this country forward again. [Applause.] I ask your help in bringing Mr. Nixon back to the beauties of California. [Applause.]" He spoke of the importance of next Tuesday's choice. "I do not ask you to choose merely between two men. I ask you to choose the kind of state of California you want, the kind of United States of America you want. What kind of an effort you will make to sustain the cause of freedom all around the globe. Mr. Nixon and I represent two wholly different parties, with wholly different records of the past, and wholly different views of the future. We disagree, and our parties disagree, on where we stand today and where we will stand tomorrow. During the past two years, and in the fourteen years that we have served in the government, we have made known our views on these matters. Mr. Nixon and the Republicans stand for the past. We stand for the future. [Applause.] Mr. Nixon represents the Republican Party which has put up in recent years Mr. Dewey, Mr. Landon, Mr. Coolidge, Mr. Harding, Mr. Taft, Mr. McKinley. I represent the party which has run Woodrow Wilson and Franklin Roosevelt [applause] and Harry Truman [applause] and Adlai Stevenson. [Applause.]" Kennedy deplored the decline in America's prestige abroad and said, "I want the people of the world and Mr. Khrushchev to know that a new generation of Americans has taken leadership of this country and that this free society speaks with power, force, and decision. [Applause.]" It was pure Kennedy. The contrast with Stevenson could hardly have been greater. Nor could Stevenson's allusion to Cicero and Demosthenes have been more apt.

Kennedy headed East for the final week of the campaign in the crucial states. Stevenson stayed West, and his schedule was remarkably light. He had nothing scheduled on Wednesday and sent Benton a note about the Britannica. On Thursday he left Los Angeles late in the morning for San Francisco and there was busy but not importantly so—appeared briefly on a television interview program, attended receptions, and spoke to the presentation of the Lasker Awards at a meeting of the American Public Health Association, quoting from his own position paper on health issued from San Francisco in the 1956 campaign and saying it was still relevant.

On that day Agnes Meyer, back from a walk in her woods, sent him a long letter about his future. *"I know you will be offered the job of Secty of St. You must accept or I will murder you.* The country needs your diplomatic skill and knowledge. Don't make too many conditions. Say 'OK, Jack. We are bound to have our differences. But we are grown-up men and we can iron them out. You are the President and I shall defer to you'—that little play to his natural vanity won't hurt you a bit."

At midday on Friday, November 4, Stevenson spoke to the Commonwealth Club in San Francisco on monetary and fiscal and foreign policy. He did not mention Kennedy (nor had he at the Lasker Awards dinner). That night in Chicago, Kennedy was riding in a torchlight parade to the Chicago Stadium for the traditional Democratic campaign windup in Illinois. Stevenson had not been invited. He made one more speech—on Saturday night, the last Saturday night before the election—to a rally in Fresno. Then he returned to Chicago. En route, he wrote to Marietta Tree, "Fresno last night was a happy end—in a flood of love and excitement. . . . After the rally—an endless crushing buffet supper. . . . And back to SF by charter plane at 2 A.M.! Now Chicago is beneath."

On Monday, November 7, the day before the election, George Ball, Tom Finletter, and J. R. Schaetzel arrived in the morning for an all-day conference with Stevenson on the foreign policy task force report and other postelection plans, assuming a Kennedy victory.

Stevenson voted at Half Day and spent Election Day at Libertyville, working on a draft of the foreign policy task force report. Jane Dick wrote to him that day: "On this day of days I can't help but write a few words from my heart. It hurts me more than I can ever express to anyone—even perhaps to you—that circumstances and timing have been such as to deny America its potentially greatest president—and to deny to my most beloved friend the opportunity to serve—and lead!—in this capacity my emotions are mixed—just as mixed as yours. . . . Because you are you, and the very fact that it has *not* been public office, or a public forum that have made you the world figure that you are but *you* yourself,—the profoundness of your thinking, the validity of your ideas, your extraordinary prescience, and your extraordinary ability to lift hearts while you are articulating them—means that, with or without public office, you will continue to grow in stature and leave a lasting impress of the thought, the morals, and the ideals of this and succeeding generations."

Marlene Dietrich telephoned Stevenson, and he wrote to her, "Your telephone calls delighted me. I am flattered and grateful—and all I ask now is that you stop off for a visit with me." That night he went to a dinner party at Adlai III's and Nancy's and later to Bill Blair's apartment to watch the election returns on television. The election result turned out to be an extremely narrow victory for John F. Kennedy and made him a minority President. He received 34,221,349 votes (including Alabama votes also cast for unpledged electors, five of whom voted for Kennedy and six of whom voted for Senator Harry Flood Byrd of Virginia). This was only 112,803 more votes than Nixon's 34,108,546. It was the smallest popular vote margin in the twentieth century up to that time. In eleven states a shift of less than one per cent of the vote would have switched the state's electoral votes. (Kennedy's margin in the electoral college was far bigger —303 to 219.) The Kennedy-Johnson ticket carried twenty-three states— a coalition of Eastern states (including New York, Pennsylvania, and New Jersey), Midwest states (Illinois, Michigan, Minnesota), and some Southern states (including Texas). The ticket lost almost the entire West, including California and the farm belt, and some Southern states. Kennedy carried Illinois by less than 9,000 votes (out of 4,757,000 cast). He received 49.71 per cent of the popular vote to 49.55 per cent for Nixon.

In campaigning for Kennedy, Stevenson had concentrated on California and New York; Kennedy carried New York but lost California. Although in the present account Stevenson has naturally been the central figure, a study of the 1960 campaign as such would not emphasize his role. Kennedy considered him helpful, as many others were, but peripheral. In an election so close it is always possible to argue that a single factor made the difference between victory and defeat but even here it would be hard to show that Stevenson's role was critical.

35.

So it was over for Stevenson—he would never be President. It remained to be seen what role if any he would play in the Kennedy administration.

The day after the election he telephoned Kennedy, Johnson, George Ball (and Suzie Zurcher twice). He spent most of the afternoon and most of the next day working on the foreign policy task force report. He sent to Robert Kennedy an application from a naval officer he knew who wanted to be the President's naval aide. (He began his letter, "Dear Bobby: Sure, and it's a glorious day!") A friend reported attending a diplomatic dinner at which a foreign guest murmured something about Kennedy's appointing Stevenson Secretary of State, whereupon Dean Acheson turned on him and announced, "That would be disastrous." Television cameramen called on Stevenson the day after the election; on Friday a *Time* photographer called. He worked all that day on the foreign policy report while a man from George Ball's office waited for the manuscript. He finally finished his editing, dictated a letter to Kennedy, and about 4 P.M. gave the report to Ball's man. In his covering letter to Kennedy, Stevenson said he was asking John Sharon to deliver the report in person. He said the report had been reviewed by Fulbright, Bowles, and Bruce "with general approval." He wrote, "I suggest two broad new lines of policy—in the field of foreign economic policy, and for nuclear cooperation within NATO—and also a new emphasis on disarmament. At a time when Cuba, the Congo and Laos concentrate attention on the grave problems of the world south of the Equator, the emphasis on strengthening the Atlantic Community may seem disproportionate, but I believe that it is indispensable." He found fault with his own report—it lacked detail of nuclear sharing, disarmament, East-West negotiation, and how foreign aid could be shifted from military cooperation to economic development. It dealt inadequately with reorganization of the State Department and personnel problems; he now added his view that more policy should be made by ambassadors abroad than by the Department in Washington: "Good men are not content to sit at the end of a cable line waiting for orders from country desks. . . . Also," he said, "some of the statements sound more emphatic and categorical than my convictions warrant."

The task force report said that Kennedy's greatest opportunity to develop new lines of foreign policy would come in the first three months after the inauguration. Preparatory work must start at once. Kennedy should appoint his Secretary of State promptly and also a director of disarmament in the State Department. The report mentioned a situation "of special urgency," Algeria, and listed several places where "explosions may break out" before Kennedy's inauguration—Cuba, Laos, the Congo, the Dominican Republic, and Iran. It recommended that Kennedy appoint a task force on foreign economic policy (George Ball's field) and that he reclaim for State various activities over which it had lost control to Defense and Treasury. Kennedy should get control of State itself (he never felt he did).

The Atlantic Alliance must be strengthened. Emerging nations should be given freedom of choice of political and economic systems. America could best win them to her side by an example of success. All Western industrialized nations should contribute to their economic development. After developing a foreign economic policy to meet the needs of the underdeveloped nations and adopting a comprehensive plan to restore the purpose of NATO, the West should negotiate with the Communist nations on arms control and disarmament.

America must be prepared for a state of "permanent negotiation." Kennedy might find himself called upon to agree to a summit meeting in the late spring or summer (he was); before agreeing to one, he should ask Congress for more military strength, strengthen the Western Alliance and reach agreement on Berlin, and make certain that the area of discussion with Khrushchev was as broad as possible, not restricted to Berlin. If agreement on nuclear sharing could be reached with the allies, it might be possible to propose to the Soviet Union a moratorium on European manufacture of nuclear material and weapons, a nuclear-free zone of several hundred miles in Central Europe with inspection, a nuclear test-ban treaty (negotiations were already in progress), and a land corridor to Berlin. To the paper were attached several annexes—a paper on foreign economic policy, one on partnership between a united Europe and America, one on sub-Sahara Africa, one on the organization of the State Department. The one on China said that the United States could not forever prevent the UN from even discussing admitting Peking—the new African states were restive—and the United States could not afford, for the sake of its international prestige, a defeat in the UN on the China question. The paper on Latin America said we had consistently downgraded Latin America until the recent Bogotá Conference, we should identify ourselves with the forces of freedom and peaceful revolution there, we should understand that the Castro revolution was a symbol of hope to millions of Latin Americans, we should help Latin American rulers promote social reform and economic progress among their peoples. Thus would we counter Soviet influence.

The task force report ran to some 150 pages. John Sharon took it to Palm Beach, Florida, and there at breakfast on Monday, November 14, presented it to Kennedy. He suggested that Kennedy might want to read the first seventeen pages of the report. Kennedy said he wanted to read it "right now" and did so. (He was a speed reader.) While reading the recommendation that he appoint a Secretary of State promptly, Kennedy asked how many jobs in the Department he would have to fill. Sharon did not know, thought it was a little over a dozen, and said Stevenson would provide him with a list of jobs and their descriptions. Kennedy said this would be "most helpful" and asked that Stevenson give him a list of "your people" whom he considered qualified to hold "key" positions in foreign policy. He said he had asked his brother-in-law, Sarge Shriver, to prepare a list of all the jobs throughout the government that he would have to fill and to prepare lists of names of qualified people, Democrats, Republicans, and independents. Reading the section on the Director of United States Disarmament Administration, he said he resented the Eisenhower administration's establishment of a Disarmament Administration late in the campaign. He discussed with Sharon the question of a "Peace Agency" and wondered whether it would require legislation. He went on to say that he hoped to bring good Republicans into the foreign policy field but said that when one had named Rockefeller, Dillon, and McCloy, one had about exhausted the supply of "good Republicans." Reading the passage on OECD, Kennedy said he had been unable to keep up with such subjects during the campaign and needed more information. Sharon proposed that Stevenson prepare a more detailed memorandum, and Kennedy approved. Kennedy wondered if the report was accurate in saying the economic embargo on Cuba had been "ineffective"; Kennedy wanted more facts. Sharon said Stevenson would look into it though he lacked access to diplomatic cables and intelligence reports. Kennedy wondered about the possibility of a rapprochement with Castro. When he finished reading, according to Sharon, Kennedy said, "Very good. Terrific. This is excellent. Just what I needed." He said he would send Stevenson a personal note and probably would want more help. He asked who had worked on the report. Sharon said Stevenson had worked with Ball and others, and Stevenson would tell him who the others were. Kennedy asked who had copies. Sharon said Stevenson, Ball, Fulbright, Bowles, and David Bruce. He approved and asked if Bruce had worked on the report. He had.

Stevenson gave Marietta Tree a list of his qualifications to be Secretary of State. He wanted her to use it in talking to people who might influence Kennedy's choice. The paper said:

1. Decisiveness—As Gov. of Ill. so decisive and effective (with a Rep legislature) that he was drafted for Pres—after he had refused Truman's request that he be a candidate (because he was a candidate for Governor) which Truman never could forgive him for.

2. Competence—life time interest in foreign affairs; extensive writing and publication abroad; travel and acquaintance unequalled in Dem Party's experience here and abroad in diplomacy during and after war. Knows Russia and Russians. Record of being right and in advance of general thinking going back to support of aid for Britain activity before last war. Seven years experience in Fed Gov. in Agriculture, Navy and State Depts going back to 1933.

3. Influence, respect, popularity—unequalled abroad by any American, including Ike!

4. Position at home. Twice nominee virtually without opposition. Respect evidenced by draft movement culminating in Los Angeles ovations—after keeping out of politics completely, except for DAC, for four years and out of the country much of time.

5. What has he done for me (JFK)? Between 60–75 speeches in 12 states during campaign. Host and speaker at fund raising affairs.

Gave JK first national prominence by invitation to nominate AES in 1956 and throwing Vice Pres. open to give him chance without offending Kefauver's followers. Keeping out of the contest and strictly neutral for four years; doing *nothing* to encourage draft.

Cyrus Eaton, the Cleveland industrialist, had sent Stevenson a telegram at election time saying he was going to Russia and offering to carry "an oral word of greeting to Khrushchev" from Stevenson. Stevenson replied, "I hope you will tell the Premier [and Mikoyan and Gromyko] that I look forward hopefully and confidently to improved Soviet-American relations, and that I am sure that with good will and sincere purpose on both sides we can now move toward a safer, saner world." Subsequently Eaton told Stevenson he had delivered the messages to the three Russians "and each asked me to convey warmest greetings to you. They all obviously hold your intellect and integrity in highest respect."

Stevenson went to Alicia Patterson's plantation in Georgia to spend three days, then to Ruth Field's plantation in South Carolina, accompanied by Alicia Patterson. He was there for Thanksgiving. He worked part of the time at both places. On November 18, Bill Benton sent him a curt memorandum: "You mentioned the transmission of your report to Jack Kennedy. Is there anything so secret about this report that I cannot be exposed to it? Indeed, I am curious as to why I haven't been exposed to it." Stevenson replied, "You'll be exposed to it Monday lunch (November 28, in New York). Meanwhile Kennedy has asked me for more and more—so instead of shooting quail and relaxing, I'm still working for him. What the hell!"

On November 22, Stevenson, in Georgia, sent a long letter to "Dear Jack" Kennedy recounting his recent conversations in New York with an American industrialist with interests in Guinea, with a Chilean official, and with Ambassador Menshikov of the Soviet Union. Menshikov had brought Stevenson a long personal message from Khrushchev. Khrushchev declared that war must be avoided, that he had high hopes of reaching agreement with Kennedy soon on nuclear testing, that agreement on disarmament would settle everything, that Berlin could not be internationalized, that Peking China would never accept the idea of two Chinas. Stevenson's Chilean visitor called Latin America "explosive" and urged the new Administration to appeal to the masses there, not the rulers. As for Guinea, the American industrialists, hoping to persuade Sekou Touré to postpone agreement with the Soviet Union on building an important dam, had assured him that the new Administration would give the project prompt and sympathetic attention. The tone of Stevenson's letter to Kennedy suggested that he had private sources on world affairs that could be valuable to Kennedy; he seemed to suggest that Kennedy send him to meet privately with Khrushchev since Khrushchev preferred such unofficial channels.

A few days before that letter, Kennedy wrote a long letter to John

Sharon. (He later decided not to mail it and telephoned Sharon to super-sede it but a carbon copy went to Chet Bowles together with a note from Kennedy, asking him to work with the Stevenson task force.) Kennedy wrote that he had read the Stevenson task force report "with great benefit." He wanted task forces set up to make specific recommendations for dramatic proposals to be made early in 1961 on Latin America and Africa. He wanted other task forces to study State Department personnel in the field, to study cultural and student exchanges and the USIA, and more; and he wanted them to make concrete recommendations and to do it by year's end.

On November 23, the day Stevenson went from Alicia Patterson's to Ruth Field's plantation, Kennedy telephoned John Sharon in Washington and asked that task force reports be prepared at once on Latin America, Africa, and USIA. He wanted to explore the possibility of the United States' sponsoring a hemispheric meeting in Panama, Puerto Rico, or else-where. (This turned into the Punta del Este meeting in the summer of 1961 where the Alliance for Progress was established.) Sharon suggested a further paper on foreign economic policy. Paul Nitze had asked Sharon for a copy of the letter from Kennedy to Sharon, and Sharon now asked if Kennedy wanted the Sharon-Stevenson-Ball group to coordinate with Nitze. Kennedy replied emphatically he did not. That same day Kennedy sent a note to Stevenson thanking him for his reports—"they are excellent and will be most useful"—and saying he had asked Sharon to obtain Stevenson's help on more reports. Kennedy said he expected to return to Washington about the first of December and hoped to see Stevenson shortly thereafter.

36.

In the midst of all this, Suzie Zurcher wrote to Stevenson on November 21, "Will you twirl at the December Ball on the 9th?" Agnes Meyer wrote from Israel, "Am already full to the brim with information that can be of use to you and other members of the new Gov-administration. . . . Am giving Kennedy's unconscious the long distance treatment—with Phil's help." Barbara Ward wrote criticizing rumored Kennedy appointments of David Bruce, John McCloy ("a banker's soul"), and Eugene Black (the prominent banker): "We are not going to find the route to Utopia by way of eight percent—at least, not if the Russians are offering two." If Kennedy really wanted to know what was going on in Africa he should talk to her husband, Sir Robert Jackson.

On the Saturday after Thanksgiving, November 26, Stevenson went to Washington. He spent Sunday there working on the task force reports and that night went on to New York. He wrote to C. K. McClatchy to thank

him for his newspaper's proposal that Stevenson be made Secretary of
State. "I'm sure you realize that I don't want a 'job'—especially *that* job—
unless he wants me, and badly." In New York he had lunch with Benton
and saw Ambassador Menshikov twice. He wrote a summary of these new
conversations with Menshikov and sent it to George Ball along with a
testy letter saying he had had no acknowledgment from Kennedy of his
previous report on a talk with Menshikov. This time Menshikov reported
that Khrushchev had been highly gratified by Stevenson's previous response to his message. Khrushchev then went on to elaborate his views on
various issues. On disarmament, he said that weapons were now so destructive that "general and complete disarmament" was the only solution, that
the United States and Soviet Union must stop the further production of nuclear weapons, prohibit their use, and destroy those that existed. If the
West would agree to "general and complete disarmament" the Soviet
Union would accept any control and inspection system worked out by the
West. He proposed a special session of the UN General Assembly in the
spring on disarmament alone. On Germany, he said the only solution was
peace treaties with the two German states, and the U.S.S.R. was prepared
to sign them, thus recognizing the permanent division of Germany. West
Berlin should be transformed into a free city under UN and four-power
guarantees. On colonialism, the U.S.S.R. intended to help former colonies
get and keep their independence. Menshikov solicited Stevenson's reactions; Stevenson said he saw hope in what Khrushchev said about disarmament but his repetition of Russian views on Berlin was not encouraging;
colonialism was virtually ended already. Menshikov requested a second
audience; it produced little. (These meetings took place November 28 and
29 in Stevenson's New York law office.)

On November 30, Stevenson returned to Chicago. He went to the funeral of his old friend and opponent on isolationism, Clay Judson. He
thanked Kennedy for his note about the task force report, told him he had
suggested names for further task force work to Sharon and Ball, and
offered to be "of further help at any time." The crucial question of the
week was his role in the Kennedy administration, a question now coming
to a head.

Sargent Shriver—and others—had been on a talent hunt, trying to
match people to jobs for Kennedy; and now at his home in Washington's
Georgetown section Kennedy was calling in men, offering them jobs, and
announcing them from the doorstep to waiting reporters. But he had not
yet appointed a Secretary of State.

Newt Minow once said that Stevenson underestimated Bill Blair and
took him for granted. Now in December of 1960 Blair performed a final
crucial mission for Stevenson: he negotiated on his behalf with President-
elect Kennedy. On Monday, December 5, Blair went to Washington and
on Tuesday saw Kennedy. He telephoned Stevenson from the Metro-

politan Club to say that Kennedy would appoint him to his choice of three jobs—Attorney General, Ambassador to the United Kingdom, or Ambassador to the United Nations.

Stevenson said, "How many times do I have to tell you I won't be Ambassador to the UN?"

Blair reported that Kennedy had said he was not prepared to appoint Stevenson Secretary of State because he was, as a leading Democrat, too "controversial" a figure. Kennedy, as a minority President, would have trouble enough with Congress without saddling his Administration with a partisan Secretary of State. He recalled the difficulties Acheson had had with Congress under Truman. He needed a non-controversial figure. This was no reflection on Stevenson's qualification or capabilities. It was purely a political matter. Kennedy was considering Fulbright, Bruce, and Dean Rusk. He had a high opinion of Fulbright. He thought well of Bruce but he had "no fire in his belly." He did not know Rusk. He would not appoint Bowles Secretary—he, too, was controversial—but might make him an undersecretary. He wanted Stevenson in his administration and thought that the post for which he was best suited was Ambassador to the United Nations. He regarded State, Treasury, Defense, and the UN ambassadorship as the four most important jobs in his Administration. G. Mennen Williams, as Assistant Secretary of State for African Affairs, would be more important than Abraham Ribicoff, who would be a cabinet minister (Secretary for Health, Education and Welfare). As UN Ambassador, Stevenson would sit with the Cabinet and have cabinet rank. Kennedy had heard talk that the UN would have nothing to do with policy. This was absurd; Stevenson would make policy in any job. He would have the President's ear. He would have a free hand in choosing the U.S. delegation to the UN. Khrushchev might come to the United States in the spring; it would be all the more important to have Stevenson at the UN. Kennedy laughed off a recent column by Joseph Alsop saying that Kennedy would not appoint Stevenson Secretary because, during their earlier Hyannis meeting, Stevenson had urged "the kind of compromise at Berlin which would have left the freedom of the city quite largely dependent on the reliability and good faith of the Soviet guarantees." Kennedy spoke of Alsop's mendacity, then sounded a note of patriotic responsibility and urged Stevenson to come to Washington Thursday afternoon to see him and make it possible for Kennedy to announce the appointment.

Newt Minow drove Stevenson home to Libertyville that night. Stevenson was angry because Kennedy had made the offer through Blair. He did not want to be Attorney General. He did not want to be Ambassador at the UN either. (He seems not to have seriously considered the ambassadorship to London.) "I'm not going to take it," he told Minow.

Minow asked why.

He said, "I had that job fifteen years ago."

"Good night," Minow said, "it isn't the same job it was then. You were never chief U. S. Ambassador. The world has changed. You've developed. The job is critical. You're the best there is for it."

Stevenson said, "My God, I'm not going to argue for things without a chance to decide what they're going to be," that is, plead for a policy which he had not helped formulate.

"What are you going to do instead?"

"I'm going to continue as we are—speeches, articles," Stevenson said.

Said Minow, "Also you'll be on page forty-six in the New York *Times* with three lines of space." Minow thought later that this hit home. Stevenson said he would think about it.

The next day, Wednesday, December 7, Blair called Stevenson again. So did Minow. And Marietta Tree, Lloyd Garrison, Sid Yates, Suzie Zurcher, and Mrs. Ives. Stevenson talked to Wirtz. He telephoned, among others, Mike Monroney, Hubert Humphrey, and George Ball. He had Jack Arvey for lunch, sandwiches at Stevenson's desk.

Ball told him that as Secretary of State he would be opposed by conservative Catholics, Nixon, and McCarthyites. He would be out in front, something which brought out jealousy and sniping. The whole Truman White House group was opposed to him as Secretary—Acheson, Charles Murphy, Nitze. At the UN, however, he would bring strength to the Administration. Bowles would not; he would instead bring more controversy and hurt the UN. Stevenson should consider whom he could work with. Who would be Secretary of State? Secretary of Defense? And what was his public responsibility? Could he play a useful role, make a unique contribution? If after a year he was not being effective and felt he had subordinated his own best interests, he could resign, having been a good soldier for a time. If he refused the job because he had wanted to be Secretary of State, he would be considered a bad sport. Furthermore, within six months he would feel frustrated and out of things. Fulbright would take the job in a minute. Perhaps Stevenson should attach conditions before accepting the UN—the right to name the U.S. delegation to the UN, the right to name junior Ambassadors and Ministers in the U. S. Mission. Perhaps he should ask who would be Secretary of State and Defense, who would be in charge of disarmament, who would be Undersecretary of State for Political Affairs.

Wirtz told Stevenson it was only natural that Kennedy wanted to be the Number One man in his own Administration; if Kennedy made Stevenson Secretary of State, many people in the Administration would think Stevenson the larger man, and abroad Kennedy would be considered a little boy being guided by a senior statesman. It was probable that Fulbright could do more good in the Senate. Stevenson would do more for the United States in the UN than anyone else. Wirtz considered the argument that he was too controversial to be Secretary "poppycock." But if he turned down the UN it would be called sour grapes. Stevenson was under no obligation to Kennedy. But the world would be a better and safer place if Stevenson was at the UN.

Hubert Humphrey told Stevenson he had talked to Kennedy this same day, Wednesday, and Kennedy had asked him whom he would appoint as Secretary of State. Humphrey replied that he was not in Kennedy's position but he himself would appoint Stevenson. Kennedy said he had great respect and admiration for Stevenson but "I have political problems and may not be able to do it," and explained that Stevenson was too "controversial." Humphrey asked, "What about Chester [Bowles]?" Kennedy said, "No, I can't do that." Humphrey suggested Rusk. Kennedy said he had no clear impression of Rusk. What about Bruce? Kennedy did not feel his background in Latin America, Asia, and other underdeveloped areas was strong enough. What about Fulbright? Kennedy thought Fulbright's best place was chairman of the Senate Foreign Relations Committee; Fulbright's record as a segregationist on civil rights (made necessary by his Arkansas constituency) would hurt him abroad. Humphrey told Stevenson he thought Stevenson should be Secretary but he also thought Kennedy was inclined to "look around" more for a Secretary. He urged Stevenson to accept the UN job. New nations had entered the UN, it was more important than ever. Stevenson had built up a reservoir of good will abroad and it was his patriotic duty to accept. He would have an "up front" role in the Administration. The Ambassador to the UN would be a central figure in the world if he were Stevenson.

Marietta Tree told Stevenson the Kennedy family was against him because he had refused to nominate Kennedy at the convention. She told Stevenson it was his responsibility to accept the UN job and be a good soldier. He would be miserable if he retired. He could not allow bitterness to decide; he would be destroyed by his own bitterness. He should not take the UN job in a spirit of doing it only because he felt he ought to but rather as an important responsibility.

Jack Arvey suggested that, to increase Stevenson's effectiveness at the UN, Kennedy should announce that Stevenson would have a hand in policy making. Lloyd Garrison told Stevenson that he had talked with "the deciding group," the senior partners of the law firm, and they all felt he should accept. They were full of sympathy for his predicament but predicted that at the UN he would be at least co-equal with the Secretary. He would also have freedom to shape policy and to travel. He would be at the center of things. He would be not only a national but a world figure. If he declined, he would feel frustrated. He could take a leave of absence from the firm.

Mike Monroney told him how important the UN was. He would be our Ambassador there at the time when Communist China was admitted. The Secretary of State's job was now a factory management job. At the UN he would not be saddled with all the problems of the civil service bureaucracy. He would need an understanding with Kennedy on how he would communicate with him on policy.

Blair told Stevenson that Kennedy would see him at 3 P.M. next day at Kennedy's house. Blair told him he was pre-eminently fitted for the job and would find Kennedy "very amenable" to suggestions about the job.

Late that afternoon, Wednesday, December 7, Stevenson took a plane to Washington. He and George Ball sat up till 2 A.M. talking. "He said he was going to turn it down because he'd been that route," Ball later recalled. "I gave him all the arguments for taking it—which he wanted to hear. I told him he was temperamentally incapable of taking himself out of public life. No one knew how things were going to go. He had a great role to play in the UN. This was a new administration; if he became a part of it, over a period of time there was no telling what could turn out of it; I told him not to be an Agamemnon. I had no doubt that he would take it finally."

Next morning Stevenson saw Sharon and called on Walter Lippmann. He learned that Acheson had proposed Rusk for Secretary of State, that Kennedy could not take Fulbright because of his record on civil rights and that, asked about Stevenson, Kennedy had replied, "Oh, he's got too many enemies—they'll chew him alive. They'll call him an appeaser, a Communist—that'll be their attack on him." Kennedy thought perhaps the best place for Stevenson was the UN, where his world-wide prestige could be useful.

Stevenson went to Kennedy's house that afternoon. According to his own notes, he told Kennedy he would be frank and say that he had expected to be appointed Secretary of State. He wanted to do something of value to Kennedy and the country. But administration and policy making, not representation, were his interests. Kennedy said that the UN job was a most difficult assignment. Ninety-nine nations were members, and the United States was in trouble everywhere. He mentioned the Soviet attack on the UN, the UN's budgetary problems, Africa, China, colonialism, disarmament, AID, Cuba, and the Congo. "Save UN!" Stevenson's notes read. "Will depend on U.S. Have used up good will on China. *All* policies affect UN—Made *here*—stuck *there*. Cabinet?—policy making—Asst Sec'y hardly adequate—Strong enough to fight battles. What policy participation? *Name*—base in Wash—bureau. Ans charges—freedom of action. More senior help and money—if necessary. Need 2 or 3 top pros—Russians. . . . Sec.—Under Sec—policy—Econ—Defense [—] Disarmament [—] *Ball*." They discussed the Alsop column about Stevenson's position on Germany. Stevenson wanted to know who would be Secretary of State; he needed to know whether he could work with him. Kennedy could not say with certainty but seemed to be leaning toward Rusk. Stevenson said he would not go to the UN if, as was being rumored, Kennedy appointed McGeorge Bundy Secretary of State—"I won't work for that young Republican." Kennedy had met that morning for the first time with

Dean Rusk. Kennedy said, "I'll be your boss. You can have a direct line to me."

They emerged from the meeting and stood on the stoop of Kennedy's red brick house in Georgetown. A pro-Stevenson crowd, mostly George-town University students, applauded from across the street and held up placards urging Stevenson's appointment as Secretary of State. Newspaper-men crowded around. Kennedy said, "I have asked Governor Stevenson to accept the position of Ambassador to the United Nations for the United States. . . . I can think of no American who would fill this responsibility with greater distinction. . . . I regard this as one of the three or four most important jobs in the entire Administration. The ambassadorship and the mission to the United Nations must be strengthened. We must place more senior officers at the United Nations. The mission must be expanded. The Ambassador to the United Nations, the United States Ambassador to the United Nations, must play a greater role in policy making as well as in presenting our foreign policy views at the United Nations in New York, it-self. The job is part of the Cabinet and it is my hope, if Governor Steven-son accepts the position, that he will attend cabinet meetings and will serve as a strong voice in foreign policy over its entire range. He has always an-swered the call of duty on every other occasion in his life, and I am hope-ful that he will find it possible to serve the United States in this most vital position."

Stevenson then said, "I appreciate Senator Kennedy's confidence, and I share his view about the difficulty and the importance of this assignment. The United Nations is the very center of our foreign policy, and its effec-tiveness is indispensable to the peace and the security of the world. While I have not sought this assignment, I want to be helpful. I have some mat-ters both of organization of the work and of ways and means of strengthening that I want to consider and want to discuss with him further. This I hope to do in the very near future."

A reporter asked, "Are we to understand you have not accepted it?" "I have not accepted it," Stevenson replied, "pending a further talk . . . which I hope will be very soon." Kennedy said, "I hope it will be before the mid-dle of next week." Stevenson left almost immediately for Chicago.

Bill Blair had warned Kennedy that Stevenson might not accept immedi-ately. His principal reason, as he told Adlai III, was, "How can I accept it before I know who will be Secretary of State?" Nevertheless, Robert F. Kennedy said later, "The President was shocked. Of all the conversations he ever had with major figures over a period of five years, one of the most unsatisfactory was when he invited Stevenson to become Ambassador to the UN. He was absolutely furious. He said, 'He should say he wants it or he doesn't want it—but to act petulant, to say he was going to think it over, and again raising the question of he couldn't make up his mind.'" Robert Kennedy believed that this incident, coming as it did after the unsatisfactory conversation Kennedy had had with Stevenson in Libertyville during the primaries, seriously undermined their relationship. As Ted Sorensen put it, "During the campaign Stevenson loyally campaigned for Kennedy, and Kennedy appreciated it. But there was a strong effort made by Stevenson people to put pressure on Kennedy to say during the campaign that if elected he would appoint Stevenson Secretary of State. He refused to do it or to promise anything to anybody during the campaign. So when he won, he owed no debt to Stevenson. Stevenson was not ever seriously considered for Secretary of State. Stevenson asked what the [UN] job entailed, who would be Secretary, said he'd like to think it over, all that sort of thing. This was a different reaction from the reaction from everyone else in the country that was going to the President. Everyone else was accepting with pride and pleasure. So this naturally also impaired their relationship. All this is essential to understand their relationship later. Stevenson's chances to be Secretary of State ended definitely at the 1960 convention."

Jane Dick thought Stevenson's disappointment at not being appointed Secretary was in some ways worse than his 1952 and 1956 election defeats. About 1964, Stevenson said to Arthur Schlesinger, "Of course I expected to be Secretary, and it was a great blow." Ruth Field thought Stevenson lifelong had seen himself as Secretary, not as President. Leading newspapers expressed editorially the hope that Stevenson would accept the UN job. Most of them said that his delay was due not to policy differences with Kennedy but to the fact that he wanted to know who would be Secretary before he accepted. Friends expressed disappointment but hoped that he would accept.

Back home, Stevenson wrote out in longhand a set of "conditions," as he called them, under which he would accept the UN ambassadorship. They were:

1. Adm recognizes UN as center of our foreign policy (needs strengthening—USSR attack)

1A. Some voice in policy making. No important decisions without an opportunity to express my views. How? Upgrade asst secy? firmer base in [State] Dept?

2. At least a veto on appointments to his staff in Wash & N.Y.

3. When NSC considers foreign policy matters should have option to attend.

4. To win support of less developed and smaller powers—hold more conf at all levels under auspices of UN. (Disarm cttee of 10 with Sec Gen) One way to counter Soviet attack on UN.

5. Increase the portion of our aid channeled thru UN.

6. Our pol is to end the cold war as soon as possible.

7. Our aid directed not against anyone or system.[17]

8. Strengthen mission by assigning several senior officers.

9. Adequate quarters and representation allowance

10. Reconsideration of composition of Gen Ass. deleg to assure more experience competence & continuity (½ of our deleg. had no dip. exp. ag. toughest team K could send)

11. Will be consulted about organization and direction of our disarm. efforts. Negotiations should be resp. of Sec State—not head of any disarm agency.

12. Something to say about machinery of coordination between State and Defense. Many decisions by Defense embarrassing or late at UN.

On Saturday, December 10, Ralph McGill, editor of the Atlanta *Constitution,* and William Baggs, editor of the Miami *News,* both Southern liberals, telephoned Stevenson to tell him that people expected him to accept the ambassadorship. Senator Sparkman of Alabama called to suggest the appointment of a friend to the UN Mission and to say that he had hoped Stevenson would become Secretary of State but hoped he would accept the ambassadorship. Chet Bowles called and said he had had no word of an appointment from Kennedy—"wants a job so bad!" Stevenson noted. (Kennedy soon appointed Bowles Undersecretary of State.) Philip Graham urged Stevenson to call Kennedy and say he was ready to go to work —he thought a good relationship between Stevenson and Kennedy imperative. At about 1 P.M. Stevenson telephoned Kennedy in Palm Beach, the Kennedy family's winter home where Kennedy had gone for the weekend, and told Kennedy that Kennedy could discuss Stevenson's "conditions" with the new Secretary and if they were acceptable to him Kennedy could announce Stevenson's acceptance. Kennedy said that was fine, he hoped to choose his Secretary tomorrow night and would telephone Stevenson. Stevenson recited his "conditions" and believed that Kennedy took notes on them. Kennedy said he had encountered opposition to Fulbright as Secretary and was inclined toward Rusk.

Stevenson wrote out in longhand notes about his further negotiations with Kennedy on Sunday. (He fastened this document to others already noted and headed it "Notes on negotiations with Senator Kennedy regarding UN post.") He noted that he told Kennedy he wanted to "have something to say about" the job before he accepted it and that he was not sure he could do the job or wanted to but was willing to try if Kennedy and Secretary Rusk were "sympathetic" to the notion that Stevenson would be a member of the Cabinet, would attend important meetings of the National

[17] Stevenson added the following footnote: "but to create conditions in which countries can keep their indep. improve living stds and reduce illiteracy poverty etc. *Pro* improvement rather than *anti* communist."

Security Council, would be in the "mainstream" of policy making, would meet at least once a week with the Secretary of State, would control the senior members of his own staff, would be consulted on disarmament, and would be able to "upgrade" the office of the Assistant Secretary for International Affairs. More substantively, he told Kennedy, according to his notes, that the UN must become the "center of our foreign policy," not merely something used "occasionally, in desperation," as Dulles had used it; that we should use the UN to win the support of underdeveloped countries, to focus our policy toward the Soviet Union, to end the cold war, to channel our foreign aid; and that U.S. policy should not be purely defensive and anti-Communist but affirmative and pro-improvement of life in the rest of the world.

Kennedy announced the appointment of Rusk as Secretary and Stevenson as Ambassador. Despite all of Stevenson's negotiations, in the end Kennedy got his way: he got Stevenson at the UN on his own terms.

37.

On Monday, December 12, Stevenson held a press conference in his office—said he was glad to serve with Kennedy and Rusk and Bowles. Then he had a long lunch with his Chicago law partners to discuss the firm's future. Soon Kennedy appointed Bill Wirtz Undersecretary of Labor (he later became Secretary), Newt Minow chairman of the Federal Communications Commission, and Bill Blair Ambassador to Denmark. Stevenson said, "I regret that I have but one law firm to give to my country."

He took Mrs. Paepcke to the Quadrangle Club at the University of Chicago for a dinner and theater party. (At about this time Stevenson was beginning to see Mrs. Paepcke more frequently and Suzie Zurcher less. Mrs. Paepcke, by then widowed, was Paul Nitze's sister.) He told Jonathan Daniels, "I have undertaken this tough assignment at the UN with the hope that I can contribute something in a trying and dangerous time for us and that organization." Agnes Meyer told him, "I write to tell you that I feel the greatest era of your great life is about to begin and I want you to feel it too." She spoke well of Rusk but admonished Stevenson, "Never forget—where you sit is the head of the table. Nobody else brings the respect of the entire world to this new administration."

On December 13, Stevenson went to New York. He talked with people he knew at the U. S. Mission to the UN, had lunch with Dag Hammarskjold, talked again with Ambassador Menshikov. George Kennan and he discussed relations with the Soviet Union. He had a talk with Krishna Menon of India. He met with his New York partners and decided he must resign from the firm. Dean Rusk and Stevenson held a joint press conference at Stevenson's law office. Rusk said Stevenson would "play a key role" in the formulation of foreign policy. He said it was Kennedy's wish that Stevenson take an active part in cabinet deliberations. He praised

Acheson and said he intended to consult him. Stevenson said he and Rusk had been in agreement for many years on the need to preserve and strengthen the UN. (Rusk had once been Assistant Secretary of State for International Organizations.) Stevenson said he hoped the UN would help end, not intensify, the cold war. Rusk said he and Stevenson were "friends and future colleagues" and would meet often between now and Kennedy's inauguration on January 20. He said Stevenson probably knew more about the UN than any other American.

Back in Chicago, Stevenson received charts and memoranda on the USUN (United States Mission to the United Nations). One said that the USUN needed "a fairly thorough house-cleaning from top to bottom" because it contained too many people appointed by Ambassador Henry Cabot Lodge, who lacked previous experience in State. During each General Assembly a delegation consisting of inexperienced private citizens was appointed for the three- or four-month session; professional diplomats should be appointed instead. Stevenson's penciled notes on the memoranda indicate that he was considering Dorothy Fosdick, Charles Yost, Ambassador to Morocco, Francis T. P. Plimpton, Barry Bingham, Marietta Tree, Phil Klutznick of Chicago, and Ellsworth Bunker (an experienced diplomat) for key positions. One memorandum recommended that the present operating staff of the mission be almost completely replaced. Stevenson did not do it, though considerable turnover occurred gradually. The same could be said of the bureau in the State Department in Washington to which Stevenson would report, the office of the Assistant Secretary of State for International Organizations, called "IO" by bureaucrats.

On December 21, Stevenson sent Rusk copies of his memoranda of conversations with Ambassador Menshikov as well as a memorandum from Harrison Salisbury of the New York *Times* about his own talks with Menshikov. Stevenson told Rusk, "In my last talk—December 15th—the note of anxiety to proceed with disarmament persisted. He asked me specifically to review the Soviet proposals submitted to the General Assembly by Mr. Khrushchev on September 23rd and to 'give him my reaction to these proposals.' . . . He did not talk to me about a summit meeting, as he evidently did to Mr. Salisbury."

Stevenson recommended that he himself meet soon with Rusk to discuss how to handle future discussions with Menshikov and how to upgrade IO in the Department and the delegation in New York. At the same time Stevenson sent Menshikov a pamphlet containing a Russian translation of a portion of a book by Grenville Clark and Louis B. Sohn, *World Peace Through World Law*. Stevenson had delivered a copy of the American edition to Khrushchev in 1958 with the suggestion that it be translated and published in Russia. He now asked Menshikov to send the Russian translation to Khrushchev with a renewed suggestion that it be published in Russia. He wrote, "I will appreciate it also if you will be good enough to extend my regards and greetings to Mr. Khrushchev, together with my very warm thanks for the delightful Christmas gift which has arrived. Such elegant Russian spirits and caviar are a most welcome addition to our Christmas festivities." The next night Stevenson went to a white-tie dinner and to the Passavant Cotillion, a fashionable white-tie Christmas ball given by Chicago and North Shore society for the benefit of Passavant Hospital. He attracted as much attention as the debutantes.

Hubert Humphrey said how pleased he was with Stevenson's appointment—"the combination of Rusk, Stevenson, and Bowles is outstanding." Stevenson, thanking him, hoped they could talk soon—"I need counsel and comfort!" He asked David Bruce, who also had congratulated him, for advice on the two or three top-level people to be appointed as Ambassadors to the UN with rank just below Stevenson's. Mrs. Roosevelt sent him a list of able women for UN jobs and another list of women to be avoided. Stevenson asked the opinion of Jack Fischer of *Harper's* about Harlan Cleveland and said he was considering him for Assistant Secretary of State for IO. (This, of course, was a presidential appointment but Stevenson evidently felt he had Kennedy's support in choosing.) Cleveland was indeed appointed Assistant Secretary for IO.

Stevenson seemed at this time to regard Chet Bowles as his closest ally in the Department in Washington. He telephoned him repeatedly rather than Rusk. On December 23 he told John Sharon it appeared likely that either George Ball or Dean Edward Mason would be appointed Undersecretary of State for Economic Affairs. (Ball was; later he became the highest-ranking Undersecretary, second only to Rusk.)

On December 23, Stevenson drove to Bloomington to spend Christmas. Mrs. Ives had opened the old house on Washington Street and gave a party in his honor that evening for about 200 people. On Christmas afternoon he drove back to Chicago and had supper with Adlai III, Nancy, Borden, and the grandchildren.

Adlai III and Nancy had had Ellen Stevenson for lunch that day. According to Nancy's court testimony, they opened their presents, talked for a while, then went in to lunch. Ellen looked at the sideboard and saw two candlesticks. They had been in Ellen's mother's house at 1020 Lake Shore Drive. When Ellen's Art Center there was closed, its furnishings had been auctioned off. The candlesticks had not been sold, and Ellen's mother, Mrs. Carpenter, had later given them to Nancy. Now at lunch Ellen Stevenson pointed to them and said, "You are a thief. You have stolen my candlesticks."

Nancy tried to explain but Ellen kept interrupting and calling her a thief. The children were seated at the table, silent, waiting for Nancy to bring in the soup. Weeping, she went to the kitchen to get the soup and pull herself together. When she returned she said, "I'm sorry. There's been a misunderstanding, and I don't care that much about the candlesticks, of course, and please, won't you take them?"

Ellen called her a thief and a son of a bitch and a liar.

Nancy said again there was a misunderstanding. Ellen kept on calling her a thief and liar. Nancy said, "Please, this is Christmas and the children are here and let's sit down and have lunch and please let's not mention this again during Christmas." They did. When Ellen left, Nancy gave her the candlesticks and she took them. A few days later Nancy found them on the doorstep.

Hamilton Fish Armstrong recommended Charles Yost to Stevenson for a senior post at the USUN. Henry Cabot Lodge, who had been Eisenhower's Ambassador to the UN until he was nominated for Vice President on the Nixon ticket in 1960, had congratulated Stevenson on his appointment; Stevenson thanked him belatedly and arranged to meet with him to discuss UN problems. Averell Harriman wrote to Stevenson on behalf of Jonathan Bingham of New York; Stevenson said he hoped he could use him. (He did.) Pierre Mendès-France congratulated him.

Stevenson was uncertain of his own access to Kennedy—James P. Warburg sent him suggestions for Kennedy's inaugural address and asked him to forward them to Kennedy, and Stevenson did but told Warburg, "I think it will get through to him, although I am by no means sure what happens in Palm Beach. Most things, I hear, end up on Sorensen's desk." Stevenson drafted the letter to Kennedy in longhand. Sorensen asked Stevenson—as he asked other members of the new Administration—for suggestions for the inaugural address. On December 30, Stevenson wrote to "Dear Mr. Sorensen." He thought the inaugural should contain "a frank acknowledgment of the changing equilibrium in the world and the grave dangers and difficulties which the West faces"; "all-out support" of the UN; "unequivocal commitment" to disarmament; recognition that the first order of business was to halt the proliferation of nuclear weapons; "unequivocal commitment" to the Western Alliance; cooperation by the industrialized nations toward "lifting the living standards of the underprivileged peoples"; recognition of "a special U.S. responsibility for Latin America"; eagerness to reduce tensions over Germany, the Formosa Strait, the Middle East, the Congo, Cuba, Laos; "*perhaps* a conditioned hint of re-examination of our China policy." More generally, he wrote, "The main thing, of course is to create the impression of new, bold, imaginative, purposeful leadership; to de-emphasize the bi-polar power struggle; and to emphasize the affirmative approaches to peace." He hoped "Jack" would mention, in the State of the Union speech if not the inaugural, Stevenson's proposal of an omnibus foreign aid bill. Stevenson enclosed "some hurried paragraphs" covering some of those points in speech language. Several ideas in them, if not precise language, turned up in Kennedy's famous inaugural address, such as, "We dare not tempt them with weakness"; "united for common purposes, there is little we cannot do to advance peace and well-being; disunited, there is little we can do"; "we cannot deal with the Communist challenge divided and in disarray"; "if the free way of life doesn't help the many poor of this world it will never save the few rich." Stevenson sent copies of his letter to Rusk and Bowles.

Jane Dick sent him a New Year's letter, saying she hoped he would visit old friends in Lake Forest and Libertyville whenever "you felt that *home* would restore your sanity." She hoped he could find a job she could do for him at the UN. At about the same time Alicia Patterson advised Stevenson to have Jane Dick appointed to the pre-eminent woman's position in his Mission to the UN, telling him she could be of great help and comfort to him and would undertake mundane tasks as the more glamorous Marietta Tree would not. Jane, she wrote, had been a loyal friend through many long and difficult years; such friends were hard to find. In the end, Stevenson found room for both Jane and Marietta at the UN.

Barbara Ward wrote to him from London on January 4, "Now that the Kennedy team is assembled it seems to me long on competence, but possibly short on vision. . . . Will you and Chet [Bowles] have enough influence on policy?" Stevenson told her, "There is some disquiet about the large conservative Republican influence in the new Administration. . . . There are some unkind words from some Democrats who feel that maybe taking positions and being 'controversial' is precisely what we need. But who am I to say?" Because of deferred decisions and past errors, his task at the UN would be "appalling, in view of the sad decline in American prestige and influence in this past year." To her, as to others, he said that "snatching the fat out of the fire is a blistering job!" Shortly thereafter she wrote a passage in a letter which Stevenson underlined heavily: "Isn't it possible that the new Administration may behave *too* cautiously vis-à-vis Khrushchev and thus lose a possible initiative? There are two sides, no, *three* sides to this risk. The first is that K. may well be the most reasonable Communist available at this moment and he may therefore be worth encouraging in his own power struggle with the Moscow-Peking Stalinists. The second is that uncommitted opinion (which alas! is less uncommitted than it was a year ago) has seen the Kremlin take the initiative for over 5 and possibly 8 years. To recapture the world's imagination is one of Jack's first jobs. . . . In this situation, isn't it worth America's while to explore at once with K. the sort of things he *will* do jointly? I mean—joint commissions for geo-physics, for medical research, for probing outer space and controlling satellites, water research, desert development. . . . I don't believe we can 'win' the Cold War by getting ex-colonial nations 'on our side.' We *can* perhaps keep them on nobody's side. But this means a *modus vivendi* with the Russians. . . . I think America ought to find out at once where the limits of agreement lie and let it be Russia, not Kennedy, that says: Nyet, nyet." It was a policy line Stevenson advocated. Clayton Fritchey, who went to the USUN as Stevenson's press officer, said that Barbara Ward had more influence on Stevenson's policy views during his UN years than anyone else.

Stevenson had sent a note to Jacqueline Kennedy upon the birth of her son, and on January 5 she thanked him, addressing him as "Dear Governor—or, rather, Excellence: The tumult and the shouting will never die down—for a few years, at least—but I rather enjoy it when it's about John F. Kennedy, Jr. Thank you for your nice note about his arrival—and I shall be seeing you very soon, in that tranquil, peaceful period lying ahead, January 20th."

His days were crowded with UN staffing, phone calls, and well-wishers. On January 12 he took all members of his Chicago law firm to lunch at the Attic Club. He left the office early to hold a farewell press conference at the Ambassador Hotel and to attend a large reception there in his honor. The reception was given jointly by the Chicago Council on Foreign Relations and the Chicago branch of the American Association for the United Nations, and the Guildhall of the Ambassador was crowded with people who had been associated with him in the campaigns of 1948, 1952, and 1956. It was a sentimental day, and he stayed that night at Mrs. Welling's. Agnes Meyer sent $3,000 to pay the expenses of the foreign policy task force; Stevenson sent it on to George Ball.

The day after the reception, Friday, January 13, was Stevenson's last in his law office in Chicago. The principal staff officer of the Senate Foreign Relations Committee telephoned to request his presence at a hearing on his nomination to be Ambassador to the UN on January 18, the following Wednesday. Stevenson spent the day dictating, telephoning, talking with his partners and friends, and packing up papers and pictures and bric-a-brac. Sidney Lens, a non-Communist leftist and pacifist Chicago writer and union leader, came in to report on his recent visit to Cuba.

Stevenson telephoned Kennedy and Rusk. He mentioned the Cuban conversation to Kennedy but most of their conversation was about appointments. Stevenson said he wanted "to put in a word for my friend, Tom Finletter, for that NATO post, again." Kennedy said, "Yes. That looks all set." They discussed a place for Brooks Hays of Arkansas. Then Stevenson said, "I have had a lot of communications from Sarge [Shriver] regarding Phil Klutznick. I like him, and I think I can use one senior Jew without too much trouble with the Arabs. But I would like to feel it along a little bit before I do that." Klutznick might not want to serve in the UN Mission unless he had the title of Ambassador; Kennedy did not want to commit himself. (As things turned out, Stevenson came to value Klutznick highly at the UN and as a close friend.) Thus far Stevenson had "signed up" Harlan Cleveland, Jonathan Bingham, Francis Plimpton, Klutznick, and Charles Noyes, whom Stevenson had known in the UN's early days. He described Plimpton as "a senior lawyer in New York of my generation." He had not yet chosen a senior Ambassador—"Ellsworth Bunker is not up to it." (Bunker outlived Stevenson by many years and served as Ambassador to Vietnam under Presidents Johnson and Nixon, among other difficult posts.) Stevenson recommended an old friend, Jonathan Daniels, for a job. Kennedy was noncommittal. Stevenson suggested making Mrs. Roosevelt a member of the delegation to the resumed session of the General Assembly which would meet in March; Kennedy thought it fine. They discussed other women candidates for UN posts—Marietta Tree, Gladys Tillett, Mary Lord, Margaret Price, Eugenie Anderson. Kennedy was inclined to leave it to "your final judgment" but felt that the best would be Marietta Tree and Gladys Tillett of North Carolina. Stevenson seemed to agree. Neither mentioned Jane Dick.

Then Stevenson told Kennedy that "the most important first thing" the Kennedy administration must do was to "discover what is in [Khrushchev's] mind." He thought this could only be done by a man who would go to Moscow as Kennedy's personal emissary for informal talks soon after the inauguration. He should not be a professional diplomat but, rather, "someone who corresponds to Khrushchev's concept of power," that is, "a political figure rather than a diplomatic one." He thought it important to find out what Khrushchev's troubles were, to explore ours with him, to learn more about Khrushchev's health—Stevenson thought it might not be good—and about his problem with extremists in Peking and Moscow. "I think we will not find anyone easier to deal with than K is. I think it is important to find out whether he wants to expand the cold war —if we make proposals on general and complete disarmament—how are we going to proceed—does he want an effective U.N., or is he determined to destroy it? I know how he reveals himself in conversation—and it could be this could determine quite a good deal, especially if he wants to do business. . . . It would be helpful if Zorin at the U.N. got some new instructions and we could have a more profitable meeting in the Spring than we had in the Fall. I think they have been taking the initiative too long now. This would recapture the world's imagination which is one of the first jobs to be done—and I don't think we can do it by being too cautious. I think this is one of the things that you should talk over—I haven't been able to get Dean [Rusk]."

Kennedy thought perhaps he should bring Ambassador Thompson home from Moscow right away and talk to him about the idea. He asked, "Who would be [the] best one to talk to K?" Stevenson replied, "I think the unhappy thing is the best one is me. But I haven't wanted to suggest this and it would come at an awkward time—but I would do this if it were deemed wise and helpful—and I would put other things aside. The alternative would be Harriman—he has disadvantages in view of the fact he always insists on talking—and has difficulty in hearing. I think it would be best to send someone K knows and with whom he has had dealings before —someone he would be quite sure would represent you—someone influential—not just a personal diplomat." Kennedy replied, "Good. We will have a chance to talk before we come to a final judgment on this? . . . I'll see you at the inauguration and then the cabinet lunch-eon." Nothing came of this—unfortunately, in view of the difficulty of Kennedy's summit meeting with Khrushchev in Vienna a few months later.

Stevenson signed and sent to Dick Daley a recommendation that he make Jane Dick national committeewoman from Illinois. He gave up his law clients and resigned formally as chairman of the Executive Committee of Encyclopaedia Britannica Films, Inc. He would continue as a member of the Board. He told Fulbright he had arranged to bring Brooks Hays to the USUN until Rusk decided to use him as Assistant Secretary of State for Congressional Relations, a post which Stevenson had recommended. And then late in the afternoon that Friday he left his law office for good.

38.

On Wednesday morning, January 18, he appeared in Washington before the Senate Foreign Relations Committee for his confirmation hearing. To the committee he read a long prepared statement expressing his pleasure at the prospect of the UN post, outlining his background in UN affairs, and discussing the UN today. Developing nations attached even greater impor-tance to the UN than did the United States, he said. The UN was "partly a debating society—but let us not denigrate the importance of debating, on the world's platform." The UN was also "an operation" in such places as the Gaza Strip and the Congo. It functioned, too, as a way of sorting out complex issues involving many nations. Multilateral diplomacy comple-mented bilateral diplomacy. Finally, the UN took part in "everyman's struggle against 'poverty, hunger, desperation and chaos.'" The United States should "cherish, preserve, strengthen this great experiment in inter-national collaboration. . . . We should use it not as a device in this cold war . . . but affirmatively." The UN was at its best not in promoting sta-bility but as a framework for change.

The Senators' opening questions were friendly. Humphrey asked if Stevenson thought the UN might be used to establish a multilateral pro-gram of foreign economic aid. Stevenson did. Humphrey asked about his place in the State Department structure. He replied, "I am clear that I am expected, and intend, to the limit of my ability, to spend more time myself on these matters in Washington than has been the practice in the past." Senator Wiley (R-Wis.) asked how Stevenson estimated Khrushchev's in-tentions. Stevenson said Khrushchev's objective was "one Communist world" but that the means he preferred were peaceful. "He does not want the consequences of nuclear war. This implies, Senator . . . an economic, political, and psychological competition with the Communist bloc for years to come."

Wiley asked whether Stevenson thought "Communist China" should be admitted to the UN. Stevenson said he could not anticipate the new Administration's policy but said support was steadily declining for U.S. opposition and admission might prove inevitable. Senator Sparkman asked if he thought the United States should "work toward some kind of disarmament or arms control." Stevenson said, "It should be a first priority in American foreign policy," and added that there were two "transcendent" problems in the world—the proliferation of nuclear weapons and the disparity in living standards between the rich and the poor in the world.

Senator Hickenlooper, the Iowa Republican leader, asked more searching questions. Did Stevenson think he would have "an enlarged field in the determination of foreign policy over and above what other Ambassadors to the United Nations have held?" Stevenson evaded: "I am not sufficiently informed about the conditions that have prevailed in the past to be able to answer that 'Yes' or 'No.' I can say that, as to my own situation, my understanding is that policy matters, especially those which relate to the execution of my office in New York, will come to my attention. I will be a consultant. I will have an opportunity to express my views on policy formation." At the UN, would he exercise his own judgment without advance "guidance and approval" from State and the President? Stevenson replied, "I would hope that I could always have the guidance of the Secretary and the President, where necessary, in matters of that kind," although if the United States were attacked in debate he could "do whatever my judgment indicated as the commander in the field." Hickenlooper pressed him—would he at the UN have a veto over positions taken by the Secretary of State? Emphatically not, Stevenson said. Hickenlooper asked if it was true that Stevenson had consistently advocated admission of "Red China" to the UN. Stevenson said he had never taken that position. Hickenlooper quoted from Stevenson's own article in *Foreign Affairs* to prove he had, then asked if, as Ambassador to the UN, Stevenson would advocate the evacuation of Quemoy and Matsu and the inclusion of Korea and Japan in an atom-free zone. Stevenson said he did not know what policy was going to be. Hickenlooper quoted Rusk as saying Stevenson would play "a key role" in planning foreign policy; Hickenlooper interpreted that to mean "something more than acting in an advisory capacity." Stevenson replied, "A key advisory capacity."

Senator Lausche, a conservative Democrat from Ohio, suggested the possibility of a coalition government in Laos and asked Stevenson what he thought of coalition governments. Stevenson said he was not informed about Laos, though coalition governments were better than Communist governments and served a useful purpose in some instances but all too often became Communist governments. Lausche asked his views on emerging nations whose people were incapable of governing themselves and where chaos might develop. "I suspect," Stevenson said, "that for a long time we would have to anticipate that such countries could only be run by a strong non-democratic central government until education made democratic government possible."

Chairman Fulbright led him back to the gap between United States affluence and overseas poverty and asked whether our affluence was necessarily a source of strength in the contest for "these lean and hungry nations" in the world. "I think our ideals are of much greater influence in these new nations than our economic well-being . . ." Stevenson replied. "I think the most important export commodity we have is not wheat, is not even surplus agricultural commodities, but it is the ideals of freedom and independence, the ideals embodied in the Declaration of Independence, which have swept the world." Senator Lausche interjected, "I have time and again said that our greatest strength, our economic riches, is our greatest weakness. We are the champions, we are at the top of the ladder, and when people are living in squalor and distress, you can understand that they look with envy upon us. . . . And we aggravate the situation by our perfumed couches, and by our vessels of gold and silver out of which we drink, and the dancing we do and the coats we wear, and that is especially true of those who are representing us around the world. If we have a weakness, that is where it lies." Stevenson responded, "Wealth is a heavy burden, sir, I agree," and Fulbright quickly closed the meeting. The committee recommended that the Senate confirm Stevenson's appointment, and it promptly did so.

The following day, January 19, Stevenson sent Rusk a memorandum on things he wanted to discuss with him soon—selection of a deputy to Stevenson (the experienced diplomats under consideration were Philip Bonsal, Jacob Beam, Charles Yost, and James Riddleberger); the future of the incumbent Ambassador to the UN, James Wadsworth; announcement of Harlan Cleveland's selection as Assistant Secretary for IO; consideration of Bill Benton for London; appointments of women to the Human Rights Commission and the Commission on the Status of Women and the Social Commission (Stevenson asked if Rusk had "any plans" for Dorothy Fosdick and wondered whether Marietta Tree's husband's British citizenship would matter); the public relations staff at the USUN in New York; appointment of a Negro to the staff; composition of the U.S. delegation to the resumed General Assembly in March; and a table of organization of the USUN.

On that day the inauguration festivities began—receptions for Governors and "special distinguished guests," receptions for individuals, a reception at Phil Graham's (one of the most sought-after invitations), a concert, a jamboree. The celebration continued through the next day, January 20, inauguration day, and the day after that. After the inauguration ceremonies at noon on Capitol Hill, the Cabinet met for lunch. Then came the parade, a California cocktail party, a cocktail party for Senator Douglas, an ILGWU reception, a cocktail party of Chet Bowles's, a reception for Mrs. Roosevelt, a dinner, the inaugural balls all over town.

Stevenson moved through the affairs with dignity and outward good humor. Crowds attended his movements, though naturally nothing like the crowds that attended the Kennedys'. His own admirers accompanied him. The new crowd, the Kennedy crowd, were strangers to many of the Stevenson people. Once Stevenson told a friend, "The thing that really annoys me is to see that Peter Lawford"—President Kennedy's brother-in-law—"has announced that he's paying off my campaign deficits." It snowed hard the day before the inaugural, and the weather was cold and traffic was disrupted. With the others designated to be cabinet members, Stevenson sat on the platform to watch President Kennedy sworn in. After the ceremony he alone, of all the Cabinet, had no limousine to pick him up. He blamed the "Irish Mafia" of Kennedy's staff. Afoot he started out to make his way in the biting wind up Pennsylvania Avenue to the reviewing stand at the White House. It pleased him to note that the crowds on the sidewalk gave only perfunctory applause to Kennedy and the dignitaries who drove by in the parade but when they recognized Stevenson on foot among them they cheered. The day after the inauguration Stevenson went to a "recuperative brunch" at the Phil Sterns' in Alexandria, and so did Ball and Wirtz and Blair and Wyatt and Martin and a host of other Stevenson friends and supporters from past campaigns, and in midafternoon Stevenson led some of the others out of the Sterns' and to the White House to be sworn into office. During the picture-taking of the President and his Cabinet, Kennedy made a point of having Rusk stand on one side of him and Stevenson on the other; and when an aide arrived with word that, as a gesture of good will, the Soviet Union was releasing an American-held prisoner, Kennedy again made a point of beckoning both Rusk and Stevenson to him to consult on his response. More festivities that Saturday, and on Sunday at 3:50 P.M. Stevenson flew to New York to take up his new duties at the USUN. His day as national political leader had passed; his new career had begun as the voice of America to the world.

PART TWO
THE WORLD

CHAPTER FOUR

Ambassador Stevenson, Secretary Rusk, and President Kennedy 1961–1963

For the first few months of his ambassadorship Stevenson and the rest of the United States Mission occupied headquarters at 2 Park Avenue; but in May they moved into a new building on UN Plaza across the street from the UN itself. Stevenson's office was a pleasant suite of rooms well carpeted, overlooking the broad avenue and the East River and the UN, equipped with a loudspeaker over which he could listen to debate in the Security Council and General Assembly.

The UN Secretariat building across the street seemed by day a slab, a thin slice of structural glass and steel reared high against the sky. By night lights burned late in its upper reaches where the Secretary General and his principal aides had offices. Below it lay the squat dome-shaped building housing the General Assembly, the Security Council, and facilities for delegates. The Security Council's forum looked like a cockpit—a large doughnut-shaped table at which the delegates sat backed up by two rows of aides. Translators sat above behind glass partitions. Outside the heavy doors was a bank of telephones which delegates could use to telephone for instructions. The General Assembly, that huge deliberative body sometimes called the parliament of man, contained at that time the delegations of ninety-nine nations. The General Assembly met in a chamber somewhat resembling the United States House of Representatives, though more brightly lit and richer. Outside down a corridor was the bare delegates' lounge, a bar at one end. Stevenson almost never went there—American tourists would besiege him.

He lived at the U. S. Embassy, Apartment 42A of the Waldorf Towers, a large and gracious apartment high above Manhattan, with a magnificent view of the city, spectacularly lit at night. During his tenure some of the finest art in America graced the embassy. Stevenson had original letters by

Jefferson and Lafayette framed and hung on the living-room wall. All in all, it was a pleasant place to work and live.

The UN works on an academic year. Ordinarily, the General Assembly session begins in September and lasts until about Christmas. The Security Council meets on call all year to consider crises. Thus Stevenson's year fell into a pattern. In the fall he would be busy in New York with the General Assembly. In the winter and spring he would be occupied there with the Security Council. In early summer, activity suspended, except in unusual circumstances, and he usually went to Europe (and so did Marietta Tree —ECOSOC, the Economic and Social Council, met there in early summer). In August he would meet with his staff in New York and, in Washington, with the President, Secretary Rusk, and Harlan Cleveland, Assistant Secretary for International Organizations (called IO at State), to lay plans for United States moves in the coming General Assembly. And so in September the year would begin again.

The United States Ambassador to the UN is the only U. S. Ambassador who is obliged to look constantly at the world as a whole. An Ambassador to, say, India, is principally concerned with "his" county (and with other countries as they directly affect India); he sometimes becomes almost a lobbyist for India. But the Ambassador to the UN must take into account the world at large, and in this respect he, and he alone among Ambassadors, resembles the Secretary of State. Herein lies an inherent problem: to the extent that the Ambassador to the UN deals with the world, he becomes, in a sense, a rival of the Secretary of State. He can never rival the Secretary in any real sense—there can be, after all, only one Secretary of State, as there can be only one President. But their jurisdictions, their areas of interest, match.

Stevenson's official title was United States Permanent Representative to the UN but he carried the rank of Ambassador, was so addressed, and was chief of mission. His deputy was Francis T. P. Plimpton, his old friend from law school, a distinguished New York lawyer, an intelligent gentle man. Charles W. Yost, a career diplomat, was his deputy representative in the Security Council, with the rank of Ambassador. At the UN, he was Stevenson's principal operational officer. (He later became U. S. Permanent Representative.)

Phil Klutznick of Chicago became representative in the Economic and Social Council, with the rank of Ambassador. Jonathan Bingham of New York, formerly with Harriman in the State Department, was representative in the Trusteeship Council; Charles P. Noyes, a Foreign Service officer, was counselor of mission; Richard Pedersen, another FSO, was head of the political section. In all, the Mission consisted of about 125 people, including clerical help. Of the 125, perhaps 30 were Foreign Service officers. Marietta Tree, Jane Dick, and Gladys Tillett were the highest-ranking women. Marietta sat for a year behind Sidney Yates, appointed U.S. representative to the UN Trusteeship Council after his defeat for a Senate seat in 1962. In 1964 Yates went back to Congress, and Marietta was appointed to take his place and given the personal rank of Ambassador. Stevenson hand-picked his senior staff as well as many of lower rank. An impression got around in the State Department that, to assuage his disappointment at not being appointed Secretary, he was getting the first pick of the Department for his UN staff.

Except for emergencies when instantaneous reaction was essential, speeches, including Stevenson's, were cleared in Washington and frequently drafted there. About a dozen people were involved. Sometimes the speech was finished only minutes before Stevenson had to deliver it. Sometimes even debate rebuttal speeches were written in Washington. At times IO sent experts up to New York to stay with Stevenson and his staff during a crisis. Yost, Pedersen, a political officer, and Stevenson himself wrote speech drafts. Extemporaneous speeches were sometimes scribbled out in the debating chamber by Stevenson and an adviser at his side. In the Security Council, Stevenson often occupied the U.S. chair with four advisers behind him—Yost and Pedersen, or Plimpton and Pedersen, plus two political officer specialists. Between crises the political officers worked on papers on their assigned subjects and geographical areas, often working with other friendly delegations, especially the British.

At the UN the underdeveloped countries claimed Stevenson's attention, and for three reasons: that was where the problems were—the Congo, Cuba, Angola, Goa, Vietnam, Dominican Republic; that was where the votes were in the General Assembly; and that was where his personal interest lay. As new nations gained independence they joined the UN and brought their problems to it. Moreover, the accession of new nations in Africa and Asia to UN membership swelled that membership, and each such nation had the same single vote in the General Assembly as the United States or the U.S.S.R. Thus the opposing superpowers, the United States and the U.S.S.R., had to compete for votes among the small new nations. Votes shifted often, became "swirling majorities." Stevenson assiduously courted the new nations, particularly the African ones, and the Latin Americans too. Yost once said, "We had persistent differences with the Department on Africa. We had a different viewpoint. The Africans were a nuisance to the Department but they meant votes to us. We kept the Department interested by saying it would affect Chirep [State Department word for the question of Peking China's representation in the United Nations] and other things that the Department was interested in."

Yost once said Stevenson gave his staff "a good deal of discretion" in their work, "especially those not dealing with the big conspicuous issues." Klutznick, for example, served for two years at ECOSOC and "pretty much ran things himself." At least once Stevenson's delegation of authority had an unfortunate affect: Stevenson did not get into the Article 19 problem—Russia's and others' refusal to pay peace-keeping assessments—until too late. "He didn't realize that it would mushroom the way it did.

None of us realized it." The staff members Stevenson worked with most were on the eleventh floor—Plimpton, Yost, and Noyes. He also saw Clayton Fritchey, his director of public relations, often. He left the other three main sections to themselves—Klutznick at ECOSOC, Jonathan Bingham at trusteeship, and administration.

Stevenson did a good deal of business direct, by telephone to the White House and to Secretary Rusk, Undersecretary Ball, and, constantly, Assistant Secretary Cleveland. His was a rather free-wheeling Mission. "We tried to spare him everything we could," Yost said. "He led an appallingly busy life. He did more than he should have. He had all his other activities and obligations—the Field Foundation, the Eleanor Roosevelt Memorial Foundation, and all sorts of committees. Then there were all his friends— political and social friends of all kinds. All this was not entirely good. Sometimes Noyes or I would try to get him to receive the Foreign Minister of X country but no, he had to see John Doe, an old friend or political supporter who was in town only for that day. It was not in his nature to run a systematic office." He had no buffer, nobody to play Bill Blair's old role. He tried several young men from the Department but they never gained his confidence. His calendar was nearly always hopelessly crowded. All the while he grumbled about it yet enjoyed it secretly, as always.

When the General Assembly was in session it was possible to outline everyone's duties neatly. The Assembly met in plenary session and in seven committees. Committee One was political, Committee One-A a special political subcommittee on Palestine, Committee Two economics, Three social, Four trusteeship and colonial, Five financial and budget, Six legal. Staff people were assigned to each committee. But special problems kept cropping up, such as disarmament in the First Committee, which was handled from Washington by William C. Foster's Arms Control and Disarmament Agency. Plimpton was assigned outer space and Palestine refugees. Stevenson himself handled Berlin. Plimpton once said, "He was not the greatest organizer in the world. You couldn't make a chart of the mission and its members' responsibilities. It was a staff joke that you could never tell if there would be a staff meeting—but if you saw Stevenson's door open you walked in and that was the staff meeting."

One might expect that Stevenson would have been interested in human rights but, preoccupied with big political crises, he left it to subordinates. Plimpton thought Stevenson spent too much time on speeches outside the UN. Most of them were not cleared by the Department. He had writers in New York and Washington. "He was contemptuous of writers and of the clearance process," Plimpton said. "The important speeches—for example, the American speech in general debate at the opening of the General Assembly, which would be made by the President or Stevenson—a speech like that would be drafted in Washington, cabled up to New York, pawed over in New York, then sent back and forth between Washington and New York, then finally Stevenson would get into it and get in the middle of it and moan and groan and rewrite and rewrite and finally finish it. Technically it was cleared in Washington. But he'd keep changing it up to the time he delivered it, even while he was waiting his turn to speak. This used to worry Washington." Assistant Secretary Harlan Cleveland in Washington and his deputy, Joseph Sisco, often monitored Stevenson's speeches in New York over a loudspeaker connection, worrying. By and large, he followed his prepared text.

Plimpton has said, "One complaint was that Stevenson was never seen at the UN. He never hung around the delegates' lounge. I did it for him. He was very poor about going to diplomatic receptions. He didn't like it. He asked me to go. You had to prod him with a cattle goad to get him to go. He had a vigorous social life too—if there is a criticism of him, I would think it was that. Adlai used to love to go to first nights and go backstage and be greeted by the lady star. He was the number one dinner guest of everyone in New York City." Stevenson talked to other ranking Ambassadors in his own office whenever possible, though some of them insisted on reciprocity, as when the Mexican Ambassador asked if the next meeting on peace keeping could be held in his embassy—his superiors did not like his always going to the North Americans. "The Latin Americans loved him," Plimpton said, "though he didn't use the heart and flowers that they like or observe their *dignidad*. I guess it was his ebullience that they liked, his natural warmth." He occasionally saw Ambassadors for private talks in his embassy at 42A in the Waldorf. The British usually came to him.

Richard N. Gardner, member of the Mission under Stevenson, once said, "One of the disappointments about the Governor was that he found very little time for non-political matters. Of course he had all he could do to keep his head above water. But in the long run, the long-range things may be more important. For example, economic development, staffing the UN Secretariat with first-rate Americans, and so on. I never could understand why he found so little time for these things. The 1960s were announced as the Development Decade at the UN, and he had a natural disposition to be interested in development. But he never got into it. I could get him on outer space once a year when I brought a text up to him. He'd say it was wonderful and he was sorry he didn't have more time to go into it. I guess—well, basically, he was not a good administrator. He couldn't say no to his old friends who would call him up. He did not know how to husband his time. He took too many speaking engagements. His vast constituency was a liability as well as an asset."

When Stevenson was appointed to the UN his detractors remarked that it was a good place for him—the UN did nothing but talk, and he was a good speaker. Was it true? Was the UN really just talk? Or did it have real meaning? Many people have asked those questions. Certainly the UN was out of the action line, out of both the policy line and the operations line, in United States foreign policy. The geographical bureaus at State made more policy than IO. Debates were everything at the UN, and it served as a world-wide sounding board and, occasionally, as a real keeper of the peace, as in the Congo. It shepherded small nations and underdeveloped nations. When a real confrontation occurred between the great powers, however, especially between the United States and the Soviet Union, the UN was powerless. The small nations appealed to the UN for help but the UN had to appeal to the big nations for help. Thus when the Cuban missile crisis occurred, the Secretary General appealed to the United States and the U.S.S.R. to resolve it.

A sense that the UN was merely talk may have contributed to what various people have described as Stevenson's sense of frustration during these years. Anybody who has read many diplomatic cables is struck by the difference between the long and thoughtful cables sent between the UN Mission and the Department, on the one hand, and, on the other hand, the terse action cables between the Department's geographical bureaus and individual embassies around the world. Real power lay in the White House and the Kremlin, not the UN. A study of Harlan Cleveland's papers reveals that the White House, operating in the dirty, bloody arena of power, was always messing up the neat designs of Stevenson, IO, and the UN for world order. Power is always disorderly. At the same time Stevenson at the UN sometimes functioned as a one-man Voice of America. During the Cuban missile crisis, while Kennedy and Khrushchev were struggling secretly, the White House simply could not speak. Only Stevenson could speak. His was the only voice of America that Americans and the world could hear during those critical days. He helped prepare world opinion for the Kennedy position, he made the United States case to the world. It was a significant contribution.

To an outsider accustomed to using power, the UN sometimes seems almost the ultimate bureaucracy, producing acres of papers, developing an arcane vocabulary of its own, developing elaborate systems for identifying documents, burying vital issues under almost unreadable titles, referring to the most searing problems of the times as "items" and "questions" ("Question of the incidents in the Gulf of Tonkin"), debating procedural matters endlessly, quarreling over the language of resolutions that really call for no action, following parliamentary procedures without a constituency or real authority, politicizing without power or a body politic. At times it seems almost as if all this were deliberately designed to obfuscate the issues, conceal things from laymen, and insulate the lofty institution and its practitioners from the dirty street brawl of power politics. Thus it is all the more shocking when the street brawl crashes into the orderly chamber, as during Khrushchevs' shoe-pounding or Castro's antics or Stevenson's angry "hell freezes over" speech during the missile crisis. Tons and tons of paper; billions and billions of words; yet it is all we have. Once Stevenson, impatient to go to Libertyville, was told by the Department that a crisis was coming and he should not go. He said irritably, "Do I have to stay here for more of that yak-yak? It doesn't mean a thing."

Richard Gardner once summarized in a book favorable to the UN the criticisms often made of it—it had not brought peace; it cost too much; its voting procedures were unreasonable and inimical to the United States; Afro-Asian nations were irresponsible on colonial issues; our desire to please them had divided NATO; the UN controlled U.S. foreign policy; the United States should rely on the Atlantic Community, not the UN, to promote its national interests; the UN's peace-keeping role was dangerous because it might someday be used against the United States. Gardner, while acknowledging that the UN was not perfect, argued that it nonetheless performed valuable functions—it was a world forum for debate, a place for negotiation of differences through quiet diplomacy, and a place for action, both in the economic and social fields and in peace keeping by means of mediation, conciliation, observation, fact finding, and the actual use of UN international military forces. Gardner pointed out that the UN spent more money and energy on promoting the general welfare of nations than on political and military operations. Some have called the UN, weak as it is, the world's last best hope for peace. Again, history alone will tell.

2.

When Stevenson began at the UN he hoped to have a major voice in making the foreign policy of the United States. The importance of his post (the embassy to the UN is perhaps our most important one), his cabinet rank, and his own personal prestige promised much. During his first months at the UN he went to Washington and saw the President frequently. Upon occasion, especially when the UN itself was directly involved, as in the Congo, he clearly did help shape United States policy. Throughout his tenure he was involved in all the big foreign policy decisions; but because they were big they also involved the President and the Secretary, and so Stevenson was almost reduced to defending U.S. interests at the UN. In the main, policy was made in Washington, not in New York. He became frustrated, the mere conveyor of what Washington decided, with little to say about what was decided. He began going to Washington only when invited or when he had something he wanted urgently to discuss—to speak, almost, only when spoken to. As time passed he increasingly withdrew, seeing the President less and less often, until by the time of his death in 1965 those at the heart of the policy-making process felt that his over-all influence on policy was slight—largely indirect and atmospheric.

His position was difficult. The men in the White House close to Kennedy were many years younger than Stevenson. He refused to take part in

White House infighting. McGeorge Bundy, national security adviser to Presidents Kennedy and Johnson, was not only young; he was a Republican and had voted twice for Eisenhower against Stevenson. Secretary Rusk had been a foundation executive and a junior civil servant at the time Stevenson had been a presidential candidate of world renown. Stevenson had seventeen more years' experience of life than President Kennedy himself. Nearly all the instructions Stevenson received from Washington were written by Harlan Cleveland, the Assistant Secretary, or by Cleveland's deputy, Joseph Sisco, or by some lower-ranking Foreign Service officer—all of whom Stevenson regarded as working for him; yet they were giving him his instructions. A study of Department papers shows clearly that the Department kept Stevenson under tight rein. Each of his major speeches at the UN had a large backup file at the Department —drafts written in Washington by Tom Wilson, Schlesinger, Cleveland, Sisco.

The relationship between Stevenson and Kennedy was uncomfortable and sometimes almost painful. The generation gap, old political rivalry, striking personality differences—their relationship was scarred at the outset. Kennedy, Rusk, Ball, and the others tended to think of themselves as living in the world of reality and power. They tended to think of Stevenson as living in the UN dream world. When Kennedy gathered together Rusk and his other advisers in the cabinet room, the meeting was intensely operational—what, for example, should the Administration say publicly about the overthrow of a Latin American government a few hours earlier, and who should say it? Rusk? A Department spokesman? Kennedy? A White House spokesman? Stevenson preferred more philosophical, statesmanlike discussions of long-range problems, such as disarmament, which he considered the ultimate reality that mattered. Sometimes at policy meetings with the President, Stevenson gave those present the impression that he was a whiner, a hand-wringer. Time and again he urged the others to reconsider a decision already taken. That irritated Kennedy. Sometimes in a meeting he would talk about the issue at hand in the discursive, ruminative way he had. Kennedy disliked few things more. He wanted crisp concise statements. Sometimes Stevenson was hastily summoned into the middle of a series of meetings at the White House and arrived ignorant of proposals that had already been discarded; the result was that he irritated Kennedy by seeming to argue for positions already rejected; others at the meeting, being better informed, seemed more on target, less diffuse than he. Stevenson felt himself the equal of everyone in the room. Once, in the White House for a policy meeting, he took Joe Sisco up to the second floor —the President's living quarters—and showed him around almost as if they were in his own apartment. Stevenson seems to have thought Kennedy cold-blooded, even heartless. He gave one friend the impression that he found Robert Kennedy warmer than the President. He sometimes said that President Kennedy treated him with a cruel wit. He thought Kennedy's decisive approach to problems led him to such disasters as the Bay of Pigs and said that one of these decisive and impulsive young men could bumble us into nuclear war. He thought Kennedy too sure of himself. He sometimes talked openly to friends in a derogatory way about the Kennedys. Word of this got back to the Kennedys. The young men around Kennedy, impatient with Stevenson, fell into the habit of talking about him disparagingly. Once President Kennedy pulled McGeorge Bundy up short, saying, "Let's not talk this way about Stevenson; he is indispensable."

President Kennedy himself, more than many around him, appreciated Stevenson's worth. He worked hard to improve their relationship. Every now and then his wife, Jacqueline, who thought Stevenson wonderful, would go up to New York to dine or go to the theater with him (perhaps to escape those very realities in the White House); President Kennedy encouraged her to. He was careful to invite Stevenson to state dinners and social functions at his glittering White House. And when Kennedy gave Stevenson his marching orders—his instructions—Stevenson carried them out with full vigor whether he agreed or not; Kennedy appreciated and respected that. Harlan Cleveland tried in vain to improve the relationship between Kennedy and Stevenson, and after a time Kennedy gave Schlesinger the unenviable task of performing liaison between them.

Courage was an important quality in Adlai Stevenson, especially courage in adversity, as in defeat in 1952 and 1956, or in public humiliation, as at the time of the Bay of Pigs and the Cuban missile crisis, or in the disasters of his private life. He grumbled least when he had the most reason to grumble. He had an inner toughness. He was at his best in adversity. It is odd that President Kennedy, who admired courage above all else, missed this quality in Stevenson most of the time. Perhaps he missed it because Stevenson did not show his best qualities to Kennedy. Once Kennedy caught it—during the Cuban missile crisis Stevenson walked into a meeting with the President and such men as McNamara and Rusk and Bundy. The meeting was deciding to challenge the Soviet Union with a blockade and, in the face of negativism and even hostility, Stevenson argued ardently and ably and at length for a different policy, one that would give up our base at Guantánamo and our missiles in Turkey. Even though Kennedy decided against him, he said privately how greatly he admired Stevenson's courage.

Occasionally Stevenson sent a memorandum to the President on some particular issue, such as disarmament or policy toward the Soviet Union. Some of these papers were disappointing. They offered little that was new, did not really try to direct policy. They resembled the papers on NATO and, many years earlier, the introductions he had delivered at the Chicago Council on Foreign Relations. They were discursive, speculative, almost, as George Ball once said, the work of a dilettante. Once Stevenson saw De Gaulle, and the telegram he sent reporting the interview was soft, imprecise, wandering. Ball saw De Gaulle at about the same time, and his telegram was pointed and operational. Other papers Stevenson sent to the Department were well argued and very much to the point. But then the problem was that his views, however cogent, were unacceptable to the President, the Secretary, and the other men who were running our foreign policy at that time and who considered themselves pragmatists. It is possible, of course, that it was Stevenson, with his preoccupation with such large questions as disarmament and the third world, who was the true pragmatist, the true realist, and that the others were distracted by day-to-day problems of little ultimate importance.

Stevenson's relations with Secretary Rusk were no better than with Kennedy, perhaps worse. The documents make it clear that Rusk and Cleveland were at great pains to say nothing to Stevenson that might offend. They seemed to feel that he was very sensitive; they went out of their way to be nice to him. But they had the power, and he did not, and he chafed in the situation. Early in his term at the UN, Stevenson said of Rusk, "He's just a good technician." But on another occasion, after speaking in a derogatory way of Rusk, he added, "Discount what I say—I wanted to be Secretary of State and he got it." Rusk was almost as inflexible and moralistic as Dulles. With him, the "when-in-doubt policy" was firmness. Stevenson was more flexible, less certain. Stevenson was concerned with such large abstract questions as the future of the third world. Rusk avoided such questions, preferring to deal with the concrete prickly questions of the day. Stevenson once said he found Rusk "wooden." He was shocked when Rusk told him that the hardest decision he, Rusk, ever had to make was to give up a career in the Army. Rusk underrated the UN, Stevenson overrated it.

At the beginning of each meeting of the General Assembly in September, it is customary for Foreign Ministers and sometimes chiefs of state to come to New York; and the session begins with a long "general debate" during which nations state their positions to the world. During this period, too, nations engage in bilateral discussions in private meetings in New York outside the UN itself; the nations usually speak through their Foreign Ministers, who, of course, outrank their representatives to the UN. All this is considered highly important diplomacy. Not once did Rusk upstage Stevenson. When Secretary Dulles had visited the UN, there was no doubt he was boss. But Rusk would say, "I'd like to stay out of the way on UN matters, Stevenson is welcome at the bilaterals, but I'm not going into the General Assembly hall at all—if I do, I have to take the first seat and Stevenson would take second." At no time during Stevenson's tenure did Rusk make a General Assembly speech as other Foreign Ministers did. Either Stevenson or President Kennedy himself spoke for the United States. Rusk wanted it so.

As had happened previously, Stevenson at the UN had difficulties with the so-called Eastern establishment. Carl McGowan said, "The establishment had it in for Stevenson. McCloy and those guys. Forrestal earlier

wouldn't let FDR appoint Stevenson Assistant Secretary of the Navy.
Acheson compounded the problems in 1952. Acheson hated the test ban
treaty. He's hard as nails." George Ball has said, "Acheson took a hard
line on the Soviet Union and thought Stevenson soupy on Africa. Acheson
cared nothing for Africa. Acheson was a Europeanist. I'm considered one,
too. But I am concerned with power, and it happens that power is in the
Western European littoral, not in India. Stevenson felt otherwise. The only
two great wars in history started in the heart of Europe. Acheson and I
feel that Vietnam is on the periphery. So while it may be justified as a
holding action, it's nothing more than that. Stevenson hated to think in
power terms. He liked to think in terms of the requirements of people—
their aspirations—how did you move to fulfill them? The whole third
world. He was early on it. The revolution of rising expectations." Dick
Gardner, while agreeing, has recalled that toward the end of his life Stevenson was "getting fed up with the Mali-Ghana-Guinea crowd." (And yet
Acheson, about two years before he died, after Stevenson died, told Carl
McGowan he had urged Truman to work for Stevenson's nomination for
President in 1960.)

All this leads to a curious view of Stevenson. While Ball and others considered him a non-Europeanist with an exaggerated concern for the underdeveloped countries, Klutznick complained that he couldn't get Stevenson
interested in the economic development of those countries. "I couldn't get
to him. Stevenson wouldn't get involved" in ECOSOC. What, then, was
Stevenson interested in? It is a paradox more apparent than real. Klutznick was talking about his inability to interest Stevenson in specific UN
economic programs. Stevenson was interested in the politics of the underdeveloped countries and the needs of their people. He said time and again
that the problem was not underdeveloped economies but underdeveloped
people, that nothing was possible with underdeveloped people but anything was possible if they developed. He derived his views on anti-
colonialism from America's deepest historic traditions. So, of course, did
Ball, Kennedy, and everyone else. The difference was that Stevenson emphasized the underdeveloped countries more than the Europeanists, who
were, as they admitted, interested in power. Several times while Stevenson
was at the UN the United States was forced to choose between a European
ally and its African colony or former colony, as between Portugal and
Angolan nationalists, and Stevenson always argued for siding with the
colony while the Acheson crowd favored siding with the European ally.
Averell Harriman said, "I was against the Ball-Acheson-McCloy group
that thought NATO was the most important thing on earth and we
couldn't turn against our friends. I was very strongly for a good strong position on Angola in the UN. But I was not quite as anxious to spit in
Salazar's eye as Adlai." (António de Oliveira Salazar, the long-time dictator of Portugal, strongly resisted Angolan independence from Portugal.)
While Harriman's and Stevenson's views usually coincided, somehow

when Harriman put them in words to Kennedy they sounded tougher and more realistic than when Stevenson did, and he was more persuasive to Kennedy than Stevenson. (Harriman was called "The Crocodile" around the Department.)

In the corridors of the UN, Stevenson was effective, particularly with the Africans and Latin Americans, and when he spoke in the Security Council great weight was given his words and he advanced America's cause greatly. But when he reported to the Department he did not always seem at grips with the issues, and his advice to the President did not seem the crisp, hard-driving advice so dear to the hearts of the New Frontiersmen. At such times, and especially toward the end of his life, he seemed almost a great statesman without a constituency, a great personage but nothing more, a ceremonial figure.

And yet at times of great crisis, such as the Cuban missiles, Stevenson displayed an iron nerve and when he spoke in the UN he advocated the American position with an effectiveness no one else could have mustered. President Kennedy praised him highly for it. Stevenson was particularly effective, during his first couple of years at the UN, under President Kennedy. It was later, under President Johnson, during the last two years of his life, that he seemed remote, ineffectual, uninterested.

And something more must be said: his words at the UN moved millions, advanced the American interest, and strengthened the United Nations. Indeed, herein may have lain his greatest contribution. He did not enlarge the role of U. S. Ambassador to the UN, because he could not. But he did play another role, and in the long run perhaps a more important one: that of unofficial UN Ambassador *to* the United States. He gave the UN a standing with the American people that it had never enjoyed before (and has not since). He worked consciously at the task of selling the UN to the American people, and worked at it successfully. It takes nothing away from them to say that not Henry Cabot Lodge or Warren Austin or Arthur Goldberg or any other U.S. representative gave the UN the impact on the American people that Stevenson gave it. For none personified so well before the American people the ideal of world order to which the UN aspired.

3.

Stevenson's approach to diplomacy was personal. Yost has recalled, "There were people at the UN that he simply couldn't stand. It was very hard to get him to see them, even when it was important that he see them." He enjoyed several delegates, including Chief Adebo, Hugh Foot, James Plimsoll, Patrick Dean, Quaison-Sackey, the Argentine and Pakistani representatives. Walking through the UN corridors, he surprised many of these people by calling them by name. He was conscientious about having them to lunch and seeing them in his office. He had one of the qualities of a good physician—he may only give you five minutes of his time, but during those five minutes you think that nothing else in the world matters so much to him as your problem. Marietta Tree thought he was "a good soldier" about going to the endless cocktail parties of diplomatic life. He did not, however, mix with the UN people much privately. He would attend cocktail parties or give dinners for a group of diplomats but these were official, or semi-official, functions. He spent his free time with his own friends. He was fond of saying that diplomacy was composed of equal parts of protocol, alcohol, and Geritol. A member of one rather minor mission to which Stevenson paid assiduous attention called Stevenson "a kind of house mother to the UN" and said his epitaph should read, "Once upon a time there was an American diplomat." Stevenson, told of this, was touched. Stevenson said the Africans lacked parliamentary training and he tried to help them. This did not go unnoticed. Robert Kennedy said, "President Kennedy always thought he did a good job of keeping people happy at the UN. He did not make mistakes. He represented in an articulate way the United States in foreign eyes as well as could be. He was the best Ambassador we could have had there."

Some of Stevenson's Chicago-Lake Forest friends felt he neglected them after he went to the UN. He disliked losing friends but wished they could understand pressures of work which made him give them up. He continued to see Jim Oates, by now living in New York himself. Not often, but, Oates said, "frequently enough so I didn't feel we were getting separated." He saw Steve Hord occasionally, and Hord thought he was "nervous and had trouble quieting down" during these last years. Jane Dick thought he was lonely in New York. She thought it was loneliness that made him attend so many parties and travel so much to other countries. Carl McGowan, however, thought Stevenson enjoyed being at the UN. "He'd rather have done that than practice law on LaSalle Street or the other alternatives available. He was a Wilsonian and so he loved the UN and wanted it to succeed." Archibald MacLeish saw a lot of Stevenson in New York. "His life was intensely social and active," MacLeish once said. "He used to get fed up with it. Every now and then we'd get an appeal to come in [from Conway, in the Berkshires]. Sometimes he'd have a party for us, sometimes we'd see him alone. Once he urged us to come on a Sunday afternoon for supper. He said he was too tired to hold his head up. We found his secretary had invited Burton and Liz. It was a wonderful evening. Adlai came in, so tired he could hardly sit up. He immediately took the center of the stage and talked till eleven-thirty, completely relaxed, lying back, laughing his head off. He rejoiced in the company of pretty women." He rejoiced less in solitary pursuits. The last time Stevenson visited MacLeish in Antigua, John and Jane Gunther were there. One evening Gunther and MacLeish talked for a long time about books, and Stevenson was listening and finally said, "My God, what an ignoramus I am—I

haven't read one of those you've been talking about for the last fifteen
minutes."

Adlai III once said, "He was always grumbling, though less as Governor
—I think he liked being Governor best of all. At the UN you'd hear him
say, 'Oh, God, this is where I came in.' He'd groan about the parties he
had to go to—and go to more than he really had to. He would complain
about how lonely he was—no family around. But it was good for him to
be in New York rather than Washington. In New York he was number
one. He had good times there. He had friends around, and he liked that."

Often Stevenson took one of his sons to UN receptions. John Fell
recalled, "He always wanted us to go with him. Usually I thought it was
sort of a bore." He discussed his prospects for remarrying with them. John
Fell said, "All three of us would be there and he would bring it up—these
girls—he would jokingly poll us; which one would we vote for. We and
he disagreed. I'd say that Alicia was great. Borden and Ad would say
Ruthie Field. Dad would say that Marietta was awful nice. Somehow I
never thought he was going to remarry." Lifelong he was interested in,
affectionate toward, and attractive to women. Lifelong, too, he was interested in the lives of the daughters of his friends, such as Marietta's daughter Frankie, Ruth Field's daughter Fiona, Kay Graham's daughter Lally,
Martin's daughter Cindy, Dutch Smith's daughter Adele, and many others.
"They all felt he was concerned—and he was," Adlai III said.

In fact, Benton thought all of Stevenson's closest friends were women.
Schlesinger, too, had the impression that Stevenson's best friends in New
York during the UN years were women. Mrs. Welling once said, "There
were lots of women crazy about him but not he, because of his experience
with Ellen. It would make anybody gunshy." He kept himself surrounded
with people. Mrs. Welling once visited him for a week at 42A in the Waldorf and did not see him alone "for one second."

His sons had the impression that he hoped to marry Marietta Tree.
Marietta, who has refused to discuss this, once said, "He used to talk all
the time about getting married. He'd read off the list of a dozen names of
women and give the arguments for and against each one. He called it his
harem. I used to tell him, 'You're not going to go through that again, it's
such a bore.' He used to tell me what other women said to him—and I
never asked what he did to provoke the sentiments. He couldn't believe he
was attractive to women. He was, though." His letters to Marietta contained lyric descriptions of scenery, poems, and personal notes as well as
UN issues. They were *written,* in a writer's sense of the word. He had a
rather arch style at times, writing that "we repaired" to the Red and Green
Rooms after dinner at the White House. In letters, Stevenson sent
Marietta the same poem three times, and each time he underlined the
same last line: "Humankind cannot bear very much reality." He was close
to Marietta's daughter Frankie. He once disapproved of a boy friend of

Frankie's and went to some lengths trying to get him transferred out of the country.

He encouraged Marietta to deliver public speeches. "I was afraid. I thought I just couldn't do it. The first thirty or fifty times I couldn't eat beforehand, and the palms of my hands sweat. He was terribly good about getting people to do things. He sent me to a meeting of the UN Commission on Human Rights and said, 'Of course you can do it.' After about a year he heard me make a speech and wrote me a letter about it." The letter said, "M—Excellent. And for one so young and beautiful! Its not fair that you could have so many talents and most so few. I protest—on behalf of the common man! But I bow humbly when I hear how much you have given—and without any help or counsel from me! But 1) the word is 'administer'—not 'administrate.' 2) With larger type could you forgo the glasses? Or are they a 'property' to reduce dazzle?" Marietta once said, "He forced people to develop. That was one of his great contributions. He was marvelous to me. He gently pressed me to do things that I never had known I could do before, like organizing an office and raising money."

Mrs. Ives wanted him to marry Ruth Field. "She played tennis, she liked to shoot, she was interested in him for himself, and was interested in politics, she had money. He liked his rich friends. So do we all." Adlai III said that Ruth Field was not a "romantic figure" in Stevenson's life but would have made the best wife for him. "She was devoted to Dad, really devoted." Stevenson became deeply involved in her personal family problems as well as with the Field Foundation. She remained loyal to him after his death, contributing generously to the Adlai Stevenson Institute. Mrs. Field believed that "he was a man who existed because he lived his life in compartments. Mine was a personal relationship. He visited me in Maine and South Carolina. He would dine here alone or I would dine with him alone. Once I remember he dropped off to sleep on my sofa. It wasn't very flattering to me but it was what I wanted for him."

Stevenson's private secretary at the UN, Roxane Eberlein, has recalled that he liked to spend quiet weekends at Ruth Field's estate on Long Island, playing tennis and resting. Sometimes he went upstate to Mary Lasker's place at Amenia, New York, and sometimes to Francis Plimpton's home. Ruth Field thought him "remarkably dangerous" with a gun and recalled an occasion when he went hunting and the gamekeeper screamed a warning at him. Mrs. Field thought his parents had handled him well at the time when, as a child, he had accidentally killed another child, else he would not have been so casual with a gun. He told her, "I think you know me better than anybody." She said, "He was a deeply insecure person. He was deeply distressed about the failure of his marriage. On several occasions he said, 'I *was* a good husband.' Twice he asked, 'Could I be a good husband? Could I? Tell me.'" Why did he not remarry? Mrs. Field said, "He suggested it about several persons, including me. I think he never even hinted at marriage with the person he was talking to unless he was pretty darned sure that he wouldn't be taken up on it. He was much more lonely than people thought. I loved him very much. I'm a truncated person myself. I'm not in good shape, I have a thin veneer. He knew he'd be bored by constant association with any one person, and yet he was too romantic to accept the idea of a 'compartmentalized' marriage —it wouldn't fit that tantalizing dream of 'being a good husband.' Once he asked me. I told him he kept things compartmentalized. He said, 'No, I want it all.' " He kept a picture of Ruth Field on his desk.

He kept in almost constant touch with Barbara Ward. Once Stevenson, at the last minute, and at Barbara Ward's suggestion, inserted into a speech an endorsement of a new international monetary unit only to learn on the same day the President had said he opposed it. It was left to Fritchey to explain it away to the press. Fritchey once said, "Whenever he exceeded instructions, it was her doing." Miss Ward once called him "an intelligent layman" in economics. "He had an intuitive grasp of the areas where the needs of the economy and public policy meet. He was basically pre-Keynesian. He came around to it, though. Initially he was very skeptical. He came around before Walter Heller had sold it to President Kennedy, a little ahead of U.S. official policy. His economics were very conservative by instinct but by intelligence very liberal."

Stevenson enjoyed taking Jacqueline Kennedy to dinner or the theater. For a time he saw Joan Fontaine, the actress, and the newspapers made much of it, possibly influenced by a theatrical press agent; once he gave her a Tiffany box which contained only a lapel pin—a shoe with a hole in it—from the 1952 campaign. He saw and corresponded warmly with Evelyn Houston of California and Babs Caulkins of New York. That first spring at the UN, Suzie Zurcher broke off her relationship with him, and on April 6 he sent her a longhand note saying he was just back from exhausting meetings in Washington, he feared his mind had wandered far from NATO but never farther than Chicago and her, he wanted to thank her and say he had been preoccupied of late but was grateful to her for not having treated him cruelly, and "now to sleep with the help of God and seconal." It was one of his few relationships with women that came to a clean break.

He went to a great many parties, sometimes three or four in one evening. Barbara Ward thought it was a device for self-protection. His friend Beth Currie remarked that, when he arrived at a party to which he was looking forward with pleasure, he entered the room "like a ship under full sail"—radiated an extraordinary magnetism, seemed taller than he really was, looked about him with eyes so bottomlessly blue they were almost purple; then took charge, looked around the room, gathered everyone in it and held them all "in the palm of his hand. He could do anything he liked when he was in this mood. To see how he controlled a multifaceted conversation was fascinating. It went exactly where he wanted it to. He could make you feel that you were absolutely alone with him in a room full of people."

He saw Bill Benton frequently and played tennis and went to the theater and the River Club with him. Soon Stevenson joined the River Club, a fashionable and expensive one not far from the UN overlooking the East River; he used it for tennis and business lunches. Because of his weight he slowed down on the tennis court, but Benton remembered always losing the first set to him before his weight began to tell—"he was a terrific tennis player, big belly and all, particularly at getting up to the net." Once Stevenson met Huntington Hartford, a somewhat flamboyant financier and art patron, and was impressed. Marietta Tree commented, "That house in Bloomington explains so much. He really was a small-town boy. He *would* be impressed by Huntington Hartford, by a name like that. Sometimes you wondered if he really did know what was important."

When Stevenson went to Washington he usually stayed with the Magnusons, sometimes at the Metropolitan Club. In Washington he led a "frenetic" social life, John Steele once observed. Steele thought he looked "haggard." He was met at the airport by a small car from the Department —not one of the big Cadillacs the Secretary and Undersecretaries used. "Then he would hit the Georgetown circuit," Steele said. Mrs. Magnuson said that the last few times he visited her he said repeatedly, "I'm so tired all the time." And yet, she recalled, "He'd go chasing around to a party if someone called him." If the Magnusons were away he simply used their house—he had a key. Sometimes visiting Mrs. Magnuson during a crisis, he would bemoan the trouble, rub his face, complain that he could get no sleep for press of work. "I don't think he ever took things easily. Nothing rolled off his shoulders." Yet, like many others, she later enjoyed recalling anecdotes about him. He brightened her life.

Some years earlier, in 1950, Stevenson had told T. S. Matthews, "The pace does not change, nor do I propose to do anything to change it. If I did I might be unhappy, lonesome—even indiscreet." The feeling that he dared not change his pace may have had something to do with his almost frantic social life in New York. There he adopted an Eastern crowd not unlike the Lake Forest crowd of his early years as a young lawyer—people with money, some of them interested in public questions, all living well. The Easterners had more leverage on national and international affairs than the Lake Foresters, who were more closely devoted to business or the law. The Easterners were closer to government and more influential on it —compare Mary Lasker and Jane Dick, Tom Finletter and Dutch Smith. More of the Easterners were Democrats. But they were essentially the same sort of people.

George Ball felt that during the UN years Stevenson "sort of went to seed." He said Stevenson "used" his rich friends, going on their yachts and staying at their villas, even thought he felt no respect for some of them. Once on a cruise Stevenson said to Ball, "Let's get off this God damned yacht and go somewhere—I can't stand it." Ball has said, "This business of living in New York with all these middle-aged women—all of them very rich—some of them public figures—he loved the fact that he couldn't walk through the streets of New York without being recognized. He loved the fact that he got great adulation from very rich women. That was his destruction. I had a funny sense about Adlai. It was symbolic. He—well, you don't get lean and healthy from adulation—you get overweight and despairing. There was a certain self-destruction in Adlai's early death. I used to tease him about it a little—tell him he was letting himself go because he really didn't have it any longer. And he knew it was a very phony life—the UN—divorced from the reality of politics—living in the uncritical adulation of these women all the time—adulation largely on the part of people that didn't count—and not being where the real decisions were being made. It was a study in futility. Yet he couldn't break free of it. He had no alternatives. What he really needed was a wife to say to him, 'Stop overdramatizing yourself' or 'Your constant complaining about being put upon is getting tiresome,' or even 'Your speech last night went on forever. When will you ever learn when to stop?'"

He was, until near the end, a light drinker but a heavy eater. Marietta Tree said, "He sneaked food like an alcoholic and then pretended he didn't know he'd done it." He doted on his grandchildren. "He talked about them incessantly, he had their pictures around, he came back here to see them, but it could wear thin," Adlai III said. "They were too young for him to be with long." Adlai III and Nancy saw Stevenson infrequently in New York, usually at breakfast, but Stevenson often went out to Chicago and Libertyville for a long weekend, sometimes taking Marietta Tree or Barbara Ward with him, and Adlai III and Nancy would visit them, with the children. Stevenson fostered Adlai III's entry into politics. Adlai III and his family lived in the house in Libertyville summers, and sometimes Stevenson joined them there. "The trip was almost always cut short by some crisis," Adlai III recalled. The crises came from the world and from within. "He'd come out and bask in the sun. Go around almost naked, play a lot of tennis. He'd walk, pick up fallen limbs, taking care of his beloved trees, walk the grounds with Frank [the caretaker], keep an eye on the place. He often talked about coming back to Libertyville. Then he'd get there, relax the first day or two, sleep well—but soon he'd get restless. He'd show irritability over little things, the farm, something the kids would do, and soon wonder aloud what was going on in New York and Washington, and then take the next plane back. His friends weren't there any more"—that is, were not in Libertyville and Lake Forest. "He enjoyed seeing them, but they were not part of his life any more. They weren't the people he could discuss the problems of the world with. The grandchildren and the farm were the big attraction. But after a few days, he had had enough. He could relax at Desbarats, sun-bathe, take canoe trips, but by Desbarats standards he was not relaxing. He always wanted

to take a trip or play tennis, or do something, running everybody ragged."
Sometimes he stayed with Adlai III and Nancy after they bought a house
on the Near North Side of Chicago, the neighborhood where Stevenson
had started his own career and had lived for a time with Ellen. Marietta
Tree once said, "He adored going to Libertyville and sitting in the shade
but he really would have died doing that for long—he couldn't stand it."

After Stevenson died, Adlai III found an envelope in the drawer of a
desk beside his father's bed in 42A in the Waldorf. It was the stationery of
the U. S. Mission to the UN. On it Stevenson had written in longhand:
"Beauty—Tender Bits." Inside was a collection of bits of poetry and prose
quotations on love by various writers, most of them sent to Stevenson by
the women in his life, all sentimental. As Adlai III saw it, "He liked to
have these bits of love around him." It was, sadly, love at arms' length,
quotations on love by other writers sent through the mail. He led a lonely
life high in the Waldorf Towers.

4.

President Kennedy had been inaugurated on Friday, January 20, and
Stevenson sworn into office on Saturday. On Monday, January 23, in New
York, Stevenson took charge of the United States Mission to the UN and
at noon he presented his credentials to Secretary General Dag Hammarskjold in the Secretariat building. After the ceremony they had a long private talk in Hammarskjold's office. Most of the conversation dealt with the
Congo, at that time the most serious crisis before the UN. It would continue to occupy Stevenson's attention—as well as President Kennedy's—
for many months.

The Congo, that great heart of Africa, had become independent of Belgium the previous June 30, in 1960. On that occasion, in the presence of
the King of the Belgians, the Congo's first Prime Minister, Patrice
Lumumba, a former postal clerk and an African nationalist, had delivered
a blistering speech denouncing the colonial legacy of "atrocious sufferings"
and "humiliating bondage," filled with "ironies, insults, blows which we
had to endure morning, noon, and night because we were 'Negroes.'"
Westerners and President Joseph Kasavubu were shocked. Within a few
days the new state was in chaos. Tribal violence had begun, the Congolese
troops had mutinied against their Belgian officers, terror-stricken refugees had begun streaming over the Congo's borders, and on July 9 against
the wishes of the Congo government Belgian paratroopers began flying
back to restore order and protect Belgian lives.

President Moise Tshombe of the province of Katanga proclaimed Katanga independent, in part an act of angry nationalism; in part a political
move to preserve the mineral wealth of Katanga, the lives of the Belgian
residents, and the interests of foreign investors in Union Minière du Haut-

Katanga (UMHK), a powerful mining company which paid some $60 million in taxes to the Belgian government in 1959 alone.

Lumumba asked the United States to intervene militarily because of Belgian "aggression" and Belgian support of the Katangan secession. President Eisenhower advised him to seek UN help. Lumumba thereupon asked help from Khrushchev, who sent military equipment and several hundred Russian "technicians." On July 14 the UN voted to send an international force to the Congo to assist the Congolese Central Government and called upon Belgium to withdraw its troops.

Around the world between 1945 and 1962 some thirty-eight wars occurred, with an average duration of 5.8 years, but never before 1960, except in Korea, had the UN authorized peace-keeping missions involving military personnel for other than observation or police functions. Now it sent nearly 20,000 troops from some thirty different countries. Soon Lumumba and Dag Hammarskjold disagreed over the proper role of the UN force in the Congo. Lumumba sought more Soviet help to move against the Katangan secessionist, Tshombe. This put him in opposition to his more conservative President, Kasavubu. In September, Kasavubu dismissed Lumumba and appointed Joseph Ileo as the new Prime Minister. Lumumba went through the gesture of dismissing Kasavubu in turn but failed, and Colonel Joseph Mobutu, Chief of Staff of the new Congolese National Army, arrested Lumumba and moved for power himself.

With their own man, Lumumba, in jail, the Soviets attacked Secretary General Hammarskjold heavily. In September, Khrushchev, visiting New York, called upon Hammarskjold to resign, charged that he had been guilty of "arbitrary and lawless behavior" in carrying out his Congo mandate, said he had supported the "colonialists," and demanded that the one-man Secretary General be replaced by a three-man secretariat, the famous "troika," one man representing the Communist camp, one the Western camp, and one the neutralists, each with a veto. Thus by the time Stevenson reached the United Nations the Congo was in chaos, with the pro-Western Kasavubu government in Leopoldville, the pro-Soviet Lumumba in jail, the pro-Belgian secessionists of Tshombe in Elisabethville, and yet another secessionist group led by Antoine Gizenga in Stanleyville. And in New York the Soviet Union was continuing to use the Congo as a weapon against the UN itself.

In the Congo the UN force operated in a political vacuum under the greatest difficulties. In Washington and other capitals diplomats were deeply concerned lest the Congo explode in a full-scale confrontation between the Soviet Union and the United States. So urgent was the situation that Secretary Rusk met on inauguration day with the United Kingdom Ambassadors to the United States and to the UN. Rusk thought continued efforts must be made to solve the Congo problem through the UN. The UN operations should be strengthened. The UN might have to run the

Congo behind a Congolese mask. President Kennedy ordered a prompt restudy of the entire Congo problem.

Presenting his credentials, Stevenson found Hammarskjold more optimistic about the Congo than he had expected. He thought that a moratorium on cold war rhetoric for two or three months could save the Congo. It was hard to get facts. Hammarskjold thought little of Gizenga. But Lumumba, he thought, was a man of authority, shrewd, able, one to reckon with.

On the very day that Stevenson took over the Mission, President Kwame Nkrumah of the Republic of Ghana wrote to Stevenson appealing to him to "use your good offices" to "secure the immediate release of Mr. Lumumba," who, he said, symbolized to Africans "the will of the Congolese people for freedom and independence." And, "We in Africa are very confident of the contribution that you can personally make." Stevenson replied on February 6, after policy lines had been laid down inside the United States Government, saying he was "touched and honored" by Nkrumah's letter, saying the United States was trying to find the best way to avoid civil war and restore unity and peace in the Congo, but avoiding the question of Lumumba's release. "I will always look to *you* especially for enlightenment and constructive leadership in the complex affairs of emerging Africa." He closed with personal messages.

Stevenson received briefings on the Congo, Laos, and other matters from UN officials and began his weary round of protocol calls on other nations' UN representatives. Noyes gave him a list of topics the Department wanted him to discuss with Hammarskjold—the Congo, Laos, New Guinea, South Africa, Soviet nationals in the Secretariat, and outer space.

Stevenson lunched with Hammarskjold on Wednesday, January 25, and talked with him for three hours. After the talk he dictated notes, and a telegram was drafted from them and sent to Washington next day. Hammarskjold had talked at length about the resumed session of the General Assembly due to begin in March. On the Congo, he considered a session of the Security Council early the next week inevitable and also useless. The "Casablanca Powers"—Morocco, United Arab Republic (U.A.R.— Egypt), Guinea, Mali, the Algerian Provisional Government, Libya, Ceylon, and Ghana—had met at Casablanca in January and adopted a series of resolutions critical of UN actions in the Congo. They supported the Stanleyville regime of Gizenga as the true successor to Lumumba and had resolved to withdraw their troops from the UN force in the Congo. Hammarskjold would have to replace them. The Casablanca Powers would demand a Security Council meeting and attack Hammarskjold. Hammarskjold urged the United States to keep out of the discussion and let the small powers defend him. Both the United States and Russia would be well advised to fade from the Congo picture, he thought. They could never agree formally. "In darkness both sides could climb down."

Yet he did not consider the situation hopeless, for by now the Russians

realized they could not have their way in the Congo, since the West was
still strong in Africa. Hammarskjold advised Stevenson never to try to
force the Russians to publicly relinquish power or prestige positions.
Rather, he thought, a quiet direct approach to Khrushchev on a cold war
truce in the Congo might be profitable. Hammarskjold discerned an effort
to get the UN out of the Congo and hoped for "a strenuous diplomatic
effort" by the United States to keep it there.

Stevenson reported all this and more in his first long substantive telegrams to the Department. On Thursday morning, January 26, he attended
the first meeting of the Kennedy Cabinet. On the agenda were the international situation by Rusk, the domestic economy by Walter Heller, and the
budget by Dave Bell; but Stevenson had written out in longhand a great
many notes from which he spoke. Rusk spoke first, a dull tour of the horizon, followed by Stevenson. His notes began, "As senior—let me say
briefly what I know is in the hearts of all of us as we meet here today for
the first time. We congratulate you—honored to serve with you. We
pledge you our loyalty and our labor to the end that your administration
will meet the great demands and solve the staggering problems that
confront our country and you as its President." With his sense of history
he signed that first page of notes "AES." There followed six pages on "the
problems I find" at the UN. On the Congo, he followed the Hammarskjold
line. On Laos, he suggested a neutralist government. At the UN itself, he
said, the U.S. position had deteriorated because of the rise of new nations,
the rise of Soviet power and prestige, and "our own mistakes and unpopular positions"—military emphasis, intolerance of neutralism, support
for colonialism, China policy, preoccupation with the cold war when most
uncommitted peoples were more interested in development. The UN itself
was bankrupt, the Secretary General was under heavy attack. Often the
new nations behaved irresponsibly. They were suspicious of the West and
impressed by Soviet achievements. We must recapture their confidence.
Stevenson's speech was brief, eloquent, and moving, and Fred Dutton
thought Stevenson stole the show from everyone but President Kennedy.

In New York the next day, Friday, January 27, Stevenson held his first
press conference. In his opening remarks he called for an end to name
calling and propaganda rhetoric. (In the months to come Stevenson himself would violate this canon.) He said we wanted to end, not fight, the
cold war at the UN. We would not try to impose our system on others but
favored freedom and self-determination for all peoples. We viewed "with
satisfaction" the revolutionary independence of former colonial powers.
Together with the United Kingdom and France, we wanted an orderly
transition to self-government. Hence we regretted deeply the "disaster that
has befallen the Congo." He spoke of economic development, of "quiet diplomacy" at the UN, and of the "integrity of the office" of the Secretary
General. He invited questions, but answered them more carefully and

evasively than he had at press conferences when he was a candidate for office.

5.

On Monday morning, January 30, Stevenson and Plimpton called on Ambassador Zorin of the Soviet Union. Stevenson expressed hope for improved relations and an end to public acrimony. Zorin said his government would drop a complaint against U.S. overflights of the U.S.S.R. and proposed that the United States drop the items on Hungary and Tibet. Stevenson said the United States had not cosponsored the Tibet item—Zorin said it had influenced the cosponsors—but said he was sure the Department would want to consider his suggestion. Stevenson emphasized the "vigor and seriousness" with which the new Administration was tackling disarmament and suggested the U.S.S.R. also review its positions, especially on controls and inspection. Zorin wanted to make it clear he was talking about "general and complete disarmament," not arms control. Prospects for agreement at the resumed Assembly would be good if the United States discarded its previous proposals and accepted a draft resolution proposed by neutrals. The Russians could support this resolution. Stevenson said merely that agreement on such matters was more attainable through private exchanges than public debate. Zorin agreed.

On the Congo, Stevenson said that "speaking personally"—diplomatic language to make it clear he was not speaking under official government instruction—he believed the United States would favor early establishment of constitutional government, prohibition of assistance except for the UN, and full support for the Secretary General's efforts. Zorin said that he too would welcome a return to legal government, particularly by Lumumba, and said that the only outside interference was coming from Belgium. The Soviets were interested in obtaining a new embassy in New York and Stevenson offered to help. "My general impression," he reported, "was that Zorin clearly reflects [the] desire of his Government to establish more friendly relations between us. But in his remarks Zorin gave no indication of softening of Soviet views on either disarmament or Congo."

In response to President Kennedy's request for a review of Congo policy, Joe Sisco of IO had drafted a new United States policy paper. The paper said that at present events were drifting toward fragmentation in the Congo that would solidify Gizenga's control over Orientale Province, turn that area into a Communist stronghold, and permit the expansion of Communism to other parts of the Congo. Tshombe was forced to rely increasingly on Belgian help. The ineptness of the Kasavubu-Mobutu leadership together with the increase of open Belgian activity had resulted in identifying United States policy with the colonialists. This had hurt us in Africa and the world generally. The impending withdrawal of troops would weaken the UN force. The UN itself might be seriously damaged. Khrushchev's attacks might bring down Hammarskjold. The paper suggested, therefore, that the United States seek a new broader Congo mandate from the UN, one that would provide for the establishment of a broadly based Congolese government including all principal Congolese political elements. Stevenson suggested that that position—a government including all Congolese political elements—be regarded as a fallback position, to be taken only after we had failed in efforts to use our influence with the Belgians, Kasavubu, and others to establish a middle-of-the-road government under Ileo. IO adopted his suggestion, Secretary Rusk had approved the paper, and by January 31, IO planned to submit it to the President within the next twenty-four hours.

That same day Stevenson talked to Hammarskjold, then, at 4:35 P.M., telephoned Cleveland in Washington. He said Hammarskjold believed that the real difficulty was "the ANC mob"—the armed remnants of the Congolese Army—and it had to be controlled. Hammarskjold wanted a Kasavubu government with Ileo as Prime Minister. Only after the Congo forces had been controlled and the Ileo government established should all political prisoners, including Lumumba, be released. Parliament should be called later. After reporting this, Stevenson told Cleveland he thought he should ask the President for a "discretionary document"—one that would leave him room for maneuver in negotiating the composition of the proposed new Congolese government.

IO made final changes and sent the paper to the President. Woodruff Wallner of IO sent Stevenson a copy on February 1. The revised paper proposed that the United States, behind the Afro-Asians, seek a new Congo mandate from the UN, giving it authority to bring all military elements in the Congo under control, undertake a training program for Congolese troops, step up efforts to prevent outside assistance, and use force if necessary to insure military neutralization of the Congo. The United States would press Kasavubu to establish as soon as possible a middle-of-the-road government with Ileo as Prime Minister. If that failed the United States, as a fallback, would support the establishment of a broadly based Congolese government which would include Lumumba elements but not Lumumba himself as Prime Minister. Thus had Stevenson influenced policy. One of the principal purposes of the new policy was to gain for the United States support of world opinion, especially Afro-Asian. (Some in the Pentagon and CIA argued for a different policy, one of encouraging the Mobutu forces under Kasavubu to attack Lumumba-controlled forces and Tshombe's separatist Katanga. Stevenson argued that such a policy would result in endless civil war with the real possibility of outside intervention and wider crisis. So, characteristically, did he seek a political, not a military, solution.)

Stevenson and Yost saw Hammarskjold that afternoon to discuss the

Department's paper. Stevenson said that the Department's thinking was moving more or less parallel with that of Hammarskjold, though a final decision by the President had not yet been taken. Hammarskjold unfolded an elaborate Congo scenario which followed the United States policy paper rather closely. Congo policy was being made. It seems clear that Stevenson was indeed exerting influence.

On February 1, Chiang Kai-shek sent a letter to President Kennedy on U.S.-Formosa relations and Moscow-Peking relations. The Kennedy administration's review of the China problem began. It would figure importantly in Stevenson's work.

On that February 1, a Wednesday, Stevenson made his first appearance in the Security Council. The U.K. representative, Sir Patrick Dean, president that month, welcomed Stevenson to the Council, saying, "He is, happily, so distinguished that it would be quite superfluous for me to remind members of the Council of the high qualities of intelligence and character and of the wide experience of world affairs which he brings to his important post." There followed an extraordinary outpouring of praise for Stevenson from other Council members, including the representatives of France, China, Chile, Ecuador, the Soviet Union, Liberia, United Arab Republic, Ceylon, and Turkey; and Ambassador Zorin of Russia expressed hope for agreement among the permanent members, including the United States and Soviet Union.

Stevenson, responding, said, "I deeply appreciate, Mr. President, the kind words and good wishes of you and of my colleagues," and used his old joke, "I have sometimes said that flattery is all right, Mr. President, if you do not inhale," then set forth principles which guided the United States. As "the oldest anti-colonial power," the United States favored freedom and self-determination for all peoples. It sought no military allies among them nor wished to impose its system on them. It hoped the transition from colonialism to freedom could be orderly and peaceful. "And we applaud the efforts of this Council to assist the orderly transition in the Congo through the Secretary General." Equally important was the promotion of economic development. The United States would help. The United States was "giving its most earnest attention to the impasse over disarmament." Finally, he said, the UN must be "properly financed," "the integrity of the office of the Secretary General and of the Secretariat must be preserved," and members should debate freely but avoid "useless recrimination."

The President approved the new Congo policy. Now the United States was closely aligned with the Hammarskjold policy. The United Kingdom disagreed with a part of it—the effort to neutralize the Congolese Army. So did France.

The Cabinet met in Washington on February 2. It dealt mainly with congressional relations and anti-recession measures, and Stevenson did not attend. That evening Stevenson gave his first large diplomatic dinner. The guests were the representatives of Latin American states, together with members of the U. S. Mission. Mrs. Ives was Stevenson's hostess.

Shortly, the Security Council met on the Congo. The Casablanca Powers presented their views and the Russian representative denounced the Secretary General and Belgian "aggression." Stevenson did not speak. Instead, on February 3, he and his subordinates launched a quiet diplomatic offensive in the corridors and embassies, trying to enlist support for U.S. Congo policy. On February 3 senior officers of the Mission called on nineteen delegations to outline U.S. policy. Stevenson telephoned the U.K. and the French. The U.K. was favorably disposed, the French raised vigorous objections. Yost talked to the Moroccans, the Tunisians, the Congolese. Stevenson called on the Indian and the Ghana chargés, both of whom demanded the release of Lumumba. Stevenson saw two Nigerians. Their views seemed in substantial conformity with the U.S. views and they seemed willing to take the initiative. They said Ethiopia, Sudan, and Tunisia were behind them and they thought Senegal would be helpful. Stevenson asked about the possibility of getting support from Ghana and Guinea. They said Nkrumah was a practical politician and would go in the direction the winds were blowing. If Nigeria took the lead and received backing, Ghana would move in the same direction, and then Guinea would pose no problem.

Day after day the consultations continued. On February 7 a Nigerian told a Mission officer that the Ghana position on Lumumba had shifted in the past twenty-four hours away from complete support. By this time various delegations were beginning to receive instructions from their home offices. Hammarskjold informed Stevenson that the Indians seemed prepared to follow procedures that Hammarskjold recommended. Persuading the Nigerians and Indians to agree to the general lines of U.S. policy was a diplomatic victory. Previously they had often turned up on the Soviet side. When Ambassador Zorin of Russia learned of it, he was shocked.

Jha of India told Stevenson he was working on a Congo resolution with the Casablanca group; when they had a draft, they would seek agreement from the United States and the U.S.S.R. The Nigerians were becoming increasingly important. On February 8, Stevenson and Yost called on them and discussed a resolution they might introduce. The Casablanca group was to meet on February 9. As the days passed, activity became increasingly intense. What hurried Stevenson and his colleagues was fear that the Congo would break up and some of the small states resulting would come under the influence of the U.S.S.R. or the United Arab Republic, tearing to pieces the whole center of Africa.

In the end they succeeded beyond their wildest hopes—the Congo remained united and its own armed forces resumed control. The episode was an example of what is often the hidden purpose of foreign policy—to prevent something from happening. (The Cuban missile crisis and the

Dominican intervention of 1965 were other examples.) But in February of 1961, when Stevenson was undergoing this baptism of fire, the outlook was bleak.

6.

Other problems claimed Stevenson's attention, including the troika, the Soviet proposal to replace the Secretary General with a three-man board. As the United Kingdom and United States saw it, this would transform the UN into an instrument of Soviet policy or, failing that, destroy it. On February 4, Stevenson and his colleagues met with Arthur Dean and John J. McCloy on how to handle the question of disarmament at the resumed General Assembly. The Soviets had proposed a special General Assembly devoted exclusively to disarmament. The United States opposed this and favored negotiations with a limited number of parties.

Despite these activities, Stevenson still found time for social life. On February 4 he was host at his own sixty-first birthday party at 42A in the Waldorf and the guest list included old friends from both his private and his political lives. As a birthday gift, Ambassador Zorin sent him a book of reproductions of paintings in the Hermitage, the great art museum in Leningrad, together with an assortment of wines and vodka and a note, "I wish you good health, many years to live as well as successes in your activity in the interests of strengthening the universal peace." Alicia Patterson and Jack Arvey sent Stevenson birthday telegrams. Carl McGowan told his wife after the party, "I'm glad we came, because he won't be here long. If word of this gets back to Kennedy, he'll cut off his head." At the party Stevenson had been belittling Kennedy and bemoaning his own fate. "He kept saying, 'It won't work, I'm on the wrong end of the telephone, I don't know why I took this job, it was a terrible idea,' all that sort of thing." The talk did get back to Kennedy, and Kennedy said, in effect, "Why can't Stevenson be patient? Why does he have to talk this way? He has a great contribution to make to the country and to the Administration."

Stevenson asked authorization from the Department to urge the Nigerians to take the lead in developing a Congo resolution for submission to the Security Council. The Department approved, and on February 7 and 8, Stevenson and Yost met with the Nigerians. (The United States often persuaded a friendly nation to introduce a resolution which the United States wanted adopted, rather than introduce it itself.) On February 6, Hammarskjold had told Stevenson he was trying to persuade the radical Africans, who were preoccupied with Lumumba, that the first essential step was to restore order by removing the Congolese armed forces from politics. Until that was done, conciliation was impossible. Lumumba had no valid role to play until the conciliation stage was reached. Stevenson asked about tactics in the Security Council. Hammarskjold said the United

States should allow the radical Africans to speak first, then encourage responsible Africans, starting with Nigeria, to speak out. He thought that after two days of this the time would be ripe for the United States to speak on Thursday, February 9. Stevenson called on Zorin and Morozov of the U.S.S.R. and outlined the U.S. approach to the Congo. Zorin doubted it would work and said that immediate elimination from the Congo of all Belgian influence was a necessary first step for pacification.

John J. McCloy had lunch with Ambassador Menshikov and told him that President Kennedy was sincere in his desire for a nuclear test-ban agreement, provided it contained reasonable safeguards, and that the U.S. disarmament program was not yet ready. Menshikov said Stevenson had indicated the United States might make new concessions in connection with the test ban. McCloy did not think this could be true. Menshikov said that Stevenson had said one thing and Secretary Rusk another. McCloy suggested he ask Rusk.

The Chinese Embassy asked the State Department to arrange a meeting between Stevenson and Ambassador T. F. Tsiang, who was going home for consultation. The Department tried to postpone the meeting. But in New York, Tsiang insisted and succeeded in seeing Stevenson on February 10. Tsiang said that Stevenson's testimony before the Senate Foreign Relations Committee had given rise to the feeling in Formosa that Stevenson was being "defeatist" on preventing the admission of Peking China to the UN. Stevenson said it was necessary to face the facts, no matter how unpleasant, and if one calculated that it was impossible to win he should be prepared to retreat without falling into disarray. Stevenson said it was "obvious" to him that the votes for refusing admission were going down steadily year by year and it was "only a matter of time" before present strategy would fail. Was there any other way to deal with the question—to salvage something out of defeat? Tsiang asked if he had in mind the two-China approach. Stevenson said that, personally, he thought this was a "possibility worth exploring." Tsiang said his government was not prepared to accept the two-China concept. Stevenson asked for other alternatives. Tsiang had none. Reporting to the Department, Stevenson thought it only prudent to give the problem high priority and hoped he would have a chance to discuss it in Washington soon.

On February 9 in Washington, Stevenson attended a meeting of the National Security Council, riding to the White House with Secretary Rusk. Next day the Katanga authorities who had been holding Lumumba prisoner announced that he had escaped. Lumumba had become the symbol of black African nationalism. Immediately rumors swept the UN that he had been or soon would be killed.

Back in his New York office, Stevenson at noon received Ambassador Zorin of the U.S.S.R. Zorin said that the purported escape of Lumumba increased the urgent need for Security Council action. He found a measure of agreement between the United States and U.S.S.R. on three points—

release of political prisoners, convening Parliament, Belgian withdrawal. But Zorin said Lumumba's disappearance, Kasavubu's creation of a new Ileo government, and America's favorable reaction to the Ileo government all proved that the colonial powers wanted to confront the Security Council with a fait accompli. Zorin predicted that if Lumumba was killed the atmosphere in the Security Council would be "extremely unpleasant" and the situation in the Congo "uncontrollable." Stevenson said he would "deeply deplore" Lumumba's death. He assumed the U.S.S.R. would agree that a change from a military junta to a provisional government was a favorable development. He rejected Zorin's contention of the fait accompli. As to immediate release of prisoners, the question was how to do it—the United States favored disarming all troops first.

After lunch Stevenson hurried to see Hammarskjold. Hammarskjold said that, if Lumumba was dead, the UN must temporarily take over the Congo. He planned to seize airports and transport facilities as emergency measures, to establish a protective guard for all political leaders in the Congo, and to take more drastic steps to protect Belgian citizens. Kasavubu himself would ask for protection, he thought. He did not believe Mobutu's troops would resist UN action. He would also call for a Security Council meeting to report his actions and would ask for a new mandate. He conceded he would be on thin ice but thought there was no other course. Stevenson and his colleagues were not sure that any of this would be acceptable to Kasavubu. Hammarskjold even thought the UN might take Lumumba into protective custody.

After further probes, the Mission on Saturday, February 11, sent a summary of the situation to the Department. They still did not know whether Lumumba was dead or alive but either his death or escape was likely to aggravate the situation and make prompt action urgent. If he was dead, many Afro-Asians would believe the Belgians and French had stalled Security Council action by buttressing Kasavubu and Tshombe and getting rid of Lumumba; some might suspect that the U.S. plan had been a smoke screen to cover the operation. If Lumumba had escaped and rejoined his allies, civil war was likely and some countries might recognize a separate Lumumba government at Stanleyville. The French at the UN were marshaling their friends for a barrage of pro-Kasavubu speeches on Monday which would be directed against the new U.S. policy. The Nigerians and Indians had separately been negotiating constructive programs along U.S. lines and reported the Casablanca Powers moving away from an extreme pro-Lumumba position. These efforts, however, would be set back by Lumumba's escape or death.

Stevenson found time that Saturday to send a letter to President Kennedy, via Kenny O'Donnell, the President's appointment secretary, recommending three appointments to commissions created by ECOSOC—Mrs. Gladys Tillett to the Commission on the Status of Women, Jane Dick to the Social Commission, and Marietta Tree to the Human Rights Commission. The appointments were becoming imperative; the Human Rights Commission would meet February 20 and, "although I suspect it will do very little as usual, it is important that we have the new member present."

On Sunday, Yost saw the Nigerians. They assumed Lumumba had been assassinated and considered the Congo problem drastically altered. Before this happened, India and Ghana had agreed with them to support the U.S. line, Morocco and the U.A.R. had acquiesced, and the U.S.S.R. had hesitated to oppose. But now this coalition was likely to break up, with bitter recrimination against the Belgians, French, Tshombe, and Kasavubu. There was serious danger that all Casablanca Powers troops would be withdrawn from the UN command and even used to help Lumumba forces wreak vengeance on Kasavubu and Tshombe. If that happened, Nigeria could not instruct its troops to fall on the Casablanca troops. The only hope of maintaining a UN initiative and preventing full-scale civil war was to proceed with a resolution on two points: effective neutralization of all Congolese troops and maintenance of law and order by the UN until Parliament could meet and a new government be formed; immediate withdrawal of all Belgian and French military personnel, with Belgian civilian advisers going under UN control. The Nigerians had planned to speak in the Security Council the next day along lines Stevenson had suggested but now would either sit silent or speak in a very reserved way. It was clear that Lumumba's fate had derailed the elaborate plan of action which the United States had been promoting.

Stevenson played tennis that day and had drinks with Agnes Meyer. On Monday, February 13, Katanga authorities announced that Lumumba had been killed while trying to escape. The U. S. Mission promptly called on the Security Council to meet and asked to be permitted to speak first. The Council met at 11 A.M. Just before it came to order, several Russians argued with the secretary of the Security Council—they wanted to speak first. Stevenson made his initial speech in the Security Council and went directly to the point without preliminary remarks. He said President Kennedy was "deeply shocked" by the death of Lumumba. The United States hoped that all concerned would now seek reconciliation, not recrimination or revenge. Efforts of the past week to find a consensus must now be accelerated. "We earnestly appeal" to all governments not to inflame the situation and to give full support to the UN and its mission in the Congo. He spoke for only a few minutes.

Zorin was next. He denounced the "most terrible crimes committed by the colonialists against the Congolese people," "the criminal farce which has been played out in the last few days before the whole world," and "the hypocritical maneuvers which have been going on here in the Council during the last few days." He termed Lumumba "a national hero of the Congolese people and of all Africa." No one could any longer have confidence in the Secretary General or his staff. "While the Security Council is dragging out its discussions here, on Congolese soil the colonialists are committing their crimes with impunity." Any discussion in the Security Council was pointless before all governments had been able to examine the situation afresh.

Stevenson had invited Zorin and several aides to lunch. Viola, who had come from Libertyville to be his embassy housekeeper, was setting the table when a courier arrived from the Soviet Embassy with a note. It said that the press of business made it impossible for the Russians to have lunch. Thus Stevenson learned, if he had not learned it from the Security Council debate, that Zorin was suddenly taking a hard line. Stevenson had come to the UN determined to avoid cold war rhetoric and to try to establish good personal relations with the Soviets and their friends, hoping to help ease international tensions and end the cold war itself. He had enjoyed some success, as the birthday gift from Zorin suggested, and they had seemed close to agreement on eliminating useless cold war items from the agenda of the General Assembly. Now all that was changed. The murder of Lumumba gave the Soviets a weapon, and they proposed to use it against the Secretary General, the UN, and the United States. They announced they would no longer recognize Hammarskjold as Secretary General, declaring that he was an "organizer" of Lumumba's assassination.

Stevenson saw Hammarskjold. He seemed unconcerned about the Russian's declaration that they would no longer recognize him—except that it made likely a Soviet veto of any resolution. He thought five things were needed now: a full-scale investigation of the death of Lumumba, clear endorsement of UN responsibility to protect civilians, UN intervention "by peaceful means" to prevent clashes between armed units, adherence to the earlier objective of getting the Congolese Army out of politics, and getting the Belgians out of the country.

Hammarskjold instructed the UN forces in the Congo to stop all military action by Congolese. The UN was taking control of airfields and sending troops to Stanleyville. Stevenson urgently consulted various Afro-Asian delegates.

Next day, February 14, was Valentine's Day. Stevenson sent a longhand note to Alicia Patterson: "Give me the keys to the Black River—so I can mope and dream too." That day the Peking government denounced the murder of Lumumba. Diallo Telli of Guinea called on Stevenson at his request, said his government had been disappointed that Stevenson's statement in the Security Council had not contained a strong anti-colonial declaration, and said that under instructions of Sekou Touré he would have to attack Hammarskjold in his speech in the Security Council next day even though he and Touré were personal friends of Hammarskjold— Hammarskjold had mishandled the Congo mandate. Stevenson strongly urged him not to do it, saying it would only weaken the UN and play into Soviet hands. Such pressure from Africans reinforced Stevenson's own anti-colonial sentiments and helped push him to anti-colonial positions which sometimes put him in opposition to other policies of the United States Government.

At noon Stevenson saw Hammarskjold, who gave him the instruction he had sent to the UN force in the Congo—it should prevent armed conflict by all means other than armed force and should use force if necessary to protect unarmed groups, civilians, political leaders, and refugees and to prevent outside force from entering. Plimpton called on the Ambassadors of Turkey, Sudan, France, and Liberia to test sentiment. Hammarskjold told Stevenson of messages from various chiefs of state, including Nehru, Nkrumah, Touré, and Selassie, describing Touré's as a straightforward "go to hell" message accusing Hammarskjold of personal responsibility for Lumumba's murder.

The Security Council met on Wednesday, February 15, at 11 A.M. The Liberian representative, under instructions, asked that the question of Angola, a Portuguese colony in Africa, be added to the agenda, accusing Portugal of using "tyranny and oppression" in putting down efforts to achieve independence and proclaiming that "the rising tide of African nationalism cannot be curled back like the waters of the Red Sea as it reaches the Angolan border." The Russians supported him, proposing that the Security Council take up Angola after it had dealt with the Congo.

The Council faced the Congo question; and Stevenson spoke first, his first substantive speech to the UN Security Council. It was a long, cold war speech. He called the Soviet statement and resolution on the Congo "virtually a declaration of war on the United Nations." Russia, he said, proposed abandoning UN efforts to keep peace in the Congo. "Does this Council . . . favor abandoning security for insecurity and anarchy?" The United States did not. "We believe that the only way to keep the cold war out of the Congo is to keep the United Nations in the Congo. . . . The issue, then, is simply this. Shall the United Nations survive?" Stevenson said the United States could look out after its own interests but smaller states should defend the UN. He set forth "fundamental principles" which the United States supported—the unity, territorial integrity, and political independence of the Congo; no "cold or a hot war" there; UN peace keeping; and freedom for the Congolese people to reach their own political settlement by peaceful means. What, then, needed to be done? First, all foreign military intervention except for UN, and including Belgian, should cease immediately. UN troops should take measures to avert the extension of civil war and protect the lives of civilians and refugees. The Congolese Army should be unified, reorganized, and retrained. Political prisoners should be released once law and order had been restored. The Secretary General should press an investigation of the death of Lumumba. Congolese constitutional processes should be restored, the base of the Congolese government broadened, and Parliament convened as soon as possible.

Zorin spoke next, accusing Stevenson of holding "the old attitudes and

approaches which, you all know, have already led to regrettable consequences in the whole train of events in the Congo," and said Stevenson
had offered no "constructive approach" to solving the Congolese problem.
The Security Council adjourned at 1:45 P.M. to resume at 3 P.M.

At that time Hammarskjold defended himself and the UN's role in the
Congo. He said he would resign if any UN member withdrew its
confidence in him but for the fact the U.S.S.R. had made it clear that if he
did resign no new Secretary General could be appointed and the world
"would have to bow to the wish of the Soviet Union to have this organization . . . run by a triumvirate which could not function." He then reported on his instructions to the UN force in the Congo since the death of
Lumumba.

From a hideaway office in the Secretariat building, Stevenson telephoned President Kennedy, who was to hold a nationally televised press
conference that night. Stevenson recommended that he open it with a
tough statement on the Congo, warning against any unilateral intervention
and strongly supporting the UN. Kennedy did. Later he told a visitor he
had been pleasantly surprised by Stevenson's telephone call. He said,
"Adlai's got an iron ass and, my God, in this job, he's got the nerve of a
burglar."

After adjournment, members of the U. S. Mission sought out members
of other delegations to test the wind. The Ambassador of Mali told Yost
that Stevenson's speech had made a good impression among Afro-Asians
and he had moderated his own speech in consequence. The Madagascan
said the same thing. The Cuban said the speech was excellent, the Philippine said it was superb. Warm praise came too from New Zealand,
Sweden, China, and Senegal. A man from Ghana was disappointed and
thought the speech added nothing new.

Agnes Meyer wrote to Stevenson, saying Eleanor Roosevelt had told her
that he had already "transformed" the UN attitude toward himself and the
United States. She asked him to promise that "if you are ever tempted to
resign, you will talk it over with Eleanor before doing anything." A few
days later Mrs. Paepcke wrote to him about his trials in the UN and said
she was worried about him: "I could hardly bear to watch your face. To
me it seems an anachronism that anyone in the present NOW should think
that it is important to listen to Senator Goldwater. . . . I mention the
Senator particularly because last night Lake Forest ran like mad to the
Academy to listen to its deepest convictions confirmed by the Senator in
person. . . . No, you must not answer this letter. This is not the time to
be polite or kind to friends. I only wanted to let you know that I put my
arms around you in all times of trouble. Now. P."

In the Security Council meeting at 11 A.M. on February 16, African nationalists angrily denounced the murder of Lumumba and some denounced Hammarskjold. The representative of Mali rejected the proposals
Stevenson had made the day before. Stevenson courteously corrected him

on one point. Stevenson had the Indians and Nigerians to lunch. Next day the Security Council met until 12:30 P.M. and convened again at 3 P.M. Its members reached no consensus, and Stevenson supported a suggestion that it adjourn until Monday (over U.S.S.R. objection) to give more time for quiet consultation.

After the meeting Stevenson met with Liberia, Ceylon, and the U.A.R. His efforts to build an Afro-Asian consensus around his own and Hammarskjold's positions were failing. Those three countries submitted a resolution to the Security Council that they knew was unacceptable to the United States. The death of Lumumba plus pressure from radical Africans was drawing the moderates to the Soviet side. Stevenson did not believe we should give up, however. The governments of these delegations, knowing the Congo could be settled only with U.S. support, might still make changes in their position that their delegates at the UN could not make. Stevenson therefore recommended "urgent approaches . . . at highest level" to the home governments of India, Nigeria, and Liberia in time for their effects to be felt by Monday morning's Security Council meeting. This was, in effect, an appeal to Kennedy and Rusk to approach those three countries' chiefs of state and Foreign Ministers directly.

It may have been at about this point that, in the evening, George Ball went to see Kennedy. "He decided that we ought to get Stevenson," Ball recalled. "I went to the phone on the wall and talked to Stevenson. I guess I was a little bit tough on him. Then I said, 'Just a minute, Adlai, I want to speak to the President.' Kennedy said to me, 'Look, George, he lives in a microcosm that's totally different from the world of reality we live in here. Don't be as tough as you are with him. He's got to live in his microcosm and we've got to live in this world and we've all got to work these things out.' "

That same day Stevenson met with a group of African representatives who wanted to postpone the Congo debate until March. Stevenson told them the Congo situation was too precarious for delay—collapse seemed imminent, and with it might go the UN. He gave them his proposals for modifying the Ceylon-Liberia-U.A.R. resolution. A total of twenty-nine words was involved. They promised to cable his views home immediately and to meet with him again on Monday morning before the Security Council met. All through the weekend Stevenson and Mission officers consulted furiously with other delegations. The Congo crisis was moving to a climax.

On Monday, February 20, Stevenson's secretary had noted on his calendar pad, "Director General of UNESCO wants appt. today." It was an example of why Stevenson neglected non-political matters: he was in the Security Council all day and indeed nearly all night. The Security Council met at 10:30 A.M. At the outset Hammarskjold reported "with revolt and shock" the execution of six Congolese by the secessionist government. The Liberian delegate asked the Security Council to recess at once until 3 P.M.

to permit African countries to consult about the news. Stevenson agreed to the adjournment, expressed his government's "shock, its revulsion and its indignation," and said action was all the more imperative. The U.A.R. agreed. Zorin of the U.S.S.R., noting that his country's "worst fears . . . have been realized" and denouncing anew "Belgian aggression" and the "terrorist regime" of "Kasavubu-Mobutu-Tshombe," did not object to a recess but warned that further delay invited disaster.

At the resumed meeting at 3 P.M., representatives of the U.A.R., Ceylon, and Liberia spoke on behalf of the three-power resolution. Liberia also introduced a new resolution calling for the Security Council to hold its next meeting in the Congo. The Council president announced that the U.A.R., Liberia, and Ceylon had submitted a new draft resolution and asked that it be given priority. While it was being circulated, debate continued on the original three-power resolution. The Indian said that the UN was in the "greatest crisis" in its history.

Stevenson gave a lengthy speech. He agreed that the UN as well as the Congo was in crisis. He supported the Liberian proposal to move the Security Council to Africa and offered the United States Air Force for transport. The United States would support the three-power resolution, but he argued for three points the United States wanted inserted into the resolution and "humbly" suggested amended language. All that evening and far into the next morning the debate went on. The Council voted on a long string of resolutions and amendments, and slowly a pattern emerged: the votes represented one defeat after another for the Soviet Union. Twice Zorin and Stevenson fell into a wrangle. Finally a three-power resolution was adopted which Secretary General Hammarskjold welcomed. On this note the Security Council adjourned. It was 4:20 A.M. It had been, on the whole, a victory for Stevenson and the United States, and it gave promise of saving the Congo.

7.

The last part of February and March and the first part of April were weeks of almost frantic activity for Stevenson. The convening of the resumed General Assembly brought to New York a variety of foreign diplomats and dignitaries, including Gromyko of the Soviet Union and Nkrumah of Ghana, both of whom Stevenson saw privately. At the same time the Security Council was meeting and, throughout March, Stevenson served as its president, adding to his burdens. His calendar was crowded with diplomatic affairs—meetings with Hammarskjold and various Ambassadors, luncheons and dinners and receptions. It was crowded too with personal engagements. He gave the lunch for the Soviet group postponed during the Congo crisis. He saw newspapermen and columnists privately and individually, including Scotty Reston of the New York *Times* and

Walter Lippmann. He met with the U.S. delegation to the General Assembly and entertained them. He took Mrs. Field to a dinner with the Nigerians and spent a quiet weekend at her place in the country. He went to Washington fives times, something less than once a week, and met with, among others, President Kennedy, Vice President Johnson, and Prime Minister Macmillan.

Evelyn Houston of California was hurt because he did not write to her —"If you would make peace in the Congo, can you not find charity for one of your own?" Stevenson answered with a handwritten note, and she thanked him. He made several attempts to arrange a "rendezvous" with Alicia Patterson; she seemed evasive. He tried to resolve a conflict between a dinner date with Nan McEvoy and one with Chancellor Adenauer at the German Embassy in Washington.

He invited Kathryn Lewis, widow of the author Lloyd Lewis, to stay with him at 42A. Jane Dick reported to him on his family in Chicago and her own new commission at the UN—"I have seen . . . your house, hugged three maples for you, thrown a kiss to Merlin [his dog]."

During this period he received huge amounts of publicity, more than anybody except President Kennedy himself, so much that the President suspected he was making foreign policy independently. Kennedy had not regarded the UN as central to the policy-making process but suddenly Stevenson made it seem so. Eventually, however, Kennedy traced the policy back to Rusk and Cleveland. At this point Kennedy said he wanted to be told in advance of all important coming events in the UN, not read about them in the New York *Times*. As a result, Cleveland, Schlesinger, and Bundy worked out a scheme to give Kennedy memos, for his night reading before going to bed, on anything at the UN that seemed likely to make the front page of the *Times*. Once Jack Arvey told Stevenson, "Both the Chicago *Tribune* and the Chicago *American* have been saying nice things about you. What have you done wrong, now?"

Stevenson involved himself in recommending people for appointments as Ambassadors. The Washington *Afro American* criticized Stevenson harshly, saying he had no Negro at the mission. (He had one, of middle rank.) Lloyd Garrison wrote a long letter to the editor defending Stevenson but privately sent Stevenson a report on other Negro disaffection— Negroes mistrusted him, and Garrison recommended adding one or more Negroes to the Mission staff and delegation.

During this period Stevenson was handling issues of great importance— Chinese admission to the UN, the Congo, the Article 19 controversy, disarmament, Angola, Laos, African policy, and Cuba. More often than not they had to be handled on an emergency basis. Phil Klutznick told Newt Minow, "The constant danger here is that emergencies take on a priority to a point where everyone loses perspective. The Governor is having to fight this with himself—he must win this battle or else he will lose his

Washington strength." The Congo was a relatively quiet issue in the UN from the time the Security Council passed its resolution near dawn on February 21 until the resumed session of the General Assembly began debate on March 21. (The Congo itself was less quiet—in March, Sudanese troops in the UN command clashed with Mobutu's troops and two were killed, the Sudan withdrew its troops, weakening the UN force, and African political leaders, including Kasavubu and Tshombe of Katanga, at a conference in the Malagasy Republic, reached tentative agreement on the confederation of all Congolese states. A crisis at the UN did not always correspond to what was happening in the dust and blood of the Congo itself, and vice versa.)

Stevenson had told the Department that the Security Council vote giving the UN more authority in the Congo had bought time to avert a still threatened collapse of the UN's position there. The issue lay nearly dormant in New York until March 21, when Soviet Foreign Minister Gromyko, speaking in the General Assembly, again criticized the UN's Congo operation and called for its end in one month. He also repeated charges against the Secretary General and Belgian "aggression."

Stevenson replied on the same day. He said he was "frankly astonished" to hear Gromyko open the debate with a speech which was "in the worst and most destructive traditions of the cold war. I am afraid that we must take this as further evidence that the Soviet Union does not regard our Organization as a means of international cooperation but simply as an instrument of international discord." The reason for the large and expensive UN effort in the Congo was not to impose a solution on the Congolese but, rather, to help them establish a government of their own choice. The Soviet Union, "by its wild and irresponsible and absurd attacks," was only making the Secretary General's task harder. The United States respected the Secretary General and his office. He appealed for an end to the incessant debate in New York which had attended the first nine months of the UN operation. "We must stop, I suggest, pulling up the roots of this fragile plant every few days to see if it is growing. That is the best way to kill a plant, and I suspect that that may be the objective of these incessant attacks." The UN had its mandate from the Security Council. It needed to carry it out. The Soviet Union did not want the UN to succeed in the Congo. It demanded the resignation of the Secretary General. The United States would "oppose this demand with all our strength." The Soviet Union had demanded that the UN withdraw from the Congo within one month. The United States was "totally opposed" to this surrender to anarchy. Both the Congo and the UN "desperately" needed a period of quiet and constructive cooperation to help the Congolese.

Newsweek reported that President Kennedy was pleased with that speech, and Stevenson tore the clipping out of *Newsweek* and put it in his desk, where it was found after he died more than four years later. The plenary debate in the General Assembly continued day after day, far into April, and so did meetings of foreign diplomats with Stevenson, Rusk, and other U.S. officials, both in Washington and in New York.

At this same General Assembly session the United States launched something called "the African initiative," an effort to spur the development of Africa, which in the end came to little more than rhetoric.

Angola, a smoldering issue for some time, burst into flame that spring. Angola was a large Portuguese "overseas territory," or colony, lying just south of the Congo. For some time independence-seeking rebels had been fighting Portuguese authority and appealing to world opinion. It posed a cruel issue for the United States (and for the United Kingdom and other Western Allies too). Portugal was a NATO ally; it was therefore essential to maintain good relations with Portugal for the sake of Western unity. But Portugal, unlike England and France, was determined to keep her colonial empire, or all of it that she could, and this put Portugal on a collision course with the over-all American policy of encouraging the freedom of colonial peoples. In the State Department the Europeanists in the Western Europe Bureau tended to support Portugal, while friends of African nationalism in the African Bureau supported the Angola rebels. At the UN, the issue was ready made for Russian meddling—the Russians could use it to win favor with the African delegations and to split the Western Allies.

During the night of February 4 several hundred people calling themselves Angolan nationalists attacked a Portuguese police station in Luanda, the capital of Angola, and were repulsed with heavy losses on both sides. Later clashes between police and civilians occurred during funeral services for some of the attackers. At the same time disturbances broke out in the interior in protest against Portuguese agricultural policy. In the course of a Security Council debate on the Congo on February 15, the Liberian representative referred to the violence and requested that the problem be considered immediately. It was not on the agenda and he was ruled out of order. But the U.S.S.R., the U.A.R., and Ceylon told the Security Council it should take up the question soon. The Portuguese representative argued that the Security Council could not take up Angola—it was a purely domestic affair. He lost, and on March 10 the Security Council met to consider "the Angola item."

On March 14 a draft resolution was offered by Ceylon, Liberia, and the U.A.R. which would call upon Portugal to consider urgently reforms in Angola to permit the Angolan people to exercise the right of self-determination and would establish a UN subcommittee to report on conditions in Angola. Stevenson spoke the next day, March 15. He said the situation in Angola did not immediately imperil the general peace but might later on. He deplored the violence and loss of life in Luanda. He said Angola

was "but a part of the over-all picture of evolution on the African continent." The United States Declaration of Independence asserted that governments derive "their just powers" from the consent of the governed.
These were still the guiding lights of American policy, he said. "The
United States would be remiss in its duties as a friend of Portugal if it
failed to express honestly its conviction that step-by-step planning within
Portuguese territories and the acceleration thereof is now imperative for
the successful political, economic, and social advancement of all inhabitants under Portuguese administration—advancement, in brief, towards full
self-determination." The resolution failed—nobody opposed it, and five
nations voted for it (the three sponsors plus both the United States and
the U.S.S.R.), but six abstained, and so it did not receive the required
seven votes.

The U.S. position was a reversal of past U.S. policy, a break with the
Eisenhower line. After the vote the press printed opinions that the U.S.
position had been hasty and ill considered. The Mission press officer said
on March 17 that the U.S. position had been taken only after thorough
consultation between Stevenson and the Department and after approval by
Secretary Rusk and the President. "Our allies were informed in advance.
We have a deep and continuing common interest with them. The difficulty
and complexity of African questions are, however, such that there are and
may continue to be differences in approach on some of them." Robert D.
Murphy, a former Undersecretary of State with a reputation as a hard-line
Europeanist and cold warrior, told Stevenson privately on March 21 that
he viewed the U.S. position on Angola "with dismay." "The spectacle," he
said, of the United States' voting with the Soviet Union against her own
NATO allies was "a matter of deep concern" to anyone valuing the Atlantic Alliance. He viewed the Soviet attack on our European allies for their
colonialism as a smoke screen to mask its basic target—Europe itself.
Stevenson said he was sorry Murphy disagreed with the U.S. position but
believed it was correct. He wrote, "I hope that neither you nor your colleagues [at the American Council on NATO] have any doubts about my
own or the Administration's recognition of the fundamental importance of
NATO. . . . At the same time I am sure you will agree that the age of colonial rule in Africa is coming rapidly to an end."

This, however, was by no means the end of the Angola question. Hol-
den Roberto, leader of the Angolan independence movement, came to
New York and on March 19 deplored the "extreme violence" of Africans
against Portuguese settlers in one Angolan province but said the killings
were an "expression of desperation against Portuguese terrorism over the
past five hundred years." He wanted to plead the cause of independence
with the UN and the United States. He was thirty-six years old, fluent in
English, French, and Portuguese. He said he wanted to avoid "another
Congo." He told the State Department his movement had been forced to
violence after non-violence—mainly pressure on the UN—had proved

ineffectual. His movement would continue fighting; there was no hope of voluntary change under Salazar. The only thing his people would accept was a publicly announced date for independence within two or three years. He asked for U.S. financial and military aid.

U.S. officers gave him no commitment and told him there would be danger for all concerned if the United States became identified with his movement. The United States, "while fully supporting the orderly progress of dependent areas to full self-government," could not condone violence. Roberto said he understood the U.S. position but needed more than moral support. He personally preferred negotiated peaceable solutions but they were no longer possible in Angola. If he counseled non-violence, he would be replaced as leader. His movement was firmly anti-Communist, he said, but there were two Communist-oriented movements in Angola and he himself had been approached by the Soviet delegation to the UN in New York. The U.S. officers asked if he was pro-Western or pro-Communist. "Roberto said he was neither, that he was an African nationalist who was only 'pro-Angola.'"

Subsequently Roberto submitted a memorandum to the Security Council on behalf of his liberation movement, setting forth the facts as he saw them. Widespread disorders broke out in northern Angola, and Africans attacked Portuguese villages and plantations. Large loss of life and extreme brutality were reported. Forty Afro-Asian members insisted that the situation in Angola be put on the agenda. On March 23 the Portuguese representative again vigorously denied the UN's jurisdiction, rejected "with indignation" the assertion that human rights had been denied in Angola, and led his delegation out of the General Assembly.

8.

Disarmament negotiation was an enormously complex and highly technical matter. At this time it was divided into two segments—the Geneva Conference on the Discontinuance of Nuclear Weapons Tests and general disarmament negotiations. The Geneva Conference on nuclear testing was in recess when Kennedy took office. It resumed work on March 21 and remained in session until September 9. Ambassador Arthur H. Dean represented the United States at the Geneva Conference. John J. McCloy represented the United States in the general disarmament negotiations in Washington, Moscow, and New York during the summer and fall. Stevenson's formal role was limited to handling UN aspects of the matters, chiefly the resolution on general disarmament.

He did, however, participate in several policy meetings on disarmament. On March 18 he met with President Kennedy, Vice President Johnson, McCloy, Nitze, Bundy, and others. Ed Gullion, soon to become U. S. Ambassador to the Congo, said at the time that the meeting was not very productive but may have revealed to the President the basic conflict of attitudes toward disarmament within his administration. It was the old split between the Europeanists and the anti-colonialists—according to Gullion, "a disagreement between those who think of the world in terms of 1945—in terms essentially of NATO; and those who are concerned with the emerging nations of Asia and Africa." Stevenson argued that any retreat from "complete and general disarmament" would be disastrous in terms of the UN and world opinion. McCloy, Lovett, Acheson, and others of that tradition cared less about what the UN thought. Similarly, opinion divided between those who favored general and complete disarmament and those who favored stabilized nuclear deterrence. Stevenson and Gullion favored disarmament; Wiesner and Rostow favored progress toward disarmament through transitional stages of stabilized deterrence; Kissinger favored stabilized deterrence; and McCloy favored what he called "the rule of law," which could mean the maintenance of strength. Two days after the White House meeting President Kennedy told Walter Lippmann and Arthur Schlesinger that he had been greatly impressed by Stevenson and his performance at the UN. He said that at the White House meeting Stevenson seemed to be far more precise and specific than McCloy and to have all the better of the argument. (President Kennedy added, "Stevenson could be appointed [Secretary] now; he isn't so controversial a figure as he was before the Congo debate." Schlesinger discounted this somewhat, since the President knew he liked Stevenson.)

9.

The admission of mainland China into the UN was another issue that came to the forefront in the spring of 1961. The question had been raised in the UN every year since 1950. In recent years the United States had succeeded in avoiding a showdown by means of the moratorium formula —the General Assembly decided for the duration of the session not to consider any proposals to exclude the Formosa government or to seat the Peking government. But support appeared to be growing for full discussion and it was doubtful the formula could succeed again.

At meetings late in February and early in March with the Prime Ministers of Australia and New Zealand, Secretary Rusk said the mainland Chinese were as hostile as ever and the United States would not consider their recognition seriously. In the UN, the United States would try to avoid damaging Formosa and at the same time avoid a hopeless moratorium battle. President Kennedy spoke of the "deep feeling" which the China issue engendered in the United States in both political parties, stressed that it should not be dealt with in a way that would cause harmful division and controversy here, and said that, if mainland China were seated in the UN, American support for the UN might be forfeited.

On March 10, Rusk sent to Stevenson a paper originally prepared for President Kennedy, taking note of press rumors that the new Administration would move to a "two-China" policy and pointing out that Peking had repeatedly rejected any such policy. (Formosa, of course, rejected it too.) Great Britain already recognized Peking. Secretary Rusk thought it "tragic" that American and British policy diverged. But at present the United States saw no prospect of recognizing Peking unless it changed its hostile ways. In the UN our objective would be to put ourselves in a "reasonable" light but it was fundamental to U.S. policy that Formosa retain a seat in the UN. It was possible the UN could pass a resolution saying that what is now one country had become two countries.

On March 17, Rusk, on his own initiative, told Ambassador Yeh of the Formosa Chinese that he was not surprised China hoped to continue the moratorium but he thought China should consider alternatives. Rusk emphasized that the United States itself would continue to recognize Formosa; there was no chance it would recognize Peking. But the UN problem was more complicated. A parliamentary danger was that a bare majority would decide it was a matter of credentials. Rusk indicated that the United States should try to get away from the deadlock and get onto more advantageous ground. Formosa should consider a key question: what was its choice between an all-or-nothing stance and the determination to remain a member of the UN? If Formosa took an all-or-nothing position, it was likely that a majority would insist on dealing with the issue as a credentials question (and Peking might win). If on the other hand Formosa concentrated on retaining its position in the UN, the prospect was that Peking would refuse membership and a deadlock would ensue for which Peking would bear responsibility. Rusk said that if the issue were decided to be an "important matter," in the language of the UN Charter, a two-thirds vote would be necessary for any solution, and the chances were against getting two-thirds for any solution at this time.

Thus the United States was resisting pressure from Great Britain and two Commonwealth countries to soften its opposition to Peking and, at the same time, urging the Formosa Chinese to soften their own position. All this was preliminary to the forthcoming visit of Prime Minister Macmillan on April 5 and to the General Assembly session next fall.

On April 2, Ambassador Yeh returned from Formosa with a letter from Chiang Kai-shek to President Kennedy. It was filled with cold war rhetoric and expressed intransigent opposition to the "so-called 'two Chinas'" policy. Yeh suggested that if moratorium failed we try to have the issue treated as an "important question," requiring a two-thirds vote. President Kennedy, replying, said that it was U.S. policy to maintain the status of Formosa as a member of the UN, that the United States had indicated to Ambassador Yeh its serious doubt that sufficient support remained for the moratorium, and that the United States was giving urgent consideration to other tactics.

When Stevenson returned from Chicago after the Easter weekend, Noyes gave him a memorandum representing the staff thinking—that Harlan Cleveland's proposed two-Chinas policy was unrealistic—and told him he was not sure whether there was still time to modify the U.S. position, since President Kennedy and Stevenson were seeing Macmillan the next day.

Kennedy met with Macmillan at lunch on April 5 at the White House and again in the afternoon. At the afternoon meeting Rusk, Stevenson, and other American and British officials were present and so was Dean Acheson. A great deal of preparation had preceded the meetings. Staff members in the Department, the White House, and the UN Mission had drawn up papers for their senior officers. The papers for Stevenson had emphasized colonial issues, such as Angola, where the U.S. and U.K. positions differed. A paper prepared for the President by McGeorge Bundy had listed the following points for discussion with Macmillan: British entry into the European Common Market (the single biggest question, handled by George Ball), commercial policy, the Atlantic community and Western cooperation, the UN (Chinese representation and colonial policy, especially with respect to Portugal), East-West relations, including Khrushchev's attacks on Hammarskjold, Berlin, and "such interesting areas of Soviet pressure as Afghanistan and Iran." The agenda illustrates well the point that whereas Stevenson (rightly) concentrated on UN matters, Kennedy (also rightly) was obliged to consider a far wider range of problems. And Rusk was obliged to take still a third approach.

The main emphasis of the meeting was on Berlin, with Acheson taking a hard line and Stevenson saying little. Discussion of China was inconclusive, since the U.S. position was not yet firm. Again, Stevenson contributed little. For a long time he had been concerned about the unrealistic policy of pretending that mainland China did not exist and he had been drawn toward the two-Chinas policy; perhaps Noyes's view that Cleveland's two-China policy was also unrealistic made Stevenson reluctant to speak out. He had been in Chicago during the last few days and had had little or no opportunity to make his views known in advance of the meeting. Yet had he wanted to he could have arranged it—he had known since April 1 that he would attend the Kennedy-Macmillan talks and could have gone to Washington instead of to Libertyville for Easter weekend. Even at the last minute his staff seems to have wanted him to intervene. All this gives the impression that Cleveland and others were more eager to be policy makers than Stevenson. One wonders whether he had become reluctant to take strong positions. Once he wrote a paper on the resumption of nuclear testing, presenting the "moral" case against it but taking no position. One wonders whether he often refused to take a position but simply presented pros and cons and let Kennedy decide. Sorensen thought so. Yost, Bundy, and Schlesinger disagreed. Bundy added, "But he only spoke when he cared."

10.

The Mission was busy with other issues as well, but all others faded into insignificance on April 8 when Arthur Schlesinger, Jr., a man from the CIA, and a man from the State Department went to New York to brief Stevenson on the Cuban adventure that soon became known to the world as the Bay of Pigs invasion.

A "Cuban item" was already on the General Assembly's agenda. Cuba had complained the previous fall at the General Assembly of "various plans of aggression and acts of intervention" by the United States against Cuba. The matter had been carried forward to the spring. In March and April the Mission had informed Latin American delegations that the United States was strongly opposed to any General Assembly resolution on the Cuban complaint. Even a simple resolution calling on the United States and Cuba to settle the dispute peacefully would lend credence to the Cuban charges. In order not to inflame the issue, the United States had refrained from asking the UN to focus on what was, in the U.S. view, the real problem—Cuban willingness to serve as a base for Communist intervention in other Latin American countries.

All this had had an air of shadow boxing about it. Castro had for months been loudly alerting his people to the imminence of a U.S. invasion. Many people had believed it a fake, designed to distract the attention of the Cuban people from domestic difficulties. Now suddenly, secretly, the real thing was at hand. According to members of the Kennedy administration, President Eisenhower, early in his last year in office, 1960, had directed the CIA to bring together Cuban exiles, excluding Batistianos and Communists, into unified political opposition to the Castro regime and to recruit and train a Cuban exile force capable of guerrilla action against the Castro regime. As time passed the plan became one to train and equip a force of exiles to make a direct amphibious assault, complete with air cover, on the Cuban coast. Some of the principal exiles were men who had fought with Castro in the Sierra Maestra, then broken with him when, in their view, he betrayed his revolution to the Communists. The exiles were trained in Guatemala. B-26s were provided. Allen Dulles of the CIA told President-elect Kennedy about it shortly after the election. Kennedy told him to continue with the project.

At that point Kennedy had not committed himself to the enterprise; he merely wanted to have the alternative of an invasion force in dealing with Castro when he took office. But such projects have a life and momentum of their own, and by early 1961 pressures were rising to carry out the scheme. The President of Guatemala complained that the presence of the exiles, whose training was becoming known, was a mounting embarrassment—they must leave by the end of April. The exiles themselves were anxious to move; postponement would erode their morale. The rainy season soon would bring training to a stop. The CIA had reports that Castro was to receive jet aircraft from the Soviet Union and Cuban pilots trained in Czechoslovakia to fly them; after June 1, nothing short of the U. S. Air Force and U. S. Marines could overthrow Castro.

By the middle of March, Kennedy was confronted with a now-or-never choice. For a time he resisted. The CIA argued that if the project was called off the CIA would have a "disposal problem"—it could hardly take the exiles out of training in Guatemala and bring them back to the United States to let them tell the world what had been going on. Moreover, many of them would wander through Latin America, embittered and talkative, saying that the United States had lost its nerve. Slowly Kennedy came around to the view that the best thing to do would be to let the exiles go where they wanted to go—to Cuba. Senator Fulbright, almost alone among Kennedy's advisers, opposed the project—it would violate the spirit if not the letter of the OAS Charter, hemisphere treaties, and U.S. laws; it would be denounced throughout Latin America as *imperialismo yanqui;* it would make trouble in the UN; it would commit the United States to making a success of the post-Castro Cuban regime; and if the invasion seemed about to fail, the United States, with its prestige already committed, would be tempted to use its own armed force. The whole operation, Fulbright said, was wildly out of proportion to the threat and would compromise America's moral position in the world, making it impossible for us to denounce treaty violations committed by the Soviet Union. But Kennedy had become a prisoner of events. He did reserve the right to veto the operation up to twenty-four hours before it began. He scaled it down somewhat. And he did stipulate that no Americans should be directly involved. (Actually, the first man ashore at the Bay of Pigs was an American.)

In order to conceal the American role the CIA had prepared a cover story. Before the invasion B-26s flying from Nicaragua would hit Cuban airfields in order to knock out Castro's planes. At the same time another B-26, with the insignia of the Castro air force painted on it, would fly straight from Nicaragua to Florida, and its pilot would announce that he was a defector from Castro's air force, that he had just bombed Castro's airfields, and that he wanted asylum in the United States.

On Friday, April 7, Kennedy told Schlesinger to go to New York and brief Stevenson on the Bay of Pigs. He said, "The integrity and credibility of Adlai Stevenson constitute one of our great national assets. I don't want anything to be done which might jeopardize that." He talked with Schlesinger about Stevenson's forthcoming speech on the old "Cuban item." Schlesinger thought it ought to lay down the main lines of Administration policy toward Cuba—not to see Cuba return to a Batista dictatorship but to help restore the original purity of the Castro revolution as it had begun in the Sierra Maestra, a non-Communist leftist revolutionary regime.

On Saturday morning, April 8, Schlesinger saw Rusk, who had misgivings about the project but who also seemed unable to halt it, then went to New York to brief Stevenson. Schlesinger has recalled, "We told him about the exile group. We told him we were training them, supplying weapons, I'm not sure that we told him that there would be U.S. planes, but we told him there would be no U.S. combat troops involved. We told him that the Cubans were armed by us and the money had come from the United States, and it was going to take place. But there was a failure of communication. I fear we inadvertently left him with the impression that it would not take place until the General Assembly adjourned. It was set up so it could be called back. Maybe I hoped it would be called back. We gave Stevenson no date. We knew it would go ahead in the next week or ten days, but no date had yet been set." They did not tell Stevenson about the CIA cover story involving the plane with false insignia. A State Department man who accompanied Schlesinger said, "Stevenson was very much against the operation. Right from the very beginning. He wondered whether President Kennedy had really thought this thing through. Whether he had considered if the consequences of winning or losing were worth it. He got no straightforward answers. There were two weeks left in the session of the General Assembly. He said, 'Look, I don't like this. If I were calling the shots, I wouldn't do it. But this is Kennedy's show. All I ask is three things: First, don't do anything till the Assembly adjourns. Second, nobody leaves from the U.S. territory. Third, no American participation.'"

They talked with Stevenson all morning, then had lunch with him and Harlan Cleveland and Clayton Fritchey at the Century club. Schlesinger noted in his journal, "AES made it clear that he wholly disapproves of the project, objects to the fact that he was given no opportunity to comment on it, and believes it will cause infinite trouble. However, he is substantially a good soldier about it and is prepared to try and make the best possible US case."

On Wednesday, April 12, the Department was still struggling with the draft of Stevenson's speech, which was a reply to the anticipated charges by Cuba in the Political Committee. Cleveland discussed the draft with Chet Bowles and Abe Chayes, the Department's legal counselor, then sent Secretary Rusk a revised draft. He told Rusk he was troubled by the passages concerning the activities of Cuban exiles in the United States and American participation in military action against Cuba. He recommended that Rusk and President Kennedy, who knew more about the project than Cleveland, give Stevenson guidance. He added that he wondered whether the Cuban matter had not been held so closely for security reasons that a really adequate review of its foreign policy implications was impossible.

Even before the invasion, those concerned with the UN had serious misgivings about the project and about the fact that they were operating in the dark. Finally, at 6 P.M. that day, the Stevenson speech was cleared by the Secretary and portions of it were approved by the President and the text was wired to Stevenson in New York. It was overtaken by events—before Stevenson could deliver it, the Bay of Pigs invasion had occurred and made much of it obsolete.

The same day, April 12, President Kennedy held a press conference. The first question was on "how far this country will be willing to go in helping an anti-Castro uprising or invasion of Cuba." Kennedy replied, "First, I want to say that there will not be, under any conditions, an intervention in Cuba by the United States armed forces. This government will do everything it possibly can, and I think it can meet its responsibilities, to make sure that there are no Americans involved in any actions inside Cuba. . . . The basic issue in Cuba is not one between the United States and Cuba. It is between the Cubans themselves."

On Friday, April 14, Stevenson spoke in the General Assembly on the Congo. The next day at ten-thirty, Saturday, April 15, when the General Assembly met to continue the Congo debate, the Cuban Foreign Minister, Dr. Raul Roa, said at the outset of the session, "I have asked for the floor on a matter which is not a point of order, but is of vital concern to the General Assembly, the organ of the United Nations responsible for dealing with all questions bearing on international peace and security. I should like to inform this Assembly, which is the supreme forum for the expression of the international conscience, that this morning, at 6:30 A.M., United States aircraft—"

The Assembly president, Frederick H. Boland, interrupted him: "I hope that the distinguished Foreign Minister of Cuba will cooperate with the Chair and will understand that the Chair is bound by the rules of procedure. The distinguished Foreign Minister has asked for the floor on a point of order; but the point he is now making is not a point of order, but is one of substance. . . . I am afraid he is out of order."

"Thank you, Mr. President," Roa said. "But really I do not know which is of greater interest to the United Nations General Assembly, a purely procedural question or a breach of international peace. I have made my point and shall withdraw." Ambassador Zorin of the Soviet Union spoke immediately on a "point of order"—"I consider it necessary to draw the attention of the General Assembly to the statement just made by the Cuban Minister for Foreign Affairs, and I think that we should now change the order of the General Assembly's proceedings and discuss immediately the question of the aggression against Cuba." The president said that the "Cuban item" was already on the agenda of the Political Committee. Zorin said let the Political Committee meet that afternoon "to discuss this question as a matter of urgency." The president said that during the morning he would consult with the chairman of the Political Committee and try to arrange for it to meet in the afternoon. Thus did the Bay of Pigs come to the United Nations.

Stevenson had Alicia Patterson to lunch that day in 42A. The Assembly concluded its debate on the Congo that afternoon and at long last voted on four resolutions, adopting three and rejecting one, a mixed result from the U.S. point of view.[1] The Assembly also congratulated the Soviet Union on a successful flight in space, and Stevenson congratulated it on behalf of the United States.

Outside the UN a crowd of Castro sympathizers, members of the Fair Play for Cuba Committee, were marching up and down, waving placards denouncing the United States as "Murder, Inc." and shouting, *"Cuba sí, yanqui no."* At seven o'clock that morning a bullet-riddled B-26 bearing the markings of Castro's air force had made an emergency landing at Key West. It was one of the planes which had bombed Cuban airfields after taking off from Nicaragua. It had been hit and could not get home. At about the same time another B-26, also bearing the insignia of Castro, landed at Miami International Airport. One of its engines was dead and the fuselage was pierced by bullets. The Cuban pilot was taken away by U.S. immigration officials. Soon the director of the Immigration and Naturalization Service in Miami issued a statement supposedly drafted by the pilot. It said that he and three of his comrades had defected from Castro's air force in stolen planes. Two of the planes were hit by anti-aircraft fire and were low on gas and so had flown to Florida. When reporters asked for the fliers' names the Immigration Service refused, in order to protect their families in Cuba, it said. When reporters suggested that Castro would know the names of his own pilots, the Immigration Service simply said they had asked that their names be kept secret. This was the CIA cover story. The brigade of invaders was already at sea, en route to the Cuban south coast.

In Washington, Harlan Cleveland, seeking the facts, called the Bureau of Latin American Affairs, which in turn called the CIA. Word promptly came back that the bombing was the work of defectors. Cleveland had a speech drafted and sent to New York. Pedersen went over it. It contained the CIA cover story—that "defectors" had bombed the airfields. Pedersen had no way of knowing it was a cover story. He accepted it as fact. His colleague, Joe Sisco, became suspicious and called Robert Sayre of the Bureau of Latin American Affairs in Washington and asked if he could make a change in language. Sayre confirmed to Sisco that the bombing was by

[1] The resolutions adopted called for withdrawal of all foreign forces from the Congo except for the UN command, called on the Congolese to desist from force and resolve their differences peaceably, and called for an "immediate and impartial investigation" of the death of Lumumba. (The United States favored the second.) A Soviet resolution calling for the convening of the Congolese Parliament within twenty-one days was rejected (the United States voted against).

defectors—"No, you can't change one word." Stevenson, Pedersen, and Sisco—none of the three knew it was a cover story. Stevenson went to the Political Committee to speak.

Foreign Minister Roa, on instructions from Castro, denounced the U.S. "aggression" and said it was a prelude to a long-planned invasion. Stevenson replied, "We have heard a number of charges by Dr. Roa and now, if I may, I should like to impose on the committee long enough to report a few facts." He said that Castro's air force chief and his private pilot had defected the day before and landed at Jacksonville, Florida. (This was true. It had nothing to do with the Bay of Pigs operation and was pure coincidence—coincidence which helped confuse the situation and appears to have confused even Secretary Rusk briefly.) Stevenson went on to discuss reports of bombing and rocket attacks on Cuban airfields that morning. He then rejected Roa's charges "categorically" as "without foundation" and said:

"First, as the President of the United States said a few days ago, there will not be under any conditions—and I repeat, any conditions—any intervention in Cuba by the United States armed forces.

"Secondly, the United States will do everything it possibly can to make sure that no Americans participate in any actions against Cuba.

"Thirdly, regarding the events which have reportedly occurred this morning and yesterday, the United States will consider, in accordance with its usual practices, the request for political asylum. . . .

"Fourthly, regarding the two aircraft which landed in Florida today, they were piloted by Cuban Air Force pilots. These pilots and certain other crew members have apparently defected from Castro's tyranny. No United States personnel participated. No United States Government airplanes of any kind participated. These two planes to the best of our knowledge were Castro's own air force planes and, according to the pilots, they took off from Castro's own air force fields." He closed by repeating what Kennedy had said—that the basic issue in Cuba was not between the United States and Cuba but among Cubans themselves.

Thus did Stevenson swallow whole—and all unknowing—the CIA cover story.

At midnight the Department sent the Mission a revision of the speech it had sent to Stevenson on April 12. It sent a substitute paragraph for the declaration that "no American citizens [would] take part in military action against Cuba." The new paragraph read: "I want to say now and clearly: the United States has no aggressive purposes against Cuba. We naturally sympathize with the desire of the people of Cuba—including those in exile, who do not stop being Cubans merely because they could no longer stand to live under Castro's tyranny—to seek Cuban independence and freedom. We hope that the Cuban people will succeed in doing what Castro's revolution never really tried to do: that is, to bring democratic processes to Cuba. But as President Kennedy has already said, 'There will not, under any conditions, be an intervention in Cuba by United States armed forces.' This government will do everything it possibly can to make sure that there are no Americans involved in any actions in Cuba."

The Department told Stevenson that a decision had been made not to produce the defecting fliers or to reveal their identities. It sent him language on the pilots he could use if he wished. Finally, "The Cuban representative, Dr. Roa, has charged that the United States is directly and criminally responsible for attacks on Cuban air bases. The United States Government formally and categorically denies this charge. The attack did not proceed from the United States. It was not made by the United States' pilots." Thus the Department, at midnight on Saturday, was still sticking to the CIA cover story.

But the CIA cover story began to break down. It had never been very good. Why did the United States Government continue to withhold the names of the pilots even after newspaper photographs showing their faces were published? What about the rocket fragments bearing the inscription "U.S.A." which Castro said he had recovered after the attack? What about two auxiliary fuel tanks recovered twelve miles off the north coast near Havana? Did not that prove that the planes came from some distant point? The Cuban Revolutionary Council in New York announced that six planes took part in the bombings. Then why did the pilot in Miami say only four had defected? As Robert F. Kennedy remarked later, "Things were beginning to surface." By Sunday, Stevenson and his colleagues at the Mission realized he had been trapped into making false statements to the UN.

"He was disgusted," one of his colleagues recalled. "Upset. He was a man who was very jealous of his image—and rightly. And he felt that this had tarnished his image."

About midnight on Sunday, April 16, the exile brigade began to go ashore at the Bay of Pigs. Pedersen was notified at 7 A.M. on Monday. He telephoned Stevenson at 42A in the Waldorf. Stevenson said, "Yes, I know, Bundy is here." McGeorge Bundy had been sent to New York to tell Stevenson what was going on. He told him everything, including the CIA cover story. "We had breakfast that morning," Bundy said later. "He'd been out the night before to a Democratic party. I told him all about it. We should have done that a week earlier. It was most difficult for him. He was very decent about it. He did *not* fuss about the box he was in. All he wanted was more information so he would not dig deeper holes." It was another instance of Stevenson's behaving courageously instead of grumbling—at a time when he had a good deal to grumble about.

That day, while the brigade was fighting on the beach, Stevenson spoke at length on Cuba to the Political Committee. Dr. Roa had just charged the United States with aggression against Cuba—an invasion coming from Florida. Stevenson said, "These charges are totally false and I deny them categorically. The United States has committed no aggression against Cuba and no offensive has been launched from Florida or from any other part of the United States." He then declared that the United States "would be opposed to the use of our territory for mounting an offensive against any foreign government." Stevenson recalled the great American sympathy for the early Castro cause and accused Castro of the "methodical and shameless" betrayal of his own revolution. He said, "If the Castro regime is perishing it is from self-inflicted wounds. What Dr. Roa seeks from us today is the protection of the Castro regime from the natural wrath of the Cuban people." The exiles who sought Castro's overthrow would not "turn the clock back" to Batista's tyranny. They "stand for a new and brighter Cuba which will genuinely realize the pledge which Dr. Castro has so fanatically betrayed—the pledge of bread with freedom."

The invasion had gone badly from the start. It immediately lost the element of surprise. Its men had known nothing in advance of coral reefs which obstructed or sank their boats as they attempted to go ashore. By 4 A.M. the invasion was faltering. Soon its supply ship, laden with munitions and gasoline, was grounded and abandoned, a target for Castro's planes, which were strafing the beach. Presently a rocket hit another supply ship, blowing it up. Castro himself had been awakened at 3:15 A.M. and had gone to the beach to direct the defense.

That day Rusk held a press conference. He spoke of the debate in the UN, said information was incomplete on what was happening in Cuba but said "serious unrest and disorders are to be found in all parts of the country," and said the United States was not intervening in Cuba nor would it. He refused to answer questions or otherwise go beyond his prepared statement.

During this critical day UN machinery continued to grind away. Telegrams went out on the Cameroons and the Congo. Hammarskjold summoned Dean of the United Kingdom, and Yost, to deplore what he considered a lack of U.S.-U.K. support for Kasavubu. The Moroccan representative asked Yost what the U.S. position would be on admission of Mauritania. Two Israeli delegates met with Plimpton to express their displeasure with a U.S. decision on another pending resolution. The Mission informed the Secretary General of a Soviet arms shipment seen in Ghana and reported destined for the Congo.

At the meeting of the Political Committee on Tuesday, April 18, Ambassador Zorin read the text of a message from Premier Khrushchev to President Kennedy, warning that the U.S.S.R. would give the Cuban government all necessary assistance in repelling the attack.

Later in the day Stevenson read Kennedy's reply. Kennedy told Khrushchev that he was "under a serious misapprehension" about Cuba. For months resistance to Castro had increased inside Cuba and more than 100,000 refugees had fled Cuba. Many of them hoped to overthrow Castro, although they had fought for him earlier. The United States "intends no military intervention in Cuba." If any outside force intervened militarily "we will immediately honor our obligations under the inter-

American system to protect this hemisphere against external aggression." Kennedy had taken "careful note" of Khrushchev's statement that events in Cuba might affect peace in all parts of the world. "I trust that this does not mean that the Soviet government, using the situation in Cuba as a pretext, is planning to inflame other areas of the world."

Other delegates seemed in no hurry to deal with the issue. Many assumed that the United States would invade militarily and that then the task would be one of somehow burying the problem, just as had happened when the Russians suppressed the Hungarian revolt.

That night, April 18, Stevenson, having spoken at a college banquet, arrived at the Political Committee about nine-fifteen and spoke again at length. "I have listened here," he said, "to every kind of epitaph [epithet?] and abuse of my country. All of the familiar Communist words have been poured in a torrent on a nation that has fought in the two world wars to defeat the designs of tyrants and protect your freedom as well as ours, a nation that bore the greatest burden of the first great battle for collective security in Korea and the protection of a small country from cynical and unprovoked attack by its neighbor, a nation that has poured out its treasure to aid the reconstruction and rehabilitation, the defense and prosperity, of friends and foes alike, with a magnanimity without historical precedence [precedents?]. And for our pains the words that reverberate in this chamber are too often 'greedy monopolists,' 'mercenaries,' 'economic imperialists,' 'exploiters,' 'pirates,' 'aggressors' and all the familiar Communist jargon, including the worst of all, 'counterrevolutionary,' which of course means anti-Communist. And I must say that after listening to this that I welcome the healthy and wholesome suggestion of the representative of Ecuador that we declare a moratorium on epithets and poison in our discussion."

Cuba, he said, had confiscated American property, denounced America repeatedly, closed the American Embassy, persecuted American citizens, and then complained because America would not buy her sugar at a price above the world market. "I am reminded," Stevenson said, "of the little boy who killed his mother and his father and then pleaded for clemency on the ground that he was an orphan." Cuba was no orphan. She had "a new and powerful friend" which, having taken over the Cuban revolution, now denied the right of revolution to the Cuban people. He repeated, "No invasion has taken place from Florida or any other part of the United States."

Roa had produced "not one bit of evidence of United States involvement," he said. The world knew that since Castro had betrayed his revolution a tide of discontent and resistance had been rising inside Cuba. Roa had produced photographs of U.S. armaments found in Cuba after the assaults. Stevenson declared that these armaments were widely distributed throughout Latin America, Europe, and most of the world and could be bought on private arms markets. Roa had said that the United States was trying to force Cuba back to the constitution of 1940, which he called an expression of colonial economic structure. But Castro himself had made the constitution of 1940 a "cornerstone" of his revolutionary movement before he took power. Stevenson read from the Declaration of Sierra Maestra of 1957, in which Castro outlined the aims of his revolution, and then described, point by point, how, after taking power, Castro had betrayed his own ideals, destroying freedom. He closed, "The United States sincerely hopes that any difficulties which we or other American countries may have with Cuba will be settled peacefully. We have committed no aggression against Cuba. We have no aggressive purposes against Cuba. We intend no military intervention in Cuba. We seek to see a restoration of the friendly relations which once prevailed between Cuba and the United States." Zorin spoke. The debate was long and bitter.

By Wednesday, April 19, it was clear that the Bay of Pigs invasion had failed. Kennedy refused to intervene with American force to save it. The men on the beach were being captured or killed. Castro was said to be rounding up some 200,000 Cubans suspected of sympathy toward the invaders. A little after 4 P.M. on Wednesday the men on the beach at the Bay of Pigs sent a final message, then destroyed their radio and fled into the swamps.

Early that morning—indeed, in the middle of the night—the Department sent Stevenson voting instructions. Its first preference would be for the debate to conclude without a vote on any resolution but it realized this was probably impossible. A seven-power Latin American resolution continued to be the best. Stevenson was authorized to actively mobilize support for it. A U.S.S.R. resolution was so extreme it probably would not be adopted; the United States should oppose it. A Rumanian resolution was less extreme but still bad. The Mexican draft was, however, the most difficult to deal with. It might split the Latin Americans. Stevenson could vote against it or could abstain, whichever he considered best tactically.

The plenary session of the General Assembly that day debated Angola. By now Stevenson was so deeply embroiled in Cuba that Yost made the United States speech on Angola. (The Assembly at length adopted the Angola resolution which the Security Council had rejected—the Ceylon-Liberia-U.A.R. resolution calling on Portugal to consider urgently reforms to permit the Angolan people to exercise the right of self-determination and establishing a UN subcommittee to report on conditions in Angola. The vote was 73 [including the United States] to 2 [Spain, Union of South Africa] with 2 abstentions.[2])

President Kennedy spoke to the American Society of Newspaper Editors

[2] Henceforward, for brevity, I shall indicate on which side the United States and Russia voted thus: 73 (U.S.) to 5 (U.S.S.R.).

that day. He emphasized that the Cuban affair was "a struggle of Cuban patriots against a Cuban dictator." American unilateral intervention would have been "contrary to our traditions and to our international obligations," he said. "But let the record show that our restraint is not inexhaustible. Should it ever appear that the inter-American doctrine of non-interference merely conceals or excuses a policy of non-action—if the nations of this hemisphere should fail to meet their commitments against out-side Communist penetration—then I want it clearly understood that this government will not hesitate in meeting its primary obligations, which are to the security of our nation." Cuba itself was no threat to the United States. But Cuba was a base for "subverting" other nations throughout the hemisphere. And "it is clearer than ever that we face a relentless struggle in every corner of the globe that goes far beyond the clash of armies or even nuclear armaments. The armies are there, and in large number. The nuclear armaments are there. But they serve primarily as the shield behind which subversion, infiltration, and a host of other tactics steadily advance, picking off vulnerable areas one by one in situations which do not permit our own armed intervention. . . . We dare not fail to see the insidious na-ture of this new and deeper struggle . . . whether in Cuba or South Viet-nam. . . . The message of Cuba, of Laos, of the rising din of Communist voices in Asia and Latin America—these messages are all the same. The complacent, the self-indulgent, the soft societies are about to be swept away with the debris of history. Only the strong, only the industrious, only the determined, only the courageous, only the visionary who determine the real nature of our struggle can possibly survive. . . . Too long we have fixed our eyes on traditional military needs, on armies prepared to cross borders, on missiles poised for flight. Now it should be clear that this is no longer enough—that our security may be lost piece by piece, country by country, without the firing of a single missile or the crossing of a single border. . . . We intend to re-examine and reorient our forces of all kinds."

Ambassador Menshikov had been scheduled to breakfast with Steven-son next morning but broke the appointment. Stevenson telephoned Harlan Cleveland in Washington. Cleveland had attended a meeting on tactics with President Kennedy. Stevenson set forth the "scenario" for that night's meeting of the Political Committee. Stevenson thought if he could get priority consideration of the seven-power Latin American resolution, all would be well. The Mexican resolution, however, troubled him. The U.K. delegation presently had instructions to abstain. Stevenson suggested the Department try to persuade the British and the Mexicans. How strongly did President Kennedy feel about the issue?

Cleveland replied that the President believed U.S. prestige and his own personal prestige and that of the presidency were at stake. Stevenson saw only two things to be done—approach the U.K. and Mexico quickly. Cleveland decided to approach the British by having Ambassador Foy

Kohler get in touch with the British Ambassador, Caccia, and to approach the Mexicans through the Mexican Ambassador in Washington, all on instructions of the President.

The meeting in the Political Committee that night resembled an armed camp. Phil Klutznick was embattled in the Fifth Committee, which was considering UN financing and the Russians' refusal to pay their assessment. He had only one political officer helping him and he sent the man to Stevenson to ask for more help. The political officer reported that every other official on the staff was in the First Committee, helping Stevenson, watching everybody in the room, spotting votes. Klutznick left his man in the chair and went himself to plead with Stevenson. "He was fighting a battle," Klutznick said. "He hadn't got the word from Washington. The seats were loaded. I got behind him and told him we were in trouble [in the Fifth Committee] and were not going to get our two-thirds vote and I needed help." Stevenson asked how badly we would lose. By three or four votes, Klutznick said. Stevenson said the financing question would still have to go to the General Assembly and told him to go back and lose gracefully—Stevenson needed all hands in the First Committee.

Stevenson spoke at length, beginning, "Although I am loath to speak so often or as long as the representative of the Soviet Union, this is, after all, an item that involves the United States and not the U.S.S.R. So I have some final words." He repeated what he had said before about the abuse of the United States, then asked "—if this was a United States military operation, do you think it would succeed or fail? How long do you think Cuba could resist the military power of the United States? Perhaps the best evidence of the falsity of the shrill charges of American aggression in Cuba is the melancholy fact that this blow for freedom has not yet succeeded. And if the United States had been in charge I submit that fighting would hardly have broken out on the day debate was to start in this committee." He replied to charges of "economic slavery" by describing the Alliance for Progress. He sought to rally Latin American opinion by warning against Soviet penetration in the hemisphere. "The free nations of the world cannot permit political conquest any more than they can tolerate military aggression." He quoted President Kennedy's speech of that afternoon, asking, "Can we ignore what is happening in a small country like Vietnam whose freedom is in danger [endangered?] by guerrilla forces operating under Communist direction from the north and are seeking to overthrow the freely elected government of that country?" He said the United States would vote for the Latin American resolution and against the Soviet and Rumanian resolutions. He termed the Mexican resolution "unacceptable" because it ignored the OAS. He closed by paying tribute to the Cuban exiles.

Throughout the debate, Mission officers negotiated with the Mexicans and others, and telegrams and telephone calls went back and forth between the Mission and Cleveland, discussing various resolutions, amend-

ments to them, tactics. In the committee, the Latin American resolution
was amended and passed 61 (U.S.) to 27, with 10 abstentions. The Mexican resolution was adopted 42 to 31 (U.S.) with 25 abstentions. The
U.S.S.R. and Rumania withdrew their resolutions. When the remaining
resolutions went to the General Assembly the next day, the Latin American resolution was amended, then adopted by 59 (U.S.) to 13 (Soviet
bloc and Cuba), and the Mexican resolution failed to receive the necessary two-thirds vote—the vote was 41 (U.S.S.R. and Cuba) to 35 (U.S.)
with 20 abstentions. The session did not end till 6 A.M. At that time the
resumed session of the General Assembly adjourned. That day, too, President Kennedy at a press conference took full responsibility for the Bay of
Pigs in his memorable statement: "There's an old saying that victory has a
hundred fathers and defeat is an orphan. . . . I'm the responsible officer
of the government."

On April 24, Harlan Cleveland sent congratulations to Stevenson and
his colleagues, said it was an inspiration to watch Stevenson work and fun
to work with him.

The day after the Assembly ended, Saturday, April 22, Stevenson slept
only from 6:30 A.M. to 8:30 A.M. Then he telephoned Washington and
talked with President Kennedy in lieu of attending a National Security
Council meeting. After that he dictated letters and talked by telephone
with Agnes Meyer, Dean Rusk, Bill Wirtz, and Bill Blair. (He told Blair,
"They've got the damnedest bunch of boy commandos running around
down there [Washington] you ever saw.") He had lunch with Barbara
Ward and at about two-thirty left with her in a car sent by Ruth Field to
spend a quiet weekend at Mrs. Field's place, Caumsett. Worn out, he went
to bed at 9 P.M. and slept until ten the next morning. Mrs. Field recalled,
"I never saw a more exhausted man. He and Barbara and I walked on the
beach. He lay down on a rock and went sound asleep." He went back to
New York to attend a farewell lunch at Mrs. Lasker's town house for Bill
Blair, leaving for Denmark as Ambassador.

The Bay of Pigs had taxed Stevenson severely—and would continue to
do so. He had been personally humiliated, had, albeit unwittingly, lied to
the United Nations. "At first he thought that his credibility and usefulness
had been destroyed," Yost once said. In the end, however, Yost came to
feel that Stevenson's credibility was not gone. "It simply didn't happen. It
passed away very quickly. There was a lot of sympathy for the United
States and it came to the surface at that time. If the invasion attempt had
succeeded, we would have been in worse shape. But it was such a tragic
failure—and President Kennedy and the Governor took the responsibility
quickly. We got amazingly little flack under the circumstances." Other
Ambassadors at the UN did not believe Stevenson was a liar, and told him
so privately, even the Russians. Many of them had been lied to by their
governments in the past; they sympathized with Stevenson. Several weeks
later, on a mission to Latin America, Stevenson spoke of the Bay of Pigs

in a businesslike way to his companion, Lincoln Gordon (later Assistant
Secretary of State for Latin America), not complaining about the position
it had put him in (though he did refer to Kennedy as "that immature
young man" who was inexperienced and somewhat rash, in need of advice
from older men).

But a week or so after the Bay of Pigs, Stevenson, in Washington on
business, stopped in at Schlesinger's White House office and said he had
been greatly "hurt" by the failure of Washington to consult him in advance
about the Bay of Pigs. Although he had accepted the job on the understanding that he would be brought into major policy decisions, no one in
Washington had asked his advice about anything, until recently when the
President, at a National Security Council meeting, had unexpectedly asked
him what he thought should be done about Laos. Schlesinger advised him
to give the President advice when he had something on his mind, even if
not specifically asked. Stevenson said he had given up hope of being
consulted by Rusk. He spoke more irritably than angrily, Schlesinger
thought.

If the Bay of Pigs had not undermined his credibility at the UN, it had
clearly and publicly demonstrated that Stevenson was not consulted by
Kennedy and Rusk on secret matters of great import. This hurt. Robert
Kennedy felt that the Bay of Pigs worsened relations between President
Kennedy and Stevenson. Stevenson and Marietta Tree had been saying repeatedly that Stevenson, not Kennedy, should have been President. Kennedy heard of it. The Bay of Pigs fiasco seemed to prove to Stevenson's
friends that he, not Kennedy, should have been President. His age and
wisdom would have averted danger. The President was aware they held
this feeling.

Jane Dick thought Stevenson very close to resigning because of the Bay
of Pigs. When the CIA cover story was exposed, she had encountered him
in an elevator at the Waldorf. "I said 'Hello' and he just dashed past me. I
could see he'd had a frightful shock. I thought he was very ill or else Ellen
had jumped off the roof. Or some terrible family illness had happened. I
was so concerned that I turned around and went to 42A. I said to him,
'Adlai, what in heaven's name has happened?' He said, 'You heard my
speech today? Well, I did not tell the whole truth; I did not know the
whole truth. I took this job at the President's request on the understanding
that I would be consulted and kept fully informed on everything. I spoke
in the United Nations in good faith on that understanding. Now, my credibility has been compromised, and therefore my usefulness.' He kept repeating, 'I've got to resign—there's nothing I can do but resign.' Then he'd
say, 'But I can't resign—can't—the young President and the country are
in enough trouble.' "

He told Agnes Meyer on May 14, "The Cuban absurdity made me sick
for a week . . . but I've been surprised how little it seems to have affected
my *personal* regard." Barbara Ward suggested Stevenson propose to Ken-

nedy that he, Stevenson, go on a trip around Latin America soon in order to repair relations. Stevenson and Kennedy discussed such a trip the week after the Bay of Pigs. Stevenson recommended that Kennedy send Muñoz Marín, Governor of Puerto Rico. In the end, however, he sent Stevenson.

The whole affair of the Bay of Pigs is rather muddled. But U.S. responsibility for the adventure cannot be doubted: American agents trained the invaders, armed them, provided them with planes, and dominated their political leadership. Much of this Stevenson knew in advance, though not in complete detail, and he opposed it. But he was not consulted; he was informed. And he was incompletely informed—he was not told of the CIA cover story designed to prove that the Cuban Air Force had begun insurrection inside Cuba. That is what got him into trouble at the UN; that is where he unwittingly misled the UN. He himself had been unintentionally misled by a failure of communication with Schlesinger (and others); the error was compounded by the United States Government's own "need-to-know" security rule. Stevenson did need to know about the CIA's cover story; but the CIA decided, wrongly, that he did not. As a consequence, it appeared briefly that the Bay of Pigs might bring Stevenson down with it. That that did not happen is a tribute to his own prestige. The Bay of Pigs was, nonetheless, one of the worst foreign policy disasters of recent years, redeemed only by the role its memory played in strengthening Kennedy's skepticism about the Joint Chiefs and the CIA and in urging prudence on the Administration a year and a half later at the time of the Cuban missile crisis. Some have thought that Stevenson, once he learned he had been compromised by the CIA cover story, should have abandoned the entire defense of the U.S. position. They forget the old saying: "An Ambassador is an honest man sent to lie abroad for the commonwealth." The adage is overstated—one does not always have to lie, but simply to put the best possible face on what his country does—yet it contains an element of truth, as Stevenson would realize (if he had not before) as his time passed at the UN.

11.

Between the end of April and his June departure for Latin America, Stevenson was occupied with plans for his trip and with plans for next fall's session of the General Assembly, although Cleveland and others in the Department were more concerned than Stevenson with the next session. (Phil Klutznick warned him that it was not too soon to consider the problem of financing the UN operation in the Congo, an early warning of serious trouble, but neither Stevenson nor the Department paid much heed at this time.) Stevenson carried on a busy social life, part of it the unavoidable diplomatic dinners and cocktail parties, part of it with friends. He spent weekends at Mrs. Vincent Astor's, Mary Lasker's, Ruth Field's. Pussy Paepcke visited him for several days and he took her to diplomatic functions. He entertained Jane Dick at a family dinner. The Rev. Mr. Graebel visited him. He went to the theater with Mary Lasker, had his postponed breakfast with Ambassador Menshikov, spent a weekend late in May at Libertyville.

He saw President Kennedy several times during this period. Kennedy was looking for an Assistant Secretary of State for Latin America, and Stevenson suggested three names—Albion Patterson, De Lesseps Morrison, and John Moors Cabot. (None was appointed.) When, on May 1, Kennedy asked for Stevenson's views on Laos, he responded promptly with a memorandum, drafted by Yost and revised by Stevenson.

Just before Kennedy took office, President Eisenhower had spent more time with him discussing Laos than any other subject. Pathet Lao Communist forces were moving against the royal Laotian government. Some in the United States Government thought the United States should go into Laos militarily against the Communists. Others thought we should appeal to the UN Security Council. Others wanted to allow time for the machinery established by the Geneva Conference to bring about a cease-fire.

Stevenson thought it impossible to convince the French, British, Indians, and others that immediate action was necessary unless the Communists made further advances against the two capitals and the river ports. He therefore recommended against immediate military or Security Council action. If the Communist offensive was resumed, he recommended acting in the Security Council and moving SEATO forces to the Thai side of the Mekong River across from the threatened Laotian cities and, if the Communist offensive continued, that the United States "be prepared" to move SEATO forces across the river into Laos. He warned that American military action "would almost certainly provoke" military reaction by North Vietnam and "probably" mainland China. The best the United States could hope for would be a division of Laos. Even assuming an early cease-fire, "you confront a prolonged period of tough diplomatic bargaining and of political and covert warfare on the ground." The result could be a neutral Laos, a Communist Laos, or a partitioned Laos. Given the geographical position of Laos and the temper of America's allies and neutrals, "the U.S. almost certainly does *not* have the capability to maintain its commitment to Laos in the broadest sense, without risks far out of proportion to the ends to be achieved." The real question was, therefore, whether to play safe with a divided Laos or to gamble on maintaining a neutral Laos. Stevenson recommended doing nothing for the moment and waiting to see what happened after a cease-fire was achieved but making it clear by "concrete political and military measures to demonstrate that we will defend, if attacked, Thailand, South Vietnam and Cambodia, and South Laos if the country should be divided."

Two weeks before he was to leave for Latin America he expressed to a Department official misgivings about going. If it was to be merely a "good will" trip, he would not go. If, however, he was to sell a U.S. Latin American policy in which he concurred, he would go. He complained he never had seen National Security Council papers on Latin America. He met with various U.S. and Latin American diplomats. Barbara Ward urged that the United States reach some sort of accommodation with Castro, perhaps buying his sugar above world prices. She opposed trying to isolate Castro in the hemisphere.

Kennedy was preparing to go to Europe to meet with Khrushchev, De Gaulle, and others. Stevenson was not satisfied with the way American relations with the Soviet Union were being handled. He felt that way throughout his tenure at the UN and prepared several papers on it. On May 24 he had a long meeting with President Kennedy, together with Secretary Rusk and Assistant Secretary Cleveland, and Stevenson gave Kennedy a paper on the forthcoming meetings. While Kennedy would wish to discuss such specific questions as disarmament, Berlin, Laos, and Cuba, he should concentrate if possible on "the basic question which governs all of these—the Soviet interpretation of 'peaceful coexistence.'" Stevenson said that from his own talks with Khrushchev and others he gathered that the Soviets demanded an absolute taboo on Western intervention inside the Communist bloc but a free hand for themselves, short of provoking general war, to aid "wars of liberation" outside the bloc. The Soviets also demanded a veto on international action both inside and outside the Communist bloc. Khrushchev, he said, would not concede this but Kennedy might say that peaceful coexistence could not last long within this framework. Despite De Gaulle's scorn of the UN, Stevenson recommended that Kennedy suggest to him that it was the best place to try to attract the uncommitted Afro-Asians to the Western side. He hoped Kennedy would show his disappointment that France had refused to contribute to the UN expenses in the Congo, thus aligning herself with Russia. (Kennedy would later this same day ask Stevenson to prepare another more detailed memo on how the Soviet leaders viewed the world.)

On Chinese representation in the UN, Secretary Rusk gave Kennedy a "talking paper" for a meeting with Henry Luce of *Time*. (Kennedy rarely made much use of such papers.) Luce was one of several important U.S. "opinion makers"—Roy Howard of Scripps-Howard newspapers was another—whom Kennedy or other high officials planned to ask to support a shift in U.S. China policy. Kennedy turned to Stevenson and asked what he "really" thought about mainland China—should we want them in the UN? Stevenson replied that he did not want them in the UN but on this issue the United States should not suffer a major defeat. Kennedy understood the Formosa Chinese were in real danger of being ejected from the UN, the United States was committed to keeping them in, and the two-

Chinas formula might be the best way to keep them in. But, he said, the United States could not take the lead in promoting a two-Chinas formula —it would stir up political controversy in the United States, hurting the foreign aid bill and other Administration projects. Therefore, while informal discussions could proceed in diplomatic channels and with key figures in the United States, including Eisenhower, Kennedy thought the government could not bring the problem to the surface formally for at least several months. Rusk said the Australian Ambassador had volunteered to float the two-Chinas proposal. Kennedy thought it would be useful if both Australia and Great Britain floated it. He suggested further conversations with the Chinese Ambassadors to the UN and to the United States. He emphasized again "the political dynamite locked up in this issue." On Latin America, Kennedy said emphatically that Stevenson's trip there should not be to encourage common action against Cuba or explain the Bay of Pigs but, rather, to lay the groundwork for further inter-American meetings on the Alliance for Progress, to seek ways to improve hemispheric economic and social and political cooperation, and to consult with Latin American leaders on UN matters. Kennedy thought the less said about Cuba the better.

On Saturday, May 27, Stevenson met with Kennedy and Harlan Cleveland and Pierre Salinger. Kennedy asked what line he should take with Khrushchev on Berlin, a crucial issue. Stevenson said he thought it might be useful to renew the proposal of some sort of unification of Berlin. He also mentioned the possibility of other proposals which would make West Berlin less physically and militarily untenable, including a corridor of access from West Germany.

At this meeting Stevenson handed President Kennedy the long memorandum Kennedy had requested on "the way Soviet leaders see things." He said Karl Marx had taught that capitalist governments would make increasingly dangerous war on each other and would make every effort to destroy any revolutionary socialist regime. During the lifetimes of the men ruling the Kremlin, the Western European democracies had done much to prove him right. They had started two world wars "which could justly be called imperialist," betrayed the League of Nations Covenant by permitting the conquest of Manchuria, Abyssinia, Spain, Austria, and Czechoslovakia, and given constant proof of their "deep and sustained hostility to the Soviet regime," starting with the intervention of 1917–21 and ending with the expulsion of Russia from the League in 1939. It was therefore not surprising that the Kremlin leaders regarded the West with suspicion. Moreover the United States had rejected its own disarmament proposals in 1955 after the Russians had accepted them, and the crises of Suez, Lebanon, the U-2, and the Bay of Pigs had not helped. Since 1955, Khrushchev had campaigned for disarmament. The West had accepted his ultimate objective of "general and complete disarmament" only on condition that a UN international force be created to enforce it. At the Garst farm in Iowa in 1959, Khrushchev had told Stevenson he would consider an international police force "at the end of the disarmament road."

Meanwhile, the UN had been called into the Congo, and Hammarskjold had done things there that Khrushchev disliked, no doubt raising in Khrushchev's mind doubts about the UN role in a disarmed world. It could be hostile to the Soviet Union, he might think. Indeed, in his speech to the UN on September 23, 1960, Khrushchev had made it clear that this was in fact the origin of his troika proposal. Hammarskjold did not feel that Khrushchev's attacks had been personal; they had been aimed at the idea of having a Secretary General exclusively control a UN force that might, under disarmament agreements, become extremely important. Stevenson suggested putting the UN force under a commander chosen from among smaller powers and directly responsible not to the Secretary General but to the General Assembly through a standing commission. A similar system might resolve the present deadlock in the Conference on Nuclear Tests. It must also be understood that the Kremlin believed the Communist bloc was seriously underrepresented in the Secretariat and in the various UN councils.

But did the men in the Kremlin genuinely want disarmament and peaceful coexistence? Their basic objectives probably were to develop economic and political strength inside the U.S.S.R. and the Communist bloc and to expand the Soviet empire without seriously risking general war or seriously impairing the impression that theirs was a "progressive" regime after Stalin's. Peking's influence often supported Communist expansion, since that regime was still in a fanatical phase of development and its extremism increased its power within the Communist bloc. It must also be remembered that Khrushchev and other Russian leaders insisted upon having absolute equality in world affairs because of their "inferiority-superiority complex."

In view of all this, Stevenson thought, the Soviet leaders presumably did desire a "substantial measure" of disarmament—the danger of nuclear war threatened their objective of improving their position, they saw no point in general war since they confidently expected to defeat the West by other means, they would like to reduce the enormous economic burden of the arms race, and the Communist Party would be happy to diminish the power of the military officer corps. At the same time, the Kremlin leaders, like other leaders, were unwilling to disarm to a point or in a way which would jeopardize their national security or domestic political power. They still believed a "closed society" essential and so probably would not agree to the extensive inspection that the United States had heretofore insisted on. They might sincerely believe the West would use inspections to spy.

Whether the West and Russia could ever agree on significant disarmament probably would depend on whether they could resolve five other issues: inspection, military equality between the Soviet Union and the

United States, Chinese cooperation, an end to Communist assistance to "wars of liberation," and international policing after disarmament. The best hope lay in convincing the Soviets that peaceful change, not violent revolution, was the way of progress and in convincing the Western democracies that they must treat the Soviet Union as an equal. The West must view inspection as surveillance, not as airtight control. The Soviets, under Chinese pressure, probably had decided to merge the negotiating of a nuclear test ban with general disarmament. They probably would welcome the U.S. resumption of nuclear tests—it would permit them to resume, free the Chinese to commence, and put the international onus on the United States.

The President announced Stevenson's Latin American trip on May 29. Privately he gave Stevenson a message for Janio Quadros of Brazil—Quadros was making things "very difficult" for the United States by declaring political neutrality at a time when he was seeking financial assistance from the United States. Stevenson told Arthur Schlesinger that some Latin Americans resented U.S. disinterest in their "cultural and intellectual ferment," that disinterest had arisen during the years when anti-intellectuals controlled our government, and that now "Harvard on the Potomac" could transform the United States' attitude. He was taking with him Ellis Briggs, a senior career Foreign Service officer, at that time Ambassador to Greece but experienced in Latin America; Lincoln Gordon, who had headed the Kennedy task force that produced the Alliance for Progress proposals; Borden; Roxane Eberlein; aides, and newspapermen. He offered to buy aquamarines or tourmalines for Barbara Ward as he had for Mrs. Ives during his last trip to Brazil. He would start out by commercial jet and later ride a U.S. military plane.

The last few days before the party left were frenzied. Stevenson had heard that the United States was proposing to establish a missile tracking station in the Union of South Africa and to sell South Africa arms, including fighter aircraft. He opposed it to Rusk because feeling against apartheid was rising. "I hardly need add that relations with the rest of Africa, and especially the new states, are important to our security, too." In Washington on June 2 he went through a briefing on Latin America, but it was confused because Trujillo, dictator of the Dominican Republic, had just been assassinated—the Latin American Bureau of the Department was in an uproar.

Steve Mitchell had asked Stevenson's support for a federal judgeship. Stevenson told Mitchell he had written to Robert Kennedy, the Attorney General, about him. At the same time Stevenson recommended Carl McGowan and R. Hunter Pierson of Alexandria, Louisiana, to Attorney General Kennedy for federal judgeships. (Of McGowan he said, "This man is of Supreme Court quality," a judgment in which many people would have concurred. McGowan was appointed to the U. S. Circuit Court of Appeals in Washington.) Declining an invitation to an affair in

honor of his old associate Fred Hoehler in Chicago—he would be in South
America—Stevenson said, "It all reminds me of the boy who wrote home
from Palestine in the first war and said to his folks: 'Here I am in Palestine where Christ was born, and I wish to Christ I was in Evanston where
I was born!'" David Riesman, the social scientist, had written Stevenson
sympathetically after the Bay of Pigs, recalling how he had refused to support Kennedy in 1960 because he feared his "jingoism and impetuosity"
toward Cuba. He reminded Stevenson that he still had a "devoted constituency" which recognized that he must support his country's position at the
UN or resign—it would support him whatever he chose to do, including
resign. Now on the eve of his departure Stevenson replied, "I had my troubles as you know, and begin to wonder how long it takes to 'season' some
of the young liberals. . . . I may need that 'devoted constituency' more
than ever!"

12.

He was in South America nearly three weeks. He visited every South
American country (but none in the Caribbean or Central America). At
the outset, according to Lincoln Gordon, he was unenthusiastic about the
trip but later came to feel he had a role to play, was not merely an errand
boy for President Kennedy. The trip was not unlike his earlier private
travels—embassy briefings, meetings with Foreign Ministers and chiefs of
state and influential people, official dinners and receptions, press conferences—but now he did less sightseeing and talked with officials not
about generalities but about hard political and economic problems—the
amount of American aid, inter-American action on Cuba and the Dominican Republic, the admission of mainland China into the UN, the Latin
American seat on the Security Council. Once he wrote, in Venezuela,
"Large reception—3 hrs on my poor feet talking, talking, talking. Shades
of every Embassy across the world!" And again, landing at La Paz,
"Llama on the airstrip!" But most of his notes were on politics and economics.

The inter-American meeting at Punta del Este which would establish the
Alliance for Progress was only a few months away; everywhere Stevenson
found officials wondering whether Kennedy would attend; it became the
key question. Some chiefs of state viewed the meeting with uncertainty;
some wanted it postponed. President Quadros of Brazil wanted a Latin
American summit meeting with Kennedy. He told Stevenson northeast
Brazil and Bolivia were the two most dangerous places in the hemisphere.
(Betancourt of Venezuela, on the Caribbean, was more worried about
Cuba and the Dominican Republic.) In many countries students were riot-
ing, and news that one had been killed by the police was brought to the
Bolivian President, Victor Paz Estenssoro, and Stevenson while they were

meeting. Troops lined the streets of La Paz and ringed the hotel when Stevenson arrived.

Stevenson had been urged to avoid Paraguay because of its dictator, Stroessner. Stevenson's plane stopped there briefly en route to Buenos Aires and, "to my discomfiture," the Foreign Minister was at the airport. Later Stevenson decided to pay an official visit to Paraguay, and did, and found Stroessner "v. German looking & pleasant. Very defensive re regime. . . . Dinner at FM & jolliest evening of trip. . . . Wish I didn't like these warm, eager poor Paraguayans so much. . . . Sad situation—but not as totally repressive as I had expected." Everywhere he saw the consequences of the Bay of Pigs: as Quadros told him, the great prestige of the Kennedy administration had been "spoiled" by it, and another attempt at invasion would be "fatal." From Santiago, Stevenson talked by telephone with Chet Bowles and strongly recommended that Kennedy appoint Lincoln Gordon Assistant Secretary for Latin America. (Gordon did become Assistant Secretary, but not until after he had served as Kennedy's Ambassador to Brazil.) In Bogotá, his last stop before leaving for home on June 22, "Dinner alone with Pres. Lleras Camargo—4 hrs!—best leader in continent!!"

13.

While Stevenson was in South America his colleagues at the Mission and Department were working on Chinese representation, disarmament, Angola, and Berlin, on which Khrushchev had taken a hard line with Kennedy at Vienna. On China, Rusk was telling foreign diplomats that the United States had not reached a formal position but did not think the moratorium would succeed and thought Formosa's stubborn all-or-nothing policy might well end up with Peking in and Formosa out of the UN. By June 23 the New York *Times* was reporting that the United States was studying a two-Chinas policy. Pressures were building up on Berlin. Senior American diplomats in Washington considered this the most serious Berlin crisis yet. They consulted with French and British and Germans. The crisis became increasingly inflamed and by late July and August had reached the point where Kennedy was calling up reserves and Khrushchev was accusing him, in a conversation with McCloy, of issuing an ultimatum which amounted to a "preliminary" declaration of war against the Soviet Union. Indeed, the Berlin crisis of that late summer was probably the most dangerous President Kennedy ever faced, not excepting the Cuban missile crisis, since the vital interests of both the United States and the U.S.S.R. were engaged, while in Cuba only those of the United States were engaged.

During that same time preparations went forward for disarmament and nuclear testing negotiations. Some in the government wanted the United States to resume testing. Others, including Stevenson, were opposed. And during this same period the Angola problem also continued to occupy the diplomats.

Stevenson returned to Washington from South America on June 22, a Thursday. He spent the weekend at the Magnusons', working on a speech and on his report to President Kennedy, meeting with Secretary Rusk on Chinese representation, and meeting in the White House with President Kennedy, Rusk, Bowles, and others to report orally on his trip.

He delivered the speech on Monday to the National Press Club, speaking from notes. He said nearly every Latin American country he visited was under democratic control. Political stability was "under severe strain." Communist and other extreme leftists had gained strength. And the danger of right-wing coups was evident.[3]

Everywhere, he said, Communist penetration had increased since 1960. "A good deal" of propaganda material was being imported from Cuba. Cuba's alignment with the Communist movement had strengthened Communism, which now could appear as an indigenous Latin American revolutionary movement. Sympathy was widespread for the proclaimed goals of the Cuban revolution. The Bay of Pigs had not enhanced America's reputation—non-intervention was still important. But some Latins were disappointed that the invasion failed, though they did not say so publicly. Latins were mostly unaware of Castro's repression, terror, and betrayal of his revolution. Cuba was of concern to all American nations, not just the United States. Stevenson thought it "quite possible" that some Latin American leaders at the Alliance for Progress meeting would want to "deal with this new form of outside intervention." Such action would have to be supported by Argentina, Brazil, and Mexico. Mexican support did not seem likely. Much must be done to promote the democratic cause among intellectuals in Latin America. Government ministers complained of the lack of cheap paperback translations of American books, "including

[3] In Argentina, President Frondizi's regime was gaining strength. In Brazil, President Quadros was less popular than formerly because of his austerity measures to combat inflation. Communist agitation in northeastern Brazil was increasingly vigorous and dangerous. In Uruguay social and economic conditions were good. Venezuela feared leftist violence in the Caracas slums and a right-wing coup. In Paraguay, General Stroessner was "clearly in command." His was not a totalitarian police state but he seemed "reluctant" to fulfill his pledges of democratization. "But I have great hope for Paraguay." Chile continued to enjoy its traditional devotion to democracy, though a danger signal was the recent swing of peasant votes to the extreme left. Bolivia was in "an acute and dangerous state," and President Paz Estenssoro was maintaining authority only "by a tenuous thread." In Peru political circles were preoccupied with next year's presidential election; the opposition front runner appeared to be Fernando Belaúnde Terry, "an attractive and vigorous younger man." In Ecuador, Communists had lost control of the student movement for the first time in sixteen years. The present leadership of Colombia was "excellent" but stability depended on finding a conservative presidential candidate to carry on between 1962 and 1966. Banditry and violence remained serious. But President Lleras Camargo was carrying out a domestic program in accord with the Alliance for Progress.

[said Stevenson] my own." Communist tracts were everywhere. He had encountered, however, "a unanimous and intense" interest in the Alliance for Progress. The Alliance meeting next month in Uruguay would succeed, though some Latin American nations viewed it only as "the cutting of an aid melon." In long-term economic and social development, Colombia, Chile, Brazil, "and perhaps" Venezuela seemed well ahead of other countries. Several countries were interested in negotiations with the European Common Market.

Answering questions, he said, "The great thing about South America, like all of the world, is that the masses of the people are on the move now." He was "shocked" by the proportion of national budgets spent on the military. But military men, once the bulwark of dictatorships, were now "showing increasing signs of responsibility, of democratic conviction."

That same afternoon Stevenson appeared before the House Foreign Affairs Committee. Woodruff Wallner and others in IO were urging Stevenson to press the China question. They thought it important to warn Congress that the moratorium position could not be maintained and a new policy was imperative.

At five o'clock, Stevenson and Secretary Rusk met with President Kennedy in the White House to discuss Chinese representation. The time was approaching when a decision must be taken. By now, President Kennedy considered Communist China's admission to the UN inevitable and was prepared to adopt the successor-state formula. He felt, however, that nothing should be said until the foreign aid bill passed Congress—any shift in China policy might endanger the bill. That meant a long delay—and the General Assembly would convene on September 19. Kennedy asked for a fresh country-by-country survey of votes for and against the moratorium. He instructed Stevenson to tell the Senate committee, if asked, that Administration policy was to keep the Chinese Communists out of the UN but that the Administration had grave misgivings about whether the moratorium could prevail again. He instructed Stevenson to talk to former UN Ambassadors Lodge and Wadsworth, to Roy Howard, and to an associate of Henry Luce. He would instruct the U. S. Ambassador to prepare to take a firm position with Chiang. He requested a memorandum explaining the successor-state approach; Stevenson would prepare one.

Rusk left the meeting early. Stevenson stayed. He told Kennedy he felt the United States should seize the initiative on disarmament in the General Assembly. Bilateral talks between McCloy and Zorin seemed unlikely to lead to the resumption of multilateral negotiations on July 31; Zorin had made it clear that multilateral negotiations could only be resumed if there were prior agreement between the United States and U.S.S.R. on the substance of the Soviet plan for general and complete disarmament. Stevenson thought the Soviet objective was to launch "another propaganda onslaught" at the next General Assembly. He thought that if Kennedy addressed the General Assembly he should speak on disarmament, saying it was "our top-priority national interest." He should ask that the UN Disarmament Commission (which consisted of all ninety-nine UN members) be convened. He should submit an item on disarmament for the Assembly. "The United States must appear second to none in its desire for disarmament."

Stevenson left the meeting with the impression that he had authority to proceed with a new approach to China policy and he testified the next day, June 27, before the Senate Foreign Relations Committee. But Rusk had a different impression. Rusk called in Chet Bowles, Alexis Johnson, Walter McConaughy, and Woodruff Wallner and told them it was dangerous to proclaim a policy of keeping Peking out of the UN and at the same time surreptitiously peddle a successor-state resolution. At least it was dangerous until the foreign aid bill had passed Congress. He rejected Wallner's argument that it was risky to wait until September. He too asked for an up-to-date estimate of the moratorium vote. He did not want any moves made that would in any way indicate the United States favored the successor-state approach or any other alternative to the moratorium. He instructed them to stand fast on three points—support for Nationalist Chinese representation at the UN, opposition to entry of the Chinese Communists, and no decision on tactics. The United States, he said, must maintain this position until just before the General Assembly met. Just as Kennedy feared to endanger the foreign aid bill by shifting China policy, so did Rusk fear to endanger Berlin policy that way—if the United States changed its China policy, he thought, Khrushchev might misinterpret it as a lack of steadfastness to commitments, which could be dangerous at Berlin. Furthermore, the sharp crisis over Berlin, caused by Soviet belligerence, would increase free-world support for the United States on China. Rusk also asked for a quiet reassessment of all alternatives to the moratorium approach. He ruled out nothing. At a press conference he took occasion to deny reports that the United States was changing its China policy, obscuring the issue in a discussion of parliamentary tactics in the Assembly and saying the United States was discussing "many" alternatives and had reached no decision.

Wallner felt Rusk had been somewhat harsh with him and he talked to Stevenson about it just before Stevenson left for New York. Stevenson was "quite disturbed." Wallner thought IO and the Mission were like "field generals who ask for four divisions and ammunition for a forty-eight-hour barrage prior to the assault, and are told by headquarters that they can have two divisions and a twenty-four-hour barrage, but are damned well expected to achieve their objectives anyway." In this case headquarters had to consider both the foreign aid bill and the coming Assembly session, and it had chosen to protect the objective most immediately threatened, the bill. But Wallner did not believe the United States could maintain the "freeze" on public debate until September.

Stevenson spent the rest of that week in New York, seeing diplomats, attending cocktail parties, completing his report to Kennedy, and carrying out the assignments Kennedy had given him. He spoke to Arthur Goldberg, Secretary of Labor, about the request of the union leaders, George Meany and Walter Reuther, to serve on the delegation to the UN—they would be welcome as advisers but the Administration was converting the delegation itself into a professional one with two Congressmen as the only exceptions. He estimated for President Kennedy the vote on moratorium —31 for, 43 against, 25 abstaining. Roy Howard suggested that Madame Chiang be invited to visit Kennedy. Howard offered to advise Ambassador Yeh to urge Formosa to "keep its shirt on." Henry Cabot Lodge was less helpful. Like Luce, he urged the Administration to press vigorously for the moratorium and, if it failed, to introduce a resolution that the Assembly would be willing in the future to consider representation from Peking when Peking changed its ways (he cited Korea, Tibet, Formosa Straits). Lodge, Stevenson thought, had a two-Chinas policy in mind as the ultimate result but was trying to postpone "the evil day" at least a year. He was assuming that a major U.S. effort spearheaded by Kennedy could win the moratorium. The Mission thought him wrong. Stevenson wrote, "In conclusion, from the international point of view we stand to gain much more and lose much less by going straight to the successor-state approach without trying the moratorium. . . . In domestic politics there are political disadvantages no matter which approach is used." Stevenson added a draft of a proposed statement by President Kennedy:

"The attitude of the United States concerning Chinese representation in the United Nations is that the Republic of China is a founding member and is, of course, entitled to retain its seat in the United Nations. In view of Communist China's continued belligerent attitude, we are still opposed to discussion in the United Nations as to whether or not Communist China is entitled to participate. When the Communist Chinese manifest a willingness to comply with the United Nations Charter and refrain from the use of force, the United States would be prepared to recognize that they are also entitled to a seat." Stevenson recommended that, because of congressional interest, Kennedy make the statement soon—it implied the United States would fight for the moratorium again in the fall but did not commit us to do so, and it foreshadowed a shift to a successor-state solution on condition that Peking observe the Charter.

Stevenson also sent Kennedy a long memo on disarmament, again urging him to take the initiative. (He sent a copy to McCloy, who was in Russia talking to Khrushchev.) "If a disarmament control organization is ever created, it will be potentially the greatest advance in international organization since the creation of the UN. It should be built very tightly into the UN itself, though not subject to veto." On Berlin, Stevenson thought Kennedy's efforts to convince Khrushchev of our determination to maintain our Berlin position were already bearing fruit—Khrushchev's most recent statement was "slightly milder" than earlier ones. These efforts should be continued, "but I would hope not in such frantic fashion as to create the impression we expect general war in the fall, or as to distort our treatment of other critical issues we face." An example was the Joint Chiefs of Staff proposal that we support Portugal on Angola because of our Azores bases, which they said would be essential if we became involved in a military crisis over Berlin. "I have often had the impression that, whenever the Soviets want to steal a march on us in one or two other places, they heat up the Berlin situation on the confident expectation that we will become so obsessed with it as to neglect or minimize most everything else."

14.

On Monday, July 3, Stevenson flew to Geneva. On the night before he wrote a check for $450 and told Mrs. John F. Kennedy that he wanted to buy a Victorian settee and two side chairs which had been owned by President Lincoln and have them put in the White House Lincoln Room, "where I have slept!" Several weeks later Mrs. Kennedy returned his check: "I am just heartbroken to be writing you this—because you were so fantastic to respond so quickly and generously . . . but the sad thing is I got someone to give them [previously]. . . . Please forgive my predatory instincts for the White House—I did think of asking you but then decided I didn't dare—as it would be imposing—I hope Lincoln will forgive me—and that you will too—" She signed herself, "Always affectionately, Jackie."

Stevenson had been in the United States only about ten days after his South American trip. He would spend July in Europe. The principal reason—or excuse—for his going was to make a speech to the UN Economic and Social Council (ECOSOC) at Geneva. With some difficulty, Phil Klutznick had persuaded him to do it. Stevenson told Bill Benton he was "miserably tired after my ordeal" in South America "and would really like to go home." He could not join Benton's yacht cruise among the Greek islands. Klutznick had announced at Geneva that Stevenson would speak for the United States, and delegates had besieged Klutznick for appointments with the famous man. Stevenson stayed in Switzerland a little less than two weeks. For the first few days he met with the American delegation to ECOSOC but soon dropped out. Klutznick and other delegates gave elaborate parties for Stevenson, and he had a good time. He went off for a weekend to Gstaad "at Karim Khan's beautiful chalet," as he noted on his appointment sheet. "Alpine wildflowers—incredible view of Alps. Walk thru village in P.M." He saw Nicolas Nabokov, the composer, and Averell Harriman arrived in Geneva for meetings on Laos and Stevenson dined with him. Between social gatherings he tried to keep in touch with what was going on in the Department and Mission about disarmament and China.

On July 10 he delivered his speech to ECOSOC. He spoke of his trip and broadened the topic beyond Latin America. He seemed to capture the flavor of the Kennedy years and the echoes of his own 1956 campaign when he said, "For no one anywhere, any longer, will passively accept the idea that hunger, misery, and disease are the immutable destiny of man. For everyone, everywhere, realizes that in this historic century man has routed the four horsemen of the apocalypse, and that for the first time in human history the ancient evil specters of pestilence and famine have been exorcised. We are crossing a great watershed in history to a time when enough food, shelter, clothing are within the reach of all and new dimensions in human wants and needs are emerging." The words were not stale then as they later became during President Johnson's war on poverty and the war in Vietnam; they were Stevensonian and Kennedyesque words of new hope. He spoke of America's economic growth in the 1960s and her pledge to "do all in our power to make the sixties a decade of development not only for ourselves, but, we hope, for our fellow men everywhere." Disarmament would not harm the American economy, America would welcome it. America would increase her participation in multilateral aid programs. He said, "The United States has no ambition to determine the future of the rest of the world." Stagnant, status-quo systems must yield to peaceful change. The "revolution of rising expectations" had accelerated beyond anyone's dreams. "Mr. President, we have just crossed the threshold of a new decade. Let us so chart our course that this decade may be remembered, not as a period of power struggle, but as the decade of great triumphs in the age-old struggle to provide a better life for men everywhere."

On July 15, Stevenson left Geneva by train for Milan, arrived there too late to catch a train to Florence, and was taken to Florence by a consular car, arriving at Buffie Ives's villa at 1 A.M. Chet Bowles telephoned Stevenson and said Kennedy was about to fire him or force him to resign, and Stevenson sent a telegram of protest to President Kennedy. (Kennedy liked Bowles but became impatient with him. Bowles, a thoughtful meditative man, belonged more to the Stevensonian school of liberalism in foreign policy than to the New Frontier school, and it was a slightly old-fashioned New Dealish school that tended to irritate the New Frontiersmen. Bowles, in talking with the President, gave long discursive thoughtful statements, not the crisp decisive operational declarations the New Frontiersmen wanted. To them he seemed indecisive. And Kennedy did not like to be lectured on things he already knew. Moreover, Bowles's relations with Rusk were not good. And by recommending the appointment of Ambassadors from academia, he had made enemies among the career men in the Department. Nor had he taken hold in running the Department—in the view of Bowles's friends, Rusk would neither run the Department nor allow Bowles to run it. Kennedy decided to replace him with Ball and to offer Bowles an Embassy. But the word leaked, and Bowles's liberal friends in Georgetown exploded, and the matter became a political issue, with Bowles's friends arguing that in firing him Kennedy was getting rid of the only man in the State Department who had, rightly, opposed the Bay of Pigs adventure. Kennedy reprieved Bowles. But that fall he moved him out of the Undersecretary job and made him a roving Ambassador dealing with underdeveloped nations. Later Bowles returned to India as Ambassador.)

Stevenson spent ten days with Buffie Ives at Florence, visiting Italian nobility in ancient villas and castles (in one of which, he noted, Boccaccio had died in 1313). He visited a music school and listened to Segovia conduct classes in classical guitar. A letter from Hubert Humphrey said that Humphrey had talked with President Kennedy—"in the main he shares your point of view" Humphrey wrote, "I only wish you would talk to him more often. If I were your manager I would get you into that White House at least once a week for a personal talk with the President. . . . Accept every invitation and insist upon a few extra." Stevenson replied, "Perhaps you are right about pressing for more opportunities to talk with him. Maybe I will do it, but it doesn't come easily. Not that I don't enjoy it, but I feel that if he wants my point of view he will ask for it."

On July 27, Stevenson went to Turin and Nice. Word came the next day that he could see De Gaulle at 5:30 P.M. and he flew to Paris.

De Gaulle told Stevenson he was entirely in accord with President Kennedy's speech on Berlin. De Gaulle did not think the Berlin problem could be solved in isolation—the German problem was a large one and would take many years to solve. It could not be solved in the present charged atmosphere of East-West relationships. Stevenson asked whether De Gaulle thought an acknowledgement by the Federal Republic of Germany of the Oder-Neisse as its eastern border, the creation of a neutralized zone in Eastern Europe, and a non-nuclear Germany might contribute to détente with the U.S.S.R. De Gaulle did not think it would help much.

They spoke of Tunisia. Fighting had broken out on July 19 between French and Tunisian forces near Bizerte, where France had a military base, and Tunisia had complained of French "aggression." The Security Council on July 22 had called for an immediate cease-fire and return of all forces to their original positions. But the forces had not returned, and on July 27 Tunisia had again requested Security Council consideration. The Council had been unable to agree on a resolution, and Liberia had asked for a special session of the General Assembly. Over U.S. objection, the General Assembly had been called and would convene on August 21.

Now on July 28, Stevenson asked De Gaulle why President Bourguiba had taken the initiative in attacking the French base at Bizerte. De Gaulle laughed and said Bourguiba liked the limelight. When Tunisia achieved independence in 1956 the French and Tunisians had agreed to put the question of Bizerte to one side. France had only 3,000 troops left in Bizerte, and they were leaving. But Bourguiba, seeking the limelight, told De Gaulle the French had to get out immediately. De Gaulle said he would not be pushed around. France would go to the UN but would not be bound by any resolutions adopted there. Eventually Bourguiba would realize that bilateral discussions were the only solution.

Stevenson asked how discussions with the FLN, the Algerian rebels, were going. De Gaulle said France was determined to end the Algerian affair this year, one way or another. Either the French and the Algerians would reach agreement on an independent Algeria or the French would resettle the million French residents in Algiers and Oran and leave the rest of Algeria to chaos. Stevenson supposed these areas would be considered a part of metropolitan France. De Gaulle was evasive. He said France was no longer greatly interested in the sovereignty of any overseas area. Stevenson asked what would happen to the Sahara. De Gaulle said that France had never been very interested in sovereignty over the Sahara. She wished to divest herself of all overseas regions.

Stevenson was about to leave when De Gaulle said, "You realize that the Atlantic Alliance is at stake. If we are not strong on Berlin, we will lose Germany. If you do not support France, you will lose France." Stevenson asked what he meant. De Gaulle said he was thinking of the "Bourguiba affair" and added, "We supported you in Cuba. Our situation in Bizerte is like yours in Cuba. We are not in Bizerte for our pleasure. You were not in Cuba for your pleasure." As Stevenson left, De Gaulle said it was always a pleasure to see him—"always so full of life, spirit, ideas, and hope. Notice," he added, "I did not say full of illusions."

Stevenson cabled an account of the conversation to the Department and on July 30 telephoned Harlan Cleveland, said he was slightly confused, asked what he was supposed to do about Bizerte, and asked whether anybody had told Bourguiba confidentially that the French communiqué embodied the principle of evacuation. Cleveland said that Yost had told Ambassador Slim of Tunisia but neither Tunisia nor France had any maneuverability. Stevenson intended to see Maurice Couve de Murville, the French Foreign Minister, in the morning. He said that neither Tunisia nor France should win a victory over Bizerte, and certainly not Tunisia— De Gaulle would never accept that.

15.

Back in New York on Wednesday, August 2, Stevenson interrupted briefings on Bizerte by his staff to attend the funeral of his sister-in-law, Betty Hines. That day, too, he talked with UN Ambassador Armand Bérard of France, who proposed a new formula on Bizerte. The French would agree to pull back their troops to their base at a certain hour; the

Tunisians would promise not to interfere with normal communications with French units outside the base. After that the French would enter into negotiations on the future of Bizerte on the basis of De Gaulle's statement that the French did not intend to remain in Bizerte forever. Stevenson told Bérard that he was somewhat impatient with both sides.

While he was in Europe the Department and the President had been occupied with China, disarmament, and Berlin, especially Berlin. Indeed, Yost complained to Stevenson that the highest U.S. officials had been so preoccupied with Berlin that they were sacrificing to it "crucial U.S. positions elsewhere in the world." Yost believed the Administration did not yet understand the importance of the admission of Outer Mongolia and Mauritania. If China denied them admission, other important issues would be affected, including Chinese representation, Berlin, disarmament, and troika. At a meeting in the White House on July 28, Secretary Rusk had recommended that the United States move to have Chinese representation declared an "important question," which would require a two-thirds vote to admit Peking. President Kennedy had asked what Stevenson's views were. The successor-state formula, Cleveland had said. The President had been anxious to have Stevenson's agreement on any proposal. Vice President Ch'en of (Formosa) China was in the United States. President Kennedy had laid out U.S. policy to him—to keep the Chinese Communists from entering the UN, but how? "We don't want to be beaten in the United Nations by a few votes." On August 1, the day Stevenson returned from Europe, President Kennedy told Vice President Ch'en that the Chinese must recognize the close relationship between the admission of Outer Mongolia and Mauritania and the retention of China's UN seat: "You can't have everything." At a separate meeting with Rusk, Vice President Ch'en read a paper saying the Chinese government "felt that the time had come to make no more concessions" and would bar Outer Mongolia's admission. Rusk said that in this case he had nothing more to say except that the United States would preserve its own freedom of action.

It was at this point, on August 2, that Ch'en gave a dinner for Kennedy which Stevenson attended. There, Kennedy gave Ch'en a message for Chiang Kai-shek: the United States Government would do its utmost to maintain China's position in the UN and prevent Peking's entry but the United States "must not be defeated" on this issue. Ch'en replied that China would not take any steps that might result in injury to the U.S. position.

The next morning Stevenson, at breakfast with Arthur Schlesinger, described his talk with De Gaulle and said he was struck by De Gaulle's extraordinary combination of great nobility and elevation, on the one hand, and, on the other, meanness and irritability. Stevenson and Rusk saw President Kennedy at 11 A.M.—Kennedy wanted Stevenson's views on China and on the United States' new comprehensive disarmament proposals.

Stevenson had lunch with Rusk, Ball, Cleveland, Joe Sisco, and several

Tunisian diplomats, to discuss Bizerte. Rusk said the United States' ability to influence De Gaulle was limited; the United States was, however, committed to support the independence of Tunisia. The United States wanted to preserve its friendship with both France and Tunisia. Stevenson said his recent talk with De Gaulle had convinced him that the French ultimately intended to evacuate the Bizerte base completely. He was convinced, too, that though they knew they could have no victory there they did not want the Tunisians to have one either. The word "evacuation" stung De Gaulle's pride and should be eliminated. A Tunisian asked if the French had told the United States they intended to leave Bizerte. Stevenson said they had, and Rusk backed him up. But, Rusk said, since U.S. prestige was now engaged, both France and Tunisia must realize that any violation of the cease-fire would be viewed "very sternly" by us. Rusk left to attend a cabinet meeting, leaving Stevenson to try to persuade the Tunisians to abandon the emergency meeting of the General Assembly in favor of quiet mediation.

On Saturday, August 5, Stevenson and Cleveland went to Hyannisport to meet with Kennedy and Schlesinger. Kennedy had given Schlesinger a new assignment: to be the White House staff man on the UN in preparation for the General Assembly. Actually, he served thereafter as go-between for Kennedy and Stevenson. He wrote in his journal, "I imagine that this will put me unhappily in the middle between JFK and AES, but I have been through this before and guess I can survive." It was a gray, dreary day. They talked for a time in the house, then about twelve-thirty went out on Kennedy's boat, the sky overcast with a cold wind rising. Kennedy expressed great concern about making a good record on disarmament at the UN. He said he did not think it was much of an issue in the United States—he had not been able to whip up congressional support for a bill to set up a disarmament administration—but he was well aware of how vital an issue it was in the rest of the world. It was also an issue on which the United States could show itself to advantage in contrast to the Russians. They were not ready to approve inspection, the United States was ready, and we should take advantage of that. Stevenson said, "Yes, this is the position we want to put them in. But we can't do that effectively if we equivocate ourselves. Your first decision, Mr. President, is to make sure that you yourself are genuinely for general and complete disarmament. We must go for that. Everything else in our program derives from it. Only total disarmament will save the world from the horror of nuclear war, as well as from the mounting expense of the arms race. Your basic decision must be to show a readiness to identify yourself with a new approach to disarmament. This must be our principal initiative in the United Nations."

Kennedy listened with interest but with skepticism. Then Kennedy said he well understood the "propaganda" importance of being all out for disarmament. This offended Stevenson. Stevenson had spent years speaking about the dangers of nuclear holocaust if the arms race was not halted. He had meant what he said. To him disarmament was not "propaganda" but a life-and-death matter. He was a crusader about nuclear war, and he demanded of Kennedy greater passion than Kennedy could muster. A practical man, Kennedy saw little prospect of serious disarmament negotiations and therefore thought that the United States should concentrate on disarmament as a weapon of international political warfare. Kennedy was also wary of Phase III in the Administration's new disarmament proposals, which seemed to lead straight to world government. Stevenson now made derisive remarks about John J. McCloy and his "balderdash" on disarmament, including his effort to substitute "total and universal disarmament" for Khrushchev's "general and complete disarmament." Stevenson and Kennedy discussed whom to have represent the United States in the UN disarmament debate. Stevenson seemed willing to have an outsider rather than himself but resisted the appointment of Arthur Dean because Dean had been too identified with the Eisenhower administration and lack of progress on disarmament.

They went on to other issues. India came up, and Kennedy said, "I'm getting increasingly tired of the Indians. They are a collection of sanctimonious bastards. I believe that they have a deal of some sort with the Soviet Union as against both China and Pakistan." He regarded the arms deal with Pakistan as a great mistake. Of Vice President Ch'en he said, "Either he is the most mysterious Chinese I have ever met, or he is gone mentally. All he did was to repeat instructions. We never had any communication." Kennedy said he had pressed the Chinese as hard as he could on Outer Mongolia and thought there was a reasonable chance of persuading them merely to abstain. Cleveland thought the best proposal so far advanced on Chinese representation was to make it an "important question," which would permit the United States to maintain a blocking one third. Rusk, who knew the UN well, had proposed this idea a few weeks earlier and had asked Joe Sisco to study all aspects of it. He would add to it a study commission to report within a year. Stevenson considered this approach too "transparent" an effort at stalling. Kennedy said, "If we can buy twelve months, it will be more than worth it. We may be preparing the way for admission of Peking in another year; but in another year things will be different." He turned to Stevenson and said, "What do you think we ought to do? If you're not for this policy, we shouldn't try and do it." Stevenson seemed embarrassed and said, "I will be for it if you decide it's the policy." Kennedy finally said he would write to Chiang Kai-shek and remarked on Chiang's *"Götterdämmerung"* mood. Stevenson said he did not believe any of this—the Chinese had been making the same threat for a long time and, if history showed anything about the Chinese, it showed their boundless instinct for self-preservation. But Kennedy now made it clear he did not want to make a policy change that year. He felt the issue was not sufficiently important to risk trouble with Congress and

Formosa. Moreover, Kennedy had been elected by a narrow plurality and now feared that a loud debate over China might split the country. It was, in the end, domestic political considerations that made him postpone everything, first for a year, and then until his second term. Stevenson concurred that the present policy, irrational though it was, had to be continued. Kennedy intended to make the policy switch a year later. But, as George Ball once said, "Then we got into Vietnam and that poisoned everything."

They discussed other issues, and Kennedy gave Stevenson a paper on Berlin strategy by Acheson and asked for comment. As the day passed, Schlesinger felt that the atmosphere grew steadily more relaxed. The only tension had come over disarmament. Cleveland later recalled that in one discussion with Stevenson, when Kennedy referred to disarmament as propaganda, "I thought Adlai Stevenson was going through the floor. You could almost see what was going through his mind—'Oh, my God, I've been devoting my life to this, I built my 1956 campaign around it, and here I've got to educate this kid all over.' His reaction was all wrong. He said, 'Jack, you've got to have faith.' It was one of the few times he called the President Jack. They had a long discussion. I tried to be the mediator —to say that the Soviets were getting away with murder for years by calling for general and complete disarmament while we had been talking about next steps. I said, 'Let's reverse it.' This worked with Kennedy. He saw it as an interesting and practical problem in politics. Stevenson was still talking about how 'you've got to believe in this.' But over a period of time Stevenson moved toward thinking of it as a tactical problem—since you couldn't bring it off, you could use tactics to influence world opinion. And Kennedy, as he learned more about the nuclear problem, came to believe that there was no alternative to peace any more [as he said in the American University speech in 1963]. They moved together, though Kennedy always more practically, Stevenson with a tinge of emotional identification." Robert Kennedy later observed he could imagine that if President Kennedy called disarmament "propaganda" in a discussion with Stevenson it was because "he didn't want to be lectured."

Stevenson participated in organizing the forum for disarmament discussions at Geneva, and he occasionally made a speech on the subject, but he never participated directly in the negotiations. This disappointed him. He had spent years talking about disarmament; now, as a high-ranking government official, he was shut off from it.

16.

On Tuesday, August 8, Stevenson had lunch with Hammarskjold. He found him indignant with the French over Bizerte and skeptical of American efforts to bring about a settlement. He was unequivocally partial to

the Tunisian position. The Russians, he thought, would make little headway with their efforts to restructure the Secretariat. He deplored constant
U.S. talk about keeping Peking out of the UN; it would only make failure
seem a worse defeat. The United States, he urged, should declare its objective to be "legal, decent, and equitable treatment for Nationalist China";
he was skeptical about the value of the "important-question" proposal, saw
value in the study commission, and liked the successor-state approach.

Stevenson sent Fanfani of Italy "a rather hasty and superficial report I
made to the President on my return" from South America. (By now
Stevenson used such self-deprecating language almost unthinkingly. Surely
it did not occur to him what Fanfani might have thought of his giving the
President of the United States a hasty, superficial report.)

On August 9, Stevenson, after talking with Ambassador Tsiang of
China, sent Kennedy a suggested draft of a letter he might send to Chiang
Kai-shek, asking him flatly to reconsider his decision to veto the admission
of Outer Mongolia and presenting the arguments. Stevenson had been surprised when Kennedy backed away from the two-Chinas formula; now
Stevenson was trying to rescue Outer Mongolia-Mauritania admission not
for their sake but for his own—he would need all the votes he could get to
make Peking's admission an important question.

On August 11, Stevenson sent McGeorge Bundy a detailed critique of
new disarmament proposals advanced by McCloy. The changes he proposed revealed no major policy disagreement with McCloy. Stevenson also
proposed a plan of action. The United States should ask for inscription of
disarmament on the Assembly agenda before Russia did. President Kennedy, in a major speech to the Assembly, should unveil the new disarmament plan. President Kennedy approved the McCloy plan on August 17,
adopting some though not all of Stevenson's changes. Arthur Dean would
handle it.

On August 12, Stevenson told Barbara Ward, "My frustration about the
failure of my negotiations on Bizerte is boundless." He was still trying to
get William Stevenson an ambassadorship. (He was appointed Ambassador to the Philippines.) Newt Minow told Stevenson that Martin had been
proposed for Ambassador to the Dominican Republic and asked Stevenson to write to Rusk in Martin's behalf (though, as Minow said, "why he
wants to go there is beyond me"). Stevenson wrote to Rusk. Stevenson
told Dutch Smith he hoped to get to Desbarats over Labor Day but "my
prospects get dimmer every day, what with the procession of crises that
seem to afflict my life."

On August 13 the wall went up in Berlin. The United States Government was taken by surprise. All year the government had been divided
over Berlin. Acheson and other hard-liners had urged that the United
States maintain the freedom of West Berlin, keep Western troops there,
and insist on access to the city; and to indicate our firmness Acheson tentatively recommended sending a division down the *Autobahn* across East

Germany to Berlin. (At one point Acheson argued for a proclamation of national emergency.) Others, including Stevenson and Harriman and Ambassador Thompson, had favored more emphasis on diplomatic and less on military moves. President Kennedy adopted Acheson's objectives but not all his methods. Yost said, "In 1961 the Governor considered Acheson a warmonger on Berlin. The two men bristled at each other. The Governor didn't think you could resolve diplomatic questions by being bellicose." Stevenson, however, did not take part in the front-line fighting inside the government on the issue. Kennedy and Rusk rarely consulted him on Berlin. The Berlin task force, appointed by Kennedy, did not include Stevenson. It met urgently during these last weeks of August, when nuclear war seemed imminent. Rusk conferred in Paris with NATO allies. Then suddenly the crisis ebbed and, in October, Khrushchev said that since the Western powers "were showing some understanding of the situation, and were inclined to seek a solution," the Soviet Union would not insist on signing a German peace treaty before December 31 (which would have canceled all U.S. rights of occupation and access). The crisis was over.

On August 14, Stevenson began a busy, typical week which took him to San Francisco to make a speech and see John Fell; to Chicago to visit grandchildren, friends, and a doctor; to Washington for talks in the State Department. He wrote Marietta Tree that it was difficult to leave John Fell: "Sometimes he tugs at my heart the hardest of all." He had always felt an especially warm affection for his youngest son. Anniversaries were beginning to crowd in. He noted: "It was 20 years ago today that my name first appeared on the front page of the N.Y. Times—in connection with the seizure by the Navy of the Kearney Shipyards. What a 20 years it has been—and curiously not half as long as the past week."

He wrote at length in response to Kennedy's request for comment on Acheson's paper on Berlin. He thought Kennedy had avoided excesses and "damped down the fires in the Berlin military planning." The important thing now was for the United States to show no reluctance to talk with the Soviets about Germany and Berlin. Rusk had spoken of calling for negotiations about September 1. Stevenson disliked waiting that long, favored an almost immediate call.

He wrote: "It would be extremely dangerous for us to allow our attention to be so absorbed by Berlin that we overlook attitudes in Asia, Africa and Latin America, or take decisions or public positions based on the exigencies of our NATO Allies rather than the exigencies of those areas. To do so would, in my view, play into the Soviet-Chicom[4] hands by sacrificing ground in what they consider to be the decisive areas of struggle in order to hold the line in Europe."

Stevenson told Kennedy that Chet Bowles would like to leave the De-

---

[4] "Chicom" is State Department jargon for Chinese Communists, or mainland China.

partment if he could be appointed head of the new AID agency, as Stevenson recommended. Finally, Stevenson offered to help lobby in Congress for an education bill in which he had been interested for many years. It was an interesting letter, showing a desire to be helpful, betraying no residual rancor over the Bay of Pigs, demonstrating his interest in underdeveloped countries as against Europe, and indicating that he felt free to involve himself in political matters, such as the education bill, outside the UN.

He told Marietta Tree he feared that if the Afro-Asians pushed an extreme resolution on Bizerte the United States would have to abstain, thereby losing friends among the Afro-Asians "to gain what in Paris?? The expense of De Gaulle's friendship is getting intolerable."

Next day, Monday, August 21, the emergency session of the General Assembly on Bizerte began. It lasted a week. France boycotted it. It appeared likely that Afro-Asians would introduce an extreme resolution condemning France. Stevenson favored supporting it as part of his anti-colonial position. The European Bureau in the Department thought the United States should abstain, not wishing to offend France. President Kennedy decided: De Gaulle's position was shaky, Bizerte could trigger a revolt against him by his own rightist generals, the United States sympathized with anti-colonialism but that cause would not be helped by the overthrow of De Gaulle, nor would the United States' position in Berlin. The United States would abstain. Schlesinger went up to New York on August 23 to discuss Bizerte with Stevenson. Stevenson was unimpressed with the argument that support of Tunisia might overturn De Gaulle. He thought rather that the Department wanted to placate De Gaulle because of Berlin. He accepted his instructions, however. In the end a resolution was adopted which noted that France had not complied fully with the Security Council's resolution, called the presence of French troops a violation of Tunisian sovereignty endangering international peace, and called on both sides to enter into immediate negotiations looking to a peaceful settlement and the withdrawal of all French troops from Tunisia. The United States abstained—Stevenson's efforts had helped effect a compromise but not enough. Within a year the French were out of Bizerte and Franco-Tunisian relations restored.

17.

The neutral nations were about to meet in Belgrade. On August 23, in response to a request by President Kennedy, Stevenson sent Kennedy a "hastily prepared" memorandum on the attitude of the neutral nations. He said he shared the President's annoyance that the neutrals seemed to apply different standards when judging the conduct of the U.S.S.R. and the United States. The neutrals were inclined to equate American firmness with belligerence, American moderation with weakness. On questions appearing to raise the danger of general war but not involving their own interests, such as Berlin, the neutrals almost always favored compromise between the Western and Communist positions with little regard to right and wrong. Neutrals expected the Soviets to be belligerent; they expected the United States to be decent and moderate. Moreover, most neutrals were formerly colonial areas and their anti-colonialism set them against the United States because of her alliance with former colonial powers, a situation the Russians exploited. "I suspect we have no choice but to be patient and philosophical about this astigmatism" but it could be ameliorated by patient explanations to neutrals and allies, behavior in the UN based not on expediency but on right and justice. Abstention on Bizerte "cost us dearly" because it was contrary to right and justice and had come after the U.S. reversal on its decision to recognize Outer Mongolia. As to Germany specifically, our military build-up may have been helpful in Congress and the country but not at the UN.

Kennedy was often annoyed with the neutrals. He felt he was losing votes in Congress by trying to appease them; at the same time they were denouncing him at Belgrade.

The Waldorf was pressing the government for an increase in rent. Stevenson feared the government would not meet its demands and he might have to give up his two guest rooms. He appealed to Henry Crown, the Chicago industrialist. He was considering bringing a butler-valet from Italy and told the hotel he could do some of the work ordinarily done by hotel maids. The Waldorf wanted to increase the rent from $30,000 a year to $45,000. Henry Crown thought the apartment should bring $75,000 but, to help Stevenson, he telephoned Conrad Hilton, a Republican who owned the hotel, and told him he could not expect to get money out of the impoverished Democrats. The rent was not raised.

On August 31 the Soviet Union announced it would resume nuclear testing. Stevenson promptly sent a memorandum to President Kennedy and Secretary Rusk proposing that the United States call for a meeting of the Security Council to deal with this "threat to peace and security." The United States should jointly with the United Kingdom introduce a resolution calling on the U.S.S.R. to rescind its decision, calling on all others to refrain from testing, and calling for an early completion of the testing agreement with adequate inspection. The U.S.S.R. would veto the resolution. The United States could then move to have the General Assembly take up the question. President Kennedy, in his speech to the Assembly, should cover the subject extensively. Stevenson should speak on it during the general debate. Immediately after the vote in the Assembly, probably in mid-October, the United States and United Kingdom should send a final appeal to the Soviets calling for compliance. When they rejected this President Kennedy should announce he had decided to resume testing in self-protection.

Others in the Administration, including Edward R. Murrow of USIA, had the same idea. John J. McCloy, who had just returned from Russia, opposed it; he thought the United States should promptly resume nuclear testing itself. He believed that action in the UN would result in a resolution calling for uncontrolled test cessation, thus departing from "the most fundamental principle" on which disarmament must be based—the principle of control. He also questioned the wisdom of pressing too eagerly our propaganda advantage. The Soviet action had not gone unnoticed.

President Kennedy decided against Stevenson's plan. Instead, on September 3, after the Soviets had exploded a huge device in the atmosphere over central Asia, Kennedy joined with Prime Minister Macmillan in proposing to Khrushchev that their three governments agree not to conduct tests in the atmosphere which produced radioactive fallout. The United States and Great Britain were prepared to rely on existing means of detection and did not suggest additional control. They reaffirmed "their serious desire" to conclude a nuclear test-ban treaty and "regret that the Soviet Government has blocked such an agreement." Stevenson told Barbara Ward that "a major initiative of the United States in the Assembly is going to be disarmament—thank Heavens!"

Stevenson went to Libertyville for the Labor Day weekend, spent Friday evening with his grandchildren, had the comedian Mort Sahl and others out for cocktails on Saturday, then went to see Sahl's show in the evening with Adlai and Nancy and Marietta Tree. On Tuesday, September 5, he was in Washington to meet with Rusk and with the President. That same day the Soviets exploded another nuclear device, and Kennedy, his patience exhausted, ordered a resumption of nuclear tests, but only in the laboratory and underground, not in the atmosphere where fallout was dangerous. The first explosion took place ten days later at the testing site in Nevada.

In the meeting with Kennedy, Rusk began by describing the need for a presidential speech at the UN. The President broke in and asked Stevenson, "What do you think of the idea of moving the UN to West Berlin?" Stevenson was dubious—the United States as the UN's host country should not initiate such a move, the UN in West Berlin would be almost a hostage behind East German lines, the idea seemed hazardous unless East and West Berlin were reunited as an international city. Kennedy pursued the idea and proposed a four-point program for Berlin negotiations that might be included in his speech to the UN—the submission of the legal dispute over Berlin to the World Court, transfer of the UN to Berlin, internationalization of the *Autobahn* to Berlin under UN control, and a UN plebiscite in Berlin. Stevenson said all these ideas sounded good to him but he wondered if there ought not be prior emphasis on unification and demilitarization. Kennedy suggested we could restate the size of armed forces in both Germanys, the permitted size of foreign forces, provisions for nuclear weapons, and a non-aggression pact between the NATO and Warsaw powers. Stevenson thought these ideas excellent but suggested they might better be reserved for private negotiations than used in a public address; and Rusk agreed.

Stevenson said, "The fact is we have to negotiate our way out of the Berlin crisis. Our position does not have strong support. No one in Western Europe wants to fight over Berlin." He questioned the tradition of deference to Adenauer and suggested a unilateral U.S. declaration of willingness to discuss the future of Germany. Kennedy said he would be glad to make such a statement. Stevenson urged a special press conference in which Kennedy could emphasize his interest in negotiation and, at the same time, unveil the new U.S. disarmament plan. Then Stevenson expressed his personal regret over the decision to resume nuclear testing.

The President said tartly, "What choice did we have? They had spit in our eye three times. We couldn't possibly sit back and do nothing at all. We had to do this."

Stevenson said, "But we were ahead in the propaganda battle."

Kennedy said, "What does that mean? I don't hear of any windows broken because of the Soviet decision. The neutrals have been terrible. The Russians made two tests *after* our note calling for a ban on atmospheric testing. Maybe they couldn't have stopped the first, but they could have stopped the second. All this makes Khrushchev look pretty tough. He has had a succession of apparent victories—space, Cuba, the wall. He wants to give out the feeling that he has us on the run. The third nuclear test was a contemptuous response to our note. Anyway, the decision has been made. I'm not saying that it was the right decision. Who the hell knows? But it is the decision which has been taken."

Rusk said the new U.S. disarmament plan was hardly good enough for a dramatic unveiling. They talked about neutral leaders who might come to the United States from the Belgrade conference. Kennedy said, "Khrushchev certainly drew the pick of the litter," meaning Nehru and Nkrumah. He and Stevenson expressed their disappointment over Nkrumah's Belgrade performance, and Stevenson said the United States might consider suspending aid to the Volta River project. The talk returned to moving the UN to Berlin. Rusk said that doing so would mean a great shift of prestige to the East. Stevenson heartily agreed. But Kennedy said: "There are two possibilities about Berlin—war, or losing West Berlin gradually to the Communists. I don't think enough of the UN not to be prepared to trade it for a nuclear war."

The talk turned to China. Kennedy expressed his great sympathy with Stevenson's difficulties. "You have the hardest thing in the world to sell," he said. "It really doesn't make any sense—the idea that Taiwan [Formosa] represents China. But, if we lose this fight, if Red China comes into the UN during our first year in town, yours and mine"—he was talking directly to Stevenson—"they'll run us both out of town. We have to lick them this year. We'll take our chances next year. It may be an election year; but we can delay the admission of Red China till after the election. So far as this year is concerned, you must do everything you can to keep them out. Whatever is required is okay by me."

Stevenson asked, "Do you mean to keep them out permanently or for a year?"

Kennedy said, "For a year. I am for any strategy which works. You can vote on Outer Mongolia as you think best. I am going to send a new letter to Chiang Kai-shek—this one based on what is good for us, not what is good for Formosa. We'll get Cabot Lodge to talk to Luce—Adlai to talk to Roy Howard—I will talk to Walter Judd [Congressman from Minnesota]. We'll have to get all these people to make it clear to Chiang that he can't expect to make a domestic political issue out of our strategy in the UN."

On September 11, Stevenson went back to Washington for the swearing in of the U.S. delegation to the General Assembly. The ceremony was at the White House, with the delegates' families present. Kennedy had a speech ready to deliver. Stevenson took charge, however, and presented the delegation to the President. Rusk was standing in the rear, having come in late. Stevenson started to adjourn the ceremony without calling on Rusk. Kennedy said the Secretary was here and perhaps they should have a word from him.

On the night of the eleventh, Stevenson had dinner at Chet Bowles's house with Galbraith, Schlesinger, and George McGhee. They talked about the neutral nations. Stevenson became impatient when Schlesinger argued that our sympathetic policy toward the neutrals meant that, in anxiety to avoid war, they would always favor the unreasonable over the reasonable nation—that is, Russia over the United States. Stevenson and the others felt that the policy of friendship was producing important results. They also thought it had been a great error to resume nuclear testing so quickly. (Kennedy had confided to Bundy after the Belgrade conference, "Do you know who the real losers of this weekend have been? Bowles and Stevenson." Stevenson did not know it.)

On September 12, President Kennedy gave Stevenson his instructions on China for the General Assembly. He was to induce several countries to inscribe on the agenda an item on "Representation of China." He could use his own judgment as to the countries and the title of the item. He should attempt to get the General Assembly to declare, by a simple majority, that any change in representation of China was an "important question" which would require a two-thirds vote. He was to persuade the Assembly to appoint a committee to consider criteria for membership and the composition of the Security Council and ECOSOC and report back a year later. He was authorized to say privately, if he deemed it essential, that the United States did not exclude the possibility that the study committee would recommend the successor-state approach to the China problem. Kennedy's objective was to head off any consideration of the representation of China as a credentials question. When the application of Outer Mongolia and Mauritania came before the Security Council, Stevenson was authorized to abstain or vote for the admission of Outer Mongolia and to assist the election of Mauritania, provided the vote took place at a time when he deemed the support of the French African states necessary in the China question. Rusk forwarded the instructions with a warm note: "We will be guided by your tactical judgments on this issue from here on in."

On September 14, Stevenson had breakfast with Sukarno of Indonesia. Stevenson tried to impress Sukarno with his disappointment in the Belgrade conference. He said Sukarno could achieve leadership of the neutrals only if he unfailingly criticized both sides in the cold war when justified. Sukarno defended his failure to condemn Soviet nuclear testing on the ground that the role of the neutrals was to bring East and West together and this could not be done by criticizing either side. Stevenson said Indonesia had not failed to criticize the United States about Cuba. If Sukarno was to oppose colonialism he must also oppose the new form of colonialism in Eastern Europe. Sukarno replied that the United States had failed to support his claim to the part of New Guinea he called West Irian, had backed revolutionary attempts at dismemberment of Indonesia, and had been less generous than the Soviets in economic and military aid. The United States failed to understand the immediacy of the problem of old forms of colonialism; to the people of Angola and Algeria who faced a daily life-and-death struggle, the danger of nuclear war seemed remote. Stevenson said the United States had not failed in any way to uphold the rights of colonial peoples to self-determination. He also pointed out that Indonesia and Mali had joined the Soviet bloc in opposing inscription of the item on Hungary, the only Afro-Asians to do so, a striking example of new colonialism. Sukarno said that in his travels in East Europe and Communist China he had seen in the eyes of the people no resentment or oppression, only enthusiasm. Stevenson reported to the Department, "Despite my best efforts, I regretfully conclude I made no headway with Sukarno."

Sukarno was only one of the world figures who arrived in New York just before the Assembly convened. As the time approached, Stevenson's schedule became increasingly crowded. He sent Evelyn Houston his schedule for late September (on the twenty-third he was "obliged to dine with the President of Peru"). She arrived September 24 and he took her to a dinner party at Ruth Field's and to the theater afterward. Departing, she sent him a note from the airport saying she desperately wanted to stay and saying she loved him. The day before the Assembly opened, Stevenson sent a memo to all members of the U.S. delegation instructing them on the line they were to take in talking about China at cocktail parties, dinner parties, the UN corridors.

Contrary to all expectations, the Soviet Union proposed that the U.S. draft resolution on disarmament be adopted.

On September 18, Dag Hammarskjold was killed in an airplane crash in the Congo.

18.

During the summer the Congolese Parliament had convened; Kasavubu had named Cyrille Adoula as Prime Minister-designate; and for the first time since the dismissal of Lumumba eleven months earlier the Congo had a legal, widely recognized central government. Antoine Gizenga was named Vice President in Adoula's government. He stopped pretending to head the government in Stanleyville.

Only the Katanga parliamentarians failed to attend the meeting. Tshombe's Katanga secession was a year old. Cyrille Adoula now said that the secession did "great harm" to the country. Katanga was full of mercenaries in the pay of the Katanga secessionists. In August, Kasavubu called for their expulsion. On August 28 the UN command "took energetic measures" to get rid of them, occupying Radio Katanga, stationing forces at other key points in Elisabethville, and calling for the surrender and repatriation of all mercenaries. Only about 80 of 500 were actually removed from the Congo, however; the rest rejoined the Katanga gendarmerie, inciting it to resist the UN and arming tribal warriors. September 9 was set as the deadline for evacuation. But more than a hundred refused to leave. Meanwhile, the attitude of the Katanga authorities became increasingly hostile to the UN command. After a series of incidents, UN authorities met with Tshombe on September 12 but could not persuade him to get rid of the mercenaries, to halt a campaign of terror against one tribe, and to reconcile his differences with the central government peaceably. On September 13, UN troops again seized the radio station and post office and were fired upon in doing so. They returned fire. Tshombe and other Katanga leaders believed they could force the UN out of the Congo. The UN sought a cease-fire. Tshombe issued a cease-fire order on September 13 but it was disregarded by the Katangan troops. Several sharp clashes took place, with light casualties. In Jadotville a company of UN troops surrendered. The Katanga air force had acquired four jet trainer aircraft earlier. One was still operating. Since the UN had no fighter planes, this single foreign-piloted jet trainer was able to gain complete control of the Congolese air. In one week it destroyed seven UN transport planes on the ground and virtually destroyed the UN ability to fly reinforcements and supplies to Elisabethville.

Hammarskjold had been on his way to the Congo to carry out a promise to Prime Minister Adoula when fighting broke out on September 13. Upon arrival he took personal charge of the efforts to get a cease-fire. At mid-

night on September 16 UN officials in Elisabethville received word that
Tshombe wanted to meet with a UN representative in northern Rhodesia.
Hammarskjold immediately agreed to meet with Tshombe at Ndola. Even
before Tshombe responded, Hammarskjold took off in a DC-6B, a chartered plane. It had been shot up on take-off at Elisabethville that day but
had been repaired. It left for Ndola at 5 P.M., traveling by night in order
to avoid attack by the Katangan jet. In circumstances never made wholly
clear, it crashed about nine miles from the airfield at Ndola at about 1
A.M. Hammarskjold and thirteen of the fourteen aides aboard were killed
and the fourteenth died a few days later.

Hammarskjold's death plunged the UN into a constitutional crisis.
Stevenson and Yost dropped everything else to concentrate on the question of Hammarskjold's successor and the future of the UN. The Soviets
would undoubtedly seize the opportunity to press their demands for a
troika. The United States would ask for the selection of an "outstanding
world leader" to succeed Hammarskjold.

President Kennedy, in his speech on September 25, described the problem as "not the death of one man" but "the life of this organization." The
Russian troika received no support outside the Soviet bloc but other countries, trying to placate the U.S.S.R., proposed various alternative arrangements. Negotiations became intensive and lasted nearly two months. Finally, on November 1, Stevenson announced that the U.S. objective of
preserving "the integrity of the Charter and the efficiency of the office of
the Secretary General" had been achieved, and on November 3 the Security Council met in private and unanimously recommended to the General
Assembly that Ambassador U Thant of Burma be appointed Acting Secretary General for the unexpired portion of Hammarskjold's term, running
until April 10, 1963. The Assembly concurred. The question had occupied
most of Stevenson's time for nearly two months. U Thant's selection was
regarded as an important Stevenson success.

During the long negotiations the United States had made a list of candidates for the job who were acceptable and had begun quiet talks, being
careful to avoid pushing its real choices, letting neutrals take the lead.
Thant was one of those acceptable, though he was not the United States'
first choice—Boland of Ireland and Slim of Tunisia were more favored.
Prior to his appointment Thant had been Burma's representative to the
UN. From 1954 to 1957 he had been a member of Prime Minister U Nu's
staff. In welcoming his appointment, Stevenson emphasized that the Secretary General's office under him would not be weakened—"he will have the
full powers and responsibilities of that office." Stevenson had known
Thant as the Burmese representative but had not known him well. After
Thant became Secretary General he developed a good relationship with
Stevenson, though the two were not so close as Stevenson and Hammarskjold had been. Thant had great respect for Stevenson. He was basically
pro-Western, in Stevenson's opinion. Stevenson felt Thant, a gentle man,

very polite, stood up well to the Soviet Union's pressures. Rusk was less enthusiastic about Thant and sometimes treated him roughly.

General debate opened in the Assembly on September 22. President Kennedy addressed it on Monday, September 25. He praised Hammar- skjold, said a troika must not succeed him, proclaimed the life of the UN, and said that war "appeals no longer as a rational alternative." He said that for fifteen years the UN had sought disarmament. "Now that goal is no longer a dream—it is a practical matter of life or death. The risks in- herent in disarmament pale in comparison to the risks inherent in an un- limited arms race." The United States and the Soviet Union had jointly presented an agreement on a new statement of newly agreed principles for negotiation looking toward general and complete disarmament. But princi- ples alone were not enough. "It is therefore our intention to challenge the Soviet Union, not to an arms race, but to a peace race—to advance to- gether step by step, stage by stage, until general and complete disarma- ment has been achieved. We invite them now to go beyond agreement in principle to reach agreement on actual plans. . . . The logical place to begin is a treaty assuring the end of nuclear tests of all kinds, in every en- vironment, under workable controls."

Kennedy spoke of "the smoldering coals of war in Southeast Asia." South Vietnam was already "under attack." The borders of Burma, Cam- bodia, and India had been "repeatedly violated." The people of Laos were "in danger of losing [their] independence." He said, "No one can call these 'wars of liberation.'" If measures could not be devised to protect small and weak states, if aggression succeeded in Laos and South Viet- nam, "the gates will be opened wide."

Of Germany and Berlin, Kennedy said, "If there is a crisis it is because an existing peace is under threat, because an existing island of free people is under pressure, because solemn agreements are being treated with indifference. . . . If there is a dangerous crisis in Berlin—and there is—it is because of threats against the vital interests and the deep commitments of the Western powers, and the freedom of West Berlin. We cannot yield these interests. We cannot fail these commitments. We cannot surrender the freedom of these people for whom we are responsible." The events and decisions of the next ten months "may well decide the fate of man for the next ten thousand years. . . . I pledge you every effort this nation possesses. I pledge you that we shall neither commit nor provoke aggres- sion, that we shall neither flee nor invoke the threat of force, that we shall never negotiate out of fear, we shall never fear to negotiate. Terror is not a new weapon. Throughout history it has been used by those who could not prevail, either by persuasion or example. But inevitably they fail, either because men are not afraid to die for a life worth living, or because the terrorists themselves came to realize that free men cannot be frightened by threats, and that aggression would meet its own response. And it is in the light of that history that every nation today should know, be he friend or foe, that the United States has both the will and the weapons to join free men in standing up to their responsibilities. . . . But however close we sometimes seem to that dark and final abyss, let no man of peace and freedom despair. For he does not stand alone. If we all can persevere, if we can in every land and office look beyond our own shores and ambitions, then surely the age will dawn in which the strong are just and the weak secure and the peace preserved."

19.

Stevenson spoke in the Security Council on September 26 on the admission of Sierra Leone, a brief acerbic exchange with Zorin on a procedural question. The applications of Outer Mongolia and Mauritania were also under consideration. They were admitted after many debates and votes. China declared she remained "convinced that Outer Mongolia is utterly unqualified for membership" but would not oppose because she did not want her opposition to become the excuse for the denial of admission to Mauritania. U.S. pressure on Chiang had prevailed.

On September 28, Stevenson went to Sweden to attend funeral services for Hammarskjold. A memorial service was held at the UN; Stevenson and Zorin were so absorbed in bargaining over the appointment of a successor to Hammarskjold that they nearly missed the service in his honor. John Steinbeck told Stevenson that when he asked Hammarskjold shortly before he died if there was anything he could do for him in the course of a world tour, Hammarskjold had replied, "Yes—there is. Sit on the ground and talk to people." Stevenson thought the remark was "the echo of a head and heart too long battered by the babble of the great, and after almost a year of consorting with one kind of people here at the UN, I am feeling a little bit the same way."

General debate in the Assembly continued through mid-October. So did Stevenson's talks with visiting Foreign Ministers and chiefs of state and UN Ambassadors; so did his social life, cocktail parties, dinner parties, theater parties, white-tie functions, sometimes frivolously with friends, sometimes dutifully with diplomats. Barbara Ward came to town. Stevenson dined with Mrs. Roosevelt, with Marietta Tree, with the actor and actress Alfred Lunt and Lynn Fontanne. He saw Alicia Patterson and Jane Dick. He took Borden to Ruth Field's Long Island estate for a quiet weekend. He flew to San Francisco to make a speech on UN Day and saw John Fell. He received an honorary degree from Brandeis University. Evelyn Houston thanked him from Madrid for "a magical weekend." At the suggestion of Stanley Frankel and Arnold Michaelis, two publicists who admired Stevenson, he began a series of television programs on the UN called "Adlai Stevenson Reports." (The programs won a Peabody award.) He sent Marietta Tree a poem. He sent a note to Alicia Patterson on her birthday: "I love you, even if you are a little more than mature!" Agnes Meyer tried to help solve his chronic speech-writing problem, sending a young writer to him. Carol Evans passed through New York on her way to take up a job with the Britannica in California; Stevenson did not see her and sent her a note—"I am distressed I missed you."

Benton often presented gifts to Stevenson, including a painting by Ben Shahn, and sent him now a pair of cuff links. Thanking him, Stevenson reported he had lost the gold money clip Benton gave him, which Stevenson said "was a reminder every day of our 'collaboration' which means so much to me." Later Stevenson found the money clip but by then Benton had already ordered a new one. He thanked Benton for making him a firm offer: to quit the UN, come back to Britannica and "your educational destiny," take his stock back, accept a big raise in salary from both companies, "concentrate on taking off thirty pounds, and live twenty years longer." Stevenson wrote, "Certainly I never had a business relationship that I enjoyed more." He wrote to Congressman Walter Judd to deny that he had, as Judd had been quoted as saying, caused cancellation of U.S. air cover for the Bay of Pigs invasion. General James A. Van Fleet made a similar statement, and Stevenson asked him to correct it, and he did.

Schlesinger visited Stevenson at the UN and wrote in his journal, "It is essential to visit the UN from time to time in order to reacquaint oneself with what is a separate world—and a world so vivid and hectic and compelling, so filled with excitement and crisis, that those who dwell in it all the time begin to believe that nothing else exists. We spent Wednesday afternoon in Stevenson's office; and the flow and variety of business were irresistible. This was the afternoon that the African nations persuaded the General Assembly to pass a vote of censure against Eric Louw of South Africa for his defense of *apartheid*. Stevenson's reaction was strong and clear—that the right of untrammeled expression in the General Assembly had to be preserved (and that the African nations had to be taught that they couldn't run everything in terms of their own emotions). I was caught up in the excitement and helped work on Stevenson's statement. And yet I cannot resist the feeling that the UN world is really an immense and picturesque form of make-believe, and that its problems and crises are remote from the serious issues of the day. I am sure that this feeling is wrong; certainly it is wrong in the long run; but it enables me to understand the inevitable gap between Washington and New York. Considering the fact that JFK is surrounded every day by State Dept people who believe essentially in bilateral diplomacy, and by generals and admirals, who don't believe in diplomacy at all, I think he does exceedingly well to keep the UN as considerably in the forefront of his attention as he does."

Stevenson sometimes chafed under Department instructions. During negotiations over a successor to Hammarskjold, he telephoned Rusk to complain that it was "impossible" to do his work under the tight rein the Department kept on him. Rusk said Stevenson should have the Department's "thinking" but should use his own judgment. Stevenson said he knew what the Department was thinking—he was told "every hour by phone." Sometimes Stevenson dealt with Rusk as though their roles were reversed, as when, reporting that the Prime Minister of Ceylon wanted to visit the United States, he told Rusk, "I assume you will see that this is considered in the proper quarters." In a letter to Mrs. Ives, Stevenson complained of "the everlasting backbiting and negativism of Dean Acheson."

Although the question of a successor to Hammarskjold dominated the Assembly that fall, other important issues were considered. Early in October, Stevenson proposed a new initiative on disarmament. He proposed the President announce within the next few days that, if the Soviet Union would discontinue nuclear testing immediately and conclude a treaty within thirty days, the United States would institute a thirty-day moratorium on testing. If the Soviets rejected the offer, the United States would be obliged to press forward with tests in all environments.

William C. Foster, head of the Arms Control and Disarmament Agency, opposed the Stevenson proposal. He said that such a statement made now would pre-empt the General Assembly debate on nuclear testing, which the United States itself had proposed. Moreover, if the Soviets accepted the proposal, negotiations would be set back to where they had been three years ago when the United States offered a one-year moratorium, and if they rejected it the United States would find it hard to oppose the addition of a moratorium to the U.S.-U.K. draft resolution later on. Foster believed the best U.S. position was to take a clear stand against any moratorium on the ground that the Soviets had broken the previous moratorium and a full moratorium was uncontrollable. The Stevenson proposal, he thought, blurred this position. Harlan Cleveland agreed with Foster, thus undermining Stevenson's position. Glenn Seaborg, chairman of the Atomic Energy Commission, also opposed a moratorium and urged an early meeting of the principals.

That meeting was held on October 10 at the White House—and Stevenson was not invited. His proposal received scant attention; the principals accepted Foster's objections. Secretary McNamara offered a Defense Department proposal to resume atmospheric testing early in November. Bundy opposed tests for the sake of demonstrating our power and insisted on the principle that we must never test in the atmosphere unless required to do so in order to ensure our military security. Everyone agreed with this except Paul Nitze, who argued for atmospheric testing in order to prevent the world from believing that the U.S.S.R. was gaining so unbeatable a lead that there was no point in resisting further.

Schlesinger and Cleveland went up to New York to see Stevenson the next day, October 11. They found him "considerably irritated," as Schlesinger put it, because his proposal had received little consideration.

He went to work on a paper designed to revive his proposal. Cleveland worked with him—but watered his paper down until it approached the Washington position.

On October 12, Stevenson sent a long memorandum to President Kennedy, repeating his proposal, noting that the principals had rejected it, and saying that the principals had agreed the United States would continue to be willing to negotiate a treaty but would not agree to a moratorium during the negotiations. "The proposal that we test in the atmosphere almost at once, for demonstration rather than technical purposes, was rejected—thank God!" Stevenson said he was not questioning the decision taken in Washington. What he did "urgently" recommend was "an immediate statement from you or me offering to sign the present draft treaty or to return now to the negotiation table" either in Geneva or New York. Stevenson pressed hard—asked Kennedy for "your authorization to make a statement here within a very few days." A week later Stevenson again appealed to the President: he was "disturbed" by signs that the United States was contemplating a new series of tests at the Eniwetok proving grounds. This would be a "grievous error," he felt. The inhabitants were Micronesians living on a Pacific island of which the United States was a trustee. They had bitterly resented earlier tests. "The moral question is even more serious and should really control," he wrote. Testing would cause us "great damage here at the UN even among our friends and allies."

Stevenson was overruled. On October 19 he was obliged to state the U.S. position officially in the Political Committee. The United States stood ready to negotiate a test-ban treaty with effective controls and believed one could be signed in thirty days but, until it was concluded, reserved the right, as a matter of self-protection, to make preparations to test in the atmosphere as well as underground. He said the Soviet Union's tests had created an "emergency" and that it had not negotiated at Geneva in good faith because even while negotiations had been progressing there the Soviets had been preparing to test in the atmosphere. Ambassador Arthur Dean would present the U.S. views in detail; this was only a preliminary statement. "I have claimed the privilege of making this declaration for the United States because few delegates, I dare say, feel more deeply about this matter than I do, in part, perhaps, because I proposed that nuclear tests be stopped almost six years ago—and lost a great many votes in the 1956 presidential election as a result. . . . I pray we do not lose still another chance to meet the challenge of our time and stop this death dance. I confess a feeling of futility when I consider the immensity of the problems which confront us and the feebleness of our efforts to deal properly with them." Thus did he not only announce a U.S. policy he privately opposed but also supported it with his personal prestige. He was, as Bundy observed, a good soldier.

Khrushchev had announced he would explode a 50-megaton weapon, working toward one of 100 megatons. Stevenson called such huge weapons militarily useless and dangerously poisonous to the atmosphere. On October 27 the General Assembly adopted a resolution appealing to the U.S.S.R. not to do it. On Monday, October 30, Stevenson spoke again in the Political Committee. That morning he had heard "the shocking news" that the U.S.S.R. had exploded a bomb even larger than one producing 50 megatons of force. "This, Mr. Chairman, is a solemn day in the history of the United Nations . . . a display of violence on a scale unheard of in human history to this time." Khrushchev had "cynically" disregarded the UN. The Russians had broken the moratorium on testing, had raised atmospheric pollution, had started "a new race for more deadly weapons," had "spurned the humanitarian appeal" of the UN. The U.S. delegation, he said, "deeply deplores this contempt for world opinion."

Stevenson and others spent a great deal of time in the early weeks of the Assembly seeking support for the American position on Chinese representation. By the end of September, Secretary Rusk told the Formosan Chinese that a new count showed the "important-question" issue would receive a tie vote, 46 to 46, with the rest abstaining—the situation was "very grave." In October the White House proposed to issue a statement on the issue and sent it to Stevenson for comment. He said, "The timing . . . could not be worse." It would be interpreted as excluding the chance of a compromise next year and as proving that the U.S. proposal for a study commission was only a device to postpone. On October 19, Stevenson told Rusk the study commission was "critical" to U.S. efforts—without it, the United States would be suspected of rounding up a perpetual blocking third on the "important question." When Outer Mongolia was admitted to the UN toward the end of October, Stevenson and his staff increased their consultations on China.

At the same time, on November 1, David Popper of the Mission gave Stevenson a memorandum saying that McNamara had not made a good case for nuclear testing and so the principals had not decided to start testing (though they would prepare). Popper hoped Stevenson would renew his objections to testing. On November 2, three days after the Soviets had exploded their superbomb in Asia, the National Security Council met at the White House. Stevenson attended (and afterward rode back to New York on the President's plane). Upon McNamara's request, the President authorized preparations for nuclear tests "in case it becomes necessary to conduct them." At the same time he declared that no test would be undertaken in the atmosphere for "psychological or political reasons" but only if essential to security and only if fallout could be restricted to "an absolute minimum." The President announced the decision that same day. Nevertheless Stevenson, Jerome Wiesner, and others continued to fight a delaying action into December (as did Harold Macmillan), arguing that testing was basically a political matter, not a technical one critical to the nation's security. Kennedy seemed to be leaning toward their view. But throughout the government the mood hardened, as though a decision to actually conduct tests had already been taken. Then President Kennedy's adviser on science, Jerome Wiesner, and John McNaughton, general counsel for the Defense Department, carried the arguments against testing. Stevenson was simply not in the room where the decisions were being taken.

He did, however, attempt to present his views, and he handled some aspects of disarmament at the UN. On November 1 he prepared a memo for President Kennedy complaining about the rearming of Germany and saying, "I wonder sometimes if we get the deeper insight and the higher truth from the kind of would-be cynical analysis coming out of the Rand Corporation, for example, where, as in so many large bureaucracies with an electronic bias, man has disappeared, and digits and theories and weapons systems take his empty place." This barb was almost certainly aimed at McNamara, whose views on Berlin were weighty—and usually opposed by Stevenson.

Stevenson and Zorin spoke to the Political Committee on disarmament on November 15. Stevenson called Zorin's speech "misleading and frequently abusive" and said the Berlin problem had been "created by the Soviet Union for its own purposes." In the past, he said, wars had produced winners as well as losers; they would not in the future. All would lose. War must be abolished. He accused the Russians of frustrating good British and American intentions to that end, most recently by resuming atmospheric testing. The Soviets, he said, would agree to a ban on nuclear tests only as part of an agreement, for general and complete disarmament, despite General Assembly calls for the urgent resumption of negotiations to outlaw nuclear tests. He reviewed the new U.S. proposals for "general and complete disarmament." On only one point was the U.S. position inflexible: "The familiar question of verification." This was indispensable, the heart of the matter. The Soviet Union rejected the inspection as espionage. He hoped the Soviets would not persist in that attitude.

20.

The Congo came to the fore again. On November 7, Rusk, Stevenson, Ball, Williams, and Cleveland met with the British Ambassador, Sir David Ormsby-Gore. Ormsby-Gore feared the UN might move militarily against Tshombe's mercenaries; this could divide Britain and the United States. Stevenson agreed that the last thing wanted was to resolve the issue by force of arms. He added that "we are on the verge of ruin" in the Congo because the UN was "about to leave the Congo with its tail between its legs unless we can bring this Tshombe to heel." Ormsby-Gore kept pressing for an effort to bring Adoula and Tshombe together. Ball finally agreed to try.

The Security Council met on the Congo eight times between November 13 and 24. Stevenson, already nearly exhausted by the struggle over the successor to Dag Hammarskjold, spoke at almost every meeting, trying to blunt Soviet and extremist Afro-Asian demands for a mandate requiring the UN command to support the Congolese Army militarily against Katanga. Ceylon, Liberia, and the U.A.R. submitted a resolution which condemned Katangan secession and authorized the Secretary General to use force against it. Stevenson introduced amendments intended to soften the resolution and emphasize peaceful reintegration of Katanga. Spaak of Belgium talked to President Kennedy and Secretary Rusk. The situation both on the ground in the Congo and in the UN was touch and go, the difficulties of orchestrating U.S. moves enormous. In the end, although not all of its amendments were adopted, the United States voted for the resolution. France and the United Kingdom abstained.

Now the State Department's Policy Planning Council prepared a long report on Communist tactics in South Vietnam. It concluded that there was a "clear and present danger of Communist conquest" of South Vietnam by the North and that such a conquest would "seal the fate" of Laos and subject Cambodia's "precarious neutrality" to "heavy and steadily increasing pressure," and would threaten Thailand and other small states. Responsibility for defeating aggression lay primarily with the South Vietnamese people. But it was "too much to expect" them to succeed without help; the North had "the full backing of Moscow, Peiping, and the rest of the communist world." The United States and other friendly countries had already contributed much to South Vietnam's military and economic programs. More assistance, the report said, "may" be needed. At this time Stevenson was not closely informed about Vietnam.

On November 22 the Security Council met to consider a complaint by Cuba that American warships were threatening the sovereignty of the Dominican Republic. The background: after Trujillo was assassinated in May, his sons and brothers had sought to retain power. The United States had been trying to negotiate them out or, failing that, to threaten to throw them out. The United States favored a restoration of non-dictatorial constitutional rule through representative democracy. In October, President Balaguer of the Dominican Republic, Trujillo's last puppet President, had addressed the UN and later had gone to Stevenson's embassy at 42A in the Waldorf to meet secretly with George Ball. Stevenson himself was not present during the discussion but knew about it and said afterward he hoped the Department would not do business with the Trujillos.[5] Now matters had come to a climax on November 19, when the Trujillo family moved to seize power and American warships appeared on the horizon while American diplomats told the Trujillos the game was up. Cuba seized on the incident as a way to embarrass the United States in the UN. Her

<hr/>

[5] President Kennedy had sent John Bartlow Martin to the Dominican Republic on a fact-finding mission in September. Martin helped arrange the Balaguer-Ball meeting in Stevenson's embassy at the Waldorf and talked to Stevenson after it.

Foreign Minister now charged in the Security Council that the United States was obstructing a popular movement against dictatorship and asked that the Security Council condemn the United States as an aggressor and demand the withdrawal of its forces. Stevenson replied that it was "little short of incredible" that the Security Council's time should be wasted by "such irresponsible accusations." He asked why at this time, "of all times," when the Dominican people were trying to free themselves from a thirty-one-year-old dictatorship, the Cubans should bring unwarranted charges. He declared that American warships and warplanes had not entered the territorial waters or air space of the Dominican Republic and that their "friendly presence" on the nearby seas was undertaken "with the full knowledge of the constitutional authorities and the responsible leaders of the Dominican Republic." He found it "strange" that the accusation against the United States was made not by Dominicans but by Cubans. He said "these absurd charges," if made at all, should have been made in the OAS.

The Dominican representative said the Cuban complaint had been lodged without the Dominicans' knowledge, asked for time to reply to its substance, said the Dominicans would tolerate no interference by Cuba in Dominican affairs. He said Cuba was using the Dominican Republic as a "pawn" in its quarrel with the United States.

Ambassador Zorin of the U.S.S.R. supported the Cuban complaint and asked why the United States, a great power, wanted to intervene in Dominican affairs or, if she did not want to intervene, why she had dispatched the warships. He derided the idea that events in the Dominican Republic might threaten U.S. security. Under the UN Charter, he said, no state had a right to intervene in the domestic affairs of another state. He also charged that U.S. warplanes had violated Dominican air space. Stevenson in reply asked what Cuba had to do with the Dominican question and why Cuba and the Soviet Union were "so deeply concerned with the protection of the Trujillo regime." The Cuban replied that the Dominicans should decide their own internal questions. Stevenson asked why Cuba had sent an invasion force to the Dominican Republic in 1959. The Cuban replied that Cuba did not "export revolution" and revolutionary movements were national movements. The Dominican representative said that were the matter not so serious he would be "highly amused"—the Dominican Republic did not "feel itself threatened."

The next day was Thanksgiving, and Stevenson went to Bill Benton's for lunch. On Friday morning, November 24, he appeared again before the Security Council on the question of the Dominican Republic, and so did a Dominican who said in a long oration, "Blessed be the moment when the United States fleet reached Dominican waters." The Cuban spoke again, bitterly, and the Council adjourned without taking action. The next day, Saturday, November 25, at Rusk's request, Stevenson left by plane for Trinidad to meet with President Frondizi of Argentina, who was beginning a world tour and had requested the meeting.

On Sunday, November 26, from Hyannis, Kennedy sent a cable to Stevenson in Port of Spain, saying he had attempted to reach him by telephone to discuss a State Department personnel shuffle. This was the famous "Thanksgiving Day Massacre" of 1961 in which Chester Bowles was removed as Undersecretary and made the President's adviser on underdeveloped countries with rank of Ambassador, a position without real power.[6]

Stevenson returned from Trinidad on November 27 and next day attended the third and last meeting of the Security Council on the Dominican question. The representatives of Ceylon, the U.A.R., Chile, Ecuador, and Liberia spoke—and none associated himself with the Cuban complaint. Stevenson said, "My government is opposed to dictatorship, be it dictatorship of the right or of the left, in this hemisphere, and has tried to give moral encouragement to those forces in the Dominican Republic which are attempting to restore normal democratic processes in an orderly and a peaceful way. . . . We are frankly proud that the moral support of the United States has aided in these accomplishments." The Council ended the debate without taking action. The United States had come off well. Frequently accused of opposing Communist dictatorships only, this time it had used the fleet to oppose a dictatorship of the right. As in Angola, it had come down on the side that Stevenson and other liberals favored. Stevenson would fare less well three and a half years later in defending another American intervention in Dominican affairs.

21.

In December, with adjournment only three weeks away, the General Assembly moved toward decisions on questions it had been struggling with all fall. It was a frantically busy time for Stevenson. He told Mrs. Ives, "I work almost literally all of the time, and the results are spotty. Tonight I am off to Washington for a session at the State Department and a visit with Kennedy, followed by a dance with [old friends], the Thorons. My visits have been infrequent lately, due to the pressure of work here, but I hope I can get a better liaison with the Department established somehow

[6] Ball replaced Bowles as Undersecretary. George McGhee became the number two Undersecretary (for Political Affairs). Walt Rostow took McGhee's place as counselor to the Department and chairman of the Policy Planning Council. Fred Dutton became Assistant Secretary for Congressional Affairs, replacing Brooks Hays, who joined the White House staff as a Special Assistant to the President. Averell Harriman replaced Walter P. McConaughy as Assistant Secretary for Far Eastern Affairs. Dick Goodwin left the White House to become Deputy Assistant Secretary of State for Latin America. The key move was Bowles's.

in the future." He was planning a big party in Libertyville for old friends over the Christmas holidays.

Earlier, the Soviet Union had submitted a resolution on Chinese representation which would have expelled the Formosa Chinese and replaced them with Peking Chinese. It was a tough resolution, referring to the Formosa government as the "Chiang Kai-shek clique" which was "unlawfully" occupying the China seat. Now on December 1 the United States, together with Australia, Colombia, Italy, and Japan, introduced another resolution declaring that any proposal to change the representation of China was an "important question" requiring a two-thirds vote. Stevenson advocated it in a long and lofty speech.

Next morning, Saturday, December 2, Stevenson went to Washington. He saw President Kennedy for an hour, then, after lunching with Secretary Rusk and having meetings in the Department and attending "Dancing Class" at the Thorons' in the evening, on Sunday went with Kennedy to Glen Ora, Kennedy's weekend retreat, and had lunch with him and talked from 11:10 A.M. to 3:10 P.M. It was a conversation important to their relationship and revelatory of Stevenson's method of operation. Stevenson complained about his relations with the Department and the President. He also talked about running for the Senate from Illinois. Senator Dirksen, a Republican, would be up for re-election next year. The Illinois Democratic machine would meet during December to slate its candidate to run against Dirksen. Kennedy gave Stevenson his views. Afterward he said, "I told Adlai that he would be even more frustrated as a junior Senator than he is in the UN. I reminded him about Alben Barkley, who came back to the Senate [after being Vice President] with much fanfare, and a week later was just another junior Senator at the bottom of the list. I told him we needed him in the UN and that I counted on him to stay on."

When Kennedy returned to the White House, Carl Kaysen of his staff saw him, and Kennedy started ruminating about Stevenson. Kaysen later recalled that Kennedy said, "I don't understand that man and I never have understood him. He's talking about being Senator from Illinois— well, if he wants to do that I wish him well. But I don't understand why he wants to be one among one hundred. He does much more at the UN. I know he's mad because I never offered him Secretary—but why didn't he ask me for it?" Schlesinger had the impression that Dick Daley wanted Stevenson to run. Newt Minow has said that Daley told Stevenson they had an opening for the Senate nomination and asked if Stevenson were interested. Sorensen thought the incident further impaired the Stevenson-Kennedy relationship. He thought Stevenson did not want to run because he feared he would lose and therefore put the decision up to Kennedy. Kennedy was subsequently criticized by some of Stevenson's friends for having "prevented" Stevenson from running—or, on the other hand, of trying to ease Stevenson out of the UN and "throw him to the wolves" in a hopeless race against Dirksen. Most of Stevenson's close friends and advisers opposed his running, if only because they feared Dirksen would beat him. Senator Douglas, however, told Stevenson, "I hope, for Illinois' sake, you can be persuaded." Bill Benton thought Stevenson should have run and years later was still critical of him for "not having the nerve" to do it.

Stevenson returned to New York that same day, Sunday, December 3. Despite a full UN schedule on Monday, he discussed with Clayton Fritchey a statement the President might issue requesting Stevenson to remain at the UN. On Tuesday, Arthur Krock reported in the New York *Times* that Stevenson had said some things at the dance on Saturday night which indicated that Kennedy and Stevenson were increasingly incompatible over such issues as Cuba and Chinese representation. Krock speculated that Kennedy had urged Mayor Daley to offer to slate Stevenson for the Senate. Early that morning Kennedy called Schlesinger's attention to the Krock column and asked who had planted such a story. Schlesinger consulted Fritchey. Fritchey said he and Stevenson proposed that Kennedy issue a statement asking Stevenson to stay at the UN. Schlesinger suggested that this statement be followed by one from Stevenson rejecting the senatorial candidacy. He and Fritchey worked out language. But Kennedy thought it looked silly for him to be pleading publicly with Stevenson to stay on. He suggested that the Stevenson statement be issued first, with Kennedy's to follow. Stevenson and Fritchey agreed. Stevenson issued his statement that day, saying Kennedy had recently "greatly reinforced my view" that he could best serve the country "in the field of foreign policy." Kennedy followed with his own: "I am delighted with Governor Stevenson's decision. I expressed to him this week-end my emphatic hope that he will continue at the United Nations and play an expanding role in the making and execution of our foreign policy. I believe that his work is vital to the cause of peace and of top importance to the country."

Schlesinger noted in his journal that Kennedy "was not mad at anyone and emphasized that AES could go as far as he liked in his statement in indicating that presidential pressure was causing him to stay in the UN. He said that he wished that the Governor would stop belly-aching around town—a sentiment heartily echoed later in the day by Clayton and by Marietta. Adlai caused a great deal of his own trouble this time by his unguarded remarks Saturday night."

James Wechsler talked to Stevenson that day, too, and Stevenson said he had never heard the President so eloquent and articulate as when he urged Stevenson not to run for the Senate. Wechsler asked how the week-end stories about Kennedy's wanting him out of the UN had started. Stevenson replied darkly, "Joe Alsop," which was wholly unlikely since Alsop was away from Washington until Sunday and would have published the tales himself rather than wholesale them to Krock and Doris Fleeson.

Stevenson wrote to Bill Blair that day, December 5, "I have just withstood the blandishments of Dick Daley, Jack Arvey, et al, and decided to stick with this ship which, in spite of my best efforts, is still afloat. I must say I was a little tempted to be my own boss again, but the President was very good about it and may make my life a little easier than it is at present."

By this time the rumors he himself had started were getting back to him, and on December 6 he sent a long letter of explanation to the President: "I hear you were distressed by reports from Washington about 'what I said' following our meeting on Saturday last." He said that in response to inquiries he had told friends there were three reasons why he would "consider" returning to Illinois—the Senate would be an easier job "at my age"; it would give him more time in Illinois near his family; it would give him "greater independence." He said he had also added "I think *in every case*" that the work at the UN is "incomparably more important" than being another Senator. He said he had made "no criticism whatever" of his relations with the President, with Rusk, "or anyone else," though "I did suggest to one or two of the more informed people that I thought the traditional practice of the State Department in sending minute instructions to the Mission in New York could well be modified in the direction of greater autonomy. If these remarks have been distorted and caused you any concern, please know that I am distressed. I don't believe I was indiscreet, but if I can only ask your forgiveness. . . . Your expression of gratitude was most reassuring. . . . Thanks, too, for that delightful visit at Glen Ora with my beloved Jackie!" Stevenson told Schlesinger privately he had suggested to Daley that the Democrats nominate Bill Wirtz for the Senate.

After those weekend meetings with Stevenson, Kennedy told Schlesinger he was dissatisfied with liaison between Stevenson and the White House. He said that he had not been kept informed about votes and that, when State and Stevenson disagreed, he had not heard a full presentation of the Stevenson case. He mentioned an example (which Stevenson had cited to him). This, Schlesinger felt, was his own, Schlesinger's, fault.

On Monday evening, December 4, Cleveland asked Stevenson what he and Kennedy had discussed at Glen Ora—he had been getting inquiries all day. Stevenson replied, "I told him I wanted a lot more autonomy and authority than in the past. I don't think there is a damned thing you can do. One of our problems here is . . . too much instructions on details and not enough of the main things, such as long-range policy projections. I am going to write him [President Kennedy] a memorandum. I think we have to think through well in advance the issues of the UN. I am thinking particularly of the nuclear testing business. We really muffed this. . . . Walt Rostow is the bloodthirstiest of all. . . . Little by little, he [the President] is learning he cannot be his own Secretary of State."

Cleveland said Bundy had visited the Department and suggested that a Department staff man from IO be attached to the White House. Stevenson said, "I can fix that. I am going to send a memo to him about the advantages of resolution planning. I told him a staff man just doesn't seem necessary. I've got the best in Harlan Cleveland. My problem is to use Harlan more effectively, and what can you do without going through the Secretary's office? . . . I guess I am not equipped for this job, maybe should go to Illinois. . . . Basically, I want to make my own decisions, particularly those that don't relate so much to the national policy. Most of the time I don't know what our policy is, what with so many papers coming up here."

Stevenson went on, "And, as a result, my outer space speech today . . . Dick [Gardner] worked two days and nights on it and I spent most of last night on it. Then today I started out, the last pages weren't even typed." Cleveland pointed out that the problem in that case had been writing (or typing), not policy. Stevenson went on, "We haven't laid the groundwork for good press relations and other things. I don't have the staff I need. There I can get help from you all. You have writers and people who are thoughtful about these matters. I think I made it clear to him [the President] that I wanted a much higher degree of autonomy and exercise of my own judgment on many of these things and . . . a desire to participate more in what goes on down there. . . . If we could by-pass Rusk, maybe we could by-pass a lot of this other stuff."

Cleveland suggested it would be wise to have an understanding among Stevenson, Rusk, himself, and all concerned. Stevenson said, "I know generally, of course, what the objectives are, but I don't have to be told every day what should be done. Just somebody wasting a lot of time writing telegrams, which I often don't have time to read, anyway. Half of them I don't read. Just give me broad general instructions on what we're trying to do and leave it to me to do it." Cleveland said perhaps they could work out a new system. Stevenson suggested they have lunch on Thursday at a club where they could "talk this thing through in peace and quiet." Stevenson probably disliked putting an IO staff man in the White House because he would be under Bundy, and that meant getting Bundy involved in UN affairs, which Stevenson opposed.

On the next day, Tuesday, December 5, the same day the statements on the Senate race were worked out, Schlesinger discussed with Stevenson "a clandestine appellate procedure" by which Stevenson could privately alert Schlesinger in case of need. That evening Schlesinger went to State to discuss the problem with Woodruff Wallner of Cleveland's staff. He noted in his journal, "An hour's consideration of the situation resulted only in persuading us that it was all very baffling." He wrote, "The problem is how to devise administrative procedures which would serve and satisfy three disparate personalities (Kennedy, Rusk, Stevenson) and at the same time not disrupt the normal administrative processes of the White House and State. The general feeling is that the most difficult relationship is that between Stevenson and Rusk."

On Thursday, December 7, Cleveland and Schlesinger went up to New York and spent the day with Stevenson working out a statement of the relationship among State, the USUN Mission, and the White House. Their task was to increase the flow of information to the White House and increase Stevenson's tactical flexibility. Stevenson drafted a statement which increased his flexibility, and Cleveland accepted it with a few amendments. On White House-Mission relations, Schlesinger provided for the appellate procedure, to which Cleveland added the sentence, "On behalf of the Department, IO (Harlan Cleveland) will keep the White House (Arthur Schlesinger) currently informed on major UN issues." Cleveland was trying to keep IO as the sole channel to the White House, and, asleep at the switch, Schlesinger let it go by. On Saturday, when he showed the draft to Bundy, he had become aware of the problem and said that the language did not carry out the President's intention, to increase the flow of information from Stevenson to the White House. Bundy suggested adding the following: "The White House staff will also keep informed, as the President may desire, by direct contact with USUN; and Ambassador Stevenson, as the President's personal representative, will keep the President appropriately informed of the general situation at the UN." Schlesinger read this language to Cleveland, who said, "This means there will be two IOs, in which case I might as well give up what I am doing and go to work for the Department of Agriculture." He said the procedure would violate Stevenson's assurance to Cleveland before he took his job. Furthermore, it would represent a challenge to State's entire control over foreign policy. Schlesinger tried to reassure him that no one in the White House wanted to make life difficult for him. Cleveland finally said he would not object if these things happened once in a while but he was "greatly concerned"— and knew Rusk would be—over the "constitutional implications." Cleveland had already shown the paper to Rusk without Bundy's amendment. Even without that amendment the paper got a cool reception from Rusk, who said he wanted to hold everything in abeyance until he returned from Paris; and on Saturday morning Rusk telephoned Schlesinger to repeat that instruction. He said he was troubled by language which seemed to transfer policy-making power from State to the Mission. Cleveland had not told him about the proposed Bundy language, nor did Schlesinger. Stevenson penciled into one draft the sentence, "If major disagreements arise between [the Mission] and Department the matter may be presented at the WH level by Amb. Stevenson."

The whole charade, including Stevenson's talks with Kennedy and the negotiations among Stevenson, Schlesinger, and Cleveland, resembled negotiations among mutually suspicious foreign powers, as bureaucratic negotiations within the government frequently do. Anybody who has ever tried to grapple with the elephantine bureaucracy of State must sympathize with Stevenson. At the same time, it appears Stevenson never was quite able to accept the fact that he was neither President nor Secretary. He seems to have used the proffer of the senatorial nomination as leverage in a devious effort to extract greater autonomy from the President and State, thus: he wanted to run for the Senate, Kennedy wanted him to stay at UN, he would stay if Kennedy would give him more autonomy and a greater role in policy making. It was a skillful—and risky—political operation.

22.

While all this was going on, the General Assembly continued its debate on Chinese representation, and the United States came under heavy attack. Secretary Rusk asked Ambassador Ormsby-Gore how the British estimated the chances of "getting some sense into Tshombe's head," a vigorous locution characteristic of Rusk's private conversations and entirely at variance with the austere reserve he presented to the public. The Assembly continued its consideration of China on December 5. In the Congo that day, fighting broke out anew between the UN and the Katanga forces of Tshombe. Katanga troops had set up road blocks at Elisabethville between headquarters of the UN command and the airport; UN forces set out on December 5 to clear them. One UN officer was killed and four men wounded; thirty-eight Katanga men and two mercenaries were killed. The UN held its position. UN troops throughout the city were attacked, and mortar fire hit the headquarters. On the sixth, Mennen Williams came to New York and he and Stevenson told U Thant he could count on political and material support from the United States in the Congo provided he had a practicable and politically realistic plan of action. The UN must move fast. During the ensuing week the UN tried to prevent the reinforcement of the Katanga forces and built up its own forces for a major thrust.

On December 8, Portugal brought a new crisis to the UN. As early as September, Portugal had told the Security Council that three Portuguese territorial enclaves, Goa, Damão, and Diu, on the Indian subcontinent were being threatened by India, which was preparing to use force to take them away from Portugal. Now Portugal informed the Security Council that India had launched a violent campaign of false charges and that Indian troops were being concentrated on the frontier. The Goa incident again posed special difficulties for the United States. The United States wanted to support Portugal, our NATO ally, but it opposed colonialism; on the other hand it wanted India's friendship but was bound to oppose India's threatened use of force. It could hardly win. The Goa affair, which would come briefly and sharply to climax and conclusion in December, aroused Stevenson greatly. India had always played the somewhat sanctimonious role of a peaceable nation forswearing force; here she was employing force herself against a tiny enclave. Yost once said, "He took it much too hard. He was very morally stirred. He was terribly indignant. He was offended that the Indians, who were always so moral and so reproachful of us, should indulge in this sort of thing. He made a very bitter speech in the Security Council."

On Saturday, December 9, Cleveland sent a memo to Rusk about China. The British delegation was presently under instructions to vote for the Russian resolution on China if it could not prevent the resolution's coming to a vote. Stevenson and Cleveland wanted Rusk to approach the British Foreign Minister, Lord Home, and try to get the British instruction changed. British support now for the Soviet resolution would reveal a deep split between the United Kingdom and the United States on an important foreign policy issue which was closely watched in the United States.

Stevenson saw Bill Attwood in his office that day. Attwood had gone to Guinea as U. S. Ambassador and now, recovering from poliomyelitis, had been reassigned to the UN Mission. While ostensibly he would work on the African states for Stevenson, actually he spent a good deal of time writing speeches and trying secretly to arrange a normalization of relations between the United States and Cuba, an initiative, like others, that died with President Kennedy.

On December 11 the Assembly discussed human rights and, again, China. That day the Ambassador of Portugal to the United States told Acting Secretary Ball in Washington that the news from Goa seemed to be getting worse and he thought it likely that India had decided to attack. Ball said Ambassador Galbraith was informing Nehru that day that "we would look with great concern on the use of force in this dispute." Ball added that we did not know how much influence we had on Nehru. The Portuguese Ambassador told Ball the Portuguese forces in Goa were small and courageous, but a war would be short. He said Portugal had always resisted independence for Goa because it was too small. India intended not independence for Goa but incorporation into India of a people spiritually, morally, and ethnically different from the Indians. The Ambassador thought if the "strong light" of public opinion could be focused on Goa, Nehru would hesitate.

On December 11, Stevenson was still fighting for his own autonomy. He sent a letter to President Kennedy reminding him that during their last meeting he had said he felt the Department's instructions should be more generalized and permit greater flexibility for the Mission, and there should be more advance planning on "large and enduring issues" that affected the U.S. "image." He said that, with Cleveland and Schlesinger, he had drafted an "outline of understanding" and presumed they would present it to Kennedy and Rusk. He attached a long memo to illustrate the problem —the record of nuclear weapons votes during the present Assembly, which made the United States appear to be fighting for the use of nuclear weapons, their proliferation, and the possibility of their use on any continent. This was, of course, inaccurate. But many African and Asian delegations, and some Latin Americans, believed it. The United States, Stevenson thought, must emerge as "the foremost apostle of disarmament" and this took long-range planning, not resolution-by-resolution voting. Year by year new resolutions on disarmament and nuclear weapons would be introduced. The United States could not merely choke them off or defeat them. It must adjust to them. Its basic position on them was as good as its basic position on colonialism. Yet too often decisions were made at the last minute in Washington with little regard for the political situation at the UN. Stevenson would call on Kennedy "for help as needed."

On December 14, Stevenson spoke at length in the General Assembly on China. The Assembly, meeting steadily for nearly two weeks, had heard some fifty speakers. A vote was near. Stevenson said the UN must look at all "the relevant and current realities." The first was that the Peking regime did not "in any meaningful way" represent the Chinese people but subjugated them by mass executions and iron controls. Second, the Peking regime had already made a record of aggression against its neighbors in Korea, Tibet, India, and Southeast Asia. Third, it was dedicated as a matter of high policy to war and violent revolution. Fourth, the Republic of China was a founding member of the UN. Fifth, the Charter set forth the requirements for membership and expulsion. Sixth, the Russian proposal would "throw out" a founding member who was guilty of nothing, would seat in its stead another delegation, and would present that new delegation with a "special license to commit armed aggression" against the ejected member. Zorin followed him, counterattacking, and others spoke and the session did not end until 12:25 A.M.

By December 14 the UN command in the Congo had completed reinforcing its troops at Elisabethville and begun an attack around the periphery of the city. At 4:30 P.M., Woodruff Wallner telephoned Harlan Cleveland from George Ball's office to say that President Kennedy had received a telegram from Tshombe saying he was willing to meet with Adoula. Kennedy had replied that he was looking into the possibilities. Stevenson was talking with U Thant in New York. The President planned to announce his reply in a half hour, at 5 P.M. He intended to propose a forty-eight-hour cease-fire and the appointment of Ralph Bunche as mediator. Stevenson tried to work this out with U Thant. He reported that U Thant was willing to designate Bunche and Robert Gardiner to act on behalf of the UN but Bunche seemed to think Adoula would refuse to meet with Tshombe if one of the purposes of the talks was to arrange a cease-fire. The UN command's advance had probably pressured Tshombe into sending his message to Kennedy. Stevenson telephoned the White House several times, the last time at 8 P.M. The day ended with nothing firmly arranged. Next day the Mission reported that Bunche was dubious about the meeting. Tshombe would want a cease-fire, Adoula would not. Any cease-fire would have to be arranged on the ground in Elisabethville between the UN command and Katanga forces. Adoula and Tshombe should discuss the reintegration of Katanga into the Congo. While they were talking the UN command would cease firing.

Chinese representation came to a climax on December 15. A vote was due that day. In Washington a British diplomat told the Department that, despite Secretary Rusk's conversation with Lord Home, the British UN delegation's instructions remained unchanged—to vote for the American "important question" resolution but also to vote for that part of the Soviet resolution which invited Peking to take a seat in the UN (though to vote against the part to expel the Formosa Chinese.) Cleveland telephoned Yost in New York and suggested he tell the chief British representative that the United States regarded as binding a verbal commitment which Lord Home had given Rusk that the U.K. delegation "probably" could vote against the entire Soviet resolution.

In New York that afternoon the General Assembly proceeded to vote. The Assembly adopted the "important question" resolution by a vote of 61 (U.S.) to 34 (U.S.S.R.). The Assembly voted against a proposed amendment to the Soviet resolution which the United States opposed. (The United Kingdom voted for it.) Finally the Assembly rejected the Soviet resolution itself by 37 (U.K., U.S.S.R.) to 48 (U.S.) with 19 abstentions. The United States won. In all instances the majority voted with the United States.

That evening President Kennedy sent Stevenson a telegram: "Today's votes on Chinese representation are further evidence of your outstanding skill and leadership in the UN. I am grateful for your eloquent and effective support on this issue. With esteem and warm regards." George Ball wrote, "Let me add one more voice of congratulations to the vote on the Chirep matter. This is universally regarded as a Stevenson *tour de force* of first magnitude." All the long tortured months of planning and negotiating had finally produced success. Formosa China's seat was safe for another year and a two-thirds vote would now be needed to change Chinese representation. Stevenson's victory had been in a cause in which he did not believe. That night he had two parties scheduled—a party at the UN given by U Thant and Mongi Slim from nine-thirty to midnight and a dance at Mary Lasker's for Marietta Tree which lasted till 3 A.M.

By December 16 the UN command in the Congo had cleared roads leading to the Elisabethville airport and to the Rhodesian frontier, had seized the main gendarmerie base in Elisabethville, and captured a strategic tunnel under a railroad bridge. A British diplomat that day called on Ball and McGhee in order to arrange a joint approach "to keep Tshombe from being destroyed." The British felt that if matters continued neither the UN nor Tshombe would be in control. Tshombe was essential to law and order. The British consul in Elisabethville reported that Tshombe had left the city; his whereabouts were unknown. Ball indicated that the United States knew where Tshombe was, said we were confident the UN would not crush Tshombe, said U Thant had already assured us that he had no intention of moving UN troops beyond Elisabethville, and U Thant saw no need for the British and Americans to do anything. Ball could afford to be confident: Tshombe was finally en route to a meeting with Adoula arranged by President Kennedy, the UN, and the U. S. Ambassador to the Congo, Gullion.

On December 17 the UN force stormed Union Minière installations in Elisabethville, and by the eighteenth Elisabethville was in UN hands. At 8 A.M. next day Tshombe boarded a U.S. plane in northern Rhodesia and arrived at the UN base at Kitona, near the mouth of the Congo River, to talk with Adoula. After two days of bargaining Tshombe signed an eight-point declaration which settled the issue of Katanga's secession in princi-ple. Under it Tshombe recognized the "indissoluble unity" of the Congo, recognized Kasavubu as chief of state, recognized the authority of the cen-tral government over the whole Congo, agreed to Katangan participation in redrafting the constitution, pledged the return of Katangese repre-sentatives to Parliament, placed the Katangan army under the chief of state, and indicated he would respect UN resolutions. In a private note to Bunche, however, Tshombe said he would have to consult competent au-thorities in Katanga to ratify the agreement. At the end of the year he was calling the Katangan Assembly into session to consider the Kitona Agreement.

Pussy Paepcke arrived in New York for several days and went to diplomatic functions with Stevenson. She wrote him later, "I had a lovely time. It may be that were the background against which we play not so grim—our fun could not be so light-hearted." One of the times she may have had in mind was the Security Council's meeting on Goa on Monday, December 18. That day the Portuguese representative reported that Indian troops had launched a full-scale attack on Goa (and Damão and Diu as well).

He requested an immediate meeting of the Security Council to order a cease-fire and the withdrawal of invading forces. The office of the Prime Minister of Portugal said that Indian ground forces had crossed the Goa frontier at midnight; Indian planes had carried out "indiscriminate" bomb-ing; and one Indian raid on an airport hit a commercial plane embarking women and children for evacuation.

Ambassador C. Burke Elbrick telephoned from Portugal to say that the Portuguese Prime Minister, Nogueira, would go to New York to appear at the UN and ask that the Indians be condemned for their "unprovoked ag-gression." A message from President Kennedy to New Delhi urging peace-ful settlement of the dispute was overtaken by events. Joe Sisco said, "Only at the last minute did we go to India—and ineffectually. We should have done it early."

When the Security Council met that afternoon the Portuguese and In-dian representatives exchanged accusations. Stevenson spoke next. "It was one of his most famous speeches," Clayton Fritchey said. "The speech we prepared was one thing. The one he gave was different. He got carried away. I was shocked. It is one of the few instances where Stevenson was a demagogue. There couldn't be a more smug country than India, but we were worse. He exceeded his instructions, but the Department was delighted." Stevenson began on a somber note: "I should like to express the views of the United States at this fateful hour in the life of the United Nations. I will not detain you long, but long enough, I hope, to make clear our anxiety for the future of this Organization as a result of this incident." Acts of violence anywhere endangered the peace and caused alarm. The Security Council had "an urgent duty to act." The "winds of change" must not be allowed to become the "bugles of war." The Charter said that the peoples of the world were determined "to save succeeding generations from the scourge of war" and to live together as good neighbors. In that connection, all at the UN owed "much" to India; and he recounted India's contributions to UN peace keeping. All this made India's behavior "harder to understand and condone. . . . So here we are, confronted with the shocking news of this armed attack, and that the Indian Minister of Defense [Krishna Menon]—so well known in these halls for his advice on matters of peace and his tireless enjoinders to everyone else to seek the way of compromise—was on the borders of Goa inspecting his troops at the zero hour of invasion. Let it be perfectly clear what is at stake here; it is the question of the use of armed force by one state against another." What was at issue now was not colonialism. It was, rather, "a bold violation" of a basic UN principle: force was prohibited. No one questioned the depth of disagreement between Portugal and India. But if the UN Charter meant anything it meant that states were obligated to renounce force and seek peaceful solutions to differences. "Mr. Nehru, the Prime Minister, has often said himself that no right end can be served by a wrong means. The Indian tradition of non-violence has inspired the whole world, but this act of force with which we are confronted today mocks the good faith of India's frequent declarations of exalted principle. It is a lamentable departure not only from the Charter but from India's own professions of faith. What is the world to do if every state whose territorial claims are unsatisfied should resort with impunity to the rule of armed might to get its way? . . . If [the UN] is to survive . . . we cannot condone the use of force in this instance and thus pave the way for forceful solutions of other disputes which exist in Latin America, in Africa, in Asia, and in Europe." He "earnestly" urged India to withdraw its forces and appealed for a cease-fire and negotiations. "There is not one law for one part of the world and another law for the rest of the world; there is one law for the whole world, and it is the duty of this Council to uphold it."

Zorin of the Soviet Union, trying to exploit the issue—to curry favor with the Afro-Asians for his own political purposes—said the problem was one of colonialism. The other nations chose sides, and when, after a dinner recess, the Council reconvened at 8:45 P.M., debate grew sharp. Stevenson declared again that the issue was not colonialism but the illegal use of force by India: "We are against colonialism and we are against war; we are for the Charter." He introduced a resolution calling for an immediate cessation of hostilities, calling on India to withdraw its forces immediately, urging the parties to work out a permanent solution by peaceful means, and requesting the Secretary General to provide "appropriate" assistance. He hoped the Council could vote yet tonight.

More speeches, more resolutions; then Liberia proposed an adjournment until the next afternoon. Stevenson spoke in opposition: "I see no need whatever for any further delay in reaching a vote. This is an urgent and pressing matter. This is war. People are being killed." The motion to adjourn lost. Debate continued. Finally the president put an Afro-Asian resolution to a vote. It was defeated 7 (U.S.) to 4 (U.S.S.R.). He put the United States resolution to a vote. Seven nations voted for it—Chile, China, Ecuador, France, Turkey, United Kingdom, and United States, enough for passage. Only four voted against it—Ceylon, Liberia, U.A.R., and U.S.S.R. The Russian negative vote constituted a veto. Plainly the Security Council could not act on Goa. Stevenson spoke at once, beginning abruptly:

"I believe I am the only representative at this table who was present at the birth of the United Nations. Tonight we are witnessing the first act in a drama which could end with the death of the Organization. The League of Nations died, I remind you, when its members no longer resisted the use of aggressive force. So it is with a most heavy heart that I must add a word of epilogue to this fateful discussion, by far the most important in which I have participated since this Organization was founded sixteen years ago." The Security Council's failure to call for a cease-fire was a failure of the UN, he said; the Soviet veto was consistent with its "long role of obstruction."

Zorin again denounced colonialism. The Portuguese said, "History will judge which member state has tonight not only shamed the United Nations but indeed the whole of mankind." The Council adjourned at 12:50 A.M.

Jane Dick, arranging a party in Libertyville for Stevenson, warned he would have too many unattached women and so proposed several men. Stevenson replied on December 19, rejecting some of the men she proposed as "just too much" and saying, "Let's let it go as it is—and I'll dance with two girls at the same time. Love."

Prime Minister Nehru, in a seven-page single-spaced typewritten letter to President Kennedy, said it was "a matter of regret to me" that they had been unable to agree on Goa and said, "I confess that I have been deeply hurt by the rather extraordinary and bitter attitude of Mr. Adlai Stevenson and some others." Kennedy, replying at length, did not mention Stevenson. Nor did he consult Stevenson or IO.

For five years, ever since the U.S.S.R. put down rebellion in Hungary in 1956, the UN had been discussing Hungary and had adopted several resolutions censuring the Soviet and Hungarian governments for repression and violation of human rights. The U.S.S.R. had ignored them. It was a "cold war issue," and the UN was incapable of acting effectively on it. Stevenson now said he wanted to allay or end the cold war, but he deplored continuing "repression" in Hungary. Zorin belittled the issue. A vote was taken on a resolution sponsored by the United States and fifteen other nations deploring the fact that Russia and Hungary had repeatedly ignored UN resolutions censuring them for suppressing the 1956 uprising. The resolution was adopted 49 (U.S.) to 17 (U.S.S.R.) with 32 abstentions. After that the Assembly adjourned at 12:50 A.M. until January 15.

On that last night of the General Assembly, Krishna Menon of India paid a "courtesy" call on Stevenson at his own request. At the beginning he slumped into a chair and went into a moody silence, broken occasionally by small talk. Stevenson finally said he believed Menon had asked to see him. Menon replied that he merely wanted to make a courtesy call. Stevenson thanked him, then said that Indian action in Goa had "profoundly" disturbed U.S. public opinion. If we could not count on India to adhere to the Charter, on what state could we count? He warned Menon that, if he spoke on Goa in the General Assembly, Stevenson would be obliged to reply along the lines of his speech to the Security Council.

Menon said he did not plan to speak on Goa. The issue was dead. India would not raise it. He thought Americans were badly informed. He said several times that India had not violated the Charter. He claimed that Goa was inherently part of India; India did not recognize Portuguese sovereignty. The Portuguese had refused to negotiate. They had long tortured Goans. The United States had said nothing about any of that. Law and order had broken down. Goans were Indians. The Portuguese in Goa had mined roads and blown up bridges. They had recently crossed the frontier into India. India had not wanted to use force but finally had no alternative. Menon objected to Stevenson's remark in the Security Council that Menon had been inspecting troops at the frontier—he had been in Delhi throughout.

Stevenson apologized if he had been wrong. He went on to say he did not want to become the defender of Portuguese policy. The United States had made its attitude toward colonialism clear. It had taken a forthright position on Angola. India had never brought the Goa problem to the UN. Whether India was right or wrong, she should not have used force. India had made no attempt to negotiate. Instead, India had rebuffed President Kennedy, the UN, and others who urged negotiation. Menon said India always respected the views of the United States even when it disagreed, and he would report Stevenson's views to his government. It was a long uncomfortable conversation.

The day after adjournment, on December 21, Stevenson held a press conference. He said that the General Assembly had convened in the shadow of the death of Dag Hammarskjold. It faced several virtually insuperable "life-and-death" problems—the choice of a successor to Hammarskjold and the maintenance of the integrity of his office, the pressure to expel Nationalist China and seat Communist China, the danger of financial ruin of the UN because of the unpaid bills of the Congo and Suez operations, secession and fighting in Katanga which could have resulted in "chaos, Balkanization, and Communism" in the Congo. All these problems had been dealt with successfully. The Congo operation might well be judged by history the "greatest single creative political act" of the UN. He did not interpret these achievements as victories for the United States but rather for the UN. Stevenson then listed fifteen achievements of the 16th General Assembly and said none would have been possible without support from the countries of Africa and Asia, which now made up nearly half of the UN membership. He then spoke of Goa, though without naming it. There could be only one law, applying equally to all, he said. "If the use of force against territory under the control of other states is to be condoned for anti-colonial reasons, it can be condoned for other reasons, and we will have opened Pandora's box. . . . The central purpose of this body is to keep the peace. . . . It is painfully evident that the rule of law and order requires the means for enforcing the law—that peaceful change and the settlement of disputes require machinery for effecting change and containing dispute. And it is painfully evident that we have neither used as well as we might the existing procedures for peaceful settlements and the peace-keeping machinery of the United Nations, nor have we used them frequently enough. . . . This is not a mechanical or organizational problem. It is a problem of the human heart and mind and will. . . . It is a question of moral choice. . . . What has happened in the last week is a warning to all of us."

23.

Stevenson told Bill Blair, "The Senate race in Illinois was really no temptation, but I wanted to pay Daley and the people out there the courtesy of serious consideration, and give the President his opportunity if he wanted it. Things have worked out very well and I think relations with the Department and the White House have been, on the whole, improved."

But December 22 he sent Cleveland a note: "As I leave for Illinois, I find that I have had no response to the 'treaty' which we worked out with you and Arthur Schlesinger. I hope it will be possible to get this cleared up soon." To Bill Benton: "We have the Assembly behind us at last, and I can't remember three worse months since the 1956 campaign." On Saturday, December 23, three days after the General Assembly recessed, Stevenson, delayed by a storm in Chicago, went home to Libertyville with Borden.

His holiday schedule was full of parties with old friends—a dinner dance given by the Kelloggs on St. Mary's Road, Christmas Eve with Harriet Welling and her daughter and with Ruth Winter, Christmas Day with his own family at Libertyville, a dinner at the Dicks' and at the William Graham Coles' (he was president of Lake Forest College), a visit by Ruth Field, a party at Onwentsia Club, and a single appointment in the city—lunch with Mayor Daley. He told Mrs. Welling that for the first time in his life he was doing something he did not want to do, and she told him he'd had a good press and said, "Come clean—isn't it satisfying to know you're doing a job well?" He confessed it was. He sent Christmas messages to President Kennedy, Agnes Meyer, Ruth Field, Barbara Ward, Pussy Paepcke, Suzie Zurcher, others.

During the holidays John Fell took his grandmother, Mrs. Carpenter, to visit his mother.[7] At the door, according to court testimony, Mrs. Carpenter gave Ellen Stevenson a gift, a purse; Ellen said something to the effect that it was the only thing her mother had ever given her. Mrs. Carpenter and John Fell went into Ellen's apartment. The two women sat down on sofas facing each other; John Fell stood between them at the fireplace. Suddenly Ellen picked up a silver cigarette box and cocked her arm to throw it at her mother. John Fell stepped in front of her and took the cigarette box out of her hand. She jumped to her feet and began to scream curses at her mother. Mrs. Carpenter, frightened, tried to leave the room. Ellen followed her into the hall, struck at her head, and tried to choke her. John Fell managed to get between them and hold Ellen's wrists. But as soon as he let her go, thinking her calmed, she hit him. He forced her into a chair in the hall and asked her to calm down, to relax. He let her go. Again she leaped up and attacked her mother. He had to subdue her again. Later she talked about the incident repeatedly, accusing John Fell of almost breaking her arms.

On Saturday night, December 30, Stevenson gave his own large party at Libertyville for old friends and family. He wrote to Marietta, "I've had no word save the New Year cable, so that was all the more precious. Thanks for starting the year with 'happiest and best.' I pray and pray it will be and that in this dark world there is inward light. 'The person who can face both life and love with confidence and courage—and give himself for the sheer joy of giving—is sure to find joy and contentment. For loving *is* living.' It sounds well—and is, no doubt, but my trouble seems to be that 'life' is so dependent on love. The holiday in the snowbound house has been glorious with all assembled in a squalor of toys, disorder and conges-

---

[7] The account of this incident, like the accounts of others involving Ellen, is drawn from testimony taken at the hearing on her incompetence.

tion with babes and dogs everywhere . . . my party, which was a triumph of overcrowding and gaiety with dancing in the basement."

24.

Stevenson traveled a good deal during that first half of 1962. He commuted often to Washington, seeing President Kennedy a dozen times, sometimes alone, sometimes at cabinet or National Security Council meetings, sometimes at state dinners. Once he lunched with Kennedy and U Thant. He went to Chicago for a few days in January and on to Bloomington on January 23, where he attended a *Pantagraph* luncheon. A member of the *Pantagraph* staff thought he never seemed comfortable in Bloomington during these years. On February 16 he flew to San Francisco and Big Sur for John Fell's wedding. He stayed three days and attended a round of parties and receptions, seeing old political friends as well as the young friends of John Fell. It was a gay time. One evening he and his sister went to a night club to hear Mort Sahl, the comedian. A front table had been reserved. Stevenson fell asleep during Sahl's performance, embarrassing Mrs. Ives. She once said that during these later years of Stevenson's life she sometimes worried about his drinking. Ellen Stevenson attended the wedding. John Fell said, "It went surprisingly well. There were only a few outbursts. She was sore because the press was taking [Dad's] picture, not hers, then she was sore when they wanted her picture." Stevenson and his divorced wife gave a wedding dinner at Carmel and it came off well. The flowers and napery cost about $1,900. (Ellen ordered them; Stevenson was outraged and wanted to protest the bill.) They used a rented limousine and chartered a plane to take the guests to Monterey.

In March, Stevenson spoke at Colgate and at North Carolina State College; he spent weekends at Libertyville; and time in Chicago. Late in May he attended the wedding of Ruth Field's daughter Fiona. Early in June he spoke at Boston College, Tufts, and Rutgers and attended his Princeton class dinner. In mid-June he went to Oregon and Washington to see John Fell and his bride and to speak at the Seattle Exposition. At the end of June he went to Europe. His almost incessant travels during these years seemed to repeat a pattern established early in his life with his parents.

During that same period he saw, as usual, a large collection of notables, not only other UN Ambassadors but personages visiting the United States briefly, including Adoula of the Congo, Madame Pandit of India, the Shah of Iran, Prime Minister Macmillan, Anthony Eden, Trygve Lie, Archbishop Makarios of Cyprus, the President of Panama. He went to a dinner at the White House in honor of André Malraux. He corresponded with Mrs. Kennedy about arranging to have Andres Segovia, his favorite musician, appear at the White House during the Brazilian President's visit. Stevenson almost never dined or lunched alone during those months and often he transacted business or entertained friends at breakfast. Once his calendar showed that he was free for lunch; he put a large question mark beside the notation.

He suggested to Barbara Ward that they get together on his birthday, February 5. President and Mrs. Kennedy sent him a birthday telegram. Bertrande Benoist sent him verses all spring. Evelyn Houston wrote several times, once apologizing for being "impertinent"—"Are we still friends? If not, I'll wither." He invited her to stay with him at 42A. Pussy Paepcke, traveling in Africa, thanked him for helping make the trip possible. Agnes Meyer advised him to marry to avoid a lonely old age. Once she took him severely to task: "It is all very well for you to tell me in confidence that you are fed up with your job in the UN but this rumor is now all over Washington and I don't think it is good." She was planning a yachting cruise in the Mediterranean and Adriatic in the summer and changed the sailing date to accommodate Stevenson. Ruth Field, planning to visit Buffie Ives at Villa Capponi in Florence that summer, told Stevenson it would not be the same without him and said she thought that next year he should include her in his vacation entourage. Stevenson asked the Aga Khan if he could use his chalet at Gstaad near Geneva while he was there in July. (He could.)

That spring the stock market slumped badly, and Ellen Stevenson telephoned Adlai III, who was visiting his father at 42A, and told him she feared banks would sell her stock held as collateral for her loans. She telephoned him as many as ten times a day. He discovered that she was selling her furniture to a dealer. Thereafter the family bought whatever she did not want. Borden had his telephone delisted in order to avoid his mother's calls. Ellen often telephoned the wife of the farmer at Libertyville and told her that Adlai III was "insane" and he and his brothers and her own mother were trying to murder her. Once she told Adlai III's son and namesake, who was about five at the time, that she had ordered a cobra for him and it would arrive at any time—"It was a real, live snake and that it was quite large now, but would grow to be bigger and bigger and when he opened the cage and let it out . . . it was going to eat his mommy and daddy."

John Fell and his bride went to South America on their honeymoon, then visited Stevenson in New York, and he gave a party for them. He saw Borden often and Adlai III too. Once he attended a party of young people on a Saturday night at a house Borden had taken on Long Island, spent the night with him, went swimming and had lunch at the beach club. A few years earlier Stevenson had resisted the idea of psychoanalysis, saying once, "If you have a problem, it's like a cockroach trotting across the kitchen floor, you step on it," but by now he seemed not only to accept Borden's being in analysis but also to become curious about it himself. He sometimes referred in letters to Borden's superior knowledge of emotional disturbance and family problems. Several times he described his own dreams to Borden and asked him to interpret them.

Stevenson involved himself with a project to obtain, either as gifts or loans, works of art to redecorate both 42A and the new Mission building. Some of the paintings were lent with the stipulation that they would be returned upon Stevenson's departure from the Mission. A Gallup poll showed that Stevenson, in 1961, ranked fourth among the "Most Admired Men." (He had first achieved Gallup notice in 1952, when he was in fifth place.)

Dick Daley's son visited New York, and Stevenson had him to breakfast; Daley was grateful. Adlai III wanted to go into politics, and Stevenson asked Daley to look after him. (In 1966, after Stevenson's death, Daley's Democratic machine slated Adlai III for state treasurer and helped elect him. In 1970 it slated him for U. S. Senator and helped elect him.)

The Democratic National Committee was planning a major fund-raising "birthday salute" to President Kennedy at Madison Square Garden on May 19. Richard Maguire, acting treasurer of the National Committee, asked Stevenson if he could give a cocktail party in Stevenson's honor for big New York contributors. Stevenson agreed. He later described the affair in a letter to Mary Lasker: "The fund raising gala for the President worked out well—altogether too well for me. I got home from the [Arthur] Krims' at 3 o'clock in the morning, after several perilous encounters with Marilyn Monroe, dressed in what she calls 'skin and beads.' I didn't see the beads! My encounters, however, were only after breaking through the strong defenses established by Robert Kennedy. . . . The show at the Garden was spotty, the hall was too big for [Maria] Callas and hardly big enough for some of those screamers from Hollywood, but the Robbins ballet, Nichols and May, Elliott Reid, etc., were marvelous. The dinner beforehand found me with [Paul] Hoffman, Andre Meyer, and the Rosenberg family—ex-Anna, who was as busy as a terrier organizing everybody and everything. And she and Krim evidently did a hell of a job, although they fell way short of the million dollar mark, Krim tells me. I sat in the box with the President, vice President, about a dozen Kennedys, and—Jim Farley! You can imagine how I enjoyed that proximity. . . . De Gaulle's telegram to the President, as read by Nichols and May, said: 'Congratulations on your birthday. And if I weren't so busy, I would walk across to see you.' I feel the same way!"

Stevenson was suffering from insomnia. He began to read again, something he had not done for years, trying to read himself to sleep. He was seeing a New York physician, Dr. Henry Lax, frequently that spring. He had first seen Dr. Lax in January of 1962, and the doctor had found him suffering from arteriosclerotic heart disease with hypertension and marked obesity. He had prescribed a diet to reduce the weight and medication to lower the blood pressure. During this spring Stevenson took his medicine and kept to his diet, and he responded well to the treatment—he lost thirteen pounds, and his blood pressure became normal. Later, however, in 1963 he became uncooperative—did not take his medicine, missed his appointments frequently, and allowed his condition to continue unchecked for months on end.

His old friend, John Paulding Brown, whom Stevenson years ago had tried to help several times, wrote to him from Washington on Metropolitan Club stationery: "I have not been an asiduous correspondent, but I have followed your goings up and down in the world closely and with the deepest interest. . . . I miss not ever seeing you but that can't be helped now that you are such a thumping Olympian. . . . Charlotte Phinney has been talking about seeing you but I told her to forget you and dry her eyes. . . . I suppose you know that dear old Lawrence Houghteling died a month ago. . . . I called him up on a Saturday to take him for a drive and the maid said he had just died. . . . Do take care of yourself, old boy, if that is at all possible. We are not indestructible."

25.

Stevenson delivered more than a dozen speeches outside the UN that spring, far more than the year before. His themes were nearly always foreign affairs and, more especially, the United Nations. In accepting an award from the Anti-Defamation League of B'nai B'rith in New York, he discussed the notion that the United Nations was "a big Communist plot" —"some plot," he said, "to organize all those votes against yourself!" He spoke of dangers facing the world—that demagogues would exploit hunger for a better life in underdeveloped nations, that the Atlantic nations would fail to concert their energies, that racial prejudice and tribal chauvinism would weaken Afro-Asia and even Latin America, that the final chapters of the European colonial era "will be written in violence and chaos," that Americans would lose faith in the UN. To the Bloomington Association of Commerce he acknowledged the UN's imperfections and frustrations, conceding it could coerce neither the United States nor the U.S.S.R., but said the Soviet veto had been circumvented, the Secretary General had become a powerful figure, the UN had saved the Congo despite the Soviets, and it was in the United States' interest to support the UN financially. At the fortieth reunion of the Princeton Class of 1922 he talked about UN critics who demanded "victory" without specifying what victory meant and asked "what good would 'victory' be if the winner sat amid radioactive ashes, scarcely able to bury his dead?"

Harlan Cleveland once said that, while Stevenson was constantly preoccupied with East-West and North-South relations, his fundamental preoccupation was with the United Nations itself—the principles, the Charter, the prestige, the influence, and the operational capacity of the Organization which represented to him the best alternative to the institution of war and violence. He was consistently a powerful advocate of U.S. policy at the UN. But somehow he belonged to the UN itself in a way that perhaps no other delegate could or did. Other representatives, even the opposition, respected him. "Surely it is not exaggerating to say," Cleveland said, "that he was beloved by most of them." This was in part because his government was the principal supporter of the UN and he was its spokesman, partly because he seemed "the universal man" who spoke not only for his country but for all men, and partly because of the endless hours, the patience, and the tact which he devoted to personal diplomacy. "I doubt very much," Cleveland said, "if Adlai Stevenson had a peer in the game of personal diplomacy." There was something peculiarly apt in Secretary Rusk's statement to the UN after Stevenson's death: "Three Presidents of the United States sent Adlai Stevenson to the United Nations. They sent you our best."

26.

The UN had need of support in the United States. On April 2, Mike Mansfield, the Democratic leader in the Senate, made a speech on the floor on the "crisis" in the United Nations. He said that the one-state, one-vote formula in the General Assembly distorted the UN, giving to small new nations the power to make decisions but not the responsibility of enforcing them. The result was "the air of detachment from reality" at the UN. Vote victories in the General Assembly "have only little relevance to the great and fundamental questions." The Security Council had for years made only "minor contributions" to world order and stability and indeed had become, not an instrument for solving international tensions, but, rather, "a center for exacerbating them," "an arena for staging the wars of violent words, with the whole world as an audience." At the time of the Korean War the United States had taken the lead in shifting political questions from the stalemated Security Council to the General Assembly. It had seemed wise at the time. But since then new nations had gained control of the Assembly, and it had become increasingly "a marketplace for the trading of votes." The Security Council was "moribund." The Assembly had diminished its moral force by attempting to perform the enforcement functions intended for the Security Council.

Stevenson quickly wrote to Mansfield, whom he had seen shortly before, and said that "evidently I failed to answer any questions that you might have about the United Nations." He urged Mansfield to visit him or, alternatively, offered to visit him in Washington. "This is as difficult a job as I have ever undertaken," he wrote, "and I hoped to have my friends behind us." Mansfield replied, "I fully appreciate the difficulties of your job and I want to assure you of my confidence and support."

This, however, was as nothing compared to the furor over a speech Senator Henry M. "Scoop" Jackson made before the National Press Club in Washington on March 20. Jackson, another powerful Democrat, said the UN should be an "important avenue" of American foreign policy. "Yet practices have developed which, I believe, lead to an undue influence of UN considerations in our national decision-making. Indeed it is necessary to ask whether the involvement of the UN in our policy-making has not at times hampered the wise definition of our national interests and the development of sound policies for their advancement." (Stevenson put a question mark beside that passage.) "The truth is . . . that the best hope for peace with justice does not lie in the United Nations. . . . The best hope for the United Nations lies in the maintenance of peace. In our deeply divided world, peace depends on the power and unity of the Atlantic Community and on the skill of our direct diplomacy." (Here Stevenson penciled in, "Peace depends on many things—the power of the West and effectiveness of UN in many places—New Guinea, Middle East, Congo, Cuba, Laos. In long run it will depend on the friendly relations of the nonaligned and the West—and the UN is the principal forum in which those political relations are developed so US not isolated. Will depend on economic development of these countries with help of West.")

Jackson said the conduct of UN affairs absorbed a "disproportionate amount of the energy" of the President and Secretary of State. The Secretary of State had called the UN a forum in which almost every aspect of foreign policy arose—but, Jackson asked, should it? He thought the United States should "take a more restricted view" of the UN's capacity to be helpful. The cold war might destroy the UN but the UN could not end the cold war. It might be more prudent, though less dramatic, "not to push the UN into the fireman's suit" at every crisis, not to ask it "to shoulder responsibilities it cannot meet." (Stevenson noted, "Congo? Suez?") Jackson was skeptical about plans to increase the "UN presences"—to use it to help halt guerrilla infiltration across frontiers and internal subversion instigated by a foreign power. The UN was useful in serving as a link between the West and the newly independent states, in supplying technical assistance and financial aid to underdeveloped countries, and perhaps in peacefully resolving disputes of concern to new states. But there were too many votes on too many issues at the UN and too much time and energy spent in lobbying for votes. And too much talk—the Secretary of State, being responsible, must carefully weigh his words, and so made little news, while UN members, lacking responsibility, could talk extravagantly, and so create news. If the UN were quieter it might accomplish more. Jackson then asked if the United States delegation to the UN should play a larger role in policy making than its representatives to NATO and major world capitals. Stevenson wrote "Of course!" in the margin but Jackson answered no—the "embassy in New York" should play the same role in policy making as any other important embassy, and no more. Jackson thought it "unfortunate" that Eisenhower and Kennedy had given the Ambassador to the UN cabinet rank—he was not "a second Secretary of State." Negotiation on such complex and important matters as disarmament required unified guidance and instructions, and the instructions should come from the President or the Secretary. Jackson went on, "The concept of world opinion has been, I fear, much abused." He asked, too, whether the U.S. delegation was "properly manned." In sum, Jackson said, "We need to take another look at our role in the United Nations. . . . We should have a top-level review conducted under the authority of the President and the Secretary of State."

Stevenson heard about the speech the day Jackson gave it and telephoned him to ask for a copy and suggest they meet to discuss it. He asked Pedersen to prepare an analysis of it. Pedersen thought Jackson held two basic ideas: that U.S. interests in the UN and NATO were more often in conflict than in accord, and that specific UN policies had put us in conflict with one or another European ally—Belgium in the Congo, Portugal in Angola, Britain and France at the Suez in 1956, and France in Algeria before De Gaulle. These issues were colonial issues. On all, the United States had parted company with one or more European ally.

The speech caused an uproar. On March 21, the day after the speech, President Kennedy was scheduled to have a press conference. Harlan Cleveland drafted a reply to an anticipated question. Stevenson worked on the Cleveland draft. It contained this passage, heavily edited by Stevenson: "When I urged Ambassador Stevenson to head our Delegation to the United Nations, I told him that I also wanted the benefit of his exceptional experience and views on the whole range of foreign policy problems—not only at the United Nations but across the board. He is making valuable and constructive contributions in those roles as well as in relations with 104 nations at the UN." Kennedy, however, while reaffirming his support for both the UN and NATO did not mention Stevenson's name.

Stevenson told Schlesinger the Jackson speech was "the most damaging personal attack" that had been made since he went to the UN. Jackson's speech contained the clear suggestion that Stevenson was playing far too influential a role in the formulation of foreign policy. Schlesinger noted in his journal that Stevenson regarded the speech as part "of a well-coordinated movement, going back to Dean Acheson a dozen years ago and deriving its momentum today from the Pentagon, the European division of State, and the Dulles-line diplomats, to favor Europe over the new states." Stevenson considered the Jackson speech a deliberate part of an Acheson-Nitze plot and recalled bitterly that he had campaigned for Jackson from Spokane to the Pacific.

Schlesinger mentioned Stevenson's distress to President Kennedy. Kennedy said no one took Jackson seriously, he had made the speech to make headlines, and neither Stevenson nor Kennedy should dignify him by making a serious reply. "Adlai Stevenson doesn't have to be protected from

Scoop Jackson," he said. The Administration soon would need Jackson's vote on a UN bond issue so Kennedy did not want to start a quarrel. The most effective way of dealing with him now would be to get his Eastern campaign contributors to protest to him. The New York *Times* denounced the speech as harmful to the UN in general and to the UN bond issue in particular.

Presently it began to be said that Jackson's speech had been drafted by Bob Tufts and Dorothy Fosdick. She was on Jackson's Senate staff; later that year she became staff director of a Senate subcommittee on national security and international operations which Jackson headed, and Tufts became a consultant to the subcommittee. Schlesinger thought Tufts and Dorothy Fosdick had "put Jackson up" to making the speech, in part for personal reasons, in part because they really believed it.

Stevenson saw Jackson and gave him a copy of Pedersen's analysis of his speech. Jackson read it and rejected it as inaccurate. Stevenson talked with several other Senators, including Sparkman and Humphrey, trying to marshal support.

In a letter of March 29, President Kennedy told Stevenson, "I hope that Senator Jackson's speech has not given you serious concern. I have felt it better not to take it seriously, but you ought to know that when I commented on it in my press conference last week, I was not aware of Jackson's direct criticism of the position of the US Ambassador at the UN. I disagree with him on that and on other points, but I don't want to build up his criticism by too much notice—and I also have to bear in mind that he has been a very strong and consistent supporter of our whole program in Congress. Now we are watching to see how he votes on the [UN] bond issue; my bet is that his voice is worse than his vote."

Stevenson, however, did not let the matter rest. On April 13 he told Jackson he was glad Jackson had not intended to imply any conflict between the UN and NATO but feared his speech had given that impression and suggested Jackson "publicly correct this impression." Stevenson sent copies of that letter to Bob Tufts and Dorothy Fosdick, asking their advice and inviting Tufts to bring his family to the Waldorf for an overnight visit. Jackson replied with some acerbity on April 16, denied he had ever said the UN and NATO were incompatible, and reiterated that our whole role in the UN ought to be rigorously re-examined. Tufts and Dorothy Fosdick responded too. On April 20, Miss Fosdick wrote to "Dear Adlai": "Thanks for your note of April 12 with its enclosure. At the moment, my one suggestion is for you people to take seriously the concern of the internationally minded Senators about the relation of our operations in the UN to the making and executing of our national security policies. You may not agree with particular criticisms, but the warning signals are up. Senators like Aiken, Jackson, and Mansfield have unimpeachable credentials. . . . What Senator Jackson had to say was considered by him to be serious and constructive. . . . A strategy of distorting this concern and retaliating with assorted brickbats is no answer." She signed it, "Regards."

Tufts sent Stevenson a long letter on April 21. He said he had been "mystified by reports of your unhappiness" over the speech. He would have expected Stevenson "to make almost the same points" as a result of his experiences at the UN. Tufts could find "no implication" in the speech that our interests in the UN were more often than not in conflict with our interests in NATO. But the truth was that on particular issues conflict did arise, as in West New Guinea, where we "gave insufficient weight to NATO." He wrote, "The most regrettable aspect of this whole affair, in my judgment, has been the defensive reactions of some people in Washington. . . . If Senators like Fulbright, Jackson, Aiken, and Mansfield are troubled, this is itself an important reality, whether or not their worries are justified. I can not believe that it is helpful in dealing with this reality to distort their statements, impugn their motives, and call for high level retaliation (how naive!). . . . Senator Jackson hoped and thought that he was engaged in constructive criticism. . . . As to the origin of the speech, it lies, I believe, in Senator Jackson's concern about the questions he raised. . . . He consulted widely, I know, and I was one of these consulted." He closed, "Jean [his wife] and the girls would be delighted, as I would be, to visit you and I hope we may sometime accept your invitation —but I am selfish enough to hope that we may have a chance to talk even sooner."

Marietta Tree thought Dorothy Fosdick may have persuaded Jackson to make the speech. Stevenson believed Tufts had done so and spoke sharply of him.

On April 19, Bill Benton wrote to Jackson: "Dear Scoop, May I," he began, "as a contributor of $1,000 to your 1958 campaign, volunteer a comment? For the last two or three weeks, I have been collecting comments on your recent speech about the U.S. delegation at the U.N. I do not claim that I circulate in all the right circles. I can only tell you that you have lost many friends in those circles in which I happen to circulate." A note on the carbon copy by Roxane Eberlein, Stevenson's personal secretary, indicated that the Benton letter had been shown to Stevenson in advance and, in fact, had been mailed from Stevenson's office. Jackson responded to Benton that he was troubled because some of his liberal friends, who had asserted over the years the right to dissent, now denied it when it was directed to a subject of special interest to them, such as the UN.

On April 26, Stevenson told Schlesinger, "The Jackson matter continues to cause trouble, and arose today in my talks with the Secretary General and Narasimhan [U Thant's *chef de cabinet*]. I hope the President will find an opportunity to set the matter straight and also advise Jackson that he does not agree with him." As late as May 31, more than two months after the speech, Stevenson was still writing to Bob Tufts about it.

27.

The Mansfield and Jackson speeches came, as noted, while Congress was considering a United Nations bond issue. When U Thant took office he faced a financial crisis. The UN had unpaid obligations of about $110 million by December 31, 1961, and unpaid assessments totaling about $80 million. One of the main difficulties was the refusal of the Soviet Union to pay its assessments to support the UN forces in the Congo and the Middle East. (France and other countries were also in arrears.) The United States had conceived the idea of having the General Assembly ask the International Court of Justice whether the special assessments constituted "expenses of the Organization" and of having the Assembly authorize the Secretary General to sell $200 million worth of bonds to member states. The United States had concealed its role. U Thant had adopted the plan and so had the General Assembly.

President Kennedy had urged Congress in his State of the Union speech to approve the purchase of UN bonds by the United States. Rusk testified for the proposal on February 6 and Stevenson on February 7. Some of their testimony on the purposes of the bond issue seemed to conflict with what the President had said. As a result, by March the bond issue was in trouble in the Senate; and at that point Jackson made his speech. Kennedy told Ted Sorensen to call Jackson, and Sorensen did. Jackson said the State Department had made a poor presentation to the committee. The Administration had to get the bill passed, Sorensen said. Jackson promised to help. After a series of meetings with various Senators, including Sparkman, Aiken, Mansfield, Jackson, Fulbright, and Dirksen, the bond issue did pass the Senate. It later got in trouble in the House and once more the White House helped State get it passed. Stevenson lobbied for it in both houses. He was not an expert on the issue, however, and did not always help his own cause. The issue was an awkward one, since it enabled critics of the UN to make all their misgivings public. Such speeches as Jackson's fed the flames. It was a bad time for Stevenson.

During this same period Stevenson was dealing with other issues, old and new, including disarmament, Angola, Kashmir, the Congo, Cuba, the Middle East, and Southern Rhodesia. Stevenson told Marietta Tree that President Kennedy expected him to "sell" the resumption of nuclear testing to the world "for obvious reasons." Resumption seemed almost inevitable. Prime Minister Macmillan, however, while telling Kennedy that the Americans could use Christmas Island in the Pacific as a testing site, asked for full consultation before a decision was actually taken to resume testing. He warned somberly that, if the United States and British tested, the Soviets undoubtedly would test again and the West would respond and so would the Russians, and so on indefinitely; but costs would be so great that at some point one side or the other might be tempted to end the competition by using the weapons. He urged on Kennedy a "supreme effort" to reach agreement on disarmament with the Russians through a meeting of Foreign Ministers or of heads of government.

Stevenson, apprised of Macmillan's letter, prepared a memorandum to Kennedy calling Macmillan's proposal "thoughtful and imaginative," worthy of something better than a "dusty answer." Stevenson "strongly" urged consultations among the United States, United Kingdom, France, and Germany followed by a "very private, very high-level exploratory" approach to Khrushchev to see if he would be interested in an early high-level meeting. (It is likely that Stevenson thought of himself as the one who might make that approach.) Stevenson saw Kennedy on January 13 and gave him the memorandum.

As always, Stevenson was rather optimistic about the climate in the Soviet Union, though he did not explain why. Stevenson also suggested Kennedy consider speaking at the Geneva disarmament conference. Ted Sorensen thought that, since there was little or no chance of the conference succeeding, it was a mistake to risk a rebuff. He thought Stevenson was always too eager to risk the presidential prestige. On January 16, Stevenson complained to Secretary Rusk about "the atmosphere of defeatism as to general and complete disarmament."

In another memorandum on February 22, Stevenson made the "moral" case against resumption of testing.

Rusk gave the President a memorandum containing his personal view that the United States could not accept the risk of failing to test.

For weeks, Stevenson continued to fight a delaying action against it, sometimes with weak arguments, sometimes seeming almost desperate to reach the President.

On March 2, President Kennedy, in a television speech to the nation, announced the United States would resume testing at Christmas Island. He said that the tests could be halted if Khrushchev were willing to accept a comprehensive test-ban treaty at Geneva. Khrushchev quickly declined.

Stevenson continued to urge his views; now, though accepting the decision, he sought to moderate its impact. When William Foster of the Disarmament Agency stated the U.S. position on television March 5, Stevenson did not like what he said and next day protested to Kennedy, Rusk, and Foster—the United States should take a "much more flexible approach" than Foster had.

When the United States resumed testing at Christmas Island on April 25, Stevenson issued a statement: "The announcement . . . is the melancholy consequence of the Soviet Union's insistence on pursuing the nuclear arms race. The implications of an intensified competition in nuclear weaponry are obvious and grim. . . . As President Kennedy has indicated, testing can be stopped if the Soviet Union will join in concluding an effective agreement to stop tests and end the fears of fallout."

On May 11, Stevenson, at the White House dinner in honor of André Malraux, gave President Kennedy a paper which began, "I want to record again my disappointment that in the disarmament talks at Geneva we have not been willing to propose a test ban on all tests except underground tests, without international inspection and control but with reliance on national detection systems only." This proposal, not original at this time, became the essence of the subsequent Limited Nuclear Test Ban Treaty later actually signed. Stevenson recommended "a good, hard look" at our position on nuclear testing. He recommended that we examine a proposal to bar weapons of mass destruction from orbit. He recommended that we press the Soviets on measures to reduce the risk of accidental war and "take a further look at" the establishment of denuclearized zones in Africa and Latin America.

Kennedy answered promptly. Stevenson's paper was "most helpful and pertinent." He agreed that the time might indeed be approaching when we should make a new test-ban proposal. Kennedy shared Stevenson's feelings about the consequence of "round after round" of tests. Three of Stevenson's proposals were now being pressed by the American delegation at Geneva—reducing the risk of war, establishing denuclearized zones, and preventing the spread of nuclear weapons (Kennedy preferred to discuss this last in connection with Berlin). The delegation had proposed discussion of another Stevenson proposal, an agreement to bar weapons of mass destruction from orbit, but the U.S.S.R. refused. Kennedy concluded, "While the prospects for early agreement in any of these areas are not encouraging, I entirely agree that we must continue to do what we can to change the Soviet attitude towards these problems."

28.

When the resumed General Assembly convened on January 15 it took up Angola at once. Bulgaria and Poland introduced an extremist anti-Portugal resolution. Forty-five Afro-Asians introduced a milder one affirming the right of the people of Angola to independence and urging Portugal to undertake extensive reforms.

The debate was long and bitter. The Portuguese Ambassador led his delegation from the Assembly hall. Stevenson's speech publicly stated the U.S. position: the solution must be based on self-determination for the Angolan people. Privately he succeeded in persuading the Afro-Asians to substitute "self-determination" for "independence" in their resolution—self-determination might or might not end up as independence. Thereupon the Afro-Asian resolution passed overwhelmingly (and the Bulgaria-Poland resolution was defeated). The Department called Stevenson's handling of Angola "brilliant."

That ended the Assembly's consideration of Angola at this session. But it did not end the problem inside the United States Government. The U.S.

position in the UN, being an anti-colonial position sympathetic to the Angolan nationalists, clashed head on with another important American policy, cooperation with Portugal, a NATO ally. This reversal of Eisenhower policy had the previous fall brought repercussions inside the Department and in U.S.-Portuguese relations and brought them even more sharply now. For in 1962 an agreement was about to expire that gave the United States military bases in the Azores, islands belonging to Portugal. Obviously, when negotiations to renew the agreement began, Portugal would use the Azores to try to force the United States to reverse its position on Angola.

On April 18, President Kennedy asked Stevenson for his views. On April 25, Dean Acheson, at Secretary Rusk's request, submitted his own views. Among other things, Acheson said Rusk should "obtain the President's support in directing the executive branch to stay out of the debates, or drafting of resolutions, on Angola in the General Assembly." That seemed directed at Stevenson.

Stevenson sent his own views to Kennedy on April 26. We should, he said, "firmly resist" Portuguese efforts to link the Azores to U.S. policy on Angola. Rather, we should insist that the Azores base was vital not only to the defense of the United States but to all of NATO, including Portugal. We should, therefore, treat it as a NATO matter and seek the support of other NATO governments.

The lines were clearly drawn for a struggle between two factions inside the United States Government. It was the old quarrel between the Europeanists, such as Rusk and Kohler and Acheson, and the anticolonialists, led by Stevenson and G. Mennen Williams and Wayne Fredericks. It was also to some extent a confrontation between the military and the political view of United States policy. And, though less clearly, it was a confrontation between Stevenson and the men of the Eastern establishment who had always considered him soft.

On May 10, having seen the Acheson paper, Stevenson wrote another for Kennedy. He pointedly disagreed with Acheson's suggestion that we stay out of debates on Angola—to do so would, in effect, reverse our policy. He went on to propose a scenario for negotiation involving our NATO partners, to take a hard line against the moldy colonialism of Salazar's Portugal, and to make a spirited defense of our anti-colonialist policy. It did Stevenson much credit.

A month later, after many further memos and discussions, the Department made its formal policy recommendation to the President. That memo straddled the Stevenson and Acheson views. It rejected Stevenson's hard line against colonialism. But it also rejected Acheson's recommendation that the United States desist from supporting anti-colonial resolutions in the UN. It adopted Stevenson's suggestion of making the Azores a NATO matter and accepted his unwavering commitment to self-determination. It became policy. In the end, Portugal extended American access to the Azores base without formally renewing the agreement.

29.

Ever since India and Pakistan had become independent nations in 1947 they had quarreled over Kashmir, a lovely wedge of land between them on the China border to the north. On January 11, 1962, Pakistan requested an urgent meeting of the Security Council, calling recent Indian statements a "grave threat" to the peace. The Security Council considered the question over many months. After much jockeying for position, the Pakistanis finally gave two resolutions to the United States and said they would try to get Ireland to sponsor one. Stevenson left on a trip to Oregon and Seattle, spending a weekend with friends at a lodge on the eastern slope of the Cascades, making a speech in Seattle, then going to Chicago. President Kennedy was concerned about Kashmir, and on June 21 he asked Schlesinger, with considerable asperity, what he knew about U.S. sponsorship of a Kashmir resolution. He had just been informed that the Irish and Venezuelans, who had been expected to sponsor a resolution, had desisted under Indian pressure. Now he was told the United States would sponsor one. But this friendly gesture to Pakistan, he said, would undermine our efforts to prevent the Indians from buying Soviet MIGs. Schlesinger knew nothing about it. Moreover, Stevenson was in Libertyville, preparing to leave for Europe. This compounded Kennedy's vexation. He kept saying, "If only someone had told me about this a week ago, I could have kept in both the Irish and the Venezuelans." He had also read in the newspapers an announcement of a $175 million U.S. loan to India, and this increased his conviction that the government was running off in all directions without telling him.

Schlesinger ascertained that State had instructed the Mission to support the Pakistan resolution even if, in the last resort, support meant sponsorship. Previously it had looked as if Ireland and Venezuela would sponsor. Meanwhile, nobody had told Stevenson or the Mission of the rising importance of the MIG negotiations in New Delhi. Then the Indians had begun saying that sponsorship would be an unfriendly act. To the Latin Americans they said that sponsorship would compel India to reopen the question of two Latin American seats on the Security Council. To the Irish, who had tried to maintain ties to the Afro-Asians, they said that sponsorship would align them irrevocably with the Americans. Since Stevenson was out of town, and Plimpton diffident, and Cleveland uninformed on the MIG negotiations, all this was allowed to proceed. No one thought of consulting the President.

On June 22, as a result of Kennedy's direct intervention with the Irish Ambassador, the Irish sponsored the resolution. It urged India and Pakistan to enter into early negotiations, to take all possible steps to create a favorable atmosphere, to refrain from any statements or actions which might aggravate the situation; and it requested the Secretary General to provide them with whatever services they needed. The Indians opposed any resolution. The Russians said the resolution was intended to produce a plebiscite on Kashmir which would constitute flagrant interference in Indian affairs and indicated they would veto the resolution if necessary.

Stevenson came back to New York that day. Cleveland had prepared a draft of his speech to celebrate the hundredth Russian veto. Schlesinger and Robert Komer, the White House staff man assigned to Pakistan-Indian affairs, went over the speech, then showed it to the President. He thought Stevenson should not give it—the U.S. hand had already begun to show as a result of the vacillation of the last forty-eight hours, and his speaking would only make matters worse. They persuaded him that Stevenson should speak if all allusions to the substance of the vetoed resolution were omitted. Later that afternoon Schlesinger saw Kennedy again, and Ralph Dungan joined them. Dungan was one of Kennedy's White House staffers, and Kennedy blamed him for not informing him about the Indian loan as he blamed Schlesinger for not informing him about the resolution. Kennedy began a rumination about the impossibility of running a government. Then he returned to the UN. "Where the hell was Stevenson?" he asked, and, told, said, "Out in Libertyville doing his income tax! The Pakistan resolution could not have been more important—and who handled it for us? Francis Plimpton. The only one I have confidence in is Stevenson. If he can't be around, then he better get a deputy who can do a decent job of representing the United States. If I were a delegate from a small country, and Francis Plimpton asked me to vote one way, and Krishna Menon asked me to vote another—hell, the United States wouldn't stand a chance." (This did not represent Kennedy's final view of Plimpton, for whom he came to have high regard.) He told Schlesinger to telephone Stevenson and tell him all this. Schlesinger did, and Stevenson contended that no one had ever told him or the Mission anything about the MIG deal or its import for U.S. policy on Kashmir. In moving toward sponsorship, the Mission had simply followed a directive received from State weeks earlier. As for Plimpton, Stevenson defended him, though weakly.

Russia did veto the resolution and Stevenson did speak on that hundredth Soviet veto, "this historic day in the Security Council." The Russian representative objected that Stevenson was out of order. The President ruled for Stevenson. The meeting deteriorated into a procedural wrangle.

30.

Exchanges of fire between Israel and Syria along the eastern shore of Lake Tiberias occurred frequently in February and early March of 1962, and, on the night of March 16–17, Israeli forces carried out a large-scale raid on Syrian positions on or near the Armistice Demarcation Line of the demilitarized zone. The UN command arranged a cease-fire. The Syrians complained to the Security Council, charging Israel with aggression. The Israelis countercharged aggression. The UN command could not determine who had started the fighting but was clear that Israel had taken the initiative in the major incident of March 16–17. Stevenson spoke in the Security Council, saying that whatever the facts they did not justify Israel's reversion to the policy of retaliatory raids which had increased tensions in 1955 and 1956. If UN machinery had been unable to prevent hostilities, the remedy lay in improving the machinery, not in retaliatory raids in violation of the armistice.

Almost at once an outcry arose from Jews in the United States. Phil Klutznick said: "Everybody was calling him a traitor. He called me in and showed me letters from Chicago" and said, "You don't think that do you?"

Klutznick said, "I got letters too. 'You shouldn't have said that—you really called Israel an aggressor and you didn't have to'—they could take it from Russia but not from us."

Stevenson asked, "What should I do?" Klutznick said nothing. Stevenson said, "How can I take this kind of mail? It's not right."

Klutznick saw Kennedy and told him that nobody was blaming Kennedy but that Stevenson was "having a rough time."

Kennedy remarked, "If it has to be him or me, it's him." Kennedy said he had known the issue was difficult and had deliberately told Stevenson to handle it. He said he was not sure the Department's advice on the Middle East was right.

Hubert Humphrey, whose constituency included American Jews, told Secretary Rusk on April 2, "I feel the need to add an urgent note of caution about Stevenson's speech." He said he could understand a desire to condemn retaliation. But provocation should be equally condemned. "It would be a serious mistake to condemn Israel more energetically than Syria." The letter was passed on to Stevenson. He told Humphrey, "I hope before you express any views that are comforting to the Zionists you will let us fully explain what was done in the Security Council and why. I don't need to tell you about my own long and sympathetic record with Israel, but perhaps you don't know how much we did to temper the action of the Security Council."

The Syrian representative proposed that the Council adopt a resolution condemning Israel. The Israeli proposed a counterresolution. The United States and United Kingdom jointly introduced a compromise resolution, and it passed.

After the voting Stevenson wrote to Rabbi Weinstein in Chicago:

Dear Jake:

   Lou Kohn has sent me your complaint about the Syria-Israel resolution in the United Nations. . . . This was the mildest of the four resolutions that have been adopted by the Security Council about Israel's use of retaliatory force, although the force was the greatest. . . . Then to be criticized so extensively by the Jewish community of the United States is a bitter pill, but I am sure that you, with your taste for justice and concern for facts, would not administer the same.

31.

Despite Schlesinger's numerous efforts, the Stevenson-Kennedy relationship continued to be strained. They met on May 2, and Schlesinger was present. It was shortly after the President had castigated the steel industry for raising prices.

Stevenson began by saying, "Well, you've had some trouble with business lately."

Kennedy replied, "Yes, they are a bunch of bastards—and I'm saying this on my own now, not just because my father told it to me." He went on to say that he would never again appear before the United States Chamber of Commerce. He mentioned a speech Senator Harry Byrd had made and said he regarded Byrd as one of the "greatest phonies" in the Senate. Then he laughed and said, "I'm beginning to sound like Harry Truman."

Stevenson said the hostility of business was inescapable for any Democratic President but added that he hoped Kennedy could find an opportunity to take an equally dramatic anti-labor position.

Kennedy said it was unlikely—after all, labor had already agreed to forgo a wage rise in the steel case and no one gave them credit for it.

Schlesinger, observing the rest of the conversation, was struck by "the curious effect," as he put it in his journal, that Kennedy had on Stevenson. In New York the day before, Stevenson had been at his best—relaxed, funny, quick, pungent, informal, saying, of Plimpton, "Francis is my oldest friend but he has all the political sex appeal of a dead mouse." But in Washington with the President, Schlesinger noted, Stevenson was "solemn, prissy, verbose and insistent. That tight little lip-smile, which used to be so unbearable on television (during the campaigns), came into play. The President was equable and courteous. He said to me later, 'Adlai seemed in good form today.' I weakly agreed; but the fact is that Adlai was not in good form at all. I wish that they had become friends before they became rivals. I do not think that JFK has ever seen Adlai at his best."

Kennedy rather frequently asked Stevenson for his views. Once he asked for Stevenson's suggestions as to what he might say to the President of Mexico on his forthcoming trip there.

In June he asked Stevenson to suggest an alternative to the use of force in Laos. Stevenson replied with a memorandum proposing that the next time a violation of the cease-fire occurred the United States dramatically propose an enlargement of the supervision of the cease-fire and try to get

India's cooperation in doing so. In sending the memorandum to Schlesinger, Stevenson asked him to see that it reached the President "at the proper time—before the military planning becomes too rigid." He sent a copy to Cleveland.

The President was planning a National Security Council review of American foreign policy on June 26. Early in June he asked Stevenson to plan to make a one-hour presentation to the NSC on UN considerations in NSC policy. Stevenson asked Pedersen to produce a first draft. Earlier, Walt Rostow of the Policy Planning Council in State had prepared a long paper on basic national security policy and a copy had been sent to Stevenson for comment. His comments, drafted by Yost, were long and critical. He was troubled by the paper's almost total concentration on the contest with Communism and how to win it. Even in that restricted framework, "disproportionate emphasis is laid on the military factor." No one would deny that the struggle with Communism was central to our national security and purposes, or that "a very strong" military deterrent was essential. But "other equally important elements are passed over very cursorily." Stevenson thought the UN offered great opportunities. Even if one were interested only in the struggle against Communism, "certainly" the orientation of the Afro-Asians and Latin Americans could be "most significant" in a hot war and "decisive" in a prolonged cold war. The two chief instruments for influencing them were economic and military aid and our policies and tactics in the UN. Rostow's original draft had "touched on the UN only in the most sketchy fashion" and had dealt inadequately with nuclear arms control, Stevenson thought.

Meanwhile, Stevenson had been working on his own paper for the National Security Council. In White House meetings Stevenson sometimes disappointed his colleagues at IO. Joe Sisco said, "He was best when we had time in advance with him so that he could get his thoughts organized precisely. He tended to make presentations hand-wringing and bemoaning the situation, not crisp alternatives. He unburdened himself, rather than seeming to be an Ambassador laying it out crisply." Cleveland was worried about this coming meeting. He told Stevenson that "the most important impression for you to leave on your audience Tuesday is that you think of the UN as an instrument of US policy." Stevenson took the drafts and worked them over, rewriting heavily, inserting phrases and whole paragraphs written out in longhand on a white ruled tablet and on Waldorf stationery. The result was a large disorderly manuscript from which, at length, emerged the long paper he delivered to the NSC at the White House on June 26. Entitled "U.S. Foreign Policy as seen from New York," it was Stevenson's most extended and carefully considered view of what he thought about the UN's role in American policy.

He said the questions that come before the United Nations include almost every aspect of American foreign policy. The basic objectives of U.S. policy were two. First came the security of the United States and world peace. They could be promoted by maintaining our nuclear deterrent; by balanced NATO defenses in Europe; by improving the anti-guerrilla and anti-subversion capabilities of the United States and its allies and friends; by the earliest possible control, reduction, and elimination of nuclear weapons, and by improving international peace-keeping machinery. Only the last two heavily involved the UN.

The second U.S. objective was "peaceful evolution in freedom and diversity," and it should be pursued by strengthening international institutions until it was politically unacceptable to use force in international relations; by strengthening the solidarity of the Atlantic community; and by helping Asia, Africa, and Latin America to throw off colonialism, develop, and mature.

What could the UN do about all this? It could help settle or cool off international disputes, improve the political climate, provide physical "presences" to avert or stop conflicts as in the Congo, and use the influence of the Secretary General. These resources were available nowhere else.

Stevenson turned to criticism of the UN. A small group of "die-hard isolationists" opposed the UN on principle. A larger group distrusted it because it believed the Soviets had somehow seized control of the UN. Some people were concerned about the preoccupation of the new Asian and African states with colonialism and the problems this created for the United States in its relations with its European friends. But this would be a problem even if there were no UN. The most recent General Assembly had made a better record on colonial issues than its predecessor. Even new members were learning moderation. The impression that the Afro-Asians leaned toward the U.S.S.R. was erroneous. Of the fifty-four members from Africa and Asia, eight were formally allied with the West. South Africa remained firmly anti-Communist. The twelve French African states were Western-oriented, as were Liberia and, in the Far East, Malaya. The remainder ranged from the moderate neutrals to the left-leaning extremists. The fact that Gabon had the same one vote in the General Assembly as the United States "does not cause me the great concern it does some others." The United Nations was based on the principle of the sovereign equality of all its members. Though we did not always win in the General Assembly, he said, the action taken had usually been acceptable to us, and where it had not been, it had offered no real threat to our national interests—the Assembly had only recommendatory powers, after all. No suitable alternative to the one-nation, one-vote principle had yet been devised.

"Perhaps the most important single impression that I want to leave with you," he said, "is that we should think of the UN not just as a convenient repository for insoluble problems, but rather as an instrument of United States policy which we should use to further our objectives." (Thus did he take Cleveland's advice.) It was a complicated instrument, since it was also an instrument of the foreign policy of 108 other countries, and it was a limited instrument: if we wanted to defend Europe, the UN was largely irrelevant and NATO essential, but if we wanted to relate to Asia, Africa, and Latin America, the UN was essential and NATO irrelevant. One should distinguish between what was symbolic and what was real in the UN. It was unlikely that any power would violate what it regarded as its own security interests to bow to a majority of the UN. Yet the UN stood for a free and diverse world, one diametrically opposed to the Soviet vision of a Communist one-world. Therefore, normally the United States could agree with the majority of the members and the Soviet Union normally could not. For these reasons, the Soviet Union had cast a hundred vetoes in the Security Council while the United States had yet to cast one.

"To conclude, let me say that building the UN is the world's toughest, most complex, most delicate, most advanced task of institution-building in the world. . . .

"If we sometimes become frustrated by the inability of the UN to find a solution, or by the fact that the solution it does find is a compromise or an inferior decision, we must remember that the UN is essentially a fire brigade. We are trying to solve issues that have become insoluble through traditional diplomacy. It is sometimes the court of last resort before force is used. . . .

"And the stake is no less than a future system of world order in which the United States can find long-term security in the postcolonial age of atoms and outer space. In a small way, we are learning some of the essential operational lessons that would make it possible to organize a world order—if we can ever get anywhere in the disarmament negotiations."

Arthur Schlesinger was present at the NSC meeting. He recalled later, "Stevenson was terrible. He flopped. It was a lost opportunity." Stevenson complained later to Schlesinger that he had not been told in advance what had been expected of him. The truth was, however, as we have seen, that he was very well prepared and had put a great deal of time and effort into his paper, as had Cleveland and others. Ted Sorensen, who was also present, was more charitable. "I was impressed with his paper and so, I think, was the President. It had a slightly academic air—and that's not derogatory—and gave us a good picture of the UN's role." The members of the NSC did not react to the paper; it raised no issue that required reaction. Sorensen thought the paper accorded with Kennedy's thinking about the UN in general. "But there is simply a different atmosphere between First Avenue and Pennsylvania Avenue. The world looks very different from each place. How to approach the problems of the world—voting majorities in the UN and world opinion and the voices of neutrals compared with allies all weigh much more heavily in New York than Washington."

John Steele saw Stevenson at this time. He reported: "Adlai Stevenson looks much older these days. The pudginess is still there. But the eyes are a tired, baleful blue; the eyebrows whitening perceptibly; the hair no less, but amply streaked with silver. He talks in a hoarse semi-whisper. The tone bespeaks age and a sort of I've-been-through-it-once-too-often attitude." Stevenson, Steele thought, had had a "rewarding but fatiguing" year at the UN. "The pressures have been monstrous, the political and party pace frantic for a man of his advanced years." He had few regrets and felt that he had had "a good deal" of independence to make on-the-spot decisions. At the same time he regretted he had not had time to participate in broad policy decisions made in Washington. He said, just after his NSC presentation, "I just don't feel I'm at the center of the stream of things." Kennedy, he felt, had met the commitments he had given Stevenson upon appointing him.

The Russians had made trouble. Stevenson called Zorin and Morozov "two of the nastiest bastards I've ever dealt with." He remembered Vishinsky and Gromyko fondly as men with some humor and courtesy. Even Dobrynin and Tsarapkin, the Soviet Ambassador to the United States and the disarmament negotiator in Geneva, were civilized. Stevenson considered Zorin and Morozov extremely able and hard-working—"I think they stay up all night sharpening their knives." He spoke sarcastically of the Indians, especially Menon and Nehru. He was irritated with the Africans, who insisted on having parties so they could meet the U.S. chief representative—the Europeans were more sophisticated and knew the "real U.S. chiefs are all in Washington." He also was irritated with Congressmen who joined the delegation—"they spend six weeks looking for the toilets before they can function properly." Stevenson was concerned about financing the UN and about the Afro-Asians' irresponsibility and he was intemperate: "When the last black-faced comedian has quit preaching about colonialism, and we've laid this issue to rest once and for all, only then will the UN be liberated to deal with those truer and more compelling issues of our time like disarmament."

32.

On June 28, Stevenson told Kennedy he was leaving New York in two days to attend the ECOSOC meeting in Geneva, to spend a few days in Rome "with the new Foreign Minister and my friend, Prime Minister Fanfani," and to "join Agnes Meyer for a holiday, yachting in the Adriatic for a fortnight." He would stop in Madrid for a few days "at the suggestion of our Ambassador"; things were "simmering" in Spain. He would return to New York on August 8. "If you have any missions you wish me to perform while abroad, I will gladly do so," and he underlined the sentence. Upon return he would report to Kennedy in Washington and arrange to review plans for the 17th General Assembly, which would convene on September 18. It was a curious letter. Its opening sounded eager for a vacation. He did not appear to have addressed himself to the facts—things

were not simmering in Spain—and Schlesinger had strongly opposed his
going there under Franco. The rest of the long letter concerned coming issues in the UN; it was prolix and obvious and suggested that he feared the
opening on vacation plans sounded frivolous and so he was obliged to give
the President something of substance.

Stevenson left New York by plane on Saturday, June 30. In Rome the
next morning he went to the beach and lunch, then left by private plane
and car for Florence, and Buffie and Ernest Ives at Villa Capponi. He had
sent an advance note to Buffie:

> Here is the first wave of the invasion. I suggest you put Alicia in "my
> room," me in the same room I had before. Alice and husband in the
> "Hutchins room." John Fell and Natalie in the corner room. Sarah
> Plimpton (25) is coming with us. Maybe she could go in the other
> large room on the street. Viva!
>
>   AES.

Sarah Plimpton was the young daughter of Francis Plimpton; henceforward she saw a good deal of Stevenson. The Mayor came to call at Villa
Capponi, and former Queen Helen of Romania came to dinner.

On July 4, Stevenson flew to Geneva in a private plane, stopping at Nice
to drop Marietta Tree off, and at Geneva was met by the Klutznicks, the
Roger Tubbys, and others. The Klutznicks took him to dinner at a new
"luxury" hotel which Stevenson described as "an expensive horror." Next
day he went to the Aga Khan's chalet at Gstaad for a long weekend, taking the Klutznicks and Marietta and her daughter. Klutznick would resign
soon. Stevenson spoke to ECOSOC in Geneva on Monday, July 9, a good
speech on the UN's world development decade.

Former Vice President Nixon had visited Denmark, and Bill Blair reported to Stevenson: "Nixon has come and gone, leaving a trail of bitterness and bad feeling. It is extraordinary how he can come into a country
like Denmark, stir everyone up and for the first time inject partisan political controversy in Denmark's celebration of the Fourth of July. . . . I
suppose I am prejudiced, but I couldn't abide Mr. Nixon. . . ." The Disarmament Conference opened in Geneva, and Stevenson wrote to President Kennedy: "Once more the Russians got the jump on us." He said he
had hoped that, after all the talk in Washington, Arthur Dean would be
able to make constructive proposals representing some advance in our
thinking. But Dean told him that Foster had only promised him some
helpful decisions soon. Stevenson urged that we quickly offer something
difficult for the Russians to refuse—the neutrals were with us, except for
India, but we would lose them if we did not move quickly. "I hope you
will see to it that we suffer no further . . . delays." The last sentence
sounded almost as though their roles were reversed. At the same time
Stevenson dictated a memorandum to himself—a reminder to take up with

the President and the Secretary the need for a UN man in all major United States embassies. Adlai III sent bad news about Ellen's finances.

After another ten days of dinners and luncheons and receptions at Geneva and another weekend at Gstaad, Stevenson picked up Alicia Patterson and Alice and Jim Hoge[8] and all drove to Villa Balbianello, the Plimptons' place on Lake Como, where he found Sarah Plimpton. He spent five days there, then left for Florence in two cars accompanied by Alicia, the Hoges, and John Fell and Natalie, arriving at Buffie's villa in time for dinner. He spent a day wandering around Florence with the young people and shopping, then on July 24 went to Rome with Alicia. He had lunch with Outerbridge Horsey, counselor of the embassy, and met with Fanfani, who was pessimistic about détente with the Soviet Union and thought Khrushchev did not have so much freedom of action as the West thought and was under constant pressure from Stalinists and the Chinese to prove that he was tough. The greatest single difficulty was the Russians' fear of Germany.

On July 25, Stevenson left for Athens, met the American Ambassador, had a long visit with the Greek President and Foreign Minister, received complaints about reduced American aid, and sent a message to Secretary Rusk urging him to "carefully review" the reduction. He went to dinner with Agnes Meyer and her yachting party—Stevenson complained about the formal dinner "when we might have been at a bistro!"—and went late aboard Mrs. Meyer's chartered yacht, the *Lisboa*. It sailed the next day on a ten-day cruise.[9]

On the first day out on the yacht, they visited Delphi—"at last!!!" Stevenson noted. They arrived at Corfu early on the next morning, July 27, and went for a swim on the opposite side of the island. "Most marvelous crisp salty water. Huge lobsters for lunch. Afternoon rowing & swimming & climbing around with Louise Pierson & other girls." On July 28 they climbed up to an old Turkish citadel. On Sunday, Stevenson started by car for the interior of Montenegro over "murderous" roads to Titograd. From there he sent a postcard to Ruth Field: "I suppose this is a familiar bay to Ruth. We anchored here last night & tonight I'm by a trout stream in the wildest mountains of Montenegro—a region that changed hands 22 times in the war! Downstairs the comrades are whooping it up with accordions, violins, song & wild Partisan shouts—and I'm thinking of Florence —the 'Villa'—and all of you!" Lifelong, visiting one person, he wrote to another, giving the impression he longed to be elsewhere. From Titograd, they drove on into the mountains and an "appalling ceremonial lunch in rough frontier hotel full of slovenly workers on vacation." Lally Graham

8 Alice Albright Hoge was Alicia Patterson's niece; her husband became editor of the Chicago *Sun-Times;* they were later divorced.
9 Among those aboard were the Drew Pearsons, the Bill Attwoods, Alicia Patterson, Chief Justice and Mrs. Earl Warren, Clayton Fritchey, and Lally Graham.

was too sick to go on. They went to a lake to fish and "I was only one to catch one small trout."

Next day, July 30, they sailed for Hercegnovi; he went to bed early. On July 31 they reached Dubrovnik on the beautiful Dalmatian coast of Yugoslavia in time to visit the old city and swim from a nearby island. Mrs. Meyer learned later that the Adriatic was full of sharks and was horrified that Justice Warren and Stevenson had gone swimming. An embassy officer from Belgrade arrived—Marshal Tito invited Stevenson to visit him on August 3. Stevenson was ill with dysentery and a fever on August 1 and part of the following day. On the second, he had dinner alone with the U. S. Ambassador to Yugoslavia, George Kennan, at Villa Dubrovnik. Kennan accompanied him the next day on his visit to Tito.

They arose at 6 A.M., went to the airport, and took off at 8:30 A.M. in Tito's private plane to Pala. "Beautiful flight along coast," Stevenson noted. "By motor boat to Brioni. Shades of 1953! Short stop & on to little islands . . . where Tito now has his personal residence." Tito greeted them, accompanied by several Yugoslav officials. "Visit to gardens in hot sun and then by golf cart to wine cellar for wine (very good!) and long talk. Back to loggia of villa for fancy lunch and more talk. Very cordial and friendly. Left at 3:15 for trip home. . . . Arrived at ship at 7 P.M."

Ambassador Kennan reported to the Department on his personal impressions of the visit, impressions which, he said, differed considerably from Stevenson's. Kennan said he thought Tito seemed "nervous, uncertain, and highly emotional," as though he had recently been through serious trials over policy. He was affable toward Stevenson but uneasy and uncommunicative toward Kennan. During the four-hour talks he addressed only one remark to Kennan. Tito was preoccupied with "expensive playthings" and improvements at his summer home, which embarrassed some of the other Yugoslavs present. Tito showed no disposition to talk about U.S.-Yugoslav relations or any other important subject. What he said, however, confirmed Kennan's belief that Yugoslavia would not return to the Soviet bloc but was determined to free itself of American aid as soon as possible and to look in other directions for major economic ties and political understanding. His subordinates seemed to accept these ideas reluctantly.

Kennan thought they originated in Tito's long ideological aversion to the United States, his sense of humiliation over his long dependence on us, his feeling that our influence was spreading among his people and had contributed to recent Communist intellectuals' aberrations. Demonstrations of congressional ill will had made matters worse. Kennan was convinced that Tito's age, suspiciousness, stubborn ideology, and lack of feel for the outside world were beginning to worsen the relationship between him and his subordinates. The Yugoslav people themselves were strongly pro-American and so were some of his senior colleagues. "Their views may override Tito's sooner than most people think," Kennan said.

On Saturday, August 4, Stevenson wrote, "Dubrovnik—Hamlet in the castle under the stars at night." The next day, Sunday, August 5, he and Alicia flew to Rome, picking up mail there. On the plane Stevenson sent a two-page letter to Marietta Tree, who was on another Greek island. The people on the yacht were "v. agreeable" but he was glad to be leaving and anxious to get home, "diverted with work." The "Adriatic Odyssy was good" but "I've had enough of idleness & thinking, post card writing and thinking, trying to work and thinking. So it will be good to get home and *have* to work. To do nothing is quite different from having nothing to do; so are serenity and idleness. Yachts are confining and I've been idle without being serene." It was a revealing passage; some inner emptiness had driven him to work for many years. He told Marietta that, in this part of the world, the United States created the impression of being more interested in winning wars than in preventing them. "I'm so glad I have a few years to give to the latter. And I ache to contrive better ways to do it— and to be able to execute them. Perhaps we can talk of this sometime." His letters for years had contained that last sentence, to almost everybody, on almost every subject.

He thanked Agnes Meyer "for one of the happiest interludes in my life." Accompanied by Alicia, he flew on to Madrid that same day, August 5, where they were met by Ambassador and Mrs. Woodward and Spanish officials. The U. S. Air Force staged an alert at its base in Madrid for him —"B49s," he noted, "very impressive." They flew on to San Sebastian in a U. S. Air Force plane and dined at a waterfront cafe with the Woodwards ("marvellous fish"). Next day they drove along the coast to a resort and "fine beach" and a fiesta, then back to San Sebastian for an official lunch at the residence of the Foreign Minister. "Finest food I've *ever* had! Never expected to be exchanging toasts with Falangists but toast was as eloquent & graceful as anything I've ever heard about myself." In the afternoon he went to a bullfight, which he thought poor, then went to an official dinner and an evening of Basque and Spanish singing and dancing. Happily, he wrote, *"One of best days of my life!"* Ambassador Woodward told the Department that Stevenson's visit had been "very useful."

33.

Upon his return Stevenson went almost immediately into a hospital for dental surgery. Harlan Cleveland was in New York, as were Schlesinger, Chayes, and Richard Gardner, and conferred with Stevenson in the hospital. Gardner tried to induce Stevenson to testify on the communications satellite, then pending in Congress. Stevenson said, "I wish I had time to get into this sort of thing." But he never did.

Adlai and Nancy visited him for several days. Stevenson told Lady Spears, "We have reached a new crisis with Ellen, who has squandered, I fear, all of her resources and now must be supported. It seems that the family's disasters repeat themselves over and over, and the scenario of her story is almost identical with John's [John Borden, Ellen's father]. But thank heaven I now have some grown and competent sons to help deal with these harrowing crises."

When Carl McGowan was appointed to the United States Court of Appeals in Washington, Stevenson congratulated him warmly. McGowan replied that "but for you this could never have happened. I'm sure that you—more than anyone else—have always known that this is how I hoped to end up in the law and the public service."

In mid-August the bilateral diplomatic rounds were starting in New York. Secretary Rusk went to New York on August 16 and had lunch with Stevenson and U Thant and spent the afternoon talking with Stevenson. They agreed with U Thant on a plan for national reconciliation in the Congo which U Thant soon unveiled as his own. That day George Ball sent a paper drafted by Harlan Cleveland to President Kennedy outlining U.S. strategy in the forthcoming General Assembly. The paper said the UN needed "a breathing spell" to consolidate its strength, get its finances in order, and improve its executive capacity. Therefore the United States should not burden it with new initiatives.

On August 21, Stevenson went to Washington and met from 4 P.M. until nearly six with President Kennedy, Rusk, Cleveland, Schlesinger, and others. Stevenson had made notes in preparation for the meeting. He would talk about "my trip abroad." It had been "a good idea" for him to attend ECOSOC meetings, indicating the importance we attached to the development decade. His impressions of Tito were not so different from Kennan's after all, except that he was less sure than Kennan that Tito would look elsewhere for economic ties.

Schlesinger thought the meeting with Kennedy "rather disappointing." The year before at Hyannisport, Stevenson and Kennedy had had a frank and full discussion. This time, however, Rusk took over. "[Stevenson] gave the impression of having an appointment somewhere else which he was anxious to make." Schlesinger had hoped for a methodical examination of a previously prepared strategy paper. "Instead, Rusk roamed through the paper in a brisk and helter-skelter way, going quickly and apparently at random from one item to another, ignoring a number of items and preventing exhaustive discussion of any."

That evening the Schlesingers gave a dinner for Stevenson at their rented house in Georgetown. Among the guests were Hubert Humphrey, Dave Bell, Harlan Cleveland, and Abe Chayes. They talked about how hard it was for a new administration to change things, to take new imaginative initiatives. Schlesinger and Chayes agreed that the "age of free wheeling" was gone, that the springtime of the Kennedy administration was over, and that ice was forming over the Administration. It was a morose conversation.

William Foster held a press background briefing on a new U.S. policy— to seek a limited ban on nuclear tests, not a comprehensive one, an important decision.

The House passed the UN bond issue bill, and Stevenson issued a statement praising the Congress. This, however, was only the tip of an iceberg —an iceberg that later almost sank the UN itself. The Administration had promised Congress to force the Soviets and French and others to pay their peace-keeping assessments if the Congress passed the bond issue. Those commitments, together with a decision to refer to the World Court members' obligations to pay, later led to a confrontation with the U.S.S.R. and France and threatened to break up the UN. In these early stages, however, Stevenson considered the matter purely budgetary and administrative and paid little attention to it. Not until about early 1964, when the confrontation was already impending, did he become fully conscious of its significance.

The General Assembly convened its seventeenth session on September 18. Schlesinger went up to New York to work on Stevenson's speech to the General Assembly. He noted that Stevenson edited it with all his old skill, turning out a crisp and effective final draft. Schlesinger did note, however, the reason why all diplomats' speeches were filled with clichés— diplomats hesitated to say anything in a fresh way because new language might indicate unsuspected shifts in policy. The only safe course was to repeat what had already been said.

Stevenson's speech on September 20 reaffirmed "the high significance" which the United States attached to the UN. He welcomed the addition to membership of Trinidad and Tobago, Jamaica, Rwanda and Burundi. He reviewed the past year—an end to the Algerian war, settlement of the dispute between the Netherlands and Indonesia over West New Guinea, a cease-fire in Laos, progress in the Congo, disarmament negotiations in a new forum. Yet all was not well. Berlin, subversive activity directed from Cuba, "unprovoked aggression" by North Vietnam, Chinese Communist provocation and subversion, the Middle East, repression in East Europe, the wrench of emergence from colonialism, world poverty, and, "most ominous of all," the suicidal arms race—all these problems and more indicated the world's troubles. "If the United Nations has not succeeded in bringing the great powers together," he said, "it has often succeeded in keeping them apart." The United Nations' most serious needs were to improve its peace-keeping capability and solve its financial problems. The United States was prepared to stop testing nuclear devices in the atmosphere, oceans, and space without inspection.

On the next day, September 21, Stevenson spoke again in the plenary session of the Assembly, this time to reply to speeches by representatives of Cuba and the Soviet Union. Stevenson referred to various "hysterical" charges Cuba had made of U.S. plans for intervention in Cuba. He accused Gromyko of "hypocrisy" in denouncing American plans to intervene in Cuba while his own government "holds in thrall all of Eastern Europe. . . . Now, in direct answer, let me say to the representatives of the Soviet Union and Cuba that we are not taking and will not take offensive action in this hemisphere, neither will we permit aggression in this hemisphere." (For some time, American intelligence had reported unusually heavy shipments to Cuba. It believed the equipment was defensive and might include surface-to-air missiles which could not be armed with nuclear warheads.) He said, "The threat to the peace in Cuba comes not from the United States but from the Soviet Union. The threat arises from the extraordinary and unnecessary flood of Soviet arms and military personnel pouring into Cuba. It is this foreign military intervention in the Western Hemisphere which is creating grave concern. For what purpose is this great military build-up in Cuba intended? No one can be sure, but all of Cuba's neighbors are justified in feeling themselves threatened and anxious. If the Soviet Union genuinely desires to keep the peace in the Caribbean, let it stop this warlike posturing, this stuffing of Cuba with rockets, military aircraft, advanced electronic equipment, and other armament all out of proportion to any legitimate needs."

On September 22, Stevenson spoke at ceremonies at the Lincoln Memorial in Washington commemorating Lincoln's Emancipation Proclamation. Rusk went to New York for a week, and Stevenson was busy with him. On the twenty-fifth, Stevenson narrated "Lincoln Portrait" with the Philadelphia Symphony at the new Lincoln Center in New York. Receptions and dinners for visiting dignitaries kept his schedule crowded day and night.

Reports from the Congo were turning ominous. Tshombe seemed to be balking at the new federal constitution, to be veering back toward secession. Stevenson worked hard for pressure on Tshombe from the British and Belgians. Stevenson thought matters were near a real crisis, with civil war again possible.

On September 26, Stevenson sent his first weekly progress report to Schlesinger. The General Assembly had opened. Stevenson was concerned because the Hungarian item, which the United States espoused, had been placed on the agenda by a much closer vote than the previous year, owing to a shift of French African votes to the Soviet side. Gromyko and the Cuban representative had spoken at length about Cuba; they would make it a major issue. Cleveland insisted on receiving Stevenson's report, to be incorporated into Cleveland's own weekly report to Kennedy. But Stevenson continued to send a copy of his reports to Schlesinger throughout Kennedy's administration. Cleveland spoke acidly of "overlapping memoranda."

On September 30, Rusk met with several Latin American Foreign Ministers to discuss what to do about Soviet military aid to Cuba. Stevenson did not attend—he was at Ruth Field's Long Island estate—yet he sometimes expressed resentment at not being invited to Rusk's New York meetings. Later he seems to have reached an understanding with Rusk, for he took to checking Rusk's schedule each morning and putting some of Rusk's meetings on his own schedule. Stevenson went to Washington on October 2 and told President Kennedy it would be helpful if he could be involved in such affairs as the previous Sunday's White House lunch for Lord Home. President Kennedy "indicated," as Cleveland put it in a memorandum, that State should suggest including Stevenson when it seemed "relevant and appropriate."

34.

At the morning session of the Assembly on October 8, President Dorticós of Cuba delivered a long stormy attack on the United States. It was a tumultuous meeting, with several interruptions from the galleries, and at one point Dorticós said, "Interruptions of this sort do not worry us any more. During the few days which we have spent in this country, we have been constantly harassed, and this is clear proof of the fact that this is a country which does not offer adequate safeguards for the functioning of the United Nations." When he finished, Stevenson rose to a point of order and said, "For seventeen years we have come to expect that when a chief of state asks for the privilege of this podium he has an obligation not to abuse it and not to demean the United Nations and the dialogue of diplomacy, but to speak here in a constructive and statesmanlike manner. But the President of Cuba . . . has seen fit to use this rostrum to attack my country, with unparalleled calumnies, slanders, and misrepresentations, for one hour and forty-five minutes. Yet I will not claim a right of reply from this platform this morning. Instead, I shall respond to his intemperate and false charges outside of this hall, and at once." Some present thought that Dorticós seemed alarmed, that he thought Stevenson was going to assault him physically in the corridor outside the chamber. Stevenson meant he would issue a statement.

In his statement Stevenson repeated that the United States would not commit aggression against Cuba but neither would it "tolerate aggression" in the hemisphere and that Cuba "has been opened to a flood of Soviet weapons and 'technicians'. . . . What we cannot accept—and will never accept—is that Cuba has become the springboard for aggressive and subversive efforts to destroy the inter-American system, to overthrow the governments of the Americas, and to obstruct the peaceful, democratic evolution of this hemisphere toward social justice and economic development."

At 6:30 P.M. on Sunday, October 14, Stevenson met President Kennedy at Idlewild Airport and rode with him to the Carlyle Hotel in Manhattan. Kennedy had been campaigning. That same day a U-2 plane of the CIA was flying over Cuba taking reconnaissance photographs. Late the next afternoon the intelligence community finished processing the pictures and identified a launching pad, a series of buildings for ballistic missiles, and one missile on the ground in San Cristóbal. (These were not the innocent SAMs—surface-to-air missiles—previously identified and useful only in defense. These were offensive ground-to-ground missiles and they could be fitted with nuclear warheads and targeted on American cities.) The CIA informed McGeorge Bundy at about eight-thirty that Monday night. Bundy knew Kennedy would demand photographs and supporting interpretation to make sure it was no mistake. It would take all night to prepare the evidence. He decided not to tell the President until next morning, Tuesday, October 16. The great Cuban missile crisis, the first direct confrontation of nuclear powers in history, had begun.

Stevenson left for Washington at 9 A.M. that day. He was to make a speech there and to attend a state luncheon at the White House for the Crown Prince of Libya. Stevenson had intended to return to New York that afternoon, but after lunch Kennedy showed him the photographic evidence of the missiles in Cuba and asked him to stay over in Washington and to join a conference at State that afternoon with Secretary Rusk and others. Stevenson did.

A group of the highest officials in government had met that morning at the White House to discuss the Cuban crisis. They continued to meet almost continuously for the next twelve days and almost daily for some six weeks thereafter. They later became known as "Ex-Comm"—the Executive Committee of the National Security Council.[10] Ex-Comm's purpose was to discuss policy alternatives and recommend a course of action to the President. President Kennedy had decided not to call a meeting of the full National Security Council—it was too big, he wanted the photographic evidence and secret discussions closely held. He had also decided not to meet with Ex-Comm himself—its discussion would be freer if he was absent. He would meet with them when they were prepared to recommend a course of action. He continued campaigning around the country and they kept as many regular appointments as possible, all in order to avoid causing talk. At least once a large number of them piled into a single limousine

---

[10] They included Secretary Rusk, Secretary McNamara, John McCone (director of the CIA), Secretary Dillon, Bundy, Sorensen, George Ball, U. Alexis Johnson (Deputy Undersecretary of State), Maxwell Taylor (chairman of the Joint Chiefs of Staff), Ed Martin (Assistant Secretary of State for Latin America), Roswell Gilpatric (Deputy Secretary of Defense,) Paul Nitze (Assistant Secretary of Defense), and Robert F. Kennedy. Chip Bohlen left after the first day to become Ambassador to France and was succeeded by Llewellyn Thompson as the Russian expert. Stevenson attended that first meeting and others but not all sessions. Vice President Johnson, Kenneth O'Donnell, and Don Wilson (Deputy Director of the USIA) attended some meetings, and so did others. Dean Acheson, Robert A. Lovett, and John J. McCloy were consulted.

to go to the White House in order to avoid attracting attention to a fleet of limousines. Had Kennedy been obliged to make the photographs public, opinion in the United States probably would have forced an invasion or at least an air strike to knock the missiles out. Secrecy gave him time to consider carefully before deciding on a course of action. It did not give him unlimited time—more photographs on Wednesday showed new installations, at least sixteen and possibly thirty-two missiles of over a thousand-mile range. Military experts advised that these missiles could be in operation within a week.

The men of Ex-Comm had several alternative courses of action, ranging in ascending order from doing nothing, through undertaking quiet diplomacy at the UN or OAS or directly with Khrushchev, through a secret approach to Castro, through a blockade or quarantine to stop further shipments of Soviet equipment and men, through a "surgical air strike" pinpointed at the missiles, to launching a full-scale invasion of Cuba. At various times most of the individual members of Ex-Comm changed their positions, some swinging 180 degrees from an extremely militant (or "hawk") position to a pacific (or "dove") position, or vice versa. The discussions through that long first week were not among men with fixed positions but among men examining an extremely complex problem that offered few good solutions and posed frightful dangers of nuclear war. Kennedy, as always, wanted not merely proposed solutions but powerful arguments for them, for in the end he alone would make the ultimate decision.

Stevenson attended the Ex-Comm meeting on Wednesday. Robert Kennedy came to serve as chairman and became the single most influential member of Ex-Comm. At this point several members argued for an air strike. Secretary McNamara opposed, arguing for a blockade. George Ball supported him and so did Robert Kennedy, saying that his brother was not going to be responsible for an American Pearl Harbor. Acheson thought the analogy false—the Soviets had had ample warning. Stevenson pointed out that little had been done to work out the political-diplomatic side of the program, yet such groundwork was essential if we were to obtain OAS and Allied approval. He proposed going to the UN before the Russians did and introducing a resolution. Stevenson also seemed to favor a high-level secret emissary to Khrushchev. He gave the President a rather ambiguous note, written in the context of the air strike:

"The national security must come first. . . . If they won't remove the missiles and restore the status quo ante, we will have to do it ourselves—and then we will be ready to discuss bases in the context of a disarmament treaty or anything else. . . . [But] to risk starting a nuclear war is bound to be divisive at best and the judgments of history seldom coincide with the tempers of the moment. . . . I feel you should have made it clear that the existence of nuclear missile bases anywhere is negotiable before we start anything. . . . I confess I have many misgivings about the proposed course of action." The note annoyed President Kennedy, according to Sorensen.

That Wednesday afternoon at four o'clock Stevenson took the air shuttle back to New York in order to attend the General Assembly's general debate on Thursday. The missile crisis was still secret. On Thursday, Ex-Comm seemed to be leaning toward a blockade, or quarantine. (The word "quarantine" was substituted for "blockade," which in international law is an act of war.)

It had become obvious that one element of American action would be a speech by the President to the nation, announcing the discovery of the missiles and declaring American policy. Stevenson wrote a proposed passage in the President's speech: "Ambassador Stevenson will propose to the Security Council tomorrow a resolution whereby the UN would dispatch immediately observation teams to all strategic nuclear missile sites maintained on the territory of any country other than the three major nuclear powers. These observation teams, which would be placed in Cuba, Italy, and Turkey, would insure that no surprise attack could be mounted in any of these countries pending a permanent solution of the problem of foreign missile bases." It said the United States would agree, together with the other American states, to guarantee the territorial integrity of Cuba and propose the dispatch of a UN force to Cuba to implement that guarantee. To ensure the security of the hemisphere, the United States would "insist on the prompt dismantling of these missile sites in Cuba and the withdrawal of all Soviet military personnel." Concurrently, the United States would evacuate its base at Guantánamo. The Soviet Union's clandestine action in Cuba had endangered the whole world and demanded that we all hasten disarmament "before it is too late." The United States stood ready to consider elimination of NATO strategic bases in Italy and Turkey "and all other bases" in the context of disarmament.

So Stevenson proposed specifically to abandon Guantánamo and offered to negotiate the elimination of the NATO bases in Italy and Turkey. Moreover, he wanted to place the entire matter within the framework of disarmament negotiations. It was characteristic of him that he wanted to broaden the crisis and use it as a means of achieving global détente with the Soviet Union. It was equally characteristic of Kennedy's intense pragmatism that he kept his eyes tightly fixed on a single objective—getting the Soviet missiles out of Cuba. Thus the discussion that arose later over who was a hawk and who a dove put the matter in the wrong framework. It was not a question of hawk or dove; it was a question of one's approach to problems. Stevenson's approach was quite different from Kennedy's.

On Friday afternoon, October 19, Stevenson went to Washington. President Kennedy was campaigning in Illinois for Sid Yates, running for the Senate, and was to speak that night at a Democratic dinner in Chicago which Stevenson was to have attended. That morning the Joint Chiefs had urged on Kennedy an air strike or invasion. Other advisers who had favored a blockade began to have misgivings. Kennedy, talking to Sorensen before departing for Chicago, seemed discouraged. He wanted to act on Sunday if possible. During the Ex-Comm meetings that day, however, a program built around a blockade was developed, and Sorensen worked late that night on a draft of the President's speech. On Saturday morning the program and the draft were generally approved by Ex-Comm and the President called back from Chicago. The climactic meeting of Ex-Comm would be held that afternoon.

Upon arriving in Washington on Friday, Stevenson had phoned Schlesinger and they had agreed to meet early Saturday morning and drive to work together. It was a measure of how secret the meetings had been that when Stevenson and Schlesinger met, Schlesinger knew nothing about the meetings or the crisis. Stevenson told Schlesinger that pressures for an air strike appeared to be subsiding and that a blockade, or quarantine, probably would be substituted. He would have to speak in the Security Council early next week and asked Schlesinger to begin work on a draft.

At that critical meeting of Ex-Comm with the President on Saturday afternoon General Taylor presented the case for the "Bundy plan," an air strike. Dillon and McCone also favored it, though with qualifications. McNamara took the lead in arguing for a blockade instead, with Gilpatric and Robert Kennedy supporting him. Stevenson seemed silent but near the end opposed the air strike, favored the blockade, and proposed a trade of Guantánamo and of Turkish and Italian missile bases for the Soviet missiles in Cuba. (McNamara too had mentioned this as a possibility.) In addition Stevenson proposed a guarantee of the territorial integrity of Cuba. He proposed sending UN inspection teams to Cuba, Turkey, and Italy and a UN-supervised standstill of military activity on both sides—thus leaving the missiles in. He also mentioned a summit meeting. It is not clear whether he argued for the complete neutralization of Cuba or only for its demilitarization. (Neutralization would presumably have meant changes in the Castro government and in its foreign policy orientation.)

Several men attacked Stevenson's proposals sharply. Stevenson defended his position ably, to Kennedy's admiration. Kennedy, however, rejected Stevenson's proposals. He wanted to concentrate on getting the missiles out of Cuba. He felt that concessions might confirm our European allies' suspicions that we would sacrifice their security to protect our interest in an area of no concern to them. Instead of being on the defense, we should be indicting the Soviet Union for duplicity and for threatening the peace. Kennedy did, however, order that the political aspects of his speech be strengthened.

Sorensen once said that since Stevenson had not attended all meetings of Ex-Comm he did not realize that its members had moved beyond the point where his course might have been possible. He said the attacks on Stevenson were severe, the more so because Stevenson at times seemed apologetic, almost as though it were the United States, not the U.S.S.R., which was threatening world peace. "It was a grim meeting," Sorensen said. At one point Robert Kennedy talked privately to Stevenson in a side room about Guantánamo. Stevenson felt the Soviets would not submit to the quarantine and withdraw their missiles unless they were offered the Guantánamo base plus a no-invasion guarantee. Afterward on the porch, President Kennedy told Sorensen, "You have to admire him for sticking to it." By doing so, Stevenson got some of his point of view into the President's speech. Kennedy seemed somewhat surprised that Stevenson argued so forcibly for his views; it did not accord with the President's previous view of Stevenson as wishy-washy. At one point in the meeting Stevenson was instructed to draft the Turkey-Guantánamo proposal (as others had drafted other proposals). Douglas Dillon, though he opposed the Stevenson proposals, said later that they had not deviated from the Ex-Comm style—everyone had presented different views at different times. He himself had favored immediate military action until he heard Robert Kennedy's speech about how an air strike would look to history. Stevenson, he said, had his own constituency in New York and presented the case for a full try at negotiation, as he should have. George Ball thought Stevenson was right "in logic" but wrong from the point of view of power. Carl Kaysen recalled that President Kennedy said afterward, "There's a lot of talk about Adlai Stevenson but it took a lot of guts to come in here and say what he thought was right."

That night Jim Rowe and his wife gave a dance on their twenty-fifth wedding anniversary. Everyone there was watching everyone else; bureau chiefs and editors began making telephone calls. The crisis was beginning to leak. At the dance Stevenson tried to persuade Kenny O'Donnell that the course decided upon had been wrong. Stevenson also talked that weekend to Robert Lovett, who subsequently telephoned President Kennedy, told him he was worried about Stevenson, and suggested sending someone up to New York to stiffen him at the UN. Kennedy considered sending Lovett but ended by calling John J. McCloy home from Europe and sending him to New York to be with Stevenson. By the end of the weekend Stevenson was reconciled to the program. The President had heard him out; he could do no more. At 10 P.M. on Sunday, October 21, Stevenson went back to New York.

Now the second phase would begin, and Stevenson would become the key figure. President Kennedy spoke to the nation on Monday night, and the missile crisis became public. The President set forth what would be his initial steps (making clear that others might follow): a quarantine on all offensive military equipment under shipment to Cuba; an intensified surveillance of Cuba; a declaration that any missile launched from Cuba would be regarded as an attack by the Soviet Union on the United States itself, requiring full retaliatory response; an immediate convening of the OAS; an emergency meeting of the UN Security Council; and an appeal to

Chairman Khrushchev "to abandon this course of world domination, and to join in an historic effort to end the perilous arms race and to transform the history of man."

Shortly before Kennedy spoke to the nation the United States had informed its allies and friends in Europe and the hemisphere, asked OAS approval of the quarantine, sent Dean Acheson to see De Gaulle and Adenauer, obtained Macmillan's support, and deployed troops, ships, and airplanes to support the quarantine and, if necessary, mount an attack. Secretary Rusk had called in Ambassador Dobrynin and told him of the speech. The President had met with leaders of Congress. And then after Kennedy spoke, the White House was obliged to remain silent and await reaction. The spotlight swung to the UN.

Stevenson had watched the President's speech Monday night on television at the Mission. Stevenson's office during the ensuing days resembled a political headquarters at a convention, with staff members rushing in and out, telephones ringing, arrangements being made for consultation with other Ambassadors and delegations. President Kennedy had sent Schlesinger to New York on Monday to work on Stevenson's speech to the Security Council. He had intended to stay one night but actually did not leave until Friday. Before he left Robert Kennedy told him, "We're counting on you to watch things in New York. That fellow [Stevenson] is ready to give everything away. We will have to make a deal at the end; but we must stand firm now."[11] Stevenson had argued that the eventual political settlement should be included in his initial UN presentation. President Kennedy had refused. By Monday evening, Schlesinger thought, Stevenson was "in good shape," accepting the President's judgment and ready to carry out his instructions. Schlesinger later recalled, "He was damn good that week."

McCloy arrived in New York late Monday night. A Republican with a reputation as a hard-liner on the cold war, he would both strengthen the U.S. effort at the UN and give it an air of bipartisanship. He had initially favored a military attack on Cuba and so would balance Stevenson's position. Stevenson was not happy with his arrival. As it turned out, however, they got along well.

Stevenson had requested a meeting of the Security Council. The U.S.S.R. and Cuba had made counterrequests. It happened that Ambassador Zorin of the U.S.S.R was the president of the Security Council at that time. The Council met at 4 P.M. on Tuesday and Zorin, opening it, used

---

11 Kennedy later modified his view. In his book, *Thirteen Days,* he wrote, "Stevenson has since been criticized publicly for the position he took at this [Saturday] meeting. I think it should be emphasized that he was presenting a point of view from a different perspective than the others, one which was therefore important for the President to consider. Although I disagreed strongly with his recommendations, I thought he was courageous to make them, and I might add they made as much sense as some others considered during that period of time."

the presentation of the agenda as an excuse to say, "The Soviet Union considers the question raised by the United States . . . to be made up out of whole cloth. The action taken by the United States to bring the matter before the Security Council is a clumsy attempt to cover up the unprecedented aggressive acts carried out by the United States against Cuba—the arbitrary and illegal naval blockade of the Republic of Cuba. In actual fact, the substance of the matter is that the United States—"

Stevenson interrupted: "Point of order, please. Are you speaking on the adoption of the agenda or are you making a speech?"

Zorin replied, "Yes, I am speaking in connection with the adoption of the agenda, and nothing else. My statement will be brief." He spoke for two more paragraphs, then went through the procedural motions of adopting the agenda and agreeing to consider all three complaints simultaneously. Then Stevenson spoke.

Now it was Kennedy's turn to watch television. Stevenson began by saying he had asked for the meeting to consider "a grave threat to the Western Hemisphere and to the peace of the world." Nearly four years ago, he said, Castro had made his revolution. He had not restored the constitution or held elections. He had instituted repression and transformed Cuba into "a Communist satellite and a police state." All this would not, if kept within the confines of Cuba, constitute a direct threat to the peace and independence of other states. The threat lay in the submission of the Castro regime to the will of an aggressive foreign power. The issue was not revolution, or reform, or socialism, or dictatorship: the issue was the invasion of the hemisphere. "The crucial fact is that Cuba has given the Soviet Union a bridgehead and staging area in this hemisphere; that it has invited an extra-continental, anti-democratic, and expansionist power into the bosom of the American family; that it has made itself an accomplice in the Communist enterprise of world dominion."

Some would equate the presence of Soviet bases in Cuba with NATO bases in areas near the Soviet Union. This was a fallacious idea. The Soviet action in Cuba had created a "new and dangerous situation." The missile sites in NATO countries were defensive, established in response to missiles in the U.S.S.R. directed at NATO countries. They were installed openly, after free negotiations and without concealment. Russia had moved secretly and with offensive, not defensive, missiles.

Furthermore, Stevenson said, the U.S.S.R. was striking at the principle of the territorial integrity of the Western Hemisphere. Despite Castro's past provocations, the hemisphere had treated him with forbearance. Castro himself had taken Cuba out of the hemispheric family. Only three countries in the hemisphere still had Ambassadors in Havana. The American states had declared unanimously that the Castro regime was incompatible with the principles of the OAS. All this had happened *before* Soviet arms and technicians moved into Cuba.

There were, however, limits to forbearance. They had been reached. "If the United States and the other nations of the Western Hemisphere should accept this basic disturbance of the world's structure of power we would invite a new surge of aggression at every point along the frontier. If we do not stand firm here our adversaries may think that we will stand firm nowhere. . . . We hope that Chairman Khrushchev has not made a miscalculation, that he has not mistaken forbearance for weakness. We cannot believe that he has deluded himself into supposing that, though we have power, we lack nerve; that, though we have weapons, we are without the will to use them." The United States still hoped and prayed that "the worst may be avoided—that the Soviet leadership will call an end to this ominous adventure." For that reason President Kennedy had initiated a quarantine. The OAS was meeting now to consider it. Meanwhile, Stevenson was submitting a draft resolution to the Security Council. The resolution called for the "immediate dismantling and withdrawal" from Cuba of all missiles and other offensive weapons; authorized and requested the Secretary General to send to Cuba a UN observer corps to report on compliance; called for termination of the quarantine once the weapons had been withdrawn, and "urgently" recommended that the United States and the U.S.S.R. "confer promptly on measures to remove the existing threat" to peace and security, and report to the Security Council.

The OAS had been meeting since 9 A.M., delaying because some Ambassadors had not received instructions. While Stevenson was still speaking, it unanimously adopted a resolution providing a legal basis for the quarantine. Ed Martin, Assistant Secretary of State for Latin America, notified Harlan Cleveland promptly. Cleveland telephoned Sisco in New York. Watching Stevenson on television, Cleveland could see Sisco leave the chamber to take the call, then in a moment return and place the resolution on the desk in front of Stevenson. Stevenson, absorbed in his speech, talked on. President Kennedy, who was watching television, called Cleveland and asked whether Stevenson knew about the OAS action. Cleveland said the message had been sent to him. Just then on the TV screen Stevenson reached for the paper which Sisco had laid before him. Kennedy said, "I guess he has it now."

Stevenson, immediately after reading the resolution he was introducing into the Security Council, said, "I have just been informed that the Organization of American States this afternoon adopted a resolution by 19 affirmative votes"[12] which called for the immediate dismantling and withdrawal from Cuba of all missiles and other offensive weapons, and recommended that the member states "take all measures, individually and collectively, including the use of armed force, which they may deem necessary to ensure that the Government of Cuba cannot continue to receive from the Sino-Soviet Power military material and related supplies which may threaten the peace and the security of the Continent, and to prevent the

12 Uruguay, which had not received instructions in time for the vote, abstained. Next day it changed its vote to affirmative.

missiles in Cuba with offensive capability from ever becoming an active threat to the peace and security of the Continent." The OAS also resolved to report to the Security Council of the UN and expressed the hope that the Security Council would send UN observers to Cuba.

Stevenson concluded: "Since the end of the Second World War, there has been no threat to the vision of peace so profound—no challenge to the world of the Charter so fateful. The hopes of mankind are concentrated in this room. The action we take may determine the future of civilization. . . . There is a road to peace. The beginning of that road is marked out in the draft resolution I have submitted for your consideration. If we act promptly, we will have another chance to take up again the dreadful questions of nuclear arms and military bases and the means and causes of aggression and of war—to take them up and do something about them. This is, I believe, a solemn and significant day for the life of the United Nations and the hope of the world community. Let it be remembered not as the day when the world came to the edge of nuclear war, but as the day when men resolved to let nothing thereafter stop them in their quest for peace."

President Kennedy sent Stevenson the following telegram:

Dear Adlai: I watched your speech this afternoon with great satisfaction. It has given our cause a great start. . . . The United States is fortunate to have your advocacy. You have my warm and personal thanks.

When Stevenson finished, the Cuban representative denounced the "blockade" as an "act of war" and said that the Cuban people had answered the "imminent armed attack" by the United States with general mobilization. He asked the Council to call for the immediate withdrawal of all troops, ships, and planes deployed on the approaches to Cuban shores, and for the cessation of all "interventionist" measures. He also contended that the United States had no right to ask for dismantling and disarmament and that UN observers should be sent to the U.S. bases "from which invaders and pirates emerge to punish and harass a small state." He said Cuba "will not accept any kind of observers in matters which fall within our domestic jurisdiction."

Ambassador Zorin said that the U.S. charges were an attempt to cover up aggressive actions. He called the quarantine a "new and extremely dangerous act of aggression" and "undisguised piracy." U.S. charges that the U.S.S.R. had set up offensive armaments in Cuba were false. He submitted a statement published by the Soviet Government during the day. It addressed a "serious warning to the United States Government, to advise it that, in carrying out the measures announced by President Kennedy, it is taking on itself a heavy responsibility for the fate of the world." It said the Soviet Government would do "everything in its power to frustrate the aggressive designs of United States imperialist circles." Zorin introduced a resolution condemning the United States for violating the Charter and "increasing the threat of war," insisting that the United States revoke the quarantine, and calling on the United States, Cuba, and the U.S.S.R. to negotiate a peaceful settlement.

The Security Council adjourned at 8:30 P.M. Stevenson issued a statement to the press less than half an hour later. He said the U.S.S.R. had not denied that missiles had been "secretly installed" in Cuba, thus admitting, in effect, that previous protestations by the Soviet Government that it had no need to install missiles beyond its own borders were "deliberate deceit." Thus the U.S.S.R. had "fully confirmed . . . the urgent necessity" of the measures the United States had taken. All this should put the world "on the alert about all protestations of innocence which we may expect to hear in the next few days."

Mission officers roamed the corridors late that night, seeking reaction to Stevenson's speech. A Yugoslav said the United States had acted too rapidly without disclosing information about the missiles. A Turk was very pleased with the strong U.S. stand but pleaded for great care lest Turkey's rights be jeopardized. Several Africans wanted more proof that the missiles really threatened the United States. They seemed to want to be helpful but were confused as to what to do. A large number of neutrals, perhaps as many as forty, met for two hours and decided provisionally to ask the Secretary General to call upon the United States, U.S.S.R., and Cuba to do nothing further pending UN action. They would likely bring pressure on the United States to lift its quarantine.

Jane Dick told Stevenson, "How I wish there were some way I could be of use to you now. You were superb today, and I was proud of you as always. . . . As I sat in the S.C. Chamber with my private thoughts, waiting to hear you, I marvelled at the extraordinary fate that has put me at your side or in the wings during every single crisis of your adult life: the day you decided to run for Governor, the evening you won; the day Ellen told you of her decision, the night the Tribune broke the news of the divorce; the historic night of the 1952 nomination, the equally historic night (alas!)—in Springfield—of your defeat. The night in Libertyville four years later when it happened again; both the boys' marriages; even the evening that you got the news that it would be the U.N. Ambassador rather than the Sec'y of State. And now, mirabile dictu, and by the chance of timing of an item on Committee III's agenda, I am here today. I've always been proud of you, A, never more than today. I wish there were something I could do at this time of trouble for you and of peril for the world."

On Wednesday Stevenson heard that U Thant was about to take an initiative. He telephoned for an appointment but Thant was out to lunch. Stevenson got him on the phone at 2:30 P.M. Thant said he was sending an appeal to Kennedy and Khrushchev proposing a two-week voluntary suspension of all shipments of arms to Cuba, the lifting of the quarantine, and immediate negotiations—a standstill agreement. He intended to send the messages by 6 P.M. and to make a similar proposal to the Security Council. Stevenson asked him to wait twenty-four hours. He declined.

Stevenson hurriedly reported to Rusk and President Kennedy. Kennedy said Thant was asking the United States to lift the quarantine and to accept the Soviets' word that they would not ship arms. But, inside Cuba, construction was continuing. Stevenson suggested language Kennedy might use in replying to Thant. Kennedy told Stevenson that six ships had already turned back. Tankers were proceeding. Kennedy did not know whether the tankers would submit to search or would simply drive ahead. The quarantine might be successful. Could not Thant wait until the next day? Stevenson said, "He plans to do it tonight and I believe we should answer it promptly and politely." The Cubans were refusing to permit UN inspection teams to enter Cuba, and, Stevenson said, Russian promises were worthless unless we had some means of verification. He and Kennedy discussed the matter further and Kennedy said he would talk to Rusk and call Stevenson later.

About 5 P.M., Stevenson, accompanied by Yost, called on Thant to try to change his appeal to Kennedy and Khrushchev. Thant said it had already been sent—about 3 P.M. by commercial telegram. The United States received it about five-thirty, the U.S.S.R. about six-thirty. On Stevenson's urging, Thant did agree to include in his statement to the Security Council that night a sentence about stopping military construction inside Cuba. He declined to include a reference to the missiles already in place. Thant had the impression that Stevenson was sympathetic to his standstill proposal but Washington was not.

The Security Council met that night and heard speeches by other members. France, Chiang's China, and Chile supported the U.S. position. The U.A.R. and Ghana could not "condone" the quarantine and submitted a draft resolution of their own. At the end of the meeting Thant disclosed his appeal to Kennedy and Khrushchev. He also appealed to Cuba to suspend military construction during negotiations.

Schlesinger told Stevenson that he had talked to Averell Harriman and that Harriman believed Khrushchev was sending us "desperate" signals pleading with us to help him find a way out. Khrushchev had instructed Soviet ships to change their course, had sent a message to Bertrand Russell (the British philosopher then critical of American policy), had appeared the night before at an American concert in Moscow. Harriman believed that Khrushchev had been under heavy pressure from Kremlin hawks to establish a missile base in Cuba as a counter to American bases in Turkey. Harriman had long believed the United States should do everything possible to reduce the influence of the Kremlin hawks. He now thought the United States should somehow make it possible for Khrushchev to save his own face and to blame the Russian hawks for the Cuban adventure. We should do nothing to escalate the crisis—stopping Soviet ships would hurt Soviet pride and reduce the chances of peaceful settlement.

At 8:30 A.M. on the next day, Thursday, October 25, Stevenson received instructions from Ball to tell U Thant that the United States hoped Khrushchev would keep his ships out of the quarantine interception area for a limited time in order to permit discussion. The United States did not want any incidents. Stevenson was told, for his information, that the Administration was ready to discuss the "modalities" Thant had suggested but must not give Thant any impression that we would agree to voluntary suspension of the quarantine without UN observation.

Stevenson saw U Thant promptly, and Thant said he would transmit the U.S. views to Khrushchev confidentially. Zorin had not liked U Thant's remarks to the Security Council—he considered the quarantine illegal. Thant had told him he did not care about legality but was trying to avert an explosion. The Afro-Asians were putting pressure on Zorin to accept Thant's standstill proposal, but Thant did not think he would. Stevenson reported this to Rusk. About 2 P.M., Thant did send a second message to Khrushchev. He transmitted Kennedy's wish to avoid a confrontation, said that he too was most concerned about a confrontation, and asked Khrushchev to tell his ships to stay away from the quarantine area. He now appealed to Kennedy to instruct U.S. vessels to do everything possible to avoid confrontation. If Kennedy responded, Thant would tell Khrushchev he had Kennedy's assurance of cooperation in avoiding a confrontation.

Stevenson had been sending suggestions to Kennedy, through the Department, for an answer to Thant's standstill proposal. He was anxious that the United States not appear to reject Thant's appeal. Cleveland and others in the Department had also been making suggestions. That afternoon President Kennedy sent his reply to U Thant via Stevenson: "I deeply appreciate the spirit which prompted your message of yesterday. As we made clear in the Security Council, the existing threat was created by the secret introduction of offensive weapons into Cuba, and the answer lies in the removal of such weapons. . . . You have made certain suggestions and have invited preliminary talks. . . . Ambassador Stevenson is ready to discuss promptly these arrangements with you. I can assure you of our desire to reach a satisfactory and peaceful solution of this matter."

Khrushchev replied to Thant that same day: "I have received your appeal and carefully studied the proposal it contains. I welcome your initiative. I understand your anxiety over the situation obtaining in the Caribbean, since the Soviet Government also regards the situation as highly dangerous and calling for immediate intervention by the United Nations. I declare that I agree with your proposal, which accords with the interests of peace." (Khrushchev told Thant this before he informed Zorin, his own Ambassador, who had, in a private conversation with Thant, rejected Thant's standstill.) Thus it appeared that the initial moves undertaken by

Thant had brought promising results though they had settled nothing—Kennedy's reminder that the crisis could be ended only by the removal of Soviet missiles still stood.

By midday Thursday the U. S. Mission reported increasing evidence that the U.S.S.R. and Soviet block nations were surprised and impressed by the firmness of the U.S. stand. The Poles were encouraging the Soviets to seek a peaceful solution. The Yugoslavs feared nothing short of war would prevent the Soviets from continuing their Cuban adventure. An Indian delegate expressed approval of U.S. action. A Nigerian was confident that Kennedy and Khrushchev would work things out. Everybody was wondering what the United States would do after the Soviets vetoed the U.S. resolution in the Security Council. Late that afternoon in Washington, Secretary Dillon and other members of Ex-Comm met to discuss a paper on an air strike against Cuba. They concluded that the air strike could not be made until the Soviets had vetoed the U.S. resolution in the Security Council and there was evidence that the Soviets were continuing their build-up in Cuba.

By now all members of the Security Council had spoken once. Stevenson spoke first in rebuttal. His tone at the outset was conciliatory. He welcomed the U.S.S.R.'s decision to avoid confrontation, Khrushchev's assurance to Bertrand Russell that the Soviet Union would do nothing reckless, and "most of all" the "report" that Khrushchev had agreed to Thant's proposals. He proceeded to rebut things Zorin, Khrushchev, and others had said—that the peace was threatened by the United States. "We are here today . . . because the Soviet Union secretly introduced this menacing offensive military build-up into the island of Cuba while assuring the world that nothing was further from its thoughts. . . . This is the first time, I confess, that I have ever heard it said that the crime is not the burglary but the discovery of the burglary." Some said that the quarantine was an "inappropriate and extreme remedy. . . . Were we to do nothing until the knife was sharpened? Were we to stand idly by until it was at our throats?" And he told the old political story: "To those who say that a limited quarantine was too much . . . let me tell them a story, attributed, like so many stories of America, to Abraham Lincoln. It is a story about a passer-by in my part of the country who was charged by a farmer's ferocious boar. He picked up a pitchfork and met the boar head on and it died. The irate farmer denounced him and asked him why he did not use the blunt end of the pitchfork. The man replied by asking, 'Why did the boar not attack me with his blunt end?' " Nothing which had been said by the Communist states altered the basic situation. The one action in the last few days which had strengthened the peace was Thant's standstill proposal. He concluded by reading President Kennedy's response to Thant's appeal.

Ambassador Zorin spoke at some length. The United States had no evidence to prove its contentions. The "aggressive intentions of the United

States" were opposed by "the overwhelming majority" of delegations to the UN. Thus Stevenson had been "forced to change his tone," to become defensive. Neutral nations believed that the "blockade" was illegal, that Cuba had a right to self-defense and independence. Zorin quoted from Kennedy's speech to the nation. He had said he had "unmistakable evidence" of the missiles by October 16—yet he had seen Foreign Minister Gromyko two days later and had said nothing about it. Why? "Because there is no such evidence." The only evidence the United States possessed was "fake." He read the text of Khrushchev's reply to Thant.

Stevenson then said, "I want to say to you, Mr. Zorin, that I do not have your talent for obfuscation, for distortion, for confusing language, and for double-talk—and I must confess to you that I am glad I do not. But, if I understood what you said, you said that my position has changed; that today I was defensive because we do not have the evidence. . . . We have it, and it is clear and incontrovertible. And let me say something else: those weapons must be taken out of Cuba.

"Next, let me say to you that, if I understood you, you said—with a trespass on credulity that excells your best—that our position had changed since I spoke here the other day because of the pressures of world opinion and a majority of the United Nations. Well, let me say to you, sir: you are wrong again. We came here today to indicate our willingness to discuss U Thant's proposals—and that is the only change that has taken place.

"But let me also say to you, sir, that there has been a change. You, the Soviet Union, have sent these weapons to Cuba. You, the Soviet Union, have upset the balance of power in the world. You, the Soviet Union, have created this new danger—not the United States. . . .

"Finally, Mr. Zorin, I remind you that the other day you did not deny the existence of these weapons. Instead, we heard that they had suddenly become defensive weapons. But today—again, if I heard you correctly— you say that they do not exist, or that we have not proved they exist—and you say this with another fine flood of rhetorical scorn. All right, sir, let me ask you one simple question: do you, Ambassador Zorin, deny that the U.S.S.R. has placed and is placing medium- and intermediate-range missiles and sites in Cuba? Yes or no? Do not wait for the interpretation. Yes or no?"

Zorin said, "I am not in an American court of law, and therefore do not wish to answer a question put to me in the manner of a prosecuting counsel. You will receive the answer in due course in my capacity as representative of the Soviet Union."

Stevenson said, "You are in the courtroom of world opinion right now, and you can answer 'Yes' or 'No.' You have denied that they exist—and I want to know whether I have understood you correctly."

Zorin said, "Please continue your statement, Mr. Stevenson. You will receive the answer in due course."

Stevenson said, "I am prepared to wait for my answer until hell freezes over, if that is your decision. I am also prepared to present the evidence in this room."

Zorin called on the Chilean representative, who said, "Mr. President, I had not expected the incident which has just occurred, and I should prefer to speak after you have replied, if you deem it necessary, to the comments or questions addressed to you by the United States representative. I should be glad to yield the floor to you for that purpose."

Stevenson interjected, "I had not finished my statement. I asked *you* a question, Mr. President, and I have had no reply to that question. I will now proceed, if I may, to finish my statement."

"By all means, you may proceed," Zorin said.

Stevenson said, "I doubt whether anyone in this room, except possibly the representative of the Soviet Union, has any doubt about the facts, but in view of his statements, and the statements of the Soviet Government up until last Thursday, when Mr. Gromyko denied the existence of or any intention of installing such weapons in Cuba, I am going to make a portion of the evidence available right now. If you will indulge me for a moment, we will set up an easel here," and he proceeded to display and explain a series of maps and aerial photographs of the missile sites in Cuba.

The Ghanaian representative, next in turn, said he would prefer to speak later. The U.A.R. representative said his delegation "cannot help but hail" President Kennedy's response to Thant's appeal. "We also welcome" Khrushchev's response, he said. (Ghana and the U.A.R. often supported the U.S.S.R.) Zorin then proceeded to "venture" a few words of reply to Stevenson. Stevenson had asked him a question but then had displayed " 'evidence' " to justify the United States "aggressive actions." He would be brief. The answer to Stevenson had already been given in a Tass statement of September 11: the government of the Soviet Union had authorized Tass to state that, so powerful was its nuclear arsenal, the Soviet Union had no need to transfer nuclear weapons to any other country, such as Cuba. As for Stevenson's photographic evidence, Zorin said, "Similar methods were used by Mr. Stevenson, though without success, in April 1961," at the time of the Bay of Pigs. Now Stevenson was using the Security Council "as a show for the display of your photographs. I consider that this procedure lacks seriousness. I had a higher opinion of you personally." All this "play acting" was designed to distract the Security Council from the main issue—the United States' violation of the Charter and international law by establishing a blockade which constituted an act of war. Therefore Zorin would not discuss the photographs. He supposed "it will be necessary" for us to exchange views, as U Thant had proposed. He then gave the floor again to Stevenson.

Stevenson said, "I have not had a direct answer to my question. . . . As to the authenticity of the photographs . . . I wonder if the Soviet Union would ask their Cuban colleagues to permit a United Nations team to go to these sites. If so, Mr. Zorin, I can assure you that we can direct them to the proper places very quickly. And now I hope that we can get down to business, that we can stop this sparring. We know the facts, Mr. Zorin, and so do you, and we are ready to talk about them. Our job here is not to score debating points: our job, Mr. Zorin, is to save the peace. If you are ready to try, we are."

The "hell freezes over" speech was by all odds the most popular one Stevenson ever made. Roxane Eberlein told Buffie Ives next day, "Yesterday was a great day for the Governor, as you can imagine. Everyone is saying he could have been elected President on the spot, and everyone who calls in says the whole city is discussing and praising what he did to Zorin last night." Walter Reuther congratulated him on his "magnificent performance." Jack Arvey thought the speech illustrated why Truman had won in 1948 and Stevenson had lost in 1952—the truck driver, the locomotive engineer, everybody could understand the hell-freezes-over speech as they could understand Truman in 1948 but not Stevenson in 1952. Bloomington loved him for it; for once, nobody in Bloomington snickered at greatness. Even Republicans in Lake Forest loved it. Jane Dick once said, "They had always thought him too liberal. Then came this speech. They thought, 'At long last he's got some guts and stature.' Suddenly he was their champion." One of Stevenson's old Lake Forest friends always had a New Year's eggnog party. Usually Stevenson would arrive and be greeted pleasantly—but no more. The other guests were little interested in his political activities. Their interests lay in bridge, canasta, horseback riding, golf, and business, usually finance. Stevenson was barely a part of all that—and only because of their long relationship. But that New Year's of 1963, after the Cuban missile crisis, when Stevenson came in, everybody rushed up to him and said, "We're so glad to see you—congratulations—what a marvelous job you've done at the UN." It was the "hell freezes over" speech that did it.

Actually, if examined closely, the logic of the "hell freezes over" speech was faulty: waiting, whether till hell froze over or for a somewhat lesser period, was precisely what the United States was not prepared to do. It wanted the Soviet missiles out urgently. But though faulty in logic, its political effect was enormous. The net impression was that at last somebody had told the Communists to go to hell.

After Stevenson made the speech he went to Ruth Field's for dinner. Jane Dick was there and so were Borden and Adlai III. Mrs. Dick recalled later, "He told us about the events of the day in a side-splitting way. There was a twinkle in his eye. It had been devastatingly grim during the day, but it was fun by now. He seemed like a person who'd been purged of something. He was sitting on top of the world—to hell with it—he thought he had taken a long shot and it had worked. He was exhilarated."

A few days later, when some of the pressure was off the missile crisis,

President Kennedy wrote: "I want to tell you how deeply and personally I appreciate the contribution you have made to the security of the United States and the peace of the world in the last week. Your vindication of American policy before the United Nations was superb; and I know that it accounts in great measure for the understanding and support that policy has received from our friends abroad."

35.

When the Security Council adjourned, the Cuban missile crisis moved into its third stage: quiet diplomacy, both at the UN and in Washington. Stevenson was very busy. He went to Washington and saw the President. He telephoned the President. He met with allies. He talked often with Thant. Messages flowed out from Thant to Kennedy, Khrushchev, and Castro; replies came back. Delegations consulted with one another. Mission officers reported corridor conversations. The Department instructed Stevenson closely. But, although the UN representatives were busy, they seemed optimistic, feeling that discussions had been started by U Thant and that a way out of the crisis would be found.

The real negotiations, however, were not conducted in New York. They were conducted directly and secretly between Kennedy and Khrushchev. The people who mattered now were not men and women at the UN but the men in the Kremlin and in Ex-Comm. And there tension did not relax. Indeed, Robert Kennedy thought that the time of greatest danger came over the weekend following the Security Council meeting. For on Friday an armed party boarded the first ship bound for Cuba.

That day the feeling in the White House grew that the crisis was not going to pass, that direct military confrontation between the United States and U.S.S.R. was inevitable. President Kennedy ordered the State Department to prepare to conduct civil government in Cuba after the invasion and occupation. The Pentagon said the United States could expect very heavy casualties in an invasion. Then Khrushchev sent a long emotional letter to Kennedy, apparently written by Khrushchev himself. He offered to desist in sending weapons to Cuba and to withdraw or destroy those already there; in return the United States would withdraw its blockade and guarantee not to invade Cuba. A private message sent through John Scali, then a television reporter and later Ambassador to the UN, confirmed the offer.

But on Saturday the FBI reported that Soviet personnel in New York were apparently preparing to destroy all sensitive documents. A second letter came from Khrushchev, this one formal and harsh, demanding removal of U.S. missiles from Turkey in return for getting Soviet missiles out of Cuba. Reconnaissance showed that the Russians in Cuba were working night and day on the missile sites and on airstrips for IL-28 bombers.

Robert Kennedy felt that the ensuing twenty-four hours were the most difficult of the crisis. The Joint Chiefs recommended an air strike on Monday followed shortly afterward by an invasion. On Saturday, too, an American U-2 plane was shot down over Cuba and its pilot killed. Another U-2 accidentally flew over Soviet territory near Alaska. Ex-Comm seemed inclined to attack early Sunday morning. President Kennedy drew back. That evening, on Robert Kennedy's recommendation, he replied to Khrushchev's first letter, ignoring his second, and accepting Khrushchev's first offer. (Actually, the letter was diffuse and contained no clear-cut offer. Kennedy and others deduced the "offer" from the context.) Ex-Comm approved the letter. On President Kennedy's instructions, Sorensen telephoned Stevenson and read it to him. Stevenson made one or two suggestions, softening the letter a bit, and Sorensen accepted them. Robert Kennedy saw Ambassador Dobrynin, told him of the Kennedy letter being transmitted, and told him time was running out—the United States needed an answer next day. That night, he wrote, "what hope there was now rested with Khrushchev's revising his course within the next few hours. It was a hope, not an expectation. The expectation was a military confrontation by Tuesday and possibly tomorrow." But on Sunday, October 28, a message came through from Khrushchev: he agreed to dismantle and withdraw the missiles under adequate supervision and inspection. The crisis was over but for the mopping up.

A good portion of that mopping up fell to Stevenson (and to U Thant—he continued to send messages to the parties involved, and his was the unrewarding task of visiting Havana to confront an unyielding Castro. Not until Mikoyan went to Cuba did Castro reluctantly accede). Stevenson's principal task was to negotiate arrangements for the International Committee of the Red Cross to inspect incoming shipments to Cuba, arrangements for verifying that the missiles had been dismantled and removed, and removing the Soviet IL-28 bombers from Cuba. President Kennedy, partly in order to give the Republicans a share of the responsibility for the settlement and partly to stiffen Stevenson's hand, again sent McCloy to negotiate alongside him with the Russians. At the outset this made trouble, particularly when the Soviet negotiator, V. V. Kuznetsov, invited McCloy, not Stevenson, to dine with Mikoyan. Yost, reporting the difficulty to Schlesinger, said Stevenson was willing to relinquish the Cuban negotiations to McCloy but Mikoyan could bring up other matters with which McCloy might not be familiar. Schlesinger discussed it with President Kennedy. Kennedy said sharply that McCloy was to confine himself strictly to Cuba. He did not want anybody to discuss other matters with the Russians until Cuba was settled. Stevenson seemed affable about the whole matter, Schlesinger thought, far less irritable than in recent weeks.

Kuznetsov, First Deputy Minister of Foreign Affairs of the U.S.S.R., was sent by Khrushchev to New York to conclude the Cuban settlement. After the meeting Stevenson reported in a detailed telegram to the Department.

He said Kuznetsov was very pleased that the United States would accept Red Cross inspection of incoming ships. He assured Stevenson that the weapons would be dismantled and removed and that we could count on it and have any verification we wanted. When Stevenson said surveillance was necessary, Kuznetsov found it hard to believe that the United States would doubt the Russians' word. He asked if we could not fly high-level reconnaissance along the coast outside Cuban territorial waters. Stevenson doubted this would be adequate. Kuznetsov suggested that reconnaissance planes could be transferred to the UN and manned by neutrals or even by Cuban, Russian, and American crews. He was worried about Cuban objections to overflights.

Kuznetsov, Stevenson reported, was "very eager" to discuss disarmament and other bases and to explore any other possibilities for broader talks. He asked why he and Stevenson should not discuss the whole range of problems and proposed a toast to disarmament and further talks between them. Several times he mentioned dismantling of American bases which threatened the Soviet Union. The meeting, Stevenson reported, was "extremely cordial." They talked about previous meetings and about Stevenson's writings on the Soviet Union. Kuznetsov was familiar with them. He spoke with "great candor" about the U.S.S.R.'s agricultural problem and the slow development of the virgin lands project and brought Stevenson friendly messages from Mikoyan and Khrushchev.

It is clear from his telegram that Stevenson considered the Cuban affair all but ended and was eager to get on with things that interested him more, especially nuclear testing and disarmament He also seemed to be wandering in his conversation with Kuznetsov and, as always, laying great stress on personal relationships. President Kennedy, upon receiving this telegram, reined Stevenson in sharply. In a telegram approved by Ex-Comm and the President, the Department instructed Stevenson and McCloy that their "entire purpose" was to get the Russians' offensive weapons out of Cuba with verification—not discuss disarmament, bases, or anything else. They should try to reach a solution to the practical problems of dismantling and removal. The telegram went into great detail on what must be removed and how removal must be verified. It was a long, tight instruction, giving Stevenson and McCloy little leeway.

The exchange of telegrams once again made clear the difference between Kennedy and Stevenson. Stevenson, thoughtful and friendly, was preoccupied with global concerns and emphasized personal diplomacy. Kennedy, hardheaded and pragmatic, still concentrated on one problem only: getting the missiles and bombers out of Cuba; and he was coldly impersonal in pursuing his objective.

Stevenson's problem as a negotiator was that he was inclined to leave his opponent thinking he had a deal when he did not. Stevenson was not always careful to tie down an agreement with precision. He could see the other point of view too well. Kennedy once said he spent more time worrying about Stevenson and McCloy than about the Russians. It was during the period of the negotiations with Kuznetsov, not during the Cuban crisis proper, that Kennedy became irritated with Stevenson. McGeorge Bundy once said the President thought Stevenson was too easily affected by "the New York climate." Kennedy saw the IL-28 bombers as a serious political problem; Stevenson, Bundy thought, did not. (Some thought Kennedy took the IL-28s too seriously and was in some danger of reviving the crisis.) "The President and I were irritated about our tactical instructions being carried out," Bundy recalled. Stevenson, on the other hand, said irritably that the White House was pressing too hard on the question of verification.

The negotiations dragged on for weeks, even into 1963. Stevenson and McCloy met with Kuznetsov and Zorin dozens of times, sometimes at the Soviet Embassy on Long Island or at the Soviet Mission headquarters in New York, sometimes at the U. S. Mission or in 42A. McCloy and Stevenson developed a good working relationship. The meetings were a bore, sometimes bogging down over technicalities, sometimes over substantive disagreement. Many times the President and the Department sent Stevenson and McCloy firm and detailed instructions. Sometimes it was Stevenson who took a strong position with the Soviets, McCloy who attempted to understand the Soviet viewpoint. At least once Kuznetsov told Stevenson he sounded as if he were issuing an ultimatum.

Since Cuba refused to permit on-the-ground inspection and verification, the United States used aerial reconnaissance, and the Russians protested it as a violation of Cuban sovereignty; it became one of the more difficult points in the negotiations, as did removal of the IL-28 bombers. Negotiating sessions lasted hours. Stevenson showed great patience. The dialogue was for the most part courteous. The Soviet position was always very firm, American probes quickly hit a wall; but the same was true of the American position. Stevenson repeatedly tried to widen the area of agreement, quickly agreeing to anything Kuznetsov said he was able to agree to. Because both sides were under tight instructions, the dialogue sometimes seemed unreal, dehumanized. Documents Stevenson drew up show that he was working hard and in a lawyer-like manner, choosing words with the greatest care. Once Stevenson drafted a proposed letter to Kuznetsov, and Rusk thought it "an admirably clear restatement of the US position." Each side accused the other of stalling. Mikoyan entered the negotiations and defended the Cuban position.

Progress was made piecemeal on the various issues—surveillance, dismantling, removal, lifting the quarantine, Soviet troop withdrawal, guaranteeing against an invasion of Cuba. The negotiators never reached complete agreement. It was McCloy, not Stevenson, who wound up the negotiation. The two sides eventually, on January 7, 1963, jointly informed the Security Council that, while not all problems had been resolved, they believed that, in view of the degree of understanding achieved and progress in implementing that understanding, it was no longer necessary for the Cuban item to remain before the Council.

The missile crisis illustrated both the usefulness and the limitations of the United Nations and, therefore, of Stevenson himself. The UN served the United States well as a forum for presenting the facts about Cuba, for exposing Soviet duplicity, and for enlisting diplomatic support for the United States. The Secretary General provided a point of contact for international consultation during the early days of the crisis. The UN could have provided on-the-spot inspection and verification services had Castro permitted. And the UN assisted in the mop-up in other ways. All this was useful, and because of it Stevenson played an important role in the crisis. He was particularly effective during the period of White House-Kremlin secret negotiations—his was the only American voice that could be heard in the world, and he used it effectively.

He could not, however, greatly influence the key moves that set American policy, and neither could the UN. The decision to put the missiles into Cuba had been Khrushchev's; just so, the decision to force them out was Kennedy's. Had Khrushchev refused to remove them, no speech at the UN could have availed—nor could it have if Kennedy had decided to invade Cuba. In the final analysis, at the stage of international cooperation at that time, a great power did what it thought it had to do to protect its vital interests. The UN could not change that. For this reason, Stevenson could not decide U.S. policy. He could offer advice, as could other presidential advisers. He could carry out instructions. He could serve as a powerful and articulate advocate of his country's policy. But he could not decide. Only the President could do that.

Mikoyan's wife died while he was in Havana negotiating with Castro, and Stevenson, in the midst of his own negotiations with Kuznetsov, had sent his condolences: "I was distressed to hear the sad news about your wife. . . . That it should come at such a time adds, I know, to your anguish. You and your sons have my utmost sympathy."

Stevenson gave Ralph McGill three reasons why, he believed, Khrushchev had backed down: the threat of U.S. military action, the solidarity of the hemisphere, and "the sudden realization that, after the Security Council confrontation and the exposure of the plot, he risked losing the confidence and good will so painstakingly developed over many years among the non-aligned Afro-Asians. And perhaps the latter was the most important of all. . . . It is only through the UN that the exposure could be dramatized and made indeed visible to all the Afro-Asians." It is a revealing letter.

No doubt most people, if asked what they remembered about Stevenson's tenure at the UN, would mention the Cuban missile crisis first, especially his hell-freezes-over speech. That confrontation had been a triumph. Indeed, the missile crisis had recouped whatever Stevenson had lost at the Bay of Pigs, and his prestige was high and so were his spirits. It was therefore all the more unfortunate that he once more had bad luck: Stewart Alsop and Charles Bartlett, two Washington reporters, published an article in the *Saturday Evening Post,* describing the deliberations of Ex-Comm during the crisis. A blurb on the article said, "An opponent charges, 'Adlai wanted a Munich. He wanted to trade U.S. bases for Cuban bases.'" A caption said, "Stevenson was strong during the UN debate, but inside the White House the hard-liners thought he was soft." The article said that, during the five days leading up to President Kennedy's decision, the members of Ex-Comm had at first divided into hawks and doves but at the end, except for Stevenson, the hawks had become less bellicose and the doves tougher, reaching a consensus that excluded only him. The article quoted an unnamed "nonadmiring" official as saying that, at the climactic meeting of Ex-Comm with the President on Saturday, "Adlai wanted a Munich. He wanted to trade the Turkish, Italian and British missile bases for the Cuban bases." Alsop and Bartlett quoted "the Stevenson camp" as maintaining that Stevenson was willing to discuss Guantánamo and the European bases with the Communists only after a neutralization of the Cuban missiles. Alsop and Bartlett wrote, "But there seems to be no doubt that he preferred political negotiation to the alternative of military action. . . . In any case, the President heard Stevenson out politely, and then gave his semifinal approval to the McNamara plan."

The article itself was not so bad but the "Munich" blurb and attendant publicity were devastating, raising yet again all the old notions that Stevenson was "soft" and "ineffectual" and "starry-eyed." Even worse, Charles Bartlett was known to be a close friend of President Kennedy. Everybody would think that Kennedy had been the source of the story.

On Saturday, December 1, Clayton Fritchey, Stevenson's press secretary, received an advance copy of the magazine. Stevenson was out of town. Much concerned, Fritchey telephoned Schlesinger. Schlesinger had been told of the article earlier that day by President Kennedy, who had been warned that the Washington *Post* would publish an article on it on Monday and who wanted Stevenson informed that he had not talked to Bartlett or any other reporter about Cuba and wanted him told that the article did not represent the President's views. Schlesinger had a collection of memoranda about Cuba which Stevenson had given him, written in the first few days of the crisis and before the decision had been taken. Schlesinger and Kennedy had gone over them. They indicated that, at that time, Stevenson had opposed any introduction of the Turkish and Italian bases into the negotiations but had favored a demilitarization or even neutralization of Cuba.

On Sunday morning, by telephone, Schlesinger and Fritchey started checking the *Saturday Evening Post* story. It seemed wrong in several ways. It suggested that Stevenson was the one person who deviated from the Ex-Comm consensus, whereas in fact most of its members had at one time or another changed their views. It said that he wanted to trade the Turkish, Italian, and British bases for the Soviet bases, whereas in fact nobody had ever mentioned the British bases and Stevenson's memoranda showed that he had opposed involving the Turkish and Italian bases. With this in mind, Schlesinger and Fritchey drafted a statement to be released by a "Stevenson spokesman." Schlesinger sent it to the President, who made a few minor changes and suggested Schlesinger check the minutes of the climactic Ex-Comm meeting on October 20 to ensure accuracy. Schlesinger would do so as soon as possible—it was Sunday. But that night Fritchey called Chalmers Roberts of the Washington *Post,* learned he intended to break the story in Monday morning's *Post,* and gave him the statement by the Stevenson spokesman so that the rebuttal could appear with the original charge.

Apprised of the situation, Stevenson was greatly upset. Next morning he broke an appointment with Kuznetsov, who was to come to 42A for lunch, and, taking Fritchey with him, went to Washington to attend a meeting of Ex-Comm in order to signalize disdain for the *Post* charges. After the meeting he and Fritchey talked with President Kennedy and agreed on a statement which Pierre Salinger would issue at the regular noon news briefing at the White House. The statement said, "The proceedings of the National Security Council have been secret since its founding in 1947 and will continue to be. The various positions of members of the National Security Council taken during deliberations must also remain secret in order to permit access by the President to the frank expression of views. I can state flatly, however, that Ambassador Stevenson strongly supported the decision taken by the President on the quarantine and brilliantly developed the United States position at the United Nations during the days which followed. He also played the key role in the negotiations at the United Nations on the Cuban matter."

Stevenson seemed satisfied that morning with the statement and so indicated to Schlesinger. Almost no one else was. Even when he read the statement, Salinger received hostile questions from the press. Pressed hard, Salinger finally said that the statement had been prepared and cleared with the knowledge and advice of the President. As background, he said that the President had never discussed the Cuban Ex-Comm deliberations with any reporter, including Bartlett and Alsop. The White House had not seen the *Post* article in advance. Bartlett had never used any inside White House information in his writings. The Washington *Post* had been inaccurate in saying that once during the crisis Bartlett had carried a message between the White House and the Soviet Embassy. Salinger had no idea where Alsop and Bartlett had received their information. The reporters were not satisfied, and one said, "I can only say that Stevenson's advisers described this job as a hatchet job and they are completely flabbergasted by it, and I don't think your statement begins to cover the sort of thing that Stevenson will need if he is going to stay on."

The trouble with Salinger's statement, of course, was that it did not deny the *Post* article. It spoke of Stevenson's support of the quarantine policy, not of whether he favored or opposed it before it was adopted. Sorensen once explained that Kennedy could not deny publicly what was false in the article without admitting what was true, which, Sorensen thought, would have damaged Stevenson even more. And if he spoke at all he would be violating his own stricture to other members of Ex-Comm not to talk to the press. By late that afternoon, people in Washington were regarding the whole affair as a planned White House effort to force Stevenson's resignation. They recalled that an adverse Bartlett article had preceded Chester Bowles's dismissal. Kennedy would have to go much further, gossip said, lest his silence be construed as conspiracy. Now Stevenson seemed deeply discouraged.

President Kennedy and Schlesinger went over the minutes of the crucial Ex-Comm meeting. They found that Stevenson had indeed proposed a trade of the Turkish, Italian, and Guantánamo (but not the British) bases for the Soviet missiles, contrary to what Stevenson's own memoranda indicated. This made the problem more difficult. Although, as President Kennedy pointed out, nearly every member of Ex-Comm changed his mind during the deliberations and Stevenson's position on October 20 seemed perfectly arguable, the fact that he had argued for it made impossible an all-out denial of the *Post* story.

Kennedy and Kenny O'Donnell recalled that Stevenson had argued against the quarantine until the political route had been tried, and said that in a sense Stevenson did seem to be the sole dissenter—he had seemed depressed and emotionally out of tune with the others, who were pleased and relieved at having found what looked like a workable solution. Schlesinger suggested that sometimes Stevenson seemed querulous, seemed to wish in a fussy and superficial way that things would be done slightly differently. This, he thought, did not necessarily imply substantive disagreement. As the President talked, Schlesinger was struck by what seemed to him a slightly greater sympathy for the predicament of Bartlett than for the predicament of Stevenson. Schlesinger finally told him that everybody in town thought that the Bartlett article was a signal from the White House that Kennedy wanted to get rid of Stevenson. They were drawing the parallel between this case and the Bowles case. If Kennedy really wanted Stevenson's resignation, all he had to do was ask for it. Kennedy swore violently and said, "Of course I don't want Stevenson to resign. I would regard his resignation as a disaster. Look at it logically. What in the world would I have to gain from his resignation? In the first place, where could I possibly get anyone who could do half as good a job at the UN? Look at the possible alternatives—Adlai would do a far better job than any of the others. In the second place, from a realistic political viewpoint, it is better for me to have Adlai in the government than out. In the third place, if I were trying to get him out, Charley Bartlett would be the last medium I would use. The difference is that I wanted to get rid of Chester and I don't want to get rid of Adlai."

Stevenson and Fritchey headed for New York but fog stopped air traffic so they went to Schlesinger's house for a drink. Stevenson went to dinner with Agnes Meyer. They met later that evening at Averell Harriman's. Stevenson seemed depressed and discouraged, unwontedly silent and unhappy. Schlesinger told him what the President had said. He commented, "That's fine—but will he say it publicly?" Harriman, without success, urged him to fight back. He seemed plainly let down by the absence of direct presidential support and more than half believed the conspiracy stories. Doris Fleeson joined them; even this cheered him little. He and Fritchey took a late train to New York. He had been talking about resigning even before this affair. Now it seemed he really might do it. Lincoln Gordon, who saw him at the time, said he "looked like the wrath of God."

Fritchey called Schlesinger next morning to point out the headline in the New York *Daily News:* ADLAI ON SKIDS OVER PACIFIST STAND IN CUBA. Much of the press was taking the same line. Fritchey said that Stevenson's morale was very low and that he now believed it was all a White House plot. Schlesinger sent the *News* to President Kennedy with a note saying that Kennedy ought to consider doing something further. Kennedy said, "This goes on all the time. Why should Adlai get so upset? Just tell him to sit tight and everything will subside. This is one of those forty-eight-hour wonders. Tell them about all those fights in the New Deal. Just get them to relax." He had asked Sorensen to draft a personal letter from him to Stevenson. He would go no further.

That afternoon Fritchey reported with great concern that Stevenson might well resign. Harlan Cleveland, who was in New York, told Schlesinger that public action by the President was absolutely essential to restore both Stevenson's personal morale and his position at the UN. He said Stevenson was convinced that the Alsop-Bartlett article was part of a deliberate plan and that the President must have known about it. Cleveland himself seemed to think the same thing.

Early Wednesday morning President Kennedy called Newt Minow and asked, "About your leader, what do you suggest I do about this? God damn it, why would I leak a thing like that? What the hell would I want to have trouble with my own Cabinet for?" Minow suggested he say that to Stevenson face to face. Kennedy said he had already written a letter to Stevenson. Minow said, "You have to give him some tangible public evi-

dence. Why not invite him to the White House and then issue a statement?" Minow asked if Kennedy wanted him to do anything. Kennedy
said no, but Minow telephoned Stevenson anyway. Stevenson said, "I can't
talk, I'm on my way to NBC to do the 'Today' show," an early morning interview program on national TV. Minow said, "For Christ's sake, don't do
anything hasty—the President wants to solve this." Stevenson said, "I'm
mad." Minow said, "Don't do anything that's argumentative—try to keep
it on a high plane." Stevenson said he would. His performance on the
"Today" show was, Minow thought, "terrible." "From his [Stevenson's]
point of view it was good but it emphasized the rift with the Administration."

Kennedy was furious. He had grudgingly authorized Schlesinger to draft
a statement he might issue but now he burst out, "Those people in New
York must be crazy. Will you please call Clayton [Fritchey] and ask him
for me whether he has lost his fucking mind? Everything was beginning to
subside, and now Adlai has brought it all to life again. Worse than that, he
has changed it from a local New York-Washington story, of interest to a
few politicians and newspapermen, into a great national scandal. Millions
of people who had never heard about the attack on Adlai now know that
he is in trouble. Why the hell couldn't he have kept quiet?" Schlesinger
urged the statement again but Kennedy replied, "I don't want to issue a
statement. It will only give the newspapers something more, and keep the
whole thing going for a few more days." At this point Sorensen arrived
with the letter from Kennedy to Stevenson and it was decided that
Schlesinger should deliver it personally in New York. The letter said:

"This is just a note to tell you again how deeply I regret the unfortunate
fuss which has arisen over the statements contained in the *Saturday Evening Post* article. I think you know how greatly we have all admired your
performance at the United Nations in general and during the Security
Council debate and private negotiations connected with the Cuban crises
in particular. Both of us are accustomed to receiving the slings and arrows
of those in the press or elsewhere who delight in stirring needless controversy—and I know you share my confidence that this furor will pass as
have all the others.

"The fact that Charley Bartlett was a co-author of this piece has made
this particularly difficult for me—perhaps you have had the same problem
with personal friends in the newspaper profession. In this particular case, I
did not discuss the Cuban crisis or any of the events surrounding it with
any newspapermen—and I am certain that the quotations in the *Saturday
Evening Post* article with respect to your role did not come from the White
House, as is clear from its obvious inaccuracies alone. While I realized
when Bartlett started this piece that everything controversial in his article
would be laid at my door, whether I talked to him or not, I did not feel I
could tell him or any other friend in the press what subject to write or *not*
write about.

"However, both of us have much more important matters to concern us and the continued success and significance of your role at the UN will soon wash out any doubts others may be trying to plant."

When Schlesinger arrived in New York, Fritchey said that Salinger had called to say the White House had come around to the view that word of the Kennedy letter should be leaked to the press. Fritchey and Schlesinger re-examined it in that light. It was apparent that the newspapermen would demand that the text be released. It would be futile to release excerpts. Therefore, since the full text would have to be released, references in the letter to Bartlett would have to be deleted. They also decided to add a sentence saying, "Meanwhile, it goes without saying that you have my fullest confidence and my best wishes." They proposed this to Stevenson. He added another paragraph: "I have, of course, valued your advice very highly. That we have eliminated the nuclear menace from Cuba is the best evidence of the wisdom of our policy and its execution, in which you played such an active part." They then telephoned President Kennedy. He wanted to delete all references to the press and to make the letter a simple and strong affirmation of confidence in Stevenson. They rewrote and called him back. He felt the concluding paragraph was weak and dictated the strongest statement himself: ". . . and your continued work at the UN will be of inestimable value." He wanted to change "fuss" to "stir" and to substitute "prudence" for "wisdom," which he considered too self-serving.[13]

They telephoned the final text to Salinger, and Fritchey immediately began leaking word to the press of its existence, supposedly mailed from Washington the preceding afternoon and received in New York around noon today. Soon the letter was on the teletype, released in Washington by Salinger. Stevenson replied to the letter on December 8, thanking Kennedy for his letters and statements and saying they had "served to allay any misgivings among the people with whom I have to work."

Stevenson went to Washington with McCloy and Schlesinger next day and that night performed brilliantly as toastmaster at a dinner of the Joseph P. Kennedy Jr. Foundation. Sargent Shriver introduced Stevenson as "by common consent a great American," and the President led a standing ovation. A few nights later Stevenson and Marietta Tree went to a

---

[13] The final text read: "This is just a note to tell you again how deeply I regret the unfortunate stir which has arisen over the statements contained in the *Saturday Evening Post* article. I think you know how greatly we have all admired your performance at the UN in general and during the Security Council discussions and private negotiations connected with the Cuban crisis in particular. I have, of course, valued your advice very highly. That we have eliminated the nuclear menace from Cuba is the best evidence of the prudence of our policy and its execution, in which you played such an active part.

"Our government has many important challenges in the days ahead; and your continued work at the UN will be of inestimable value. Meanwhile, it goes without saying that you have my fullest confidence and best wishes."

concert at Constitution Hall, and, when they were about to take their places in the box traditionally occupied by the President and First Lady if they were present, the audience, including diplomats from some thirty-five nations, burst into applause.

To a friend who sent condolences, Stevenson wrote, "You were good to write me about this latest assault—which set a new record for malice and falsehood. But I'm such an old and battle-scarred veteran that I think I'll survive! And the President's indignation seems to exceed mine."

But he really was not battle-scarred or, if he was, the scar tissue made his skin no thicker than it had been when he was young. In this affair, as in others throughout his life, he seemed remarkably touchy for a politician. Oddly, he never mentioned the incident to Adlai III. He did not resign because, as he once told Beth Currie, "they have me over a barrel—if I quit now it will look as if Kennedy dumped me. Or it will look as if there were a split in the party or in policy. And if I do quit, there will be a split in the party."

Where Bartlett and Alsop got the story has never been made entirely clear. Guesses of their source have included Dean Acheson, Paul Nitze, McGeorge Bundy. Bundy thought they got the story "all over town." He said, "I saw them. A lot of other people did too." Schlesinger and nearly everybody else felt sure that President Kennedy had not given them the story. But Robert F. Kennedy once said, "I think it came from a conversation between President Kennedy and Bartlett. But the article was misinterpreted and out of context. What developed was not what was intended by President Kennedy. He was aghast at what developed. I'm sure he did talk to Bartlett—that he told him that Stevenson didn't behave very well—he might have said something that Bartlett talked to others about and put together. So he does bear some responsibility for this."

On December 22, Stevenson thanked Kennedy for a book about the White House and took occasion to say, "At the end of another year of your Administration, I want to say again that I have enjoyed my work rather more than I expected to, and my association with you fully as much as I expected to. I wish you well, and please command me for any service I can perform. I hope there will be time in the coming year for some more leisurely talks about the future and all of the problems that you confront and manage so wisely and gallantly. With best wishes to you and dear Jackie for the New Year."

President Kennedy had privately predicted several times that Stevenson would come out of the affair better than he. Schlesinger thought he might be right. Many people thought the President had been forced to repudiate an anti-Stevenson cabal within his own official family. And many thought that if Stevenson had, by his dovelike posture, helped save the peace, more power to him.

But the effect on Stevenson personally was serious. George Ball said, "After the Cuban missile crisis Adlai was only going through the motions.

His role had become ritualistic. From then on he knew he was not going to have an impact on foreign policy—which was what was most important to him. Washington was a force of its own and he was not part of it. He was a member of the Cabinet but not really. He'd call me up and say, 'I can't change anybody's view. The President is being misled and getting bad advice.' But he didn't think for a minute that anything he said was going to change anything. It was an unhappy life, certainly not his finest hour. I loved Adlai but by the time he died I felt he was almost a caricature of himself—a hollow man. He was going through the motions, making speeches, yet with a feeling in his heart that it didn't make any difference to the world if he fell over and had a heart attack. I found it unattractive and terribly sad. Why should he spend his time with Marietta Tree and Ruth Field and Mary Lasker? They gave him adulation—they gave him the best food in New York—he went to every first night—it was an unhealthy business. So then he finally fell over and died. Ten days before he died, he had lunch with Rusk. I joined them for coffee. I said to him 'Stevenson, you're so fat you're a slug.' He patted his stomach. Rusk was paying no attention to him that day. Adlai was a terribly unhappy man. History had passed him by. His life had passed him by. He had no place to go. He talked about leaving the UN but he had no place to go."

Although what Ball said contained truth, he was to some extent employing hyperbole. Stevenson probably realized much earlier, perhaps as early as the Bay of Pigs, that he would not exert decisive influence on much of policy. He continued to try, however. The defeatist mood that Ball was describing did not dominate until the last half year or so of his life.

36.

The mid-term congressional elections resulted in a Democratic victory. The Democrats gained four Senate seats and held their losses to four in the House. The New York *Times* regarded the election as evidence of national support for President Kennedy's Cuban policies.

Mrs. Roosevelt was dying. Stevenson went to her home to see her and bent over and spoke loving words to her with his lips close to her ear. In the husky breathy voice that was his in private, he asked if she had heard him and she said, "Yes, my dearest." He was deeply moved. He had always called her "Mrs. Roosevelt." She died, and he spoke in tribute to her at the UN:

"Yesterday I said I had lost more than a friend. I had lost an inspiration. She would rather light candles than curse the darkness, and her glow has warmed the world." He went to the funeral at Hyde Park, where under rainy skies she was buried in the rose garden beside her husband. Presidents Truman, Eisenhower, and Kennedy were there. Stevenson spoke a week later at a memorial service for her at the Cathedral of St.

John the Divine in New York City. He met with a small group in the White House to form a committee to promote the major interests to which she had devoted her life. It became the Eleanor Roosevelt Foundation, and from that time on, Stevenson spent great amounts of time and energy on it.

A new criticism broke out. Stevenson wrote a sharp letter to Senator Barry Goldwater and made it public. He said Goldwater had quoted him out of context when he said, "I am more concerned over a civilian like *Adlai Stevenson telling the United Nations that we are prepared to take 'risks' to lessen the chance of an intensified arms race with Russia* than I am about military men who regard the Soviets as an implacable foe which will never deal in honor." Stevenson said what he had said was this: "We have demonstrated again and again during long negotiations that we are prepared to take certain risks to lessen the chance of an intensified arms race. *But we are not prepared to risk our survival.* If other nations permit —as we have agreed to do—the degree of international inspection techni- cally required for mutual security, we can end the arms race. *But we can- not stake our national existence on blind trust—especially on blind trust in a great and powerful nation which repeatedly declares its fundamental hostility to the basic values of free society.*" Stevenson wrote to Gold- water, "I hope that as a United States Senator you feel some obligation to be accurate and responsible in your public statements, and I trust you will keep that in mind if you have occasion to refer to any speech of mine again." Goldwater replied with equal acerbity: Stevenson's further re- marks did "not in the least modify my concern."

37.

As the General Assembly moved to adjournment the Congo blew up again. The Kitona accord approved by Adoula and Tshombe a year earlier had never worked. U Thant's Plan for National Reconciliation could not be fully implemented—Adoula of the Central Government accepted it; Tshombe of Katanga refused. At the same time, military incidents in- creased and tensions mounted. By November 26, Stevenson was telling Rusk that the UN had now reached a point where it had its last chance to solve the Congo problem. An easy middle course was no longer possible; the UN must end Katangan secession or get out of the Congo.

On December 13, Cleveland drafted a memorandum in which he recom- mended building up the UN command militarily to a point where Tshombe would not dare challenge it. The UN had sufficient ground forces but needed more fighter planes. They might come from Sweden, Italy, Iran, or Ethiopia. But an American fighter unit would have to be put into the Congo, too, and it should remain under United States command.

The White House moved into control of Congo policy. The debate centered around whether the United States should put a fighter squadron of its own into the Congo. It was a hard decision. Stevenson, after some hesitation, advocated using the squadron, manned by American pilots, against Tshombe. Mennen Williams and Chet Bowles agreed.

At this point aircraft became crucial. Swedish planes, virtually the only ones available to the UN command, threatened to pull out. Ball and Williams and Kaysen, who had been holding back on support for the UN, swung around to the offer of the U.S. fighter squadron.

On December 15, a Saturday, Stevenson saw Thant, told him the United States thought the time had come to act decisively to end the Katangan secession, and suggested that if a U.S. fighter contingent was put into the Congo Tshombe would realize that a great power was backing the UN and that resistance was useless. Thant expressed his thanks for this "magnificent, historic and epochal" gesture by the United States. He could not, however, accept the offer without approval of the Security Council—and the U.S.S.R. would never agree. The circumstances would be quite different if Adoula "asked" for the U.S. military unit. Thant wanted the United States to give him a memorandum on the nature and purpose of the U.S. force and its relationship to the UN command and he, in turn, would draft a letter for Adoula to send.

Stevenson took this proposal to the President and the Ex-Comm on the Congo. Kennedy approved Thant's plan and authorized sending a military mission to the Congo immediately to determine the UN's needs. That mission, publicly announced, was headed by Lieutenant General L. W. Truman.

On Saturday, December 22, Stevenson went home to Libertyville for the Christmas holidays with old friends. He received a long letter from Albert Schweitzer defending the Katangan secession and calling General Truman's mission incredible.

On the night of December 27–28 the heaviest fighting in more than a year broke out in the Congo at Elisabethville. Most of the firing came from the Katangese troops. Tshombe agreed to halt it but early in the morning it became heavier—and Tshombe remained unwilling or unable to stop the shooting. In the afternoon on December 28 the UN attacked, moving to clear the road blocks and restore its own freedom of movement. By the end of the day the Katangan gendarmerie were in full flight and the UN troops were trying to reassure the populace.

Little was known about the situation in the Congo. It often took twenty-four hours or longer to get a telegram out. The American consul at Elisabethville had to go out and look around, then report on what was going on to the embassy in Leopoldville. Leopoldville would cable the State Department in Washington. The Department would cable the Mission in New York, and it would tell Thant what his army was doing. By now, Kaysen and others were irritated at the whole preposterous situation.

They were also a little irritated at Stevenson—"we thought he ought to tell U Thant that he was running a war," Kaysen said.

The UN command, however, was reacting strongly. It ordered an air strike against the Katanga planes and airfields, and Swedish Saabs destroyed three planes on the ground and set fuel stores burning at Kolwezi. UN troops seemed to be pushing on beyond Elisabethville. For a year Tshombe had held the world at bay but now his bluff was being called. In Washington on Saturday, Secretary Rusk, with Stevenson on an extension telephone, called Ralph Bunche at the UN in New York. (Bunche had been handling the Congo for U Thant for some time.) Rusk asked if the UN was sure its commanders understood their mission. It was not to annihilate Tshombe and his government. Its political objectives were reconciliation and reintegration of Katanga into the Congo. Rusk feared Tshombe might misunderstand and think he was in a trap from which there was no escape. Bunche said Thant planned to issue a statement, probably on Monday, on the UN's political objectives. Stevenson said he would like to talk to Thant before he issued it. Rusk said the UN, as a peace-keeping instrumentality, should let it be known as soon as possible that its objective was peace.

Stevenson caught a morning plane that Sunday, December 30, to New York. That day UN troops entered Kipushi, twenty-five miles outside Elisabethville, and small UN units patrolled ten to fifteen miles out of Elisabethville on the road to Jadotville, moves beyond the force's mandate. The UN in New York demanded an explanation of its forces in the field. Stevenson saw Bunche. He said UN forces had not been authorized to enter Kipushi nor did the UN plan to move to Jadotville. Bunche said the first phase was over. Thant now would try again to implement his Reconciliation Plan. If it made no progress with Tshombe in about two weeks, UN troops would march on Jadotville and Kolwezi. The UN command was under orders not to undertake further military moves without approval from New York. Stevenson asked if this meant there would be no further air attacks by the UN. Bunche said apparently there were no more targets.

It was New Year's Eve. Stevenson sent a longhand note to Marietta Tree: "Called back to Wash—now N.Y.—and oh so cold. *Happiest* New Year from all your admirers at USUN, including The Boss!"

Once more, communication between the UN and its force in the Congo broke down. The UN troops reached the Lufira River a few miles outside Jadotville and, finding a bridge span intact and resistance slight, put a small group across it. Unaware of the troops' position, the UN in New York issued an order to halt at the Lufira. This order was received in the early evening. Since night had fallen, it would have been risky to undertake a night withdrawal under fire. Accordingly, though it meant exceeding instructions, the men holding the bridgehead had to move ahead and clean out the sole remaining pocket of Katangan resistance. They did and, on January 3, UN troops entered Jadotville unopposed, with the assistance of the Mayor and local officials. Thant was embarrassed—but of a sudden Katangan secession had ended. The United States Government issued a statement emphasizing the UN's peaceful purposes and Rusk privately scolded Thant for letting his troops get out of hand. But Stevenson's own comments were almost exultant and rhapsodic as he congratulated all hands on the Congo victory. New Year's Eve, Stevenson took Newt and Jo Minow and Francis Plimpton's young daughter Sarah to see a movie, *Lawrence of Arabia.*

38.

Almost everything at the UN—and sometimes more—came to Stevenson. He received appeals for help from refugees. Such requests were usually dropped into the maw of the State Department bureaucracy, though occasionally Stevenson involved himself. The New York *Journal-American* published a series of sensational stories about a "ring of international call girls operating in and out of the UN," as Stevenson put it in a letter to Secretary Rusk; the Mission asked the FBI to investigate. British Guiana requested a technical mission from the UN composed only of Soviet bloc experts to investigate its bauxite resources; R. S. Reynolds, of the Reynolds Company, called it to Stevenson's attention. A Jewish leader, backed by Senator Javits, told Stevenson a Mission officer had said at a briefing that the Mission's work was complicated by the presence in the United States of "this important Jewish vote" and some Zionists who were "almost more Zionist than American"; Stevenson arranged to meet with the Jewish leader. U Thant and other UN diplomats requested autographed photographs of President Kennedy, and Stevenson forwarded their requests. The New York *Daily News* earlier had published a story about a traffic jam caused by the car of the chief of state of the Cameroon. The Cameroon Ambassador protested strongly to Stevenson against the "unfriendly intentions" and "absolutely discourteous" attitude of the *News* toward the Cameroon; he sent Stevenson a letter to the editor of the *News* and asked Stevenson to "intervene" and have it published "in the same place and position."

Ambassador Zorin of the U.S.S.R. was leaving. Stevenson wrote to him: "I deeply regret that I have not had an opportunity to call upon you and Madame Zorin to bid you farewell. Our service here together for the past two years has given me a warm respect for your powers of advocacy and presentation, and great admiration for your tireless representation of your country." A member of the Soviet delegation died, and Stevenson expressed his sympathy in a speech. He was always, or nearly always, courteous, even courtly at times. He sent a long letter, prepared by his staff, to a State Representative in Illinois, enumerating the UN's achievements, for use against those in Illinois who wanted to forbid flying the UN flag on public buildings. During a cabinet meeting Robert Kennedy asked Stevenson for a list of useful acquaintances in Alabama; Stevenson promised to furnish it. Robert Kennedy pushed the appointment of a Negro to the Mission, and Stevenson agreed. A columnist for the *Amsterdam News,* a Negro newspaper, wrote that Stevenson belonged to the River Club which, he said, forbade Negro guests. Clayton Fritchey wrote a long protest to the editor. Congressman Adam Clayton Powell delivered an irresponsible speech saying Stevenson had refused to hire Negroes at the Mission and, when forced to do so by the White House, had insisted they be light-skinned. Stevenson, denying the report, added that the White House had not put any pressure on him. The next day President Kennedy said to Schlesinger, "I don't see why Adlai had to put in that bit about the White House not having brought pressure to hire Negroes. We've been doing that everywhere." Subsequently Stevenson said irritably, "I was disappointed that the White House did not issue a statement."

Lou Kohn, Stevenson's old friend and original supporter in Illinois, had a severe cerebral hemorrhage which crippled him. Stevenson went to see him. Don Forsyth of Springfield was going to Portugal and Spain, and at his request Stevenson wrote letters of introduction to Spain, saying his recommendations in Lisbon would be self-defeating because of his position on Angola. Ed McDougal and his wife were going to Scotland, and Stevenson asked Ambassador Bruce in London to include them in whatever "royal revelry" might be taking place in Edinburgh. Ronald Tree asked Stevenson if he could bring to the attention of the Reynolds brothers the fact that Reynolds Metals of Jamaica had pledged $30,000 a year for five years to the University College of the West Indies but had not kept its pledge. Stevenson did.

He asked former President Eisenhower to be an honorary trustee of the Eleanor Roosevelt Foundation, and Eisenhower declined. Agnes Meyer would give a big dinner for Ambassador Dobrynin and in a lengthy correspondence consulted Stevenson about the guest list. She wanted him near, too, because the emotional condition of her son-in-law, Phil Graham, was deteriorating. Stevenson, fond of him and his wife Kay and their daughter Lally as well as of Kay's mother, Agnes Meyer, offered to help in any way he could. (Graham later committed suicide.)

39.

Stevenson's relations with President Kennedy and his Administration and the Congress continued to be uneasy. Stevenson told Secretary Rusk that U Thant and some of his senior officers were becoming "increasingly sensitive" about any suggestion that what they did was unduly influenced by the United States. At about this time Stevenson made notes for himself:

"Too much pressure on SYG [Secretary General]. Counterproductive. . . . Too many Pres. letters. Getting a little manic." Fred Dutton worked hard to bring Stevenson together with congressional leaders, with mixed results. Stevenson was photographed with Mrs. Joseph P. Kennedy at a Mission reception and sent her a note and received a gracious reply. Stevenson saw Kennedy half a dozen times in the first half of 1963. Kennedy contributed a preface to a new collection of Stevenson speeches and papers, *Looking Outward.*

Stevenson wrote to Barbara Ward early in 1963, "I sometimes despair of ever getting on top of it all and finding a moment for rest and reflection." It was an old complaint but had a new depth of despair. A Gallup poll showed that people overwhelmingly approved of his work at the UN, but he marked the percentage of disapproval (11 per cent nationwide, 6 per cent among Democrats). He told his friend Beth Currie he did not expect fair treatment by historians—"history is not noted for being kind to the losers." Theodore White, the journalist, saw him several times at large official parties at 42A. "He had a melancholy air. His loneliness impressed me. There was never a moment when we could sit down quietly and contemplate." The members of small missions and newspapermen complained that Stevenson did not go to enough diplomatic receptions, luncheons, and dinners. He did as much as he could, probably more than he should. He was sixty-three. Richard Gardner observed, "By 1963 he would go to sleep at three or four in the afternoon. He slowed down a lot. He couldn't give to the job the total discipline that's needed. He would go into meetings half prepared and relying on the Stevenson charm. We never could be sure he would get it right. I sensed a lack of confidence—maybe the marriage, the two campaigns. Maybe this was why he was a less good negotiator than some people. [Arthur] Goldberg is dogmatic and argumentative. Stevenson was not. Also there was a lack of personal discipline in running his life. In organizing his time. Too often he was pushed by the flow of events. If a phone call happened to come in, that determined how the next hour was going to be spent. JFK loved detail—for example, on Chinese representation, how the two-third vote works, and so forth. But Stevenson was not interested in details. If it could be certified as liberal or helping world order, then it was all right—he didn't probe too deep into the substance."

Those closest to him noted an extreme fatigue. Adlai III: "He did more grumbling. He slowed down. Sometimes he fell asleep at cocktail parties. I have seen him literally staggering with fatigue late in the evening, clutching at chairs and walls and tables. Borden saw this and we talked about it. Dad always got very upset because Borden would never come around to see him in New York. Borden says he would go and Dad wouldn't be there. Dad used to fret about it. He tried endless ways to get him jobs. He could never understand that this was not something where reason could prevail. The only thing he could do was leave him alone—and he didn't understand that. The idea of doing nothing jarred his old-fashioned notions. On trips that he used to take, Dad would be up at the crack of dawn to go to the market or climb the nearest mountain—Borden wouldn't get out of bed."

For several months toward the end of Stevenson's life, Borden lived in one of the guest rooms of the Waldorf suite 42A, called Apartment 42F. Borden once said, "He killed himself going to all these parties. He'd come home to Apartment F to see me and we'd sit down with a drink. I could almost time it when he would conk out. He wanted desperately to talk. We would chat just about things in general. I tried to keep him talking about things of the day that he was interested in. And I could almost time it when his glass would fall down on the rug. Then Viola would come in and cart him off or I'd wake him up and walk him back to bed. It was total exhaustion. He wanted to sleep but he was so wound up that he couldn't sleep. But the old piston would finally give up and he would go to bed. In the last year when I lived up there I thought I learned what he was all about. He'd never opened up to me before. I guess I never did anything much until after he died. Then I felt somewhat free."

One reason Stevenson seemed so fatigued was his travel. During 1963 he traveled incessantly, almost compulsively. He made twenty-four trips to Washington, ten to Chicago and Libertyville, three to Europe, one to Antigua (to visit the Archibald MacLeishes), one to Desbarats (to visit the Dutch Smiths), one to Vancouver (to receive an honorary degree), two to the West Coast, one to Dallas, and more. Sometimes he would arrive home one evening and leave early next morning on another trip, home only long enough to repack. Often he went back and forth to Washington in a day, on the shuttle. While in New York his evenings were hopelessly crowded. Some of the travel, and some of the parties, were official and inescapable. But much of it was not.

It probably was of 1963, and perhaps the later years too, that George Ball was thinking when he once said, "Toward the end he sort of went to seed."

By 1963, Stevenson had become more interested in his own pleasure and comfort, less interested in his work. Too, 1963 was not a big exciting year at the UN, as 1961 and 1962 had been; there were no Cubas, no Bays of Pigs, no Congos.

The problem of Ellen, his former wife, grew worse. Ellen had received $5,000 from her Aunt Lucy's estate. She had bills totaling more than $10,000 and asked her mother, Mrs. Carpenter, for a loan of $15,000. Adlai III paid a $920 debt. Stevenson told her aunt, Mary Spears, "Things have not been well with Ellen at all lately, and we are all confronted now with contriving some means of getting her on a tolerable living standard, and then providing the standard." Ellen told her mother that her estate had decreased by half under Stevenson's management during their marriage. Once Ellen visited Adlai III and, he was obliged to testify, "started accusing me of having stolen papers from her, and my brothers having stolen papers from her, of my father having swindled her out of his home in Libertyville, of trying to destroy her and to take her property from her." Stevenson told Barbara Ward, "Things with Ellen have deteriorated and the situation becomes more acute and difficult for all concerned. Perhaps we are approaching a climax which may lead to court proceedings." Dutch Smith was advising Adlai III about his mother. Stevenson made more than one trip to Chicago about the problem. He considered asking a court to appoint a conservator to manage her financial affairs, a course subsequently adopted. (Without a conservator, he feared, she would squander the support he provided.) He told Dutch Smith, "I rather feel that the most important thing for me now is to try to help make life tolerable for the boys." Stevenson thought about the problem a great deal that spring and summer, mentioning it to various people.

Bill Benton was planning another summer yacht cruise. Stevenson declined to go. He feared he might lose Yost for financial reasons—the cost of living in New York—and talked to Benton about supplementing Yost's pay with $3,000. Benton, who was in Europe, responded with a check. A little later a newspaper story said Yost was being appointed Ambassador to Yugoslavia. The fact is that Kennedy did offer Yost the embassy in Yugoslavia, but Stevenson asked Yost to stay with him, and Yost did, to Kennedy's surprise and irritation.

On January 4, Jane Dick sent Stevenson a memorandum labeled "CONFIDENTIAL AND IMPORTANT—in fact, *urgent.*" She wrote, "I have now served for two years as Representative on the [Social] Commission. I believe it absolutely imperative that I finally have an interview with you *as soon as possible.*" She renewed her request on January 26, asking for the evening before his birthday party. In May she sent him a memorandum, "Is there *any* way I can get you to set up the meetings which you suggested, and which I consider absolutely *essential,* between you, Harlan, Dick Gardner and me? . . . It is quite impossible for me or anyone to do an effective job as your representative under the circumstances currently prevailing in the State Department and the Mission!" Stevenson finally arranged the meeting at the Department and thought it useful.

He wrote to Alicia Patterson, describing the Gridiron dinner and a dance at the White House, "a fine collection of lovely doves and assorted gentlemen, including a few older ones who managed to get home by 3 A.M. Yes, each trip to Washington makes me feel more like a benign old man!"

Jacqueline Kennedy visited New York and Stevenson gave a party for her on February 3. Afterward Mrs. Kennedy sent him a long affectionate letter: "How could I ever thank you for the gayest, happiest evening imaginable—I would rather have the memory of it than anything I can think of. You know you spoiled everyone who was there—for everytime they go out after this it will be a big sad anticlimax." She sent him a sketch she had done.

(Stevenson wrote in bold longhand "Mrs. John Kennedy" below her scrawled "Jackie.") He took her and her sister Princess Radziwill to lunch at the UN. She sent him a birthday letter and called the lunch "really fascinating." She wrote:

Lee, that fickle creature, came there adoring the Greek Ambassador and left in love with Dr. Bunche! I was so lucky to have that chance to meet U Thant—and I loved him. But I'm not fickle—so it is to you that I send all my thanks and love for making possible the two high points of my week in New York—(or of any other week I can ever remember). . . .

love

Jackie

Stevenson responded: "Thank you for your dear note, and for all that you did for my Mission, and for better relations with the whole cockeyed world! When things get bad again—please come again. Indeed, please come again and again whether things get bad or not!" Stevenson went to a party at the White House March 8 and sat next to Mrs. Kennedy and later wrote:

I've been trying to think if I ever a) had a better time, b) saw a lovelier party, and c) ever had a better seat at dinner. While I'm loathe to make such boyish confessions, the answer in each case is NO!—and especially item c)—a shock from which I hope *never* to recover. Thanks, blessings—and love ever—

Adlai

40.

Stevenson saw Marietta Tree frequently. Many times he wrote at the bottom of his daily schedule sheet, below a dinner appointment, "MT after." When one or the other of them was away he wrote to her. It was to Marietta more than to others that he expressed his inner feelings during this period, as, earlier, he had to Alicia Patterson. On a Saturday night, February 16, "very late," he noted, he wrote to Marietta from Libertyville, which she had apparently just left. He was alone. The house was still. His dog Merlin was asleep on the rug by the step leading to the front door. He wished he could sit still but could not, he kept walking around the house, fingering the cans in the kitchen cupboard. He had made his own supper —pea soup, swiss cheese, toast, bourbon; breakfast would be nearly the same, orange sections, swiss cheese, toast, though no bourbon. He kept listening to her ghost. He thought to play a record of his own eulogy to Mrs. Roosevelt on the phonograph but if he did he would weep. And there was a speech to write for the Council on Foreign Relations, and he had to get at

it, because tomorrow the children would arrive and so would applicants
for the farmer's job. He had been busy last week—with Benton and others
to dine and hear Lena Horne and hear recitations by Basil Rathbone; he
had gone to Washington to see the President, had gone to Princeton to receive a Woodrow Wilson Award and $1,000; but it all meant little, and to-
night for him alone "this wistful house . . . buzzes with silence." There
had been a time long ago when he liked solitude, lonely work, reflection.
No more—it made him feel unsafe, insecure, and insecurity in the heart
should be reserved for the young and resilient. He wrote awhile to her,
and after a time thought he could go to sleep. She could always sleep, a
blessing; he could not, perhaps because of inner conflicts, strivings, he
thought. So he went off to bed wearing Nkrumah's toga. In the morning,
feeling better, he added a postscript: "Sunday AM—Refreshed—slept.
Maudlin self pity and worry down—self confidence up. So to work!" That
was Stevenson alone.

On March 3, a Sunday, he wrote a note to Marietta from outside New
York: "M—welcome—and how! I am at Jock Whitney's [John Hay
Whitney] in the country for lunch and should be back in 42A by 4:00.
Viola is away for the week-end. Please call me as soon as you can. . . . If
you have your key and just come and wait it would be even better and
perhaps save a few minutes that get more precious daily."

March 10, on the Washington shuttle, he wrote a long better to "M."
(Strikingly, he addressed her by the initial of her first name as he had
addressed Alicia Patterson "E.") He described a White House dinner
dance at which President Kennedy had called on him to speak and the
Gridiron dinner "of (spurious) good fellowship, poor skits and splendid
speeches—[George] Romney was good; Hubert terrific and Kennedy
very relaxed, witty and for the first time master of the scene. . . . Felt
very much like a respected, indeed beloved, and amiable elder statesman.
Horrors!" He described the next day's parties and receptions and said,
"The evening concluded with the *best of all!* Mary McGrory's. It was like
an underground meeting of the IRA, and I laughed to the danger point. It
all started when she told me she had gone to a German hairdresser and
asked for some blond streaks in her muddy hair. Instead she came out
with some brown streaks in blond head! So when I arrived en route to airport with bag and baggage—the dizzy blonde shouted put 'im in the bedroom and lock the door,' and the evening was off! And so was I at 9:30 to
get the 10 shuttle. . . ."

In June he sent Marietta another long letter describing his activities—
crises at the UN, a speech in Memphis picketed by members of the John
Birch Society, a trip to Libertyville. He left his briefcase on the plane—
contrary to regulations, he often carried classified documents in it. "Emergency return to N.Y. Sunday afternoon for S.C. meeting on Yemen,
demanded by the Russians. Monday—frantic negotiating—lunch with
Pres. of India and dinner party at 42A for Willy Brandt went well. . . .

Tues Off to Boston on a 6 P.M. shuttle. Dinner with Smiths, Adele and large group of young faculty in bare little house decorated only by wit, intellect and dreary food—but well warmed by passionate supporters. . . . Brief appearance at [someone's] party for her daughter. Wed—rain!—ceremony in Sanders theatre and great success with speech (enclosed) followed by trustees lunch and talk with Schlesinger, Sr.—deeply anxious about Arthur and Marion and pleading tearfully for help." (The junior Schlesingers were subsequently divorced.) There was more, much more—visits to friends, an appearance at a wedding reception of a friend's daughter, a call on the Governor of Massachusetts (Marietta's brother), "hilarious" overnight with other friends, a lecture at the Naval War College, back to New York by Navy plane, where he went to a theatrical opening. ("But why Burton! And why! ah why! Elizabeth Taylor. But she does have *two* assets and uses them both effectively and continuously.") It was all frantic. He was writing to her every few days.

Early that year, while Marietta was in Barbados, Stevenson wrote to her daughter by a previous marriage, Frances FitzGerald, in Paris. Addressing her "Frankie darling," he said he was going to Paris soon "to inspect the winter's ravages, your progress in wine tasting, literature and boulevard beating. . . . Perhaps we can arrange the details in the Ritz bar." A little later he wrote again, asking her to "save Friday evening, March 22," for him: "I hope you are not off skiing or wine-tasting with some golden boys, and will have a moment to exhibit your apartment, report on your work, your writings and state of heart and mind."

41.

This year Sarah Plimpton wrote to Stevenson often. She was living in Paris, writing a novel, and she sent Stevenson a letter nearly every week. Her letters began a few days after she spent New Year's Eve with him and the Minows at the end of 1962. She was, as Stevenson had told her, something of a rebel. Her letters had a funny and fey quality, not unlike those of his wife long ago; they were young and gay, filled with imagery. On February 19, at about the time Stevenson was suggesting to Miss Fitz-Gerald that they meet in the Ritz bar in Paris, Sarah wrote again, saying that she and her friends in Paris were trying to free Frankie FitzGerald from the conscience that drove her to work constantly. (Evidently they did not succeed: Miss FitzGerald later wrote a book, *Fire in the Lake,* that won a Pulitzer prize.) Stevenson told Sarah he was coming to Paris; she was excited and would meet him anywhere—the Tuileries, the Louvre, the Eiffel Tower, even her room, which she might even straighten up in honor of his visit.

He did see her when he was in Europe in March and April, and she wrote later declaring that he was always in her thoughts whether she was

going to church or taking a bath or looking at a manuscript. She wrote of
Visigoths in Spain, visions of the planes bombing Guernica, sherry casks
and suede coats and bathtubs with clawed feet—and, always, Stevenson.
She sent him a quotation from Nietzsche about love. (Stevenson sent it to
Marietta Tree a little later, misspelling Nietzsche, not saying where he had
got it.) Sarah said she suspected his eager middle-aged lady friends and
was inventing imaginary fates for them. At times she seemed to have been
in love with him, or in love with the idea of being in love with him, and a
few times mentioned marriage, though she seemed to think it unlikely or
even impossible. Once she asked how long he would be in Europe and
whether he would be traveling with companions. He would, as always: she
could not have him to herself any more than others could. Her later letters
continued in their imaginative free-form style and, though Stevenson once
said ungallantly to a friend he could not make head or tail of what she
wrote, he enjoyed them. Sarah Plimpton did not write to him about public
questions; she wrote only of private feelings.

Once more, it is impossible to know precisely the depth of feeling implied by a generous and affectionate exchange of letters and visits.

42.

Preparations for Stevenson's spring trip to Europe occupied a good deal
of his time during the first few months of 1963. He had originally been invited to address the NATO War College in Paris on March 25 but his
itinerary blossomed because of diplomatic needs and his own pleasure. Instead of arranging his trip through the State Department, Stevenson was
making his own arrangements, either directly with U. S. Ambassadors in
Europe or through the UN delegations. This troubled career diplomats. In
England, Stevenson wanted to make a major speech in the Midlands, but
career diplomats opposed, and the speech did not come off—the career
officers could neither find nor devise a suitable occasion. Schlesinger opposed Stevenson's going to Spain, fearing it would be taken as an endorsement of the Franco regime and would dishearten Franco's opposition, and
Cleveland and Carl Kaysen agreed, and even Secretary Rusk demurred,
but Stevenson went to Spain anyway, because he wanted to.

At this time General de Gaulle was undertaking to lead France to nuclear, economic, and political independence. This entailed preventing
Great Britain from entering the European Common Market and rejecting
the United States' proposal of a multilateral nuclear force (MLF). President Kennedy was interested in Stevenson's exploring the prospects for
both the European Common Market and the MLF with European leaders.
This became the primary purpose of Stevenson's trip. Stevenson's mission
was not of paramount importance—indeed, McGeorge Bundy hardly
knew about it, and Schlesinger once described it as part of Kennedy's pro-

gram of keeping people busy and happy by sending them on trips—but Harlan Cleveland considered it important, and the Department produced a mass of briefing papers for Stevenson.

Before going Stevenson wrote a long memorandum for President Kennedy and Secretary Rusk on the future of NATO. He recalled that NATO, established in 1949–50 under the impact of the Berlin blockade and Korea, had in the past had as its primary objective military security. Today the question arose whether its emphasis should not shift to the political and economic. Studies were now under way to determine whether the MLF within the NATO framework was desirable and feasible. If so, NATO's military role would be renewed. If not, it would decline. De Gaulle had just thrown serious obstacles in the way of European economic and political unification. A determined U.S. drive to give NATO more political content would both strengthen the Atlantic community and turn De Gaulle's flank by building around him a growing structure of European unity which he could neither dominate nor ignore.

Thus Stevenson opposed MLF and favored what he regarded as a political solution. At that time the Administration was pro-MLF. A few months later Kennedy began to view MLF with great reserve. Later, in 1964, the Johnson administration made a halfhearted effort to establish MLF and failed. Schlesinger's opinion is that, although Stevenson's proposal may have been wiser, it was too general and was irrelevant to what was up for decision at the time. "A lot of Stevenson's things came in too early or too late. They did not dovetail with what was being decided. Seventy per cent of this problem was a function of simply not being in the room. Thirty per cent was the problem that, even when he was in the room, Stevenson was not quite putting a legitimate point in a framework that would relate to the machine of government. He was almost always right and Rusk wrong. But he spoke generally and sentimentally. Stevenson had against him the whole apparatus of the Department of State, except for Harlan Cleveland intermittently. Stevenson did understand that Rusk was his great enemy in government. He told me so. But I was never sure whether he said it because he knew of my differences with Rusk."

Stevenson left New York on March 20 and returned on April 14. He visited Paris, London, Brussels, Bonn, Berlin, Madrid, Rabat, Marrakech, Fez, and Seville. Everywhere, he was entertained; everywhere, he met political and diplomatic leaders. He delivered arrival and departure statements in various countries, held press conferences, addressed the Berlin House of Representatives, had drinks with British editors, saw numerous correspondents, and visited the Berlin wall.

He cabled home accounts of his talks with European leaders as he had them, and at the end sent a long summary report to President Kennedy. He thought that, while not much had yet come of efforts to move the Common Market forward in the face of De Gaulle's opposition, it would succeed in the long run. He thought France's separatism and England's failure to join the Common Market unfortunate and unrealistic. He himself would have preferred a non-proliferation agreement with the Russians to MLF but "with much hesitation" concluded that the MLF effort was useful for now. As always, he opposed isolationism—whether European or American—and favored increasing internationalism. "Anything that leads us backwards to the old tribalisms leads us back to war." Stevenson was always interested in the long term.

The trip was not all official business; it was in part a lark. He dined with Frankie FitzGerald. He saw Sarah Plimpton. He saw Ava Gardner, a guest in Madrid of the rich Ricardo Sicres. An Air Force plane took him to Rabat, Morocco, and he went sightseeing in the Medina, and King Hassan's plane took him to Marrakech and on to Fez and entertainment by belly dancers provided by the Minister of Tourism—"three terrifying belly dancers," says Marietta Tree, who was with him. "I was so embarrassed. Adlai thought it was funny. He was not nearly as shocked as I had hoped he'd be. Then we had a banquet and a lunch. We had nine courses at lunch that day, and the Gov ate every one, including snails in consomme." Back in Spain at Jerez de la Frontera, they visited *bodegas* and sniffed sherry four hundred years old. Marietta recalled, "At Jerez de la Frontera we went out to a pig-sticking contest. The Gov was very brave and got on a horse but nothing happened except that the poor little pig came out of the bushes and then went back in." They returned to Seville and went to a private bullfight and watched flamenco dancers—"all for me," he wrote.

43.

Stevenson's speeches that year were of uneven quality. He went home to Chicago and addressed the fortieth-anniversary lunch of the Chicago Council on Foreign Relations, his old home base: "But the room is full of ghosts and I mourn the many familiar faces and co-workers who are no longer with us. I've always thought of the Council as my introduction to public life. Certainly I must have fallen in love with my own voice here." He expanded on the theme of the UN's utility in a statement to a subcommittee of the Senate Foreign Relations Committee—he argued powerfully for the UN. On the other hand, his speech to the OAS was disappointing, filled with bureaucratic platitudes. Many of his speeches used old themes running far back in his life—the UN was essential, political dialogue should educate the people. He received several awards. Everywhere he went, including to Memphis to dedicate the airport, he preached the UN gospel. Because of his prominence, Adlai Stevenson presented the State Department with more problems than most Ambassadors—Harlan Cleveland knew Stevenson would be interviewed by the local press and therefore had to prepare briefing papers for him.

44.

The issues of apartheid in South Africa and self-determination for the Portuguese colonies were coming to the fore again. On June 12, Mennen Williams wrote a memorandum for Secretary Rusk saying the time had come when the United States could no longer merely condemn apartheid but must take "a more vigorous stand" with "meaningful action."

On the other hand, U. Alexis Johnson said in a memorandum to Secretary Rusk, "Much as we disapprove of . . . apartheid . . . I suggest that it is important we also take into consideration the following factors before moving toward a full embargo on the supply of arms to South Africa"— South Africa was "friendly and cooperative with us" in port and dock facilities, landing rights, seismographic and missile tracking stations. Earlier, Secretary Rusk had given the President a memorandum recommending an indication of U.S. willingness to sell two or three conventional submarines to South Africa.

Thus, as it had been before on Angola, the Department was split, with the African Bureau favoring stronger measures against apartheid and others resisting. On June 15, Secretary Rusk decided. In a memorandum, Rusk said that the heart of the matter was the question of how we related to countries whose internal practices were repugnant to us. In general, the United States should use its influence steadily and persistently in the direction of the principles of the UN Charter as well as our own basic commitments to human rights and constitutional processes. But it was "another question" to extend that influence into the field of an arms embargo of South Africa, as some urged. We had "the strongest objections" to apartheid. We had said so repeatedly. But there were other states where "obnoxious" practices existed, including Bulgaria, Burma, China, Czechoslovakia, Ghana, Haiti, Hungary, Indonesia, Korea, Laos, Paraguay, Poland, Portugal, Romania, Saudi Arabia, South Africa, Spain, Turkey, U.S.S.R., U.A.R., Vietnam, Yugoslavia, and various small African and Arab states. Should we precipitate sharp crises with them or try to work toward the decent world community we wanted? "I will admit that apartheid presents a case of unusual difficulty, but I would not put it ahead of violation of human rights within the Communist bloc." Rusk would "draw a sharp distinction" between our concern over racial discrimination inside the United States and the way we "crusade" on that issue abroad. "The United States is *our* responsibility. . . . But . . . we are not the self-elected gendarmes for the political and social problems of other states."

Stevenson saw the matter differently. In a memo to the President on June 26 he said that African leaders were calling on us to choose between

Africa and European colonial powers. They were critical of our own racial policies. Increasingly they were demanding sanctions against and expulsion of South Africa from the UN. In the Security Council they would present a resolution for far-reaching sanctions against Portugal and South Africa; we would oppose because we did not believe it in accord with the Charter; and the ire of the Africans would shift from Portugal and South Africa to us. What to do? "The minimum answer I can see is for us to support, in the Council, resolutions which would contain (a) 'condemnation' of their policies, (b) 'recommendations' against arms supplies that could be used to enforce those policies, and (c) provisions for a 'meaningful' United Nations function." The nature of the "meaningful" UN function was not yet clear. Africans wanted to know whether, in a showdown, we would stand for self-determination and human rights and "the mind of Africa" or for our Azores base and our missile tracking stations in South Africa. "It seems to me that when such risks must be faced—and I fear they will have to be faced this summer—your decisions should favor our future relations with the people of Africa."

So saying, Stevenson on June 30 went back to Europe.

45.

He told the President he would return July 25. The Security Council probably would meet about July 22. If there were things to be done in Europe, he could stay longer. If the Security Council met sooner, he could return. Why did he go to Europe at this juncture, with a critical confrontation looming? He had two official purposes: his annual address to ECOSOC in Geneva, and meetings in Paris with Finletter and other NATO Ambassadors on Portugal. Actually, it was more of a vacation trip with Marietta and others than anything else. McGeorge Bundy, commenting on George Ball's remark that Stevenson had "gone to seed" in his last years, once said, "He was fat, we thought. And he was always in a hurry to get away from the meeting. I do think that, except when he was on stage, he did not have the United States Government on the top of his mind towards the end."

Stevenson was not due to speak at ECOSOC in Geneva until July 12 but he left for Paris on June 30, intending to stay at the Ritz until July 4 or 5. As usual he had planned carefully and privately—asked again for the Aga Khan's chalet at Gstaad for a weekend ("I have the telephone number at the villa, and if I don't hear from you I will call the servants after I get to the Hotel des Bergues in Geneva"), given Ambassador Bohlen his arrival time in Paris and asked if a car could meet him at the airport, arranged to be taken to visit the Plimptons at Villa Balbianello and Mrs. Ives in Florence. He had told Sarah Plimpton he was coming, and she asked if she should meet him at the airport or would there be others there with an official car?

The trip began badly: because of a strike at Orly, his plane could not land in Paris and was diverted to Brussels, whence he had to take a train to Paris on July 1. He worked at the embassy and at a Development Assistance Committee meeting that day. On July 3, Jane Dick and Ruth Field telephoned him separately from America: Alicia Patterson had died the night before.

Stevenson sent a telegram to her husband, Harry Guggenheim:

She was my oldest dearest friend. Returning if possible. Deepest sympathy. Adlai.

He did not go to the funeral. Jane Dick sent him a long report on it. She described the flowers (including some she had sent in his name), the overflowing cathedral, the crowd, and the Episcopal service: "I also found it hard to pray that she should 'rest among His saints.' But when the ritual ended and the organ peeled out the Battle Hymn of the Republic it was all Alicia!" She wished he could have shared "in these moments of deeply loving tribute and farewell to her."

Stevenson replied to "My dear Jane": "I have read and re-read your letter about the funeral. Somehow, in a few words, you have brought the whole thing to life. It sounds like a suitable *conclusion,* but *why* was a conclusion necessary! It seems unthinkable that she is gone and I, for one, will have a hard time reconciling myself to life without the comforting assurance that she would always be there when needed. I hope when I get back we can talk about her and what she meant to us all—gaily!"

In Paris, Stevenson telephoned Sarah Plimpton, and she sent him a letter filled with references to *Alice in Wonderland,* to Stevenson's blue eyes, and laughter.

Harlan Cleveland came to Paris, and he and Stevenson and Finletter met with other NATO Ambassadors to discuss the Portuguese territories and apartheid. Stevenson, Cleveland, and Finletter proposed that NATO governments warn Portugal of a tough resolution from the African Foreign Ministers. They said the United States was considering an alternative resolution and suggested that other NATO governments might want to urge Portugal to accept the principle of self-determination.

A week later in Lisbon a Portuguese official told an American Embassy officer that his government knew Stevenson's approaches to various European powers were designed to put pressure on Portugal. Obviously at least one of the governments Stevenson had consulted was leaking information to Portugal; Cleveland suspected it was France. At about the same time the Portuguese Ambassador to NATO called on Finletter to ask if Stevenson had been making any moves in Paris with NATO Ambassadors. Finletter refused to tell him. A couple of days later, the Portuguese Foreign Minister, Franco Nogueira, complained to the American Ambassador to Portugal that Stevenson had come to Europe to urge NATO governments to put pressure on Portugal. The U. S. Ambassador replied stiffly. Clearly trouble lay ahead.

Stevenson spoke to ECOSOC at Geneva, went sightseeing with Marietta Tree and Barbara Ward, spent two long weekends at the Aga Khan's chalet at Gstaad, and on July 15 went to Francis Plimpton's Villa Balbianello at Lake Como, meeting Sarah Plimpton at Milan on the way. He had intended to spend several days at Como, then go to Florence to visit Mrs. Ives, but on his second day at Como he received a call from Washington: he must return at once to discuss Angola and apartheid with President Kennedy and others. He noted on his schedule, "Spent day on phone cancelling plans and making new ones. No vacation—again!"

46.

On Wednesday, July 17, Stevenson stopped briefly in New York, went on to Washington, held long preliminary meetings with Secretary Rusk and Harlan Cleveland and other Department officials, and late the next afternoon joined them in a climactic meeting with President Kennedy on Portugal-Angola and South African apartheid.

Those issues were coming before the Security Council the next Monday. Stevenson and Cleveland wanted to maintain the former hard-won United States "liberal" position—a hard line against both apartheid and Portuguese colonialism, sympathy for black African nationalists.

But now the world situation was different. Disagreement over the MLF and the European Common Market were threatening to split the Western Alliance. Averell Harriman was in Moscow with a good chance to negotiate a nuclear test-ban treaty. If he did, the Administration would have to obtain Senate ratification. With all these problems, President Kennedy wanted no trouble over the Azores. To lose our base there might mean to lose Senate ratification of the test-ban treaty and to split NATO deeply.

Kennedy and Rusk had already virtually decided what our position would be on South Africa—we would oppose an extremist African resolution that would call for economic sanctions and an immediate arms embargo against South Africa and might call for South Africa's expulsion from the UN; we would initiate or support a compromise resolution reaffirming our strong opposition to apartheid, recommending that the Secretary General appoint a special representative to discuss racial policies with the South Africans, and calling on member states to refrain from supplying arms that could be used to enforce apartheid. We would oppose an economic boycott. We would announce that we ourselves were unilaterally ending all arms shipments to South Africa after the end of 1963.

That left Angola policy up for decision, and President Kennedy had not wanted to take that decision without consulting Stevenson. Their meeting had before it a draft resolution hammered out in the Department—one that would reaffirm the timely exercise of self-determination by Portuguese territories, call on Portugal and African nationalist leaders to discuss how this could be achieved, ask the Secretary General to facilitate those talks, and request that member states refrain from providing Portugal with arms for use in its territories.

Secretary Rusk opened the meeting by saying something had to be done to take the steam out of the African drive but at the same time we had to protect the basic elements of our relationship with Portugal and prevent sanctions and expulsion.

Stevenson said we must do our best to preserve our presently favorable position in Africa without losing the Azores. The draft resolution would not, in his judgment, involve serious risk to the Azores. It would not preserve our present position in Africa either, he thought, but would not seriously damage it.

The President wondered why we had to take the initiative at all. It would only get us in trouble with the Portuguese. What if we hung back, did nothing, and let nature take its course?

Stevenson replied that this might leave the field clear for an extremist resolution. He said the draft resolution did not worry him so far as the Portuguese were concerned but it did worry him so far as the Africans were concerned—they would expect us to go further than we had gone before.

The President nonetheless insisted that we take it easy. He seemed to be moved not by military arguments about the Azores but by his own sense of the political consequences of losing the Azores. He succeeded in dampening the aggressive strategy favored by Cleveland and Stevenson. Stevenson did not seem too disconcerted. He went back to New York.

On July 22 the Security Council met on Angola. It continued to meet until July 31. Angola was an emotional issue made to order for Russian troublemakers. The meetings opened with general anti-colonial statements by the Soviet Union and Africans. Stevenson attended the meetings and met urgently behind the scenes with other Ambassadors, both African and Western. Three Afro-Asian nations introduced a draft resolution which condemned Portugal, said the situation in its territories was endangering the peace in Africa, called on all nations to forbid the sale of arms to Portugal that might be used in "repression" in its territories. Stevenson set to work to moderate the resolution's language and to bring France and the United Kingdom along with him. Kennedy and Rusk followed his progress closely, kept him under tight instructions. He felt he was making progress, was obtaining amendments to the Afro-Asian resolution that made it acceptable to Portugal, the Afro-Asians, and the United States. But when the amended resolution came to a vote on July 31, President Kennedy at the last minute decided the United States should abstain. The resolution was adopted 8–0 with the United States, United Kingdom, and France abstaining. Stevenson was disgusted. He suspected Kennedy was allowing the British to influence him unduly.

After the vote Stevenson and Foreign Minister Nogueira of Portugal engaged in a sharp nasty exchange in private, with Nogueira denouncing the United States for always conciliating the Africans at the expense of its European friends. Stevenson reported to the Department and telephoned Rusk, and Rusk was shocked, and late that afternoon Averell Harriman in Washington called in the Portuguese Ambassador to the United States, said he was doing so at the instruction of the President, and told him the President was "outraged" at Portugal's attitude. That rebuke was about all Stevenson salvaged out of the unhappy affair.

Stevenson had somewhat better luck on South African apartheid, which the Security Council debated from July 31 to August 7. He publicly reaffirmed U.S. devotion to human rights, said apartheid was a proper concern of the UN and was inconsistent with the Charter, announced that the United States would end the sale of all military equipment to South Africa by the end of 1963, but argued against severe mandatory sanctions by the UN. Once again three Afro-Asian nations introduced a tough resolution; once again, on instruction, Stevenson worked privately to moderate it. He succeeded—a paragraph calling for an economic boycott and arms embargo was removed. The amended resolution was adopted 9–0 on August 7.

By that time, however, Stevenson was in Moscow to attend the signing of the Limited Nuclear Test Ban Treaty. When the formal test-ban talks had seemed to be getting nowhere, President Kennedy and Prime Minister Macmillan had made private approaches to Premier Khrushchev. On June 10, at American University, in one of the most important speeches of his presidency, Kennedy had announced that Khrushchev, Macmillan, and he had agreed to begin high-level discussions in Moscow looking toward early agreement on a comprehensive test-ban treaty. He also announced that the United States would not conduct nuclear tests in the atmosphere so long as other states did not do so: "We will not be the first to resume." Harriman, Gromyko, and Lord Hailsham of the United Kingdom initialed a treaty banning nuclear tests in the atmosphere, in outer space, and under water. Next day President Kennedy addressed the nation and Stevenson spoke in the Security Council (as did Fedorenko of the U.S.S.R. and others). Stevenson spoke of his own "very personal gratification."

The movement toward a treaty had been glacial. International conferences had gone on inside and outside the UN for many years. Ultimately the treaty resulted. Politically, it had begun in the United States with Stevenson's 1956 campaign, when the issue was risky. He had made several contributions in the UN. But by the time the treaty was made he had little to do with it. Only a President, and he only rarely, can dramatically affect the course of great glacial movements; and Stevenson was never President. He did, however, commence the movement.

On August 2, while the Security Council was still discussing apartheid, Stevenson flew to Washington, went to a dinner party along with Harriman, and at 11 P.M. left for Moscow as a member of the U.S. delegation to sign the treaty. Secretary Rusk led the delegation.[14] The plane stopped in Copenhagen, and Bill and Deeda Blair met it, and Stevenson drove around town with Deeda, then the plane went on to Moscow, arriving at 5:55 P.M. on August 3, a Saturday, and being met by Gromyko, Zorin, and others dignitaries. They had dinner at the American Embassy in Moscow, and at eleven-thirty Stevenson went to the Leningrad Station "to talk with 'people,'" as he noted, along with the Humphreys and others.

Monday, August 5, was signing day. In the morning a U.S. group called on Khrushchev. Stevenson made notes. Khrushchev told Stevenson, "You have changed since you went to the UN"—that is, had become more the cold warrior. (It was not Stevenson that had changed but his position.) Khrushchev said the treaty was a "small beginning." Previously the United States and U.S.S.R. had used "expressions of enmity" toward each other. He hoped that hereafter he would "neither utter nor hear expressions of enmity." War no longer solved questions. The arms race could lead to catastrophe. Russia was doing everything it could to stop the arms race. It should move forward with the United States. The most "drastic" question was Germany.

Rusk said that we agreed Germany was a very important question. We were willing to discuss with Soviet diplomats how to move it toward a solution. We too were concerned with the stability of Eastern Europe after two wars. We thought there had been a relaxation of tensions in Eastern Europe. Prospects were better than three or four years ago.

They had a "huge lunch," Stevenson noted, in the Grand Kremlin Palace. At four-thirty the signing ceremony took place in Catherine Hall of the Kremlin, with speeches and toasts. At five-thirty a reception was held in St. George's Hall in the Kremlin, and Khrushchev spoke. In the evening they attended a performance of *Scheherazade* and two other ballets in the Stanislavsky Theater, then Stevenson again visited the Leningrad Station "to talk to people" with the Humphreys and others. "12:00 To Bed—dead," he noted.

Back in New York, he told Barbara Ward, "Moscow—a memorable experience which brought back poignant memories of the bitter attacks of seven years ago. To see all the faces on the bandwagon, and to hear their enthusiastic endorsements, was a little ironic. A few newspaper writers and

[14] Among the other passengers were William C. Foster, Ambassador Llewellyn Thompson, Glenn Seaborg of the Atomic Energy Commission, Arthur Dean, William Bundy, and Senators Fulbright, Sparkman, Saltonstall, Humphrey, Pastore, and Aiken.

commentators have evoked the past, but precious few. My dear friend, John Steinbeck, has reminded me of the dangers of getting seven years ahead of history. And there have been a few letters from friends around the country who remember." One who remembered was John Steele. He wrote to Stevenson, "Last week's events in Moscow brought back very poignantly to me some of the events of the 1956 campaign. Seems a long time ago but still the memories persist of the bitter attacks made against you from many quarters on the test moratorium issue." Stevenson replied, "Thank you for your letter. It touched me deeply. The memories of the test ban issue in the '56 campaign have been persistent and poignant during the past several weeks. That few seem to even remember the abusive attacks —let alone compare them with the present utterances and public attitude —makes your letter and your memory all the more precious to me." He told Mary Spears and Mrs. Ives the same things about the test-ban issue and added that Ellen's difficulties were approaching a climax.

47.

Sarah Plimpton sent Stevenson a long letter describing her own development as a child and in school, trying to say what he meant to her. Some years ago she had entered into scientific study of plants and animals. She had gone to medical school but had done poorly. She had painted for a time, then gone to Europe to write. Lately, she said, her perception and her writing had improved, a change she attributed to her knowing Stevenson.

She sent him two poems by Michelangelo, written, she said, after he was sixty-three. She wrote to him every few days from Lake Como, long descriptions of the lake and its moods, long passages filled with love imagery. Stevenson put a check mark beside some of them. She sent a long description of a gay nightlong party in Venice with her brother, George Plimpton, the writer, and his friends, complete with movie stars and *Life* photographer and launches and yachts. Stevenson sent her a postcard from Moscow. She quoted Blake to him:

> To see the world in a grain of sand,
> And a heaven in a wild flower;
> Hold infinity in the palm of your hand,
> And eternity in an hour.

48.

Estes Kefauver died and, on August 13, Stevenson joined a group of Congressmen who went to the funeral in Tennessee. He noted on his schedule, "At old family farmhouse. Large crowd—Heat!" He wrote to

Mrs. Kefauver, "Your bouyant spirit turned a funeral into a bright memory for all of us. I think Estes would have liked it just that way." Marshall Field, publisher of the Chicago *Sun-Times,* and his wife, Kay, were divorced. Stevenson sent his sympathy to both.

Planning was beginning for the fall session of the General Assembly. At the time the test-ban treaty was initialed, Stevenson had suggested to Kennedy that, if the three powers ratified the treaty by the opening of the Assembly or soon afterward, it might be well if Kennedy, Khrushchev, and Macmillan spoke briefly to the Assembly and had a registration ceremony at the UN in order to induce other countries to adhere—it would emphasize U.S. leadership in disarmament, increase public support for the UN, pave the way for periodic low-key summit meetings. "Nor," he wrote, "do I overlook the political implications, which seem to me overwhelmingly on the credit side for your Administration." He was, as he had during the Cuban missile crisis, trying to broaden the issue. Now in August he again urged Kennedy to come to the Assembly.

Kennedy, pondering the matter one day, said to Arthur Schlesinger, almost shyly: "I don't think that Adlai has written to Jackie, and she is upset about it. Everyone else who ought to write has written [notes of consolation regarding her baby's death]—she got a very nice letter from you —except Adlai. I can't believe that he didn't write, but, if he hasn't, I wish you would tell him to send her a letter. Don't mention that this came from me."

Stevenson got a vacation—six days in Maine—and then, after a one-day stopover in New York to speak in the Security Council on the Israel-Syria dispute, five days at Desbarats with Dutch and Ellen Smith. The first day was gloomy and overcast, and he "worked and walked around the cranberry bog in wet woods," as he noted, but the weather turned fine and they sailed to an island for a picnic, a swim, and a walk in the woods.

He went to Washington and on September 8 met with President Kennedy, together with Rusk, Ball, Harriman, Cleveland, and Sisco. They discussed issues at the forthcoming Assembly—the Congo, Chinese representation, the three cold war issues (Tibet, Korea, and Hungary), colonial issues, human rights, Article 19 and UN finances, disarmament. The President would speak on September 20. Rusk suggested as a theme an "Alliance for Man" in which the United States, the U.S.S.R. and other nations would work together on such non-political matters as health, nutrition, resources, agricultural productivity. The President made it clear he wanted to keep UN troops in the Congo and would say so in his speech. He volunteered to send letters to several African heads of state if Stevenson thought it a good idea. They discussed selling submarines to South Africa. Stevenson felt it would cause trouble at the UN but the President wanted to get $100 million in foreign exchange. Kennedy said, "If the Africans are going to be mad for three days, we can take it. If they are going to stay mad, it may not be worth $100 million."

The next day a full account of the meeting appeared in the New York *Times*. Kennedy was furious. Since the story cast Stevenson in a leading role, he assumed it was Stevenson who had leaked it. He called Schlesinger. Schlesinger had lunched with Carroll Kilpatrick of the *Post* and Tom Wicker of the *Times*. He had talked about the meeting to them, not expecting them to publish what he said. He checked with Sisco and Stevenson; both said they had not leaked it. Schlesinger was sure Rusk, Harriman, and Ball would not have, and Cleveland had gone to Paris. During the day other White House aides remarked at how upset the President was, one reporting that he probably would cancel the UN speech. Schlesinger sent him a memo assuming full responsibility. At the end of the day he greeted Schlesinger amiably and said, "It doesn't matter." He was less concerned with the substance than with the fact of the leak. When he saw that this leak could not be traced either to State or the U. S. Mission in New York, his concern vanished.

Later Kilpatrick of the *Post* told Schlesinger that Tom Wicker had repeated what Schlesinger had said to Scotty Reston of the *Times* in Washington, and Reston had called Stevenson in New York and got the story from him.

Schlesinger set to work on a draft of Kennedy's speech to the Assembly. Cleveland had already produced one draft. Because Rusk had pushed his "Alliance for Man" enthusiastically, Schlesinger had called a conference on it but it had produced few ideas. As he labored on the draft, he felt the material was soft. Then the idea of Kennedy's proposing a joint trip to the moon with the U.S.S.R. occurred to him and he wrote it into the speech. As he reworked the draft, the joint moon venture became increasingly prominent and the Alliance for Man faded. He talked about the idea with Dick Gardner. Gardner had previously pushed the same idea but failed— State would not request such a study, and the space agency felt it could not undertake it on its own. Established procedures nearly always prevent anything new from happening; in the main, only by such end runs as Schlesinger's can new things be accomplished. Schlesinger gave the speech to Sorensen and Bundy, and the President asked for a copy. Schlesinger gave him one, warning that the moon proposal had been cleared nowhere. President Kennedy liked it. He discussed it with the head of the space agency. He called a meeting of State, Defense, and the Arms Control agency. Nobody objected.

The General Assembly opened on September 17, and on September 20 President Kennedy addressed it. He referred to various UN accomplishments, in the Congo and elsewhere, and hailed the nuclear test-ban treaty. "The world has not escaped from the darkness. . . . But we meet today in an atmosphere of rising hope, and at a moment of comparative calm. My presence here today is not a sign of crisis but of confidence." He spoke of the differences and the agreements between the United States and the U.S.S.R. and of further, future agreements which were possible—to keep weapons of mass destruction out of outer space (this was achieved during this Assembly), to agree on comprehensive disarmament, and, finally, to make a joint expedition to the moon.

Stevenson's life in New York was hectic. Secretary Rusk was there, meeting with other Foreign Ministers and delegation leaders and sometimes with chiefs of state or heads of government, a meeting every hour through a ten- or twelve-hour day, giving dinners and receptions and cocktail parties and luncheons; and Stevenson often attended. He had his own duties to take care of—lunching one day with Gromyko, appearing on the television interview program, "Face the Nation," going to Washington for a state dinner at the White House in honor of Emperor Haile Selassie, meeting with U Thant and delegation heads on current UN business. He sat through the interminable debates in the General Assembly.

The government of Juan Bosch was overthrown in the Dominican Republic. The new head of government, installed by the military and seeking respectability and U.S. recognition, came to New York to address the plenary session of the Assembly. The plenary session debated colonialism. At the same time, in October, the political committee took up disarmament, and Stevenson spoke on October 16. The Soviet cosmonauts were introduced to the plenary session, and Chinese representation was discussed —Stevenson spoke on it on October 16 and 17. He spoke on outer space in the plenary session on October 17, too. He made a major speech on human rights in the Third Committee, his only appearance there. He spoke on the nuclear test-ban treaty in the political committee on October 15 and 16. And he made other speeches—to a Planned Parenthood group in New York; a statement commemorating UN Day; a tribute to Eleanor Roosevelt; a program to put Peace Corps veterans to work in the United States, under Roosevelt Foundation auspices.

He told Mrs. Ives, "Things have been hell here for the last month, but I think there is some light on the horizon." He also wrote, "The Ellen problem seems to be getting progressively worse and more harrowing for Adlai and the boys." By now, Adlai III had made Ellen gifts and loans totaling $11,000, some of them on his own, some on behalf of the family. Ellen telephoned Arthur Schlesinger one night and began by asking him to stop persecuting her, then said it was a joke but later returned to the theme. She said that she admired only George Orwell and Dwight Macdonald, that she was an anarchist, that she hated Stevenson, that he was a "fussy sissy," and that the Soviet Union disposed of heterodox writers by sending them to the insane asylum. She said her children had signed papers to put her away but she had sent her own papers to two historians and was not going without protest. A little later her sons and her mother did file the petition in the Circuit Court of Cook County for the appointment of a conservator of her estate. It was not easy. When the petition was filed, Steven-

son had tears in his eyes. The case was tried by a jury, with counsel
appointed for Ellen. She did not appear. She was declared incompetent,
and the Continental Bank was appointed conservator of her estate. She appealed but the decision was upheld. (Later another suit was brought by a
social case worker to force her to submit to a psychiatric examination in a
hospital. The court ordered it but she fled the jurisdiction of the court.)

Stevenson, planning a trip to Dallas and Los Angeles and San Francisco, asked that his Los Angeles schedule be sent to Evelyn Houston and
that she be invited to attend a reception with him. He left New York on
October 24, United Nations Day, and arrived at Dallas late in the morning. He spoke to a UN luncheon at the Sheraton-Dallas, held a press conference in the afternoon, spoke at an Eleanor Roosevelt Foundation reception and dinner, and delivered a televised speech at a UN meeting.

The day before, the National Indignation Convention, a radical rightist
group, had held a rival "United States Day" with Governor Connally's
sanction and with General Edwin A. Walker, the main speaker, denouncing the UN. On the morning Stevenson arrived, Dallas was flooded with
handbills bearing a photograph of President Kennedy and the message:
"WANTED FOR TREASON." While Stevenson was speaking, Walker's patriots heckled him hard, silencing him several times, and fist fights broke
out in the audience. When the police removed one heckler, Stevenson said,
"I believe in the forgiveness of sin and the redemption of ignorance." Finished speaking, he walked through a crowd of pickets to his car. They
shoved him, and a woman screamed at him, he stopped to reason with her,
and the mob closed in. Another woman hit him on the head with a sign.
Two men spat in his face. Wiping his face with a handkerchief, he said,
"Are these human beings or are these animals?" The police rescued him.
He asked them not to arrest the woman who had hit him: "I don't want to
send her to jail, I want to send her to school."

Next day President Kennedy told Schlesinger to telephone Stevenson
and give him the President's sympathy and his opinion that Stevenson had
behaved admirably. Schlesinger did, and Stevenson joked about the incident. "But," you know, he said, "there was something very ugly and
frightening about the atmosphere. Later I talked with some of the leading
people out there. They wondered whether the President should go to
Dallas," as planned for a month later, "and so do I."

Schlesinger, however, was reluctant to convey this to Kennedy—he
feared it might lead the President to think Stevenson unduly apprehensive.
A few days later Stevenson asked Schlesinger if he had spoken to the President and, told he had not, expressed relief—it would be out of character
for Kennedy to fear physical danger and, moreover, he had received reassurance from a leading Dallas businessman that the incident had outraged
Dallas.

Indeed, so it seemed—the day after the incident, the *Times Herald* published an editorial under the headline "DALLAS DISGRACED": "There is no

other way to view the storm trooper actions of last night's frightening attack on Adlai Stevenson. Must our city be given the reputation around the world of being a place where your life is physically endangered if you express any idea of which a belligerent minority mob disapproves? The inability of some of the residents of Dallas to tolerate those with whom they disagree is the very opposite of democracy and this misguided brand of patriotism is dragging the name of Dallas through the slime of national dishonor. This is not political, it is psychotic." Many people in Dallas telephoned or telegraphed Stevenson's office in New York to express sympathy and denounce the attack. The City Council made an official apology to Stevenson. The Mayor called on the city to redeem itself next month when President Kennedy visited Dallas.

Stevenson's friends sent sympathy. Jane Dick wrote, "Welcome—and thank God the placard was only made of cardboard! You handled it beautifully—just as I would have known you would." She added that her only real concern was "about the heart flutter" and asked if it was alarming and urged him to tell his doctor about it. Agnes Meyer wrote, "Darling Adlai: I am suffering so deeply for you that I simply have to express it." He minimized the incident: "Actually, I never had a warmer or more enthusiastic reception anywhere, and the idiot fringe was small if vocal and violent." Barbara Ward wrote, ". . . there is nobody like you and once again you gave the American people a lesson in good principles, good manners and good humour. You do more for the American image by being beaten over the head than most politicians in a lifetime of aspiring oratory!"

Stevenson did not take the incident seriously. He did forward to Kenny O'Donnell, President Kennedy's aide, a thoughtful letter from someone in Dallas in connection with the President's forthcoming trip. Stevenson wrote, however, "I do doubt [the letter writer's] gloomy conclusion that the idiot fringe is in fact 'winning their fight in Dallas.' On the contrary, my guess is that the President will have an enthusiastic and sincere reception."

He told Barbara Ward that this was the "dullest" Assembly on record. Despite tranquillity at the UN, however, the U. S. Mission was as busy as ever—"the thundering herd still mills around these offices day and night, leaving me little time for trips to Washington, which I miss, and trips to Illinois, which I miss still more." John Fell and Natalie were visiting him for a few days; next week Adlai III and Nancy would arrive. He had held talks with Nogueira and African leaders about Angola without much progress, "and the Africans are whipping each other up to new emotional heights in the Fourth Committee. Yesterday Tanganyika . . . even charged us with conducting underground nuclear tests with South Africa. I went into the committee this morning and let 'em have it, which I've decided is the only way to treat this sort of extremism which is increasing right and left. It is clear now that the African target is no longer Portugal, South Africa and Southern Rhodesia, but the US and the UK. . . .

"At home, I think Nixon is emerging as a probably compromise candidate after Rockefeller destroys Goldwater, which I am sure he is determined to do at any cost. Political prophecy this early is hazardous, but a replay of Kennedy versus Nixon seems to me likely [in 1964], with the probable result that Kennedy will win by something better than an eyelash this time. The disaffection of the South and the rising irritation among the whites, however, may be assuming formidable proportions. I don't include the right wing lunatic fringe (that spit on the Ambassador to the UN), because I can't believe they are numerous enough to be significant."

49.

At 1:15 P.M. on November 22, Stevenson went to a lunch given by the Chilean Ambassador for about fifty delegates in the delegates' dining room at the UN. Twenty-five minutes later, his press aide, Frank Carpenter, suddenly appeared and whispered to Stevenson. When Carpenter told him John Kennedy had been shot, he said, "Oh no," and then, "I had better get back to the office." They went across the street to the Mission. As they entered it, Stevenson sighed and said, "That Dallas! I should have *insisted* that he not go there." They went up to Stevenson's office and rolled a television set into the room and turned on a radio too. Several Mission officers gathered there.

U Thant called to ask Stevenson what had happened and to ask if he wanted the three o'clock meeting of the General Assembly postponed or if he wanted to address it briefly and then have it adjourned. Stevenson asked his staff to ask the Situation Room in Washington about the President's condition. His secretary, Norma Garaventa, called Washington. The people there thought Kennedy was recovering. While she was talking to them the radio in Stevenson's outer office said that Kennedy was dead. Stevenson told Thant he did not wish to make a speech and hoped Thant could convene the Assembly for a moment of silence and then adjourn, as it had when Dag Hammarskjold died. Stevenson dictated a telegram to Mrs. Kennedy: "I pray for you and all of us. Devotedly Adlai."

At a few minutes before three, Stevenson left the Mission and, with his entire delegation, the nine other delegates and alternates, following, walked across the street. A taxi driver who had stopped for the traffic signal recognized Stevenson, stuck his head out, stuck his arm out, palm up to the sky, and said, "Jesus Christ!" Stevenson and the others hurried across the street. The flags at the UN were coming down. In the General Assembly, the Assembly's president, Carlos Sosa Rodriguez of Venezuela, said, "It is my sad duty to announce to the General Assembly the tragic death of President Kennedy, who was assassinated at Dallas, Texas, this afternoon. I know that I speak for a unanimous Assembly in expressing our profound sorrow to Ambassador Stevenson and in asking him to convey our condolences to Mrs. Kennedy, to Vice President Lyndon Johnson and to the other members of the late President's family."

Stevenson sent a telegram to Mr. and Mrs. Robert F. Kennedy:

DEAR ETHEL AND BOB, A FEW MINUTES AGO IN THE GENERAL ASSEMBLY WE STOOD IN SILENT PRAYER. THERE WERE TEARS IN THE EYES OF ALL OF US, AND THAT'S THE WAY THE WHOLE WORLD IS TODAY. MY OWN SORROW IS IMMEASURABLE, SO I CAN IMAGINE YOURS. ADLAI E. STEVENSON.

He sent a telegram to President Johnson:

YOU HAVE MY PRAYERS AND WHATEVER STRENGTH I HAVE IS AT YOUR COMMAND ALWAYS—ADLAI E. STEVENSON.

Jane Dick drafted telegrams for him to send to the Joseph Kennedys, Pat Lawford, and Ted and Joan Kennedy. Stevenson had dinner alone with Marietta Tree at 42A; she cooked and he sat in the kitchen and talked. He took the nine o'clock shuttle to Washington and stayed with the Harrimans. Some people who saw him that night, both in New York and Washington—some of them partisans of Kennedy, some partisans of Stevenson—thought, as one put it, "He did not look grief-stricken."

It rained heavily in Washington on Saturday, November 23. At 11 A.M., Stevenson went to the White House to view the casket, which lay in state in the East Room surrounded by an honor guard. Stevenson went next to the Department and worked on his eulogy to be delivered Tuesday at the UN, and on President Johnson's speech to the joint session of Congress. Rusk, as Stevenson's notes indicated, and at President Johnson's direction, instructed all Ambassadors not to submit resignations but to remain at their posts and to display full confidence in the continuity of American foreign policy.

At two-fifteen, President Johnson held his first cabinet meeting. Stevenson said (he had written it out in longhand and had had the text retyped on a speech typewriter):

"Mr. President,

"When President Kennedy's Cabinet met for the first time following his inauguration, I presumed to speak on behalf of my colleagues, in view of my background and seniority, if that is the word, in the party and its leadership. I said to him that while of course we were all subject to the frailties of mortal men, he could count on us to discharge our assignments to the best of our abilities, and execute his decisions with absolute fidelity to him.

"Except for three changes, the same group of men surrounds you, Mr. President, on this sad and dismal afternoon. All of us suffer with you the same grief at the cruel and untimely death of the leader we, like you, respected, obeyed, and loved. All of us served him loyally.

"While we cannot obscure our grief and sense of loss, we are, I know, mindful, too, that there can only be a moment's pause in the nation's business and that the brutal burden of leadership has suddenly fallen on your shoulders.

"To share as best we can that crushing burden is our task now, Mr. President. And I know I can say again that your will is our command, and that we will serve you with the same fidelity we served your predecessor.

"Finally, Mr. President, let me echo what Dean Rusk has said. Your unique qualities of character, wisdom, and experience are a blessing to our country in this critical hour, and our confidence in your leadership is total. Seasoned by three years of the stark reality of responsibility, we trust we have deserved the confidence that you have so graciously expressed—and I speak with certainty, Mr. President, when I promise you we will all do our damnedest to merit it in the future."

That Saturday afternoon Stevenson returned to New York to help make arrangements for heads of state to go to the funeral. He returned to Washington on Sunday morning, November 24, and met in the rotunda of the Capitol with the Cabinet, renting a cutaway and mourning clothes.

The funeral was held on Monday. Stevenson and other cabinet members joined the Kennedy family and guests in the slow sad walk from the White House to St. Matthew's and then rode to Arlington for the burial. That day he sent his draft for President Johnson's forthcoming speech to Congress to George Reedy, Johnson's press secretary, saying he was doing so at the suggestion of George Ball. He sent copies to Rusk, Ball, Harriman, Rostow, and Ernest K. Lindley. Among other things, the draft asked for civil rights legislation and a tax cut and a foreign aid bill. His draft was not used; Sorensen wrote the speech Johnson delivered.

In the afternoon the State Department gave a reception for visiting dignitaries. President Johnson spent a few minutes with U Thant, Stevenson, and Cleveland and said he would discuss with Stevenson inviting U Thant to Washington soon to have lunch with him. Johnson told Stevenson, too, that he wanted to carry out Kennedy's policy of international cooperation in outer space, on which Stevenson was scheduled to speak soon at the UN. He told Stevenson to say whatever he wished in his eulogy of Kennedy at the UN but to "make it strong." U Thant remarked that Johnson seemed to support the UN strongly. Johnson replied that his support of the UN was "total" and said something like this: "It would be hard to be a more vigorous and effective supporter of the UN than President Kennedy was, but if I can manage it, that's what I will be." He told his office to give Cleveland and Stevenson copies of his own previous speeches on the UN.

That night after the funeral, Monday, November 25, Stevenson returned to New York with King Baudouin of the Belgians. Next day he sent a note to Ted Sorensen: "I don't know what you are going to do or want to do. But if you want to get away from Washington for a bit, I would be overjoyed to have you in the U. S. Mission. Yours, Adlai E. Stevenson— 11/26/63 (written in the General Assembly!)"

The Assembly was meeting in plenary session to hear tributes to Kennedy from many Ambassadors. Stevenson spoke last. "My privilege in this sad hour is to convey to you, Mr. President, and to you, Mr. Secretary General, and to you, the assembled representatives of the world community, the profound gratitude of the people of my country for what has been done and for what has been said here today. Our grief is the more bearable because it is so widely and so genuinely shared; and for this we can only say, simply, but from the depths of our full hearts: thank you. President Kennedy was so contemporary a man, so involved in our world, so immersed in our times, so responsive to its challenges, so intense a participant in the great events and the great decisions of our day, that he seemed the very symbol of the vitality and exuberance that is the essence of life itself. Never once did he lose his way in the maze; never once did he falter in the storm of spears; never once was he intimidated. . . . He made us proud to be Americans. . . .

"We shall not soon forget that, as the leader of a great nation, he met and mastered his responsibility to wield great power with great restraint. . . . We shall not soon forget that he held fast to a vision of a world in which the peace is secure; in which inevitable conflicts are reconciled by pacific means; in which nations devote their energies to the welfare of all their citizens; and in which the vast and colorful diversity of human society can flourish in a restless, competitive search for a better society. We shall not soon forget that by word and by deed he gave proof of profound confidence in the present value and the future promise of this great Organization, the United Nations. . . . Now he is gone. Today we mourn him. Tomorrow and tomorrow we shall miss him. So we shall never know how different the world might have been had fate permitted this blazing talent to live and labor longer at man's unfinished agenda for peace and progress for all. Yet for the rest of us life goes on; our agenda remains unfinished. . . . President Johnson has directed me to affirm to this Assembly that there will be no Johnson policy towards the United Nations, any more than there was a Kennedy policy. There was, and is, only a United States policy. That too outlasts violence and outlives men. . . .

"Finally, let me say that John Kennedy never believed that he or any man was indispensable. As several speakers have reminded us this afternoon, he said of Dag Hammarskjold's death: 'The problem is not the death of one man—the problem is the life of this Organization.' But he did believe passionately that peace and justice are indispensable and he believed, as he told this Assembly in 1961, '. . . in the development of this Organization rests the only true alternative to war. . . .' So, my friends, we shall honor him in the best way that lies open to us—and the way he would want—by getting on with the everlasting search for peace and justice, for which all mankind is praying."

The next day, Wednesday, November 27, Stevenson flew to Washington to attend the joint session of Congress which President Johnson addressed. From there he flew to Charlotte, North Carolina, where he was met by

Ruth Field, Adlai III, Nancy, and Borden and taken to Mrs. Field's Chelsea plantation. Buffie and Ernest Ives were already there. The next day was Thanksgiving, and Stevenson got up at 5:30 and went duck shooting with Borden, Adlai III, and Nancy—"got 12!" he noted on his schedule—and, after a picnic, went quail shooting in the afternoon. "7:30 Thanksgiving dinner," he noted. "Charades—sleep!"

CHAPTER FIVE

"... Engaged in His Country's Business and Mankind's" 1963-1965

On the day President Kennedy was buried Stevenson talked alone with President Johnson. He wrote on his schedule that Johnson said, "You should be sitting here. You carried the banner when the going was hard."

At that time and in the days ahead, President Johnson spoke movingly and with great humility both to Kennedy White House staffers and men with line responsibility. Tall and rangy, speaking quietly with head bowed down, Johnson seemed almost Lincolnesque. He asked the help of all.

Arthur Schlesinger, Jr., recalls, "The Governor came to my office after his talk with Johnson, who had given him the business about, 'You should be sitting here instead of me—you kept your word to me that you would stay out of the campaign of 1960, and that is why I am sitting here instead of you—and you know more about foreign policy than anyone in the party —you will be my man on foreign relations.' Stevenson said to me that he thought he would play a much larger role in foreign policy than he had been permitted to play under Kennedy. I think he felt that his own generation was coming back to power, and that those bright, hard, definite young men who made him vaguely uneasy would fade out of the picture. In a way he appreciated Kennedy—his eulogy of Kennedy at the UN was marvelous—but he was not given to generous remarks about him. I suppose he never overcame a certain resentment about Kennedy's being years younger and denying him first the presidency and then the Secretary of State. Now he thought his time had come. In the Kennedy years his ambition seemed to have lapsed. He did his job brilliantly but went to too many parties and didn't watch his weight. I guess he saw the Kennedy administration as something of a blind alley for himself. Now his ambition revived. By the summer of 1964 he was even, I am told, making a serious effort to become Vice President. Soon he realized that Rusk would be more powerful in foreign affairs, that Johnson had been stringing him along."

In his first months in office Johnson felt the need of experienced and influential confidants and advisers. Later, and especially after his 1964 landslide, he would become far more self-confident. At the outset he did talk with Stevenson for hours. But their relationship would begin to deteriorate shortly before the 1964 convention and to worsen during the remaining year of Stevenson's life. Harlan Cleveland said, "At the time of the assassination Stevenson said, 'I've known Johnson for years, it'll be quite a different relationship.' That relationship didn't work either. The relationship, in the end, was not as good with Johnson as with Kennedy."

At one point during the day's funeral ceremonies, Johnson, U Thant, and Stevenson found themselves sitting together. Stevenson said half jokingly (U Thant thought), "Mr. President, don't you think you ought to move me somewhere else?" President Johnson replied, "You're doing a fine job where you are, don't you think so, Mr. Secretary General?" Thant agreed. They separated, and Stevenson told Thant, "It may surprise you but I am on better terms with Johnson than I was with Kennedy." Thant believed that after Kennedy's assassination Stevenson hoped to become Secretary of State or Vice President.

"After the assassination," Newt Minow recalled, "Johnson told Stevenson, 'Anything you want—anything you want—tell me—you deal directly with me. I want your advice. You and I have been friends for thirty years and we are going to show these young people how to do things.' The Governor really liked Lady Bird and vice versa. The Governor regarded LBJ as very crafty but I never heard him say anything bad about LBJ."

"After Johnson came in Stevenson was deceived," McGeorge Bundy recalled. "He thought he was going to be heard at last. He wasn't." Schlesinger said, "Stevenson was laboring under a delusion. It turned out that he was in worse shape with Johnson than he had been with Kennedy because Rusk quickly got more power."

Stevenson had talked previously with Klutznick about resigning. "He was tired," Klutznick once said. "He was a world figure and he was accepted in the finest circles of society and the arts. Once I said, 'I'm going back home—I've had it—I can't take it any longer—I haven't read a book in a year and a half.' He said, 'I haven't read a book in five years.' I thought after the assassination it was logical to withdraw. He talked about a law partnership—time to write and see things—but shortly after that he got a new lease on life. He was close to Johnson. He hoped Johnson would make him Secretary of State, or at least would take him into his confidence. He wanted to be at the center of decision making. It did not work out. Some of it was his own fault." In 1964, Stevenson told Beth Currie he had asked Johnson about being Secretary of State but "he says I'm too old for the job." By 1965, Stevenson was reduced to asking Hubert Hum-

19 On a dreary day in August 1961, Ambassador Stevenson and Harlan
Cleveland (then Assistant Secretary for International Organizations) met
with President Kennedy at his home in Hyannis Port to plan their course
in the UN General Assembly. Stevenson pressed the disarmament issue. To
Stevenson's dismay, Kennedy dismissed it as a "propaganda" issue. Kennedy also decided to postpone American agreement to the admission of
Peking China to the UN. It was not a happy meeting.

20 More photographic evidence: here Stevenson presents to the UN Security Council in October 1962 photos made by American spy planes of Soviet missile bases in Cuba. His was a masterly presentation—he arraigned Ambassador Zorin of Russia in the court of world opinion with his famous "hell freezes over" speech—and he helped mightily to swing world opinion behind the United States in the world's first nuclear confrontation.

21 After the Cuban missile crisis, word leaked that Stevenson had opposed a hard line with Russia and urged appeasement on President Kennedy. It was not so, but it soured their triumph and worsened their relations. Stevenson thought to resign. This is the first photo of them together after their confrontation. The occasion: the awards dinner of the Joseph P. Kennedy, Jr., Foundation. The President's brother-in-law, Sargent Shriver, referred to Stevenson as "a great American," and the President led a standing ovation. Jacqueline Kennedy was Stevenson's friend. Such occasions, glamorous yet charged with political drama, created the legend of Camelot.

22 Ambassador Stevenson's life at the UN included what is usually called "a hectic round of social engagements." Here he is shown greeting the Shah of Iran and his wife at a reception Stevenson gave in their honor at his embassy residence at suite 42A in the Waldorf.

23 At the UN, Stevenson was surrounded by feminine friends, none more important in his life than Marietta Tree. Here in 1961 he watches Mrs. Tree sworn in as U.S. representative to the UN Commission on Human Rights.

24 Another of his lady friends and advisers during the late 1950s and the UN years—Barbara Ward (Lady Jackson), a British economist and writer. She provided Stevenson with ideas, speech material, and spiritual sustenance.

25 While he was at the UN, Stevenson incessantly yearned to enjoy the peace and quiet of his home in Libertyville, Illinois, and the simple pleasures of family life. Whenever he could he sneaked off there, as he is shown doing here with his son Adlai III and Adlai III's children. But after a few days he would become bored, would restlessly telephone Washington and New York, and soon would go back to that larger world.

26 Robert F. Kennedy and Stevenson did not much admire each other but they worked together, as when Kennedy returned from a mission to Malaysia, Indonesia, and the Philippines early in 1964 and held a press conference at Stevenson's UN Embassy in New York.

27 At the Berlin Wall. This photo was taken in 1963. On an earlier trip, Stevenson had crossed into East Germany and been (briefly) arrested. In the 1950s he had often spoken publicly of the reunification of Germany and of Europe but had known in his heart it was not to be, at least not in his time.

28 In some ways the triumph of Stevenson's life is here symbolized: the signing of the Limited Nuclear Test Ban Treaty in 1963. He had laid the groundwork for it in his 1956 campaign—and been denounced for it. The American delegation to the signing in Moscow, left to right: Senator William Fulbright (D-Ark.), Senator George Aiken (R-Vt.), Senator Leverett Saltonstall (R-Mass.), Senator Hubert Humphrey (D-Minn.), and AES, shown with Secretary General of the UN U Thant and Premier Khrushchev of the Soviet Union.

29 Believed to be the last photograph of Adlai Stevenson, taken in front of the American Embassy in London. Forty-five minutes later he collapsed and died of a heart attack.

30 After the funeral in the National Cathedral in Washington, after a ceremony in the state capitol in Springfield, Illinois, Adlai Stevenson's body was taken home to Bloomington. President and Mrs. Johnson went to the graveside service. In front of the President sits Stevenson's sister, Buffie Ives, and, beside her, folding the flag that draped his casket, is his son Borden. A newspaper headline read: "First Gentleman of the World Dies."

phrey how to reach Johnson. Humphrey advised him to work through Johnson's aide, Bill Moyers.

After that first cabinet meeting Johnson sent a letter to Stevenson:

No one else could have said so perfectly just what I needed to hear. Your pledge of your prayers and whatever strength you have during these trying times helped provide the strength, courage and comfort I needed. I shall cherish those words in the days ahead. With profound respect and appreciation I extend to you my warmest personal regards.

Sincerely, Lyndon

For some weeks Stevenson, in his own speeches, quoted Johnson repeatedly. In a single-spaced letter four pages long, Stevenson asked President and Mrs. Johnson to become honorary trustees of the Eleanor Roosevelt Foundation and to participate in various Foundation activities. President Johnson accepted in an effusive reply.

Subsequently Stevenson put pressure on Mrs. Johnson (whom he addressed as "Dear Lady Bird") to attend a Foundation lunch because the Foundation's fund-raising campaign was running into competition from the Kennedy Library fund-raising campaign. She finally agreed—"For the last several days I've been keeping your letter on the top of my desk and in the forefront of my mind trying to work out a way to [attend]. At last, I can accept." Stevenson, too, replied effusively.

In late December, on "Meet the Press," Stevenson said, in response to a question, that "of course" he would accept the nomination for Vice President if President Johnson asked him to but he would not seek the nomination. After the program he said he thought the chances were "very remote" of Johnson's asking him to run. Bill Blair visited Stevenson and subsequently wrote, "Nothing, but nothing, would make me happier than to see you Vice President (if we have to settle for that!) but I do hope you will not be involved by some of your friends in what might appear to be a campaign for the Vice Presidency carrying your blessing." The President, he said, would pick the candidate depending on whom the Republicans nominated and the mood of the country and would be little influenced by candidates' committees. "I would hate to see you involved (against your will, I know, but still involved) in the grubby business. . . . It just seems to me that your position and prestige will be enhanced if you can remove yourself from the political arena as much as possible." He suggested that Stevenson "pay deference to" the younger men in the party, such as Eugene McCarthy, Sargent Shriver, and Robert Kennedy. It was sound advice. Benton sent Stevenson a long account of a conversation he had had with Hubert Humphrey. Humphrey said he had told Stevenson, probably about two weeks after Kennedy's assassination, that he himself would make no effort to get the vice presidency though he was "receptive" to it and had advised Stevenson to think about it for himself. He thought Johnson would make up his mind late and would pick the man who he thought would help him most in winning re-election. Humphrey did not think he would take Robert Kennedy and thought Kennedy would soon leave government. Humphrey emphasized that the first three months of the Johnson administration were "critical" and "formative" and he hoped Stevenson would spend as much time as possible with the President, whether he was invited or not. Stevenson replied, "Thus far, things have gone very well. Lyndon, as you know, has agreed at my instance to come up to the United Nations [to speak] on the closing day of the Assembly. I think it could be very helpful to his 'image' abroad. At his instance, I have had quite a bit to do with his speech." Earlier, indeed on the very day Kennedy was buried, Benton had written to Stevenson, "I fear we will lose with Lyndon. Are you interested? The time to get going is now. Or should we get behind Hubert? Or is the fight all out of us?"

Stevenson had breakfast with President Johnson at the White House on December 11. Johnson had ordered a review of U.S. policy to see if we could take additional moves to further isolate and restrict Castro. At a cabinet meeting that afternoon President Johnson gave Stevenson a note: "Gov—at conclusion of McNamara presentation please give brief report on U.N. Lyndon." After he made his speech to the joint session of Congress, Johnson asked Stevenson for any suggestions he might have on foreign policy and, on December 10, Stevenson sent him a memorandum drafted by Yost on the "requirements of Western security." Stevenson wrote, "You will understand that in the press of work this memorandum has been hastily contrived. I have given copies to no one else."

At Stevenson's suggestion, Johnson spoke to the General Assembly on December 17, its last day. Stevenson had sent Johnson a "very quick, rough first draft" and given various people the impression he had had an important hand in the speech, but what Johnson actually delivered was written, for the most part, by Sorensen, who had a copy of the Stevenson draft. The speech began, "We meet in a time of mourning, but in a moment of rededication. My nation has lost a great leader. This organization has lost a great friend. World peace has lost a great champion. . . . I have come here today to make it unmistakably clear that the assassin's bullet which took his life did not alter his nation's purpose. We are more than ever opposed to the doctrines of hate and violence, in our own land and around the world. We are more than ever committed to the rule of law, in our own land and around the world. We believe more than ever in the rights of man, all men of every color, in our own land and around the world. And more than ever we support the United Nations as the best instrument yet devised to promote the peace of the world and to promote the well-being of mankind." He declared the United States wanted to see the cold war end "once and for all," to prevent the spread of nuclear weapons, to "press on" with arms control, and "to conquer everywhere the ancient enemies of mankind—hunger, and disease and ignorance."

After his speech Johnson had lunch at 42A with Stevenson, U Thant, other members of the Secretariat and of the U. S. Mission, several Senators including Fulbright and Hickenlooper and Humphrey, several Congressmen, the president of the General Assembly, and representatives of the countries on the Security Council. In the next days Stevenson and Johnson exchanged highly complimentary letters.

The Assembly adjourned the night of December 17 after hearing Johnson's speech. Next day Stevenson held his usual summarizing press conference. He said the "aggressive, lone-wolf foreign policy of Communist China" had become more threatening than ever. The Assembly had both reflected and contributed to the easing of cold war tensions. The Assembly's record on colonial matters was a mixture of provocative words and, for the most part, sober actions. He reviewed the UN's peace-keeping activities in the Congo, Middle East, Yemen, Kashmir, and Korea. This work, he said, was still "threatened" by the refusal of the U.S.S.R. and others to pay their assessments.

A reporter, referring to the attack on Stevenson in Dallas and Kennedy's murder there, asked his view of the danger of rightist extremist movements. He replied, "I have had a feeling that the effect of this tragedy that has befallen this country and the world has been to sober somewhat the extremist view. . . . I think it is the better part of caution, however, to anticipate that we shall never be wholly without extremist views in this country."

Asked if there was any possibility that the United States might recognize the Peking Chinese, Stevenson replied, "I think the problem of China rests in Peking, not in Washington. . . . I refer to the fact that the war still goes on in Korea, that they have encouraged and are encouraging the Viet Cong, that they are stirring up the Pathet Lao, and that this continuous behavior is of Peking manufacture—not of Washington." A reporter asked if this meant that the United States was "giving up your two-China theory." Stevenson said, "I didn't know we ever had one!" Would he participate in the election campaign next fall? He said he could not because he was "engaged in the conduct of foreign policy." Would he accept the vice presidential nomination? He said, "It seems to me this is where I came in ten years ago! I think my job is to stay here and mind the shop across the street for the President and do the best job I can for President Johnson and for my country."

President Kennedy's widow sent Stevenson a silver campaign shoe she had found in President Kennedy's effects:

> I was going through Jack's things—he had so little that was of any value—I had wanted to give people something to remember him by—but there is so little. In the stud box I gave him—which was always in his top bureau drawer, the box he kept the few nice things he had in—I found this silver shoe. It must be from your campaign. I would like you to have it back—How much has happened since those days.
>
> With my love
> Jackie

Stevenson went home on December 23, writing on his schedule, "Liber-
tyville!" All three boys were due to join him. He spent Christmas with
John Fell and Natalie and their son, Adlai III and Nancy and all four of
their children, their nurse, Borden, and Viola. He noted, "What a day!"
The day after Christmas he took Borden and John Fell and his family to
Bloomington, had lunch with Mrs. Ives at the old house on Washington
Street, had cocktails at the Bud Merwins', and had dinner at Tim Ives's.
They tried to visit Joe Bohrer but he was out.

Between Christmas and New Year's, from Libertyville, he sent Marietta
Tree a long poem by Matthew Arnold copied out in longhand (asking,
"Have I sent you that before?" He had). He told her, "A frenzied day preparing for Christmas, a glorious, exhausting Christmas with all the young
and younger. A day & night—Bloomington . . . much telephoning to
N.Y. re Cyprus-Greece . . . a reprieve until Monday at least. This morning we go hunting at −2°—but the sun is bright and the snow, and *moon*
so white. The ghost, and the creak at the top of the stair, is always there."

2.

In New York on the morning of January 10, with Sarah Plimpton, he
went to Kennedy Airport, intending to fly to Jamaica to visit Jane and
Edison Dick, but at the airport he was called back: a crisis had erupted in
Panama. He returned to midtown and that evening spoke in the Security
Council. The next day he and Sarah left for Jamaica. Stevenson's notes
emphasized the rain, wind, and fog which prevailed during his weeklong
visit. One day they took a drive around the west end of the island and pic-
nicked on the beach; another day they were escorted by police in a Land
Rover to visit the Maroon country.
    The visit frustrated and disappointed Jane Dick greatly. After he and
Sarah had left, she sent him a long document—not a letter, she said, but
"my end of an *important conversation* we couldn't have." As she wrote,
the sun was now warm and the sky cloudless, the little house flung wide
open and no longer shuttered against raging seas and gloomy skies. She
resented it. From the beginning she had conceived the house as a "small
gay cottage" to house grandchildren and "maybe *especially* as a little
haven for you" where he could escape New York's pressures and relax
with old friends. She had built it with his criticisms of other places in mind
—too airless, too windy, too many parties, too confining. She had so
looked forward to his visits—golf, tennis, swimming, siestas, soaking up
the sun, exploring the islands, fishing, riding, Jamaican music. Instead,
throughout his visit, the weather had been foul, a cocktail party that was

usually "amusing" had been boring, and so had the "endless conversation" of other guests. Christmas and other distractions had prevented her from collecting the books, magazines, short stories, and parlor games that she usually took to Jamaica; therefore, "rainy day resources" were lacking. "The other disasters—the Count's barking dog, the Thomases' gardener's new motorcycle . . . —hardly need to be recounted." She wrote, "It was against this background of total hostess despair . . . that I overheard your reply to the question of your admirer at Half Moon about whether you'd had a good time: 'Oh, only so-so.' It was a perfectly natural reply and an honest one. I guess I just longed to hear something like, 'Well, the weather's been foul but I've loved being with old friends.' Anyway it was the straw that did it. I found myself weeping uncontrollably." She discussed two projects they had in view—organizing his papers and writing an article about him. She said the article would be "an enormously helpful kick-off," in what campaign she did not say, but she (and he) may have had in mind the vice presidency or a New York Senate seat in 1964. A few weeks later Jane managed to write a funny account of the visit for presentation at the party at Marietta Tree's celebrating Stevenson's sixty-fourth birthday.

He returned to New York January 18, troubled about a speech—it was scheduled at a time when he was tentatively committed to join Agnes Meyer's yacht in the West Indies. As he wrote Barbara Ward: "I have had little success with her regarding money I had hoped to get for the Eleanor Roosevelt Foundation, and promised her a long time ago that I would try to find time to join her cruise for a few days." He added, "I can hardly tell you the headache the Foundation has become. I shall have to see it through for a few more months. The Kennedys are now going out for 10 million dollars for their library which of course cuts across my bows and causes me no end of trouble. What with the Library, the Cultural Center, and all the other memorials, I think there is increasing restlessness in this country—especially since there has never been a memorial to Franklin Roosevelt yet." He had lunch with Kenneth Royall, once Truman's Secretary of Defense and a "Stevenson fan," according to Stevenson, and Royall was "determined I *must* be VP—no one else even remotely possible," he told Marietta. He saw Dr. Lax for a checkup.

He went to Chicago, hoping to spend several days at Libertyville, but Harlan Cleveland called him back—the Cyprus problem was nearing the point of UN involvement, he thought, and Stevenson should make the U.S. speech on Kashmir in the Security Council. Those issues occupied him during the winter and early spring. Chet Bowles, now Ambassador to India, told Stevenson, "I sympathize with you in our Pakistan-India Donnybrook" over Kashmir. Bowles then wrote, "What really worries me, Adlai, is the Southeast Asia situation, which if my antenna are at all accurate could easily move from the present uncertain impasse with a sudden collapse of our entire position. It is fantastic to think that Ho Chi Minh and the group around him, operating with ill-equipped Vietnamese peasants, were able first to lick the French Army (in spite of the fact that we put more money behind them than we spent on the whole Marshall Plan in France), and are now successfully eroding a still larger Vietnamese force which has all-out United States support. [It was not yet all-out.] We have just not learned to recognize the forces which move these situations. . . . If Southeast Asia does go, South Asia will be in the front line, and judging from this distance, there are too few people back home who understand this, and a smaller number still who are prepared to do something about it."

Stevenson replied, "The anguish at the Cabinet level over South Vietnam is acute, and I suspect we have a bear by the tail, indeed. I have often wondered if the basic assumptions, as you imply, were correct. But that's not my only misgiving about the direction of things. How nice it is to be in the opposition!"

In a letter to Marietta Tree in March he mentioned a rumor about Rusk's resigning. "He always hoped to be Secretary," Marietta once said, "but not with his head—he didn't think he really would be."

After conferring with the President, Rusk, Cleveland, and others, Stevenson on March 6 opened talks with Ambassador Fedorenko of the U.S.S.R. about the conduct and financing of UN peace-keeping operations. The Russians' assessments for the Congo and Middle East operations were by now two years in arrears. This would inevitably raise the question when the next General Assembly convened of whether the Soviets would lose their vote under Article 19 of the Charter. An enormous amount of work went into the Article 19 problem, as it came to be called. It was extremely difficult. Stevenson and others, in testifying before the United States Senate on the UN bond issue, had pledged themselves to insist that Article 19 be applied against the Russians, costing them their vote, if they did not pay up—he hoped to reduce Senate wariness about buying UN bonds when the Soviets did not meet their obligations. Stevenson had promised the Senate, "We shall be extremely stubborn about this."

But the Soviet Union proved to be equally stubborn, maintaining that the General Assembly had usurped the Security Council's powers in ordering the peace-keeping missions; and it soon became plain that the UN faced a constitutional crisis that threatened to destroy it. Throughout most of the year Stevenson and others at the Mission were preoccupied with the issue, and so were Cleveland and others in the Department. The talks in New York dragged on and on. Neither Stevenson nor others at the Mission had foreseen the prolonged struggle. He and the Department devised various formulas to allay the Russians' fear that they would become liable for future operations of which they disapproved. But the question remained: Would Russia be deprived of her vote in the forthcoming General

Assembly? Ultimately, by general agreement, and in part because of the American presidential election, the convening of the Assembly was postponed from September to December, for no one really wanted to deprive Russia of its vote, and when the Assembly did convene it put no issue to a vote but took its actions by unanimous consent, arranged in backstage bargaining sessions. An air of unreality deeper than ever thus hung over the UN throughout 1964.

On March 12, Stevenson and Borden flew to Antigua to join Agnes Meyer's West Indies yacht cruise. "No yacht to meet me," he noted. "Mill Reef Club for the night for only $100!" It was one of the few hotel bills he had paid in recent years. He finally located the yacht at St. Lucia. "'Panda,'" he noted, "was a beautiful refitted 3 mast schooner formerly belonging to Emperor Bao Dai of Viet Nam—shades of my visit to him in the jungle in 1953 and dining on Gaur meat! Mrs. Meyer, feeble and insecure after her eye operation and illness, Luvie Pierson [Pearson]—Drew was at Caracas for inauguration of new Pres—Leoni (why didn't U.S. send me, everyone asked, when I knew retiring Pres. Bettancourt & Venez. so well) Dr. David Paton—eye doc. from Johns Hopkins and pretty wife —Joan. Delightful, gay young couple & good companions for Borden. After look around St. Lucia we sailed over to Martinique—anchored in pretty bay for swim and night. Next day sailed around so. coast—under canvas—to Fort de France."

The weather was sunny and fine. He slept the night on deck under the stars, and next day they sailed up the west coast of Martinique. He was reading *Bitter Lemons,* Durrell's "fine" book about Cyprus, and a book by Charlie Yost and a "great thriller," *The Spy Who Came in from the Cold.* Harlan Cleveland telephoned about Cyprus. Stevenson noted, "Why are all W. Indian towns so squalid! Slums of Empire." On a Dutch island a remote house bore a sign, "Welcome Adlai," and they stopped to visit with a man and his wife who were old Stevenson fans from Connecticut.

Afterward Stevenson thanked Agnes for "that heavenly interval with you on the Panda . . . even if Borden has now acquired a fatal addiction to expensive yachts." She had promised to contribute another $25,000 that year to the Eleanor Roosevelt Fund. He hoped she would give similar amounts in 1965 and 1966.

From time to time Stevenson recommended people to President Johnson for appointments. He recommended Newt Minow for the Communications Satellite Corporation Board and Seymour Harris for the Federal Reserve Board; neither was appointed. He contributed to the Kennedy Library.

He wrote to Marietta on March 22, "Tomorrow a hideous two weeks begins—speeches, travels, income tax etc. How I wish you were going to be with me; but its evident now that in the future I'll be travelling with you —if we have a future."

3.

Stevenson delivered several speeches that spring but none so important as one on March 23, the Dag Hammarskjold Memorial Lecture at Princeton. It was his most original speech in years. Tom Wilson of the Department contributed many of its ideas. He drew a contrast between the world of today—1964—and of 1961, when Hammarskjold died in Africa. The "overwhelming reality" of 1961 had been the division of the world into opposing and rigid military alliances led by two superpowers. Today the world was "no longer bipolar" but rather one "in which multiple centers of power and influence have come into being." Today the world was "at long last" approaching the end of "the historic struggle for military superiority." Imperialism and paternalism were dying. Traditional trade and monetary systems were "being challenged and changed." The world was "both fabulously rich and desperately poor" and was seeing much of its progress wiped out by the population explosion. Fundamental issues of human rights were "out in the open and high on the agenda of human affairs."

He recalled George Kennan's policy of "containment," proposed in 1947. The nation could take pride in what it had accomplished through containment in Berlin, in Korea, in Cuba, and elsewhere. But containment had encouraged the simplistic view of the world as divided into Good Guys and Bad Guys and it had been essentially a negative doctrine. It was relevant to a world that was divided into two parts and "may not yet have outlived its usefulness," particularly with respect to Communist China. "But as anyone willing to see clearly already knows, the current course of world affairs calls for something more than a 'policy of containment.'" He believed the world was moving from something like "limited war" to something like "limited peace"—from a policy of containment to a "policy of cease-fire, and peaceful change." The proof lay in the fact that although international disputes were numerous none had led to war. And only a few decades ago, once war started it had to be prosecuted to "victory." Victory in the conventional sense could no longer be achieved. Cease-fires had replaced the drive for victory. Some twenty conflicts had broken out since World War II, and eight could be classed as invasions, and yet only one, the Indian invasion of Goa, had been settled in the traditional way with "victory." Minor fighting had broken out on at least another twenty occasions and the current agenda of the Security Council listed fifty-seven international disputes. "This record of violence-without-war suggests, then, that we may have slipped almost imperceptibly into an era of peaceful settlement of disputes—or at least an era of cease-fires while disputes are pursued by other than military means." He suggested that Korea was "the end of the road for classical armed aggression against one's next-door neighbor; that perhaps Suez was the end of the road for colonial-type military solutions; and that *perhaps* Cuba was the end of the road for nuclear confrontation."

What could be done to make sure that we had indeed entered an era of peaceful settlement? The consensus favoring non-violent solutions must be pursued. The peace-keeping machinery of the UN should be strengthened and made ready for speedy action—it was perhaps too early to contemplate a fixed UN international force but we should move in that direction. Finally, a simple cease-fire was not good enough, since it merely returned to the status quo ante, but must be improved through "a *dynamic* system of order," how he did not say: "It is easier to write this prescription than to fill it." Stevenson was urging a policy beyond containment.

4.

President Johnson's wife attended an Eleanor Roosevelt Foundation lunch in New York, as she had promised, and Stevenson thanked her effusively, and they engaged in a bantering, somewhat arch correspondence. At about this time, on April 11, Adlai III had a long telephone conversation with his mother. It was a rambling, hostile conversation, almost entirely one-sided, a painful persecuted thing. There were others. It was at this time, on May 15, that Adlai III, his brothers, and Ellen's mother filed the legal petition for the appointment of a conservator for Ellen.

Jane Dick had written the "human interest" article about Stevenson which they had discussed in Jamaica and now in April sent it to him. She hoped it would "warm up your public image to those who feel you are admirable but remote." Stevenson thought it "marvellous!" He wrote, "If I have any criticism it is . . . about the portion towards the end, which seems to overlook entirely that much of my problem in New York is official dinners, lunches, etc., which I *have* to go to. But you must write as you think." He wished she would make the point that "my interest has been in foreign policy *per se* more than in its execution or annunciation. I have had, as you must know, many frustrations and controversies with the Department, but have tried to stick scrupulously to the State Department line even though it does not always coincide with my own views." He had another thought: she might say he had "been asked" by party leaders to run for the Senate from two big states in two years, Illinois and New York; thus "my political demise has been voluntary rather than involuntary." They correspond at length about the piece, and Jane denied several things he said. It was curious how Stevenson sometimes seemed to quarrel with Jane Dick and Ruth Field in the way that couples long married quarreled, without venom but in a nagging reproachful way. Such notes did not appear in his correspondence with Sarah, Marietta, and Alicia.

On April 30 he issued a statement declining to run for Senator from New York. There was talk around New York about his running, and President Johnson in his memoirs said Stevenson wanted to run and was disappointed when Johnson told him he would support Robert F. Kennedy. And Johnson told an aide at the time that after he refused his support for the Senate nomination Stevenson never again smiled at him. But there is no evidence in Stevenson's papers that Stevenson was considering the nomination very seriously. By the time Stevenson issued his statement declining to run, Kennedy was already making moves preliminary to running. Kennedy calculated that Stevenson would fear to risk defeat.

Stevenson went to Urbana to receive an honorary degree from the University of Illinois—"made excellent speech on education for leisure"— then went back to Chicago and Lake Forest for Dutch Smith's birthday party. On May 2, a beautiful day with, he noted, "jonquils out, emerald grass, carpets of spring beauties beneath the maples in tiny leaf," and with "children glorious," he played tennis with the Smiths, then at three-fifteen "bid reluctant farewell" and flew to New York where he repacked his suitcase and boarded an 8:30 P.M. Pan American plane, finding Marietta already aboard, and they flew to Rome.

The ostensible reason for his trip to Europe was to speak at the NATO Defense College and the Imperial Defense College. The real reason was a yacht cruise in the Mediterranean with the Ricardo Sicres, Marietta Tree, and Ava Gardner. From Rome on May 3 he flew to Naples where he boarded the yacht *Rampager* and set sail for Capri.

Stevenson wrote in his notebook: "Naples blooming—what a contrast to those cold, dark days during the war—November, December 1943—and all the horrible destruction in the port and industries and that cold, damp villa near the barracks where we slept in misery. Up anchor— and out of the little port in brisk wind & bright sunshine—dead tired after journey. Sailed past great US supply ship over to Capri. Giovanni Agnelli's beautiful sloop moored near by. Sailed around island—great cliffs —Augustus threw his enemies off?—past the huge rocks—the tunnel, the blue grotto—memories of 1953," when he had stopped here briefly on his round-the-world trip. "Took taxi up to town for walk around. . . . Walked back to ship—and there was Ava Gardner—arrived by helicopter from Naples! . . . Late dinner."

On Monday, May 4, he awoke refreshed by a long sleep. The ship was under way for Positano. With Ricardo Sicre and Marietta he climbed up past a villa he had had in 1953 and explored the town. The day was bright and warm. He swam off the boat. "Huge lobsters for lunch on deck. Very gay. Up anchor and away to Amalfi. Sun bath on top deck. . . . Dinner was a splendid pasta with sausages & meat balls & glorious sauce—very piquante—cooked by Ava, who then went to bed afraid to face it & anxious about our reaction! Strange, lovely, lush girl. (Last night she climbed alone up to Capri in the middle of the night)." Next day they anchored off Stromboli, a smoking volcano.

And so his journal went—delicious meals and splendid swimming, unpredictable Ava Gardner, castles explored and tombs visited, unspoiled towns and water skiing, siestas on deck in the hot sun and dreamless nights in port, Greek history and legend, ancient artisans and laughing young girls. He worked a little on papers he had brought along. On May 11 he and Marietta left the yacht and flew to Rome. There he ran into Dick Daley and his wife on their first European tour. They talked politics, and Stevenson recommended Bill Wirtz for the Illinois delegation to the Democratic National Convention. Daley seemed favorable and said Stevenson would be a delegate at large.

Marietta went to Teheran and Kabul for meetings of the Human Rights Commission; Stevenson went to Stockholm to make a speech and took with him Sarah Plimpton. In London he had a number of engagements but, past midnight of his first full day there, May 19, Secretary Rusk telephoned from Washington and asked him to return to New York at once—"trouble in SC re S E Asia," Stevenson noted on his schedule. He spent the next morning canceling engagements and issuing a statement on his "emergency return" to the United States and left for New York at noon. He had told Marietta Tree, "So ends another bobtailed visit to Europe. Now for Cambodia, Laos and Vietnam—a quicksand I urged JFK to keep out of in early 1961 and thereby invited the patronizing scorn of 'the group.'" The next day, Thursday, May 21, the Security Council met on Southeast Asia.

5.

Vietnam came to the UN Security Council on complaint of Cambodia in 1964 but the United States had been involved there since Eisenhower was President in the 1950s. (Indeed, Indochina had been on President Roosevelt's mind during World War II: he opposed returning it to French rule after it was liberated from Japanese occupation.) The 1954 Geneva accords had failed to resolve the political conflicts in Indochina and by 1961, in our official view, the Communist regime of North Vietnam was supporting Viet Cong guerrilla operations against U.S.-backed governments in Laos and Vietnam. In 1961 a cease-fire was agreed to in Laos. In South Vietnam, Vice President Johnson visited Saigon to dramatize U.S. support for President Diem, and later that year President Kennedy agreed to increase substantially U.S. military as well as economic aid to South Vietnam.

In 1962, under President Kennedy, the scale of military aid rose rapidly —several thousand U.S. troops undertook to train the forces of President

Diem and assist them in countering the Communist guerrilla Viet Cong. The Diem regime became increasingly repressive and following public protest over the repression of the Buddhists—and with U.S. encouragement, or at least acquiescence—military leaders overthrew Diem; together with his brother, the chief of the secret police, he was killed in November of 1963 (three weeks before President Kennedy was killed). The United States quickly announced its support of a provisional government, hoping it could rally the country against the Viet Cong. By now the United States appeared fully committed to winning the war and rejected De Gaulle's offer of French aid for a reunited and neutralized Vietnam. But General Nguyen Khanh, who had overthrown the junta that had overthrown the Diem regime, was unable to win broad political support for his war against the Communists and, in consequence, turned increasingly toward dictatorship.

Meanwhile, the new Johnson administration had moved to support Khanh with increased U.S. military aid. Soon there were 16,000 American troops in South Vietnam, serving as military advisers to the South Vietnamese troops, and the Administration planned to add 5,000 and was considering attacking North Vietnam by air.

It was at about this point that, on May 13, 1964, the Cambodian representative to the UN requested a meeting of the Security Council to consider "acts of aggression" by the armed forces of South Vietnam and the United States—"terrorist raids" into Cambodia on May 7 and other border violations. Thus the war in Southeast Asia came to the United Nations, and to Stevenson.

When the Cambodians lodged their complaint, the U. S. Mission in New York asked the Department whether or not U.S. advisers had accompanied South Vietnamese troops on their border incursion of May 7. The Security Council met on May 19, while Stevenson was still in Europe, and the Cambodians presented their case and asked for a return to the Geneva Conference. The Soviet representative denounced South Vietnam and the United States. Ambassador Yost replied briefly, denying that there was any basis for the charge of U.S. aggression or hostility toward Cambodia. He said that recent events had occurred because the Viet Cong sought sanctuary in Cambodia. The United States was prepared to consider new UN machinery to help stabilize the frontier.

U Thant asked the U. S. Mission for a confidential account of what really happened on the border on May 7 and 8. The Department replied that its information was incomplete and it was sending out inquiries. The South Vietnamese said that several of its troop elements unknowingly, in the heat of battle and in hot pursuit of Viet Cong, had crossed the border into Cambodia and killed seven Cambodians and wounded three more. South Vietnam expressed regrets and asked for bilateral agreement to cooperate in border areas. The Cambodians displayed the bodies, and the South Vietnamese protested. The Department believed that no U.S. personnel had accompanied the South Vietnamese across the border. Yost briefed U Thant, who was considering sending a UN observer team. The British wanted the United States to make a proposal. The French would try to find out what the Cambodians wanted of the UN. The Department sent out inquiries to the American Ambassadors in Phnom Penh and Saigon, asking for suggestions as to what the UN might do. The embassies pointed out the difficulties of observing, let alone patrolling, 350 miles of jungle border. Nevertheless, the United States was moving toward a new course —proposing that the UN get involved actively in observing or even patrolling the border. In retrospect, it appears that 1964 and the early months of 1965 were crucial to America's involvement in Southeast Asia. It was then that the decisions were taken to introduce ground combat troops into South Vietnam and to bomb North Vietnam. This Cambodian complaint in the Security Council in May was the curtain raiser on the wider drama.

On May 21, having returned hastily from London, Stevenson went into the Security Council to speak on Cambodia, a speech which used the occasion for a full-dress defense of the U.S. position in South Vietnam and which laid down the new U.S. proposal of UN observers at the border, something that remained policy for years to come. The Cambodian representative asked for a reconvening of the Geneva Conference. He did not feel that new UN machinery could produce a solution, though he did favor sending UN observers with a limited role. The Soviet representative supported the Cambodian position and stressed the "acts of aggression" by the United States against the peoples of Indochina. The South Vietnamese representative said that his government had never denied the incidents complained of and had apologized for them and offered indemnity and had offered to engage in bilateral discussions of the "root" of the problem —the use of Cambodia as sanctuary for the Viet Cong.

The position Stevenson took had been hammered out by the Department and approved by the President. In his speech he reviewed the border incidents and pointed out that they had been "mistakes." "But these incidents can only be assessed intelligently in the light of the surrounding facts: namely, the armed conspiracy which seeks to destroy not only the government of Vietnam but the very society of Vietnam itself." He described the "aggression" against Vietnam directed from outside its border. He declared the major elements of U.S. policy. First, the United States had no "national military objective anywhere in Southeast Asia" but only wanted to restore peace. Second, the United States was "involved . . . only because the Republic of Vietnam requested the help of the United States and of other governments to defend itself against armed attack fomented, equipped, and directed from the outside." He said that the Indochinese Communists had made it clear as early as 1951 that their aim was "to take control of all of Indochina." That was still their goal, he said.

"Hanoi seeks to accomplish this purpose in South Vietnam through subversive guerrilla warfare directed, controlled, and supplied by North Vietnam. . . . Infiltration of military personnel and supplies from North Vietnam to South Vietnam has been carried out steadily over the past several years. . . . Introduction of Communist weapons into South Vietnam has also grown steadily. . . . We all know that Southeast Asia has been the victim of almost incessant violence for more than a decade and a half. Yet despite this fact, it has been suggested that we should give up helping the people of Vietnam to defend themselves and seek only a political solution.

"But a political solution is just what we have already had, and it is in defense—in support—of that political solution that Vietnam is fighting today. The United States has never been against political solutions. Indeed, we have faithfully supported the political solutions that were agreed upon at Geneva in 1954 and again in 1962. The threat to peace in the area stems from the fact that others have not done likewise. . . . There is a very easy way to restore order in Southeast Asia. . . . Let all foreign troops withdraw from Laos. Let all states in that area make and abide by the simple decision to leave their neighbors alone. Stop the secret subversion of other people's independence. Stop the clandestine and illegal transit of national frontiers. Stop the export of revolution and the doctrine of violence. Stop the violations of the political agreements reached at Geneva."

Stevenson suggested that the Security Council request the two parties to establish a bilateral military force to patrol the frontier and report to the Secretary General. Such a force could be augmented by UN observers and even placed under UN command. Or an all-UN force could be dispatched.

Thus Stevenson's speech, written in the Department, anticipated later utterances by President Johnson and Secretary Rusk. The Department tried to push the Stevenson initiative—told the American Embassy at Phnom Penh to urge the solutions he suggested on the Cambodian government in lieu of reconvening the Geneva Conference.

Near the end of May the Department told Stevenson that a statement by U Thant was "outrageously offside" and could be "damaging." Thant had said that the question of a UN peace-keeping force in Southeast Asia was under discussion but that, "personally speaking," he felt the problem was primarily political, not military, and "I have my own doubts" about the UN's ability to do what was proposed. The Department told Stevenson the afternoon papers were already interpreting what Thant said as direct opposition to Stevenson's proposal for a UN force on the frontier. But it had larger implications, the Department said—it was not the Secretary General's job to decide what was the capacity of the UN for keeping the peace. The capacity of the UN was the capacity of the membership to act. The Secretary General should await instructions from the Security Council. The Department asked Stevenson personally to speak strongly to Thant, asking him to state publicly that he was not commenting on the Vietnamese proposal for a UN force on the Cambodian border.

Stevenson and Yost did talk to Thant on May 27. Thant feared the UN was moving toward establishment of a full-scale UN force along the entire Vietnamese border—Cambodian, Laotian, and North Vietnamese. Thant would oppose this. He also thought a UN force, along the Cambodian border alone, impractical because of financial problems and the difficulty of obtaining troops. He repeated his feeling that solutions in Southeast Asia should be found in the fourteen-power Geneva framework. And he had a specific political solution in mind. Noting that many eminent Vietnamese leaders who had fled before 1954 were now in exile in Paris and elsewhere, he suggested that a government of national conciliation be brought together through a round-table conference, including the exiles, in Thailand or Malaysia. He had already talked about it to the Canadians. He hoped such a move would lead to free elections that would make Vietnam a showplace of democracy.

What he said seemed visionary. Stevenson and Yost told him that such conciliation might be helpful in the long run but at present Vietnam could not divert its energies from its military problems. They opposed a Geneva Conference not because this was an election year in the United States but because they feared that such a step would damage morale in Vietnam, Thailand, and other places. A call for a round-table conference could have the same effect. Yost said something might be done if military pressures were removed. Stevenson said if the Communists continued their military pressures the United States would have no alternative but to step up its own military effort, a significant statement.

On May 28, Stevenson attended a Democratic fund-raising party at the home of Arthur Krim in New York and while there handed President Johnson a memorandum on Southeast Asia. It can be taken to represent definitively his own views at that time.

He wrote, *"We must demonstrate to the world that all peaceful remedies through the United Nations have been exhausted before resorting to escalation of United States military action."* As for Cambodia, he saw no present possibility of a large and effective UN force to protect the border. But a commission to inquire into the situation seemed likely, and this would at least "get a UN foot into the door." The resolution would call on all states, especially the Geneva powers, to respect the neutrality of Cambodia. The resolution would contain no reference to a Geneva Conference on Cambodia, which Prince Sihanouk wanted and the United States opposed because the Conference would become involved in Laos and Vietnam as well. Eventually, however, there would be another Geneva Conference on some part of the Indochina problem.

As to Laos, if the French supported us, we should encourage Souvanna Phouma of Laos to appeal to the Security Council for aid; the United

States should endorse his appeal and indicate that in the absence of UN aid we were prepared to take other steps; a Security Council resolution would provide for a cease-fire and standstill, UN observers to check on cease-fire and standstill, a Geneva Conference to restore a coalition government or, failing that, to partition Laos. If the Council was unable to act because of a Soviet veto, we should move U.S. forces into the Mekong Valley but not beyond, and use the U. S. Air Force against Communist advances and bases in Laos; and we should also consider the possibility, if the Soviets vetoed, of going to a special session of the General Assembly before using U.S. ground troops and air power. If the French did not support UN action, we should take the military steps set out above, based on a request from Souvanna Phouma; announce publicly our objectives and call for the establishment of UN observer arrangements so we could withdraw; call for a Security Council session to explain our moves. We should discuss all this in advance with the French and the United Kingdom. Our objective should be to get the UN into Laos, if possible without prior U.S. involvement, if necessary after it. We would have to overcome U Thant's vigorous opposition. Our objectives should be to introduce the United Nations into Laos with sufficient physical presence and political will to make any further Pathet Lao military action politically costly, and to build the basis for a political settlement.

As to Vietnam, regardless of how serious the situation seemed to us, "world opinion is simply not sufficiently prepared for either U.S. military action in North Viet Nam or a U.S. appeal to the United Nations." Military action would be considered an irresponsible escalation of the war likely to bring in Communist China. An appeal to the UN would not produce a useful Security Council resolution because most members still believed the war essentially a civil war and Hanoi assistance only secondary. Indeed, if we took Vietnam to the Security Council, we would be more likely to get a UN resolution against us than one for us. "There is grave question in my mind whether US armed intervention in North Viet Nam, consisting of more than sabotage and harassment, makes military sense. However, if the situation in North Viet Nam is so grave that military reaction against North Viet Nam is the only way out, much more political preparation is necessary. This could best be done either by bringing the Laos situation promptly to the UN, as suggested above, or by going to a Geneva Conference on Laos in conjunction with a threat or fact of US military action there. In either case, South Viet Nam could join in the complaint against Hanoi concerning use of Lao territory for attack on Viet Nam. If over a period of time at the UN or in Geneva we can demonstrate clearly that it is Hanoi which keeps the Viet Nam war going, we can perhaps build up the necessary support for UN action or justification for US action."

It was a mixed policy for a complicated situation, neither all-out "hawk" nor all-out "dove," as oversimplifications would have it. In his memorandum, Stevenson proposed to exhaust all political remedies at the UN first; but if politics failed, he did not shrink from the use of force. As always, he was concerned about world opinion. And, as always, he did not lose sight of larger considerations, in this case the danger of provoking mainland China.

By the end of May it seemed clear that Prince Sihanouk of Cambodia, although he had brought the complaint to the Security Council, would reject any UN involvement there. This irritated the Department, which felt that bringing a complaint to the Security Council was a serious matter, not to be subsequently abandoned capriciously, and it instructed the Mission to work with other Ambassadors on a Cambodian resolution. Finally, on June 4, the Security Council voted 9 to 0, with the U.S.S.R. and Czechoslovakia abstaining, to adopt the key fifth paragraph of an Ivory Coast-Morocco resolution which decided that the Security Council would send three of its members to Cambodia and South Vietnam "in order to consider such measures as may prevent any recurrence of such incidents" and to report within forty-five days. The U.S.S.R. objected because the International Control Commission established by the Geneva accords already existed and the new mission was not needed. Stevenson, on the other hand, wished the Council had taken farther-reaching steps.

On June 5, George Ball, in Paris, on President Johnson's instructions, sought the views of Couve de Murville and General de Gaulle and telegraphed a report to President Johnson and Secretary Rusk. De Gaulle believed there was no effective government in South Vietnam and the United States could not create one. He believed that "white men" had "no business" fighting a war in Asia and the United States was under "special disability" because it was easily turned into the focus of Asian resentment. He thought the problem of South Vietnam was "fundamentally psychological and political." It could not be solved by military force. He believed the more the United States exerted military force, the more the fight would be looked upon as our own. This would make trouble throughout all of Asia. Since we could not strengthen the government of South Vietnam, any effort to carry the war to the North would invite "incalculable consequences." Therefore, France would not participate in any Asian war that might result from our efforts in North Vietnam. Since he thought the problem political, he thought it could be resolved only that way, and he strongly urged us to try a large negotiation involving Moscow, Peking, and Hanoi. This would look toward the maintenance of South Vietnam's independence. As long as such a big conference was going on, Hanoi would have to call off the Viet Cong. The conference could go on for a year or more. During that time the situation could be stabilized. De Gaulle said the United States had taken to itself the responsibility the French had borne. He recognized what we hoped to do but simply did not believe we could do it. "He says that we cannot win out there, even if we do have more aircraft, cannons and other arms." The people regarded the United

States as a big foreign power, and the more we became involved the more they would turn against us.

We, of course, did not see it that way at the time. Later events, however, proved De Gaulle right in a deeper sense, something America discovered only after prolonged agony: that America could not win that war in Southeast Asia, any more than the French had been able to. A copy of Ball's report went to Stevenson; there is no direct evidence he acted on it —no action was called for—but he himself had talked to De Gaulle, and De Gaulle's views must have informed his thinking.

At about this same time President Johnson asked the CIA whether the loss of South Vietnam and Laos would precipitate a domino effect in the Far East. The CIA's Board of National Estimates concluded that it would not. That is, the loss of South Vietnam and Laos would not be followed by the rapid successive communization of the other states of the Far East, with the possible exception of Cambodia. Moreover, a continuation of the spread of Communism in the area would not be inexorable. Any spread would take time. In that time, everything might change.

The loss of South Vietnam and Laos, however, would be "profoundly damaging" to the U.S. position in the Far East, especially because the United States had publicly and repeatedly committed itself to preventing a Communist takeover of Laos and South Vietnam. Failure would seriously undermine the credibility of United States will and capability to contain the spread of Communism elsewhere. Our enemies would be encouraged; friendly states would move toward the Communist orbit. Sihanouk probably would accelerate his movement toward accommodation with the Communists. Thailand would shift to neutralism. Burma would be less affected, having already virtually severed ties with the United States. Indonesia would be emboldened. Malaysia would seek a clear U.S. commitment to help defend against Indonesia. Philippine policy probably would not change and Philippine subversion or nationalism could be dealt with. On Formosa, Chiang would be disheartened but would hardly seek accommodation with the Communists. In Japan, neutralist sentiment would increase, but basic policy probably would not change. In Communist Asia, the prestige and self-confidence of Peking as the leader of world Communism would receive an enormous boost. It would contrast Peking's boldness with Moscow's caution and encourage revolutions in other parts of the underdeveloped world.

6.

Stevenson found time for other concerns. He asked Ambassador McGhee in Bonn to have a car meet Buffie Ives on her arrival and wrote to her, "I see no reason for your paying for what is absolutely standard service to any Foreign Service officer, let alone *you,* anywhere." In the midst of the Cambodia problem he wrote to Marietta Tree: "It is Sunday midnight—a State USUN gang on S.E. Asia have just cleared out and I'm prostrate from fatigue, heat, anxiety and lonliness. What have you done to me!" Next day Lady Bird Johnson and forty guests would appear at a museum dinner. There was "some talk about drafting me for the Senate race," that is, for the race in New York which Robert Kennedy would make. "Not much response to the Kennedy trial balloon and negative edits in NYT & Post. Everyone, repeat, knows about Ava & me; I hope you can think of some way to let the Sicres know what the consequences were— not that she is disreputable but that I'm supposed to be a serious person crushed with weighty problems. And God knows I am! S E Asia is a morass of trouble with no end even over the horizon."

Stevenson spent a Saturday night at Caumsett with Ruth Field and a Sunday at Mary Lasker's farm. He made a speech in Washington, stayed at the White House, went to a party at Scottie Lanahan's (daughter of F. Scott Fitzgerald and prominent in Washington social life), and had breakfast in the White House with President Johnson. He was keeping a "Vice President 1964" folder. It contained various Gallup polls. The latest, taken in May, showed that Robert Kennedy's percentage among rank-and-file Democrats had dropped from 47 per cent in April to 41 per cent in May, while Stevenson's had risen from 18 per cent to 26 per cent (though this left Stevenson where he had been in January). Stevenson suggested to Clayton Fritchey that a columnist be encouraged to write a story about his "being urged to run for the Senate from Illinois and N.Y. in 2 years?— and declining both to stick to the field of foreign affairs?" Stevenson appeared on "Face the Nation" and afterward told Fritchey, "I have had letters and comments from several people about how deathly sick and tired I always look on television. . . . I wonder if there is some way we could experiment with make-up to improve this gargoyle?"

On June 16, Stevenson wrote an unsolicited memorandum to the President on Laos and Vietnam. As to Laos, he warned that "our various signals" might well not deter Hanoi and Peking and we should watch for their signals. We should be prepared to occupy and hold the Laotian river towns but be wary of trying to hold with American troops the central Plaine des Jarres and Luang Prabang. We should not try to drive the Communists out of Laos but, rather, to hold them where they were and make their presence costly. The best means of combating Communist military action in Laos, Stevenson thought, was "certainly by air strikes" by "'Laotian'" planes. These air strikes might bring about increased Viet Minh and perhaps Chinese intervention on the ground, but that should not deter us.

As to Vietnam, Stevenson assumed that attack by ground forces north of the 17th Parallel would be "counter-productive" but suggested air attacks in the north by "'South Viet Namese'" planes might be feasible. Direct, avowed U.S. bombing would "almost oblige" China to respond in a "very substantial" way. As to targets, the destruction of new factories would be "impressive" but they were probably close to population centers and so should be sabotaged rather than bombed. Ports would involve ships of other nations. Lines of communication would probably be the best target.

That memorandum came close to proposing, in the early summer of 1964, part of the program which President Johnson adopted in 1965 and for which Johnson and later Nixon were so severely criticized. But it did not go quite that far. Yost, who had been Ambassador to Laos in the 1950s and who produced the rough draft of Stevenson's memorandum, perceived clear differences between the situations in Laos and Vietnam. Laos, in his view, was the object of external aggression by hated foreigners, the Vietnamese, and if her cities on the Mekong should be occupied, the threat to Thailand would be serious. On the other hand, Vietnam was engaged in a civil war in which American involvement seemed to Yost both less justified and less likely to prevail. In 1965, Johnson bombed Vietnam with U.S. bombers and sent into South Vietnam large numbers of U.S. ground troops—steps Stevenson did not advocate in his 1964 memorandum.

Stevenson told Barbara Ward on June 18, "Cyprus and Viet Nam are [President Johnson's] worst problems, of course, and I seem to be up to my ears in both of them with the usual minimal opportunities for consultation. They did, however, unanimously agree on my scenario for Viet Nam, including reversing the instant rejection of the Polish proposal." (The Poles had proposed consultation among the Geneva powers.)

The Security Council met on June 18–19 to consider extending the UN force in Cyprus, and Stevenson spoke, calling the recent importation of arms to Cyprus "most serious" and urging Greece and Turkey to take steps promptly to set the stage for a negotiated solution.

Spending the weekend of June 20–21 at Caumsett with Ruth Field, Stevenson wrote to Marietta Tree, describing a Kennedy Library dinner, saying he had not been invited to a party afterward at Steve Smith's. "Buffy berated me re Ava Gardner and Liz Taylor. . . . If you see any prospects of ERF [Eleanor Roosevelt Foundation] money there please, please bore in. . . . Also don't forget Adlai needs money for his statewide campaign [for the Illinois legislature] if you see any about. I'm telling Johnson thru Abe Fortas that I'm not going to run for Senator from NY & want to be relieved from this job next March after the G.A." At about the same time, and on other occasions that winter, Stevenson told Yost he intended to resign when the General Assembly ended. Yost had grown accustomed to Stevenson's grumbling about leaving; he regarded this as more serious. Later, in the light of events, he thought it a pity Stevenson had not kept to his resolve.

He took Evelyn Houston to cocktails and dinner and after-dinner entertainment at the Spanish Pavilion at the World's Fair. He described that evening at length to Marietta, not saying he had taken Evelyn Houston but saying instead it had reminded him of Marietta, as Spain always did. His letter-writing life went on, in full measure, but his handwriting, never easy to read, was getting worse as he aged. Sometimes what he wrote made little sense, perhaps because he usually wrote late at night.

He went to Libertyville for a long Fourth of July family weekend, entertaining Adlai III and Nancy and his grandchildren, playing tennis with the Dutch Smiths, watching the fireworks at Onwentsia. From Libertyville he sent a long letter to Marietta, describing the large numbers of children at Libertyville and the various activities. He had, he said, "reflected a bit on the ordered elegance of your life and the gay happy squalor of mine—or rather Adlai's & Nancy's!" He would have "one more glorious day [at Libertyville] of green fields, grazing sheep, cool breezes, bright son and rollicking babes, kittens, puppies and happy confusion. AES III generally conceded to win—only question whether he will lead ticket. Hard at work, well organized, flooded with invitations from downstate for speaking." (All candidates for the Illinois General Assembly that year had to run at large owing to the legislature's failure to redistrict the state.) Beset though Stevenson was by affairs, and threatened by the advancing symptoms of ill-health, he never failed to brighten when he saw his family.

Back in New York, he had a long lunch with Hubert Humphrey on July 10 and talked about the vice presidency, the New York senatorial election, and the Secretaryship of State. Stevenson noted, "He thinks LBJ will not give him V-P, but two more clerks & a larger office as whip!! Also thinks he will put on a Catholic if the Republicans do" but not Robert Kennedy. Humphrey thought the odds were against his own nomination for Vice President and, if that was true, he favored Stevenson. But he thought the chance of his and Stevenson's being nominated were, put together, no better than fifty-fifty. Bill Benton, who was present, urged Stevenson to send Abe Fortas to talk to the President on Stevenson's behalf and, right after the convention, to "sit down with the President and tell him you've got to plan your own future." New York politicians were telling Stevenson that, if Johnson did not put a Catholic on the ticket for Vice President, they might have to run Robert Wagner, a Catholic, for the Senate from New York. On the other hand, if Johnson did put a Catholic on the ticket with himself, pressure on Stevenson to run for the Senate would increase. Stevenson thought the Democrats should hold open hearings on their platform in order to attack the Republican platform. He would be the principal witness, he thought.

U Thant said at a press conference on July 8, "I still feel that a return to the Geneva conference table, though perhaps belated, may produce some useful results." He said, "Whenever I read of the death of an American or the death of a Vietnamese, my heart bleeds."

But the United States still opposed reconvening the Geneva Conference, and Stevenson told Thant this emphatically. Thant said he understood the

U.S. position but disagreed. He thought that the longer the war continued and the deeper U.S. involvement became, the weaker its cause would become. The South Vietnamese would become fed up and fearful. Desertions would increase. Democratic institutions in Saigon, already weak, would grow weaker. All this would weaken the American bargaining position. Chou En-lai had told Thant years ago that Americans were encircling China and China would not stand by idly but would have to destroy the American position in Indochina. Thant pointed out that, once Burma stopped receiving U.S. aid, China let it alone. Ne Win of Burma was in contact with all the parties concerned, and Thant intended to talk to him in Rangoon. Stevenson asked if Thant would express his views when he went to Washington for a state dinner at the White House. He said he would.

Sarah Plimpton wrote to Stevenson about her plans for the summer at Lake Como. She was coming home to New York at the end of October. Mercedes McCambridge wrote: she had *"never* had anything to do with that nonsense that appears in those poopy columns now and then. Good heavens, I've never even been near most of the restaurants in which we are 'seen'! I DID say, and *Time* printed it, that for me 'there are two kinds of people in the world—everybody else, and Adlai Stevenson.' . . . How weary you must be of dog-like devotion." On July 17, Stevenson had Ava Gardner to lunch. Three days later he spent several hours with Alex Rose and James Wechsler, and in a letter to Barbara Ward he wrote, "I'm extricating myself from the Senate race in N.Y.—somehow!" On July 21 he told Marietta Tree he was going to Washington for several days and would tell President Johnson he was not going to run for the Senate and would talk to him about his role in the campaign—"some say he might ask me to resign after the Convention and campaign full time."

He described his Washington visit to Marietta: "McNamara did his lecture [at a cabinet meeting] on savings in the Defense Dept with countless charts, diagrams, graphs, samples etc—articulate, impressive & reminiscent of board meetings at the Britannica. LBJ followed with a lecture on economy; then a lecture on *the* economy; then, warmed up, he talked—and well—about the political situation leaving the (calculated) impression that he was in real trouble in the south, the middle west & perhaps California. As always, he had a secret poll in every pocket. Not content with this fight talk he wandered off into an unnecessary explanation of his relations with Bobby Baker, the history of the TV station in Texas etc. Afterward we talked alone. He agreed again to appoint you to succeed [Sid] Yates. . . . Then he said 'That McNamara is a hell of a fellow, isn't he.' I agreed, and he added—'Yes, he's in just the right place.'!!! There followed some talk about what the FBI had on the negro leaders (remind me) & an unresponsive attitude to my plea [that Johnson] do a TV fireside on law observance etc. After suddenly autographing 3 photos I had not asked for & offering me a bed for the night, I departed for Kay Graham's fun dinner—

with Lally & a lot of beaux and Arthur Schlesinger—and the usual incessant talk about Goldwater. Arthur walked home to Averill's with me & confirmed the rumor, now widespread, that B. Kennedy wants my job at the UN—or he'll go to England 'to live & read' for a year." He had seen a number of prominent Democratic politicians. He reported that Congressmen and Senators seemed to favor Humphrey for Vice President. "LBJ talks to everyone & reveals nothing." (Johnson at that time was toying with the politicians and the press over whom he would choose as his running mate. It was the only drama in the Democratic situation that year.)

"Growing comment that it need not be a Catholic & now—180° degree change in few weeks—almost no one considers B. Kennedy even possible. Meanwhile I do *nothing*—to Tony Celebrezze's & Luther Hodges discomfiture. Odd how he—practical Italian pol & turns out to be sudden passionate friend. But I *really* don't give a damn! Do you?" Muñoz Marín had asked Stevenson to represent the United States at Puerto Rico's anniversary but he had declined. "All I seem to want now is rest & recreation, & find my self secretly hoping that I can get a proper holiday in Sept & won't even have to campaign. But I suspect a few speeches to non-political meetings . . . are indicated. . . . The skies have cleared; the moon is high, full and brilliant over the silver sea. Up the valley the Spitzbarn is sparkling in the moonlight. You won't step out on the balcony to wonder at the beauty of the night for fear of prying eyes at Tournesse. So we stand in the shadow just inside the door—very close. Breath is short and the heart fast in the struggle between looking and wondering, lying and wondering. Now I will go to sleep and dream of July days and nights—from shuttered windows above the twinkling lights of Florence to lush mountain pastures & blue lakes beneath soaring white cumuli. And so it has been *every* night in this long meaningful month. Pray God it will be ever so in July; and pray God it stops on August 11! I *know* there's a letter waiting me in N.Y.—and I'm impatient now to get back. For idleness is not diverting, just painful." He said he had planned to convey all the gossip about Goldwater but could only sum it up by saying that Goldwater's supporters reminded him of the frustrated people who used to sing,

"The working class can kiss my ass,
I've got the foreman's job at last."

On July 27 the Security Council Mission to Cambodia and Vietnam recommended that the Security Council send to Cambodia a group of UN observers, that it try to arrange talks between Cambodia and Vietnam, that it take note of various assurances given by Vietnam. Vietnam accepted these proposals; Cambodia did not. The United States considered them "practical" but "limited" steps toward UN peace keeping in Southeast Asia.

On July 29, a Wednesday, Stevenson sent a longhand note to Newt Minow:

"Reflections on our telephone talk re V-P. I really haven't been much interested and *really* don't care much what happens. Hence it has been hard to get active. But I would like Johnson to know some sensible people have a good opinion of me. Hence anything Kappel[1] would say in response to a telephone call from, say, Walter Jenkins[2] or Abe Fortas[3] would be helpful, I'm sure.

"Another one—if favorable to me—who might be effective is, I'm told, Joe Block.[4] But how to pass the word from him I don't know.

"And, finally, I suppose the Pres. would be interested in what a big insurance executive might think—i.e., Jim Oates. I hate to approach him myself, but I'm sure Clarence Ross[5] would have no hesitation.

"I've sent my suggestions for the satellite corp. direct to the Pres."

Clearly, Stevenson was quietly campaigning for the vice presidential nomination. On the same day he sent that note he went to Dark Harbor, Maine, to spend ten days with Ruth Field and other friends. The next day, a beautiful warm day, he played tennis, went swimming, talked with the White House about guests at the forthcoming dinner for U Thant, and after lunch went sailing. Returning from sailing about 5 P.M. he found telephone calls waiting for him from Jim Rowe and Luther Hodges in Washington. They had called at the President's request. President Johnson was announcing unexpectedly that he would not have as his vice presidential running mate "any member of the Cabinet or any of those who meet regularly with the Cabinet." Reading his announcement to reporters in the Fish Room of the White House at 6 P.M., Johnson said he had informed Rusk, McNamara, Robert Kennedy, Orville Freeman, Stevenson, and Shriver. "In this manner, the list has been considerably narrowed." It certainly had. Robert Kennedy, at whom the President's statement was principally aimed, remarked that he was sorry to take so many nice fellows over the side with him.[6]

The best evidence that Stevenson had wanted the vice presidential nomination is his own calendar for July 30, the day he was notified at Dark Harbor of Johnson's statement. He wrote in longhand: "Telephone calls

---

[1] Frederick Russell Kappel, then chairman of the board and chief executive officer of AT&T.

[2] A Johnson staff aide who specialized in politics.

[3] A Washington lawyer, then a confidant of and adviser to President Johnson.

[4] Joseph L. Block, chairman and chief executive officer of Inland Steel.

[5] Lake Forest lawyer and utilities executive, partner in the law firm that had included Oates and Carl McGowan.

[6] President Johnson wrote in his memoirs that he barred the Cabinet from the vice presidency in order to prevent them from performing their duties with an eye to the nomination and in order to allay the impression that everybody was running for office and nobody was running the government.

from Luther Hodges and Jim Rowe at President's request re his statement on Vice President. Disappointed, of course; but also relieved that I don't have to face another campaign! Did he do it now because of rumor that Jackie would return from Adriatic to help Bobby at convention?" Stevenson telephoned Hubert Humphrey at once and offered to help him get the nomination. A few days later he told John Steele he felt that Johnson had been "abrupt" in writing off the Cabinet and others. He wondered why, if the Cabinet was so poor, Johnson kept it. Nan McEvoy told Stevenson, "It seems a grievous shame that President found you in the same bath tub as bad Bobby." Stevenson replied, "Better to have never been mentioned at all than to be thus dismissed."

Robert Kennedy reacted to the President's move by announcing his own candidacy for the New York Senate seat. Stevenson reacted differently. Arthur Schlesinger said, "Johnson had been stringing him along. After this, I think he felt, 'What the hell?' He kept talking about resigning. But he decided to enjoy himself. He always rose to the big thing, the big occasion. But that was all. He had worked very hard for Kennedy. Then he thought he was coming into his own. Then somehow the mainspring broke after the vice presidency." Agnes Meyer once said, "Toward the end at the UN he was not happy. He had to do so many things he didn't approve of." It was not only Vietnam or, later, the Dominican intervention that troubled him. He was also, for example, opposed to the multilateral force which, after 1964, became once more a prime Administration objective. He had already thought of resigning from the UN; he considered it more seriously now. Already he had considered forming a syndicate to buy one of several newspapers that were for sale or were about to go on sale.

Beth Currie saw him at a party at the Mission about this time. He stood beside her chair, swaying with fatigue, and she told him to sit down before he fell down, and he collapsed into a chair and said, "I *am* tired," and stared glassy-eyed into space. She told him, "Adlai, you'll kill yourself," and he reassured her he was all right and then said, "But what can I do? It's this damned job." She urged him to resign before the job killed him. He said he could not—he had promised Johnson to stay until the convention, and after the convention the new General Assembly would meet, and a new man could not prepare for it. She asked if he couldn't quit next spring for reasons of health. He said, "Who would believe that?" He feared his resignation would be taken as a repudiation of Johnson's policies. He felt trapped, and said so. He told Beth Currie he was worried about his health, something new to him, and said he was having trouble sleeping. "And I have the most terrible dreams when I do get to sleep." One recalls that Suzie Zurcher said earlier he took Seconal tablets to sleep and told her he had nightmares about the world blowing up. He told Beth Currie he was haunted by "the death of mankind, the end of life on this planet."

7.

On the following Monday, August 3, Stevenson went cruising with Ruth Field to have lunch with the Walter Lippmanns. He noted on his schedule, "Papers report N. Viet Nam PT boats have attacked U.S. destroyer in Gulf of Tonkin in international waters!" This was the Gulf of Tonkin incident, and next day Secretary Rusk telephoned and told Stevenson to return to New York, he might have to go before the Security Council the next day on Vietnam. He left and, by boat, taxi, Air Force helicopter, and Air Force jet returned to LaGuardia Airport. The next day he was sick, a recurrence of his kidney trouble. He saw his doctor and lay down for a few hours before appearing in the Security Council.

President Johnson had already instructed the Navy to take retaliatory action in the Gulf of Tonkin and had reported to the people on television and radio on August 4: "Aggression by terror against the peaceful villagers of South Vietnam has now been joined by open aggression on the high seas against the United States of America. The determination of all Americans to carry out our full commitment to the people and to the government of South Vietnam will be redoubled by this outrage. Yet our response, for the present, will be limited and fitting. We Americans know, although others appear to forget, the risks of spreading conflict. We still seek no wider war."

He had met with congressional leaders. Next day at Syracuse University, a few hours before Stevenson went before the Security Council, the President announced that a destroyer had been attacked on August 2 and that two destroyers had been hit on August 4:

"The attacks were deliberate.

"The attacks were unprovoked.

"The attacks have been answered.

"Throughout last night and within the last twelve hours, air units of the United States Seventh Fleet have sought out the hostile vessels and certain of their supporting facilities. Appropriate armed action has been taken against them. The United States is now asking that this be brought immediately and urgently before the Security Council of the United Nations." President Johnson sent a special message to Congress asking it to adopt a resolution expressing the support of the Congress for "all necessary action to protect our armed forces and to assist nations covered by the SEATO Treaty. At the same time, I assure the Congress that we shall continue readily to explore any avenues of political solution." Stevenson had no hand in developing policy on the Tonkin Gulf incident. Rather, to him fell the task of making the United States' case in world opinion at the UN. At the onset of the crisis, talking to someone in the Department, probably

Cleveland, Stevenson said with heavy emphasis, *"But are our hands clean? What the hell were our ships doing there in the first place?"*

The Department sent Stevenson instructions and the text of a Tonkin Gulf resolution. The Council met at 3 P.M. on August 5. Stevenson described the facts about the attacks on the destroyers *Maddox* and *C. Turner Joy,* as provided by the Department,[7] and called the affair "deliberate aggression" in international waters. U.S. retaliation had been a "limited and measured response fitted precisely to the attack"—aerial strikes against North Vietnamese torpedo boats and their bases. He said, "This is a single action designed to make unmistakably clear that the United States cannot be diverted by military attack from its obligations to help its friends establish and protect their independence. . . . As President Johnson said last night, 'We seek no wider war.' "

Ambassador Platon Morozov of the U.S.S.R. referred to the American strike against the torpedo boat bases as "acts of aggression." The Security Council adjourned without acting. After considerable backstage maneuvering, the Security Council met again on August 7. The Czech representative said that the United States had on July 30 and August 1 carried out aggressive and provocative actions against North Vietnam and that North Vietnam considered the U.S. account of the torpedo boat attacks "sheer fabrication." In reply, Stevenson denied that U.S. ships had intruded into territorial waters or shelled North Vietnamese islands, as charged. He said the torpedo boat attacks were "very real indeed." The governments of North and South Vietnam furnished information to the Security Council. Though the issue sputtered on for several weeks, the U. S. Mission advised against pressing for Security Council action, and it took none. The incident was important principally as proof in the 1964 American presidential election that the Johnson administration was committed to "limited, measured" responses in Southeast Asia as contrasted to the more belligerent policies advocated by Senator Goldwater.

On the morning of August 6, Stevenson accompanied U Thant and his official party by U. S. Air Force plane from New York to Andrews Air Force Base in Maryland and then by helicopter to the White House lawn, where President and Mrs. Johnson welcomed Thant to an official visit to Washington. Thant had just returned from a trip to Burma, Paris, Moscow, and elsewhere. Following preliminary meetings with Rusk and others, Stevenson and Thant met with President Johnson and high Administration officials. Stevenson had encouraged Thant to convey his views to Johnson, and he did. Thant said that, when he and the Prime Minister of Burma visited Hanoi and Peking in 1954, they thought Ho Chi Minh was deeply influenced by French culture and was not a Communist or even pro-Communist. Thant recognized this had been ten years ago but still thought it

7 Those facts have since been called into question.

might be worth while to attempt a private probe with Ho. He thought Ho was now probably pro-Moscow rather than pro-Peking. He referred again to his previous experience in Burma with Chinese Communists. In 1947 the Chinese had told the Burmese government they would not help the Burmese Communists if Burma allowed no Western bases. For seventeen years now they had kept their word and given no help to the Burmese Communists.

Bundy commented that if what Thant was saying was that the Chinese thought the problem of Southeast Asia was getting the Americans out, the United States could agree heartily—we wanted nothing more than to leave Southeast Asia "under proper conditions." President Johnson reinforced this: "We are ready to get out tomorrow if they will behave."

Thant said he had talked to Secretary Dulles at the time of the Geneva accords in 1954 about internationally sponsored neutrality for Southeast Asia but had found that Dulles "didn't believe in neutrality." Thant still thought that internationally guaranteed neutrality was the best solution and repeated that it was not too late to probe Ho's private feelings.

U Thant's remarks about his experiences in Peking and Hanoi in 1954 constituted a sort of speech that he was willing to give "at the drop of the hat," according to Yost, and when he gave it now at the White House he left an impression of "great naïveté"—"he was too ready to believe that the North Vietnamese were Titoists. This must have prejudiced the Secretary and maybe the President."

Nonetheless, Thant came away from that August trip to Washington convinced that the President and Rusk were receptive to the idea of private conversations between Washington and Hanoi. Accordingly, Thant sent a longhand letter to Ho Chi Minh (probably through a Russian), saying that President Johnson wanted meaningful negotiations as quickly as possible and that the only alternative to mounting destruction was peace talks, the sooner the better—and he proposed immediate secret talks as a prelude to formal negotiations. He assured Ho that if he sent an emissary it would be kept secret. Some three weeks later he received a favorable reply from Ho: North Vietnam accepted his proposal and was willing to enter into secret talks. Thant told Stevenson.

What happened after that is not clear. One report has it that Stevenson immediately went to Washington to convey the good news to Rusk and seek instructions. No entry on Stevenson's calendar confirms that view. But at some time he did convey Thant's message to Rusk orally. The idea lay dormant for several months, into early 1965, when it came to life again in odd circumstances. Why it was so long ignored can only be conjectured. At this time, early August of 1964, the Democratic National Convention was only two weeks away. During the campaign the President was insulated from developments in Vietnam. Word went out to keep hard decisions away from the White House and to avoid new policy initiatives that would complicate the President's campaigning. Thus during September and October and early November a deteriorating situation in Saigon and misgivings at middle levels of the Administration were kept from Johnson. It may well be that one of the initiatives which got lost in the political whirlpool that fall was the U Thant move with Ho. It is difficult to overemphasize the holiday from government that envelops Washington, that most political of cities, every four autumns.[8]

On August 7, the day he returned to New York from the U Thant visit, Stevenson wrote to Bill Moyers. "I don't know who is doing what about the foreign affairs plank for the [Democratic] platform. I prepared the enclosed hastily with a view to getting some of the points on paper for elaboration—or contraction!" He enclosed his first draft of a "peace and defense" plank, dated August 5. The Vietnam splinter in his plank read: "We shall continue to assist by all necessary means those nations which are under armed Communist attack as long as they desire our assistance and are willing to fight for themselves. This assurance applies particularly at the present time to the republic of Viet-Nam and the Kingdom of Laos. . . . We view with the utmost gravity the expansionist actions and designs of the Communist Chinese regime and its Asian allies. . . . At the same time we shall always be prepared to negotiate peaceful settlements, on the basis of the United Nations Charter and pertinent international agreements."

On Saturday, August 8, Stevenson went to visit the Angier Biddle Dukes at Southampton but, late that afternoon, to his annoyance, he was ordered back to New York for an emergency Security Council meeting on Cyprus which lasted until 1:25 A.M. En route to New York, he expressed his annoyance in a letter to Marietta Tree. He told her that the room next to his at the Atlantic City convention hotel was reserved for her. He added to the letter later in the evening while in the Security Council meeting: "I'm getting so sick of this place & this job and 'public life.' I don't like watersheds; I've had too many in life and now I'm on another one—blinded by the sunset and groping for the path down."

At 1 A.M. he was given "the happy news" that Cuba was calling for a Security Council meeting on Monday.

The Council resumed discussion of Cyprus the next day, on Sunday (and again on Tuesday). Stevenson sent another note to Marietta: "Turks

[8] President Johnson said in his memoirs that, in September, U Thant told Stevenson of Thant's belief, based on "third party sources" (as Johnson put it) that Hanoi was willing to talk to an American emissary. President Johnson reported, "The offer was rejected by the United States since the latest report of Blair Seaborn [the Canadian member of the International Control Commission for Vietnam] indicated Hanoi was not prepared for serious talks to end its aggression in South Viet Nam. Hanoi later denied that it had suggested any negotiations to U Thant." The President did not say to whom Stevenson relayed the U Thant message or how. Johnson evidently did not consider the incident important—did not discuss it in his text but only listed it in the notes in the Appendix as "Vietnam: Major Peace Initiatives."

still attacking by air; Cyps threatening general attack on all Turks; fleet loading for invasion. Oh, what a beautiful sunny, brisk summer day! It would be lovely on the river." He added a verse:

> "We have changed since, but the remembered spring
> Can change no more, even in the autumn smokes
> We cannot help the havoc of the *heart,*
> But my *mind* remembers half the spring,
> And shall—'till winter falls."

He wrote to her again on Monday night: "Archie [MacLeish] and Ada are here. Last night I staggered back for dinner with them and [Richard] Burton and [Elizabeth] Taylor—no one else—and it was about the most amusing night of my life in 42A. Even Liz took my fancy." He wrote about New York politics: "Yes, Senate is hot again. Bobby is mad to run now and Steve Smith is making unctuous calls daily about getting together. 'He doesn't want to do anything if I'm interested' etc. Bob Wagner is holding out but the K's have unleashed the mafia. I stalled him just not to give them any satisfaction. . . . The averice of the K's really makes me sick. I'd almost like to do it to challenge him. But *starting* a new career now is senseless; instead I'm going to *end* me." New York University had invited him to occupy a new chair as "distinguished professor"—"occasional lectures, serious and limitless aid on my 'book,' plus 3 mos. holiday—*and* a house in the Mews! I said I was doubtful about the Chair but interested in the house." The UN achieved a cease-fire at Cyprus.

On August 12, President Johnson addressed the American Bar Association in New York, and Stevenson drove with him to the airport afterward to talk about the New York Senate campaign. The next afternoon he met with Alex Rose about the Senate and that evening was the principal speaker at the Bar Association's annual banquet. He remarked upon the then current Republican declaration that the voters deserved "a voice, not an echo," and said that, while the dominant viewpoints of the two major parties had been readily distinguishable, at the same time the American political system derived its strength from the absence of extremist views. He said he hoped for a serious "political dialogue," not exchanges of slogans, in the forthcoming campaign. He attacked the view that Communism must be pursued and threatened even with nuclear punishment until it was defeated. He attacked extremism and thus, by inference, Goldwater, though he did not mention his name. He quoted President Johnson's declaration at Syracuse that "aggression unchallenged is aggression unleashed . . . there can be no peace by aggression and no immunity from reply." He said, "And let me tell you, gentlemen, that the decision as to whether United States power must be used—and when—and where—and at what level—is the heaviest responsibility of government in this day. For the consequences of one false step are incalculable—one hasty response—one impulsive or ignorant reaction—one failure to communicate clearly the purposes of a national action." Clearly he was exploiting Goldwater's impulsiveness.

It was the first of a handful of political speeches Stevenson would deliver that year. Barbara Ward had furnished the basic draft; Stevenson had rewritten it heavily. He told her on August 14 that it was "a triumph. . . . I suspect Goldwater will have me in his sights pretty quick—because the subtlety was not very subtle!" He described New York politics: "Bobby has reconsidered his Sherman statement and had moved back into New York with all his troops to seize the Senatorship with little opposition, in view of my reluctance to leave my present post at this time. . . . Johnson has asked me to stick to my post during the campaign. I had offered to resign. I suspect my role will be to make thinly-veiled speeches to non-political gatherings which has at least the saving grace of reducing the wear and tear, although I can see the restlessness of a retired race horse when the trumpets blow in the adjoining field. As to my future 'plans'—frankly, now that Johnson has thrown out the baby and all the Cabinet with the bath water, I don't see any—unless Rusk resigns. For that I have only rumors and no evidence, nor any assurance that Johnson would want me in any event."

He told Mary Lasker, who was in France at the time, that Alex Rose's Liberal Party, the Roosevelt-Lehman Reform Democrats, and labor all opposed Robert Kennedy's entry into the New York Senate campaign "but you can't stop somebody with nobody, and I have refused to alter my position. So, of course, he can get the nomination, but winning is another matter what with the widespread disaffection. . . . Meanwhile, I promised to have a talk with him, and perhaps I can be helpful in improving the 'image,' and getting some of the dissidents to go along with some consideration on his part."

On August 16, Stevenson went to Washington and testified before the Democratic Platform Committee at the Shoreham. He had lunch at State with George Ball, who was sure Dean Rusk wanted to stay on as Secretary. After lunch he met with Rusk and noted on his schedule: "Conf with Rusk—(re RFK and being an Ambassador. . . . Also Dean wired N.Y. Delegation in 1960 to vote for Stevenson. Also Bobby hostile—knows [Rusk] thinks him young & in need of seasoning.) Current Dangers— *Greek-Turkish* war; more anti-US in *Indonesia*-Malaysia US. properties, *Chinese may explode nuclear device* in Gobi desert—(Chiang against use of nuclear weapons in Asia). *Escalation of war in S.E. Asia.* No evidence of Chinese intervention in *Viet Nam*—but violent talk." Those notes contain no hint that Stevenson discussed the U Thant initiative with Rusk.

Delegates and other Democrats including Stevenson gathered at Atlantic City that ensuing Sunday, August 23. (It was only twelve years since he himself had first been nominated.) He was much sought after at receptions and parties, some given by figures of the past—the California Young Democrats for Brown and Salinger, Mayor Daley, Emmett Dedmon and the Chicago *Sun-Times* staff, Perle Mesta, Barry Bingham, the Harrimans for Mrs. Kennedy, Bill Wirtz—and he delivered a eulogy to Mrs. Roosevelt to the convention and performed various ceremonial functions. Adlai III and Nancy, John Fell and Natalie were with him, and so were Marietta Tree, Pussy Paepcke, the Minows, Wirtzes, Dicks, and others. But it was wholly unlike 1952 and 1956, even 1960, for by now it had long been plain that he had no future as a candidate for President or Vice President, the photographers and reporters and staff members and curiosity seekers and party hangers-on did not follow his every move, crowd around him every time he appeared. He felt left out.

The convention was inherently uninteresting, except for the ovation Robert Kennedy received when, near the end, he spoke about President Kennedy. President Johnson was, of course, nominated for re-election and he in turn recommended that the convention nominate Hubert Humphrey for Vice President, and it did. Evelyn Houston wrote Stevenson, "Be content. As Kempton said, there'll always be for some of us a Stevenson government-in-exile. . . . That evening at the Spanish Pavilion when the . . . minstrels spread their capes [ahead of us] all the way down the stairway for your lady to tread on. . . . It was for you and for you alone. . . . I told my brother that I usually feel like Cinderella when I'm with you, but for one moment that evening I wasn't Cinderella but Queen Isabella." She once recalled that she had been taken aback when the minstrels spread their capes, but Stevenson strode along "as if he had been walking on flung capes all his life." The day after the convention ended, Jane Dick wrote from a hotel as she and her husband were leaving Atlantic City: "I'm sorry indeed if my small request gave you the impression that I was angry or that I didn't think the evening great fun. I was *far* from angry, and what could have been gayer than a night on the town with those special people! But I confess that I found this Convention a traumatic experience—a lot of my gaiety the whole week was, as I'm sure yours was, skin deep. When Humphrey spoke I kept thinking it might have been you. When Johnson spoke I thought—it *should* have been you. To me 'Hail to the Chief' is still your song. . . . I kept thinking of what you lost, and what America & the world lost, and I was profoundly sad. And then all the memories of the great days came flooding back, starting with the evening. . . we waited for the motorcade to take you to make *your* first great acceptance speech. And suddenly I wanted to recapture the *goodness* and *fun* of those days." His relationship with Jane Dick became somewhat strained in 1964—as did his relations with others—but at the end of his life it was as good as ever. By the time Mrs. Dick wrote the letter, Stevenson had left Atlantic City for New York with John Fell and Natalie and Borden and Marietta Tree. They all went to the theater that night.

He wrote Mary Lasker that Atlantic City had been "full of ghosts of the past and there were many things about it I didn't like—and many I did, most of all Hubert's nomination. My little piece about Mrs. Roosevelt was timed to follow the emotional outburst accompanying the Kennedy film. But the reception was warm and the audience attentive. Perhaps I found my greatest comfort in the crowds along the boardwalk and in the lobbies where the affection and frenzy, especially among the young people, was almost undiminished. But certainly my part in the Convention was muted and meager." He told Mrs. Lasker he was "a little disappointed that you rushed into the [Robert] Kennedy endorsement [for Senator] so quickly. . . . As you know, many people, especially among the 'Lehman-Roosevelt' reformers, are extremely apprehensive about the implications for the future should he be elected." (Many other New York liberals, of course, supported Kennedy wholeheartedly.) He told John Steele that one more General Assembly would be enough—he would resign, perhaps as early as next March.

8.

Upon returning from Atlantic City, Stevenson found a copy of a letter Senator Vance Hartke had written to the Nobel Committee proposing Stevenson for the Nobel Peace Prize. Stevenson wrote, "I am deeply touched and more grateful than I can tell you. I was disappointed that there was no reference at the Convention to the fact that I first proposed a nuclear test ban treaty as a national policy in 1956—and few embraced it then. Now, everyone does! If others sent similar letters, I could make some suggestion for inclusion, but it is you I shall always thank for even thinking of such a recommendation. I confess I had not thought of it myself!" Bill Benton promptly drafted a seconding letter, and it included reference to Stevenson's test-ban proposal of 1956. Hartke's was an apt suggestion, and indeed in retrospect it seems odd that the Nobel Committee passed Stevenson over. (Its peace award in 1964 went to Martin Luther King and in 1965 to the United Nations Children's Fund.)

The Chicago *Tribune* reported that Ambassador Fedorenko of the U.S.S.R. told Stevenson in great secrecy that the Soviets were eager to do anything possible to help Johnson defeat Goldwater. Stevenson, according to the *Tribune,* passed the offer along orally to Johnson, who told him to decline it firmly but politely. Stevenson watched Adlai III's campaign for the Illinois legislature with great interest, and when he won and led the Democratic ticket in Illinois, Stevenson behaved "like a school kid," as Adlai III put it. "I heard—he never told me—that after that he often pulled out clippings and told people about the great victory here. He had his pride in his son and his name—it was a triumph for him, too, after bad defeats in Illinois." Adlai III not only led his ticket; he polled more votes than the leading Republican, a brother of former President Eisenhower. Later, when Adlai III was serving in the state legislature, Stevenson counseled him to be cautious and not make radical proposals which would alienate the regular organization Democrats.

Stevenson spoke in the Security Council on September 10 on the dispute between Malaysia and Indonesia. Malaysia and Cyprus, together with political speeches, occupied most of Stevenson's time in September and October. He told Barbara Ward, "All I want to do is unpack for keeps. But instead the campaign is upon us and I shall have to be going around the country quite a bit." He was, he said, sure "that Hubert has had his just deserts at last. . . . I only hope that very zest, generosity and gaiety which we admire doesn't get too exuberant and embarrass him." He thought Robert Kennedy would win although he noted "much opposition even within the Democratic party" and sympathy for his opponent, Kenneth Keating. He sent Hubert Humphrey a memorandum on his proposal, made in the 1956 campaign, to replace the draft with a professional army, a proposal now being studied by the Administration and endorsed by Goldwater. He also sent Humphrey a $1,000 campaign contribution and entertained his children in New York. Humphrey wrote, "You are a dear friend, Adlai, and I owe you much thanks for many things."

Stevenson welcomed Jacqueline Kennedy to New York: "I hope you can find some peace here. I haven't!" He invited her to hear "a remarkable young pianist" at 42A on October 18. (The pianist was Eugene Indjic, then a protégé of Mrs. Carpenter, Ellen Stevenson's mother. It was a measure of his detachment from the campaign. Robert Kennedy presented Stevenson with $25,000 for the Eleanor Roosevelt Foundation. Sarah Plimpton wrote several times from Paris, mood writing, imagery, love. Ruth Field sent him a long unhappy letter: "Our troubles are our own fault—probably my fault." Stevenson's old law firm was giving a dinner in honor of Ed Austin. Stevenson could not go but sent Austin a long affectionate letter recalling his early days at the firm.

Stevenson made a few appearances in the New York campaign. President Johnson, through Bill Moyers, asked him to do everything possible for Kennedy. Stevenson made his first important campaign speech outside New York on September 24 in Philadelphia, to the World Affairs Council. He discussed the basic course of American foreign policy and, near the end, said, "In any event, there *is* a clear choice between the American foreign policy which has evolved by broad consensus over the postwar years and a more militant, minority view of the world."

He started an extended campaign swing on October 2. In Cleveland he held a press conference, made three television appearances, went to a cocktail party, and delivered a major speech at the Mayor's luncheon. He mentioned recent political charges against the Administration, including one that it was responsible "for lies and lives" in Vietnam. He said President Johnson had made it clear that Communist expansionism would be resisted but "will not be permitted to goad us into any rash acts." Stevenson noted on his schedule: "Largest luncheon ever held in Cleveland—

2800! Speech great success—fine editorials." He left Cleveland that afternoon and went on to Chicago where he called on Mayor Daley to discuss the Illinois and national campaigns—"very flattering about Adlai." Marietta Tree arrived and went to Libertyville with Stevenson for, as he noted, a "beautiful autumn afternoon with whole family except BS [Borden Stevenson] who returned to N.Y. after his deposition in case of conservator for Ellen."

He spent Sunday, the next day, working on speeches at Libertyville and walking with Marietta. His dog got into a fight with a neighbor's dog, and Marietta told him to seize his dog's collar. He did, and the dog jumped, and the index finger of Stevenson's right hand was broken badly. He wrote to Marietta's daughter Penelope Tree, "Do you like my penmanship? If not try writing with your thumb and forefinger with a 2 pound bandage on the rest of your hand. I broke my finger—in pieces—trying to keep peace between some dogs and am just back from 3 hours on the operating table. . . . And reflect on the perils of peacekeeping!!!"

On October 6 he went to St. Louis, where he visited his aged aunts and delivered a speech to the St. Louis Bar Association. Again, reviewing basic American postwar foreign policy, he emphasized its courage tempered by restraint. In all these speeches and more, he used long passages over and over, thus abandoning his insistence of 1952 and 1956 upon having a wholly fresh speech for each occasion.

On October 29, as the campaign neared its end, he made a television appearance for Robert Kennedy, then left for Los Angeles, where he held an airport press conference, visited the Los Angeles *Times,* went to a dinner for Pierre Salinger, the Democratic senatorial candidate, and next day spoke at noon to the World Affairs Council in the Biltmore. "Great success!" he noted. "Large crowd—ovation before and after." He began "I have come here not to make a campaign speech, but to make a non-partisan talk in behalf of a bipartisan foreign policy—one that has been supported for twenty years by both major parties. I would not want to pretend, however, that I am wholly indifferent to the outcome of this election. After all, Congressman Miller [Goldwater's vice presidential running mate] has announced that I will be fired five minutes after Goldwater takes office. To that, I can only say that he will be at least four minutes too late."

9.

That ended Stevenson's part in the 1964 campaign. A few hours after he spoke in Los Angeles he left by plane for Santiago, Chile, where he would lead the U.S. delegation—Marietta was a member—attending the inauguration of President Eduardo Frei Montalvo on November 3. He went first to Mexico and next day visited the pyramids near Mexico City, noting, "Amazing excavation & restoration since Ellen and I came here in 1936!" He visited the Foreign Minister and President López Mateos, then stopped at Panama, where he discussed with the U. S. Ambassador and the Panamanian Foreign Minister the danger of a recurrence of the violence of the previous January. President Johnson's big jet arrived and Stevenson joined other members of the delegation aboard it and headed for Chile, arriving on Monday, November 2. From then until Friday, Stevenson went through the usual ceremonies attending an inauguration.

He had, however, another mission. It was believed almost certain that President Frei would open diplomatic relations with Russia. The United States disapproved. It had, however, been resigned to it until mid-October, when Khrushchev fell. This seemed to present an opportunity to at least urge Frei to wait to see who succeeded Khrushchev. Therefore Stevenson was instructed to press Frei not to establish diplomatic relations with Russia at this time. He did so on Monday morning, his first day in Santiago. The Foreign Minister-designate, Gabriel Valdés Subercaseaux, was present, as was the American Chargé d'Affaires, John Jova. Frei was a liberal, a believer in the Alliance for Progress, and a leader of the non-Communist left in Latin America, the first member of the Christian Democratic Party ever elected President. The choice of Stevenson to represent Johnson at Frei's inaugural was an excellent one. The two men might have formed a firm friendly relationship—but for Stevenson's instructions.

After a polite exchange on Chile's problems and prospects, Stevenson moved to the point—said he understood that Frei planned to resume relations with the U.S.S.R. Without wanting in any way to interfere with Chile's affairs, he advised caution and said that relations with Russia had caused difficulties in Argentina, Brazil, Uruguay, and other countries. Frei asked what the United States thought would be the policies of the new regime in Moscow. Stevenson said his own talks with Fedorenko and Dobrynin and Mikoyan's son, and Kohler's talks with Kosygin, indicated that de-Stalinization would continue and there would be no change in Soviet policy on Cuba. Therefore, Stevenson said, Latin America would continue to be threatened.

Frei said he was grateful for all this but had always felt Chile should have relations with the Iron Curtain countries and he himself had a long record of political commitment on the question. Other nations, including those of Western Europe and the United States itself, had relations with the U.S.S.R. Chile felt it had the sovereign right to have such relations abroad as it pleased. He assured Stevenson that Chile would take all due precautions so that Curtain diplomatic missions would not carry out improper activities.

Stevenson pressed him harder. According to Foreign Minister Valdés, Stevenson never actually threatened Frei but he gave the impression that the threat was there. Valdés once recalled that although Stevenson did not lose his "composure" he did lose his "diplomatic touch" and became a somewhat harsh advocate of his viewpoint. Toward the end of the interview both Frei and Stevenson were talking at the same time. Frei ended the interview abruptly by thanking Stevenson for his observations but repeating Chile's intention of renewing relations according to plan. Valdés did not think Stevenson understood Chileans or Latin Americans generally, especially their determination to maintain national identity. (It was a common Latin American complaint about North Americans. Actually, Stevenson did understand Latins' fiercely held national identity, but on this occasion his instructions overrode his understanding.) Stevenson, Valdés thought, was naturally a Europeanist, preoccupied with East-West relations, disarmament, nuclear testing, coexistence, and other global issues. The widespread admiration for Stevenson in Latin America made his contretemps with Frei all the more regrettable, Valdés thought.

Before leaving the country Stevenson told the Chilean press that, while Chile would of course take its own decision, opening relations with Moscow would worry many groups and, moreover, nobody knew what was going on in Moscow at this time. The Socialist press criticized him. Not long afterward, Chile and the U.S.S.R. did re-establish diplomatic relations.

The day of Frei's inaugural was the day of the presidential election in the United States. Stevenson had hoped to spend Election Night with Adlai III. Instead he was receiving the returns in Santiago. Then he sent cables. He told President Johnson, who won by a landslide: "Congratulations. If I have to drink any more toasts to El Presidente Johnson I may disgrace you. Coming home." To Humphrey: "You were just elected Vice President of United States and Chile. President Frei sends regards and congratulations and so do I." He told Robert Kennedy: "I wasn't surprised when the good news came in from New York. But I was mighty relieved, all the same! And the jubilation among the Chileans would have warmed your weary heart." To John Brademas, re-elected to Congress, he called: "It was a great day for Chile, the United States—and *South Bend.* Congratulations and blessings my dear friend." He told Dick Daley, "In Santiago, Chile, there was loud jubilation when the news filtered in from Illinois. And at least one visitor from abroad knew that it took a lot more than President Johnson! And thanks for all you did for Adlai Jr." He telephoned Adlai III to congratulate him.

10.

A presidential election is a watershed. If one can believe the Pentagon Papers, there were those in the Johnson administration who believed as early as September 7 that the United States probably would have to launch air attacks against North Vietnam. But, with President Johnson campaigning as the apostle of moderation and restraint against Goldwater's militaristic extremism, the Administration held back. On Election Day detailed planning for the bombing campaign began. According to the Pentagon Papers, now, during the last weeks of 1964 and the early weeks of 1965, President Johnson, with his enormous popular mandate in hand, firmly took his fateful decisions to escalate. Less than one hundred days after the election, on February 8, 1965, he ordered new reprisal strikes and five days later gave the order for the sustained bombing of the North.

Stevenson was probably not involved in those decisions of November 1964. He did, however, on November 18, after returning from Chile, give the President a long memorandum reviewing our foreign policy. Entitled "A re-assessment of United States foreign policy 1965–70," it was requested by the President and originally drafted by Yost. Stevenson changed it little. He regarded it, however, as a major effort and sent copies to Humphrey, Rusk, and Cleveland. It is one of the fullest expositions of his views of foreign policy ever set down.

The memorandum began by discussing how America had shouldered unprecedented burdens as the leading world power during the first decade after World War II and how changes had since then occurred that would make the policies which were triumphant in the 1950s obsolete before 1970—the Sino-Soviet split, the disarray of the Western Alliance, global polycentrism which tended toward international anarchy, shifts in strategic military capability. In the near future, neither the United States alone, the West as a whole, nor existing international institutions would possess the authority to prevent calamity. It was doubtful that a further increase in U.S. or Western armaments was useful, that NATO had an important military future, or that the Soviet Union (whose people and leaders were increasingly shifting their attention from their global role to their domestic needs) would remain intractable. Rather, the principal threat to world peace and Western security would almost surely be "Communist China." It was aggressive and resolute; it was already militarily stronger than any other Asian state except the Soviet Union; its prestige among "colored peoples" would increase and it would tend to create maximum disorder in Asia and Africa.

From all this flowed two consequences: first, we should mobilize far stronger forces in Asia to contain China than we had now; and, second, we should explore partial military disengagement in Europe and political relaxation there in order to make possible joint East-West containment of China.

To those ends, we should encourage India and Japan to counterbalance China; encourage Britain, Australia, and New Zealand to do the same; encourage Russia to do the same (by lessening tensions in Central Europe and improving bilateral Soviet-U.S. relations through increased trade).

We could not, however, tighten "the ring" around China if we did not demonstrate that the ring was directed against Chinese aggression, not against the Chinese people or even Chinese domestic Communism. We should remain ready to negotiate a settlement whenever Peking was ready to behave. This meant more vigorous efforts to develop a meaningful dialogue with Peking. We could not keep Peking out of the UN forever.

In sum, Stevenson was advocating a fundamental shift of emphasis from Europe to the Far East.

As for disarmament, we should try to check nuclear proliferation but probably could not persuade China or France to renounce nuclear weapons. Therefore the United States and U.S.S.R. should move rapidly at Geneva to control and reduce nuclear arms before the Chinese developed their own.

But the immediate threat to the peace lay not in either nuclear or large-scale conventional war. It lay instead in war between middle or small powers (Israel-Arab, India-Pakistan, Malaysia-Indonesia, Ethiopia-Somalia, Greece-Turkey) which could spread and involve great powers, and in wars of "liberation."

Peace keeping by regional organizations should be encouraged. And so should increased peace-keeping machinery by the UN.

Meanwhile, the widening gap between the developed and under-developed nations—a North-South split—was extremely dangerous. If development failed in the South, extremist regimes would emerge to attack white bastions in Asia and Africa. An eventual North-South confrontation might be more bloody than an East-West confrontation. And exploding populations in the South compounded the problem.

The memorandum summed up: the United States should "shift the center of containment from Europe to the Far East" and broaden containment's base; encourage rapprochement with the Chinese; push vigorously for nuclear arms control and reduction; rapidly develop improved regional and UN peace keeping; substantially expand economic development, trade, and investment with the third world.

It was a significant memorandum. An extrapolation of the policy of containment from the heart of Europe—for which it was devised—to Southeast Asia had led us into Vietnam. Some months earlier in a speech at Princeton, Stevenson had said that containment had been "useful and appropriate" in the bipolar world of 1951 but was no longer sufficient. He had added, however, that containment "may not yet have outlived its usefulness," particularly with respect to mainland China. Now he was proposing an extension of containment in the Far East and refinements on the policy. In doing so, he predicted conflicts that later occurred, such as those between Israel and the Arab states, India and Pakistan. And at the same time he broadened the discussion to disarmament and world order. As always, he both widened policy and gave it political emphasis.

Stevenson gave the memorandum to Johnson personally on November

18. McGeorge Bundy said, "This memo's fate was like all after the election. After the election everybody assumed that there was a mandate for Johnson to do as he pleased." It also got lost because the ballooning of our involvement in Vietnam smothered nearly everything else.

Giving a copy to Humphrey, Stevenson said, "It is so hard for me to find time to talk to anyone in Washington about the futures when there are so many presents—yes, and always so *many present!*" He also asked Humphrey, if the occasion arose, to "tell the President that you doubt if I am prepared to stay on this assignment indefinitely."

11.

At last, on December 1, the General Assembly opened. It met almost until Christmas Eve, day after day of plenary debate, but Stevenson spoke only once, a minor effort on Cuba. At the same time the Security Council was meeting on Syria-Israel and on a new crisis in the Congo, and Stevenson spoke there. In the midst of all the talk, anti-Castro Cubans fired a bazooka shell across the East River at the UN, and dynamite was discovered not far away.

Christmas at Libertyville: "Home with Buffy & Ernest, Adlai, Nancy & children, John Fell & Natalie & Mao [John Fell's baby's nickname] & Borden," he wrote on his schedule. "Dicks for late supper after Ruth Winters" on Christmas Eve. They spent Christmas Day at Libertyville—"house lovely—tree—whole family—Granny Carpenter joined us for Christmas dinner. Afternoon nap—and cleaning up the mess!" Ed McDougal's wife gave him a pin cushion for Christmas, embroidered, "Adlai, son of Illinois, man of vision, friend of mankind, wise counselor." Next day he went hunting with Adlai and Borden at a club near Crystal Lake and got 120 birds, quail, chukkar, and pheasant. They had a family supper that night and he had a "good" talk with Mrs. Ives. On Sunday, the twenty-seventh, they lunched with the Dicks and had old friends in for cocktails. On the following day, Monday, December 28, he was called back to New York—"as usual!" he noted irritably. There he joined a Security Council meeting on the Congo. He spoke on Wednesday, the thirtieth, had his broken finger X-rayed the next day, and went back to Chicago on the five o'clock plane—"riotous & huge party at Kelloggs. . . . How many memorable parties at the Kelloggs!! . . . New Year Eve at Kelloggs!"

12.

Vietnam—Stevenson was plagued with the Article 19 crisis over unpaid assessments and the Dominican intervention but during the winter and spring of 1965 it was Vietnam that overwhelmed him and the rest of the

Administration. It was during this spring that President Johnson began bombing the North and sent ground combat troops into South Vietnam. It was the beginning of America's agony. Although Vietnam was not officially on the agenda of either the Security Council or the General Assembly, it overshadowed everything the UN did as it overshadowed everything the Administration and the Congress did.

On Monday, January 4, Stevenson went to Washington to listen to President Johnson's State of the Union speech ("Our goal is peace in Southeast Asia. That will come only when the aggressors leave their neighbors in peace"). President Johnson asked him to come to see him, and Stevenson did the following afternoon. Johnson told him he had done a "brilliant" job at the UN and could never be replaced. Johnson said he hated to think what might have happened to the UN without Stevenson and said he wanted to make a statement of "appreciation, admiration, gratitude, and hope that you will continue throughout my administration."

Stevenson said he appreciated the President's confidence but felt that after four years he might want to resign after the forthcoming General Assembly. He suggested he had little part in policy consultations. He told the President that others could handle his domestic program—the President should concentrate on foreign affairs himself.

Johnson said he agreed "eighty per cent" but he intended to try to drive his huge legislative program through before he got in trouble with Congress. The President proposed what Stevenson called a "bicker session," the phrase Stevenson had learned as a Princeton undergraduate—a meeting of the President, Stevenson, McNamara, Rusk, and Bundy to survey the world situation. The President wanted ideas about China. As he rambled on, he referred repeatedly to Vietnam. He said the military proposed nothing but "bomb, bomb, bomb." The Senate would no doubt debate Vietnam, a bad thing. He talked about communicating with Ho Chi Minh and asked what Stevenson suggested. He asked Stevenson to talk to Senator Wayne Morse, the leading exponent of involving the UN in Vietnam, and to remind Morse that Johnson had put him on the Foreign Relations Committee the day he switched to the Democratic Party.

Stevenson replied that Morse had said so many nasty things about him that he doubted he would have much influence. Johnson observed that Morse had said nasty things about everyone except his wife.

The President described British Prime Minister Harold Wilson's visit and said that the State Department was trying to "shove MLF down his throat or else." He felt sorry for Wilson, with a narrow parliamentary majority and a run on the pound, and had told State to treat him gently, and it had, and Johnson had made a friend. He talked about the past year—eighty-five heads of state had come for President Kennedy's funeral and thirty-three more since. He wanted to make as few changes as possible in the Cabinet and other top jobs. He valued McNamara and Wirtz highest among the cabinet officers. Wirtz had settled difficult strikes and pulled the

State of the Union speech together. Mrs. Johnson and the family "loved" him. Johnson was having trouble with Senator Mansfield, whom he considered "mean and small," who would not give Humphrey's wife a ticket to the State of the Union ceremonies, who refused to give Vice President Humphrey a suitable office in the Capitol, and who had told Johnson that he, Mansfield, would run the Senate and that if Johnson sent Humphrey to run it Mansfield would oppose him. He compared Congress to a country dog—"if you stand still you get screwed to death and if you run they chew you out." Johnson said he intended to pile work onto Humphrey and make him his closest adviser in the public eye.

Stevenson noted, "Resentment of way JFK treated him very clear." Kennedy had called him a buffoon, Johnson said.

Johnson doubted if an advisory consultant position would be congenial for Stevenson—he would constantly encounter the Secretary of State in Washington and Ambassadors abroad. Johnson thought Rusk and Ball conscientious and able "but never a new idea." At the end of their talk Johnson called in reporters and photographers and told them that he and Stevenson had been having "another of our periodical talks over five continents" and said they had discussed especially Article 19, Africa, and Vietnam. He pressed two cigarette lighters and a tie clasp on Stevenson as he departed. They had talked for an hour and ten minutes.

Article 19 was claiming more and more of Stevenson's time and energy and beginning to match the Congo "for total time expenditure and frustration," as he told Barbara Ward. He was beginning to lose interest in his work. Francis Plimpton once said, "It's an awful beating. I know that after four and a half years I was ready to quit. And there's a certain repetitiveness about it. Adlai would say, 'I can't face another debate on Palestine refugees.' " Jane Dick thought he tired of the social routine, too. His broken finger was not healing properly and all spring gave him considerable pain, which contributed to his fatigue. To some of his friends he seemed weary in some fundamental way. Agnes Meyer urged him to dictate his memoirs as part of an oral history project at Princeton which she would support. He said he supposed he would "get around to it sometime" but he never did. (He did give many of his private papers to Princeton, however, and Mrs. Meyer contributed to the cost of organizing them. Shortly before he died he talked to John Bartlow Martin about working with him on his memoirs.)

He had been trying to write a draft for President Johnson's inaugural address. He sent it to Dick Goodwin on January 5, describing the interruptions which had impeded his work and saying, "But some tired old cliches fell from my palsied lips. Here they are—unedited! Perhaps you could salvage a word here or there. Please don't try to do a rhetorical 'jewel.' It would sound too contrived and, *I think*, diminish him." Stevenson's draft included a sentence Stevenson himself used more than once, "We, the human race, we are, if you like, already fellow travelers on a tiny space ship spinning through unimaginable distance. We can wreck our ship." A paraphrase of it survived in the President's final draft. He submitted a list of women who might be considered for places in the Johnson administration; one of them was Dorothy Fosdick. On January 8, McGeorge Bundy telephoned him on behalf of President Johnson and told him how much the President hoped Stevenson would stay on. The country, he said, had never had Stevenson's kind of representation at the UN. Could he announce that he had no present intention of resigning? Stevenson said yes —agreed to permit Bundy to generate a statement by Reedy, the press secretary, saying that President Johnson had asked him to stay on and he had said he had no present intention of leaving.

On January 8, Stevenson went to Chicago, spent the weekend at Libertyville, and on Monday, January 11, went to Springfield for the inauguration of Governor Kerner. He wrote on his calendar, "Memories of 16 years ago today!" when he himself had been inaugurated Governor. Jack Arvey wrote, "Inasmuch as we both are bald and past 60, I cannot understand why the ladies all greet you with a kiss and give me a formal 'hello.' Someday I would like to have you give me your secret." Stevenson thanked him for helping Adlai III—"he is curiously diffident about imposing on my old friends."

The General Assembly opened on January 18 and the next day Stevenson went to Washington for the Johnson inaugural, attending numerous ceremonies. He escorted Marietta Tree to the inaugural ball at the Sheraton Park Hotel and, discovering that only one seat remained vacant in the President's box, took it himself and abandoned Marietta. Arthur Schlesinger was leaving the White House staff; and, at a State Department reception, Stevenson urged John Bartlow Martin to take Schlesinger's place so that Stevenson would have his own man at the White House for liaison with President Johnson. It was a measure of his relationship with the President.

The General Assembly debated Cyprus for nearly a month, from January 19 to February 16. Stevenson was spending a great deal of time on Article 19. The United States was still holding firm to the position that Russia could not vote until it paid its assessments, although it had softened the position somewhat by agreeing to permit the Assembly to act by unanimous consent without votes. Stevenson spoke during general debate in the Assembly, comparing Russia's refusal now to pay its assessments to its effort earlier to impose a troika on the UN.

Libertyville was struck by a terrible ice storm and the farmer, Richard, told Stevenson that the farm, strewn with the broken limbs of elms and maples, looked like a battlefield. Stevenson replied, "I am heartsick." He went to Washington and saw the President and afterward sent the President a memorandum on the Near East arms race.

The Oateses and Dicks gave the annual birthday party, Stevenson's sixty-fifth, at the River Club in New York. Ruth Field wrote to him: "The really important point is the one [your son] Adlai made: 'You won't live' —This *should* make the decision easy: 'OUT'! Adlai is right, of course. You *can't* risk your life. . . . No one can stand the pace you set indefinitely without a long break. . . . So the questions about whether it's good or not good for the country and the U.N. to have someone of your stature dominate the job for two terms, is irrelevant. The important angle is *you* —You *must* live."

13.

On February 6, George Ball called Stevenson: Viet Cong guerrillas had attacked a U.S. military compound at Pleiku, killing nine Americans and wounding seventy-six. The United States immediately sent American carrier-based bombers against barracks and staging areas in North Vietnam in retaliation. The raid took place only a few hours after the arrival of Soviet Premier Alexei N. Kosygin in Hanoi and it triggered events which a week later culminated in President Johnson's order for the sustained air war against North Vietnam. At the time, however, the White House called the raid merely "appropriate reprisal action . . . carefully limited." The Department sent Stevenson a draft of a letter to the president of the Security Council informing the Council of the attack on Pleiku and Tuy Hoa and of U.S. retaliation. The letter closed, "Our objective is a peaceful settlement. This would require both the self-restraint of the regime to the north and the presence of effective international peacekeeping machinery to make sure that promises are kept." Stevenson sent the letter as instructed. At the same time President Johnson announced that he was ordering American dependents withdrawn from South Vietnam.

Harlan Cleveland told Stevenson to indicate to other Ambassadors that the United States planned no further retaliation for the time being. Cleveland asked the Mission to send its political officers into the corridors to get a report on UN reaction to the U.S. bombing. Several Communist-bloc delegates thought the action meant a long and futile struggle, might have been a deliberate attempt to involve the Soviets more deeply, and must have pleased Mao since it proved his charges of U.S. gangsterism and damaged the Soviet Union, which was willing to negotiate with the United States.

On February 11, Stevenson met with his staff on Vietnam, then took the shuttle to Washington, delayed an hour by fog, writing on his schedule, "What to do about Viet Nam!!" He attended a cabinet meeting on Vietnam. Talking from notes, he urged a political settlement and careful consideration of using the Security Council to start negotiations. He thought the United States should pursue a "peace track" alongside military action.

Rusk seemed to prefer a call to a conference by the chairman of the International Control Commission; Stevenson noted, "But for years State has been trying to avoid Geneva Conf!" He noted on his schedule, "Why do McNamara & Bundy make such guarded and optimistic statements about military situation in Viet Nam!!!" At the end of the meeting the President requested a memorandum on a political settlement. Stevenson prepared it. He thought the United States should first increase its military efforts in South Vietnam to "give clear evidence of our firm purpose," then go to the Security Council and ask for a fact-finding UN group to report on infiltration and ways of enforcing the 1954 Geneva accords. We could also call for another Geneva Conference. "Would [a conference] loosen up negotiations with the Chicoms? Isn't it time to end the freeze in Southeast Asia? . . . Would not Chinese admission to the UN be tolerable through this avenue if they promised to stop interference in VN and Laos and joined in any international guarantees resulting from a new conference?" (Once more he was broadening the issue.) Resort to the peaceful track "would enhance confidence in the UN and demonstrate US respect for it." Again he was thinking of the UN as such. "Also, it would still the critics, domestic and foreign, who say don't pull out but negotiate, before we get into a major war in the wrong place and alone." He was thinking too of politics. North Vietnam might deny the UN's competence. The Soviets might veto. But something must be done. "Can we go on fighting the war without (a) agreeing to negotiate or (B) raising the level of the war? . . . How long can the Administration stand with a rising domestic pressure to end the war on the one hand, or to step up the war on the other?" He left the paper unfinished and flew that night to Ruth Field's Chelsea plantation. Harlan Cleveland reworked the paper, turning it into a scenario for Security Council action on Vietnam, and George Ball discussed it with President Johnson in Stevenson's absence.

Next morning, February 12, Stevenson walked about the land with Mrs. Field and went for a swim. It was a warm day, and they had lunch in the woods and went quail hunting in the afternoon. At five-thirty he received a telephone call from Harlan Cleveland: he must return at once—U Thant had made a statement recommending a negotiated settlement and a new Geneva Conference. The President must say something promptly. They had to plan a scenario for UN action. They would send an Air Force plane for him. That night a violent storm struck and knocked the telephone out. Next morning, a dismal Saturday, Stevenson received word from Washington that he need not return until Monday. On Sunday, February 14, he took an overnight train to Washington and went on to New York.

It had been a bad weekend. On Friday, U Thant had unexpectedly issued a statement saying he was "greatly disturbed" by "the seriously deteriorating situation in Vietnam." He thought that if the dangerous escalation got out of control it "would obviously pose the gravest threat to the peace." He believed only political and diplomatic negotiations, not military moves, could achieve peace. He had previously urged a reconvening of the Geneva Conference. He said he did not now know what would be the best means of reaching a settlement but he did feel "very strongly" that "means must be found and found urgently."

Regardless of what Stevenson thought, the State Department at that time did not want a new Geneva Conference. Nor did it believe the UN could effectively intervene: any resolution acceptable to the United States would be vetoed by the Russians in the Security Council and could not muster a two-thirds majority in the Assembly. Indeed, during this first quarter of 1965, the United States Government did not appear to want negotiations of any kind over Vietnam.

After U Thant issued his unexpected statement Ralph Bunche called Yost to explain why he had done it—the press and various delegations had insisted on knowing why he was doing nothing on such a vital question. On the following day, Saturday, February 13, Bunche telephoned Yost and said he thought it would be helpful if Stevenson and Thant would have an immediate talk. Yost said that Stevenson was out of town (at Ruth Field's) until Tuesday. Bunche then suggested it would be useful if Yost saw Thant that day. About noon Yost went with Plimpton and Pedersen to see Thant and Bunche. Thant said he and Stevenson had had some very confidential talks about Vietnam over a period of time. He said that a third party was willing to play host to talks between the United States and North Vietnam. Since his talks with Stevenson had been very private he was not sure how much more he should say now and perhaps should wait for Stevenson's return. But he went on to say he thought a Geneva-type conference ought to be tried—and the "modalities" of bringing one about had already been recommended to Stevenson. He said he had talked to Stevenson about it in August and again in November and December. He said he was now waiting for a reply from the President as a result of his latest talk with Stevenson.

Yost, Plimpton, and Pedersen were flabbergasted by all this. Stevenson had told none of them about his secret talks with Thant or of Thant's favorable reply from Ho Chi Minh. Nor had he put anything about it in writing. When Pedersen wrote a memo on the talk with Thant, it was the first time anything had been put on paper by the United States Government on the Thant initiative. Yost now told Thant that he was not aware of "all the details" of Thant's talks with Stevenson but it was useful to have this explanation. Thant did not tell Yost of Ho's favorable reply nor of Burma's willingness to act as host to secret negotiations. Yost, incompletely informed by Stevenson and Thant, was unable to report fully to the Department. Had Stevenson himself been on hand, he would instantly have understood the full implications of Thant's call for a new Geneva Conference—that Thant now had reason to believe such a call would succeed—and he would have fully informed the Department. But he was in Georgia till Monday, having been told by the Department he need not return till then. And so Cleveland and others in the Department had no real comprehension of what was behind Thant's statement.

Later, Pedersen and George Ball, working with Yost, tried to piece together the history of the whole Thant initiative. Thant had begun making proposals for bilateral talks to Stevenson as early as late 1963. Stevenson had reported them to the Department, which had not deemed them feasible. Thant said he had never received a reply to them. In August of 1964, when he made his state visit to Washington, Thant had presented his "proposals" and, encouraged by President Johnson's evident desire for peace, had subsequently approached Ho Chi Minh through the Soviets. Receiving a favorable reply, he informed Stevenson, probably in early September. Throughout September and October and early November he awaited a reply in vain. Late in November (according to Thant), Stevenson had asked him where the meeting with Hanoi would take place and what would be the level of representation. Thant mentioned Cambodia, Burma, Pakistan, and France as possible meeting places and expressed a preference for Burma. Stevenson agreed. Thereafter Thant asked General Ne Win of Burma whether such a meeting could be held in Rangoon. Ne Win agreed. Thant so informed Stevenson late in December and recommended that, in order to maintain secrecy, the United States not send a special representative to Rangoon but simply authorize the U. S. Ambassador there to meet with the North Vietnamese Consul General. Stevenson was enthusiastic, according to Thant, and said he would report to Washington. But in January, according to Thant (or early February), nearly six months after Thant's original move, Stevenson told Thant that this was not the time for such an initiative. He also told Thant that it would be difficult for the United States to negotiate without South Vietnam's presence—to do so would undermine morale in the Saigon government. (He was probably acting on instructions from Rusk.) Thant discussed the alternatives of a Geneva Conference and of a seven-power conference—the four great powers plus the two Vietnams and the Viet Cong. Stevenson had not responded.

Thant, indeed, had had little response from Washington to any of this. He began to feel ill used by Washington and it impaired their relationship (although not Thant's relations with Stevenson). Soon he began issuing public statements on Vietnam, and Washington, in its turn, began to feel ill used by Thant. Pedersen and Yost in retrospect considered the whole affair unfortunate. They believed that the wasted initiative was the result of a long series of misunderstandings.

Why had Washington seemed to throw cold water on the initiative? No doubt for several reasons. Its position in Vietnam at that time was weak and it did not want to negotiate from weakness. Late in November, according to a Department chronology, Thant told Stevenson that he himself had held up his proposals pending the U.S. election. Shortly after that Rusk had talked to Stevenson, and Rusk's reaction was "not particularly encouraging," according to a chronology compiled by George Ball. By that time Thant had named his source, a Russian who had relayed Hanoi's willingness to talk. Secretary Rusk received the impression that neither the Soviet Ambassador to the United States nor their Ambassador to the UN knew about the maneuver. The Russian with whom Thant had been dealing was considered a KGB man, that is, an agent of the secret police. For this reason Rusk was not greatly interested. Later Thant indicated that Gromyko had known about the maneuver. Had Rusk known this at the time he might have reacted differently. So far as is known, the proposal never reached President Johnson, at least not at that time, in part, perhaps, because of his order to hold up new policy initiatives until after the election. And apparently Secretary Rusk, on the basis of his own private discussions with high-level Russians, came to the conclusion that there was no message from Hanoi and that U Thant had been working on the basis of a misunderstanding of some sort. In addition, Rusk—and probably Johnson as well—seems to have taken the general view that Thant was soft, wobbly, and imprecise and to have lacked wholehearted confidence in him as an intermediary.

Arthur Schlesinger once said, "Stevenson was so beaten down by Rusk's saying it was all just propaganda that he didn't do anything more about it. I don't think he took it to President Johnson. He felt defeated." Harlan Cleveland knew nothing about the initiative until Yost and Plimpton and Pedersen learned of it in February. He later said Stevenson was "very resentful" that Washington had not followed up the Thant initiative. Like Thant, Stevenson took it seriously, Cleveland thought. "Down here [in Washington] it got the brush-off. The reason is clear—it was only one of twenty or twenty-five efforts by volunteer mediators to create a procedure for us and Hanoi to talk. Adlai handled it wrong procedurally. Rusk thought he had responded—he asked Stevenson, 'What are we going to talk about?'" at Rangoon, that is. "Stevenson didn't want to tell U Thant, 'Your idea didn't get the time of day.' So he stalled." Cleveland's deputy, Joe Sisco, later concluded that both Rusk and Stevenson had perhaps been imprecise—there was confusion in communication between them. It might be added that Thant too had erred—had failed to give his move at the time the added authority of Gromyko's knowledge.

Sisco recalled that when he, Sisco, learned of the Thant initiative, Rusk said he had told Stevenson there was no use in pursuing the opening at that time but he should keep the Thant channel open. Sisco said, "Stevenson doubted if we were really willing to explore the opening since there was a lot of talk about not negotiating from weakness. He was deeply suspicious on this matter. He often said, 'We ought to get out, had no business being there, ought to get out, I don't know how we got into this pickle.'"

McGeorge Bundy, who also learned about the initiative later, said,

"Washington thought it did not amount to anything. We were talking all the time to them about their points," that is, talking to Hanoi about their preconditions for negotiations. "Rusk was saying that the UN is noisy and the thing will leak to Saigon. This was correct. But there should have been a way to explain this to Stevenson and to U Thant. The problem arose from a misunderstanding between U Thant and the Secretary and between Stevenson and the Secretary. I don't think Stevenson raised it at the White House."

George Ball said, "What happened was this: U Thant talked to Stevenson. Stevenson called Rusk on the telephone. Rusk thought this was one of Stevenson's imprecise conversations. He didn't keep any notes. There was no monitor on the call. It never occurred to Rusk for a moment that it was anything very serious. At the time there were several other things cooking. Rusk never thought it was any more than the kind of fuzzy thing he got out of Stevenson all the time. I myself don't think it was a serious initiative. It was the kind of thing U Thant thought gave him a great opportunity to be the great central figure. There was nothing in it to make any of us think it was serious. I think Stevenson was more encouraging to U Thant than to Rusk. He was a very poor communicator." Ball was positive that Stevenson had gone only to Rusk with the Thant initiative, not to the President. "Stevenson thought this was top-level stuff. Rusk didn't. He was totally astonished when people later thought it was important. I don't believe that Rusk and the President blew one here. There wasn't anything to blow."

Nicholas de B. Katzenbach, later Undersecretary of State, said, "I can imagine a busy Secretary missing this *unless* Stevenson pushed it. So I don't think he did. And he would have if he had thought it was for real." But Yost said, "Stevenson thought that it was a great tragedy that we never took it up. He couldn't understand why we didn't." Nobody will ever know whether anything might have resulted had the opening been pursued vigorously. Most authorities doubt it.

14.

On February 13, while Stevenson was still at Ruth Field's, Cleveland and Sisco drafted a memorandum setting out a UN scenario on Vietnam. At about this time a great many memos were drafted in the Department and the Mission, a reflection of the imminent escalation on the ground in Vietnam.

Stevenson, when he returned, made undated notes, apparently on various talks with U Thant and designed to be discussed with Rusk. One set of notes indicated that Stevenson thought the United States would accept negotiations if Hanoi would—and if they did not we would continue bombing them. One difficulty was that the United States and the Soviets could agree but the Soviets could not bring Peking along. All the notes reflected Stevenson's deep concern over Vietnam.

On February 15, the day Stevenson returned to New York, he began drafting a speech which argued that the National Liberation Front, or Viet Cong, a "creature" of the Communist Party that controlled the regime in Hanoi, was not engaged in a "war of national liberation" but was an arm of Hanoi's military forces conducting "an international war of aggression." This "clandestine war of aggression" was an open violation of the Geneva accords. Next day he talked to Thant and afterward dictated a long memorandum on the conversation and had it telephoned to Cleveland's office in Washington. Stevenson also sent a copy to Horace Busby of the White House staff for President Johnson. He began the memorandum by, for the first time, putting the Thant initiative on paper.

Stevenson said that "for more than a year" U Thant had been urging bilateral talks between the United States and North Vietnam to explore a negotiated settlement. He said that "all these proposals" had been reported to the Department "but not deemed feasible." Thant himself had renewed his proposal during his state visit to Washington in August of 1964. In December, he had informed Stevenson that through the Soviet Union he had made a sounding in Hanoi and Hanoi was ready and willing to talk. (Most chronologies date this several months later.) Thant said that General Ne Win would offer Rangoon as a place for the talks. He also proposed Pakistan as perhaps the best available intermediary with Hanoi. On Friday, Stevenson noted, Thant had told Yost he was still waiting to hear from Stevenson about his suggestion, having received a "positive" response from Hanoi. Now Stevenson saw Thant on February 16 and the following, Stevenson reported, is what he said:

Thant did not think a Security Council meeting on Vietnam "realistic" at this time, though sentiment for such a meeting was rising. He thought Russia would deny the jurisdiction of the UN, would say it was a war of liberation, and veto any resolution calling for a cease-fire and negotiations. But he felt "very strongly" that further attempts at a negotiated solution should be made, "because there is a definite discernible trend toward closer rapprochement between Peking and Moscow." Moreover, many Afro-Asians were very critical of the bombing.

If the United States hesitated to propose negotiations for fear of seeming weak, or because the Congress or South Vietnam would cause difficulty, Thant himself would do it. He liked the idea of a seven-power meeting— the two Vietnams, mainland China, the Soviet Union, France, the United Kingdom, and the United States. Geneva might be better than Rangoon. Hanoi would respond—it was anxious not to become a vassal of China. Thant would not include in his proposal reference to infiltration or cease-fire but would speak of "a more congenial climate." If agreement was reached, he saw the possibility of a useful UN involvement.

The next day Stevenson wrote a letter to the President. "I have admired greatly your prudent and careful approach to this critical situation and the choices that are very difficult. But at least our purpose in Viet Nam is clear and firm: to end the aggression and secure the genuine independence of the Republic of Viet Nam—by peaceful means if possible, by military means if necessary. I do not believe that we should pursue a harder military line with all the risks it involves without at the same time making it emphatically clear that we prefer a peaceful solution and that we are ready to negotiate. Moreover, I believe that escalation of the war would diminish our maneuverability and that we should move quickly." He described his talk with U Thant the day before. Stevenson then proposed a course of action for Johnson's consideration. First, he suggested an early statement by the President expressing our firm intention to continue all necessary military measures to stop "the aggression" but indicating our readiness to explore the willingness of the Communists to accept a peaceful solution. This statement would be circulated to the Security Council, possibly accompanied by a full documented exposition of Communist aggression and infiltration. (Stevenson attached a draft.) Second, he suggested that Thant follow up the President's statement with an appeal to the seven powers to open discussions.

All this, Stevenson wrote, should be done within "a very few days," since military actions could soon make it harder to move to negotiations. It should not be accompanied by preconditions. It would have broad support at home and abroad. It would give the U.S.S.R. ammunition in Peking and Hanoi. It would be harder for the Communists to reject than a proposal by the United States. It would move toward internationalizing the problem. It would not give the impression that the United States was "suing for peace." It would set us on "a diplomatic-military track which cannot be attacked as either unlimited expansion of the war or appeasement." It could be presented persuasively to Saigon and other Asian allies "as the political adjunct of our military step-up and not as a sign of weakened resolve." Hanoi and Peking might not "bite." If they did, we could talk. If they did not, they would bear the onus.

Stevenson sent a copy of the letter to Secretary Rusk. Rusk and George Ball, however, regarded Stevenson's proposal as one that would cut across other negotiations then in progress, as Ball said, and nothing came of it. Yost recalled that Stevenson worked repeatedly on the problem "until he hit a stone wall." At one point he had a detailed cease-fire program worked out with U Thant but Washington was skeptical about how it could be supervised, and it never was presented to the Security Council. "The whole thing petered out," Yost said.

That same day, Wednesday, February 17, Stevenson cabled Jane and Edison Dick in Jamaica:

ARRIVING KINGSTON FRIDAY PAA 221 6:45 WITH JANE GUNTHER WHO LEAVES FOR SOUTH AMERICA MONDAY HOPE YOU CAN PUT HER UP SUNDAY STOP US CHARGÉ RESERVING TWO HOTEL ROOMS.

On Thursday the General Assembly adjourned after Stevenson helped defeat an Albanian effort to force a showdown on Article 19. During the final meeting the Assembly had been picketed noisily by anti-war groups. Next day Stevenson left for Jamaica.

It is unusual for an Ambassador to leave his post unless he feels certain it will remain quiet while he is gone. Stevenson had every reason to expect important matters to arise, especially Vietnam. True, he had agreed to speak at the University of the West Indies in Kingston on February 19. But he stayed the rest of the week with the Dicks. He arrived at Kingston barely in time for the Governor General's dinner for the Queen Mother at King's House. He spoke at graduation ceremonies out of doors to 9,000 people. His speech was on education, one of his great themes. Wednesday evening Secretary Rusk and Harlan Cleveland telephoned from Washington: U Thant had issued another statement, Stevenson must return at once. He did, on Thursday, February 25, but not before he had sent word by the Queen Mother's equerry that he would be unable to call on her "alas," not before Ruth Field telephoned him about a party next week, and Marietta Tree called about going to Barbados for Lady Churchill's visit. A police escort took him to the airport, and he flew to Washington via Miami, arriving there at seven-thirty and talking about Vietnam with Rusk, Ball, and Cleveland until eleven-thirty, then spending the night at the Magnusons'.

The day before, U Thant had said that he had been conducting private discussions on Vietnam "for a long time." He praised President Johnson's "moderation" and "sensitivity" to world opinion. Then he said, "I am sure the great American people, if only they knew the true facts and background of developments in South Vietnam, will agree with me that further bloodshed is unnecessary." While he saw no immediate prospect of useful discussion in the Security Council, he still advocated informal and confidential dialogues and had already approached all the "principal parties" with "concrete ideas and proposals" which included negotiations.

George Reedy, the White House press secretary, promptly denied, somewhat irrelevantly, that the President was "contemplating" negotiations and said the Thant proposal was "not before the President." But what really touched off an explosion in Washington was Thant's implication that the American people were not being told the truth. That same night, about ten o'clock, Secretary Rusk telephoned Thant. Thant asked repeatedly why the United States had virtually ignored his initiative. Rusk brushed the initiative aside as merely procedural and, indeed, dangerous, since nobody knew what might result from the procedure; and he went on to upbraid Thant for saying the Americans were not being told the truth by their government.

At the same time Cleveland sent Yost instructions on what Rusk wanted him to tell Thant the next morning. Yost was to say that Thant seemed to single out the American people and address remarks to them over the head of their government and to avoid the central issue of aggression. The United States Government saw no indication that Hanoi or Peking was interested in discussing a peaceful settlement on a realistic basis. If a new Geneva Conference blew up in anger, peaceful settlement would be even further away. Therefore the United States thought it better to find out whether there was a reasonable possibility of success before considering any negotiation process. If Hanoi would "leave its neighbors alone," the United States would withdraw immediately. There was much more, none of it new.

Next morning, February 25, Yost read the full text of his instructions to Thant and Bunche with occasional comments. Later that day Thant issued a renewed public appeal for negotiations and, at the same time, said he had not intended in his previous statement to suggest that the American people were not being told the truth by their government. Secretary Rusk at a press conference of his own ruled out negotiations with North Vietnam so long as North Vietnam refused to let its neighbors alone, though he said that political channels were being kept open.

It was to this atmosphere that Stevenson was called back from Jamaica. He spent the morning of Friday, February 26, in the Department, then had lunch at one-thirty alone with President Johnson and discussed Vietnam until 3:45 P.M. He noted on his schedule, "Military situation worse than I thought. . . . Anger with U Thant—press conference. Fear of China coming in." The start of sustained bombing of the North, designed to break Hanoi's will, was only four days away.

The Department sent Stevenson instructions that same day for his meeting with U Thant on Saturday, February 27. It followed the Rusk line. He was instructed to say that what was missing in Vietnam was any indication that Hanoi was ready to talk about calling off its efforts to take over South Vietnam. Purely procedural suggestions of who might talk to whom were relevant only if they included an indication that serious substantive talks were also possible. There were many communication lines open and active and several political tracks had already been tried. In view of this, the United States Government did not think that a public call for a Geneva Conference or a seven-power conference was promising.

Next morning, Saturday, February 27, Stevenson and Yost saw U Thant and Bunche for two hours. Stevenson took an extremely hard line, harder than his instructions. At the outset he said that he had assumed his conversations with Thant were strictly confidential and Thant's disclosure of them at a press conference created "very serious doubts" whether confidential exchanges were possible; that, contrary to what Thant said, Burma had been receiving secret U.S. military aid for many years and Congress knew it. He then covered the points set forth by the State Department. He added that President Johnson was especially distressed by Thant's remark about the truth. We were going to continue measured response, not going to escalate substantially. But if this did not succeed, we would consider other and more dangerous steps. Stevenson asked Thant if he knew anything about the North's intentions.

Thant replied that he had always been guided by the idea that the United States should not bring about an agreement between Peking and Moscow. Moscow would join Peking only if the United States pushed too hard in Vietnam. Thant had always felt that Hanoi did not want to be tied to Peking and it still was not too late to draw it away. He also had always felt that the important thing was the mood and attitude of Asian countries. More and more Asian opinion was turning against the United States for racial reasons. Everybody except Thailand thought that the worse things got in Vietnam the more the Communists would win. For all these reasons, he had tried to help; he reviewed his proposals, then explained his press conference and said he very much regretted putting Stevenson and Washington in an embarrassing position. He expressed admiration for Johnson and asked Stevenson to talk to him about not helping Moscow and Peking get together.

Stevenson said we agreed on this, but how? We had hoped Kosygin would restrain Hanoi when he went there, but they had trapped him, and he had promised more aid. Stevenson said negotiations should take up stopping infiltration from the North and guaranteeing the independence of South Vietnam. Stevenson said the UN's prestige in Washington was at an all-time low. It would be very difficult to talk international affairs frankly with the Secretariat in the future. Stevenson did say he wanted to keep the channel to Thant open.

It was, however, an unusually harsh statement for Stevenson to make to U Thant. Nothing else quite like it appears in the record.

At the same time Stevenson transmitted to the president of the Security Council a document called "Aggression from the North," a State Department White Paper which sought to document with photographs and case histories the American contention that the war in South Vietnam was not a civil war or a war of "liberation" but an aggressive war "inspired, directed, supplied, and controlled by the Communist regime in Hanoi!"— "a totally new brand of aggression."

It was, secretly, the eve of sustained bombing of the North, according to the Pentagon Papers, and ground combat forces were soon to come. Policy was moving toward a military "solution."

15.

Stevenson attended a performance of a musical, *The Sound of Music*, and afterward at supper sat next to "Julie Andrews, the star," as he noted. Despite his own fame he was still star-struck.

On the evening of March 3, Secretary Rusk called Stevenson and relayed President Johnson's request that he go to Vienna the next day for the funeral of the President of Austria. Stevenson agreed reluctantly. He took the 9 A.M. shuttle to Washington, went to Capitol Hill, narrated a re-enactment of Lincoln's second inauguration, had lunch with a group of Senators, called Dave Bell about an appointment for Borden, met with George Ball and Harlan Cleveland, picked up funeral clothes, visited the Austrian Ambassador, and took off from Andrews Air Force Base for Vienna—alone in a huge presidential jet. He wrote on his schedule, "Over Vienna at 8:50 AM—airfield closed in—circled for 2 hours! Wild ride with motor cycle escort to Parliament arriving at 12—just in time for funeral ceremony. Stood with visiting dignitaries and diplomatic corps. Ceremony consisted of biographical speech by Chancellor Kraus & fine music."

On Saturday he continued his notes in Vienna: "Saturday morning—6 inches of snow! Beautiful & clear. Stopped for look at St Stephen's church. Airport at 12 and off to Paris in my huge Air Force jet. Clear and crisp—Paris—no snow." He had lunch with the Finletters and Chip Bohlen and a long talk about Vietnam, De Gaulle, and other affairs. He went to see Sarah Plimpton at her "shabby apt house—old city on Left Bank" but dis-covered she was still in India. (She had told him she would be; he had evidently forgotten.) Not finding her, he went for a long walk alone. On Sunday he talked with Finletter, our Ambassador to NATO, who, he noted, was going home in a few days "determined to resign" because he was "discontented with Rusk & support from State." Stevenson flew back to New York on March 7.

A "spokesman" for U Thant issued a statement: "This is the first time that there has been an official U.S. reaction to the SYG's [Secretary General's] proposals regarding Viet-Nam." To Stevenson and Cleveland it seemed to imply that Thant had been getting no official reaction from Stevenson. Cleveland, after talking with George Ball, sent a note to McGeorge Bundy saying that the "battle of the spokesmen" had gone on long enough, press secretaries should be silent, we did not think Thant's proposals relevant or helpful now.

On March 12, Stevenson and Rusk and Cleveland saw President John-son about proposed amendments to the UN Charter. They also talked at length about racial troubles in Selma, Alabama, and about the voting rights bill. Stevenson gave the President a memorandum on Vietnam. "Forgive me for deluging you with unsolicited memos—especially about Viet Nam, on which I have received no information. But you have asked for my views from time to time, and I think the conditions that Sec Rusk has attached to any talk about peaceful settlement is unrealistic and un-supported by the illustrations he uses." It was the first time he had broken with Rusk's policy. To no avail—next day the President said at a press conference, "Our policy is still the same, and that is to any armed attack our forces will reply. To any in Southeast Asia who ask for help in defending their freedom, we are going to give it, and that means we are going to continue to give it."

One evening Stevenson gave a reception for Middle East delegates, and the eminent actors Fredric March and Florence Eldridge recited excerpts from several plays. Afterward they returned to 42A, and Barbara Ward joined them and so did Marietta Tree and Carl McGowan and his son. They sat up until 1 A.M., and McGowan remembered it as a wonderful time. McGowan and his son stayed overnight and had breakfast with Stevenson next morning. McGowan recalled, "He was a little more subdued than usual. During the evening before he had been his usual charming self but at breakfast he looked older, he moved with less bounce. He told me he had a heart condition. But he was in fairly good spirits." That morning Stevenson left for the Caribbean to join Brooke Astor's cruise aboard the yacht *Rara Avis.*

For nine days they cruised among the Virgin Islands and the British West Indies. The weather was fine, blue sky and white clouds with a high trade wind. They made rough crossings in the open sea between islands and anchored in still blue sheltered bays. They swam and went picnicking ashore. On some islands they called on friends in palatial homes. Stevenson described the scenery meticulously, as always. He read histories of the islands and observed historical sites. Sometimes they went to dinner ashore at "very swank" hotels, as he put it, with dancing on the terrace afterward. He went snorkeling. Once he wrote, "Back to Gorda Sound for the night. Reflected at length—as I do every night, damn it, about the future—the job at UN, resignation, love, retirement and writing 'the book,' the children, especially Borden, marriage. (Feel ever more confident that I did the right thing to decline the Presidency of Geo Wash. University and the Motion Picture Producers Assoc.—however seductive the latter salary of $150,000 etc.)" He was reading a book about Joseph P. Kennedy "and his remorseless, ruthless ambition for money—any way to get it—and status. Power?"

16.

While he was gone, opposition to the Vietnam War produced the first "teach-ins," debates over the war. Stevenson put down some thoughts of his own about the war, emphasizing that he still hoped for a political solution: "Military track runs into dead end. . . . How get on parallel track. . . . No reason for insisting on preconditions—have estab. our position—won't permit SVN to be taken over. As we have altered our pos. on mil. side, should attack on pol. side. Could change entire climate of world opinion. Ready to discuss means of settlement that will protect all sides—re-establish basic elements of Geneva Accords."

At a reception for American astronauts Stevenson asked U Thant about rumors of his possible trip to Hanoi and Saigon. (The Department instructed him not to seek out Thant to inquire about this; the instruction arrived too late.) Thant replied that he doubted the legality and propriety of such a trip unless he was directed to go by "the proper organ" of the UN, presumably the Security Council, although he would "study" the matter. Stevenson said he saw no objection if Thant wished to make a personal attempt to mediate without authorization or encouragement from the United States.

Bunche told Stevenson that Thant had discussed the idea of sending identical messages to the United States and the two Vietnams—the "three governments directly involved militarily." (This meant Thant accepted the U.S. claim that Hanoi was engaged, something Hanoi itself denied.) His message would say the war might escalate beyond control with "incalculable" dangers to world peace, solution must be found at the conference table, not on the battlefield, and to create a favorable climate the fighting must stop quickly. Therefore he would appeal to the three governments directly involved to stop military activity across the 17th Parallel for three months—an appeal to the United States to stop bombing the North and to Hanoi to stop infiltrating the South.

Joe Sisco told Secretary Rusk he considered Thant's latest proposal "surprisingly good" in several respects. It would meet the U.S. requirement that there must be an indication by the other side of a readiness to leave their neighbors alone. It did not call for withdrawal of the Viet Cong but neither did it call for a withdrawal of U.S. forces. The probe could take place without tying our hands militarily. It came at a time when the United States was not negotiating from a position of weakness—its recent bombing had "convinced the world of our resolve." Hanoi was unlikely to accept the proposal but it would bear the onus of frustrating it. It might provide a handle for the U.S.S.R. in its struggle with Peking over Hanoi. True, the proposal entailed risks—the United States would have to cease its air strikes but could not be sure infiltration had actually stopped, and the proposal did not cover Viet Cong activity within South Vietnam. Nevertheless, Sisco did not feel the proposal should be rejected out of hand. Harlan Cleveland concurred. At the same time the president of the Security Council pressed Stevenson for Security Council consideration of Vietnam. Also at the same time, seventeen neutrals appealed publicly to all parties for peace talks without preconditions. Thus pressures were rising for a settlement.

On April 2, Cleveland sent a draft instruction to Stevenson before he had cleared it with Rusk or President Johnson. It suggested that Thant delay action—though we thought his explorations might be helpful later—until Hanoi had answered the seventeen-nation appeal. We ourselves expected to be "quite forthcoming" to the seventeen and hoped Saigon would too. As to the substance of Thant's proposal, the United States wanted to include infiltration through Laos (a possibility Thant had left open) and to establish machinery to inspect the suspension of infiltration. But a more fundamental difficulty existed—organized Viet Cong activity in the South. "All these complexities" made it "difficult and inadvisable" to tell Thant now in detail just what language might be acceptable to the United States. The main point to make to him at that time was our belief that somehow military activity in South Vietnam must be bracketed with stopping infiltration. In sum, Cleveland wanted to preserve Thant as a useful channel for quiet diplomacy.

By telephone, Rusk asked Stevenson's views of that draft instruction. Stevenson thought that Thant, if asked to, would postpone his private move or abandon it. Rusk responded that we did not want Thant, as of now, to forsake any role whatever. Stevenson said he felt it important to give Thant a precise reply.

Rusk wanted any firm instruction to Stevenson to be cleared with himself and the President. Stevenson had an appointment with Thant at three o'clock that afternoon and intended to leave at five for Libertyville. Cleveland told Rusk that if Rusk wanted to stop Stevenson from seeing Thant without firm instructions he would have to let Cleveland know by 2:45 P.M. Rusk did not do so. Instead, Stevenson and Yost saw Thant and Bunche and conveyed to them the sense of Rusk's telephone message, saying that they might have a more detailed response later. Thant seemed pleased and satisfied and disposed to follow the course we wanted.

Stevenson left for Libertyville, a family weekend. While he was gone, the Department told the Mission in New York our reply to the seventeen would be made early that week. Thant told the United States that he had received a message from Chou En-lai through the Algerians that the UN should not be involved in Southeast Asia and that Peking had no interest in a visit by Thant. Hanoi also had sent word that he would not be welcome in Hanoi.

When Stevenson returned to his office on April 7 he received telephone calls about a speech President Johnson made that day at Johns Hopkins University. It was the clearest and most authoritative statement of U.S. policy in Vietnam up to that time. In it, the President said, "We are there because we have a promise to keep . . . we have made a national pledge to help South Vietnam defend its independence. . . . We are also there to strengthen world order. . . . To leave Vietnam to its fate would shake the confidence of people around the globe in the value of an American commitment. . . . We are also there because there are great stakes in the balance. Let no one think for a moment that retreat from Vietnam would bring an end to the conflict. The battle would be renewed in one country and then another. . . . The central lesson of our time is that the appetite of aggression is never satisfied. . . . We will not be defeated. We will not grow tired. We will not withdraw, either openly or under the cloak of a meaningless agreement. . . . We hope that peace will come swiftly. But that is in the hands of others. . . . The only path for reasonable men is the path of peaceful settlement. Such peace demands an independent South Vietnam—securely guaranteed and able to shape its own relationships to all others—free from outside interference—tied to no alliance —a military base for no other country. These are the essentials of any final settlement. . . ." The President also said the United States remained ready for "unconditional discussions."

The speech was well received, and for a time it appeared that the President had taken an initiative which might break the bloody stalemate. But after a while hope subsided, and the U.S. troop buildup continued, and more North Vietnamese units went south. In 1965, indeed, U.S. troops in South Vietnam increased from 23,000 to 184,314. And during that spring, too, protests from various peace groups rose at the U. S. Mission.

17.

Sarah Plimpton sent Stevenson a loving letter. Ruth Field sent him a long handwritten letter about her problems with the Field Foundation. Jacqueline Kennedy wrote a teasing note about his girl friends, showing a surprisingly good knowledge of them.

On April 14, Stevenson learned that Chou En-lai had told President Ben Bella of Algeria that Peking did not want U Thant to visit Peking or to intervene in Vietnam. Peking would support anything the Viet Cong did on negotiations. Chou was critical of the seventeen-nation appeal because it failed to mention the 1954 Geneva agreements and called for negotiation without precondition; and the withdrawal of U.S. forces was a necessary precondition (although he had not given the last point much stress). Stevenson heard that U Thant intended, in a speech on April 15, to call for a cessation of hostilities. Stevenson asked Bunche to ask Thant to desist. Bunche reported that Thant, somewhat reluctantly, had agreed to say nothing. But he had instructed Bunche to say that he had now delayed his cease-fire proposal twice at Stevenson's request and wanted it understood that he would be obliged to make an appeal sometime because it was his primary responsibility to do what he could to stop the fighting.

On April 23, Stevenson, on instructions, told U Thant that the United States had tried to find out publicly and privately if suspending the bombing of North Vietnam would lead to an end to aggression from the North. There had been no response. If we thought it would advance the cause of an honorable peace, Stevenson said, we would stop the bombing immediately, but our best judgment now told us it would encourage the aggressor. Thant said that if the United States stopped bombing or indicated it intended to, Hanoi, Peking, and Moscow might be willing to begin negotiations. This was only his private speculation, but he thought the United States ought to try it, if only to encourage the seventeen neutrals to press their appeal.

18.

Stevenson had an appointment with President Johnson at five o'clock on Wednesday, April 28, to discuss Vietnam. He said that, although Thant had so far deferred to our wishes and delayed his appeal for a cease-fire, "I cannot be sure that he will defer some action indefinitely." Thant was "acutely conscious" of his responsibilities, troubled by criticism that he as Secretary General and the UN as an institution had not been able to contribute to a solution in Vietnam, and strongly convinced that the continued use of force held no promise of a settlement but only the ever increasing danger of wider warfare and Peking-Moscow collaboration. Therefore Stevenson presented the advantages and disadvantages of acquiescing in an appeal by Thant for a cessation of hostilities.

The advantages: If we were receptive, we would be in a good position to influence what Thant said and when. A favorable U.S. response conditional on one from North Vietnam would continue the improvement of the U.S. image begun by the President's Johns Hopkins speech. Rejection of Thant's appeal by North Vietnam would seriously damage its international standing and justify continuing our bombing. An appeal from Thant would put him on record as implicitly admitting that North Vietnam was using force against South Vietnam. Such an appeal would make Thant a center of the effort to end the war and facilitate a later move by us to involve the UN in supervising a negotiated settlement.

The disadvantages: International pressure on the United States to stop bombing the North would probably increase rather than decrease. A favorable U.S. response might be interpreted as a sign of weakness, though this could easily be disproved. Temporary cessation of air strikes against the North might damage the morale of the South Vietnamese. If we stopped air strikes because of Thant's appeal, we would be under pressure not to resume them even if the North continued infiltration. Our judgment and his was that unilateral surveillance by the United States and South Vietnam was the only practicable present means of policing a cessation of hostilities. We were dubious that surveillance by some international body would serve our interests—it could easily determine whether air strikes had been stopped but checking on infiltration would be difficult if not impossible.

Stevenson said the broad objective of U.S. policy was to demonstrate that Communist conquests, including wars of liberation, could not be carried out successfully. In particular, we wanted to contain the Chinese Communists' ambitions to dominate Southeast Asia and North Vietnam's ambitions to absorb South Vietnam. "The United States has the force to carry out these tasks *if* the American people have the steadfastness to pursue them over many years." We should, however, attempt to rally an Asian consensus so we would not have to bear the burden alone.

Thus did Stevenson subscribe to the objective of containing mainland China—and succumb to the temptation of stating what we imagined was in the minds of the North Vietnamese and Chinese Communist leaders, people with whom we had almost no contact. George Ball, who had opposed intervention in Vietnam from the very beginning, was now urging withdrawal, but the President was heeding the counsel of General Westmoreland and others to embark on a full-scale ground war.

A little before Stevenson's five o'clock meeting, the President was meeting with Rusk, McNamara, and Bundy on Vietnam when a cable came in from the Ambassador in Santo Domingo. A rebellion planned by the followers of Juan Bosch had broken out in the Dominican Republic four days earlier. Communist leaders had joined it. So had elements of the Dominican armed forces. Over the weekend a blood bath occurred and the rebels seized control of the central city. By Tuesday government troops seemed to be gaining the upper hand, and rebel leaders asked the U. S. Ambassador to intercede and try to arrange a settlement. He declined. Thereupon the civilian rebel leaders—Bosch's political followers—went into asylum in various foreign embassies. But the military rebels, led by Colonel Francisco Caamaño Deño, went back to the streets to fight, knowing it was fight or die. At this point virtually the only political advice available to Caamaño and the other soldiers came from Communists and other extremists. By Wednesday the rebels seemed to be winning—government forces had retreated to an air base outside the city, and the police had informed the U. S. Ambassador they could no longer guarantee the safety of Americans. The Ambassador believed there was danger of another Castro in the Caribbean and, by cable, transmitted a request from the governing junta for American military intervention. A little after 5 P.M. he followed with a cable saying that in his opinion the time had come to send the Marines. The President sent them at once. Stevenson stayed in the White House until 9 P.M. discussing Vietnam and the Dominican Republic. That evening the President went on nationwide television and radio to say that Americans were in danger in the Dominican Republic; Dominican authorities could not safeguard them and we were evacuating them; four hundred Marines had already landed; we had "appealed repeatedly in recent days for a cease-fire" between the contending Dominican forces. The Dominican Ambassador had informed the Council of the OAS of all this. President Johnson himself appealed for a cease-fire. The U. S. Ambassador to the OAS, Ellsworth Bunker, asked the OAS for a special emergency meeting. Stevenson had proposed that the President include in his speech a reference to the danger of a Communist takeover but the President decided against it.

Next morning Stevenson testified before the Senate Foreign Relations Committee on proposed UN Charter amendments, then took the shuttle to New York. Clearly he was not at the policy-making center on either the Dominican Republic or Vietnam at this critical time. Instead, he attended diplomatic functions that evening. On Friday, April 30, the Security Council met on Southern Rhodesia, and Stevenson attended Edward R. Murrow's funeral. He spent the weekend in Libertyville; the jonquils were out. On Monday, May 3, the Security Council met on the Dominican crisis—and it continued to meet on it for weeks. Indeed, although Vietnam always hovered in the background, the Dominican Republic claimed much of Stevenson's time.

Some of his associates have said the Dominican crisis troubled him more than anything that happened during his time at the UN. He once told a correspondent that the Dominican intervention had taken years off his life. Sending troops troubled him because it struck at the principle of peaceful international settlements and alienated Latin American opinion. And yet his files on the Dominican intervention are singularly barren, containing no indication of what he thought of it, no scribbled notes such as he made repeatedly on Vietnam when he was trying to sort out his thoughts. Moreover, one searches in vain through his private correspondence for comments on the Dominican intervention. He spoke time and time again in the Security Council as the debate raged through May and June. But he took relatively little part in the corridor conversations. It was almost as if he were not personally engaged, was merely serving as the United States Government's official spokesman. President Johnson sent John Bartlow Martin to the Dominican Republic to try to get a cease-fire and reach a political solution. When Martin returned he saw Stevenson in Washington at Kay Graham's house and found him perplexed by our intervention but not upset. Stevenson asked what we were doing in the Dominican Republic, and Martin explained, and Stevenson seemed to accept the explanation. Of that occasion he wrote in his own notes, "Lunch at Kay's with John Bartlow Martin, BW [Barbara Ward], Florence Mahoney. Conference with John re Dominican Republic—there as Pres. personal rep to make peace!! V. [very] interesting." Arthur Schlesinger had refused to help the President explain his policy to Latin Americans because he thought the policy wrong and sent Stevenson a copy of a letter criticizing it. Stevenson responded, "Nothing has caused me as much trouble since the Bay of Pigs and it goes on and on."

The Dominican intervention,[9] coming as it did while the Vietnam War

[9] The Dominican intervention was exceedingly complex. Those interested can find opposing accounts of it in John Bartlow Martin's book, *Overtaken by Events,* and in a book by Theodore Draper, *The Dominican Revolt.* Martin was Ambassador to the Dominican Republic from 1962 to 1964. He had been retired to private life for more than a year when the Dominican civil war broke out and President Johnson sent troops. He returned briefly as President Johnson's envoy during the intervention.

was being escalated, touched off widespread criticism of the Administration both in the United States and abroad. To many, it seemed proof that the United States was recklessly bent on policing the world. President Johnson's utterances on the Dominican case sometimes seemed inaccurate, contradictory, and evasive; they contributed to—indeed, they opened—the "credibility gap" which ultimately brought him down. Inevitably the reaction in the UN was one of dismay. At the very outset, the day after the President sent the troops, the Mission reported that a Brazilian lamented the intervention and said the Communists would take advantage of it, while a Costa Rican was convinced that the Castro movement was taking advantage of the situation with danger to the whole area. Later the Mission reported that most Latin Americans had been guarded in their comments but what they did say indicated "a sense of shock at the suddenness of U.S. action and regret that we did not get OAS blessing." One diplomat reported the Mexican Foreign Office was privately relieved at the intervention but took a different public position for domestic political reasons. Later, throughout the hemisphere, various diplomats said the same thing.

Stevenson placed the Dominican problem before the UN on April 29, the day after the first troops landed. He informed the Security Council that President Johnson had ordered American troops into the Republic to protect and evacuate American citizens and that the United States had asked for a meeting of the OAS. On April 30 the Cuban Foreign Minister sent a letter to U Thant calling our intervention aggression.

On May 1 the Soviet Union requested an urgent meeting of the Security Council to consider "the armed interference by the United States in the internal affairs of the Dominican Republic."

Cuba asked to participate in the Council debate without the right to vote. Stevenson said that "we should be glad to hear the Cuban representative explain his country's role in this matter" and reminded the Council that this was "the same Cuba" which "conspired" with Russia to put missiles in the hemisphere and which stood "charged with aggression" by the OAS. He thought it "extremely interesting" that Cuba wanted to participate because "it emphasizes again the close relationship between the Communist movement and what is going on in the Dominican Republic today."

Ambassador Fedorenko spoke to the Council first. He accused the United States of violating "fundamental principles" of the UN Charter by embarking on an "armed intervention in the Dominican Republic with openly imperialistic aims." It was, he said, "open aggression." "United States imperialism is dealing barbarously with the people of a sovereign country who have risen against a bloody dictatorship." U.S. troops had "taken over" Santo Domingo, supported by air and naval forces. Protecting American lives was only a "false pretext." The United States' aim was to "suppress, by the force of foreign bayonets, the desire of the Dominican people for freedom and independence." To carry it out we had put "a whole invading army" ashore, not the few hundred Marines which would have sufficed to evacuate American citizens. The United States had not bothered to consult the OAS beforehand. Since the fall of Trujillo in 1961, the United States had done everything possible to restore the dictatorship. It had given aid to the military junta which had overthrown President Bosch in part to protect American investments and "monopolies." Fedorenko called on the Security Council to condemn the intervention as a breach of international peace and an act incompatible with Charter obligations and to call on the United States to withdraw its forces from the Republic immediately.

Stevenson replied. "I used to marvel at the audacity of the Soviet Union in pointing an accusing finger at others—the Soviet Union, which signed a pact with Hitler, which forcibly added 264,000 square miles and over 24 million people to its own territory and population in the aftermath of the Second World War, which subjugated all of Eastern Europe, which crushed the uprisings in East Germany and Hungary and which has persistently sought to enlarge its domination elsewhere beyond its borders."

He said the OAS had "for several days" been "dealing with the situation" in the Dominican Republic. Since the U.S.S.R. could not make propaganda attacks in the OAS, it tried to bring disputes to the UN where it could. The Dominican Republic would continue to enjoy sovereignty and independence "if the agents of foreign powers do not succeed in first exploiting and then taking over a democratic revolution as they did in Cuba and as they have tried and are trying to do in Venezuela and in other countries of the region."

Stevenson said that "the great majority" of the rebels in the Dominican Republic were not Communists. Bosch was not; neither were his party's followers. But "a small group of well-known Communists . . . quickly attempted to seize control of the revolution and of the armed bands in the streets." They were acting "in conformity with directives" from Havana. President Johnson had sent the troops only after governmental authority had collapsed. The police and government could no longer guarantee the safety of Americans or other foreigners, they had said that only an immediate landing could protect American and other lives and property, the United States Embassy was under fire, the death toll had reached 400, hospitals were unable to care for the wounded, medical supplies were running out, the power supply had broken down, and a food shortage threatened. The troops had evacuated foreigners. The United States had reported fully to the OAS, and the OAS had sent a commission to Santo Domingo. The United States had proposed that other American states make military forces available under OAS command. The OAS had called for an immediate cease-fire on all sides and the establishment of an international neutral zone of refuge surrounding foreign embassies and had sent its Secretary General to the Dominican Republic. A cease-fire was now in force, though not wholly effective, largely because of shooting by

"Communist leaders, many trained in Cuba." The OAS, not the UN, should deal with the matter. He declared, "The American nations will not permit the establishment of another Communist government in the Western Hemisphere." Stevenson entertained private doubts about the imminent danger of a Communist takeover, according to Pedersen.

Fighting broke out again on May 14, and the Security Council adopted a Jordanian resolution under which Thant sent a representative to the Dominican Republic in order to prepare a report to the Security Council. This annoyed the OAS Commission, and for weeks UN and OAS officials quarreled. The OAS established an inter-American force and a Brazilian general took command of U.S. troops and token forces sent by Brazil, Honduras, Costa Rica, Nicaragua, and Paraguay. Finally a Soviet resolution was rejected and a French one adopted which did not mention the OAS and said the Security Council expressed concern over the situation and asked that the truce be transformed into an immediate cease-fire. The United States abstained.

None of this affected the situation on the ground in the Dominican Republic. At times the State Department and UN Mission seemed light-years away from the street realities in Santo Domingo. Stevenson was wearily involved to the end. The Security Council ended its consideration of the situation on May 24. It reopened the question on June 7 upon complaint by the Dominican rebels that the international force was violating the cease-fire. At length the issue died.

19.

In May, while Stevenson was busy with the Dominican Republic, he continued his usual social rounds—a surprise party for Theodore White, a weekend at the Astors', a weekend in Virginia at Mrs. Graham's, tennis and supper with Scotty Reston and his wife, various diplomatic receptions, a picnic lunch at William Paley's, a weekend with Borden. On May 3, in the first days of the Dominican crisis, he told Lyndon Johnson, "I am deeply grateful to you for the inscribed photographs—and while I am not sure how 'comforting it is to have me *near*'—it is more than comforting to me to have you *there!*" He consulted people about business prospects for Borden and John Fell. He sent out a form letter on behalf of the United Nations Association, proselytizing for the UN.

He went to see Dr. Lax. To the doctor he seemed tired, run down, and depressed. He told Dr. Lax he was going to parties almost every night. He had not been taking his prescribed medication or adhering to his diet. Dr. Lax talked with him at length. The doctor said, "Governor, it cannot go on like this. You have to stop this way of living, even if it means to resign as an Ambassador; you are on a suicidal course." Stevenson looked at him and, with a smile, replied, "How do you know that I want to live long? My father died at the age of sixty, my mother at sixty-five. I am now sixty-five, that will be enough for me."

Ruth Field wrote to him about her problems—the Foundation, her family, her own inability to do anything without direction. "I was so touched," she wrote, "by your note received Wed—it is extraordinary how you manage to think of your friends & give them cheer, & confidence, & support— Perhaps that is the difference, the uniqueness, that puts you above the other 'greats'—You are so human—you keep that quality despite the pressures."

Jane Dick, after consulting Stevenson, went to Washington to explore means by which Stevenson's influence on Administration policy might be increased. A cabinet member and a newspaper columnist confirmed what she had thought—that President Johnson really consulted only three people in the Administration—Rusk, McNamara, and Bundy, that he was uncomfortable in the presence of "intellectuals" such as Stevenson, that he was determined to make a great record and might reorganize his administration to do it (the implication was that he might appoint a new Secretary of State), that his other closest friends and most influential advisers were Abe Fortas and Clark Clifford. She said the columnist reported that Stevenson recently had told him he was depressed and had given up and was resigned to the notion that we were in an era when China was expanding her influence throughout the world and nothing could be done about it. Mrs. Dick told him, "You *mustn't* believe this, A. dear. . . . When you give up no great voice will be left to speak for the verities by which we must live and *prevail.*"

He had not given up. He was exceedingly busy—one day he took the 9 A.M. shuttle to Washington, attended a cabinet meeting on Vietnam, and took the shuttle back to New York in time for a Security Council meeting on the Dominican Republic. He sent a letter on disarmament to Senator Fulbright. He met at length with U Thant on Article 19 and UN financing. He worked tirelessly on these problems and on peace keeping, evidence of his dedication to the UN.

Evelyn Houston, making a date with Stevenson for June 18, wrote, "I'm starting to grow old, my love. Are you? Sometimes I think life isn't worth living; other times I think I can't bear the thought of its ever ending. . . . You lost your parents some years ago, but I lost my last parent somewhat later than average, as I'd lost the other one a good deal earlier than average, when I was six, and it is like moving up in the firing line: so long as a parent lived there was the feeling, primitive, primordial, of being at one remove from the unknown, in a sheltered position, with still a row ahead to go down before one's own turn came. But when the row has gone down one feels suddenly so vulnerable." Stevenson marked that passage.

Talking with Thant one day in May about Vietnam, Stevenson said he had been seriously disturbed by our bombing the North. That day, he said, the United States was announcing a pause in the bombing of North Vietnam that would last six days in hope of getting talks started. Thant said that the previous September, when he made his first sounding about private peace talks, Ho Chi Minh had been ready to talk with the United States and South Vietnam alone, but now Hanoi had adopted the Peking position that North Vietnam should be represented exclusively by the Viet Cong. Thant in March had asked Algeria to tell the Viet Cong and Hanoi representatives in Algiers that it was "unrealistic" to insist on this. He had received no answer. But he did believe that if the United States refused to talk with the Viet Cong no talks would take place. He and Stevenson discussed ways to get around the problem.

At this same time Rusk told Dobrynin we were looking for a response from Hanoi. On May 12, Ambassador Kohler tried to deliver the message to Hanoi's representative in Moscow. His message was returned the next day unopened. Several other approaches were made and, although none were acknowledged, the United States felt certain Hanoi had received the message one way or another. On May 18 a Hanoi delegate in Paris told the French Foreign Office that the Indian proposal to police the border of the two Vietnams was unacceptable and, reiterated four points as the "best base for settlement." The United States concluded to make no response through the French except to tell Hanoi that the French had passed the message to us. We also decided against direct contact with Hanoi because we thought the time was not right. The Department still liked the Indians' proposal. It wanted no dealings with the Viet Cong— treating it as a valid party would recognize the war as a civil war. The French believed Hanoi was the key, though some thought Peking was. If anything was to be done, it would be through very secret talks or some form of reciprocal actions.

Stevenson discussed Vietnam on May 25 with the Italian Foreign Minister, Fanfani. Stevenson said that despite his urging the Soviets had been unable to pressure Hanoi toward negotiations for fear of exposing themselves to criticism from Peking. Instead they were competing with Peking to support Hanoi without direct involvement against the United States and were lighting fires where they could, including the Dominican Republic. Hanoi felt no pressure to negotiate from either Peking or Moscow. They were also inhibited by a split between the more conciliatory Ho Chi Minh and the hard-liner General Giap and, further, by a fear of negotiating behind the backs of the Viet Cong. Stevenson also reported that a Russian official in the UN Secretariat was gloomy over U.S.-Soviet relations and had accused the United States of forcing the Soviets to close ranks with Peking. During a recent visit to Moscow, Stevenson had found that he and others who favored a U.S.S.R.-U.S. détente were in a very difficult position, accused of being "apologists of American imperialism." He said that Ambassador Dobrynin, too, was depressed.

Late in May, Stevenson saw his doctor once more. The doctor found he had gained an additional five pounds. Dr. Lax was dissatisfied with his general condition. But when he said so, Stevenson looked at him and shrugged his shoulders.

On May 28, Stevenson went to Toronto and Ottawa for the weekend, taking Borden with him. On this trip he told Borden he had a heart condition. He spoke at the University of Toronto and received an honorary degree. Students had protested awarding him the degree because of American policy in Vietnam but the university Senate had overruled them. When Stevenson appeared, they picketed him. In his speech he said that the danger in the continents emerging from colonialism lay not in outright war but in the Communists' "wars of national liberation." "General Giap, Minister of Defense of North Vietnam, describes the war [in Vietnam] as a test case for the Communist doctrine of 'wars of national liberation.' We made the mistake thirty years ago of not taking seriously the harsh, cruel, aggressive ideology that Hitler openly professed. We cannot afford to repeat that mistake." Any government faced with armed violence it could not control would appeal for outside help. And this was all too likely to be the United States. And if international organizations could not respond quickly, national power would be called in. Yet national power was the most costly, dangerous, and least desirable kind of peace keeping. What was the alternative? The UN had been "surprisingly successful" in dealing with the crises by improvisation. But there was yet no permanent, reliable system of dealing swiftly and certainly with aggression.

Stevenson had not, he said, "come here to defend" America's role in Vietnam and the Dominican Republic. We wanted a swift peaceful settlement in both places. In the Dominican Republic, while the OAS force kept them from each other's throats, we hoped the factions could agree on a centrist government that would arrange popular elections as soon as possible. "In Vietnam, President Johnson has asked publicly and privately again and again, for a peaceful settlement—to no avail. He has offered negotiations without preconditions—to no avail. It was said the North could not negotiate while the bombing was going on. So he suspended the bombing—to no avail." It must be apparent by now to even the most skeptical that it was not Saigon or the United States that would not negotiate or even meet, but Peking and Hanoi. "Yet I seem to detect more complaints about what we, defenders, are doing, than about what Hanoi and Peking, aggressors, are doing. It is all a little perplexing. But the war in Vietnam is only a steppingstone to something better or much worse in Southeast Asia. It seems to me—and I speak for myself only—that the only solution to Southeast Asia compatible with the postcolonial world we are trying to build is to give these states between the Chinese and the Indian colossi international security guarantees, impartially policed frontiers, long-term development and broad framework of social and economic cooperation." The audience rose to applaud him.

After the speech Stevenson felt ill and faint. He pulled himself together and went on to functions as scheduled. But he told Marietta Tree he had never before felt so ill. Returning to Washington on Sunday, May 30, in the Prime Minister's plane, he described his trip in a letter to Marietta (who was briefly in Africa on a UN trip). "I have *never* had more fulsome, extravagant introductions at all the public appearances—doubtless inflated to compensate for the hostile pickets—which were not very hostile to an old veteran of Dallas' hawks—and the demonstrations which may have been noisy for Canada but were muted for us. . . . The speech . . . went off gloriously and I had what they said was the only standing ovation in the experience of their convocations. The luncheon by the PM & the afternoon with Mike Pearson at his country retreat were all easy, relaxed, agreeable & useful. The dinner with 2000 alumni in the great hall . . . was done with great style & dignity and the utterances about me very moving. Last night the US Ambass. dinner in Ottawa was heavier but tolerable in spite of exhaustion." He added: "Monday—all went well in Wash—clips enclosed—and now I'm back in the office on Decoration Day and the loveliest day I've ever seen in N.Y.! When—oh God—when can I roll in the grass and look at the sky thru the leaves—with a hand in mine for the fullest measure."

He added yet another passage: "Tues night—1:20 AM—Decoration Day went like all the rest—no, gloriously!—as I struggled to get thru the day's office work and then a speech for this morning in Atlantic City to the Rotary International. I flew off in a small plane with Luther Hodges & Borden & reentered that great hall full of shades & horrors of last summer's convention . . . to find 12,000!—literally—people waiting for me. The speech worked—why I don't know—and I flew back to N.Y., again content . . . but with that uncomfortable questioning—what am I doing all this for—for me? for you? for who? Tonight it was two receptions and then a dinner for Erhard & a reply to his speech. Now—at 1 A.M.—George McGhee has left and I'm done—at last—with nothing except these blank pages and a speech to do for Arkansas day after tomorrow—and no time tomorrow. But this whimper of self pity is unworthy."

Later, Marietta blamed his awful schedule in May and June for his death. One wonders if he might have lightened his schedule had he wished to survive.

Criticism of the war in Vietnam and the Dominican intervention was rising. Murray Kempton, then of the New York *World-Telegram and Sun,* told Stevenson on June 2 he had been asked by pacifist friends to join them in signing a petition to Stevenson. He wrote privately to him instead —he could not bring himself to address Stevenson in the tone of a manifesto because he admired him so. Kempton said he could appreciate that remaining at the UN might seem to Stevenson a duty. But the government had spent May lying to the people, and, at such a time, "the private man is our one essential resource. . . . The need now is for commoners, for men out of office and we have only Mr. Nixon. I know that I am asking you to do one more messy and exhausting thing; but could you [resign and] come out here and lead us?"

Jane Dick visited him and left a note: "You are a loved and honored man. If America is in trouble it's *in spite* of you. I know what a ghastly spot you're in at the moment, but thank God you're 'philosophical,' if low at the moment. Take heart—come home for the summer, or as much of it as you can, and plunge your feet into the deep fecund soil of Illinois. . . . Dear Abe!!—Come home for awhile—*feel* America—the real America again."

On June 3, Stevenson went to Arkansas to speak to the state Bar Association, then went to Chicago to spend the weekend at Libertyville with Adlai, Nancy, and the children. He noted "Talk with Adlai." They discussed rewriting Stevenson's will (and Adlai III did indeed rewrite it, but Stevenson would not live to sign it).[10] He went to a wedding and a reception at Onwentsia and "saw many old friends." On Monday, June 7, he returned to New York in time to have a sandwich in his office and attend a Security Council meeting on the Dominican Republic.

A former Congressman who had worked for Stevenson's election to the presidency wrote, "Many of us who worked for a handful of eloquent leaders such as you feel almost betrayed. We think that your great name and potential is being destroyed. . . . We understand the ways of compromise and negotiation but feel that your role as spokesman for United States . . . for several years has on critical occasions completely disregarded the very principles advanced so ably by you in earlier years. . . . In your place, I would have long since resigned. . . . Privately, I now urge you to do so."

On June 8, Stevenson told Roxane Eberlein he had to break an appointment with Dr. Lax (it was not the first one he had broken): "Pls apologize—I'll be in touch with him when the dust settles after July 1 and *promise* to come in then." The White House announced that General Westmoreland had been given authority to use American troops "in support of Vietnamese forces faced with aggressive attack." A little later Westmoreland's authority was extended—he could commit Americans to battle whenever he deemed it necessary to strengthen South Vietnamese forces.

Stevenson wrote Lady Spears, "Actually, things are moving to a conclusion in Ellen's case—we hope! When I was last in Illinois it looked as though the Court would enter a finding of incompetence and make the appointment of the Conservator permanent. Meanwhile, all the mortgages on her house and farm are being foreclosed and I fear there will be nothing left, even for the unsecured creditors. It is all very sad but inevitable as

---

[10] When Stevenson died, he left an estate of $1,256,386.99. He bequeathed it to his three sons, except for a gift of $5,000 to Frank Holland, the farmer, and $3,000 each to Viola, Roxane Eberlein, and Carol Evans. He designated young Adlai and Newton Minow co-executors.

long as she declines to accept any arrangements in her behalf and insists on fighting everything to the bitter end. All my plans for a visit in London have been abandoned in view of circumstances here."

McGeorge Bundy asked Cleveland for a memorandum on why the United States had not wanted to go to the UN on Vietnam. Cleveland responded that it was because of possible demoralizing effect on Saigon, a preference for quiet diplomatic channels to reach the Soviets, the likelihood that the Soviets would veto any proposal in the Security Council and that the United States could not obtain a two-thirds majority in the General Assembly, a feeling that a veto in the Security Council might produce a special session of the Assembly which the United States did not want because of the Article 19 problem, UN impotence might build up overwhelming pressure for a new Geneva Conference which the United States did not want, and a desire to hold the UN in reserve until the time when UN machinery might be used to police a settlement. All these reasons, Cleveland thought, had been eroded by time.

True, going to the UN entailed risks—it might push Moscow and Peking and Hanoi closer together, it would produce strong pressure for a one-sided halt to air strikes, the Security Council would insist we accept the Viet Cong in negotiations, we would be criticized heavily for our military efforts, and no UN action would likely result. Nonetheless, Cleveland thought that, on balance, the advantages outweighed the risks. He outlined a detailed course of action and sent a copy to Secretary Rusk with the comment, "If this is a serious prospect, as I think it should be, we ought to bring Stevenson into the discussion right away."

John Fell and Natalie were visiting Stevenson. He was making summer plans. He told Buffie Ives, "I had hoped to stay at Libertyville for a while and get a good rest and tend to my papers in the basement. There is talk now, however, of the necessity of a major speech at the Economic and Social Council meeting in Geneva. . . . I might come to see you [in Italy] for a few days or go to London. . . . As for shirts, if you can get one yellow one—more yellow than cream—and a blue one identical with the last one, please do so." He had begun his letter: "I have had a hideous month, but the end is in sight. . . ."

Stevenson delivered a commencement address at Williams College and received an honorary degree. He went to Harvard to receive another honorary degree—one which he had long wanted. It was a gala occasion, including a cocktail party at the Galbraiths' and a "large and splendid" dinner at President Pusey's home. Commencement Day was a "perfect cloudless cool day." Some 10,000 people assembled in Harvard Yard. "Enormous academic procession," Stevenson noted, "clapping as I passed by!—awarding degrees—standing ovation when I was presented. . . . Precedent shattered by Pusey's announcement that I would speak in afternoon. Speech—Great success—standing ovation again." Returning to New York on June 18, he had a dinner date with Evelyn Houston. She had arrived in New York with four evening dresses and later wrote to him, "The last thing I had counted on was dinner alone at your apartment with your housekeeper absent. At first startled, even a little disappointed, having looked forward to a festive evening, maybe the theater, my second reaction was to misunderstand. . . . Although I regret the cost to *your* nervous system . . . I love you peacefully now. There won't be any more torment. . . . But love you I still do. . . . After . . . 4½ [years] of bondage to something that was never real but seemed more so than what was, I am free at last."

Dwight Macdonald, Kay Boyle, Paul Goodman, and others were forming a group called Artists and Writers Dissent to protest the Vietnam War and the Dominican intervention; and on June 21 a delegation of them called on Stevenson. He defended Administration policy. A few days later they denounced him publicly and picketed the U. S. Mission, carrying placards demanding his resignation.

20.

The UN was celebrating its twentieth anniversary with elaborate ceremonies in San Francisco on June 24–26. Stevenson was eager to have President Johnson go. Various staff members prepared speech drafts for the President. They advised him to pledge to shift the U.S. position on Article 19 so the General Assembly could transact business. But word of this leaked to the New York *Times* and the *Times* published it, and so the President removed it from his speech.

He said the UN "must be concerned" about Southeast Asia where the "willful aggressors" refused peaceful settlement. Bilateral diplomacy had yielded no result. The machinery of the Geneva Conference was paralyzed. Resort to the Security Council had been rejected. U Thant's efforts had been "rebuffed." An appeal for unconditional discussion "was met with contempt." A bombing pause "was called an insult." The concern of the Commonwealth Prime Ministers was ignored. "Therefore . . . I now call upon this gathering of the nations of the world to use all their influence, individually and collectively, to bring to the tables those who seem determined to make war. We will support your efforts."

Yost, at Stevenson's request, had drafted the rhetoric about the UN for the President's speech, and Stevenson had sent it to the President. He forgot he had done so and used the rhetoric himself in a speech in Chicago on his way west. When he heard the President at San Francisco uttering the same words, he asked Yost, "Where did he get that?" Yost replied, "You gave it to him." Stevenson noted, "LBJ speech—partly by me!" Stevenson found a number of delegates disappointed in the President's speech. This resulted from Johnson's having omitted the Article 19 material, which the delegates had been led to expect him to deliver. What remained was little more than rhetoric. "The whole episode was a disaster," Yost recalled. Ruth Field thought Johnson had "betrayed" Stevenson.

Stevenson stayed on through the weekend in San Francisco, going fishing early Sunday morning outside the Golden Gate with Chief Justice Earl Warren, Governor Brown, John Fell, and others. That afternoon he appeared on "Meet the Press." On Monday he took a ride around the harbor with John Fell on a hydrofoil and in the evening went to a night club called the "hungry i" to hear Dick Gregory. He raised $35,000 through Brown Brothers Harriman "to make another investment with Mr. Swig" (of the Fairmont Hotel), as he told Roxane Eberlein. He asked her to again postpone an appointment with Dr. Lax and to make a reservation for him to Geneva leaving New York on July 5.

On Tuesday, June 29, he met Marietta Tree in Chicago and went to Libertyville for two days—"glorious day at farm," he noted. He had hoped to stay on through the long Fourth of July weekend but was obliged to return to New York on the first and go to Washington on Friday, July 2, to discuss with Secretary Rusk the latest American position on Article 19 and financing. "Still not final!" he noted. And, "Rusk says LBJ thinks my first priority is to stay in Wash. and lobby with assorted Senators rather than go to Geneva for ECOSOC and weekend at Chequers with Harold Wilson." He saw Scotty Reston, and Reston later recalled, "He was down in the dumps. I asked what he wanted to drink. He said, 'Straight vodka.' He took a big hooker of vodka. Then he talked about his troubles. He said the opposite of what he told Paul Goodman of Artists and Writers Dissent"—said he did not support the Administration on Vietnam. "He did not himself have a solution. He was quite modest and fair to the President. He kept saying what a mess it is—he didn't know how to get out either."

Stevenson told Phil Klutznick he was thinking about resigning. Klutznick recalled, "He said, 'The Department of State won't listen—the President won't listen—I've had it. I think I ought to quit.' He was talking about Vietnam. Then he said, 'You haven't said a word.'

"I said, 'There's nothing to say. You won't quit.'

"He asked why not?

"I said, 'If you do, you'll have to explain. No one will believe it. At sixty-five you're not taking on another fight.'"

Stevenson went back to Chicago that evening, met Barbara Ward at O'Hare Airport, and spent the weekend at Libertyville with the children. "Work at desk and around place." He made a list of things to do before going to Europe. It included telephoning Jane Gunther, Pussy Paepcke, Mary Lasker, Kay Graham, Ruth Field, Joe Sisco (he misspelled it), Phil Klutznick, Betty Beale (a Washington writer), Alice Hoge; giving Borden introductions; notifying Benton and Roger Tubby and Sarah Plimpton of his forthcoming trip to Europe; asking Roxane to arrange several appointments; seeing John Steele in Washington; writing a letter on behalf of one of John Fell's business ventures. The Dicks and Ellises came Saturday night to supper and all went to a concert at Ravinia, an outdoor concert park in Highland Park. Jane Dick recalled, "You can't imagine so many people—Adlai and Nancy and their four children and a niece of Nancy's and the maid—frogs and toads and dogs the boys had collected—then Barbara Ward came out—the house was overflowing—we all lived a joint life for four days. We took the overflow. Adlai called and asked us to dinner. He was going to carve the lamb. He adored to carve his own lamb. During supper he kept being called to the phone. He said, 'I had wanted to take off the whole month here but this is it, I've got to go to ECOSOC the day after tomorrow and stop in Washington on the way and come back via London.' We asked when he would be back. He said in mid-July—'I'll be back as fast as I can.' He looked sad. We said, 'Adlai, why do you have to do this? Can't you say no?' He said no. Well, we went to Ravinia. We had three tickets plus two general admission tickets. He said, 'I want to go in the park and lie on the blanket under the stars and rest with the old folks.' We insisted on his staying for the first half inside." Ravinia concerts are given in an orchestra shell surrounded by a park. "The park was filled. The sky was beautiful, it was a beautiful night. The temperature was perfect, it was a beautiful concert, Adlai was in ecstasy. Then intermission came. We couldn't get out—everybody rushed up to him, he was surrounded. The park was so filled we couldn't find the young people. So he had to come back inside and sit through the rest of it. But it was great."

On Sunday, July 4, he worked at his desk and on the farm, played tennis and went with Barbara Ward to Edison Dick's sixty-fifth birthday party. In the evening he took the grandchildren to a fireworks display at Onwentsia. He complained of heart palpitations to Adlai III and said Dr. Lax had advised him to "take it easier." Adlai III asked, "Why don't you?" Adlai III once recalled, "I tried to plead with him, we'd been going through this as long as I can remember. He'd seen Dr. Riba in Chicago. He was overweight and working too hard for a guy his age—that's what the doctor told him."

Stevenson told Adlai III that many people had urged him to resign in protest against the Administration's Vietnam policy but he resented their assumptions that he disagreed with the policy and, further, he felt that even if he did disagree it was by no means certain that the most effective act was resignation—it might be better to stay and try to influence policy.

Criticism of U.S. policy in Vietnam and the Dominican Republic was multiplying, pacifists had demonstrated at the Pentagon, Stevenson was receiving an increasing number of letters from liberals who wanted him to resign in protest. Before June 30 such letters had averaged from eight to ten a week. About July 1 the number of printed or mimeographed petitions increased but the number of individually written letters decreased. In Connecticut a group sprang up called "Volunteers for Stevenson—1965" and "dedicated to the ideals spelled out by Governor Stevenson in his Presidential campaigns of 1952 and 1956; and in his reluctant bid for the nomination in 1960. 'LET'S TALK SENSE TO THE AMERICAN PEOPLE.'"

Artists and Writers Dissent now included Kay Boyle, Maxwell Geismar, Paul Goodman, Helen Merrell Lynd, Dwight Macdonald, A. J. Muste, David Dempsey, Rockwell Kent, Norman Mailer, Robert Osborn, Philip Roth, and Lyle Stuart. They sent Stevenson a printed declaration saying, "We have watched in dismay as our government—by its actions in Viet Nam and the Dominican Republic—has clearly violated the United Nations Charter, international law, and those fundamental principles of human decency which alone can prevent a terrifying, world-wide escalation of suffering and death. We urgently ask you, as our government's representative in the United Nations and as a man who has in the past stood for the best hopes of realizing American ideals, to consider your complicity in what this government is doing. . . . *We urge you to resign as United States Ambassador to the United Nations,* and, having done that, to become a spokesman again for that which is humane in the traditions and in the people of America."

Ralph Ginzburg, editor and publisher of the magazine *Fact,* told Stevenson in a personal letter, "Many of your great admirers—myself included—are losing heart over your failure to strike a firm blow in behalf of world peace. . . . If you fear that quitting your UN post in protest over Vietnam would bring your personal career to an inglorious end, I can only say that I believe that by continuing your present hypocritical stance you will bring even greater ignominy to yourself."

James Farrell, who had been asked to join the Artists and Writers Dissent, refused and told Stevenson he considered them "politically irresponsible." Stevenson, thanking him on July 2, wrote, "The fight is not so lonely when one has friends like you!" Others wrote letters urging Stevenson to refuse to resign. A Californian urged him not to "let this sort of thing influence you. . . . These people may talk to you of resigning and of 'complicity' but you have my little vote of confidence and, I think, the whole Nation's." A man in New York wrote, after reading of efforts to persuade Stevenson to resign, "Because I have long admired you but at the same time because I feel very strongly that President Johnson has adopted a policy that is best for the United States, I urge you to continue to represent us in the U.N. and not to give way to pressures from certain 'Liberals.'" A man in St. Louis wrote, "Those who urge you to resign are wrong. I agree that the game is not played that way. I urge you to stay at your post and do whatever you can to lead our country down the right path, regardless of rebuffs."

At Libertyville over the Fourth of July weekend, Stevenson and Barbara Ward prepared a long thoughtful reply to Paul Goodman of the Artists and Writers Dissent. It said, "Thank you for your letter. Its arguments, I think, rest on a simple pre-supposition: that I share your belief in the disastrous trend of American foreign policy and that I must therefore resign to underline my disagreement, rally public opinion against it and nail the 'lies' in which it is being presented to the people. But it is precisely this pre-supposition that I do not share with you, and I would like to send you my reasons for believing that, whatever criticisms may be made over the detail and emphasis of American foreign policy, its purpose and direction are sound."

Our purpose, he wrote, was to avoid war. But we lived "in a state of international anarchy" in which each nation claimed absolute sovereignty and great powers still believed they could enforce their interests. In these circumstances nuclear disaster could be avoided only by two clear lines of policy: "The *first* is to establish a tacitly agreed frontier between Communist and non-Communist areas of influence on the understanding that neither power system will use force to change the status quo. . . . The *second* is to move from this position of precarious stability toward international procedures for settling differences, towards the building of an international juridical and policing system and toward a whole variety of policies designed to turn our small vulnerable planet into a genuine economic and social community."

Between 1947 and 1962, he said, such a dividing line was achieved with the Soviets in Europe and in the Western Hemisphere. But we had no such line with the Chinese. The line we were holding was at the 17th parallel across Vietnam. Should we hold it? The answer depended on one's view of Chinese power.

In the past some Chinese dynasties had been aggressive, Stevenson wrote. The new Communist regime "has not been particularly unaggressive," having swallowed Tibet, attacked India, and sought "national liberation" for Malays. Today "the apparatus of infiltration and aggression" was at work in north Thailand. Chinese maps showed China's frontiers at the farthest reach of the old empire. So it was not irrational to check Chinese power. Not to do so would be to set off on "the old, old route whereby expansive powers push at more and more doors, believing they will be open until, at the ultimate door, resistance is unavoidable and major war breaks out." The French Revolution had led to prolonged war before the limits of French power were established. The Chinese revolution might follow the same course. "My hope in Viet Nam is that relatively small scale resistance now may establish the [point] that changes in Asia are not to be precipitated by outside force. This was the point of the Korean War. This is the point of the conflict in Viet Nam. I believe Asia will be more [stable] if the outcome is the same in both—a negotiated line and a negotiated peace."

As to the second line of policy, moving toward a world order of law and peace, "I believe that we must seek a negotiated peace in Viet Nam based upon the internationalization of the whole area's security, on a big effort to develop under the U.N. the resources of the Mekong River and guarantee that Viet Nam, North and South, can choose, again under international supervision, the kind of governments, the form of association and . . . the type of reunification of the two states they genuinely want to establish."

Such an achievement would "begin to establish procedures by which local revolutionary movements such as the rising in the Dominican Republic and . . . Zanzibar are *not* automatically a prey to outside intervention" and would end spheres of influence as empires were already ended. Retreat in Asia would not advance the cause of peace and world order. "It is my conviction that American policy is groping its way towards this difficult but essential ideal. . . .

"Now it is possible for honest men to differ on every aspect of this interpretation. You may believe that Communist Powers are not expansive. Or you may believe that the changes they seek to support by violence are beneficient changes which can be achieved by no other route. Again, you may believe that a return to some form of non-involvement in world affairs is the best posture for America. Or you may genuinely believe that America is in Viet Nam 'for sheer capitalist greed.' These are all possible attitudes and I do not impugn the good faith of those who hold them. I would only ask them, in the name of the courtesies and decencies of a free society, that they should equally refrain from impugning mine."

It was a hard line, harder, Clayton Fritchey thought, than Stevenson would have drafted if left to himself.

On July 6, Stevenson left Libertyville and flew to Washington where he had lunch with Rusk and saw George Ball, who told him he was too fat, then went on to New York. In Washington he left a copy of his letter to Paul Goodman with Joe Sisco for the Department to review. Sisco would send it, together with any changes the Department made, to Clayton Fritchey. In New York, Stevenson gave Fritchey a memorandum asking him to see that the letter was sent after the Department had cleared it. He thought perhaps the letter should be published. Fritchey, disturbed because the letter was so strong, held it up. Some have questioned whether the letter truly reflected Stevenson's thinking. Dick Pedersen and Charles Yost thought Stevenson believed our policy in Vietnam at that time basically correct, though he was troubled by our bombing the North.

It is difficult to know precisely what Stevenson thought about Vietnam. At that time the escalation had just begun (we had more troops in the Dominican Republic than in Vietnam). Many people in the government had grave misgivings about where our policy in Southeast Asia might lead, but at that time Vietnam was simply not a subject on which a thoughtful man could have an unswervable opinion. Stevenson, like many others, probably was ambivalent.

He spent the afternoon and early evening packing and clearing his desk and making notes of things for Roxane Eberlein to do—inquire about income tax, make a $1,000 interest-free loan to Viola to refurbish her house

—then at nine-fifteen left for Geneva via Swissair. Martha Gelhorn, a writer and former wife of Ernest Hemingway, had written from London. Stevenson put the letter in his pocket. He took with him a briefcase full of reading material, unanswered correspondence, and newspaper clippings. He sent a hurried note to Evelyn Houston, "Tues. I go back to Wash., Tues. night to Geneva, then to London—and then I don't know what."

21.

He arrived at Geneva after a sleepless night and was met by Roger Tubby and others. He went to the embassy residence for telephone calls and a brief nap and at eleven-thirty talked about Vietnam to U Thant, who thought Hanoi would insist we negotiate with the Viet Cong. He had lunch at the Australian Ambassador's house and in the afternoon reported by telephone to Rusk on his talk with Thant. He worked on a cable and on a speech and on plans for a visit to London, attended a reception at Tubby's, dined with Bill Benton, walked about in the rain, and went to bed "at last" at eleven-thirty. Next day, Thursday, July 8, he met again with Thant and wrote on his schedule, " 'We cannot negotiate with Viet Cong!' (I wonder how long that position will hold!)" He telephoned Ambassador Bruce in London and Buffie Ives in Florence. He had lunch with an ECOSOC group, visited with the Aga Khan, and dined with a British cabinet minister. On Friday, July 9, he delivered his annual speech to ECOSOC. It was a "great success," he noted, " 'splendid,' 'excellent,' 'marvelous'—'one of the best you ever gave.' " Then lunch with friends at a hotel—"memories of lunch parties at same table every summer I came to Geneva with MT." Roger Tubby thought him dispirited about the difficulty in getting through to the White House and the impossibility of carrying on meaningful dialogues with Russia and China. He told Tubby he was reading Barbara Tuchman's *The Guns of August* and felt that once again, as in the early twentieth century, the world was caught up in an inexorable drift to war.

At breakfast with the Tubbys on the day he left Geneva he suddenly stopped talking, put both hands on the table, and said, "I'm a bit dizzy." It passed.

He told the Aga Khan he could not use his chalet at Gstaad that weekend after all. That evening, July 9, he flew to Paris and had dinner with Mr. and Mrs. Averell Harriman, Sarah Plimpton, and David Schoenbrun, a television reporter. Stevenson complained about his lot at the UN—he had to defend U.S. policy in Vietnam and the Dominican Republic, a "massive blunder." Schoenbrun later reported it publicly. Still later Harriman said he thought Schoenbrun's report was an "outrageous" betrayal of a confidence given at a private dinner; "Adlai was just doing his normal grousing," Harriman said. "There was nothing special about it." Plimpton agreed—"Sarah said that Adlai was just saying the sort of thing he always said, things like, 'What am I doing here at the UN?' but she attached no importance to it nor would anybody who knew him well. Schoenbrun did not know him very well."

Stevenson went to London the next day, Saturday, July 10, met Benton, who had preceded him to London from Geneva, and they went to Chequers to spend the day with Harold Wilson. On Sunday he and Benton drove up to have lunch with Lady Spears and on for dinner with Lord Franks, the Provost of Worcester College, returning to London late that night. Riding in the car that day, Stevenson told Benton he wanted to resign from the UN after next fall's meeting of the General Assembly. Benton told him he could not leave until he had found a successor. Stevenson discussed several possibilities—Senator Eugene McCarthy, Senator John Sherman Cooper, Chet Bowles, in that order. He told Benton the Garrison law firm wanted him to return when he left the UN and give it 80 per cent of his time. Benton told him that was absurd and offered him $100,000 a year in salary plus $100,000 a year in expenses if he would work for Britannica as "the greatest ornament" the Britannica had. Stevenson said he would discuss it at Benton's home next weekend. In ensuing days he met with Britannica executives.

Marietta Tree was to call him about lunch on Monday. He appeared on a television show that Sunday night and went to a buffet supper given in his honor by the British Broadcasting Corporation. On television, he said a military solution was impossible in Vietnam; we must have a political solution. But, asked if he was "not altogether happy" with President Johnson's policy, he replied, "Well, I've heard those reports, indeed I had many letters and petitions and representations and delegations and even pickets and so on, but I think it's unfortunate because actually I don't share this—any misgiving about the direction of our policy, especially with respect to Vietnam. . . . As we did in Europe, we shall have to draw a line between the Communist and the non-Communist world areas, so that neither power system can force a change by force." He thought he would have to publish these views when he returned home.

He was staying at the American Embassy residence. So was Kay Graham. He went there to wait for her, taking Eric Sevareid (the television commentator) with him, and, waiting for Mrs. Graham, fell into conversation with Sevareid in the library. He complained again about his lot at the UN, criticizing the execution though not the fundamentals of American policy in Vietnam and the Dominican Republic, and said he wanted to resign, go back to Libertyville to see his grandchildren and practice a little law, and "for a while, I'd really just like to sit in the shade with a glass of wine in my hand and watch the people dance."

Mrs. Graham came home, saw the two of them engaged in what she took to be business conversation, and went to bed. Later Sevareid published an account of the interview. He had the impression Stevenson was clinging to him in order to unburden himself; actually Stevenson was killing time while waiting for Mrs. Graham, and next morning was irritated at Mrs. Graham for not interrupting them and for leaving him with "that bore Sevareid."[11]

People close to Stevenson had no doubt he said the things Sevareid reported but considered them nothing more than his habitual grumbling.

On Wednesday, July 14, he saw a British diplomat and went to a lunch given by Bill Benton. Leaving, he asked Benton for the key to his hotel suite, saying he had some interviews and did not want to use the embassy residence. He gave an interview to a BBC reporter and again defended America's Vietnam policy. He started to walk with Marietta Tree. He told her he wanted to save Bill Benton one night's rent and went to the hotel and turned in the key. Then he and Marietta went walking in Grosvenor Square near the United States Embassy. It was a bright warm afternoon. He wanted to show Marietta the house in the mews where he had lived with Ellen and the boys many years ago while he was working at the UN Preparatory Commission. He found the place, but the house had been demolished and replaced with a building of modern architecture. He sighed and said, "That makes me feel very old." They walked on. He was grumbling because he couldn't arrange a tennis game. They headed toward Hyde Park past the American Embassy. Several slow strollers impeded their progress, and Marietta skipped into the street to by-pass them, and Stevenson followed, rejoining her on the sidewalk. In a moment he asked her to slow down and said he felt very tired. Then unaccountably he said, "Keep your head high." She did not know what he meant. He said to her, "I am going to faint." She looked into a building entrance, hoping to find something he could sit down on; she felt his arm brush hers, and he fell over backward, and his head hit the pavement with a heavy thud. She thought he had fractured his skull, ran to a nearby club, and asked a man to call a doctor. She returned to Stevenson; someone gave her water and a blanket, and she covered him, then knelt helplessly beside him.

A stranger came along, a heart doctor, and started massaging Stevenson's heart and instructed Marietta in how to give Stevenson mouth-to-mouth resuscitation—"the kiss of life," the British call it. Presently Stevenson started breathing again. She asked a stranger to send for Ambassador Bruce, not saying who had fallen—she did not think Stevenson would want it publicized. A guard from the embassy finally appeared without Bruce; Marietta asked him to tell the Minister, Philip Kaiser, that Mrs. Tree wanted him to come as quickly as possible. She asked for an ambulance. Kaiser and the ambulance arrived almost together. Men put Stevenson into the ambulance, and she and Kaiser got in behind him; but she no-

---

11 Almost surely this did not represent Stevenson's true feelings toward Sevareid, whom he had known and liked for a long time. Rather, he was probably ingratiating himself with Mrs. Graham. He did it often. Once, in front of the Ricardo Sicres, he referred to Marietta Tree as "that lump." He could not have meant that either.

ticed some pink State Department classified cables on the sidewalk where he had fallen; evidently they had come out of his pockets. She got out and retrieved them, and they went to the hospital. A few minutes after they took Stevenson into the hospital the doctor told Marietta and Kaiser that he was dead of a heart attack. They went back to the embassy and, with Kay Graham and Sevareid, to Ambassador Bruce's office to tell him and his wife what had happened. On the embassy steps Ruth Field said, "How fortunate Alicia Patterson was. She died before Adlai." That day Secretary McNamara went to Saigon, and three days later President Johnson decided to increase American troop strength in Vietnam from 75,000 to 125,000.

An American delegation headed by Vice President Humphrey and including Dick Daley, George Ball, Bill Wirtz, and a congressional group, taking with them Adlai III and Borden and John Fell and others, flew in a presidential jet to London and brought Stevenson's body back to Washington. President Johnson, Secretary Rusk, and others met the plane. In National Cathedral a funeral service was held. Flying to it from Bloomington, his cousin Bud—Loring Merwin—said, "It never occurred to us kids that Adlai would be a great man. That darned Adlai," smiling and shaking his head, "wouldn't you know he'd die walking with a beautiful woman?"

Stevenson had expected to die young and hoped to die quickly. He often had talked to Marietta about his funeral—he wanted it held in a big cathedral and a requiem mass sung. (The last proved impractical.) His family was there. So were President Johnson and other officials. The Rev. Dr. Graebel from Springfield conducted the services. Carl McGowan delivered the eulogy: "He died as he would have wished, engaged in his country's business, and mankind's." Then his family and some of his friends took his body, again on a presidential jet, to Springfield where it lay in state on Lincoln's bier in the rotunda of the Capitol while Governor Kerner pronounced a eulogy—"Adlai Stevenson of Illinois has returned."

The United States Congress and the United Nations devoted a day to eulogies. His old supporters and opponents in the Chicago Democratic machine named an expressway for him. His friends and relatives planned the Adlai E. Stevenson Institute of International Affairs in Chicago. His family took his body to Bloomington. There a final service was held at the Unitarian Church. President Johnson and his family attended and called on the Iveses in the old family home on Washington Street. Adlai Stevenson was buried in the quiet Bloomington cemetery near the graves of his forebears.

ACKNOWLEDGMENTS

Adlai E. Stevenson died in July of 1965. In December of that year I undertook to write his biography. I have worked at it ever since, at Princeton, Washington, New York, Lake Como, Springfield, Chicago and its suburbs, and other places he frequented. When we began the research, my family and I lived for a few months in the house in Libertyville that he loved. We had visited him there often during his lifetime, and that winter it was at first hard to realize that we would not see his slightly dumpy figure waddling up the sloping field from the Des Plaines River, picking up dead tree branches as he came; to enter through the sun porch, blue eyes wide, cross the living room and, looking slightly perplexed, hesitate by the fireplace; then, grumbling about "this appalling task," go into his study to work on a speech.

The place was not quite the same that winter as when he left it. For one thing, the sheep were gone. He had raised sheep on his seventy acres (to save the cost of cutting hay and grass I suspected). Adlai III, his eldest son, had had the sheep butchered and given to his father's friends that first Christmas of his father's death, a hard thing for him.

Well, to work. A researcher and I catalogued his library. It was a working library—reference books and bound copies of his own speeches nearest his desk. But genealogies and family histories were not far away, nor were the Lincoln shelves. He was a man of Illinois, always; even after he belonged to the world, Illinois history, the Illinois prairies, and above all these seventy acres held him. Scattered about were gorgeous pictures of a cruise on a private yacht during the UN years; a bust of President Kennedy and an autographed photograph of President Johnson; plaques and awards, gavels and a collection of plaster donkeys; exotic mementos of his travels. (He used to have a basement room full of travel mementos and at Christmas gave them to friends—keys to cities, spears, oriental bric-a-brac.) Under his desk blotter was a scrap of paper containing in his handwriting a notation that Artie, his Dalmatian, was buried by a tree outside his study window.

The living room, like the study, was comfortable. The upholstered chairs and sofa that flanked the fireplace were frayed. Yet the whole house was light and airy, filled with sunshine, cheering. The house was bigger than it looked from the outside, where trees and shrubbery screened it. It sat far back from a gravel road. In later years hundreds of tourists found their way here, and even if he was working in seclusion, he received them courteously. He always called the place "the farm" and dutifully reported its profit or loss on his income tax returns.

We searched the house, a search, really, for Stevenson. And, merely in using it, found traces of him, too—his highball glasses were decorated with Princeton's orange and black tiger and "22," his class. He was only somewhat less a Princetonian than an Illinoisan. The freezer was full of lamb and mutton. Over the big double bed in the master bedroom hung two gilded cupids, melancholy when one reflected on his disastrous marriage. On the night table beside his bed lay a book—the Social Register. So many of his Social Register friends voted against him for President.

On a telephone note pad Stevenson had written "Penelope is 21," a reminder. Lifelong he was good to his friends' children, helped raise them, in a way. He was thoughtful and affectionate. Forgetful, too—we found nine identical trench coats in a downstairs closet, bought no doubt while traveling, having forgotten to bring a coat.

On the wall of the basement stair was a lithograph from the campaign of 1892, when Stevenson's grandfather and namesake was elected Vice President, the running mate of Cleveland. And another from the campaign of 1900, when he lost with Bryan. In the basement we found an old filing cabinet. One drawer was stuck tight. I finally pried it open—and found Stevenson's daily appointment books covering his entire four years as Governor.

One wintry day Adlai III and I sat in front of the fireplace with my agent and publisher and worked out the contracts for the biography. As a writer and lawyer, Stevenson would have enjoyed that. Then we had a drink, and he would have enjoyed that too. Soon I moved on, to Washington, and he would have approved.

Stevenson was a string-saver; he almost literally never threw anything away. Among his papers one can find not only the longhand first drafts of famous speeches but also football game ticket stubs and old dance programs. His archive is enormous. We copied several hundred thousand pages of his papers. We indexed the copies, making an average of perhaps a thousand index cards on each of the sixty-five years of his life. To fill in gaps, I interviewed about a hundred people who had been close to him. In using the material, I have usually let it speak for itself, though occasionally I have felt it necessary to intervene. It has not always been possible to unravel all the complexities and resolve all the ambiguities of his life, for he was a complex and sometimes ambiguous man. But I think the important questions have been answered.

A great many people helped in the making of this book.

I had the cooperation of Stevenson's family—his sister, Mrs. Ernest Ives, and his three sons, Adlai III, Borden, and John Fell. They gave me free access to Stevenson's private papers. I consulted them at various stages of the project. It is only fair to them, however, to absolve them of any responsibility for the book that has resulted. It is my book, not theirs; its interpretation of Adlai Stevenson is mine, not theirs. I am deeply grateful for their help.

For supporting the project in various ways, I wish to express my gratitude to Lake Forest College, the Woodrow Wilson School of Princeton University, the Graduate Center of the City University of New York, the Medill School of Northwestern University, and the Rockefeller Foundation—and to their presidents, deans, professors, and librarians. And to the First National Bank of Highland Park, Illinois.

I am grateful to the memory of Louis A. Kohn and to his widow, Mary Jane Kohn, for introducing me to Adlai Stevenson in the first place, while he was still Governor.

Many people kindly gave me permission to quote from their own letters, private journals, or other writings.

The reader should know that the passage on Stevenson's feelings about Richard Nixon was written long before Nixon's disgrace and resignation.

Quotations from unpublished letters, journals, and other writings are reprinted by permission of their authors (or their authors' estates), as follows:

Jacob M. Arvey, William Attwood, Edwin Austin, George W. Ball, William Benton, William McCormick Blair, Chester Bowles, Kenneth F. Burgess, William J. Campbell, Cass Canfield, Benjamin V. Cohen, Norman Cousins, John Cowles, Henry Crown, Beth Currie, Harry S Truman, Mrs. Clifton Daniel, Jane Warner Dick, Paul H. Douglas, William O. Douglas, James Doyle, Roxane Eberlein, Carol Evans, Mrs. Kellogg Fairbank, Ruth Field, Gay Finletter, Thomas K. Finletter, Dorothy Fosdick, J. W. Fulbright, John Kenneth Galbraith, Lloyd Garrison, Averell Harriman, Barnet Hodes, Chester Holifield, Evelyn Houston, Hubert H. Humphrey, Walter Johnson, Clay Judson, Murray Kempton, George Kennan, Robert F. Kennedy, Louis A. Kohn, Henry Lax, David Lloyd, Archibald MacLeish, Donald MacPherson, Mercedes McCambridge, Nan McEvoy, Carl McGowan, Davis Merwin, Loring Merwin, Louis Merwin, Agnes Meyer, Eugene Meyer, John S. Miller, Newton N. Minow, Charles Murphy, Jacqueline Kennedy Onassis, Mrs. Walter Paepcke, Francis T. P. Plimpton, David Riesman, James Reston, William Rivkin, Eugene Rostow, James Rowe, Dean Rusk, Dore Schary, Arthur M. Schlesinger, Jr., R. Sargent Shriver, William Sidley, Hermon Dunlap Smith, Mrs. Smith, John Steele, Richard K. Stevens, Roger Stevens, Adlai E. Stevenson and Ellen Stevenson, Adlai E. Stevenson III, Borden Stevenson, John Fell Stevenson, Nancy Stevenson, Stuart Symington, Robert W. Tufts, Barbara Ward, Jacob Weinstein, Harriet Welling, Theodore White, Wilson W. Wyatt, Suzie Zurcher.

Francis S. Nipp served as Research Director of the project for the first two years. Roxane Eberlein, who was formerly Stevenson's private secretary, took over thereafter. Alton B. Smith arranged the typing of various drafts of the manuscript. My wife helped research and edit the book through all the years. To their fidelity, I owe much. And to my understanding and patient and skillful editors and agents—Samuel S. Vaughan, Kenneth McCormick, and Eric Larrabee, all of Doubleday, and Ivan Von Auw and Dorothy Olding of Harold Ober Associates.

I am grateful to Stevenson's friends and associates who submitted to interviews, most of them more than once. I am not listing them here because they are quoted in the text. I am grateful, too, to several private citizens and to several of my own graduate students who volunteered help with research and other chores—I especially want to mention Cynthia Brilliant, Dave Gollust, William King, Lee Knauerhaze, Suzanne Meldman, and Nancy Szokan.

PHOTO CREDITS

SOURCE NOTES

The principal sources I have used in writing this book are Adlai Stevenson's public and private papers. They exist, for the most part, in three locations. Those relating to his ambassadorship are in the Department of State archives in Washington, D.C., and in the chancery of the United States Mission to the United Nations in New York. The rest are in Firestone Library at Princeton University in Princeton, New Jersey. In addition, his family and friends retain possession of a relatively small number of papers.

Some of Stevenson's papers are in the process of being published in a multi-volume Selected Papers under the editorship of Walter Johnson.

I have interviewed most of the principals in Stevenson's life and used miscellaneous other papers. Transcripts of the interviews are in my possession. In these notes I will locate the miscellaneous papers.

Often the source of a sentence in the book is stated explicitly in the text, as when Stevenson wrote a letter to a certain person on a given date. It would be tedious to repeat such citations in these notes. Moreover, individual documents cannot at this time be precisely located for scholars within libraries; the documents are in the process of being rearranged by archivists. Scholars will readily find ordinary material, such as the proceedings of the United Nations, Stevenson's speeches during the presidential campaign, or Stevenson's letters. And of course, on matters of general knowledge, I have used such standard reference works as Who's Who, the Columbia Encyclopedia, and various publications by the United States Government and the United Nations and Congressional Quarterly; scholars will not need citations to them. Therefore, in these notes, I shall in the main cite only unusual sources, such as private journals or interviews—material not readily identified or found.

One caveat: the system just explained results in a certain distortion. That is to say, by far the most important sources of this book are AES's own speeches, correspondence, official papers, diaries, statements, press conference transcripts, and so on. Since, as I say, I am not citing them here, a cursory inspection of the Source Notes would suggest that interviews and several private journals other than AES's own had an importance far greater than they actually do have. One should remember that the basic sources are AES's own utterances.

In citing sources below, chapter by chapter, section by section, I have used the following abbreviations:

AES-Adlai Ewing Stevenson, Governor of Illinois, 1949–53; presidential candidate, 1952 and 1956; Ambassador to the United Nations, 1961–65.
ESI-his sister, Elizabeth Stevenson Ives.
EBS-his wife, Ellen Borden Stevenson.
AES III-his eldest son, Adlai Ewing Stevenson III, United States Senator from Illinois, 1971– .

BS-his second son, Borden Stevenson.
JFS-his youngest son, John Fell Stevenson.
JBM-John Bartlow Martin
HHH-Hubert H. Humphrey
PFL-Princeton Firestone Library.

On an important Stevenson speech, I have used, if it was available, a transcript of AES's words as actually uttered. As a second choice, I have used his reading copy; as a third, the mimeographed text released to the press in advance; as a fourth, the text as subsequently published in a book.

CHAPTER 1: 1952-1955

Principal sources not ordinarily cited in detail are AES speeches, writings, correspondence, calendars, travel diaries, press conference transcripts, and appointment sheets, all at PFL.

SECTION TWO:
Election condolences: Newton Minow interview.

SECTION THREE:
Closing up headquarters: Minow interview.
AES re-entering Sidley firm: Ed Austin interview.
Schlesinger visit: Arthur M. Schlesinger, Jr., journal, in his possession.
AES/HST relations: letter, Truman to AES, Nov. 21, 1952, and telegrams Nov. 7, Nov. 12, at PFL.
Schlesinger on McCarthyism: letter, Schlesinger, Jr., to AES, Nov. 21, 1952, at PFL.

SECTION FOUR:
Marietta Tree background: Marietta Tree interview.

SECTION FIVE:
AES visit to the White House: letter, AES to Jane Dick, Dec. 4, 1952, at PFL, in typed transcript; contemporary clippings.

SECTION SIX:
AES on writing magazine pieces from world tour: letter, AES to Garrison, Dec. 29, 1952, at PFL.
Stratton's inauguration: contemporary clippings; letter, Rev. Mr. Graebel to AES, Jan. 13, 1953, at PFL.

SECTION SEVEN:
AES peak in 1948: Carl McGowan interview.
AES recreating the Democratic Party: Barbara Ward, Jack Arvey interviews.
AES young Volunteers: Bill Rivkin, Abner Mikva interviews.
AES "a compulsive writer": Bill Benton interview.
AES political importance: James "Scotty" Reston, Newton Minow interviews; Carl McGowan speech to the Law and Legal Clubs, Chicago, Mar. 11, 1966.
AES/Eastern establishment: James Reston, Newt Minow, Agnes Meyer, Carl McGowan, George Ball interviews; and a confidential source.
AES/Libertyville: Glen Lloyd interview.
AES multilevel life: Carl McGowan interview and speech cited above; Draper Daniels, Jim Oates interviews.
AES remarrying: Bill Benton, Newt Minow, Bill Blair interviews.
AES and women: Bill Benton, Mrs. Ives interviews.

SECTION EIGHT:
Lyndon Johnson in the Senate: Schlesinger, Jr., interview.

Johnson/AES: letter, James Rowe to McGowan, Jan. 29, 1953.
AES/Mayor Clark: letter, Clark to AES, Jan. 22, 1953.
Barbados: Marietta Tree interview.
AES speech book intro: Newton Minow interview; *Life,* Mar. 2, 1953.
AES New York speech: letter, Gov. Dennis J. Roberts to AES, Feb. 16, 1953; letter, George Ball to Reston, Feb. 17, 1953; contemporary clips; letter, Harry S Truman to AES, Feb. 19, 1953; wire, Truman to David D. Lloyd, Feb. 16, 1953.
AES Washington trip: AES schedule at PFL.
Democrats in Illinois: letter, Larry Irvin to JBM, 1972; letter, AES to Mayor Richard J. Daley, Mar. 1, 1953.

SECTION NINE:
Girls on AES's ship abroad: AES III interview; letter, AES to Ellen Davies, Jan. 15, 1954.
AES in Hawaii: brown "Handy Note Book" with black top-flip binding, penciled on cover, "Japan-Korea," at PFL.
AES in Japan: same notebook as above; Walter Johnson's journal, dictaphone tapes at PFL; letter, AES to Mrs. Ives, undated, but with envelope attached postmarked Mar. 14, 1953; postcard, AES to the Smiths from Kyoto, in possession of the Smiths; AES speech at meeting of the Japan-American Society at Tokyo Kaiken, Tokyo, Mar. 12, 1953.
AES in Korea: same notebook as above.
AES in Formosa: brown "Handy Note Book" with black top-flip binding, penciled on cover "Formosa, Hong Kong," at PFL; Walter Johnson journal on dictaphone tapes at PFL, tapes 12–23; Barry Bingham's memorandum of conversation, headnoted "Taipeh, March 21, 1953," at PFL.

SECTION TEN:
AES in the Philippines: brown "Handy Note Book" with black top-flip binding with "Phillipines" (sic) on cover; William Attwood journal, in his possession.

SECTION ELEVEN:
AES in Vietnam: brown spiral notebook with side flip headed "Indo-China" with "Malay Singapor" (sic) crossed out on top; Robert McClintock Memorandum of Conversation with Bao Dai at Banmethuot, April 2, 1953, headed in right corner "Copy for Mr. Stevenson," at PFL; undated postcard, AES to Ruth Winter, in her possession; letter, AES to Jane Dick, April 7, 1953; Walter Johnson journal, dictaphone tape 56; *Look,* June 2, 1953.

SECTION TWELVE:
AES in Indonesia: plain brown notebook with black side-flip binding, with "Indonesia" written on front, at PFL; letter, Arthur Schlesinger, Jr., to AES, April 8, 1953; letter, Chester Bowles, to AES, June 5, 1953; Walter Johnson journal, dictaphone tape 64 at PFL.
AES in Singapore: Walter Johnson journal, dictaphone tapes 76–77 at PFL.
AES in Malaya: Walter Johnson journal, dictaphone tapes 77–81, at PFL; letter, AES to Mrs. Ives, undated on stationery headed with a crown and "King's House, Kuala Lumpur, Malaya."

AES helicopter problems in Malaya: Walter Johnson journal, dictaphone tape 83, at PFL; Federal Government Press Statement ⅍4/53/162, dated April 16, 1953.

AES with Malayan university students: Walter Johnson journal, dictaphone tapes 87–88 at PFL.

AES with pro-Chiang Chinese: Walter Johnson journal, dictaphone tapes 87–88 at PFL.

AES in Thailand: Walter Johnson journal, dictaphone tapes 91–98.

AES and the floating market: Walter Johnson journal, dictaphone tape 94 at PFL.

AES meeting U Thant: U Thant interview.

SECTION THIRTEEN:

AES in India: brown notebook called "the spiral" with "INDIA" written on it, at PFL, and brown notebook with black side binding with "India(cont)" and "Pakistan" labeling it, at PFL; letters, AES to Ambassador George Allen, Aug. 23, 1953, Sept. 5, 1953 and reverse, Aug. 28, 1953, at PFL; telegram, Dulles to AES, July 15, 1953; letter, AES to Jane Dick, dated Rashtrapati, Bhaven, New Delhi, Ap. 5, with pencil notation "May 5, 1953" on top; letter, AES to Jane Dick, April 7, 1953.

AES in Pakistan: brown notebook with black side binding labeled "India(cont.), Pakistan," at PFL; Walter Johnson journal, dictaphone tapes 130–32, at PFL; letter, Arthur Schlesinger, Jr., to AES, May 11, 1953, May 26, 1953.

SECTION FOURTEEN:

AES in Saudi Arabia: brown "the spiral" notebook with top spiral flip, labeled "Saudi Arabia," at PFL; letter, AES to Jane Dick, May 26, 1953; Walter Johnson journal, dictaphone tapes 136–37 at PFL.

AES in Egypt: brown "the spiral" notebook labeled "Egypt, Lebanon, Jordan, Israel," at PFL.

AES in Lebanon: same brown notebook.

AES in Jordan: same notebook.

AES in Israel: same notebook plus green-patterned "El-Amir Writing Block," top flip, labeled "Israel (cont.)-Cyprus," at PFL; note, AES to Jane Dick, undated.

SECTION FIFTEEN:

AES in Cyprus: same green "El-Amir Writing Block" described above; Walter Johnson journal, dictaphone tape 162, at PFL; letter, Stephen Mitchell to AES on Mitchell and Conway stationery, May 28, 1953; letter, Bill Blair to Stephen Mitchell, dated "Catsellia Dome Hotel Kyrenia," June 15, 1953.

AES in Turkey: green-patterned "El-Amir Writing Block" with top flip, labeled "Turkey," at PFL.

AES in Yugoslavia: blue-patterned "El-Amir Writing Block" labeled "Yugoslavia."

AES in Greece: blue-patterned "El-Amir Writing Block" labeled Greece, at PFL.

SECTION SIXTEEN:

AES in Italy: green-patterned "El-Amir Writing Block" labeled "Italy Austria" at PFL; John Fell Stevenson interview; letter, AES to Bingham, dated Vienna, Austria, July 9, 1953.

AES in Austria: same notebook as in above note; "Message Broadcast by Mr. Adlai Stevenson on Radio Free Europe to the Peoples Living Under Communist Dictatorship," undated, at PFL.

AES in Germany: green-patterned top-flip "El-Amir Writing Block" labeled "Germany France" at PFL.

AES/East German confrontation: William Attwood journal, in his possession.

AES in France: same notebook; Theodore White interview; letter, Jane Dick to AES, dated July 20, 1953.

SECTION SEVENTEEN:

AES in England: red flip-top "Century Notebook" labeled "England," at PFL; William Attwood journal, in his possession; *Look,* Sept. 22, 1953.

AES with Churchill: red notebook noted above.

SECTION EIGHTEEN:

Richard Rovere article: *New York Times Magazine,* Sept. 13, 1953, pp. 1–44.

AES/Truman dinner: Arthur Schlesinger, Jr., journal, in his possession.

Chicago Civic Opera: Arthur Schlesinger, Jr., journal, in his possession.

SECTION NINETEEN:

Study group: contemporary correspondence; JBM journal, in his possession; Arthur Schlesinger, Jr., journal, in his possession; Arthur Schlesinger, Jr., Thomas K. Finletter, and W. Averell Harriman interviews.

Exposing AES to issues and ideas: Schlesinger, Jr., interview.

Shadow cabinet: Thomas K. Finletter interview.

Sharon group: letter, Sharon to Wilson Wyatt, Sept. 28, 1953; letter, Sharon to AES, Nov. 24, 1953; letter, AES to Wyatt, Oct. 29, 1953; letter, Wyatt to AES, Oct. 21, 1953; letter, AES to Sharon, Feb. 2, 1954; letter, Sharon to AES, Jan. 27, 1954.

AES defense speech: JBM journal, in his possession.

Finletter Group first meeting: Thomas K. Finletter Papers, in his possession.

Finletter Group early papers (1953–54): Thomas K. Finletter Papers, in his possession.

Finletter Group meetings: George Ball, Arthur Schlesinger, Jr., interviews.

SECTION TWENTY:

Reorganizing the Chicago machine: letter, Henry S. Blum to AES, Sept. 17, 1953; reverse, Sept. 22, 1953.

AES new law firm: letter, Schlesinger, Jr., to AES, Sept. 20, 1953; reverse, Sept. 23, 1953.

New Picture of AES: *Wall Street Journal,* Sept. 23, 1953.

AES visit with Eisenhower: letter, AES to Hon. Stanley Woodward, Sept. 17, 1953; letter, John Foster Dulles to AES, Oct. 21, 1953; reverse, Oct. 13, 1953; Dwight David Eisenhower, *Public Papers of the President, 1953,* p. 648; JBM notes on visit to Libertyville, October 1953, in his possession.

SECTION TWENTY-ONE:

HUAC subpoenas: Earl Latham, *The Communist Controversy in Washington* (Cambridge: Harvard University Press, 1966), pp. 369ff.

Holding Eisenhower responsible for his subordinates: letter, James Boyd to AES, Oct. 28, 1953; reverse, Nov. 20, 1953.

Relations with Alicia Patterson: letter, AES to Alicia Patterson, postmarked Dec. 4, 1953.

Scrapbooks for AES: letter, AES to Miss Edith Gifford, Dec. 7, 1953.

AES in Philadelphia; Marietta Tree interview; letter, Richard Stevens to AES III, July 15, 1966.

SECTION TWENTY-TWO:

Democratic Party changes in mid-1950s: Arthur Schlesinger, Jr., interview.

AES/Mitchell/ADA: correspondence at PFL.

AES/Kefauver/LBJ: correspondence at PFL.

AES in Miami: Thomas K. Finletter Papers, in his possession.

Finletter defense budget analysis: Finletter Papers, in his possession.

Rowe analysis of Democratic Party/AES: letter, Rowe to Carl McGowan, Jan. 27, 1954.

LBJ savage toward AES: Arthur Schlesinger, Jr., interview.

AES spring schedule: letters, Blair to Schlesinger, Jr., Jan. 27, 1954; reverse, Jan. 14, 1954.

SECTION TWENTY-THREE:

AES in Miami: McGowan speech to the Law and Legal Clubs, Mar. 11, 1966.

SECTION TWENTY-FOUR

Godkin lectures: *Harvard Alumni Bulletin*, April 3, 1954.

AES/Barbara Ward; Barbara Ward, Marietta Tree, Clayton Fritchey, George Ball interviews.

AES surrounded by intellectual resources: Rostow policy essays, at PFL; JBM conversation with JFK.

SECTION TWENTY-FIVE:

Tufts critique of Dulles' policy: letter, Tufts to AES, Mar. 16, 1954; reverse, April 6, 1954.

AES kidney operation: JBM journal, in his possession.

AES need for an agent: JBM journal, in his possession.

AES/hydrogen bombs: JBM journal, in his possession; letter, Lewis Mumford to AES with enclosed New York *Times* clip, April 1, 1954; reverse, May 19, 1954.

Dienbienphu: letter, William J. vanden Heuvel to AES, April 19, 1954; reverse, April 28, 1954.

AES to Alicia Patterson: letter, AES to Alicia Patterson, envelope dated May 19, 1954, with *Newsday* cover sheet.

AES/Truman birthday dinner: correspondence at PFL.

Marriage proposals: correspondence in "T" file at PFL, to AES, May 7, 1954; letter, Carol Evans to Miss "T," undated.

AES/Oppenheimer case: letter, Lloyd Garrison to AES, May 10, 1954; reverse, May 11, 1954.

Jefferson-Jackson Day dinner: letter, AES to Lyndon Johnson, May 12, 1954; reverse, April 14, 1954.

AES/Truman birthday speech: letter, AES to Truman, May 12, 1954; reverse, May 17, 1954.

AES/desegregation speech: Marietta Tree interview; Mrs. Currie's notes, in her possession.

AES/civil rights: Mrs. Currie's notes, in her possession.

AES/congressional elections advice: letter, AES to Truman, May 19, 1954; reverse, May 24, 1954.

Elmo Roper job: letter, Schlesinger, Jr., to Blair, May 20, 1954; reverse, May 25, 1954.

Southeast Asia statement: letter, Chester Bowles to AES, May 20, 1954; reverse, May 28, 1954.

AES/Agnes Meyer: Agnes Meyer interview; letter, Agnes Meyer to AES, June 20, 1955.

SECTION TWENTY-SIX:

AES wire to Truman on hospital stay: day letter, AES to Truman, June 21, 1954.

AES Alaska trip: letter, AES to Jane Dick; John Fell Stevenson interview; letter, Mrs. Robbins Milbank to AES, Aug. 17, 1954; reverse, Sept. 2, 1954.

AES in Montana: AES speech notes titled "Adlai Stevenson, Great Falls, Montana, August 2, 1954," at PFL.

AES plane incident: letter, Bert Tracey to AES, Aug. 8, 1954; reverse, Sept. 11, 1954.

AES III homecoming: AES III and Nancy Anderson Stevenson testimony, EBS competency hearings, 1966.

SECTION TWENTY-SEVEN:

AES pre-campaigning days: letter, Agnes Meyer to AES, June 30, 1954; reverse, Aug. 10, 1954.

Rowe on Mitchell resignation: letter, Schlesinger, Jr., to Blair, Aug. 16, 1954; reverse, Aug. 20, 1954.

AES speaking style vs. Paul Douglas': JBM journal, in his possession.

AES/Dietrich: letter, Marlene Dietrich to AES, dated only Sunday, with address at top left.

AES/Mrs. Bogart (Lauren Bacall): letter, AES to Mrs. Bogart, Aug. 19, 1954.

AES/mood: Arthur Schlesinger, Jr., journal, in his possession.

Adlai III/Nancy's engagement party: letter, AES to Nancy Anderson, Sept. 19, 1954; letter, AES to Warwick Anderson, Sept. 19, 1954.

Indianapolis speech: letter, Truman to AES, Sept. 20, 1954; reverse, Sept. 22, 1954.

Post-election plans: Thomas K. Finletter Papers, in his possession; Newton Minow interview.

Hollywood Bowl speech: letter, Emanuel Celler to AES, Sept. 29, 1954; reverse, Oct. 11, 1954.

Final Eastern campaign swing: Averell Harriman interview; letter, Blair to Alicia Patterson, Nov. 2, 1954; Marietta Tree, Bill Blair interviews; JBM journal, in his possession.

SECTION TWENTY-EIGHT

AES/Marietta talk about 1956: Marietta Tree interview.

Bill Benton visit: William Benton, George Ball, Newton Minow interviews; letter, Benton to Francis Nipp, Aug. 4, 1966.

Democratic National Committee meeting: Edward Doyle, ed., *As We Knew Adlai* (New York: Harper & Row, 1966), p. 87; John Brademas, William Rivkin, Arthur Schlesinger, Jr., Jacob Arvey interviews; Rowland Evans and Robert Novak, *Lyndon B. Johnson: The Exercise of Power* (New York: The New American Library, 1966), p. 185; AES speech to the committee; roll call at meeting of the Democratic National Committee, at PFL; JBM journal, in his possession.

Fulbright congressional meeting suggestion: letter, Fulbright to AES, Dec. 11, 1954; Nov. 23, 1954; reverse, Dec. 13, 1954.

AES/RCA/anti-trust case: letter, John D. McConnell to AES, Nov. 6, 1954; reverse, Dec. 11, 1954.

Christmas: AES III interview; AES III testimony, EBS competency hearings, 1966; Nancy Anderson Stevenson testimony, ibid.

SECTION TWENTY-NINE:

AES law firm and office: John Bartlow Martin, "Adlai Girds for Battle," *Saturday Evening Post*, Oct. 22, 1955, p. 28; partnership agreements and income statements are at PFL; Newton Minow interview.

RCA case: "Adlai Girds for Battle," op. cit.; Minow interview.

AES correspondence: correspondence and messages are at PFL.

AES life style: appointment sheets and calendars are at PFL; "Adlai Girds for Battle," op. cit.

AES self-deprecation as a gambit: Newton Minow interview; letter, Penelope Tree to AES.

Nancy Anderson: letter, Nancy to AES, Jan. 30, marked "12/30/54"; reverse, Jan. 4, 1954, marked "1955."

SECTION THIRTY:

Administration and the Far East: letter, AES to Ben Cohen, Jan. 10, 1955.

AES on Costa Rica and the whooping crane: letter, AES to Arthur Schlesinger, Jr., Jan. 19, 1955.

1955 election campaign: "Adlai Girds for Battle," op. cit.; JBM journal; miscellaneous correspondence at PFL; contemporary clippings; AES Feb. 1, 1955 statement, at PFL; AES speech at PFL.

Finletter Group finances: letter, Garrison to AES, Jan. 24, 1955; letter, Bill Benton to Bill Blair, Feb. 9, 1955.

AES for President Committee: memo, Stevenson for President Committee, Feb. 14, 1955, at PFL; letter, Arthur Schlesinger, Jr., to AES, Feb. 15, 1955; letter, Agnes Meyer to AES, Feb. 5, 1955; reverse, Feb. 17, 1955; John Steele files, in his possession.

Arvey Miami Beach dinner: Jack Arvey interview.

Daley's election: letter, Jasper S. King to AES, April 4, 1955; reverse, April 6, 1955; letter, Mrs. Charles E. Merriam to AES, undated; reverse, April 13, 1955.

SECTION THIRTY-ONE:

Quemoy and Matsu: John Steele files, in his possession; letter, AES to Chester Bowles, Mar. 28, 1955; phone conversations, undated, at PFL.

AES III wedding problems: letter, AES to AES III, April 6, 1955; reverse, dated "April, 1955"; letter, AES III to AES, dated "April, 1955"; reverse, April 8, 1955; letter, AES to Warwick Anderson, April 8, 1955; reverse, dated "Wednesday morning," undated.

AES opinion of the Quemoy-Matsu speech: "Adlai Girds for Battle," op. cit.

AES in Washington: black leather notebook, unlabeled, "Africa trip 1955" on inside page in pencil, at PFL; appointment sheets, at PFL; letter, AES III to AES, undated.

SECTION THIRTY-TWO:

Africa departure: black leather notebook unlabeled with "Africa trip 1955" on inside page in pencil, at PFL.

Garrisons in Africa: Lloyd Garrison interview.

AES in Kenya: Garrison interview.

AES in Uganda: Canfield account.

AES in South Africa: Garrison interview; AES press conference at Jan Smuts Airport, May 8, 1955, statement at PFL; local press clippings at PFL.

AES in the Gold Coast: letter, AES to Quame (sic) Nkrumah, May 23, 1955; Barbara Ward interview.

AES/Barbara Ward: letter, Barbara Ward to AES, May 15, 1955.

AES return: "Memo to the Boys on the month in Africa," longhand, May 1955, at PFL.

SECTION THIRTY-THREE:

Political situation on AES's return: John Steele files, in his possession.

AES more gusto than 1952: John Steele files, in his possession.

Political miscellaneous: letter with clipping, Sargent Shriver to AES, undated; reverse, June 9, 1955.

Stevenson Steering Committee: contribution lists at PFL; letter, AES to Barbara Ward, June 21, 1955; letter AES to Robert Jackson, June 21, 1955; "Report on Stevenson Steering Committee Receipts and Disbursements" to July 31, 1955; letter, Edward W. Cooke to Robert Hutchins, June 3, 1955; memo probably from Raskin to Bill Blair, June 16, 1955; letter, Violet M. Gunther, to Arthur Schlesinger, Jr., June 16, 1955; appointment sheets at PFL; letters, AES to Jim Finnegan, June 21, 1955; letter, Blair to Finnegan, July 5, 1955.

AES III wedding: AES III testimony, EBS competency hearings, 1966; letter, Mrs. Ives to Carol Evans, June 29, 1955; reverse, June 27, 1955.

SECTION THIRTY-FOUR:

AES/Agnes Meyer: letter, AES to Agnes Meyer, June 14, 1955; Agnes Meyer interview; letters, Agnes Meyer to AES, June 3, 1955; June 16, 1955; June 20, 1955; June 3, 1955; undated.

AES/Truman: letter, AES to Truman, July 5, 1955; reverse, July 6, 1955.

AES/Johnson's illness: letter, AES to Mrs. Lyndon Johnson, July 5, 1955; reverse, July 9, 1955.

AES/federal appropriations desegregation rider: letter, Garrison to AES, July 15, 1955; reverse, July 20, 1955; letter, Hubert H. Humphrey to AES, July 8, 1955; reverse, July 15, 1955.

AES/1956 presidency: letter, AES to Truman, July 18, 1955; reverse, July 19, 1955.

AES education speech: wire, Agnes Meyer to AES, July 7, 1955; letter, Agnes Meyer to AES, July 7, 1955; reverse, July 10, 1955.

AES health: note, Mrs. Ives to Carol Evans, undated.

What I Think: letter, AES to Cass Canfield, dictated July 15, 1955.
Harriman campaigning: letter, Agnes Meyer to AES, July 26, 1955; reverse, Aug. 2, 1955.

SECTION THIRTY-FIVE:
AES strategy meeting, Aug. 5, 1955: Blair's meeting agenda, Blair's meeting notes, Minow's meeting notes, all at PFL; Minow interview.
Finletter Group Paper, "The Central Issue for 1956," at PFL.
Blair memo: Blair memo, untitled, undated, at PFL.
AES/Agnes Meyer: letters, Agnes Meyer to AES, Aug. 5, 1955; Aug. 9, 1955; reverse, dictated, Aug. 12, 1955.
John Fell's travels: letter, John Fell to AES, July 17, 1955; reverse, Aug. 12, 1955.
Rowe pleased with Finnegan: letter, Rowe to Blair, Aug. 12, 1955.

SECTION THIRTY-SIX:
Dulles' Middle East speech: letter and speech, Dulles to AES, Aug. 24, 1955; reverse, Aug. 25, 1955; letter, AES to Henry Fisher, Aug. 25, 1955; reverse, Aug. 31, 1955.
AES/LeRoy Collins: letter, Collins to AES, Sept. 1, 1955; reverse, Sept. 7, 1955.
Johnson for President: letter, Benton to Blair, Sept. 7, 1955.
Finletter Group meeting: Thomas K. Finletter Papers, in his possession.
AES/Agnes Meyer: letter, AES to Agnes Meyer, Sept. 9, 1955 from Jamaica; reverse, Sept. 9, 1955, marked "First Letter"; Agnes Meyer to AES, Sept. 12, 1955, marked "Third Letter."
Finletter Paper: Finletter Papers, in his possession.
Ashmore memorandum: Harry Ashmore memorandum, dated Sept. 20, 1955, at PFL.
Eisenhower's heart attack: Minow interview.
Harriman and the presidency: letter, Agnes Meyer to AES, Sept. 20, 1955, dated "Tuesday."
Agnes Meyer and AES domestic problems; letter, Agnes Meyer to AES, Sept. 25, 1955.
AES/Harriman presidency understanding: Arthur Schlesinger, Jr., journal, in his possession.

SECTION THIRTY-SEVEN:
AES trip to Dallas: Minow interview.
AES and the primaries: Minow interview.
AES nomination problem: JBM journal.
AES office space expanding: JBM notes, in his possession.
AES/Agnes Meyer: letters, Agnes Meyer to AES, Sept. 27, 1955, Oct. 1, 1955; reverse, Oct. 3, 1955, Oct. 5, 1955; letter, Agnes Meyer to AES, Oct. 8, 1955.
Truman/Harriman: Finletter Papers, in his possession.
Reactivating the Volunteers: Marietta Tree interview.
Schlesinger memo: letter, Schlesinger to AES, Oct. 10, 1955.
New York events irk AES: letter, AES to Alicia Patterson, postmarked Oct. 11, 1955.
ES and the nomination: letter, AES to Rev. William T. Levy, Oct. 11, 1955.

SECTION THIRTY-EIGHT:

California primary: letter, Pat Brown to AES, Oct. 11, 1955; reverse, Oct. 14, 1955.

Political policy line: John Sharon memorandum of Oct. 14, 1955 conference at the Hay-Adams Hotel, at PFL.

AES in Cambridge: Arthur Schlesinger, Jr., journal, in his possession.

AES in New York: Finletter Papers, in his possession.

Roger Kent: letter, Kent to AES, Oct. 5, 1955.

AES/Truman Chicago meeting: Mrs. Currie's notes, in her possession.

AES/JFK: letter, Kennedy to AES, Oct. 21, 1955; reverse, Oct. 29, 1955.

AES/Harriman: "Miscellaneous Political Notes," undated, unsigned, marked "Top Secret"; *Time* interview with Averell Harriman, at PFL.

AES/Humphrey in Minnesota: letter, AES to Humphrey, Nov. 2, 1955; reverse, Nov. 4, 1955.

AES/Freeman in Minnesota: letter, AES to Freeman, Nov. 2, 1955.

Agnes Meyer/Truman: letter, Agnes Meyer to Truman, Nov. 1, 1955; reverse, Oct. 27, 1955; letter, Agnes Meyer to AES, Nov. 2, 1955; reverse, Nov. 3, 1955.

AES political intelligence: Arthur Schlesinger, Jr., journal, in his possession.

AES/Kefauver meeting cancellation: Chicago *Tribune*, Nov. 8, 1955; wire, AES to Kefauver, Nov. 8, 1955.

Eisenhower developments: letter, John Steele to Blair, Nov. 8, 1955.

Nov. 19 Democratic affair: letter, AES to AES III, Nov. 9, 1955.

Humphrey estimation of AES: letter, HHH to Blair, Nov. 11, 1955.

SECTION THIRTY-NINE:

AES announcement: letter, AES to Mrs. Hines, Nov. 16, 1955; letter, AES to Richard Spencer, Nov. 16, 1955.

AES Nov. 19 speech: letter, Mrs. Ives to Carol Evans, undated, headed "Memo about Berkeley, Cal."

Post-dinner correspondence: letter, AES to Agnes Meyer, Nov. 21, 1955; letter, AES to Lyndon Johnson, Nov. 21, 1955; reverse, Nov. 9, 1955; memorandum, John Sharon to Wirtz, Blair, Ashmore, and Tubby, Nov. 21, 1955; "Report from Texas," cover sheet to Blair from Schlesinger, undated.

CHAPTER 2: 1956

Once again, I have relied principally upon AES's statements, press conference transcripts, appointment sheets, program papers, and speeches, all at PFL. The important speeches and program papers were published in *The New America*, edited by Seymour Harris, JBM, and Arthur Schlesinger, Jr. (New York: Harper, 1957). Other important sources include contemporary newspapers, Schlesinger's journal, JBM's journal and related documents, and *Public Papers of the Presidents of the United States—Dwight D. Eisenhower, 1956* (Washington: U. S. Government Printing Office, 1958). Schlesinger and Martin are in possession of their respective journals.

SECTION ONE:

Opening discussion of 1956 campaign, up to Robert Kennedy's comments: JBM journal.

Kennedy comments: Robert F. Kennedy interview.

Relations with John and Robert Kennedy, Libertyville strategy meeting: Newton Minow interview.

"Am I not master in my own house?": JBM journal; New York *Times,* Sept. 16, 1956.

Advice of pros vs. semi-pros: JBM journal; letter, Arthur Schlesinger, Jr., to JBM, Jan. 11, 1972.

SECTION TWO:

Views on Israel-Arab problem: letter, Agnes Meyer to AES, Dec. 2, 1955.

Barbara Ward report: letter, Barbara Ward to AES, Dec. 5, 1955.

Meeting with Eban, Potofsky, Lilienthal; "anti-Israel" stand: David Lilienthal journal, in PFL.

SECTION THREE:

Remarks to Mrs. Ives: letter, AES to Mrs. Ernest L. Ives, Dec. 16, 1955.

Wechsler letter and the Till case: letter, AES to Arthur Schlesinger, Jr., Dec. 19, 1955.

Meeting with Wilkins and Powell: letter, AES to Arthur Schlesinger, Jr., Dec. 13, 1955.

Meeting with John B. Oakes: letter, AES to Manning Hathaway, Dec. 13, 1955.

Remarks on John Fell: letter, AES to Eleanor Roosevelt, Dec. 30, 1955.

The "most affectionate" call: letter, AES to Dore Schary, Dec. 30, 1955.

SECTION FOUR:

Reston/Patrick correspondence on DDE: Thomas K. Finletter Papers, in his possession.

Murray wanting to talk to AES: Thomas K. Finletter Papers, in his possession.

Speech advice: letter, Dore Schary to AES, Dec. 2, 1955; reverse, Dec. 30, 1955.

MacArthur and presidential politics: letter, Chester Bowles to AES, Dec. 30, 1955, marked Jan. 3, 1956.

AES and the primaries: JBM journal.

AES fund raising: Roger Stevens interview; campaign fund memo at PFL.

Disagreements between Stevens and McCloskey: Roger Stevens interview.

Campaign effects on AES's law firm: fees received during 1956 at PFL.

AES/show business supporters: staff list of AES fans in the arts and show business, at PFL.

AES/Truman Southeast Asia trip: letter, AES to Truman, Jan. 3, 1956; reverse, Jan. 7, 1956.

Humphrey on Israel: letter, HHH to AES, Nov. 28, 1955; reverse, Jan. 4, 1956.

John Fell's recovery: letter, AES to Mrs. Ives, Jan. 6, 1956; card, AES to Agnes Meyer, Jan. 6, 1956, in the Agnes Meyer files at PFL; reverse, Jan. 2, 1956.

James Roosevelt offer of California primary support: letter, James Roosevelt to AES, Jan. 3, 1956; reverse, Jan. 6, 1956.

Wallace support offer: letter, Henry Wallace to AES, Dec. 10, 1955; reverse, Jan. 6, 1956.

CBS-TV "Face the Nation": transcript at PFL; Arthur Schlesinger, Jr., journal, in his possession.

Lehman on Harriman: letter, Senator Herbert Lehman to AES, Jan. 5, 1956.

De Sapio: Thomas K. Finletter Papers, in his possession.

Schlesinger, Jr., on California: letter, Arthur Schlesinger, Jr., to AES, Jan. 17, 1956.

Kefauver Florida strategy plans: letter, Seymour Harris to Schlesinger, Jr., Jan. 17, 1956; attached memo, Schlesinger to Blair, undated.

Kefauver gains in Florida: letter, Bobby Baker to Harry Ashmore, Jan. 17, 1956; reverse, Jan. 23, 1956; letter, Baker to Ashmore, Jan. 25, 1956; reverse, Jan. 31, 1956.

Agar and "The Image of America": letter, AES to Herbert Agar, Jan. 18, 1956.

Anti-AES mail samples: letter, Jacob Arvey to James Finnegan, Jan. 26, 1956.

AES and the Jewish vote: Rabbi Jacob J. Weinstein, "Adlai, as a Friend Remembers Him," Chicago *Sun-Times*, July 10, 1966.

AES and foreign defense speech: Thomas K. Finletter Papers, in his possession; memo to Governor Stevenson from T. K. Finletter, Jan. 30, 1956.

AES accused as "creature of the party bosses": letter, Charles Brien to Blair, Jan. 27, 1956; letter, HHH to AES, Jan. 28, 1956.

"The Fresno Fiasco": Blair interview; letter, Eugene Meyer to AES, Feb. 11, 1956; reverse, Feb. 8, 1956; letter, AES to Mrs. Meyer, Feb. 8, 1956; letter, Pat Brown to AES, Feb. 17, 1956; letter, AES to Lauren Bacall, Feb. 20, 1956; letter, Leonard B. Hirsch to AES, Feb. 9, 1956; reverse, Feb. 20, 1956; letter, Mrs. A. L. Grey, Jr., to AES, Feb. 6, 1956; letter, Gilbert A. Harrison to AES, Feb. 7, 1956; reverse, Feb. 23, 1956, dictated Feb. 20, 1956.

AES at Hillcrest Country Club: Roger Stevens, Newton Minow interviews.

AES "waspish" memo: this memo, AES to Harry Ashmore, Feb. 8, 1956, as well as all other memos to and from AES and campaign staff are at PFL.

AES on desegregation: letter, Leonard B. Hirsch to AES, Feb. 9, 1956.

AES thoughts on his California trip: letter, AES to Cecil R. King, Feb. 8, 1956.

Kefauver on desegregation: letter, AES to Agnes Meyer, Feb. 8, 1956.

Alicia Patterson and Harriman: letter, Alicia to AES, undated; reverse, Feb. 8, 1956.

SECTION EIGHT:

Minnesota: letter, Ken Hechler to John Horne, Feb. 7, 1956.

New York: letter, Finletter to Blair, Feb. 7, 1956.

AES birthday greetings: letters, AES III and Nancy Stevenson to AES, Feb. 1, 1956.

AES on civil rights: letter, Mrs. Eleanor Roosevelt to AES, Feb. 11, 1956; letter, Sen. Herbert Lehman to AES, Feb. 11, 1956; letter, Alicia Patterson to AES, undated, with attached undated editorial; Eric Sevareid CBS Radio News Analysis, Feb. 14, 1956.

SECTION NINE:

Agnes Meyer/Mrs. Ives friendship: letter, AES to Agnes Meyer, Feb. 20, 1956.

AES opinion of California speeches: letter, AES to Alan Cranston, Feb. 21, 1956; reverse, Mar. 14, 1956.

AES opinion of his desegregation speeches: letter, AES to Bill Dawson, Feb. 22, 1956.

Wolf Ladejinsky: letter, AES to Mr. Curt R. Schaefer, Feb. 24, 1956; reverse, Feb. 17, 1956; cablegram from Schaefer, Feb. 7, 1956.

Massachusetts presidential preference poll: letter, JFK to Blair, Feb. 15, 1956.

AES pre-Minnesota advice letters: letter, AES to Geoffrey Crowther, Mar. 1, 1956; letter, Fulbright to AES, Mar. 1, 1956.

AES extemporaneous speeches: transcripts of most of AES's extemporaneous Minnesota speeches are at PFL.

Minnesota reaction to AES: John Steele files, in his possession.

SECTION TEN:

Finletter/Rose/De Sapio lunch: Thomas K. Finletter Papers, in his possession.

AES scheduling problems: Newton Minow interview.

AES III/Nancy's baby: letter, AES III to AES, Mar. 5, 1956, in AES III's possession.

Greater Moorhead Days speech: wire, Kefauver to AES, Mar. 10, 1956; interoffice memorandum from Marilyn Stone, Mar. 10, 1956; Blair dictated statement, Mar. 13, 1956, headed "WB+Minn."; wire, AES to Kefauver, Mar. 13, 1956.

Democratic leader endorsements: letter, John F. Simms, Jr., to AES, Jan. 20, 1956; reverse, Mar. 12, 1956; JBM journal.

Harassment of Ellen B. Stevenson: letter, AES III to AES, Mar. 8, 1956; reverse, Mar. 13, 1956.

New Hampshire: Thomas K. Finletter Papers, in his possession.

Southern Manifesto: postcard, AES to Agnes Meyer, Mar. 13, 1956, in Agnes Meyer files at PFL.

AES/AEC: letter, AES to Thomas E. Murray, Mar. 14, 1956; reverse, April 17, 1956.

Bowles foreign policy issues group: letter, Chester Bowles to AES, Feb. 16, 1956; Thomas K. Finletter Papers, in his possession.

GOP attitude on foreign policy and AES: letter, AES to George Kennan, March 14, 1956.

AES/foreign policy: letter, AES to James P. Warburg, Mar. 14, 1956.

AES/Sen. Bricker: letter to AES signed "Bill," Mar. 14, 1956, with handwritten headnote to Ken Hechler.

SECTION ELEVEN:

Last Minnesota week activities: letter, AES to Marietta Tree, undated, marked "March, 1956"; JBM journal.

Election Day: letter, AES to Fritz Rosenberg, Mar. 20, 1956; JBM journal.

Minnesota defeat reaction: letter, Herbert Lehman to Finletter, Mar. 22, 1956; wire, JFK to AES, Mar. 22, 1956; reverse letter, Mar. 23, 1956; letter, Sanford Schwartz to Blair, Mar. 24, 1956; reverse, Mar. 26, 1956; Averell Harriman interview.

SECTION TWELVE:

AES speech writing: JBM journal.

Wyatt and the campaign: JBM journal.

Diminishing Minnesota's effect: JBM journal.

AES/nuclear testing declaration idea: letter, Frank Altschul to AES, Mar. 1, 1956; reverse, Mar. 26, 1956; Thomas K. Finletter Papers, in his possession.

AES/Chicago organization: letter, Arthur Schlesinger, Jr., to AES, Mar. 23, 1956; reverse, Mar. 26, 1956.

Further Minnesota reaction: letter, AES to William H. Davis, Mar. 27, 1956.

AES LA speech: JBM journal.

AES California trip: JBM journal.

SECTION THIRTEEN:

Minnesota recoup plans: JBM journal; letter, Paul H. Douglas to AES, Mar. 29, 1956; memo, Newt Minow to AES, Mar. 30, 1956; confidential memo, Minow to AES about Illinois primary, Mar. 30, 1956.

Kefauver Florida speech: JBM journal.

AES/Israel position: JBM journal.

AES and Cloud Nine: JBM journal.

SECTION FOURTEEN:

AES Florida trip: JBM journal.

Chicago national Stevenson for President Committee speech: Arthur Schlesinger, Jr., journal, in his possession; Marietta Tree interview.

AES/New York liberal speech: Arthur Schlesinger, Jr., journal.

Highland Park high school reception: JBM journal.

Illinois primary eve: JBM journal.

Oregon primary: letter, Richard L. Neuberger to Newton Minow, April 10, 1956.
Illinois primary: JBM journal.

SECTION FIFTEEN:
Tampa: letter, John Popham to AES, at PFL.
Wyoming delegation: letter, JFK to Newton Minow, April 16, 1956.
Overwhelming campaign schedule: JBM journal.
Using Brademas files for speeches: JBM journal.

SECTION SIXTEEN:
ASNE speech on H-bomb: all documents tracing exegesis are at PFL.
ASNE speech reactions: letter, AES to Ben Cohen, April 26, 1956, April 29, 1956; letter, AES to Walter Lippmann, April 27, 1956; letter, AES to Arthur Schlesinger, Jr., April 28, 1956.
"Meet the Press": transcript at PFL.

SECTION SEVENTEEN:
AES help on television speaking: transcript on Encyclopaedia Britannica stationery, undated, at PFL.
AES asking Finletter to help with test ban and missile program reconciliation: Thomas K. Finletter Papers, in his possession.
Martin in L.A.: JBM journal.
AES/Jane Dick correspondence: letters, Jane Dick to AES, April 28, 1956.

SECTION EIGHTEEN:
AES California campaign, May 1–13: JBM journal; Newton Minow comment on Barkley funeral is from JBM interview with Minow; AES/LBJ exchange transcript is at PFL.

SECTION NINETEEN:
HHH opinion on AES nomination: letter, HHH to AES, May 4, 1956; reverse, May 14, 1956.
Last week of Florida campaign: JBM journal.
Downstate Illinois Democrats: memorandum, Newt Minow to AES, May 26, 1956.
California campaign May 28–29: JBM journal.
Florida results: JBM journal.

SECTION TWENTY:
Final week of California campaign: JBM journal and related documents in his possession.
Foreign policy as an issue: JBM journal; letter, AES to Sen. J. W. Fulbright, June 15, 1956.
Issue planning instead of delegate hunting: letter, AES to HHH, June 15, 1956.
AES view of the primaries: letter, AES to the Warwick Andersons, June 12, 1956.
Getting nominated on the first ballot: Newton Minow interview.
Post-California ranch rest: Marietta Tree interview.
California congratulations: wire, Estes Kefauver to AES, June 5, 1956; reverse, June 6, 1956.

Roger Stevens finance problems: letter, Stevens to AES, June 5, 1956, and attached memorandum, undated.

AES opinion of Eisenhower: letter, AES to Archibald MacLeish, June 12, 1956; letter, AES to Gerald Johnson, June 12, 1956; letter, AES to Ralph McGill, June 15, 1956; letter, AES to Eugene Rostow, June 12, 1956.

AES staff changes: JBM journal.

Acceptance speech drafts: JBM journal.

Desegregation plank for platform drafting: JBM journal; letter, AES to Mrs. Eleanor Roosevelt, June 15, 1956; letter, Lloyd Garrison to Blair, June 12, 1956.

AES/Kefauver rapprochement: JBM journal; interoffice memorandum from Blair, June 20, 1956, marked "Kefauver, Estes"; letter, Arthur Schlesinger, Jr., to AES, June 19, 1956; wire, Kefauver to AES, June 18, 1956; letter, AES to Kefauver, June 21, 1956; reverse, June 29, 1956, June 24, 1956, June 28, 1956.

The New American Revolution: JBM journal.

Catholic Vice President: letter, AES to Agnes Meyer, June 24, 1956, in Agnes Meyer files at PFL.

Early July nomination confidence: Arthur Schlesinger, Jr., journal, in his possession.

Delegate hunting in early July: JBM journal; Newton Minow interview.

Fall campaign planning: JBM journal.

Schlesinger and opinion poll surveys: JBM journal.

July 26 strategy meeting: JBM journal.

Eisenhower's health as a campaign issue: JBM journal; letter, AES to Truman, July 30, 1956; reverse.

AES/Agnes Meyer correspondence: letter, Agnes Meyer to AES, July 16, 1956.

Suez Canal issue: letter, AES to Stuart Gerry Brown, April 28, 1958.

Kefauver withdrawal: JBM journal; letter, Agnes Meyer to AES, Aug. 1, 1956; reverse, Aug. 6, 1956.

Preconvention week: Marietta Tree interview; Finletter memo of Aug. 18, Finletter Papers, in his possession; John Steele files, in his possession.

Sunday reception: copy of invitation at PFL.

Last week delegate hunting: JBM journal: John Steele files, in his possession.

Nomination speech: Arthur Schlesinger, Jr., journal, in his possession; JBM journal; Arthur Schlesinger, Jr., interview; John Steele files, in his possession; Newton Minow interview.

AES drafting his acceptance speech: JBM journal.

AES considering Vice President nomination: Theodore Sorensen, Newton Minow interviews; Arthur Schlesinger, Jr., journal, in his possession.

AES/Truman meeting: John Steele files, in his possession.

JFK/Kefauver people contest for vice presidential nomination: Arthur Schlesinger, Jr., journal, in his possession.

AES watching convention on television: JBM journal.

Kefauver nomination and reaction: John Steele files, in his possession; Theodore Sorensen, Kathryn Lewis interviews.

AES acceptance speech and aftermath: Arthur Schlesinger, Jr., journal, in his possession; JBM journal.

Replacing Paul Butler as national chairman issue: Arthur Schlesinger, Jr., journal, in his possession; Marietta Tree interview; John Steel files, in his possession.

Libertyville welcome and rest: John Steele files, in his possession.

SECTION TWENTY-THREE:

1956 campaign atmosphere: Arthur Schlesinger, Jr., Jack Arvey interviews; JBM journal.

Campaigning from Washington: JBM journal.

AES view of his chances in New York: letter, AES to Alicia Patterson, Aug. 20, 1956.

AES asking JFK to speak in Philadelphia: wire, AES to JFK, Aug. 23, 1956.

JFK plans to help in Massachusetts: letter, JFK to AES, Oct. 3, 1956.

Campaign opening: letter, AES to Agnes Meyer, Aug. 26, 1956; letter, AES to Francis Biddle, Sept. 14, 1956; letter, Dean Acheson to AES, Aug. 23, 1956; reverse, Aug. 26, 1956.

Campaign tone compared with 1952: memorandum, William Rivkin to Arthur Schlesinger, Jr., undated, with Sept. 10, 1956 newsclipping attached, in JBM's possession.

Mid-October campaign lost momentum: letter, AES to Jack Kroll, Oct. 16, 1956; letter, Eugene Rostow to AES, Oct. 9, 1956; letter, Agnes Meyer to AES, Sept. 17, 1956.

1956 ideas vs. 1952 ideas: Carl McGowan, James Reston, Barbara Ward interviews.

Eisenhower unbeatable, AES campaign spiritless: James Reston, Barbara Ward, Jane Dick, George Ball interviews.

Eisenhower's indestructible popularity: Adlai E. Stevenson, *The New America*, edited by Seymour E. Harris, John Bartlow Martin, and Arthur Schlesinger, Jr. (New York: Harper & Brothers, 1957), p. xxv.

AES and adulation: Mrs. Currie's notes, in her possession.

SECTION TWENTY-FOUR:

Substance of AES campaign: AES speeches, most of them published in *The New America*, pp. 237–43.

Schlesinger and Harris on significance of national defeats: ibid., p. xxvii.

SECTION TWENTY-FIVE:

AES speaking on foreign policy: letter, AES to Dean Acheson, Oct. 13, 1956; letter, Bill McMillan to LBJ, Sept. 20, 1956; LBJ to AES, Sept. 24, 1956; AES to both, Oct. 13, 1956.

AES resents criticism of his draft and H-bomb proposals: Mrs. Currie's notes, in her possession.

SECTION TWENTY-SIX:

AES weary and depressed last two weeks of the campaign: JBM journal; Arthur Schlesinger, Jr., journal.

Washington cloak-and-dagger campaign aspects: JBM journal.

AES getting equal time after Eisenhower Suez speech: Newton Minow interview; letter, Frank Stanton to Newton Minow, Jan. 28, 1972, in Minow's possession.

Birth of AES's first grandson: Mrs. Currie notes, in her possession; Jim Oates interview.

McCarthy/JFK speech Election Eve: JBM journal.

AES inferentially predicts Eisenhower's death: JBM journal; Arthur Schlesinger, Jr., interview.

SECTION TWENTY-SEVEN:

AES on effect of Suez on election: John Brademas interview.

Losing bigger than in 1952: Newton Minow, Marietta Tree interviews.

SECTION TWENTY-EIGHT:

Scotty Reston's son: wire, AES to James Reston, undated; letters, AES to Tommy Reston, Nov. 13, 1956; reverse, Nov. 14, 1956, all in Reston's possession.

Postelection immediate correspondence: letter, AES to Harry Truman, Nov. 9, 1956.

Thanksgiving: AES III testimony, Ellen Borden Stevenson Estate—court hearings, 1966.

Post article suggestion: letter, AES to Agnes Meyer, Nov. 18, 1956, in Agnes Meyer files, at PFL.

Gratitude to JFK: letter, AES to JFK, Nov. 18, 1956.

Statement that AES would not run again for President: statement Dec. 4, 1956, at PFL; Newton Minow interview; letter, AES to Mrs. Robbins Milbank, Dec. 8, 1956.

Princeton presidency: letter, Harold H. Helm to JBM, Jan., 1972, in JBM's possession.

AES other enterprises besides law: letter, AES to Alicia Patterson, Dec. 8, 1956; letter, AES to Glenn Adcox, Dec. 12, 1956; letter, J. W. Fulbright to Ed Pauley, Nov. 10, 1956; letter, AES to Morris Ernst, Dec. 8, 1956.

Attending first DAC meeting: letter, AES to Kefauver, Dec. 9, 1956.

CHAPTER 3: 1957–1960

Principal sources are AES's correspondence, speeches, statements, travel note-books, appointment sheets, and law firm records, all at PFL; plus JBM interviews, in JBM's possession.

SECTION ONE:
AES quarrel with LBJ and Sam Rayburn: letter, AES to Gerald Johnson, Jan. 21, 1957.
AES/Democratic Advisory Council: Thomas K. Finletter, Charles Tyroler interviews.
Statements of the Democratic Advisory Council are at PFL.
Reaction to DAC: Thomas Finletter, James Reston interviews.
AES/Dean Acheson and Acheson/DAC: Carl McGowan, Newton Minow, Averell Harriman interviews.

SECTION TWO:
Warburg proposal: letter, James P. Warburg to AES, Dec. 26, 1956; reverse, Jan. 20, 1957.
AES/forming a power group: Mrs. Currie's notes, in her possession.
AES/Encyclopaedia Britannica: letter, William Benton to AES, Jan. 28, 1957, reverse Jan. 10–11, 1957.
AES/his law firm, buying a newspaper: letter, AES to Allen Kander, Jan. 11, 1957.
AES/Reynolds Metals, aluminum: letter, AES to Richard S. Reynolds, Jr., Jan. 17, 1957.
Mary Lasker-AES marriage rumor: letter, AES to Mrs. Ives, Jan. 28, 1957.
Schaefer/AES III: letter, Walter Schaefer to AES III, Feb. 7, 1957; reverse, Feb. 8, 1957.
Barbados vacation: Marietta Tree interview; letters, from Arthur Schlesinger, Jr., and Barry Bingham to JBM.

SECTION THREE:
Garrison/Stevenson law firm and Minow/AES visits to New York: Newton Minow interview.
Transcript of May 5 appearance of AES on "Meet the Press" is at PFL.
Thoughts on AES's possible marriage: letter, AES to Agnes Meyer, May 10, 1957, at Agnes Meyer collection at PFL; reverse, May 13, 1957.

SECTION FOUR:
John Fell's job on steamship: letter, George Killion to AES, May 16, 1957.
Summer, 1957, trip to Europe and Africa: AES notes in brown memo book with black binding on left edge, labeled "Adlai E. Stevenson, Europe-Africa 1957" at PFL.
AES/Oxford degree: letter, Barbara Ward to Jane Dick, June 4, 1957.
Reynolds Metals interests in Ghana: letter, AES to Walter L. Rice, June 6, 1957; reverse, June 18, 1957.

AES report to the J. Henry Schroder Banking Corp.: letter, AES to Vala Lada-Mocarski, June 7, 1957.

Advice to aluminum companies in Africa: letter, AES to Richard Reynolds, May 26, 1959.

AES/Marietta Tree and Alicia Patterson: AES III interview.

South African recollections: AES III interview.

Race problems in Africa: letter, AES to Geoffrey Crowther, June 21, 1957.

Kennedy criticism of U.S. policy: John F. Kennedy, *The Strategy of Peace* (New York: Harper & Brothers, 1960), pp. 65–80.

AES/Servan-Schreiber meeting: Arthur Schlesinger, Jr., interview.

SECTION FIVE:

Borden Stevenson/AES: letter, AES to Mrs. Ernst Ives, Aug. 25, 1957.

SECTION SIX:

Transcript of AES's Sept. 8, 1957 appearance on "Face the Nation" is at PFL.

AES/presidential Commission on Civil Rights: AES notes headed "Dean" and "Tom" at PFL; telegram, Arthur Schlesinger, Jr., to AES, Oct. 9, 1957.

SECTION SEVEN:

Papers relating to AES's work for John Foster Dulles on NATO are at PFL. Additional material is from George Ball interview and John Steele's files.

SECTION EIGHT:

Christmas, 1957, gifts: Newton Minow interview.

SECTION NINE:

AES III plans: AES III interview.

AES III concern for Ellen Stevenson's competence: testimony from EBS competency hearings, 1966.

Speech to President's Conference on foreign aid: Feb. 25, 1958; text is at PFL.

AES Mar. 30, 1958, appearance on "Look Here": text is at PFL.

Agnes Meyer comments: letters, Agnes Meyer to AES, Mar. 30, 1958 and April 15, 1958.

SECTION TEN:

Travel as U.S.S.R. official guest: letter, AES to Menshikov, April 30, 1958; reverse, May 5, 1958.

AES in London: red leather "travel notes" notebook, with address of AES inside, at PFL.

AES in Brussels: letter, AES to Marietta Tree, June 28, 1958; red notebook, op. cit.

AES in Norway: letter, AES to Marietta Tree, July 1, 1958; red notebook, op. cit.

Three strikes against JFK for President: letter, Blair to JFK, Aug. 7, 1958.

AES in Finland: letter, AES to Marietta Tree, July 10, 1958; red notebook, op. cit.

AES in Moscow: brown notebook with black side binding, labeled "Russia 1958 Adlai E. Stevenson," at PFL.

B. Ward working papers: letter, Barbara Ward to AES, July 19, 1958.

Style of AES Russia trip: Jane Dick interview.
AES in Bern: letter, AES to Marietta Tree, Aug. 12, 1958.

SECTION ELEVEN:
AES/congressional campaign speeches: JBM journal.
Quemoy-Matsu speech: letter, Dutton to AES; JBM to Dutton, Oct. 30, 1958.
AES/Proxmire and Nelson speech, Oct. 18, 1958, at PFL.

SECTION TWELVE:
Assessing others for 1960: letter, AES to Senator Joseph S. Clark, Dec. 29, 1958.
Geoffrey Crowther's dinner party in Chicago: letter, AES to Crowther, Dec. 28, 1958.
David Lawrence/AES "ablest statesman"; clipping marked "Hartford, 12/12/58; letter, AES to Lawrence, Dec. 30, 1958.
Mrs. Ives reminisces about past: letter, Mrs. Ives to AES, Dec. 1958, but dated "December, 1956."

SECTION THIRTEEN:
Presidency of the Field Foundation: Ruth Field interview.
AES/Suzie Zurcher: Suzie Zurcher, Marieta Tree interviews.
Presidential support from an Oregon woman: letter, AES to Marietta Tree, May 9, 1959.
Sentimentality about Illinois: letter, AES to Mme. André Brochart, May 9, 1959.
AES house a cottage: letter, Agnes Meyer to AES, June 10, 1959.

SECTION FOURTEEN:
AES reluctance about 1960 nomination: John Steele files, in his possession.
Butler: letter, Rowe to Blair, Feb. 16, 1959.
AES replacing Dulles: letter, AES to Gerald Johnson, Mar. 30, 1959.
Steele believing AES will be nominated: letter, John Steele to AES, April 14, 1959.
May 1 Steele dispatch on presidential prospects: John Steele files, in his possession.
HHH asking access to AES's political files: letter, Rowe to AES, May 13, 1959.

SECTION FIFTEEN:
University of Illinois foreign policy speech: letter, J. William Fulbright to AES, May 20, 1959.

SECTION SIXTEEN:
AES/Benton relationship: letter, Benton to AES, Jan. 20, 1959; William Benton interview.
AES/Marlborough's bed: Suzie Zurcher interview.
Visit with the John Steinbecks: Mrs. Currie's notes, in her possession; brown notebook, with black side binding, labeled "Europe 1959–1963," at PFL.
AES at Wimbledon: brown "Europe" notebook, at PFL.
Yacht cruise activities and relaxation: letter, AES to Agnes Meyer, July 20, 1959, Agnes Meyer files at PFL.

Flying Clipper cruise: itinerary and guest list are at PFL. Also William Benton Oral History at Columbia University; William Benton, John Fell Stevenson, Suzie Zurcher interviews; letter, AES to Mrs. Ives, July 13, 1959.

Eugene Meyer's death: letter, AES to Agnes Meyer, July 20, 1959, in Agnes Meyer files at PFL.

Democratic Party interest from "the sidelines": BBC interview transcript at PFL.

SECTION SEVENTEEN:

Britannica Canada trip idea: letter, AES to Benton, Aug. 31, 1959.

John Steele memo to AES: John Steele files, in his possession; Steele memorandum via "Memo to Newton Minow," Aug. 25, 1959.

Bowles: letter, Bowles to AES, Aug. 26, 1959; reverse, Sept. 2, 1959.

Alicia Patterson: letter, AES to Alicia Patterson, Sept. 4, 1959; reverse, undated, probably late Sept. 1959.

AES speaking in Madison: letter, AES to James Doyle, Sept. 10, 1959, and reverse.

Group forming to advocate AES 1960 candidacy: Ruth Field interview; plus correspondence with Stuart Gerry Brown, at PFL.

AES speech help from Barbara Ward: correspondence at PFL.

AES visit on Iowa farm with Khrushchev: Newton Minow interview.

AES trip to Madison: appointment sheets, at PFL; Newton Minow interview.

AES article for *Foreign Affairs:* letter, AES to Barbara Ward, Sept. 30, 1959.

Meany: letter, James Rowe to Blair, Wirtz, Minow, Oct. 13, 1959.

SECTION EIGHTEEN:

"Open End": transcript at PFL.

AES Boston: Arthur Schlesinger, Jr., journal, in his possession.

Time finding latent AES strength: John Steele files, in his possession.

Schlesinger difficulty deciding between JFK and HHH: Schlesinger, Jr., interview.

SECTION NINETEEN:

Ellen Borden Stevenson's telephone conversation with Jane Dick: memo entitled "Telephone Conversation with EBS, Oct. 24, 1958." supplied by AES family.

Touré dinner: Newton Minow interview; AES time sheet; letter, AES to Agnes Meyer, Oct. 31, 1959.

SECTION TWENTY:

All presidential candidates wanting to summon U.S.A.; John Steele files, in his possession.

AES denounces U.S. stagnation: memo, AES to Blair, Nov. 4, 1959.

National draft-AES movement: letter, James Doyle to Blair, Nov. 6, 1959.

Significance of AES sentiment: letter, James Doyle to Blair, Nov. 16, 1959.

Sharon's lunch: letter, John Sharon to Blair, Nov. 19, 1959.

Nevins suggestion of an AES/JFK ticket: letter, Nevins to AES, Nov. 22, 1959; reverse, Nov. 30, 1959.

Arthur Schlesinger, Jr., visits to Washington and Libertyville: Arthur Schlesinger, Jr., journal, in his possession.

Angier Biddle Duke: letter, Duke to AES, Dec. 4, 1959; reverse, Dec. 20, 1959.

SECTION TWENTY-ONE:
AES opinion of Nixon: letter, AES to Lady Spears, Jan. 7, 1960.
Early 1960 relations with JFK: letters, JFK to AES, Jan. 5, 1960; reverse, Jan. 8, 1960; Robert Kennedy interview.
Lewis Stevens: letter, Stevens to Blair, Jan. 8, 1960; reverse, Jan. 11, 1960.
Nixon "bad" for the country: letter, Amy Heffernan to AES, Jan. 6, 1960; reverse, Jan. 12, 1960.
Stevenson for President draft movement: letter, Agnes Meyer to AES, undated, probably Jan. 10 or Jan. 17; letter, Sharon to Blair, Jan. 15, 1960.
AES/Menshikov conversation: memcon of AES/Menshikov conversation supplied by AES family.
AES demeanor in Washington: John Steele files, in his possession.

SECTION TWENTY-TWO:
AES/Attwood: letter, AES to Agnes Meyer, Jan. 20, 1960; letter, AES to Attwood, Jan. 25, 1960.
National draft-AES movement: John Steele files, in his possession.
Ellen Stevenson and 1020 Lake Shore: testimony of Gary Kent Anderson, EBS competency hearings, 1966; memorandum, Carol Evans to AES, at PFL.
AES III/Nancy visited by Ellen Stevenson: Nancy Anderson Stevenson testimony, EBS competency hearings, 1966.
AES 60th Birthday: invitations to AES's 60th Birthday are at PFL; AES appointment sheets, at PFL.

SECTION TWENTY-THREE:
AES Latin America trip: description relies heavily on AES's brown notebook with black side binding labeled "Latin America 1960," at PFL.
John Fell photographer: John Fell Stevenson interview.
Latin America trip finances: William Benton interview.
AES visiting Cuba: letter, Rev. Mr. Graebel to AES, Feb. 9, 1960.
JFK campaign funds: cable, AES to Catledge, Feb. 19, 1960.
"Fantastic reception" in Bogotá: letter, Blair to Agnes Meyer, undated, probably Jan. 24.
Jim Doyle political report: letter, Doyle to Blair and Minow, Feb. 25, 1960.
AES calls trip a South American primary: letter, AES to Marietta Tree, Feb. 24, 1960.
AES in South America Feb. 28, 1960 to Mar. 16, 1960: description drawn heavily from AES brown notebook with black side binding labeled "South America 1960 II," at PFL.
New York AES-for-President Committee and Washington command post: unpublished study, "Citizens in Politics: The 1960 Campaign to Nominate Adlai E. Stevenson for the Presidency," Robert S. Hirschfield, Hunter College, City University of New York, in possession of author.
Draft groups intercommunication and with Doyle: Hirschfield study, op. cit.
Doyle reports: letter, Doyle to Blair and Minow, Mar. 3, 1960.
AES/JFK "informal secret understanding": Washington *Post*, Feb. 25, 1960; memo, Rowe to Minow and Wirtz, Feb. 25, 1960; letter, Wirtz to

Blair, Feb. 26, 1960; reverse, Mar. 7, 1960; AES appointment sheets, at PFL.

AES making important speeches after his trip: memorandum, Minow to Blair and AES, Mar. 9, 1960.

AES "hurt" by *Post:* letter, AES to Agnes Meyer, Mar. 10, 1960.

AES in Latin America, Mar. 16, 1960 to end: description heavily taken from AES brown notebook with black side binding, labeled "South America 1960 vol. III," at PFL.

Agnes Meyer visit with JFK: letter, Agnes Meyer to AES, Mar. 23, 1960.

Steele/Bean sampling: John Steele files, in his possession.

Schlesinger/Lubell meeting: Arthur Schlesinger, Jr., journal, in his possession.

Barbara Ward political advice: letter, Barbara Ward to AES, Mar. 26, 1960.

"Terrible contriver": letter, Agnes Meyer to AES, Mar. 30, 1960.

Jim Doyle on Kennedy: letter, Doyle to Blair and Minow, Mar. 31, 1960.

AES in Barbados: Marietta Tree interview.

Jane Dick political advice: letter, Jane Dick to AES, April 1960, probably April 10, 1960.

SECTION TWENTY-FOUR:

AES should go no further in renouncing nomination: letter, Paul L. Kelley to Minow, April 21, 1960.

Pressure to renounce further: JBM observation at the time.

"Meet the Press" transcript at PFL.

Financing Bean survey: letter, Sharon to Minow and Blair, May 3, 1960.

Barbara Ward on JFK/AES relations: letter, Barbara Ward to AES, May 1, 1960 or May 11, 1960.

SECTION TWENTY-FIVE:

RFK urging AES to come out for JFK: Minow interview.

Kennedy thinking AES was a candidate: Arthur Schlesinger, Jr., journal, in his possession.

AES post-West Virginia reflections: Arthur Schlesinger, Jr., journal, in his possession.

AES testimony on candidates' free time: "Statement of the Honorable Adlai E. Stevenson before the Subcommittee on Communications of the Senate Committee on Interstate and Foreign Commerce," Washington, June 16, 1960, at PFL.

AES/LBJ Washington conversation: John Steele files, in his possession; Newton Minow, Arthur Schlesinger, Jr., AES III interviews.

AES/Rowe Washington visit: John Steele files, in his possession.

Monroney scouting activities: John Steele files, in his possession; Rowland Evans and Robert Novak, *Lyndon B. Johnson: The Exercise of Power,* (New York: New American Library, 1966), pp. 261–62; Hirschfield study, op. cit., in author's possession.

AES/Justice Douglas breakfast and Khrushchev cable: memorandum for file, by AES, May 17, 1960; cablegram to Khrushchev May 17, 1960, signed by Rayburn, LBJ, AES.

AES/"America must quit Berlin" interview: telephone message from State to Blair, May 16, 1960; telegram dictated by Blair to Lincoln White, May 17, 1960.

Boulay/Nixon aide: letter, AES to Lisagor, June 2, 1960; letter, AES to Childs, June 1, 1960; wire, AES to Cramer, May 20, 1960; letter, AES to Stoneman, May 27, 1960; cable, Minow to Blair, June 1, 1960; letter, AES to Vanden Heuvel, July 8, 1960; reverse, July 14, 1960.

SECTION TWENTY-SIX:

Elmo Roper/JFK correspondence: letters, Roper to AES, May 17, 1960; JFK to Roper, Jan. 21, 1960, Feb. 11, 1960; Roper to JFK, Feb. 1, 1960, Feb. 16, 1960; AES to Roper, June 7, 1960.

AES/Steele flight to Chicago: John Steele files, in his possession.

AES nightmares of world blowing up: Suzie Zurcher interview.

Cook County Democratic Committee dinner speech: telegram, Frances Murray to AES, May 20, 1960; wire, Holifield to AES, May 20, 1960; letter, Holifield to AES, May 20, 1960.

SECTION TWENTY-SEVEN:

JFK/AES Libertyville post-Oregon meeting: Minow, Robert F. Kennedy, AES III, Ted Sorensen interviews; letter, AES to Schlesinger, Jr., May 21, 1960; Theodore Sorensen, *Kennedy* (New York: Harper & Row, 1965), p. 148; Arthur Schlesinger, Jr., journal, in his possession.

AES memo on "stopping JFK": memorandum, AES to Minow, May 31, 1960.

SECTION TWENTY-EIGHT:

New York *Times* ad: Hirschfield study, op. cit., in author's possession.

New York volunteer groups for AES: Hirschfield study, in author's possession.

Reluctance of regulars and reform Dems: Hirschfield study, in author's possession.

Telling Sharon AES L.A. hotel, *if* he goes to convention: letter, Minow to Sharon, June 1, 1960.

AES gratified by Boston airport reception: Arthur Schlesinger, Jr., journal, in his possession.

Finletter endorsement of AES: Arthur Schlesinger, Jr., journal, in his possession.

Schlesinger, Jr.'s endorsement: Arthur Schlesinger, Jr., journal, in his possession; letter, AES to Schlesinger, Jr., June 9, 1960; reverse, Mar. 2, 1960; letter, AES to Jeppson, June 14, 1960.

Schlesinger/Galbraith at Hyannisport: Arthur Schlesinger, Jr., interview.

AES not resenting desertions to JFK: Arthur Schlesinger, Jr., interview.

SECTION TWENTY-NINE:

Mrs. Roosevelt pressure: Theodore White, *The Making of the President 1960* (New York: Atheneum Publishers, 1961), pp. 119–22.

Mrs. Roosevelt endorsement and result: AES statement, June 12, 1960, at PFL; John Steele files, in his possession.

New York draft committee: Hirschfield study, op. cit., in author's possession.

Brown's estimate of JFK in California: letter, Brown to Agnes Meyer, June 13, 1960; Agnes Meyer to AES, June 13, 1960.

AES thinks "our young friend" could be nominated on the first ballot: letter, AES to Agnes Meyer, June 21, 1960.

Draft-AES leaders meeting to coordinate: Hirschfield study, op. cit., in author's possession; Donald Murray "The Stevenson Campaign at the 1960 Democratic Convention," unpublished manuscript, in author's possession.

Ryan believing Russian missiles were in Cuba: letter, Ryan to AES, June 22, 1960; reverse, June 27, 1960.

Bowles form letter for JFK: letter, Bowles to AES, June 27, 1960.

AES hotels in L.A.: letter, Blair to Benton, June 27, 1960.

Agnes Meyer Pasadena informal AES base: letter, Agnes Meyer to AES, June 28, 1960.

Frontier endorsement: letter, Phil Kerby to AES, July 1, 1960; reverse, July 6, 1960.

Preconvention CBS interview: interview transcript at PFL.

SECTION THIRTY:

AES workers Biltmore Hotel space: John Steele files, in his possession.

Preconvention supporters working: JBM journal and Hirschfield study, op. cit., in author's possession.

Airport arrival of AES: Hirschfield study, in author's possession.

Galbraith as a "personal betrayal": Arthur M. Schlesinger, Jr., *A Thousand Days,* (Boston: Houghton Mifflin Co., 1965), p. 34.

Graham discussion with AES of JFK nomination: White, op. cit., p. 408.

Labor endorses JFK: Hirschfield study, in author's possession.

Monroney/Sharon/Finney urging AES: Hirschfield study, in author's possession.

Illinois going for JFK: Newton Minow interview.

AES overwhelmed by his headquarters activities: Hirschfield study, in author's possession.

"Face the Nation": transcript of July 10, 1960 broadcast is at PFL.

Illinois caucus results: White, op. cit., p. 160.

Mrs. Roosevelt phoning Daley for AES support: Newton Minow interview.

Daley/asking AES to declare candidacy: Newton Minow interview.

Blair/Minow/Arvey/Lawrence meeting: Jacob Arvey interview.

Lawrence urging AES withdrawal: letter, Lawrence to Schlesinger, Jr., Dec. 30, 1965.

Visiting the New York delegation: Newton Minow interview.

AES/Minnesota caucus: Schlesinger, *A Thousand Days,* p. 37.

Kansas/Iowa released to JFK: Hirschfield study, in author's possession.

Opening night AES supporters chants: White, op. cit., pp. 162–63.

An explosion, not a demonstration: ibid.

Biltmore Bowl press conference persuasion: Hirschfield study, in author's possession.

AES taking convention seat: Marietta Tree interview.

Galleries going "mad" at AES appearance: White, op. cit., pp. 162–64.

AES flat appearance: ibid., p. 164. Hirschfield study, in author's possession.

Agnes Meyer anger at AES convention behavior: Agnes Meyer interview.

Benton recollection: William Benton interview.

Leaders of AES draft: Donald Murray study, in author's possession.

California caucus: White, op. cit., p. 162.

Unit-rule states: ibid., p. 164.

New York reassessing AES: ibid., p. 164; Hirschfield study, in author's possession; Murray study, in author's possession.

HHH declaring for AES/RFK meeting/JFK bandwagon faltering: White, op. cit., pp. 167–68.

AES phoning Daley: Arvey interview; White, op. cit., p. 167.

AES name in nomination: Mrs. Currie's notes, in her possession.

AES allowing it: AES III, Robert F. Kennedy interviews.

Convention widening JFK/AES gulf: Theodore Sorensen interview.

McCarthy: Schlesinger, Jr., Minow interviews.

AES managers packing the galleries: Hirschfield study, in author's possession.

Post-AES nomination speech demonstration: Hirschfield study, in author's possession; White, op. cit., p. 166.

Willkie: Hirschfield study, in author's possession.

AES watching balloting: Laura Magnuson interview.

JFK/vice presidency: Newton Minow interview; Mrs. Currie's notes, in her possession.

Humphrey: Humphrey interview.

SECTION THIRTY-ONE:

AES exhaustion: Suzie Zurcher interview.

Santa Barbara and drive: AES appointment sheets, pp. 156–57, at PFL.

AES/Secretary of State: James Reston interview.

Blair/winning election: letter, William Blair to John Steinbeck, July 22, 1960, in Steinbeck's possession.

Benton invitation: telegram, William Benton to AES, July 18, 1960; letter, AES to Benton, July 25, 1960.

Hutchins/Secretary of State: letter, Robert Hutchins to AES, July 20, 1960; reverse, July 25, 1960.

AES/Kennedy administration: letter, AES to Gerald Johnson, July 26, 1960; letter, AES to Harry M. Ayers, July 26, 1960; letter, AES to Lady Mary Spears, July 28, 1960; all at PFL.

Chain-letter campaign: letter, W. Willard Wirtz to Mrs. Andrew Winton Roth, July 29, 1960.

AES plans re Kennedy administration: letter, AES to Barbara Ward, July 29, 1960.

Hyannis reception: AES's appointment sheets.

AES/Schlesinger talk: Arthur Schlesinger, Jr., journal, in his possession.

Lunch with Kennedys: AES appointment sheets, p. 160; letter, AES to Marietta Tree, Aug. 2(?), 1960.

AES/Kennedy visit: Schlesinger, *A Thousand Days*, p. 64.

Draft of Kennedy statement re AES is at PFL.

AES in East: letter, AES to Marietta Tree, Aug. 7 and Aug. 8, 1960.

Agnes Meyer/Kennedy: letters, Agnes Meyer to AES, Aug. 2, 1960, Aug. 10, 1960.

McKeever/Secretary of State candidates: letter, Porter McKeever to William Blair, July 27, 1960; reverse, Aug. 2, 1960.

Foreign policy task force report: Richard Gardner, Theodore White, Ted Sorensen, George Ball interviews.

AES description of task force: letter, AES to Barbara Ward, Aug. 11, 1960.

National security study appointments: letter, AES to David Bruce, Sept. 5, 1960; reverse, Sept. 10, 1960.

AES/Ball papers: letters, AES to George Ball, Sept. 12 and Sept. 19, 1960.
AES/Kennedy/Bowles/Secretary of State: letter, AES to William Benton, Aug. 13, 1960; also, letter, AES to Marietta Tree, Aug. 13, 1960.
Mrs. Roosevelt's talk with Kennedy of August 1960, at PFL.
AES memo of conversation, August 15, 1960, with Mrs. Roosevelt is at PFL.
AES supporters working for Kennedy: letter, Jack Fischer to AES, Aug. 19, 1960; reverse, Aug. 29, 1960.
AES/Congo and Katanga: letter, AES to Harry Hochschild, Aug. 19, 1960.
Catholic issue: letter, Agnes Meyer to AES, Aug. 24, 1960.
AES/JFK paper on age and experience issue is at PFL.
Kennedy/AES partisans/Secretary of State: letter, Robert Dickinson to John Kennedy, July 18, 1960; letter, John Kennedy to Richard Holtz, Aug. 30, 1960.
AES draft of JFK statement is at PFL.

SECTION THIRTY-TWO:
Kennedy's campaign: observations of JBM.
AES/Marietta Tree correspondence: Marietta Tree interview.
Van Dusen/Kennedy rumors: letters, AES to Dr. Henry Van Dusen, Sept. 13, 1960; Arthur Schlesinger, Jr., to AES, Sept. 4, 1960; Van Dusen to AES, Aug. 2, 1960; John Bennetto to Van Dusen, Aug. 1, 1960; AES to Van Dusen, Aug. 11, 1960; Van Dusen to AES, Aug. 28, 1960. At PFL.
JFK campaign speeches were published by U. S. Government as companion to Senate committee report.

SECTION THIRTY-THREE:
AES Liberal Party speech: letter, Robert Benjamin to AES, Sept. 20, 1960; letter, Alex Rose to AES, Sept. 16, 1960; reverse, Sept. 19, 1960.
AES "shilly-shallying": letter, Agnes Meyer to AES, Sept. 16, 1960; reverse, Sept. 20, 1960.
Support for AES for Secretary of State: letter, AES to Mrs. Andrew G. Carey, Sept. 19, 1960; reverse, Sept. 13, 1960; letter, Mrs. Carey to Mrs. A. David Owen, Aug. 31, 1960.
Catholics/AES appointment: letter, AES to William Benton, Sept. 20, 1960; reverse, Sept. 7, 1960.
Phil Graham/JFK victory, AES appointment: letter, Agnes Meyer to AES, Sept. 22, 1960, from Agnes Meyer collection at PFL.
AES/religious issue: letter, AES to Barbara Ward, Sept. 20, 1960; letter, AES to Harry I. Golden, Sept. 23, 1960.
AES/defense, peace emphases: letter, AES to Thomas K. Finletter, Sept. 24, 1960.
Doyle in California: letter, James Doyle to Robert Kennedy, Sept. 26, 1960.
AES/Hall of Fame: at PFL.
Bowles/AES as Secretary of State: memo, Newton Minow to AES, Oct. 13, 1960.

SECTION THIRTY-FOUR:
Benton/Rusk/Secretary of State: letter, William Benton to Dr. Henry M. Wriston, Oct. 19, 1960.
Benton/Ambassadorship to Great Britain: letter, William Benton to AES, Oct. 20, 1960.

AES re Kennedy victory: letter, AES to Barbara Ward, Oct. 28, 1960.
AES re his activities in campaign: letter, AES to Marietta Tree, Nov. 1(?), 1960, in Mrs. Tree's possession.
AES re Fresno: letter, AES to Marietta Tree, Nov. 6, 1960, in Mrs. Tree's possession.

SECTION THIRTY-FIVE:
Acheson/AES as Secretary: John Steele files, in his possession.
A copy of the task force report on foreign policy is at PFL.
Sharon delivery of task force report to Kennedy: memo, John Sharon to AES, dated Nov. 16, 1960, on Nov. 14, 1960 meeting with John Kennedy.
AES paper giving reasons he should be Secretary of State: undated longhand paper given to Marietta Tree in Nov. 1960, in her possession.
Cyrus Eaton/AES-Russia messages: letter, AES to Cyrus Eaton, Nov. 17, 1960; reverse, Nov. 14, 1960; telegrams, Eaton to AES, Nov. 9, 1960 and Dec. 9, 1960; letter, Eaton to AES, Dec. 10, 1960; reverse, Dec. 13, 1960.
Kennedy/task forces: letter, John Kennedy to John Sharon, Nov. 18, 1960.
Kennedy telephone call to John Sharon: memo, John Sharon to AES, Nov. 23, 1960.
JFK/task force report: note, JFK to AES, Nov. 23, 1960.

SECTION THIRTY-SIX:
Agnes Meyer/information for new Administration: letter, Agnes Meyer to AES, Nov. 23, 1960.
AES/newspaper support for Secretary: letter, AES to C. K. McClatchy, Nov. 20, 1960.
Report on AES's meeting with Ambassador Menshikov is at PFL.
AES offer of help to Kennedy: letter, AES to John Kennedy, Dec. 1, 1960.
Newton Minow re Blair: Newton Minow interview.
Blair-Kennedy negotiations re AES: William Blair interview; AES time sheets.
Minow-AES conversation on way to Libertyville re UN Ambassador: Newton Minow interview.
Advice to AES on Ambassador is noted in longhand sheets dated Dec. 7, 1960, at PFL.
AES conversation with George Ball: George Ball interview.
AES visit to JFK: AES notes on negotiations with JFK are at PFL
AES/Kennedy comments outside JFK's Georgetown home re UN ambassadorship: New York *Times,* Dec. 9, 1960.
Bill Blair warning to Kennedy: Blair interview.
AES reason for not accepting UN post: AES III interview.
Kennedy reaction to AES not accepting immediately: Robert Kennedy interview.
Sorensen/Kennedy debt to AES: Theodore Sorensen interview.
AES reaction: Jane Dick, Arthur Schlesinger, Jr., Ruth Field interviews.
Longhand list of AES's conditions for acceptance of UN ambassadorship is at PFL. So are notes of other AES consultations about ambassadorship.

SECTION THIRTY-SEVEN:
Congratulations on UN appointment/AES reaction: letter, AES to Daniels, Dec. 12, 1960; letter, Agnes Meyer to AES, Dec. 14, 1960.
Rusk/AES press conference in New York: New York *Times,* Dec. 13, 1960.

AES receiving USUN charts and information: all at PFL.

AES congratulations/asking appointment advice: letter, HHH to AES, Dec. 12, 1960; letter, AES to Bruce, Dec. 22, 1960; letter, Mrs. Eleanor Roosevelt to AES, Dec. 12, 1960.

AES III/Nancy/Ellen Stevenson Dec. 23 lunch: Nancy Anderson Stevenson testimony, EBS competency hearings, 1966.

Male adviser suggestions: letter, Armstrong to AES, Jan. 3, 1961; letter, Harriman to AES, Dec. 23, 1960.

More congratulations: letter, Lodge to AES, Dec. 12, 1960; letter, Mendès-France to AES, Dec. 20, 1960; letter, Stowe to AES, Dec. 26, 1960; reverse, Dec. 29, 1960.

AES uncertain of access to JFK: letter, AES to Warburg, Dec. 30, 1960; letter, AES to JFK, Dec. 30, 1960.

AES/inaugural speech: wire, Sorensen to AES, Dec. 23, 1960.

Administration too cautious vis-à-vis Khrushchev: letter, Barbara Ward to AES, Jan. 6, 1961.

Barbara Ward's influence on AES: Clayton Fritchey interview.

AES/JFK appointments conversation: "Telephone Conversation AES/JFK," Jan. 13, 1961, at PFL.

SECTION THIRTY-EIGHT:

AES appearance for his confirmation hearing: Hearings of the Senate Committee on Foreign Relations, Jan. 18, 1961.

AES in Washington at the Inauguration: JBM observation at the time; John Steele files, in his possession.

Two principal sources for Sections Twelve and Thirteen are the official documents of the United Nations—printed transcripts of proceedings of the Security Council and General Assembly, for example—and the archives of the Department of State. I have not cited them individually—the United Nations documents can be found at UN headquarters in New York (or in the UN's depositories around the world); the State Department documents are at the Department in Washington and the chancery of the United States Mission to the United Nations in New York. Useful summaries are the annual *U. S. Participation in the UN Report by the President to the Congress* . . . , published by the U. S. Government Printing Office at Washington, and the *Annual Report of the Secretary-General on the Work of the Organization* . . . , published by the United Nations at New York. I have not cited those documents in full detail. Other important sources are AES's correspondence, both private and official, statements, press conference transcripts, travel notebooks, speeches both in the UN and outside it, and calendars and appointment sheets, all at PFL and not cited if clearly identified in the text. Interviews are cited. The public papers of Presidents Kennedy and Johnson are not.

SECTION ONE:

AES/Tree appointment: Mrs. Tree interview.

AES/Workings of UN Mission: Mrs. Tree, Plimpton, Yost, Klutznick, Thant, Pedersen, Gardner, Cleveland, Sisco, Fritchey, Ball interviews; Richard N. Gardner, *In Pursuit of World Order* (New York: Praeger, 1966).

SECTION TWO:

AES/UN/Washington relationship: McGeorge Bundy, Ball, Sisco, Sorensen, Gardner, RFK, Yost, McGowan, Cleveland, Klutznick, Mrs. Magnuson, Steele interviews.

AES/JFK relationship: Ball, AES III, Mrs. Meyer, Lippmann, Mrs. Field, McGeorge Bundy, Barbara Ward, Schlesinger, Yost, Cleveland, RFK, Sorensen, Sisco interviews.

AES/Rusk relationship: Theodore White, McGeorge Bundy, Ball, Minow, AES III, Klutznick, Sisco, Yost interviews.

AES/Eastern establishment relationship: McGowan, Ball, Sisco, Gardner, Klutznick, Harriman, Schlesinger interviews.

SECTION THREE:

AES/diplomacy: Yost, Mrs. Tree, Rivkin, RFK, Schlesinger interviews.

AES/NY/women/friends: Jim Oates, Stephen Hord, Mrs. Dick, McGowan, Archibald MacLeish, Arvey, Mrs. Magnuson, AES III, Lippmann, John Fell, Benton, Mrs. Welling, Schlesinger, Mrs. Tree, ESI, Mrs. Field, Roxane Eberlein, Barbara Ward, Fritchey, Mrs. Zurcher, Henry Crown, T. S. Matthews, Ball, Borden Stevenson interviews: Mrs. Currie's notes, in her possession.

AES's life style: Mrs. Tree, AES III interviews.

SECTION FOUR:

Congo background: *Report by the President to the Congress* and other documents cited in headnote to this chapter; Ernest W. Lefever, *Crisis in the Congo* (Washington, D.C.: The Brookings Institution, 1965); Schlesinger, *A Thousand Days;* AES correspondence with Nkrumah, Jan. 23, 1961, and Feb. 6, 1961.

AES's notes for first cabinet meeting are at PFL.

SECTION SIX:

AES/Zorin: Zorin to AES, Feb. 4, 1961; AES to Zorin, Feb. 7, 1961, at PFL.

AES's complaints against UN appointment and JFK: McGowan interview.

Union Minière du Haut-Katanga: Security Council records cited in headnote to this chapter.

AES/Zorin/Hammarskjold: John Steele files, Feb. 17, 1961, from New York, in his possession; official Security Council records cited above.

JFK/AES's "iron ass": John Steele files cited above.

SECTION SEVEN:

AES/correspondence with women: letters, Evelyn Houston to AES, Mar. 1, Mar. 19, 1961, at PFL; letter, Jane Dick to AES, Mar. 6, 1961.

AES/publicity: letter, Arvey to AES, Mar. 23, 1961, at PFL.

AES/*Afro American* criticism: Washington *Afro American*, Feb. 25, 1961; letter, Lloyd Garrison to AES, Mar. 8, 1961; letter, Garrison to C. Sumner Stone, Jr., editor, Washington *Afro American,* all at PFL.

UN/emergencies/AES: letter, Klutznick to Minow, Feb. 26, 1961, in Minow's possession.

SECTION EIGHT:

AES/disarmament meetings: Schlesinger, Jr., journal, Mar. 1961, in his possession.

JFK/AES as Secretary of State: Schlesinger, Jr., journal, Mar. 1961, cited above, in his possession.

SECTION NINE:

AES/recommendations to JFK: Sorensen, Schlesinger, Yost, McGeorge Bundy interviews.

SECTION TEN:

Cuban background: official UN and State Department documents cited in headnote to this chapter; Sorensen, *Kennedy;* Schlesinger, *A Thousand Days;* Haynes Johnson, *The Bay of Pigs* (New York: W. W. Norton, 1964).

Schlesinger/AES briefing on Bay of Pigs: Schlesinger interview; Schlesinger, Jr., journal, in his possession.

AES recognizes entrapment: Pedersen interview.

AES reaction to revelation: Pedersen, and McGeorge Bundy interviews.

Description of Political Committee meeting: Klutznick interview.

Cleveland congratulates AES: letter, Cleveland to AES, April 24, 1961.

AES reaction after Bay of Pigs: Mrs. Field, Yost, Lincoln Gordon, RFK, Jane

Dick interviews; Doyle, ed., *As We Knew Adlai* (New York: Harper & Row, 1966), p. 286; letter, AES to Agnes Meyer, May 14, 1961; reverse, April 1961, both at PFL; letter, Barbara Ward to AES, April 1961.

SECTION ELEVEN:

Barbara Ward advice re Castro: letter, Barbara Ward to AES, May 23, 1961, at PFL.

JFK/"talking papers": Sorensen interview.

AES appraisal of Latin American resentment: letter, AES to Schlesinger, May 31, 1961, at PFL.

AES plans for Latin American trip: letter, AES to Barbara Ward, May 31, 1961, at PFL.

AES/Mitchell's federal judgeship: letter, Mitchell to AES, May 24, 1961; reverse, June 3, 1961, both at PFL.

AES/McGowan appointment: letter, AES to RFK, June 3, 1961, at PFL.

AES's Palestine joke: letter, AES to Robert L. Farwell, June 3, 1961, at PFL.

AES/JFK/Riesman/Bay of Pigs: letter, AES to David Riesman, June 3, 1961, at PFL.

SECTION TWELVE:

AES/Latin American trip: AES's small black leather notebook with his handwritten notes is at PFL; most of the description of trip is drawn from it.

SECTION THIRTEEN:

AES/successor-state approach to China question: Yost interview.

SECTION FOURTEEN:

AES/Lincoln furniture for White House: letter, AES to Mrs. JFK; letter, AES to White House Fine Arts Committee, July 3, 1961; letter, Mrs. JFK to AES, July 24, 1961, all at PFL.

AES/Benton's yacht trip to Greek islands: letter, AES to Benton, July 6, 1961, at PFL.

AES/ECOSOC meeting in Geneva: Klutznick interview.

AES's relations with JFK: letter, Hubert Humphrey to AES, July 19; reverse, July 26, 1961, at PFL.

AES/talk with De Gaulle: Schlesinger, Jr., journal, Aug. 6, 1961, in his possession.

SECTION FIFTEEN:

AES/JFK/meeting on UN: Cleveland, Schlesinger, Sisco, RFK interviews.

SECTION SIXTEEN:

AES/William Stevenson appointment: letter, AES to Stevenson, Aug. 12; reverse, Aug. 24, 1961, at PFL.

AES/Martin appointment: letter, Minow to AES, Aug. 14, 1961, at PFL.

AES/Labor Day plans: letter, AES to Dutch Smith, Aug. 14, 1961, at PFL.

AES/anniversary: letter, AES to Mrs. Tree, Aug. 18, 1961.

AES/Bizerte: letter, AES to Mrs. Tree, Aug. 20, 1961.

AES/Tunisia/De Gaulle: Schlesinger journal, in his possession.

SECTION SEVENTEEN:

AES/Waldorf accommodations: Henry Crown interview; letter, AES to ESI, Aug. 26, 1961, at PFL.

AES/JFK meeting on nuclear tests: official records cited in headnote to this chapter; Schlesinger, Jr., journal, in his possession.

AES/swearing in of UN delegates: Klutznick interview.

SECTION EIGHTEEN:

AES/U Thant: interviews with Thant, Yost, Pedersen, and others at mission.

SECTION NINETEEN:

AES/Hammarskjold: letter, John Steinbeck to AES, Sept. 23, 1961; reverse, Oct. 20, 1961, at PFL.

AES/speech-writing problem: letter, Agnes Meyer to AES, Oct. 6, 1961, at PFL.

AES/Benton gifts: AES-Benton correspondence, Oct. and Nov. 1961, is at PFL.

AES/Benton offer of Britannica position: AES-Benton correspondence cited above.

AES/Bay of Pigs: letter, AES to Walter Judd, Oct. 20, 1961, at PFL; letter, AES to Van Fleet, Oct. 31; letter, Van Fleet to AES; New York _Times_, Nov. 2, 1961, all at PFL.

AES/Acheson: letter, AES to ESI, Oct. 19, 1961, at PFL.

Schlesinger/Cleveland/AES meeting on nuclear tests: Schlesinger, Jr., journal, in his possession.

SECTION TWENTY-ONE:

AES/pressure of work: letter, AES to ESI, Dec. 1, 1961, at PFL.

AES/JFK meeting at Glen Ora: Schlesinger, Carl Kaysen, Minow, Sorensen interviews.

AES/Senate nomination in Illinois: RFK, Minow, Benton, Sorensen interviews; letter, Paul Douglas to AES, Sept. 12, 1961, at PFL; letter, AES to Blair, Dec. 5, 1961, at PFL; letter, AES to JFK, Dec. 6, 1961, at PFL.

AES/relationship with State Department and White House: Schlesinger, Jr., journal, in his possession; AES typewritten memo entitled "Proposed Procedures for Handling UN Affairs" and dated Dec. 7, 1961, is at PFL.

SECTION TWENTY-TWO:

AES/Attwood duties at UN: William Attwood, _The Reds and the Blacks_ (New York: Harper & Row, 1967).

AES/vote on Chinese representation: letter, Ball to AES, Dec. 21, 1961; JFK telegram to AES, Dec. 15, 1961; both at PFL.

UN/Goa: Sisco interview.

AES speech on Goa: Fritchey interview.

SECTION TWENTY-THREE:

AES/Illinois Senate race: letter, AES to Blair, Dec. 18, 1961, at PFL.

AES/General Assembly: letter, AES to Benton, Dec. 22, 1961, at PFL.

AES complaints to Mrs. Welling: Mrs. Welling interview.

John Fell's visit to EBS: Transcript of EBS competency hearings, 1966.

AES/New Year's: letter, AES to Marietta Tree, undated, but later dated by AES "Dec. 1961."

SECTION TWENTY-FOUR:

John Fell's wedding: ESI interview; transcript of EBS competency hearings, 1966.

AES/correspondence with women: letters, Evelyn Houston to AES, Mar. 13, April 27, 1962; letter, Agnes Meyer to AES, Feb. 27, 1962, at PFL; letter, Ruth Field to AES, June or July 1962.

AES/Aga Khan: letter, AES to Aga Khan, June 6, 1962; reverse, June 18, 1962, both at PFL.

Problems with EBS: AES III testimony, EBS competency hearings, 1966.

AES/Borden and John Fell: AES's schedules are at PFL; Borden Stevenson interview.

AES/redecorating apartment and Mission: memos and correspondence among AES, F. L. Mewshaw, Stanley Woodward and Woodward Foundation, dated Jan. and Feb. 1962, are at PFL.

AES/Daley: letter, Daley to AES, Mar. 19, 1962; letter, Daley, Jr., to AES, Mar. 20, 1962, both at PFL.

AES's description of JFK Gala at Madison Square Garden: letter, AES to Mary Lasker, May 21, 1962, at PFL.

AES/insomnia and medication: Mrs. Currie's notes, in her possession.

AES/Lax: letter, Lax to JBM, April 25, 1972.

AES/old friend, John Paulding Brown: letter, Brown to AES, June 14, 1962, at PFL.

SECTION TWENTY-FIVE:

AES/preoccupation with UN: letter, Harlan Cleveland to JBM, May 2, 1966.

SECTION TWENTY-SIX:

AES/Mansfield: letter, AES to Mansfield, April 7, 1962, at PFL.

AES/Scoop Jackson: Schlesinger, Jr., journal, in his possession; Mrs. Tree interview; mimeo text press release from Jackson's office, AES's marked copy is at PFL; memo, Pedersen to AES, Mar. 23, 1962, at PFL; memo, Cleveland to Ball, Mar. 21, 1962, at PFL; letter, Jackson to AES, Mar. 28, 1962, at PFL; letter, AES to Jackson, April 13, 1962, at PFL; letter, Jackson to AES, April 16, 1962, at PFL; letter, Dorothy Fosdick to AES, April 20, 1962, at PFL; letter, Tufts to AES, April 21, 1962, at PFL; letter, Benton to Jackson, April 19, 1962, at PFL; reverse, May 16, 1962, at PFL; letter, AES to Schlesinger, April 26, 1962, at PFL.

SECTION TWENTY-SEVEN:

JFK/UN bonds: Sorensen interview; Senate Foreign Relations Committee hearings.

AES/nuclear test resumption: Mrs. Tree, George Ball interviews.

AES/disarmament: Sorensen interview; letter, AES to Rusk, Jan. 16, 1962, at PFL.

SECTION THIRTY:

AES/Middle East: Klutznick interview; Mrs. Currie's notes, in her possession; letter, AES to Humphrey, April 16, 1962, at PFL; letter, AES to Weinstein, April 30, 1962, at PFL.

SECTION THIRTY-ONE:

AES/JFK relations: Schlesinger, Jr., journal, in his possession.

AES/NSC meeting: Schlesinger, Sorensen interviews; Steele files, in his possession.

SECTION THIRTY-TWO:
AES/trip to Florence: undated longhand note, AES to ESI, at PFL.
AES/Geneva and Gstaad: Klutznick interview.
Nixon visit to Denmark: letter, Blair to AES, July 16, 1962, at PFL.
EBS's finances: letter, AES to ESI, July 10, 1962, at PFL.
AES/Disarmament Conference: letter, AES to Schlesinger, July 17, 1962.
AES/UN personnel abroad: memo, AES to himself, July 17, 1962, at PFL.
AES/women: undated postcard, to Ruth Field, at PFL.
AES/visit with Tito: AES handwritten notebooks on these travels are at PFL.
AES correspondence with Agnes Meyer is at PFL.

SECTION THIRTY-THREE:
AES/testimony on communications satellite: Gardner interview.
EBS's crisis: letter, AES to Lady Mary Spears, Aug. 27, 1962, at PFL.
AES/McGowan appointment: letter, McGowan to AES, Aug. 25, 1962, at
    PFL, as is AES to McGowan, Aug. 20, 1962.
AES/JFK meeting: Schlesinger, Jr., journal, in his possession.
AES/weekly Assembly reports: Schlesinger interview.
AES/Rusk schedules: Roxane Eberlein interview.

SECTION THIRTY-FOUR:
Cuban missile crisis: account drawn from Department of State and UN docu-
    ments; interviews as noted; Schlesinger, *A Thousand Days,* cited above;
    Sorensen, *Kennedy,* cited above; Robert F. Kennedy, *Thirteen Days*
    (New York: W. W. Norton & Company, 1969); Elie Abel, *The Missile
    Crisis* (Philadelphia and New York: J. B. Lippincott Company, 1966).

Certain specific items:

AES memo, four pages of longhand notes marked "Cuba—Memo to Self for
    Conf. Sept.–Oct. 17," is at PFL.
AES note to JFK: Sorensen interview.
Saturday afternoon meeting of Ex-Comm: Sorensen, RFK, Katzenbach,
    George Ball, Carl Kaysen interviews.
Concern over AES's dissent: Schlesinger, Jr., journal, in his possession;
    Schlesinger, RFK interviews.
Reaction to AES speeches: longhand letter, Jane Dick to AES, Oct. 23, 1962,
    at PFL; Jane Dick, Arvey interviews; letter, Roxane Eberlein to ESI,
    Oct. 26, 1962, at PFL; letter, Reuther to AES, Nov. 1, 1962, at PFL.
AES made his famous "hell freezes over" speech at the 1,025th meeting of the
    Security Council, held in New York on Thursday, Oct. 25, 1962, at 4 P.M.
AES reaction to speech success: Mrs. Dick, Mrs. Field interviews.
JFK to AES, Oct. 29, 1962, at PFL.

SECTION THIRTY-FIVE:
Continuing tension: Kennedy, *Thirteen Days,* cited above.
AES/JFK letter to Khrushchev: Sorensen interview.
AES/McCloy/Soviet negotiation: Schlesinger, Jr., journal, in his possession;
    McGowan, Sorensen, McGeorge Bundy, RFK interviews.

AES/Mikoyan: letter, AES to Mikoyan, Nov. 6, 1962, at PFL.

AES explanation of Khrushchev retreat: letter, AES to Ralph McGill, Nov. 21, 1962, at PFL.

AES/*Saturday Evening Post* article: account drawn from the files of John Steele, in his possession; Schlesinger, Jr., journal, in his possession; transcripts of contemporary news conferences; contemporary newspaper and magazine clippings; the Public Papers of President Kennedy; Schlesinger, Sorensen, Mrs. Field, Lincoln Gordon, Minow, AES III, RFK, McGeorge Bundy interviews; volumes of related correspondence are at PFL.

SECTION THIRTY-SIX:

AES/Mrs. Roosevelt: Mrs. Tree interview; AES memorial speeches are at PFL; letter, Meyer Feldman to AES, Nov. 14, and telegram, JFK to AES, Nov. 14, 1962, are at PFL.

AES/Goldwater attack: letter, AES to Goldwater, Nov. 13, reverse, Nov. 26, 1962, at PFL.

SECTION THIRTY-SEVEN:

AES/Congo: official documents at UN and State Department; Sorensen and Kaysen interviews; letter, Schweitzer to AES, Dec. 27, 1962, at PFL.

AES/New Year's: letter, AES to Mrs. Tree, Dec. 31, 1962; AES's schedules are at PFL; Minow interview.

SECTION THIRTY-EIGHT:

AES/Zorin departure: letter, AES to Zorin, Jan. 2, 1963, at PFL.

AES speech on Soviet delegate's death, April 24, 1963, is at PFL.

AES/defense of UN: letter, AES to Representative Elward of Illinois, March 15, 1963, at PFL.

AES/RFK/appointments: letters, AES to RFK, May 22, 1963, Jan. 18, 1963, at PFL.

AES/*Amsterdam News* attack: *Amsterdam News*, June 1, 1963; letter, Fritchey to *Afro American News*, June 14; letter, Fritchey to James L. Hicks, editor, *Amsterdam News*, June 13, 1963, at PFL.

AES/Reynolds Metals: letter, Marietta Tree to AES, Jan. 17; letter, AES to Richard Reynolds, Feb. 7, 1963, at PFL; AES draft of letter to JFK and letter, JFK to AES, June 21, 1963, at PFL.

AES/Phil Graham: Agnes Meyer-AES correspondence is at PFL.

SECTION THIRTY-NINE:

AES/JFK: letter, AES to Mrs. Joseph Kennedy, Feb. 23, 1963; reverse, Feb. 28, 1963, at PFL.

AES/fatigue/despair: letter, AES to Barbara Ward, Jan. 17, 1963, at PFL; Mrs. Currie's notes, in her possession; Theodore White, Gardner, Adlai III, Borden, George Ball interviews.

EBS problems: AES III testimony, EBS competency hearings, 1966; letter, AES to Mary Spears, Jan. 18, 1963; letter, EBS to Mrs. Carpenter, Jan. 30, 1963; letter, AES to Barbara Ward, July 29, 1963; letter, AES to Dutch Smith, Aug. 15, 1963, all at PFL.

AES/staff financing: letter, AES to Benton, May 2; letters, Benton to AES,

May 8 and July 11; AES to Benton, undated longhand scrawl, and related correspondence; all at PFL.

AES/Gridiron dinner: letter, AES to Alicia Patterson, Mar. 11, 1963, at PFL.

AES/Jacqueline Kennedy: AES-Mrs. JFK correspondence is at PFL.

SECTION FORTY:

AES/Mrs. Tree: letters, AES to Mrs. Tree, Feb. 16, 1963, and Mar. 3, 1963, supplied by AES III; letter, AES to Mrs. Tree, Mar. 10, 1963, supplied by Mrs. Tree; AES to Mrs. Tree, June 13, 1963, supplied by AES III; AES to Mrs. Tree, June 19, 1963, supplied by Mrs. Tree; AES notes to Frances FitzGerald are at PFL.

SECTION FORTY-ONE:

AES/Sarah Plimpton: letters, Sarah to AES, Jan. 2, 1963; undated, probably Jan. 1963; Jan. 26, 1963; Feb. 8, 1963; Feb. 19, 1963; Feb. 26, 1963; April 29, 1963; May 1963; May 6, 1963; May 18, 1963.

SECTION FORTY-TWO:

AES/Midlands speech: letter, Ambassador Bruce to AES, Mar. 7, 1963, at PFL.

AES/MLF: McGeorge Bundy, Schlesinger interviews.

AES plans Seville trip: letter, AES to S. Roger Tyler, Jr., Mar. 27, 1963, at PFL.

AES/Ava Gardner: letter, AES to Ava Gardner, April 8, 1963, at PFL.

AES/Ricardo Sicre: letter, AES to Princeton Admissions, May 22, 1963, at PFL.

AES/Morocco and Seville: AES's notes on his schedule are at PFL; Mrs. Tree interview; AES to Manuel María González, Aug. 27, 1963, at PFL.

SECTION FORTY-THREE:

AES speech to the Center for the Study of Democratic Institutions: Jan. 22, 1963, mimeo text USUN press release ✗4145 is at PFL.

AES speech at Notre Dame: Feb. 15, 1963, mimeo text USUN press release is at PFL.

AES speech to Chicago Council on Foreign Relations: Feb. 21, 1963, USUN press release ✗4151 is at PFL.

AES speech to OAS: April 15, 1963, mimeo text of USUN press release ✗4179 is at PFL.

AES speech to Red Cross: May 8, 1963, USUN press release ✗4200 is at PFL.

AES speech to DePaul University: May 9, 1963, USUN press release ✗4203 is at PFL.

AES speech to UN groups: May 13, 1963, USUN press release ✗4205 is at PFL.

AES speech to American Jewish Committee: May 18, 1963; USUN press release ✗4209 dated May 21, 1963, is at PFL.

SECTION FORTY-FIVE:

AES/travels: McGeorge Bundy interview; letter, AES to Aga Khan, June 19, 1963, at PFL; AES's notes on schedules; letter, AES to Ambassador Bohlen, June 19, 1963; letter, Sarah Plimpton to AES, June 15, 1963.

AES/Alicia Patterson's death: AES correspondence with Harry Guggenheim, Mrs. Ivan Albright, Jane Dick, Agnes Meyer, ESI, and Mrs. Paepcke, July 1963, is at PFL.
AES/Sarah Plimpton: letter, Sarah to AES, July 5, 1963.
AES/complaints of official duties: letter, AES to ESI, July 17, 1963, at PFL.

SECTION FORTY-SIX:
AES/meeting with JFK on Portuguese territories: AES schedule at PFL; Schlesinger, Jr., journal, in his possession.
AES/Moscow trip: AES schedules and notes are at PFL.
AES recalls 1956 attacks on him over nuclear test issue: letter, AES to Barbara Ward, Aug. 15, 1963; letter, John Steele to AES, Aug. 13, 1963; reverse, Aug. 15, 1963; letter, AES to Lady Spears, Aug. 8, 1963; AES to ESI, Aug. 8, 1963; all at PFL.

SECTION FORTY-SEVEN:
AES/Sarah Plimpton: letters, Sarah to AES, July 18, July 23, Aug. 3, Aug. 8, Aug. 10, 1963.

SECTION FORTY-EIGHT:
AES/death of Kennedy baby: Schlesinger, Jr., journal, in his possession.
AES speech in Security Council on Israel-Syria: letter, Arvey to AES, Aug. 30, 1963, at PFL.
AES's annotated schedules are at PFL.
AES/New York *Times* leak: Schlesinger, Jr., journal, in his possession.
EBS's problems: letter, AES to ESI, Oct. 3, 1963; transcript of EBS competency hearings, 1966; AES III, Klutznick, Schlesinger interviews.
AES/attack in Dallas: contemporary newspaper clippings; Schlesinger, Jr., journal, in his possession; letter, Jane Dick to AES, Oct. 27, 1963; letter, Agnes Meyer to AES, Oct. 26, 1963; reverse, Nov. 1, 1963, at PFL; letter, Barbara Ward to AES, Nov. 6, 1963, at PFL.
Copy of letter from Dallas man which AES forwarded to Kenny O'Donnell is at PFL.
AES/UN affairs: letter, AES to Barbara Ward, Nov. 12, 1963, at PFL.

SECTION FORTY-NINE:
JFK assassination: contemporary newspaper clippings; AES schedules, annotated, are at PFL; AES public statements and telegrams to members of Kennedy family are all at PFL; records of General Assembly 1,263rd plenary session are at USUN; Schlesinger, Mrs. Tree interviews; AES's longhand notes, undated except for Nov. 1963, are at PFL; AES speech at first Johnson cabinet meeting, reading copy at PFL; copy of AES note to Sorensen, Nov. 26, 1963, is at PFL.

CHAPTER 5: 1963-1965

See headnote for Chapter Four.

SECTION ONE:
AES/meeting with LBJ: AES's hand-annotated schedules are at PFL.
AES/relationship with LBJ: Schlesinger, Cleveland, Thant, Minow, McGeorge Bundy, Klutznick interviews; Mrs. Currie's notes, in her possession; Rowland Evans and Robert Novak, *Lyndon B. Johnson: The Exercise of Power*, cited above.
AES/first LBJ cabinet meeting: letter, LBJ to AES, Dec. 9, 1963, at PFL; AES notes.
AES/LBJ/Eleanor Roosevelt Memorial Foundation: letter, AES to LBJ, Dec. 2, 1963; letter, AES to Mrs. Johnson, Jan. 25, 1964; letter, Mrs. Johnson to AES, Feb. 10, 1964; letter, AES to Mrs. Johnson, Feb. 17, 1964; all at PFL.
AES/vice presidency: NBC, "Meet the Press," Dec. 22, 1963; contemporary newspaper clippings; letter, Blair to AES, Dec. 12, 1963, at PFL; letter, Benton to AES, Dec. 10, 1963, at PFL; letter, AES to Benton, Dec. 14, 1963, at PFL.
AES/presidency: letter, Benton to AES, Nov. 25, 1963, at PFL.
AES/cabinet meeting, Dec. 11, 1964; LBJ handwritten note on White House note paper, dated Dec. 11 by AES, is at PFL.
AES/LBJ/foreign policy: memo and letter, AES to LBJ, Dec. 10, 1963, at PFL.
AES/LBJ speech to General Assembly: letter, AES to LBJ, Dec. 11, 1963; letter, LBJ to AES, Dec. 21, 1963, both at PFL; Sorensen interview.
AES/Mrs. JFK: letter, Mrs. JFK to AES, Dec. 4, 1963.
AES/Christmas: letter, AES to Mrs. Tree, Dec. 28, 1963.

SECTION TWO:
AES/Jane Dick/Jamaica: letter, Jane Dick to AES, Jan. 19, 1964; "For Adlai Stevenson's 64th Birthday Celebrated January 31, 1964, from Jane Dick."
AES/correspondence with women: letter, AES to Barbara Ward (re Roosevelt Foundation), Jan. 23, 1964, at PFL; letter, AES to Mrs. Tree, Feb. 3, 1964.
AES/rumors of Rusk resignation: letter, AES to Mrs. Tree, Mar. 21, 1964; Mrs. Tree interview.
AES/West Indian cruise; AES's annotated schedules and diaries are at PFL.
AES/recommendations for federal appointments: letter, AES to Minow, Mar. 25, 1964; letter, AES to Walter Jenkins, Jan. 11, 1964; both at PFL.

SECTION FOUR:
AES/Mrs. LBJ: correspondence between them, April 1964, at PFL.
AES/EBS's problems: testimony at EBS competency hearings, 1966.
AES/Jane Dick's "human interest" article: voluminous correspondence beginning with Jane Dick telegram to AES, April 13, 1964, and continuing through May 1964, is at PFL.

AES/New York Senate race: RFK conversation with JBM at the time; Sorensen interview; Lyndon Baines Johnson, *The Vantage Point, Perspectives of the Presidency 1963–1969* (New York: Holt, Rinehart and Winston, 1971).

AES/trip to Europe: AES travel notebooks and diaries are at PFL; letter, Sarah Plimpton to AES, May 21, 1964; letter, AES to Mrs. Tree, May 19, 1964.

SECTION SIX:

AES/diplomatic courtesies: letters, AES to ESI, May 23, May 30, 1964, at PFL.

AES/"Vice President 1964" file: copy of Gallup poll, May 31, 1964, at PFL.

AES/Senate race: memo, AES to Fritchey, June 1964, at PFL.

AES/television appearance: memo, AES to Fritchey, June 18, 1964, at PFL.

AES/Roosevelt Foundation/Adlai III fund raising/future plans: letter, AES to Mrs. Tree, June 1964.

AES/family life/Senate race/future plans: letter, AES to Mrs. Tree, July 5, 1964.

AES/vice presidency: letter, HHH to AES, July 7, 1964, containing AES longhand notes on conversation, at PFL; letter, Benton to AES, July 13, 1964 at PFL.

AES/Senate race/platform hearings: letter, AES to Barbara Ward, July 11, 1964, at PFL.

AES/Sarah Plimpton: letter, Sarah to AES, dated in AES's longhand July 12, 1964.

AES/Mercedes McCambridge: letter, Mercedes McCambridge to AES, July 18, 1964, at PFL.

AES/Washington trip/meeting with LBJ: letter, AES to Mrs. Tree, July 25, 1964.

AES's campaign for vice presidential nomination: longhand note, AES to Minow, July 29, 1964, copy supplied by Mr. Minow, who has the original in his possession.

AES's reaction to LBJ announcement: Schlesinger and Minow interviews; AES's annotated calendar for July 30, 1964, at PFL; John Steele's files, in his possession; letter, Nan McEvoy to AES, July 31, 1964; reverse, Aug. 10, 1964, at PFL; Agnes Meyer and Barbara Ward interviews.

AES/health/fatigue: Mrs. Currie's notes, in her possession.

SECTION SEVEN:

AES/news of Gulf of Tonkin: AES schedules, with longhand notations, are at PFL.

AES/U Thant/LBJ meeting/Thant negotiation with North Vietnam: Yost, U Thant, Rusk, Ball, Pedersen interviews. AES calendar, with notations, at PFL; *Look,* July 29, 1969; Townsend Hoopes, *The Limits of Intervention* (New York: David McKay Company, Inc., 1969); Lyndon Baines Johnson, *The Vantage Point,* cited above.

AES/"sick of public life": letter, AES to Mrs. Tree, Aug. 8, 1964.

AES/RFK/New York Senate nomination: letter, AES to Mrs. Lasker, Aug. 14, 1964, at PFL.

AES/meeting with Rusk: notes on AES schedule for Aug. 17, 1964, at PFL.
AES/HHH vice presidential nomination: letter, Evelyn Houston to AES, Aug. 25, 1964; letter, AES to Mrs. Lasker, Aug. 29, 1964, at PFL.
AES's intention to resign: John Steele files, Aug. 31, 1964, in his possession.

SECTION EIGHT:
AES/Nobel Peace Prize: letter, AES to Hartke, Aug. 29, 1964; letter, Benton to the Norwegian Nobel Committee, Aug. 31, 1964.
AES on AES III's victory: AES III interview.
AES wanting to rest: letter, AES to Barbara Ward, Sept. 10, 1964.
AES professional army idea: letter, AES to HHH, Sept. 15, 1964.
AES campaign contribution to HHH: letter, AES to HHH, Sept. 22, 1964; reverse, Sept. 22, Sept. 28, 1964.
AES welcomes Mrs. JFK: letter, AES to Mrs. Kennedy, Sept. 16, 1964.
Sarah Plimpton's letters from Paris: letters, Sarah to AES, Sept. 17, 1964; Sept 23, 1964.
AES/Ruth Field: letters, Mrs. Field to AES, Oct. 1964; Nov. 1964 on RF stationery.
AES/law firm dinner for Ed Austin: letter, AES to Austin, Oct. 27, 1964.
LBJ request that AES help Kennedy: letter, Bill Moyers to AES, Oct. 16, 1964.
AES's broken finger: AES schedule; Mrs. Ives and Marietta Tree interviews; letter, AES to Penelope Tree, Oct. 15, 1964.

SECTION NINE:
AES trip to Chile: AES schedule; Gabriel Valdés Subercaseaux interview.

SECTION TEN:
Johnson's consensus and Vietnam developments: *Pentagon Papers.*
AES post-Chile memorandum to LBJ: letter, AES to HHH, Nov. 24, 1964; McGeorge Bundy interview.

SECTION ELEVEN:
AES Christmas activities. AES schedule at PFL.

SECTION TWELVE:
AES talk with LBJ: AES schedule at PFL; letter, AES to Barbara Ward, Jan. 8, 1965.
AES thoughts of retiring from UN: letter, AES to Barbara Ward, Jan. 8, 1965; Francis Plimpton, Jane Dick interviews; letters, Agnes Meyer to AES, Dec. 29, 1964; Jan. 5, 1965; letter, AES to Agnes Meyer, Jan. 1965.
AES/Illinois: letter, Arvey to AES, Jan. 14, 1965; reverse, Jan. 19, 1965.
AES at LBJ inaugural: AES schedule at PFL; JBM observation at the time.
Libertyville ice storm: letter, Richard to AES, Jan. 28, 1965; reverse, Feb. 1, 1965.
AES birthday party: letter, Ruth Field to AES, dated Feb. 1965.

SECTION THIRTEEN:
AES at cabinet meeting: AES longhand notes at PFL, dated Feb. 18, 1965.
U Thant's Vietnam initiatives: Schlesinger, Cleveland, Sisco, Bundy, Ball, Nicholas de B. Katzenbach, Yost interviews; documents.

SECTION FOURTEEN:
AES concern over Vietnam: documents; letter, Jane Gunther to JBM, Jan. 14, 1972; interviews as above.

SECTION FIFTEEN:
AES Vienna trip: letter, Sarah Plimpton to AES, Mar. 20, 1965.
AES reception for Middle East delegates: McGowan interview.
Caribbean cruise: appointments sheets March 19–28 at PFL.

SECTION SEVENTEEN:
AES correspondence: letter, Sarah Plimpton to AES, dated April 1965; letter, Ruth Field to AES, dated April 1965; letter, Mrs. JFK to AES, dated April 1965.

SECTION EIGHTEEN:
Dominican crisis and AES: Sisco and Klutznick interviews; letter, Schlesinger to AES, May 10, 1965; reverse, May 14, 1965; Pedersen interview.

SECTION NINETEEN:
AES health and schedule: letter, Dr. Lax to JBM, April 25, 1972.
AES correspondence: letter, Ruth Field to AES, May 1965.
AES sending Jane Dick to Washington: letter, Jane Dick to AES, May 25, 1965.
AES/Evelyn Houston: letter, Evelyn Houston to AES, May 14, 1965.
AES health after University of Toronto speech: Roxane Eberlein memo of Aug. 30, 1965 in AES schedule, at PFL.
AES hectic schedule in May and June: Marietta Tree interview.
Jane Dick on America's troubles: letter, Jane Dick to AES, June 3, 1965.
AES Arkansas/Libertyville trip: AES III interview.
Former Congressman asking AES to resign: letter, William H. Meyer to AES, June 7, 1965.
Ellen Stevenson case: letter, AES to Lady Mary Spears, June 9, 1965.
AES summer plans: letter, AES to Mrs. Ives, June 16, 1965.
Honorary degree at Williams College: AES schedule at PFL.
Honorary degree at Harvard: AES schedule at PFL.
Dinner with Evelyn Houston: letter, Evelyn Houston to AES, June, 1965.

SECTION TWENTY:
LBJ UN anniversary speech: Yost, Ruth Field interviews.
AES depression/resignation: Reston, Klutznick interviews.
AES at Ravinia: Jane Dick interview.
AES health: AES III interview.
Letters from liberals asking AES to resign over Vietnam: memo to Clayton Fritchey from Marjorie Reitz; printed "Declaration to Ambassador Adlai Stevenson" at PFL; letter, Ralph Ginzburg to AES, July 2, 1965; letter, James Farrell to AES, June 28, 1965; reverse, July 2, 1965; letter, Donald C. Skone Palmer to AES, July 7, 1965; letter, Walter J. Schloss to AES, June 28, 1965; letter, Betty Kelly to AES, June 30, 1965; letter, Warren F. Milius to AES, June 30, 1965; letter, AES to Paul Goodman, undated, but early July 1965; Fritchey interview; AES note to Fritchey, July 6, 1965, at PFL; Yost and Pedersen interviews.

SECTION TWENTY-ONE:

AES dispirited about getting through to White House: letter, Roger Tubby to JBM, Feb. 26, 1970.

AES not using Khan's chalet: letter, AES to Aga Khan, July 9, 1965.

AES dinner with Harrimans et al.: Harriman interview; Washington *Post*, July 16, 1965; Plimpton interview.

AES in London: William Benton oral history at Columbia University; transcription from a TV telediphone recording of "Panorama ⚡2025," BBC, July 12, 1965; Eric Sevareid article, *Look*, Nov. 30, 1965; Schlesinger interview.

AES death: William Benton oral history at Columbia University; letter, Marietta Tree to JBM, Jan. 4, 1972; Marietta Tree interview.

AES funeral: Mrs. Currie's notes, in her possession; Marietta Tree interview; JBM observation at the time.

INDEX